DICTIONARY OF THE RUSSIAN REVOLUTION

DICTIONARY OF THE
RUSSIAN
REVOLUTION

GEORGE JACKSON, Editor-in-Chief

ROBERT DEVLIN, Assistant Editor

GREENWOOD PRESS

NEW YORK · WESTPORT, CONNECTICUT · LONDON

Library of Congress Cataloging-in-Publication Data

Dictionary of the Russian Revolution / George Jackson, editor-in-chief
 ; Robert Devlin, assistant editor.
    p. cm.
    Includes bibliographies and index.
    ISBN 0–313–21131–0 (lib. bdg. : alk. paper)
    1. Soviet Union—History—Revolution, 1917–1921—Dictionaries.
I. Jackson, George D. II. Devlin, Robert James, 1941–
DK265.D49 1989
947.084′1′00321—dc19   88–17771

British Library Cataloguing in Publication Data is available.

Library of Congress Catalog Card Number: 88–17771
ISBN: 0–313–21131–0

First published in 1989

Greenwood Press, Inc.
88 Post Road West, Westport, Connecticut 06881

Printed in the United States of America

The paper used in this book complies with the
Permanent Paper Standard issued by the National
Information Standards Organization (Z39.48–1984).

10 9 8 7 6 5 4 3 2 1

Copyright Acknowledgment

Grateful acknowledgment is made for permission to reprint material from AN ATLAS OF RUSSIAN
AND EAST EUROPEAN HISTORY, Arthur E. Adams, Ian M. Matley, and William O. McCagg
(Praeger Publishers, New York, 1967). Copyright © 1967 by Frederick A. Praeger, Inc. Reprinted
with permission.

TO KAREN

This book is dedicated to my wife Karen. Her love and patience helped to sustain me during the many trying years it has taken to complete this book. She gave more than warmth and support; the book could not have been completed without her contribution. It has truly been a collaboration and a partnership because she shared equally in the burdens of editing, typing, and completing the final manuscript.

George Jackson

CONTENTS

PREFACE

I have tried in this reference book to provide a one volume guide to the major institutions, people, and movements associated with the Russian Revolutions of 1917–21. As far as I know, no other convenient guide exists in English, though there are several written from the Soviet point of view in Russian. I have assembled nearly one hundred contributors from the United States, Canada, Great Britain, France, Holland, and Australia. In my opinion they are some of the finest specialists in the field. Reluctantly, I decided not to ask for contributions from our Soviet colleagues, not out of a lack of respect for their expert quali- fications, but because I recognized when I began the book that at that time they would have been compelled to write within strictures that might have embarrassed them and us.

In any such endeavor, one of the most important questions is the principle of selection. For our English-speaking readers that presented a problem. For them the first three great political revolutions of the Western world are the English Revolution of 1688, the American Revolution of 1776, and the French Revolution of 1789, because they all grow out of the same body of political theory, em- phasizing rule by law, representative political institutions, social contract, and popular sovereignty. Although the Bolshevik Seizure of Power in 1917 also grew out of European political theory, it is in certain ways a different body of theory, emphasizing economic determinism and social democracy, rather than political democracy, and an explicit rejection of many of the ideals that prompted the other three revolutions. Because the Russian Revolution ended differently from the other three, we in the non-communist world have been tempted to see it as an isolated event, departing from the course set by its predecessors, and owing more to the unique features of the Russian historical experience than to the European. Some scholars have even denied that it had any significant popular support in Russia.[1]

This has led in the West to a rather stilted view of the Russian Revolution as a movement without antecedents or consequences. By depriving the Russian Revolution of its legitimate origins and its momentous worldwide consequences, we have tended to deprive it also of its history. As so many historians have pointed out, history is the study of both the aberrations and the deep regularities of the past. It *is* necessary to see the unique qualities of the Russian Revolution, but it is also necessary to see the ways in which it relates to broader developments in the rest of the world, and to the aspirations of the Russian people as well.

With these considerations in mind, we tried to choose subjects and authors that would treat institutions and personalities in the Russian Revolution from both perspectives. We did not try to impose any party line on our contributors, but we did press them to express not only their own perspectives, but also to articulate other possible interpretations that have appeared in the research literature. The greatest division of opinion among historians, as pointed out above and in the article on historiography, is not between Western and Soviet scholars, for both tend to see the Bolshevik Seizure of Power in 1917 as an elitist phenomenon in which Lenin and his supposedly disciplined Bolshevik Party seized power by successful organization and leadership, unscrupulously manipulating the politically naive interest groups that emerged during 1917 in Russia. Rather, the difference of opinion lies between that elitist view and another view, which sees the Bolshevik Revolution as a response to the needs and aspirations of self-conscious mass movements which sought a leadership congruent with their own views. As Louis Menashe has stated the latter view, the Bolsheviks were "objects as well as agents of mass radicalism."[2] In the first perspective the Bolsheviks are portrayed as a well disciplined, but unscrupulous conspiratorial elite that concealed its agenda and adopted the right propaganda slogans to manipulate the discontent of politically naive mass organizations. In the second perspective mass movements consciously choose the Bolsheviks, not only for their propaganda slogans, but also because in many significant ways the Bolsheviks possessed an identity and quality of character and a known agenda that corresponded to their own needs.

Because the history of the Russian Revolution is now being written from the "bottom up," as well as "from the top down," we have tried to include articles not only on conventional subjects like revolutionary leaders and governing institutions, but also on those pertaining to social classes and social problems: workers, peasants, the agrarian question, the national question, the army, the navy, and the trade unions. We have tried to give considerable space to subjects frequently slighted in scholarly monographs, such as individual national minorities and their geographic areas, religion, and new international institutions like the Comintern, the Profintern, and the Krestintern. We have asked the authors of our major articles to try to keep their contributions to approximately 2500 words, although many were longer when completed.

The system of transliteration used was developed by the Library of Congress, although I am using it without the special diacritical marks that their system calls for. This is a convention that many authors follow. It means, however, that except for certain well known personal and geographical names in English, like Trotsky (should be Trotskii) or Kerensky (should be Kerenskii), I may be using a spelling that is different from other sources. In the system I am using, for example, names which frequently appear in English with a Y (such as Yaroslavskii, Yudenich) will appear with an I (Iaroslavskii and Iudenich). There is a system for geographic names which I am not using because their spellings are inconsistent with the Library of Congress. I will be using the spelling Enisei, for example, while many maps will be spelling that province and river Yenisei.

For the names of people and places among ethnic minorities or countries like Poland and Lithuania, there is no simple solution. I am not a scholar of the numerous Turkic or Finno-Ugric languages in Russia. In those cases where the figure is primarily a local person, I have tried to use the spelling proper to that national group. In those cases where there were doubts, I have tried to use the conventions of my sources. In those cases where it is a member of a national minority who becomes a national politician, like Dzerzhinskii, I have used the Russian version of the name (rather than the Polish Dzerzynsky) because that is the way it appears in most English language sources. My choices with regard to spelling will not please everyone, but that is the nature of the field. There is no "H" or "J" in Russian, so I have usually changed the spelling of ethnic names to conform to the Russian version (Hummet or Himmat to Gummet), though with "Jadid" I have used the most familiar spelling in English.

The Russian Social Democratic Workers' Party was technically one party until 1917. Therefore, although the Bolshevik and Menshevik factions often had separate newspapers and organizations, they are not separate parties and not all members belong to one faction or another. Therefore, I will sometimes simply use the label Russian Social Democratic Workers' Party to designate membership during those years. Technically the Russian Social Democratic Workers' Party (Bolshevik) is the name of that party until the Seventh Party Congress in March 1918, at which time the party becomes the Russian Communist Party (Bolshevik). In referring to the Central Committee of the Russian Social Democratic Workers' Party (Bolshevik) it is necessary to add (*see* the Central Committee of the Russian Communist party [Bolshevik]), because that is the label I chose for the Central Committee. A further note—in Russian the party name is spelled a little differently as Russian Social Democratic Workers' Party (bol'shevik). I have not chosen to follow that convention. At the Fourteenth Party Congress in December 1925 the name was changed to the All-Union Communist Party (Bolshevik), though Western sources rarely observe that distinction.

Although the most prominent Soviet personalities, like Lenin and Stalin, are listed by their pseudonyms, which are more familiar than their correct family names, lesser individuals are listed under their true names and are cross listed by their pseudonyms. For spelling of well known names that frequently appear in English in a form that is different from the Library of Congress transliteration system, such as Trotsky and Kerensky, I have used the more familiar spelling.

Bibliographies for individual articles normally do not include the standard reference works, but as they are valuable for information for all articles, I would like to list them here.

Bolshaia Sovetskaia entsiklopedia (3rd ed.) 31 vols. 1960–81. Available in English
      translation as *The Great Soviet Encyclopedia*. 31 vols. 1973–1983.
Sovetskaia istoricheskaia entsiklopediia. 16 vols. (1961–1976).
Velikaia Oktiabr'skaia sotsialisticheskaia revoliutsiia: entsiklopediia. 1977.
Wyczynski, J. *Modern Encyclopedia of Russian and Soviet History*. 1976-   . 45 vols.
      to date.

Notes

1. For a full discussion of the shifts in attitudes among Western scholars of the Russian Revolution, see the article on Historiography.

2. Louis Menashe, "Demystifying the Russian Revolution," *Radical History Review*, 18 (Fall 1978), p. 149.

ACKNOWLEDGMENTS

It is always a pleasure when presenting academic research to the general public to acknowledge one's debt to those who have helped to make the book possible. Although I wish to express my gratitude for the help of the following, I do not mean to imply that these institutions or individuals bear any responsibility for the final results. Whatever shortcomings or errors that may have occurred are the sole responsibility of the editor and his contributors. First of all, I would like to thank my assistant, Professor Robert Devlin for his help in the original planning of the book and the recruitment of contributors. We conceived the book together and I regret that he was not able to continue providing his skills and knowledge in the final editing of articles by outside contributors, putting the book together, and composing the remaining articles. The book would not have been possible without several visits to the Summer Research Institute at the University of Illinois. I would like to express my gratitude to the university, where I originally planned the book and recruited many of our contributors, for its generous support of that enterprise, and to Ralph T. Fisher, upon whose initiative the summer institute was created and has continued to thrive despite several threats to its existence. I would also like to thank the staff of the Slavic Library at the University of Illinois for their patience and considerable assistance in locating source material for the short articles appearing in the book. I would like to thank Hofstra University for its financial support and grants of research time in order to complete the arduous task of writing, editing, and typing the final manuscript. Finally, I want to thank Greenwood Press and its History Editor Cynthia Harris for her patience during the ten-year period that was required to organize and complete the work.

George Jackson

CONTRIBUTORS

GEORGE JACKSON, Editor-in Chief, is Professor of History at Hofstra University. He is the author of *Comintern and Peasant in East Europe, 1919–30* and of articles on numerous topics in East European and Russian history

ROBERT DEVLIN, Assistant Editor, is Associate Professor at Adelphi University

HARVEY ASHER, Department of History, Drury College

ANITA BAKER, University College, University of Maryland

SAMUEL H. BARON, Department of History (emeritus), University of North Carolina

STEPHEN BLANK, Air University, Maxwell Air Force Base, Alabama

GEORGE BRINKLEY, Department of Government and International Studies, University of Notre Dame

ROBERT P. BROWDER, Department of History, University of Arizona

PAUL E. BURNS, Department of History, University of Nevada

WILLIAM CHASE, Department of History, University of Pittsburgh

BARBARA CLEMENTS, Department of History, University of Akron

ANTHONY D'AGOSTINO, Department of History, San Francisco State University

ROBERT V. DANIELS, Department of History, University of Vermont

RICHARD DEBO, Department of History, Simon Fraser University, British Columbia

ALTON S. DONNELLY, Department of History, State University of New York at Binghampton

PATRICK DRINAN, Department of Political Science, University of California at San Diego

CHARLES DUVAL, Department of History, New Mexico State University (deceased)

ROBERT EDELMAN, Department of History, University of California at San Diego

CHARLES M. EDMONDSON, Department of History, Rollins College

CARTER ELWOOD, Department of History, Ithaca College

ANDREW EZERGAILIS, Department of History, Ithaca College

MARC FERRO, Centre d'Etudes Sur l'URSS, Ecole des Hautes Etudes, Paris

MICHAEL J. FONTENOT, Department of History, Southern University

DAVID J. FOOTMAN, St. Antony College, Oxford University

ZIVA GALILI Y GARCIA, Department of History, Rutgers University

NORBERT GAWOREK, University of Wisconsin

LENNARD GERSON, Department of History and Political Science, Nassau Community College

J. ARCH GETTY, Department of History, University of California at Riverside

ISRAEL GETZLER, Department of Russian Studies, Hebrew University of Jerusalem

GRAEME GILL, Department of Government, University of Sydney

WILLIAM GLEASON, Doane College

MICHAEL HAMM, Department of History, Centre College

SIDNEY S. HARCAVE, Department of History (emeritus), State University of New York at Binghampton

J. DANE HARTGROVE, U.S. National Archives, Washington

TSUYOSHI HASEGAWA, Slavic Research Center, Hokkaido University

RONALD HAYASHIDA, School of American and International Studies, Ramapo College of New Jersey

MYRON HEDLIN, Silver Springs, Maryland

MALVIN M. HELGESEN, Central Intelligence Agency

TARAS HUNCZAK, Department of History, Rutgers University

PETER H. JUVILER, Department of Political Science, Columbia University

FREDERICK I. KAPLAN, Department of Humanities, Michigan State University

JOHN KEEP, Department of History, University of Toronto

PETER KENEZ, Adlai E. Stevenson College, University of California at Santa Cruz

ESTHER KINGSTON-MANN, Department of History, University of Massachusetts at Boston

D. G. KIRBY, School of Slavonic and East European Studies, University of London

DIANE KOENKER, Department of History, University of Illinois

LAWRENCE LERNER, Jackson School of International Studies, University of Washington

JOHN LONG, Department of History, Rider College

DAVID MACEY, Department of History, Middlebury College

DAVID MANDEL, Department de science politique, Universite du Quebec a Montreal

LOUIS MENASHE, Polytechnic Institute of New York

CHRISTOPHER MENDOZA, Indiana University

EMANUEL NODEL, Department of History, Western Michigan University

MATTHEW L. O'LEARY, Department of History, University of Washington

ALEXANDER ORBACH, Department of Religious Studies, University of Pittsburgh

WILLIAM H. PARSONS, Department of Russian Studies, Eckerd College

MAUREEN PERRIE, Centre for Russian and East European Studies, Birmingham, England

ALEXANDER RABINOWITCH, Office of International Programs, Indiana University

THOMAS H. RIGBY, Research School of the Social Sciences, Australian National University, Canberra

RUTH ROOSA, Harriman Institute, Columbia University

WILLIAM ROSENBERG, Department of History, University of Michigan

BERNICE GLATZER ROSENTHAL, Department of History, Fordham University

NORMAN SAUL, Department of History, University of Kansas

ALFRED E. SENN, Department of History, University of Wisconsin

ROBERT SERVICE, School of Slavonic and East European Studies, University of London

MICHAEL SHAW, Department of History, William Patterson College

LEWIS SIEGELBAUM, Department of History, Michigan State University

WILLIAM B. SIMONS, Legal Counsel, Fike Corporation; formerly, Faculty of Law, University of Leyden, The Netherlands

BARRY SMIRNOFF, Oceanside, New York

RUSSEL SNOW, Freeport, New York

PAUL D. STEEVES, Department of History, Stetson University

RONALD GREGOR SUNY, Department of History, University of Michigan

RICHARD TAYLOR, Department of Political Theory and Government, University College of Swansea, Wales

ELIZABETH VALKENIER, Harriman Institute, Columbia University

MARK LOUIS VON HAGEN, Department of History, Columbia University

REX WADE, Department of History, George Mason University

ROBERT D. WARTH, Department of History, University of Kentucky

ROBERT WESSON, Department of International Relations, University of Californian at Santa Barbara

ALLAN WILDMAN, Department of History, Ohio State University

K. PAUL ZYGAS, School of Architecture, Arizona State University

DICTIONARY OF THE RUSSIAN REVOLUTION

A

Adalet (Justice) Party. Adalet was a forerunner of the Persian Communist Party.

Founded in 1916 in Baku by some Iranian leaders from Tabriz and Teheran, it was helped in 1917 by Gummet*, and both organizations came under the influence of the Russian Social Democratic Workers' Party (Bolshevik)*. Its leaders were Asadulla Kafar Zade and Haidar Khan Amuoglu. It became the Persian Communist Party on June 20, 1920.

Agrarian Policy, 1917–1921. The policy of any Russian government toward the peasantry and the use of agricultural land was bound to be of crucial importance in determining the outcome of the 1917 revolutions because the majority of the population were peasants.

Soviet agrarian policy in and shortly after the Revolution was a complex interplay of a desire to secure peasant support or at least tolerance, doctrinaire socialism with faith in collectivism and controls, the immediate need to secure food, and concessions to economic realism. V. I. Lenin* was much impressed with the revolutionary potential of the peasant masses, who constituted a large majority of the population. An appeal to their land hunger was a large part of his program—"Peace, land, and bread"—upon his return to Russia in April 1917. Although peasants already held a large majority of the arable land, they dreamed of more and began attacking estates soon after the Tsar abdicated in February; violence in the countryside increased steadily in the following months. The more moderate parties felt unable to sanction the peasants' self-help because they feared the resultant loss of production through disorganization and destruction and because the land-grabbing drive contributed to the breakup of the army— peasant soldiers did not want to be left out—and made difficult the continuation of the war with Germany. For Lenin and his followers, these were good reasons to urge the peasants on. From March to October, while a million soldiers left the army to participate in the semi-revolution in the countryside, the Provisional

Government* could only exhort the impatient peasants to wait for the much postponed Constituent Assembly*, and as late as September, Prime Minister A. F. Kerensky* was threatening village lawbreakers with dire punishment. Not surprisingly, in October the peasants in uniform listened to the Bolsheviks (*see* Russian Social Democratic Workers' Party [Bolshevik]) and declined to fight for the Kerensky government.

Yet it was only later that Lenin made a real effort to appeal to the peasants. In his April Theses* he called for nationalization of the land, but he wanted it to become not individual but collective property. Large estates were to be made into model farms run by the state—a daydream under the circumstances. In July he still warned of peasant landholding, in the Marxist tradition, as a bourgeois evil. But desire for revolutionary action prevailed over socialist principles, and in August Lenin appropriated, without thanks, the program of the peasant party, the Socialist-Revolutionary Party*, for simply turning land over to the working peasantry.

This promise was fulfilled in the Decree on Land (*see* Agriculture) promulgated by the new Soviet government on its first day. Land was nationalized and large holdings were turned over to peasant committees to parcel out, peasant debts were cancelled, and hiring of labor was prohibited. Lenin afterwards spoke of the division of the land into small holdings as contrary to Bolshevik principles, but he hoped that the peasants would proceed to join collectives. In fact, he had no real choice. The Bolshevik organization hardly penetrated into the countryside; where they did, they were generally city dwellers with no esteem for the peasants and little understanding of their psychology and problems. The Socialist–Revolutionaries (S–R's) overwhelmed the Bolsheviks in the election to the Constituent Assembly a few weeks after the Revolution. In any case, the redistribution of land was largely spontaneous, but it was effective and took not only big estates but above-average peasant holdings. The Russian countryside became more egalitarian in 1917–1921 than ever before or after.

As far as the Bolsheviks could claim to represent the peasant majority of the country, it was by virtue of their coalition with the peasant-based Left Socialist–Revolutionaries (*see* Left Socialist-Revolutionary Party), who joined Lenin's government in December 1917. The Left S–R's, however, were never given a real share of power, and since they represented primarily peasant interests, they soon came into conflict with the Bolsheviks. In March 1918 they withdrew in protest against the Treaty of Brest-Litovsk* with Germany as well as the increasing squeezing of the peasants through the state grain monopoly established in February. In July they took up arms against the Soviet government and, concurrently with rightists who had taken refuge in the South, began the Civil War (*see* Civil War in Russia).

The Bolsheviks, having lost their allies in the countryside, pressed coercive measures and class warfare. In May 1918 a decree sanctioned the requisition of ill-defined peasant surpluses by force. In June the government ordered the organization of Committees of the Poor*, somewhat irregularly appointed bodies that supplanted the land committees dominated by the Socialist–Revolutionaries. They divided the peasantry and weakened the sector less disposed to favor the Bolsheviks. With armed detachments of workers or soldiers, they confiscated grain, tools, and livestock from the richer peasants; the take was divided between the committees, armed detachments, and the state grain reserves. This was politically expedient since it divided the peasantry and made both poor peasants and workers accomplices in Soviet coercion. But it was economically counter-productive because requisition often amounted to plunder, provoked hundreds of local uprisings, and caused great losses. The authorities saw the whole problem as getting hold of vast stocks of grain held by the well-to-do peasants (*kulaks*), but the supposed hoards were not found, and production suffered. Although Lenin held the poorest peasants to be true proletarians, the committees were checked in August, were dissolved during the Civil War, and were replaced by new Bolshevik-controlled local soviets including middle as well as poor peasants.

The Committees of the Poor were also intended to promote the collectivization of agriculture. The old aspiration was never forgotten, and many Bolsheviks were convinced that for the survival of socialism, that is, of their state, it was necessary to socialize the peasant majority. Some believed that the way to leap to pure communism was by joining in communal farms. However, only a handful of agricultural communes, in which members worked and lived together, were set up in the months after the October Seizure of Power; a decree of February 1918 calling for collectivization as a way to a socialist economy had no apparent results. However, after June, several hundred collective farms were established monthly, with more or less support from the Committees of the Poor. Through 1918 there was much eager propaganda for collectives, especially those of the commune type, which stressed communal consumption and did away with almost all private ownership. In the summer of 1918 the Soviet government spent a substantial amount of its very limited funds to promote communes which fulfilled the communist ideal by full sharing in production and consumption, and favored them in allocating land. Some thought the Soviet state had to be a huge federation of communes. Lenin frequently called for "socialized working of the land," and in October 1918 it was officially predicted that Russia would be covered with communes by the next spring.

The advocacy of communes, however, came mostly from idealistic leftists, not from the top ranks of the Leninists who were more concerned with control than egalitarianism. Lenin strongly preferred state farms, in which the peasants became hired workers, over peasant communities, which smacked of the popular old *mir* (village commune) with its considerable communal institutions and custom of periodic land redistribution, and which was revived or made more frequent after the Revolution. A decree of February 1919 still spoke of the necessary transition to collective farming, but by this time official support was less, and the number of collectives—communes plus the *artels* (which produced collectively but retained private households) and *tozes* (which shared equipment that collectivized production but not consumption)—increased only slowly and remained trivial compared to the mass of individual farming households, with 3 percent of production in 1920. A number of state farms (some 3,000 in 1918) were also set up, but the Soviet state lacked personnel to operate them and machinery to make them useful, and the peasants saw them as estates under new management.

Engaged in a struggle for survival in the Civil War, the government increasingly concentrated on the primary purpose of getting food for the cities. The requisitioning of 1918 produced only about a tenth as much grain as had been freely marketed in previous years, and the Bolsheviks saw the problem as one of collection, not production. The apparatus was improved sufficiently for requisitions to double in 1919 and increased further in 1920, but city rations were at or below the level of starvation throughout the Civil War. Probably a majority of the city dwellers fled to the countryside to be nearer a source of food. Under these circumstances, Lenin declared that it was criminal for a peasant to regard the grain he produced as his own.

It was not surprising that food supplies were much diminished. Before the Revolution 70 percent of marketed grain came from farms of landlords and wealthier peasants, the so-called *kulaks,* classes now more or less liquidated. Peasants were given virtually no return for their produce and had little incentive to produce more than they could store (very likely out of fear that it would be lost to rot, rodents, or requisitions). Cultivated acreage decreased by half or more in many places, and numbers of livestock declined by about one-fourth in the period 1918–1920. Nonetheless, peasants did produce, and despite much unpleasantness, they generally supported the Bolsheviks in the Civil War. The anti-Bolshevik forces mostly stood by the landlords; where White armies (*see* White Movement) came back, peasants were punished for land seizures. The Bolsheviks seemed the lesser evil, and the confiscating detachments could be excused as a wartime necessity. Some peasants organized as "Greens," (such as Nestor Makhno's* bands in the Ukraine) independent of both Reds and Whites. They fought against the Whites only to be destroyed in turn by the Bolsheviks.

The end of the Civil War brought a new crisis. Demobilization of the Red Army*, beginning in September 1920, sent millions of trained soldiers home to the villages, and peasants, no longer fearing return of the landlords, increasingly resisted requisitioning. But it was difficult for the Soviet leadership to change its approach. To allow peasants to sell their grain was free trade and capitalism, hence inadmissible. Communists thought that compelling the peasants to do their share was part of class warfare and necessary for the building of socialism. Even though the immediate effect was bad, they reasoned that the ultimate result would be good because socialism was good. Requisitioning was pushed strongly during the last months of 1920; in December there was even an attempt to set up committees to control sowing and harvesting by 20 million households. Collective farming was still seen as the way of the future, and in October Lenin demanded that it be promoted while military methods were used to collect grain.

It became increasingly evident in the first months of 1921, however, that change was necessary to save the Revolution. There was a serious strike wave in Petrograd. At the end of February a mutiny began at the Kronstadt naval base (*see* Kronstadt), gravely threatening the Soviet state. There were widespread peasant uprisings, the largest of which covered Tambov and several neighboring provinces and involved some 20,000 rebel fighters. A proposal submitted in February to abolish requisitioning was at first rejected, but under pressure of circumstances, on March 21, the forced delivery (*see* Agriculture; Peasants in the Russian Revolution) of supposed surpluses was replaced by a fixed tax in kind, and after paying it the peasant could freely sell his produce.

This amounted to a breach in the whole policy of War Communism*. Freedom of trade was still seen as dangerous, but once admitted for grain, the logic carried forward. In succeeding months, artisans and small industries were permitted to produce and sell for the market; Lenin's New Economic Policy* was in full swing, leading to economic revival under a mixed capitalist–socialist system. However, two drought years, in addition to disruptions of Civil War and strife, brought a great famine; in the summer of 1921 the Soviet government made another ideological retreat in permitting Hoover's American Relief Administration to distribute food to some 10 million Russians. Special favors were also withdrawn from the collective farms, and they languished until Stalin moved again toward collectivization in 1928. The new policies gave the peasants freedom of action, security, and incentives; recovery was rapid thereafter *see also* Agriculture.

Robert Wesson

Bibliography

Carr, Edward H. *A History of Soviet Russia*. Vol. 2. 1950.
Chamberlin, William H. *The Russian Revolution, 1917–1921*. 1935.
Jasny, Naum. *Socialized Agriculture of the USSR: Plans and Performance*. 1965.
Liashchenko, Peter Ivanovich. *Sotsial'naia ekonomiia sel'skogo khoziaistva*. 1930.
Volin, Lazar. *A Century of Russian Agriculture*. 1970.
Wesson, Robert G. *Soviet Communes*. 1963.

Agriculture. In Russia the system of agricultural production and land tenure strongly influenced the attitude of the peasants and other social groups toward their government and social change. It also was an important factor in any program for rapid national economic growth.

At the beginning of the twentieth century, agriculture constituted the single largest sector of the Russian economy, producing approximately one-half of the national income and employing two-thirds to three-quarters of Russia's population. Peasants were not only important in economic terms, however. They also had long played a key role in the revolutionary ideology of both Populists and Social Democrats. When the Revolution finally arrived, peasants played an equally critical role in practice. Above all, the realization of the peasants' age-old dream of black repartition (*chernyi peredel*), or a final redistribution of all privately owned lands to those who worked them, was a major factor in consolidating Bolshevik legitimacy. In their turn, the political and social changes that followed the installation of the new regime were to have a similarly powerful impact on the peasant way of life. The revolutions' immediate impact on both agriculture proper and on land-use practices was, however, relatively minor, serving merely either to retard or accelerate pre-existing trends rather than to rupture them and initiate new patterns of development. Moreover, those changes that did take place flowed out of the disruptions accompanying World War I* and then the Civil War (*see* Civil War in Russia) rather than any specifically revolutionary acts. By 1927, indeed, most of agriculture's prewar trends had reasserted themselves.

At the end of the nineteenth century, Russian agriculture as a whole was perhaps the most backward in Europe, and it has long been argued that Russia was in the midst of a major agricultural crisis. Structurally, close to 95 percent of its arable land was devoted to grain production. Of the four major crops, rye was the principal item of peasant consumption and absorbed one-third of the sown area. Wheat, one of the two major export items, accounted for another quarter. Of the other two, both of which were used to alternate with rye and wheat in the prevailing three-field pattern of crop rotation, barley was grown almost exclusively for export and occupied another 10 percent, and oats, grown primarily for animal fodder, took up a further 20 percent. Altogether, cereals produced just under 50 percent of net agricultural income.

Beyond its backward structure, Russian agriculture also suffered from extremely low levels of capital investment and technological development. Tools and implements were primitive by any standard, having changed little over the preceding centuries, and more advanced types of machinery were extremely rare. Manuring and the use of chemical fertilizers was also relatively insignificant. It was the same with methods of cultivation. Less than two-thirds of the arable land was under crops in any given year as a consequence of the three-field pattern of rotation. Moreover, in conjunction with the almost universal system of open-field strip cultivation that was based on the peasant commune (*obshchina*), both repartitional and non-repartitional, such rotation was compulsory for all members of a peasant community.

The other major area of agricultural activity was livestock production, which contributed slightly more than a quarter of total agricultural income, though less than a fifth of gross output. It, too, was notoriously backward, both quantitatively and qualitatively, and is frequently considered to have been in a state of crisis. In part, this was a consequence of the low level of arable farming and the lack of resources devoted to the cultivation of animal fodder. Meadows and pasture-land amounted to only one-third of the total area of arable land. Thus livestock was heavily dependent on fallow grazing. Both systems, however, failed to provide adequately either for the long winter or for the critical periods between sowing the fallow and harvesting.

The remainder of the cultivated area, meanwhile, was devoted to more intensive forms of agriculture, including the cultivation of industrial crops, viticulture, fruit growing, and vegetable gardening. Together, these activities contributed almost a quarter of total agricultural income. The balance was provided by forestry and fishing industries.

Despite the government's somewhat belated attempts to rationalize peasant agriculture and increase its productivity through the passage of the agrarian reforms of P. A. Stolypin beginning in 1906, the basic outlines of this picture had not changed substantially by the outbreak of the war in 1914. Compared to the rest of Europe, however, Russia had fallen even further behind. Yet viewed within an exclusively Russian context, the situation was not as dismal as it appeared. Indeed, during the final half-century of tsarist rule, the agricultural economy had become increasingly diversified and intensified as its emphasis shifted gradually from subsistence or consumption-oriented production to production directly for the market.

Stimulating these changes were, first, the rapid growth in the population, which increased by some 40 percent between the 1897 census and the revolution, reaching about 170 million; second, the tremendous expansion in the railroad network, which more than doubled in length between 1895 and the revolution, when some 50,000 miles were in use; and third, the expansion of the domestic market that accompanied the commercialization of the economy as a whole. Attempts to evaluate the impact of these changes are hindered by long-standing disputes over the accuracy of Russia's prewar statistics. However, the value of the agricultural product appears to have increased by more than a third between 1900 and the outbreak of the war, measured in constant 1900 prices, and the gross harvest of all crops by some 40 percent. The source of this increase was divided between extensification and intensification. Thus during this period, the sown area increased by some 15 percent, so by 1914 more than 100 million *desiatins* were under cultivation. At the same time, the yields of all principal crops increased by some 25 percent, although yields continued to remain far below the rest of Europe. Overall, agricultural production grew approximately 2 percent per annum between the emancipation of the serfs in 1861 and the war, just slightly ahead of population growth. There were, therefore, only minor increases in per capita output. Nonetheless, in sheer bulk alone, Russia's contribution to world agricultural production was impressive, providing a quarter of its wheat and more than half of its rye, a third of its barley, and a quarter of its oats. Only livestock production failed to keep pace, and although the absolute size of Russia's herds increased, they did so more slowly than the rate of increase in population and cultivated area.

Within these global figures, there were also important shifts in both the output of specific crops and the relative balance between them as well as a marked increase in geographical specialization. The most significant change was a 30 percent growth in the sown area of wheat, which now replaced rye as the principal crop. By 1914 wheat thus accounted for slightly more than 30 percent of the sown area, rye for slightly less, although the absolute area under rye remained virtually unchanged. Even so, rye continued to outpace wheat in the size of its net harvest due to its higher and more consistent yields. Even more spectacular was the 30 percent increase in the area under barley and the 80 percent increase in its net harvest. As a result, barley and wheat together comprised two-thirds of the total grain export market to which they contributed approximately equal proportions. The area under oats also expanded, though by a more moderate 10 percent. As in the case of rye, however, the relative proportions of the sown area held by both barley and oats also declined. Nonetheless, these four grains continued to dominate about 85 percent of the sown area. The secondary grains and legumes accounted for half of the remaining sown area. Of the grains, buckwheat, millet, and maize (corn) all expanded their output, although the first two were actually cultivated on a smaller absolute area. Spelt, meanwhile, decreased both its sown area and output, but peas, lentils, and beans increased output from a smaller given area.

Occupying 3.5 percent of the sown area, the most important crop after the principal grains was potatoes, not only because of its increasing role as a food item among the peasantry, for whom it provided much higher caloric yields per unit sown than cereal grains, but also for the production of starch, sugar, and alcohol, in the latter instance virtually displacing grain. The potato output was also a sign of increasing crop intensification. Between 1900 and 1914, the land area in potatoes increased by one-fifth and the total output by more than one-third. After potatoes, flax and hemp were the most significant crops both in terms of area sown and as exports. They each occupied approximately 1.5 percent of the sown area. However, in the years before the war both crops suffered a decrease in area sown, with an increase in net output. Of the other industrial crops, sugar beets was next in importance with 1 percent of the sown area. During the final two decades before the war, the area in sugar beets increased by 40 percent and the output by 70 percent—one of the notable success stories and a further sign of agricultural intensification. Cotton, too, increased in importance, with its area of cultivation expanded by 70 percent, although output increased by only 45 percent. Tobacco, on the other hand, underwent a decline in land area but an increase in yield. There was also a moderate expansion in the production of sunflower seeds, hops, rice, tea, and in viticulture. Altogether, the technical crops increased the value of their output by some 30 percent. Finally, there was an expansion in the production of vegetables—including cabbages, onions, cucumbers, and chicory—and fruit—including melons, apples, apricots, plums, and pears.

Beyond the shift to wheat and toward the increased cultivation of root crops such as potatoes and sugar beets, the other major indicator of agricultural intensification was an expansion in the land area devoted to fodder grasses, which nearly doubled in European Russia between 1901 and 1914 and totaled 1.7 million *desiatins* for the entire empire—an area equivalent to more than 1 percent of the sown area. Equally important for livestock production, the land area used for and the output of hay also increased during this period.

Agricultural progress was also reflected in the changing pattern of regional specialization. The axis of change in Russia runs from northwest to southeast, from the traditional centers of population settlement in the northern black-earth and non-black-earth regions to the zone of colonization in the southern black-earth and steppe areas. Moving along this line, one passes from a zone where an increasing proportion of the land was being devoted to technical and specialized industrial and market crops to a zone where the proportion of land devoted to grain, especially wheat, was increasing. Traditionally, it is the latter region that has been the area of agricultural growth and expansion. However, since the beginning of the century, this could be accomplished only at the expense of either pasture or fallow. As a consequence, the zone of growth shifted to the southeastern steppe, which extended beyond the Volga into Central Asia, to the northern Caucasus and to Siberia, both east and west.

Despite the relative backwardness of livestock production compared to arable farming, it, too, managed to increase the total value of its output during the prewar years, expanding by 25 percent. Moreover, as with land, most of the herds were owned by the peasantry—in this case approximately 95 percent. The number of horses, cattle, and oxen each increased by some 10 percent to a total of 36 million and 52 million head, respectively. The number of pigs also increased slightly to some 17 million. Sheep, however, declined by some 20 percent to around 81 million head. In addition, there were approximately 5.5 million goats and an unknown number of chickens, the latter particularly important both as a source of protein in the countryside and for the production of eggs, Russia's most important export item among animal products.

There were regional differences along the same northwest to southeast axis that, for cattle, marked a gradual shift from an economy that focused on the production of milk for the market to one focused on the production of meat. There were also sharp differences in the proportion of cattle to both sown area and population, with low ratios characteristic of the more densely populated and more intensively cultivated zones. The highest ratios and the greatest absolute numbers of cattle were in the areas beyond the Volga in the southeastern and Asian steppes and Siberia. Mirroring the changing state of arable farming, the quantity of livestock had declined in the southern Ukraine and lower Volga areas, due to the expansion of arable land there, and had increased in the West and North, reflecting that area's gradual agricultural intensification and the increased use of root crops and fodder grasses. The overall balance between the two zones, however, remained unchanged.

A final indication of agricultural progress is to be found in the increasing levels of capital investment, although the incidence of such improvements was not very great and was limited to a small proportion of prosperous peasants and to non-peasant properties. Nonetheless, the importation and domestic production of agricultural machinery increased some 350 percent in value between 1906 and 1913, while fertilizer use was up 250 percent. In addition, and in conjunction with the government's program of agrarian reform and the expansion of interest in agriculture on the part of the local *zemstvo* organs of self-government, advances were made toward the development of a full array of agronomical extension services designed to increase both the quantity and quality of peasant inventory, fertilizer, seed, and livestock as well as to introduce more intensive systems of rotation and encourage the formation of cooperative associations.

Perhaps the most noticeable trend, and one that reflected both the general orientation of government policy as well as more powerful economic and cultural forces, was the continued increase in proportion of land cultivated by the peasantry on its own account, whether through purchase or renting. Indeed, this trend accelerated with the turn of the new century, and by the eve of the war the peasantry was directly cultivating some 90 percent of the total sown area. Moreover, because peasants cultivated their own lands more intensively than they did land they worked for non-peasant owners, their lower absolute yields per sown area were transformed into higher net yields per total area of arable land. As a consequence, by 1914 the peasantry also provided four-fifths of the exported grain. The one area in which noble landowners maintained a near monopoly, producing 90 percent of the total output, was sugar beet production, which required very high levels of investment.

Despite the various signs of progress, Russian agriculture continued to be beset by chronic instabilities in yearly output, with totals regularly varying in range by up to 30 percent in a single decade (without allowing for major crop failures). However, this was less the result either of the three-field system or the level of development, although they certainly contributed their share, than it was of the notorious unreliability of Russia's climate. The critical factor here was the heat-moisture balance. Unfortunately, it varied along the same north-west–southeast axis in inverse proportion to what the crops required, with low heat and high moisture toward the northern end of the line and high heat and low moisture in the South.

The impact of World War I* on this basic picture was, as has already been suggested, remarkably insignificant even though the mobilization of some 10 million rural dwellers, constituting approximately half of the adult male workers between the ages of twenty and fifty, and one-fifth of the work horses removed a vast quantity of labor power from the village. Thus by the spring of 1917 the overall sown area had been reduced only by 10 percent over prewar levels, somewhat more in the North and South than in the center, compensated for, in part, by a slight increase in Siberia. The total harvest, meanwhile, had decreased by a quarter. In terms of crop structure, the major changes introduced by the war were increases in the production of flax and oats, needed to supply the army, and a decrease in the overall proportion of fodder crops. On the other hand, the war had certain positive effects, for by removing such large numbers of human and animal mouths, it vastly reduced the competition for the otherwise limited supply of food among those who remained behind. In addition, the prohibition of alcohol consumption left a higher proportion of the reduced output of both grain and potatoes available for consumption.

The war also produced changes in marketing patterns, first, by shifting surplus grain away from export markets, which were virtually eliminated, to the military. At the same time, the proportion of agricultural produce going to the market declined 25 percent to about two-thirds of the smaller total. Later, the war brought on a sharp decline in the production of consumer goods, in part because of the wartime labor shortage, as well as the breakdown of the transportation network. Together, these changes succeeded in rupturing those still tenuous links between the grain-producing areas of the South and East with their surpluses and the grain-consuming areas of the North and West with their deficits, not to mention the links between town and country generally. The curtailment of both export and domestic markets had a disastrous impact both on the war effort itself and on urban standards of living. However, the gradual "naturalization" of the peasant economy and the return of the countryside to its traditional isolation and self-sufficiency actually led, in some cases and areas, to improvements in peasant well-being.

The impact of the war on gentry agriculture was much more serious—above all, because it removed the gentry's labor force. The mobilization of prisoners of war and refugees did not provide an adequate alternative. Insofar as the overall agricultural picture was concerned, however, the sharp decline in the area and output of gentry sowing was in large part compensated for by an expansion in direct peasant cultivation. Thus the fate of gentry agriculture during the war years only represented a further stage in its long decline and gradual replacement by small-scale peasant cultivation. The final elimination of a gentry agriculture during 1917–1918 and the reversion of the peasantry to communal forms of land use (except in the Northwest) merely served as a capstone to this long drawn-out process. Moreover, since the final *coup de grace* now involved only a very small proportion of the agricultural economy and its output, the long-feared disruption to both the agricultural and national economy never transpired.

Favorable weather conditions in 1917 and 1918 further contributed to Russia's ability to survive both the wartime devastation and the subsequent political chaos. Moreover, those changes that did occur were a consequence rather of the continuing disruption of industrial production, capped by the anarchic decree on workers' control and the abolition of private trade. Yet even these political acts were but the de jure recognition of a de facto situation and merely served to accelerate further the existing trends toward peasant self-sufficiency by denying them the goods for which they would be willing to exchange their surplus produce. Thus despite the instantaneous appearance of a black market, the new regime found itself with no alternative but to resort to forcible grain collections (*prodrazverstki*) in order to supply the cities and the new Red Army* with food. It was this resurgence of the coercive, interventionist state that was, in fact, to dominate the years down to the onset of the New Economic Policy *(NEP) in 1921 when compulsory requisitions were replaced by a tax in kind and the impersonal and seemingly voluntary market mechanism. The intervening years only served to emphasize the underlying conflict of interest between the new regime's production-oriented concerns and the peasantry's consumption-oriented ones.

Viewing the period of war, revolution, and civil war as a whole, Russian agriculture went through a long period of regression that reached its lowest point in 1922 and that, in conjunction with the severe drought of the previous year, helped produce one of the worst famines Russia has experienced in modern times. During this entire eight-year period, agriculture shifted with increasing rapidity away from labor-intensive and more specialized industrial and cash crops and toward the more traditional, consumption-oriented production of grain. In the process, both the regional specialization and the overall diversification of the prewar years began to break down. These developments were accompanied by a 60 percent decline in peasant handicraft production. Even more critical was the almost total disruption in the supply of agricultural machinery and implements since this not only undermined agriculture's technological basis but also placed severe strains on the village's ability to absorb the flow of population from the cities and the army and provide its new residents with the inventory necessary to support themselves.

Looked at in terms of admittedly somewhat flawed statistics, it appears that by 1921 the sown area had declined to two-thirds of what it had been in 1913 and by 1922, to 55 percent. Total agricultural output decreased equally precipitously, reaching a low point in the same year of only 45 percent of the prewar level. Similarly, the output of flax and hemp declined by 80 percent, sugar beets by 95 percent, potatoes by 83 percent, and cotton by 92 percent. Not surprisingly, yields also decreased by some 30 to 40 percent overall. In the area directly affected by the drought (41 percent of the sown area), they declined to a quarter of their former level. Regardless of these special conditions, however, the South and Southeast experienced greater declines than the North and Northwest, where yields were only marginally reduced.

Measured by sown area, there were also significant variations among the different crops. Thus comparing the worst year, 1922 in most cases, with 1913, the proportion of land sown with rye decreased by 30 percent; wheat by 75 percent; oats by 55 percent; barley by 70 percent; and buckwheat by only 12 percent. Spelt, on the other hand, increased its share by more than 50 percent. The tale was similar with regard to root crops, with potatoes declining by more than a half and sugar beets by more than three-quarters. Industrial crops such as flax and hemp each declined by two-thirds, cotton by 90 percent, peas by two-thirds, lentils and beans by 60 percent, and tobacco and fodder grasses declined almost to zero. Following a slight increase through 1916 similar to that of flax and oats, sunflower seed production also declined, though only by one-fifth. Two crops expanded their share of the sown area: maize (corn), which increased by 250 percent over its prewar level, and millet, which increased by nearly 80 percent. These changes also led to shifts in the relative importance of the different crops. In particular, rye recaptured its former dominance over wheat, expanding its share of the sown area within European Russia to 37 percent of the total. Altogether, there was a significant shift from fodder and root crops to consumption-oriented grain production, indicating a sharp decline in the intensity of cultivation in the crisis years following the revolution.

Insofar as other areas of the economy are concerned, there are no data available for fruit production, although viticulture experienced a decrease in sown area by more than a third. Beekeeping, sericulture, and chicken farming also experienced sharp declines. Finally, there were marked declines in livestock production. During the first years of the war, the reduction of herds was relatively moderate, the number of horses decreasing by 20 percent, cattle and oxen by 10 percent, and sheep by 7 percent. The two exceptions were goats, which decreased by more than half to 2.7 million, and pigs, which increased by almost a quarter to nearly 21.0 million. However, during the civil war (*see* Civil War in Russia), the losses became even sharper. By 1921 the total livestock population constituted only 65 percent of its 1916 level. The losses became even worse during the final famine year of 1922. At that time, horses numbered only 60 percent of their 1916 level; cattle and oxen, 66 percent; sheep, 48 percent; pigs, 54 percent; goats, 32 percent.

The period of revolution and civil war was not wholly negative, however. Most important, by 1922 agriculture's contribution to the national income had declined only by about 35 percent, considerably less than for other sectors of the economy. Moreover, the bleakness of the picture was counterposed by two trends in the realm of land-use patterns that not only indicated a revival of prewar patterns of development but would also present contrasting policy alternatives to the new regime as it sought a solution to the underlying problem of productivity in the future. Thus on the one hand, there was a resurgence of popular pressure for the rationalization and intensification of agriculture on individualistic principles of small-scale peasant land use and, on the other hand, a revival of the Cooperative Movement (*see* Cooperative Movement, 1917–1921) and the further application of its principles to labor and to cultivation itself, thereby opening a path to the formation of large-scale agricultural units capable of using advanced agricultural machinery. At the same time, the new regime was establishing state farms to take over the cultivation of specialized and capital-intensive crops, particularly sugar beets.

The subsequent history of agriculture during the NEP years of the 1920s was a story of considerable success with a gradual revival of earlier developments toward intensification, diversification, and specialization and a nearly complete return to prewar levels of sown area, output, and yields. By 1926–1927 agriculture contributed about 5 percent more to the national income than it had in 1913, measured in 1913 rubles. The failure to restore the grain export market, however, led to some permanent changes in crop structure, in particular a reduction in the proportion of wheat sown. Yet, even during these relatively good years, the wartime phenomena of both a scissors crisis and a goods famine initiated a new grain-supply crisis, leading the government to adopt a new round of coercive taxation and the complete collectivization of agriculture at the end of the 1920s (*see* Agrarian Policy, 1917–1921; Soviets [Councils] of Workers', Soldiers', and Peasants' Deputies; Peasants in the Russian Revolution).

David A. J. Macey

Bibliography

Anfimov, A. M. *Rossiiskaia derevnia v gody pervoi mirovoi voiny (1914-fevral' 1917 g.).* 1962.
Antsiferov, Alexis N., Batshev, M. O., and Ivantsov, P. N. *Russian Agriculture during the War.* 1968.
Chelintsev, A. N. *Sel'sko-khoziaistvennaia geografiia Rossii.* 1923.
Dubrovskii, S. M. *Sel'skoe khoziaistvo i krestianstvo Rossii v period imperializma.* 1975.
Gordeev, G. S. *Sel'skoe khoziaistvo v voine i revoliutsii.* 1925.
Karnaukhova, E. S. *Razmeshchenie selskogo khoziaistva Rossii v period kapitalizma (1860–1914 gg.).* 1951.
Knipovich, V. N. *Glavnye cherty Sel.-Khoz. Evoliutsii Evropeiskoi Rossii v 1916–1921 gg.* 1923.
Oganovskii, N. P. *Sel'skoe khoziaistvo Rossii v XX veke. Sbornik statistiko-ekonomicheskikh svedenii za 1901–1922 gg.* 1923.
Pavlovsky, George. *Agricultural Russia on the Eve of the Revolution.* 1968.
Volin, Lazar. *A Century of Russian Agriculture: From Alexander II to Khrushchev.* 1970.

Akselrod, Pavel Borisovich (1850–1928). Akselrod was a prominent Menshevik leader, one of the founders of Russian Social Democracy.

Born in a small village in Chernigov Province, he had an impoverished childhood. He studied at Kiev University. During the 1870s Akselrod was an adherent of the *narodnik* movement, for whose publications he worked as editor. He left Russia in 1880 and, in 1883 with G. V. Plekhanov* and others, founded Gruppa Osvobozhdeniia Truda (Group for the Liberation of Labor), forerunner of the Russian Social Democratic Workers' Party (Bolshevik)*. He served as theorist and publicist for the Russian Marxist movement and as editor of the journal *Iskra* (*Spark*) after 1900. He was active in the Second International.

After 1905 Akselrod was characterized as a "liquidator" by the Bolsheviks for advocating legal work among trade unions instead of revolutionary activity. During World War I* he was a centrist. After the February Revolution* he became a member of the Executive Committee of the Petrograd Soviet* and supported the Provisional Government*. He emigrated after the October Seizure of Power and died in Berlin (*see* Russian Social Democratic Workers' Party [Menshevik]).

Bibliography

Israel Getzler. *Martov.* 1967.

Alash-Orda. The Alash-Orda was the major nationalist movement among the Kazakhs and Kirghiz in Kazakhstan in 1917. (*see* Kazakhstan, Revolution in).

It was a Kazakh–Kirghiz nationalist political movement founded at the First All-Kazakh Congress in Orenburg, July 21–26, 1917. It grew out of the activity of those Kazakh intellectuals taking part in the activities of the newspaper *Kazakh* from 1911 to 1917, including A. B. Baitursinov, A. Bukeikhanov, and Kh. Dosmukhammedov. Although the Kazakhs and Kirghiz were ethnically and linguistically Turkic, they favored Westernization and the political philosophy of the Constitutional Democratic Party—Cadet* because of its emphasis on cultural self-determination. That posture lost them the support of some Moslem intellectuals, such as Amangeldy Imanov, to more radical movements. The goal of Alash-Orda was to mobilize Kazakh nationalism against both the threat of Russian settlers and of the economically, culturally, and religiously dominant Tatars. In 1916 they played a leading role in the Kazakh revolt against the tsarist government.

The name "Alash" refers to the mythical founder of the Kazakh–Kirghiz tribes; "Orda" refers to the seat of government of the ancient Kazakh sultans. The movement established close contact with the Bashkirs and the Orenburg Cossacks*, and by the summer of 1917 it was calling for territorial autonomy for each national group. Russian colonists in Kazakhstan, located primarily in the cities, tended to gravitate toward the budding Bolshevik movement as a bulwark against the native nationalist movements.

The October Seizure of Power* did not have much immediate impact on the Kazakhs, but in December 1917 the Third All-Kazakh Congress met in Orenburg under the protection of General A. I. Dutov* and his Cossacks and proclaimed a Kazakh republic under the Alash-Orda leaders. Semipalitinsk became one of the new capitals in the East under Bukeikhanov, and Jambeitu became a second capital city in the West under Dosmukhammedov. During the Civil War (*see* Civil War in Russia) Dosmukhammedov collaborated with the Ural Cossacks and Bukeikhanov with the Whites (*see* White Movement) in Siberia. In 1919, facing defeat, the Alash-Orda leaders defected to the Bolsheviks, and in July 1919 many of them joined the Kirrevkom (the Kirghiz–Kazakh Revolutionary Committee), the core of the future Kazakh Soviet government. In the absence of Kazakh Bolsheviks, the Alash-Orda leaders assumed a significant role in Kirrevkom. But the role of native nationalists, in particular the Alash-Orda leader Baitursinov, was reduced when the Kirghiz Autonomous Republic was created on August 26, 1920. Of the ten members of the new Kirrevkom formed at that juncture, only five were Turkish. The Bolshevik agrarian reforms reduced native dissatisfaction by redistributing Cossack, state, and church lands. Nonetheless, the Alash-Orda leaders played an important role in the Soviet leadership in Kazakhstan for the next five years and continued to defend Kazakh nationalist positions (*see* Central Asia, Revolution in; Kazakhstan, Revolution in.)

Bibliography

Bennigsen, Alexandre A., and Wimbush, S. Enders. *Muslim National Communism in the Soviet Union*. 1979.
Zenkovsky, S. A. *Pan-Turkism and Islam in Russia*. 1960.

Aleksandrov, Mikhail Stepanov (1863–1933; party name, Ol'minsky). Aleksandrov was a prominent Old Bolshevik (*see* Russian Social Democratic Workers' Party [Bolshevik]) who took part in the preparation for the Soviet seizure of power in Petrograd and Moscow and later became a prominent historian of the Revolution. He was born in Voronezh into an aristocratic family. He joined the peasant political movement, or Populists (The Peoples' Will), in 1885 while attending the University of St. Petersburg. In 1894 he was arrested for publishing and distributing a workers' newspaper in St. Petersburg. He was sentenced to eight years in prison, the first three to be served in solitary confinement. During his exile Aleksandrov became a Marxist and an accomplished writer.

In 1905 he returned from exile and immigrated to Switzerland, becoming a leading propagandist for the Bolsheviks. He was one of the founders of the first legal Bolsheviks newspaper, *Pravda* (Truth), in 1912 in St. Petersburg.

After the February Revolution* in 1917 Aleksandrov helped to create the Bolshevik daily newspaper *Sotsial-demokrat* in Moscow, where he worked on and off until the Bolsheviks took power. After the October Seizure of Power* Aleksandrov served a brief stint as Deputy Minister of Finance but had to resign because of ill health. When he returned to full-time active party work in 1919, he was appointed as chief editor of the official commission charged with writing the history of the October Revolution (*Istpart*). To a large extent, he is responsible for the invaluable series of memoirs of party members published in the 1970s chiefly in the historical journal *Proletarskaia Revoliutsiia*. These memoirs remain among the most useful sources of information to historians all over the world who wish to piece together the role of the Bolsheviks in the events of 1917. In 1922 Aleksandrov established the Society of Old Bolsheviks.

In 1922 those who disagreed with Aleksandrov's approach to party history and the history of the October Revolution, that is, his emphasis on source materials and memoirs rather than the work of professional historians, unseated him as chief editor of *Istpart*. Although in semiretirement, Aleksandrov continued to struggle against the sanitization and politicization of party history and the growing cult of Lenin. During the Stalin* era the place of the Old Bolsheviks in party history all but vanished as the exaggeration of Stalin's role in the Revolution continued to grow. After Stalin's death in 1952 and Khrushchev's de-Stalinization speech in 1956 at the Twentieth Party Congress, there was a renewed interest in Aleksandrov's approach to the Bolshevik past (*see* Historiography).

Bibliography

Amiantov Iu, *Rytsar bol'shevizma*. 1960.
Lezhava, O. A., and Nelidov, N. V. *M.S. Ol'minskii*. 1962.

Allied Blockade. Russia's economic isolation began in August 1914. During the following seven years, Russia was virtually cut off from international trade.

Before World War I*, Russia's main link to the international economy was Germany, from which in 1913 half of its imports—particularly machinery, electrical supplies, agricultural machines, instruments, chemicals and medicines, and other complex finished products—had come. Wartime Allied loans and assistance, consisting primarily of military supplies, did not offset this loss. Indeed, while the Allies extended and perfected their economic war against the Central Powers, they also separated Russia from the world. Already in 1915 it was apparent that Russia's backward economy, inadequate social and political organization, and inefficient administration could meet neither the rapidly growing demands of modern war nor the needs of the civilian population. Russia was about to enter a new "time of troubles."

After the October Seizure of Power* the Allied leaders were worried about the consequences of the eastern front's collapse and uncertain about the resolution of Russia's latest political turmoil. Informed of growing hostility toward the Soviet regime, they immediately sought to remedy a dangerous situation, particularly the breach in the economic encirclement of Germany, by extending the blockade to territories controlled by the new Soviet government to forestall Germany's suspected designs to dominate and exploit Russia. All financial transactions were stopped, the Russian goods and assets were seized, and an embargo was placed on all goods to Russia. At first, a few shipments of nonmilitary goods were still sent because the Allies wished to keep their vague promise to aid the Russian people. Eventually, however, Great Britain assumed the leadership in economic matters and declared even food a contraband, despite the opposition of the United States. Other countries were persuaded or coerced into joining the blockade.

The Allied governments attempted to retrieve supplies located in neutral countries and in Russia. Efforts to secure goods within Russia through purchase or exchange generally failed because the Allies had to negotiate with the Soviet regime and because a state of undeclared war existed between the Allies and Soviet Russia. After the Brest-Litovsk* Treaty was signed, the Allies occupied Vladivostok, Murmansk, and Archangel and seized huge stocks of mostly Allied goods, thus denying them to Germany and Soviet Russia. With the exception of the German–Soviet connection, the Allies succeeded in isolating Soviet Russia by the middle of 1918. The Allies were resolved to vanquish both Germany and Soviet Russia.

Allied military and economic assistance to the Whites (*see* White Movement) increased sharply toward the end of 1918. The Allies were now committed to assist in the formation of a liberal-democratic Russia through military intervention and, favored particularly by the United States, implementation of a policy of economic reconstruction.

After the end of the war in Europe, the Allies decided to maintain the blockade of Germany until the peace treaty was signed. The maintenance of the blockade

of Germany provided the pretext for completing the blockade of Soviet Russia.
Allied navies now also controlled the Baltic, Black, and Caspian seas. Before
1918 ended, Allied troops occupied additional areas in Russia. In November
1918 Admiral A. V. Kolchak* had become "Supreme Ruler" of White Russian
forces, promising to unite all anti-Bolshevik movements and, with Allied support,
to put an end to the Soviet regime.

In 1919, while gradually dismantling wartime economic restrictions, the Allies
maintained the blockade of Soviet Russia. Concerned about the spread of communism—which they regarded as a product of misery and desperation against
which even large armies might not prevail—and recognizing that they could not
continue military intervention partially because of growing domestic opposition,
the Allies increasingly turned to non-military solutions: they provided counterrevolutionary White Russian forces with more relief, consumer goods, and military aid; they intended to demonstrate the contrast between a poor and a contented
Russia and sought to make the latter attractive to people living in Soviet Russia.

The blockade issue became controversial again after the signing of the peace
treaty with Germany in June 1919. While military intervention was gradually
ending, the Allies were searching for ways to maintain the blockade particularly
because the White armies appeared to be making good headway. Even British
War Office officials believed that Bolshevism could now be defeated by primarily
economic rather than military means.

These propitious circumstances made Allied unity again a necessity, and the
British government led the way toward achieving a common Russian policy.
After lengthy debates in October 1919, the Allies asked all other governments
to join in comprehensive international economic sanctions against Soviet Russia,
which included a physical blockade of land and sea routes, an embargo on all
trade, and prohibitions of travel and communications. This effort to strengthen,
perpetuate, and legitimize Soviet Russia's isolation, while the policy to aid the
Whites and the emerging border states continued, was the clearest expression
yet of an Allied–Russian policy. It was a compromise between France's demand
for still stronger action and the more moderate position of the United States,
which was plagued by doubts about the scheme's legality and the motives of
the major Allies.

Most governments readily agreed to participate; only Sweden and Germany
balked, questioning the efficacy of the enterprise. In the meantime, however,
the Civil War (*see* Civil War in Russia) turned decisively against the Whites on
all fronts. These two events dashed Allied efforts. Great Britain's Prime Minister
Lloyd George quickly adjusted to the new circumstances. He proposed encouraging peace negotiations between Soviet Russia and the border states, exchanging
prisoners, easing tensions, and resuming trade relations. His new initiative was
all the more understandable because he had been concerned for some time about
Great Britain's and Europe's dependence on expensive American raw materials
and food supplies, growing domestic discontent, the bankruptcy of previous
Allied policies, and the fear shared by many high-ranking officials that Germany

LIBRARY MEDIA CENTER
ALBUQUERQUE ACADEMY

or the United States might attain a dominant position in the Russian economy. Lloyd George now announced that he was convinced that the restoration of trade would lead to more normal conditions in Russia, including a more moderate regime; he now considered trade a solvent of extremism. Restoring a sound Russian economy would improve the social and political climate of Soviet Russia. Force had failed; perhaps Russia could be saved through trade.

In January 1920 Lloyd George persuaded the Allies to lift the blockade and authorize the resumption of trade through Russia's cooperative societies, which, however, were already controlled by the Soviet government. Only the United States, suspicious of this new development, did not take part in this decision and moved further away from her Allies, eventually formulating its own Russian policy announced in mid–1920 by Secretary of State Bainbridge Colby.

In essence, the new gambit was a continuation of the old policy by other means; it, too, was based on faulty information and erroneous assumptions and, like other policies before, was destined to fail. For Soviet Russia, however, the lifting of the blockade meant the removal of a major barrier, actual and symbolic, to the resumption of commercial and political relations with other countries, providing new opportunities at home and abroad, and diminishing the prospects of a renewed Allied offensive undertaking.

The blockade abetted the reduction of Russia's foreign trade to negligible amounts and values (1919: 3 million gold rubles) and exacerbated its economic, social, and political difficulties. Yet it did not induce the collapse of Soviet Russia. Beyond this, there is little agreement about the blockade's efficacy and its impact on economic and political development of Soviet Russia.

Norbert Gaworek

Bibliography

Bukharin, N. I. *Ekonomika perekhodnogo perioda.* 1920.
Committee for the Regeneration of Russia. *The Blockade of Soviet Russia.* 1920.
Ioffe, Ia. A. *Organisatsiia interventsii i blokady sovetskoi respubliki, 1918–1920.* 1930.
Kaverin, I. N. *Za kulisami angliiskoi blokady: iz istorii pervoi mirovoi voiny.* 1955.
Larin, Iu., and Kristman, L. *Wirtschaftsleben und wirtschaftlicher Aufbau in Sowjet-Russland, 1917–1920.* 1921.
Narodnyi komissariat inostrannikh del. *Délégation de Russie à Gênes, Máteriaux et documents sur l'intervention, le blocus, et les dommages causés par eux à la Russie.* 1924.
Nolde, Boris E. *Russia in the Economic War.* 1928.
Sutton, Anthony C. *Western Technology and Soviet Economic Development, 1917–1930.* 1968.

All Power to the Soviets. All Power to the Soviets was the Bolshevik slogan in 1917.

Surely the most famous slogan of the Russian Revolution, "All Power to the Soviets" was first articulated by V. I. Lenin* in his April Theses*. Lenin envisioned a republic of soviets as the political form of the dictatorship of the proletariat. The specific content of the slogan changed in 1917. From April through June, during the so-called peaceful development of the Revolution, the slogan called for the end of the "Dual Power"* through the peaceful transfer of governance from the Provisional Government* to the soviets as organs of the revolutionary democracy. At this time leadership of the soviets was in the hands of the Mensheviks (*see* Russian Social Democratic Workers' Party [Menshevik]) and the Socialist–Revolutionaries (*see* Socialist-Revolutionary Party) with the Bolsheviks (*see* Russian Social Democratic Workers' Party [Bolshevik]) constituting a minority opposition party.

Given the resistance to the idea of a socialist government by the Menshevik and the Socialist–Revolutionary (S–R) forces dominating the Central Executive Committee of the All-Russian Congress of Soviets (*see* All-Russian Central Executive Committee), and as a consequence of the "July Days"*, the slogan was temporarily abandoned at the Bolshevik Sixth Party Congress (July 26-August 3, 1917). It was replaced by a new, rather vague slogan proposed by Lenin advocating a dictatorship of the proletariat and the poorer peasants. In the aftermath of the aborted coup by General L. G. Kornilov (*see* Kornilov Revolt) and the subsequent Bolshevik victories in the Petrograd, Moscow, and other soviets, "All Power to the Soviets" was resurrected. Implicit now, from Lenin's point of view, was a violent overthrow of the Provisional Government and a dominant position for the Bolshevik Party in the resulting Soviet government. The October Seizure of Power* in Petrograd was ratified by the Second All-Russian Congress of Soviets, although there was considerable opposition both within and outside the Bolshevik Party to the exclusion of Mensheviks, S–R's, and other parties from the revolutionary government, the Council of Peoples' Commissars*.

Bibliography

Daniels, R. V. *Red October*. 1967.
Rabinowitch, A. *The Bolsheviks Come to Power*. 1976.

All-Russian Association of Soviets of Worker's and Soldier's Deputies. *See* Soviets (Councils) of Workers', Soldiers', and Peasants' Deputies.

All-Russian Central Council of Trade Unions (ACCTU) (Vserossiiskii tsentral'nyi sovet professional'nykh soiuzov). The All-Russian Central Council of Trade Unions was the elected leadership organ of the trade union movement in Russia.

The ACCTU was created by the Third All-Russian Conference of Trade Unions, which met in Petrograd, June 20–28, 1917. The conference delegates, 211 representing 967 unions with nearly 1.5 million members, were almost evenly divided between Bolsheviks and Mensheviks. This was reflected in the Executive Committee elections, which yielded 5 Mensheviks and 4 Bolsheviks. The chairman was the Menshevik V. Grinevich. Before the October Revolution (*see* October Seizure of Power), neither Mensheviks nor Bolsheviks succeeded in establishing dominance in the ACCTU, and that body played no real part in the October seizure.

Following the seizure of power, Bolshevik influence in the trade unions increased. At the First All-Russian Congress of Trade Unions, January 7–14, 1918, seven of the nine members of the ACCTU were Bolsheviks, with the Bolsheviks G. E. Zinoviev* named chairman and V. V. Shmidt named secretary. In March M. P. Tomsky was elected chairman. The ACCTU did not restrict itself only to traditional trade union concerns. In this period it participated in administering nationalized enterprises and the creation of the Red Army*. During the Civil War (*see* Civil War in Russia) it sought to coordinate labor's contribution to the defense of the Revolution.

In 1924 the organization's name was changed to All-Union Central Council of Trade Unions under which name it continues to operate. (*see* Trade Unions in the Russian Revolution.)

All-Russian Central Executive Committee (Vserossiiskii tsentral'nyi ispolnitel'nyi komitet [VTsIK]). The All-Russian Central Executive Committee of Soviets of Workers' and Soldiers' Deputies (VTsIK) was created by the First All-Russian Congress of Soviets on June 17, 1917. Its formation was largely due to the demand from provincial and regional soviets for some body that could provide general supervision for provincial soviets and coordinate policy throughout Russia. For example, the All-Russian Conference (Soveshchanie) of Soviets (March 29-April 3) had instructed all regional congresses of soviets to elect regional executive committees that could coordinate Soviet policy in the provinces, supply new soviets with literature and personnel, and help organize an All-Russian congress of soviets. The All-Russian Congress of Soviets, in turn, was to create a permanent all-Russian central organ of soviets of workers' and soldiers' deputies. This demand for a national executive committee had been supported by many soviets, including the influential Moscow Regional Bureau of Soviets and the Petrograd Soviet*.

According to its founding decrees, VTsIK remained responsible for its actions before all-Russian congresses of soviets, which ratified the actions of VTsIK. In the interim between Soviet congresses, however, VTsIK was to direct the forces of "revolutionary democracy" in Russia, protect the victories of the Revolution, conduct revolutionary propaganda, and supervise the socialist ministers in the Provisional Government*. These ministers were to remain responsible to VTsIK for their statements on both foreign and domestic questions. The decrees of VTsIK were to be binding on all soviets of workers' and soldiers' deputies until the next All-Russian Congress of Soviets. The first VTsIK, elected on the basis of proportional representation from all delegations at the First All-Russian Congress of Soviets, included 150 representatives who resided in Petrograd, 100 members who were to be sent to the provinces to work, and specific representatives from nine political parties. VTsIK could also coopt additional representatives from socialist organizations at its discretion. In addition to those elected by the Soviet congress, VTsIK included representatives from the trade unions, the All-Russian Railway Union (*see* All-Russian Executive Committee of the Union of Railwaymen), and the Executive Committee of the Petrograd Soviet. At the first plenum of VTsIK on June 21, N. S. Chkheidze* was unanimously elected chairman. At the same meeting VTsIK selected a presidium of nine people from the three major political factions—Bolsheviks, Mensheviks, and Socialist–Revolutionaries (*see* Russian Social Democratic Workers' Party [Bolshevik]; Russian Social Democratic Workers' Party [Menshevik]; Socialist-Revolutionary Party)—and a bureau of fifty people, which included the presidium and representatives from political delegations of at least five people. VTsIK members working in the provinces were to have a "deciding vote" in all VTsIK plenums but only a "consultative vote" in the regional bureaus in which they worked.

On June 27 VTsIK decreed that the plenum was to direct all activities, reviewing and confirming all decisions of its bureau, concerning major political issues. The plenum was to meet not less than once a week with a quorum of 50 percent of those VTsIK members who resided in Petrograd. The bureau, on the other hand, was to act as the executive organ of the plenum, conducting all business work of VTsIK and implementing political and organizational decisions. If for some reason a plenum could not be convened, the bureau could make emergency decisions. These actions, however, were subject to review by the next plenary meeting. The bureau was to meet daily with a quorum of two members from the presidium plus one-third of the members of the bureau. The Mensheviks, who had twenty-one representatives, and the Socialist–Revolutionaries, who had nineteen members, dominated this key inner group of VTsIK. Bolshevik representation in the bureau totaled seven delegates. The last subgroup was the VTsIK presidium, which could make emergency decisions only if the bureau could not be convened. This presidium was split evenly between Mensheviks and Socialist–Revolutionaries, each of which had four representatives, while the Bolsheviks were given one representative.

The VTsIK bureau met frequently during the early part of 1917 and considered questions such as the state of military affairs in the Ukraine, the authorization of military commissars, the election of a central committee for the Russian navy, and the progress of a campaign against anti-Semitism in the provinces. The delegation of powers at the national level was imitated by provincial soviets, which also elected executive committees with plenums, bureaus, and presidiums. By the beginning of July, VTsIK began to meet jointly with the All-Russian Executive Committee of the Soviet of Peasants' Deputies. The national peasant executive committee, while participating in these sessions, successfully thwarted efforts by VTsIK to merge the two bodies and retained its own sovereignty.

VTsIK played an important role in both the "July Days"* and in the subsequent "mutiny" of L. G. Kornilov (*see* Kornilov Revolt) in late August. In the first case, thousands of demonstrators, led by the First Machine Gun Regiment of Kronstadt, demanded on July 3 that power be transferred to the soviets from the faltering Provisional Government. A joint meeting of VTsIK and the national peasant executive committee condemned these disturbances as dangerous to the Revolution. The joint resolution on July 3 called for "quick and resolute measures" to protect revolutionary order and freedom. The demonstrators were not to be put off, however, and invaded the Tauride Palace where the executive committees were in session, demanding that they take power. VTsIK held firm, however, and, after an all-night meeting, issued the appeal "To All Workers and Soldiers of Petrograd." This statement blamed the demonstration on "unknown people" who were bent upon destroying the will of all socialist parties. It branded as "traitors" all those who persisted in the armed demonstration. Having condemned the disturbances, VTsIK, on July 5, also issued an ultimatum to the Kronstadt sailors to either surrender and leave Petrograd or be disarmed by force. VTsIK also supported indirectly the military attack against Bolshevik headquarters, ordered by the Provisional Government and carried out by loyal troops. The moderate leadership of VTsIK was also able to pass a motion that called for a plenum of the executive committee (meeting jointly with the national peasant executive committee) to decide the question of reconstructing the Provisional Government. Until that time, soviets were to give their support to the existing government. Should it be decided to transfer power to the soviets, only a full meeting of the two executive committees had the power to make the decision legal.

VTsIK also responded to the attempt by Kornilov in late August to depose the established order and form a strongman government. After a report by I. G. Tsereteli* on August 27, VTsIK and the national peasant Executive Committee passed a resolution that instructed A. F. Kerensky* to form a new government, the central task of which was to defeat the mutinous general. They also instructed railway workers to avert any unnecessary bloodshed by disrupting troop movements toward Petrograd, a task that the railroad men successfully carried out. By the beginning of September 1917, in response to the Kornilov affair, VTsIK established a special committee for the struggle against counterrevolution.

As the more radical political parties (Bolshevik Party; Left Socialist-Revolutionary Party) began to increase in strength and capture strategic soviets in the fall of 1917, the Menshevik and Socialist–Revolutionary leaders of VTsIK found themselves increasingly on the defensive. By October VTsIK was unable to prevent an important congress of soviets of the northern region, which had been called by the Helsingfors Soviet rather than the VTsIK bureau. VTsIK also tried to retain control over the preparations for the Second All-Russian Congress of Soviets. The VTsIK bureau claimed that only it and a special VTsIK commission had the right to call such a congress, establish the electoral rules that governed such a gathering, and prepare an agenda. On October 19 VTsIK warned workers and soldiers not to respond to any calls for demonstrations, blaming them on "dark forces" that aimed to subvert the Revolution. When the Second All-Russian Congress of Soviets finally met in Petrograd on October 25, it deposed the VTsIK dominated by Mensheviks and Socialist–Revolutionaries and elected a new national executive committee of 102 full members and 34 candidate members. Among the Bolsheviks' 62 full members and 29 candidate members were V. I. Lenin*, L. D. Trotsky*, G. E. Zinoviev*, L. B. Kamenev*, I. V. Stalin*, Ia. M. Sverdlov*, and F. E. Dzerzhinskii*; the Left Socialist-Revolutionary Party* delegation of 30 members and 5 candidate members included M. A. Spiridonova, B. V. Kamkov, and V. A. Karelin. The only other major political factions were the United Social Democratic Internationalists (6 members), Ukrainian socialists (3 representatives), and S–R Maximalists (1 delegate).

This VTsIK confronted several obstacles. The "old" VTsIK, dissolved by the Second All-Russian Congress of Soviets, refused to die. It continued to meet and issue appeals that opposed the Second Soviet Congress, the new VTsIK, and the Council of Peoples' Commissars* (Sovnarkom). Merging with and financing the Committee for the Salvation of the Motherland and Revolution*, the "old" VTsIK continued to meet throughout 1917, passing resolutions against the government and supporting the Constituent Assembly.

A second issue was the demand for a broader-based government of all socialist parties. This demand, presented by the executive committee of the All-Russian Executive Committee of the Union of Railwaymen* (Vikzhel), was supported by the Left Socialist–Revolutionaries, Menshevik Internationalists, and many Bolsheviks, including the moderate chairman of VTsIK, L. B. Kamenev. Kamenev shared the view that only a socialist coalition could retain power and supported negotiations with Vikzhel representatives. On November 4, however, these Bolsheviks, who were in a minority in the Central Committee, were given an ultimatum by the majority to either submit to party discipline on this question or face expulsion. Kamenev (and others) resigned from the Central Committee in protest, but he continued in his capacity as VTsIK chairman to work for a socialist coalition. This arrangement did not please Lenin, who, using the Central Committee of the Bolsheviks (see Central Committee of the Russian Communist Party [Bolshevik]), removed Kamenev from his post. The new chairman was Ia. M. Sverdlov, a young "professional revolutionary," a staunch Leninist, and director of the Bolshevik Secretariat. This change, ratified by VTsIK on November 8, undermined the chances for a coalition government of socialists. The growing military threat to the government superceded this demand, and it was finally dropped.

The relationship between VTsIK and the government, represented by the Council of Peoples' Commissars (Sovnarkom), was not clearly defined. In theory, VTsIK, as the supreme power between all-Russian congresses of soviets, had the right to confirm or reject any decree issued by the Sovnarkom. It could also request periodic reports on the activities of the Sovnarkom. The Sovnarkom, on the other hand, was to battle counterrevolution directly. In practice, the working scheme was for matters of major political importance to pass through the executive committee for review and authorization. After the election of Sverdlov as chairman of VTsIK, he and the Bolshevik majority were not prepared to check the independent policy-making of the Sovnarkom. In fact, the Bolshevik majority began to use VTsIK to confer legitimacy on Sovnarkom decrees, which originated in the Bolshevik Central Committee. This situation was not altered by the merger on November 15 of the National Peasant Executive Committee with VTsIK and the entry of the Left Socialist–Revolutionaries into the Sovnarkom. This merger gave equal representation to peasant delegates (108 seats by this time) but deprived the Left S–R's of an independent executive committee and made them responsible for Sovnarkom decrees. The Left S–R's soon found that they were unable to repeal in VTsIK extralegal decrees such as the closure of opposition newspapers, the establishment of revolutionary tribunals, and the dissolution of the Petrograd City Duma, all of which had been issued by Sovnarkom without VTsIK authorization.

The structure of VTsIK itself began to change after November 1917. The presidium, formerly the least prestigious inner committee within VTsIK, gradually evolved into the real center of power and eclipsed the authority of the plenum. On December 12 a new presidium was elected and contained twelve Bolsheviks, seven Left S–R's, and one United Social Democrat Internationalist. Smaller political delegations were denied representation by the electoral rules. Despite the absence of a delineation of its functions in the 1918 constitution, the presidium became the chief policy-making body within VTsIK. It played a crucial role in the victory of the Leninists in the controversy over the Brest-Litovsk Treaty (when it was again expanded and its powers broadened), the arrest of the Moscow anarchists, and the exclusion from VTsIK of the Mensheviks and Right and Center Socialist–Revolutionaries on grounds of counterrevolutionary activity. After the Left S–R revolt at the Fifth All-Russian Congress of Soviets (July 1918), the new VTsIK elected by that congress was completely in the hands of the communists, who had 157 members out of a total of approximately 200. The only other representatives were Left S–R's who had condemned the revolt by their Central Committee (11 delegates), S–R Maximalists (4 representatives), and 6 "non-elected" (*nedovyb*) members. After July 1918 there was rarely genuine debate over policy and appearances of Sovnarkom representatives became little more than a formality. VTsIK abandoned all pretense of equality with the Sovnarkom and simply enforced the decrees of the latter within the soviet apparatus. The presidium, whose functions were finally defined by the Seventh All-Russian Congress of Soviets in December 1919, retained its privileged position within VTsIK and continued to implement the policies of the Bolshevik Central Committee through VTsIK.

Charles Duval

Bibliography

Avdeev, N. et al., eds. *Revoliutsiia 1917 goda: khronika sobytii*. Vols. 3–6. 1923–1930.

Chamberlin, William H. *The Russian Revolution, 1917–1921*. 2 vols. 1957.

Fedorov, K. G. *VTsIK v pervye gody sovetskoi vlasti, 1917–1920 gg*. 1957.

Gorin, P. O., ed. *Organizatsiia i stroitel'stvo sovetov RD V 1917 gody*. 1928.

Keep, John L. H. *The Russian Revolution: A Study in Mass Mobilization.* 1976.
Kleandrova, V. M. *Organizatsiia i formy deiatel'nosti VTsIK (1917–1924 gg.).* 1968.
Protokoly zasedanii VTsIKa sovetov R., S., Kr., i Kaz. deputatov II sozyva. 1918.
Rabinowitch, Alexander. *The Bolsheviks Come to Power: The Revolution of 1917 in Petrograd.* 1976.
Radkey, Oliver H. *The Sickle under the Hammer: The Russian Socialist Revolutionaries in the Early Years.* 1963.
Razgon, A. I. *VTsIK sovetov v pervye mesiatsy diktatury proletariata.* 1977.

All-Russian Communist Party of the Soviet Union. *See* Russian Social Democratic Workers' Party (Bolshevik).

All-Russian Congresses. *See* appropriate organizations.

All-Russian Constituent Assembly. *See* Constituent Assembly.

All-Russian Council of People's Commissars. *See* Council of People's Commissars, 1917–1922.

All-Russian Democratic Council. *See* Democratic Conference.

All-Russian Executive Committee of the Union of Railwaymen (Vserossiiskii Ispolnitel'nyi Komitet Zheleznodorozhnego Souiza). The Union of Railwaymen, of which this was the executive organ, was one of the most extreme examples of syndicalism in action during the Russian Revolution. Not only did the union embrace every railway worker and literally take over the operation of Russia's railroads, but it also nearly succeeded in forcing the Bolsheviks (*see* Russian Social Democratic Workers' Party [Bolshevik]) to create a genuine coalition government after the October Seizure of Power*.

The All-Russian Executive Committee of the Union of Railwaymen (Vikzhel) was created at the First All-Russian Congress of Railwaymen between July 15 and August 25, 1917. Five hundred delegates gathered for that meeting with the Left Socialist–Revolutionaries (*see* Left Socialist-Revolutionary Party) clearly dominating the meeting. Of the 500 delegates, only 2 were Bolsheviks and 2 were members of the Interdistrict Committee* (Mezhraiontsyi). Of the 40 members elected to the new Executive Committee (Vikzhel), only 2 were Bolsheviks, although those 2 did come from the strategically located Moscow branch of the union. The mood of the congress was optimistic,and it promised the Provisional Government* its full support in the expectation that its own influence on that government would insure continued progress toward socialism and democracy.

An All-Russian Union of Railwaymen had been created in the 1905 Revolution (*see* Nineteen-Five Revolution), and it had played a decisive role in the October general strike in that year, but the union vanished after the failure of the December uprising. However, the memory of a successful general strike of railroad workers lived on and influenced the decisions of the railwaymen in 1917 about the structure of the new union. The new All-Russian Union of Railwaymen was created on April 6, 1917, at the First All-Russian Conference of Railwaymen in Moscow. The 200 delegates who attended that meeting decided to create a mass union rather than separate craft unions. From the beginning, the new union was dominated by moderate socialists who formed the organization on democratic principles and rigorous adherence to the principles of decentralization and self-government, which in practice made it extremely difficult for the organization to mobilize its members effectively for the pursuit of any single program of action. This also made them less effective than they might have been in implementing successfully their goal of workers' control when it was within their reach.

Vikzhel had inner divisions as well. Its left wing consisted of fifteen members who were Left Socialist–Revolutionaries, Bolsheviks, or Menshevik-Internationalists (*see* Russian Social Democratic Workers' Party [Menshevik]; Internationalists), and its right wing consisted of Mensheviks, Right Wing Socialist–Revolutionaries, and Popular Socialists. The remainder of the members of the Executive Committee tended to support the right wing, although they had no firm party affiliation. On September 15 a Left Socialist–Revolutionary, A. L. Malitskii, became chairman of Vikzhel. The Bolsheviks made little headway in winning significant support in the union and its Executive Committee, perhaps because of their emphasis on centralization, whereas the railwaymen were strongly in favor of workers' control.

After the October Seizure of Power in Petrograd only one organization seemed able to mediate between the right-wing socialists, who wanted an all-socialist coalition democratic government, and the radical Left socialists around Lenin, who had seized the reins of power.

When L. B. Kamenev* appeared before the Second Congress of Soviets on October 26 and read a list of the new members of the Council of Peoples' Commissars (the all-Bolshevik cabinet that would now govern Russia), a delegate from Vikzhel asked for the floor. After first being denied the opportunity to speak, he was finally allowed to read a statement in which he announced that his organization was opposed to the seizure of political power by any single party and that therefore it would take over the operation and administration of Russia's railroads itself until a genuine revolutionary socialist government was formed that was "responsible to the plenipotentiary organ of the whole revolutionary democracy." If the Bolshevik government took any punitive action against the railwaymen, he said, they would cut off all supplies going into Petrograd. Vikzhel called a conference of socialist parties on October 29 and threatened to call a general railroad strike if there was no truce in the fighting in Petrograd. Feeling extremely vulnerable in this desperate situation, the Bolsheviks agreed to attend the conference, but the fighting for control of Petrograd continued.

A coalition of moderates took shape, including leaders from the Left Socialist–Revolutionaries, the Menshevik–Internationalists, the Petrograd Trade Union Soviet, and the Central Soviet of Factory Shop Committees. They gradually abandoned the notion of removing the Bolsheviks from positions of power and began to negotiate between October 29 and 31, with Vikzhel asking for an all-socialist government that would include Bolsheviks, with the exception of Lenin and Trotsky.

By October 31, however, the military threat to Petrograd and the Bolshevik government from General P. N. Krasnov and his Cossacks* had ended. Between October 29 and 31 the Bolsheviks sent negotiators who were somewhat sympathetic to the Vikzhel position. But during that period Vikzhel scarcely seemed responsive to proposals from the Bolsheviks. When the crisis ended, however, it was the Bolsheviks' turn to display indifference. Lenin and Trotsky, no longer distracted by the military crisis, returned to party meetings on November 1 and told party delegates to demonstrate the impossibility of collaborating with the moderates and to bring the negotiations to a halt as soon as possible. The negotiations dragged on until, finally, on November 10 at the All-Russian Congress of Peasant Deputies in Petrograd, Vikzhel accepted a one-sided compromise by which three Left Socialist–Revolutionaries were admitted to the Council of Peoples' Commissars, and a member of Vikzhel became Commissar of Communications. Later, when the Constituent Assembly* was about to meet in January 1918, Vikzhel gave that institution a vote of confidence, once again hoping to intervene to preserve some vestige of representative government, but to no avail.

Although Lenin's drive for dominance of the new Soviet government was not in doubt, the shortcomings of Vikzhel, the last hope for a more representative government, was also clear. By entering the Provisional Government, the leaders of the non-Bolshevik socialist parties and Vikzhel compromised their ability to use strikes to obtain the wage demands of their constituents, in effect weakening their own popular support. By imposing workers' control of the railroads, Vikzhel also weakened its ability to take any concerted action for higher wages or against the all-Bolshevik government. Finally, by failing to make a binding agreement with the Bolsheviks at the opportune moment when Petrograd was still under siege between October 29 and 31, Vikzhel allowed that moment to pass and with it the possibility for a more balanced all-socialist government.

As a postscript, in 1918 the moderate leaders of Vikzhel overestimated their ability to influence the new Soviet government and found themselves adrift without any organizations. When Vikzhel gave its vote of confidence to the stillborn Constituent Assembly*, the railwaymen who favored the Bolsheviks seceded from the union and formed their own Railway Workers' Congress. That meeting, from January 5 to 30, formed its own All-Russian Executive Committee of the Union of Railwaymen (Vserossiiskii ispolnitel'nyi komitet zheleznodorozhnikov, or Vikzhedor), which had a membership of twenty-five Bolsheviks, twelve Left Socialist–Revolutionaries, and three independents. On January 10,

1918, the Soviet government turned over the operation of Russia's railroads to this new pro-Bolshevik organization when it was being formed. Vikzhel was destroyed in the end partially by its own actions during the revolutionary crisis and partially through the actions of the new Soviet government. Once Vikzhedor had undermined Vikzhel, the Soviet government dropped its endorsement of syndicalism. On March 23, 1918, the Council of People's Commissars issued a decree giving itself dictatorial power over the operation of Russia's railroads.

Bibliography

Bunyan, James, and Fisher, H. H. *The Bolshevik Revolution, 1917–18: Documents and Materials.* 1934.

Carr, E. H. *The Bolshevik Revolution, 1917–23.* Vol. 2. 1950.

Daniels, Robert V. *Red October.* 1967.

Haimson, Leopold, ed. *The Mensheviks.* 1974.

Metel'kov, P. F. *Zheleznodorozhniki v Revoliutsii.* 1970.

Rabinowitch, Alexander. *The Bolsheviks Come to Power.* 1976.

Vompe, P. A. *Tri goda revoliutsionnogo dvizheniia na zheleznykh dorogakh Rossiiskoi Sovetskoi Respubliki (1917–20).* 1920.

Vompe, P. A. *Dni Oktiabr'skoi revoliutsii i zheleznodorozhniki.* 1924.

The All-Russian Extraordinary Commission for Combatting Counterrevolution and Sabotage (Vserossssiiskaia Chrezvychainaia Kommissia Bor'ba s Kontrrevoliutsiei i Sabotazha, or Cheka). The state security organization created by the Soviet state.

The Cheka was established on December 7, 1917, some six weeks after the October Seizure of Power*. Its roots lay in the Petrograd Military Revolutionary Committee, and its head was Feliks Edmundovich Dzerzhinskii*, who had been military commandant at the Smolnyi Institute at the time of the October Revolution. The Cheka was originally charged with uncovering acts of sabotage and counterrevolution. It was to conduct preliminary investigations and hand perpetrators over to revolutionary tribunals for trial. E. H. Carr observed that "the development of the Cheka was a gradual and largely unpremeditated process. It grew out of a series of emergencies" (Carr 1966, I: 168). In the absence of a tradition of rule by law the Russian government had never been able to set limits to the activities of the state security police (they were called the *Okhrana* under the tsarist regime). This proved even more difficult under the Soviet regime because the Cheka was charged with responsibility for rooting out all opposition to the primary goal of the Soviet system (the achievement of socialism), and after the Revolution there were no legal, customary, or institutional limits to their pursuit of that goal. From the outset the Chekists displayed a tendency to take over the whole political system. An early spur to the expansion of the Cheka's activities was the breakdown of peace talks with Germany in February 1918. In response to the resumption of the advance of German troops, a Soviet proclamation declared that "the socialist fatherland is in danger," and the Cheka was ordered to uncover and shoot enemy agents, counterrevolutionary activists, and speculators. The transfer of the Soviet government to Moscow in March was the occasion for establishing Cheka headquarters on the premises of a large insurance company located on what was then known as Lubianka Square. The square has since been renamed Dzerzhinskii Square, but the security forces' headquarters continues to be known as "The Lubianka." Red terror on a wide scale only began in July 1918 in response to a succession of blows to the precarious Soviet regime. These blows included armed uprisings in Iaroslavl and Murom, the landing of Allied troops on Russian soil in the North, the Japanese landing in Siberia, the revolt of the Czechoslovak Legion*, and its seizure of the Trans-Siberian Railroad. The Cheka's role increased as the regime's survival was imperiled. Assassinations of Soviet officials claimed V. Volodarskii* and M. S. Uritskii*, and V. I. Lenin* was severely wounded on August 30 in Moscow. This last event prompted government decrees on September 3 and 5 calling for mass terror, hostage taking, and the establishment of concentration camps for the "enemies of the people." There were numerous victims of the terror. Three hundred fifty people were executed after the abortive Iaroslavl rising, 35 at Viatka, and more than 500 in Petrograd in September 1918. However, the terror was applied rather idiosyncratically. Publications of the outlawed Constitutional Democratic Party*-Cadets* continued to appear months later, and anarchists, and even Mensheviks (*see* Russian Social Democratic Workers' Party [Menshevik]) continued to operate openly.

Many historians have drawn analogies between the terror of the Russian Revolution and the French Revolution of 1789–1794. In the Russian case it has been estimated that as many as 250,000 perished compared with 17,000 in the French Revolution.

The operations, and what many regarded as the excesses of the Cheka, were the subject of frequent discussions and debate. In the fall of 1919 the Sixth All-Russian Congress of Soviets passed a resolution "on revolutionary legality" intended to curb the heavy-handed use of force on the part of the Cheka. However, as E. H. Carr has observed, this and other measures amounted to "sincere, though ultimately unavailing attempts to check the arbitrary power by the security organs and to confine them within the limits of legality" (Carr 1973). Lenin, for his part, usually supported the Cheka against those who "sobbed or fussed" over mistakes, but he also chastised those within the Cheka, like M. Latsis, who favored forceful measures on a class basis, whether or not there was opposition to the regime (p. 179). Robert Conquest in his work *The Great Terror* noted that Lenin and others feared that "alien elements" might have penetrated the Cheka and contributed to some of its brutal excesses. Latsis himself is quoted as agreeing and noted further:

> Work in the Cheka, conducted in an atmosphere of physical coercion, attracts corrupt and outright criminal elements. . . . However honest a man is, however crystal clear his heart, work in the Cheka, which is carried on with almost unlimited rights and conditions greatly affecting the nervous system, begins to tell. Few escape the effect of the conditions under which they work. (Conquest 1973, p. 544)

In February 1922 with the end of the Civil War in Russia* and the introduction of the New Economic Policy* (NEP), the Cheka was abolished, many of its agents dismissed, and a new security organ fashioned under the control and supervision of the Peoples' Commissariat of Internal Affairs (NKVD). The name of the new organization was the State Security Administration (GPU). In succeeding years the agency that inherited the responsibilities of the Cheka would be known by a number of different acronyms, based on changes in the Russian name of the organizations, such as OGPU, MVD, and KGB. During the period 1934–1938 Stalin inaugurated the Great Purges, during which, in the words of Seweryn Bialer, "terror functioned principally, not as a tool of social change, but as a normal method rule of governance" (Bialer 1980, p. 12). The state security police had control of several armed divisions of their own, a vast system of prison camps and forced labor camps, and a huge, powerful administrative apparatus throughout Russia. At present, despite de-Stalinization, the term *Chekist* is regarded as a high accolade in official circles and in Soviet publications.

Bibliography

Bialer, S. *Stalin's Successors*. 1980.
Carr, E. H. *The Bolshevik Revolution, 1917–21*. Vol. 1. 1973.
Conquest, Robert. *The Great Terror*. 1973.
Gerson, Lennard. *The Secret Police in Lenin's Russia*. 1976.
Latsis, M. Ia. *Chrezvychainnyie kommissiia po borby s kontrrevoliutsiei*. 1921.
———. *Dva goda bor'by na vnutrennoi fronte*. 1920.
Leggett, G. *The Cheka*. 1981.
Wolin, ?, and Slusser, R. M. *The Soviet Secret Police*. 1957.

All-Russian Moslem Congress. *See* All-Russian Moslem Council.

All-Russian Moslem Council (All-Russian Moslem Soviet, or Milii Merkezi Shuro). The executive organ of the All-Russian Moslem Movement during the Revolutions of 1917.

The All-Russian Moslem Council was created by the First All-Russian Moslem Congress in May 1917 in Moscow. Its first chairman was Akhmed Tsalikov, a Daghestani Social Democrat who was also a member of the Petrograd Soviet*.

Soon after the abdication of Nicholas II* in 1917 the leaders of the liberal Moslem intelligentsia who had served in the Duma (*see* Duma and Revolution) and who were organized into the political movement Ittifak called a conference of Moslems in Petrograd. The conference took place from March 15 to 17, 1917, and elected the Provisional Central Bureau of Russian Moslems. It was this latter organization that issued the call for an All-Russian Moslem Congress to meet in Moscow in May 1917. Akhmed Tsalikov was elected chairman of the Provisional Central Bureau. When the congress met, Russia's Moslems proved to be divided into three major groups: the conservatives who were closely allied with religious leaders and who were strongest in Central Asia (*see* Central Asia, Revolution in); the moderate liberals, formerly organized in Ittifak and now

reorganized under Ittihad-ve Tarakki*; and the Moslem Left in which the strongest group was the Moslem Socialist–Revolutionaries. In the end these divisions
would weaken all efforts to create a single united Moslem movement in Russia.

There were about 900 delegates to the First All-Russian Moslem Congress.
After bitter debate the participants adopted a plan for an autonomous federation
of secularized, democratic Moslem republics within a Russian state. The congress
also voted to present a single slate of candidates for the Constituent Assembly
to represent Russia's Moslems and to be called the Moslem Democratic Bloc.
They also voted to establish the Provisional National Central Moslem Council
(Milii merkezi shuro). Because of the political differences between Moslem
political movements, the Moslem Council was never in a position to provide
centralized leadership for Russia's Moslems.

The Second All-Russian Moslem Congress met in Kazan on July 21, and its
character demonstrated that the divisions between the separate Moslem movements had widened. Although the congress claimed to represent all of Russia's
Moslems, the delegates attending came only from the Volga and Ural regions.
At the same time that the Second All-Russian Moslem Congress took place, the
All-Russian Moslem Military Congress was held in Kazan to represent Moslem
military units in the Russian army. The Military Congress elected the All-Russian
Moslem Central Military Council (Harbi Shuro). This latter organization began
to form special Moslem military units with the permission of the Provisional
Government*. The Second All-Russian Moslem Congress also created a com-
mission (Milii Medzhili, or Milii Meclis), which called a national assembly in
Ufa on November 20, 1917. The National Assembly chose three ministries for
all-Russian Moslem territories: education, religion, and finances.

At the time appointed for the first meeting of the Constituent Assembly, Stalin
recruited three Moslem leaders who came to Petrograd to attend. With their help
he created a rival center for Moslem political activity, a Commissariat for Moslem
Affairs under the Commissariat of Nationalities. The Commissariat for Moslem
Affairs was intended to coopt the Shuro and draw all-Russian Moslems under
Soviet control. The Moslem leaders who agreed to work with I. V. Stalin* were
the Tatar Mulla Nur Vakhitov* (who became Commissar for Moslem Affairs),
the Tatar Galimjan Ibragimov*, and a Bashkir deputy, Serif Manatov. When
the Shuro in Kazan tried to establish an autonomous government in February
1917, it was dissolved by Russian troops and its members were arrested. Akhmed
Tsalikov, like Vakhitov, joined the Communist Party and became a Soviet official.

Bibliography

Pipes, R. *The Formation of the Soviet Union*. Rev. ed. 1968.
Zenkovsky, S. *Pan-Turkism and Islam in Russia*. 1960.

All-Russian Moslem Military Congress. *See* All-Russian Moslem Council.

All-Russian Union of Towns and All-Russian Union of Zemstvos. The story of the All-Russian Union of Towns and All-Russian Union of Zemstvos illustrates three dimensions of Imperial Russian society on the eve of its demise: (1) the determination of a segment of the educated public to save tsarism from military collapse; (2) the ascendancy of the technical and professional intelligentsia within local government during the last years of the old regime; and (3) the political consequence of the division within local government between enfranchised elements (in particular those professional people hired by the town and *zemstvo* councils to staff hospitals, schools, and other public facilities) coming almost exclusively from large propertied groups and everyone else.

The unions originated at the inception of World War I*. Fashioned spontaneously by the Moscow municipal and *zemstvo* councils, the unions were voluntary associations of local self-governing units engaged in medical relief work on an empirewide scale. M. V. Chelnokov, mayor of Moscow from 1914 to 1917, headed the union of towns. Prince G. E. L'vov*, chairman of the Tula provincial *zemstvo* who went on in 1917 to lead the first Provisional Government*, directed the Union of Zemstvos. The official tasks of the unions were identical: to staff hospitals for the sick and wounded, to expedite the evacuation of soldiers and civilians from the war zone, and to provide medical supplies for the army. Except for the stricture of the imperial decree, which limited their existence to the period of the war and placed the unions under the Red Cross, there were no restrictions either on membership or makeup. Not until 1916 was legislation introduced to clarify the relationship between the unions and the State Duma (*see* Duma and Revolution), but the Council of Ministers failed to act on that bill before the 1917 February Revolution*.

Since the unions represented the towns and *zemstvos,* one would expect that their work in the provinces would have been carried out by the established institutions of local government. This was not the case. The unions simply could not function on the basis of the prewar local franchise, however great the enthusiasm of the civic-minded nobility or burgher-bureaucrats. Union notables, both at headquarters in Moscow and in the provinces, had to seek expert advice because they themselves were not versed in the complexities of hospital management and public health care. The result was employment of professionals who were, however, debarred by law from voting in the local assemblies. By 1916, for example, two-thirds of the membership of the union of towns belonged to the professions. Once enrolled, these specialists acquired authority concerning the organization of various services, for example, the vaccination of soldiers against contagious disease. Ad hoc committees, consisting of doctors, statisticians, and sanitation engineers, soon emerged and functioned side by side with the regular institutions.

The de facto transformation of the social composition of local government was underscored by the willingness of the tsarist regime, usually at the insistence of the army high command, to permit the unions to discharge duties that properly were the responsibility of the state. That development is easily explained. Everyone in Russia had assumed in August 1914 that a heavy struggle under terrible conditions would be settled in less than six months. Neither the high command, the dynasty, nor the general public was prepared for a protracted conflict. Thus it soon became evident that there were no plans for the evacuation of wounded and for medical provisions beyond points immediately adjacent to the battlefield and that the army medical staff could not operate with the facilities at its disposal. Consequently, in September 1914 the Council of Ministers turned in desperation to the unions for the purpose of organizing victory in the rear. For the first six months that entailed the provisioning of hospitals and medical workers for the entire home front. During the same half-year period the army threw itself on the mercy of the unions for the running and maintenance of evacuation carriers, including trains, inside the war zone. By 1915 the Union of Zemstvos maintained fifty trains that carried as many as 16,000 sick and wounded at one time. Most of the cost of this operation was borne by the government, which channeled funds through a special agency within the army General Staff.

As the unions entered the area of battle, the army implored them to extend their operations as far as possible. Eventually, the network of services ranged from the Zemgor, a joint committee of the unions to increase the flow of small arms and munitions, to schemes to improve the cleanliness of the troops and to the procurement of meat for army consumption. Some of the programs, in particular the Zemgor, were poorly conceived and never amounted to much. In other instances, such as the transportation of wounded from the front, the unions acquitted themselves well, and it was only through their efforts that anything close to adequacy was achieved in ambulance work. Finally, when it came to the care of refugees in the war zone, the unions, acting together, provided the only element of civil administration.

By 1916 the unions controlled thousands of employees and monthly budgets that ran into the tens of millions of rubles. The responses of the unions to the problems engendered by the war—in the form of professional initiatives and programs—revealed the dynamic of educated society and its potential for development. Certainly, the government took note. From its perspective the unions clearly served as agents for change in the structure and functioning of the old order of society. B. V. Shturmer, chairman of the Council of Ministers in 1916, put it this way:

> If a permanently active . . . Municipal Union was formed, Russia would have two governments, of which the public one would be independent not only of governmental authority, but also in general of the state. . . . furthermore . . . town life—in its economic and administrative entirety—would be completely in the hands of the lawyers, technicians, and others from the best segments of the urban population. (Emmons 1983, p. 371).

During the first eighteen months of fighting, the government watched with growing alarm the proliferation of practical public initiative. Yet since it was impossible to win the war without accepting a degree of popular assistance, the ministers displayed an ambivalent attitude toward the unions, alternating between heartfelt effusions for the help received and dark suggestions that union leaders were maneuvering to destroy the regime's credibility. When at last it became apparent that the unions were going to press forward on key issues such as refugees and the organization of food supplies, thereby indirectly challenging the government's authority, the government stepped up its attack. An effort was made to curtail the number of union meetings, and in April 1916 a ban was placed on public conferences. In December, when members of both unions gathered in Moscow to propose remedies for the spreading food shortages in the major northern cities, the government resorted to strong-arm police tactics. In a stormy confrontation, the meetings were shut down and the delegates forcibly dispersed.

The government's fear of the unions was partially justified: they had thousands of civilians under their jurisdiction; they conducted their business at all levels of society and in all areas of the empire; and unlike the State Duma, they operated year round and could not be dismissed without an inexcusable increase in human distress. Even more important, there was no precedent for the intimate relationship in the war zone between military and civilian elites. Because of the army's jurisdiction and its pronounced preference for union-sponsored programs, the public organizations operated independently. Therefore, if so inclined, union leaders could have demanded the democratization of the towns and *zemstvos* as the price for continued support of the Tsar. They could have backed these demands with threats of work stoppages in the field. They even could have appealed to the high command for support, insisting that this was an act of patriotism.

In the end, however, union leaders refused to exploit their organizational leverage for political purposes. A portion of their disdain for such activity was traceable to the war itself: the unions were patriotic organizations dedicated to victory and to the proposition that the needs of the army took precedence over everything else. Much of the restrained political outlook, however, transcended the war. Simply put, it was grounded in the opposition of entrenched political elites—the founders of the unions—to the drive for equality by municipal and *zemstvo* employees. For example, the employees of the Moscow provincial *zemstvo* banded together with white-collar workers from the Union of Towns to demand a voice in civic affairs commensurate with their role in local government. Their avowed aim was to take advantage of the unique opportunity provided by the war to secure legislative enactment of a new municipal and *zemstvo* franchise.

Efforts by the professional intelligentsia to stir the conscience of union leaders on the question of voting rights came to naught, with the result that the intelligentsia did not support the unions. In April 1916 the Pirogov Society, the arm of Russia's medical profession, called for the introduction of universal suffrage and castigated the unions for neglect of this issue. Simultaneously, doctors and hospital orderlies of the Union of Zemstvos stopped work along a section of the western front to protest the class-dominated unions. In August groups of doctors and statisticians of the union of towns resigned their posts in Moscow, Kiev, and Petrograd. By the end of the year, union employees in Moscow were meeting in secret for the purpose of spreading antiwar propaganda. Confrontation with union leaders was averted by the downfall of the monarchy two months later.

The unions survived the February Revolution* and in 1917 were radically restructured to meet the democratic demands of the Provisional Government*. Nevertheless, from a functional standpoint the unions had ceased to exist by the end of 1916: many field workers had left the committees, and operations in the war zone had fallen off considerably. The unions finally were dissolved in January 1918 by decree of the Bolsheviks.

Years later, in exile, union leaders argued that their organizations were the most nearly successful attempt before the Revolution to give the towns and *zemstvos* a more influential place in the Russian polity. It is clear, however, that the unions did not constitute a viable alternative to the existing political order. The contribution of the Russian professional classes to the wartime mobilization, made manifest in the unions, served only to whet their appetite for power. Their presence in the unions threatened the status of union leaders who proved unwilling to bridge the gap that separated privileged society from its restless majority. Fear of democracy overrode the opposition of the unions to the autocracy and drove their spokesmen into a tacit alliance with a reactionary officialdom. In the unions the reality of class in time overshadowed that of dedication to a common cause, thus foreshadowing the shape of things to come once the empire gave way.

William Gleason

Bibliography

Emmons, T., and Vucinich, W., eds. *The Zemstvo: An Experiment in Local Self-Government*. 1983.
Polner, Tikhon. *Russian Local Government during the War and the Union of Zemstvos*. 1930.

All-Russian Union of Zemstvos. *See* the All-Russian Union of Towns and All-Russian Union of Zemstvos.

Anarchism. Together with the Spanish events of 1936–1939, the Russian Revolution has represented a *götterdammerung* for the anarchist idea. Nineteenth-century anarchism had been influential in the labor movements of various European countries and especially in Latin Europe. Russian anarchists had sensed great possibilities in their own country, whose background bore a certain resemblance to that of lands where anarchism had taken root. An absolute monarchy, lacking the experience of a reformation or a constitutional tradition, Russia seemed good soil for an anti-clerical, anti-state ideology. Two Russian exiles, Mikhail A. Bakunin and Peter A. Kropotkin, had given shape to anarchist revolutionism and helped prepare European opinion for the inevitable explosion of revolt against the tsardom. Yet when the Revolution came, satisfying the wildest hopes for spontaneous mass action against every form of authority, its outcome crushed the anarchist's dream mercilessly.

Anarchism and Marxism were old opponents. But in 1917 the Bolsheviks did not see anarchism as an enemy but rather as a barometer by which to measure the popular mood. For their part, most anarchists saw in Bolshevism a fresh departure from the parliamentary Marxism they had known. Since the days of Bakunin's struggle with Marx for preeminence in the First International, Marxist Social Democracy had stood for peaceful, legal, trade union, and political activity, having more in common with the English New Model Trade Unionism than with that of Bakunin's International Brotherhood, which preached the economic general strike. The Second International had excluded anarchists and ignored the general strike. V. I. Lenin's* Bolshevism also seemed closer to the anarchists on an array of tactical questions and even on the theory of the state. Lenin was later to admit, in *Left-Wing Communism: An Infantile Disorder,* that the anarchist criticism of the Social Democratic theory of the state had been correct. In 1917 many anarchists concluded that Lenin had abandoned Marxism.

The anarchist intellectual tradition was itself divided about Marxism. Bakunin had accepted Marx's political economy, its critique of capitalism, the doctrine of the class struggle, and the imperative of organizing the labor movement, for which he is commonly regarded as an important forebearer of revolutionary syndicalism. After Bakunin's death in 1876, Kropotkin developed the Italian idea of anarchist communism as a leap into a society of distribution according to need, without a transition period of administration by labor organizations, which were not entirely trusted. His disciple, Errico Malatesta, had harbored the interesting premonition that anarcho-syndicalism could turn out to be a Left cover for "trade unionism pure and simple." Both anarcho-syndicalism and anarchist communism derided Marxism's metaphysical idea of dialectics, its gradualism, and its "knouto-German" state worship. Some anarchists even broadened the plebeian prejudice against intellectuals into the theory that Marxism was actually the doctrine of the intelligentsia. Following the Polish anarchist J. W. Machajski, who traced Marx's favor of the intellectuals back to the "doctrine of the perpetual incommensurability of social product by social income" in volume two of *Capital,* they warned of the menace posed by the development of Western-style parliamentary democracy. Strictly speaking, anarchism seeks not merely a classless society but also a society without division of labor (here it shares a preoccupation of the young Marx). However, those anarchists who put class struggle in a prominent position were more likely to support the Bolshevik plans for a "transition period" than were those who warned about the corrupting influence of the labor organizations.

A tacit anarchist "bloc" with Bolshevism began with their defeatist position in World War I*. The most famous anarchists—Kropotkin, V. N. Cherkezov, Jean Grave, James Guillaume, and others—had supported the Russian war effort, like G. V. Plekhanov*, primarily to defend France, "the *foyer* of free thought, of socialism, and of anarchy." But most of the young generation were defeatist. In 1915 the *International Anarchist Manifesto on the War* signed by Alexander Berkman, William Shatov, and others, called for turning the imperialist war into a civil war, a position for which Lenin had experienced great difficulty finding support at Zimmerwald (*see* World War I). Cooperation with the Bolsheviks after the fall of the Tsar extended from this common defeatism to all questions involving spontaneous mass action, with the important footnote that, unlike the Bolsheviks, the anarchists saw these matters as questions of principle. House committees, factory committees, soviets (*see* Soviets of Workers', Soldiers', and Peasants' Deputies), trade unions*, and cooperatives (*see* Cooperative Movement, 1917–1921) were, for the anarchist press, evidence of "constructive anarchism" among the masses. The anarchist–communist newspaper *Kommuna* (*Commune*), and later *Svobodnaia Kommuna* (*Free Commune*), saw the most potential in residential organizations such as the house committees but encouraged action in industry and urged the workers to seize control of factories and shops and to run them for themselves. The anarcho-syndicalists who rallied around *Golos Truda* (*Voice of Labor*), among them Vsevolod Eikhenbaum (Volin), Grigorii P., Maksimov, A. M. Shapiro, and Bill Shatov, could not arrive at a clear idea of the meaning of the slogan "Worker's Control" (*see* Workers in the Revolution, Role of), which had appeared among Petrograd factory committees. They had been organized in advance of the trade unions, a fact that presented certain problems for anarchist theory.

Traditional syndicalism had seen trade unions as fighting units and organizations around which to arrange production in the stateless society. The soviets, which had arisen during the 1905 Revolution (*see* Nineteen-Five Revolution) had been seen as a Russian version of the French *bourses du travail* of the 1890s. Syndicalists such as Volin, who clung to the tradition, were depressed by Menshevik (*see* Russian Social Democratic Workers' Party [Menshevik]) influence in the trade unions and by that of political parties in the soviets. They began to attribute statist tendencies of the soviets to the absence of a mature labor movement of the Western type. This interesting idea, so subversive of anarchism, appears prominently in Volin's history *La Revolution inconnue* (1945). Other anarcho-syndicalists tried to adjust to the factory committees and soviets. Maksimov argued that factory committees were superior to trade unions and soviets to parliaments. Workers' control should stop short of outright seizure in order to create the institutions for a "transition period" of "labor dictatorship." For this, the soviet seemed heaven-sent, in Maksimov's imagination, a "production-consumption commune." Here we have a synthesis of the Bakunin and Kropotkin traditions and, ironically, a program aligning anarchists solidly with Bolshevism.

In 1917 Lenin had no reason to object to the opposition of factory committees and soviets to trade unions and parliaments, although by 1920 he would struggle mightily, in *Left-Wing Communism,* against Hermann Gorter's and Anton Pannekoek's espousal of a similar idea. This subsequent change of heart was a result of Lenin's recognition that the revolutionary chances in the West had passed, and for the time being Russia would need to go it alone.

In 1917 anarchists judged mass action from below to be sufficiently powerful to drag all of the parties, Bolsheviks included, in its wake. In June they defended the dacha of P. N. Durnovo in Petrograd's Vyborg district, seized in the aftermath of the February Revolution* against the Provisional Government* and soviet, as Lenin condemned the government's action. The fiery speeches of the anarchist–communist I. N. Bleikhman roused the First Machine-Gun Regiment to initiate the armed demonstrations of the July Days*. Anarchists opposed the patriotic call of the Moscow State Conference* in August, even while Kropotkin joined in issuing it. They supported the Red Guards'* resistance to the coup of Kornilov (*see* Kornilov Revolt) and opposed A. F. Kerensky's* call for a Democratic Conference* in October. On the threshold of destroying the Provisional Government, *Golos Truda* warned that an uprising led by the Bolsheviks would not abolish the state but resolved to follow the masses.

Bolshevik policy changed after October. It favored trade unions over factory committees and coordinated economic life, as best it could, under the Supreme Council of the National Economy* (Vesenkha). The anarchists, already unhappy about the granting of freedom to the nationalities, were by turns delighted and appalled, first by the closing of the Constituent Assembly* (in which they assisted) and then by the Peace of Brest-Litovsk* and the implementation of the new economic measures, which by the spring included compulsory grain requisitions. Desire for continuation of the maximalism of 1917 came increasingly to be expressed in the call for a "third revolution," which coincided with the insurrectionary mood of the Left Socialist–Revolutionaires (S–R's) (*see* Left Socialist-Revolutionary Party). Inside the Bolshevik Party, not yet fully regimented, there were increased accusations that the leadership aimed only at "state capitalism." N. I. Bukharin*, who led the criticism, proclaimed to Volin his agreement with the Left S–R's and anarchists but bemoaned his weakness before Lenin in party councils. Lenin's factional victory over these "Left Communists" coincided with the Soviet government's attack on the Moscow House of Anarchy and its Black Guards on April 11–12, 1918. In May most anarchist papers were closed down, and most of the important anarchists left Moscow to work in the free soviets in the localities. They did not include Maksimov and the Left anarcho-syndicalists who resolved to continue the fight for free soviets against "Bolshevik state capitalism" in the main urban centers and, at the same time, to support the Bolsheviks against the Whites (*see* White Movement). This proved to be impossible. By 1919 anarchists had been forced to choose between working for the government and being imprisoned by it. Most prominent anarchists chose the former, but Maksimov and a number of others ended up in prison for making anarchist propaganda in the Red Army*.

A few urban anarchists, among them Volin and Petr Arshinov, made their way to the Ukraine to assist Nestor Makhno's anarchist guerilla army. Makhno had led the peasant war around his village of Guliai Pole in the southeastern Ukraine during 1917. German and Austrian occupation cut this short, and Makhno fled to Moscow for advice. Lenin encouraged Makhno's return to resume the fight, seeing an advantage in anarchist sentiment among the Ukrainian peasants. Makhno's partisans fought the occupiers and followers of S. M. Petliura* in 1918, the Red Army and then A. I. Denikin* (in alliance with the Red Army) in 1919, the Red Army and then P. N. Wrangel* (in another alliance with the Red Army in 1920), and after Wrangel's defeat, the Red Army alone. Where the Maknovshchina held sway, communes, free soviets, and Ferrer schools flourished, but Makhno insisted that his army was not anarchist. It merely prepared the way for "constructive anarchism." Volin, who rode with Makhno, thought this could only mean "united anarchism," which combined the different libertarian traditions. Maksimov condemned Volin's "synthesis" as mere Kropotkinism adapted to the needs of the Ukrainian smallholder. Most anarchist supporters of the Bolsheviks nevertheless admired Makhno, but some, such as Alexander Berkman, deplored his fighting the Bolsheviks. Not Makhno's defeat but the suppression of the Kronstadt Revolt (*see* Kronstadt, 1917–1921) was the last straw for this kind of anarchist, and it set the seal on his deep disillusionment with the Soviet regime.

In general, anarchists tended to support the Bolsheviks throughout the period of the Civil War (*see* Civil War in Russia). But for them the Bolshevik suppression of the Kronstadt Revolt was the last straw. They had not led the revolt or, with a few exceptions, even participated in it, but they hailed the sailors' Petropavlovsk manifesto, with its call for free soviets and an end to party control over the armed forces. They saw the "Kronstadt commune" as a chapter in the "third revolution," which they hoped would end the rule of the commissars.

Occasional anarchist leaflets continued to appear at least until 1924. In exile anarchists constructed their notions of the lessons of the Revolution in terms of their divergent intellectual traditions, to which were now added *Makhnovshchina* (which profoundly influenced Bueneventura Durruti), United Anarchism, Maksimov's Left Syndicalism, and Arshinov's "Anarcho-Bolshevism." Soviet writers such as Iu. M. Steklov freely admitted during the twenties that anarchism was a working-class trend, even judging Bakunin to have been the "first founder of the idea of Soviet power," but after the rise of Stalinism, the line changed, and it came to be regarded as petty-bourgeois and counterrevolutionary. Today it is still regarded as petty-bourgeois but not always counterrevolutionary.

Anthony D'Agostino

Bibliography

Arshinov, Petr. *A History of the Makhno Movement, 1918–21*. Translated by L. Perlman and F. Perlman. 1973.
Avrich, Paul, ed. *The Anarchists in the Russian Revolution*. 1973.

D'Agostino, Anthony. *Marxism and the Russian Anarchists*. 1977.
Gorev, B. I. *Anarkhizm v rossii: ot Bakunina do Makhno*. 1930.
Kanev, S. N. *Oktiabr'skaia revoliutsiia i krakh anarkhizma: bor'ba partii bolshevikov protiv anarkhizma, 1917–1922 gg.* 1974.
Maksimov, G. P. *The Guillotine at Work: Twenty Years of Terror in Russia*. 1940.
Steklov, Iu. M. *Mikhail Aleksandrovich Bakunin: ego zhizn i deiatel'nost', 1914–1876.* 4 vols. 1926–1927.
Volin (V. Eikhenbaum), *The Unknown Revolution, 1917–21*. Translated by H. Cantine, F. Perlman, et al. 1974.

Anthems. The tsarist national anthem "God Preserve the Tsar" ("Bozhe Tsaria Khrani"), reflected well the ideology of Imperial Russia. God was invoked to preserve the orthodox tsar in his glorious rule over the Russian people. The anthem emphasized the close relationship between church and state and the autocratic power of the sovereign. The poet Vasilii A. Zhukovskii, a strong supporter of autocracy, wrote the words in 1833. In 1814 Zhukovskii had written an earlier version to the music of the English national anthem "God Save the King," and in 1816 Alexander S. Pushkin added two more stanzas, but these initial verses did not receive official approval. Aleksei F. Lvov, on orders from Nicholas I, composed the melody in 1833, and "Bozhe Tsaria Khrani" became the official anthem in December of that year.

This anthem was widely performed in tsarist Russia. It was popular with the army and was heard on ceremonial state occasions. The chimes of the Spasskii Gate in Moscow played its melody, and in St. Petersburg it was heard on the bells of the Peter–Paul Cathedral. During the Revolution of 1905 (*see* Nineteen-Five Revolution), the icon-carrying marchers were singing it just before the Cossacks* opened fire on the "Bloody Sunday" demonstration. After the fall of the monarchy in 1917, the tsarist anthem also had to be replaced.

Three songs, each representing a different constituency, competed for the honor of becoming the new national anthem. A hymn written by Dimitrii S. Bortnianskii, "Glory to the Lord" ("Kol slaven"), was the favorite for many who opposed the Tsar but who remained loyal to the traditions of the orthodox religion and Russian traditions. This hymn is now the unofficial anthem for most of the Russian emigré community around the world. The "Marseillaise" was a second anthem associated with the period of the Provisional Government*. As an instrumental rendition it represented well the republican virtues of "liberty, equality, and fraternity" associated with the French Revolution. The words best known in Russia came from a lyric by the famous Populist Peter Lavrov called "The Workers' Marseillaise." This song became popular among revolutionary workers, but it never matched the popularity of the official anthem of Marxist socialism, the "Internationale," which became the official national anthem of Soviet Russia after the Bolshevik victory.

The French revolutionary poet Eugene Pottier wrote the words for the "Internationale" during the period of the Paris Commune in 1871. The melody was composed by Pierre Degeyter, a French wood carver, in 1888. Although the song was banned in tsarist Russia, it was translated by A. Ia. Kots in 1902 and circulated among Russia's revolutionaries at home and abroad.

The words of the "Internationale" speak of a struggle between the hungry and enslaved workers of the world against the privileged old order. There are promises to build a new world on the ruins of the old. John Reed, an American journalist sympathetic to the Bolshevik Revolution, described the enthusiasm of the revolutionaries as they sang the "Internationale" at the Congress of Soviets on October 25: "Suddenly, by common impulse, we found ourselves on our feet, mumbling together into the smooth lifting unison of the *Internationale*. A grizzled old soldier was sobbing like a child. Aleksandra M. Kollontai* (an Old Bolshevik revolutionary) rapidly winked the tears back. The immense sound rolled through the hall, burst windows and doors and seared into the quiet sky" (Reed 1919, p. 132).

The only change that was made in the text after the Revolution occurred in the chorus. Pottier's original words placed the struggle in the future, but the Russian Bolsheviks were now successful. They no longer sang "It *will be* our last and decisive battle" but rather sang "It *is* our last and decisive battle."

The "Internationale" served as the official anthem of Soviet Russia until 1943.

William H. Parsons

Bibliography

Reed, John. *Ten Days That Shook the World*. 1919.
Shaw, M. F. *National Anthems of the World*. 1978.

Anti-Semitism. Anti-Jewish sentiments at both the popular and governmental levels can be traced to the Kievan and Moscovite periods in Russian history. Not only were Jews barred from settling on Russian lands, but since the days of Ivan IV, Jews had been expelled systematically from those new lands added to the realm. However, after the partitions of Poland, when lands containing more than 1 million Jews were added to the Empire, a new Jewish policy was initiated by the tsarist government. Rather than expel such a sizable population, thereby disrupting the economic underpinnings of the region, Russian officials decided to confine Jewish life to the newly annexed territories. Thus the origins of the Pale of Settlement, the westernmost provinces of the Empire to which Jewish residence was confined, can be traced to tsarist policies at the close of the eighteenth century.

The reign of Alexander II (1856–1881) marked a shift in the Jewish policies of the government. In his efforts to modernize his realm and so increase Russia's ability to compete both economically and militarily with the Western and Central European states, Alexander II removed a number of restrictions theretofore imposed on the Russian–Jewish population. Alexander's initial efforts offered the hope that during his reign a gradual progression would begin that would ultimately culminate in the final emancipation of Russia's Jewish community. It was in the first half of the 1860s that selective categories of the Jewish population received permission to leave the Pale in order to settle in the heartland of the Empire, including the capital cities of Moscow and St. Petersburg.

However, the assassination of the emperor in March 1881 revealed that Russian policymakers continued to identify the Jews as a foreign element detrimental to the general welfare of the Russian population. Police responses to the pogrom movement that raged through the southern Ukraine in April 1881 was slow and law and order was restored only after the rioting had gone on for several days. Furthermore, official inquiries into the causes of the pogroms concluded that the Jews were responsible for the assaults that befell them since their economic activities in the Russian countryside aroused such animosity among the local peasantry. As a result, the government introduced a new series of laws further restricting Jewish life in the Empire. These laws, known as the Temporary Laws or the May Laws of 1882, were intended to segregate Jewish life even further and to diminish contacts between the Jews of the Pale and the local populations there. These laws remained in existence to the end of the tsarist period. Thus not only was the road to emancipation formally abandoned, but Jews, after the events of 1881, found themselves even more confined geographically and more restricted economically as well as socially.

Subsequently, Russia's Jewish community continued to suffer further reversals at the hands of the government. In 1887 Jewish enrollments at Russian schools from the elementary through the university level were curtailed. The number of Jewish students could no longer exceed established quotas set by the government for all schools in the Empire. The introduction of this *numerus clausus* shut off the primary means by which Jews had formerly escaped the Pale for opportunities in the interior of the country. Continuing its anti-Jewish policy, the government also began to return to the Pale categories of the Jewish population that had been permitted in the previous regime to take up residence in the countryside outside of the Pale. The mass expulsion of Jews from Moscow in March 1891 was an especially brutal act that focused Western attention on the plight of Russian Jewry and gave an added impetus to the Jewish emigration movement from both Russia and Poland to the West, mainly to the United States.

The pogrom in Kishenev in the spring of 1903 once again unleashed a reign of terror directed against the Jews of southern Russia. Pogroms against the Jewish community continued sporadically in 1904, 1905, and into 1906. The worst riot occurred in the city of Odessa in October 1905. More than 300 Jews were killed in that violent assault. In the same period, elements from within the Russian right, aided by official agencies, first fabricated and then disseminated the text of what was to become the basis for the infamous *Protocols of the Elders of Zion*. Ostensibly a verbatim transcript of a clandestine Jewish meeting, the *Protocols* reported the existence of a worldwide Jewish conspiracy directed against the Christian world. According to this document, Jewish goals were to be furthered through the manipulation of both revolutionary movements and commercial and monetary exchanges—in short, through subterfuge and chicanery. The actual purpose of the document, produced by the tsarist secret police in France for distribution in Russia, was to discredit the Russian revolutionary movement by implying that the movement was, in fact, a means being used by world Jewry for the overthrow of the Empire as part of a diabolical plan. Clearly, too, existing popular anti-Semitic sentiments and persuasions were being stimulated by the counterrevolutionary forces whose membership included members of the royal family.

The appeal to base anti-Semitic views did not stop there. In 1911 at the direction of the Ministry of Justice, a Jew living in Russia, Mendel Beilis, was accused of the murder of a Christian youth for the purpose of using the child's blood for Jewish ceremonial needs. After two years, Beilis was finally tried on the charge, only to be acquitted by a local jury in Kiev that could not accept the government's case in spite of all of the anti-Semitic propaganda associated with the proceedings. The last decades of tsarist rule, then, were characterized by a deliberate intensification and a calculated exploitation of popular anti-Semitic views that had been latent within Russian culture since the formative years of Russian life.

Alexander Orbach

Bibliography

Kochan, L., ed. *The Jews in Soviet Russia Since 1917.* 1952.
Pinson, K. S., ed. *Antisemitism.* 1946.
Schwarz, Solomon M. *Antisemitizm v Sovetskom soiuze.* 1962.
Tcherikower, Elias. *Di ukrainer pogromen.* 1965.

Antonov-Ovseenko, Vladimir Aleksandrovich (1884–1939) (pseudonyms, "Shtyk" [Bayonet], A. Gal'skii). One of the foremost military experts among Social Democrats and one of the leaders of the October Seizure of Power* in Petrograd.

Born in Chernigov, Antonov-Ovseenko was the son of a military officer who was an impoverished landowner. He graduated from Voronezh Military School in 1901 and in the same year entered the revolutionary movement, having developed a strong disgust for militarism. He became involved with a Social Democratic student circle in Warsaw and joined the Russian Social Democratic Workers' Party (RSDWP; *see* Russian Social Democratic Workers' Party [Bolshevik]) in 1903. In 1904 he graduated from St. Petersburg Military Academy. He was active in the 1905 Revolution (*see* Nineteen-Five Revolution) and was an organizer of military uprisings in Novo-Aleksandriia (Poland) and Sevastopol during 1905–1906. Arrested in Sevastopol, he was sentenced to death, but later the sentence was commuted to twenty years' hard labor. He escaped on June 1907 and worked in Finland, St. Petersburg, and later Moscow.

Antonov-Ovseenko immigrated to France in 1910 and joined with the Mensheviks. He was a forceful and outspoken opponent of V. I. Lenin* and the Bolsheviks. During World War I* he was an Internationalist*. In exile he edited

the newspapers *Golos* (*Voice*) and *Nashe Slovo* (*Our Word*) and was close to
L. D. Trotsky* and the Mezhraiontsyi (*see* Interdistrict Committee).

He returned to Russia in May 1917 and joined the Bolsheviks. Active in
Helsinki and Petrograd as an agitator, editor, and organizer, he was imprisoned
in July by the Provisional Government*. A member of a number of military and
civil bodies, he was in the Finnish Regional Commission, represented the Northern Front in the Constituent Assembly*, and was Secretary of the Committee
of the Northern Soviets and of the Petrograd Military Revolutionary Committee.
He was largely responsible for coordinating the October Seizure of Power in
Petrograd, the taking of the Winter Palace, and the arrest of the Provisional
Government. At the Second All-Russian Congress of Soviets he was elected a
member of the first Council of People's Commissars (Sovnarkom) and of the
Committee on Military and Naval Affairs.

He held military command during the Civil War in Russia*, commanding the
Ukrainian front from December 1918 to June 1919. During 1920–1921 he served
briefly as a member of the Collegium of the People's Commissariat for Labor
and of the NKVD. In 1921 he led the suppression of the Tambov peasant revolt.

In 1922 at the Eleventh Party Congress he attacked the New Economic Policy*
(NEP) as surrender to the *kulaks* (rich peasants) and foreign capitalists. During
1923–1927 he associated with the Trotsky opposition. In 1928 he broke with it
and joined I. V. Stalin's* camp. From the mid–1920s he was involved in diplomatic work: Czechoslovakia (1925), Lithuania (1928), and Poland (1930). In
1936 he served as Soviet Consul General in Barcelona during the Spanish Civil
War and was recalled in 1937. In 1938 he was named Commissar for Justice.
He was arrested shortly thereafter and was shot in 1939 without trial. He was
rehabilitated in 1956.

Bibliography

Haupt, Georges, and Marie, Jean-Jaques. *Makers of the Russian Revolution*. 1974.

April Conference. *See* Russian Social Democratic Workers' Party (Bolshevik).

April Theses. Proposals for changes in Bolshevik policy presented by V. I.
Lenin* upon his return to revolutionary Russia in April 1917.

"April Theses" is the name given to the radical proposals advanced by Lenin
on his return to Russia from Switzerland. Lenin's ideas were first enunciated on
the night of April 3, 1917, at the Finland Station in Petrograd and later published
in the Bolshevik newspaper *Pravda* (*Truth*) on April 7 under the title "On the
Tasks of the Proletariat in the Present Revolution." The main points advanced
were that the World War (*see* World War I) was a conflict between capitalist,
imperialist powers; that the Russian Provisional Government* served the interests
of the capitalist class in Russia; and that, therefore, to bring the war to an end
it was necessary to transfer state power to the soviets of workers' and peasants'
deputies. To this end Lenin advocated non-support of the Provisional Government

and advanced the slogan "All Power to the Soviets"*. In addition, the Theses called for confiscation of all landed estates and the nationalization of all lands; amalgamation and state control over all banking institutions; control by the soviets of workers' deputies over "social production and the distribution of products"; and the abolition of the police and army and their replacement by the arming of the entire population. Finally, Lenin proposed that the Russian Social Democratic Workers' Party (Bolshevik)* (RSDWP [B]) change its name to the Communist Party to set itself apart from the international Social Democratic movement that he regarded as having betrayed the working classes (*see* World War I).

A member of the Bolshevik Petersburg Committee has stated that Lenin's April Theses had the effect of an "exploding bomb." The Bolshevik Party leadership was thrown into confusion and disarray. Before Lenin's return, the leading Bolsheviks in Petrograd, notably I. V. Stalin* and L. B. Kamenev*, had lent qualified Bolshevik support to the Provisional Government and had embraced the position of revolutionary "defensism"* on the question of the continuation of Russia's participation in the World War. Furthermore, there were moves being made to effect a reconciliation between the Bolshevik, Menshevik (*see* Russian Social Democratic Workers' Party [Menshevik]), and other factions of the RSDWP. Lenin's views ran so strongly against the grain of the other Bolshevik leaders' views that when Lenin's *Pravda* article appeared, it was presented as an individual's view, without any official standing, and was accompanied by a statement of the newspaper's editors that Lenin's general scheme seemed "unacceptable." The Menshevik* leader I. G. Tsereteli*, for his part, accused Lenin of being an anarchist, "a new Bakunin," and charged that he threatened civil war in Russia.

To put the basis of the controversy in the Marxist terms of the day, both the Bolshevik and Menshevik factions assumed that socialism for Russia was possible only in the distant future. Lenin argued, on the other hand, that Russia was in a transition between the bourgeois and proletarian stages of the Revolution. Therefore, Lenin contended, the Bolshevik Party was to assume the task of facilitating that transition and leading the country to the assumption of power by the proletariat and poor peasants. To the argument that Russia was not sufficiently advanced industrially to permit socialism, Lenin argued that Europe was ripe for revolution and revolution in Russia would precipitate a successful worldwide socialist revolution that, in turn, would aid Russia in its transition to socialism.

As far as Bolshevik tactics were concerned, Lenin recognized that his position represented a minority view in the country. He thus counseled the Bolshevik Party: to explain the error of the defensists to them with special thoroughness, persistence and patience. In short order Lenin succeeded in winning the party to his position, which became the touchstone of Bolshevik policy during 1917.

Bibliography

Meyer, Alfred. *Leninism.* 1957.
Possony, Stefan. *The Lenin Reader.* 1966.
Sukhanov, N. N. *The Russian Revolution, 1917.* Vol. 1. 1962.

Architecture and the Revolution. The attempt to translate social and political radicalism into architectural form emerges late in the eighteenth century in French projects such as the Ideal City of Chaux by Claude-Nicholas Ledoux (1736–1806) and the megalomaniac proposals of Etienne-Louis Boulles (1728–1799). However, throughout the nineteenth century European social reformers continued to find traditional neo-Gothic or neoclassical imagery symbolically adequate, and the architecture inspired by the aspirations of the French Revolution remained forgotten or ignored.

Concurrently, as mass production made iron and glass increasingly cheaper and more plentiful, these materials became strongly associated with architectural visions of a progressive and industrialized mass society. Numerous world fairs, especially the Great Exhibition of All Nations (London, 1851) and the Paris Exhibition of 1889 (marking the centennial of the French Revolution), celebrated these materials in astonishing structures like the "Crystal Palace" (1851) and the Eiffel Tower (1889). By the end of the nineteenth century, certain architects consolidated the relation of a politically engaged architecture with glass and iron by exploiting these materials in art nouveau designs for socialist clients, as, for instance, the Maison du Peuple of 1896–1899 in Brussels by Victor Horta (1861–1947).

Reinforced concrete acquired similar associations when Toni Garnier (1869–1948) published the 1904–1917 drawings for a *Cite Industrielle* and Antonio Sant'Elia (1888–1916) exhibited his futurist visions as the *Citta Nuova* in 1914. Both projects demonstrated that reinforced concrete could be the preeminent building material for the industrialized urban societies of the imminent future. Thus before the advent of World War I*, correlations had become established between glass, iron, reinforced concrete and certain architectural forms that signified a designer's or client's political convictions.

After World War I, as disenchantment with the preexisting political order became commonplace, the prevailing dissatisfaction with established values came to include discontent with traditional architecture as well. Given this mental climate, modern architecture could find support throughout Europe.

Modern architecture rejected traditional forms and imagery as passionately as it embraced the diluted socialist programs that were to be celebrated in an environment of glass, iron, and reinforced concrete. When these materials were unavailable, customary building materials and methods were used to convey the iconography of a new age through machine imagery and industrial metaphors. As these developments were geographically widespread, the Soviet version of modern architecture should be seen as but one episode of a much larger phenomenon. However, there was an important difference. Modern architecture in Soviet Russia attended to a society in the throes of a pervasive social transformation. In Western Europe, by contrast, modern architecture attended to more stable societies and its ambitious, socialist agenda generally remained implicit and unfulfilled.

Of all post–1917 Russian architectural projects, the Monument to the Third Communist International by Vladimir Tatlin (1885–1953), familiarly known as

"Tatlin's Tower," is perhaps the most startling. This 1920 design intended to glorify the anticipated Soviet world order in the tradition of nineteenth-century glass and iron megastructures, especially the Eiffel Tower, which it meant to outdo by an additional 100 meters. Tatlin's Tower enclosed four immense glass volumes within a conical steel network stiffened by two, external intertwining spirals. The interior's multistory glass cube, pyramid, cylinder, and hemisphere rotated at progressively faster speeds (once a year, month, day) and were intended for the Comintern's (*see* Communist International) legislative, executive, and information bureaus, respectively. Although an altogether arresting scheme, Tatlin's proposal remained unbuilt. Its remarkable features confounded contemporary observers, and although it continues to haunt the imagination, Tatlin's Tower had surprisingly little direct influence on Soviet architecture during the 1920s.

The most potent and influential concentration of architectural activity initially centered in the Higher State Artistic-Technical Studios (Vysshii Gosudarstvennye Khudozhestvenno—tekhnicheskie Masterskie [Vkhutemas]), an art, architecture, and design school organized in 1920; consolidated as Vkhutenin in 1926; and closed in 1930. Various student projects—for instance, the Communal House by M. A. Turkus, Cliff Restaurant by V. Simbiritsev, Covered Market by I. I. Volodko, and Skyscraper by S. Lopatin—demonstrate that as early as 1922–1923 modern architecture in Soviet Russia was establishing its own distinctive character. This was in large part due to the influence of N. A. Ladovsky (1881–1941) whose studio exercises stressed perceptual clarity and formal dynamics. Even designers unaffiliated with the Vkhutemas or differing with the "rationalists" in the Association of New Architects (Assotsiatsiia Novykh Arkhitektorov [Asnova]), founded by Ladovsky in 1923, were affected by his approach. Like-minded architects soon developed "rationalist" design methods and popularized them in well-known projects, for instance, the 1924 "Cloud-Hanger" skyscraper project by El Lissitzky (1890–1941) and the 1925 USSR Pavilion by Constantin Melnikov (1890–1974) erected at the International *Exposition des Arts Decoratifs* in Paris.

Although older, established architects generally remained apart from the new directions, several attempted the new architectural idioms with considerable success. The first venture of the Vesnin brothers—Viktor (1882–1950), Leonid (1880–1933), Aleksandr (1883–1959)—was the uneven but influential design for the unexecuted 1923 Palace of Labor. Shortly thereafter, their masterly 1924 project for the Leningrad *Pravda* building became a key image of "constructivist" architecture. When the opportunities came for actual building, the Vesnins provided innovative designs as diverse as the 1927 Mostorg store and the collaboratively designed 1927–1932 Dniepr Dam. Other notable examples of modern buildings by senior architects include the 1925–1927 *Izvestiia* building by G. Barkhin (1880–1969) as well as the 1930–1934 *Pravda* building by P. Golosov (1882–1945). Finally, and most conspicuously, the 1924–1930 Lenin Mausoleum by A. V. Shchusev (1873–1949) exemplifies the extent to which the highest circles of the ruling elite had once relied on modern architecture to provide the Soviet state with its official public imagery.

Throughout the 1920s numerous architectural competitions were held in the Soviet Union. Several important competitions, are the Palace of Labor (1923), USSR Pavilion (1924), Lenin Library (1927), *Tsentrosoyuz* building (1928), and Palace of the Soviets (1932). Although they did not always result in executed buildings, the competitions were invaluable for stimulating the rapid development of Soviet architecture and for providing a wide spectrum of architectural alternatives to the sponsoring agencies. The breadth of architectural responses also indicate that, despite agreement on ideological fundamentals, opinion was far from unanimous regarding what was to be most distinctive about Soviet architecture. The matter was hotly debated in Soviet architectural periodicals and partially resolved in executed buildings that meant to put social theory into actual practice.

As the pace of architectural activity quickened in the latter 1920s, it reached particular intensity around 1927 when the Soviet government, municipal agencies, factories, and professional societies commissioned buildings to celebrate the Soviet Revolution's tenth anniversary. Consequently, numerous public buildings, workers' clubs, hostels, theaters, stores, offices, and communal housing complexes of varying quality appeared in response. Of the many examples, K. Melnikov's 1927–1929 Rusakov Club, I. A. Golosov's 1926–1928 Zuev Club, and the 1928–1929 Narkomfin Building by M. Ginzburg and I. Milnis are among the best of their kind. These edifices represent building types meant to be "social condensers," that is, physical instruments precipitating the transformation of the entire society into the desired communist mold.

Soviet architectural publications played an indispensable part in defining architecture's general role and in establishing the building types required for the anticipated social transformations. In retrospect, the magazine *SA* (*Sovremennaia arkhitektura,* or *Contemporary Architecture*) published from 1926 to 1930 by the Society of Contemporary Architects (Obshchestvo Sovremennykh arkhitektorov [OSA]) appears to have exerted the most influence by virtue of its relative longevity, its steadfast editorial position, and its consistent architectural preferences. Edited primarily by M. Ginzburg (1892–1946), *SA* established "constructivist" architecture as the most influential architectural movement generated under Soviet auspices to date.

Seen from the perspective of the Western avant-garde about 1930, Soviet architecture appeared to have reached an enviable position. It seemed to enjoy the support of the State, which had commissioned a considerable number of important competitions as well as a diverse range of completed modern buildings. Although architectural opinion spanned a wide spectrum, most practitioners strongly supported state policies and sustained high levels of prolonged, intensive effort for the public good. In this sense, the "constructivists," the "rationalists," and also the traditionalists were all heirs of an *engagé* architectural tradition begun with the French Revolution. Furthermore, in the 1920s the Western avant-garde was particularly struck by the unending stream of Soviet radical designs startling in their formal inventiveness. For example, in the late 1920s unclassifiable talents such as I. Leonidov (1902–1959) and Ia. Chernikhov (1889–1951) clearly demonstrated that the architectural imagery dependent on glass, steel, and reinforced concrete was far richer than hitherto suspected. But the sanguine cultural environment that made constant innovation possible changed quickly for the worse in the early 1930s with the Soviet government's prohibition of modernism in all schools, publications, and professional organizations. The winning entries of the landmark 1932 Palace of the Soviets competition announced the unequivocal end for modern architecture in Soviet Russia. Thereafter, the Soviet government supported theatrical versions of neoclassical architecture as its official imagery.

K. P. Zygas

Bibliography

Barkhin M. G., ed. *Mastera sovetskoi arkhitektury ob arkhitekture*. 2 vols. 1975.
Khazanova, V. E. *Iz istorii sovetskoi arkhitektury 1917–1925; Iz istorii sovetskoi arkhitektury 1926–1932*. 2 vols. 1963, 1970.
————. *Sovetskaia arkhitektura pervykh let Oktiabria, 1917–1925 gg*. 1970.
Kirillov, V. V. *Put poiska i eksperimenta*. 1974.
Kopp, Anatole. *Town and Revolution: Soviet Architecture and City Planning, 1917–1935*. Translated by T. E. Burton. 1970.
Lissitzky, El. *Russia: An Architecture for World Revolution*. Translated by E. Dluhosch. 1970.
Miliutin, N. A. *Sotsgorod: The Problem of Building Socialist Cities*. Translated by A. Sprague. 1974.
Senkevich, Anatole, Jr. *Soviet Architecture, 1917–1962: A Bibliographic Guide to Source Material*. 1974.
Shvidkovsky, O. A., ed. *Building in the USSR, 1917–1932*. 1971.
Starr, Frederick S. *Melnikov: Solo Architect in a Mass Society*. 1978.

Arkhiv russkoi revoliutsii (*Archives of the Russian Revolution*). Published in twenty-two volumes, from 1922 to 1937, in Berlin. Edited by I. V. Gessen, it was the major emigré historical journal. It contains Russian-language memoirs and primary source material on the Revolution, Allied intervention, and the Civil War (*see* Civil War in Russia).

Armand (nee Steffen), Inessa Feodorovna (1875–1920). Armand was a prominent Bolshevik and feminist leader.

Inessa Armand was born in Paris of an English father and a French mother who were both in the theater. Her father died when she was young, and she was sent by her mother to live with her grandmother, a governess in Moscow, where she could enjoy a more settled existence. The family where Inessa's grandmother served were wealthy industrialists named Armand, and they raised and educated her as one of the family. She married the oldest son, Alexander, and bore him four children. Between 1901 and 1903 Inessa left her husband to live with his youngest brother, Vladimir. During that same period she became interested in social problems, including prostitution, and became a feminist and revolutionary socialist. According to official sources, she joined the Russian Social Democratic Workers' Party (Bolshevik)* in 1904. When she was arrested in 1907 the police believed her to be a Socialist–Revolutionary (see Socialist-Revolutionary Party).

Sent to Siberia in 1907, she escaped and fled to Finland where her lover, Vladimir Armand, succumbed to tuberculosis. She moved to Brussels in 1909 and probably met V. I. Lenin* at that time. Robert H. McNeal, the biographer of Lenin's wife, N. K. Krupskaia*, believes that she and Lenin were lovers between 1911 and 1912 and from 1914 to 1915. In any case, Lenin asked her to teach in his school for Bolsheviks in Longjumeau in 1911. She and Lenin were leading members during 1910–1911 in the Paris group of the emigré organization of the party, and Inessa became secretary of the Executive Committee of all groups of Russian Social Democrats. In 1912 Lenin went to Cracow, and Inessa went to southern France and then to underground work in Russia where she was arrested and sent to prison.

Inessa escaped from Russia in 1913 and joined Lenin and Krupskaia in Cracow. Together with Krupskaia she was foreign editor of *Rabotnitsa (Woman Worker)*, a socialist newspaper for women to be published in Russia. From 1914 to 1916 Inessa and Lenin closely collaborated with one another. In 1916 she left for France and did not rejoin Lenin until the trip back to Russia with him and Krupskaia in April 1917. From 1914 to 1918 she participated as a representative of the Bolsheviks in the Berne Conference of Bolsheviks, the International Conference of Women and Youth, and the Zimmerwald and Kienthal Conferences of Internationalists*. She represented the Bolsheviks at the International Socialist Bureau in Brussels.

After returning to Russia in 1917 Inessa settled in Moscow where she became a member of the Executive Commission of the Moscow Committee of the Russian Social Democratic Workers' Party (Bolshevik) (RSDWP [B]). She was a delegate to the Seventh Conference and the Sixth Congress of the RSDWP (B). Following the October Seizure of Power she served as a member of the Bureau of the Moscow Guberniia Council of People's Commissars and of the All-Russian Central Executive Committee of the Russian Communist Party (Bolshevik). From 1918 she was Chairperson of the Woman's Section of the Central Committee of the Communist Party. In 1920 she served as delegate to the Second Congress of the Communist International*, and she organized the First International Conference of Communist Women. In 1920 she died of cholera in the Caucasus (see Women in the Russian Revolution, Role of).

Armenia, Revolution in. The Armenian people constituted somewhat less than 1 percent of the population of the Russian state in 1897, and most of them lived in the Southwest corner of the Caucasus. By 1916 there were about 1,860,000 Armenians in the Empire. Like the Georgians, the Armenians had adopted Christianity in the fourth century, which set them apart from the Moslem nationalities of the Middle East. Those Armenians living in Russia were absorbed into the Empire during the first part of the nineteenth century, although the majority of them remained under Turkish control in the Ottoman Empire. The Armenians had no separate political institutions at the beginning of 1917 but were ruled by a Governor General of the Caucasus. The Armenian national movement was dominated by a desire to free their brethren from Turkish control and was less socialist than the other Caucasian national movements. One of the earliest such movements was the Dashnaktsutiun, or Dashnaks*, which used terror in its struggle with the Ottoman government. In its political program it bore some resemblance to the Socialist-Revolutionary Party*. At the time of the February Revolution*, General N. N. Iudenich* took command, and civil power was placed in the hands of the Special Transcaucasian Committee, or Ozakom (Osobyi Zakavkazskii Komitet), which introduced zemstvos at the local level. The other source of political power in the Caucasus was the soviets. The Dashnaks shared political power with the Mensheviks (see Russian Social Democratic Workers' Party [Menshevik]) and the Musavats (see Moslem Democratic Party) in the Baku Soviet. All of the soviets were united, and a regional center in Tiflis and Ozakom usually approved their decisions.

The Armenian Dashnaks joined the Russian army during World War I* by organizing voluntary detachments to fight the Turks and by encouraging their brethren in Turkey to rebel. The Turks responded by ordering the Armenians to be forcibly removed to Mesopotamia. Up to a million Armenians were massacred in prison. The Dashnak Regional Congress in April 1917 supported the Provisional Government*.

In September the Armenian National Council in Tiflis created the Armenian National Conference and organized 3,000 Armenian volunteers into the Armenian Corps with the permission of the Provisional Government.

When the Provisional Government fell in October, the Transcaucasian Commissariat, or executive body, including two Dashnaks within it, was created to administer the Caucasus until the Constituent Assembly* created a new government. When the Constituent Assembly was dissolved by the Bolsheviks, the Caucasian deputies returned to organize a Transcaucasian seim (diet or legislature) in Tiflis (Zakavkazskii Seim). In April 1918 the whole area, now possessing its own executive and legislative organization, seceded from Russia in order to negotiate separately with the Turks for independence. The new state was called the Transcaucasian Federal Republic.

In March 1918 fierce fighting began in Baku between the Baku Soviet, dominated by Dashnaks and pro-communist Russian deserters, and the Moslems in the city, clearing the path for the formation of a Bolshevik (see Russian Social Democratic Workers' Party [Bolshevik]) government in Baku in April. The Dashnaks were ordered to disband their separate military detachments and their national soviet. When the Baku Commune voted to appoint a tsarist general as its commander-in-chief and asked for British help against the invading Turks and Azerbaijani, the communists resigned from the government. In their wake the Centro-Caspian Military Flotilla was created, dominated by Russian Socialist–Revolutionaries (*see* Socialist-Revolutionary Party). It fell to the Turks in September 1918.

The Armenian Republic lost two-thirds of its territory to the invading Turks. It lacked any strong allies to support its claim to independence, although it collaborated for a while with General A. I. Denikin* and the White forces (*see* White Movement). In May 1919 it announced the annexation of Turkish Armenia. (Although the Allied Supreme Council in Paris recognized the independence of Azerbaijan, Georgia, and Armenia in January 1920, they were not able to sustain themselves). In November 1920 Soviet forces crossed into Armenia from Azerbaijan ostensibly to forestall the Turkish occupation of Erevan. The independent Dashnak government of the Armenian Republic hastily agreed to a joint communist–Dashnak government. By December 1920 Armenia had become part of the Soviet Union (*see* Transcaucasia, Revolution in).

Bibliography

Hovannisian, R. G. *The Republic of Armenia*. 1971.

Katz, Zev; Rogers, Rosemarie; and Harned, Frederic. *Handbook of Major Soviet Nationalities*. 1975.

Lang, D. M. *Armenia, Cradle of Civilization*. 1978.

Matossian, M. K. *The Impact of Soviet Policies in Armenia*. 1962.

Pipes, R. *The Formation of the Soviet Union*. Rev. ed. 1964.

Suny, R. G. *Armenia in the Twentieth Century*. 1983.

Army of Imperial Russia in World War I. The Russian army that fought against the Central Powers in 1914 was still recovering from the dual disaster of the Russo–Japanese War and the Revolution of 1905 (*see* Nineteen-Five Revolution). A demoralized army of more than a million mobilized reservists had returned to European Russia at the height of political events in late 1905 and early 1906 over the Trans-Siberian Railroad, which was largely under the control of revolutionary "republics." In 1906–1907 peasant soldiers had often been used to suppress peasant unrest, occasionally resulting in mutinies and the circulation of revolutionary agitation in the army. Only the rapid discharging of veterans and the intensive recruitment of younger soldiers allowed discipline and training to recover somewhat from 1909 onward. Nevertheless, with the mobilization in 1914 of all reservists up to the age of forty-three, nearly 1,800,000 of the mobilized army of 5,350,000 had served in 1904–1907. Moreover, they were overwhelmingly family men for whom being torn away again from fragile peasant households was bitterly resented. They frequently expressed this in riots at induction centers or in desertions. The cadre arm of 1,500,000 younger soldiers had been well trained and well equipped and, contrary to common opinion, fought well even against Germans in the early months of the war.

The Russian officers corps, including a significant share of the higher leadership, had become considerably professionalized and penetrated by the nonnoble orders in the decades before 1914. Of the 45,500 career officers in 1914, exactly half were classified as of nonnoble origin, closer to 60 percent in infantry units. Most (around 55 percent) had been trained in the junker schools attached to the military districts, to which any soldier with the equivalent of six years of education could be admitted regardless of social origin. The regular professional military schools, which supplied less than half the required annual number of commissioned officers, still formally required noble origin for admission and drew primarily from the cadet corps schools but accepted ever larger numbers from civilian gymnasia, many of the latter, in fact, from the urbanized professional and middle classes. In addition, there were 20,700 mobilized reserve officers who had served as civilian "volunteers" before the war. Volunteers were mainly youths from the educated classes who wished to escape conscription (a four-year term and eighteen years in the reserves as soldiers) and, with shorter terms of training (only six months for university graduates), would obtain a reserve commission to be called on only in wartime. Thus many educated civilians of radical political persuasion entered the wartime officer corps, many of them playing a significant role in soldiers' committees in 1917.

Although the high nobility through the Corps of Pages and service in the Imperial Guards continued to have favored careers in the army, the Academy of the General Staff prepared an increasing number of products of the junker schools for higher military positions, so a fair number of talented generals in World War I* were of nonnoble, even peasant, origin (e.g., A. I. Denikin*, M. V. Alekseev). A new generation of general staff officers was responsible for a program of reforms between 1908 and 1914, which included improved training in infantry and artillery tactics, an effective mobilization plan, and needed improvements in organization and weaponry. But favoritism and seniority kept many incompetent types, grand dukes, and superannuated officers in top posts. Thus the aged, ambitious General A. A. Sukhomlinov retained Nicholas II's* favor as War Minister from 1909 to 1915 in spite of his lamentable performance. The key office of Chief of the General Staff was held by six occupants in the decade before the First World War, none of them contributing significantly to the positive work of the General Staff.

In spite of the decimation of Samsonov's Second Army at Tannenberg (the loss of the better part of three corps or more than 100,000 men), the Russian army performed quite well in the first six months of the war, conquering Galicia and the Carpathian passes from Austria–Hungary and holding its own against the Germans at Lodz and on the lower Vistula. However, the unprecedented scale of the fighting resulted within six months in the virtual halving of the trained prewar army and the exhaustion of existing stocks of artillery shells, rifles, and ammunition. By January 1915 the Russian army had lost approximately 396,000 in fatalities, 918,000 in wounded, and 486,000 in captured, a total of 1.8 million men (this awesome rate of attrition continued until the end of the

Great Retreat in September 1915). Some 2.0 million replacements in 1915 were given only the most rudimentary training without the benefit of rifles and sent off to the front. The ammunition crisis was due to faulty staff planning before the war: norms were based on a short war of maneuver on the scale of the Russo–Japanese War, and the Artillery Department and the War Ministry refused to believe field reports on the phenomenal expenditure of shells. Thus civilian industry was retooled only late in the year, and orders were not placed abroad until the catastrophe was already upon them. Rifle production had ceased before the war in favor of machine guns because of a large surplus of guns in relation to the number of trained reserves, but none was on hand for the 1915 replacements. Other belligerent nations faced similar problems but were able to adjust their more mature industrial economies and perceived the need more quickly. The Russian army paid very heavily for its deficiencies in casualties throughout 1915.

On April 18, 1915, a German army under General Mackensen broke through at Gorlice, Austria, in the rear of the Russian army occupying the Carpathians, setting off a retreat that was to last four and a half months and end in the surrender of all of Poland, Courland, conquered Galicia, and most of White Russia to the enemy. In the first two months the retreat was measured and orderly but at the price of enormous losses among the freshly called up replacements, who were obliged to obtain rifles from fallen comrades. But after the fall of Warsaw and the key fortresses of Novo-Geogievsk and Ivanogorod in July, the retreat turned into a rout, with hundreds of thousands of Polish, Jewish, and White Russian refugees intermingling with deserters and disorganized units on the few roads through the White Russian forests. In September the line stabilized from Riga southward along the line of the Dvina, Minsk, and the Galician border. From this point onward the war of maneuver was over, and two years of bitter trench warfare set in. At the front both officers and soldiers blamed their misfortunes on treason in the rear on the part of ministers, courtiers, and generals with German-sounding names but, above all, on War Minister Sukhomlinov and his former protégé Colonel Miasoedov, who was executed for allegedly betraying the plans of a fortress to the enemy.

To placate the aroused public, Nicholas dismissed his most hated ministers (among them Sukhomlinov), called the Duma (*see* Duma and Revolution) back in session, and authorized public organizations to help in war production and rear services to the army (War Industry Committees*, Red Cross, and the All-Russian Union of Towns and All-Russian Union of Zemstvos*). But against all advice, he dismissed the popular Grand Duke Nicholas as Commander-in-Chief and assumed the post himself, leaving the supervision of domestic matters to his imperious consort Aleksandra and the unscrupulous holy man Grigorii Rasputin*. At front headquarters Nicholas left all practical military matters to his chief of staff, General Alekseev, which was undoubtedly an improvement over the greatly overrated Grand Duke Nicholas and his incompetent chief of staff, General N. N. Ianushkevich. In 1916 the deficiencies in supply were largely overcome, making possible the startlingly successful, but unplanned, offensive on the southwestern front under General A. A. Brusilov*, which in a few weeks gained a depth of 30 to 40 miles along a 200-mile front. But the effort could not be sustained due to the enormous casualties, lack of replacements, and strong counterattacks by primarily German units. Nor was any strategic gain registered by the entry of Romania into the war in August 1916, as its rapid collapse only added to the burden of the Russian armies by extending the front an additional 350 miles.

The attempt to mount a new offensive in June 1917, after the front army had been shaken by revolutionary upheaval, ended in complete failure. The four armies of the southwestern front retreated 150 miles to the rear. In August a new German offensive captured Riga and key islands at the juncture of the Riga and Finnish gulfs, exposing Petrograd to attack. Plagued by massive desertions and the clamor not to spend another winter in the trenches, the Russian army was no longer in a condition to fight. The great majority of the front soldiers welcomed the proclamation of Soviet power and the opening of peace negotiations, which ended in the Peace of Brest-Litovsk*.

Approximately 15.5 million men were brought under arms in Russia during the war, virtually the entire healthy male population between the ages of nineteen and forty-three, except for those with special exemptions. Most of the latter were workers in critical industries (slightly over 1 million), but more than half a million were from the middle and upper classes, many of them with soft berths in the "public organizations" (*zemgussary*). The Central Powers took 2.4 million prisoners, somewhere between 1.6 million and 1.8 million were fatalities, and around 3 million were seriously wounded or sick and never returned to the ranks. Estimates of the number of deserters run as high as 2 million, but the figures are likely inaccurate since most desertions were temporary until after the June offensive of 1917. The call-up of the last category of family men in the autumn of 1915 (sole breadwinners) led to serious riots that autumn as did that of the "over-forties" in 1916; the latter became a particularly turbulent element prone to desertion and "Bolshevism" in 1917. The unprecedented rate of casualties occasioned by Brusilov's misguided efforts to renew the offensive in the autumn of 1916 led to a series of mutinies of entire regiments and divisions that were suppressed by force and executions. Persistent rumors of peace, deflated by Nicholas's Manifesto of mid-December declaring them to be false, helped crystallize a particularly bitter mood at the front by the end of the year. Likewise, a sharp curtailment in food rations, combined with news of the wild inflation back home and the treason of the "German Party" to which Aleksandra and Rasputin were linked, contributed to a sharp decline in respect for political authority and the dynasty, preparing the way for the cataclysm of March 1917 (*see* February Revolution; Soldiers and Soldiers' Committees).

Allan K. Wildman

Bibliography

Danilov, General Iu. N. *Rossiia v mirovoi voine, 1914–15 g.g.* 1924.
Golovin, General N. N. *Voennye usiliia v mirovoi voine.* 2 vols. 1924.

Knox, General Alfred. *With the Russian Army, 1914–1917.* 2 vols. 1921.
Stone, Norman. *The Eastern Front, 1914–1917.* 1975.
Tsentral'noe Statisticheskoe Upravlenie. *Rossiia v mirovoi voine, 1914–1918 goda (v tsifrakh).* 1925.
Wildman, Allan K. *The End of the Russian Imperial Army. The Old Army and the Soldier's Revolt (March-April 1917).* 1980.
———. *The End of the Russian Imperial Army. The Road to Soviet Power and Peace.* 1987.

Art and the October Revolution. The October Revolution transformed the artistic scene in two respects. It swept away existing institutions and catapulted the avant-garde into prominence.

The liberation of the administrative setting was a deliberate policy of the Bolshevik government, a necessary component of the new order. The efflorescence of innovative currents, however, was not the result of official sponsorship. Rather, it arose from the spontaneous identification of the modernists with the political and social transformation of the country.

In prerevolutionary Russia the Imperial Academy of Arts epitomized an elaborate system of state support and supervision that encouraged conservatism and bred privilege. Operating under the jurisdiction of the Palace Ministry, the academy not only was the apex of all training in the fine arts but also functioned as the Ministry of Arts, supervising art education and museums throughout the Empire, dispensing state subsidies and commissions, sponsoring exhibits, and granting professional recognition and titles.

Countering this tsarist legacy, the Bolshevik government sought to introduce maximum autonomy and opportunity. Although it did not set up a separate Commissariat of Art, it created the Fine Arts Department (IZO) and the Department of Museums and the Preservation of Antiquities within the People's Commissariat of Education headed by Anatolii V. Lunacharskii*. The Imperial Academy was abolished in April 1918, and its massive building in Petrograd was transformed into the Free Art Studios (Svomas) that were open to any applicant over the age of sixteen, regardless of educational background. Any artist could now apply for a teaching position, subject to approval by the students, while they in turn could study with professors of their own choice or independently. The entire system of art education was similarly decentralized. Other art schools were converted into free art studios with flexible administrative rules, instructional programs, and graduation requirements.

Further measures sought to democratize and to revitalize artistic life. To make exhibits easily accessible, the IZO organized and subsidized a series of juryless Exhibits of All Artistic Trends. In distributing state commissions, it tried to be fair in patronizing both the modernists and the traditionalists. However, the sizable purchasing fund was deliberately used to redress prerevolutionary favoritism and to diversify museum holdings. As a result, Soviet museums were the first in Europe to display modern art on an extensive scale.

Despite extensive government support of the arts, there was no party policy regarding style. The writings of Marx provided little guidance since he had never tackled the question of an art appropriate for the proletarian epoch other than to assert that the whole complex of culture was part of the superstructure erected by a particular economic system. Although Aleksandr Bogdanov and other pro-Bolshevik intellectuals propounded various theories about the nature of proletarian art, ranging from esoteric to pragmatic, V. I. Lenin* never came up with any definitive pronouncement. His own tastes, like those of most Bolshevik leaders, were conservative, and in private he expressed dismay with the formal experimentations of the *futurists* (a generic, derogatory term for all innovative trends of the time). But he never publicly advocated any comprehensive interference by the state to curtail freedom of artistic expression.

This policy was shared and fairly administered by Lunacharskii. During his tenure as Commissar of Education (1917–1929), he resisted the repeated attempts by various coteries to gain official recognition as *the* exponent of revolutionary or Soviet art. He eloquently argued that giving free rein to a variety of trends created the best preconditions for the eventual emergence of art forms appropriate for the future proletarian society. The single party statement concerning style— the Central Committee's letter in 1920 chastizing the futurists for imparting perverse artistic tastes to the masses—cannot be equated with an official condemnation of nonobjective art, even though it has been interpreted as such both by advocates of state control and by critics of Stalinist cultural policies. In the context of contemporary issues, this pronouncement was meant to undercut the claims of Proletarian Culture (Proletkult)—an educational organization that rejected traditions—to be the only bearer of the new culture and to assert the party's authority over the course of cultural development. Neither in intention nor in effect was it a decree specifying an official style.

The Bolsheviks had no reservations, however, about turning art into an instrument of political agitation. In April 1918 the party issued two decrees, one calling for razing the ''monuments created in honor of tsars and their servants'' and the other launching the Program of Monumental Propaganda to commemorate various progressive figures, ranging from Spartacus and Pugachev to Marx. Unveilings were the occasion for political festivities to glorify and confirm the revolutionary cause. The program also called for the transformation of public buildings, streets, and squares into striking displays of agitational slogans that would be even more effective than revolutionary perorations.

On the educational level, the regime committed itself to bringing art to the people. The public was invited to express its preferences and to vote on what monuments were worthy of state purchase. In Petrograd the winter residence of the tsars was turned into the Palace of Arts where free performances, concerts, and lectures were held. Those collections, like the Hermitage where attendance had been restricted, were now open to all. Every museum was staffed with guides so that the new, semiliterate mass visitors could be properly instructed. New museums of artistic culture, intended to popularize revolutionary art concepts, were set up as well as an extensive network of art classes and exhibits for soldiers and workers. In short, responsive to the socialist tradition, the regime fostered cultural uplift for the masses.

Lunacharskii invited all artists, without distinction, to help liberalize and activate the artistic life. While the established figures set up a virtual boycott, the leftists responded with enthusiasm. Unsuccessful and derided critics of bourgeoisie culture before World War I*, they were now eager to implement their iconoclastic ideas in support of political and social revolution. Because of this response and not because the authorities gave them carte blanche, the avant-garde came to exercise a virtual dictatorship. Occupying most of the administrative posts, they tended to monopolize the tribune, to initiate and carry out various mass spectacles, and to found and staff the new teaching centers and research institutes. Nikolai Punin, the radical critic, headed the Free Art Studios in Petrograd; the modernist artists David Shternberg and Vladimir Tatlin headed, respectively, the Petrograd and the Moscow sections of IZO; Vasilii Kandinsky and Alexander Rodchenko founded the Institute of Artistic Culture (Inkhuk) devoted both to theoretical research and to applied arts. Marc Chagall and Kasimir Malevich directed an experimental art school in Vitebsk.

The needs of the time and the identification of the innovators with the cause of the Revolution relegated traditional art to the background. Little easel painting was produced, but many new forms of expression were invented, especially in the mass media. Art left the studio and moved into the streets, the front lines, or the factories. Painters designed mass political festivities for city squares; elaborated a new, terse language for war and propaganda posters; decorated agitational trains and boats that took revolutionary slogans to the countryside via rail and river; and wrote visionary tracts on how the application of modern design to architecture (*see* Architecture and the Revolution) and industrial production was going to change society.

The predominance of the avant-garde did not last beyond 1920–1921, very few of the monuments and displays have survived, and many visionary projects could not be realized during those times of privation and strife. But the new theories about the forms and functions of art—spawned by the October Revolution and expressed in part by Tatlin's constructivism, Rodchenko's productionalism, and Malevich's suprematism—have left tangible and lasting results. They gave impetus, both in Russia and abroad, to new techniques in mass media; to novel industrial, graphic, and stage design; and to new concepts in architecture and urban planning.

Elizabeth Valkeneir

Bibliography

Bojko, Szymon. *New Graphic Design in Revolutionary Russia.* 1972.
Bowlt, John E. *Russian Art of the Avant-Garde: Theory and Criticism, 1902–1934.* 1976.
Gray, Camilla. *The Russian Experiment in Art, 1863–1922.* 1962.
Guerman, Mikhail. *Art of the October Revolution.* 1979.
Lobanov, V. *Khudozhestennye gruppirovki za poslednie 25 let.* 1930.

Matsa, Ivan L., ed. *Sovetskoe iskusstvo za 15 let; materialy i documentatsiya*. 1933.
Shidkovsky, O. A., ed. *Building in the USSR, 1917–1932*. 1971.
Tugenhold, Ya. *Iskusstvo oktiabr'skoe epokhi*. 1930.

Aurora. Baltic Fleet cruiser whose crew of 578 men participated in the October Seizure of Power* in Petrograd.

Brought into service in 1903, it was part of the Second Pacific Squadron during 1904–1905 and participated in the Tsushima Battle. In 1916 it was under repair at the Franco–Russian plant in Petrograd.

Aurora sailors were active in the February Revolution* and formed ship committees. By October the Bolsheviks numbered forty-two members on ship. On October 22 the ship committee agreed not to carry out orders of the Provisional Government*.

On October 25 at 3:30 a.m. the *Aurora* and its crew, on orders of the Petrograd Military Revolutionary Council, took control of the Nikolaevskii Bridge. At 9:40 p.m. the *Aurora* received the command and fired a blank round to signal the assault on the Winter Palace, one of the few remaining points held by the Provisional Government.

The cruiser served in the Baltic during World War II. In 1948 it assumed permanent mooring in the Neva in Leningrad as a monument of the October Revolution, and in 1957 it was incorporated as a museum.

Avksent'ev, Nikolai Dmitrievich (1878–1943). Socialist–Revolutionary (S–R) (*see* Socialist-Revolutionary Party), member of the Provisional Government*, and opponent of the October Revolution (*see* October Seizure of Power).

Avksent'ev was a member of the Central Committee of the Socialist-Revolutionary Party and a leading representative of the party's right wing, defending legal activities and opposing terrorism. He spent 1907–1917 in emigration, mostly in Paris. During World War I* he adopted a pro-French, anti-German "defensist" position (*see* Defensism) and represented the most rigorous pro-war stance among the S–R's. He wrote for the periodicals *Za rubezhom* (*Abroad*) and *Novosti* (*News*) and was among the editors of the Paris-based newspaper *Prizyv* (*The Call*), a prowar publication expressing the views of the S–R and Menshevik (*see* Russian Social Democratic Workers' Party [Menshevik]) right wings. Avksent'ev returned to Russia in early April following the February Revolution*. He soon became a member of the Executive Committee of the Petrograd Soviet* and chairman of the Executive Committee of the All-Russian Council of Peasants' Deputies. He favored the principle of class collaboration, thus opposing the initial refusal of the leadership of the Petrograd Soviet to enter into coalition with the bourgeois parties of the Provisional Government. In July-August 1917 Avksent'ev served as Minister of Internal Affairs in the second coalition of the Provisional Government. In October he was chairman of the Pre-parliament. (*see* Democratic Conference). He strongly opposed the Bolsheviks and the October Revolution and became chairman of the Committee for the Salvation of the Motherland and Revolution*, which was partially responsible for the abortive October 29, 1917, uprising in Petrograd. In 1918 he was one of the organizers of the counterrevolution in the Volga Region and Siberia and was a member of the Ufa Directory*. He emigrated at the end of 1918. In the 1930s Avksent'ev, long a freemason, headed the emigrant Masonic Lodge Severanai zvezda (Northern Star), which Soviet sources allege engaged in anti-Soviet activities.

Bibliography

Radkey, O. *The Agrarian Foes of Bolshevism*. 1958.
Rakey, O. *The Sickle Under the Hammer*. 1963.

Azbuka. Azbuka (Alphabet) was an intelligence service for the White Movement* operating in South Russia during the Civil War (*see* Civil War in Russia). It was formed in mid–1918 by V. V. Shulgin and reflected its creator's monarchist, Great Russian nationalist and anti-Semitic views (*see* Anti-Semitism).

Azbuka was originally funded by two Moscow counterrevolutionary groups, the Right Center and the National Center. Early in 1919 Shulgin threw in his lot with A. I. Denikin* and the White Volunteer Army (*see* White Movement). Thereafter Azbuka was funded, albeit parsimoneously, by Denikin. Although never numbering more than 100 agents, the service was credited with being accurate and reliable in its reports on the public mood and political developments in South Russia. Although apparently unsuccessful in penetrating Soviet institutions, it infiltrated the movements of S. M. Petliura* and P. P. Skoropadskii. There were apparently some cases of sabotage in Soviet occupied areas. In December 1919 Azbuka was compelled to cease operations for lack of financial support.

Azerbaijan, Revolution in. Azerbaijan was one of the crucial areas in the revolutionary movement in the Caucasus. The Azerbaijani were a relatively small group of Turkic-Moslem peoples inhabiting the Southeastern Caucasus Mountains in 1917. They were strategically located in and around the city of Baku, the oil-producing capital of prerevolutionary Russia. Modern oil wells were first erected in Azerbaijan in the 1870s, and by 1900 the Baku oil fields were producing 50 percent of the world's oil. Baku became a sprawling Westernized city surrounded by a sea of peasants. The Azerbaijani constituted about a third of the total number of workers in and around Baku, although they were more likely to be the unskilled workers in any industrial enterprise. Traditional Azerbaijan had been strongly influenced by Iranian language and literature until the eleventh century, when "turkization" began. By 1916 about 60 percent of the Moslem population had become members of the Shiite Moslem sect as a result of renewed Persian influence. The Azerbaijani villages remained conservative and religious, giving their unswerving allegiance to their Moslem landlords and their pro-Persian Shiite clergy. They were the least revolutionary peasant group in Transcaucasia and represented a sharp contrast to the pro-Turkish Westernized intelligentsia in the cities.

In 1904 the first socialist group was formed among the Azerbaijani: Gummet* (Endeavor). Like the Jewish Bund*, Gummet attempted to unite all of the workers of one nationality. Gummet was a Pan-Turkic organization that sought to give the Azerbaijani workers some leverage against the nationalist Armenian parties that had organized the Armenian workers. After the Revolution of 1905 (see Nineteen-Five Revolution) many of the former leaders drifted away and in 1911 formed a new political party called Musavat (Equality) (see Moslem Democratic Party), a movement that called for the unification of all Moslem people along with their Westernization. The program of Musavat did not represent any systematic ideology but rather a nostalgic urge to return to the former greatness and unity of the Moslem world. But unlike the Tatar Pan-Islamic movement, the Azerbaijani wanted a federal state structure secularization of the state and a moderate socialism. Musavat's program was popular among the urban intellectuals and the workers, but the Moslem Shiite clergy and the peasants were more inclined toward traditional and conservative Pan-Islamic movements.

Like the other nationalist movements in Transcaucasia, those of the Azerbaijani were able to realize their aspirations from 1918 to 1920 while their former Russian masters were preoccupied with fighting one another during the Civil War (see Civil War in Russia), and the White armies (see White Movement) formed a protective cushion in the Northern Caucasus. In May 1917 the First All-Russian Moslem Congress met in Moscow and accepted the proposals of the Musavat leader Resul Zade for independence for Azerbaijan and the other Russian–Turkish territories within a Russian democratic republican federation. When an Azerbaijani parliament was elected in the fall of 1918, Musavat elected the largest number of delegates from any one party, 38 deputies out of 180.

Following the creation of a Soviet government in Russia in 1917, on May 28, 1918, Azerbaijan proclaimed its independence. The decision was defensive and followed the slaughter of Moslems in the city of Baku in March 1918 by the Armenian Dashnaks* during the short-lived Baku Commune. The Azerbaijani turned toward the Turks, who helped them to retake the city, and the Moslems conducted their own pogrom against the Armenians. In November 1918, with the armistice that brought an end to World War I*, the Turks withdrew from Baku, and the British took the city, holding it until August 1919. At this point the Musavat and the extreme Moslem nationalist party Ittihad-ve Tarakki* began to make overtures to Moscow.

The reasons for this shift were tactical rather than ideological. General A. I. Denikin's* Volunteer Army was rapidly losing its strength toward the end of 1920 after a string of defeats. Finally, with the withdrawal of the British, the small new states of the Caucasus were confronted with the threat of invasion by the communist behemoth in the North. Anastas Mikoian had already organized the Azerbaijani Communist Party in 1918 at the same time that he rejuvenated the Baku Committee. There was some friction between the Left Baku organization, which had close ties to Moscow, and the rightist Tiflis Regional Committee, which opposed the creation of the Communist Party of Azerbaijan and its call for a Soviet Azerbaijan republic. By January 1920 Moscow intervened in favor of its disciples in Baku, and in February 1920 the Communist Party of Azerbaijan, claiming 4,000 members, held its first congress and called for the creation of the Azerbaijan Soviet Republic. The close collaboration between the Soviet government and Kemal Pasha (Ataturk) strengthened the decision of Moscow nationalists to seek closer ties with Russia. In April 1920 the Caucasian Bureau* (Kavbruo) and the Central Committee of the Communist Party of Azerbaijan sent an ultimatum to the government of Azerbaijan demanding that Azerbaijan become a Soviet republic. The Azerbaijan parliament, surrounded by Baku communists and threatened by Red Army troops under G. K. Ordzhonikidzhe*, accepted the ultimatum. The following day the Red Army entered Baku without firing a single shot. The chairmanship to the Council of Ministers of the new Azerbaijan Soviet Republic was given to Nariman Narimanov*, an Azerbaijan Social Democrat and ex-president of Gummet who had served as an official in the Soviet government (*see* Transcaucasia, Revolution in).

Bibliography

Katz, Zev; Rogers, Rosemarie; and Harned, Frederic. *Handbook of Major Soviet Nationalities*. 1975.
Pipes, R. *The Formation of the Soviet Union*. Rev. ed. 1964.
Swietochowski, T. *Russian Azerbaijan, 1905–20*. 1983.

Azizbekov, Meshadi Azim-bek-ogly (1876–1918). A Bolshevik who participated in the Soviet seizure of power in Baku; one of twenty-six commissars of the Baku Soviet.

The son of a bricklayer, Azizbekov graduated from St. Petersburg Technological Institute. He joined the Social Democratic movement in 1898 and was one of the leaders of the Social Democratic group and Gummet*. He played an active role in the 1905–1907 Revolution in Baku, was elected to the Baku City Duma, and after 1917 was a member of the Baku Soviet and the Russian Social Democratic Workers' Party (Bolshevik)*.

In September 1917 he led a general strike in the Baku oil fields. He participated in the Soviet seizure of power in Baku and the suppression of the Musavat (*see* Moslem Democratic Party) in March 1918. Azizbekov was Guberniia Commissar, Deputy Commissar of Internal Affairs in the Baku Council of People's Commissars, and chairman of the Executive Committee of the Baku Soviet of Peasant Deputies. He was one of the organizers of the defense of Baku against the Turks and was arrested and shot after the fall of Baku.

B

Baku Commune. *See* Transcaucasia, Revolution in; Azerbaijan, Revolution in; Armenia, Revolution in; Georgia, Revolution in.

Bashkiria, Revolution in. Bashkiria was a part of Russia where economic backwardness, nationalism, and the Moslem religion served as barriers to communism.

The Bashkirs are a semi-nomadic Turkic people closely related to the Tatars (*see* Tatars, Revolution Among the). They live in the Southeast Ural Region. In 1897 they numbered 1,493,900, or 1.2 percent of the population of the Russian Empire. The Bashkirs settled in this area as early as the sixth century. In 1789 they acquired considerable independence when the Bashkir Military District was created under a Russian Imperial governor. Despite the close cultural relations to the Tatars, the Bashkirs were more backward and rural, and they resented the Tatars for their disdainful attitude toward them.

When the Moslem independence movement seemed to be reaching its apogee at the beginning of 1918, I. V. Stalin*, People's Commissar for Nationalities, began to launch an attack on it by attempting to coopt its leaders. With the help of a few native recruits, he organized a Tatar–Bashkir state in May 1918. The Bashkirs never expressed much enthusiasm for the arrangements, and when Stalin's chief Moslem agent, M. Vakhitov, was killed in the autumn of 1918, the new state fell apart.

Ahmed Zeki Validov, the most prominent nationalist Bashkir leader in the revolutionary period, moved into the vacuum created by the failures of both the All-Russian independent Moslem movement and Stalin's Tatar–Bashkir state by organizing an independent Bashkir army. Validov had already called a Bashkir pre-parliament in Orenburg on November 8, 1917, and announced an independent and autonomous Bashkiria, although the Moslems constituted by this time only about 20 to 30 percent of the population in that area. In 1917 and in 1918 Validov tended to ally himself to the anti-Soviet Committee of Members of the Constituent Assembly* (Komuch) in Samara. With the destruction of Komuch by A. V. Kolchak* in November 1918, Validov began to move back toward the Soviet government. In February 1919 Validov came to an agreement with the Soviet regime to create an independent Bashkir republic. Validov was asked to place his 6,500 Bashkir soldiers at the disposal of the Red Army* and to create the Bashkir Revolutionary Committee (Bashrevkom) to govern until the Bashkir Congress of Soviets could be called. Bashkir railroads, factories, mines, and armed forces were to be subordinated to the All-Russian Soviet government, although Bashkir soldiers were to remain in their own units. Other functions of government would be assumed by Bashrevkom. Validov subsequently joined the Russian Communist Party (*see* Russian Social Democratic Workers' Party [Bolshevik]) along with approximately 200 other Bashkir intellectuals.

The Bashrevkom headed by Validov made plans to create an autonomous Bashkir Communist Party and to transfer all land held by non-Moslems to Bashkir peasants. Most of the soviets that took shape in Bashkiria, however, were Great Russian in membership, and they tended to redistribute confiscated land among Russian colonists. The Bolshevik Party (*see* Russian Social Democratic Workers' Party [Bolshevik]) itself was not enthusiastic about the idea of a separate Bashkir republic. By September 1919 the Executive Committee of the Russian Communist Party (Bolshevik) at Ufa, mostly Russian in its membership, had taken control of most of Bashkiria with help from the Red Army. The Executive Committee simply ignored Bashkir institutions and the agreement calling for an independent Bashkiria. The Bashrevkom recovered its control only with a great deal of effort. In November 1919 the First Bashkir Regional Communist Party Conference was called, and it elected the Regional Committee of the party (Obkom) dominated by Great Russian and Tatar communists. The Obkom ultimately put an end to Bashkir autonomy. It created the Society for Aid to Bashkiria (Bashkiropomoshch), to be administered by F. A. Artem, a right-wing leader of the Communist Party of the Ukraine (Bolshevik) (*see* Ukraine, Revolution in). Using its position as the chief instrument for funneling Soviet aid to the native Bashkirs, the Bashkiropomoshch created its own network of Bolshevik cells throughout the country. When the Bashrevkom tried in January 1920 to arrest several Tatar members of the Obkom, the latter called in the Red Army. With its help the Obkom subordinated Bashrevkom to its control.

In March 1920 L. D. Trotsky* held several conferences in the area to try to reconcile the Bashrevkom and the Obkom. A special commission was set up in Moscow under Trotsky, Stalin, and L. B. Kamenev* to deal with future disagreements. However, in May 1920, when the Soviet government no longer needed the Bashrevkom, it published a decree ending most of the special privileges of Bashrevkom. The Bashkir government officials decided to fight for their independence. The Soviet government called in the Red Army again, and the Russian colonists inaugurated a reign of terror, seizing Bashkir land and cattle. At the same time many Bashkirs were eliminated from the state and party apparatus. The first Congress of Soviets of Bashkiria elected a government for Bashkiria that had no Bashkir members (*see* Central Asia, Revolution in).

Bibliography

Pipes, Richard. *The Formation of the Soviet Union*. Rev. ed. 1964.
Tipeev S. *Kistorii natsional'nogo dvizheniia v Bashkirii*. 1929.
Zenkovsky, Serge A. *Pan-Turkism and Islam in Russia*. 1960.

Basmachi. The major conservative political movement among the nomadic tribes in Central Asia (*see* Central Asia, Revolution in).

The Basmachi opposed both Bolshevism and Pan-Turkism. They wanted to preserve the old Islamic way of life, including the tribal social order and strict adherence to Islamic teachings. The movement started as little more than bandit hordes among the various tribes of Fergana opposed to Soviet rule in Turkestan. It spread to other parts of Central Asia when it became apparent that Moslems were not adequately represented in the Tashkent Soviet government and after the Bolsheviks suppressed the Moslem Kokand Autonomous Government (*see* Kokand, Autonomous Government of) in February 1918. Some of the Moslem leaders who fled from Kokand joined the Basmachi. From the very beginning the movement lacked the bond of a coherent program or common nationalist or ethnic base. Although the Bolsheviks in Moscow ordered local Soviet officials to assign deputies in such a way as to give the native nationalities representation, local officials were slow to respond, which limited the effective participation by Moslem groups. To a large extent Bolshevism in Central Asia was an urban and Russian phenomenon, and there was a fear that the Moslem groups might give the countryside and the native nationalities too much political leverage. The Fifth Regional Congress of Soviets at the end of April 1918 was the first one in which Moslems and Russians were both represented, and it proclaimed the Autonomous Republic of Turkestan (*see* Turkestan, Revolution in). But the native nationalities were still not represented in the local government for another two years.

The Tashkent Soviet tended to continue the traditional policy of the tsarist government in confining the Kazakhs to the poorer land, with the Russians often exploiting them as day laborers. The Tashkent Soviet also made high financial exactions on the Moslem inhabitants of the city. Famine and breakdown of all civil services persuaded many Moslem peasants to join in guerilla warfare against the Bolshevik authorities. The movement became known as Basmachestvo, or Basmachism. Its slogans were "Turkestan for the Natives" and "Turkestan without Oppressors." The movement had considerable support from the Moslem native population and reached its zenith between 1920 and 1922.

In the autumn of 1919 the Basmachi held their own Constituent Assembly and formed the Fergana Provisional Government*. Although a special Turkestan Commission was formed by the Soviet government under the command of M. V. Frunze*, the movement was not successfully wiped out that year. Frunze attempted to coopt the movement by recruiting communist Basmachi units, adopting a more tolerant attitude toward Islam, and stepping up efforts to give the native nationalities genuine representative government.

The character of the Basmachi movement itself began to change. Tribal conflicts, especially between the Kirghiz and Uzbek Basmachi, began to appear, and defeated conservative elements from other movements began to infiltrate the Basmachi. Unity was restored to the Basmachi when Enver Pasha* assumed command of the movement in November 1921. He called for the creation of a Great Central Asian Moslem state. In May 1922 he sent an ultimatum to the Soviet government demanding that it evacuate Khiva, Turkestan, and Bukhara. The Soviets responded by intensifying efforts to recruit a Moslem Red Militia. In June 1922 Enver Pasha was defeated by a Red Army* special force with modern weapons and was killed in August. In 1922 the Turkestan Bureau (Turkburo) of the Central Committee of the Russian Communist Party (Bolshevik) and the Turk Commission initiated significant reforms designed to make the Soviet government more palatable to Central Asian Moslems. Discriminatory land policies were abolished, and religious schools and courts reopened. The New Economic Policy* allowed a return to private trading. As a result, the Basmachi movement began to lose strength and gradually disappeared during 1923–1924 (see Central Asia, Revolution in).

Bibliography

Pipes, Richard. *The Formation of the Soviet Union*. Rev. ed. 1964.
Zenkovsky, Serge A. *Pan-Turkism and Islam in Russia*. 1960.

Bauman, Karl Ianovich (1892–1937). Bolshevik (*see* Russian Social Democratic Workers' Party [Bolshevik]); state and party activist; active in the October Revolution in Kiev.

Bauman was born in Vilkan township (Volost), Latvia, into a peasant family. In 1906 he enrolled in Pskov agricultural school where he was influenced by Social Democratic ideas. He joined the Russian Social Democratic Workers' Party (Bolshevik) in 1907 in Pskov and carried out party activities in Pskov, Kiev, and Saratov. He graduated from the Kiev Commercial Institute. In 1917 Bauman was one of the organizers of the Latvian Social Democratic organization in Kiev, a subdivision of the Bolshevik organization, and was active in the trade union of bank employees. After the October Seizure of Power* he was elected Latvian People's Commissar in Kiev, Commissar for Nationalization of Private Banks, and Deputy to the Kiev Soviet. Bauman was active during the Civil War (*see* Civil War in Russia) and became People's Commissar of Finance in the Ukraine. He contracted pneumonia and typhus during the Civil War period. In 1920 he began his work in the apparatus of the Central Committee of the Russian Communist Party (Bolshevik)* (*see* Russian Social Democratic Workers' Party [Bolshevik]), of which he was a member from 1925 to 1937. He was a purge victim.

Bibliography

Levytsky, Borys. *The Stalinist Terror in the Thirties.* 1974.

Belorussia, Revolution in. The Belorussians, or White Russians, are one of the three major Slavic peoples in Russia. In 1897 Belorussians constituted 4.7 percent of the population of the empire. They occupy the northwestern portion of European Russia between Poland, the Baltic States, and Great Russia.

The Belorussian movement for national independence began with the organization of clubs for the study of Belorussian life by Belorussian students in Russian cities in the 1890s. In 1902, under the leadership of Ivan Lutskevich, it took on a political character with the formation of the Belorussian Socialist Party (Hramada) in Petrograd by a group of students who had been members of the Polish Socialist Party. During the 1905 Revolution (*see* Nineteen-Five Revolution), the Belorussian masses became involved for the first time in the nationalist movement. A peasant convention was convoked in Minsk in March 1905 and began to organize its own revolutionary forces. In 1906 the Hramada held its second congress and formulated a political program calling for federal autonomy within the Russian Empire and a national assembly in Vilna. There was a Marxist movement also, but it was confined to minority groups, like Catholics and Jews, and was not associated with the Belorussian nationalist movement. At the same time a more conservative nationalist movement began in Roman Catholic seminaries led by Epimach Shypillo, subsequently one of the founders of the Christian Democratic Party. All of this political activity was confined to a small group of urban intellectuals.

Belorussia remained economically backward before 1917, with only about 60,000 industrial workers, more than 90 percent of whom worked in enterprises with fewer than 100 people. The nationalist movement fared better than the labor movement. Between 1906 and 1914 the Belorussian cultural revolution made great strides, especially with the appearance and rapid growth of the Belorussian newspaper *Nashe Niva* (*Our Field*). The Belorussian Peoples' Theater began to send troupes around the country. Belorussia was in the middle of the battle zone during World War I* and experienced all of the confusion and destruction that it entailed, along with occupation by foreign troops. When the country was occupied by the Germans, the nationalist leaders were offered the opportunity by the occupying authorities to form an independent Belorussian state. On December 19, 1915, a "Universal" calling for an independent Belorussia and Lithuania was published by them in Belorussian, Polish, and Yiddish languages. Within the Lithuanian state created by the Germans in 1916 with Vilna as its capital, Belorussia was not granted independence, however. Rather, Belorussian people were expected to accept provisional status within a greater Lithuania.

With the February Revolution* of 1917 in Russia the Belorussian National Committee was formed in Petrograd. The Belorussian Socialist Hramada believed that the Petrograd Committee was an awkward competitor rather than an ally and in March 1917 rejected it, but it was able to find no more than fifteen people to attend its own second congress shortly thereafter. The platform of the Hramada was close to that of the Russian Socialist-Revolutionary Party*. In June 1917 some members of the Hramada under A. V. Cherviakov formed a Belorussian section of the Bolshevik Party (*see* Russian Social Democratic Workers' Party [Bolshevik]). The Bolsheviks were militantly opposed to the Hramada, and in March 1917 M. V. Frunze* became chairman of the Executive Committee of the Soviet of Workers' and Soldiers' Deputies in Minsk. He called for the formation of a Soviet of Peasants' Deputies. The First Congress of Belorussian Peasants' Deputies met in May and called for the formation of a Soviet of Peasants' Deputies with Frunze as chairman. While Frunze organized the soviets, A. F. Miasnikov created the Belorussian Communist Party. The Bolshevik organization in Minsk had only about forty members, most of whom were ethnic Russians, not Belorussians. However, the Belorussian Bolshevik movement grew rapidly. By June the Bolsheviks in Belorussia claimed about 500 members, although most of them were still Russians. In August the Belorussian Bolsheviks began to publish their own newspaper, *Zvezda* (*Star*), edited by A. F. Miasnikov. Although the party claimed about 28,000 members by that time, it remained almost entirely Russian in its membership.

The non-Bolshevik parties were also active. In March 1917 a Belorussian National Committee had been formed in Minsk after a national congress called by the Hramada. In June 1917 the Hramada gave its approval and support to the Provisional Government* and expressed a willingness to join its cabinet. In July 1917 a second national congress of Belorussian political parties met in Minsk and called for the formation of the Belorussian Central Rada. The Central Rada of Belorussia, intended as the leading organization of the Belorussian national movement, was created in Minsk at the end of July. It selected an electoral committee of nine people to press for agrarian reform and federal autonomy for Belorussia.

The October Seizure of Power* in Petrograd took place on October 24–25. Shortly thereafter, on October 27, the Military Revolutionary Committee was formed by the Bolsheviks in Minsk. It claimed to be the supreme organ of political power in Belorussia. A. F. Miasnikov was elected as its chairman with V. G. Knorin and K. I. Landeras as members. The other opposing political parties organized the Committee to Save the Revolution and the Fatherland as a united front against the Bolsheviks. On November 2 an armored train arrived in Minsk to support the Minsk Soviet, and a Belorussian government was formed in December with K. I. Landeras as chairman of the Council of People's Commissars. The new Soviet-style government eschewed nationalism and thus avoided the use of the term *Belorussia,* calling itself, rather, the Soviet of People's Commissars of the Western Regions and the Front. The opposition parties, operating through the Central Rada, responded by calling the First Belorussian National Convention. In Minsk on December 14, 1,872 convention delegates voted to recognize the Soviet government. The convention delegates were divided, however, on the question of independence for Belorussia. On December 17 the Soviet government responded by sending in the Red Army* to dissolve the Congress forcibly.

The Treaty of Brest-Litovsk* on February 19, 1918, left most of Belorussia, including Minsk, in the hands of the Germans and spelled the end of the first Belorussian Soviet Socialist Republic. On February 21 the non-Bolshevik political parties in Minsk formed a provisional government, and on March 22, 1918, the Executive Committee of the Rada proclaimed a Belorussian national republic. But the occupying German forces who entered Minsk on February 28 announced that they recognized a rival Belorussian government created in Vilna on February 18. On March 25, 1918, the two governments joined forces and announced the creation of the Belorussian National Republic with the official approval this time of the German High Command. But German indifference to Belorussian national sentiment until this time and German-forced requisition of food had already driven many Belorussian politicians into the arms of the Bolsheviks. In any case, the end of World War I* marked the end of the German occupation. On November 26, 1918, German occupation forces moved out, and on November 29 the Soviet regime decided to create a second Belorussian Soviet Republic. In keeping with new efforts to recognize Belorussian national sentiment, the local communist party met on December 30 and changed its name from the Northwest Regional Committee of the Russian Communist Party (Bolshevik) to the Communist Party (Bolshevik) of Belorussia. This meeting became known as the First Congress of the Belorussian Communist Party. The formation of the Belorussian Soviet Socialist Republic was announced on January 1, 1919, and was ratified by the First All-Belorussian Congress of Soviets on February 1, 1919, which annexed Lithuania during that month. One observer stated that Stalin personally selected the candidates for the government of the republic.

There was one brief setback to these plans when the army of the newly independent Polish Republic marched into Belorussia in April 1919 and its commander, Marshal Pilsudski, offered the Belorussians federal status in a union with Poland, but he proceeded to ignore those promises in the Belorussian territory he conquered. However, before any formal recognition of Belorussian autonomy could be granted, peace negotiations were initiated between Poland and Soviet Russia. By August 1920 the Poles were defeated and the Belorussian Soviet Socialist Republic (in its third incarnation) was restored. The Treaty of Riga between Poland and the USSR, signed on March 12, 1921, left 40,000 square miles of western Belorussia in Polish hands and much of eastern Belorussia was subsequently incorporated into the Russian Soviet Socialist Republic. Some Belorussian historians refer to this as the partition of Belorussia, although the country had never enjoyed genuine stability or autonomy.

Bibliography

Istoriia BSSR. 2d ed. 2 vols. 1961.
Ivan S. Lubachenko, *Belorussia under Soviet Rule, 1917–1957.* 1972.

Richard Pipes. *The Formation of the Soviet Union: Communism and Nationalism, 1917–23*. 1968.
Nicholas Vakar. *Belorussia: The Making of a Nation*. 1956.

Bessarabia (Moldavia), Revolution in. Bessarabia was one of those provinces in Russia in which the seizure of power by the soviets failed.

Before World War I* Bessarabia was a Russian province consisting of about 16,000 square miles and about 2.8 million people. It was located between the Danube, the Black Seas, the Dniester, and the Pruth. The territory became part of the Russian Empire in 1812 when Turkey ceded it in the Treaty of Bucharest at the end of the Russo–Turkish War. Bessarabia was a rich farming country, producing wheat and wine grapes. Although the population of the province was originally Romanian—in 1816 about 92 percent of the population—by 1920 the ratio of Romanians had declined to about 55 percent of the population, and the Slavic population, mostly Ukrainian, had increased to about 20 percent.

After the February Revolution* in Russia in 1917, two other revolutionary movements occurred. A nationalist agrarian revolution occurred in Bessarabia among those speaking the Romanian language. Because the Romanian peasants in Bessarabia had seized about two-thirds of the land held in large estates, the nationalist leaders opposed union with Romania, because they believed that Romania was controlled by aristocratic landowners who would try to reverse the land reforms. A second revolutionary movement took shape among the urban workers in Bessarabia, who were chiefly Russian and Ukrainian, and among the soldiers, who were chiefly Russian. A soviet of workers' and soldiers' deputies was formed in Kishinev on March 9, 1917, but it did not include any native Romanians. To try to keep the Bessarabians within the Russian orbit, A. F. Kerensky* sent a personal emissary, Sokolov, to the First Congress of Soviets in Kishinev in May 1920. He also sent John Inculetz, who would become the first president of the independent Bessarabian Republic, to the Second Congress of Peasant Soviets on August 17. The movement for Bessarabian independence began on April 3 when the National Moldavian Party, representing the Romanian majority, was formed. It called for federal autonomy for Bessarabia within the Russian state, with a Provincial Romanian Diet, or Sfatul Tarii (Council of the Country). The National Moldavian Party called for the use of the local language in administration, the courts, and education and for an end to Russian colonization.

On May 8, 1917, the Bessarabian Diet was called into session, and on November 14, 1917, the Diet announced the formation of the Democratic Moldavian Republic to be a part of the new federal democratic Russian state. But the nationalist Moldavian Diet was threatened by strong internal and external pressures. The Slavic-dominated urban soviet threatened to deliver Bessarabia to the Russian communists and crush the Diet. Both the Ukraine and Romania claimed sovereignty over Bessarabia and hoped to annex it. In November a soviet was formed in Kishinev. In January the Bessarabian Diet invited the Romanian army in to put down the soviets. On April 9, 1918, the Romanian majority in the Bessarabian Diet voted for union with Romania, providing the radical land reform conducted by the Romanian peasants be accepted by the Romanian state.

Bessarabia provided a conduit for revolutionary ideas from Russia to Romania. The more radical Bessarabian land reform served as a spur for the peasant political movement in Romania. The leading figure in Romanian Marxist socialism was Constantine Dobrogeanu-Gherea, a Russian emigré who thought that the advent of capitalism in Romania made things worse, not better, for the Romanian peasants, creating what he called "neo-serfdom." Another prominent Marxist leader, Bulgarian-born Kh. G. Rakovskii*, was active in the Romanian Marxist movement until he became president of the Ukrainian Council of People's Commissars in 1919. Russian Populism (the narodnik movement) had some influence on the Romanian peasant political movement through the activities of the Bessarabian aristocrat Constantine Stere, who had spent some time in exile in Siberia. In Romania social unrest reached its peak with the general strike of October 20–28, 1920. The strike was called to protest the arrest of social democratic and labor leaders, but the government broke it up in seven days. This led to a split between the Social Democrats and the communists in 1921. The Romanian Communist Party did not make much headway in the 1920s, however, because of vigorous persecution by the Romanian government. In 1924 the Romanian Communist Party was outlawed completely. In the same year the Soviet Union expressed its conviction that Bessarabia was its *irridenta* by authorizing the creation within the Ukrainian Soviet Socialist Republic of the Autonomous Moldavian Soviet Socialist Republic (SSR) on the West Bank of the Dniester. At the end of World War II in June 1940, Bessarabia was returned to the Russian state to join with the Autonomous Moldavian SSR and became the Moldavian Soviet Socialist Republic.

Bibliography

Clark, Charles Upson. *Bessarabia: Russia and Romania on the Black Sea*. 1923.
Mitrany, David. *The Land and the Peasant in Romania*. 1930.
Roberts, Henry L. *Romania: The Political Problems of an Agrarian State*. 1951.

Bliukher, Vasilii Konstantinovich (1890–1938). Bliukher was a military leader and Marshall of the Soviet Union. He participated in the Soviet seizure of power in the Volga and the Ukraine.

Born in a peasant family in the village of Barshchinka, near Rybinsk, he was employed as a metal worker at the Mytishchi factory. He served as a junior officer in World War I*, was discharged from the army after being wounded in 1915, and worked at the Sormovo shipbuilding yard and the Osterman power station in Kazan. He became a member of the Russian Social Democratic Workers' Party (Bolshevik)* in 1916. In February 1917 he was ordered by the party to return to the army, and he served in the 102nd Reserve Regiment at Samara, where he was elected to the regimental committee and the City Soviet of Soldiers'

Deputies. In October 1917 he was a member of the city Soviet's Military Revolutionary Council (MRC). In November he was sent with an expeditionary force to Cheliabinsk, where he was elected chairman of the MRC of the town. He commanded the victorious Red Guard* regiments against Ataman G. P. Polkovnikov and General A. I. Dutov*. In September 1918 he was the first person to receive the Order of the Red Banner. He subsequently commanded the 51st Rifle Division against A. V. Kolchak*. In 1921–1922 he was Commander-in-Chief, War Minister, and chairman of the Far Eastern Republic*. From 1924 to 1927 he was chief military advisor to the Revolutionary Government of China at Canton, headed by Sun Yat-Sen. For the last nine years of his life he commanded the Special Red Banner Army of the Far East. He was also a member of the Central Committee of the Communist Party, a member of the Soviet Central Executive Committee, and a deputy to the Supreme Soviet of the USSR. Arrested during the Great Purges, he was executed but was posthumously rehabilitated.

Bibliography

Levytsky, Borys. *The Stalinist Terror in the Thirties*. 1974.

Blockade. *See* Allied Blockade.

Bobin'skii, Stanislav Ianovich (1882–1937). Polish Bolshevik active in Moscow during the October Seizure of Power*.

Born in Warsaw into an intelligentsia family, Bobin'skii was first arrested in 1903 while attending the Faculty of Art in Warsaw University. He took part in student demonstrations in the Revolution of 1905 (*see* Nineteen-Five Revolution), and consequently, was expelled from the university. In 1905 he joined the Social Democratic Party of Poland and Lithuania (SDPPL) and worked with F. E. Dzerzhinskii*. From 1910 he attended Jagellon University in Cracow from which he received the doctor of philosophy degree. Subsequently, he studied in the Forestry Academy in Dresden where he received a second doctorate. Bobin'skii became an engineer by profession. Returning to Warsaw in 1913, he was involved in political work in association with S. Budzynskii. He was arrested in 1915.

After May 1917 he became a representative of the SDPPL in the Moscow Committee of the Russian Social Democratic Workers' Party (Bolshevik)* (RSDWP [B]). He was a deputy of the Moscow Soviet* and a member of its Executive Committee. In June he became a member of the Executive Committee of the SDPPL in Russia. In January 1918 he was a candidate for the Constituent Assembly* and a delegate to the Sixth Congress of the RSDWP (B). He also participated in the editorship of the Petrograd-based newspaper *Trybuna* (*Tribune*). During the October days he was a member of the Military Bureau of the Moscow Committee of the RSDWP (B) and was on the reserve staff of the Military Revolutionary Committee of the Moscow Soviet. During the Seizure of Power he was one of the Bolshevik leaders in the Grodskii district (Raion).

From December 1917 to August 1918 Bobin'skii served as deputy commissar in the Polish Commissariat of the People's Commissariat for Nationalities. He represented the SDPPL at the negotiations for the Brest-Litovsk* Treaty in February 1918. In that year he also took charge of the formation of a Polish regiment for the Red Army*. From 1918 to 1920 he was a member of the All-Russian Central Executive Committee* of Soviets, and from September 1919 to May 1920 he was a member of the Polish Bureau of the Central Committee of the Communist Party. From 1925 to 1926 Bobinskii was a member of the Executive Committee of the Communist International*, and from 1929 to 1936 he served as director of the Polytechnic Museum in Moscow. He was author of a number of works on the history of the Polish and international workers' movements and memoirs of the October Revolution.

Bibliography

Levytsky, Borys. *The Stalinist Terror in the Thirties*. 1974.

Bolshevik. *See* Russian Social Democratic Workers' Party (Bolshevik).

Bonch-Bruevich, Mikhail Dmitrievich (1870–1956). M. D. Bonch-Bruevich was a tsarist military officer who also served in the Red Army*. He was a geodesist and the brother of V. D. Bonch-Bruevich.

Born in Moscow, M. D. Bonch-Bruevich was the son of a land surveyor. He was graduated in 1890 from the Surveying Institute in Moscow, in 1892 from the Moscow Infantry School, and in 1898 from the General Staff Academy. From 1898 to 1907 he served as a staff officer at Kiev Military District and, after 1907, as a lecturer in the General Staff Academy.

At the outbreak of World War I* Bonch-Bruevich served in the quartermaster corps as a lieutenant general. In March 1915 he was named chief of staff of the northern front. In 1917, following the February Revolution*, he was elected a member of the Pskov Soviet. During August–September 1917 he was Commander-in-Chief at the northern front and helped put down the Kornilov Revolt*. At the time of the October Seizure of Power* he was serving as head of the Mogilev garrison and was a member of the Mogilev Soviet. On November 7 Bonch-Bruevich became one of the first Russian generals to side with the Revolution, and on November 20 he was named Chief of Staff of the High Command. L. D. Trotsky* was Commander-in-Chief. In February 1918 Bonch-Bruevich participated in organizing the defense of Petrograd. In March he became military director of the Supreme Military Council. During June and July 1919, he headed the field staff of the Revolutionary Military Council of the republic. In March 1919 he took part in the formation of the Geodetic Administration of the Supreme Council of the National Economy* (Vesenkha), which he headed until 1923. In 1925 he created and headed the Aerial Photography Survey Bureau. He was subsequently engaged in scholarly and editing work in the area of geodetics and was author or editor of a number of major works.

Bibliography

Sovetskaia istoricheskaia entsiklopediia. Vol. 2. 1962.
Velikaia Oktiabr'skaia sotsialisticheskaia revoliutsiia: entsiklopediia. 1977.

Bonch-Bruevich, Vladimir Dmitrievich (1873–1955) (pseudonyms, "Diadia Tom," "Sverianin," and more than two dozen other names). V. D. Bonch-Bruevich was a historian, an ethnographer, a journalist, and a state and party official. He participated in the October Seizure of Power* in Petrograd and was first head of the Chancellery of the Council of People's Commissars.

Born in Moscow, he was the son of a land surveyor. He entered the Moscow Surveying Institute in 1889 but was forced to leave Moscow for his part in student disturbances. He subsequently graduated from the Kursk Surveying School, returned to Moscow, and worked for a liberal publishing house. He became associated with radical circles and engaged in illegal publishing work. In 1895 he joined the Russian Social Democratic Workers' Party (RSDWP) (*see* Russian Social Democratic Workers' Party [Bolshevik]). In 1896 he emigrated to Switzerland with his wife, V. M. Velichkina, and studied at Zurich University.

Bonch-Bruevich developed an interest in ethnography and became an authority on Russian religious sectarians. He accompanied the Dukhobers to Canada in 1899. His scholarly standing in the field became such that the Imperial Academy of Sciences commissioned him to set up a special section dealing with the sectarians. In Switzerland he became associated with the Marxist Liberation of Labor Group through P. B. Akselrod*. He wrote and did editorial work for the Marxist publications *Zhizn'* (*Life*), *Iskra* (*The Spark*), and *Rassvet* (*The Dawn*). In addition, he helped organize the central party archives in Geneva. Bonch-Bruevich first met V. I. Lenin* in Switzerland and worked closely with him, siding with the Leninist faction (*see* Russian Social Democratic Workers' Party [Bolshevik]) in the 1903 party split at the Second Congress of the RSDWP. During 1903–1905 he headed the RSDWP Central Committee group in Zurich. He returned to Russia in 1905 where he traveled extensively on party business.

Bonch-Bruevich became involved in journalistic undertakings and worked for the newspaper *Novaia Zhizn'* (*New Life*). In 1906 he organized the RSDWP newspapers *Volna* (*Wave*), *Vpered* (*Forward*), and *Ekho* (*Echo*). During the period of reaction following the 1905 Revolution (*see* Nineteen-Five Revolution), Bonch-Bruevich was arrested several times. In 1910 he helped organize the newspaper *Zvezda* (*Star*) and subsequently worked for the newspapers *Pravda* (*Truth*) and *Prosveshchenie* (*Enlightenment*). During this period he founded the publishing house *Zhizn' i Znanie* (*Life and Knowledge*), and at the same time he published a major study on the Russian religious sectarians. During the February Revolution* in 1917, Bonch-Bruevich led a detachment of soldiers in the seizure of a printing plant, which led to the publication of *Izvestiia Petrogradskogo Sovet* (*News of the Petrograd Soviet*). He served on the Editorial Board of *Izvestiia* until May when he departed over disagreements with his

Menshevik (*see* Social Democratic Workers' Party [Menshevik]) and Socialist–Revolutionary (*see* Socialist-Revolutionary Party) colleagues. Following the Kornilov Revolt*, he was associated with the newspaper *Rabochii i soldat* (*Worker and Soldier*).

During the October Seizure of Power he served as commandant of the Smolnyi-Tauride section of Petrograd. Following the seizure of power he served on several bodies concerned with consolidating power, among them the Committee for the Revolutionary Defense of Petrograd. Within days of the October Seizure of Power, V. I. Lenin made Bonch-Bruevich the head of the Chancellery of the Council of Peoples' Commissars* (Sovnarkom). As head of the Chancellery he was responsible for the establishment of the government apparatus, reflecting Lenin's very high regard for him. Also in the spring of 1918, he was in charge of transferring governmental operations from Petrograd to Moscow. He retained this high post until October 1920 when he retired. Some have suggested that abuses or improprieties were involved in his departure from office.

The remainder of his career was spent in academic and publishing pursuits. He was chief editor of *Zhizn' i znanie* from 1920 to 1936. Bonch-Bruevich also took part in the publication of the journal *Kommunist* (*Communist*) and served as director of the State Literacy Museum from 1933 to 1939. During 1944–1955 Bonch-Bruevich served as director of the Museum of Religion and Atheism. In addition to writing numerous ethnographic and historical works, he is the author of *Reminscences of V. I. Lenin* (in Russian) covering the years 1893–1920. He was a recipient of the Order of Lenin.

Bibliography

Oktiabr'skaia sotsialisticheskaia revoliutsiia: entsiklopediia. 1977.
Sovetskaia istoricheskaia entsiklopediia. Vol. 2.

Bor'ba klassov. A monthly historical journal on the history of Communist Parties and the history of the revolutionary movement, *Bor'ba klassov* was started in 1931 under the title *Ogenek* (*Light*) as an organ of the Society of Marxist historians. Its chief editor in 1931 was the famous Mikhail N. Pokrovskii*. In 1932 its name was changed to *Bor'ba klassov* (*Class struggle*), and its chief editor was B. M. Volin. The journal published articles on the history of communist parties, the Communist International*, the October Seizure of Power*, and the Civil War (*see* Civil War in Russia). In 1937 it became *Istoricheskii zhurnal* (*Historical Journal*).

Borotbisty. The Left Socialist-Revolutionary Party* in the Ukraine, (Borotbist) was formed in May 1918 when the Ukrainian Socialist-Revolutionary Party (USRP) failed to take a strong stand against the German puppet Hetman P. P. Skoropadskii. The left wing of the party took over the USRP Central Committee and the party newspaper *Borotba* (*Struggle*). Although it moved steadily toward the Left, it preserved some important differences between its program and that of the Bolsheviks (*see* Russian Social Democratic Workers' Party [Bolshevik]). The Borotbists favored a radical social program, including the expropriation and redistribution of landlord property. They also wanted national independence for the Ukraine, a Ukrainian Soviet government, and an independent Ukrainian national army. It is estimated that the Borotbisty may have had as many as a million peasant supporters.

V. I. Lenin* believed that the Bolsheviks should cooperate with the Borotbists and ordered his followers in the Ukraine to do so. But there was considerable resistance from the Communist Party (Bolshevik) of the Ukraine (CP[B]U) (*see* Ukraine, Revolution in), which did not approve of the nationalistic and peasantist orientation of the Borotbists. In 1919 the Borotbists lent some support to the colorful Cossack chieftain Ataman Grigoriev, who joined the party for a time. In January 1919 Grigoriev tried to persuade the CP(B)U to form a coalition government and accept 6,000 to 7,000 Cossacks* into the Red Army*.

In March 1929 the Borotbists, having failed in their efforts to court the CP(B)U, established themselves as a rival by adopting the name Communist Party of the Ukraine (Borotbist) or CPU(B) and applied for membership in the Communist International*. During the year Grigoriev alienated himself from both the Borotbists and the CP(B)U and finally conducted an unsuccessful rebellion against the latter. Although the rebellion failed, it served, along with other defeats, to underscore the weakness of the CP(B)U. On October 2, 1919, Moscow ordered the dissolution of the Central Committee of the CP(B)U, and the party began to disintegrate. At the Eighth Party Conference of the Russian Communist Party (Bolshevik) (*see* Russian Social Democratic Workers' Party [Bolshevik]) on December 3–5, 1919, Lenin bitterly attacked the Ukrainian communists on several counts but especially for their failure to enlist the support of the Borotbists, and he called for the creation of a wholly new central committee for the organization.

The new shadow Ukrainian Conference of the CP(B)U created as a result of the Seventh Conference of the CP(B)U included one member of the Borotbists. However, when the Bolsheviks regained power in the Ukraine in December 1919, the Borotbists were not allowed to continue as a separate political party. In March 1920 they were formally amalgamated with the CP(B)U at the Fourth Congress of the CP(B)U. Although this made it necessary for the Borotbists to compromise with the CP(B)U, individual Borotbist leaders now had some influence within the CP(B)U itself.

At the Fifth Party Conference of the CP(B)U, G. E. Zinoviev* argued that there should be no further enrollment of Borotbists in the party because it might make the party too nationalistic. The former Borotbist member of the Central Committee Vasily Blakitnyi disagreed, claiming that the CP(B)U and the Soviet Ukrainian state were dominated by non-Ukrainian petty-bourgeois bureaucrats. Blakitnyi was not reelected to the Central Committee.

In July 1921 the CP(B)U was purged. The chief targets were former Borotbists and Ukrainian nationalists. In December 1921 the last Borotbist in a high CP(B)U post, Aleksandr Shumskii, was dropped from the Central Committee. In the spring of 1922 the well-known Borotbist G. F. Grinko was dropped from his post as Commissar of Education for moving too rapidly toward Ukrainization.

Bibliography

Adams, Arthur E. *Bolsheviks in the Ukraine*. 1963.
Borys, Jury. *The Sovietization of the Ukraine, 1917–23*. 1977.
Hunczak, Taras, ed. *Borot'bism*. 1954.
Majstrenko, John S., Jr. *The Ukrainian Revolution*. 1952.
Reshetar, John S. *The Ukrainian Revolution*. 1952.

Breshko-Breshkovskaia (nee Virigo), Ekaterina Konstantinovna (1844–1934). "Grandmother of the Russian Revolution," legendary opponent of tsarism, one of the organizers and leaders of the Socialist–Revolutionary Party*, and an opponent of Bolshevism (*see* Russian Social Democratic Workers' Party [Bolshevik]) and the October Seizure of Power*.

Breshkovskaia was born into a liberal gentry family in Vitebsk Province (Guberniia). She was involved in working with the peasantry from the early 1860s through village schools and the *zemstvos*. She married Nikolai Breshko-Breshkovskaia in the 1860s. Active in local politics, she came under police surveillance. She left her husband in 1873, went to Kiev, and established the "Kiev Commune" with her sister Olga.

Breshkovskaia became a convert to the terrorist revolutionary theories of M. A. Bakunin, and she participated in the "going-to-the-people" campaign in the spring and summer of 1874. She was arrested in September, and incarcerated in the Peter-Paul Fortress. Breshkovskaia was tried and convicted in 1878 and sentenced to five years of hard labor in the Siberian mines. Her sentence was reduced after ten months in Siberian exile, from which she escaped in 1881. She was recaptured and spent four years in the mines, followed by further exile. She was not permitted to return to European Russia until 1896.

Breshkovskaia resumed propaganda and agitation work in the company of G. Ia. Gershuni. She came into contact with V. M. Chernov* and helped form the Socialist-Revolutionary (S-R) Party in 1901. Gershuni was captured in 1903, but Breshkovskaia escaped to Geneva where she assumed a position in the Central Committee of the S-R Party. During 1904 she attended the Congress of the Second International in Amsterdam and toured the United States raising money for the struggle. She returned to Russia during the 1905 Revolution (*see* Nineteen-Five Revolution) and supported the formation of a peasants' union. She participated in 1906 in the Second Peasant Congress at Nizhni-Novgorod. She was arrested in 1907 and imprisoned again in the Peter-Paul Fortress. She was tried and convicted in 1909 and sentenced to Siberian exile. She attempted to escape in 1913, was arrested, and was sentenced to a period of solitary confinement.

During her exile Breshkovskaia made the acquaintance of A. F. Kerensky* and subsequently became one of his strongest supporters. In 1917, following the February Revolution*, her return from exile was arranged by Kerensky. During 1917 she emerged as one of the leading figures in the right wing of the S-R Party and was associated with the newspaper *Volia naroda* (*Will of the People*). She vigorously supported the Provisional Government* and presented her views in many forums, among them the Peasant Congress and the Moscow State Conference. Because of her bitter opposition to the Bolsheviks, whom she regarded as German agents, and to the left wing of her own party, she found herself increasingly isolated. Although venerated in the abstract, she retained little influence, though she threatened to further fragment the S-R Party by serving its right wing.

Following the October Revolution she worked for the creation of an anti-Bolshevik Constituent Assembly*. She subsequently supported the Samara Komuch government (*see* Committee of Members of the Constituent Assembly) formed in June 1918 in the wake of the revolt of the Czechoslovak Legion*. She traveled to the United States to raise funds to carry on her work. In 1919 she testified before the U.S. Senate against the Bolsheviks. Unable to return to Russia, she spent the remainder of her life as an exile in the Ukrainian districts of Czechoslovakia where she administered two children's schools. Her memoirs, *The Little Grandmother of the Russian Revolution: Reminiscences and Letters* (1918) are available in English.

Bibliography

Rodkey, O. *The Agrarian Foes of Bolshevism*. 1958.

Brest-Litovsk. This treaty was the peace agreement between Russia and the Central Powers signed on March 3, 1918. The treaty ended Russia's participation in World War I* and was made possible by the October Seizure of Power* by the Soviets in 1917. Fulfilling their promise to the war-weary Russian population, the new leaders called for a general peace among the belligerents. Russia's allies, principally Great Britain, France, the United States, and Italy, spurned an invitation to participate in the negotiations, and the Soviet government therefore participated alone. On November 28 a cease-fire was arranged on the eastern front. Four days later formal armistice negotiations began at the Polish city of Brest-Litovsk, which, since July 1916, had served as German military headquarters for operations against Russia. The choice of a conference location was in itself eloquent testimony to the feeble bargaining power of the Russians, who would have vastly preferred a neutral site.

The Soviet delegation was headed by A. A. Ioffe, a protege of L. D. Trotsky*, the Commissar of Foreign affairs. His colleagues included L. M. Karakhan, who served as secretary to the delegation; L. B. Kamenev*; G. A. Sokol'nikov*; and five individuals whose role was purely symbolic: a female, a worker, a soldier, a sailor, and a peasant. The representatives of the Central Powers were a more conventional group. Germany's delegation was led by Major General Max Hoffman, the de facto commander of the eastern front, and Baron Richard von Kuhlmann, the foreign secretary. Austria–Hungary was represented by its foreign minister Count Ottokar Czernin, and Turkey and Bulgaria also sent delegations whose functions were necessarily circumscribed.

Germany's armistice terms were simple enough: an immediate end to hostilities and the maintenance of the military status quo until the peace conference should decide otherwise. The Soviet government had broader aspirations, of which a propaganda campaign to hasten a prospective Communist revolution in Germany was deemed the most desirable. Thus Ioffe and Kamenev attempted to use their seats at the conference table as a political forum. Hoffman declined to engage in such a debate but, perhaps unwisely, did accept the principle of publicity for the negotiations. On December 5 Ioffe admitted that he was not empowered to sign a separate armistice for Russia alone and that the Allies had refused to participate. The deliberations were then recessed to allow the Russians to return home for consultation and to proceed with the ritual of inviting the Allies to join the talks at Brest-Litovsk. No direct reply was received to this renewed invitation, and the proceedings resumed on December 13. Agreement was reached two days later, with the truce to last until January 14, 1918, and to be renewed automatically unless terminated by advance notice. Fraternization at the front, which the Soviet government had already encouraged, was reluctantly accepted by the Germans, a political mistake that opened the floodgates to a torrent of Bolshevik (*see* Russian Social Democratic Workers' Party [Bolshevik]) propaganda (*see* Propaganda and the Russian Revolution).

The peace conference opened on December 22 with a welcoming speech by Prince Leopold of Bavaria. The delegation remained approximately the same, although the Russians added the noted Marxist historian Mikhail Pokrovsky. By this time the polite phrases of conventional diplomacy were becoming a little threadbare. Nevertheless, Ioffe adhered to the largely ceremonial formula of a general rather than a separate peace, no forcible annexation of territories, no war indemnities, and political freedom for all nationalities. Despite divided counsels and the objections entertained by the Turks and the Bulgarians, whose annexationist demands were undisguised, Kuhlman's insistence that the Soviet terms be accepted in principle won out.

On Christmas Day the Central Powers surprised the Russians by declaring that the Soviet proposals furnished a reasonable basis of discussion, and the "sincerely naive" Ioffe labored for a time under the misapprehension that Germany would actually return its Polish and Baltic conquests. That reciprocity would be required—namely, the return of Allied "conquests"—had not occurred to Ioffe. It was left to the blunt-spoken Hoffman to disabuse him of Germany's beneficent intentions. The Russians, shocked and bitterly disappointed, were granted a day of recess on December 28, ostensibly to permit other Allied powers to join the peace conference. But the Soviet leadership, caught unprepared, needed time to develop a new diplomatic strategy. No satisfactory alternative was found, for a strong army—not even a weak one was available—remained the only guarantee of impressing the Germans. Some of the Bolsheviks, including

Trotsky, began to toy with the idea of a "holy war" presumably to be fought on a wave of revolutionary enthusiasm, but Lenin refused to be ensnared by demagoguery of this kind. He did, however, permit himself the illusion of a possible revolution in Germany. With that goal in mind, he insisted that Trotsky, whose agitational skills were unrivaled, should take Ioffe's position at the head of the Russian delegation.

Trotsky reluctantly accepted the assignment: "I felt as if I were being led to the torture chamber. Being with strange and alien people had always aroused my fears" (Trotsky 1970, p. 363). He was joined by Karl Radek*, a specialist on German affairs, who signaled his arrival at Brest-Litovsk by tossing propaganda material to the German troops guarding the station platform. The five ornaments of "revolutionary democracy" were left behind. Trotsky would have none of the false comraderie that had heretofore prevailed and "quarantined" his colleagues from contact with the opposing delegations except on formal occasions. Kuhlmann, temporarily discarding his customary diplomatic finesse, curtly informed the Russians at the first plenary session on January 9, 1918, that since the Entente powers were not participants, the original Soviet proposals had become null and void. But he presented no demands and seemed content to let Trotsky spin out his negotiations indefinitely, although he invariably responded to the Soviet Commissars' rhetorical sallies with suave composure and confidence borne of Germany's superior military positions. However, Hoffman and his associates grew increasingly restless as Trotsky's provocative tactics continued, and on January 18 the general displayed a large map with a blue line drawn from Brest-Litovsk to the Baltic Sea, depicting the future boundary of Germany and Russia. The frontier south of Brest-Litovsk, Hoffman indicated, would depend on a settlement with the representatives of the separatist Ukrainian government (see Ukraine, Revolution in). Aware that a German ultimatum could not be long delayed, Trotsky had already conceived of a daring but risky scheme to evade the humiliation of a peace dictated by enemy bayonets. His request for a recess to consult his government was granted, and Soviet delegates left for Petrograd on the evening of January 18.

Once back in the capital, Trotsky plunged into a round of heated discussions with other party leaders. His controversial idea, that Russia should simply declare hostilities at an end but refuse to sign a peace treaty ("no war, no peace") was based in part upon his conviction that a "pedagogical demonstration" was necessary to prove to the European proletariat the deadly enmity existing between the new Communist state and predatory German militarism. Lenin was unpersuaded, and he adamantly opposed the "holy war" concept of which the so-called Left Communists (see Left Communism) led by Nikolai I. Bukharin* were becoming increasingly enamored. Trotsky's plan seemed to offer a reasonable compromise between a hopeless war and a shameful peace. By a vote of nine to seven the Bolshevik Central Committee (see Central Committee of the Russian Communist Party [Bolshevik]) gave its approval, provided that no other means of prolonging the negotiations could be found.

The peace conference reopened on January 30. Trotsky's bargaining position was strengthened by a wave of strikes and demonstrations in Germany, and the Bolsheviks were tempted to believe that their confidence in the revolutionary potential of the German worker had not been misplaced. Unhappily for the Russians, the strike movement collapsed within a few days. Nor were they fortunate in regard to the Ukrainian question, although Soviet forces were in the process of occupying Kiev, and Trotsky had brought along the Ukrainian Bolsheviks to offset the separatists.

The Germans, ignoring the altered circumstances, signed peace terms with "their" Ukrainians on February 9. On the larger issue of peace with Russia, Germany was now less inclined to humor Trotsky. Kuhlmann succeeded in postponing an ultimatum by a veiled threat to resign, only to find that he had risked his position in vain. At the evening session of February 10, when it seemed that Trotsky was ready to capitulate after a final burst of eloquence, he suddenly announced that Russia was "going out of the war" but would "refuse to sign the peace treaty." He had thrown his verbal bombshell with skill and precision in timing, taking grim satisfaction from the stupefied amazement of his adversaries. Within a few hours the Russian delegation left Brest-Litovsk in a euphoric mood, confident that the Germans had been confounded and that the Soviet Republic had extricated itself from an impossible predicament. Once back in Petrograd, a more sober appraisal seemed warranted, and Trotsky's apparent triumph began to look like a dangerous gamble. At any rate, this was Lenin's view, and even Trotsky permitted himself a few doubts while affirming the wisdom of his policy and its efficacy in awakening the German workers to their revolutionary duty. But the prevailing mood in party circles remained incurably optimistic.

Soviet illusions were quickly dispelled. On February 17 the Germans gave formal notice of the intention to resume hostilities. Two days later their army pushed forward against only token opposition. Again the Bolshevik leaders engaged in frenzied debate culminating in a one-vote majority in the Central Committee backing Lenin's plea for immediate surrender. But Hoffman was in no hurry to accept the Russian offer. The German advance continued at a leisurely pace, and the panicky Bolsheviks, foreseeing the possible occupation of Petrograd, ordered the capital moved to Moscow. The new peace treaty terms that were finally submitted to the Soviet government were considerably harsher than those previously tendered. Lenin, declaring that the policy of "revolutionary phrases" was bankrupt, once more carried the day in the Central Committee. On February 24 another Russian delegation set out for Brest-Litovsk, this one headed by Sokolnikov (Trotsky declined an ignominious return to the scene of his "triumph" and had already resigned as Commissar of Foreign Affairs). Ostentatiously refusing to discuss the terms, the better to dramatize the dictated nature of the peace, the Soviet representatives, after a ringing protest by Sokolnikov, signed the offensive document on March 3.

The draconian peace deprived Russia of approximately a third of its population, half of its industry, and a third of its cultivated land. Territorial losses involved Poland, the Baltic Provinces, and the Ukraine as well as the Caucasian border districts of Ardahan, Kars, and Batum, ceded to Turkey. The treaty itself, though not some of its consequences, proved short lived. Nullified when Germany was defeated by the Allies in November 1918, it was formally renounced by the Central Powers in the subsequent peace settlement.

Robert D. Warth

Bibliography

Baumgart, Winifried. *Deutsche Ostpolitik, 1918.* 1966.
Debo, Richard K. *Revolution and Survival: The Foreign Policy of Soviet Russia, 1917–18.* 1979.
Deutscher, Isaac. *The Prophet Armed: Trotsky, 1879–1921.* 1954.
Kennan, George F. *Russia Leaves the War.* 1956.
Trotsky, L. *My Life.* 1970.
Warth, Robert D. *The Allies and the Russian Revolution.* 1954.
Wheeler-Bennett, John W. *The Forgotten Peace: Brest-Litovsk.* 1939.

Brusilov, Aleksei Alekseevich (1853–1926). Tsarist and Soviet military figure.

Brusilov was born in Tiflis into a military family. His father was a general. Brusilov was educated at the Corps of Pages and in 1872 began a career as a cavalry officer in the Caucasus. He participated in the Russo–Turkish War of 1877–1878. From 1906 he commanded a cavalry division and then an army corps, and from 1912 to 1913 he served in Warsaw. At the start of World War I* he commanded the Seventh Army and in March 1916 was placed in charge of the entire southwestern front. Under him Russian troops achieved major success in May 1916 in an assault on the Austro–German lines. In 1917 in the midst of the February Revolution* crisis, Brusilov and others exercised their influence to encourage Nicholas II* to step down from the throne. From May 22 to July 18 the Provisional Government* elevated him to the position of Supreme Commander of the Imperial Army (*see* Army of Imperial Russia in World War I) and chief military advisor to the Provisional Government. Following the failure of the June 1917 offensive, he was replaced by L. G. Kornilov (*see* Kornilov's Revolt) but remained military advisor to the Provisional Government. While serving as Supreme Commander, Brusilov signed the order reintroducing the death sentence at the front. After the October Revolution Brusilov, unlike a number of other leading military figures, did not come out in opposition to Soviet power. In 1920 he entered the Red Army* and served in the Peoples' Commissariat of Military Affairs as Inspector of the Cavalry. From 1924 he was assigned to special military commissions. His memoirs were published in 1929.

Bibliography

Velikaia Oktiabr'skaia sotsialisticheskaia revoliutsiia: entsiklopediia. 1977.

Bubnov, Andrei Sergeevich (1883–1940) (pseudonyms, Khimik, Iakov, A. Glotov, S. Iaslov, A.B.). Bubnov was a Bolshevik Party (*see* Russian Social Democratic Workers' Party [Bolshevik]) leader and historian and a Left Communist (*see* Left Communism) who was active in Moscow in 1917.

Born in Ivanovo-Voznesensk into a middle-class family, Bubnov was educated in the local schools and attended the Moscow Agricultural Institute (Timiriazev Academy), from which he was expelled for revolutionary work. He joined the Russian Social Democratic Workers' Party (RSDWP) in 1903 and joined the Bolshevik faction after the Second Congress of the RSDWP in 1903. In 1905 he was a member of the Ivanovo-Voznesensk Committee of the Bolsheviks and their Ivanovo-Voznesensk Bureau in 1906. Between 1905 and 1917 he was active in party work in the Central Industrial Region*. He was arrested thirteen times and experienced four years' imprisonment and exile. In 1910 he was coopted into the Bolshevik Center for Russia. At the Sixth (Prague) Conference of the RSDWP he was elected a candidate member of the Central Committee, and during 1912–1913 he worked in St. Petersburg on the staff of *Pravda** (*Truth*). He became a Bolshevik deputy to the Fourth State Duma.

In February 1917, at the time of the February Revolution*, Bubnov was a member of the Moscow Province (Oblast') Bureau of the Bolsheviks. At the Seventh (April) Conference of the RSDWP he was elected to the Central Committee (*see* Central Committee of the Russian Communist Party [Bolshevik]) and represented it in the Petrograd Committee of the RSDWP (B). At the October 10, 1917, session of the Central Committee he was elected to the Political Bureau (Politburo) and on October 16 to the Revolutionary Military Party Center for the direction of the October Revolution. He became a member of the Petersburg Military Revolutionary Committee and Commissar for the Railroads. After the Second All-Russian Congress of Soviets he was elected a member of the All-Union Central Executive Committee of Soviets and People's Commissar of Communications. During the Civil War (*see* Civil War in Russia) he played an active role as Commissar of Railroads in the military operations in South Russia. In March 1918 he became a member of the Ukrainian Soviet government and of the Ukrainian Communist Party. In 1919 he was a member of the Revolutionary Military Committee of the Ukraine and of the Fourteenth Army. After 1919 he worked in the administration of the textile industry in Moscow and returned as a member of the Moscow Committee, in the Bureau of the Moscow Committee, of the Communist Party.

Bubnov frequently found himself in opposition during the Revolution and Civil War period. He supported V. I. Lenin* on the issue of an all-Bolshevik government against the right wing of the party (G. E. Zinoviev*, A. I. Rykov*, L. B. Kamenev*, V. P. Miliutin, and V. P. Nogin*) but opposed Lenin on the issue of peace with the Germans in February 1918 (when he joined with N. I. Bukharin*, M. S. Uritskii*, and G. I. Lomov-Oppokov*). He became, therefore, a Left Communist, or member of the left wing faction within the Communist

Party. While in service in the Ukraine he led, with G. L. Piatakov, the Left Communist faction in the Ukrainian Communist Party (UCP) (see Ukraine, Revolution in) that opposed centralization and supported regional autonomy for the Ukraine. In 1920–1921 he was a member of the Democratic Centralist faction (*see* Democratic Centralists) with former friends from the Moscow Province (Oblast') Bureau, N. Osinskii*, T. V. Sapronov, and I. N. Smirnov*. This faction opposed the increasing administrative centralization that they saw taking place under War Communism*. In the Trade Unions Controversy of 1920 he opposed L. D. Trotsky's* plans for the militarization of labor, joining the ultra-Left faction of Smirnov that resisted any encroachments on the power and independence of the trade unions. His last act of public opposition was his signature to the "Declaration of 46" in 1923. This document was a full-scale attack on the party's policy on economic issues and intra-party democracy. This group blamed many of the country's woes on excessive authoritarianism and centralization in the party apparatus.

From 1922 to 1924 Bubnov directed the agitation and propaganda department of the Central Committee of the Communist Party. From 1924 to 1929 he was head of the political administration of the Red Army* and a member of the Organization Bureau (Orgburo) of the party. In 1925 he became Secretary of the Communist Party and from 1929 to 1937 People's Commissar of Education. Arrested in 1937, he was executed sometime between 1937 and 1940. He has been rehabilitated posthumously.

Bibliography

Bubnov, A. S. *Osnovne momenty v razvitie kommunisticheskoi partii v Rossii.* 1921.
Haupt, Georges, and Marie, Jean Jacques. *Makers of the Russian Revolution.* 1974.
Levytsky, Borys. *The Stalinist Terror in the Thirties.* 1974.

Budennyi, Semen Mikhailovich (1883–1973). Budennyi was a prominent military figure and Civil War hero (*see* Civil War in Russia).

He was born in Rostov Province into a family of landless peasants. He was conscripted into the army in 1903 and served in the Russo–Japanese War from 1904 to 1905. During World War I* he rose to the rank of senior non-commissioned officer. During the summer of 1917, while serving in a cavalry division, he was elected chairman of the Regimental Soldiers' Committee and deputy chairman of the Division Committee. In August 1917 he participated in the disarming of part of the forces of L. G. Kornilov's "Wild Division" (*see* Kornilov Revolt). In 1918 he formed and commanded a cavalry unit that ultimately grew to division size during the Civil War. He later led the First Horse Army, which played a large role in the defeat of the forces of A. I. Denikin* and P. N. Wrangel* liberating the Donbas and Northern Caucasus. In his military career following the Civil War he served as Inspector of the Cavalry for the Red Army* from 1924 to 1937. In 1932 he graduated from the M. V. Frunze* Academy, and in 1935 he was promoted to the rank of Marshal. In 1937 he was commander of forces of the Moscow Military District (Okrug). Budennyi was named First

Deputy People's Commissar of Defense in 1940 and from 1941 to 1945 commander of the armed forces.

Budennyi joined the Communist Party in 1919 and held numerous state and party posts. In 1920 he was a member of the All-Russian Central Executive Committee* of Soviets and in 1922 Deputy to the Supreme Soviet to which he was elected continuously for eight convocations. In 1938 he was named a member of the Presidium of the Supreme Soviet. In 1938 he was named a member of the Central Committee of the Russian Communist Party (Bolshevik) (*see* Russian Social Democratic Workers' Party [Bolshevik]) and in 1952 a candidate member. He was three times named "Hero of the Soviet Union"—1958, 1963, and 1968.

Bibliography

Sidorov, V. I. *Pervaia Konnaia armiia.* 1949.
Velikaia Oktiabr'skaia sotsialisticheskaia revoliutsiia: entsiklopediia. 1977.

Bukhara, Revolution in. Bukhara is one of the three major khanates formed in Central Asia before 1500 in the fertile Fergana River Valley. The other two were Kokand and Khiva. In all three, the Uzbeks formed the ruling aristocracy. Until 1920 these khanates were not included within the Russian Empire but were subject to the Russian Tsar and were administered by Russian officers under the Turkestan governor general in Tashkent. The native population remained outside Russian cultural influences, preserving its own language and Moslem religious culture.

By 1914 Bukhara and the other two khanates had been transformed socially and economically by the cotton trade. Westernized Bukharan intellectuals, like Ahmed Mahdunb Donish, called for the modernization of their homeland. Young Uzbek intellectuals began to organize the liberal Jadid movement*, which at that time focused primarily on modernizing education and personal life as a way of saving Moslem society. By 1910 this group moved into the political arena, calling for an end to the rule of reactionary clergymen and Uzbek chieftains. Abdul Rauf Fitrat, who had been educated in Turkey where he came into contact with the Young Turk movement, wrote the *Munizira* (*Table*), which became the chief platform of the Young Bukhara movement that would put an end to Islamic divisiveness and, therefore, its economic and military weakness. In March 1918 a liberal Bukharan, Faizullah Hojaev, obtained the support of the Tashkent Soviet of People's Commissars for an expedition to overthrow the Emir of Bukhara, but it ended in failure. Along with the Jadids, the Young Bukharans began to gravitate toward Moscow. In the summer of 1920, after the fall of the Tashkent Soviet* and near the end of the Civil War (*see* Civil War in Russia), the Red Army* began to move into Bukhara. The city was seized on August 29, and the Emir fled to the mountains. The Young Bukhara leaders entered the city with the Red Army and set up the Peoples' Republic of Bukhara. Most of the cabinet posts were given to members of two of the wealthy Bukharan merchant families, the Maksumov and the Hojaev.

The new government was liberal and Pan-Turkic rather than communist. Ottoman Turkish became the language of instruction in the upper schools, and the government promised to fight the "excesses of clericalism." Another new independent state established with the approval of the Soviet government, the Far Eastern Republic*, had abolished private property. The People's Republic of Bukhara did not. In many ways it was a foreshadowing of the peoples' democracies established in Eastern Europe after World War II, a political system intended to be a transitional stage on the path toward a communist state, embodying some of the traditional institutions and some of the new Soviet practices.

The victory of the Red Army in Bukhara was an important turning point in the relations between Moscow and Russia's Moslem population. The communists had just called the First Congress of Peoples of the East in Baku from September 1 to 9. It enabled the Soviet government to appear as the sponsor of Islam's rebellion against European imperialism and clerical domination.

The Red Army began to evacuate Eastern Bukhara, giving control to the new People's Republic. However, this permitted Basmachi* groups to move into the breach. The former Emir escaped to Afghanistan and gave his support to the Basmachi. In western Bukhara a rift appeared between the leaders of Young Bukhara and those of the new Bukharan Communist Party. In November 1921 Enver Pasha*, a Turkish general and soldier–adventurer, appeared in Bukhara at the request of the Soviet government. He defected, however, and allied himself to Ibrahim Bek, the Emir's lieutenant among the Basmachi in Bukhara. Enver Pasha became the commander-in-chief of the Basmachi and established his headquarters in Eastern Bukhara from which he launched an attack on West Bukhara. But splits between Enver Pasha and the forces supported by the Emir contributed to Pasha's defeat and death in combat in August 1922.

The Soviet government responded to the threat posed by the Basmachi and Enver Pasha by making significant religious concessions to the Moslems of Central Asia. By the end of 1923 the Basmachi movement in Bukhara had been defeated. In 1924 the Soviet government abolished the independent republics of Bukhara and Khorezm (the Far Eastern Republic had already been abolished). The land of the former Bukharan Republic was divided among the new Central Asian Soviet republics (*see* Central Asia, Revolution in). By 1923 most of the former leaders of the Young Bukhara movement had become members of the Communist Party. Some, like Abdul Kadir Mukhtidinov and Faizullah Khojaev, went on to distinguished careers in the communist movement in Central Asia until the Great Purges of the thirties.

Bibliography

Pipes, Richard. *The Formation of the Soviet Union, Communism, and Nationalism.* 1968.
Zenkovsky, Serge. *Pan Turkism and Islam in Russia.* 1960.

Bukharin, Nikolai Ivanovich (1888–1938). Bukharin was born in Moscow into a middle-class family. Both parents were primary schoolteachers. His father took an interest in his son's development and taught the boy to read and write before he was five years old. When Nikolai was five, his father accepted a job as tax inspector in Bessarabia, and for four years Bukharin and his younger brother had little formal education but spent most of their time playing out of doors. Bukharin was an avid reader, and, as he puts it, he became at the same time something of a "street urchin" during those years. In 1899 the Bukharin family returned to Moscow, but for two years the father was unemployed, and the family lived in great poverty.

Bukharin was an exceptional student and was admitted to the First Moscow Gymnasium in 1901, where he achieved a remarkable academic record. During his four years in the gymnasium Bukharin gradually became a political radical. He took part in Social Democratic political activity in Moscow during the Revolution of 1905 (*see* Nineteen-Five Revolution). In 1906 Bukharin formally entered the Russian Social Democratic Workers' Party (Bolshevik) (RSDWP [B])* and together with the future author–journalist Ilia Ehrenburg led a strike at the Sladkov Wallpaper Factory. With G. Ia. Sokolnikov* he united all of the youth groups into a single city organization and asked for a congress to create a national Social Democratic youth organization. Bukharin entered Moscow University in 1907 as a full-time professional revolutionary. He became a revolutionary leader among the students, spending little time in genuine academic work.

In 1908 he was appointed to the Moscow Committee of the Bolshevik faction, and in 1909, at the age of twenty, he was arrested and subsequently fled abroad. Although Bukharin was profoundly influenced by West European philosophical trends and leaned toward the Russian Marxist philosopher Alexander Bogdanov in the famous debate between Lenin and Bogdanov, he retained Lenin's friendship and respect, and in 1913 Lenin asked Bukharin to help I. V. Stalin* to do research in Vienna on his pamphlet *Marxism and the National Question*. Bukharin was himself opposed to Lenin's position on the national question, arguing that national self-determination should be granted only to the workers and not to the nation as a whole.

During his travels Bukharin arrived in New York in 1916 and briefly collaborated with L. D. Trotsky* on the staff of the emigré newspaper *Novyi mir* (*New World*). When the February Revolution* took place, Bukharin returned to Russia by way of Japan but was soon arrested by the Mensheviks (*see* Russian Social Democratic Workers' Party [Menshevik]) in Cheliabinsk. Bukharin managed to get away and return to his native Moscow, where he resumed his position as a member of the Bolshevik Moscow Committee and was appointed a member of the Executive Committee of the Moscow soviet* and editor of the Moscow party newspaper *Sotsial demokrat* (*Social Democrat*). During the 1917 Revolution Bukharin soon became the leader of the left wing of the Bolshevik Party, a position he would retain throughout the Civil War (*see* Civil War in Russia). Bukharin was widely regarded as the party's leading theoretician and economist and as one of its most prolific writers, although he was less talented as a political leader.

In Moscow, Bukharin renewed his collaboration with the friends of his youth, a generation of Moscow radicals that would include famous names such as N. Osinskii*, V. M. Smirnov, G. Ia. Sokol'nikov, G. I. Lomov-Oppokov*, G. A. Usievich, and D. P. Bogolepov. Along with the other leaders of the left wing of the Bolshevik movement, Bukharin saw World War I* as an opportunity for worldwide proletarian revolution and welcomed the October Seizure of Power* as the opening stage in that process. But he had opposed Lenin's position on the war at the Bern Conference in February and March of 1915 for making too many concessions to the bourgeoisie. These differences would lead Bukharin ultimately to oppose the Treaty of Brest-Litovsk*, which he saw as an unnecessary and unproductive concession to imperialist, capitalist governments of the West. Bukharin believed that the Russian Revolution could not kindle the world proletarian revolution or get its support if it made agreements with capitalist governments. Recognizing that Russia was not, in Marxist terms, ripe for revolution meant to him that the Russians needed the help of the proletarian revolution in the more highly industrialized countries of Western Europe.

These differences of opinion brought Lenin and Bukharin together in 1917 and drove them apart in 1918. In 1917 Bukharin could enthusiastically embrace Lenin's call for revolutionary action to overthrow the Provisional Government*, and he played a decisive role with his following in mobilizing the rank and file of the Moscow party against the older generation of more moderate Bolshevik leaders. He played a leading role in pushing the Moscow party toward a Soviet seizure of power. He drafted the revolutionary decrees of the Moscow soviet at the time of the October Seizure of Power, and he edited the bulletin of the Military Revolutionary Committee in Moscow appointed by the Moscow Soviet to organize the Soviet seizure of power.

In 1918 when the issue of signing a peace with Germany came to the foreground, however, Bukharin joined with Karl Radek* in opposing Lenin's position in the newspaper *Kommunist* (*Communist*). That phase in the history of the Left opposition within Bolshevism ended with the signing of the Treaty of Brest-Litovsk in March 1918. The opposition of the Left (*see* Left Communism) had fateful echoes in the 1930s when charges of opposition to Lenin would be used against them as part of an excuse for executing them as traitors. At the end of March there were also some conversations between the leaders of Left Communism and the Left Socialist–Revolutionaries (S–R's). During these talks some Left Communists even proposed the arrest of Lenin, although there does not seem to have been any widespread support for that notion. After the assassination of the German ambassador on July 6, 1918, by a Left S–R, the Left Communists denounced the other party in the press. After an abortive Left S–R rebellion in July 1918, Bukharin and his followers supported the campaign of terror against the Left S–R's.

After the period of War Communism* and the Civil War (*see* Civil War in Russia) came to an end, Bukharin and his followers shifted their criticism to Lenin's New Economic Policy (NEP)*. Their opposition to NEP was consistent with their opposition to the Treaty of Brest-Litovsk. Like Brest-Litovsk, the NEP was seen as a concession to capitalism that weakened the Soviet Union's posture as the spearhead of world revolution. Believing that Russia could not achieve socialism without help from a proletarian revolution in the more advanced capitalist countries, Bukharin concluded that Soviet actions should be directed toward the achievement of that revolution. The burden of attack passed, however, from Bukharin to Osinskii.

Gradually, Bukharin moderated his views and became convinced that the New Economic Policy, far from being a retreat, was actually a better path toward socialism for Russia. In 1918 he argued that Russia needed the support from proletarian revolutions in more advanced industrial societies because Russia was not itself at a high enough stage of development to achieve socialism without outside help. Now, after 1921, he began to argue that in the absence of international proletarian revolution Russia might achieve socialism in one country by the gradualist approach inherent in the NEP. The arguments he advanced in the 1920s for gradualism, flexibility, and voluntarism have recently been revived by dissidents in the Soviet Union to justify reform. Under the dictatorship of the proletariat, Bukharin argued, the Russian working class and peasantry might develop self-consciousness and maturity and work their way beyond the mixed capitalist–socialist economy provided by NEP.

After Lenin's death in 1924 Bukharin became the chief spokesman for the right wing of the party and for socialism in one country. He called for compromise with the peasantry and a gradual weaning of the whole population away from capitalism toward socialism, using voluntary organizations of the masses as a counterpoint to the burgeoning bureaucracy.

From 1924 to 1927 Bukharin joined Stalin in the Politburo as one of the top leaders of the Soviet Union opposing L. D. Trotsky*, G. E. Zinoviev*, and L. B. Kamenev* in the struggle for power. In 1926 Bukharin became chairman of the Executive Committee of the Communist International*. After the defeat of the Joint Opposition of Trotsky and Zinoviev, Stalin began to move toward the Left, and in August 1929, after the start of the collectivization drive that Bukharin had opposed, *Pravda* (*Truth*) began to denounce Bukharin as the leader of the "right wing deviation." On November 17, 1929, Bukharin was expelled from the Politburo.

Bukharin was restored to a minor role in the midthirties, becoming editor of the official government newspaper *Izvestiia** (*News*) and playing a major role in the composition of the "Stalin" Constitution of 1936. However, he soon emerged as a major target in the Great Purges, and on March 30, 1938, he was expelled from the party, arrested, and, following a dramatic "show" trial, tried and executed. He was rehabilitated posthumously in 1987.

Bibliography

Cohen, Stephen. *Bukharin and the Bolshevik Revolution*. 1980.
Daniels, Robert. *Conscience of Revolution*. 1969.

Haupt, Georges, and Marie, Jean Jacques. *Makers of the Russian Revolution.* 1974.
Heitman, Sidney. *Nikolai I. Bukharin: A Bibliography.* 1969.
Schapiro, Leonard. *The Origin of the Communist Autocracy.* 1963.

The Bund. The Bund was the common and popular name by which the General Jewish Workers' Union in Lithuania, Poland, and Russia was known. Founded in Vilna in 1897, the Bund played a key role in both the histories of the Russian labor movement and in the politicization of the Russian–Jewish community in the last two decades of tsarist rule.

The founders of the Bund came from a group of Jewish intellectuals and worker–activists with Marxist leaning active among the Jewish workers in the Pale since the early 1890s. Initially, there was nothing particularly Jewish in either their efforts or in the message that they were spreading among the workers. Seeking to inculcate socialist values and a proletarian consciousness among Jewish laborers, many of whom were former independent artisans or apprentices aspiring to their own shops, these propagandists used the classical socialist texts in the Russian language in their clandestine educational activities. In fact, it was their involvement in organizing educational seminars and reading circles that attracted them to the Jewish workers and contributed to their gaining a significant following within the Jewish community. However, within a very short time, these Jewish activists shifted their efforts from a simple consciousness raising to actual revolutionary agitation. In this shift, the Jewish Marxists realized that in order to reach the widest circles within the Jewish community, they would have to use the spoken Yiddish language of the masses and to incorporate into their propaganda some of the classics from the world of Yiddish literature, especially those materials that focused on the current plight of the Jewish community. This marked the transition in the evolution of this group from that of being socialists of Jewish origin to that of being Jewish socialists with a specific Jewish program. Key developments in this transition included the publication of Arkady Kremer's article "On Agitation" ("Ob agitatsii"), in 1892, in which he spelled out the new tactics that were to be adopted, and the May Day speech delivered in Vilna in 1895 by Iu. O. Martov* (Tsederbaum) in which he declared that there was a need for a formal, progressive-minded, Jewish organization to represent the Jewish community and to articulate its needs, rather than to allow the Jewish bourgeoisie to assume such a role.

By September 1897 thirteen Jewish delegates representing groups in Vilna, Minsk, Warsaw, Bialystok, and Vitebsk gathered in Vilna to consolidate these scattered Jewish labor and revolutionary groups into a highly organized movement, hereafter known as the Bund. Led by intellectuals and activists, the Bund shortly became a powerful force within the Jewish community of the Empire. At its inception the Bund's program did not go beyond the general aims of social democracy. However, by representing Jewish laborers in a separate organization, the leadership of the Bund indicated clearly to other socialist organizations that the Jewish community was to be regarded as a separate but equal partner in the general labor movement. Eager to tie their work into the general cause after the founding of their own organization, the leaders of the Bund took the initiative in working for the creation of an all-Russian workers' party with which they could affiliate. Six months later in March 1898 the Bund hosted the first meeting of the Russian Social Democratic Workers' Party (RSDWP) (*see* Russian Social Democratic Workers' Party [Bolshevik]) in Minsk.

The Bund entered the RSDWP as a fully autonomous body, the sole representative of Jewish labor, with responsibility for organizing and directing the Jewish proletariat within the Russian Empire. However, the RSDWP did not become an active organization, since most of the delegates who attended the Minsk gathering soon found themselves under arrest or in flight from the tsarist police. In the interval between the first and second national congresses of the RSDWP, 1898–1903, a number of developments within the Jewish community forced the leadership of the Bund to articulate a series of specific Jewish demands that the movement then went on to champion within the arena of Russian political life. In the main, two types of developments had the effect of moving the Bund more to especially Jewish concerns and ultimately in raising those Jewish issues to such primacy that by 1903 they had led to the estrangement of the Bund from the newly reorganized RSDWP. Among these developments were the solidification of Jewish nationalist thinking and the wave of pogroms unleashed in 1903.

The emergence of an organized Zionist movement within the Pale, including efforts at synthesizing Jewish nationalism with a socialist outlook, and the elaboration of a program that demanded Jewish cultural autonomy in the areas of Jewish residence, challenged the leaders of the Bund and forced them to respond with a national program of their own. At the Bund's fourth convention in Bialystok in 1901, delegates found themselves debating a proposition that called for the conversion of Russia into a federation of nations with the concept of "nation" being applied to the Jews as well. Although the proposal was not approved by them, the idea of Jewish cultural autonomy in a future Russia did come to be supported by the Bund as one option open for Jewish life within the context of the socialist state. Even though some of the leaders of the Bund accepted the general socialist analysis that the withering away of the bourgeois state would bring with it the full assimilation of the Jewish community, those individuals did not insist that such a process need necessarily be forced upon the Jewish community of Russia. Cultural autonomy for the Jewish community of the Empire was thus left open as one possible solution to the "Jewish Question" there.

The Kishenev pogrom of April 1903 raised for the leadership of the Bund the problem of Jewish self-defense in the wake of assaults against the community. In the earlier periods, following their orthodox Marxist teaching on the role of isolated uses of force, the Bund had condemned revolutionary violence. After Kishenev, however, local groups organized by the Bund took an active part in Jewish self-defense efforts—even to the point of launching preemptive strikes against would-be assailants. Hence while still critical of the Zionists and other

Jewish nationalists within the Jewish community, the Bund, nevertheless, developed its own independent Jewish identity with a concomitant program for future Jewish life in a revolutionized Russia.

Thus in 1903, when V. I. Lenin* and the Iskra group revived the Russian Social Democratic Workers' Party, they encountered in the Bund a major opponent to their reorganizational plans. Insisting on retaining its status as the sole representative of the Jewish working class for the whole of the Empire, and affirming a positive Jewish identity that need not necessarily disappear after the introduction of socialism, the Bund found itself at odds with Lenin's conception of its place within the party and with his commitment to the total assimilation of the Jewish community within the socialist state. Spokespersons for the Bund had been engaged in an ongoing public exchange with Lenin and the other members of the Iskra board before the convening of the Congress, with the hope that their formulations would be acceptable to the Iskra group. However, when the delegates representing the Bund at the 1903 Congress realized that their demands would be rejected, they left the Russian Social Democratic Workers' Party and established the Bund as an independent worker party for the Jewish proletariat. Clearly, the Bund's Jewish experiences had estranged the group from the official Russian Social Democratic labor movement.

Revolutionary developments in 1905 served to reunite the Bund with the Russian Social Democratic Workers' Party. The Bund was an effective agent in organizing demonstrations and strikes in the revolutionary turmoil of the period. Even though they did not abdicate their own Jewish national program, the leaders of the Bund brought their party back into the RSDWP in 1905 without any concessions being made to them on the overall structure of the party. Under the influence of the general revolutionary mood of the day, the internationalist and revolutionary motifs within the Bund program had regained ascendancy over the Jewish demands espoused earlier by the Jewish workers' party.

The Bund's radical activism declined in the period after 1905, as the government's suppression of revolutionary activity forced the Bund to concentrate more and more on education and cultural work within the Jewish community. In the period between the Revolution of 1905 (*see* Nineteen-Five Revolution) and World War I*, the program adopted by the Bund moved closer and closer to the line being taken by the Menshevik (*see* Russian Social Democratic Party [Menshevik]) branch of the RSDWP. In fact, the Bund sided with the Menshevik branch of the party at the time of the final split in 1912 between the RSDWP's Menshevik and Bolshevik branches. At the same time, Menshevik theories on the nationalities question (*see* National Question and the Russian Revolution) were also being revised, and in the summer of 1917, the Mensheviks accepted the idea of national–cultural autonomy for the nationalities of the Russian Empire after a successful socialist revolution. With that declaration, the Bund and the Mensheviks came to full agreement on this key question.

World War I* split the Bund because of the German occupation of much of the Pale. Estimates place the total Bund membership at just over 33,000 on the eve of the war. However, the strength and cohesiveness of the organization declined sharply with the onset of hostilities and the ensuing Russian reverses at the hands of the Germans. Generally, Bund policy during the period followed the Mensheviks, both being split between Internationalists and Defensists factions. While the principal leaders of the Bund opposed the Bolshevik coup in 1917, a number of prominent Bundists gravitated to the Communist Party in the period of the Civil War, especially so in the Ukraine and in parts of Belorussia (*see* Belorussia, Revolution in). In many of those areas the Red Army* and the Russian Communist Party (Bolshevik) (RCP [B]) (*see* Russian Social Democratic Workers' Party [Bolshevik]) saved the local Jewish population from savage pogroms unleashed by the counterrevolutionary nationalist forces.

After 1921 some Bundists entered the newly created Jewish sections of the Russian Communist Party (Bolshevik) where they participated in formulating the Jewish policy of revolutionary Russia as it was being developed in the first years after the Revolution. Thus by 1921 the Russian wing of the Bund had ceased to exist. On the other hand, the party's Polish wing reconstituted itself as a separate entity after the war and played a significant role in the Polish Republic during the interwar period in both Polish politics and in Jewish cultural life.

Alexander Orbach

Bibliography

Buchbinder, N. *Istoriia evreiskogo rabochego dvizhenii v Rossii.* 1925.
Gitelman, Z. *Jewish Nationality and Soviet Politics.* 1972.
Mendelsohn, E. *Class Struggle in the Pale.* 1970.
Rafes, M. *Ocherki po istorii 'bunda'.* 1923.
Tobias, H. *The Jewish Bund in Russia.* 1972.

Burtsev, Vladimir L'vovich (1842–1942). Burtsev was a political radical and publicist and an opponent of the October Seizure of Power*. He was born in Fort Aleksandrovskii and was politically active from the 1880s. In the beginning he was an adherent of the narodnik (Populist) movement. He was later closer to the Socialist-Revolutionary Party* and then the Constitutional Democratic Party—Cadet*. Burtsev was arrested in 1885, imprisoned, and later exiled to Siberia*. He escaped from Siberia in 1888 and became an advocate of the terror. In the 1890s he was involved in the publication of the journals *Svobodnaia Rossia* (*Free Russia*) and *Narodovolets* (*Member of the People's Will*), and in 1900 he began the publication of *Byloe* (*The Past*), with which he is most identified. That periodical appeared in 1900–1904, 1906–1907, and 1908–1912.

Burtsev developed an interest in the history of the revolutionary movement from which he assumed the mission of uncovering tsarist double agents among the ranks of the revolutionaries. Among his most notable successes were the exposures of Evno F. Azef, prominent in the Socialist–Revolutionaries, and R. V. Malinovskii, prominent Bolshevik and confidant of V. I. Lenin*. From

1911 to 1914 he published the newspaper *Budushchee-L'Avenir* (*The Future*) in Paris. He returned to Russia in 1915. Following the February Revolution* he published the Petrograd newspaper *Obshchee delo* (*Public Affairs*), which opposed the Bolsheviks. After the October Seizure of Power he moved the newspaper to the south of Russia and continued publication (1920–1922) after his immigration to Paris. In 1921 he took part in the formation of a National Committee made up of emigrés opposed to the Bolsheviks. He published his memoirs (in Russian) in 1923.

Bibliography

Burtsev, V. L. *Moi vospominaniia*. 1923.

C

Cadets. *See* Constitutional Democratic Party—Cadet.

Caucasian Bureau (Kavkazkoe Biuro, or Kavbiuro). The Caucasian Bureau was a special bureau formed within the Russian Communist Party (Bolshevik) (*see* Russian Social Democratic Workers' Party [Bolshevik]) for the purpose of establishing Soviet rule throughout the area of the Caucasus. The Caucasian Bureau was established within the executive agencies of the Bolshevik Party on April 8, 1920, by its Central Committee (*see* Central Committee of the Russian Communist Party [Bolshevik]). The bureau was responsible for coordinating assistance to nationalist revolutionary movements in the Caucasus and the Near East and in efforts to unify the Caucasus under communist regimes. The first chairman of the Caucasian Bureau was G. K. Ordzhonikidzhe*, a Georgian. Its vice-chairman was S. M. Kirov*, a Russian who grew up in Kazan, an area in which there was a large Moslem population. The other two members were P. G. (Budu) Mdivani and A. M. Stopani, both Georgians.

The appointment of the Caucasian Bureau meant that the Bolsheviks had lost faith in the ability of the Regional Committee of their party in Tbilisi to accomplish its assigned task, that is, to bring Soviet government to the Caucasus. Ordzhonikidzhe and Kirov favored a strong centralized government for the USSR with little autonomy for the national republics. Mdivani and Stopani were strong supporters of greater autonomy for the national republics. I. V. Stalin*, Chairman of the Commissariat of Nationalities, favored the centralists.

The Caucasian Bureau was renamed the Transcaucasian Regional Committee on March 12, 1922, when it announced the creation of the Federated Union of Socialist Republics of Transcaucasia, a highly centralized political structure that was confirmed in the All-Union Constitution approved in February 1923 (*see* Transcaucasia, Revolution in).

Central Asia, Revolution in. The revolutionary upheaval that began in Central Asia and Kazakhstan was in reality two separate, simultaneous revolutions. One took place among the Russian soldiers, workers, and peasants who had migrated into this region, and this revolution followed the pattern of events in European Russia. The other revolution was a national-colonial struggle of the native inhabitants for national identity and liberation from their imperial masters. The first revolution succeeded; the latter failed because the local peoples had not reached a sufficiently mature stage of national development to unite in their struggle against the better-organized Russians.

The area in question—the territory encompassed by the present-day Kazakh, Kirghiz, Uzbek, Tajik, and Turkmen Soviet republics—covers some 1.5 million square miles, an area equal to approximately one-half that of the continental United States. The various native peoples after whom the republics are named are basically Turkic in origin, the one major exception being the Iranian Tajiks. They were all Moslems. The Kazakhs, Kirghiz, and Turkmen were largely pastoral nomads; the Uzbeks and Tajiks were farmers who intensively cultivated the rich soil of the great river valleys of Asia through the aid of an elaborate irrigation system.

After the conquest of this region in the last half of the nineteenth century, the Russians organized the territory into the Governorship-General of the Steppe (Kazakhstan) and the Governorship-General of Turkestan (parts of Uzbekistan, Turkmenistan, Tajikstan, and Kirghizstan). The two small, backward khanates of Bukhara and Khiva were left as autonomous enclaves within the Russian Empire. The administration was entirely under the army. The Moslems did not participate.

Russians of several types moved in with and followed the conquering armies. First came the army itself, which constructed European settlements apart from the native cities where the soldiers and the military administrators lived and worked. Then, following the Stolypin reforms of 1907, peasants and Cossack farmers in large numbers moved into the Kazakh steppe. One aim of these reforms was to relieve the pressure on overcrowded Russian and Ukrainian villages, considered one of the major causes of agrarian unrest. By 1914 most of the land with agricultural value, approximately one-eighth of the Kazakh steppe, had been distributed to Russians. The construction of the Transcaspian and Ohrenburg-Tashkent railroads brought significant numbers of Russian workers and administrators into the region. They, too, lived apart from the native population.

The arrival of these foreign imperialists, alien in religion and culture, who seized land and ruled through the army, was sufficient grounds for hostility between Russians and natives in Kazakhstan. Further aggravated by the decrees drafting non-Russians for use as service troops during World War I*, the Kazakhs and Kirghiz rose in revolt in 1916. The Russians put down the revolt with great brutality.

To the south in Turkestan, World War I* also brought on a crisis. In the decades before 1914 the formerly balanced agricultural economy—completely self-sufficient in food—had been converted to the cultivation of cotton. This required the importation of grain for food, most coming from the northern Caucasus area. First the war and then the serious disruptions of the communications during the upheavals of 1917 brought great hardship. It was under such circumstances that the Revolution of 1917 came to Kazakhstan and Central Asia.

When the tsarist regime collapsed in February 1917, the newly formed Provisional Government* issued decrees that abolished all restrictive legislation relating to national minorities and placed the borderlands under special committees composed mostly of Duma (*see* Duma and Revolution) deputies of the local population. From the very beginning these committees commanded little real authority, and by mid–1917 their power was purely nominal.

Modern nationalism and political organization came late to the Moslem peoples of the Empire. The first steps relate to the establishment of Turkish-language newspapers and the "new method" schools by the Crimean and Volga Tatars (*see* Crimean Tatars; Tatars, Revolution Among the) in the late nineteenth century. During the Revolution of 1905 (*see* Nineteen-Five Revolution), the Volga Tatars organized the Moslem deputies of the Duma into an all-Russian movement (Ittifak). This group supported the Cadets (*see* Constitutional Democratic Party—Cadet). Simultaneously, separate parties of a more radical nature formed in the various regions. Where Islam was still firmly in control of the popular mind, as in Turkestan, groups composed of the Moslem clergy and the wealthy members of society sought to advance their conservative program. A middle group, liberal in orientation, generally supported the Provisional Government. More radical parties formed among young intellectuals who tended toward socialism of the Socialist-Revolutionary type (*see* Socialist-Revolutionary Party). In April the Moslem deputies in the Duma called for an All-Russian Congress of Moslems (*see* All-Russian Moslem Council) to meet in Moscow. The deputies selected at regional conferences met in May and appointed the All-Russian Moslem Council (Shura) to represent the interest of all Moslems in the Empire and to prepare measures for submission to the soon-to-meet Constituent Assembly*. A second congress met in Kazan in July, but although the organization appealed to Moslem intellectuals, the border regions were so isolated from one another and differed so greatly among the various areas that each region went its own way.

Also in April the All-Kazakh Congress in Orenburg passed a resolution calling for a return of all land to the Kazakh–Kirghiz people and the expulsion of the new Russian–Ukrainian settlers. Three months later at another congress in Orenburg the idea of territorial autonomy was broached, and a Kazakh–Kirghiz political party called the Alash-Orda* was formed.

Meanwhile, the Russian–Ukrainian settlers in Semirechie met in Vernyi (present-day Alma Ata) and voted to take all measures to maintain their position. If necessary, they thought the natives should be forced out of the country. Returning refugees from the 1916 rebellion met with the violent opposition of the Russian settlers. A Moslem source claims mass slaughters led to 83,000 deaths. In

September, with the violence at a peak, the Provisional Government placed the area under martial law.

Toward the end of 1917 as the authority of the Provisional Government faded and was replaced by the Bolshevik regime, Orenburg became the center of three political groups: the Bashkirs (see Bashkiria, Revolution in), the Alash-Orda, and the Orenburg Cossacks*. Under Ataman A. I. Dutov* they cooperated to oppose the new order in Petrograd. Bolshevik organizations did not exist in this area until 1918, and they faced a serious dilemma. Spreading their message among the military, the railroad workers, and the peasant colonists, the Bolsheviks became a consequential force. The dilemma resulted from a conflict between the highly successful Bolshevik nationalities policy of self-determination and the political aims of their Russian adherents in Kazakhstan and Central Asia. The Russian workers and peasants wanted the proletarian dictatorship to prohibit the land confiscation favored by the natives. The Bashkirs, the Alash Orda, and the Orenburg Cossacks all lost during the Civil War (see Civil War in Russia).

Like Kazakhstan, the liberals in the Turkestan Committee were ousted when their counterparts lost out in the Provisional Government. Real authority in Turkestan lay in the Tashkent Soviet, then headed by a Socialist–Revolutionary (S–R) lawyer, a body dominated by a coalition of S–R's and Mensheviks (see Russian Social Democratic Workers' Party [Menshevik]). No separate Bolshevik organizations existed in Tashkent until December 1917, and the Bolsheviks had no cells in other towns until 1918. The Tashkent Soviet represented the interests of the European population alone.

The aggressiveness of the Russians brought conflict. The Moslem leadership in the region was liberal, advocating a federal system in Russia and a return to the natives of all confiscated land. At a Congress in April they formed a Turkestan Moslem Central Committee. The council tried to negotiate with the Tashkent Soviet on a reasonable method of electing deputies to the Constituent Assembly. They offered to guarantee the Russians a certain number of seats. The Russians demanded a curial method of selecting the deputies that would insure Russian domination. When the more radical Russians seized control of the Soviet, the Moslems began to press more vigorously for autonomy.

The revolutionary temper of the Russian soldiers and workers developed more rapidly than elsewhere in the Empire, and they overthrew the Provisional Government organ. The Provisional Government dispatched military force to take over the administration, but on October 25 the railroad workers arose, and within a week the major centers of Turkestan were in the hands of a coalition of Bolsheviks and Left Socialist–Revolutionaries. The countryside was almost entirely unaffected. On November 15 the Third Regional Congress of Soviets proclaimed Soviet rule throughout Turkestan. The Turkestan Council of People's Commissars took over the administration.

On witnessing these events, the Turkestan Moslem Central Council sounded out the new ruler on the matter of autonomy. In an overwhelming vote the Congress of Soviets rejected the idea, fearing it would weaken Russian control.

To forestall the opposition of the Moslems the Soviets organized another Congress of Turkestan Moslems, largely from members of the Socialist Union of Toiling Moslems and similar bodies, and obtained approval for the actions of the Soviet.

The Moslems responded by calling a Fourth Extraordinary Congress. Because of the disorders in Tashkent and the hostility of the Russian leaders, they decided to meet in Kokand, which was some 220 miles east of Tashkent and 96 percent Moslem. The Congress met on November 28. Right S–R's, Bukharan Jews, and others opposed to the Soviet met with the Moslems. The 180 delegates decided that some form of autonomy was necessary and called for a constituent assembly to meet on March 20, 1918. Deputies were elected to a People's Council, thirty-six seats going to Moslems and eighteen to Russians. They also appointed an executive committee to counter the Tashkent Soviet. Two governments then existed in Turkestan. (*See* Kokand, the Autonomous Government of.)

Kokand tried to obtain the assistance of the Alash-Orda and the Emir of Bukhara without success. In January 1918, with only a pitiful force of a few hundred volunteers to meet the challenge of thousands of Russian veterans and mercenaries (Austrian and Hungarian prisoners of war), the Kokand government soon met defeat. Those who refused to capitulate joined the Basmachis* (originally bandits) in the countryside and mountains, and a popular resistance movement began. It was not decisively destroyed until the mid–1920s.

After taking Kokand the Soviet force marched on Bukhara but suffered a defeat. The two khanates, Bukhara and Khiva, were spared another two years before they were conquered by the Red Army*.

Alton S. Donnelly

Bibliography

Abdushukurov, R. *Oktiabr' skaia revoliutsiia: rastsvet uzbekskoi natsii i sblizhenie ee s natsiami SSR*. 1962.

Allworth E., ed. *Central Asia: A Century of Russian Rule*. 1969.

Bennigsen, A., and Lemercier-Quelquejay, C. *Islam in the Soviet Union*. 1967.

Caroe, O. *Soviet Empire*. 2d ed. 1967.

Hayit, B. *Turkestan im XX. Jahrhundert*. 1956.

Khodzaev, F. *K istorii revoliutsii v Bukhare*. 1926.

Muraveiskii, S. *Ocherki po istorii revoliutsionnogo dvizheniia v srednei Azii*. 1926.

Park, A. *Bolshevism in Turkestan, 1917–27*. 1957.

Pobeda Velikoi Oktiabr' skoi sotsialisticheskoi revoliutsii v Kazakhstane, 1917–1918 gg.: Sbornik dokumentov i materialov. 1957.

Safarov, G. *Kolonial'naia revoliutsiia, opyt Turkestana*. 1921.

Zenkovsky, Serge. *Pan-Turkism and Islam in Russia*. 1960.

Central Bureau of Communist Organizations of Peoples of the East under the Russian Communist Party (Bolshevik). The branch of the Russian Communist Party (Bolshevik) (RCP [B]) (*see* Russian Social Democratic Workers' Party [Bolshevik]) designated by Stalin to direct and control all domestic political movements among Eastern peoples. It absorbed the Central Bureau of Moslem Organizations of the RCP (B) (*see* Central Bureau of Moslem Organizations of the Russian Communist Party [Bolshevik]) as part of an effort to subordinate Moslem nationalism to the needs and discipline of the Russian party. At the Seventh Congress of the RCP (B) at the end of March 1918 it was announced that there should no longer be any distinction made between the Moslem and non-Moslem peoples of the East, and any mention of Islam itself was thenceforth prohibited. The move was also seen as an effort to reduce the popularity and political strength of M. Sultangaliev* among the Moslem communists in the USSR. In January 1921 it was reorganized as the Central Bureau of Agitation and Propaganda among Turkic Peoples under the Central Committee of the Russian Communist Party (Bolshevik) (*see also* Central Asia, Revolution in; Transcaucasia, Revolution in).

Central Bureau of the Lithuanian Section of the Russian Social Democratic Workers' Party (Bolshevik). An administrative center for Bolshevik Party work among the Lithuanians. The Central Bureau of the Lithuanian Section was proposed by Bolsheviks in Petrograd in September 1917 and approved by the Central Committee of the party on October 10, 1917, with V. S. Mickevicius-Kapsukas and Iu. Dumsha as two of its members. The First Conference of the Lithuanian Section in Petrograd took place between January 5 and January 8, 1918, with 36 delegates representing 2,400 members. The members of the Central Bureau elected at this conference were E. I. Angaretis, Dumsha, P. Kurkulas, I. Liankaitis, S. Matulaitis, P. Mitskivicius, Iu. Smol'kis, and S. Turla. In March 1918 the Central Bureau was transferred to Moscow. The organ of the Central Bureau was the newspaper *Tiesa* (*Truth*), published after April 1918 and edited by Mickevicius-Kapsukas and Matulaitis. There was also a weekly edited by Angaretis. The Central Bureau mobilized Lithuanian workers in Moscow in the struggle for Soviet power and took part in the creation of the People's Commissariat of National Affairs for Lithuanians. They recruited followers from the Lithuanians captured as prisoners of war and deserters, and set up an underground organization in occupied Lithuania. The leaders of the Central Bureau sided with the Left Communists (*see* Left Communism) on the issue of the Brest Peace (*see* Brest-Litovsk), calling for revolutionary war against Germany. The Second Conference of the Lithuanian Section in Moscow on May 26–27, 1918, consisted of 24 delegates, representing more than 540 members of the Russian Communist Party (Bolshevik). This conference raised the issue of creating a communist party of Lithuania. The new Central Bureau elected at this conference included V. S. Mickevicius-Kapsukas, I. Liankaitis, S. Matulaitis, P. Mitskivicius, R. Rosikas, K. Gedris, P. Mitskivicius, and Iu. Opanskis. When Soviet power was briefly established on December 16, 1918, Mickevicius-Kapsukas and Angaretis became the head of that revolutionary government, which lasted for months (*see* Lithuania and Russian Revolution).

Central Bureau of Moslem Organizations of the Russian Communist Party (Bolshevik). The Central Bureau of Moslem Organizations was founded in November 1918 at the First Congress of the All-Russian Party of Moslem Communists (Bolshevik) in Moscow. Its main purpose was to bring Moslem Communists under the direct control of the Russian Communist Party (Bolshevik) (*see* Russian Social Democratic Workers' Party [Bolshevik]). I. V. Stalin*, the Commissar of Nationalities for the USSR, assumed personal leadership of the new organization, and it marked the beginning of the subordination of all Moslem nationalist movements in Russia to Russian leadership. The announced aim of the new organization was to "gradually bring the revolutionary masses to an understanding of the idea of world communism." To do this it took over an earlier organization, the Department of International Propaganda for the Eastern Peoples, as its chief agency for coordinating propaganda for the Moslem people of the USSR. That department was divided into twelve sections for that purpose: Arab, Persian, Turkish, Azerbaijani, Bukharan Kirghiz, Caucasian mountaineers, Kalmyk, Chinese, Korean, Japanese, and Indian. In March 1919 the Central Bureau of Moslem Organizations of the Russian Communist Party (Bolshevik) (RCP [B]) was absorbed into a broader organization for all of the nationalities in the East called the Central Bureau of Communist Organizations of the RCP (B). This new organization also took over the work of the organization known as the Union for the Liberation of the East. The officers of the original Central Bureau of Moslem Organizations of the RCP (B) were I. V. Stalin, President, and B. Sardarov and G. Ia'lmov, Vice-Presidents. The original members of the bureau were M. Sultangaliev*, Kh. Iu. Iumagulov (Z. Validov), K. Iakubov, and candidate members D. Buniatzade, M. Dulat-Aliev, M. Konov, I. Rakhmatulin, and N. Iarullin.

The bureau published newspapers, journals, and brochures in Turkish, Persian, and other languages. It recruited among the local branches of the Russian Communist Party in Central Asia and in the revolutionary organizations: Adalet (Justice) Party*, The Turkish Party of Socialist Communists, Indian revolutionary groups, and others. The Central Bureau had several subdivisions including an international propaganda section headed by the Turkish communist M. Subkhi. The propaganda section had ten subsections for each of the major Moslem languages: a publishing-information section with subbranches for women, youth, peasants, and so on.

Central Committee. See Central Committee of the Russian Communist Party (Bolshevik).

Central Committee of the Baltic Fleet (Centrobalt; Tsentralnyi Komitet Baltiiskogo Flota; TsKBF; or Tsentrobalt). Centrobalt was the highest elective executive organ of the revolutionary sailors of the Baltic Fleet. The idea for the creation of Centrobalt came from the Bolshevik sailors of the Helsingfors (Helsinki) Soviet. It was established at a meeting of the fleet committees on the transport ship *Viola* on April 30, 1917. The first chairman of Centrobalt was the famous Bolshevik sailor P. E. Dybenko*. His deputy chairmen were F. I. Efimov and R. R. Grundman. The sailors participating in Centrobalt played an active role in the October Seizure of Power* in 1917 and in the struggles to defend Soviet power during the remainder of the year 1917. In the spring of 1918 the Soviet government disbanded Centrobalt, stating that it had been taken over by anarchists, and replaced it with the Council of Commissars of the Baltic Fleet (*see* Sailors in 1917).

Central Committee of the Caspian Military Flotilla (Centrocasp; Tsentral'nyi komitet Kaspiiskoi voennoi flotilii; or Tsentrokasp). Centrocasp seems to have been a name applied to at least three organizations of which the above is only one. According to Ronald Suny (p. 83) the first Centrocasp was created in Baku on March 13, 1917, as the executive committee of a trade union for the sailors of the commercial maritime fleet in the Caspian Sea. From the outset it was dominated by the Socialist-Revolutionary Party*, which never lost its grip on the organization. The chairman of Centrocasp was a member of the Socialist-Revolutionary Party, a Georgian doctor named I. Turkiia (or Gurkiia). His deputy was another Socialist–Revolutionary, Nadzharov. When news of the October Seizure of Power* in Petrograd reached Baku, the Executive Committee of the Baku Soviet formed the Committee of Public Safety, ostensibly to defend against counterrevolution, and Centrocasp was represented in that body. According to Suny, its real purpose was to prevent a Bolshevik (*see* Russian Social Democratic Workers' Party [Bolshevik]) takeover of the city. But the strength of the Bolsheviks in the Baku Soviet continued to grow, and the Committee of Public Safety in that city was not successful in uniting the opposition to the Bolsheviks outside of the Baku Soviet.

When an uprising among the Moslem population in the city of Baku took place in March, the divisive national hostilities manifest in the suppression of that rebellion served as a revelation of the weakness of the anti-Bolshevik coalition, and the Bolshevik-dominated Baku seized power and announced the creation of the Baku Commune, which would stay in power only until July. At the same time, the Bolshevik sailors in the Caspian military fleet met and formed their own Central Committee of the Caspian Military Fleet (a second Centrocasp), which Soviet sources described as the chief command post for Bolshevik soldiers and sailors, a minority in the armed forces. The chairman of this second Centrocasp was the Bolshevik A. M. Kuzminskii. By the end of November the anti-Bolshevik Committee of Public Safety had been disbanded by order of the Baku Soviet, but the first anti-Soviet Centrocasp continued its protest against the Bolsheviks in muted form and made contact with the nearby British military forces.

When the Turks threatened to take Baku in July 1918, the Bolshevik leaders of the Baku Commune suddenly found themselves again in a minority in the Baku Soviet on the question of asking for British help against the Turkish menace—they opposed it—and they resigned and fled the city. The first Centrocasp and other right-wing socialist groups took power from the Bolsheviks who led the Baku Commune and created a moderate socialist dictatorship in its place in the hope of preserving socialist power in Baku and uniting resistance to the invading Turkish army with the help of the British. This government is generally called the Centrocasp Dictatorship, a third common usage of the acronym. The official name of the new government was the Dictatorship of Centrocasp and the Presidium of the Provisional Executive Committee of Soviets. British forces decided, however, on September 14, 1918, to abandon the city to the invading Turkish forces, and the remaining representatives of all three Centrocasps fled.

Bibliography

Suny, Ronald Grigor. *The Baku Commune, 1917–18.* 1972.

Central Committee of the Fleet of the Arctic Ocean (Seledflot; Tsentralnyi Komitet Flotillii Severno-Ledovitogo okeana; or Tseledflot). The Central Committee of the Fleet of the Northern Arctic Ocean was formed on April 30, 1917, at a meeting of representatives of the sailors, officers, and conductors serving in the Arctic Fleet. The meeting expressed its support for the Provisional Government* and sent six delegates led by the Right Socialist–Revolutionary (*see* Socialist-Revolutionary Party) M. N. Abramov to the Central Executive Committee of the Military Fleet under the All-Russian Central Executive Committee of Soviets of Workers' and Soldiers' Deputies* (Centroflot, or Tsentroflot). Although originally a stronghold for the Socialist–Revolutionaries, the organization became dominated by the Bolsheviks between October and December 1917. With the intervention in the North (*see* North, Revolution in) in the summer of 1918, Seledflot ceased to exist.

Central Committee of the Murmansk Detachment of Ships of the Fleet of the Arctic Ocean (Centro-Mur, or Tsentromur). Centro-Mur was created in March 1917. The organization was supposed to be subordinate to the Executive Committee of the Arctic Fleet (Seledflot) and, like its parent organization, preserved a guarded attitude toward the Bolsheviks and the October Seizure of Power*. Like its parent organization, Centro-Mur ceased to exist after the intervention in the North (*see* North, Revolution in) in the middle of 1918.

Central Committee of the Russian Communist Party (Bolshevik). The Central Committee of the Russian Communist Party (Bolshevik) is theoretically the highest organ of power in the party between party congresses.

Although a central committee was elected for the Russian Social Democratic Workers' Party (Bolshevik)* (RSDWP [B]) at the Sixth (Prague) Conference in January 1912, the actual work of leading the party was conducted before April 3, 1917, by the Russian Bureau of the Central Committee of the RSDWP (B).

On April 3, 1917, when Lenin returned to Russia, the distinction between the two organizations was eliminated because most of the emigrants had returned to Russia and the members of the Central Committee could now assemble in one place. At the Seventh (April) Conference of the RSDWP (B) in 1917, the following members were elected to the Central Committee: V. I. Lenin*, G. E. Zinoviev*, L. B. Kamenev*, V. P. Miliutin*, V. P. Nogin*, Ia. M. Sverdlov*, I. T. Smilga*, I. V. Stalin*, G. F. Fedorov, and candidates A. S. Bubnov*, N. P. Glebov-Avilov, I. G. Pravdina, and I. A. Teodorovich.

At the Sixth Congress of the Russian Social Democratic Workers' Party (Bolshevik) in July-August 1917, the Central Committee was enlarged to twenty-one members and eight candidate members. The full Central Committee only met once every one or two months, and current work was carried on by a small staff of eleven elected by the plenum of the Central Committee on August 5, 1917. On August 6, 1917, this staff elected the party's first secretariat of five people.

On October 10, 1917, after hearing a report by Lenin, the Central Committee made the decision to put preparations for armed insurrection at the top of its agenda and elected the first Politburo of seven headed by Lenin. Zinoviev and Kamenev voted against the resolution but were elected to the Politburo anyway. According to Robert V. Daniels (1969), four other absent members probably would have voted against the resolution, making the opposition about one-quarter of the membership of the Central Committee. At an enlarged session of the Central Committee on October 16, 1917, it decided to prepare for armed insurrection, despite the continued opposition of Zinoviev and Kamenev and four abstentions, and the committee elected a military revolutionary center of five people to serve as a party cell in the Petrograd Military Revolutionary Committee formed on October 11 in the Petrograd Soviet*. Alexander Rabinowitch (1976) suggested that more than a third of the members of the Central Committee had strong reservations about the wisdom of preparations for an immediate insurrection. Lenin subsequently attacked the position of Zinoviev and Kamenev on this issue in a letter to the party, and Kamenev gave an interview to M. Gorkii's newspaper *Novaia zhizn'* expressing the reasons for his opposition. Kamenev resigned in protest, and a meeting of the Central Committee on October 20 agreed to accept his resignation.

On the morning of October 24 the Military Revolutionary Committee ordered the beginning of the October Seizure of Power* by driving *junkers* (students from the officer's training schools) from the Bolshevik newspaper plant Rabochii put', which they had seized during the night upon orders from the Prime Minister of the Provisional Government*, A. F. Kerensky*. On the night of October 24–25 the Central Committee met at the Smolnyi Institute under Lenin's direct leadership and approved the actions of the Military Revolutionary Committee around the city and proposed that a new government to be called the Council of People's Commissars* be presented to the imminent Second All-Russian

Congress of Soviets. One member of the Central Committee even proposed the designation of candidates.

From November to the end of January 1918 the Central Committee met almost daily, but its work was hampered by the opposition among those like Kamenev, A. I. Rykov*, G. E. Zinoviev, V. P. Miliutin, and V. P. Nogin*, who favored an all-socialist government including other political parties and those who did not. When the Russian Social Democratic Workers' Party (Bolshevik) changed its name on March 8, 1918, the Central Committee became known as the Central Committee of the Russian Communist Party (Bolshevik).

Bibliography

Daniels, Robert V., *The Conscience of the Revolution*. 1969.
Daniels, R. *Red October*. 1967.
Rabinowitch, Alexander. *The Bolsheviks Come to Power*. 1976.
Schapiro, L. *The Communist Party of the Soviet Union*. 1960.

Central Executive Committee. *See* All-Russian Central Executive Committee (VTsIK).

Central Executive Committee of the Military Fleet under the All-Russian Central Executive Committee of Soviets of Workers' and Soldiers' Deputies (Centroflot; Tsentral'nyi ispolnitel'nyi komitet voennogo flota pri VTsIK Sovetov rabochikh i soldatskikh deputatov; or Tsentroflot). The chief executive organ for the revolutionary forces in the Russian fleet. Centroflot was created at the First All-Russian Congress of Soviets in June 1917 from the delegates representing the Russian fleet. The chairman of Centroflot was the Right Socialist–Revolutionary M. N. Abramov, and the organization was dominated by non-Bolshevik parties. Centroflot participated in the Committee for the Salvation of the Motherland and Revolution*. The Bolsheviks bypassed Centroflot by creating their own Military/Naval Revolutionary Committee with a Bolshevik, I. I. Vakhrameev, at its head.

Central Executive Committee of the Soviets of Siberia (Centrosibir; Tsentral'nyi ispolnitel'nyi komitet Sovetov Sibiri; TsIK Sibiri; or Tentrosibir). Centrosibir was created by the First Congress of Soviets of Workers', Soldiers', and Peasants' Deputies of Siberia, which was held in Irkutsk on October 16–23, 1917, and lasted until August 28, 1918. Under the chairmanship of the Bolshevik B. Z. Shumiatskii, Centrosibir became the chief source of leadership for the Soviet October Seizure of Power in Siberia. (*see* Siberia, Revolution in). At first, most of the city soviets in Siberia, including that in Irkutsk, were dominated by Socialist–Revolutionaries (*see* Socialist-Revolutionary Party) and Mensheviks (*see* Russian Socialist Democratic Workers' Party [Menshevik]). The socialist parties on the Right tried to develop a counterpoise to Centrosibir by creating a Siberian Regional Duma* that would in turn create a Provisional Siberian Government until a Siberian Constituent Assembly could be elected. But the success of Centrosibir in bringing about the Soviet seizure of power in one Siberian city after another between October 1917 and January 1918 prevented the opposition from succeeding. At the Second All-Siberian Congress of Soviets in Irkutsk from February 16th to 26th, 1918 a new Centrosibir was elected with a membership of forty-four Bolsheviks and eleven Left Socialist–Revolutionaries, and a rudimentary Council of People's Commissars for all of Siberia was established. When the Czechoslovak Legion* rebelled against the Soviet government and seized most of the cities along the Trans-Siberian Railroads, the Czechs, the counterrevolutionary armies, and the foreign interventionists dissolved most of the soviets and arrested or executed most of their leaders. (*see* Siberia, Revolution in).

Bibliography

Snow, Russel. *The Bolsheviks in Siberia, 1917–18*. 1977.

Central Industrial Region. One of the most important economic regions in Russia; after Petrograd, the most highly developed industrial region in Russia. It is the region that includes Moscow and its environs and in 1913 included 16.7 percent of all industrial enterprises and 37.0 percent of the value of industrial production for the whole of Russia. By 1916 the Central Industrial Region had 33.0 percent of the industrial enterprises in Russia and by 1917 almost half (47.6 percent) of all of the industrial workers in the country. By 1917 there were about 300,000 garrison troops in the cities of this region, and in Moscow alone the Bolsheviks (*see* Russian Social Democratic Workers' Party [Bolshevik]) claimed a membership of about 70,000. The activities of the Bolsheviks in the Central Industrial Region were under the supervision of the Moscow Regional Bureau (Moskovskoe Oblastnoe Biuro; MOB). Shortly before the October Seizure of Power* in Petrograd, the soviets in many of the districts of the Central Industrial Region had already seized power, as, for example, in Ivanovo-Voznesensk, Kineshma, Kostromo, Tver, Briansk, Podolsk, Shuia, Riazan, Iaroslavl, Vladimir, Kovrov, and Serpukhov. In other areas there was more resistance from other parties and movements (*see* Moscow, Revolution in) as, for example, in the cities of Tula, Kursk, Kaluga, Orel, Voronezh, and Nizhnyi-Novgorod. It is difficult to know how significant the Soviet seizure of power was, since most of the soviets were vacillating in their political views, and Bolshevik domination of many of them was tenuous at best (*see* Central Provinces). When the Nizhnii Novgorod Soviet refused to seize power, the city was seized by its own Red Guard* on October 28, and a new soviet was chosen by the Red Guard to declare power in its own name. In Voronezh Soviet power was not proclaimed until October 30 after an armed struggle. After ''assistance'' was sent from Moscow on November 28 the Kaluga Soviet seized power. Tula and Penza were among those cities where the local soviets refused to seize power and were forced to do so on December 7 and 22. Orel declared Soviet power on November 20,

Kursk on November 26, and Tambov not until February 13, 1918. However, by January 1918 most of the Central Industrial Region was ostensibly under the control of the new Soviet government.

Bibliography

Keep, John L. H. *The Russian Revolution*. 1976.
Koenker, Diane. *Moscow Workers and the 1917 Revolution*. 1981.
Trukan, G. A. *Oktiabr' v Tsentral'noi Rossii*. 1967.

Central Provinces. The image of a ''seizure of power'' in the provinces— though pervasive in Western literature in 1917—misleads rather than illuminates, since power was not seized by the proponents of Soviet power as much as it was organized and institutionalized out of a virtual political vacuum. This is especially evident if one looks at the events in the crucial central provinces of Russia.

The creation of a new basis of authority began in late October 1917 with the October Seizure of Power* and was completed by the onset of the crisis of February-March 1918 that led to the Treaty of Brest-Litovsk*. The length of this period belies the term *October Revolution*. This period witnessed what might be considered a Soviet revolution during which the support of garrisons and segments of the working class catapulted the more radical socialists, usually Bolsheviks (*see* Russian Social Democratic Workers' Party [Bolshevik]), into control of the key urban soviets from where they consolidated their positions and extended their authority into the countryside. The success of the proponents of Soviet power was guaranteed by the tremendous popularity of the program of ''peace, bread, and land,'' adopted by the Second All-Russian Congress of Soviets (*see* Soviets of Workers', Soldiers', and Peasants' Deputies). This factor proved far more decisive than the partisan appeal of the Bolsheviks, who were surprisingly disorganized in the period but shrewdly realized that support for the ''Soviet program'' would win the workers, soldiers, and peasants away from the moderates. In this process, particularly in the countryside, the Bolsheviks reaped inestimable support from the maximalist wing of the Socialist-Revolutionary Party*, the Left Socialist–Revolutionaries (*see* Left Socialist-Revolutionary Party). Thus the traditional image of a Bolshevik seizure of power, of a ''Bolshevik Revolution'' directed from Petrograd, overlooks the real nature of the political transformation carried out through the society with considerable grass-roots support.

The process of introducing Soviet power was basically similar throughout European Russia despite the considerable diversity of the local situation in October 1917. In the initial phase, proponents of Soviet power aimed to attain dominance in the large urban soviets, which, in some of the more remote centers, took weeks or months of patient political organizing and then gained declarations of support for the principle of Soviet power, approval for the new central government, and sanction for the actualization of local soviet control, usually through

the creation of a military revolutionary committee (MRC). In the second stage—
a consolidation phase—proponents of Soviet power moved to strengthen their
hold over the major urban centers, extend their control to the smaller towns,
and gain political support from the peasantry. To accomplish this, they took
steps to neutralize their non-socialist opponents in the Committees to Save the
Revolution (*see* Committee of Public Safety—Moscow; Committee of Public
Safety—Petrograd; Committee of Public Organizations), extend control over or
liquidate existing non-Soviet administrative institutions (e.g., Dumas, *zemstvos*),
and, finally, create a hierarchy of unified worker, soldier, and peasant soviets
with a rudimentary apparatus.

Immediately after the October Seizure of Power in Petrograd, the contest for
power shifted to the major provincial soviets where the maximalists sought
support for the decisions of the Second All-Russian Congress of Soviets. Generally, the level of political radicalization was most intense in the more industrialized cities of the Central Industrial Region* while it was far less so in the
agricultural belt. This resulted in considerable disparity in the tempo of the initial
phase of creating Soviet power.

In a number of the most industrialized cities, particularly those in close proximity to the capitals, the support for the transfer of power to the soviets was
very strong from the outset. The Bolsheviks either controlled these soviets before
the Second All-Russian Congress of Soviets or the decisions of that congress
acted as a final catalyst for the process of radicalization, leading to the ascendency
of the Bolsheviks immediately after the Congress. The moderate socialists em-
ulated the tactics of their delegations at the Second Congress and walked out of
the soviets, surrendering the mantle of legitimacy to the maximalists.

In other cities, like Nizhnii-Novgorod and Riazan, the alignment of forces
was slightly less favorable to the proponents of Soviet power. The existing Soviet
executive committees remained in the hands of moderates, or they remained a
powerful force at the Soviet plenums. Here the Maximalists moved to isolate
the moderates in the soviets by using the popularity of the Soviet program. In
Riazan, local proponents of Soviet power solved their problem by organizing
an independent MRC to forestall opposition until the arrival of delegates from
the Second Congress swayed enough uncommitted deputies to the side of Soviet
power. In Nizhnii-Novgorod, the Bolsheviks not only formed a party-based
Military Revolutionary Committee but had to rely on a partial reelection of the
soviet before they were able to command a majority in the soviet in early
November.

In other cities, like Orel, Tula, Vologda, and Tambov, the scenario differed
more fundamentally. The moderate socialists not only controlled a majority in
the soviets at the time of A. F. Kerensky's* fall but also retained popular support
for a considerable time thereafter. The center of political gravity within the local
Menshevik (*see* Social Democratic Workers' Party [Menshevik]) and Socialist-
Revolutionary (*see* Socialist-Revolutionary Party) organizations lay to the Left
of that in the capitals, resulting in the continued credibility of the moderates for

weeks or months after the overthrow of the Provisional Government*. The Bolsheviks relied on tactical flexibility and patience in order eventually to win hegemony in these soviets. In several of these cities, local Bolsheviks even decided to participate in the work of temporary administrative organs created by the moderates to fill the power vacuum existing after the fall of Kerensky. Generally, the Bolsheviks and their Maximalist allies banked on the growing radicalization of the masses, facilitated by growing popular support of the Soviet program. They particularly cultivated support among the garrisons (see Soldiers and Soldiers' Committees), and when they felt sufficiently powerful, they instigated partial or complete reelections of the soviets. In most of these cities, however, the political situation remained very fluid even after such declarations, especially as soldiers dispersed after demobilization. Control over the soviets was seldom very secure even after the creation of provincial soviet institutions dominated by the Maximalists. By mid-January 1918, despite continued participation of moderate socialists in some soviets, the Maximalists had achieved declarations favoring Soviet power in all major cities in Central Russia legitimizing the transfer of power initiated in late October.

Opposition to the process of establishing Soviet power, at the same time, proved ineffectual. Where the Bolsheviks held a commanding position in October, their strength naturally precluded effective opposition. In Ivanovo-Voznesensk, for instance, the Bolsheviks not only controlled the soviet but also the City Duma. However, in most cities where the level of radicalization lagged somewhat, non-socialist opponents usually were well entrenched in the organs of municipal administration, and they became the loci for the creation of anti-Bolshevik Committees to Save the Revolution. These committees sometimes included moderate socialists as well as nonsocialist opponents, but they still failed to generate effective resistance. In nearly every case, opposition in Central Russia took a peaceful form, perhaps reflecting the erroneous expectation by Bolshevik opponents that the latter would soon fall. Instead of mounting armed resistance, the committees organized civil servants' strikes or other forms of passive resistance. Eventually, these strikes collapsed after causing minor inconvenience to the population while the committees, which had proved impotent in blocking the transfer of power, dissolved themselves, ending resistance in major cities.

In the regions where support for Soviet power was strong, the declaration and consolidation phases proved more distinct, whereas in areas where radicalization lagged, the two phases chronologically overlapped. The consolidation phase entailed a number of important steps: the extension of Soviet power to smaller cities and the countryside, the defeat of the Soviet's institutional rivals, and the creation of rudimentary regional soviets to actualize Soviet power on the provincial level.

In the countryside, the Socialist–Revolutionaries won an overwhelming victory in the elections to the Constituent Assembly*, whereas the Constitutional Democratic Party—Cadet* and the parties of the Right displayed continued support in several provincial cities and most smaller cities. However, the Soviet program accelerated the latent social revolution and won its proponents increasing support outside the major urban centers. Even the Constituent Assembly elections, which had proven an impressive though illusory victory for the Socialist–Revolutionaries, increased the visibility of the Bolsheviks, whereas the appearance of the Left Socialist–Revolutionaries as a separate party provided a more acceptable and familiar alternative for peasants who approved the Soviet program (i.e., the immediate distribution of land). Between October 1917 and January 1918 official and unofficial agitators (mostly demobilized soldiers) who preached the gospel of revolution flooded the countryside and smaller cities, acting as the nucleus for local soviets and as the most visible advocates of Soviet power. From November 1917 to February 1918 these agitators organized many local soviets, which, in turn, declared support for Soviet power, strengthening the new Soviet system by giving it roots in the countryside.

The local successes of agitators laid the groundwork for the convocation of numerous peasant congresses in December 1917 and January 1918 (*see* Peasants in the Russian Revolution) at which the maximalists again succeeded in winning the mantle of legitimacy. The Left Socialist-Revolutionary and Bolshevik alliance proved crucial to the isolation of the moderates. Although both sides called congresses to bolster their positions, the proponents of Soviet power proved far more successful in winning mass support for their positions with the Decree on Land (*see* Agrarian Policy, 1917–1921; Peasants in the Russian Revolution) apparently playing the foremost role in the success of their efforts. The peasant congresses usually also approved the merger of urban and peasant soviets and sanctioned the creation of unified provincial executive committees dominated by the radicals, thus cementing their hold on the countryside.

The congresses served the same legitimizing function as the earlier victories in the urban soviets had served, permitting the Maximalists to claim the Soviet mantle from the moderates, while taking the first steps toward creating a complete hierarchy of unified soviets.

Even after these congresses, proponents of Soviet power faced entrenched opposition outside the soviets, particularly in the *zemstvos*. Mass support based on the land decree, however, enabled the Bolsheviks and Left Socialist–Revolutionaries to win control of some local *zemstvos,* isolate others, and force many to subordinate themselves to village or county soviets. If these tactics failed, the *zemstvos* were simply abolished, by force if necessary. After the dissolution of the Constituent Assembly in January, both sides intensified the use of coercion, but despite isolated cases of violence, the alliance of Bolsheviks and Left Socialist–Revolutionaries was able to consolidate its hold on power by March 1918.

In summary, by March 1918 the maximalists succeeded in filling the power vacuum created by the overthrow of Kerensky with a hierarchy of soviets because of the popularity of the Soviet program. The Bolsheviks and, to a lesser extent, the Left Socialist–Revolutionaries played a crucial role during this Soviet Revolution, gaining the support first in the major urban soviets where the moderates' opposition to the Soviet program isolated them and then consolidating their position through the defeat of half-hearted opposition in the peasant soviets, the Dumas, and the Committees to Save the Revolution. By March 1918 passive resistance in Central Russia had collapsed and proponents of Soviet power had succeeded in taking steps to create a hierarchy of unified soviets to exercise authority in the provinces. This fragile base for Soviet power, however, would soon be severely tested from the onset of the Civil War (*see* Civil War in Russia) in the spring and summer of 1918.

Malvin Helgesen

Bibliography

Keep, John L. H. *The Russian Revolution.* 1976.
Trukan, G. A. *Oktiabr' v tsentraln'noi Rossii.* 1967.

Central Rada. The first revolutionary government in the Ukraine in 1917.

The Rada government ruled the Ukraine from March 1917 to April 1918. Its full name was the Ukrainska Tsentralna Rada, which means the Ukrainian Central Council. The word *rada* means the same thing in Ukrainian as the Russian word *soviet*. The political groups that formed the Central Rada in 1917 were primarily democratic and nationalist. The initiative for the formation of the Central Rada was taken by the Society of Ukrainian Progressives (Tovaristvo Ukrainska Postupovtsiv) led by the famous historian Michael Hrushevsky. That group decided to form the Central Rada at a meeting on March 20, 1917. The Rada was to be a union of various democratic and Ukrainian nationalist organizations. To give the organization a more representative character, the Society of Ukrainian Progressives called an All-Ukrainian National Congress in Kiev from April 17 to 21. S. Erast presided over the meeting and M. A. Sukhovkin attended as the representative of the Provisional Government*. The congress did not choose complete independence from Russia but sought national territorial autonomy within a Russian federation of democratic national states. (For details of the Ukrainian Revolution, *see* Ukraine, Revolution in.)

After frustrating negotiations with the Russian Provisional Government, the Central Rada finally declared the independence of the Ukraine in the First Universal issued on June 10, 1917. The decree did not call for an end to all relations with Russia, but asked for an All-Ukrainian Constituent Assembly to write a constitution for the Ukraine, which would then be submitted to the All-Russian Constituent Assembly for approval. The Ukraine would remain part of the Russian state, but with federal autonomy. The Rada also created a General Secretariat on June 15 with V. Vynnychenko, a Social Democrat, as its head. In June the First All-Russian Congress of Soviets of Workers' and Soldiers' Deputies supported the First Universal. On July 3, after negotiating with representatives of the Provisional Government, the General Secretariat issued a Second Universal reaffirming the principles of the First Universal and announcing that the Provisional Government had accepted those principles.

The Second Universal, however, broadened the representation of non-Ukrainian nationalities in the Central Rada, allotting them 35 percent of the seats. Despite the Rada's announced intention of staying within the Russian state, it began to create its own state apparatus and military forces and persuaded the Provisional Government to accept that fact. After the fall of the Provisional Government the Bolsheviks and the Central Rada cooperated in evicting the members of the Provisional Government from Kiev on October 31 and seizing the city.

Although the fall of the Provisional Government and the Soviet seizure of power in Petrograd led to a temporary alliance with pro-Soviet forces, on the day that the representatives of the Provisional Government were evicted the Central Rada, though still denying any intention to seek complete independence from Russia, enlarged its General Secretariat with non-Bolsheviks and announced that it was the new government of the Ukraine. This decision was announced in the Third Universal issued on November 7. January 9, 1918 was selected as the date for an All-Ukrainian Constituent Assembly.

The temporary alliance between the Central Rada and the Bolsheviks faded away in November and the two groups began competing for the allegiance of the soviets springing up all over the Ukraine. The Kievan Bolsheviks decided to call an All-Ukrainian Congress of Soviets to meet on December 4 without the approval of the Central Rada. But the Central Rada decided upon a preemptive strike and seized the city of Kiev at the end of November and expelled many of the Bolshevik leaders. Lenin decided that it was time to bring in the Red Army.

On December 3 Lenin sent the Rada an ultimatum demanding that the Rada cease forming its own army, encouraging separatism and allowing anti-Soviet military units to operate within the Ukraine. If these conditions were not met, the Soviet government would regard that response as an act of war. When the All-Ukrainian Congress of Soviets met on the same day as the ultimatum without most of their Bolshevik delegates and heard these demands, they condemned the posture of the Russian Soviet government. The Soviet government continued negotiations, but directed Red Army troops to Kharkov to use that city as the base of operations to support pro-Bolshevik insurrections in the Ukraine.

The Ukrainian Bolsheviks, after failing to win over the All-Ukrainian Congress of Workers', Soldiers' and Peasants' Soviets in Kiev on December 4, 1917, fled to Kharkov where they could enjoy the protection of pro-Soviet Russian troops and called their own miniscule All-Ukrainian Congress of Soviets on December 11–12 which elected a self-styled Ukrainian Council of People's Commissars, which, after seizing control in Kharkov, proclaimed a Ukrainian Soviet Socialist Republic on December 16. On January 4 the Kharkov government declared the Rada to be an enemy of the people and dispatched troops from that city in the direction of Kiev. Many local soviets outside of Kiev were seized by the Bolsheviks.

The genuine All-Ukrainian Congress of Soviets endorsed the Rada. When the Russian Soviet government proclaimed an armistice with Germany on behalf of all of Russia, including the Ukraine, the Rada announced it was adopting an independent position on international affairs on December 9 and the Central Powers invited a delegation from the Rada to the peace conference at Brest-Litovsk*. On January 10 when the Ukrainian Bolsheviks and the Red Army were getting close to Kiev, the Soviet delegates to Brest-Litovsk asked that Rada delegates to the peace conference be unseated and replaced with delegates from their Bolshevik Ukrainian government. On January 9, 1918, the day originally set for the convocation of the All-Ukrainian Constituent Assembly, the Rada had issued its Fourth Universal, the first of its public declarations to proclaim full independence from Russia. But the announcement came, ironically, when Kiev was about to fall into Bolshevik hands. On January 26, in one last desperate effort to save themselves from the Red Army and their own Bolshevik rebels who were then marching into Kiev, the Rada signed the first Peace Treaty of Brest-Litovsk. The Bolsheviks held Kiev for three weeks, but after the Rada signed the first Treaty of Brest-Litovsk the German army obligingly came to the rescue of the Rada by advancing on Kiev. In effect the Rada returned to Kiev in early March but its members were now clearly dependent on German military help to survive. On April 28, 1918, with the support of the German occupying forces, the Ukrainian landowner/general Paul Skoropadskii* conducted a coup d'état and dissolved the Central Rada (*see* Ukraine, Revolution in).

Bibliography

Hunczak, Taras ed. *The Ukraine 1917–21*. 1977.
Pipes, Richard. *The Formation of the Soviet Union*. 1968.
Reshetar, John S. *The Ukrainian Revolution, 1917–20*. 1952.

Centrobalt. *See* Central Committee of the Baltic Fleet.

Centrocasp. *See* Central Committee of the Caspian Military Flotilla.

Centroflot. *See* Central Executive Committee of the Military Fleet under the All-Russian Central Executive Committee of Soviets of Workers' and Soldiers' Deputies.

Centromur. *See* Central Committee of the Murmansk Detachment of Ships of the Fleet of the Arctic Ocean.

Centrosibir. *See* Central Executive Committee of the Soviets of Siberia.

Cheka. *See* All-Russian Extraordinary Commission for Combatting Counter-revolution and Sabotage.

Chernov, Viktor Mikhailovich (1873–1952). Viktor Mikhailovich Chernov was a member of the Central Committee of the Socialist-Revolutionary (S-R) Party* from the time of its formation in 1901 and the party's chief ideologist and theoretician.

Chernov was born in the town of Novouzensk, in Samara Province (*guberniia*). His father had been born in a serf peasant family but had risen to the rank of district treasurer (*uezdnyi kaznachei*) in the provincial civil service. Viktor's first interest in political ideas was as a schoolboy at Saratov high school (*gimnaziia*), where he joined the Populist discussion circles. His political interests attracted the attention of the Saratov police, and he transferred to the high school at Iur'ev (Derpt) for the last year of his secondary education. In 1892 Chernov entered the Law Faculty of Moscow University, where he joined a student group of Populist tendency and participated in the current debates with the Marxists. In the spring of 1894 he was arrested for his political activities and spent nine months imprisoned in the Peter-Paul Fortress in St. Petersburg. He was released at the beginning of 1894 and underwent a period of administrative exile in the towns of Kamyshin, Saratov, and Tambov.

In 1899, when his period of exile came to an end, Chernov went abroad to join the neo-Populist emigration. He went first to Zurich and then to Berne, where he was associated with Kh. O. Zhitlovskii's Union of Russian Socialist Revolutionaries Abroad. In 1900 Chernov moved to Paris where, with S. A. An-skii (Solomon Rappoport), E. E. Lazarev, L. E. Shishko, and F. V. Volk-hovskii, he became a founder of the Agrarian Socialist League, an organization that aimed to publish popular works of socialist propaganda for distribution to the Russian peasantry. At this time the various neo-Populist groups in Russia were moving toward the formation of a united party of Socialist–Revolutionaries, and Chernov played an active part in the negotiations in 1901–1902 that brought the emigré groups into membership of the new S-R Party. From 1902 until 1905 Chernov was coeditor with A. R. Gots of *Revoliutsionnaia Rossiia* (*Revolutionary Russia*), the chief S-R Party paper. In this period Chernov was one of the most prominent leaders of the S-R Party: he was a member of the party delegation to the Amsterdam Congress of the Socialist International in August 1904 and of the S-R delegation to the Paris Conference of Russian Opposition Parties in September 1904.

Chernov's most important contribution to the life of the party at this time was in the formulation of its distinctive version of socialist theory. He aimed to achieve a synthesis of Populism and Marxism that would be appropriate to Russian conditions. His main intellectual influences were P. L. Lavrov and N. K. Mikhailovskii. From European Social Democratic thinking he was influenced by the revisionist school of E. Bernstein. In the 1890s Chernov had contributed articles to *Russkoe bogatstvo* (*Russian Wealth*), the legal Populist journal. In a series of articles in *Revoliutsionnaia Rossiia* (*Revolutionary Russia*) in 1902–1905 he developed the views that were later embodied in the program approved by the First Party Congress in January 1906. The key concept in Chernov's sociological analysis was that of the revolutionary working class, which included not only proletarians (as in Social Democratic theory) but also peasant producers. He believed that the mass of Russian peasantry had an interest in socialism, and that S–R's should devote considerable attention to the political organization of the peasantry. Chernov accepted a two-stage model of Russia's path to socialism, but he considered that the first stage of the Revolution could go further toward the transition to socialism than the Social Democrats' perspective of a bourgeois democratic revolution implied. The S–R's minimum and maximum programs were designed for the first and second stages, respectively, of the Revolution. In the minimum program the most controversial demand was for the "social-ization" of land, that is, the abolition of private property in land and its egalitarian distribution for the use of those who worked it. Chernov regarded this as a necessary measure to prevent the growth of agrarian capitalism and to prepare the way for the collective or cooperative agricultural production of the socialist future.

After the publication of the October Manifesto of 1905, Chernov returned to Russia and helped to reorganize *Syn Otechestva* (*Son of the Fatherland*), a legal Populist newspaper, as a legal S-R Party organ published in St. Petersburg. At the First Party Congress (December 29, 1905, to January 4, 1906) in Imatra, Finland, Chernov played a leading part in the debates on the party program. He dominated the discussions and achieved a considerable personal triumph in de-fending his program against attacks both from the Left and from the Right, although the approval of the program by the congress led to the secession of the Maximalists to the Left and the Popular Socialists to the Right. After the tsarist government's suppression of *Syn Otechestva* in December 1905, Chernov lived illegally in Russia in 1906 and attempted to restore the party press. In 1907 he returned to emigré party activity. He participated in the Second (Extraordinary) Congress of the S-R Party at Tammerfors in February 1907, which discussed the party's attitude toward the Second Duma, and the First All-Party Conference in London in August 1908, which analyzed the failure of the revolutionary movement in 1905–1907. From 1910 to 1912 he edited the Paris-based party journal *Sotsialist-Revolutsioner* (*Socialist–Revolutionary*).

At the outbreak of the war in 1914 Chernov was the leading figure in the "internationalist" minority of his party. In September 1915 he was a delegate to the Zimmerwald Conference where he adopted an independent "centrist" position.

Chernov returned to Russia in April 1917 after the February Revolution*. He was elected Vice-Chairman of the Petrograd Soviet* and became an editor of the S-R newspaper *Delo Naroda* (*The Cause of the People*). He became Minister of Agriculture in the First Coalition Government, which was formed in the beginning of May. The S–R's were committed to leaving the final implementation of agrarian reforms to the Constituent Assembly*, and this prevented Chernov from taking any effective measures as Minister of Agriculture. He had to confine himself to provisional, preparatory steps, such as restricting land transactions and extending the power of the local land committees. These policies failed to stem the tide of peasant unrest in the summer of 1917 and exposed Chernov to criticism from the Left, not only from the Bolsheviks but also from the Far Left of his own party, the future Left Socialist-Revolutionary Party*. Chernov's policies as Minister of Agriculture also antagonized the Cadets (*see* Constitutional Democratic Party—Cadet) and the senior partners in the coalition government and served as the pretext for Prince Georgii Evgen'evich L'vov's* resignation as Prime Minister in July 1917. The resultant ministerial crisis provoked a split in the S-R Central Committee on the issue whether the party should renew its coalition with the Cadets or seek to form an all-socialist government. In this debate, Chernov was a spokesman for the "Left–Center" of the party, which was opposed to continuing the coalition with the liberals. Chernov continued to serve as Minister of Agriculture in the second coalition formed by A. F. Kerensky* in July, but he resigned at the end of August in protest against the suspected complicity of the Cadets in the Kornilov affair (*see* Kornilov Revolt). After the Democratic Conference* in September, and the decision of the "Right–centrist" majority of the S-R Central Committee to participate in a third coalition including Cadets, Chernov became increasingly alienated from the leadership of his party. He remained outside the last Provisional Government* and was absent from Petrograd when the Soviet seizure of power took place in October (*see* October Seizure of Power).

Chernov returned to Petrograd at the end of November 1917. He participated in the Fourth Congress of the S-R Party and in the Second All-Russian Congress of Peasant Soviets in December, both of which condemned the Bolshevik Revolution and called for the transfer of power to the Constituent Assembly*. When the Constituent Assembly, in which the S–R's had an overall majority, met on January 5, 1918, Chernov was elected its president. He presided over the only session of the assembly before its disbandment by the Bolsheviks. During 1918 Chernov played a leading role in his party's unsuccessful attempts to establish a government based on the Constituent Assembly, which could act as a "third force" between the Reds and the Whites in the Civil War in Russia*. In 1919–1920 he lived illegally in Moscow.

Chernov emigrated from Russia at the end of 1920. Between the wars he lived mainly in Prague. His last years were spent in New York. His years in emigration were devoted to literary activity: from 1920 to 1931 he edited *Revoliutsionnaia Rossiia* (*Revolutionary Russia*), a party journal of left-wing tendency. His writings included works of history and autobiography as well as socialist theory. His main theoretical writings of this period were on "constructive socialism" and stressed the need for a democratic basis for a socialist society.

Maureen Perrie

Bibliography

Chernov, V. *Zapiski Sotsialista-Revoliutsionera.* 1922.
Chernov, V. M. *Peredburei.* 1953.

Perrie, M. *The Agrarian Policy of the Russian Socialist-Revolutionary Party*. 1975.
Radkey, O. H. *The Agrarian Foes of Bolshevism*. 1958.
——. *The Sickle under the Hammer*. 1963.

Chicherin, Georgii Vasil'evich (1872–1936) (pseudonym, A. Ornatskii). Chicherin was a prominent Bolshevik (*see* Russian Social Democratic Workers' Party [Bolshevik]) and Soviet diplomat.

He was born into an old aristocratic family on the estate of his uncle, the leading Russian liberal, Boris Nikolaevich Chicherin, in Kirsanov District of Tambov Province. There was a family tradition of diplomatic service. In 1896 Chicherin graduated from the University of St. Petersburg's History and Philology Faculty. Shortly thereafter he joined the Ministry of Foreign Affairs. Infected with radical ideas from his university days, he developed sympathies for the Socialist-Revolutionary Party*. Distressed with the idea of service to the tsarist state, Chicherin emigrated to Germany in 1904. There he studied the labor movement and became a Marxist and a friend of Karl Liebknecht. In 1905 Chicherin joined the Russian Social Democratic Workers' Party (Bolshevik). During the prewar years he was associated with the Menshevik wing of the party (*see* Russian Social Democratic Workers' Party [Menshevik]). In 1908 Chicherin was in France working with the French Socialist Party. Just before World War I* he moved to England where he became a leader of the Russian emigré community in Britain and associated with the British Labor Party. During the war Chicherin developed into a militant anti-war activist and moved closer to the position of his former foe V. I. Lenin*. In September 1917 Chicherin was imprisoned by the British for alleged pro-German, anti-Allied activities.

Following the October Seizure of Power*, L. D. Trotsky*, Peoples' Commissar for Foreign Affairs, sought and obtained the release of Russian radicals held by the British. Chicherin and others were released and expelled in January 1918. Chicherin returned to revolutionary Russia, where he joined the Russian Communist Party (Bolshevik) and was promptly named Deputy Peoples' Commissar for Foreign Affairs, replacing Ivan Zalkind. Despite many years spent in the advocacy of Menshevik policies, Chicherin had much to qualify him for that government post. He knew many languages: French, German, English, Italian, Polish, and Serbian. He was an intelligent and indefatigable worker and possessed a remarkable memory. On the minus side, he was unable to delegate work. Because of insomnia, he conducted the work of the Commissariat into the small hours of the morning. As deputy commissar Chicherin oversaw the conversion of a predominantly propaganda-oriented Commissariat into a more traditional diplomatic orientation. In March 1918 Chicherin succeeded Trotsky to the chief post. He took part in the peace negotiations with Germany and signed the Brest-Litovsk* Treaty in the same month.

After the period of Civil War (*see* Civil War in Russia) and foreign intervention, Chicherin made great gains in setting Soviet foreign policy on a firm footing. During the 1921–1924 period he secured diplomatic recognition from virtually all of the great powers with the exception of the United States. He was particularly interested in the Near East and in 1921 signed treaties of friendship with Iran, Afghanistan, and Turkey. In Europe he favored a pro-German, anti-British, and anti-League of Nations orientation. Chicherin led the Soviet delegation to the Genoa Conference in 1922 and negotiated and designed the Treaty of Rapallo with Germany in April 1923. During the 1920s Chicherin struggled to make the Peoples' Commissariat of Foreign Affairs the principal face of the Soviet state to the world in opposition to the Comintern (*see* Communist International). In this he largely succeeded. After Lenin's death, Chicherin's influence in foreign-policy formulation diminished somewhat. Chicherin did not have good relations with I. V. Stalin* because the two had clashed in 1921 over national policy. Nevertheless, Chicherin was elected a member of the Communist Party's Central Committee in 1927. The same year, ill health forced him into semi-retirement. His duties were assumed by his deputy M. M. Litvinov, who succeeded him when he retired in 1930.

Chicherin spent the remaining six years of his life in seclusion pursuing a lifelong passion, the study of music. A study of Mozart by Chicherin was finally published in 1973.

Bibliography

Fischer, Louis. *The Soviets in World Affairs*. 1951.
Haupt, Georges and Maria Jean-Jacques. *Makers of the Revolution*. 1974.
Zainitskii, A. Sergeev. *Chicherin*. 1968.

Chkheidze, Nikolai Semenovich (1864–1926). Nikolai Semenovich Chkheidze was a Georgian Menshevik, little known before 1917 and not particularly note-worthy for his contribution to Marxist thought. However, he came to occupy by force of circumstance, several of the most prestigious positions within the Russian labor movement and in the Petrograd Soviet* in 1917.

Like many of the first generation of Georgia's Menshevik leaders, Chkheidze was born of a poor, noble family in western Georgia. He was expected to make a career as a civil servant, but his life changed abruptly while attending the University of Odessa (1887) and the Vetinary Institute in Kharkov (1888), where he became involved with radical student circles. Expelled from the in-stitute, he returned to Georgia and found work in a state commission fighting the phylloxera epidemic but continued to maintain close ties with other radical youths.

In December 1892 a small group of Georgian socialists met in Kvirily to lay the foundations for a political organization. The participants included many of the future leaders of Georgian Social Democracy: Noi Zhordaniia*, Mikha Tskhakaia, Isidor Ramishvili, Sil'vester Jibladze, and Chkheidze himself. A program favoring national autonomy proposed by Zhordaniia was rejected and instead an attempt was made to develop a Marxist platform critical of both populism and nationalism. The Georgian Marxists soon began to publicize their views in legal journals and were known as the *Mesame dasi* ("third generation" of the Georgian intelligentsia).

In general, Chkheidze's role in the Social Democratic movement was that of an intellectual and a "legal" propagandist rather than that of an underground activist and organizer. He favored Zhordaniia's approach of exploiting legal channels such as the press and the local elected institutions. In 1898 he moved to Batumi where he served as an elected deputy to the City Duma until 1902 and as the inspector of the Municipal Hospital from 1902 to 1905. During his first years in Batumi, Chkheidze believed that no socialist work was possible among the workers and, indeed, as the workers' movement grew in scope and militancy, he actually reduced his contacts with it. He came under severe criticism from party activists for his caution, although he remained highly respected by local workers and intellectuals, who referred to him as Batumi's "Karlo" (after Marx).

However, after the strike and demonstrations organized by I. V. Stalin* at the Rothschild plant in 1902—during which about a dozen workers were killed—Chkheidze and his fellow Marxists in Batumi were stirred from their passivity. They formed the first Social Democratic committee in the city, composed of two intellectuals (one of them Chkheidze) and three workers. In the next few years the Batumi Committee wove a network of peasant organizations into a united Marxist-led agrarian movement against Russian autocracy.

From its inception the Georgian Social Democratic movement displayed strong democratic characteristics such as elected committees, subordinate roles for intellectuals, and close personal ties between the leaders and their constituency. Thus it is not surprising that after the Bolshevik–Menshevik split most Georgian Marxists took the Menshevik side and that Chkheidze himself completely opposed Lenin, arguing that the Russian Social Democratic Workers' Party should be a workers' party rather than a party of Jacobins tied to the working class.

During the revolutionary year 1905 the Social Democrats of western Georgia enjoyed extraordinary political authority. The Batumi Committee acted as the defacto government for large areas controlled by rebel peasants and workers. Chkheidze also took a more active personal role: he organized two mass meetings outside the city, worked to prevent Armenian–Azerbaijani clashes in Batumi, and chaired a large political gathering of the revolutionary parties in the municipal theater. His position on vital issues was often too moderate for the aroused workers, for although he was skeptical about the October Manifesto, he was sympathetic to Viceroy Vorontsov's efforts to establish *zemstvos* in Transcaucasia. After the tsarist army restored Russian rule in western Georgia, Chkheidze fled to Guria. He was arrested in 1906 and moved to Chiatury and then, after a second detention by the police, to Tiflis. In early 1907 he was elected to the Tiflis City Duma.

Later that year Chkheidze found himself unexpectedly in the role of a national political figure. He was elected in 1907 as a deputy from the Province of Tiflis to the Third State Duma and was chosen to chair its small Social Democratic faction. By the time he was reelected to the Fourth Duma in 1912, political conditions had changed markedly: labor unrest was increasing, and the Social Democratic faction was the only visible leadership to which workers could turn. The Social Democratic deputies took advantage of their parliamentary immunity to establish extensive links with their workers' constituencies, and their contact with the Party of the Progressists made it appear (in 1913) as though the Social Democrats of the Duma would finally break their political isolation. But in October 1913 the Bolshevik deputies split the Social Democratic faction itself, leaving Chkheidze and what remained of the faction (seven Mensheviks) isolated from the increasingly militant workers of Petersburg. Chkheidze never forgot this "betrayal" by the Bolsheviks and the consequent loss of the loyalty and confidence of the radicalized workers.

When World War I* broke out, the Social Democratic faction refused to vote for the special wartime budget, and Chkheidze repeatedly denounced the war and publicly declared his faction's support of the Socialist–Internationalist movement, which called for the revival of the Socialist International as the only means of bringing the war to a just end. He regarded the use of military force for national purposes as unacceptable. Chkheidze at first opposed the participation of workers in the War–Industrial Committees,* but like many other Mensheviks then living in Russia, he gradually came to see the organizational opportunities offered by the Labor Groups and began collaborating with their leaders. Through his membership in the Duma and in the local lodge of Free Masons, Chkheidze also developed contacts with representatives of the various opposition groups among whom were moderate Populists, Progressists, Left Cadets (see Constitutional Democratic Party—Cadets), and leaders of "public organizations."

During the February days of 1917 (see February Revolution), the socialist deputies of the Duma were the only widely known leaders to whom the workers of the capital could turn. Chkheidze was elected Chairman of the Petrograd Soviet* and later headed the All-Russian Central Executive Committee* as well. In these capacities he was able to help I. G. Tsereteli* form the "Revolutionary Defensist" bloc in the soviet and to facilitate the passage through that body of the policies and resolutions that sought to strengthen cooperation between the soviets and the Provisional Government* and to balance a demand for a general peace without annexation and indemnities with a commitment to the defense of revolutionary Russia until such peace was achieved. Chkheidze usually refrained from involving himself in the policies outlined by the leadership, although he made an exception in persistently and effectively opposing the idea of coalition government throughout the month of April. Because of his past experience he favored cooperation between between the Soviet and the non-socialist "progressive forces" of the country (particularly the Progressists and the Left Cadets) but feared that the actual participation of the socialists in government would contribute to the workers' radicalization and their eventual disenchantment with the moderate socialists.

Once a coalition government was formed and his party assumed state responsibilities, Chkheidze came to its support while his worst fears about workers' disenchantment were being realized. In his roles as Chairman of the Soviet and President of the Democratic Conference*, which met in Petrograd in September, he contributed to the Revolutionary Defensists' efforts to save the coalition. He had condemned the Bolsheviks in the strongest terms during the July Days* and remained opposed to any cooperation with them after October.

Chkheidze's involvement in Russia's political life came to an end with the Soviet seizure of power in October. He left for Georgia where he served as chairman, first of the Transcaucasian Seim and then of the Georgian Constituent Assembly. He became a member of the Georgian mission to the Paris Peace Conference and remained there even after the Bolshevik occupation of Georgia in 1921. In Paris he eked out a meager existence for his wife and three daughters (his only son had been killed in an accident while Chkheidze was chairing an emergency meeting of the Soviet in 1917). He was in constant disagreement with his comrades in the Georgian Government in Exile (he shared Tsereteli's disdain for Zhordaniia's nationalism), and in June 1926 he committed suicide.

Ziva Galili y Garcia and Ronald Gregor Suny

Bibliography

Rechi N. S. Chkheidze. Part 1. 1917.
Uratadze, G. Vospominaniia gruzinskogo sotsial-demokrata. 1968.
Zhordania, N. Moia Zhizn'. 1968.

Chubar', Vlas Iakovlevich (1891–1939). Chubar' was a Ukrainian Bolshevik (*see* Russian Social Democratic Workers' Party [Bolshevik]) and a participant in the October Revolution (*see* October Seizure of Power) in Petrograd.

Chubar' was born in the village of Federovka, Ekaterinoslav Province, into a poor, illiterate family, one of eight children. He attended the village school until 1904 and then entered Alexandrovsk Mechanical and Technical School on a *zemstvo* scholarship, working summers in railroad shops. He graduated in 1911. During the 1905 Revolution (*see* Nineteen-Five Revolution) he returned to the village, becoming active in the peasant movement. He joined the Russian Social Democratic Workers' Party (Bolshevik) in 1907.

From 1911 to 1915 he engaged in factory work in a number of metallurgical enterprises. He was very active in the underground political movement, was arrested several times, and was imprisoned once for six months. In May 1915 he was mobilized into the army but in 1916 was reassigned to the ordnance plant in Petrograd as a lathe operator. Following the February Revolution* of 1917 Chubar' organized the workers' militia and factory committee of his enterprise and was elected chairman of the latter. He was also elected Deputy to the Petrograd Soviet* and to the All-Russian Committee of Ordinance Factory Workers. He was very active in the Petrograd factory committee movement and was elected to the Central Council of Petrograd Factory and Plant Committees in early June and to the Central Committee of the All-Russian Congress of Factory and Plant Committees in October. During the October Revolution he was Commissar of the Petrograd Military Revolutionary Committee of the Chief Artillery Administration.

After October Chubar' was very active in important economic and industrial posts. He was elected to the Soviet of Workers' Control and the Supreme Council of the National Economy (SCNE)*. In 1918–1919 he served as Chairman of the SCNE commission to reconstruct industry in the Urals. In 1920–1921 he headed the Ukrainian Supreme Council of the National Economy and in 1922 was in charge of the Donbas coal industry. From 1920 to 1934 he directed the Ukrainian Industrial Bureau. Chubar' became virtual head of the government in the Ukraine in 1923. He served as Chairman of the Council of Peoples' Commissars of the USSR from 1934 to 1938 and as People's Commissar of Finance from 1937 to 1938; in 1937 he was elected to the Supreme Soviet of the USSR. Chubar's public rise was paralleled by his rise in party ranks. In 1920 he was elected to the Central Committee of the Ukrainian Communist Party. In 1921 he was elected a candidate and then a full member of the Russian Communist Party, and from 1926 to 1930 he was a full member of the Politburo of the Communist Party. His career has been characterized as *apparatchik*. He was a consistent supporter of I. V. Stalin*, but in 1938 he was expelled from the Politburo and dismissed from government work. Subsequently, he was arrested and in 1939 was executed. He was posthumously rehabilitated by N. S. Khrushchev in 1956.

Bibliography

Haupt, Georges, and Marie, Jean Jacques. *Makers of the Russian Revolution*. 1974.
Levytsky, Borys. *The Stalinist Terror in the Thirties*. 1974.

Church and the Russian Revolution. The Russian Orthodox Church was a dominating presence in the Empire. It was the religion of 70 percent of the residents of the entire country (88 million were baptized in that faith) and 94 percent of the people in European Russia. The Russian Orthodox Church comprised more than 40,000 parishes in sixty-seven dioceses; it owned one-third of all primary schools in the empire; it possessed 3 million hectares of land. More than 1,000 monasteries and convents housed 95,000 religious persons.

Imperial law had defined the Orthodox Church as the "supreme and dominant" religious institution of Russia, and the tsar was designated the "guardian of its dogmas." In the year before the Revolution, the Church received 63 million rubles from the state budget. Orthodox doctrine, "The Law of God," was specifically taught in all schools, and until 1905 defection from Orthodoxy was a crime. But when the February Revolution* abolished the autocracy, it had been the source of such apparent favor that scant objection emanated from the Church. "The Will of God has been done," declared the first official ecclesiastical comment on the organization of the Provisional Government* (Browder and Kerensky 1961, II: 803).

Despite Orthodoxy's manifestly privileged position in the Empire, on the eve of the Revolution unrest permeated the Church. Under the structure begun by Peter I, in which the Holy Synod instead of the patriarch was the chief ecclesiastical authority, the hierarchy of the Church usually viewed itself as in bondage to a benevolent despot. For the most part, only subservient bishops were appointed to the Synod, whose actions were supervised by a bureaucrat, the Procurator General. By 1917 the Synod's composition was especially reactionary, including among its ten members both conscientious conservative monarchists (Vladimir of Kiev) and disciples of Gregory Rasputin* (Pitirim of Petrograd, Makarii of Moscow). Throughout the Church, voices called for change. Some advocated the liberation of the Church from the state by the restoration of the monarchical patriarchate; some advocated democratization of church polity, including election of priests and bishops by their subordinates; some clergy, in contrast to the bishops of the Synod, represented liberal political parties in the State Duma (*see* Duma and Revolution); and others even flirted with socialism, although the Synod forbade advocacy of radical views under threat of ecclesiastical prosecution.

When the disorders of February (*see* February Revolution) began in Petrograd, the Church showed no readiness to resist them. On February 27 the Procurator General chosen by Rasputin in 1915, N. P. Raev, proposed to the Synod that it condemn the agitation. The Synod's refusal coincided with the Duma's resistance to the Tsar's prorogation order and formation of the Executive Committee. Instead of a synodal appeal against Revolution, the clerical members of the Duma called upon "Orthodox clergy of all Russia . . . to recognize the authority of the Executive Committee" (Titlinov 1924, p. 58).

After the Provisional Government's Procurator General, V. N. L'vov, dramatized for the Synod the emancipation of the Church from the state by ordering the removal of the tsar's chair from the meeting room, the Synod responded with its announcement that the change in government was divinely ordained and called on Orthodox people to support the new leader and war effort. Significantly, Metropolitan Pitirim's name did not appear among the signatories of the resolution; he had been arrested with the Tsar's ministers. L'vov promptly expelled him from the Synod in the first of many independent actions that belied his premise of administrative freedom for the Church.

Beginning in April the new Synod began to implement the administrative autonomy the new government promised. On April 29 it announced that it would soon convene a council, a local sobor, to decide fundamental questions of Church structure. The sobor would consist of elected representatives from the entire Russian Church. A Pre-Sobor conference would begin preparation presently.

The revolutionary spirit quickly penetrated even church politics. The Synod directed that Pitirim's successor be elected by an assembly of representatives from each parish of the Petrograd diocese and that a congress of 1,603 commissioners choose Veniamin. In response to petitions from the Moscow diocese, the Synod dismissed Metropolitan Makarii: Muscovites elected Tikhon to replace him. Throughout the country diocesan congresses with laymen sitting beside clerics elected new bishops or at least gave democratic confirmation to the incumbents.

On June 4 the All-Russian Congress of Clergy and Laymen convened in Moscow. In its opening declaration, the 1,200 delegates voiced support for the Provisional Government* and a democratic political system for Russia. Furthermore, they called for transfer of land to the peasants and the establishment of "just relations between labor and capital" (Titlinov 1924, p. 58).

This congress, however, foreshadowed tensions between Church and State that became increasingly acute as the center of gravity of the Revolution shifted Left. Although the congress explicitly advocated freedom of religion, it also anticipated privileges for the Orthodox Church. The delegates denounced separation of the Church from the State; they called for continued financial support from the State for schools owned by the Church, and they declared that the "Law of God" should remain an obligatory subject in all state schools.

Conflict between Church and the Revolution could hardly be avoided. In the Church, the overwhelmingly dominant view insisted on a privileged position for orthodoxy, but the programs of all political parties represented in the government called for formal separation of Church and State. Open clash between civil and ecclesiastical authorities was muted only because the Provisional Government did not expedite full separation, leaving the question to the Constituent Assembly*. On June 12 the Provisional Government displeased the Church with its secularization of the 37,000 parish schools. The Synod protested that the Church had been deprived of its "means of exerting religious educational influence upon the Russian people" (Titlinov 1924, p. 65). As the government prepared its Law on Freedom of Conscience, the Pre-Sobor Conference, fearing further losses, enunciated the church's *desiderata* in a resolution of July 13. As the traditional religion of the majority of the Russian population, it said that the Orthodox Church must occupy the first and most privileged position among the confessions in the Russian state."[1] This primacy would include rights such as the following: ecclesiastical norms and acts would carry the force of law; the head of the government and the minister of justice would be Orthodox; Orthodox dogmas would be obligatory subjects in all schools where Orthodox children studied; the church would receive subsidies from the state budget.

The mood of increasing dissatisfaction with the Revolution was reflected in the elections of Sobor delegates held on July 30. Speeches in the election meetings voiced conservative concerns. Although democratizing forces had won the right of equal representation of laity, and each diocese was represented by three lay delegates who accompanied two elected priests and the bishop, the system of indirect voting resulted in the triumph of rightist elements. The large conservative majority of the Sobor followed the leadership of Antonii of Kharkov; a small minority, mostly theology professors, represented more liberal views.

With 564 members, the Sobor opened on August 15 in the Kremlin's Assumption Cathedral. The following day the Sobor moved to the Church of Christ the Savior, where it heard from the Provisional Government's Minister of Confessions, A. V. Kartashev, that the Sobor was authorized to determine for itself the internal affairs of the church. Subsequent working sessions of the Sobor met in the diocesan buildings on Likhov Street.

As social disintegration spread, the Sobor spoke more conservatively. It flirted with support of Kornilov's advance on Petrograd in its second week of meeting; it declared September 14 as a "National Day of Repentance and Prayer for the Salvation of the Russian State," calling the masses to cease from "plunder and anarchy, the beginnings of the horrors of civil war."[2] In mid-October it began debate on the institution of the patriarchal form of administration, which the liberal minority opposed. Goaded by the October Seizure of Power* on the 28th, the Sobor decided to restore the office of Patriarch, subordinating it constitutionally to the Russian Sobor, which was to meet periodically at his call. On October 31 the Sobor nominated three candidates for patriarch, from among whom Tikhon of Moscow was selected by lot on November 5. On November 21, the Bolsheviks (see Russian Social Democratic Workers' Party [Bolshevik]) permitted the Sobor to use the traditional site, the Cathedral of the Dormition, to enthrone the fifty-one-year-old Tikhon as the eleventh Russian Patriarch. It had been 216 years since the tenth one had died in 1701.

In addition to enthroning the Patriarch, the Sobor elected two councils as the administrative bodies of the Church. A Holy Synod comprising twelve bishops was responsible for purely religious affairs; economic and legal matters were to be the concern of the Supreme Ecclesiastical Council consisting of three bishops, five priests, one monk, and six laymen. The patriarch was president of both bodies with power of veto over their actions. Moreover, he could act administratively, apart from them, subject only to review by the Sobor.

Conflict between the Church and the new government began at once. Nationalization took away the Church's landed wealth. Churchmen spoke with almost total unanimity against the usurpers. They did not see the developments of November to be the will of God as many had declared February's revolution to be. Instead, the Sobor offered itself as the true representative of Russia. When the Bolsheviks began peace negotiations with Germany, members of the Sobor declared that they were "not the freely elected representatives of the population"; rather, the Sobor spoke as the "lawfully elected representatives of more than 100,000,000."[3]

The conflict became bloody in the latter part of January 1918. On January 19, when the Commissariat of Welfare attempted to enforce its requisition of the Nevsky Monastery by armed takeover, the archpriest Peter Shipetov was killed. The same day, Tikhon issued a virtual declaration of war, threatening the Bolsheviks with hellfire for their "Satanic deeds." The Patriarch excommunicated and anathematized the atheistic rulers and called the faithful to "stand in defense of our outraged and oppressed Holy Mother" Church (Bunyan and Fisher 1934, p. 588). When the Peoples' Commissars (see Council of

People's Commissars, 1917–1922) formally declared the separation of church and state four days later, the Sobor promptly threatened ecclesiastical punishment of any who cooperated in the implementation of the decree. It issued its battle cry: "it is better to shed one's blood and win a martyr's crown than to surrender the Orthodox faith to be abused by enemies" (Titlinov 1924, p. 121).

On January 25 the very prestigious Metropolitan Vladimir was killed at the Cave Monastery in Kiev. The Sobor established a bodyguard for the Patriarch and ordered congregations to create committees to defend church buildings against confiscation. Soon local Parish Unions of Defense numbered more than 60,000 members. Under the circumstances, further bloodshed could not be avoided. Through widely scattered violent confrontations accompanied by numerous arrests, the Revolution took the lives of more than 1,000 priests and 28 bishops before 1923.

After the Council of People's Commissars transferred to Moscow, the Sobor sent a delegation on March 14 to protest the separation of church and State to V. I. Lenin* personally. When he would not receive them, the delegates, showing no mood to compromise, left a letter declaring "that the state cannot be religionless and Russia can only be an Orthodox State" (Titlinov 1924, p. 132).

As the Civil War (*see* Civil War in Russia) developed, the church sympathized with the anti-Bolsheviks. The Sobor, which the government permitted to meet without hindrance, finally adjourned in September, renewing its appeal to the faithful to prevent "blasphemous seizures" of church property. The Patriarch marked the anniversary of the October Seizure of Power with an indictment addressed to the Council of People's Commissars, charging them with responsibility for all of Russia's bloodshed and threatening that "you who have taken the sword will perish by the sword" (Curtiss 1965, p. 65). Tikhon was soon placed under house arrest.

With the changes occurring in revolutionary Russia, the Orthodox Church lost most of its wealth, privilege, and formal influence in molding Russian culture; it gained a measure of autonomy that it had not enjoyed for centuries. In the five months after the Tsar's abdication, the gain seemed to churchmen to be the principal effect of the Revolution, and thus voices supporting the political transformation dominated within the Church. After midsummer, however, as the losses appeared more clearly, antirevolutionary impulses gained momentum, culminating in their almost total triumph in the Church by the end of the first month of 1918. Although an institution with a widely disbursed membership such as the Orthodox Church cannot speak univocally, it is possible to detect dominant motifs within it during the Revolution. Generally, the Church welcomed and defended the first government headed by L'vov; it supported Kerensky's government only ambiguously. Finally, it declared open hostility to the government of Lenin. That hostility continued for six years. Only in 1923 did the Patriarch relent enough to declare an end to the hierarchy's overt rejection of Bolshevik power. Even then, the animosity between the Revolution and a substantial portion of the Orthodox clergy remained (*see* also Religion and the Revolution).

Paul D. Steeves

Notes

1. A. V. Kartashev, "Revoliutsiia i sobor 1917–18," *Bogoslovskaia mysl'* 4 (1942): 85.
2. Ibid., p. 93.
3. Ibid., p. 99.

Bibliography

Bogolepov, Alexander A. *Church Reforms in Russia 1905–1918*. 1966.
Browder, Robert Paul, and Kerensky, Alexander F. *The Russian Provisional Government, 1917*. 1961.
Bunyon, James, and Fisher, H. H. *The Bolshevik Revolution, 1917–18*. 1934.
Curtiss, John Shelton. *The Russian Church and the Soviet State, 1917–50*. 1965.
Fletcher, William C. *A Study in Survival*. 1965.
Nichols, William C., and Stavrou, Theofanis. *Russian Orthodoxy under the Old Regime*. 1934.
Pospeilovsky, Dmitry. *The Russian Church under the Soviet Regime, 1917–82*. 1984.
Titlinov, B. V. *Tserkov vo vremia revoliutsii*. 1924.

Cinema, 1917–1921. When the Bolsheviks came to power in October 1917, cinema was already one of the most popular forms of entertainment in the towns and cities of the Russian Empire. But when Lenin remarked that "of all the arts for us the most important is the cinema," he was commenting not on its aesthetic achievements but on its potential as a weapon of agitation and propaganda (Taylor 1979, p.26). Anatolii Lunacharskii*, who as Commissar for Enlightenment (*see* Commissariat of the Enlightenment) had overall responsibility for cinema, said, "We must remember that a socialist government must imbue even film shows with a socialist spirit" (Taylor 1979, p. 41).

Prerevolutionary Russian film production, and the films imported for distribution, had fallen into the categories of "psychological drawing room dramas" and "love intrigues." They were later to be denounced as bourgeois, but they continued to attract large audiences, the kind of audiences that had previously patronized the variety theater and the music hall. The private companies responsible for most of the film production during the Civil War (*see* Civil War in Russia) period (1918–1920) went on making films of this kind: their motive was, after all, still to make a profit.

But the new government, albeit still in embryonic form, had other designs. For the moment, however, shortages—of film stock, electricity, trained personnel, expertise—forced the authorities to rely in the main on private producers. Fear of putting producers to flight delayed the nationalization decree until August 27, 1919, and even then the actual process of imposing state control was not completed until late 1920. Because of the ravages of World War I*, Revolution, and the Civil War, much of the cinema network was in disarray and disrepair. Most of the leading lights of prerevolutionary film industry had already fled abroad or to areas still controlled by the Whites (*see* White Movement), such as the Crimea (*see* Crimea, Revolution in). This accentuated already existing problems.

With these circumstances, it is tempting to ask why the Bolsheviks bothered: why did they consider cinema so important? There are several reasons. First, at least in urban areas, there existed a ready-made audience for cinema. Second, before the advent of radio and television, cinema was the only *mass* medium available. Even today it is the only such medium where the audience is alone and yet part of a crowd: the volatility of crowd behavior is reinforced by the darkness in the auditorium as a larger-than-life bright image flickers across the screen. Third, as a silent medium, cinema communicated its message simply and directly through largely or purely visual images; its impact was, therefore, both more profound and more accessible to audiences of widely varying languages and levels of literacy. Cinema was the only book that even an illiterate soul could read. Fourth, as a mechanical medium, cinema's production and distribution were highly centralized and, therefore, more reliable. Finally, cinema was a dynamic medium. Unlike a ROSTA poster, a film *moved*: "The soul of the cinema is in the movement of life" (Taylor 1979, p. 31). Small wonder, then, that Lunacharskii felt that the power of cinema was unbounded.

However, this was largely expression of faith in cinema's future rather than accurate description of its contemporary reality. With production and distribution still mainly in the hands of private enterprise and constrained by that sector, the government's hands were tied. But it took three important steps to extricate itself.

First it established, under the ultimate control of the People's Commissariat for Enlightenment and with the close collaboration of party activists, a fleet of agit-lorries, vans, steamers, and, above all, agit-trains (*see* Propaganda and the Russian Revolution). They traveled along the front lines of the Civil War and through areas newly recaptured from the Whites. They used a variety of forms and methods of agitation and propaganda, and cinema was important among them. (The Whites also used cinema in this way, but their films were supplied from the United States). Short punchy *agitky* were commissioned from state and private producers to drive the Bolshevik message home. Leading film directors, like Dziga Vertov and Lev Kuleshov, cut their cinematic teeth on these films. Leading political figures, like N. K. Krupskaia*, M. I. Kalinin*, and V. M. Molotov* represented the Communist Party's interest, and the trains were decorated by artists of the caliber of El Lissitsky, V. Maiakovskii, and Malevich.

Second, the government established the world's first State Film School in Moscow under the veteran film director Vladimir Gardin. This was largely an investment in the future, a means of ensuring adequate trained cadres for future Soviet film production. Given the shortages, nothing could be wasted: Kuleshov and his workshop spent their time rehearsing and miming so-called *fil' my bez plenki* (films without film).

Third, the People's Commissariat for Enlightenment produced a collection of essays outlining the potential of the cinema and intended as a blueprint for the future, when Lunacharskii's aim of infusing cinema with a socialist spirit could eventually be attempted, if not necessarily achieved. A state-owned cinema, he argued, "must do what nobody else is either able or willing to do."

For the moment, despite Lenin's remark, the Soviet government paid only limited attention to cinema: it had more important priorities, such as its own survival, to attend to. The Civil War period was a time of desperate struggle and compromise for the Soviet cinema, but it was also a period when foundations for its future development were firmly laid.

Richard Taylor

Bibliography

Karpinskii, V., ed. *Agitparpoezda V.Ts.I.K. 1kh istoriia, apparat, metody, i formy raboty.* Moscow, 1920.
———. *Agitpoezda V.Ts.I.K. ikh istoriia, apparat, metody, i formy raboty.* 1920.
Leyda, J. *Kino.* 3d ed. 1983.
Maksakova, L. V. *Agitpoezda Oktiabr'skaia revoliutsiia 1919-29 gg.* 1965.
Speranskaia, E. A., ed. *Agitatsionno-massovoe iskusstvo pervykh let Oktiabria.* 1971.
Taylor, R. *The Politics of the Soviet Cinema, 1917–1929.* 1979.
———, ed. *The Film Factory: Russian and Soviet Cinema in Documents.* 1987.

City in Late Imperial Russia. "Brothers we will go to Riga. In Riga life is good. In Riga golden dogs bark. And silver cocks crow." This turn-of-the-century Baltic folk tune reflects the lure of Riga, but for tens of thousands throughout the Imperial Russian countryside the burgeoning cities offered a myriad of economic opportunities.

Only St. Petersburg, Moscow, Warsaw, and Odessa had populations of at least 100,000 at the time of the emancipation of the serfs in 1861. By the eve of World War I* St. Petersburg, Moscow, and Warsaw had quadrupled in size. Riga and Odessa had quintupled, and Kiev and Lodz had grown by ten times or more. By 1914 St. Petersburg had surpassed 2 million, Moscow had approached that figure, and Warsaw had approached 900,000. Kiev and Odessa each had surpassed 600,000, and about 500,000 lived in Riga and more than 400,000 in Lodz. Tiflis, with perhaps 50,000 in 1861, had surpassed 300,000 by 1914. Oil-rich Baku, which had 15,000 people in 1885, joined Tashkent, Khar'kov, Saratov, Ekaterinoslav, and Vil'na as cities with at least 200,000 by 1914. In all, nearly three dozen cities had at least 100,000 people by 1914.

Industrial development was an obvious catalyst of urban growth. Particularly important were the textile and metalworking industries, which by 1900 ranked first and second as employers of factory labor. The former, which relied primarily on unskilled labor, was particularly important to Moscow and the surrounding cities of the Central Industrial Region*. Women became prominent in this industry, and partially for this reason, women comprised about one-third of Moscow's factory labor force by 1912.

Machine building and metalworking, which required a relatively skilled labor force, were especially important to the growth of St. Petersburg. There the number of factory workers grew from 24,500 in 1867 to 125,000 in 1908 and 195,000 in 1913. Large factories were common in cities where textile, metalworking, and machine-building industries developed. In 1908 60 percent of the workers who were subject to factory inspection in Moscow and St. Petersburg worked in plants with 500 or more employees, one-third in plants with more than 1 million. Large factories were also common in cities such as Lodz, a textile center, and Riga, an important center for the machine building, shipbuilding, rubber-tire, and railway-car industries. The number of factory hands in Riga grew from 16,000 in 1890 to 76,000 by 1913.

About 20 percent of all workers who were under the supervision of the Factory Inspectorate in 1908 worked in Moscow and St. Petersburg. Together, the capitals had more workers than the seven cities that followed in size of factory proletariat (Lodz, Riga, Warsaw, Ivanovo-Voznesensk, Odessa, Tver, and Iaroslavl). But if the importance of the capitals as industrial centers is worth noting, it is also important to note that many factories were located in the countryside. Just east of Moscow, for example, was the factory village of Orekhovo-Zuevo, where in 1908 two giant textile mills employed 26,000 workers, more factory hands than lived in the large cities of Kiev and Kharkov combined.

Thus industrial growth was not exclusively an urban phenomenon. Nor can Russia's dramatic urban growth be seen only as a result of industrialization. Kiev's 1913 population of 625,000 included only about 15,000 individuals who could legitimately be classified as factory and railway workers. Most Kievans toiled in small workshops; in the building, hauling, and service trades; or as self-employed craftsmen and entrepreneurs. Similar distributions characterized the work forces of many other cities. Moscow and St. Petersburg had a combined sales–clerical work force of about 200,000 by 1900. The impression that Moscow was a city of small-scale production and distribution was still valid in 1917 and beyond, one historian has noted. Factory production was but one important cause of urban growth. Russia's cities clearly provided a wide variety of economic opportunities.

Soviet historians have tended to view the post-emancipation city as the cauldron in which intensified class consciousness and conflict pushed Russia toward revolution. Some Western scholars have drawn a similar picture, although others stress as well the image of the city as a "big village" where rural values and traditions were commonly maintained. Urban migrants often maintained frequent contact with the countryside. Studies of Moscow and St. Petersburg reveal high levels of transience among all urban groups. Perhaps 100,000 to 150,000 migrants came to Moscow every year from 1880 to 1900, but an equivalent number left every year. Many urban migrants were peasants (Moscow and St. Petersburg were about 70 percent peasant by class designation in 1910), and peasants often settled near factories and in neighborhoods with others from their villages and districts, thereby creating informal networks that provided material assistance for newcomers and a means of perpetuating rural values and traditions.

Urban migrants did encounter a variety of associations that promoted literacy, sobriety, cultural edification, and sometimes political change. They encountered radical students and intellectuals eager to promote new concepts of justice and dignity and new attitudes toward authority. One scholar suggests that "class consciousness" was most apparent among workers who developed their own "urban identity forged by the interactions of factory and city with their own character and values." Central to this process, he concluded, were "encounters with city life, with other urban classes, with school, church, neighborhood and tavern."

High literacy rates were common in many cities. By 1910 seven out of ten residents of Moscow and St. Petersburg could read and write. In rural areas the spread of literacy was generally much slower. In rural Kiev Province in 1914, for example, *zemstvo* authorities complained that little progress was being made against illiteracy and that two-thirds of the eligible children remained out of school for one reason or another.

The printed word was much more likely to have an impact on urban society, and cities were not lacking in reading materials, legal and illegal. Presses could turn out 30,000 newspapers an hour by 1904. Kiev, which had only one newspaper in 1859, had nine newspapers and twenty-five journals in 1904. In Moscow thirteen newspapers and sixty-nine journals were in publication that year. One scholar has surmised that the quicker growth of literacy in the cities accentuated the historically sharp cultural differences between city and countryside, helping to widen the gap between the mostly urban, educated elite, and the rural masses that liberals and moderates could not bridge during the revolutionary events of 1917. Still, the degree to which elements of the urban environment helped undermine the old order and create the ideological blueprint for the new, the extent to which that environment transformed political behavior, remains open to debate.

Thanks to a number of recent works, it is possible to generalize about many facets of the late-imperial urban environment. Self-government came to most cities in 1870. The reform enactment of that year allowed for a small number of voters (based on payment of taxes) to serve on councils, which in turn were charged with developing urban services and amenities. In 1892 the narrow franchise was further restricted to a small group of income-producing property owners who generally constituted 1 or 2 percent of the urban population, and state control over city administration was strengthened.

City government nevertheless initiated a great deal of developmental progress. Especially after the upheavals of 1905, doctors, professors, engineers, and other professionals seemed to take a more active part in city affairs, and coalitions of voters, often led by professionals and calling themselves "progressives," won many city elections. These coalitions almost always called for the municipalization of services and utilities and for increased spending on public health, education, and transportation. Developmental advances continued to be concentrated in the more prosperous central districts; comparatively little developmental progress was made in the underrepresented outlying districts where the poor tended to live.

Death-rate data for most cities are scarce. In Moscow the death rate declined slightly from 27.1 per 1,000 in 1870 to 24.2 in 1910. In many cities the poor quality of water; the absence of sewers, especially outside of the central districts; and general problems of public health remained central issues in city politics until 1917. The incidence of typhus in St. Petersburg actually increased from 1880 to 1914, and the city retained its reputation as the deadliest of Europe's capitals. Cholera outbreaks continued to plague cities from Kiev to St. Petersburg, producing victims comparable in number to those of the great epidemics of the nineteenth century. Death rates from these epidemics were highest in the outlying neighborhoods. Epidemics and other miseries may have reinforced a sense of militant solidarity among the residents of these areas. One angry resident of Kiev's Shuliavka district, where a workers' republic had been suppressed in 1905, wrote an open letter to local officials during the 1907 cholera epidemic, asking rhetorically whether officials even knew where Shuliavka was.

Crowded housing was also part of Russia's urban scene. A 1904 survey showed that in parts of St. Petersburg it was common for five or more people to share a bed. In 1912 about half of Moscow's entire population lived in residences where the owner or other tenants sublet part of their living space. High rents were a source of complaint almost everywhere in urban Russia. Rents in Moscow and St. Petersburg were commonly said to be among the highest in Europe.

Given the rapid growth of urban population, it was difficult for city governments to keep pace with the expanding need for services. Yet although housing inadequacies and other shortcomings of the urban environment were often cited in petitions to city councils, and occasionally listed among grievances by strikers, the impact of urban living conditions on the growth of political dissatisfaction in Russia remains unclear.

A great deal of research remains to be done on the day laborers, service employees, and artisans (who were among the first to form unions and other protective associations), for these large groups often endured the worst living and working conditions. Kiev's tailors struck against eighteen-hour work days in the early 1900s, for example, and many of the city's bakers were still working nineteen-hour days in 1913. Was real income improving or declining for various groups of urban workers in late tsarist Russia? To what extent did rapid population growth cause a deterioration in the quality of urban life? The answers are not clear, and few definitive conclusions can be drawn about the ways in which changes in the urban environment helped undermine the old order.

Michael F. Hamm

Bibliography

Bater, James. *St. Petersburg: Industrialization and Change.* 1976.

Bonnel, Victoria. *Roots of Rebellion. Worker's Politics and Organization in St. Petersburg and Moscow, 1900–1914.* 1983.

Bradley, Joseph. *Muzhik and Muscovite Urbanization in Late Imperial Russia.* 1984.

Hamm, Michael, ed. *The City in Late Imperial Russia.* 1986.

Johnson, Robert. *Peasant and Proletarian: The Working Class of Moscow in the Late Nineteenth Century.* 1979.

Kir'ianov, In. I. *Zhiznennyi uroven' rabochikh Rossii (konets XIX-nachalo XX v.).* 1979.

McClelland, James. *Autocrats and Academics: Education, Culture, and Society in Tsarist Russia.* 1979.

Civil War in Russia. The Russian Civil War was in effect a number of wars fought over the vast Russian territory. Serious action began in January 1918 when the Bolsheviks, with such troops as they could get together, launched offensives against the Ukraine and the Don areas, where locally formed governments had proclaimed their independence. Kiev was occupied, the Don Cossack regime collapsed, and the small Volunteer Army under Generals L. G. Kornilov (*see* Kornilov Revolt) and A. I. Denikin* were forced back to the Kuban.

Meanwhile, with the breakdown of the negotiations, the Germans continued their advance into Russia. The Brest-Litovsk* Treaty signed, at last, on March 3, 1918, confirmed the independence of Finland, where General C. G. von Mannerheim with German help effectively crushed the Finnish Reds. The Ukraine became in effect a German satellite under the puppet Hetman P. Skoropadskii, and German and Austrian troops occupied the whole area. In early May, as the Germans reached Rostov, the Don Cossacks staged an uprising and established a Don Cossack state with German backing. The Volunteer Army returned from the Kuban to refit and prepare for future operations. In the Far East a young Cossack officer, G. M. Semenov*, with a handful of troops and with Japanese backing took over a station on the Manchurian frontier and began to launch raids into Soviet territory.

In the early spring of 1918 agreement had been reached for the Czechoslovak Legion*, numbering some 40,000 men, to be withdrawn from Russia and shipped to France via Vladivostok. By May their echelons were spread along 5,000 miles of the Trans-Siberian Railway. There had been friction with various Bolshevik authorities, and in late May the Czechs revolted. A few weeks later all main centers along the line were in Czech hands.

Following the evidence of Bolshevik weakness, an anti-Bolshevik government was set up in Samara, composed mainly of Socialist–Revolutionaries (S–R's) (*see* Socialist-Revolutionary Party) from the dissolved Constituent Assembly*. Another government, politically more conservative, was formed at Omsk. In the summer Czech and Samara forces took the offensive and captured Kazan together with the huge gold reserve stored there. In the North the Bolsheviks in Archangel were ejected in a bloodless coup, and town and port were occupied by Allied (mostly British) troops. In the Far East (*see* Far Eastern Republic), United States and Japanese detachments landed in Vladivostok in August, and by early autumn of 1918 the last vestiges of Bolshevik authority in Siberia and the Far East had been wiped out by Czech, Omsk, Semenov, and Japanese troops. In Transcaspia a Menshevik (*see* Russian Social Democratic Workers' Party [Menshevik]) regime was formed in Ashkhabad in defiance of the Bolsheviks in Tashkent. In August a British detachment under General L. C. Dunsterville occupied Baku. In South Russia the Volunteer Army captured Ekaterinodar and Novorossiisk.

Later in 1918 the tide turned in favor of the Reds. L. D. Trotsky's* drastic reorganization of the Red Army* was beginning to take effect. On the Volga front the Czechs were disaffected and weary of fighting what increasingly seemed to them to be someone else's war. In October the revived Red Army recaptured Kazan. In November an officer's coup d'état in Omsk brought Admiral A. V. Kolchak* to power with the title of Supreme Ruler. A few weeks later his young Siberian Army reached Perm in the northern sector, but the offensive petered out. Friction developed between the Omsk regime and the Czechoslovak Legion.

The Armistice of November 11, 1918, ending World War I* in Western Europe brought about the withdrawal of German troops from western Russia and left a power vacuum that the Western Allies had neither the means nor the will to fight. Early in 1919 a mixed force under French command occupied Odessa. On the approach of weak Red detachments, the troops refused to fight. There were mutinies, and the whole force was hurriedly embarked in early April.

Meanwhile, in March 1919 the Western Allies had confidentially agreed that all their contingents should be withdrawn from Russian soil. Accordingly, later in the year all British troops were withdrawn from Archangel, and the fate of the Northern Provisional Government* there became dependent on the outcome on other fronts. By late summer the position along the Baltic had stabilized enough to make the future of the Baltic states of Estonia (*see* Estonia and the Russian Revolution, 1917–1921), Latvia (*see* Latvia and the Russian Revolution), and Lithuania (*see* Lithuania and the Russian Revolution) seem insured.

In the summer and autumn of 1919 the decisive campaigns of the Civil War were fought on the southern and eastern fronts. The Bolshevik hold on the South had been weakened by defections and by peasant guerilla activity. Denikin, now in command of all White forces in the South, started an offensive in May. Kharkov was taken in June, Poltava in July, Odessa and Kiev in August, and Kursk in September. In October the Whites reached Orel. In the same month a small contingent of the White Army under General N. N. Iudenich* advanced along the Baltic coast to within a few miles of Petrograd but was then defeated and straggled back to the Estonian frontier. Meanwhile, Denikin had over-stretched his forces. The Reds counterattacked at Orel, and by November the Whites (*see* White Movement) were in ever more disorderly retreat. In the spring of 1920, when Denikin was succeeded by General P. N. Wrangel*, all that was left were some 40,000 dispirited troops and a horde of refugees crowded into the Crimea peninsula (*see* Crimea, Revolution in).

On the eastern front Kolchak's forces attacked in March 1919 but after some early successes had to pay the price of faulty strategy and dissipation of effort. The Reds under M. V. Frunze* counterattacked in April, reached the Urals in July, and forged steadily eastward. Well before Kolchak ordered the evacuation of Omsk in November 1919 his far-flung empire was falling to pieces not so much from pressure by the Red Army as from desertion, mutiny, partisan attacks, and its own inherent weakness. The one stable element was the Czechoslovak Legion, and Kolchak's relations with the Czechs had reached the breaking point. When his train arrived at Irkutsk station in January 1920, the legion handed him over to the local leftist political center, and he was executed three weeks later.

In the spring of 1920, with the only important White armies decisively de-feated, it might seem that the Civil War was over. But April saw the start of the Russo–Polish War, and in June Wrangel's forces broke out of the Crimea and pushed northward. However, the Russo–Polish armistice of October 12 freed overwhelming Red forces for action in the South. In early November they stormed the isthmus of Perekop, and Wrangel had no choice but to order complete evacuation of the Crimea.

In the Far East the Czechs embarked at Vladivostok and left for Europe. All American troops were evacuated, and the Japanese, under strong pressure from Washington, began a series of withdrawals. The ensuing power vacuum was filled by the first Soviet satellite, the Far Eastern Republic, proclaimed at Verkh-neudinsk in March 1920. When the last Japanese detachment left Vladivostok in the autumn of 1922, the Republic declared itself dissolved and was incor-porated into the Soviet Union.

The Russian Civil War was marked by dramatic changes of fortune. The Whites received some aid from the Western Allies, but such aid was limited, uncertain, and bedeviled by inter-Allied differences. Foreign intervention was nowhere decisive but provided a telling point for Bolshevik propaganda and has been vigorously exploited ever since.

The Reds had the advantage of interior lines and a homogenous population. The Whites on the periphery had all the problems entailed by local nationalism. They had no effective overall leadership. The White generals lacked political and administrative ability; Wrangel perhaps was an exception, but when he came to power, the war was already lost. On the other hand, in V. I. Lenin* the Reds had a leader supremely capable of dealing with problems both at home and in foreign affairs and one, moreover, always ready to jettison traditional revolu-tionary myths for the sake of practical advantage.

Russia at that time was war weary, hungry, and disorganized. Matters such as recruitment, supply, transport, and administration offered almost insuperable difficulties. It was a savage war with atrocities on both sides, although F. E. Dzerzhinskii's* Red Terror was probably more effective than the sporadic brutalities of the Whites. Finally, the Reds could count on the devotion and discipline of the Russian Communist Party members. Although only a tiny proportion of Russia's population, it may well have been their effort that turned the scales.

David Footman

Bibliography

Bradley, *Civil War in Russia, 1917–20.* 1975.
Bubnov, A. S.; Kamenev, S. S.; and Eideman, R. P. *Grazhdanskaia voina, 1918–20.* 1928–1930.
Chamberlin, William H. *The Russian Revolution, 1917–21.* 2 vols. 1935.
Footman, David. *Civil War in Russia.* 1961.
Kennan, George D. *Soviet American Relations, 1917–20.* 2 vols. 1958.
Naida, S. F.; Obichkin, G. D.; Petrov, Iu. P.; Stuchkov, A. A.; and Shatagin, N. I. *Istoriia grazhdanskoi voiny.* 1957–1960.

Coalition Government. Refers to the entry of representative members of moderate socialist parties into the Provisional Government*.

The initial response of the Mensheviks (*see* Russian Social Democratic Workers' Party [Menshevik]) and Socialist–Revolutionaries (*see* Socialist–Revolutionary Party) was to abstain from participation in the Provisional Government in 1917, the only exception being the Socialist–Revolutionary A. F. Kerensky*, who served as Minister of Justice in the original government. The crisis that followed the publication of the Miliukov Note prompted the moderate socialists to take posts in the three succeeding Provisional Government coalitions formed May 5, July 23, and September 25 (*see* Dual Power, Appendix).

Comintern (Komintern). *See* Communist International.

Commissar (Komissar). *See also* Council of People's Commissars, 1917–1922 (Sovnarkom). From the French *Commissaire*. The choice of this word as a name for the ministers of the new Soviet government was intentional. It was meant to publicize the difference between the ministers of the revolutionary government and the former ministers of the Russian imperial government. The word has a long tradition in Western Europe as well as in Russia, and it was most commonly used to indicate a special agent charged with a specific political or administrative task.

Commissariat of the Enlightenment (Komissariat Narodnogo Prosveshcheniia). *See also* Lunacharskii, Anatolii. The Commissariat of the Enlightenment was the Ministry of Education of the Soviet government.

One of the ministries created at the Second All-Russian Congress of Soviets in November 1917 immediately after the October Seizure of Power* as a commissariat under the Council of People's Commissar*. The first Commissar of Enlightenment (or Education) was Anatolii Vasilievich Lunacharskii*. Although, technically, Lunacharskii's jurisdiction was confined to the Russian Soviet Federative Socialist Republic—other Soviet republics had their own Commissariats of Education—Lunacharskii, in keeping with his theories, assumed control over all cultural activities within the Soviet Union: education, theater, cinema, publishing, and so on. During the Revolution and the Civil War period (*see* Civil War in Russia) Lunacharskii failed in his efforts to conceive and construct a system of universal, free, and compulsory education in the USSR. With the coming of the New Economic Policy*, he concluded that he would not be able to reach that goal. From 1921 to 1928 there was an attempt to rationalize the organization of his inefficient and unwieldy commissariat, but those efforts enjoyed only limited success. To his credit, Lunacharskii succeeded during his tenure in office until 1929 in preserving freedom of artistic expression and creativity (*see* Education).

Commissars of the Council of People's Commissars. Special administrative agents of the Council of People's Commissars*. They need to be distinguished from the People's Commissars (or Ministers) of the Council of People's Commissars. These commissars were Soviet officials with specific tasks in consolidating the Soviet Revolution in military and border regions. For example, among the commissars dispatched to the military were B. P. Pozern (northern front), S. M. Nakhimson (Twelfth Army), P. P. Vasianin and G. I. Chudnovskii (southwestern front), and S. G. Roshal and V. Volodarskii* (M. M. Gold'dshtein) (Black Sea Fleet). Among those dispatched to specific regions were S. G. Shaumian (Caucasus), G. K. Ordzhonikidzhe* (Ukraine), V. S. Mickevicius-Kapsukas (Lithuania), P. A. Kobozev (Urals), and A. T. Dzhangil'din (Kazakhstan).

Committee of Members of the Constituent Assembly. (Comuch; Komitet chlenov uchreditel'nogo sobraniia; Komuch). A Committee formed after the October Seizure of Power* to coordinate the efforts of all political parties opposed to the new Soviet government. It was formed in Samara on June 8, 1918, after that city had been taken by the Czechoslovak Legions*. The members of the Committee were five Social–Revolutionaries (S–R's) who had been delegates to the Constituent Assembly*, V. K. Volskii, I. M. Brushvit, P. D. Klimushkin, B. K. Fortunatov, and I. P. Nestorov. The Volga–Ural regions seemed ideal for the resurrection of the Constituent Assembly since the elections to that body had indicated strong popular support for the non-Bolshevik radical parties in that region. The local S–R leaders in particular believed that the Bolshevik dictatorship did not have enough popular support to stay in power.

On June 8 Comuch announced that it had replaced the Soviet government in Samara and that the freedom of press, assembly, and speech were restored.

Comuch soon claimed to represent the All-Russian Constituent Assembly itself and not just the Volga–Ural regions. On July 7, 1918, Comuch appointed the Czech general S. K. Cecek as Commander-in-Chief of all Czech and Russian forces in that area. On August 10, 1918, the prominent Menshevik leader I. M. Maiskii arrived in Samara and tried to widen the political base of Comuch. Maiskii was appointed as head of Comuch's Department of Labor as a conciliatory gesture to make conclusive decisions about the future structure of the Russian state. The announced program of Comuch was to establish democratic freedoms, the eight-hour working day, and free assembly for all worker and peasant organizations. The committee denied the legitimacy of Soviet power and called for the inviolability of private property, although recognizing the nationalization of land.

From June through August 1918 the committee gained control over the provinces of Samara, Simbirsk, Kazan and Ufa and part of Saratov. Unfortunately, Comuch was dependent on the Czech Legion for its survival and was in competition for the supreme leadership of the anti-Bolshevik forces with other groups further on the political Right. A conference of such groups in September decided to unite all of the rival anti-Bolshevik groups under an all-Russian provisional government as sole trustees of the sovereign authority over all territories of the Russian state. A Directorate of five was established including Avksent'ev and Zenzinov from Comuch. By October 1918 Samara was retaken by Soviet forces and Comuch fled, first to Omsk, and then to Cheliabinsk. When Admiral Kolchak assumed power over all anti-Bolshevik forces in Omsk in November, the remnants of Comuch in Cheliabinsk tried to counter by declaring Comuch to be the supreme authority in Russia under an executive committee headed by V. M. Chernov* and Volskii, but the Czechs refused to recognize Comuch's aspirations this time and expelled them from the city. Kolchak ordered the arrest of the members of the Committee for treason. Chernov decided to explore the possibility of a compromise with the Bolsheviks and opened negotiations with them about the possibility of a coalition government. On January 13, 1920, the Bolsheviks announced their terms. They would discuss some issues with the S–R's, but the Constituent Assembly and the Soviet Constitution were not negotiable. That spelled the end for Comuch. (*see* Siberia, Revolution in).

Bibliography

Chamberlin, W. H. *The Russian Revolution* I. 1935.
Malgunov, S. P. *The Bolshevik Seizure of Power*. 1972.
Rosenberg, W. *Liberals in the Russian Revolution*. 1974.

Committee of Public Organizations—Moscow (Komitet Moskovskiikh Obshchestvennykh Organizatsii). A coalition of public organizations mostly dominated by liberals created after the February Revolution* in Moscow to mobilize public opinion on behalf of the Provisional Government* and to administer the city until a new City Duma could be elected. The Committee of Public Organizations was conceived on February 28, 1917. Some Moscow liberals, including N. M. Kishkin and N. I. Astrov, met to plan a founding conference. The first meeting of the new organization took place on March 1. One hundred and sixty-five delegates attended, including sixty-four representatives of the Moscow workers (forty-four from the trade unions and twenty from the Moscow Soviet of Workers' Deputies). An executive committee was created with fifteen members, five from each of the old electoral curiae, the old City Duma, the liberal political organizations, and the workers. The two Bolsheviks (*see* Russian Social Democratic Workers' Party [Bolshevik]) who took part were V. P. Nogin* (who also became a member of the five-man Presidium) and P. G. Smidovich*.

In effect the Committee of Public Organizations became the governing body in Moscow until the new City Duma was elected on July 25. Similar organizations were created, often with the same name, in other cities in Russia. In the Moscow Duma elections the Socialist-Revolutionary Party* received 58 percent of the vote (*see* Moscow, Revolution in).

Bibliography

Chamberlin, W. H. *The Russian Revolution* I. 1935.
Malgunov, S. P. *The Bolshevik Seizure of Power*. 1972.
Rosenberg, W. *Liberals in the Russian Revolution*. 1974.

Committee of Public Safety—Moscow. A coalition of all political groups opposing the threat of a Soviet seizure of power. The Committee of Public Safety in Moscow was created by the Moscow City Duma on October 25, 1917. The meeting of the Duma was called by the Socialist-Revolutionary (*see* Socialist-Revolutionary Party) mayor of the city, V. V. Rudnev, to organize the opposition to a Soviet seizure of power and to prevent Moscow from going the way of Petrograd. Most of its members were drawn from the City Duma, rather than the Provisional Government*, although it also included delegates from the Menshevik (*see* Russian Social Democratic Workers' Party [Menshevik]) and Socialist-Revolutionary factions in the Moscow Soviets of Workers' and of Soldiers' Deputies, the staff of the Moscow military district, the railroad and postal–telegraph unions, and the *zemstvos*. The new organization claimed to be defending the Constituent Assembly* rather than the Provisional Government. When the actual fighting began in Moscow on October 27, 1917, the 6,000 troops supporting the Committee of Public Safety seemed to have all of the advantages. The tide began to turn in the other direction on October 28 and on November 2 the forces of the Committee of Public Safety surrendered and agreed to the dissolution of their organization (*see* Moscow, Revolution in).

Bibliography

Chamberlin, W. H. *The Russian Revolution* I. 1935.
Malgunov, S. P. *The Bolshevik Seizure of Power*. 1972.
Rosenberg, W. *Liberals in the Russian Revolution*. 1974.

Committee of Public Safety—Petrograd. The Committee of Public Safety was an organization formed in opposition to the October Seizure of Power* in Petrograd. The Committee of Public Safety was founded on October 24, 1917, as an organ of the Petrograd City Duma (*see* Duma and Revolution) and was headed by the Socialist-Revolutionary (*see* Socialist-Revolutionary Party) mayor of Petrograd, G. I. Shreider. The Committee opposed the October Revolution of 1917 and sought to return power to the Provisional Government*. People associated with the Committee represented the Central Executive Committee (*see* All-Russian Central Executive Committee) of the First All-Russian Congress of Soviets, the Executive Committee of the All-Russian Congress of Soviets, the Executive Committee of the All-Russian Soviet of Peasant Deputies, the army and navy general staffs, representatives of railroad and post-telegraph trade unions, and others. Although Mensheviks (*see* Russian Social Democratic Workers' Party [Menshevik]), Socialist–Revolutionaries (*see* Social-Revolutionary Party), Cadets (*see* Constitutional Democratic Party—Cadet), and members of the Jewish Bund* were associated with the Committee, the Committee was based on institutions, not on political parties. Although originating in Petrograd, the Committee had many adherents in Moscow as well. It supported the Petrograd-based Committee for the Salvation of the Motherland and Revolution* in aiding the abortive junker (students from the officer training schools) uprising of October 29 in Petrograd against the revolutionary Soviet government. The Committee of Public Safety was suppressed by the Soviet regime at the end of 1917 (*see* October Seizure of Power).

Bibliography

Chamberlin, W. H. *The Russian Revolution* I. 1935.
Malgunov, S. P. *The Bolshevik Seizure of Power*. 1972.
Rosenberg, W. *Liberals in the Russian Revolution*. 1974.

Committee of Social Democratic War Prisoners—Internationalists of the Moscow Military Okrug. This Committee of War Prisoners was formed on December 17, 1917, in Moscow and was a forerunner of the Communist International*. The delegates attending represented about 20,000 war prisoners. The movement began among a group of Austro–Hungarian war prisoners working the factory Guzhon including Friedrich Karikash, who would later become the military chief of the Hungarian Soviet Republic in 1919. The German and Austro–Hungarian war prisoners took part in the October Seizure of Power* in Moscow (see Moscow, Revolution in). Under the supervision of the Moscow Bolshevik organization, the Committee of War Prisoners returned to work among the war prisoners, creating the nucleus of future communist parties among their recruits. A conference of this group in February 1918 invited all war prisoners to join the Red Army* in its defense of Russia from the German offensive. The committee made contact with similar organizations in Nizhnii-Novgorod, Kostromo, Tambov, Saratov, Astrakhan, and so on and prepared for the All-Russian Conference of Social Democratic–Internationalist War Prisoners, which met on April

15, 1918, in Moscow with some 400 delegates claiming to represent 500,000 prisoners of war. They formed a new organization called the International Revolutionary Organization of Socialists, Workers, and Peasants, which was clearly intended to be a forerunner of the Communist International*. The Congress ended with an appeal by its chairman for the formation of the Third International. The organization was also a manifestation of Lenin's belief that the Red Army should be an international army of the world proletariat. The People's Commissariat of Nationality Affairs under I. V. Stalin* performed a similar function, organizing special departments within the Commissariat for those national groups among the war prisoners who wished to become Russian citizens. Special national sections within the Russian Communist Party (*see* Russian Social Democratic Workers' Party [Bolshevik]) were also organized for those war prisoners who wished to become communist. In May 1918 all of these efforts were placed under the supervision of Bela Kun* in a new organization called the Federation of Foreign Groups of the Russian Communist Party.

Bibliography

Lazitch, Branko, and Drachkovitch, Milorad M. *Lenin and the Comintern.* 1972.

Committee for the Salvation of the Motherland and Revolution (Komitet spaseniia rodiny i revoliutsii). This committee was a counterrevolutionary organization. It was formed on the morning of October 26, 1917, apparently at the instigation of the Socialist–Revolutionary (*see* Socialist-Revolutionary Party) mayor of Petrograd, G. I. Shreider. The Committee's formation followed an unsuccessful march of Petrograd City Duma delegates to the Winter Palace in support of the Provisional Government* on the night of October 25. The Committee was an ad hoc response to the October Seizure of Power* in Petrograd (*see* Petrograd Soviet) and represented a number of diverse interests opposed to Bolshevism. The Committee was dominated by the right-wing members of the Socialist-Revolutionary Party whose Central Committee and Military Commission provided organizational structure such as the Committee possessed. Among the prominent Socialist–Revolutionaries (S–R's) involved were N. D. Avksent'ev*, A. R. Gots*, and V. M. Zenzinov. Among other organizations associated with the Committee were the Petrograd City Duma and the All-Russian Central Executive Committee of the All-Russian Congress of Soviets, as well as Mensheviks (*see* Russian Social Democratic Workers' Party [Mensheviks]) and S–R's who had walked out of the Second All-Russian Congress of Peasant Soviets. The Committee was also supported by monarchist elements associated with V. M. Purishkevich. Colonel G. P. Polkovnikov, former head of the Petrograd Military District, was named to head the Committee.

The Committee opposed the Soviet seizure of power and sought to rally the forces needed to overthrow it. The program of the Committee, set forth in appeals and leaflets, called for a new government composed "exclusively of the revolutionary democracy." Noteworthy is the fact that the Committee rejected the proposal to act in the name of the Provisional Government due to the latter's unpopularity. It also called for the immediate transfer of all land to the land committees* and supported the proposal of a general democratic peace to be presented to all combatant powers in the World War. Tactically, the Committee sought to gain its ends by the use of force, organizing armed resistance to the new Soviet government within Petrograd in order to rise up when the forces being mustered outside the city by A. F. Kerensky* and General P. N. Krasnov were approaching the capital. The Committee was apparently in contact with Kerensky.

Politically, the Committee members proposed that Kerensky enter Petrograd as a military victor and restore the former government. The Committee would then cause the dismissal of Kerensky and all nonsocialist ministers of the Provisional Government, creating an all-socialist government but excluding the Bolsheviks. To carry off its end of the plot the Committee had at its disposal very limited forces, primarily *junkers* (officer cadets from the capital's military schools numbering between 800 and 1,500).

Bolshevik military authorities came into possession of information regarding the planned uprising, and the Committee was forced to move before the enterprise would be entirely lost. At 2:00 a.m. on October 28 the junkers moved to occupy strategic points in Petrograd, but despite initial successes, the inadequate forces were defeated, and by the afternoon the uprising had been totally suppressed. Failure of the uprising resulted in the collapse of the Committee whose members fled. Many later joined or formed other opposition groups.

Bibliography

Chamberlin, W. H. *The Russian Revolution* I. 1935.
Malgunov, S. P. *The Bolshevik Seizure of Power*. 1972.
Rosenberg, W. *Liberals in the Russian Revolution*. 1974.

Committee for Struggle against the Counterrevolution. The Committee for Struggle against the Counterrevolution was established by the Executive Committee of the Petrograd Soviet* on the night of August 27–28, 1917. Originally, it was supposed to include three members of each of the socialist parties—the Menshevik (*see* Russian Social Democratic Workers' Party [Menshevik]), the Bolshevik (*see* Russian Social Democratic Workers' Party [Bolshevik]), and the Socialist–Revolutionaries (*see* Socialist-Revolutionary Party)—and five representatives from the Presidium of the All-Russian Central Executive Committee* of Soviets, five representatives from the Executive Committee of the Soviet of Peasant Deputies, and two representatives each from the Petrograd Soviets and the Central Trade Union. On August 29 two representatives from the Interdistrict Committee were appointed to the Committee. The Committee formed a military section, a political commissariat, and an information section. Similar organizations were established by other soviets throughout the country to deal with the threat of the Kornilov uprising (*see* Kornilov Revolt). The Petrograd Committee, in particular its military section, became a general staff for those forces that were beginning to organize in opposition to the Right. During the Kornilov uprising the Committee issued regular bulletins to the entire country from the Provisional Government*, the Petrograd Soviet, and other mass organizations. Although created in the emergency brought about by the Kornilov uprising, the Committee served long after that event as an instrument for the dissemination of revolutionary propaganda using the counterrevolutionary cause as a rationale for its activities. It also took the initiative in beginning the organization of armed units of workers, in many cases with full financial support from some of the trade unions. After the defeat of Kornilov on September 4, 1917, A. F. Kerensky* ordered the dissolution of the Committee, which the Committee simply ignored. In October the functions of the Committee were taken over by the Bolshevik-sponsored Military-Revolutionary Committee, whose purpose was not to preserve the Provisional Government like its predecessor but to overthrow it and replace the Provisional Government with a Soviet government.

Bibliography

Chamberlin, W. H. *The Russian Revolution* I. 1935.
Malgunov, S. P. *The Bolshevik Seizure of Power*. 1972.
Rosenberg, W. *Liberals in the Russian Revolution*. 1974.

Committees of the Poor (Komitety bednoty, or Kombedy). Committees of poor peasants sponsored by the state and the Russian Communist Party (*see* Russian Social Democratic Workers' Party [Bolshevik]) to acquire surplus grain being withheld from the Soviet regime. On June 11, 1918, the Food Commissariat of the Soviet government, desperate for food supplies for the cities, established committees of poor peasants. These Committees of the Poor were charged, on the local level, with distributing grain, essential commodities, and agricultural implements. They also were to cooperate with local food organizations in confiscating surplus grain from the *kulaks* (rich peasants). Recruitment in the committees was encouraged by offering poor peasants a share of confiscated grain. Membership on the committees was denied to *kulaks,* employers, or hired labor and owners of surplus grain. Committees of the Poor were not numerous in the turbulent black-soil region, especially in Tambov, Tula, and Penza provinces.

On balance, Committees of the Poor were a failure. Although substantial quantities of grain were taken in, the social and political costs were high, and there were widespread abuses. The object of the campaign had been to divide the peasants of poor and middling rank from the well-to-do peasants. This had not occurred; rather, division was largely between the poorest and everyone else. This was acknowledged in a government circular of August 1918 that asserted that Committees of the Poor were not to be "organizations only of the village proletariat against all of the rest of the village population." Furthermore, what the regime came to characterize as "Dual Power"* came to exist between the committees and the village soviets. In addition to their food collection and

distribution duties, committees often usurped other functions, including the levy-
ing of taxes. There were also instances of abuses in which *kulak* farm animals
and agricultural implements were seized and divided among members of the
communities. By mid-November 1918 the need to gain the support of the middle
peasants in the gathering Civil War (*see* Civil War in Russia) prompted the
abolition of the Committees of the Poor as independent entities and their merger
with village soviets. The amalgamation of the two followed new village soviet
elections decreed by the All-Russian Central Executive Committee* of Soviets
on December 2, 1918.

Bibliography

Medvedev, Roy. *The October Revolution*. 1979.

Communist International (Comintern; Third [Communist] International) (Kom-
munistischeskii Internatsional; or Komintern). The Communist International was
the international organization based in Moscow for the coordination of the efforts
of communist parties around the world. It was founded in Moscow in March
1919 and was called the Third International to differentiate it from the Second
or Socialist International. The First International was formed in 1866 by Karl
Marx and Michael Bakunin under the name the International Workingman's
Association. At its first meeting there were sixty people representing eleven
worker–socialist movements. The First International lasted until its Fifth Congress in 1872. The Second International was formed in 1889. At its Ninth
Congress in 1912 it represented twenty-seven socialist parties in twenty-three
countries with a total membership of 3,787,000 members. The organization
foundered in World War I* when the member parties split on the question of
supporting the war efforts of their individual countries. At the wartime conferences in Zimmerwald (1915) and Kienthal (1916), V. I. Lenin* joined the minority of socialists who believed that no support should be given to their native
country's war efforts. The idea of a new international appears as early as November 1914 in a manifesto of the Central Committee (*see* Central Committee
of the Russian Communist Party [Bolshevik]) of the Russian Social Democratic
Workers' Party (Bolshevik) entitled ''The War and Social Democracy'' and in
an article by Lenin appearing in the November 1, 1914, issue of the Bolshevik
newspaper *Sotsial-demokrat*. When he returned to Russia in April 1917, Lenin
made the formation of a new socialist international one of the items on his agenda
in his famous April Theses*.

The preparations for actually creating a Third International did not begin,
however, until the end of 1918. A group of Communists who had lived in
England and America and spoke English were gathered together to form the
''Anglo-American Communist Group'' on November 28, 1918, and were
charged to begin work among the prisoners of war—which finally led to the
formation of the procommunist ''Internationalists''*—and to organize propaganda for England and America. Internationalist meetings were established for

Moscow on December 5 and in Petrograd on December 19. When the British Laborites issued an invitation for an international socialist conference in Switzerland to revive the Second International, the Central Committee of the Bolshevik Party sent a telegram on December 24 calling upon all revolutionary European socialists to boycott that conference, stating that "the Third International, in charge of the Revolution, already exists," although this was not true. V. I. Lenin sent a detailed note to G. V. Chicherin*, the Commissar of Foreign Affairs, on December 24, indicating the need to hold an international conference to set up the Third International, preferably before the scheduled socialist conference in Switzerland. Chicherin and N. I. Bukharin* were given the responsibility to frame the invitation, which was issued January 24, 1919.

A preliminary conference of sorts was held under the auspices of the People's Commissariat of Foreign Affairs on January 21, 1918. There were representatives from the Bolsheviks (including I. V. Stalin*), some of the border countries, P. Petrov (probably J. Fineberg—an Englishman working in the Commissariat of Foreign Affairs) claiming to represent the British Socialist Party, and B. Reinstein claiming to represent the Socialist-Labor Party of America, although working with Chicherin in the Commissariat of Foreign Affairs. They were charged with writing the invitation, selecting the groups to be invited, and exhorting them to send representatives. The date of the invitation, January 24, 1919, was exactly six days before the Berne Conference, which was designed to resurrect the Second International. To some extent, the Russian leaders were inspired by the formation in December of the German Communist Party.

The First Congress of the Communist International met in Moscow in March 2nd to 16th, 1919. There were sixty delegates claiming to represent communist parties or groups from nineteen countries. Most of the delegates came from Russia or Eastern Europe or were permanent residents in Moscow but of foreign origin. The real hope of Moscow was the new Communist Party of Germany represented by Hugo Eberlein. After composing a "secret" communist manifesto (seventy-one years after the first), it called upon the proletariat of the world to force their mother countries to recognize the Soviet state and withdraw all support for armed intervention against Russia. The First Congress elected an Executive Committee (Executive Committee of the Communist International [ECCI or, in Russian, IKKI]) with G. E. Zinoviev* as its president and K. Radek* as its secretary.

From the outset the power and success of the Russian leaders who headed, in their words, the only socialist state in the world and the choice of Moscow as the headquarters of the Communist International guaranteed their domination of the new organization. The only member party strong enough to resist Russian prestige at this time was German, and its representative, Hugo Eberlein, although abstaining from the resolution calling for the formation of the new international, allowed himself to be outvoted.

The initial optimism of the Russian leaders about the prospects for an international communist revolution at the time of the First Congress diminished

considerably afterwards with the failure of attempted communist uprisings in
Germany, Austria, and Hungary and with the subsequent invasion of Soviet
Russia by Pilsudski's Polish Legions. When the Second Congress met from July
19 to August 7, 1920, however, the Poles were being driven back, and the
representation from foreign communist parties was more impressive. There were
more than 200 delegates from thirty-seven countries. To strengthen the discipline
of the international movement, the Second Congress adopted the famous Twenty-
One Conditions of Membership, making all member parties conform essentially
to the rules and discipline of the Russian Party. These conditions not only
guaranteed the militancy of the international communist movement and its subordination to its Russian members but also made any rapprochement between
the communist parties and the socialist parties in their own countries impossible.

The reasons for tightening discipline at that juncture were not pessimism but
optimism about the forthcoming international proletarian revolution. It was probably the last Comintern Congress to be that optimistic. At that time it seemed
to the Russians that Poland would be the first communist state to be established
by the Red Army*. That mood did not flag when the Polish offensive ground
to a halt because the Comintern achieved its first great victory in a major industrialized country with the defection of a large number of German Socialists
to the new German Communist Party in December 1920, raising the membership
of that party to more than 350,000 people. The French Socialist Party would
soon experience a similar loss to the French Communist Party, and a somewhat
smaller Italian Communist Party would be formed in 1921.

All of these promising developments were overshadowed, however, by a
receding enthusiasm for revolutionary action in Europe and by the pressing crisis
at home in the Soviet Union. The adoption of the New Economic Policy* by
Russia in March 1921 marked the beginning of a new era in Russian foreign
policy as well as domestic. This was reflected in the mood of the Comintern in
June 1921. The watchwords were unification, stabilization, and recruitment, and
the member parties were warned not to expect imminent communist revolution.
The Comintern would continue to meet until disbanded in 1943, but its activities
would, for the most part from this time onward, be subordinated to those of the
Ministry of Foreign Affairs.

Bibliography

Borkenau, Franz. *World Communism: A History of the Communist International*. 1939.
Carr, Edward Hallet. *The Bolshevik Revolution, 1917–23*. 3 vols. 1950–1953.
Degras, Jane, ed. *The Communist International, 1919–43:Documents*. 3 vols. 1956–
    1965.
Drachkovitch, M. M., and Lazitch, Branko. *Lenin and the Comintern*. 1972.
Gruber, H. *International Communism in the Era of Lenin*. 1967.
Hulse, James. *The Forming of the Communist International*. 1964.
*Istoriia mezhdunarodnogo rabochego i natsional'no-osvoboditel'nogo dvizheniia: Vol.
    2, 1917–39*. 1962.

Lazic, B. M. *Lénine et la IIIe Internationale*. 1951.
Lazitch, Brank, and Drachkovitch, Milorad M. *Lenin and the Comintern*. 2 vols. 1972.
Sworakowski, Witold S. *The Communist International and Its Front Organizations*. 1965.

Communist International of Peasants (Kransnyi Krest'ianskii Internatsional, or Krestintern). *See* Peasant International.

Communist International of Youth (Kommunisticheskii Internatsional O Molodezhi, or KIM). An international communist youth organization created in 1919.

The founding congress of the Communist International of Youth took place in Berlin on November 20–26, 1919. The initiative for its formation came from V. I. Lenin*, who had long advocated such an organization since his disillusionment with the Second International during World War I*. At the first congress of the Russian Communist League of Youth* in October 1918, the Russian youth organization called for the creation of an international youth organization and established a central committee to carry out that task. The first congress of the Communist International of Youth included eighteen delegates, eleven from communist youth organizations of ten European countries other than Russia. These delegates claimed to represent youth organizations with a total membership of 300,000, including their Russian component. The congress established an administrative structure and a program for the Communist International of Youth and petitioned the Communist International* for membership. The Communist International of Youth soon became subordinate to its parent organization, the Communist International, which meant in turn becoming subordinate, like its parent organization, to the Russian Social Democratic Workers' Party (Bolshevik)*. All subsequent congresses of the Communist International of Youth took place in Moscow, and the organization grew to an established membership of nearly 4 million by 1935. It was disbanded in 1943 at the same time as the Comintern.

Bibliography

Cornell, Richard. *Youth and Communism*.

Communist League of Youth. *See* Russian Communist League of Youth.

Communist Party of the Soviet Union (Bolshevik). *See* Russian Social Democratic Workers' Party (Bolshevik).

Comsomol. *See* Russian Communist League of Youth.

Congresses. *See* appropriate organizations.

Constituent Assembly (Vserossiiskoe Uchreditel'noe Sobranie). The first and last freely elected national representative assembly in the history of Russia elected in mid-November 1917 after the October Seizure of Power*.

The idea of a freely elected national assembly meeting together to write a national constitution is enshrined in liberal political philosophy dating from John Locke and the historical experience of the American Revolution of 1776 and the French Revolution of 1789. Locke argued that it was "natural law" that when a government became tyrannical, that government broke a "social contract" with its people and thus destroyed its legitimacy. At that point, the people were entitled to revert to a state of nature, in which they collectively enjoyed sovereign power over themselves, and to write a new social contract, delegating power to a new government and political institutions of their own choosing. This could be done as in the case of the American Revolution with a constitutional convention or, as it was called in the French Revolution of 1789, by a Constituent Assembly.

In tsarist Russia almost all political groups, including the Bolsheviks (*see* Russian Social Democratic Workers' Party [Bolshevik]), favored the calling of an all-Russian constituent assembly. After the February Revolution* of 1917 the new Provisional Government* issued a declaration on March 21, 1917, calling for the election of a constituent assembly. An electoral commission was created to prepare procedures for the election of such an assembly. The elections were to be conducted on the basis of universal, equal, direct, and secret suffrage.

The dilatory behavior of the Electoral Commission may have been a result of fears by the members of the Constitutional Democratic—Cadet Party*, which then dominated the Provisional Government, that their party would be relegated to a minor role if the elections took place too soon. But the effect of their delay was to draw criticism to the Provisional Government from all of the other political groups. When A. F. Kerensky* became Prime Minister in midsummer, he set September 17 as the date for the elections. Once elected, the Constituent Assembly would meet on September 30. The preparations for the elections took longer than expected because he had underestimated the difficulties involved, and the day of elections was postponed to November 12.

After the October Seizure of Power the Bolsheviks, having used the slogan "All Power to the Constituent Assembly," were bound to hold the elections on schedule, despite their fears of losing the elections to the more popular Socialist-Revolutionary Party*. During the elections the other political parties were intimidated by the Bolsheviks but participated in the campaigning anyway. Despite the adverse environment provided by war, Revolution, and the Bolshevik grip on the reins of power, all of which certainly had some influence on the outcome, there was a very high turnout of eligible voters.

The results were an overwhelming victory for the Socialist-Revolutionary Party, although it was a pyrrhic victory because the Bolsheviks already held the most powerful posts in the Council of People's Commissars*, and the Socialist-Revolutionary Party was itself split into two factions, the Left Socialist–Revolutionaries (*see* Left Socialist-Revolutionary Party) who supported the new Soviet government and the Right Socialist–Revolutionaries who did not. Therefore, although the Socialist–Revolutionaries controlled more than half of the seats (57 percent) in the new Constituent Assembly, about 10 percent of those delegates were in favor of the Soviet system of government. In coalition with the other delegates opposed to Soviet power, however, the Socialist–Revolutionaries would have had an ample majority in favor of a more democratic form of government. The distribution of delegates as given by Oliver Radkey (1950) was as follows:

Distribution of Delegates to the *All-Russian Constituent Assembly*

S–R's	370
Left S–R's	40
Bolsheviks	175
Mensheviks	16
Popular Socialists	2
Cadets	17
National groups	86
Unknown	1
Total	707

After meeting for a single day, January 5, 1918, the Constituent Assembly was dissolved. Although the other political parties tried to keep the idea of the Constituent Assembly alive during the Civil War (*see* Civil War in Russia), it was never convened again (*see* Committee of Members of the Constituent Assembly).

Lenin began to criticize the Constituent Assembly even before it was convened in his December 1917 article "Theses on the Constituent Assembly." He argued that the October Seizure of Power had already created a higher democracy than could be achieved by bourgeois procedures such as free elections. Alluding to the problem of "false consciousness," which pervaded all of his arguments for the seizure of power, Lenin suggested that the elections to the Constituent Assembly had taken place before the country could understand the full implications of the seizure of power. In his article "The Proletarian Revolution and the Renegade Kautsky," Lenin contended that the elections to the Constituent Assembly were superfluous once a higher form of democracy, the Soviet government, had come to power. In Marxist terms this is a consistent argument, for universal suffrage represents an institutional solution to societal problems, which from a Marxist perspective would not fundamentally change the character of the society unless accompanied by the abolition of private property and the achievement of some kind of collective ownership of the means of production.

For many Western liberals and socialists, however, Lenin's decision to dissolve the only freely elected representative assembly in the history of Russia epitomizes the gulf between his revolution and those in France and the United States. They still believed that the election represented the will of the people and should, therefore, have prevailed. Historians are not supposed to speculate on the "might have beens" of history, but those who have done so seriously doubt that the Constituent Assembly, if it had continued, would have been able to bring peace, order, and stability to Russia, given the confusion of that period of history in Russia and the absence of a strong democratic tradition.

Bibliography

Radkey, Oliver. *The Election to the Russian Constituent Assembly of 1917.* 1950.
Znamenskii, O. N. *Vserossiiskoe uchreditel'noe sobranie.* 1976.

Constitution of the Russian Soviet Federative Socialist Republic. The first Constitution for the new Soviet state after the October Seizure of Power*.

The first Soviet Constitution, or fundamental law (*osnovnoi zakon*), comprising ninety articles and divided into six main sections, was adopted by the Fifth All-Russian Congress of Soviets on July 10, 1918, and went into force nine days later upon publication in the government newspaper *Izvestiia**. Depending on one's approach to politics, history, state, and law, the enactment of the Soviet Constitution may appear to be either an unexpected occurrence or a natural development in the history of the Russian Revolution. Karl Marx and Friedrich Engels believed in revolution rather than in the constitutions of their day as the means for the ultimate liberation of the working classes. But by 1903 the program of the Russian Social Democratic Workers' Party already contained a provision calling for a constitution to be enacted in the democratic republic that would follow the overthrow of the tsarist monarchy. Here the emphasis in the Party program was on the first stage of the revolutionary struggle, the bourgeois democratic revolution that Marx said was a necessary precondition to the proletarian revolution and the eventual establishment of a communist state.

Democracy, rather than socialism, was also the watchword in 1917 during the first weeks following the February Revolution* not only among the liberal democratic groups but also among virtually all of the revolutionary parties in Russia including the Bolsheviks (*see* Russian Social Democratic Workers' Party [Bolshevik]) and the Mensheviks (*see* Russian Social Democratic Workers' Party [Menshevik]). It was in the name of democracy in the early fall of 1917 that all of these various groups anticipated the convening of the Constituent Assembly*, the characteristic organ of bourgeois democracy. Yet even before the Assembly began its deliberations in January 1918, the duration of the bourgeois-democratic Revolution in Russia (and ultimately the fate of the Assembly itself) had become the subject of sharp debate among the revolutionary fractions. Some groups, such as the Right Socialist–Revolutionaries (S–R's) and the Mensheviks continued to believe that the October Revolution was but an interruption or perhaps a continuation of the bourgeois February Revolution,* which of necessity had to be brought to its full development and conclusion. V. I. Lenin* and others, however, referred increasingly to the immediate pursuit of the socialist revolution and characterized the October uprising as genuinely proletarian. In an article entitled "Theses on the Constituent Assembly," published anonymously in *Izvestiia* in December 1917, Lenin had already described the soviets of workers' deputies as a higher form of the democratic principle than a bourgeois republic with its Constituent Assembly.

In January 1918 the "Provisional" (as it was then officially known) Workers' and Peasants' Government had drafted the Declaration of the Rights of Working and Exploited People for consideration by the Constituent Assembly. The declaration proclaimed Russia to be a republic of soviets (councils) of workers', soldiers', and peasants' Deputies* in which "all power belongs to the Soviets"— repeating this slogan from the proclamation of the Second All-Russian Congress of Soviets of October 26, 1917—and laid the foundation for the establishment of Soviet Russia as a federation of Soviet national republics. The declaration also repeated provisions of the most important acts and decrees that had been promulgated since the October Revolution, such as nationalization of land and natural resources and workers' control over production. When the Constituent Assembly was dissolved the day after it was convened, its immediate successor was declared to be the Second All-Russian Congress of Soviets. On January 12, 1918, as one of its first official acts, the Congress adopted the declaration upon the motion of the Bolshevik fraction. Three days later, the Congress passed two resolutions that had been submitted by I. V. Stalin* on behalf of the Bolsheviks that also were to have an influence upon the Soviet Constitution. The first resolution (No. 46), on the nationalities question, repeated the principle of self-determination of peoples as enunciated by the Council of People's Commissars* on November 2, 1917. The second resolution (No. 47), "On Federal Institutions of the Russian Republic," envisaged the Soviet socialist character of the Russian Republic, a union of republics in a Russian federation headed by a congress of Soviets, the All-Russian Central Executive Committee* of Soviets, and the Council of People's Commissars and including autonomous regional soviets in areas differentiated by special custom and national character. In addition, the third resolution (No. 47) mandated the All-Russian Central Executive Committee to prepare basic constitutional provisions for submission to the next Congress of Soviets.

Although several draft texts were compiled in the various ministries (commissariats) during the first months of 1918, no final draft was ready by the time the Fourth Congress of Soviets met in March 1918. Given the many internal and external problems that beset the government of the new republic during that period of revolution, this state of affairs was probably to be expected. It was, however, only temporary. A call for renewed attention to the preparation of the Constitution was made at a meeting of the Bolshevik Party plenum on March 30, 1918, where a proposal was directed to the All-Russian Central Executive

Committee* that a constitutional commission be appointed. In its session of April 1, 1918, the All-Russian Central Executive Committee adopted the Bolshevik motion and formed a commission to be made up of nominees of the parties represented in the All-Russian Central Executive Committee on a proportional basis and of representatives from various ministries, as well as of "other comrades." By April 16 the Commission reached its final size of fifteen members.

Speaking at the All-Russian Central Executive Committee session of April 1, Sverdlov (chairman of the All-Russian Executive Committee and subsequently also appointed chairman of the constitutional commission) declared that the first period of Soviet life had more or less come to an end. However, if the establishment of Soviets of Workers' Deputies as the basic governmental form marked the end of the first phase of the Russian Revolution, the beginning of the second period was to be seen in the struggle between the various factions represented in the All-Russian Central Executive Committee to determine the direction and tenor of the new Soviet state. It was this struggle that was in part played out in the constitutional commission.

The Bolshevik Party line was based on the establishment of the dictatorship of the proletariat as one of the fundamental tasks of the state. This concept was first enshrined in the Program of the Second Congress of the Russian Social Democratic Workers' Party (Bolshevik) and was defined therein as "the conquest of political power by the proletariat enabling it to crush any resistance of the exploiters." This meant a strong central authority functioning on roughly the same democratic-centralist principle of decision making as used in the party. By contrast, the Left Socialist–Revolutionaries (*see* Left Socialist-Revolutionary Party) envisaged only a social role for the Soviets and sought to establish local institutions of self-government. Another proposal put forward to the commission provided for a state apparatus that would be but a center regulating productive and economic relationships and for a republic to be made up of a federation of socioeconomic units rather than of national republics. The Socialist–Revolutionary–Maximalists drafted a constitution of labor republics focusing on labor as the communist basis of society. These various proposals were put to a vote of the commission during its deliberations, and the Bolshevik line (as formulated in a set of theses delivered by Stalin) was adopted as a result of the numerical strength of the Bolsheviks in the commission. Stalin then presented to the commission a plan for the general provisions of the Constitution of the Russian Soviet Federative Socialist Republic which was based upon the Bolshevik theses. On April 19 this was also adopted by the commission. The General Provisions repeated the basic elements of the January Resolution No. 47, but it also called for the establishment of the dictatorship of the urban and rural proletariat in the form of a strong all-Russian Soviet order to suppress the bourgeoisie completely and to introduce socialism where there would be neither classes nor organs of state power. If there had previously been any doubt about what type of constitution would be produced by the commission's deliberations, the adoption of the General Provisions was evidence that it would ultimately be a Bolshevik socialist constitution.

In the same session at which it adopted the Bolshevik General Provisions, the commission resolved to split up into three subcommittees dealing with the structure and competency of state organs and the relationship of the local soviets with the central state apparatus, the rights and duties of workers, and the question of the right to vote and to be elected to soviets. A redactional committee was also created to provide for publication of the results of the commission's work. Although the debates of the commissions were continued in the subcommittees and several draft sections were published in the press, continued reference to the General Provisions meant that proposals such as replacing the then existing Central Executive Committee and the Council of People's Commissars with a single council for the Central Executive Committee composed of eleven collegia, or providing for secret balloting, or establishing proportional representation in elections were defeated by the full commission. The lengthy nature of these debates, however, threatened to delay completion of the commission's work in time for the Fifth Congress of Soviets. On June 28 the Council of People's Commissars instructed the commissariats to speed up work on the draft constitutions, and on the same date the Bolshevik Party Central Committee decided to form a special committee headed by Lenin to assist the All-Russian Central Executive Committee's constitutional commission.

By the end of June two draft Constitutions had been formulated: one prepared by the commission of the All-Russian Central Executive Committee, the other submitted by the Ministry of Justice under the editorship of M. A. Reisner and A. G. Goikhbarg. Both drafts were discussed at a session of the Council of People's Commissars on June 28 and at a Bolshevik Central Committee meeting on July 3. Although the two drafts did not differ greatly from each other, not surprisingly the Party Central Committee expressed a preference for the version from the commission of the All-Russian Central Executive Committee, to which the Central Committee introduced some amendments. The most important change was the insertion of the January Declaration of the Right of Working and Exploited People as the declaratory portion of the draft Constitution. When the first session of the Fifth Congress of Soviets was convened the following day, Ia. M. Sverdlov* proposed and the Congress accepted a motion to form a congress constitutional committee. This nine-member committee examined the various draft proposals and recommended to the full congress that it adopt the final All-Russian Central Executive Committee version (incorporating the last-minute Bolshevik amendments). The fact that the Bolsheviks had a two-thirds majority of delegates to the Congress helped to ensure that the Committee motion was finally adopted by the full congress at its session of July 10 as Resolution No. 2992—The Constitutions (Fundamental Law) of the Russian Soviet Federative Socialist Republic (RSFSR).

In the period that followed, although some changes were made in the RSFSR Constitution, the next milestone in the history of the Soviet Constitution would be the drafting of a new constitution to take account of the formation of the Union of Soviet Socialist Republics. The first USSR Constitution became provisionally effective in July 1923 and was formally adopted on January 31, 1924. This would in turn be followed by the "Stalin" Constitution of 1936 and the "Brezhnev" Constitution of 1977.

The first Soviet Constitution, in part, contained provisions of the most important laws and decrees that were promulgated by the Soviet government in the first eight months of the Russian Revolution, and in part, it proclaimed policies and goals to be pursued in the future. It was, in this regard, an economic and political document that could be readily understood. As a legal document, however, the first Soviet Constitution must be read as much for what it does not state as for what it does. For example, the 1918 Constitution omits any reference to observance of the Constitution, and, writing in the early 1920s, Professor G. S. Gurvich (a member of the constitutional commission of the All-Russian Central Executive Committee) even criticized the Ministry of Justice draft because it promised to deal severely with violations of the Constitution. Gurvich commented that there are times when there is nothing less constitutional than to obey a constitution and nothing more constitutional than to disregard one. Although this denies the axiom familiar in the West that a constitution should provide the rule of law and should be a predictable regulator of government and society, a view such as the one put forward by Gurvich is not inconsistent with Marxist–Leninist theories on the rule of law. Indeed, there have been periods in Soviet history when law was honored more in its breach than in its observance. In post-revolutionary Russia and later in the Soviet Union, it was and is not law that functions as the keystone of society; it was and is the Party that stands at the vanguard of the proletariat and that is the leading and guiding force of all society. This has been, and remains today, a basic principle of Soviet socialist life and the foundation upon which the Soviet Constitutions rest—a premise in the Soviet Constitutions of 1918, 1924, and 1936 that was finally stated explicitly in the Soviet Constitution of 1977. It is a rule not of law but, ultimately, of the Party. *See* appendix for Commission members and summary of the Constitution of 1918.

William B. Simons

Bibliography

Carr, E. H. *The Bolshevik Revolution, 1917–1923*. Vol. 1. 1964.

Feldbrugge, F. J. M.; van den Berg, G. P.; and Simons, W. B. *Encyclopedia of Soviet Law*. 2d rev. ed. 1985.

Gurvich, G. S. *Istoriia Sovetskoi Konstitutsiii*. 1923.

Lipatov, A. A., and Savenkov, N. T. *Istoriia Sovetskoi Konstitutsiii (v dokumentakh), 1917–1956*. 1957.

Rumiantsev, A. S. *V Vserossiiskii S''ezd Sovetov i Priniatie Pervoi Sovetskoi Konstitutsii*. 1958.

Triska, Jan F., ed. *Constitutions of the Communist-Party States*. 1968.

Constitutional Democratic Party—Cadet (Konstitutsionno Demokratiches-kaia Partiia, or Kadet Partii). Russia's liberal party, usually called the Cadet Party.

The Constitutional Democratic Party entered the 1917 Revolution fully confident of its ability and right to take up the reins of government. Organized in 1905 by progressive zemstvo figures and leading members of the liberal intelligentsia, the party included in its ranks many of Russia's best-known professors, lawyers, physicians, agronomists, and other professionals. Under the leadership of Pavel N. Miliukov* and others, the party dominated the First State Duma and struggled throughout the turbulent pre-revolutionary decade to bring Russian society under constitutional government and a rule of law. The Cadets championed civil liberties. Their party program advanced a broad nationalism in which state power would be vested in a British-type cabinet, responsible to a popularly elected legislature. It also insisted that they stood above partisan class interests and favored a broad pattern of social reforms that would recognize the legitimacy of competitive social interests.

Cadet presumption and confidence stemmed from these nonpartisan statist commitments, which seemed ideally suited to a socially backward society lacking traditions of political partisanship, but they cloaked significant political differences within party ranks, which came to dominate developments in 1917. Leading Moscow and provincial Cadets believed in conciliation with the moderate Left. They supported closer identification with popular worker and peasant interests and, before February, urged organic opposition to autocracy and the tsar. "Legalists" in Petrograd, however, dominated by Miliukov and the Central Committee, resisted "Union of Liberationist"-type ties to the Left. Instead, they hoped through the Progressive Bloc* and contacts with the Right to gain the confidence of "privileged" Russia. When the Provisional Government* took power in February, it was this group that most influenced events, Miliukov even hoped for a time that the cabinet "elected by the Revolution" would govern under the regency of Grand Duke Michael (*see* Nicholas II).

This stance tainted Cadets from the start, rather unfairly, as a party uniformly opposed to the Revolution and its social goals. As Foreign Minister and a leading figure in the first Provisional regime (*see* Provisional Government) Miliukov felt responsible in the first instance to preserve law and order, inculcate a respect for legality (*zakonnost*), and protect Russia's state interests. This meant war to complete victory, which in Miliukov's well-publicized vision included securing control over Constantinople and the straits, as promised in the secret wartime treaties. Social reforms, beyond those necessary to support the war effort, had to be postponed until the convocation of a freely elected Constituent Assembly* and the establishment of democratic rule, presumably after the war had been won. In contrast, Miliukov's Central Committee colleague Nicholas Nekrasov and others urged accommodation with Soviet leaders. They supported in principle peace "without annexations and indemnities" and encouraged immediate social reforms, including workers' control over Russia's crucial industries and the railroad. "Conciliationists" presented their views at the Seventh Cadet Congress in March, but Miliukov held sway. Substantial party support may even have encouraged the Cadet leader, shortly afterwards, to issue his famous note of April 18, precipitating the April crisis and the collapse of the first provisional regime.

At the upper levels of the party, Miliukov's note and his subsequent opposition to coalition government produced deep rifts. Only one-third of the Central Committee supported his demand for complete Cadet withdrawal from the regime during the April crisis, and some, including M. M. Vinaver, V. D. Nabokov, and N. V. Nekrasov, now had grave doubts about Russia's military ability or even the desirability of prosecuting the war "to complete victory." Nekrasov, Minister of Transport in the provisional regime, demonstratively resigned from the Central Committee threatening to split the party in two. Other leading Cadets, including the Minister of Agriculture, A. I. Shingarev, began to work more energetically on reforms, showing themselves willing to reach some accommodation with moderate Soviet leaders in return for the latter's support for continued action at the front. At lower party levels, however, among the 180 or so local Cadet organizations that had organized by May in some sixty-six provinces and regions, the party's mood was moving rapidly to the Right. The collapse of all formal right-wing parties after February (*see* February Revolution) made local Cadet organizations attractive to thousands of conservative "March Cadets" hoping to protect their interests. Some provincial organizations, particularly in Moscow, retained conciliationist orientations, but by the end of May stout opposition to any efforts at "deepening" or "broadening" the Revolution had clearly become the dominant liberal view.

Cadets under these circumstances pressed what they called the principles of "*gosudarstvennost*," or "state consciousness," hoping to rally the nation to defend state interests over sectarian ones and insisting on respect for the law. Party schism was avoided in the face of what all perceived as a more profound crisis of anarchy and social revolution. In local City Duma elections (*see* Duma and Revolution) during late May and June, however, the limits of this appeal were clear. In their strongest centers of support, Moscow and Petrograd, the liberals could garner scarcely 20 percent of the vote. Cadet candidates were regarded, moreover, as representatives of the Right, in polar opposition to the radical Bolsheviks and in contrast to the moderate socialist center, which was rapidly assuming the broad middle ground Cadet leaders had once staked out for themselves. Under these conditions, Miliukov and others thought that it was useless to continue Cadet attempts to rule. Despite the start of the long awaited military offensive in mid-June, the Cadet leader led his Central Committee in bringing party representatives out of the government in early July, when a delegation of socialist ministers under A. F. Kerensky* agreed "illegally" to allow the Ukrainian Central Rada (*see* Central Rada; Ukraine, Revolution in) full competency in local Ukrainian affairs. Immediately thereafter, Bolshevik sailors attempted to seize power in the "July Days*."

In the sustained crisis that followed, Cadet "legalists" like Miliukov, P. I. Novgorodtsev, P. D. Dolgorukov, V. A. Maklakov*, and A. V. Tyrkova moved even further to the Right, rejecting any efforts at compromise with the Soviet leadership. At the Ninth Cadet Congress in late July, they urged the reestablishment of the death penalty, the postponement of the Constituent Assembly elections, and new measures to protect landlord rights, resolving "to dedicate all forces to saving the motherland." What these forces might be soon became clear at the Congress of Public Figures and the Moscow State Conference* in August, when voices were heard urging a military dictatorship under General L. G. Kornilov (*see* Kornilov Revolt). Conciliationists like N. M. Kishkin, N. I. Astrov, and N. V. Nekrasov, meanwhile, continued efforts to work with moderate socialists and the Left, although increasingly with a sense of abandonment and isolation. In fact, Russia's rapid social polarization was depriving the liberals of any but openly right-wing support.

By mid-August Miliukov and others made it clear that they would not oppose Kornilov's attempt to "suppress Bolshevism" and "establish order" in Petrograd, which clearly meant an attack on the provisional regime. Although not active instigators or participants in the plot, many Cadets clearly abandoned the government, now under Kerensky, in their sympathy for Kornilov and wholeheartedly supported his goals. This moral culpability gave credence to Bolshevik (*see* Russian Social Democratic Workers' Party [Bolshevik]) accusations against them in the aftermath of Kornilov's disastrous failure, and Cadets subsequently entered the last weeks of the Provisional Government discredited on all sides. Miliukov and F. F. Kokoshkin left immediately for the Crimea (*see* Crimea, Revolution in) as if fleeing arrest. Maklakov took up an ambassadorial appointment in France. Tyrkova and others withdrew to their country estates. In their absence, party conciliationists—M. M. Vinaver, N. M. Kishkin, M. S. Adzhemov, D. I. Shakhovskoi, and others—finally secured a temporary position of dominance in the Central Committee and, in mid-September, joined Kerensky's last cabinet, formally committed to the implementation of a forthright socialist program. They also organized a "peasant committee" and urged cooperation with moderate socialists in forthcoming Constituent Assembly elections, even to the extent of forming electoral blocs.

At the Tenth Cadet Congress in October, however, a majority once again lined up behind the forceful Miliukov. Convinced as he was that only a consolidation of right-wing forces could protect their interests and Russia's, a full-fledged civil war mentality now prevailed, making compromise resistance to Bolshevism impossible. Within ten days, Lenin's party seized power.

In the months and years that followed, Cadets continued their divided and sometimes contradictory struggle for what they regarded as Russia's state interests, working with the anti-Bolshevik forces of General A. I. Denikin*, Admiral A. V. Kolchak*, and Baron P. N. Wrangel*, arguing among themselves about "accommodating" the Left, struggling "from the depths" to preserve their vision of a legal Russian order, and suffering enormous deprivations. The Central

Committee went underground; Kokoshkin, Shingarev, and other party leaders were arrested and some were brutally murdered; many fled abroad. In Omsk, Cadets openly supported the dictatorship of Kolchak, and in Ekaterinidar and Rostov, moderates like Astrov tried vainly to hold Denikin's regime to some semblance of constitutional commitment. Finally, in Paris in July 1921 the party formally split apart as Miliukov, ironically, now turned full circle and led the conciliationist Cadets in a "new tactic" of accommodation and cooperation with the socialists and "the broad Russian masses"—views also supported by the left-Cadet dominated "Changing landmarks" group.

Such a policy might have been effective in 1917, as Nekrasov and others had urged, and at the very least might have contained right-wing (especially Kornilovite) opposition to the Provisional regime. Democratic Russia might possibly have limped to a constituent assembly had Kornilov's coup attempt been averted, supported by some semblance of military force. It might also have been possible to withdraw from active involvement in the war, if not sign a separate peace. Here in any case, in a policy of conciliation, was an opportunity not taken for Russia's liberal party to have attained political influence disproportionate to its actual strength in numbers. Instead, it might be argued, a majority of the party's leadership attenuated the very social polarization they ostensibly wanted to avoid by allowing Cadets to become the party of privileged Russia and the Right when true liberal statesmanship might have consistently recognized the need for compromise and conciliation.

William G. Rosenberg

Bibliography

Diakin, V. A. *Russkaia burzhuaziia i tsarism v gody pervoi mirovoi voiny, 1914–1917.* 1967.
Fischer, G. *Russian Liberalism.* 1958.
Pearson, R. *Russian Moderates and the Crisis of Tsarism, 1914–1917.* 1977.
Riha, T. *A Russian European: Paul Miliukov in Russian Politics.* 1967.
Rosenberg, W. G. *Liberals in the Russian Revolution.* 1974.
Spirin, L. M. *Klassy i partii v grazdanskoi voine v Rossii.* 1966.
Timberlake, C., ed. *Essays on Russian Liberalism.* 1972.
Volobuev, P. V. *Proletariat i burzhuaziia Rossii v 1917 g.* 1964.

The Cooperative Movement, 1917–1921. The Cooperative Movement was one of the most significant social and economic developments in rural Russia before 1918.

Credit and savings–loan associations, consumer societies, and dairy associations appeared in Russia during the 1870s. Only after 1905, however, did they develop into a coherent, primarily rural movement, sponsored by a cross-section of Russian society. During World War I* the cooperatives played an important role in providing food, clothing, and raw materials to the Russian army and urban population. In providing such assistance the cooperatives widened the scope of their activities to include the production and marketing of a bewildering variety of products, from butter, dried fruits, and cured meats to macaroni, candy, and shoes. Among other things, cooperatives bought fishing boats, refrigerated rail cars, electric stations, granaries, organized seed-cleaning and equipment-rental stations, and printing establishments. By 1917 the cooperatives' work resulted in the organization of producers' and consumers' unions such as those for tar, flax, and egg producers. These unions joined with the old established ones—the Moscow People's Bank, the Moscow Union of Consumer Societies, and the Union of Siberian Dairy Societies—to form a vast network for production, marketing, and financing. By 1917 there were 25,000 cooperative societies and 5,600 unions. Their 9 million members represented one-fourth of the Russian population. The growth of unions was so rapid during the war that the Moscow Union of Consumer Societies formed an umbrella organization for all of these organizations. This was the All-Russian Central Council of Trade Unions*, or Tsentrosoiuz. It had affiliates in London, New York, Stockholm, and Constantinople and continued working through the 1920s.

It was precisely the large number of organizations, the size of their membership, the vast number of economic enterprises, and their experience in large-scale grain procurements that made the cooperatives of such vital importance to both the Provisional Government* and the Bolsheviks (*see* Russian Social Democratic Workers' Party [Bolshevik]) in 1917. At the time the cooperatives appeared to be the only viable economic organizations still functioning in rural areas.

The initial response of the leaders of cooperation to the February Revolution* was one of elation. By March the Provisional Government had lifted tsarist restrictions on the cooperatives' activities. The leaders of the various unions thereupon formed the All-Russian Congress of Cooperative Unions and Committees. During its four meetings between March and October the Congress enunciated the policies cooperatives were to follow during this stormy period. The Congress also published its own newspaper, *Izvestiia soveta vse-rossiskikh kooperativnykh s'ezdov*. At the Congress' first meeting on March 25, cooperative leaders urged their members to maintain their traditional political neutrality and to continue to concern themselves with the economic welfare of the peasantry. However, political neutrality was necessarily compromised when Minister of Agriculture A. I. Shingarev gave the cooperatives the task of marketing grain and other supplies to alleviate the food crisis. When the Commission on Food Supply was formed in March, it was dominated by representatives from the Moscow Peoples' Bank, the Moscow Union of Consumer Societies, and the All-Russian Union of Unions. In addition to coopting the cooperatives to deal with food supplies, the Provisional Government also recruited some of the movement's leaders directly. S. N. Prokopovich became Minister of Trade and Industry in March and Minister of Food Supply in September. S. L. Maslov was appointed Minister of Agriculture in September. Well-known academics and agronomists, the backbone of the Cooperative Movement, worked in various capacities for the new government, particularly in the Ministry of Agriculture. Most of the individuals belonged to the Constitutional Democratic Party—Cadet* or were Socialist–Revolutionaries (*see* Socialist-Revolutionary Party).

The Cooperative Movement became politically fragmented between March and September, and its leaders turned to partisan politics. In March workers who had already belonged to consumer cooperatives decided to form their own "class" organizations that limited membership to workers only. By August there were 124 Workers' Cooperatives in urban areas, chiefly Moscow and Petrograd, with 511,665 members. These cooperatives were led by Mensheviks (*see* Russian Social Democratic Workers' Party [Menshevik]) and moderate socialists who had been leaders in the consumer movement since its inception in the 1890s. At the Workers' Cooperatives first Congress in August, E. D. Kuskova, proposed the organization of a new political party that would run its own candidates for election to the Constituent Assembly*. The Congress opted instead to support non-Bolshevik but socialist candidates. Some cooperators across Russia, nonetheless, ran on local cooperative tickets for election and as a whole received 100,000 votes. Only one candidate was actually elected, S. N. Prokopovich in Moscow, a Constitutional Democrat.

Political tensions also appeared at the September All-Russian Congress meeting. The participants were urged to have their organizations support a coalition of political groups that supported the Constituent Assembly. All members were asked to work for the economic welfare of all social classes and for the successful completion of the war. After the meeting, the All-Russian Union of Unions spent more than 1 million rubles on the printing and distribution of pamphlets exhorting the peasants to support the Pre-parliament (*see* Democratic Conference) and the Constituent Assembly.

The Bolsheviks and the cooperatives became adversaries for a variety of reasons. Lenin realized, as had the Provisional Government, that the network of cooperatives was of potential economic importance in building the new Soviet state, specifically in providing the urban population with food. The Bolsheviks were, however, faced with a dilemma: they had ignored the movement before 1917 and did not have any grass-roots support in rural cooperatives. The Communist Party had no way of controlling thousands of rural organizations, many of which were located in hostile territory during the Civil War (*see* Civil War in Russia). Furthermore, the Workers' Cooperatives in urban areas were led by Mensheviks. They, too, were not amenable to Bolshevik control. The cooperatives' hostility was clear from the outset. At its February 1918 meeting the All-Russian Cooperative Congress flatly stated that the traditional political neutrality and independence of the movement did not allow it to support the Soviet state. The Worker's Cooperative Congress in April maintained it would not cooperate with the new government. The Workers' Cooperative maintained its hostile stance throughout its meetings in 1918 and early 1919.

The Bolshevik's early legislation on cooperatives did not help change the attitude of cooperators. The first laws on cooperatives (April 12 and November 21, 1918 and March 20, 1919) essentially deprived the organizations of the freedoms they had gained in February 1917. The laws gradually tightened central control over the activities of the cooperatives and tried to determine the conditions of the membership. They created havoc in the existing organizations by insisting that every Soviet citizen belong to a cooperative. The organizations were not able to handle the volume of new members and broke down under the strain. Vocal protests among cooperators and also the failure of the party's own newly created consumer societies, *sovetskie lavki,* forced Lenin to back down. An uneasy truce was signed. The government once again allowed the organizations to run their internal activities. In return, the cooperatives agreed to work as part of the central economic planning system, the Supreme Council of the National Economy*, and act as distributors of food and consumer products for the government. By January 27, 1920, all types of cooperatives had been incorporated into one central organization, the All-Russian Union of Unions, which in turn was placed under the aegis of the Peoples' Commissariat of Food (Narkomprod, or Narodnyi Kommissariat Prodovol'stviia). While the leaders of cooperation signed a truce in Moscow, the situation in rural areas was more complicated and varied from country to country. In some areas, local councils of workers' deputies confiscated, at their own initiative, the cooperatives' property and distributed the goods among the local peasants. In other cases, returning soldiers took over the leadership and management of the associations. In some instances, cooperative leaders were shot. Active opposition to the Bolsheviks appeared in cooperatives in three areas of Russia during 1918. In Archangel N. V. Chaikovskii, the former leader of the Union of Flax Producers, joined the British forces and called on all members to fight the Bolsheviks. In the southern Ukraine members of the Moscow Union of Consumer Societies' affiliate supplied A. I. Denikin's* troops with food, although the actual amount is not clear. The most significant resistance to the Bolsheviks came from Siberian dairy cooperatives, chiefly from one of the largest unions, the Zakoopsbyt. These Siberian cooperatives were dominated by Socialist–Revolutionaries (*see* Socialist-Revolutionary Party). They supported General A. N. Grishin-Almazov in Novonikolaevsk and A. V. Kolchak* by providing food and money to them during the Civil War. Finally, even in the foreign affiliates of the All-Russian Union of Unions, old cooperative leaders such as A. M. Berkengeim, V. N. Zel'geim, and O. Lenskaia worked actively against the new government until 1920.

The cooperative organizations possessed a vast network for agricultural collection and distribution that was of considerable importance to the Bolsheviks to acquire. Lenin himself came to this conclusion. They nevertheless remained autonomous and, therefore, troublesome organizations. Their role as real and potential sources of opposition through the 1920s sealed off their chances for survival even before Stalin consolidated his power.

Anita Baker

Bibliography

Baron, Noah. *Russian Cooperation Abroad: Foreign Trade, 1917–1928.* 1930.
Blanc, Elsie T. *The Cooperative Movement in Russia.* 1924.

Bubnoff, J. V. *The Cooperative Movement in Russia*. 1917.
Ivanov, B. V. *Sibirskaia kooperatsiia v period oktiabr'skoi revoliutsii i grazhdanskoi voiny*. 1976.
Kabanov, V. V. *Oktiabr'skaia revoliutsiia i kooperatsiia, 1917—Mart, 1919*. 1973.
Kayden, Eugene M., and Alexis N. Antiseferov. *The Cooperative Movement in Russia during the War*. 1929.
Miliutin, V. P., ed. *Kooperatisiia v SSSR za desiat' let*. 1928.
Morozov, L. F. *Ot kooperatsii burzhuaznoi k kooperatsii sotsialisticheskoi*. 1969.

Cossacks. The Cossacks were military groups with a distinctive identity and history of their own. The term *Cossack* is the anglicization of the Russian *kazak* and the Ukrainian *kozak,* both of which derive, according to George Vernadsky, from the Turkic word for a free frontiersman. Originally, Cossacks dwelled on the frontier between the Russians and the Poles and the Turkic peoples in the South and East. The largest component of the early Cossack bands were escaped serfs. By the sixteenth century Cossack groups had formed along the Dnieper and Don rivers. Cossack society was roughly democratic. Leaders, referred to as *ataman* or *hetman,* and a Cossack general assembly, called *krug* or *rada,* debated current issues. Cossacks subsisted in large part by raiding neighboring territories and developing formidable military skills.

In the mid-eighteenth century, under Hetman Bohdan Khmelnitsky, the process of bringing the Cossacks under Muscovite control was greatly advanced. Thereafter, the Cossacks exercized local autonomy over lands ceded them by the tsarist government, while acknowledging the sovereignty of Moscow and agreeing to serve in the tsarist army, although as distinct units commanded by their own officers. Self-government was retained at the village (*stanitsa*) level. Integration into the centralizing tsarist state was not a smooth process, and the sixteenth and seventeenth centuries witnessed peasant uprisings in which Cossacks were prominent. Among the Cossack leaders were the legendary S. T. Razin, K. A. Bulavin, and E. I. Pugachev.

Over the centuries new Cossack *voiska* (host or community) were established. By the early twentieth century the total Cossack population numbered approximately 4.5 million, with slightly fewer than 300,000 in military service. The eleven hosts then in existence were, in order of size of population, Don, Kuban, Orenburg, Trans-Baikal, Terek, Siberian, Ural, Amur, Semirech'e, Astrakhan, and Ussuri. The hosts differed widely in size with the largest, Don, Kuban, and Orenburg, accounting for more than three-quarters of the total Cossack population. Cossacks were particularly famed for their cavalry units, which formed the largest element of the Cossack fighting forces but also possessed many artillery batteries and a number of infantry units. The special standing of the Cossack units was reflected in their distinctive uniforms, swords, and horses, all of which they provided themselves, unlike any other units of the Russian army. In addition to maintaining their traditional military duties, Cossack units during the last decades of tsarist rule came to be relied upon increasingly for internal security purposes. For example, Cossack units were very active in putting down peasant uprisings in 1905–1906. It became common to garrison units in the neighborhood of urban centers in order to have a ready and reliable weapon against industrial and political unrest.

Cossack lands were among the most fertile in Russia, and on them Cossacks engaged in agricultural pursuits. The industrial, mining, and commercial activity carried out on Cossack lands was done by non-Cossacks, referred to as *inogorodnye* (literally, people from different towns). The great majority of *inogorodnye,* however, were impoverished peasants attracted to the fertile Cossack lands. There they leased land or toiled in Cossack fields. Although in many areas they came to outnumber the native Cossacks, the *inogorodnye* were decidedly second-class citizens possessing few legal rights in the Cossack regions. Their inferior position and exploitation led the *inogorodnye* to increasing embitterment against the defiant Cossacks. This was not the only form of social tension within the Cossack *voiska*. Social stratification also arose among the Cossacks themselves. From about the mid-nineteenth century lands held by Cossack officers were transformed into hereditary property, thus transforming the officers into a hereditary caste, much the same as existed in Russian society at large. This violation of Cossack tradition challenged the solidarity of Cossackdom in the face of all other social elements, threatening to divide richer Cossacks from poorer Cossacks.

Cossack units served in World War I* in great numbers. They, as other components of the Russian armed forces, became disaffected with tsarism, both as a result of privations and suffering at the front and communications from the rear, testifying to a high level of inefficiency, corruption, and chaos. Thus in February 1917 the Cossacks, the last bulwark of tsarism, failed to support Nicholas II*, and in Petrograd a number of Cossack units actually went over to the cause of the Revolution.

In the aftermath of the February Revolution* soviets (councils) of Cossack deputies sprang up everywhere, much as was the case with all other segments of Russian society. In March a national body purporting to represent all Cossacks arose in Petrograd that was called the Soviet of the Union of Cossack Hosts. This group systematically championed rightist, although never monarchist, positions. In September 1917 a major conference of Cossack representatives was held at Vladikavkaz. Delegates from seven of the Cossack *voiska* agreed to establish the Southwestern League. A representative government organized on federal principles was to be established at Ekaterinodar in the Kuban *voiska*. Members of this Cossack federation were to be absolutely independent in the management of internal affairs but united in their opposition to Bolshevism (*see* Russian Social Democratic Workers' Party [Bolshevik]). Nothing came of the league, but it is significant for its articulation of the Cossack political program: preservation of traditional privileges, guaranteed by internal self-rule, and freedom from any egalitarian challenge from without.

Generally, during 1917 the Cossacks supported the Provisional Government*; thus they were called up to help put down the July Days*. Primarily, however, the Cossacks' attention was focused on parochial issues. In the *voiska* antagonism between *inogorodnye* and Cossack surfaced. For example, in May a conference of *inogorodnye* representatives of the Don *voiska* called for the elimination of Cossack privileges. Similarly, in the Kuban a joint Cossack-*inogorodnye* assembly broke apart in July with the withdrawal of Cossack deputies over the issue of Cossack privilege. The revolt of General L. G. Kornilov (*see* Kornilov Revolt) in August 1917 was initially supported by Cossack leaders, including the Soviet of the Union of Cossack Hosts. These Cossacks were concerned with the radicalization of Russian society and the absence of strong leadership at the helm of government.

In the October Seizure of Power* the Cossacks were essentially neutral. In the final hours of the Provisional Government* a Cossack squadron abandoned the defense of the Winter Palace. A. F. Kerensky* succeeded in rallying General P. N. Krasnov and a force of 700 Cossacks, but this force quickly disintegrated.

Cossack attitudes toward the new Soviet power were generally divided along lines of perceived interest. The prosperous and middle strata of the Cossacks sided largely with the White (*see* White Movement) forces. These elements feared the loss of privileges and property, as well as Cossack autonomy, local self-government, and ultimately Cossack identity. At the same time, all Cossacks tended to unite against the demands of the *inogorodnye*. Cossack allegiance to the White cause in the Civil War (*see* Civil War in Russia) was generally not philosophical: Cossacks opposed the Revolution because the *inogorodnye* supported it. There was no place for Cossack privilege in the midst of an egalitarian revolution. A. M. Kaledin*, *ataman* of the Don *voiska,* was exceptional for a Cossack in his philosophical adherence to the White cause, a position at odds with most of his constituents. The day following the seizure of power in the capital, Kaledin invited the members of the Provisional Government and other anti-Bolshevik elements to repair to Novocherkassk in the Don *voiska*. General M. V. Alekseev and others responded and began to organize resistance. At this juncture the differences between Kaledin and rank-and-file Cossacks came to the fore. The average Cossack was tired of war and merely wanted to be left alone. The presence of counterrevolutionary forces on Cossack lands, it was feared, might cause the Reds to attack. In these early days Cossacks were reluctant even to defend their own territory, preferring that this be accomplished by the Whites. When they did agree to fight, it was with the understanding that they would not be called upon to leave their own territory. Resentment by the White leaders to this recalcitrance caused V. S. Zavoisko, aide to L. G. Kornilov, to seek to overthrow Kaledin as *ataman* and replace him with Kornilov, mistakenly thinking that Kaledin was responsible for the lack of Cossack bellicosity. Nor was there always solidarity among the various Cossack hosts. When the Don Cossacks were driven from their own lands into the Kuban by the Red Army* in 1919, the Kuban Cossacks opposed taking the offensive, preferring merely to defend their own *voiska*. For that matter, the Kuban Cossacks were not unified within their own ranks. They were divided between a *chernomortsy* faction that leaned toward Ukrainian separatism and a *lineitsy* faction that favored a unified Russia.

In other regions, Cossacks also lined up against the Soviet regime. The Orenburg Cossack *ataman*, A. I. Dutov*, very early declared war on the Red Guard* units and local soviets in his area. On the Manchurian frontier the notorious bandit–warlord *ataman* of the Transbaikal Cossacks G. M. Semenov* and others formed the beginnings of resistance in that region and soon gained financial support from Britain and later Japan (*see* Siberia, Revolution in).

A significant reason contributing to Cossack adherence to the White cause was British ineptitude. In the period March-May 1918 several small Soviet republics were set up on Cossack territory but were within the administrative network of the revolutionary Russian Republic. The Don, Kuban-Black Sea, and Terek Soviet Republics were dominated by Bolshevik radicals, and their institution of a Red Terror helped in a significant way to push the Cossacks into the arms of the Whites.

All of this notwithstanding, many of the lower strata of the Cossacks, especially those from the front (*frontovniki*), favored the Bolsheviks. During the Civil War, a number of Cossack units favoring the Soviet cause were formed. Among the leaders of these units were P. V. Bakhturov, M. F. Blinov, B. M. Dumenko, N. D. Kashiring, and F. K. Mironov; the most renowned was Semen M. Budennyi*.

During the Civil War, the Cossacks constituted the largest single component, between one-half and two-thirds, of the forces of the Volunteer Army (*see* Civil War). Thus Cossacks were involved in most of the military actions of the period and constituted the Volunteer Army's greatest strength. The history of the struggle is not chronicled here; however, certain distinctive characteristics of the Cossack role in the Civil War must be noted. The first has already been mentioned, the reluctance of the Cossacks to fight beyond the boundaries of their own territories. Second was the Cossack propensity to engage in looting, a hallowed Cossack tradition. Third was the carrying out of anti-Semitic pogroms. All sources agree that the Cossacks were the most vicious of all of the White elements that participated in the pogroms. The number of pogrom victims has been variously estimated at between 100,000 and a million during the Civil War. The first two weaknesses or shortcomings were greatly lamented by the White leaders because they seriously impeded the war effort by hampering mobility and generating opposition to the White cause. In their anti-Semitism*, however, the Cossacks were echoing the oft-stated views of the White leaders themselves who often treated "Jewishness" and Bolshevism as equivalent.

On February 29, 1920, there was convened in Moscow the First All-Russian Congress of Working Cossacks. At this congress it was determined that the Cossacks did not represent a separate nationality and, therefore, did not qualify for autonomous rule within the Russian Republic. As a consequence, institutions of Soviet local government were extended to Cossack lands. With this, the Cossack hosts were disbanded, the existence of the Cossacks as a separate caste ended, and the incorporation of the Cossacks into the general population began. This process was advanced mightily by the collectivization of agriculture in the 1930s. In the later 1930s Cossack military, primarily cavalry, units were revived, only to be disbanded in the midst of World War II when their efficiency against modern weaponry was shown to be limited. In the USSR today, Cossackdom possesses no official standing but remains an honored tradition.

Bibliography

Longworth, Philip. *The Cossacks*. 1970.

Council of People's Commissars, 1917–1922. The Council of People's Commissars (Sovet narodnykh kommissarov, or Sovnarkom) was also referred to in official documents as the "Government" (Pravitel'stvo) of Soviet Russia.

As such, it was the successor of the Council of Ministers (Sovet Ministrov) of the imperial regime and the Provisional Government*. The Bolshevik (*see* Russian Social Democratic Workers' Party [Bolshevik]) leadership sought to deemphasize this continuity and to signal that its worker–peasant government was something qualitatively new by calling ministers "people's commissars" and ministries "people's commissariats." (I. V. Stalin* restored their pre–1917 appellations in 1946). It was seen as the task of Sovnarkom to take over the existing governmental machine and to transform it to implement Bolshevik policy.

The creation of such a body seemed to some Bolsheviks to be a contradiction of prerevolutionary concepts of the future "republic of Soviets," as expressed, for example, in V. I. Lenin's* *State and Revolution,* and the great power it assumed was assailed by successive internal opposition groups. To offset such criticism, the subordination of Sovnarkom to the All-Russian Central Executive Committee* of Soviets was repeatedly stressed, but such subordination was never effective, nor did Lenin and his fellow leaders intend it to be.

It took some weeks for Sovnarkom to take up its assigned role, owing partially to the noncooperation of a large part of the civil service, which regarded Bolshevik rule as illegitimate; in the meantime, the main instrument of rule was the Military Revolutionary Committee of the Petrograd soviet*. By late November, however, Sovnarkom was a regularly functioning body, and by early 1918 it had effective control of the administrative machine. Patterns of operation evolved in this period were perpetuated and developed after the transfer of the seat of government to Moscow in March.

Sovnarkom under Lenin numbered eighteen to nineteen members. Except for a brief period (November 1917-March 1918), when a handful of Left Socialist–Revolutionaries (*see* Left Socialist-Revolutionary Party) entered the government, they were all Bolsheviks. Initially, most were either top party leaders (notably V. I. Lenin, L. D. Trotsky*, and I. V. Stalin*) or men prominent in the Petrograd or Moscow party committees. In time, many of these veterans of the revolutionary underground were supplanted by Bolsheviks less prominent but better qualified by their training and experience for administrative responsibilities. From the beginning, men of upper- or middle-class background predominated, and the predominance grew over time.

The fact that Lenin was Chairman of Sovnarkom and held no other executive post (e.g., in the party's Central Committee) helped make it the most important organ of the early Bolshevik regime. Lenin's apartment opened onto the corridor at the Sovnarkom offices, where he spent most of his working day. Ably helped by his first Head of chancellery, V. D. Bonch-Bruevich*, Lenin devoted much effort to establishing structures and procedures, such as rules for standing and ad hoc subcommittees, for participation in and conduct of Sovnarkom meetings, for the preparation of agendas and circulation of properly documented agenda papers, and for interdepartmental consultations. At first Sovnarkom met every evening, heavy agendas often keeping it in session until well after midnight. Meetings grew progressively shorter and less frequent, and by 1921 they were being convened once a week. This was partially due to the better organization of business and partially due to the devolution of decision-making work to the Sovnarkom "commissions," especially the Little Sovnarkom and the Defense Council.

The Little Sovnarkom (Malyi Sovnarkom), set up at the end of 1917 on the model of the prerevolutionary Little Council of Ministers (Malyi Sovet ministrov) with the purpose of freeing the Sovnarkom proper from much second-level business, especially financial matters, gradually widened its powers and by 1920–1921 was giving preliminary consideration (and often final decision) to almost all questions referred for Sovnarkom attention. A small committee of relatively junior Bolshevik administrators, the Little Sovnarkom acquired its importance primarily as a result of the high value placed upon it by Lenin, who called it his "first assistant." He did not attend its meetings but, as the Sovnarkom chairman, was empowered personally to endorse its decisions, to return them for further consideration, or to refer them to the Sovnarkom proper. The Little Sovnarkom thus gave him unique leverage over the administration and development of government policy. Its noticeable decline from the end of 1921 was clearly connected with the deterioration of Lenin's health.

The Defense Council (Sovet oborony) was set up in November 1918 and vested with virtually unlimited powers to deal with the catastrophic economic and military crisis confronting the regime. A small subcommittee of senior Sovnarkom members chaired by Lenin, it quickly became the key decision-making body for mobilizing the economy and population for waging the Civil War (*see* Civil War in Russia) but not for the conduct of actual military operations. As the military crisis receded, it was decided to retain the Defense Council as an instrument for coordinating the national economy, and in March 1920 it was renamed the Labor and Defense Council (Sovet truda i oborony, or STO).

However, it significantly declined in importance, changing in effect from a body coordinated with the Sovnarkom proper to one subordinate to it.

The effective functioning of Sovnarkom depended substantially on its Chancellery (Upravlenie delami), whose staff numbered more than 100 in 1921, two-thirds of them administrative officials and the remainder auxiliary personnel. It serviced the meetings of the Sovnarkom proper, the Labor and Defense Council, the Little Sovnarkom, and the numerous other standing and ad hoc commissions; prepared agenda papers; arranged intercommissariat consultations; and monitored the implementation of decisions. It included a small Sovnarkom secretariat, which also served as Lenin's personal secretariat. Lenin involved himself closely in the operation of the Chancellery and relied heavily on its senior officials, especially V. D. Bonch-Bruevich and Lidia Fotieva (secretary from 1918), both of whom had worked with him in Geneva many years earlier.

Given the enormous resources of will and energy that Lenin devoted daily to Sovnarkom and the fact that its very structures and operational procedures had been molded to fit his unique authority and style, it is not surprising that it began to founder when his health forced him to take longer and longer spells away from his Sovnarkom office. Lenin at first sought to deal with this by improving procedural arrangements, especially relating to the distribution of business between the Sovnarkom proper, the Little Sovnarkom, and the Labor and Defense Council and by the appointment of Deputy Chairmen: A. I. Rykov* in May 1921, A. D. Tsiurupa in December 1921, and L. B. Kamenev* in September 1922 (L. D. Trotsky* turned down Lenin's proposal that he become the fourth deputy). But without a single authoritative and dynamic figure at the helm, policy disputes and administrative and jurisdictional conflicts became more and more difficult to resolve within the Sovnarkom system, and the burden of decision making increasingly passed from it to the party Central Committee and especially its Political Bureau (Politburo).

There were, however, additional reasons for this latter development. Despite Lenin's best efforts, Sovnarkom's effectiveness was impaired by serious operational defects. The work of the Little Sovnarkom and the network of special commissions did not prevent the Sovnarkom agenda from becoming overloaded with minor issues. Even more damaging were the rules for attendance, which allowed large numbers of non-Sovnarkom members to participate in Sovnarkom meetings as ''specialists'' or representatives of departmental interests, while permitting peoples' commissars to depute proxies. The more senior peoples' commissars, including Trotsky and Stalin, virtually stopped attending, concentrating on their activities within their own executive machinery and relying on their right to appeal to the party Central Committee when Sovnarkom failed to resolve matters to their satisfaction.

The authority of the party to determine the broad lines of policy, to take the most crucial decisions, and to settle major disputes had always been recognized, but Sovnarkom (including the Defense Council during the Civil War [see Civil

War in Russia]) had been responsible not only for supervising day-to-day administration but also for making most of the decisions necessary to implement party policies. The establishment of the Politburo as an effective and constantly functioning decision-making body in 1919 did not immediately change this, but its steadily increasing use as a "court of appeal" from Sovnarkom decisions prepared the scene for a massive shift of business from Sovnarkom to the Politburo during 1921–1922. Thus Lenin's incapacitation greatly accelerated this process but was not the sole cause of it. One further factor was the growth of full-time party officialdom in the provinces and its emergent role as supervisor and co-ordinator of all locally situated regime agencies and personnel; effective government now required information from and authority over both the government and party machines, and only the top-level party body could achieve this.

Among those disturbed by these developments was Lenin himself, who saw the body he had toiled so hard to make the major instrument of Bolshevik rule being relegated to an inferior role and who strongly believed that party bodies could effectively perform their proper role of determining the broad lines of policy and resolving the most contentious issues only if they avoided becoming bogged down in day-to-day details of government. He sponsored a resolution at the Eleventh Party Congress in March-April 1922 aimed at reversing these developments, which, however, had little effect because he was incapacitated by a stroke shortly thereafter. His last brief outburst of work in his Sovnarkom office at the end of 1922 was largely aimed at restoring Sovnarkom's effectiveness and authority, but it was too late to reverse the trend. In effect, the true government of the Soviet Republic was now the Politburo, and the Sovnarkom had been reduced to what it has since remained, one of the two main executive instruments of the Politburo (the other being the party Central Committee Organization Bureau—Orgburo, or the Secretariat) handling second-order business and directing the implementation of Politburo decisions by subordinate agencies.

T. H. Rigby

Bibliography

Carr, Edward Hallett. *The Bolshevik Revolution, 1917–23*. Vol. 1. 1950.

Genkina, E. V. *Lenin-predsedatel' Sovnarkoma i STO*. 1960.

Genkina, E. V. *Gosudarstvennaia deiatel'nost' V. I. Lenina, 1921–23 gg*. 1969.

Iroshnikov, M. P. *Sozdanie sovetskogo tsentral'nogo gosudarstvennogo apparata. Sovet Narodnykh Kommissarov i narodnye kommissariaty (oktiabr' 1917 g.-ianvar' 1918 g*. 1966.

Pietsch, Walter. *Revolution und Staat. Institutionen als Traeger der Macht in Sowjetrussland*. 1969.

Rigby, T. H. *Lenin's Government: Sovnarkom, 1917–22*. 1979.

Towster, Julian. *Political Power in the USSR 1917–47*. 1948.

Van den Berg, Gerard Pieter. *De Regering van Rusland en de Sovjet-Unie*. 1977.

Council of the Republic. *See* Democratic Council.

Courts. *See* Justice and the Judicial System, 1917–1921.

Crimea, Revolution in. The Crimean Peninsula was strategically located in relation to the military campaigns of the Russian Revolution and the Civil War (*see* Civil War in Russia).

Although only about 10,000 square miles in area, the peninsula has one of the warmest climates in Russia and juts into the Black Sea, making it a superb supply point or base for embarkation. The population of the Crimea is ethnically and religiously mixed. It includes Russians, Tatars, Greeks, Armenians, and Ukrainians. In 1897 about 34 percent of the population (196,834) were Crimean Tatars and 45 percent were Russians or Ukrainians. Even Soviet sources agree that the area was economically backward and did not possess an industrial working class of any size. The efforts of Ismail Bey Gasprinskii, who published a Turkish language newspaper, *Terdzhiman (Interpretation)*, in Bakchisarai in the 1880s, had awakened the national consciousness of the Crimean Tatars.

The First Crimean Tatar Conference met in Simferopol in March 1917. At the conference a young lawyer named Chelibidzhan (Tatar name, Noman Chelibi Cihan) was named *Mufti* or leader of the Crimean Tatars. The movement he led would take shape in July 1917 in the formation of the Crimean Tatar National Party (Milli Firka). This party controlled the Crimean Tatars until 1920 and effectively excluded both the Tatar liberals and the right-wing clergy from political power. Its program called for federal autonomy for Russia's national minorities and for the redistribution of Moslem church lands and popular control over Moslem religious institutions. The Russian and Ukrainian majority controlled the Crimea through the organs of the Provisional Government* and the Constitutional Democratic Party—Cadet* at that time, but in June and July the institutions representing the two ethnic groups, the Tatars and the Slavs, came into conflict with the Provisional Government, arresting Chelibidzhan briefly at the end of July.

The Bolsheviks (*see* Russian Social Democratic Workers' Party [Bolshevik]) sent Baltic sailors to the Crimea in mid–1917, and they began to experience some success under Zh. A. Miller in winning over the sailors of the Black Sea Fleet stationed in the city of Sebastopol. When all of the indigenous political groups opposed the October Seizure of Power*, the Bolsheviks sent down a new team of Baltic sailors to mobilize the Black Sea sailors in Sebastopol for military action. The sailors managed to seize the city of Sebastopol and the Sebastopol Soviet on December 24, 1917. On November 26 the Tatars convoked their own Constituent Assembly (Kurultai) in Bakchisarai. It had confirmed Chelibidzhan as leader of the Tatars (in this instance as leader of the Tatar National Directory at Simferopol), giving him executive power over all Tatar institutions, including the military forces. The National Conference also adopted a Western-style democratic constitution for the Tatars, including in it guarantees of civil rights and the abolition of the aristocracy and the clergy. A third Crimean government was created in Simferopol in October and November by the Russians and the Ukrainians in the Crimea, and it was dominated by the Socialist–Revolutionaries (*see* Socialist-Revolutionary Party). The government it created was called the Crimean Provincial Assembly.

In January 1918 the Soviet forces came into conflict with the Tatars, defeating them and executing their leaders. Ironically, in executing Chelibidzhan they eliminated one of the few Tatar leaders ready to negotiate with the new Soviet government. Between January and April Bolshevik strength began to erode. When the Soviet government attacked the Ukraine (*see* Ukraine, Revolution in), it lost a considerable amount of its support among the sailors of the Black Sea Fleet, most of whom were Ukrainian. Therefore, the formation of a Crimean Soviet government in March proved to be an empty gesture. In the middle of April elections to the Simferopol Soviet gave popular support to the Mensheviks (*see* Russian Social Democratic Workers' Party [Menshevik]) and Socialist–Revolutionaries, rather than the Bolsheviks. When the German army advanced into the Crimea in April, the Soviet government of the Crimea proclaimed itself an independent republic—the Taurida Republic, but its members were soon forced to flee from the Germans. They were captured by Russian and Tatar military units and executed.

After the German occupation ended in November 1918, there was a reshuffling of political groups that made it easier for a new Soviet Crimean government to be formed in May 1918. A Moslem general, Suleiman Sulkiewicz, formed a Moslem Corps and helped the Germans to clear the peninsula of Bolsheviks. When the Tatar National Assembly was called, it elected Sulkiewicz as its new leader. Although the Treaty of Brest-Litovsk* assigned the Crimea to Ukrainian jurisdiction, the German high command did not honor that clause. During the German occupation the Tatar National Assembly (Kurultai) served as a Crimean national parliament. A new Russian–Ukrainian government was formed out of representatives to that National Assembly in November, ending Tatar dominance. The Bolsheviks invaded the Crimea in April 1919 and enacted decrees favorable to the Tatars. But they, too, soon lost power, this time to the White (*see* White Movement) forces of General A. I. Denikin* in the second half of 1919. Denikin's anti-Tatar policies drove the remnants of Milli Firka into the arms of the communists. The Crimean Revolutionary Committee (Crimrevcom, or Krymrevkom) was formed with former members of Milli Firka participating. By October Soviet military forces occupied the Crimean Peninsula for the third time, and Baron P. N. Wrangel*, who commanded the remnants of the White Army, was forced to evacuate his troops.

The third Soviet government in the Crimea failed to come to terms with Milli Firka, and the peasants were soon alienated by the Bolshevik land program, which preserved large-scale property in the form of state farms. In May 1921 M. Sultangaliev* presented a report to the central Soviet government in Moscow criticizing the conduct of the Crimean Bolsheviks on the question of land and calling for active recruitment of Tatars into the party. His report was accepted in November 1921, and at that point the Autonomous Crimean Socialist Soviet Republic was established with Iu. P. Gaven at its head.

Bibliography

Fisher, Alan W. *The Crimean Tatars*. 1978.
Pipes, Richard. *The Formation of the Soviet Union*. 1968.
Zenkovsky, Serge. *Pan-Turkism and Islam in Russia*. 1960.

Czechoslovak Legion. The Czechoslovak Legion, like the Latvian Riflemen (*see* Latvia and The Russian Revolution), was a foreign military group in Russia during the October Seizure of Power* that played a role in the outcome of the Revolution out of all proportion to its size. It originated as the First Czechoslovak Brigade in 1917. It was created from prisoners of war and deserters captured by the Russians. Those Czechoslovak prisoners who volunteered to fight the Central Powers on behalf of the Provisional Government of Czechoslovakia were united in a Czechoslovak Infantry Regiment in February 1916 and became a division in July 1917 and, finally, a brigade in the same year. The government that authorized the formation of the Czech units, the Provisional Government of Czechoslovakia, had been created in 1915 by the Czechoslovak National Council headed by Thomas G. Masaryk. It had established a branch inside Russia in the hope of gaining support from both the Russian imperial government and the Czechoslovak prisoners of war for the creation of an independent Czechoslovak republic by fighting the Austrian Empire and its allies.

The First Czechoslovak Brigade fought on the Ukrainian front under the command of a Russian officer, General V. N. Shokhorov. Although it was under the military command of the Russians, they had considerable autonomy and, like the rest of the Russian imperial army (*see* Army of Imperial Russia in World War I) they enjoyed considerable self-government through the formation of soviets after Army Order Number One was issued by the Petrograd Soviet*. After the February Revolution* the Czechoslovak Brigade was subject to the Czechoslovak National Council in Russia (whose Presidium consisted of Prokop Maxa, Bohumir Cernich, and Jiri Klecanda) on political and diplomatic affairs. The Czechoslovak Brigade also committed itself to non-interference in the internal affairs of Russia.

On October 9, 1917 the Prime Minister of the Provisional Government* of Russia, A. F. Kerensky*, elevated the Brigade to corps status, though it is usually referred to as the Czech Legion. The new title was the Czechoslovak Army Corps in Russia. When the October Seizure of Power took place, Masaryk telegrammed the Council of the Corps and ordered it to maintain strict neutrality. The Czechoslovak Corps did not go along, however, with Soviet efforts to achieve an armistice with the Central Powers. They declared that the Czechoslovak Army Corps, then about 40,000 troops, were still in a state of war with the Central Powers. On January 18, 1918 in Kiev, the Czech National Council in Russia declared that their forces would continue to fight until they were defeated and an independent Czechoslovak state was achieved. The French government declared that the Czechoslovak army had belligerent status and the National Council on January 22, 1918 declared that the Czechoslovak Army Corps in Russia considered itself to be part of the Czechoslovak army in France. However, both the French government and the Czechoslovak National Council in Russia agreed that the Ukraine (*see* Ukraine, Revolution in) was not defensible, and on February 18, 1918 the Czechs came to an agreement with the Soviet government to leave Russia for France, boarding seventy-two trains bound for Vladivostok and evacuating eastward through Siberia and Eastern Russia.

On March 15, 1918 the Czechoslovak leaders met with representatives of the new Soviet government, including A. A. Andreev and I. V. Stalin*. V. I. Lenin* had agreed to the plan for the evacuation of Czechoslovak troops providing that it was completed with despatch, and he ordered all local soviets to cooperate. He was eager to conclude the peace treaty with Germany, and felt that the continued presence of belligerent troops on Russian soil jeopardized the peace with Germany.

On March 20, 1918 the seventy trains of the Czechoslovak Army Corps were stopped at Omsk on orders from the local soviet. Although they were allowed to resume their movement six days later, Stalin added some new limitations, indicating that the Soviet government was having some second thoughts. He ordered that they proceed "not as fighting units, but as a group of free citizens, taking with them a certain quantity of arms for self-defense against the attacks of counter-revolutionists." (Bunyan, 1976, p. 81). They were allowed to keep only ten rifles per hundred men.

For a short time the Soviet government toyed with the idea of building the new Red Army* around the trained Czech fighting force. Encouraged by meetings with a few Czech communists, Lenin had ordered L. D. Trotsky* to begin to build the Red Army by recruiting as many members of the Czechoslovak Army Corps as possible. Trotsky announced the founding of the Red Army on March 21, 1918 and opened negotiations with the Czechoslovaks and with French leaders about the use of Czech troops as the nucleus of that army. Trotsky suggested to the French the prospect of reopening the eastern front against the Germans with the new Red Army. When Czech and French leaders refused to cooperate (the French were not sure of the reliability of the Czechs), Czech communists were sent to use peaceful persuasion with the Legion on their trains. The Soviet government was successful in recruiting war prisoners in Russian prison camps, recruiting first 15,000, then by April, approximately 20,000 prisoners of war. At that point 40 to 50 percent of the Red Army recruits were drawn from this source (*see* Internationalists). But only 150 Czech soldiers could be induced to leave the Czechoslovak Army Corps and join the Red Army.

The whole situation changed when the Japanese landed troops in Vladivostok on April 4 and the British followed with a token force of their own. Trotsky ordered the movement of the Czechs toward Vladivostok stopped on April 7,

1918. Though he rescinded that order two days later, the Czechs warned on April 14, 1918 that they were dissatisfied with the innumerable delays imposed by the Soviet government and that, therefore, they would no longer turn over their arms, and would try to obtain more arms and ammunitions and take control of the locomotives they were using and any fuel along the way. Both English and French leaders stepped up the pressure on the Western Allies to use the Czech Legion to support British and Japanese intervention in Siberia (*see* Siberia, Revolution in). At this point the Czechs were a hundred miles from the White forces of Ataman G. Semenov*. Toward the end of April Soviet authorities were approached with a different proposal, namely, that half of the Czech Legion be re-routed north to be shipped to fight on the Western Front.

These plans were interrupted by an incident in Siberia. On May 18 Moscow learned of a confrontation between the Czech troops and the local soviet in Cheliabinsk. Trotsky ordered all Czech troops to be removed from the trains and drafted into the Red Army or labor battalions. On May 24, 1918 Trotsky ordered that "Every armed Czech found on the railway is to be shot on the spot" (Bunyan, 1976, p. 96). At the time this decision was made, the Czech- oslovak Army Corps probably outnumbered the troops of the entire Red Army, which, in any case, was mostly deployed elsewhere in Russia.

The decision to try to disarm the Czechoslovak Army Corps proved to be one of the most disastrous errors made by the new Soviet government. The Czech- oslovak Army Corps was trained and armed and occupied all of the railroad stations along the Trans-Siberian Railroad. The Czechs were in a formidable strategic position in relation to the weaker military forces of the new Soviet government. Nonetheless, on May 21 Trotsky had arrested the political leaders of the Czechoslovaks in Moscow and forced them to issue an order to their troops to surrender their army to Soviet authorities. The Red Army was ordered to immediately force the Czechoslovaks into either the Red Army or labor battalions. The Czechoslovak Army Corps responded to these orders on May 21 by gathering 120 delegates in Cheliabinsk, and they decided to appoint a new three-man Provisional Executive Committee to direct the renewed movement eastward, using force against Soviet troops if necessary. The conflict between the Czechs and the Russians began on May 25, 1918 when Soviet forces attacked a Czech train near Omsk. The Czechs returned their fire, in effect, marking the beginning of the Civil War (*see* Civil War in Russia).

The uprising of the Czechoslovak Army Corps was precipitated by the bad judgment of the Soviet leaders. It placed the main artery of the Russian Empire, the Trans-Siberian Railroad, in the hands of enemy troops. The Czechoslovak Army Corps occupied most of the important cities and strategic points along the railroad and began negotiating with the anti-Soviet forces and foreign powers for help in achieving their evacuation of Russia.

Soviet historians like to portray the Czechoslovak rebellion as a conspiracy directed and financed by the Western Powers. Though it is true that Great Britain and France had allocated money for the support of the Czechoslovak Army Corps before the Soviet seizure of power, little of those funds actually reached the Czechs before their revolt. Most of their provisions had been supplied first by the imperial government, and then by the Soviet government and the local soviets in Siberia. Although the Czech rebellion did follow Japanese intervention in Siberia, and the allies discussed the possibility of using Czech troops to strengthen the intervention in the East, the Czech National Council never gave its approval to any plan except the transport of Czech troops to the Western Front. Allied effort did not bring on the rebellion of the Czechoslovak Army Corps, but it certainly encouraged the Western powers to proceed with their plans to intervene, ostensibly to rescue the Czechs, but in fact to use the Czechs as a counterpoise to the Japanese and the Bolsheviks.

By June 1918 the Czechs had seized all of the major cities and railway junctions along the Trans-Siberian Railroad, including Vladivostok, and had established a cooperative relationship with the counterrevolutionary military forces in each area and with the Japanese interventionists. The Japanese had 70,000 troops in Siberia by November 1918, in order, they said, to help the Czechs to evacuate. In August 1918 the United States landed an infantry division, also, they said, to help the Czechs to evacuate.

As the only fully organized and armed fighting force in Siberia, the Czechoslovak Army Corps became the catalyst for military actions by Japanese interventionists, Cossack adventurers, like Ataman G. Semenov, and scattered counterrevolutionary forces. Along the way the Czechs found it convenient to overthrow the local Soviet governments established along the Trans-Siberian Railway.

The armistice in World War I* in November 1918 strengthened the arguments in the West for armed intervention against the new Soviet government in Russia, but it also deprived them of their chief internal ally, the Czechoslovak Army Corps. The Czechs no longer regarded themselves as belligerents and refused to continue to fight. The Siberian All-Russian Directory (*see* Committee of Members of the Constituent Assembly; Siberia, Revolution in) which the Czechs had supported began to crumble and Admiral A. V. Kolchak* seized control of the counterrevolutionary movement.

In the end Kolchak's failures would place him at the mercy of the retreating Czechoslovak Army Corps. While fleeing from his failures in western Siberia he was forced to place himself under Czech protection. At Irkutsk the Czechs decided to surrender Kolchak to the local city government, which called itself the Political Center, in order, to obtain safe passage through the city. Kolchak was executed in Irkutsk on February 7, 1920, on the same day that the Czechoslovak Army Corps also decided to surrender the Tsar's gold reserve, which they had picked up along the way to the Soviet government to insure their agreement to Czech withdrawal. The gold reserve would remain in Irkutsk under joint Russian/Czech guard until the Czech evacuation was completed. By November 30, 1920, the evacuation was completed and more than 68,000 people left, including about 56,000 Czechoslovak soldiers.

Bibliography

Bradley, John. *La Legion tchecoslovaque en Russia.* 1965.
Bradley, John. *Allied Intervention in Russia 1917–20.* 1968.
Bradley, John. *Civil War in Russia 1917–20.* 1975.
Bunyan, James, ed. *Intervention, Civil War and Communism in Russia.* 1976.
Fic, Victor M. *The Bolsheviks and the Czechoslovak Legion.* 1978.
Fic, Victor M. *Revolutionary War for Independence and the Russian Question.* 1977.
Hoyt, Edwin P. *The Army Without a Country.* 1967.
Kennan, George F. *The Decision to Intervene.* 1967.

D

Daghestan. Daghestan was a remote mountainous province in the northeastern end of the Caucasus between the Caucasus Mountains and the Caspian Sea. One of the most backward areas in Russia, it was the home of a radical Moslem movement called Muridism, a form of Sufism. This movement sought the inspiration of divinely appointed religious leaders, *imams,* who would be granted absolute power. The hero and model for these religious leaders was the nineteenth-century leader of Moslem resistance to Russian imperialism, Shamil.

It is difficult to speak of a Daghestan national movement, since there are about thirty nationalities in the area. Various national movements attracted the more educated and urban inhabitants of the region, but the religious movements dominated the more backward and less literate peoples. The nationalists called a meeting of mountain people in September 1917 in Vladikavkaz. There they formed the Union of Mountain Peoples. Their program called for the union of all Moslem groups in the Caucasus into a single state. But the friction between this group and the more extreme religious groups frustrated the ambitions of both. By the end of 1917 full-scale war broke out between the Moslem mountain tribes and the inhabitants of the cities in the plains.

A Daghestan Social Democratic group had been formed before World War I* in Petrovsk and functioned from 1906 until 1911 under the leadership of I. V. Malygin, a member of the Russian Social Democratic Workers' Party (Bolshevik)*. Although a soviet was formed in Petrovsk-Port in May 1917, it was dominated by Socialist–Revolutionaries (*see* Socialist-Revolutionary Party) and Mensheviks (*see* Russian Social Democratic Workers' Party [Menshevik]). About this time a group calling itself the Daghestan Socialist Group was formed including D. Korkmasov among its leaders. Its membership was drawn primarily from the intelligentsia in the city and represented many different political views, including that of nonparty socialists, Left Socialist–Revolutionaries (*see* Left Socialist-Revolutionary Party), and Bolsheviks. At the end of November a Bol-

shevik, U. D. Buinaksii, persuaded the Petrovsk Soviet to form a military revolutionary committee with him at its head. Using the Daghestan Socialist Group
and the Military Revolutionary Committee of Petrovsk as a nucleus, the Bolsheviks were able to mobilize popular support behind the Red Army* when it
entered Petrovsk and Temir-Khan-Shura in April and May 1918. In July 1918
the First Congress of Soviets of Daghestan met in Temir-Khan-Shura. But by
the end of 1918 Daghestan was conquered by White forces under the command
of Colonel L. F. Bicherakovy. Forced underground, the Bolsheviks amalgamated
with the Daghestan Socialist Group to form the Daghestan Regional Committee
of the Russian Communist Party in February 1919.

White armies under General A. I. Denikin* gained control of Daghestan in
May and June of 1919 and drove the Eleventh and Twelfth Red Armies under
G. K. Ordzhonikidzhe* into the mountains. Because of his hostility toward the
national aspirations of the local inhabitants, Denikin's forces ended up in October
and November 1919 involved in a war with the local inhabitants as well as the
Red Army. His policies on the National Question* brought together groups that
would not have united in any other cause. Lenin decided in March 1920 to put
all Bolshevik operations in the Caucasus under the centralized leadership of
trusted party members and appointed the Caucasian Bureau* (Kavburo) under
the able leadership of Ordzhonikidzhe and S. M. Kirov* to carry out the task
of winning control of that area. In Daghestan they were able to capitalize on
Denikin's deficiencies and bring together North Caucasian nationalists, religious
leaders, and socialists to form a base of operations for the reconquest of the
Caucasus from the White forces (see White Movement) and the Turks. Ordzhonikidzhe promised the local inhabitants that none of their customs or traditions
would be affected by the arrival of the Red Army and urged them to unite in
the common struggle under the command of General M. N. Tukhachevskii. In
Daghestan the chief native communist figure was D. Korkmasov.

Most of the cities of Daghestan were reconquered in a major offensive launched
by the Red Army from Russia in the Spring of 1920, with political leadership
being provided by the Caucasian Committee. The Commissar of Nationalities
himself, I. V. Stalin* would visit Daghestan in the spring of 1920 to inspect the
situation and take part in the preparations for the formation of a Daghestan
Republic. In January 1921 a decree of the All-Russian Central Executive Committee* of the Russian Soviet Federative Socialist Republic (RSFSR) created the
Daghestan Autonomous Soviet Socialist Republic within the RSFSR. In the
spring of 1921 there was one last unsuccessful effort on the part of Muridism
to mobilize Moslem resistance to Soviet domination in the form of a mountaineer
uprising led by the Imam Nazhmudin of Gotzo (Gotsinski), Said-bey, and Ali
Khanov.

Bibliography

Pipes, Richard. *The Formation of the Soviet Union.* 1968.
Sovetskaia istoricheskaia entsiklopediia. Vol. 4. 1963.

Dal'biuro. *See* Far Eastern Bureau.

Dan, F. I. *See* Gur'vich, Fedor Il'ich.

Dashnaks (Dashnaktsutiun). This is the Russian name for the Armenian National Party. In Armenian the full name of the party is Haigagan Heghapokhakan Dashnaksutiun (Armenian Revolutionary Federation). The party was founded in 1890 in Tiflis. Its program resembled that of the Russian Socialist-Revolutionary Party* and, like the Socialist–Revolutionaries (S–R's), they used terror as an instrument to achieve their program. However, the Dashnaks directed their energies primarily against the Ottoman Turks in a struggle to achieve national self-determination. Before the Revolutions of 1917 the party focused its attention primarily on arming and training Turkish Armenians, originally for the purpose of self-defense, although once trained, these Armenians were eventually organized into regular military formations.

When World War I* broke out, the sympathies of the Dashnaks were clearly for Russia and the Western Allies, because they believed that the only hope of any form of independence for Armenia lay in their hands. The leading Dashnaks even formed an Organizing Committee of the Armenian Volunteer Groups in Tiflis to help the Allied cause. This was one of the reasons for the famous massacre of the Armenians of eastern Asia Minor by the Turks in 1915. In the years of the Revolution and Civil War in Russia*, the Dashnaks played an important role in the formation of the Transcaucasian Republic (*see* Armenia, Revolution in; Transcaucasia, Revolution in). By December 1920 Turkish Armenia had been annexed by Turkey, and Russian Armenia had become the Armenian Soviet Socialist Republic.

Bibliography

Hovannisian, Richard G. *Armenia on the Road to Independence.* 1967.

Decemists. *See* Democratic Centralists.

Defeatism. Defeatism or revolutionary defeatism was the position taken by V. I. Lenin* at the international socialist conference at Zimmerwald, Switzerland, in September 1915 (*see* World War I). He urged all of the socialist parties represented at the conference to turn the imperialist war into civil war, and to call for the creation of a new international that would exclude those socialist parties that supported their country's capitalist leaders in World War I. In Russia itself, Lenin argued, socialists should call for the defeat of the tsarist government and refuse to help in the war effort in any way. This argument was directed against Defensism*, the position taken by many socialists of every persuasion, including Lenin's former mentor G. V. Plekhanov* and the Menshevik (*see* Russian Social Democratic Workers' Party [Menshevik]) I. G. Tsereteli*. Many prominent socialists who were opposed to the war, like L. D. Trotsky* and N. I. Bukharin*, countered that Lenin's position was somewhat oversimplified, and they tended to adopt the more moderate slogan of a "democratic peace without annexations." Lenin also differentiated himself from the "Internationalists"* by emphasizing the right of every nationality to national self-determination (*see* National Question and the Russian Revolution).

Bibliography

Baron, Samuel H. *Plekhanov.* 1963.
Daniels, R. V. *The Conscience of the Revolution.* 1960.
Ferro, Marc. *The Great War, 1914–1918.* 1969.
Haimson, Leopold. *The Mensheviks.* 1974.

Defensism. Defensism was the position taken by most of the European socialist parties toward World War I*. They argued that they must endorse and support their own national governments in the national war effort because that was necessary to sustain the progress achieved in social programs. V. I. Lenin*, leader of the Bolsheviks (*see* Russian Social Democratic Workers' Party [Bolshevik]), opposed defeatism*, arguing that support for the war was simply support for capitalism and that both in Russia and Europe socialists should use the strains of war as an opportunity to further class conflict and revolution and turn the imperialist war into civil war. Lenin espoused his position against the majority of "Defensists" at the international socialist conference in Zimmerwald, Switzerland, in September 1915.

Lenin's former mentor G. V. Plekhanov* was one of the most prominent Russian socialist leaders to adopt a "Defensist" position from the outset. He urged Russian socialists to support the war effort in every way and to postpone the political and class struggle until the war had ended. The prominent Menshevik (*see* Russian Social Democratic Workers' Party [Menshevik]) leader I. G. Tsereteli* was able to impose his "revolutionary defensism" on the Petrograd Soviet* until the autumn of 1917. He was able to persuade the Menshevik and Socialist-Revolutionary (*see* Socialist-Revolutionary Party) members of the Soviet to join with bourgeois political leaders in the formation of a coalition government and to issue an appeal for an international socialist conference that would join in appeals to all belligerent governments to end the war.

Bibliography

Baron, Samuel H. *Plekhanov.* 1963.
Daniels, R. V. *The Conscience of the Revolution.* 1969.
Ferro, Marc. *The Great War, 1914–18.* 1969.
Haimson, Leopold. *The Mensheviks.* 1974.

Democratic Centralists (or Decemists). A faction within the Russian Communist Party (*see* Russian Social Democratic Workers' Party [Bolshevik]) in 1919. The Decemists were a faction that tried to return to the conception of democratic centralism presented by V. I. Lenin* in the Third Party Congress in

London in April 1905. At that time Lenin endorsed a decentralized political organization, pluralism, and freedom of criticism for his Marxist movement. Most of the leaders of the faction were ideologues who had been Left Communists (*see* Left Communism) in 1918. They included V. M. Smirnov*, T. V. Sapronov, V. N. Maksimovskii, N. Osinskii*, and A. S. Bubnov*.

Osinskii assumed a position of leadership in challenging the party heads on matters of party organization at the Eighth Party Congress in March 1919. Essentially, he attempted to eliminate the domination of the party Presidium and transfer power to the popularly elected soviet institutions by proposing that the party Presidium be merged with the Council of People's Commissars* (Sovnarkom) and that the All-Russian Central Executive Committee* actively employ its legislative responsibilities. Although approved in principle at the Eighth Party Conference in December 1919, his reforms were never really implemented.

At the Ninth Congress of the Russian Communist Party in March 1920, the Decemists tried to oppose both Lenin's insistence upon one-man management and L. D. Trotsky's* efforts to militarize labor at the expense of trade union autonomy, opposing those notions with their own principle of collegial leadership for all socialist institutions. Their efforts to affirm democratic principles in the new Soviet state failed at least in part because those principles were not consistent with the demands placed upon the revolutionary state by the strains of the Civil War (*see* Civil War in Russia) and also because they attempted to change the character of the Bolshevik Party by mere institutional reforms. All of the leaders of this faction were eliminated during the Great Purges of the Thirties.

Bibliography

Daniels, R. V. *The Conscience of the Opposition.* 1969.
Wolfe, B. *Three Who Made Revolution.* 1948.

Democratic Conference (or Democratic State Conference). The Democratic Conference was an effort to begin creating a permanent democratic government before the Constituent Assembly* met. After the elections to the Constituent Assembly were postponed from September to November by the cabinet of the Provisional Government* and the Kornilov Revolt* dramatized the dangers of procrastination in settling the character of the new revolutionary government, the All-Russian Central Executive Committee* of Soviets issued a call on September 3 for an assembly to be called later in the month to represent all of the popular organizations and serve in a consultative capacity to the Provisional Government. The sponsors of the proposal, chiefly Socialist–Revolutionaries (*see* Socialist-Revolutionary Party) and Mensheviks (*see* Social Democratic Workers' Party [Menshevik]), believed that such a conference would lay the groundwork for an all-socialist democratic government.

V. I. Lenin* was already persuaded, however, that the soviets could be controlled by the Bolsheviks (*see* Russian Social Democratic Workers' Party [Bolshevik]) and that the soviets could form their own government, especially after the Petrograd Soviet* endorsed a Bolshevik resolution on August 31 and the Moscow Soviet* on September 5. Despite Lenin's conviction that the calling of a Democratic Conference should not be encouraged, the Bolsheviks worked hard to gain strong representation at the meeting. In the end, though, the Bolsheviks won only about one-sixtieth of the seats. They continued to support the efforts of the Democratic Conference until they received two letters from Lenin on September 15 ordering them to prepare for an armed uprising and abandon the conference.

The Democratic Conference met from September 14 to 22, and it revealed more disagreement than agreement among the other socialist parties. In the end the conference could not decide on the question of participation by the bourgeois (or liberal) political parties in any future coalition government. With the support of the Bolshevik delegation, the meeting decided to refer that question to a new permanent representative body that would meet until the Constituent Assembly was elected. At various times this new body was called the Democratic Council*, the Pre-Parliament, or the Council of the Republic.

Bibliography

Browder, P., and Kerensky, A. *The Russian Provisional Government.* Vol. 3. 1961.
Rabinowitch, Alexander. *The Bolsheviks Come to Power.* 1976.

Democratic Council (or Pre-Parliament, Council of the Republic). A permanent representative body chosen by the Democratic Conference* from its own membership was to begin to formulate plans for a democratic government for Russia in 1917.

The question of Bolshevik (*see* Russian Social Democratic Workers' Party [Bolshevik]) participation in the Democratic Council became a stormy issue within the party. V. I Lenin* had opposed participation in the Democratic Conference and was even more adamant about participation in the Pre-Parliament. Writing from temporary exile in Finland, he urged Bolshevik leaders to boycott the forthcoming Pre-Parliament and to prepare for armed insurrection in the name of the Soviet government. The decision to add 150 representatives of the propertied classes to the 367 delegates already chosen from the Democratic Conference seemed to confirm Lenin's fears that the Pre-Parliament was simply a weapon of the Provisional Government* against a revolutionary struggle for power with the soviets.

The Central Committee of the Russian Communist Party (Bolshevik)* (*see* Russian Social Democratic Workers' Party [Bolshevik]) met on September 21, 1917, with the Bolshevik delegation to the Democratic Conference and voted in favor of participation, essentially a rejection of Lenin's request for boycott and preparations for an armed insurrection. On September 23 the All-Russian Central Executive Committee* of Soviets met with soviet delegates from the Democratic Conference and endorsed a nationwide Congress of Soviets for October 20. On September 24, 1917, the Bolshevik Central Committee ordered its delegation to the Pre-Parliament to subordinate its activity there to the mass struggle to win popular support for the transfer of power to soviets at the forthcoming nationwide Congress of Soviets. Under continued pressure from Lenin through his letters to the Central Committee and the left-wing leaders in the Central Committee, that group finally decided at a meeting on October 5 to walk out of the Pre-Parliament when it met on October 7. Only L. B. Kamenev* disagreed with this decision.

When the Pre-Parliament opened on October 7, L. D. Trotsky* denounced the Provisional Government and the Pre-Parliament and called for the transfer of power to the soviets. Then he and the whole Bolshevik delegation marched out.

On October 24 A. I. Kerensky, Prime Minister of the Provisional Government, appeared before the Democratic Council and asked for strong support to deal with the impending Bolshevik attempt to seize power in the name of the soviets. Although he received a resounding ovation, the endorsement he expected from the Pre-Parliament was not forthcoming. Once again, those meeting could not agree on a common course of action. On the following day the Pre-Parliament was dispersed by soldiers and sailors acting on the orders of the Bolshevik dominated Military Revolutionary Committee. Trotsky announced to the Petrograd Soviet that afternoon that the Provisional Government and the Democratic Council were overthrown.

Bibliography

Browder, P., and Kerensky, A. *The Provisional Government, 1917.* Vol. 3. 1961.
Rabinowitch, A. *The Bolsheviks Come to Power.* 1976.

Demography. In the decades between the death of Peter I and the first All-Russian census of 1897, the population of the Russian Empire grew rapidly due to geographic expansion and a natural increase of the Russian population. Although hard data from the period before 1897 are meager and unreliable, it has been estimated by F. Lorimer that the Russian population (defined as Russians, Belorussians, and Ukrainians) of the empire grew at an average per annum rate of 13 per 1,000 from 1895 to 1897. The nature of this demographic growth was revealed in the first systematic national census in 1897.

According to that census, the population of the Russian Empire was 125 million, 95 million of whom were defined as Russians. The vast majority (85 percent) of the population lived in rural areas. European Russia was, by far, the most densely populated region of the empire. Nationally, population density stood at 19 persons per square kilometer. But in European Russia, only the sparsely populated Northwest region had such low density. The most densely populated regions were the Northern Ukraine (55 persons per square kilometer), the Southwest (50 persons per square kilometer), and the Center (46 persons per square kilometer). Within those regions, certain provinces were very densely populated, for example, Moscow (73 per square kilometer) and Kiev (70 per square kilometer). The Siberian and Central Asian regions remained sparsely populated even though the rate of peasant migration from European to Asiatic Russia began to increase dramatically from 1880. The "high tide" of migration to Siberia in the pre-revolutionary period occurred in the first decade of the twentieth century when the per annum rate was 226,000.

Excluding geographic expansion, the rapid increase in the population of the Russian Empire in the nineteenth century was due to the maintenance of a high birth rate and a gradually declining death rate. Ascertaining a precise birth rate is impossible because births were, in all likelihood, underreported. However, in 1897 the birth rate was about fifty births per thousand; the death rate was about thirty-three per thousand. The ethnic heterogeneity of the Russian Empire meant that within its borders very different patterns of nuptiality and marital fertility could be found. A recent study by A. Coale, B. Anderson, and E. Harm has revealed that in 1897 the average age of marriage decreased as one traveled from the Baltic lands (average mean age of marriage, 25.0 years) through European Russia (average mean age of marriage, 20.0–21.0 years) to the non-Slavic south-eastern areas (average mean age of marriage, 17.0–19.6 years). In European Russia and the non-Baltic regions of the empire, marriage occurred at a younger age and among virtually all of the population, whereas in the Baltic the marital pattern adhered more closely to the West European pattern. In fact, within European Russia the proportion of the rural population that was married increased steadily as one moved from west to east.

Marital fertility in the empire was high relative to Western Europe, and, not surprisingly, the marital fertility rate in urban areas was lower than that of rural areas. In the period from 1900 to 1914, a gradual decline in the index of marital infertility occurred. This decline was sharpest in urban areas; only fifteen to twenty provinces experienced a 10 percent or more decline in this index. In the period 1897–1913, the decline in the birth rate from approximately 50 to 48 per thousand was paralleled by a slight decline in the death rate. In the fifty provinces of European Russia, the infant mortality rate dropped from 271 per 1,000 live births in 1886–1897 to 245 in 1908–1910. As a result, the rate of natural increase rose slightly.

The demographic growth of the empire in the years from the 1897 census to the outbreak of World War I* was accompanied by a rapid increase in the urban population of European Russia. The absolute and proportional rates of growth in the urban centers exceeded that of the nation as a whole. In 1898 15 percent of the population were urban dwellers; by 1913 the proportion had jumped to 18 percent. Rural–urban migration was the major stimulus to urban growth. Although a recent study of migration by Barbara Anderson (1980) has argued that rural population pressure was not a primary cause of migration, rural economic pressures surely played a role. In general, rural–urban migrants came from areas with more developed market networks and rural industries and were more likely to be literate than those who remained in the village. Whether peasant migrants were attracted by industrial jobs, as some maintain, or by employment in the service and commercial sectors that required little skill, as Robert Lewis and Richard Rowland (1979) have argued, may depend less on the occupational desires of the majority of migrants than on the nature of the economy of those nearby urban areas with the greatest employment opportunities. As Anderson has demonstrated, many recent migrants took unskilled jobs until better employment opportunities became available.

In general, urban centers acted as magnets that drew potential migrants from the surrounding rural areas: the further the distance from a given urban area, the less the attraction. Whatever the motives, the influx of peasants to urban areas accounted for an average per annum growth of 630,000 or 2.6 percent from 1897 to 1913. But this average figure masks the fact that the rate of rural–urban migration increased significantly after the Stolpin Reforms, which freed peasants from communal ties and obligation. For example, from 1870 to 1907 an average of 15,000 people per year migrated to Moscow and St. Petersburg; from 1907 to 1914, the number of migrants swelled the population of each city to an average of 50,000 per year.

With the outbreak of war in 1914, the demographic indices of the previous period began to be reversed, a process that continued unabated until the end of the Civil War (*see* Civil War in Russia). From the end of 1916 to 1923 the empire experienced an absolute demographic decline. Fifteen million males were mobilized into military service from 1914 to 1917. The majority (55 percent) were males of ages eighteen to twenty-six; almost a third (30 percent) were males aged twenty-seven to thirty-five. Peasants comprised the vast majority of soldiers, the result being that in 1917 only 43 percent of rural civilian population were males. Not surprisingly, the number of marriages declined precipitously during the war, although it increased somewhat in 1917. The transfer of young males to the front and the increased demand for military wares changed the complexion of urban areas. Not only did urban centers grow during 1914–1917 (e.g., Petrograd and Moscow's population each grew from approximately 1.5 million in 1910 to 2.0 million in 1917), but the sexual composition of cities changed dramatically. In 1912 there were some 843 females per thousand males in Moscow; by October 1917 there were 1,016 females per thousand males.

From the time of the October Seizure of Power* in 1917 until the end of the famine in 1921–1922, the population of the empire declined at a staggering rate. Because of the unavailability and unreliability of the statistics of the period, precise estimates of the numbers involved are impossible to ascertain. Estimates of the national population deficit of the country in the period from 1914 to 1923 range from 25 to 30 million. Excluding the estimated deficit of births (10 million), the total number of deaths in the period is estimated to have ranged from 15 to 20 million (or 9–12 percent of the 1917 population). Of this figure, battle and battle-related deaths during World War I account for some 4 million people. Emigration accounted for an estimated 2 million people. Disease, especially epidemic disease, flourished. During the Civil War, the country was ravaged by epidemics of typhus (which claimed some 2.3 million lives), cholera, and scarlet fever, which, along with pneumonia, are estimated to have caused some 3.3 million deaths. In all, epidemics, famine, and cold claimed approximately 7.5 million lives. The remaining deaths are attributed to those who were killed in the Revolution and, most importantly, the Civil War and intervention.

Ascertaining the rate and incidence of death in this period by geographic location is impossible, but no doubt those areas in the various theaters of battle during the Civil War suffered the worst. Urban centers experienced a sharp decline in their population. Between 1917 and 1921 the proportion of people living in the cities shrank from 18 to 15 percent. After the Decree on Land in October 1917, masses of urban dwelling peasant workers returned to the countryside to claim their share in the subsequent redistribution of village lands. As the size of ration allotments, the supply of fuel, and number of jobs in urban areas diminished, more urban dwellers migrated to the countryside. These conditions and the spread of epidemics (in 1919–1920 cholera and typhus raged in Russia) spurred the death rate in cities such as Moscow where it rose from 23.3 per 1,000 in 1912–1917 to 45.4 in 1919; in 1920 it was 36.3. In Petrograd the death rate jumped from 22.0 per 1,000 in 1914 to 47.0 in 1918 to 77.0 in 1919; in 1920 it dropped to 51.0. During this period, the number of births fell precipitously. However, if the estimates for Moscow are representative, the birth rate, after being halved between 1914 and 1918, began to rise slowly after the latter date. By 1921 the population of Moscow had declined to about 1 million; Petrograd's population was about 725,000.

The 1926 All-Union Census revealed the extent of the demographic destruction of the period 1914–1921. The depleted fertility and heightened mortality of the period revealed a substantial shortage of persons in the cohort born in 1912–1921. There was a conspicuous shortage of children ages five to nine. The 1926 census also revealed an unusually large number of widows and a significant deficit of males ages twenty-five to twenty-nine (84 males per 100 females) and males aged thirty to thirty-five (88 males per 100 females). Despite the lack of reliable statistics for the period 1914–1921, there can be no question that the devastation radically altered the demographic composition of society; its psychological impact can only be imagined.

William Chase

Bibliography

Anderson, Barbara. *Internal Migration during Modernization in Late Nineteenth Century Russia.* 1980.
Coale, Ansley; Anderson, Barbara; and Harm, Erna. *Human Fertility in Russia Since the Nineteenth Century.* 1979.
Fedor, Thomas. *Patterns of Urban Growth in the Russian Empire during the Nineteenth Century.* 1975.
Hamm, Michael. *The City in Russian History.* 1976.
Kohn, Stanislas, and Meyendorff, Alexander F. *The Cost of the War to Russia.* 1932.
Lewis, Robert, and Rowland, Richard. *Population Redistribution in the USSR.* 1979.
Lorimer, Frank. *The Population of the Soviet Union.* 1946.

Rashin, A. G. *Naselenie Rossii za 100 let.* 1956.
Vol'kov, E. Z. *Dinamika naselenii SSSR za vosem' desiat let.* 1930.
Vydro, M. Ia. *Naselenie Moskvy.* 1976.

Denikin, Anton Ivanovich (1872–1947). Denikin was a career military officer in the army (*see* Army of Imperial Russia in World War I) of the Romanov dynasty. He also played a prominent role in the military leadership of the Provisional Government*, of the White Movement*, and in the Civil War in Russia*.

Denikin was born in Warsaw Province in Russian Poland. His father was born a serf but rose to the rank of major in the Russian army; his mother was a Polish Catholic. Denikin decided early to pursue a military career. He attended a junker school in Kiev from which he graduated an ensign in 1892. In 1895 he was admitted and subsequently graduated from the General Staff Academy in St. Petersburg. He advanced steadily in his career. A captain in 1904, he rose to the rank of colonel through service in the Russo–Japanese War, and in June 1914 he was made a major-general. In World War I* Denikin received command of the Iron Brigade, later made into the Iron Division. During 1914–1915 he fought on the Austrian front. He was promoted to lieutenant-general in 1915 and in 1916 was decorated for his role in the Brusilov offensive.

Following the February Revolution* of 1917, Denikin served for a time as Chief-of-Staff of the Supreme Command. Later he was in charge of the western and southwestern fronts during the ultimately unsuccessful June-July 1917 offensive. Denikin opposed changes in the Russian army (*see* Army of Imperial Russia in World War I) wrought by the Revolution. He publicly advocated the reintroduction of the death penalty and the status and power of officers and demanded an end to the intrusions of committees and commissars into military affairs. In August 1917, although not a conspirator, he publicly expressed sympathy for the attempted military uprising of General L. G. Kornilov (*see* Kornilov Revolt). For this Denikin was arrested and imprisoned in Bykhov Prison along with Kornilov and others.

Following the October Seizure of Power* Denikin, Kornilov, and others escaped and fled to the South of Russia. There they organized the Volunteer Army, which Denikin headed from April 1918, following the death of Kornilov. In the fall of 1918, after the death of M. V. Alekseev and with the support of the Western interventionist powers, Denikin was named commander-in-chief of the armed forces of South Russia. He also assumed responsibility for civilian administration in the areas under White control in the South. When Kolchak emerged as the Supreme Ruler of Russia, Denikin was named his deputy.

Denikin was the leader of the greatest of the White military campaigns of the Civil War, the drive for Moscow during the summer and fall of 1919. After significant early successes, Denikin's 300,000-man army was halted in October by a counterattack of Red forces. Continued reverses saw the White forces pushed back to the Crimea. In April 1920 Denikin turned command of the remaining White troops over to General Baron P. N. Wrangel* and he emigrated.

Denikin was clearly the most capable of the White commanders in the Russian Civil War. As a politician he was less gifted. Denikin never formulated a political platform both because his interests did not lie in that direction and because to do so would have further divided the diverse elements that made up the White cause. He did advocate a unified Russian state whose ultimate shape and destiny was to be determined by the Russian peoples at the Constituent Assembly* following victory over the Reds. Even this minimal program caused problems with the autonomy-minded Cossacks* and the separatist national minorities (*see* National Question and the Russian Revolution). To his credit, Denikin resisted considerable pressure from pro-monarchist elements. He personally is thought to have favored a constitutional monarchy. Such political ideas as he possessed are said to have most closely paralleled those of the Constitutional Democratic Party—Cadet*. Denikin was personally honest and a deeply religious adherent to Russian orthodoxy. Nevertheless, he was an anti-Semite, as were many of his caste and station, and although the corruption that tainted the White movement was not of his doing or approval, he was very slow to denounce anti-Semitic pogroms, only speaking out in late 1919.

Denikin's life in emigration was spent mostly in France. He published his memoirs in five volumes, *Ocherki russkoi smuty* (1921–1926), and wrote and lectured but was not greatly active in emigré (*see* Emigration) politics. He did, however, in 1939 call on his fellow emigrés not to support fascist Germany in the event of war with the USSR. Denikin emigrated to the United States in 1945 and at the time of his death in 1947 resided in Ann Arbor, Michigan.

Bibliography

Brinkley, G. A. *The Volunteer Army and Allied Intervention in South Russia, 1917–21.* 1966.
Denikin, A. I. *The Russian Turmoil.* 1932.
———. *The White Army.* 1930.
Kenez, Peter. *Civil War in South Russia.* 1971.
———. *Civil War in South Russia, 1919–1920.* 1977.
Lehovich, D. V. *White against Red.* 1974.
Luckett, R. *The White Generals.* 1971.
Stewart, G. *The White Armies.* 1933.

Directory—Russia. Directory was a label borrowed from the French Revolution. From 1795 to 1799 France was ruled by a small executive committee, that was empowered to make decisions promptly in order to deal with the succession of crises facing the revolutionary government of that period.

At the national level in Russia A. I. Kerensky* contemplated the possibility of establishing a Directory in Russia during the Kornilov Revolt*. At that time the members of the Constitutional Democratic Party—Cadet* who participated in the cabinet threatened to resign if he took that step. He accepted their resignations but asked them to stay at their posts until the Kornilov crisis was over and he could form a new government. On August 27 the All-Russian Central

Executive Committee* agreed over Bolshevik (*see* Russian Social Democratic Workers' Party [Bolshevik]) protests to give Kerensky the power to adopt any form of government he chose, including the six-man Directory he requested.

On September 1, 1917, Kerensky announced the formation of the Directory. Its members were the Minister-Chairman A. F. Kerensky, the Minister of Foreign Affairs M. I. Tereshchenko, the Minister of War A. I. Verkhovskii, the Minister of the Navy D. N. Verderevskii, and the Minister of Post and Telegraph A. M. Nikitin. As a result of this decision the Bolsheviks strengthened their efforts to persuade the Soviets to form their own government, and the moderate socialists urged a speedy convocation of the Democratic Conference* that would, it was suggested, decide on the form of government. The Directory came to an end with the formation of a coalition cabinet, the Third Coalition (*see* Coalition Government) and the decision of the Democratic Conference to accept these arrangements while the newly created Democratic Council* met to consider the future form of the government in preparation for the coming Constituent Assembly*.

Many of the same leaders who met at the Democratic Conference with the exclusion of the Bolsheviks gathered again in Ufa a year later on September 10. By that time the Soviet October Seizure of Power* was complete in the center of Russia, and the Red Army* had demonstrated its strength in the Civil War in Russia* by seizing Kazan. The meeting was called the Ufa State Conference. It decided, as a compromise between all of the divergent anti-Soviet political views represented there, to form a five-man Directory to serve as a successor to the former Provisional Government*. Its members were a liberal general, V. B. Boldirev; the Prime Minister of Siberia, P. V. Vologodsky; a leader of the Constitutional Democratic Party in Siberia, V. A. Vinogradov; and two moderate Socialist–Revolutionaries, N. D. Avksent'ev* and V. M. Zenzinov.

The Directory never gained any substantial support even in the area where it was located. Although it called itself the All-Russian Directory, implying that it was the legal government of all of Russia, it lacked support from the parties represented in it and had no administrative apparatus, financial resources, or military backing. It set up housekeeping on October 9, 1918, in railroad cars in Omsk until a Constitutional Democratic Party Conference in that city in November came out forcibly in opposition to that government and in favor of one-man rule. They ended the conference on November 18 by endorsing Admiral Kolchak as the "Supreme Ruler" of all Russia. The city of Omsk was taken over by troops, and the fiction of the All-Russian Directory was replaced by the reality of Kolchak's military rule.

Bibliography

Chamberlin, W. H. *The Russian Revolution, 1917–21*. Vol. 2. 1935.
Rosenberg, W. G. *Liberals in the Russian Revolution*. 1974.

Directory—Ukraine. In the Ukraine a Directory was established out of the efforts of various national groups, including professionals, labor, cultural organizations, and student groups who hoped to influence Hetman S. Skoropadskyi to "Ukrainize" his cabinet as the German occupation forces withdrew.

In July 1918 various Ukrainian nationalist groups formed the Ukrainian National Union (Ukrainskyi Natsionalyni Soiuz). However, after dickering with the Ukrainian National Union, Skoropadski decided in the autumn of 1918 to move toward federation with Russia, and the Ukrainian National Union decided upon a coup d'état to insure Ukrainian national independence. On November 13 V. Vynnychenko organized the action against Skoropadskyi with a small group of conspirators, informing them that the alternative was for Skoropadskyi to announce the union of the Ukraine with Russia.

With the support of Skoropadskyi's well-trained Ukrainian troops, the conspirators announced the formation of a provisional revolutionary organ to lead the rebellion, the Directory, consisting of five members from the Ukrainian National Union, Vynnychenko, S. M. Petliura*, F. Shvets, O. Andriievskyi, and A. Makarenko. Vynnychenko, who led the Directory from November 15, 1918, to February 10, 1919, was a member of the Ukrainian Social Democratic Party. He had tried to curry favor with the Soviet government by promising their emissary, Kh. G. Rakovsky*, that the Communist Party in the Ukraine would be allowed to operate legally once he had come to power, and he believed that the Soviet government would remain neutral in exchange for his tolerance of the Ukrainian communists.

The Directory, operating out of Bila Tserkva, issued some radical appeals on the need to "bring back all social and political gains of revolutionary democracy" (Hunczak 1977, p. 85) in order to win support from the peasants and workers and announced the reunification of the Austrian and Russian Ukraine. It gained control of Kiev and the Ukraine on December 14 when its troops entered the city; Skoropadskyi resigned.

But the supposed agreement with the Ukrainian Communists and the Soviet state rapidly dissolved, and the Directory soon found itself trying to contend with an invasion by the Red Army* supported by the tiny Ukrainian Communist Party. Although Vynnychenko tried to rally the peasants and trade unions to the struggle for national independence against the Soviet invasion, he did not succeed. On February 6, 1919, the Red Army entered Kiev for the second time and held the city until autumn. The Directory fled the capital, and Vynnychenko resigned, but the remaining members of the Directory continued to claim to be the legitimate government of the Ukraine and played a significant role in subsequent efforts to rid the Ukraine of outsiders and create an independent Ukrainian national state. This second Council of Ministers formed under the Directory was much more moderate in its social policies and remained in place until April 1919 when it was replaced by a coalition of Ukrainian Socialist–Revolutionaries and Galician radicals. But it was not able to take advantage of the second Soviet abandonment of the Ukraine in the summer of 1919 because it came into conflict with the Galician Ukrainians in the East and General A. I. Denikin, the commander of the military forces that drove the Bolsheviks out.

Taking advantage of Denikin's heavy-handed policies in the Ukraine, the Red Army invaded the Ukraine for the third time in February 1920. Petliura, acting in the name of the Directory had signed an agreement with Poland in December 1919. The Directory joined with Marshal J. Pilsudski in an effort to drive the Red Army from the Ukraine in the spring. Despite some initial successes, the Petliura–Pilsudski campaign succumbed to the Red Army's advances in July, and Poland signed a truce in November 1920. The final treaty, the Treaty of Riga, concluded in March, ending the war, and literally surrendered most of the Ukraine to Soviet rule (*see* Poland, Revolution in). The Directory and its armed forces went into exile shortly after the truce.

Bibliography

Chamberlin, W. H. *The Russian Revolution, 1917–21*. Vol. 2. 1935.
Hunczak, T., ed. *The Ukraine, 1917–21*. 1977.
Rabinowitch, A. *The Bolsheviks Come to Power*. 1976.
Reshetar, J. S. *The Ukrainian Revolution*. 1952.

Dual Power. Between the February Revolution* and the October Seizure of Power* political power in Russia was divided between the Provisional Government* and the soviets. The Soviets (Councils) of Workers', Soldiers', and Peasants' Deputies*—especially the Petrograd Soviet*, the Moscow Soviet*, and later the All-Russian Central Executive Committee* (VTsIK) of the All-Russian Congress of Soviets—were led by the Soviet intelligentsia and commanded support from the Russian masses. The Provisional Government was thought to represent the middle class or Russian bourgeoisie. The assumption was that cooperation between the Provisional Government and the Soviets would result from their common interest in completing the democratic revolution. Dual power was a peculiar situation in which the Provisional Government, the "responsible" Russian political entity that replaced the Tsar's government in February, possessed only nominal power, whereas the soviets had no legal standing but possessed real political power through their influence over the masses that recognized them as the sole authority. A tension-filled coexistence persisted through 1917 because the Provisional Government could not function without the political support of the soviets. Menshevik (*see* Russian Social Democratic Workers' Party [Menshevik]) and Socialist-Revolutionary (S-R) (*see* Socialist-Revolutionary Party) soviet leaders, for their part, did not wish either to assume power directly themselves or to abandon the Revolution to the mercies of the bourgeoisie. Many Bolsheviks (*see* Russian Social Democratic Workers' Party [Bolshevik]), at least in the beginning before Lenin's return from abroad, also shared in the belief that all social classes should cooperate through these two sets of institutions.

Dual power arose in the earliest days of the Revolution out of necessity. On March 2 Menshevik and S-R leaders of the Petrograd Soviet rejected participation in the Provisional Government on the grounds that (1) socialism was inappropriate for Russia at that historical juncture, (2) pursuit of Russia's efforts in World War I* required the support of all segments of the population, and (3) it was feared that association with the bourgeoisie might compromise socialism in the eyes of the masses. The single exception was A. F. Kerensky* who, on his own initiative, entered the first cabinet of the Provisional Government as Minister of Justice. Furthermore, most Menshevik and S-R leaders thought that the soviets were ephemeral institutions that would not constitute a permanent or long-term element in Russian life but would permanently settle the question of government in Russia. The relationship that emerged was a result of the Petrograd Soviet's support for the Provisional Government, conditional upon enactment of political and social reforms. Soviet leaders demanded the removal of legal distinctions regarding class, religion, and ethnicity; a full range of political and civil liberties; and support for the convocation of a constituent assembly*. In addition, the Petrograd military garrison, so crucial to the success of the February Revolution, was not to be removed from the capital. To give effect to its status of "control organ of the revolutionary democracy" the Petrograd Soviet created a five-member "liason committee" to deal with the Provisional Government. The members of the soviet were not as convinced as their leaders of the transient character of the soviets and, even before the formation of the Provisional Government, had issued the famous Army Order Number 1, which called for the recognition of the primary authority of the soviets on all policy questions in relation to the armed forces. In effect this left the rank and file in the army subservient to the soviets and the officers subservient to the Provisional Government.

The awkward relationship between the soviets and the Provisional Government was partially amended in April as a consequence of the crisis wrought by the "Miliukov note" (see Foreign Policy, 1914–1921). The credibility of the Provisional Government among the masses became so strained that the Soviet leadership was faced with the dilemma of taking governmental power into its own hands or of entering into a coalition government*. The latter course was chosen with the object of transferring a portion of the soviet's authority and legitimacy to the Provisional Government. Claiming that revolutionary democracy must assume responsibility for serving the country, Menshevik and S-R leaders accepted military posts in all three coalition governments formed before the October Revolution. The Bolshevik Party, following its endorsement of V. I. Lenin's* program as initially spelled out in the April Theses*, refused to accept as valid the Dual Power formula, agitating instead for replacement of the Provisional Government by a government based on the soviets.

Soviet historiography on the question of Dual Power holds that it came to an end in July 1917. This follows the position taken by Lenin at that time. Lenin argued that because leaders of the All-Russian Congress of Soviets had failed to take the opportunity of seizing power from the Provisional Government during the July Days*, Dual Power was ended and the slogan "All Power to the Soviets"* had to be abandoned. In its stead, at the Sixth Party Congress in July, the Bolsheviks endorsed a new position that somewhat vaguely called for a "dictatorship of the proletariat and poor peasants." However, with the Bolshevik electoral victories in the Petrograd and Moscow Soviets in early September, Lenin returned to the call for a Soviet seizure of power. Ultimately, the Dual Power was resolved by the October Revolution.

Bibliography

Anweiler, O. *The Soviets: The Russian Workers', Peasants', and Soldiers' Councils.* 1974.
Fitzpatrick, Sheila. *The Russian Revolution, 1917–32.* 1984.
Rosenberg, W. G. *Liberals in the Russian Revolution.* 1974.
Sukhanov, N. N. *The Russian Revolution, 1917.* 2 vols. 1955.

Duma and Revolution. The State Duma (Gosudarstvennaia Duma) played an indirect role in the events in Russia after the formation of the Provisional Government*, since it did not meet officially after February 26, 1917. However, since many of the social and political forces at work in 1917 took shape in the Duma, its history is of the greatest importance in trying to understand the events that followed. The Revolutions of 1917 took place in a country that had limited experience with a parliamentary, semiconstitutional monarchy, resembling more the German "Rechtsstaat" than the British or French political systems.

The State Duma, Russia's first national parliament, was granted to the Russian people by Tsar Nicholas II* during the worst days of the 1905 Revolution (*see* Nineteen-Five Revolution). In an attempt to quell the revolutionary tide, Nicholas issued the Manifesto of October 17, 1905, which established "as an unbreakable rule that no law shall take force without the approval of the State Duma" whose representatives, elected by the people, were also to supervise the legality of government actions. The electorate was made up of members of the peasantry, merchants, landowners, townsmen, and the clergy. Not receiving any right to vote for deputies to the Duma were women, governors, vice-governors, soldiers, students, men under twenty-five, and nomads.

The rights and duties of the State Duma were defined in the Fundamental Laws of April 23, 1906, which is often referred to as Russia's first constitution. According to the Fundamental Laws, the Duma was to share legislative power with an upper house, the reformed State Council (*Gosudarstvennyi Sovet*). The Duma, which was elected for a five-year term, had the power to initiate legislation. However, before a bill could become law, it had to be approved by both houses and receive the signature of the Tsar. This, in effect, gave the Tsar and both houses a legislative veto even though the Fundamental Laws stated that the power of the Tsar shall remain unimpaired.

The Duma had limited means by which it could influence the government since ministers of the government were appointed by and responsible only to the Tsar. This was the cause of continual and festering dissatisfaction on the part of the moderate, liberal, and radical deputies during the Duma's history, since deputies of these political bents were all demanding a government responsible to the Duma. One tool at the disposal of the Duma was its right of interpellation (*zapros*), by which ministers and officials were called before the Duma to answer questions concerning government actions. The Duma was prohibited from legislating in the areas of foreign affairs and defense. However, through its annual budget debate, the Duma could even bring these prohibited areas within its purview.

The first two Dumas were oppositional bodies whose members on the whole had no intention of working with the existing governments; as a result, both were dismissed by Tsar Nicholas II after serving only a few months of their five-year terms. The First and Second Dumas served from April 27 to July 1906 and February 8 to June 3, 1907, respectively.

Prime Minister P. A. Stolypin, who had been named to replace I. L. Goremykin when the First Duma was dismissed in July 1906, was determined to establish a better working relationship between the government and the Duma. Therefore, he published a new electoral law along with the decree dissolving the Second Duma; the new law would guarantee the election of a more moderate Duma. The new electoral law was issued under the emergency powers of Article 87 of the Fundamental Laws, which gave the Tsar the right to issue laws when the Duma was not in session. This was an unconstitutional act since the Fundamental Laws proscribed the use of Article 87 to change the electoral laws; thus this action is often referred to as Stolypin's coup d'état of June 3, 1907. As a result, many scholars like A. Ia. Avrekh have dubbed the Duma era the "Third of June System." The label is appropriate.

The Third Duma was convened on November 1, 1907. The new electoral law achieved its goal in that the new Duma was more moderate than its predecessors, and although radical revolutionary parties were represented, the Third Duma was much more willing to work with the Prime Minister than either of the first two. Prime Minister Stolypin was able to develop a close working relationship with A. I. Guchkov*, the leader of the Third Duma's largest party, the Octobrists.

Of all of the Dumas, the third is considered to have been the most productive. It passed some 2,500 bills, including legislation on agrarian reform, education, working conditions, and labor insurance.

Stolypin's good working relationship with the Duma evaporated as a result of his handling of the western *zemstvo* bill. Stolypin established *zemstvo* institutions in the western provinces by first temporarily suspending the Duma on March 12, 1911, and then by using Article 87 to implement the bill two days later. Both the Duma and State Council considered the Prime Minister's actions to be dictatorial and refused any further cooperation with his government; even those who supported the bill objected to his unconstitutional methods. Six months later, on September 1, 1911, he was mortally wounded by an assassin's bullet. V. N. Kokovstev was named Prime Minister, a position he held for the remainder of the Third Duma and into the Fourth Duma. The Third Duma, the only Duma to serve its entire five years, ended its term on June 9, 1912.

On November 14, 1912, the newly elected Fourth Duma was opened. Although the recent elections produced a considerable shift to the right in the Duma's membership, the lower house was soon to rise in opposition to the government reminiscent of both the First and Second Dumas. From its convening in late 1912 to early 1914, the Duma was involved in numerous legislative conflicts with the upper house, the State Council, on the one hand, and the government on the other hand. Attacks on the Duma floor against the Tsarina's favorite, Gregory Rasputin*, began, and those against the government became more frequent. Relations between the government and the Duma reached their nadir in May 1913 when the two bodies stopped doing business. The trouble began with one of the deputies insulting Prime Minister Kokovtsev. He responded by stopping all communications between members of the government and the Duma. The legislative process remained at a standstill until November 1913 when the Tsar intervened. Shortly after this, Kokovtsev was dismissed in January 1914, and the Tsar once more appointed I. L. Goremykin, a choice that the Tsarina looked upon with favor.

Goremykin's appointment, which lasted until January 1916, did little to improve relations between the Duma and government. The Prime Minister had little regard for the Fundamental Laws, and he refused to answer interpellations on the grounds that the Prime Minister was only responsible to the Tsar. Consequently, there was little legislative activity from the time Goremykin was named Prime Minister to the outbreak of the World War I* on July 25, 1914.

Following the declaration of war, the Duma immediately rallied to support the government in a demonstration of patriotic fervor at a special session on July 26, 1914, the same day that Germany and Austria declared war. Goremykin showed his gratitude by recessing the Duma on that same day. The Duma was later reconvened for three days in January 1915 to approve the budget and war credits but then was not reconvened again until the summer. The Prime Minister thought that he could pursue the war effort more easily if he did not have a Duma to contend with. Goremykin preferred using Article 87 to relying on the people's representatives.

When the Duma reconvened in July 1915, opposition to the government was once more being expressed on the Duma floor. The deputies were particularly upset by the government's conduct of the war and the absence of a significant wartime role for the Duma. To increase both Duma influence on policy and participation in the war effort, 300 deputies united to form the Progressive Bloc* in August 1915. Also to emerge in August 1915 were the Duma's Special Councils, a Duma attempt to become involved in the war effort by complementing and working alongside the Union of Zemstvos and Towns (see All-Russian Union of Towns and All-Russian Union of Zemstvos) and the War Industries Committees*. The five Special Councils were those for national defense, transportation, fuel, food supply, and refugees.

Tsar Nicholas II, attempting to improve the political climate in wartime Russia, made a gesture toward the Duma and personally attended the opening of the Fourth Session on February 9, 1916. It is significant to note that this was the Tsar's only visit in the entire history of the Duma. The deputies, however, were not placated by the visit or the Tsar's recent replacement of Goremykin by the disliked B. V. Sturmer.

The Duma continued to press for an increase in participation in matters of state. By November 1916 scathing attacks against the Tsarina, Rasputin, and the government were being launched from the speaker's rostrum. The most famous of these attacks were by the liberal opposition leader P. N. Miliukov* and the extreme rightist V. M. Purishkevitch. Miliukov asked whether the government's policies could best be described as stupidity or treason. He concluded by stating that the government did not merit the confidence of the Duma and must go. Purishkevitch, always a fervent supporter of the Tsar, pleaded with Nicholas to deliver Russia from Rasputin, a task Purishkevitch himself would take on in the next month, December 1916.

Rasputin's death did not have the palliative effect expected, nor did the appointment in rapid succession of two new prime ministers, A. F. Trepov and Prince N. D. Golitsyn, and in another two months Russia would be embroiled in the February Revolution*. On February 23 demonstrations broke out in Petrograd and quickly turned violent. The Tsar's inability to deal with the situation brought down the government and created a political vacuum that the Duma willingly filled.

The Duma's involvement in the Revolution began on February 26 following the receipt of a tsarist decree proroguing the Duma. The Council of Duma Elders, a committee of leading representatives of the Duma factions, met with M. V. Rodzianko, the President of the Duma, and decided that the Duma would continue to meet unofficially. Although the Fourth Duma would never again meet as a legislative body, Duma deputies played a prominent role in shaping events during the early days of the Revolution.

The day after Rodzianko received the order of prorogation, February 27, the Duma commissioned the Council of Elders to create a provisional committee of Duma deputies for the restoration of order in the capital and for the establishment of relations between the Duma and public organizations and institutions. The committee was composed of leading deputies, many of whom would become prime actors in the events of 1917. Among its members were Rodzianko, Miliukov, V. V. Shulgin, N. V. Nekrasov, A. F. Kerensky*, N. S. Chkheidze*, A. I. Konovalov, and V. N. Lvov.

The Tauride Palace, where the Duma met, became a center of revolutionary activity and excitement. The Provisional Committee quickly became involved in the Revolution and, on February 28, decided to take power. It issued proclamations calling for a restoration of public order and declaring the committee's intentions to create a new government. The proclamations were followed by arrest orders for the ministers of the tsarist government and the committee's takeover of several public institutions, including the telegraph system, Petrograd water and electrical stations, municipal transport, railways, the State Bank, and all governmental and administrative institutions. The Provisional Committee also took control of the Military Commission, which had been formed on the previous day by the Petrograd Soviet* for the purpose of organizing the soldiers who were roaming the streets of the capital. Also on February 28 Rodzianko, whose importance on the committee would soon be dwarfed by the rising star of Miliukov, informed the military commanders that the Provisional committee had assumed power and assured them that no internal or external policy changes would take place.

On March 1 the Petrograd Soviet issued Order Number One (*see* Army of Imperial Russia in World War I), which destroyed the Duma committees' authority with the soldiers. The next day the Provisional Committee and the Executive Committee of the Petrograd Soviet met to resolve differences between the two bodies. Negotiations led to an agreement allowing the Provisional Committee to form the Provisional Government, and the Committee accepted Soviet demands on the context of the Provisional Government's program. Later that same day the Committee announced the composition of the Provisional Government.

Also on March 2, the most important day of the Revolution, the Committee sent a Duma delegation of Shul'gin and A. I. Guchkov to Pskov to obtain the abdication of Nicholas II. Instead of abdicating in favor of his son Aleksei, as expected, Nicholas II surprised the delegation by passing the throne to his brother Mikhail. The Provisional Committee of the Duma met with Mikhail the following day, however. He refused the throne and abdicated in favor of the Provisional Government and its Premier, Prince G. E. L'vov*.

The second abdication brought the Romanov dynasty to an end and gave the Provisional Government a sense of legitimacy as the interim government of Russia. Although the Provisional Committee of the Duma continued to exist for several more months, the seating of the Provisional Government marked the end of the Duma as a force in the events of the Revolution. Duma deputies did visit the front, make reports, and attend various official and unofficial meetings, but the Duma no longer had any notable influence. When the Duma was officially dissolved by the Provisional Government on October 9, 1917, only sixteen days before its term would have expired on the day that the October Seizure of Power* began, it was not even felt necessary to inform the president, M. V. Rodzianko.

Lawrence W. Lerner and Matthew L. O'Leary

Bibliography

Avrekh, A. Ia. *Raspad tret'eiunskoi sistemy*. 1986.
———. *Stolypin i tret'ia duma*. 1968.
———. *Tsarizm i IV duma*. 1981.

———. *Tsarizm i tret'eiiunskaia sistema.* 1966.

Chermenskii, E. D. *IV gosudarstvennaia duma i sverzhenie tsarizma.* 1976.

Diakin, V. A. *Russkaia burzhuaziia i tsarizm v gody pervoi mirovoi voini, 1914–1917.* 1967.

Hasegawa, T. *The February Revolution.* 1973.

Hosking, G. A. *The Russian Constitutional Experiment.* 1973.

Pearson, R. *The Russian Moderates and the Crisis of Tsarism.* 1977.

Schapiro, Leonard. *The Russian Revolutions of 1917: The Origins of Modern Communism.* 1984.

Tokmakoff, G. *P. A. Stolypin and the Third Duma.* 1981.

Dutov, Aleksandr Il'ich (1864–1921). Dutov was a Cossack* military commander and counterrevolutionary active in the southern Urals during the Civil War in Russia*.

Dutov was born into the Cossack gentry in the Orenburg Region of the southern Ural mountains. He pursued a military career, attending the Nikolai Cavalry School, and rose to the rank of colonel in World War I*. Following the February Revolution* in 1917, Dutov became involved in attempts to organize the several Cossack bands politically. This led to his election in Petrograd in June to head the All-Cossack Congress. In September Dutov traveled to Orenburg where he was elected *ataman* of the Orenburg Cossack Host. Although there is not a great deal of personal data available on Dutov, several scholars of the Russian Civil War have rendered assessments of him. The historian Peter Fleming has described Dutov as "a plump spaniel-eyed, ineffective little man" (1963, p. 84). The historian Richard Luckett asserted that Dutov sought to compensate for his lack of an engaging personality or diplomatic finesses "with brutality and low guile" (1971, p. 165).

Following the October Seizure of Power*, Dutov's Cossacks joined other Cossack bands in opposition to Russia's withdrawal from the war against Germany and in defense of Cossack interests against Bolshevik (*see* Russian Social Democratic Workers' Party [Bolshevik]) attacks. On November 15, 1917, Ataman Dutov gave effect to his sympathies by carrying out a military insurrection in Orenburg that overthrew the Orenburg Soviet and broke up the Orenburg Military Revolutionary Committee. By the end of 1917 Dutov seemed well established in Orenburg. He commanded a military force of about 7,000 Cossack troops and had established a *modus vivendi* with the Bashkir (*see* Bashkiria, Revolution in) and the Kazakh–Kirghiz (*see* Alash-Orda) nationalist forces to the south. Furthermore, the key geographical position of Orenburg meant that East–West communications, especially by rail, were severed between European Russia and Siberia and Central Asia.

In late January 1918, however, attacks by military and Red Guard* forces loyal to the Revolution, combined with strikes by Orenburg workers, led to Dutov's withdrawal from Orenburg. His forces retreated first to Verkhneural'sk and then, under pressure from Soviet troops led by V. K. Bliukher*, fled into the Turgai steppes.

The revolt of the Czechoslovak Legion* in the spring of 1918 marked a major new stage in the Russian Civil War. In June Dutov's Cossacks allied themselves with the anti-Soviet Samara government, and in September they joined the All-Russian Provisional Government. This body, known as the Directory*, was a coalition of conservatives, moderate socialists, national separatists, and Cossack elements. Internal tensions between these disparate forces led to a coup in November 1918 that transformed the body into a dictatorship under Admiral A. V. Kolchak*. Dutov supported the Kolchak government, now located in Omsk, but the Kolchak forces were not strong enough to prevent further Bolshevik victories in the winter of 1918–1919, and Dutov and his troops were again driven into the Turgai steppes.

In February 1919 Kolchak launched a major offensive. Dutov, now with the rank of general, commanded Kolchak's Southern Army, a force of 15,000 men. The offensive ultimately failed, however, in part due to the inability of Dutov's forces to link up with the White forces in the South under General A. I. Denikin*. Thus began a period of steady withdrawals and increasingly disorderly retreat eastward on the part of Dutov. The fleeing forces, swelled by the addition of wives, children, and others, came to about 150,000. In early 1920 30,000 survivors of the trek of thousands of miles entered Chinese Turkestan. On March 7, 1921, in Suidin, China, Dutov was assassinated by one of his own.

Bibliography

Fleming, Peter. *The Fate of Admiral Kolchak.* 1963.
Luckett, Richard. *The White Generals.* 1971.
Stewart, George. *The White Armies of Russia.* 1933.

Dvoevlastie. *See* Dual Power.

Dybenko, Pavel Efimovich (1889–1938). Dybenko was a prominent leader of the Bolshevik (*see* Russian Social Democratic Workers' Party [Bolshevik]) sailors. He played an important role in the October Seizure of Power* in Petrograd and in the Civil War in Russia* and was a member of the first Soviet government.

Born into a peasant family in Chernigov Province, Dybenko, as a young man, received four years of schooling and became a dock worker in Riga where he became involved in revolutionary activity in 1907. In 1911 he became a sailor in the Baltic fleet (*see* Sailors in 1917; Navy in World War I). He joined the Russian Social Democratic Workers' Party in 1912 and was one of the leaders of the revolt on the Russian ship *Emperor Paul the First* in 1915 for which he received six months' imprisonment. He subsequently served in the naval infantry and later as a storekeeper on a transport ship.

In March 1917, following the February Revolution*, Dybenko was elected a member of the Helsinki Soviet. Charismatic, imposing in height, and an excellent orator, he was elected Chairman of Centrobalt (*see* Central Committee of the Baltic Fleet) in April. He was arrested and confined to "Kresty" prison in early summer for his part in the July Days* and was released on September 4. He was again named Chairman of Centrobalt on October 3. A member of the Petrograd Military Revolutionary Council in the October Revolution (*see* October Seizure of Power), he was responsible for the dispatch of revolutionary sailor detachments to Petrograd (*see* Sailors in 1917). On October 26 he was named with V. A. Antonov-Ovseenko* and N. V. Krylenko* to the governing committee of the Peoples' Commissariat for Military and Naval Affairs. Shortly thereafter he was named People's Commissar for Naval Affairs. Of the original Peoples' Commissars, Dybenko was the youngest and probably of the humblest social origins. He commanded workers and sailor forces in the Gatchina area against the assaults of anti-revolutionary forces of P. N. Krasnov and personally arrested Krasnov on November 2. In January 1918 he led the soldiers who dispersed the Constituent Assembly*.

Together with Commissars A. M. Kollontai (his mistress), N. Osinskii* (V. V. Obolenskii), and I. N. Smirnov*, he resigned from the Soviet government over opposition to the Brest-Litovsk* Treaty. In May 1918 Dybenko was tried and acquitted of the surrender of Narva to the Germans (February 1918). It is alleged that he considered overthrowing the Soviet government about this time. Expelled from the party, he was later readmitted. During 1918–1919 he carried out military assignments in Ekaterinoslav, the Ukraine (*see* Ukraine, Revolution in), and the Crimea (*see* Crimea, Revolution in). Arrested in August 1918 in Sevastopol, he was exchanged for captive German officers. In 1919 he was named People's Commissar for Naval Affairs in the Crimean Soviet Republic. During 1919–1920 he participated in the fighting for Tsaritsyn and in the Caucasus. Together with K. E. Voroshilov* he was criticized by V. I. Lenin* for administrative shortcomings. In 1921 he aided in the suppression of the Kronstadt Revolt (*see* Kronstadt, 1917–1921).

Dybenko graduated from the Red Army* Military Academy in 1922, and in his subsequent military career he served as the commander of the military districts in the Central Asian and Volga regions and Leningrad and in a number of military commissions. His work for the Communist Party included serving on the Central Asian Bureau of the Central Committees of Uzbekistan and Tadzhikstan. In April 1938 he was arrested and executed. Three times a recipient of the Order of the Red Banner, Dybenko was posthumously rehabilitated.

Bibliography

Haupt, Georges, and Marie, Jean Jacques. *Makers of the Russian Revolution.* 1974.
Levytsky, Borys. *The Stalinist Terror in the Thirties.* 1974.
Mawdsley, Evan. *The Russian Revolution and the Baltic Fleet.* 1978.
Saul, Norman E. *Sailors in Revolt.* 1978.

Dzerzhinskii, Felix Edmundovich (1877–1926). Dzerzhinskii (in Polish, Dzierżyński) was the head of the first Soviet state security police, the All-Russian Extraordinary Commission for Combatting Counterrevolution and Sabotage*, or Cheka.

A leading Bolshevik (*see* Russian Social Democratic Workers' Party [Bolshevik]) of the Lenin era, he was born on August 30, 1877, near Vilna in Russian-occupied Poland. The Dzerzhinskii family, which was of Tatar origin, traced its Polish roots to the fifteenth century. Felix Dzerzhinskii's father was educated at the University of St. Petersburg and taught mathematics in southern Russia until illness forced him into early retirement in 1875. As was the custom among Polish families of the lesser nobility, Felix and his seven brothers and sisters were reared in a very patriotic and religious atmosphere, and as a child Felix wanted to become a Catholic priest.

Dzerzhinskii's conversion to Marxian socialism came during his seventeenth year when he was a student at the Vilna gymnasium. By his own admission, while young Dzerzhinskii was quick tempered and impulsive and was continually in a "state of war" with the gymnasium authorities. The heavy-handed efforts of the teachers to "Russify" the students led the young Dzerzhinskii to choose the path of rebel. In 1896 he quit the gymnasium to devote all of his energies to agitation and organizational work on behalf of the Lithuanian Social Democratic Party (*see* Lithuania and the Russian Revolution), a miniscule group of about 150 members under whose ideological influence he had fallen.

During his two decades in the conspiratorial movement, Dzerzhinskii's life followed the pattern of the typical professional revolutionary—feverish underground work followed by arrest, exile, and escape. He spent a total of eleven years in tsarist prisons and was arrested six times (1897, 1900, 1905, 1906, and 1921); thrice he was sentenced to Siberian exile and escaped each time, once after serving just seven days of a life sentence. Dzerzhinskii's health never completely recovered from the physical hardship of these years.

Dzerzhinskii's most notable achievement as a young revolutionary came in early 1900 when he took an active part in forming the Social Democracy of the Kingdom of Poland and Lithuania (SDKPiL), a party that unified the left-wing faction of the Lithuanian Social Democracy and the Social Democracy of the Kingdom of Poland. Dzerzhinskii quickly won the esteem of the SDKPiL rank and file for his brave and selfless dedication to the revolutionary cause, and he became one of the party's most popular figures. On the other hand, the ideological leadership of the SDKPiL, which was based in Berlin and included luminaries such as Rosa Luxemburg* and Leon Jogiches, often found Dzerzhinskii difficult. Dzerzhinskii frequently criticized the SDKPiL leadership for its isolation from the daily realities of Polish life and more than once was rebuked for his pragmatic approach to dealings with rival socialist parties. In June 1905 the SDKPiL came close to a split over Dzerzhinskii's effort to detach the "home organization" of the party in Russian Poland, which for all practical purposes he led, from its dependence on the Berlin leadership. Already Dzerzhinskii was demonstrating an unwillingness to adopt slavishly the views and policies even of those whose overall authority he readily acknowledged.

Felix Dzerzhinskii was early attracted to the Russian Social Democratic Workers' Party (Bolshevik) and was considered by his Polish comrades to be "completely Bolshevik" in body and soul. For years he was the most outspoken advocate of the Leninist position in the Polish party, and V. I. Lenin*, who had a sharp eye for potential supporters, did all in his power to keep this zealous partisan on his side. In July 1906 Dzerzhinskii became the first member of the SDKPiL to be elected as a delegate to the Central Committee of the Russian Communist Party (Bolshevik)*. Both the Menshevik (*see* Russian Social Democratic Workers' Party [Menshevik]) and Bolshevik factions hoped to benefit from Dzerzhinskii's presence on the Central Committee, but Dzerzhinskii put himself unconditionally on Lenin's side in the disputes of those days.

The year 1917 found Dzerzhinskii locked up in Moscow's Butyrki Prison. Following his sudden and dramatic release after the February Revolution*, Dzerzhinskii plunged into Bolshevik organizational work in Moscow and Petrograd. In the autumn Dzerzhinskii became a member of the Bolshevik-controlled Petrograd Military Revolutionary Committee and played a direct part in the October Seizure of Power*. The capture of the city's central post office and telegraph station was his special assignment. In the aftermath of the seizure of power Dzerzhinskii assumed personal responsibility for the security of the Smolnyi Institute and also helped supervise "revolutionary order" in the streets of Petrograd.

Unlike many of his comrades, Dzerzhinskii never showed any reluctance to shoulder the difficult and thankless duties of a revolutionary policeman. On December 7, 1917, the Council of People's Commissars* appointed Dzerzhinskii to head the All-Russian Extraordinary Commission (Cheka), the first Soviet security police organization. Entrusted with the "sword of revolution," Dzerzhinskii vigorously set about extirpating the virus of counterrevolution throughout Soviet-held territory and in the process acquired a considerable measure of fame and notoriety. In June 1918, in one of his earliest public statements as chief of the Cheka, Dzerzhinskii declared: "We stand for organized terror—this should be frankly admitted. Terror is an absolute necessity during times of revolution. . . . We terrorize the enemies of Soviet power in order to suppress crime at its roots" (Leggett, p. 68). Under Dzerzhinskii's leadership and direction the Cheka grew rapidly into a ruthless and indispensible enforcement arm of the Soviet Republic. There was hardly any facet of Soviet life that was not touched by its far-flung apparatus of repression and control. Dzerzhinskii remained at the helm of the security police until his death in 1926. Under his tutelage this institution was entrenched as a permanent part of the Soviet system.

The notoriety surrounding Felix Dzerzhinskii, the "first Chekist," has obscured the important role he simultaneously played as one of the foremost economic administrators of his day. By the end of the Civil War in Russia* Lenin had come to recognize that Dzerzhinskii's seemingly inexhaustible energy and administrative talents were as applicable to the solution of difficult economic problems as they were to the direction of a security apparatus dedicated to the relentless pursuit of all "enemies of the people." In April 1921 Dzerzhinskii was appointed Commissar of Transport and began the slow and painful reconstruction of the nation's railroad network. In February 1924, shortly after Lenin's death, Dzerzhinskii was assigned the demanding post of chairman of the Supreme Council of the National Economy* (Vesenkha), the state organ responsible for managing all Soviet industry. Dzerzhinskii was a staunch advocate of the New Economic Policy* (NEP) and fought against those in the Communist Party who were ready to sacrifice the well being of the peasant majority for the sake of the maximum development of industry. Not even his critics could deny that Dzerzhinskii was an energetic, strong, and forthright economic administrator.

It is significant that while Lenin lived, Dzerzhinskii, despite his many responsible government duties, was never brought into the Political Bureau (Politburo), the innermost sanctum of the Communist Party. (Under Lenin, Dzerzhinskii never rose beyond membership on the Central Committee.) Certain aspects of Dzerzhinskii's character and outlook may at least in part explain his exclusion from the Communist Party summit. Dzerzhinskii was not typical of the small circle of top Soviet leaders. His independence of mind, which several times brought him into conflict with Lenin over national policy and other issues, and his steadfast refusal to engage in party factionalism to advance his own political fortunes set him apart. Even Dzerzhinskii's relations with I. V. Stalin* were stormier than is generally recognized. They frequently clashed on economic matters, and Dzerzhinskii once threatened to resign as chairman of Vesenkha because of opposition from the General Secretary. In his last impassioned speech, given just hours before his death on July 20, 1926, Dzerzhinskii gave his own epitaph: "You know very well where my strength lies. I never spare myself. . . . I am never insincere; if I see something is wrong, I come down on it with all my strength." Dzerzhinskii was always very much his own man.

Felix Dzerzhinskii reached the peak of his career when Russian society, shattered and transformed as it was by the Revolution, had not yet been set in its narrow and rigid Stalinist frame. It was still possible for a man of strong opinion and forceful personality to attain a position of leadership. Dzerzhinskii was fortunate that his reputation as a revolutionary was intact when he died.

Lennard D. Gerson

Bibliography

Dzerzhinskii, F. E. *Izbrannye prioizvedeniia.* 1977.

———. *Prison Diary and Letters.* 1959.

Gerson, Lennard D. *The Secret Police in Lenin's Russia.* 1976.

Haupt, Georges, and Marie, Jean Jacques. *Makers of the Russian Revolution.* 1974.

Khatskevich, A. F. *Soldat, velikikh boev: zhizn' o deiatel' nost' F. E. Dzerzhinskioogo.* 1965.

Khromov, S. S. *F. E. Dzerzhinskii na khoziaistvennom fronte.* 1977.

———. *F. E. Dzerzhinskii vo glave metallopromyshlennosti.* 1966.

———. *Felix Edmundovich Dzerzhinskii: biografiiia.* 1977.

Leggett, George. *The Cheka.* 1981.

Tishkov, A. V. *Dzerzhinskii*. 1974.
Tishkov, A. V. *Pervyi chekhist*. 1968.

Dzhadizm. *See* Jadid Movement.

Dzhugashvili, Iosif Vissarionovich. *See* Stalin, I. V.

E

Edinstvo (*Unity*). *Edinstvo* was a daily newspaper advancing the views of the Edinstvo Group* led by G. V. Plekhanov*. Four issues of the newspaper appeared between May and June 1914. It appeared as a daily in Petrograd from March to October 1917. From December 1917 to February 19, 1918, it was published under the name *Nashe Edinstvo* (*Our Unity*) and *Nachalo* (*Beginning*). The editorial staff consisted of L. I. Akselrod, G. A. Aleksinskii, L. G. Deich, N. I. Iordanskii, G. V. Plekhanov, N. V. Vailiev, and V. I. Zasulich.

Edinstvo Group. The Edinstvo (Unity) Group was a right-wing group of Social Democrats led by G. V. Plekhanov* in 1917. The group began to form in 1914 but only took shape in 1917 following the February Revolution*. It contained several leading figures from the formative years of Russian Social Democracy. In addition to G. V. Plekhanov were A. F. Bur'ianov, N. I. Iordanskii, L. I. Aksel'rod, L. G. Deich, and V. I. Zasulich. Although it had many adherents in Petrograd, Moscow, Baku, and other cities, the group had only a small following throughout Russia as a whole. It held views on the extreme right of the socialist movement and supported the Provisional Government*, the socialist coalition with the Constitutional Democratic Party—Cadet*, and the continuation of Russia's participation in World War I* to a victorious conclusion over Germany. It vigorously opposed the Bolshevik Party and socialist Revolution. The group's views were advanced in the newspaper *Edinstvo* (*Unity*). It broke up in the summer of 1918.

Education. Public education in Russia was radically altered by the October Seizure of Power*. In October 1918 the new Soviet state adopted the Unified Labor School as the basis of its public education. This action signaled the triumph of N. K. Krupskaia's polytechnical labor school, an offshoot of the Russian progressive education movement (*see also* commissariat of the Enlightenment;

Lunacharskii, Anatolii Vasilievich). Especially after 1905 Russian progressive education, influenced by its European and American counterparts, promoted freedom, democracy, and decentralization in its struggle with the tsarist school. It proposed the cultivation of the child's individuality, creativity, and happiness; his development in a collective of peers, active and practical; instructional methods; libertarian teacher–pupil relations; and a relevant curriculum that encouraged a familiarity with labor and life. This "new" or "free" education, many of whose adherents were socialists, worked for a school system that would be popularly controlled and freely accessible to all. Krupskaia's polytechnical school was derived from this progressive legacy as well as from Marxists' precepts about the scientific basis of education, the mastery of theory and practice, and the nexus between mental and manual labor.

The tsarist state school, on the other hand, had fostered loyalty to the autocracy, the nation, and religion. Its curriculum was largely classical, and its teaching methods were authoritarian and formalistic. It discriminated against the lower classes, national minorities, and women, as well as political and religious nonconformists. The lack of uniform school types and the absence of interlocking academic tracks from the lowest to the highest institutions further impeded educational advancement. The administration of education itself was fragmented among a number of ministries, the Holy Synod, and the local *zemstvos*. A bureaucratically centralized Ministry of Public Education directed most of the state schools through the curators of its twelve educational circuits and through school directors and inspectors that supervised local primary and secondary institutions.

Considerable progress toward mass education had been made before 1917. In 1897 only 22.9 percent of the population of European Russia and western Siberia older than age nine had been literate. By 1920 literacy was raised to 33.0 percent. Much of this increase in literacy stemmed from the rapid expansion in primary schooling, especially after the State Duma passed its 1908 legislation on universal elementary education. In 1911 there were 100,295 elementary schools that served 6.1 million pupils or 3.85 percent of the population of the Russian Empire. By 1915 the total increased to 123,745 schools with 7.7 million youngsters or 5.45 percent of the population. The expansion of the schools under the Minister of Education accounted for most of this growth. In 1905 there were only 48,288 schools, but by 1915 there were 80,801, an impressive increase of 40.0 percent. But still one-half of those between the ages of eight and eleven did not receive any schooling, and two-thirds admitted to these institutions left after the first or second year.

The number and composition of secondary and higher educational institutions also rapidly changed before 1917. From 863 institutions in 1904 with 294,245 students, secondary schools increased to 1722 in 1914 with an enrollment of 556,487. If the students in specialized secondary schools are included, total attendance nearly quadrupled during this period. Secondary education, moreover, had lost its privileged status by 1914. Nearly half of the students in boys' gymnasia came from the families of workers, craftsmen, and peasants. Likewise, in 1914 the 105 higher educational institutions (VUZY) with their 127,400 students (or 0.75 percent of the population) had more than doubled in enrollment since 1904. Furthermore, 38.8 percent of the students in the universities and 44 percent of those in higher technical institutions were from the families of workers, peasants, and craftsmen.

In the aftermath of the February Revolution*, the Provisional Government's* Ministry of Education under A. A. Manuilov of the Constitutional Democratic Party—Cadet, issued a number of sweeping reforms. All discriminatory political, social, and religious restrictions were rescinded. Community representation in educational circuits, increased *zemstvo* participation in school administration, the consolidation of all schools under the ministry, and three integrated levels of vocational–technical institutions were promised. Also passed were resolutions on coeducation, voluntary religious instruction in the school, autonomy for universities, increased teaching salaries, and higher expenditures for extrascholastic education.

The Ministry of Education, however, never succeeded in establishing its authority over public education. The Socialist-Revolutionary (S-R) (*see* Socialist-Revolutionary Party) dominated All-Russian Teacher's Union (VUS), at the forefront of the progressive education movement, was instrumental in creating the State Committee for Public Education, composed of representatives of revolutionary democracy—including those of VUS, the soviets, and the *zemstvos*. By July this State Committee emerged as the counterauthority to the Ministry of Education. It demanded the complete replacement of the old educational administration and personnel, the reduction of the state's role in education, and the community control of schools and the election of teachers. In seven sessions and approximately seventy meetings of its specialized commission, the State Committee formulated more than 40 legal drafts for enactment by the Provisional Government.

The October Revolution shifted the direction of educational change from the mainstream of the progressive movement to Krupskaia's variant. A. V. Lunacharskii* (the new Commissar of Education), M. N. Pokrovskii*, and Krupskaia, with thirty Bolshevik (*see* Russian Social Democratic Workers' Party [Bolshevik])* teachers in Petrograd and thirty-four in Moscow, were confronted with three basic tasks in 1917–1918. First, they had to establish and recruit a central and local administration. Second, they had to struggle with VUS, the State Committee, and other counterrevolutionary teachers. Finally, the new polytechnical school had to be formulated.

Soviet educational administration was initially directed by a representative State Commission of Education modeled after the State Committee. Never to reach its full complement of sixteen delegates, the State Commissions occupied the old Ministry on November 18 and established the Commissariat of Education (Narkompros) on December 11, 1917. By June 1918 Sovnarkom transferred the broad general direction of education from the State Commission to Narkompros' collegium, thereby discarding the illusion of a representative leadership. By 1919 Narkompros was staffed by 3,062 administrators organized into twenty-eight departments.

Decentralization and democratization in lower educational administration were also quickly compromised. Krupskaia's popularly elected educational soviets at the *volost'* (district), *uezd* (county), *guberniia* (province), and *oblast'* (region) levels fell victims to the Ministry of Internal Affairs' opposition to such a parallel structure. By June 1918 the educational departments of the government soviets received the blessings of the Council of People's Commissars* in their direction of the lower schools' structure, and the educational soviets were relegated to advisory functions. Meanwhile, the formed educational circuits as well as the old supervisory school directors and inspectors were abolished. All administrative and teaching personnel were subject to community elections, as much to demonstrate popular support for them as to insure their loyalty to the new regime.

Narkompros' struggle with the State Committee, VUS, and counterrevolutionary teachers lasted well into 1918. The State Committee, which had refused to cooperate with Soviet power, was officially disbanded on November 23. With their 75,000 members, VUS locals in Moscow, Petrograd, and a number of other cities joined the metropolitan teachers in a December strike against Soviet power and in support of the S-R plurality in the Constituent Assembly. The dissolution of the Constituent Assembly, Narkompros' control of all educational funds, and the teachers' own sense of professionalism broke the VUS strike in January. The All-Russian Central Executive Committee* decreed the abolition of VUS on December 23, 1918. In 1919 the Internationalist Teachers were replaced by a broader professional Union of Workers of Education and Socialist Culture (Rabpros) with an enrollment of 70,000.

A series of reforms paved the way toward the formation of the polytechnical school in 1918: the creation of a network of preschool institutions; the separation of education from the Church; a secular, nonclassical curriculum and coeducation; the transference of former Church schools along with specialized and technical schools to Narkompros; the prohibition against all academic uniforms, insignias, and privileges; and the creation of national minority schools. In August 1918 Sovnarkom decreed open admission to all *vuzy* without fees or entrance examinations for anyone over sixteen.

After Narkompros moved to Moscow in March 1918, two approaches to the progressive polytechnical school began to crystallize. The Petrograd approach of Lunacharskii and L. R. Menzhinskaia defined polytechnical education as a pedagogical method of obtaining general education through the scientific study of all aspects of production. The Moscow approach of P. N. Lepeshinskii (head of Narkompros' Department of Social Reform) and V. M. Pozner (head of the Unified Labor School from 1917 to 1919) advocated a year-long school commune that would in effect supplant the family and engage the youngster in actual production labor. The September 30 "Position of the Unified Labor School" and Narkompros' October 16 "Basic Principles of the Unified Labor School" never fully resolved the difference between these two approaches. However, a one-month, week-long school of two levels (Level I, ages eight to thirteen, and Level II, ages thirteen to seventeen) was established.

From 1918 to 1920 the Unified Labor School developed slowly and adjusted to exigencies. By 1920–1921 the total number of primary and secondary schools equalled 118,390 with an enrollment of 9.7 million. Progressive principles and production labor were being worked out in a small number of children's colonies, model experimental schools, nurseries, kindergartens, and boarding schools. Harsh economic conditions and the great numbers of homeless waifs (*besprizornye*) that had to be fed, clothed, sheltered, and medically cared for made Narkompros' development of the polytechnical school even more difficult.

Also by 1920 the polytechnical school was adversely affected by the creation of three main administrations (*glavki*) for education in Narkompros. The semi-autonomous Main Administration for Vocational Education (Glavprofobr) had been forced on Narkompros by the combined pressures of the Supreme Council of the National Economy* (Vesenkha), the technical and economic commissariats, the trade unions, the Ukrainian Narkompros, and the Komsomol (*see* Russian Communist League of Youth). Glavprofobr was charged with directing all secondary vocational–technical education as well as higher educational institutions that were now duty-bound to pursue a more practical mission under the guidance of the State Scientific Council (GUS). Secondary vocational–technical education was to begin at age fifteen, thus rolling back the general polytechnical school from a nine-year course to seven years. In fact, from 1919 many factories had established schools of factory urban youths (*fabrichnoe-zavodskoe uchilishche*, or FZU). Workers' faculties (*rabfaky*) attached to higher technical institutions and universities provided worker–students with an accelerated, compensatory education for entrance into the *vuzy*.

The Main Administration for Social Education (Glavsotvos) presided over what remained of the polytechnical school and was defended by Krupskaia and Lenin against further encroachments. The Main Administration for Political Education (Glavpolitprosv bet) spread literacy, culture, and propaganda.

Ronald Hideo Hayashida

Bibliography

Allston, Patrick L. *Education and the State in Tsarist Russia*. 1969.
Anweiler, Oskar. *Geschichte der Schule un Paedogogik in Russland von Ende des Zarenreiches bis zum Beginn der Stalin-Aera*. 1964.
Fitzpatrick, Sheila. *The Commissariat of Enlightenment*. 1970.
Ignatiev, Paul N.; Odinetz, Dimitrii M.; and Novogrodtsev, Paul. *Russian Schools and Universities in the World War*. 1929.
Korolev, F. F. *Ocherki po istorii sovetskoi shkoly i pedgogiki, 1917–20*. 1958.
Krupskaia, N. K. *Pedagogicheskie sochineniia v desiat' tomakh*. 10 vols. 1957.
Pedagogicheskaia entsiklopediia 4 vols. 1964–1968.
Popova, N. V. *K istorii vserossiskogo uchitel'skogo soiuza*. 1917.

Emigration. The experience of the war was perhaps more profound for members of Russian emigration than it was for their position within the Russian Empire. Their position in Western Europe (centered mainly in Paris, Zurich, Lausanne, Berne, London, and in the Scandinavian countries) provided them with a broader perspective on the war's meaning and its impact. This perspective allowed them to remain less susceptible to the appeals of patriotism or to the visions of a German-executed apocalypse. Thus for the most part, this emigration (or its major figures and spokesmen) was unaffected by the wave of patriotism that initially swept through the opposition movement in Russia.

There were notable exceptions to this rule, however. Men such as George V. Plekhanov* and the Socialist-Revolutionary Party leaders I. A. Rubanovich, V. L. Burtsev*, and B. V. Savinkov* either reversed their positions and called for the support of the autocracy in its struggle against German "barbarism" or adopted a pro-Entente position, seeing in the victory of the Entente a progressive historical event that would bring in its wake the sought-after reforms in the Russian autocracy. These men, formerly major forces within the Russian political opposition, would, as a consequence of this position (and of the war's duration), lose much of their influence and prestige.

The initial agreement on the necessity of opposition to the war that animated the preponderant majority of the members of the various organizations of the emigration movement had, as its immediate result, a reemergent sentiment in favor of reorganization and reunification of the Russian Social Democratic Workers' Party (Bolshevik)*. This sentiment was found in divergent groups such as the Foreign Committee (Zagranichnyi komitet) of the Menshevik (*see* Russian Social Democratic Workers' Party [Menshevik]) Organizational Committee, the Vpered group, the Mezhraionka (*see* Interdistrict Committee), and even the Bolshevik (*see* Russian Social Democratic Workers' Party [Bolshevik]) organizations (N. I. Bukharin*, G. L. Piatakov, and E. B. Bosh showed initial enthusiasm for the project). The sentiment was given additional impulse by the formation of a suprafactional group whose organ (successively known as *Golos, Nashe slovo, Nachalo,* and *Novaia epokha,* this newspaper began appearing daily in Paris between September 1914 and April 1917) sought to provide a forum in which reunification could be debated and elaborated. The group's members included Iu. O. Martov*, V. A. Antonov-Ovseenko, D. Z. Manuilskii, and, from late 1914, L. D. Trotsky* among its contributors and active collaborators.

The drive for, as well as the sentiment in favor of, reunification, initially so promising, would founder by late 1915 due to the opposition of both the Menshevik Organizational Committee and V. I. Lenin's* Central Committee of the Russian Communist Party (Bolshevik)*. As the war unexpectedly dragged on, the disagreements intensified between those who, while condemning the Second International and its leaders for their pro-war positions or their passivity in the face of war, urged a policy of reconciliation after the war was ended and the more radical wing, led by Lenin, which argued that reconciliation was impossible due to the innate betrayal of these leaders to the principles of internationalism. This debate served to polarize the Zimmerwald movements as well as to threaten the unity of the anti-war movement in various European parties. By the time of the February Revolution* the anti-war opposition, while everywhere growing in strength, was itself deeply divided over the question of amnesty. This question had effectively aborted efforts at reunification among the members of the Russian emigration and had led instead to the startling collapse of the loosely structured Menshevik movement. Many individuals and groups, including Trotsky* and others, who had earlier looked to the Mensheviks as a viable counter to the organizational dogmatism of the Bolsheviks, now viewed Menshevism as a bankrupt solution. The Revolution would have the effect of convincing these individuals that the Bolshevik organization provided the only vehicle capable of reunifying the party and thereby securing the success of the Revolution.

This conclusion, which was reached only in July 1917, led to a rallying toward the Bolsheviks by Trotsky, A. V. Lunacharskii*, and other figures of the independent Inter-District Committee* (Mezhraionka). In this process, it was perhaps ironic that the Menshevik organization suffered because of its strengths. Its greater influence within Russia (during the period 1914–1917) among underground organizations and in the rank-and-file workers' movement made it more cautious in its dealing with ''social Defensist'' (see Defensism) proponents of the war effort. That influence also made it more susceptible to the pressures favoring participation in the War Industries Committees* and other forms of war-related activity involving collective work with pro-war groups. The Menshevik emigré leadership's resistance to a sharp break with those who took such positions tended to make them appear as organizationally dogmatic. They would only criticize non-Mensheviks, like the Leninists. This comparison, especially given the heterogenous nature of the Menshevik organization (more a confederation than a party), led to its actual dissolution and, more rapidly, to a loss of effective leadership among those elements and groups traditionally hostile to Lenin.

The February Revolution hastened this dissolution because, in its continued insistence on amnesty for Defensists, it also pursued a cautious policy with regard to the development of the revolutionary movement. Essentially, it followed a policy of collaboration with the Provisional Government and, therefore, of limited expectations for the revolutionary movement—making it seem as though it had abdicated in the face of the ''bourgeois revolution.''

Thus Revolution in Russia came at the end of a process of reappraisal and redefinition within the political emigration that would have startling benefits for the Bolsheviks and startling disadvantages for the Mensheviks. By February 1917 a significant number of the Russian Social Democratic leaders had already concluded that policies of reconciliation or collaboration, or moderation, would spell the defeat of the revolutionary movement in Russia and in the West. This conclusion was a part of their baggage as they boarded trains and (like Trotsky) boats to return to Petrograd. It presaged the deepening of the revolutionary crisis in Russia and, finally, the October Seizure of Power* initiated by the Bolsheviks in the name of the soviets.

Michael Shaw

Bibliography

Collart, Yves. *Le Parti socialist suisse et l'Internationale, 1914–15*. 1969.
Fainsod, Merle. *International Socialism and the World War*. 1935.
Gankin, O. H., and Fisher, H. H. *The Bolsheviks and the World War*. 1940.
Rosmer, A. *Le mouvement ouvrier pendant la guerre*. 1936.
———. *Le mouvement ouvrier pendant la premiere guerre mondiale*. 1959.
Senn, Alfred E. *The Russian Revolution in Switzerland*. 1971.
Temkin, Ia. G. *Lenin i mezhdunarodnaia sotsial-demokratiia*. 1968.

Enlightenment, Commissariat of. *See* Commissariat of the Enlightenment.

Enver Pasha (1881–1922). Enver Pasha was a prominent Turkish political and military leader who took part in the Basmachi* movement in Soviet Central Asia. He was born in Istanbul and participated in the Young Turk Revolt of 1908. Enver Pasha was a leader of the Young Turk Party and of the Committee of Union and Progress. He was trained as an army officer in the Academy of the General Staff and took part in the coup d'état of January 1913 in Turkey that brought a new triumvirate to power that included Enver Pasha, Talaat Pasha, and Jemal Pasha. During World War I* he was, in effect, commander-in-chief of the armed forces of Turkey under the Sultan. He was instrumental in bringing Turkey into the war on the side of Germany, and he espoused the ideology of Pan-Turkism. He was one of the leaders responsible for the massacre of the Armenian people during World War I*. He commanded the Turkish forces that seized Baku in 1918 and put an end to the Baku Commune (*see* Transcaucasia, Revolution in). When Turkey accepted defeat in 1918 Enver Pasha fled to Germany, and he appeared in Moscow in the autumn of 1920. In September he took part in the Congress of Eastern Peoples in Russia called by the Communist International*.

In his speeches Enver Pasha offered to join in the struggle against "Western imperialism." The Soviet government sent him to Bukhara* in 1921 to help organize the resistance to the Basmachis, hoping that he would recruit more trained Turkish officers for that task. Enver Pasha soon defected, however, and established ties with the Emir of Bukhara who ordered Ibrahim Bek to put Enver Pasha in command of the Basmachi in eastern Bukhara. Enver Pasha soon chafed at his minor role—he controlled less than a fifth of the 16,000 Basmachi rebels— and his efforts to expand his control brought him into conflict with the Emir and Ibrahim Bek. At one point he offered to return to the communist fold if the Russians would withdraw their troops from Turkestan. When Enver Pasha began to assume grandiose titles usurping the authority of the Emir, they began withdrawing support. In August 1922 he was killed in a skirmish with troops of the Red Army*. (*See* Basmachi)

Bibliography

Pipes, Richard. *The Formation of the Soviet Union.* 1968.

Estonia and the Russian Revolution, 1917–1921. The outbreak of World War I* kindled Estonia's hope for independence from Russia, and when the February Revolution* of 1917 overthrew Tsar Nicholas II* that hope was partially realized.

Under an act of the Provisional Government* of March 21, 1917, proposed by A. F. Kerensky*, which permitted national minorities to establish their own administrative agencies, the Estonian provinces were for the first time in the history of the Estonian people linked under one administration headed by Jaan Poska, the mayor of Tallinn. On July 1, 1917, the democratically elected Estonian Diet met in Tallinn. It elected its own government, called the National Council, with Konstantin Päts as its head. Simultaneously, the old Baltic Diets of the German nobility surrendered their functions to the Estonian Diet.

At the time of the establishment of a Provisional Government in Petrograd, Soviets (Councils) of Workers, Peasants, and Soldiers Deputies* were established in Tallinn, Tartu, and Narva, the three major cities in Estonia. Thus there was dual power* in Estonia, just as in Russia, with each institution claiming to be representative of the Estonian people. On July 14, 1917, the National Council met in Tallinn, in spite of the opposition of the Tallinn Soviet. As in the rest of Russia, in Estonia political movements tended to polarize, with the National Council increasingly seen as the representative of those in favor of Western-style political democracy and the soviets perceived as the representative of those urban workers who placed a higher priority on the benefits of social democracy. The National Council passed a series of resolutions: crown lands were to be expropriated and divided among the landless peasants and workers; private schools were to be abolished and a system of state schools set up with Estonian as the language of instruction. Estonia was to be a free state within a Russian democratic federation. The newly won independence of Estonia seemed somewhat precarious as the German army moved closer and closer to that country, seizing the nearby capital of Latvia, Riga, in August (*see* Latvia and the Russian Revolution). Some such as Konstantin Päts argued, however, that this only strengthened the arguments for declaring Estonia completely independent of Russia and, therefore, out of the war with Germany.

When the Bolsheviks overthrew the Provisional Government of Kerensky on October 24, 1917, the repercussions were felt in Estonia. The Tallinn Soviet declared itself the only legal government of Estonia, rejecting the authority of the National Council. But the National Council continued its work in Tallinn until forcibly removed from office by the Tallinn Red Guards on November 15, 1917. The Estonian communist leaders, Jaan Anvelt and Viktor E. Kingisepp, tried to establish themselves by declaring the newly elected assembly dissolved.

The Estonian national deputies refused to part with their mandates and formally withdrew from the Russian state on that very day. Although political power was, in fact, in the hands of the Estonian Bolsheviks, the National Council hastened to establish its claims to legitimacy by sending its delegates, Jaan Tönnisson and Ants Piip, abroad, charged with the task of gaining recognition for its cause among Western powers.

The Estonian Bolsheviks called for new elections to gain some public recognition for their seizure of power. When the vote threatened to turn against them, they called off the elections entirely and continued to rule by military force. When the German army began its advance into Estonia, the Estonian Bolsheviks fled and the National Council met and made a formal announcement of Estonia's Declaration of Independence on February 24, 1918. A temporary government under Konstantin Päts was established, and all able-bodied male Estonians were called upon to join the Estonian army. Two Estonian regiments had already been established under the rule of the Russian Provisional Government. After Estonia's Declaration of Independence this force rapidly increased to about 4,000 troops, many of them from Petrograd. This became the nucleus of the future Estonian army, which quickly attracted thousands of Estonian soldiers and officers from inside the Russian Republic.

The Estonians were able to enjoy their political independence for only a short time before the German army arrived. When the treaty negotiations between the Germans and the Russians broke down at Brest-Litovsk* on February 18, the German army began moving north from Riga, reaching Tallinn on February 25. The German military authorities suppressed Bolshevik as well as nationalist Estonians, arresting most members of the Estonian National Council. On May 4, 1918, the German army took Narva, which placed all of Estonia in its hands. The collapse of the German army on the western front made the German army in Estonia too weak to stop the Russian Red Army* from moving back to Estonia. Nevertheless, some German officers, headed by General Rudiger von der Goltz, intent upon remaining in Estonia, asked for German volunteers and more help from Germany itself. Under the Treaty of Brest-Litovsk between Soviet Russia and Germany on March 3, 1918, Soviet Russia renounced all historical and legal rights over Estonia, while Germany retained under Article 3 the right to settle its differences with the local population. With Germany's defeat on November 11, 1918, the German occupation came to an end, and on November 18 the German authorities handed over their authority to the Estonian Provisional Government. The Soviet government responded by renouncing the Treaty of Brest-Litovsk, and on November 22 Soviet forces appeared near Narva.

The Estonian National Council ordered total mobilization of its army, and British forces, which had landed in Tallinn on December 12, 1918, supplied much-needed weapons. The British gave the Estonian government two destroyers, rifles, ammunition, guns, and clothing. Within a month, a defense line north and south of Lake Peipus on the eastern border with Russia had been firmly established.

Except in the South, Estonia was free from communist rule by February 1919. On August 31, 1919, the Soviet Foreign Secretary, G. V. Chicherin*, proposed an armistice to the Estonian government. A couple of thousand volunteers from Finland, Sweden, and Denmark swelled the ranks of the new Estonian army, giving them hope and reinforcement. Under the able leadership of General Jaan Laidoner, the Estonian offensive against the communists began. Using armored trains in surprise attacks, the Estonian army was able to upset the morale of the Red Army. By grim fighting a few hundred Estonian soldiers drove 18,000 communist troops from Narva. Early in February the Red Army was expelled from Voru and Walka. On February 16 an Estonian army expedition took the largest Estonian island, Saaremaa. Finally, on February 24, 1919, General Laidoner reported to the National Council that the Estonian army, with the help of the White Russian army under General N. N. Iudenich*, had expelled the Red Army from the entire Estonian region.

While fighting the Red Army, the Estonians had another danger to face: German military units were still on Estonian soil. Under the terms of the armistice with Germany, the German forces were to withdraw gradually to the East Prussian frontier. Owing to Red Army incursions into the Baltic area, however, certain German forces were ordered by the Allies to remain in the Baltic area to protect the new Baltic republics from the Red Army. Even though the German High Commission for the Baltic signed an agreement with the Estonian government on November 18, 1919, recognizing it as an independent state, General von der Goltz promoted the formation of a German Iron Division from the local Balts. The Estonian government recognized this as a threat and decided to help the Latvians, who were engaged in a struggle with von der Goltz, to push the Germans out of the Baltic region. General von der Goltz, realizing that his position was untenable under the Versailles Treaty, handed over the control of his troops to a White Russian Colonel, P. M. Bermondt-Avalov. The failure of the Western Allies to realize that von der Goltz and Bermondt-Avalov were a real threat to the Baltic peoples' aspirations for independence nearly proved fatal to those young countries. Fortunately, the combined forces of the Latvian and Estonian armies routed the forces of von der Goltz and Bermondt-Avalov near Riga. Only then did the Allies recognize this new danger, and a British fleet sailed into Daugava and began to shell the flanks of the German forces, forcing the latter to retreat south. By the end of the year, the Germans withdrew completely from the Baltic. The Soviet government, pressed hard on all fronts, put forward peace proposals to the Estonian government on August 31, 1919. Peace negotiations began in Pscov on September 17 but soon broke off. They were resumed in Tartu on December 5, 1919, and concluded on December 31, 1919, with Soviet Russia granting full recognition of Estonia's sovereignty.

This did not bring an end, however, to the activities of the Estonian Communist Party. In November 1920 it held an illegal conference headed by Anvelt and Kingisepp. The goal of the Estonian Communist Party was the overthrow of the Estonian Democratic Republic. During the elections to the national parliament in 1923, the Estonian Communist Party received 10 percent of the votes. The Estonian Communist Party organized strikes that threatened to disrupt the Estonian economy. While the leaders of the party were arrested, some managed to flee to the Soviet Union. With the assistance of the Soviet government, several hundred Estonian communists secretly returned from the Soviet Union to organize an uprising against the Estonian state. In the early morning on December 1, 1924, the communists struck in Tallinn where they attempted to take over the main strategic military installations: the railroad station, the post office, the telegraph, the radio station, and the police and military barracks of the young cadets. They were successful in taking over the radio station, and called upon the workers and the peasants to join them in forming an Estonian Soviet republic. But they were surprised by the stiff resistance they met from the young military cadets and their lack of success in winning mass support from the Estonian people. The December 1 uprising was quickly crushed by the army and the police.

Estonia remained independent of the Soviet Union until World War II. It was relegated to the Soviet sphere of influence by the notorious Molotov–von Ribbentrop Pact of August 23, 1939, and forced into a Mutual Assistance Pact with the Soviet Union on September 24, 1939. On June 16, 1940, the Estonian government was presented with a set of demands from the Soviet Union. It was asked to form a new and more sympathetic cabinet and to grant Soviet troops the right to cross Estonian territory. When the reply of the Estonian government was deemed unsatisfactory two days later, the Red Army occupied Estonia on June 20, and on July 5 it was reincorporated into the Soviet Russian state.

Emanuel Nodel

Bibliography

Jackson, J. Hampden. *Estonia*. 1948.
Nodel, Emmanuel. *Nation on an Anvil*. 1963.
Page, Stanley. *The Formation of the Baltic States*. 1959.
Royal Institute of International Affairs. *The Baltic States*. 1938.
Rudnev, D. M. *Viktor Edvardovich Kingisepp*. 1967.
Saat. J. *Velikaia Oktiabr' skaya sotsialisticheskaia revoliutsiia v Estoniii*. 1958.
Tipner, P. *V ogne revoliutsii*. 1964.
Uustalu, Evald. *The History of the Estonian People*. 1952.
Von Rauch, Georg. *Geschichte der baltischen Staate*. 1970.
Wittram, R. *Baltische Geschichte*. 1954.

F

Famine. The role of food shortages in revolutions has received scant attention at the hands of historians. In Russia the inability of successive governments to provide an adequate food supply contributed to the loss of public confidence in each one, including the Soviet government. Although famine is usually classified as a natural disaster, in modern times food shortages and famines have usually resulted from political and economic exigencies brought on inadvertently by government policies. This was certainly true of the food-supply problem and eventually, the huge famine that plagued Russia during the Revolution and Civil War (*see* Civil War in Russia).

The seeds of the famine in Russia actually sprang from a sudden and state-induced increase in peasant prosperity at the outset of World War I*. The prosperity came in the form of the imperial government's payments to peasants for requisitioning horses and allowances for the dependents of conscripts. Combined with the termination of grain exports, these payments increased the peasant's income by an average of 18 percent while enabling him to consume more grain than in the past. Simultaneously, the war effort quickly absorbed the full productive capacity of Russian industry. This sharply limited the availability of consumer goods and drove their prices upward. Hence the peasant, whose own basic needs were fulfilled, had little significant incentive to produce and market surpluses of grain.

These developments coincided with the early failure of the railroads to maintain civilian food deliveries while bearing the burden of military shipments. This created an instant decline in the supply of food and a major increase in the cost of food in the great cities and those provinces that were net importers of grain. The government tried to alleviate these problems by inaugurating food rationing in 1915 and establishing a state monopoly in the grain trade in 1916. Because the price paid for grain was fixed, but the prices of other products were allowed to float, the peasant's flush of prosperity passed, and his incentive to produce food surpluses declined even more. The result was that both the area under cultivation and the total volume of grain production were 20 percent lower in 1917 than they had been in 1913. Such reductions could only have a severe impact on the lives of industrial workers. The urban disorders that culminated in the Tsar's abdication in February 1917 were the ultimate proof of that impact.

The food problem did not vanish with the Tsar as the Provisional Government* would discover. Its leaders came under immediate pressure to increase food deliveries to the cities and consuming provinces. Limited by the disintegration of the machinery of government, they could do little more than elaborate the state monopoly in the grain trade by empowering the State Supply Committee to fix both delivery quotas and prices for producing peasants. There was widespread recognition in 1917 that Russia had to be rescued from the threat of famine, and in the beginning of its tenure in office the Provisional Government received some expression of support from the peasants in the form of new waves of grain deliveries to the city. But in the late spring and summer, food supplies once again began to run short. A government decree of March 25, 1917, tightened the grain monopoly and called for the creation of food committees in every Volost that was charged with the responsibility of increasing the production and delivery of grain. In May the minister of agriculture sent instructions to the provincial (*guberniia*) food committee giving it the power to seize at half the fixed price any grain not delivered as required by the government's quotas. On May 5 the Ministry of Food was established to supervise and centralize all efforts to increase agricultural production.

All of these efforts, however, foundered in bureaucratic delay and inadequate implementation. Given the confusion and mass upheavals of the year 1917, it may have been beyond the powers of any government to solve the food problem. Whatever the reason, the food crisis loomed larger and larger throughout the year and played a major role in creating the unrest in Russia that led to the October Seizure of Power*. When the Provisional Government became desperate in August, it doubled the fixed price for grain. But by this time the currency had depreciated so badly and the cost of manufactured goods had soared to such heights that these measures only worsened matters. During the last three months of 1917, the cost of basic foodstuffs increased fivefold in the large cities.

The Soviet seizure of power in October was obviously facilitated by these developments. The survival of the new Soviet government, though, was largely the result, in the short run, of its ability to liquidate hunger among industrial workers by draconian measures, such as confiscating large supplies of grain in Western Siberia and commandeering freight cars to carry it to Great Russian cities. Such expedients did not, however, deal with the underlying problems. Ironically Lenin's land decree greatly complicated the problem by seeming to legitimize the frenzied distribution of land already under way, a movement that disrupted current production and proliferated the kind of small peasant holding that could rarely generate surpluses of grain even under ideal conditions.

By the time the new government was able to respond to these problems in the spring of 1918, urban hunger was so widespread that there was little opportunity for careful deliberation. Rather, the government issued a series of expedient ad hoc measures that became known as War Communism*. As early as May 1918 the masses were becoming disillusioned by the evident failure of centralized grain requisitioning and distribution. Even a sympathetic observer like the Soviet dissident historian Roy Medvedev wrote: "In general, one could say without great exaggeration that by the early summer of 1918 the Bolsheviks had lost much of the confidence they earlier won among the peasants, especially middle peasants, as well as among artisans and even a section of the industrial workers (Medvedev 1979, p. 150). He argued that the Bolsheviks should have compromised with the peasants' needs and did not. Instead, they chose the road of violence by creating the Commissariat of Food Supply and the Committees of the Poor*. In June 1918 Lenin proposed that the Red Army* be mobilized to collect grain, and nine-tenths of the work of the Commissariat of War was devoted to this effort. The death penalty was restored for use against hoarders, and terror became the chief method of grain collection. Dissatisfaction with the food supply and the mode of grain collection contributed to the anti-Bolshevik sentiment that nourished the Civil War in Russia*. In turn, the coming of the Civil War gave great momentum to the food crisis, increasing the harshness and the terror that accompanied grain collection and cutting off some of the most important sources of desperately needed grain. The Bolshevik government found itself battling for its survival, reduced at one point to effective control only over a portion of the Great Russian provinces. Under such conditions maintaining control over the cities and supplying the cities and the Red Army took precedence over everything else. Peasant resistance to such measures consisted mostly of passive retrenchment to self-sufficiency, which cut agricultural production by an estimated 30 percent annually after 1918. Not even the most draconian policy of requisitioning could offset such a decline and feed the cities. One result was that almost a third of the urban population would migrate to the countryside by early 1921. Meanwhile, a severe drought had swept much of the countryside, especially the Volga provinces in the latter half of 1920. Thus many who fled the hunger of the cities would now be confronted with the more classical pattern of rural famine.

By the summer of 1920 this new famine had expanded into the Ukraine, Transcaucasia, and parts of the Urals. More than 37 million persons inhabited these areas, and at least one-third of them were threatened by extreme starvation. The human, economic, and political danger inherent in the famine was immense, as the Kronstadt Mutiny (see Kronstadt, 1917–1921) and outbursts of peasant violence (most notably the Antonov Rebellion) clearly revealed.

The food problem was not solved until the "carrot" replaced the "stick." The introduction of the New Economic Policy* (NEP) in March 1921, as E. H. Carr pointed out, "came too late to forestall or mitigate a great natural catastrophe," but it adopted the correct solution "by guaranteeing the peasant the freedom to dispose of his surpluses" and by giving him a feeling of security in the possession of his land (Carr 1952, II: 283). The beneficial effects of NEP did not come soon enough, however, to avert the catastrophe of famine.

Soviet governmental relief measures were largely ineffective because of the strains of the Civil War and the weakness of the state apparatus and transportation system. Only a massive infusion of foreign assistance, principally through the American Relief Administration, prevented a catastrophe of epic proportion. Foreign efforts supported approximately 12 million persons and estimates of deaths still range from 3 million to 6 million. Even those relief efforts were regarded with suspicion by the Soviet government, and they were terminated in mid–1922 with more than 10 million Russians dependent upon foreign food deliveries. Early in 1923 (with foreign food relief still supporting 5 million persons), the Soviet government renewed grain exports with shipments totaling more than 8 million tons in an effort to stabilize the currency and renew foreign trade. Lenin was convinced that only through the revival of the whole Russian economy could the problems of food supply be resolved, but his decisions seemed to the outside world proof that the Bolshevik Revolution cared for the plight of the Russian people only in the abstract and was willing to ignore the suffering of the few for its perception of the good of the many (*see also* Peasants in the Russian Revolution; Agriculture; Agrarian Policy, 1917–1921).

Charles Edmondson

Bibliography

Anfimov, A. M. *Rossiiskaia derevnia vo vremia pervoi mirovoi voiny*. 1962.
Antiseferov, A. N.; Batshev, M. O.; and Irantsov, D. N. *Russian Agriculture during the War*. 1930.
Carr, E. H. *The Bolshevik Revolution, 1917–23*. Vol. 2. 1952.
Davydov, M. I. *Bor'ba za khleb*. 1971.
Fisher, H. H. *The Famine in Soviet Russia*. 1927.
Gill, G. J. *Peasants and Government in the Russian Revolution*. 1979.
Medvedev, Roy. *The October Revolution*. 1979.
Oganovskii, N. P., ed. *Sel'skoe khoziaistvo Rossiia v XX veke*. 1923.

Far Eastern Bureau (*Dal' nevostochnoe Biuro*). The Far Eastern Bureau was an executive body created under the Siberian Bureau of the Central Committee of the Russian Communist Party (*see* Russian Social Democratic Workers' Party [Bolshevik]) to take charge of efforts to establish communist control over the Russian Far East, that is, Russia east of Lake Baikal, or eastern Siberia. The Far Eastern Bureau was created on March 3, 1920, under the Siberian Bureau, but in August it was placed directly under the Central Committee of the Russian Communist Party (Bolshevik)*. The two leading figures in the Far Eastern Bureau were A. M. Krasnoshchekov*, the first President of the Far Eastern Republic* with its original base in Verkhneudinsk, and P. M. Nikoforov, based in Vladivostok. With the decline of Ataman Grigorii M. Semenov's* Cossacks* in

October 1920, these two centers of communist power in the Far East were able to unite and create the Far Eastern Republic.

In November the Far Eastern Bureau moved the capital of the Far Eastern Republic to Chita, although its members from Vladivostok favored that city as the capital. This dispute was one of the major issues in the Far Eastern Bureau, and it grew out of the personal distrust of Vladivostok communist leaders for A. M. Krasnoshchekhov and the other Verkhneudinsk communists. This was also a matter of geography, for the Verkhneudinsk communists were closer to the Siberian Bureau at Omsk and the Soviet government at Moscow, and because of communications problems, the communists at Vladivostok were accustomed to acting on their own initiative. There were also differences on the issue of immediate political goals, with some communists in the Far Eastern Bureau favoring immediate sovietization and others sharing Lenin's and Krasnoshchekhov's belief that the Far Eastern Republic should remain apparently autonomous and democratic. Most of these differences were resolved by changing the membership of the Far Eastern Bureau in the fall and winter of 1920. On December 11, 1920, the Popular Assembly in Vladivostok accepted the Chita government and the Far Eastern Bureau, and in January 1921 the Far Eastern Bureau was able to muster a sizeable majority in the voting for a constituent assembly for the Far Eastern Republic. These temporary successes were to some extent negated when a White (*see* White Movement) coup d'état took place in Vladivostok in May 1921 with the tacit support of the occupying Japanese forces, and the threat of a White Far Eastern Republic remained until the Japanese announced that they would withdraw their forces on June 24, 1922. On November 14, 1922, the Far Eastern Republic asked to become part of the Union of Soviet Socialist Republics. The Far Eastern Bureau immediately assumed less importance but continued to exist until it was eliminated on November 20, 1925. (*See* Siberia, Revolution in).

Bibliography

Nikoforov, P. M. *Zapiski premera DVR*. 1963.
Norton, Henry. *The Far Eastern Republic of Siberia*. 1923.
Smith, Canfield. *Vladivostok under Red and White Rule*. 1975.

Far Eastern Republic. A buffer state created by Russian communists in eastern Siberia on April 6, 1920 to serve as a barrier to the advance of Japanese and American troops occupying Vladivostok.

The idea of creating a Far Eastern Republic as a holding action in eastern Siberia was strongly recommended by V. I. Lenin* but was opposed by many Siberian communists, who believed that with their estimated 4,000 members they could seize power in their own right in 1920. Lenin believed that the new Soviet state in European Russia was too weak to take any military action to expand in the Far East, especially against approximately 70,000 Japanese and 12,000 American troops. The Moscow communists believed that any precipitate action by the Siberian communists might inspire attack but that a semiautonomous political entity might encourage the hope for a democratic turn in the Russian Revolution and give the Japanese and the Americans greater hope of influence in the Russian Far East.

The communists were strongest in Verkhneudinsk and Vladivostok but faced competition in Chita from Ataman Grigorii M. Semenov* and his Cossacks*, who had set up a rival Government of the Eastern Borderlands in Chita. Actually, the original idea of a democratic buffer state in eastern Siberia began with a non-Bolshevik (for Bolsheviks see Russian Social Democratic Workers' Party [Bolshevik]) organization created in 1919. When Admiral A. V. Kolchak's dictatorship over Siberia began to disintegrate in 1919, the "Political Center" in Irkutsk, dominated by Socialist–Revolutionaries (see Socialist-Revolutionary Party) and Mensheviks (see Russian Social Democratic Workers' Party [Menshevik]), claimed after they had seized power in that city on January 5, 1920, that they would form a democratic state east of Lake Baikal, and they formed a Provisional Government. Conditions in Siberia did not favor communism in the beginning, at least in part because there was no significant industry or industrial proletariat except in the rail centers and port cities. Because neither serfdom nor landed aristocracy had developed into important institutions, the Bolshevik land program (see Agrarian Policy, 1917–1921) never achieved popularity among the peasants and Cossacks of Siberia. Finally, the Japanese interventionists were strongly anti-communist and tended to support the White Movements* and Cossacks against the communists. In the long run, however, as the communist Soviet state proved its durability in the West and the various moderate and White movements were discredited by their association with the Japanese interventionists, and as the factions among the Siberian communists began to reconcile their differences, they gradually began to gain ground.

In January the communist Irkutsk Revolutionary Committee (Revcom) was invited to send a representative to the new Provisional Council in Irkutsk. The Provisional Council urged this representative to contact Lenin and arrange for a truce with the Red Army*. A. M. Krasnoshchekhov was sent on this mission. On January 21, 1920, the Irkutsk Revcom, alarmed by the advance of White forces, seized power in that city and called the Soviet of Workers', Soldiers', and Peasants' Deputies into being on January 25, 1920. One of the first decisions of this meeting was to execute Admiral Kolchak before his armed forces reached the city. By March 1920 the People's Revolutionary Army (PRA) was fighting in the name of the communist governments of Irkutsk and Vladivostok, and on March 8, 1920, the Red Army took Irkutsk. Irkutsk was annexed by the Soviet Union, and the Irkutsk Revcom was urged to form the Far Eastern Republic further east in Verkhneudinsk. On April 6, 1920, a hastily convoked Constituent Assembly met in Verkhneudinsk and announced the formation of the Far Eastern Republic, with a promise that its new constitution would guarantee civil rights and free elections under universal, direct, and equal suffrage and would encourage foreign capital.

Japanese forces agreed to recognize the new buffer state in a truce with the Red Army on July 15, 1920, in effect abandoning Semenov's Cossacks. The capital of the Far Eastern Republic was moved to Chita on December 11, 1920 and several local governments joined the new state. A provisional national assembly for the Far East met in Vladivostok on November 11 and recognized the government at Chita and set January 9, 1921, as the date for elections to the Constituent Assembly of the Far Eastern Republic. The new Constitution, which bore a marked resemblance to the American Constitution, was written and approved on April 27, 1921.

There was a temporary setback in May 26, 1921, when White forces in Vladivostok seized power with the approval of the Japanese military forces still occupying the city. They included some powerful business interests and a group calling themselves Kappelites who were mostly Russian-born workers from the Urals who had served in the White forces of General V. O. Kappel before his death in 1919. The Kappelites were moderate anti-communists most of whom simply wanted to return home. Buoyed by their victory in Vladivostok, the new White army they created moved on nearby urban centers, taking Khabarovsk in December. But neither the popular support they expected from the native population nor the arms they expected from the Japanese materialized, and the White offensive began to falter in the summer of 1921. By way of contrast, the Far Eastern Republic gained both momentum and arms from the increasingly powerful USSR. When the Japanese withdrew their armies from Russia in the summer of 1922 the People's Revolutionary Army moved in behind them and on November 15, 1922, the Far Eastern Republic was absorbed into the USSR at its own request. (*See* Siberia, Revolution in).

Bibliography

Avideva, N. A. *Dal'nevostochnaia narodnaia respublika 1920–22.* 1957.
Nikoforov, P. M. *Zapiski prem'era DVR.* 1963.
Norton, Henry K. *The Far Eastern Republic of Siberia.* 1923.
Papin, L. M. *Krakh Kolchakovshchiny i Dal'nevostochnoi respubliki.* 1957.
Shereshevskii, B. M. *V bitvakh za Dan'nyii Vostok (1920–22).* 1974.
Shishkin, S. N. *Grazhdanskaia voina na Dal'noi Vostoke 1918–22 gg..* 1957.
Smith, Canfield. *Vladivostok under Red and White Rule.* 1975.

February Revolution. The February Revolution was the explosion of the two fundamental contradictions in Russia—the revolt of the masses against the established order and the irreconcilable conflict between ''society'' and the ''state.'' World War I* initially seemed to halt the process of what Leopold Haimson called dual polarization of urban Russia, but eventually it quickened its process with ferocious force. The workers' strike movement was revitalized after the summer of 1915. Radical revolutionary activists led by the Bolsheviks (*see* Russian Social Democratic Workers' Party [Bolshevik]) extended their influence among the workers at the expense of the Menshevik (*see* Russian Social

Democratic Workers' Party [Menshevik])-led Workers' Group of the War Industries Committee*. The "sacred union" between the government and the liberals quickly turned into hostility and distrust. But the liberals could not decisively break with the government, partially because they feared that such an action might lead to a revolution from below and partially because, despite the political animosity, the liberals and bureaucracy had created a web of interdependent organizations in support of war efforts.

The February Revolution began on February 23, 1917, International Woman's Day, with the strike of women workers in the textile mills in the Vyborg District in Petrograd who went out into the streets with a single demand—*"Bread."* The strike immediately spread to the neighboring metallurgical factories and its leadership was quickly taken over by more experienced activists. At least 78,000 workers of 50 factories joined in the strike. Although the movement was mainly limited to the Vyborg District, its militancy far surpassed any of the previous strikes during the war. On February 24 the strike was no longer confined to the Vyborg District but spread to all the districts in Petrograd. At least 158,000 workers of 131 factories participated in the strike. For the first time during the war massive demonstrations were staged along Petrograd's principal thoroughfare, the Nevskii Prospekt. On the third day, February 25, the workers' movement developed into a general strike that paralyzed the normal functioning of the capital. The strike participants surpassed 200,000, the largest number since the 1905 Revolution (*see* Nineteen-Five Revolution). The demonstrators attacked police, while the Cossacks* and the soldiers remained unenthusiastic in suppressing the demonstration. Crowds controlled the Nevskii Prospekt, and political rallies were held continuously on Kazan and Znamenskaia Squares.

On February 25, however, the security authorities in Petrograd began to pursue a policy of active suppression of the unrest. The government troops systematically fired upon the demonstrators, chasing them away from the center of the city. The government's determination led even the veteran leaders of the strike movement to predict that the movement was coming to an end, but the firing order pushed the soldiers to an inevitable choice between conscience and obedience. Already, on the night of February 26, the Fourth Company of the Pavlovskii Regiment revolted. This was still an isolated event, and it was easily put down. But it was an ominous sign.

On February 27 the revolt of the Volynskii Regiment led by a few noncommissioned officers quickly spread to the Preobrazhenskii and Lithuanian Regiments and the Sixth Engineering Battalion. The soldiers' insurrection had begun. The insurgent soldiers crossed the Neva and were united with the workers in the Vyborg District. They attacked the Kresty Prison, occupied the Finland Station, burned the police station, and armed themselves after occupying the weapon factories. The entire Vyborg District fell into the hands of the insurgents. They then moved toward the Tauride Palace, site of the Duma (*see* Duma and Revolution). On the way they occupied the arsenal, seized enormous quantities of weapons and ammunition, and burned the circuit court. From then on the insurrection spread to all parts of the city. By late night, almost all the reserve battalions in the city had joined the insurrection. The insurrection, assisted by the ineptitude of the security authorities, had triumphed in Petrograd.

While lawlessness and chaos began to reign in the streets on February 27, two centers of power, the Petrograd Soviet* and the Duma Committee, were created in the Tauride Palace. The Petrograd soviet was formed on the initiative of the Menshevik leaders, who envisaged the Soviet to be no more than a center for the movement to coordinate and organize the activities of the insurgent masses. The policy of its Executive Committee was formulated by three non-party socialists, N. N. Sukhanov*, N. D. Sokolov, and Iu. M. Steklov. On the question of power, they consistently maintained that a provisional government ought to be a bourgeois government composed of representatives of the liberals. This notion was supported by a majority of the Petrograd soviet leaders, including some of the Bolsheviks, like A. G. Shliapnikov*. They believed that revolutionary power emanating solely from the insurgent masses could not possibly have a chance for survival. As punitive detachments sent from the front were approaching the capital, it seemed foolhardy to rest the future of the Revolution on those soldiers roaming in the streets defying any order and discipline and the armed workers who did not even know how to use weapons. The only way to prevent a civil war appeared to them to expand the Revolution to include the rest of society.

The challenge to this notion came from two directions. First, the overwhelming support that the Petrograd Soviet received from the insurgent masses began to transform its nature into something more than the initiators had envisaged. The masses supported the Soviet, not the Duma Committee, thereby accentuating the social content of the Revolution. The workers' militia in the workers' districts effectively established its police power, and the district soviets were quickly extending their self-governing authority in various districts. The soldiers began to form the soldiers' committees in the units, controlled weapons and finances of the units, and even began electing the officers. The insurgents thus asserted their power over immediate administrative matters without reference to any outside authorities. The majority of insurgents, however, had not yet begun to translate their aspirations into conscious revolutionary programs. They could not offer any alternative to the Executive Committee's policy toward the problem of power.

The second threat to the Soviet leaders' policy came from the small group of radical socialists led by the Bolshevik Vyborg District Committee and the Mezhraiontsy (*see* Interdistrict Committee). From the moment the insurrection had triumphed, they called for the establishment of a provisional revolutionary government in the form of a soviet and advocated the transformation of the Petrograd Soviet into a revolutionary government. Although they were still isolated from the mass of insurgents, there were signs that their slogans might receive wide acceptance. Alarmed by this possibility, the Soviet Executive Committee decided

to hasten the formation of a bourgeois provisional government by directly negotiating with the liberal representatives.

The liberals also welcomed the opportunity to reach an agreement with the
Petrograd Soviet on the question of power. The most difficult question that the
liberals faced during the February Revolution was the problem of the legitimacy
of the Provisional Government*. On the one hand, they sought to make the
Revolution itself a source of legitimacy. In fact, they had to take some revolutionary actions, despite themselves, to contain further intensification of the
Revolution. The Duma Committee sanctioned the arrests of the former tsarist
ministers, officials, and the police, while it took over the government apparatus
in the name of the Revolution but actually for the purpose of ensuring the
continuity of the governmental function. It created the city militia to replace the
old police that had disappeared and took over the Military Commission created
by the Petrograd Soviet in order to exert its influence over the insurgent soldiers.
Nevertheless, because there existed unbridgeable class barriers between the liberals and the insurgents and, more importantly, because their ultimate goals—
the restoration of order and the prevention of further revolutionary development
were in basic conflict with the aspirations of the insurgents—they failed to gain
the acceptance of the insurgents. It was for this reason that they chose to negotiate
with the leaders of the Petrograd Soviet for the conditions of transfer of power
in the hope that the Soviet would persuade the insurgents to support the Provisional Government.

This policy failed. The insurgents enforced their will without much consideration of their leaders' intentions and ideological niceties. The process in which
the soldiers issued Order Number One, the insurgent's response to the question
of weapons control, and the response of the workers' militia to the merger with
the city militia all indicated the bankruptcy of the Provisional Government's
policy of reliance on the Soviet leaders for gaining the insurgents' support.
Despite their intention to help out the Provisional Government, the Soviet leaders
could not very well give it their unconditional support without risking the loss
of their own credibility among the masses.

While pursuing the policy to gain legitimacy from the insurgents, the liberals
also sought another source of legitimacy in the legal continuity with the old
regime. The alternative of a palace coup, which they rejected before the February
Revolution, was conceived as the last defense against the further development
of the Revolution and as a measure to ensure the continuity with the old regime.
In dealing with the Tsar and the military leaders, the liberals always presented
themselves as the defenders of law and order against anarchy and demanded
Nicholas II's* abdication as the only alternative to arrest the further development
of the Revolution.

A crucial factor leading to the end of the monarchy was the attitude of the
military leaders. In the beginning of the Revolution, the high command at the
front supported Nicholas's counterrevolutionary measures because it believed
that Petrograd had been taken over by radical socialists. But as soon as it learned

that power had been transferred to the liberal forces, it fully cooperated with the Duma Committee and supported its policy to seek Nicholas's abdication, while halting General N. I. Ivanov's expeditionary detachments. What ultimately determined the actions of the military leaders was their concern with the continuation of war and the preservation of the fighting capacity of the armed forces. Met with the collective pressure of the military leaders, Nicholas agreed to abdicate in favor of his brother Grand Duke Mikhail Aleksandrovich on the night of March 2. On the following day, realizing that the preservation of the monarchy would not be acceptable to the insurgents, the Duma Committee pressured Nicholas's brother Mikhail into refusing to accept the throne. On March 4 the formation of the Provisional Government was formally proclaimed.

Ultimately, it proved impossible for the liberals to pursue two contradictory sources of legitimacy for the Provisional Government. The middle ground that they sought between the old regime and the Revolution did not exist. The liberals of the Provisional Government did not succeed in gaining the full endorsement by the Petrograd Soviet, nor could they even muster all of the strengths of the privileged society. Forced to remove surgically the monarchical system, which actually they needed for their own survival, the liberals were left a vacuum without any solid legal, social, and institutional foundations on which to base the Provisional Government.

The February Revolution in Petrograd was thus merely the beginning of a more revolutionary process. It immediately spread to Moscow and other cities, to the armed forces, and eventually to the countryside, touching off an unprecedented social cataclysm (*see also* Constitutional Democratic Party—Cadet; Nicholas II; Provisional Government).

Tsuyoshi Hasegawa

Bibliography

Burdzhalov, E. N. *Vtoraia russkaia revoliutsiia: Moskva, front, periferiia.* 1971.
———. *Vtoraia russkaia revoliutsiia: vosstanie v Petrograda.* 1967.
Ferro, Marc. *The Russian Revolution of February 1917.* 1972.
Hasegawa, Tsuyoshi.*The February Revolution: Petrograd, 1917.* 1981.
Katkov, George. *Russia 1917: The February Revolution.* 1967.
Leiborov, P. I. *Na shturm samoderzhaviia: Petrogradskii proletariat v gody pervoi mirovo voiny i fevral'skoi revoliutsii.* 1979.
Mel'gunov, S. S. *Martovskie dni 1917 goda.* 1961.
Tokarev, Iu. S. *Petrogradskii sovet rabochikh i soldatskikh deputatov.* 1976.

Finland, Revolution in. Finland was an autonomous Grand Duchy since its incorporation into the Russian Empire in 1809. By 1910 it had a population of 943,000 people, of which about 89 percent spoke Finnish and 11 percent Swedish. It was primarily an agricultural country with 85 percent of the population living in the countryside. Between 1809 and World War I the autonomy of the Grand Duchy of Finland had been undermined by a series of imperial rescripts and edicts. The Finnish government, or Senate, had become a subservient instrument of imperial policy by 1910, and the democratically elected parliament (Eduskunta), which replaced the four-estate Diet in 1906, had been reduced to impotence as a legislative body.

One of the first acts of the Russian Provisional Government* was to rescind all previous legislation that had imposed limits on Finland's autonomy and to order the convention of the Eduskunta. M. A. Stakhovich, a liberal known for his sympathies toward Finland, was appointed as the new Governor-General. The Finnish Social Democratic Party,which enjoyed wide support amongst the rural proletariat and tenant farmers as well as amongst the urban working class, won 103 of the 200 seats in the parliamentary elections of 1916. In March 1917 the party reluctantly agreed to enter the government, and a new Senate composed equally of socialists and non-socialists replaced the nonentities appointed by the Emperor.

The Provisional Government also promised a new constitutional arrangement but was reluctant to grant the Finns the degree of control over their own affairs that they had demanded. The constitutional conflict came to a head on July 18, 1917 (July 5 O.S.), when the Eduskunta passed a socialist-inspired act that transferred the exercise of sovereignty—with the exception of foreign affairs and matters of defense—to the Finnish parliament.[1] The Provisional Government, its authority temporarily strengthened following the July Days*, was able to ignore this act and to proclaim the dissolution of the Eduskunta on July 31 (July 18 O.S.). Although the Finnish Social Democrats seemed at first disposed to challenge the validity of this dissolution, they finally gave way and decided to participate in the elections for a new parliament at the beginning of October. In these elections, the Social Democrats lost their absolute majority but emerged as the largest single parliamentary group with ninety-two seats. By this time the Social Democrats had withdrawn from government and were returning to their traditional attitude of fierce class-conscious opposition. The non-socialist parties, which had been in some disarray in the spring, had drawn closer together in the face of increasing social disorder. Support for full independence for Finland had also grown in the bourgeois parties.

Growing unemployment, as war orders from Russia were cancelled and the construction of large-scale fortifications abandoned, coincided with rapid price inflation. Many essential commodities were in short supply, and food riots occurred in several Finnish towns. The presence of almost 100,000 Russian troops in the country and the large number of Russian sailors in Helsinki, which was the major base for Russia's Baltic Fleet, imposed a severe strain on Finland's meager food reserves, and the indiscipline of these men in a country lacking its own forces for the maintenance of order was a matter of growing concern. During the wave of strikes by farm workers in the spring and summer, farmers in southwestern Finland had begun to form their own vigilante groups to protect their property. In the autumn of 1917 these groups began to coalesce with units dedicated to the defense of a future independent Finland to form a civil or "White guard" (Suojeluskunta). The labor movement responded by authorizing the establishment of a workers' guard, which soon took on the title of Red Guard (Punakaarti). It also resorted to extraparliamentary means to force concessions from the new parliament, which met in November.

Although there was a general strike in November and the Russian Bolsheviks urged the Finnish Social Democrats to seize power, they still sought to resolve the crisis by parliamentary means. The passing of political reforms, including transfer of sovereignty to parliament, in the Eduskunta on November 15–16, and the reluctance of the Social Democratic leaders to stage a seizure of power led to the strike being called off on November 18.

The general strike from November 13 to 18, during which a number of disturbances and atrocities occurred, ended in a great deal of confusion, with a dissident section of the Finnish Red Guards threatening to carry on the fight. It was against this background that a nonsocialist government headed by P. E. Svinhufvud was voted into office by the Eduskunta on November 26. On December 6 the bourgeois majority of the Eduskunta authorized this government to work for the recognition of Finland's independence. The socialists did not oppose independence but argued that it could best be achieved by negotiation with the Soviet government. The reluctance of foreign governments to recognize Finland as an independent state did in fact compel the Svinhufvud government to seek recognition of independence from the Soviet of People's Commissars (see Council of People's Commissars, 1917–1922). This was duly given on December 31 (December 18 O.S.), 1917, and confirmed by the Central Executive Committee of Soviets (see All-Russian Central Executive Committee) four days later.

The Russian Bolsheviks (see Russian Social Democratic Workers' Party [Bolshevik]) had consistently supported Finland's right to national self-determination in 1917, but by the autumn of that year they were more concerned to persuade the Finnish Social Democrats to follow their example and seize power. The Finnish Social Democratic Party did not enjoy close relations with the Bolsheviks and did not seek to pursue their example of seizing power for themselves. However, increasing pressure from the militant element of the Finnish Red Guards for some sort of action and the declaration of the Svinhufvud government on January 12 to make the bourgeois civil guards their official force for the maintenance of order pushed the Social Democratic leadership into accepting the necessity of a seizure of power on January 25, 1918. Fighting between Red and White Guards had already broken out in Eastern Finland, where a large consignment of arms for the Red Guard was expected from Petrograd. The government had appointed a former Imperial Army officer, General Carl Gustaf Mannerheim, to command the new Finnish army and instructed him to disarm and intern Russian troops stationed in the country. As Mannerheim's troops began to carry out these instructions in Ostrobothnia on the night of January 27–28, Red Guards went into action in Helsinki, where a socialist Council of People's Commissars was established. Three members of the government had managed to reach Ostrobothnia before the coup, and they established the provisional headquarters of the government in Vaasa, where they were joined by several other members of the government who managed to escape arrest.

The Civil War lasted some three months. The Whites, numbering some 70,000 by the end of the war, were led by Finnish ex-Imperial Army officers, Swedish officers who volunteered for service, and Finns who had received military training in Germany during the war. The Reds, although superior in numbers, were poorly led and derived little benefit from the Russian troops who remained in Finland other than the professional advice of a handful of officers. By the end of March, all Red offensives to cut the vital east–west railway link between the Gulf of Bothnia and the Karelian Isthmus had been repulsed, and the drive southward by the Whites had begun. Mannerheim's troops took the important town of Tampere early in April, as German troops prepared to land on the southern coast in accordance with an agreement concluded in Berlin by representatives of the Vaasa government. Helsinki fell to the Germans in mid-April, and Red resistance in southern Finland finally collapsed early in May.

Although the Soviet of People's Commissars proclaimed fraternal solidarity with the Finnish Reds, its support was limited. The Treaty of Brest-Litovsk* stipulated that Russian troops be withdrawn from Finland, although those troops had been less helpful to the Finnish Reds than arms from Russia. Relations between the two revolutionary governments were cordial rather than close, and the Russo–Finnish Treaty concluded between the Soviets and the Finnish Reds on March 1 was little more than a clarification of details pertaining to the separation, although some territorial concessions were made by the Russians.

Relations between Finland and Russia remained cool for the next two years. Many Whites believed that a "war of liberation" should be carried on across the frontier to free the Karelians from Russian rule. Finland also became involved in the complex situation involving allied intervention in northern Russia, almost entering into open conflict with Britain in the summer of 1918. The Allies were slow to grant recognition of Finland's independence, partially because of the need to acknowledge the claims of the White Russian representatives to a united and indivisible Russia and partially because of the pro-German attitude of the Finnish government. New elections and the formation of a more acceptable government in 1919 eventually brought this recognition. Mannerheim's efforts to persuade the government of Finland to support the cause of intervention in Russia in the latter half of 1919 failed, and peace negotiations with Soviet Russia began in the summer of 1920. The course of those negotiations was influenced by the changing pattern of the Russo–Polish War going on at that time, (*see* Poland, Revolution in), and the appearance of a rebellion in Karelia where the Karelian Workers' Commune was established on June 8, 1920, after the allied interventionists left that area. Finland demanded that the Karelian people be given the opportunity to exercise their own right of self-determination but finally dropped that demand and signed the Soviet–Finnish Peace Treaty of Tartu on October 14, 1920.

David Kirby

Note

1. Dates in this article are given according to the Gregorian calendar that was in use in Finland but not in Russia. The Russian dates (O.S.) are included in a few instances.

Bibliography

Hodgson, John. *Communism in Finland.* 1967.
Kholodovskii, V. M. *Revoliutsiia v Finliandii i germanskaia interventsiia.* 1967.
————. *Finliandiia i Sovetskaia Rossiia, 1918–20 gg.* 1975.
Kirby, D. G. *Finland and Russia, 1808–1920.* 1975.
Paasivirta, Juhani. *The Victors in World War One and Finland.* 1965.
Siukiiainen, I. I. *Revoliutsionnye sobytiia, 1917–18 gg. v Finliandii.* 1962.

Flag. The flag of the Russian Socialist Federative Soviet Republic (RSFSR) was determined by a decree of the Russian Central Executive Committee of Soviets of Workers' and Soldiers' Deputies on April 8, 1918, as a red flag with the inscription "Russian Federative Republic" drawn by the artist S. V. Chekhonin. Traditionally, the red flag had been a warning posted when an area was under martial law, although it became associated with revolution and worker uprisings during the Paris Commune of 1871. It was used by the workers in the Revolutions of 1904–1905 in Russia. The new flag was decreed the official flag of the RSFSR in its Constitution of 1918 with the golden letters RSFSR in the upper left-hand corner. The flag of the USSR (Union of Soviet Socialist Republics) began to be worked out in 1923 in connection with the first Constitution of the USSR. On November 12, 1923, the All-Russian Central Executive Committee* of Soviets adopted a description of the new national flag that appeared as Article 71 in the new Constitution in 1924. It was to be a red or scarlet square with a golden hammer and sickle in its upper corner toward the flagpole with a red five-pointed star over it framed with a gold border.

Foreign Policy, 1914–1921. In November 1918 Lenin told his fellow Bolsheviks (*see* Russian Social Democratic Workers' Party [Bolshevik]) that the main question facing them from the very beginning of the Revolution had been foreign policy and international relations. These questions, in fact, had significantly influenced the origin, development, and ultimate outcome of the Russian Revolution. Although the Revolution arose from domestic developments, the outside world helped shape events within Russia and, in turn, was influenced by them. The foreign policies of successive Russian governments added an international dimension to the revolutionary crisis and contributed either to stabilization or destabilization of the regimes that formulated them.

The foreign policies pursued between 1914 and March 1918 were all pro- foundly destabilizing and undermined the governments that pursued them. They lowered the prestige of these governments, impaired their ability to govern, worsened economic disorganization, and promoted social disorder. Such negative consequences arose from the repeated failure of successive Russian governments to adjust their political goals to the resources available to pursue them. Russian governments repeatedly sought to do too much with too little; the result was collapse, revolution, and disintegration.

This imbalance of means and ends began with the great international crisis preceding the outbreak of World War I*. In a series of agreements dating from the previous century, Russia had promised to aid France militarily in the event of war with Germany. Although wholly unprepared for such a conflict, the tsarist regime honored this commitment when war broke out in August 1914. The resulting military disaster led within a year to the loss of Poland and other portions of the western borderlands. It did nothing to sober Russian leaders. Instead, they negotiated a series of agreements with the Western powers sanc- tioning a substantial enlargement of the Russian Empire at the end of a victorious war against Germany and its allies. Both Britain and France agreed that Russia should have the straits, Constantinople, and parts of Asia Minor, and France gave Russia full freedom to determine its western border with Germany. No agreement was reached about the future of Austria–Hungary, but Russian leaders expected, at the least, to receive Galicia at the end of the war. These objectives, however, were beyond the Russian grasp. In pursuing them the Tsar placed too great a strain on the fragile social–economic structure of his Empire, and in March 1917 the autocracy collapsed (*see* February Revolution; Nicholas II).

The fall of the monarchy accelerated the process of social–economic disin- tegration. This substantially diminished the resources available for achieving Russian foreign-policy goals, but the governments that followed the Tsar did not recognize this. P. N. Miliukov*, the first Foreign Minister of the Provisional Government*, sought exactly the same aims as Nicholas. This served to deepen the Revolution, for moderate socialists led by I. G. Tsereteli* opposed these aims and soon succeeded in driving him from power. The policies pursued by his successors, though more modest in scope, were no more successful because they still overestimated the resources available to achieve them. Thus Tsereteli sought salvation for Russia in a policy of revolutionary defensism, a continuation of the war while seeking a negotiated peace. Success depended upon a united struggle of European socialists to compel reluctant governments of both coalitions to agree to a peace of no annexations or indemnification. By August 1917 revolutionary defensism* was in shambles, smashed by the intransigence of both coalitions, the ambivalence of other socialist parties, and the sabotage of out- standing personalities in the Provisional Government such as A. F. Kerensky* and M. I. Tereshchenko. The moderate socialists, by subscribing to the July offensive (*see* July Days; World War I) helped to seal the fate of their own peace program. The ignominious failure of this offensive, the consequent rise in war weariness, and the collapse of internal order had a disastrous effect on revolutionary defensism. Russia began to disintegrate, the Allied Powers ceased to take it seriously, and the Provisional Government was left to face an overwhelming popular demand for peace without any program worthy of the name. Tsereteli and his supporters drifted into the shadows while Kerensky and Tereshchenko, hoping for an early Allied victory, attempted to bind Russia together with rhetoric. With the Bolsheviks in the wings this was impossible; in November V. I. Lenin took on himself the terrible task of extricating Russia from the war.

The first Bolshevik foreign policies proved to be just as dysfunctional and destabilizing as those pursued by previous governments. Revolutionary internationalism replaced revolutionary defensism, and the Bolsheviks sought to transcend the entire existing framework of international relations. They wished to convert the international war of state against state into an international civil war of class against class. They loudly proclaimed this ambition, published compromising documents of previous Russian governments, and sought to entangle the belligerent powers in peace negotiations. During these negotiations they hoped to put their adversaries on trial and force them to conclude a peace of no annexations, no indemnifications, and self-determination for all peoples. Such a peace, or even the mere effort of avoiding it, would serve, they believed, to destabilize existing regimes and foment revolution. Only the Central Powers, however, agreed to meet with the Bolsheviks. The Western allies ignored them, and the peace conference at Brest-Litovsk* soon reached an impasse. The Germans demanded that the Bolsheviks agree to the amputation of the western borderlands from Russia.

The failure of revolutionary internationalism led to a sharp conflict within the Bolshevik Central Committee (*see* Central Committee of the Russian Communist Party [Bolshevik]). Lenin wanted to accept the German terms; the "Left Communists*", led by N. I. Bukharin*, demanded a revolutionary war against German imperialism. In this debate the Commissar for Foreign Affairs, L. D. Trotsky*, held the balance of power, and he succeeded in convincing his reluctant colleagues to endorse a policy of "no war, no peace." Trotsky announced that Soviet Russia was leaving the war but would not sign a formal peace treaty with Germany. His policy failed immediately because the Germans refused to accept it as a basis for ending hostilities. Instead, they resumed the war and plunged even farther into Russia. Russian leaders had again failed to balance means and ends with the result that the very existence of Russia as an organized and self-determined state was in question.

In the crisis that followed, Trotsky resigned and was replaced with G. V. Chicherin*. Lenin, however, retained actual control of Soviet foreign relations and moved swiftly to implement a wholly new policy. Unlike earlier policies, this one did not overestimate the resources available for its implementation. The new policy sought to buy peace from Germany, fend off the Western allies, and consolidate Bolshevik power in Russia. It was based on the Treaty of Brest-Litovsk* (March 3, 1918) and the even more rapacious supplementary agreements to that treaty signed in Berlin on August 27, 1918. Its stark realism contributed substantially to the stabilization of the Soviet regime. Despite the most humiliating subservience to Germany, the Bolsheviks were able to cling to power.

Success in this venture earned Soviet Russia the hostility of the Allied Powers and triggered their intervention in the Civil War in Russia*. In mid–1918 they began military operations in Siberia (*see* Siberia, Revolution in) and northern Russia. The end of the war against Germany allowed the Allies to expand intervention to include South Russia, the Ukraine (*see* Ukraine, Revolution in), the Baltic (*see* North, Revolution in), the Caucasus (*see* Caucasian Bureau; Transcaucasia) and Central Asia (*see* Central Asia, Revolution in). The Bolsheviks, however, had made good use of the breathing space they had purchased so dearly from Germany and were able to deploy the Red Army* effectively against the Allies and the forces they supported. Nor did they have to pursue a single policy of survival. Due to the increasing power at their disposal they were able to contend for control of most of the territory of the former tsarist empire. They were greatly aided in this by the inability of the Western governments to interest their peoples in a new war fought in Russia or to formulate a common policy against Bolshevism. The Bolsheviks did not have to face a united opposition; their enemies were badly divided and could be dealt with one at a time.

By the end of 1919 the Bolsheviks had defeated Admiral A. V. Kolchak* in Siberia, A. I. Denikin* in South Russia, and N. N. Iudenich* near Petrograd. They had driven the Western allies from Russia, had reoccupied most of the Ukraine, and had begun to spill back to the borderlands. With the organization of the Comintern (*see* Communist International) in 1919 they opened a political offensive against the Western powers. The Comintern was designed to provide guidance for the newly emergent communist parties of the world. The Bolsheviks hoped it could sharpen class conflict in Europe and intensify nationalist opposition to colonialism in Asia. While not representing a return to the unabashed revolutionary internationalism of 1917, the Comintern did reflect the keen Bolshevik interest in the revolutionary potential offered by the highly unstable postwar world.

Lenin's policy, however, continued to stress the necessity of peace, and the Soviet government never missed an opportunity to propose it to their many enemies. Estonia (*see* Estonia and the Russian Revolution, 1917–1921) was the first to accept the Soviet invitation and was soon joined by other successor states of the Russian Empire. Negotiations for the restoration of trade with Great Britain, Germany, and Italy soon followed. France and Poland (*see* Poland, Revolution in), however, remained unreconciled to the existence of Soviet Russia and the latter, with the tacit consent of the former, invaded the Ukraine in April 1920. The Red Army repulsed this attack and launched its own invasion of Poland. In August Soviet armies were nearing Warsaw while excited delegates to the Second Comintern Congress speculated furiously about the spread of Revolution to Germany. At this moment Lenin came perilously close to overestimating the resources at his disposal and gave serious consideration to further efforts to foment the long expected, but ever elusive, world workers' revolution.

Defeat before Warsaw and the forced retreat of the Red Army proved sobering. Lenin reverted to a policy of promoting peace and commerce. The utter exhaustion of the Russian economy made this all the more necessary. In early 1921 Russia had no more capital on which to live; it had been entirely consumed by seven years of foreign and domestic conflict. On March 16, 1921, a trade agreement was signed with Great Britain. Two days later the Treaty of Riga brought to an end the war with Poland. In the spring of 1921 Soviet Russia passed uneasily into the postwar world, a world made in no small measure by the widely differing foreign policies of successive Russian governments.

Richard K. Debo

Bibliography

Carr, Edward Hallet. *A History of Soviet Russia: The Bolshevik Revolution, 1917–23.* Vol. 3. 1953.

Chubar'ian. *V. I. Lenin i formirovannie sovetskoi vneshnei politiki.* 1972.

Debo, Richard K. *Revolution and Survival.* 1979.

Kheifets, A. N. *Sovetskaia Rossiia i sopredel'nye strany vostoka v gody grazadanskoie voiny, 1918–20.* 1964.

Ministerstvo Inostrannykh Del SSSR. *Dokumenty Vneshnei Politiki SSSR.* Vols. 1–3. 1958–1959.

Oznobishin, D. V. *Ot Bresta do Iur'eva.* 1966.

Temkin, Ia. G. *Lenin i mezhdunarodnaia sotsial-demokratiia, 1914–1917.* 1968.

Uldricks, Teddy J. *Diplomacy and Ideology.* 1979.

Wandycz, Piotr S. *Soviet-Polish relations, 1917–20.* 1969.

Wade, Rex A. *The Russian Search for Peace.* 1969.

Frunze, Mikhail Vasil'evich (1885–1925). M. V. Frunze was a prominent Soviet military leader and Commissar of War.

Frunze was born in Central Asia in the city of Pishpek on January 21, 1885. His mother was a Russian and his father a Moldavian. This diverse background made Frunze a representative of several ethnic groups. He attended the gymnasium at Vernyi where he graduated in 1904 with academic honors. During his student years he was a student activist in St. Petersburg, Petrovsk, Shuia, and Ivanovo-Voznesensk. Among his early revolutionary experiences were participation in the leadership of the Ivanovo-Voznesensk textile workers strike of 1905 and the Moscow uprising of December 1905. He attended the Third Congress of the Russian Social Democratic Workers' Party in London in 1905 and the Fourth Congress at Stockholm in 1906. In 1909 he was sentenced to death by hanging, but in a retrial in 1910 he received four years in prison at Vladimir. The charge was membership in the Russian Social Democratic Workers' Party and the distribution of their political literature. Later in the year he received six years for attempted murder of a policeman, and in 1914 he was sentenced to life in Siberian exile.

In March 1916 Frunze escaped Siberia and fled to Moscow, where the Russian Social Democratic Workers' Party (Bolshevik)* sent him into the front lines to work with the troops. He was remarkably successful. At Shuia he was elected chairman of its Soviet of Workers', Peasants' and Soldiers' Deputies* and President of the Zemstvo Board. On October 28, 1917, he brought 2000 troops under his command to Moscow to take part in the siege of the Hotel Metropole and the Kremlin.

The new Soviet government appointed Frunze Military Commissar of Ivanovo-Voznesensk and Vladimir. This began a successful military career during which he reached the highest posts in the Red Army* and the Russian Social Democratic Workers' Party (Bolshevik). After crushing the anti-Soviet Iaroslav uprising, Frunze was given command of the military forces in eight provinces. By the end of 1918 he was commanding the whole eastern front and Turkestan, and by 1920 he commanded the southern front where he defeated all of the White movements* in that area. In 1921 he was elected a member of the Central Committee of the Russian Communist Party (Bolshevik) (*see* Russian Social Democratic Workers' Party [Bolshevik]) and in 1924 a member of the Politburo.

A persistent opponent of L. D. Trotsky* on military matters, Frunze rose very rapidly to replace Trotsky as Commissar of War in January 1925. Frunze's position on military theory lay between that of M. N. Tukhachevskii* and Trotsky. Frunze had opposed Trotsky's more conventional view that the traditional bourgeois military strategies were still valid, and he opposed Trotsky's mass recruitment of military specialists. Representing the views of many younger communist military commanders, Frunze believed that the whole Soviet state needed to be militarized to prepare for the coming combat with the international forces of capitalism (the doctrine of proletarian war). His ''unitary military doctrine'' called for an army that would draw its strength from the class character of the state, using guerilla warfare in the lands of its enemies with an emphasis on offensive strategy. Shortly before his death in 1925, he issued a decree on universal military service that called for the maintenance of a permanent standing army of more than 500,000 men.

Politically, Frunze was a protege of G. E. Zinoviev*. When the triumvirate of I. V. Stalin*, M. I. Kalinin*, and G. E. Zinoviev began to dissolve in 1925, Frunze found himself in a precarious position. The doctors employed by the Central Committee of the party recommended him for surgery in 1925 for stomach ulcers, a procedure opposed by Frunze's own doctors. He died on the operating table, to be replaced as Commissar of War by his friend, K. E. Voroshilov*.

Bibliography

Arkhangel'skii, V. V. *Frunze*. 1970.
Haupt, G., and Marie, J. J. *Makers of the Russian Revolution*. 1969.
Jacobs, W. D. *Frunze, the Soviet Clauswitz, 1885–1925*. 1969.
Schapiro, L. *The Origin of the Communist Autocracy*. 1965.
Whiting, K. R. *Readings in Soviet Military Theory*. 1952.

G

General Staff. During the Russian Revolution the attitude of the army was decisively important (*see* Army of Imperial Russia in World War I). How the officers lost control over their soldiers in 1917 and why some officers were willing to serve the Bolsheviks during the Civil War in Russia* while others chose to fight the revolutionaries with great determination are among the crucial questions of revolutionary history.

The nerve center of the army was the General Staff. Although it was Peter the Great who created the rudiments of this institution, it fully developed only in the second half of the nineteenth century. The military reforms of 1874 created a modern mass army and the development of the General Staff was a necessary corollary of this modernization. In this process the Russians learned a great deal from the foreign, primarily from French and German, example.

Not all graduates of the Academy of the General Staff (Genshtabisty) did staff work. In the extremely heterogeneous and largely poorly educated officer corps, the graduates of the academy stood out by their relative competence. The academy opened in 1832, and by the end of the century its graduates entirely dominated military life. At the time of World War I*, with a few exceptions, they held all major command posts. Admission to the academy was fiercely competitive and was based entirely on achievement rather than social background. As a result, some of the most powerful military leaders of the country at the time of the war came from humble families. The graduates of the academy spent years doing staff work, but after this apprenticeship, they jumped in rank over their less fortunate comrades. The Genshtabisty formed a self-conscious elite. It looked down on its less well-educated comrades, who reciprocated with resentment. Although officers of the General Staff were the most competent officers, they often lacked field command experience and suffered the consequences of having been cut off from the main stream of the life of the army for a long time.

At the outbreak of the war the newly formed General Headquarters (Stavka) took over the functions of the General Staff. It is hard to evaluate the quality of Russian staff work. On the one hand, it is clear that the defeat of the country was caused by reasons more profound than the errors of officers. On the other, it is generally agreed that the quality of staff work was below that of other belligerent countries. On one occasion, for example, it took four months to gather data on casualties. At another time, in 1916, the staff issued two reports on the size of the army, and these reports differed from one another by more than 2 million men. But most important, the staff failed to coordinate operations successfully; the railroad system was in constant disarray, and the army failed to provide munitions to those units that most desperately needed them.

In September 1915 Nicholas II* became the supreme Commander of the Army. Obviously, the Tsar was not capable of directing the military operations of an enormous army at a time of war, and this duty fell on the newly named and reasonably competent Chief of Staff, General M. V. Alekseev. It was of considerable political significance that the Tsar spent much of his time at the Stavka. During the February Revolution* in Petrograd, the senior officers of the General Staff possessed decisive influence, for the Tsar looked to them for advice. At that time the High Command was unanimous in its recommendation: the Tsar must abdicate.

This position was not motivated by the general revolutionary enthusiasm: the great majority of the officers were and remained monarchists. However, they believed that the cost of resisting the Revolution would be a civil war and, consequently, the collapse of the war effort. When they had to choose between their loyalty to the monarch and their commitment to the successful prosecution of the war, they chose the second.

It soon became clear that the officers sacrificed their monarch in vain. Revolutionary Russia was not capable of a successful prosecution of the war. The leaders of the army blamed the politicians—whether they worked for the soviets or for the Provisional Government*—for the disorganization, the collapse of authority, and the popular disillusionment in the war. The generals were wrong: the members of the Provisional Government were just as committed to the continuation of the war as they were. Nevertheless, the high command felt increasingly betrayed by politicians, and in turn, the enemies of the February Revolution came to look on the Stavka as their best hope.

The Provisional Government, in a frantic effort to improve the performance of the army and to lessen the distrust between politicians and officers, carried out a series of reorganizations at the Stavka. During 1917 the government repeatedly changed the person of the Supreme Commander. In July A. F. Kerensky* chose L. G. Kornilov (see Kornilov Revolt), a young and inexperienced general, to head the army. Kornilov, an impetuous man with little political sense, almost immediately after assuming office turned the General Headquarters into a center of conspiracy both against the soviets and the Provisional Government. He grossly overestimated his strength and therefore embarked on a venture that was to have disastrous consequences for liberal non-Bolshevik Russia. His mutiny failed with almost ridiculous ease: the soldiers would not follow their officers. This failure prepared the soil for an attempt from the Left and demoralized and confused the Right.

The bitterness generated by the collapse of the Kornilov mutiny further increased the hatred of the officers of the General Staff for the liberal-democratic politicians. This irrational hatred was at least partially why their headquarters chose to be inactive during the crucial days of the Bolshevik (*see* Russian Social Democratic Workers' Party [Bolshevik]) takeover (*see* October Seizure of Power). From the point of view of the officers, V. I. Lenin* could not be worse than Kerensky. It was only the Bolsheviks' determination to start negotiations with the Germans that brought an inevitable conflict between the new government in Petrograd and the Stavka in Mogilev. General N. N. Dukhonin, the acting Commander-in-Chief, defied Lenin's order to initiate immediate discussions with the enemy. Lenin then named Ensign N. V. Krylenko* Commander-in-Chief. Krylenko, with a small band of soldiers, occupied the Stavka on December 3, and his soldiers murdered Dukhonin.

The Soviet seizure of power destroyed the ideological homogeneity of the officers of the General Staff. The great majority of them were tired of the war and of disappointments and were willing to concede defeat to the Bolsheviks. They realized that they had lost their authority over their soldiers, and therefore, resistance to the revolutionaries, at least for the time being, was futile. They hoped the Russian people sooner or later would overthrow the Bolsheviks, but as for themselves, they wanted to be left alone.

A minority of the General Staff officers, usually the most conservative ones, heeded the call of the best-known soldiers of the country, Generals M. V. Alekseev and Kornilov, and joined the fledgling White Army (*see* White Movement). This is not to say that every General Staff officer who fought in the White Army did so voluntarily. Many escaped the Bolsheviks and hoped to sit out the storm in South Russia. As these areas came under White control, the anti-Bolsheviks drafted officers who had no choice but to obey.

The Bolsheviks, who faced numerous enemies after their rather easy victory in October 1917, soon found that contrary to their utopian notions a "revolutionary militia" was incapable of defending the country. L. D. Trotsky* took energetic steps to build a regular army (*see* Red Army), and among his steps, none was more important than his decision to use "military specialists." Within a short time the most important command posts in the Red Army were filled by graduates of the Academy of the General Staff. Trotsky's policy of employment of military specialists met considerable opposition within the Bolshevik Party. Many feared treason. Indeed, ex-generals defected from the Red Army, causing tremendous harm to the young Soviet Republic. However, Trotsky was certainly right that the Red Army needed military expertise that only trained men could provide.

According to some admittedly imprecise estimates, 75 percent of the General Staff officers who fought in the Civil War in Russia* did so on the Bolshevik side. It has been a debated issue why men who had been trained in service of the Tsar came to fight for the revolutionaries. It is self-evident that very few of them became convinced Marxists. Some historians suggested that it was the patriotism of the officers that impelled them to take arms in defense of the Soviet Republic. Lenin, after all, was the de facto head of the government, and the war against the Germans did not end until March 1918. Others had argued that the explanation must be sought in the professionalism of the officers. In this view, the General Staff officers saw that, whatever the political and social philosophy of the Bolsheviks, these were determined men who would not vacillate as members of the Provisional Government had done. The General Staff officers served in the Red Army because that ever-expanding force promised wonderful opportunities for advancement and revolutionary leadership. However, it is most likely that the best explanation is the simplest one: the majority of the officers accepted service because they feared the consequences of refusal for themselves and for their families. The large number of General Staff officers who served in the Red Army assured a considerable continuity between the Imperial and Red armies.

Peter Kenez

Bibliography

Denikin, A. I. *Staraia armiia*. 2 vols. 1929–1931.
Golovine, N. N. *The Russian Army in World War I*. 1931.
Mayzel, M. *Generals and Revolutionaries*. 1979.

Georgia, Revolution in. Georgia (Gruziia) was one of the important centers of the Russian Revolution in the Caucasus.

The Georgian people are one of the oldest ethnic groups in Russia with their own alphabet, language, literature, national territory, and a long and distinctive history. In short, long before the Russian Revolution the Georgians had all of the prerequisites for a national movement. In 1897 they had a population of about 1,260,000, or about 1 percent of the total population of the empire. The Georgian church was Christian, and according to legend, it was converted at the time of Constantine (approximately A.D. 330) by Saint Nino. Georgia was known as Iberia in the time of the Romans, when its state was conquered and occupied. Feudal institution and a native aristocracy were well established by the time of the Russian conquest in 1801.

The Marxist movement was extraordinarily successful among Georgian intellectuals, and most of Georgia's elected delegates to the imperial Duma were Marxists. Before the Revolution the Georgian Marxists had no national party but formed a regional branch of the Russian Social Democratic Workers' Party. Although the chief theoretician for the Georgian movement, Noi Zhordania*, did not advocate national autonomy for his country, believing it to be unrealistic, by 1910 the Georgian Mensheviks (*see* Russian Social Democratic Workers' Party [Menshevik]) like Zhordania who dominated the Marxist movement in Georgia advocated cultural autonomy.

When Nicholas II* was deposed in 1917, the Russian viceroy for Transcaucasia, the Grand Duke Nicholas Nikolaevich, resigned, and his powers were divided, with General N. N. Iudenich* taking over his military functions and the Special Transcaucasian Committee (Ozakom) (*see* Caucasian Bureau) his civil powers. In the capital city of Georgia, Tiflis, however, the real power rested in the Menshevik-dominated soviet. A regional center (*Kraevoi tsentr*) that coordinated the work of the Transcaucasian soviets was also located in Tiflis, and in effect, the Ozakom simply ratified the decisions of these bodies, which were then carried out by the local soviets. Georgian Menshevik social democracy became the major political manifestation of the Georgian national movement because it appealed to both the Georgian resentment of Armenian economic domination and of Russian political domination. The Armenian middle class in Tiflis supported the Dashnaks* and the Russian soldiers supported the Socialist-Revolutionaries*.

The Menshevik-dominated soviet at Tiflis originally opposed the entry of socialists in the "bourgeois" Provisional Government*, and it opposed any overt seizure of power by the soviets. After moderate socialists in Tiflis faced down a demonstration by the local garrison calling for a socialist government, they began to rethink this position. Even before they changed their minds, prominent Georgian Menshevik leaders like N. S. Chkheidze* and I. G. Tsereteli* had assumed an important role in national politics in 1917 by their leadership role in the Petrograd Soviet*. When the Provisional Government formed a coalition cabinet in May, Tsereteli was appointed to a ministerial post.

The Bolshevik (*see* Russian Social Democratic Workers' Party [Bolshevik]) movement found it difficult to make any headway against the entrenched Georgian Menshevik movement. Its successes were confined chiefly to the garrison troops among which the Socialist-Revolutionary Party* gradually lost ground to the Bolsheviks, especially after the abortive Kornilov Revolt*. But even these gains proved illusory when the Georgian Mensheviks declared martial law in Tiflis in November, seized power with their own Red Guards on November 29, 1917, and proceeded to transfer power to the local soviets. Bolshevik support in the local garrison backfired as the regular army "voted for peace with their feet" by deserting in droves and dashing all hopes for a Bolshevik seizure of power. In February 1918 the Bolshevik Party was outlawed in Tiflis.

In April 1918 all of Transcaucasia became an independent federative republic (Zakavkazshaia Federativnaia Respublika), but the invasion of Transcaucasia by the Turks led to the separation of this union into three states: Armenia, Georgia, and Azerbaijan. With the promise of German protection against the Turks, the Georgians proclaimed their independence on May 26, 1918. In terms of political experience and economic strength, the Georgians had better prospects for survival as an independent state than did the other two Transcaucasian republics. The

German army moved in to provide a protective shield until their departure in November 1918. When World War I* came to an end, British troops intervened to replace the German troops and stayed until late in 1919.

N. N. Zhordaniia became president of the new republic, and his government inaugurated a major redistribution of land, nationalized large-scale industries, and created its own 50,000-man army. Although the Civil War in Russia* raged in the northern Caucasus in 1919, the three Transcaucasian republics remained intact, and in 1920 when the White movement* collapsed, the Allied Supreme Council in Paris gave de facto recognition to the three republics.

The mineral wealth of the Caucasus, especially the oil in Baku, provided a powerful argument for the recapture of this area by the new Soviet state. The Tiflis Regional Committee of the Russian Social Democratic Committee (Bolshevik) left Tiflis at the time of the German occupation in May 1918 and fled to the Terek Region in the northern Caucasus. It found itself in conflict with the stronger Baku Committee for the leadership of the communists in the Caucasus. In January 1920 Moscow gave its support to the more radical and militant Baku communists who promptly formed the Azerbaijani Communist Party in February.

By this time the communists in the Terek Region and Daghestan* were poised to move southeast. Rapprochement between the Soviet state, Great Britain, and Turkey in the winter of 1919–1920 set the diplomatic stage for the Soviet conquest of the Caucasus. Under the military leadership of General M. N. Tukhachevskii* and the political leadership of G. K. Ordzhonikidzhe* and his Caucasian Revolutionary Committee, they began to move in March 1920. Azerbaijan was seized by a combination of an internal coup d'état and an invasion by Soviet troops on August 27, 1920. Georgian communists had attempted a similar coup d'état on May 2, 1920, and failed, forestalling a similar takeover in that state, and the Soviet Union recognized the Georgian Republic on May 7, 1920. The agreement called for the immediate release of 1,000 Georgian communists from jail, and they immediately prepared for a Soviet seizure of power. When the Armenian Republic fell to the Soviet Union on November 27, 1920, Georgia was surrounded. On January 26, 1921, the Politburo of the Russian Communist Party approved preparations for an internal revolt of Georgian communists to be assisted by an invasion of the Red Army* from neighboring Caucasian states. The communist revolt in Tiflis took place on February 11, 1921, and the Red Army took Tiflis on February 25.

Bibliography

Lang, D. M. *A Modern History of Soviet Georgia.* 1962.
Pipes, R. *The Formation of the Soviet Union.* 1968.
Suny, R. G. *Transcaucasia.* 1983.

Gorky, Maksim. *See* Peshkov, Aleksei Maksimovich.

Gots, Abram Rafailovich (1882–1937). Gots was a Socialist-Revolutionary (*see* Socialist-Revolutionary Party) leader and member of the Socialist-Revolutionary Party's Central Committee. He was a leader of the socialist movement, a strong supporter of the Provisional Government*, and an opponent of the October Seizure of Power*. A. R. Gots was born into a wealthy Jewish family. His brother M. R. Gots (1866–1906) was one of the founders of the Socialist-Revolutionary Party. In 1906 A. R. Gots became an active member in the "Battle Organization" of the Socialist-Revolutionary (S-R) Party. Gots was sentenced to eight years' penal servitude. At the time of the February Revolution* he was in Siberian exile. Upon his return to Petrograd he became a member of the S-R faction in the Executive Committee of the Petrograd Soviet*. In June Gots was named the chairman of the All-Russian Central Executive Committee* of the Congress of Soviets, a post he held until October 25. He also served as a member of the Democratic Conference* (September 14–22).

One historian of the S-R Party, O. H. Radkey, stated: "Insofar as there was a leader of the PSR [the S-R's in 1917] it was Abram Gots, but he had neither the brains, nor the stage presence, nor the prestige of the other two [V. M. Chernov* and A. F. Kerensky*]" (1958, p. 465). At the Third S-R Party Congress in May 1917 Gots received the largest number of votes in the election for the Central Committee. By the Fourth S-R Congress (December 1917) Gots's influence declined to the extent that he dropped to eleventh place in voting for Central Committee membership. Throughout 1917 Gots, as leader of the S-R Right–Center tendency, advocated socialist collaboration with the bourgeoisie. He consistently supported a coalition government* that included Constitutional Democrats (see Constitutional Democratic Party—Cadet) and was personally involved in the formation of all three coalitions that occurred in 1917. During 1917 Gots served as a buffer between Kerensky and the Petrograd Soviet and, from June, as a buffer between Kerensky and the Central Executive Committee created by the First All-Russian Congress of Soviets.

In 1920 Gots was condemned to death for attempting to organize resistance to the Bolsheviks (see Russian Social Democratic Workers' Party [Bolshevik]) along with eleven other members of the S-R Party. The sentence was reduced to five years' imprisonment, although he was not released until 1927, after which he worked in several Soviet economic agencies. In 1936 he was arrested and, according to some reports, was executed in 1937. Soviet sources state that he died in Berlin in 1940.

Bibliography

Radkey, O. H. The Agrarian Foes of Bolshevism. 1958.
Spiridovich, A. I. Zapiski zhandarma. 2d ed. 1928.

Gubel'man, Minei Izrailovich (1878–1943). Gubel'man was best known under the pseudonym Emel'ian Mikhailovich Iaroslavskii but also used Vladimir Semenovich Lapin and Stepan Krasil'nikov. He was a prominent Soviet publicist, historian, and journalist who took part in the seizure of power in Moscow.

Gubel'man's parents were the children of exiles who had settled in Siberia. His father was a peasant who became a furrier and then a teacher. His mother was a fisherman's daughter. In his official biography Gubel'man stated that he grew up among revolutionaries who had been exiled to Siberia for their political crimes in the 1860s and 1870s. Gubel'man passed the examinations for assistant pharmacist in 1898, the same year that he joined the Russian Social Democratic Workers' Party. He worked during the year on the Trans-Baikal Railroad and organized what may have been the first Marxist group among the workers on that line.

From 1899 to 1901 Gubel'man served in the Eighteenth Sharpshooter's Regiment. In 1901, upon being discharged from the army, he visited Berlin and Paris and met many of the luminaries in the European Marxist movement. In 1902 he became a member of the Chita Committee of the Russian Social Democratic Workers' Party, and in 1903 he helped to organize a trade union for the railway workers of Transbaikal. In 1903 he also went for a stay in St. Petersburg where he did party work under the name Vladimir Semenovich Lapin.

By the time of the 1905 Revolution (*see* Nineteen-Five Revolution) Gubel'man was already a veteran party worker. He started that year working in Odessa under the name Stepan Krasil'nikov and between 1905 and 1907 conducted party work in a number of places, including St. Petersburg, Tver, Iaroslavl, and Moscow. He was a delegate to the Fifth (London) Conference in 1907. In 1910 Gubel'man was arrested and sentenced to seven years in prison. He spent the next seven years in various prisons, and in 1917, at the time of the February Revolution*, he was in Iakutsk.

Gubel'man returned to Moscow, in European Russia in July 1917 and immediately became a member of the Bolsheviks' (*see* Russian Social Democratic Workers' Party [Bolshevik]) military organization and a member of the editorial board of the party's newspapers, *Sotsial-demokrat* (*Social Democrat*) and *Derevenskaiaia pravda* (*Village Truth*). He took part in the struggle for Soviet power in Moscow in October, in the creation of the Red Guard*, and in the attack on the Kremlin (*see* Moscow, Revolution in). He was a member of the Military Revolutionary Committee, and after the October Seizure of Power*, he became the first Commissar of the Moscow Military District (Okrug) and editor of the party newspaper, *Sotsial Demokrat*. He was elected a delegate to the Constituent Assembly*. In 1918 he was a "Left communist" (*see* Left Communism) closely associated with Moscow Bolsheviks including N. I. Bukharin*. During the Civil War in Russia* he was associated with the " military opposition group" that opposed the recruitment of former tsarist officers into the Red Army as military specialists. Gubel'man took part in efforts to establish Soviet power in the Urals and Siberia, and from 1920 to 1922 he was a member of the Siberian Bureau* of the Communist Party. In 1920 Gubel'man was elected a member of the Central Committee of the Russian Communist Party (Bolshevik) (*see* Russian Social Democratic Workers' Party [Bolshevik]) and Secretary to the Central Committee.

Gubel'man acquired a reputation as a Stalinist party hack in the 1930s because of his association with the editing and publishing of official party histories and as chairman of the All-Union Society of Old Bolsheviks in 1931. He also took part in the editing of *Pravda* and *Bol' shevik* and serious academic publications such as *Istorik Marksist* (*Marxist Historian*) and *Istoricheskii zhurnal* (*Historical Journal*). He was chairman of the Union of the Godless and an elder in the All-Union Society of Political Prisoners and Exiles; from 1939 he was a member of the Academy of Sciences of the USSR, a member of the Executive Board of the Institute of Leninism, and a member of the Presidium of the Central Executive Committee (*see* All-Russian Central Executive Committee) of the Congress of Soviets of the USSR and deputy to the Supreme Soviet. He is buried in Red Square in the Wall of the Kremlin along with other heroes of the October Revolution.

Bibliography

Daniels, R. V. *The Conscience of the Revolution*. 1969.
Schapiro, L. *The Origin of the Communist Autocracy*. 1955.

Guchkov, Aleksandr Ivanovich (1862–1936). Guchkov was among the most colorful public figures in late Imperial Russia. The scion of a prominent Moscow industrial family that had made a fortune in textiles, Guchkov entered national political life on the right wing of the Zemstvo movement of 1904–1905, after years of travel and adventure, and would subsequently become the leader of the Octobrist Party (*see* Duma and Revolution) and President of the Third Duma. His exploits (many duels among them), his wealth, and his self-confidence seemed characteristic of the new, dynamic, and politically ambitious Moscow bourgeoisie.

Guchkov's position as War Minister in the first Provisional Government* of 1917 was outwardly the consummation of a political career animated above all by a concern for Russian national power and military reform. Yet he had entered the cabinet reluctantly and only half-heartedly exercised his limited powers. He was disconsolate for good reason; little had gone according to his plans and hopes. He was put into office by a revolution he had sought to forestall, and once in office, he could not assert his authority against the rush of popular passions unleashed by that Revolution.

Guchkov was familiar with military affairs and battlefields, having fought against the British in the Boer War and having directed a hospital in the Far East during the Russo–Japanese War. In the Third Duma he startled government and public with his charges of irresponsibility levelled at Grand Dukes in high military office. At the start of World War I* Guchkov was at the western front as Red Cross Commissioner for the Moscow Zemstvo. By then, the Octobrist Party he had helped to organize in 1905 was in disarray. Octobrism was a movement based on propertied elements in town and country, which had backed the monarchy against revolution but had favored modernizing reforms. Guchkov still held to these principles, but the war convinced him that they could not be realized under the regime of Nicholas II*.

When industrialists were appalled at the condition of war-related production and provisioning in the spring of 1915, they formed War Industries Committees* and invited Guchkov to head the central body. He was a natural choice, given his many contacts among business and military men. In August 1916 he sent a widely circulated letter to General and Chief of Staff M. I. Alekseev in which he described the "complete disintegration" of the home front and the "rot . . . at the roots of state power." He concluded with an admission of despair that also—in a perspicacious phrase—betrayed anxiety about the possible consequence of reform efforts: "Our means of struggle are double-edged and, given the rising temper of the masses, especially the masses of workers, can act as the first spark of a conflagration the scale of which no one can forsee or contain."

Such dramatic confessions of concern were a prelude to active recruiting by Guchkov of key officers for a bloodless coup designed to remove Nicholas II from the throne. Guchkov did not share the confidence of some other public men that were a revolution to erupt, they, as men of political experience, would get a popular mandate to rule. Guchkov was determined to preclude mass involvement in the fate of Nicholas's regime, and together with Cadet (*see* Constitutional Democratic Party—Cadet) Deputy N. V. Nekrasov and M. V. Tereshchenko, Chairman of the Kiev War Industries Committee, prepared a coup timed for March 1917. The February Revolution* not only upset the plan but confirmed Guchkov's worst fears. Political matters were now in the streets. On the night of February 27–28 Guchkov and twenty-one other elected members of the State Council signed a vain last-minute appeal to Nicholas to form that old will-of-the-wisp, a ministry of "public confidence" that could govern the country in complete harmony with the representatives of the people.

On March 1 Guchkov made the rounds of the Petrograd barracks, doing his share to maintain order and mobilize support for the political forces associated with the State Duma. During this tour his good friend Prince D. L. Viazemskii was mortally wounded at Guchkov's side in an automobile—a portent of the mood in the Petrograd Garrison. Going directly to the State Duma headquarters at the Tauride Palace after this tour, Guchkov learned that the Temporary Committee of the State Duma (*see* February Revolution) had named him Minister of War and (temporarily) navy in the Provisional Government after consultations with the Executive Committee of the Petrograd Soviet*. Guchkov's name regularly appeared in lists of proposed ministries prepared by liberal circles; in this case it won only grudging support from the Soviet. In the public eye, after all, Guchkov was considered a tough-minded opponent of popular demands who had backed P. A. Stolypin's ferocious repressions after the 1905 Revolution (*see* Nineteen-Five Revolution).

During discussions at the Tauride Palace about establishing the legal foundations of the new authority, Guchkov volunteered to go to meet Nicholas, secure his abdication in favor of his son Alexei, and get his blessing for the Provisional Government. On the night of March 2 Guchkov arrived in Pskov with V. V. Shulgin, a nationalist Duma deputy. In the Tsar's railway car, Guchkov, the great-grandson of a serf-industrialist and Old Believer, received the abdication of the last Romanov. (Nicholas had abdicated in favor of his brother Michael.) Returning to Petrograd, Guchkov could not resist a triumphal public announcement. With the abdication document in hand, he described what had taken place to workers at a railway shop and proclaimed, "Long live Michael II!" The workers, however, did not share Guchkov's enthusiasm for a new monarchy. There were cries for lynching Guchkov and destroying the document—another portent of mass moods in the capital.

When Michael declared his unwillingness to take the crown, Guchkov, a convinced monarchist, had to be persuaded to overcome his reservations about joining the Provisional—and now republican—Government. From his post as Minister of War, Guchkov fought a dispirited and losing battle to restore discipline in the ranks and arouse enthusiasm for the war. During Guchkov's two-month tenure many military reforms were introduced. All national, religious, class (*soslovie*), and political restrictions or promotions in the armed forces were abolished. The eight-hour working day was introduced in government armament factories. Officer's shoulder boards were abolished in the navy. Cossack* autonomy was restored. There was also a purge of some 150 officers for reasons of efficiency and morale. But Guchkov was openly hostile to the Petrograd Soviet, and friction intensified with Guchkov's efforts to undo the disorganizing results of Army Order No. 1 (*see* Army of Imperial Russia in World War I), which destroyed the authority of officers. Several commissions formed by Guchkov to draft regulations governing soldiers' rights produced documents acceptable to the Soviet but not to Guchkov and commanders of the front.

Guchkov understood that he had no strength at his disposal in any showdown with the Soviet. There were only a handful of troops in the Petrograd garrison considered "reliable," that is, willing to back the Provisional Government in a conflict with the Soviet, and any effort to transfer troops from the capital to the front or bring in "reliable" troops from the front would have been blocked by the Soviet. With a steady flow of reports from the front about indiscipline in the ranks and alienation from war aims; with a sense of isolation from his colleagues in the cabinet who, Miliukov (*see* Miliukov, Pavel Nikolaevich) excepted, were inclined to compromise with the Soviet; with street demonstrations toward the end of April demanding "Down with the bourgeois government, down with Miliukov and Guchkov"; and with a sense that even many officers were turning coat and engaging in "revolutionary careerism," Guchkov decided to leave the Provisional Government on May 1 and rejected invitations to stay on in other capacities. He was replaced as War Minister by A. F. Kerensky*. Guchkov, in the words of V. D. Nabokov, who headed the Provisional Government Chancellory, had "from the beginning . . . felt in his soul that the cause was lost and only stayed on *par acquir de conscience*. . . . the note of utter despair and skepticism never sounded so strongly in anyone as it did in him whenever the question of the army and the fleet arose."

Guchkov's despair did not prevent him from throwing his energies into counterrevolutionary activities. Shortly after his resignation as War Minister, he
accepted the invitation of the wealthy business magnates A. I. Putilov and A. I.
Vishnegradskii to head their Society for the Economic Rebirth of Russia, a cover
for raising money and organizing anti-Soviet propaganda. During the summer
of 1917, Guchkov, with the society's 4 million rubles backing him, toured the
fronts and arranged for the publication of many leaflets and publications. Some
of the society's money was also turned over to General L. G. Kornilov* (*see*
Kornilov Revolt), who impressed Guchkov as the right man to lead a movement
to crush the Petrograd Soviet.

After the Bolshevik coup Guchkov joined various White forces (*see* White
Movement) from the Caucasus to Manchuria. In 1919 he left southern Russia,
where he was collaborating with General A. I. Denikin*, for what was to be a
final emigration to Western Europe. Settling in Paris, Guchkov, according to
his daughter, participated in some acts of anti-Soviet sabotage and possibly in
the assassination of Soviet officials. But he remained aloof from emigré politics.
Guchkov died in Paris in 1936.

His isolation in exile mirrored a certain isolation he had experienced throughout
his political career. Although respected for his political courage and adeptness
at ''practical affairs,'' Guchkov was mistrusted by the liberals for his conservative
views and despised by the right for his personal campaign against Nicholas II.
For the Right, Guchkov bears a great deal of responsibility for the success of
the February Revolution inasmuch as his plotting against the crown helped
disorient and undermine the morale of important sections of the officers' corps
at a crucial moment. For his part, Guchkov, the political realist, seems to have
been the victim of an insufficient sense of realism in 1917. On the one hand,
his views regarding the monarchy's incapacity to wage war and the urgent need
to change regimes were well founded, as was his conviction that the Provisional
Government lacked the necessary social, legal, and military base to consolidate
its position. On the other hand, his insistence on decisive, behind-the-scenes
action to counter or crush the soviet was a myopic realism in which the strength
of radical forces sweeping the country were entirely underrated.

Guchkov's personal political trajectory reflected accurately self-confidence and
then despair as well as the rise and then the ruin of the Moscow bourgeoisie
from whose ranks he sprang.

Louis Menashe

Bibliography

Browder, R. P., and Kerensky, A. F., ed. *The Russian Provisional Government, 1917.*
    3 vols. 1961.
Chermenskii, E. D. *IV Gosudarstvennaia duma i sverzhenie tsarizma v Rossiaa.* 1976.
Diakin, V. S. *Russkaia burzhuaziia i tsarizma v gody pervoi mirovoi voiny, 1914–17.*
    1967.
Guchkov, A. I. *Rechi po voprosam gosudarstvennogo oborony i ob obshchei politke,
    1908–1917.* 1917.

Medlin, V. D., and Parsons, S. L., ed. *V. D. Nabokov and the Russian Provisional Government, 1917.* 1976.
Padenie Tsarskogo Rezhima. Vol. 6. 1927.

Gummet (Hummet, Himmät). The complete name of this party was the Moslem Social Democratic Party. This was the name of the Azerbaijan Social Democratic Party that became the nucleus of the Azerbaijan Communist Party. It played an important role in the ill-fated Baku Commune (*see* Azerbaijan, Revolution in; Transcaucasia, Revolution in).

Gummet was created as a Moslem Social Democratic Group in 1904 and consisted almost entirely of Azeri Turks who were students or professional people in the city of Baku. It was closely affiliated with the Baku branch of the Russian Social Democratic Workers' Party to which some of its members already belonged. Two talented new members joined Gummet in 1905, N. N. Narimanov* and M. A. Azizbekov*. In 1906 Gummet became a separate party, although there was some fear among some of the Russian Social Democrats that it might demand special standing within the Russian Social Democratic Workers' Party, as had the Jewish Bund*. Some Moslem Social Democrats wanted separate status because they believed that the Baku Russian Social Democratic Party was dominated by Armenians. Some of the prominent members of Gummet were Narimanov, Azizbekov, S. M. Efendiev, Isa Ashurbekov, and D. Kh. Buniatzada.

In its first party program in 1909 Gummet emphasized democratic goals and made no reference to socialism or the Russian Social Democratic Workers' Party. The party seemed to die out after that, although some of its members continued to work for socialism in the Baku Russian Social Democratic Workers' Party. In March 1917 the Baku Russian Social Democratic Workers' Party decided to revive the Gummet Party in order to have an organization that could work exclusively with Azerbaijani workers. Led by Narimanov and Azizbekov, this new organization was much more Marxist than its predecessor. But it now had competition in its efforts to recruit Moslems from the Musavat Party (*see* Moslem Democratic Party). Both played an active role in the Baku Commune of 1917–1918 (*see* Transcaucasia, Revolution in). Some Gummet members, like Azizbekov and Efendiev, were appointed Commissars by the Baku Commune for Moslem Districts. Gummet survived that debacle and participated in the new parliament of an independent Azerbaijan state that began in December 1918.

The new Gummet split into Bolshevik and Menshevik factions in December 1917, but the factions were reunited in March 1919 as the fortunes of the party began to revive. The Menshevik faction tended to predominate, and therefore, the Baku Social Democratic Workers' Party sought to revive the split. By mid-1919 it succeeded. The Menshevik faction adopted the name Social Democratic Workers' Party—Gummet, and the Left called itself the Azerbaijan Communist Party—Gummet. In July 1919 the Politburo of the Russian Communist Party (*see* Russian Social Democratic Workers' Party [Bolshevik]) recognized the

Azerbaijan Communist Party—Gummet as an autonomous party and recognized Azerbaijan as an autonomous Soviet republic. The decision was somewhat academic since at that time Azerbaijan was not ruled by the communists but was at least nominally independent.

On February 13, 1920, at the request of Moscow, Adalet (the Persian Communist Party) and the Azerbaijan Communist Party—Gummet merged to form the Azerbaijan Communist Party and claimed a membership of 4,000 by April, mostly in the city of Baku. The Azerbaijan Communist Party planned to seize power on April 27, but it never had to undergo this ordeal because four troop trains arrived in the city bearing Red Army* troops. All political parties except the Azerbaijan Communist Party were immediately outlawed.

The former members of Gummet never completely lost their separatist feelings, however, and never fully merged with the Russian Communist Party. They had originally been attracted to the movements' socialism as a way of attacking the domination of Armenian merchants and Russian imperialism. This separatist sentiment caused them some difficulty as members of the Russian Communist Party. Fortunately for Narimanov, he died in bed in 1933, but many of his friends and colleagues in Gummet were purged in 1937–1939, including Efendiev, then Chairman of the Central Executive Committee of the Communist Party of Azerbaijan, Buniatzada, then Chairman of the Council of People's Commissars of the Azerbaijan Soviet Socialist Republic, and H. N. Sultanov, People's Commissar of the Interior of the Azerbaijan Soviet Socialist Republic (*see* Azerbaijan, Revolution in). They have been posthumously rehabilitated.

Bibliography

Bennigsen, Alexandre A., and Wimbush, S. Enders. *Muslim National Communism in the Soviet Union.* 1979.
Pipes, Richard. *The Formation of the Soviet Union.* 1968.
Suny, R. G. *The Baku Commune, 1917–1918.* 1972.
Swietochowski, Tadeusz. *Russian Azerbaijan, 1905–20.* 1985.
Zenkovsky, *Pan-Turkism and Islam in Russia.* 1960.

Gur'vich, Fedor Il'ich (1871–1947; pseudonym Dan). One of the most important leaders of the Mensheviks (*see* Russian Social Democratic Workers' Party [Menshevik]) during and after the October Seizure of Power*. He and Iu. O. Martov* gave their support to the new Soviet government.

Gur'vich's activities were closely associated with the city of St. Petersburg where he was born in 1871. He returned to St. Petersburg after studying medicine at the University of Dorpat in Estonia where he received a medical degree. In 1895 he participated in the formation of the Union of the Liberation of the Working Class, a group that included both V. I. Lenin* and Martov among its members. Gur'vich became especially close to the Martov family and married Martov's sister Lydia. Gur'vich was arrested in 1896 and exiled from 1896 to 1897. He spent the years from 1900 to 1902 abroad and in 1902 returned to

Russia where he was soon arrested and once again sent into exile. Escaping from eastern Siberia, he did not return to Russia until 1905 when there was a general amnesty for those accused of political crimes.

Although Gur'vich was not able to attend the Second Congress of the Russian Social Democratic Workers' Party in 1903 when the split began between the Bolshevik (*see* Russian Social Democratic Workers' Party [Bolshevik]) and Menshevik factions, he soon became a leading opponent of Lenin. Between 1907 and 1912, although spending most of his time in Western Europe, Gur'vich became one of the foremost leaders of the Mensheviks. He opposed any future revolutionary alliances with the peasants and put his faith in the prospects for an alliance with middle-class liberals in the event of a revolutionary struggle. Despite these beliefs Gur'vich opposed a complete break with the Bolsheviks in January 1908. At that time Martov wanted to read the Bolsheviks out of the socialist movement and bring them before a tribunal of the Second Socialist International. At a conference of Menshevik emigré leaders in Geneva, Gur'vich and A. S. Martynov strongly opposed that action and called for unity with the Bolsheviks at any price. In 1913, when another amnesty for those accused of political crimes was issued, Gur'vich returned to St. Petersburg and became a leading contributor to Menshevik journals.

When World War I* broke out, Gur'vich was arrested again and did not return to European Russia until February 1917. When he returned to St. Petersburg after the February Revolution*, he became vice-chairman of the Petrograd Soviet*; editor of its newspaper, *Izvestiia* (*News*); and one of the most important leaders of the Menshevik movement. Until August 1917 the Defensist (*see* Defensism) wing of the Menshevik movement to which Gur'vich adhered became increasingly powerful. With I. G. Tsereteli* and N. K. Chkheidze*, Gur'vich advocated support for the Provisional Government, alliance with the Constitutional Democratic Party—Cadet*, and Menshevik participation in a coalition government.

Gur'vich contributed to the split in Menshevik ranks that prevented that party from exploiting its unusual influence before August 1917. If he and Tsereteli had eschewed coalitionism and defensism and supported Martov's positions on peace, agrarian reform, and the immediate convocation of the Constituent Assembly*, the Mensheviks could have competed with the Bolsheviks for the allegiance of the workers and soldiers and, perhaps, formed a popular-front coalition with the Bolsheviks in October. Once the Kornilov Revolt* took place in August, that opportunity had passed, and the demise of the Mensheviks was preordained. The party was, by then, too closely associated with the policies of the government that had allowed and even encouraged someone like Kornilov to appear.

Gur'vich presided over the Second All-Russian Congress of Soviets that approved the new Soviet government. Having become disillusioned with Kerensky, Gur'vich gave his support and that of his followers to the new Soviet government and achieved a long overdue reconciliation with the left-wing Mensheviks led by Martov.

Although supporting the Soviet government, Gur'vich continued to criticize its actions under Bolshevik leadership while urging his party to join that government and share power with the Bolsheviks. At the Eighth All-Russian Congress of the Soviets in 1920 Gur'vich criticized the Cheka (*see* All-Russian Extraordinary Commission for Combatting Counterrevolution and Sabotage) and the central government for usurping the power of the local soviets. He was subjected to repeated arrests by the Cheka until, finally, he was permitted or encouraged to go into exile in 1922. Once abroad, he became one of the chief spokesmen for the Menshevik community in exile and editor of their journal, *Sotsialisticheskii vestnik* (*Socialist Herald*). In his writing Gur'vich continued to express hope that a democratic version of socialism would triumph in Russia, and he continued to offer an olive branch to the Russian Communist Party. Gur'vich's openness to communist overtures and his continued faith in the prospects for a Communist–Menshevik alliance led to his departure from the journal (Sotsialisticheskii vestnik, and he began to publish his own journal, *Novyi put'* (*New Way*), in New York in 1940.

Bibliography

Ascher, Abraham. *Pavel Axelrod and the Development of Menshevism.* 1972.

Dan, F. I. [Gur'vich]. *The Origins of Bolshevism.* 1964.

Dvinov, B. *F. I. Dan, Martov i ego blizkie. Sbornik.* 1959.

Getzler, Israel. *Martov.* 1967.

Haimson, Leopold H., ed. *The Mensheviks from the Revolution of 1917 to the Second World War.* 1974.

H

Highest Council of the National Economy (*Vesenkha*). *See* Supreme Council of the National Economy.

Himmat. *See* Gummet.

Historiography. Historiography is the study of conflicting interpretations and controversies in history and the attempt to evaluate the important secondary sources about a given historical event. The historiography of the Russian Revolution covers a broad spectrum of views, but two general categories are easily discernible. The first group of interpretations places emphasis on the contingencies of history, the accidental factors, and the unforeseen circumstances that must be understood to explain why and how the Revolution occurred as it did. The role of individual personalities is often the key to explaining events in this political approach to history. The second group consists of those interpretations that explain the Revolution as the expected, perhaps even inevitable, outcome of earlier Russian history.

Those who opposed the Revolution and those who supported the initial stages of the Revolution but opposed the Bolshevik (*see* Russian Social Democratic Workers' Party [Bolshevik]) seizure of power (*see* October Seizure of Power) frequently supported the first approach. The Revolution could have been prevented if Nicholas II* had not been under the influence of Gregory Rasputin* or the Provisional Government* could have survived if A. F. Kerensky* had acted more wisely, or if the Germans had not sent V. I. Lenin* back into Russia. Although the reasons given for Bolshevik success vary, it is clear from these accounts that the Bolsheviks were not destined to succeed because they were right or because they were supported by the masses. They were successful in their coup d'état because they took advantage of the unique circumstances that could be manipulated by their highly disciplined political party. Included in this group were the memoir–histories by A. F. Kerensky, P. N. Miliukov*, and V. M. Chernov*. The best account of this type is S. P. Melgunov's study available in English translation as *The Bolshevik Seizure of Power* (1972).

The first Western scholarly history of the Revolution belongs to William Henry Chamberlin, a correspondent for *The Christian Science Monitor* in the Soviet Union from 1922 to 1933. His two-volume study, *The Russian Revolution, 1917–21* (1935), is still considered one of the best narrative accounts of the events of 1917. A more recent contribution, couched in terms of the contingency theory and owing much to S. P. Melgunov, is Robert V. Daniel's *Red October: The Bolshevik Revolution of 1917* (1967). Daniels dramatically related the familiar story of Bolshevik success based on personal and unpredictable circumstances, bungling of anti-Bolshevik forces, vigorous Bolshevik leadership over a disciplined conspiratorial party, and sheer good luck.

Those who view the October Revolution as an expected outcome of historical forces held views very different from the first group. The Bolsheviks and their supporters explained the victory as the heroic and inevitable triumph of socialism. The people overwhelmingly supported the Revolution and felt exhilarated at the possibility of building a new society. This view is well represented by the American journalist John Reed in his *Ten Days That Shook the World* (1919) and by the Bolshevik revolutionary leader Leon Trotsky* in his *History of the Russian Revolution* (3 vols., 1932–1933). These works are considered to have literary merit and to be important contributions by participant–observers, but their value as historical analysis is limited.

Many Marxist observers who hoped for a socialist victory in Russia did not share the enthusiasm of Reed and Trotsky. Some feared that the Revolution would end badly because Russia was not ready for socialism. Karl Liebknecht, Rosa Luxemburg*, and Karl Kautsky* were German Marxists who held this view and predicted that a dictatorship in Russia would be the result. A more valuable eyewitness account written by the non-Bolshevik socialist N. N. Sukhanov* which is available in English translation as *The Russian Revolution 1917* (2 vols., 1955)—the Russian original was *Zapiski o revoliutsii* (7 vols., 1922–1923)—is generally considered the most important memoir–history of the Revolution.

Another explanation of the Revolution argues that it was deeply rooted in the Russian past but that Bolshevik victory had nothing to do with Marxism or socialism; rather, it was the natural and inevitable outcome of Russian national character. The Russian "soul," conditioned by years of autocratic government and the lack of a middle class and a democratic or liberal tradition, simply made the short-lived experiment of the Provisional Government untenable. A leading proponent of this neo-Slavophile view was Nicholas Berdiaev in his two historical works, *The Russian Revolution* (1932) and *The Origin of Russian Communism* (1937), in which he viewed 1917 as a uniquely Russian phenomenon with little significance for other countries. An opposite Western view has been advanced by Theodore Von Laue in *Why Lenin? Why Stalin? A Reappraisal of the Russian*

Revolution, 1900–1930 (1964), in which he argued that Russia's backwardness and the demands of rapid modernization can best explain the coming of and the course of the Revolution, and it is a pattern that is likely to be repeated in other societies attempting revolutionary modernization.

In the past fifteen years a new emphasis, both in the Soviet Union and in the outside world, on social history and the political power of parties and mass organizations has replaced the more traditional exclusively political interpretations of the Revolution. Several detailed monographs have argued that the Bolsheviks were successful not because they were a highly organized conspiratorial party led by dynamic personalities but rather because they were the standard-bearers for a social movement that had broad mass support. Pioneer works in this field were Alexander Rabinowitch's *Prelude to Revolution: The Petrograd Bolsheviks and the July Uprising* (1968) and *The Bolsheviks Come to Power: The Revolution of 1917 in Petrograd* (1976). His well-documented work stresses the flexibility of the Bolshevik Party and its responsiveness to the masses as the reason for its success.

Many scholars, most of whom appear in this volume, have tried to present a more detailed analysis of the common people of the major Russian cities and the outlying provinces and their relationship to the Revolution. Included in these sociohistorical studies are the following: Diane Koenker, *Moscow Workers and the 1917 Revolution* (1981); S. A. Smith, *Red Petrograd: Revolution in the Factories 1917–18;* David Mandel, *The Petrograd Workers and the Fall of the Old Regime* (1983); idem, *The Petrograd Workers and the Soviet Seizure of Power* (1984); Ronald Grigor Suny, *The Baku Commune, 1917–1918: Class and Nationality in the Russian Revolution* (1972); Allan K. Wildman, *The End of the Russian Imperial Army: The Old Army and the Soldier's Revolt (March-April 1917)* (1980); Norman E. Saul, *Sailors in Revolt* (1978); and Graeme J. Gill, *Peasants and Government in the Russian Revolution* (1979). The role of the mass organizations has also been examined more carefully by Tsuyoshi Hasegawa in the February Revolution*: *The February Revolution: Petrograd, 1917* (1980); by Oskar Anweiler for the soviets (*see* Soviets [Councils] of Workers', Soldiers', and Peasants' Deputies): *The Soviets: The Russian Workers', Peasants', and Soldiers Councils* (1974); by Rex Wade on the Red Guard*: *Red Guard and Workers' Militias* (1983); and by Marc Ferro on the entire course of 1917: *The Russian Revolution of February 1917* (1972) and *October 1917: A Social History of the Russian Revolution.* (1980). John Keep also examined the lower levels of Russian society in *The Russian Revolution: A Study in Mass Mobilization* (1976), but his detailed characterization of the Russian people as instinctual, anarchical, and easily led and manipulated by the Bolsheviks tends to support the earlier explanations for the Bolshevik success as a conspiratorial party. Finally, attention has been given to the social composition and programs of the unsuccessful political parties in a blending of social and political history by Oliver H. Radkey, *The Agrarian Foes of Bolshevism: Promise and Default of the Russian Socialist Revolutionaries February to October 1917* (1958); by

William H. Rosenberg, *Liberals in the Russian Revolution: The Constitutional Democratic Party, 1917–21* (1974); and by Leopold H. Haimson, ed., *The Mensheviks: From the Revolution of 1917 to the Second World War* (1974).

Although no consensus has emerged among Western historians on the reasons for the Bolshevik victory, the debate has become more sophisticated with the appearance of the new monographs in social and sociopolitical history. Two recent surveys on the Revolution—John M. Thompson's overview of 1917, *Revolutionary Russia, 1917* (1981), and Sheila Fitzpatrick's summary of events from 1917 to 1932, *The Russian Revolution* (1982)—both reflect the results of the new scholarship, although Thompson's work concentrates more on political history.

In Soviet historiography a consensus has been in place for a number of years because of the nature of the historical establishment in the Soviet Union, but the past two decades have seen an expanded interest in social history similar to that in the West. In the Soviet Union historiography is a specialized discipline of the historical sciences because official ideology demands a Marxist–Leninist view of all historical events, showing that they conform to the historical laws discovered by Karl Marx in the nineteenth century. Historical interpretation contrary to this view, therefore, must be exposed as incorrect "falsification" of history. Soviet historical writings on the Russian Revolution show this emphasis, but even more clearly they document the influence of political considerations in the determination of what is historically acceptable.

V. I. Lenin is a key figure in Soviet historiography of the Revolution. Although he did not write his own history of 1917, he did engage in polemical writings against what he considered to be mistaken ideas about the Revolution. Thus Lenin himself set the pattern for the Soviet campaign against "incorrect" interpretations with attacks on G. V. Plekhanov*, Karl Kautsky, and N. N. Sukhanov. Lenin contributed three main ideas that became the cornerstone of subsequent Soviet writings. First, he insisted that the February Revolution was not a spontaneous revolution but one that had been prepared in advance by the Bolsheviks. Second, he suggested a formula for explaining the "growing over" (*pererastanie*) process in which the bourgeois-democratic February Revolution of 1917 led directly and inevitably to the socialist October Revolution. Finally, he argued that the October Seizure of Power was a true socialist revolution that corresponded to historical laws, thus having significance worldwide as a model for revolution.

The 1920s witnessed a great outpouring of Soviet writings on the Revolution. In 1921 the Commission for the Collection and Study of Materials on the History of the October Revolution had been organized under the direction of M. S. Ol'minskii (*see* Aleksandrov, Mikhail Stepanov), and by the end of the decade it had published scores of valuable source materials and memoirs. The historians S. A. Piontkovskii, M. N. Pokrovskii*, and A. G. Shliapnikov* had written their own secondary works attempting to put the Revolution in a correct Marxist–Leninist framework. With Stalin's rise to power, however, these attempts were found inadequate, and in 1931 the party commissioned a new attempt to write an authoritative account of the Revolution and Civil War in Russia*. The first volume of *The History of the Civil War in the U.S.S.R.* (1935) attempted to correct the so-called errors of the earlier works. For the first time Lenin's periodizations and interpretations were followed completely, but now I. V. Stalin's* role in the events of 1917 was greatly exaggerated, and L. D. Trotsky almost disappeared from the scene. A Stalinist work imbued with this same "cult of the personality" was the *History of the Communist Party: Short Course* (1938). The role of individuals other than Stalin, both Bolshevik and non-Bolshevik, and the role of other political movements in determining events nearly disappeared from published accounts of the revolution. As long as Stalin ruled in the Soviet Union, there would be little progress in reaching a more objective account.

During the "thaw" following Stalin's death in 1953, the historians were among the leaders in pushing the limits of the new freedom. E. N. Burdzhalov for one challenged the Stalinist historiography on the question of spontaneity in the February Revolution, and lost his position on the historical journal *Voprosy istorii* when the more conservative members of the historical establishment reasserted their position. Burdzhalov later did publish a lengthy study of the February Revolution, *Vtoraia russkaia revoliutsiia* (2 vols. 1967–71).

Khrushchev's secret speech of 1956 denouncing Stalin (which still has not been published in the Soviet Union), and the subsequent de-Stalinization campaign led to a re-evaluation and condemnation of many aspects of the Stalinist historiography of the Revolution and to a new flurry of historical research. During the next decade more than 150 collections of primary source materials were published, including the ten-volume collection of documents *Velikaia Oktiabr'skaia sotsialisticheskaia revoliutsiia* (1957–63) edited by A. L. Sidorov.

The most authoritative synthesis of recent Soviet historiography is the three-volume, 3,088-page official saga of the Revolution by academician I. I. Mints, *Istoriia Velikogo Oktiabria* (1967–1972). Mints added a great deal of factual material to the story, but he used the new information to support the earlier Leninist periodization and explanations. Lenin himself appears as a larger-than-life hero, while Trotsky and Stalin are shown as minor figures in the narrative, and most other prominent personalities occupy a minor place, although many Old Bolsheviks executed in Stalin's purges in the thirties have reemerged. Although the demythologizing of Stalin is certainly appropriate, the unwillingness to give credit to Trotsky's role in 1917 is one of the most obvious shortcomings of all Soviet historiography since the 1920s.

The most recent Soviet historiography continues to devote central attention to demonstrating the correctness of Leninist ideas about the Revolution and to the treatment of the role of Lenin and the Communist Party in the Revolution. In a recent review of the Soviet historiography of the Revolution, the new works of "Leniniana" of the October revolutionary period was stressed, including the fourth volume of Lenin's biographical chronicle, which records the daily and often hourly account of the leader's activities: *Vladimir Il'ich Lenin: Biografi-*

cheskaia Khronika (vol. 4, 1973). Many monographs were also published on the theme of Lenin's leadership of the revolutionary movement.

It is ironic that Soviet historiography, which is based on the Marxist philosophy of history, would put such great stress until very recently on the role of one individual and on the political significance of the Bolshevik Party, paradoxically paralleling the interpretations most commonly found in Western historical literature in the same period. Like their Western counterparts, some Soviet historians have embarked in new directions away from the prevailing orthodoxy toward an emphasis on social history. Among some of the new Soviet studies in social history are L. S. Gaponenko's *Rabochii klass v 1917 godu* (1970) on the history of the industrial working class, G. L. Sobolev's *Revoliutsionnoe soznanie rabochikh i soldat Petrograda v 1917 godu* (1973) on the state of mind of the workers and soldiers of Petrograd in 1917, and N. A. Kravchuk's *Massovoe krest'ianskoe dvizhenie v Rossii nakanune Oktiabria* on mass peasant movements on the eve of the October Seizure of Power. Finally, the Russian bourgeoisie has been studied by P. V. Volobuev in *Proletariat i burzhuaziia v 1917 godu* (1964); V. I. Startsev, *Russkaia burzhuaziia i samoderzhavie v 1905–1917 gg;* E. D. Chermenskii, *Burzhuaziia i tsarizm v pervoi russkoi revoliutsii* (1970); and idem, *IV gosudarstvennaia duma i sverzhenie tsarizma v Rossii* (1977). Even some of the defeated political movements have been studied recently, if only to be castigated, in K. Gusev's *Krakh partii levykh eserov* (1971) on the breakup of the alliance between the Bolsheviks and the Left Socialist–Revolutionaries (*see* Left Socialist-Revolutionary Party) and N. V. Ruban's *Oktiabr'skaia revoliutsiia i krakh menshevizma* (1968) on the role of the Mensheviks (*see* Social Democratic Workers' Party [Menshevik]) in 1917.

The late 1970s and early 1980s did not witness much new official Soviet writing on the revolution, but the advent of Gorbachev and his policy of "glasnost" promised new approaches to the Soviet past. As opposed to the Khrushchev thaw, however, the movement for more openness in evaluating the past seems to be coming from journalists, like the editors of Moscow News and Ogonek, rather than from the professional historians themselves. So far there has been more attention to the Stalinist period, and to a re-evaluation of Bukharin and some of the other old Bolsheviks. Perhaps if "glasnost" does become more firmly entrenched, we will see a greater variety of Soviet historiography on a variety of topics.

Soviet historiography has often been accused of a "whig" approach to history, meaning that Soviet historians have written the history of the Revolution to justify the present Soviet political system. They interpret the past by showing how it has led directly, and perhaps inevitably, to the present. This interpretation could also explain how the Soviet historians might be called on by Gorbachev to support his current policies of "glasnost".

In a variation on this theme, Stephen Cohen has recently accused many Western sovietologists of reading into the Russian Revolution their aversion to what came later under Stalinist totalitarianism (*see* Bibliography). This inverted "Whig consensus'' has been challenged by Cohen and much of the recent social and social–political history monographs that show the Revolution a popular social movement with the Bolsheviks leading not as a conspiratorial party but as popular standard-bearers for the movement. No Western consensus has emerged, but our understanding of the Revolution has certainly been enriched by this new revisionist literature.

William Parsons

Bibliography

Cohen, Stephen F. *Rethinking the Soviet Experience: Politics and History Since 1917.* 1985.
Laquer, Walter. *The Fate of the Revolution: Interpretations of Soviet History.* 1967.
Sovetskaia istoriografiia velikoi Oktiabrskoi sotsialisticheskoi revoliutsii. 1981.
Sovetskoi istoriografiia Fevral'skoi burzhuazno-demokraticheskoi revoliutsii. 1979.

Himmät. *See* Gummet.

Hummet. *See* Gummet.

I

Iakovleva, Varvara Nikolaevna (1885–1944). V. N. Iakovleva was a prominent Bolshevik (*see* Russian Social Democratic Workers' Party [Bolshevik]) leader in Moscow during the October Seizure of Power*. She was born in Moscow into an upper-middle-class family. She studied in the Higher Women's Courses (or Ger'e Courses) in the Mathematics and Physics Faculty of Moscow University. In 1904 she joined the Russian Social Democratic Workers' Party. She and her brother Nikolai Nikolaevich Iakovlev and her husband, P. K. Shternberg, were among the group of young intellectuals clustered around N. I. Bukharin*. She was a participant in the 1905 Revolution (*see* Nineteen-Five Revolution). Between 1908 and 1910, while a teacher in Moscow, Iakovleva was arrested and sentenced to four years in exile in Narym Krai in Siberia. Escaping in 1912, she returned to European Russia and became a member of the Central Committee of the Russian Social Democratic Workers' Party (Bolshevik) (*see* Central Committee of the Russian Communist Party [Bolshevik]). She was arrested again in 1913 and sent to Astrakhan until 1916. In that year she was made a member of the Moscow Committee of the Bolshevik Party and then secretary of the Moscow Regional (Oblast') Bureau of the Bolshevik Party.

During 1917 Iakovleva was a member of the Party Center directing the October Seizure of Power and of the Military Revolutionary Committee in that city. During the Civil War in Russia* she was one of the leading Left Communists (*see* Left Communism). When Lenin began to press for an end to the war with Germany in January 1918, Iakovleva and the Moscow Oblast' Bureau became the center of opposition, calling instead for continuing the struggle with Germany and fanning the flames of international communist revolution (*see* Left Communism). When the Communist Party voted for peace with Germany on February 18, Bukharin, Iakovleva (by this time a candidate member of the Central Committee), G. K. Piatakov, and V. M. Smirnov resigned their government posts and threatened to go among the party members to organize their opposition to peace. When that controversy subsided, Iakovleva and many other members of the Left Communists continued to oppose Lenin's "state capitalism" of April-May 1918, his rapprochement with former capitalists and bureaucrats against which they pitted the need for workers' (*see* Workers in the Russian Revolution) control, socialization of industry, large-scale farming, and power to the local economic soviets. After the death of her husband, she married a prominent representative of Left Communism, V. M. Smirnov. As late as 1923 she signed the "Platform of 46," which criticized the economic consequences of the New Economic Policy*. From 1919 to 1921 Iakovleva was a member of the Collegium of the People's Commissariat of Food Supplies, and she held several important party posts: member of the Siberian Bureau* of the Central Committee, secretary of the Moscow Committee, and member of the Siberian Oblast' Bureau of the Central Committee. From 1922 to 1929 she was People's Commissar for Education of the Russian Socialist Federative Soviet Republic (RSFSR). In 1929 she became People's Commissar of Finance of the RSFSR. She was a member of the All-Union Central Executive Committee of the Congress of Soviets. As part of the Great Purges of the mid–1930s, she was arrested and tried along with the other Left Communists and apparently died in jail. The dissident Soviet historian Roy Medvedev (1971) stated that although she was forced to make a public confession during the Purge Trials of 1938, she asked that her fellow prisoners who survived reveal her innocence once they had escaped or had been set free. Iakovleva has been posthumously rehabilitated.

Bibliography

Cohen, Stephen. *Bukharin and the Bolshevik Revolution*. 1971.
Daniels, Robert. *The Conscience of the Revolution*. 1960.
Medvedev, Roy. *Let History Judge*. 1971.

Iaroslavskii. *See* Gubel'man, Minei Izrailovich.

Ibragimov, Galimjan (1887–1938). Ibragimov was a prominent Crimean Tatar novelist and linguist and a nationalist leader who became one of the top Moslem Communist leaders.

Ibragimov was not a communist at the time of the October Seizure of Power*. He was born the son of a mullah in the village of Sultamuratovo near Ufa and educated in the madrasa of Galia of Ufa, a Moslem theological seminary with a reformist curriculum. He became one of the anti-Turkish leaders of the Islah* (Reform) movement. During the 1905 Revolution (*see* Nineteen-Five Revolution) he was close to the left wing of the Russian Socialist-Revolutionary Party* in Ufa. He was a popular novelist and journalist who wrote in the Tatar tongue. Ibragimov denied that Tatar national identity was the same as Turkic national identity and called for the development of the Tatar, rather than Turkish, language as a literary tongue for Tatars. He supported the secularization of education for

Tatars as a way of reaching that goal. Until 1917 he worked primarily as a Tatar language teacher and writer.

After the February Revolution*, Ibragimov differed from other Jadid (*see* Jadid Movement) reformers by moving closer to the socialist movements. In the spring of 1917 he began to publish the Socialist-Revolutionary newspaper *Irek* in the Tatar language. He was elected as a Socialist-Revolutionary delegate to the Constituent Assembly*. At the Third All-Russian Congress of Soviets in 1918 he was appointed to the new Central Commissariat for Moslem Affairs along with Mullanur Vakhitov* and Sharif Manatov. Ibragimov and Vakhitov signed a decree in March 1918 calling for the creation of a Tatar–Bashkir republic, (*see* Bashkiria, Revolution in), which effectively diverted the enthusiasm of Tatar nationalists away from the non-Bolshevik movements. Ibragimov was apparently hoping for a relatively independent Moslem communist movement in which Tatars would play a leading role. When the Tatar Autonomous Soviet Socialist Republic was finally proclaimed in May 1920, it excluded Bashkiria, which was a blow to Ibragimov's ambitions. Nevertheless, he became chairman of the Academic Center for the People's Commissariat of Education in the Tatar Republic, and from 1920 to 1929 he dominated Tatar cultural life.

Although he formally joined the Communist Party in 1920 and remained an orthodox Marxist, he also remained a staunch supporter of linguistic nationalism. In June 1927 his pamphlet "Which Way Will Tatar Culture Go" called for the purification and preservation of a distinctive Tatar language. It was denounced by the Tatar Provincial Committees as "nationalistic." From 1927 to 1937 he was in poor health but continued to be active in Tatar cultural affairs. In 1937 he was arrested and put in jail, where he died in 1938. He was rehabilitated after 1954.

Bibliography

Bennigsen, Alexandre A., and Wimbush, S. Enders. *Muslim National Communism in the Soviet Union.* 1979.
Zenzinov, *Pan-Turkism and Islam in Russia.* 1960.

Industrialists and the Russian Revolution. The role of the industrialists of Imperial Russia in the Revolution, which ultimately deprived them of their position in the Russian economy, has received relatively little attention in published scholarship in English.

The industrialists first appeared on the Russian national scene in an active public capacity during the Revolution of 1905 (*see* Nineteen-Five Revolution). At that time the leading enterprises in most of the major industries of Russia were already organized in a variety of "representative" organizations designed to promote their interests within bureaucratic circles and the articulate public. One result of the 1905 Revolution was the decision in 1906 of the leaders of large-scale industry to unite in an empirewide federation, the Association of Industry and Trade (Sovet S'ezdov Predstavitelei Promyshlennosti i Torgovli).

It was based in St. Petersburg and, from its founding until the collapse of the Empire, was recognized as the spokesman for "united industry," although the many differences among its members on issues of economic policy often seemed to belie this reputation.

The most influential groups within the Association were those representing heavy industry. Most notable was the Association of Southern Mine Owners (Sovet S' ezda Predstavitelei Gornopromyshlennikov Iuga Rossii), which represented the coal and metallurgical interests of the Donbas and Krivoi Rog. Its former president, N. S. Avdakov, soon became president of the Association of Industry and Trade, serving from 1907 until his death in 1915. Other major groupings included the oil interests of Baku, the Ural mining industrialists, the sugar refiners, and the various industrialists of St. Petersburg, Moscow, and the Central Industrial Region. Many of these member organizations were closely related to syndicates operating in their fields and also had ties with foreign capital.

During the years before World War I* the Association actively promoted the interests of large-scale industry through its publications, especially in its fortnightly journal *Industry and Trade (Promyshlennost' i Torgovlia)* and its annual congresses. Its ties with the government, particularly with the Ministries of Finance and of Trade and Industry, were close, although the industrialists frequently complained of their own failure to exercise sufficiently effective influence on official policies. Their numerous grievances against the government resulted from the close degree of regulation and supervision of private industry that was maintained and also the government's growing role as the owner of competing industrial enterprises. But many branches of industry were heavily dependent on the government for orders and contracts as well as for the supply of raw materials and other services. The Association continuously lobbied for additional governmental aid to industry in the form of increased tariff protection, support for greater inflow of capital from abroad, development of transport facilities, and the expansion of foreign markets, particularly in the Middle and Far East.

The Association was also an active proponent of the modernization of Russia along Western lines through a system of economic planning focused on the further growth of heavy industry. It sought to reduce industry's dependence on governmental purchases through an expansion of the Russian home market. In this connection it supported P. A. Stolypin's program of agrarian reform as a means of increasing both the productivity of agriculture and the domestic consumption of industrial goods. At the same time it called for a policy of austerity with regard to consumer goods. It was opposed to free competition in domestic as well as in foreign policy and favored the organized participation of the major elements in economic life in the form of cooperatives, labor unions, and industrial syndicates.

The Association's labor policies included not only recognition of labor unions but also support for the workers' accident and health insurance that were enacted into law in 1912. It also called for increased educational opportunities for the working class. However, it generally resisted increases in wages and reductions in working hours. In this area industrial interests were seriously divided among themselves, and the formation of unified policies that all of industry could support were sometimes impossible.

During the Stolypin period the industrialists participation in political life was minimal. This, no doubt, was in part a reflection of the failure of their efforts to win significant representation in the First Duma through their own political parties and a recognition both of continued lack of support among other elements in the population and of the diversity of political views within their own class. The industrialists' support for the principle of a national representative legislature, however, was firm. A majority of industrialists supported the Octobrist Party although they also had representation among the Constitutional Democratic Party—Cadet* and a scattered array of right-wing parties. Beginning with the Fourth Duma in 1912 the industrialists became politically more active as their conflict with the government about issues of "state socialists" and the role of monopolies in the current wave of inflation and goods shortages escalated. The leaders of this movement were a group of liberal industrialists in Moscow organized in the Progressist Party under the direction of P. P. Riabushinskii and A. I. Konovalov. Both were active in the Association, and Konovalov was a member of the Third and Fourth Dumas.

The outbreak of World War I was nevertheless marked by declarations of solidarity with the government on the part of industry's leaders. Despite their early awareness of the economic difficulties Russia would face, they welcomed the war as a means of freeing their country from its growing dependence on Germany. They also sought the acquisition of Constantinople and the Straits of Daradanelles as a guarantee of free access to the Mediterranean for commercial shipping.

Increasing economic difficulties as the war progressed soon provided the momentum for the transformation of industry's economic grievances against the government into a renewal and escalation of political antagonism. The government's early refusal to allow industrialists to share in the formulation of wartime economic policies was a particular source of irritation. The critical shortage of arms and munitions during the spring of 1915 brought the conflict to a head, with the resultant decisions by the Ninth Congress of the Association in May of this year to undertake the "self-mobilization" of industry. The result was the creation of a Central War Industries Committee (*see* War Industries Committees) to direct a network of similar committees throughout the country for the purpose of increasing production and organizing distribution for the war effort. After an initial period of organization by the Association, leadership of the War Industries Committees passed to A. I. Guchkov*, a leader of the Octobrist Party and a member of an established family of Moscow industrialists, and A. I. Konovalov as chairman and vice-chairman, respectively. However, the necessary governmental cooperation in the form of war contracts and assurance of needed supplies of materials was never sufficiently forthcoming, and the results of the committees' work was, on the whole, disappointing. Official attitudes toward the committee were colored by the fear that they served as a screen for antigovernmental political action, a fear that was heightened by the decision of the First Congress of War Industries Committees in July 1915 to admit a delegation of workers' representatives to membership in the Central Committee. Most industrialists did indeed aspire to constitutional reform but for the most part only as one of the benefits to be derived from a victorious war.

During the summer of 1915 the industrialists joined with the Octobrists, the Cadets, the Progressists, and other centrist parties in demanding a government that would have the confidence of the country; in August the association gave its support to the Progressive Bloc*. But although some circles of industrialists, especially those involving the Progressist Party, continued to be politically active until the end of the Empire, in general they failed to take any significant action after the summer of 1915. Governmental harassment, political divisions among the industrialists themselves, and the desire for profits and government contracts as well as a growing fear of the labor movement accounted in a large part for their passivity. But although some industrialists were not above catering to Rasputin* in return for economic favors, Guchkov, among others, plotted to remove Nicholas from the throne and replace him with a more satisfactory ruler. During the final weeks of 1916 and early 1917 a new movement of protest was clearly emerging among the industrialists as a whole and also within the association itself.

The collapse of the Empire in February 1917 (*see* February Revolution) was welcomed by the industrialists, although the majority would have preferred a limited monarchy over a republican form of government. With the creation of the "first" Provisional Government*, which survived only until May, the industrialists assumed a leading role. Guchkov served as Minister of War, Konovalov as Minister of Trade and Industry, and M. I. Tereshchenko, a wealthy, but little known sugar producer from Kiev, as Minister of Finance. After the May crisis, Guchkov lost his post, and shortly afterward Konovalov resigned because of differences with the government over economic policy. Konovalov was later reappointed by Kerensky, and in September he assumed the responsibilities of deputy prime minister. Tereshchenko replaced P. N. Miliukov* as Minister of Foreign Affairs and continued to occupy that post until the October Seizure of Power by the Bolsheviks.

During the months between the February and October revolutions most industrialists supported the Cadet Party, which became the rallying point for centrist and liberal feeling. Despite general agreement regarding the necessity to counter the rising power of labor and to establish an effective government, as well as support for the Constituent Assembly* and the foreign policy aims of the old regime, there were numerous tactical disagreements among the industrialists. Despite early differences with regard to the workers' demands they soon yielded to a generally common approach toward labor and the Soviets. During August many Moscow industrialists sympathized with the Kornilov Revolt* although few gave it active support. The proliferation of entrepreneurial organizations during the interrevolutionary months, although designed to achieve a measure of class solidarity, actually served to make their many differences, and particularly the differences between the Moscow and Petrograd industrialists, even more apparent.

Although Konovalov and Tereshchenko, as members of the Provisional Government, were arrested by the Bolsheviks during the October Seizure of Power, they were later released and, along with most large-scale industrialists, found their way to the West. In Paris the former industrialists founded an organization known as the Russian Financial, Industrial, and Commercial Association (L'Association financiere, industrielle et commerciale russe), which held meetings and published materials on the Soviet economy. It remained active until well into the 1930s.

Ruth Amende Roosa

Bibliography

Berlin, P. A. *Russkaia burzhaziia v staroe i novoe vremia.* 1922.
Buryshkin, P. A. *Moskva Kupecheskaia.* 1954.
Diakin, V. S. *Russkaia burzhuaziia i tsarizm v gody pervoi mirovoi voiny.* 1967.
Rieber, A. J. *Merchants and Entrepreneurs in Imperial Russia.* 1982.
Volobuev, P. V. *Proletariat i burzhuaziia Rossii v 1917 g.* 1964.

Interdistrict Committee (Mezhraiontsy). The Interdistrict Committee was the name of L. D. Trotsky's* faction in the Russian Social Democratic Workers' Party (Bolshevik)* in 1917, one of the most important internationalist* factions in the Russian Social Democratic movement.

Until the end of 1914, the full name of this organization was the Inter-District Commission of the Russian Social Democratic Workers' Party. Among those belonging to this group were the followers of Trotsky, some Mensheviks (*see* Russian Social Democratic Workers' Party [Menshevik]), some members of the "Vpered group," and some Bolsheviks (*see* Russian Social Democratic Workers' Party [Bolshevik]) who were called "conciliators." The goal of the group was to bring together the various factions in the Russian Social Democratic Workers' Party into a united organization, although they only succeeded in creating yet another faction.

The group had taken shape in 1913 and had not started as an effort to create a new party. In the beginning it had opposed the war and had support only in a few working-class districts. Its members included some brilliant intellectuals, such as A. V. Lunacharskii*, D. B. Riazanov, D. Z. Manuilskii, A. A. Ioffe*, and M. N. Pokrovskii*. When Trotsky returned to Russia, he was greeted as their natural leader, and a joint reception was held for him on May 7, 1917, arranged by both the Bolsheviks and the Interdistrict Committee. At a meeting with the Bolsheviks on May 10, Lenin asked Trotsky and his group to join the Bolshevik Party and offered them positions on the Editorial Board of *Pravda* and in the leading organs of the party. Lenin wrote at the time that there were no major disagreements between the programs of the two groups, although Trotsky's biographer Isaac Deutscher indicated that it was Lenin who had come over to Trotsky's views, rather than the other way around. At the Sixth Congress of the Bolshevik Party in July the Interdistrict Committee, some 4,000 strong, formally joined the Bolshevik Party.

Bibliography

Daniels, Robert. *The Conscience of the Revolution.* 1960.
Deutscher, Isaac. *The Prophet Armed.* 1954.

Internationale. *See* Anthems.

Internationalists. The internationalists were those factions in the Russian Social Democratic Workers movement that opposed World War I*. They found themselves in opposition to most European socialists who tended to adopt a Defensist (*see* Defensism) position, that is, that socialists should support the national war effort in their own countries to sustain the progress achieved in social programs. The internationalists in Russian Social Democracy ranged from Menshevik–Internationalists (*see* Russian Social Democratic Workers' Party [Menshevik]) such as Iu. O. Martov* to L. D. Trotsky* and his Interdistrict Committee*. But the leading internationalist faction in Russian Social Democracy was Lenin's Bolshevik Party (*see* Russian Social Democratic Workers' Party [Bolshevik]), enabling Lenin* eventually to recruit support from the individual internationalists from all of the other factions in the Social Democratic movement in 1917. The famous meeting of European socialists who opposed the war in Zimmerwald on September 5, 1915 (*see* World War I), included representatives from all of the "internationalists" in the Russian Social Democratic movement. Although they all agreed to endorse the Zimmerwald Manifesto that Trotsky drafted, the non-Bolsheviks feared domination by Lenin at that time and could not fall into line with his views completely. Lenin called for defeatism*, that is, for turning the imperialist war into civil war, and called for the creation of a new antiwar socialist international. Although most non-Bolsheviks found those views unacceptable in 1915, many, like Trotsky, would move closer to Lenin in 1917 (*see* World War I; Trotsky; Interdistrict Committee).

Bibliography

Daniels, Robert V. *The Conscience of the Revolution.* 1960.
Deutscher, Isaac. *The Prophet Armed.* 1954.
Ferro, Marc. *The Great War, 1914–18.* 1973.

Internationalists. (*Internatsionalisty*). This term is also used to describe those who joined the Bolsheviks (*see* Russian Social Democratic Workers' Party [Bolshevik]) during the Civil War in Russia* and were born outside the borders of Imperial Russia. Soviet sources claim that there were more than 4 million foreigners in Russia in 1917, including more than 100,000 Chinese and Koreans. They were said to have provided the Red Army* with more than a quarter of a million troops, many from the prisoners of war captured during World War I by the imperial army. Many of these soldiers remained in Russia after the war. Some, like the Hungarian B. Kun, the Czech A. Muna, the Austrian K. Tomann, and the Yugoslav C. Copic went home and became leaders in the formation of Communist Parties in their own countries.

Bibliography

Mints, I. I. *Uchastie trudiashchiakhsia zarubezhnykh stran v Oktiabr' skoi revoliutsii.* 1967.

Ioffe, Adolf Abramovich. (1883–1927; pseudonym, V. Krymsky). A. A. Ioffe was a prominent member of the Interdistrict Committee* who joined the Bolsheviks (*see* Russian Social Democratic Workers' Party [Bolshevik]) in 1917 and became a prominent Bolshevik leader, taking part in the October Seizure of Power*.

Ioffe was born into a middle-class Karaite Jewish family in Simferopol in the Crimea and joined the Russian Social Democratic Workers' Party in 1902, but did not join either the Bolshevik or Menshevik faction in 1903. When he graduated from the gymnasium in 1903, he was deemed politically "unreliable" and, therefore, had to go abroad to pursue his medical studies. In Berlin he participated in both the German and the Russian Social Democratic movements. He took part in the 1905 Revolution (*see* Nineteen-Five Revolution) in the Crimea and then left for Zurich where he began legal studies. In 1908 he settled in Vienna and began his long collaboration with L. D. Trotsky* helping to finance Trotsky's political activities with his personal fortune.

While he was living in Vienna, Ioffe was treated by the famous psychoanalyst Alfred Adler for a nervous disorder that would plague him for the rest of his life. In 1912 he was arrested in Odessa and imprisoned until February 1917. In Petrograd he joined the Bolsheviks along with the other members of the Interdistrict Committee and became a Bolshevik delegate to the Petrograd City Duma, to the Petrograd Soviet*, to its Central Executive Committee, to the Democratic Conference*, to the Pre-Parliament, and to the Constituent Assembly*. He was elected a member of the Central Committee of the Russian Social Democratic Workers' Party (Bolshevik) (*see* Central Committee of the Russian Communist Party [Bolshevik]) in July 1917 at the Sixth Party Congress. In October 1917 he was chairman of the Military Revolutionary Committee in Petrograd. He was in charge of the negotiations for the Treaty of Brest-Litovsk* with Germany. He was subsequently appointed Soviet Russia's first ambassador to Germany, although they refused to accept him. Until 1925 he was involved with many important diplomatic assignments for the Commissariat of Foreign Affairs.

From 1925 to 1927 he was involved in the struggle for power as a member of Trotsky's faction, opposing the growing power of Stalin. In 1927 he committed suicide, and about 4,000 people attended his funeral, which became the last public demonstration of support for Trotsky's opposition group.

Bibliography

Haupt, Georges, and Marie, Jean-Jacques. *Makers of the Russian Revolution*. 1974.

Islah (Reform; in Arabic, Islah Komitesi, or Committee for Reform). Islah was a major Islamic group devoted to reform in the Tatar regions. It was created in 1905 by a small group of Tatar intellectuals who came from the more radical wing of the Jadid movement*. Its members were opposed to Russian influence and to the conservatism of the Moslem religious leaders. The members of the group did not form any coherent political party, although they were clearly drawn to the methods and program of the Russian Socialist-Revolutionary Party* and, especially, to the idea of direct action, including terrorism, to achieve Tatar national goals. After the October Seizure of Power* some members of this group, like Gallimjan Ibragimov* and Ayaz Iskhaki, joined the Bolsheviks (*see* Russian Social Democratic Workers' Party [Bolshevik]).

Bibliography

Bennigsen, Alexandre A., and Wimbush, S. Enders. *Muslim National Communism in the Soviet Union*. 1979.
Zenkovsky, Serge A. *Pan-Turkism and Islam in Russia*. 1960.

Ittihad-ve Tarakki (Unity and Progress). A secret political group said to have been formed in the 1920s by leaders such as the Tatar M. S. Sultangaliev*, the Bashkir A. Z. Validov, and the Uzbek Jadid (*see* Jadid Movement) leaders Tursun Khojaev and Turar Ryskulov*. Soviet sources claim that the Kazakh leader A. B. Baitursunov and the Russian M. S. Sedel'nikov were also members, although S. A. Zenkovsky doubts it. Soviet writers claim that the Ittihad program called for the infiltration of the Communist Party by Turkic militants, an attempt to seize control of educational institutions in the Moslem areas, establishing connections with counterrevolutionary organizations like the Basmachis*, and the creation of a bourgeois Pan-Turkic state in place of the Moslem Soviet republics. All that is really certain is that the political leaders named here wanted greater autonomy for the Moslem republics. Most of these leaders went into exile, disappeared, or were executed during the Great Purges of the 1930s.

Bibliography

Bennigsen, A. A., and Wimbush, S. Enders. *Muslim National Communism in the Soviet Union*. 1979.
Zenkovsky, S. A. *Pan-Turkism and Islam in Russia*. 1960.

Iudenich, Nikolai Nikolaevich (1862–1933). Iudenich was a general of the infantry in the Russian Imperial Army and commander of the counterrevolutionary forces in northwestern Russia during the Civil War (*see* Civil War in

Russia). He was born in a noble family in Minsk and graduated from the Alexander Military School in 1881. During the Russo–Japanese War in 1905 he commanded a regiment. In 1912 he was appointed chief of staff of the Kazan Military District and in 1913 of the Caucasian Military District. At the outset of World War I* Iudenich was named Chief of Staff of the Army of the Caucasus, and he conducted several successful operations.

After the February Revolution* Iudenich retired and in 1918 emigrated to Finland. On June 15, 1919 he took command of the White Guard Northwestern Army in Estonia and became a member of the Northwestern Government. After his attempt to take Petrograd failed in October and November 1919, he retreated to Estonia and then went into exile in England. Throughout the Revolution and the Civil War his public political statements ranged from liberal to conservative, with no consistent orientation. In exile he remained outside of emigré politics.

Bibliography

Bradley, John. *Civil War in Russia*. 1975.
Luckett, Richard. *The White Generals*. 1971.
Stewart, George. *The White Armies of Russia*. 1933.

Izvestiia. The official newspaper of the Petrograd Soviet* that became the official newspaper of the present Soviet government. *Izvestiia (News)* began publication during the 1905 Revolution (*see* Nineteen-Five Revolution) when it was published on an irregular basis as the official newspaper of the St. Petersburg Soviet during that period. During 1917 the first issue appearing on February 28 with the title *Izvestiia Petrogradskaia Soveta rabochikh deputatov (News of the Petrograd Soviet of Workers' Deputies)*.

In the beginning the newspaper reflected the balance of political forces in the Petrograd Soviet, with a Menshevik Internationalist*, Iurii M. Steklov, as the chief editor and an editorial board that included the Mensheviks (*see* Russian Social Democratic Workers' Party [Menshevik]) F. I. Dan (*see* Gur'vich, F. I.), and N. N. Sukhanov*, the Socialist–Populist V. B. Stankevich, and the Bolsheviks (*see* Russian Social Democratic Workers' Party [Bolshevik]) N. P. Avilov and V. D. Bonch-Bruevich*. The newspaper tended to support the Provisional Government*.

After the October Seizure of Power* *Izvestiia* became the official newspaper of the new Soviet government, and Steklov converted to Bolshevism and kept his post as chief editor. After the capital was moved to Moscow *Izvestiia* was published in that city, starting with the March 12, 1918, issue.

J

Jadid Movement. The Jadid Movement was a Pan-Islamic modernizing movement among the Turkish population of Russian Central Asia.

The efforts of a Russian, N. I. Ilminsky, a professor at the Kazan Orthodox Theological Seminary who tried to develop a new type of school for the Moslem natives of the Russian Empire, were the original inspiration for the Jadid movement. Ilminsky wanted to provide a new curriculum for the Russian–Tatar schools sponsored by the tsarist government. His schools would include instruction in Russian civilization and other non-Islamic subjects in the native language, and at the upper level the students would begin to learn Russian, the administrative language of the empire. The goal was to end the parochialism fostered by the more traditional Moslem schools and to socialize Russia's Moslem people.

But Tatar intellectuals and clergymen saw Ilminsky's schools as an effort at Russianization and opposed him by modernizing their own schools, by teaching Ottoman Turkic rather than Arabic, and by adding secular subjects to the traditional religious curriculum. The pioneer in this effort was Ismail bey Gasprinsky (1851–1914). His Tatar schools were called "New Method" (Usul-Jadid) schools, and the Tatar leaders in the movement came to be known as Jadids (innovators). Gasprinsky was strongly influenced by the Pan-Slavs, although he looked more to Constantinople than to Moscow for inspiration.

The movement became very popular among the Tatar bourgeoisie who supported the schools financially. The Tatar Jadids began to spread their message to other Turks in the Russian Empire like the Kazakhs and the Uzbeks. Jadid schools were opened in Kazakhstan, Tashkent, and Samarkand. After the 1905 Revolution (*see* Nineteen-Five Revolution) several Jadid publications began to appear in Tashkent, at first sponsored by Tatars and then by Uzbek publishing houses. In 1909 the Jadids organized a cultural society, "The Aid." The tsarist government supported the more conservative Moslem movements against the Jadids, whom they tended to regard as dangerous revolutionary nationalists.

The Jadids also moved into the Khanate of Bukhara, and a Jadid school opened in Bukhara in 1908 with the permission of the Emir. The language of instruction was Tajik. By 1913 there were ten such schools in Bukhara. In 1914 all of them were closed by order of the emir at the request of the Moslem clergy.

Many of the leaders of the emerging liberal Pan-Islamic Young Bukharan Movement (*see* Bukhara, Revolution in) came out of Jadid schools. The Young Bukharans attacked the superstition and fanaticism encouraged by the more conservative Moslem schools. When the Emir banned the Jadid schools in 1914, the Young Bukharans fled for a time to Constantinople, but they soon returned to Tashkent.

During 1917 and 1918 Bolshevik (*see* Russian Social Democratic Workers' Party [Bolshevik]) influence in Central Asia was limited (*see* Central Asia, Revolution in). The stronghold of radicalism in Central Asia was the Tashkent Soviet, which was dominated by Europeans who were mostly members of the Socialist-Revolutionary Party* and the Menshevik Party (*see* Russian Social Democratic Workers' Party [Menshevik]). The Moslems created a rival center, the Kokand Autonomous government (*see* Kokand, the Autonomous Government of), which was crushed by the Red Army* in January 1918. I. V. Stalin*, People's Commissar of Nationalities, began to build an apparatus for winning over the Moslems in the form of the Central Bureau of Moslem Organizations of the Russian Social Democratic Workers' Party (Bolshevik)* under his control. Although the Red Army began gaining ground in Central Asia, the Soviet government became aware that it would not be able to base its power on the non-Moslem Tashkent Soviet, which was viewed by the native Moslem population as a new instrument for Russian imperialism. A wider search for Moslem allies began.

Many of the Uzbek Jadids who fled from the persecution of the Emir of Bukhara allied themselves with the communists after 1917, and some of them—men such as Turar Ryskulov*, and N. Khojaev—later joined the Communist Party. They became members of the eleven-man Regional Bureau of the party at its Third Regional Party Congress in June 1919 in Tashkent. Three months later a Moslem majority was elected to the Turkestan Central Committee by the Eighth Congress of Central Asian Soviets. Another Jadid, Tursan Khojaev, was named the General Secretary of the party's Regional Bureau. Once in power, the Jadids began to agitate for the fulfillment of their original program, the unification of all Russian Turkic peoples under Moslem self-rule.

In 1919 the Russian Communist Party appointed the Special Turkestan Commission including figures such as M. V. Frunze*, Sh. Z. Eliava, and Ia. Z. Rudzutak to consolidate Soviet power against the threat posed by the Basmachi* movement in the area and build up some popular support by more lenient policies toward Turkic nationalism and the Moslem faith. The Turkestan Commission purged those who opposed the Jadids, only to discover their mistake a few months later. Although the Uzbek Jadids opposed colonialism, feudalism, and clericalism, they did not support the idea of a class struggle and were really

Pan-Turkish nationalists rather than Marxists. At the request of Frunze a new Turkestan commission was formed with no Russian or Moslem members, and it adopted a hard line toward the Jadid Communists. The new commission first purged Russian anti-communists and then removed the Jadid Communists from positions of power. They were accused of supporting the patriarchal feudal heritage. A new Regional Bureau was elected with few Jadid intellectuals in it. To prevent the formation of a large Turkish Central Asian state, in 1924 the Soviet Union combined the Khanates of Khiva and Bukhara with Turkestan to form the Autonomous Soviet Socialist Republic (ASSR) of Turkestan, and Uzbekistan became a separate union republic. The Tajiks were left as an Autonomous Republic under the Uzbek ASSR. This effectively ended the Pan-Turkic movement in Central Asia.

Bibliography

Pipes, Richard. *The Formation of the Soviet Union.* 1954.
Zenkovsky, S. A. *Pan-Turkism and Islam in Russia.* 1960.

Jewry, 1905–1921. At the beginning of World War I*, the Jewish population of tsarist Russia was the largest Jewish community in the world. According to the official census of 1897, some 5,189,000 Jews, constituting 4.13 percent of the total population of the empire, were to be found in territories governed by Nicholas II*. Although the total Russian–Jewish population may not in itself have been of great numerical significance, the geographical location and the economic development of the Jewish community in the nineteenth and early twentieth centuries made that community an important consideration for both tsarist administrators and Soviet officials. Because of the residential and economic restrictions imposed upon them, 95 percent of the Russian–Jewish population found themselves residing in the Pale of Settlement, an area defined by tsarist legislation during the nineteenth century. In that region, which included major areas within Lithuania, the Western Ukraine, and Belorussia, as well as all of the Congress Kingdom of Poland, the Jewish community constituted a significant 11.5 percent of the total population.

The extent of Jewish concentration in the region and its overall economic importance there becomes even further accentuated when one considers the other demographic aspects of those western borderlands. Most striking is the degree of Jewish urbanization in that zone. In 1897 more than half of the urban population of Belorussia and Lithuania were Jewish, and in the Ukraine Jews constituted nearly one-third of the urban population. For example, Jews made up more than 75 percent of the population of Bialystok, more than 50 percent of the residents in Minsk, 45 percent of the population of Vilna, and more than 30 percent of the inhabitants of Lodz, Odessa, and Warsaw. Economically, the Jewish population was categorized as a middle-class group; approximately 75 percent of the community was employed or associated with commercial and mercantile professions or trades. Thus in an area that was ethnically heterogenous and was predominantly rural and agricultural in its economic development, the Jews, by virtue of their occupations, places of residence, and cultural folkways, stood out within the general populace.

As the Russian Empire was undergoing a major economic transformation in the second half of the nineteenth century, the Jewish community found itself in many positions that were becoming critical to the development of a modern industrial state. On the whole, while beneficial to individual members of the Jewish community who were able to gain personally from the new economic circumstances of the last third of the nineteenth century, the rapid transformation of Russian society and the economy adversely affected most of the Jewish community. Especially hard hit were those who were not able to leave the Pale of Settlement in search of opportunities in the heartland of the empire.

Increased competition for urban jobs from former serfs and peasants fleeing the countryside for new opportunities in the cities, together with the maintenance of legal prohibitions against Jewish residence outside the Pale for all but the privileged few, created a severe economic crisis for Russia's Jewish population. The early 1880s through the first years of the twentieth century constituted a period of growing congestion within the Pale. This caused economic difficulties that were further exacerbated by episodes of mob violence directed against the Jews of the Pale, leading rapidly to the impoverishment of the Jewish community there. Together, the economic crisis and the physical insecurities induced nearly 2 million Jews to emigrate from Russian territory in the period 1881–1914.

In its cultural development, the Jewish community of Russia had evolved along a number of paths. Unlike the modernization of Western and Central European Jewry, the growing secularization of Russian Jewry in the second half of the nineteenth century did not bring with it a cultural integration into the surrounding majority culture. Although the trend to Russification did exist, it was being challenged vigorously by alternative models, namely, the growth and development of both a Yiddish-based and a Hebrew-based secular culture. Daily, weekly, and monthly periodicals, literary and scholarly journals, as well as novels, collections of poetry, and monographs on a variety of themes were appearing in increasing numbers in both Yiddish and Hebrew for what was apparently an insatiable reading public.

In short, by 1914 Russia's Jews had gone through a process of becoming more and more secular but not necessarily more and more Russian. The community was composed of religious Jews and secularists; Jewish nationalists of liberal as well as socialist persuasions; Jewish socialists committed to a Marxist ideology, as well as those whose socialism was based on a different set of economic perspectives; and artisans, workers, and middle-class merchants. Common to all groups and ideological perspectives, though, was an adherence to a Jewish identity that, though hard to define, was clearly differentiated from the other national identities then in existence within the multinational empire of the tsars.

These economic, social, and cultural developments shaped the nature of Jewish political activity in the period 1905–1921. Jewish political attitudes, as expressed by both middle-class liberals and left-wing socialists, emphasized the need for some form of national or cultural rights in addition to individual civil rights in order to ameliorate the immediate economic and social problems then besetting the community. Although the Jewish parties were not able to gain meaningful representation in any of the four Dumas elected in the period before the Revolution, individual Jews, representing Russian liberal and socialist movements, were elected to each of the Dumas (*see* Duma and Revolution), and some of those individuals used their positions to speak out on behalf of Jewish interests. By and large though, Jewish-related matters did not receive much of a public hearing in any of the Dumas, and no real improvement in Jewish status or in the quality of Jewish life occurred during the last decade of tsarist rule. Quite the contrary, the period from 1905 to World War I was one of increased anti-Jewish sentiment and activity (*see* Anti-Semitism).

The battle lines of World War I divided Russia's Jews nearly in half, with part of the community falling under German occupation and the remainder under Russian control. Not only were the established lines of communication and exchange severed by the war, but the combat zone, which went through the very heart of the Pale, brought massive dislocations and physical destruction to the Russian–Jewish community. Although official attitudes to Jews continued to remain hostile during the wartime period, with Jewish loyalty to the empire being questioned, the exigencies of the war forced the government to abolish most of the residential restrictions imposed on the Jews. Thus in August 1915 a large number of Jews were permitted to escape the front and to find refuge in the interior of the country.

The February Revolution* in 1917 brought with it full emancipation for all, thus eliminating the remaining restrictions that had been imposed on Jewish life. Also, the upheaval and the ensuing politicization of life among the various nationalities of the former tsarist empire stimulated Jewish politicians to prepare their own political program for the Jews in some new Russian state to evolve in the future. In the spring and early summer of 1917, a number of Jewish groups laid the groundwork for the convening of a Russian–Jewish Congress that was to be the first effort toward the securing of national autonomy for the Jewish community of the future Russian state. That congress, scheduled to meet in the autumn of 1917, never did convene because of the battlefield reverses and the October Seizure of Power* by the Bolsheviks (*see* Russian Social Democratic Workers' Party [Bolshevik]). However, Jewish political efforts were not confined to the idea of a congress. Jewish political leaders also made plans for the forthcoming Constituent Assembly*, which was to shape the contours of the future Russian state. Thus the summer of 1917 saw the full flowering of Jewish national sentiments with every expectation that these hopes for Jewish national or cultural autonomy would be realized within the very near future. National consciousness among the Jewish population of Russia was further stimulated in November 1917 when the British Wartime Cabinet issued the Balfour Declaration recognizing Palestine as a future Jewish national home.

The Soviet Seizure of Power in October came as a jolt to these Jewish hopes. First, the Bolshevik commitment to a socialized economy raised grave fears within the Jewish community, which, after all, was middle class and mainly involved in the mercantile trades. Jewish leaders worried that the new government would close down the shops and stalls that were the mainstay of Jewish economic life at the time. Furthermore, the ideological antagonism expressed by the Bolshevik leadership to organized religion was, in the view of many Jews, threatening to the future of Judaism in that country. Finally, while developing their revolutionary ideology in the first decades of the twentieth century, V. I. Lenin* and other Bolshevik leaders expressed themselves in opposition to the idea of Jewish national identity. Following traditional Marxist thinking, the Bolshevik leadership identified the Jewish community as part of the middle class, and it postulated that with the triumph of socialism and the establishment of a classless society, the Jewish community would disappear. Thus Jewish nationalists and others anxious for some form of Jewish cultural autonomy were apprehensive about the prospects for such status under a Soviet government. Theoretically, then, the ideological positions of the new Soviet government threatened the existing Jewish economic structure, the foundations of Judaism, and any national status in a future Soviet Russia.

Hence, the Soviet Revolution did not elicit any real support from the organized Jewish community. On the other hand, Jews did not move quickly into the ranks of the opposition determined to overthrow Bolshevism, mainly because many of those groups most active in combatting Bolshevism were themselves engaged in violent anti-Semitic activities. Thus Lenin's denunciation of anti-Semitism as a counterrevolutionary activity and his call for its immediate suppression with prosecution of all who indulged in it had the effect of neutralizing Jewish opposition to the new regime. Not only that, but in some areas, principally in the pogrom-ravaged Ukraine and in parts of Belorussia, the Red Army*, by rescuing Jews from the Pogromists, emerged as the physical savior of Jewish life there and thus secured Jewish support for itself and the new regime as against those groups intent on restoring the *ancien regime*. So although the organized Jewish community did not support Bolshevism, many individual Jews did so in order to safeguard many of the gains made in the period since the fall of tsarism.

As the Civil War (*see* Civil War in Russia) period came to an end and the New Economic Policy* was introduced to give Russian society respite from the ravages of the previous half-decade, the Jewish community found itself with mixed hopes and fears for the future. Bolshevik policies since 1918 had implicitly recognized the Jews as a national entity. Perhaps positive developments would be forthcoming, and Jewish cultural life could be rebuilt within the context of a Bolshevik Soviet society. Furthermore, with the introduction of the New Economic Policy, an opportunity was being created for the Jews, as well as other Soviet citizens, to repair the bases of their shattered economic life. In addition, the eradication of residence and other discriminatory legislation of the tsarist period now afforded the opportunity to those Jews interested in associating themselves with the new society to do so and to advance as far as their talents and skills would take them. Only time would tell how long the policies and the attitudes in effect in 1921 would last.

Alexander Orbach

Bibliography

Aronson, C., and J. Frumkin, eds. *Russian Jewry, 1860–1917.* 1966.
Aronson, C., and J. Frumkin, eds. *Russian Jewry, 1917–67.* 1969.
Baron, S. *The Russian Jew under Tsars and Soviet.* 2d rev. ed. 1976.
Dubnow, S. M. *A History of the Jews in Poland and Russia.* 1916.
Kochan, L., ed. *The Jews in Soviet Russia Since 1917.* 1970.
Maro, Y. *The Jewish Question in the Liberal and Revolutionary Movement in Russia, 1890–1914.* (in Hebrew). 1964.
Schwarz, S. M. *The Jews in the Soviet Union.* 1951.

July Days. During the chaotic July Days between the February and October Revolutions (*see* February Revolution; October Seizure of Power), an abortive mass uprising against the Provisional Government* took place in Petrograd.

The fundamental cause of this uprising was a genuine, widespread, spiraling impatience and dissatisfaction on the part of Petrograd factory workers (*see* Workers in the Russian Revolution) and soldiers (*see* Soldiers and Soldiers' Committees) and Baltic fleet sailors (*see* Sailors in 1917) with continued maintenance of the war effort and the meager social and economic results of the February Revolution. Deteriorating economic conditions had helped trigger the overthrow of the old order in the first place, and the Revolution had done little to alleviate the situation. On the contrary, administrative confusion increased in March and April, and this, in addition to the continued deterioration of transportation, led to a significant worsening of the supply situation. The increased shortages of raw materials and fuel that developed forced factory workers to curtail production and led to extensive layoffs. Simultaneously, food deliveries also continued to decline; attempts by the government to introduce an effective food pricing and rationing system failed to ease the strains caused by these shortages. In the spring of 1917 workers in a number of industries had received substantial wage increases. However, skyrocketing prices quickly offset these gains, so that by early summer Petrograd factory workers, generally, were no better off economically than they had been in February.

An immediate contributing factor leading to the July eruption was the launching by the Provisional Government in mid-June of a major new Military offensive on the western front. The soldiers of the war-inflated Petrograd garrison had played a prominent part in the overthrow of the Tsar. They had hailed the basic changes in the armed forces brought about by the February Revolution and had confidently awaited arrangement of a compromise peace that would free them to return home to share in the Revolution's fruits. Efforts by the government to restore a semblance of traditional order in the army, which greatly increased the likelihood of early transfer to the front, drove many of those soldiers into a frenzy.

By late spring, massive numbers of Petrograd factory workers, soldiers, and sailors had already concluded that the Provisional Government was an instrument of the propertied classes opposed to fundamental political change and uninterested in the needs of ordinary people. No small part in the crystallization of such views was played by the radically inclined Bolsheviks (*see* Russian Social Democratic Workers' Party [Bolshevik]), led by V. I. Lenin*. On the other hand, although the lowest strata of the Petrograd population subjected the moderate socialists to increasing criticism for their support of the government and the war effort, the soviets* were nonetheless contrasted positively with the Provisional Government and viewed as genuinely democratic institutions of popular self-rule—hence the enormous attraction of the chief political slogan of the Bolsheviks, "All Power to the Soviets."

Popular disenchantment with the Provisional Government was reflected initially during the April Crisis (*see* Miliukov, P. N.) of April 20 and 21, when thousands of workers, soldiers, and sailors took to the streets to protest Foreign Minister P. N. Miliukov's* obvious intention of pursuing the war effort to a "victorious conclusion." Significantly, the crowds ended these demonstrations only at the request of the Petrograd Soviet* after openly ignoring government orders to disperse.

In the wake of the April Crisis, two of the ministers most closely associated with the government's unpopular foreign and military policies, Miliukov and A. I. Guchkov*, the War Minister, had withdrawn from the cabinet. At that time, the first liberal socialist coalition government, under G. E. L'vov*, had been formed. These personnel changes, however, did not significantly alter the government's orientation. An antigovernment demonstration organized by the Bolsheviks for June 10 was cancelled, in part due to last-minute intervention by the moderate socialist leadership of the Soviet. However, popular sentiment in the capital was manifested anew on June 18, when the Bolsheviks successfully transformed a mass demonstration designed by the moderate socialists as an endorsement of their policies into an impressive display of support for an exclusively socialist Soviet government.

The July uprising, two weeks later, was touched off by soldiers of the First Machine Gun Regiment, one of the most militantly inclined military units based in Petrograd. The machine gunners had earlier received orders for sizeable shipments of men and arms to the front. On the afternoon of July 3, one or two of their number were dispatched to every major factory and military unit, where, more often than not, their appeals for immediate insurrection were greeted with enthusiasm. By early evening upper-class citizens disappeared from downtown streets, and thousands of soldiers in full battle dress and workers carrying banners, many of the latter accompanied by their families, were demonstrating outside the Marinskii and Tauride Palaces, headquarters of the Provisional Government and the Soviet, respectively. This popular explosion aside, the national political situation at this point in the Revolution was especially clouded by the resignation of several Constitutional Democrats (*see* Constitutional Democratic Party—Cadet) from the cabinet because of differences with socialist ministers over nationality policy (*see* National Question and the Russian Revolution).

The start of the July uprising found Lenin taking a brief, much-needed respite from political activity in the Finnish countryside. He returned hurriedly to Petrograd the morning of July 4, arriving in the capital in time to greet representatives of some 10,000 Bolshevik-led Kronstadt sailors, most of whom were armed and battle hungry. The July Days reached their peak the afternoon of July 4. At that time, insurrectionary elements controlled the psychologically and strategically important Peter and Paul fortress. The number of demonstrators may have reached as high as 400,000. Numerous incidents of shooting and looting, which the authorities were helpless to control, occurred in widely scattered parts of the city. Indeed, the membership of the Provisional Government and participants in the First All-Russian Congress of Workers' and Soldiers' Deputies (*see* Soviets [Councils] of Workers', Soldiers', and Peasants' Deputies), which had just recently completed its deliberations, then meeting in the capital, were both completely at the mercy of rampaging demonstrators. Throughout the crisis, however, the Menshevik (*see* Russian Social Democratic Workers' Party [Menshevik]) and Socialist-Revolutionary (*see* Socialist-Revolutionary Party) leaders in the Soviet remained determined not to yield to mass pressure. They were convinced, probably with good reason, that at that time, neither the provincial population nor the army at the front would support a transfer of power to the soviets; they also thought that it was necessary for all of the people to work together in the interest of the war effort and the survival of the Revolution.

As it turned out, the insurgents shied away from taking the decisive step of arresting the government. The July uprising petered out during the night of July 4–5, after it became known that loyal troops were on the way to the capital from the northern front and after government officials successfully convinced previously neutral garrison units that Lenin was an agent of enemy Germany.

The precise role of the Bolsheviks in the preparation and organization of the July uprising has been the subject of considerable dispute. In the immediate aftermath of the insurrection, it was widely assumed that it had been part of an abortive conspiracy by the Bolsheviks, working hand in hand with the Germans, to seize power. This view is reflected in many Western interpretations. The Bolsheviks claimed at the time that the July events were a spontaneous, essentially peaceful outburst of mass indignation with the Provisional Government, not unlike the June 18 demonstration, to which the party sought to give an organized character. This is the view still propounded in Soviet accounts.

Reliable evidence suggests a somewhat more complex picture. It is clear that the July movement was in part an outgrowth of months of anti-government propaganda (*see* Propaganda and the Russian Revolution). Rank-and-file Bolsheviks from Petrograd factories and military regiments appear to have played a leading role in its organization. Most interesting, it seems that leaders of two important auxiliary arms of the party, the Bolshevik Military Organization (*see* Military Opposition) and the Bolshevik Petersburg Committee, responsive to their militant constituencies, encouraged the insurrection against the wishes of Lenin and a majority of the Central Committee (*see* Central Committee of the Russian Communist Party [Bolshevik]) who considered such action premature. Once the street demonstrations had begun, the central party leadership was left with little alternative but to endorse them, which it did late the night of July 3– 4. The next day, with the party already gravely compromised and with the moderate socialists adamantly refusing to acquiesce in the creation of a Soviet national government, Lenin and other top Bolsheviks momentarily considered the possibility of seizing power independently of and in opposition to the soviets. However, developments later that evening—that is, the dispatch of loyal troops from the front and the abrupt shift in the mood of garrison regiments—quickly dampened such thinking and, instead, impelled the Central Committee to issue a public call for an immediate end to the street movement.

The July Days ended in an apparent defeat for the Bolsheviks. The main party newspapers were shut down, Bolshevik offices were ransacked, Lenin was forced to flee the capital in disgrace, and many top party leaders, including a significant portion of the military organization leadership cadre from the Petrograd garrison, were arrested and jailed. Sizeable groups of workers appeared to be turning against the party, the Bolsheviks' numerical growth was temporarily halted, and even in the central Soviet institutions, the party was the subject of the most bitter reproaches.

Taking advantage of this changed atmosphere, A. F. Kerensky*, who became Prime Minister soon after the July uprising, loudly proclaimed his determination to crush the Bolsheviks and to restore governmental authority and order throughout the country. However, for a variety of reasons Kerensky's efforts came to naught. By early August, well before the abortive Kornilov rightist putsch (*see* Kornilov Revolt), there were already clear signs that the party, with its apparatus intact, had embarked on a new period of growth. Indeed, with the perspective of more than seventy years, what appears most significant is not the Bolsheviks' temporary defeat and eclipse in July but rather the great popularity of the Bolshevik program demonstrated during the July Days. In the period between the beginning of August and the formation of the first Bolshevik government in October, when the expectations of the Russian masses remained practically unlimited and when all other major political groups were insisting on patience and sacrifice in the interests of the war effort (*see* World War I), the revolutionary political and social program of the Bolsheviks was to be a major factor in the party's increasing influence and strength.

Alexander Rabinowitch

Bibliography

Chamberlin, W. H. *The Russian Revolution, 1917–21*. Vol. 1. 1935.

Kudelli, P. F., ed. *Pervyi legal'nyi Peterburgskii komitet bol'shevikov v 1917 godu*. 1927.

Rabinowitch, Alexander. *Prelude to Revolution*. 1968.
Revoliutsionnoe dvizhenie v Rossii v iule 1917 g. 1959.
Znamenskii, O. N. *Iul'skii krizis 1917 goda*. 1964.

Justice and the Judicial System 1917–1921. The Revolutions of 1917 began
sweeping zigzags of change in the administration of justice. Under the Provisional
Government* (February-October 1917), justice moved closer to Western liberal
ideals of equality under the law and judicial independence. The Bolsheviks (*see*
Russian Social Democratic Workers' Party [Bolshevik]) rejected such ideals,
unlike most other Russian socialists, and moved justice under Soviet rule sharply
in the opposite direction in 1917–1918. They decreed class inequality under the
law, a political judiciary, and a simplified and popularized system of justice and
law. Actually, considering the separate system of political justice under the secret
police, the Bolsheviks established two systems, as under the tsars. Between 1919
and 1921 the Soviet government again reversed course toward a centralized and
complex justice system.

Histories of the Russian revolutionary period all too often overlook the vigorous and extensive judicial reforms of the Provisional Government following
its takeover from the collapsed tsarist regime. A flurry of decrees between March
and June 1917 eliminated the repressive and socially discriminating features of
the imperial administration of justice, in the spirit of the much-vitiated Judicial
Reforms of 1864. The Provisional Government eliminated special political
courts, released political prisoners and ended capital punishment (it was restored
at the front in July). Perhaps unwisely for its own good, the government abolished
the notorious tsarist secret police (Okhrana) and the gendarmerie. It replaced all
police with a single state militia shorn of repressive powers, such as extrajudicial
arrest and administrative exile. Among other reforms, the government restored
the electoral basis of local courts, ended discrimination in the law professions
against Jews and other non-Christians, and admitted women to the bar. An
eminent commission under the renowned jurist A. F. Koni set about restoring
to practice principles of the Judicial Reform of 1864 such as independence of
the judiciary, equality of all before the law, public trials, and jury trials for
felonies.

By and large, justice under the Provisional Government still rested on the
1864 reforms. Its first track consisted of local elected courts (urban justice of
the peace courts and peasant courts) trying cases of petty disputes and misde-
meanors. Among the local courts existed also an incipient network of children's
courts modeled on the pioneering U.S. children's court of Cook County, Illinois.

The second track contained appointed general courts trying larger disputes
and felonies in more than 100 circuit courts with appeals to about 14 judicial
chambers. Both tracks, local and general courts, ended in the Governing Senate
as a supreme court. The Ministry of Justice contained the Procurator General's
Office and ran separate departments for prosecution, pretrial investigation, and
courts. The prisons, under the Ministry of the Interior, operated with regimes
lagging far behind the thinking of many Russian criminologists such as M. N.

Gernet and penologists such as O. I. Liublinskii, an expert with close ties to the international penological community. The thinking of such experts left its mark in the reform decrees of March and April 1917 intended to end prison brutality and Siberian exile. Gernet, Liublinskii, and the accomplished statistician of justice E. M. Tarnovskii continued to serve under the successor Soviet government after it took over in the Bolshevik Revolution of October 24–26, 1917, but the system of justice they served changed drastically.

V. I. Lenin*, leader of the Russian Social Democratic Workers' Party (Bolshevik) and head of the new Soviet government of the RSFSR (Russian Soviet Federative Socialist Republic), was a jurist trained in tsarist law, as were the leading officials working with him to reshape justice such as P. I. Stuchka, *Narkomiust* (commissar of justice) in 1917 and again in 1918 and a leading theorist of law; D. I. Kurskii, Stuchka's successor as *Narkomiust* from 1918 to 1928, and N. V. Krylenko, their energetic collaborator. Although these officials' legal training readied them to administer justice, their radical brand of Marxism prepared them also to regard all preexisting justice and law as repressive instruments serving the interests of the dominant class in society. Hence they viewed the justice system inherited from the old order as irredeemably counterrevolutionary, a system they must dismantle, not reform.

Dismantle they did, beginning with the first decree on the courts of November 24, 1917, which abolished the existing bar and courts, replacing the courts with a dual system of people's courts and revolutionary tribunals. The decree ordered judges to recognize only those old laws not repealed by revolutionary acts and only insofar as they did not conflict with the judges' "revolutionary conscience and revolutionary concept of justice." This policy of dismantling brought its Bolshevik authors into conflict with many jurists of the old school, like the Left Socialist–Revolutionary (*see* Left Socialist-Revolutionary Party) I. N. Shteinberg, briefly *Narkomiust* during the coalition of Left Socialist–Revolutionaries (S–R's) and Bolsheviks from December to March 1918.

With the old system dismantled, the question became what to erect in its place. Lenin and his leading justice officials shared the Marxist vision, restated by Lenin in *State and Revolution* (August-September 1917), that the victory of the working people and their government over the dominant elites would set the stage for a classless society. In it there would be no more poverty or class conflict and exploitation, hence no more crime and no more need for police, courts, or jails. In fact, the Soviet state as the organized instrument of the working class, the state of the dictatorship of the proletariat, would lose its coercive functions and, over time, wither away. Lenin and his aides accepted as a model for their temporary courts the rudimentary and popularized tribunals established by the short-lived Paris Commune of 1871. This model of simple tribunals accessible to the ordinary people inspired the first court decree just mentioned. The only higher court set up by the decree took the form of Councils of People's Court Judges, authorized to review decisions of the People's Courts in their regions.

One of the few structural reminders of the old system turned up under the second decree on the courts of February 15, 1918, as people's circuit courts. They tried the more serious and complicated cases as well as the cases held over from the circuit courts of the old regime.

Returning to office after Shteinberg's term as *Narkomiust,* Stuchka promoted a resimplification of the courts by issuing a third court decree on July 10, 1918. Stuchka's successor as *Narkomiust,* Kurskii, signed a fourth court decree of November 30, 1918, ordering courts to stop applying all pre-Bolshevik laws. The only consolidations of new laws into codes available to the courts appeared in October 1918 as the Code of Laws on Registration of Civil States and Marriage, Family, and Guardianship and in December 1918 as the Labor Code.

The popularist features of justice appearing during the weeks of experimentation before the first court decree of November 24, 1917, have been preserved, at least in form, to this day. They include the participation of lay judges on trial benches alongside professional judges, the election of judges to trial courts, informal procedures and rules of evidence, and opportunities for public participation, as accusers or defenders. No evidence has ever surfaced, however, to indicate that, after the earliest days of Soviet justice, public participation slipped free of the control of the full-time jurists.

By 1919 the Soviet framers of new justice had carried the simplification of justice to its farthest point. The Communist Party's new program, issued that year, proclaimed to the world that "the Soviet government has replaced the former endless series of courts of justice with their various divisions, by a very simplified uniform system of People's Courts, accessible to the population, and freed of all useless formalities of procedure" (Hazard 1960, p. 62).

This review of Soviet justice would not be complete, though, without reference also to the other side of the picture—the statist and centrist features of Soviet justice and, beginning as early as 1919, its growing complexity. Just before the October Seizure of Power* Lenin signaled clearly his readiness to build as strong a Soviet state as would be politically necessary: "When the state will be proletarian, when it will be a machine for proletarian violence against the bourgeoisie, then we are unconditionally for strong state power and centralism."[1]

Among its instruments of strong state power and centralism by 1918, the Soviet government wielded a purged militia (police), the Revolutionary Tribunals, the Red Army*, and a new political police formed December 7, 1917, as the All-Russian Extraordinary Commission for Combatting Counterrevolution and Sabotage* (Vecheka, or Vserossiiskaia chrezvychainaia kommissia po bor'be kontrrevoliutsiei i sabotazhe), popularly known as the Cheka.

The Cheka developed its own independent justice system. It arrested, interrogated, investigated, tried, sentenced, exiled, imprisoned, and shot real or imagined foes. The pace of its activities quickened after the declaration of "Red Terror" on September 5, 1918, in response to armed uprising and armed attacks on Soviet leaders. The Cheka's ruthlessness figured among the reasons for the disillusionment of the radical sailors of the naval garrison of the fortress of

Kronstadt (*see* Kronstadt, 1917–1921) guarding the maritime approaches to Petrograd (formerly St. Petersburg). One of the proclamations issuing from their rebellion (bloodily put down in March 1921) called Soviet power more oppressive than that of the tsars: "the power of the police and the gendarme passed into the hands of the Communist usurpers, who, instead of giving the people freedom, instilled in them the fear of falling into the torture chambers of the Cheka, which in horrors far exceed the gendarme administration of the tsarist regime" (translated from the original, by Paul Avrich in *Kronstadt 1921*. 1970, p. 241).

Beginning in 1919 the Cheka's head, F. E. Dzerzhinskii*, headed the People's Commissariat of Internal Affairs as well. The commissariat ran "labor camps" with a mixed inmate population, about 35 percent political prisoners. The Cheka ran places of confinement it called "concentration camps." Those grim places emerged in Alexander Solzhenitsyn's *Gulag Archipelago* as forerunners of Stalin's labor camp empire, which would grow to thirty times the size of Cheka's Northern Camps of Special Purpose (SLON).

Toward children Dzerzhinskii and the Cheka acted as helpers rather than oppressors. The Cheka along with education and welfare agencies responded to the desperate plight of the *besprizornye*, the "untended ones," or homeless children cast out to wander the streets in the wake of war's devastation and the 1921 famine. Their number is estimated at 4 million by 1921; later it reached 7 million (Juviler 1976, p. 276, n. 22). The *besprizornye* worsened an already serious crime problem. In 1921 Dzerzhinskii created a network of Commissions to Improve the Life of Children headed by Cheka officials.

On the legal front, Lenin pushed through, over opposition, a decree of January 14, 1918, raising the minimum age of juvenile criminal responsibility from ten to seventeen. But as crimes by *besprizornye* mounted, the Bolsheviks retreated partially from their principle of "no courts or jails for children." The minimum age of criminals decreased from seventeen to fourteen in 1919.

The treatment of young waifs and criminals roaming Russia, the Ukraine, and the Caucasus presented vivid contrasts. On the one hand, millions remained homeless: hellish conditions prevailed in many children's shelters, overcrowded with starving children; lack of juvenile facilities caused young convicts to be housed with adults. On the other hand, special agencies existed to hear cases of child offenders under the age of criminal liability. Called Commissions for Juveniles, they were decreed on January 1, 1918, to replace the abolished children's courts. As early as 1918 some devoted innovators in the People's Commissariat of Enlightenment (*see* Commissariat of the Enlightenment) set up open "children's labor communes" against seemingly overwhelming odds. Outstanding examples in this early period were the commune founded by Mirandov in 1918 on the Volga at Uliankovsk and the commune set up by A. S. Makarenko outside Poltava in 1920. Communes like Makarenko's, eventually sponsored by the Cheka and its successor Obedinennoe Gosudarstvennoe Politicheskoe Upravlenie (OGPU), gained international fame. I. V. Stalin* liquidated them in 1936 (along with their secret police sponsors, G. G. Iagoda and his aides) but left Makarenko alive to write about his family upbringing.

In 1919, in regard to the treatment of adults, those not deemed class enemies also faced reduced punishment as compared with tsarist penalties. The 1919 Guiding Principles of Criminal Law of the Russian Soviet Federative Socialist Republic (RSFSR) enjoined courts to avoid sentences and confinement where possible and to cause the criminal "as little suffering as possible" commensurate with the tasks of social defense. Officials advocating the penology of rehabilitation, like the criminologist E. Shervindt (eventually the director of Corrections in the Commissariat of the Interior), tried to humanize the prisons inherited from the tsars.

Some Soviet jurists proposed ending punishment altogether. But Lenin and his aides, like Ia. Berman, confronting the rampant disorder in their backward, poverty-stricken country, thought that would be rushing communism. M. I. Kozlovskii, a high justice official and co-author with Stuchka of the 1919 Guiding Principles of Criminal Law, spoke for Lenin and others when he insisted that the Soviet government would need firm measures of "terror and isolation" during the long time it would take to build socialism and eliminate "remnants of the past" and the need for punishment. Responding to such stern sentiments, the Russian Soviet Federative Socialist Republic (RSFSR) government restored capital punishment in 1918 after its abolition against Lenin's wishes at the Second Congress of Soviets on October 25, 1917. The government briefly abolished capital punishment again between January 17 and May 4, 1920. Since then the death penalty has been available for a changing menu of crimes, except when abolished again from 1947 to 1950. Bans or no bans, the Cheka carried out executions as it pleased. M. Ia. Latsis, an aide to Dzerzhinskii, stated that when the Cheka had no formal right, "life itself legalized the right to execute" (Gerson 1976, p. 31).

Reorganizations of justice between 1919 and 1921 reflected three competing influences: ideals of simplicity and popularity, imperatives of central control, and the growing need for predictable and professionally competent adjudication.

During 1919 the Soviet government, under military siege from east, west and south, strengthened central authority over local police and courts. As the Civil War in Russia* neared its end by mid–1920 and the communists imposed Soviet rule over substantial portions of the former empire, Soviet judicial policy revealed a growing preoccupation with the quality and uniformity of justice. Commissar of Justice Kurskii continued to proclaim the simplicity principle of a "single people's court." Yet in practice he and his colleagues incorporated into the People's Court Act of October 21, 1920, further departures from that principle through measures proposed at the Fourth Congress of Administrators of Justice meeting in June 1920. The Act added a second tier of regular courts, "special sessions" of the People's Courts, for serious cases, with specially qualified judges and lay judges on call, special investigators attached to these new courts, and a special staff of professional accusers (prosecutors). Only in its abolition of full-time attorneys did the 1920 Act hark back to simplicity (and this innovation turned out to be temporary).

The advent of the New Economic Policy* (NEP) in 1921 brought a shift in priorities from defense to economic reconstruction in the devastated land. Concessions to private enterprise spurred a recovery of commerce, farming, and production, creating an urgent need for predictable and competent justice. A decree of March 10, 1921, created a department of "supreme court control" in the Commissariat of Justice—a forerunner of the republic supreme courts to come the following year. Looking beyond 1921 we can see how changes in justice until then prepared the path for the elaborate system legislated by 1922 in the RSFSR as a model for the other Soviet republics (joined together as the USSR on December 31 of that year). The Cheka was renamed the OGPU in 1922 and lost its special courts (February 6). The RSFSR Judiciary Act of October 31, 1922, brought the Soviet justice system close to its present form. The Act established regional bar associations of full-time attorneys to give advice and act in court, a central prosecutors' office (not without some unease and opposition in the government), and a republic supreme court combining the roles of "supreme court control" and the Supreme Revolutionary Tribunal.

Codifying the jumble of existing statutes began with the first work on a Criminal Code as early as 1920. That code appeared in 1922 followed by the new Land Code, Labor Code, and Civil Code—all models for similar codes in other Soviet republics. Capping this rebuilding of justice was the organization of the USSR Supreme Court and other national agencies of justice in 1923 after the formation of the USSR.

All of this elaboration would prompt great debate among theorists of law about how to interpret and justify the Soviet departures from original legitimizing ideals of simplicity. Was Soviet law, as Stuchka maintained in 1921, the expression of working class will and interests, a new "proletarian" Soviet law, destined to flourish as long as needed? (Stuchka, quoted in Lenin, Stuchka, et al., 1951, pp. 17–69). Or was Soviet law still bourgeois law, the law of the marketplace, as E. B. Pashukanis depicted it (Beirne and Sharlett 1980)? Was Soviet law not likely, therefore, to be a short-lived expedient? Such views brought Pashukanis first fame and dominance in legal scholarship and then purging and death in 1937 as a legal "nihilist" and enemy of the people.

In 1921 *Narkomiust* D. S. Kurskii expressed the essence of Soviet developments in justice and law: "We are leaving behind the short slogans in the field of law and are going on to a complicated system of laws" (quoted in Hazard 1960, p. 148). Despite their cherished vision of a future communist society without policemen, courts, and lawyers, Soviet jurists had erected by 1921 much of what would emerge during NEP as the elaborate system of Soviet codes, courts, and judicial agencies basically similar to those of today.

Peter Juviler

Note

1. V. I. Lenin, "Will the Bolsheviks Retain State Power?" in *Polnoe sobrannie sochinennii,* 5th ed., pp. 34, 318.

Bibliography

Beirne, Piers, and Sharlet, Robert, eds. *Pashukanis: Selected Writings on Marxism and Law*. 1980.

Bowen, James. *Soviet Education, Anton Makarenko, and the Years of Experiment*. 1961.

Browder, Robert Paul, and Kerensky, Alexander F., eds. *The Provisional Government, 1917: Documents*. Vol. 1. 1961.

Davydov, N. V., and Polianskii, N. N., eds. *Sudebnaia reforma*. 2 vols. 1915.

Gerson, Leonard A. *The Secret Police in Lenin's Russia*. 1976.

Goliakov, I. T., ed. *Sbornik dokumentov po istorii ugolovnogo zakonodatel'stva SSSR i RSFSR, 1917–52*. 1953.

Hazard, John. *Settling Disputes in Soviet Society*. 1960.

Juviler, Peter M. *Revolutionary Law and Order*. 1976.

Kucherov, S. *Courts, Trials, and Lawyers under the Last Three Tsars*. 1953.

Lenin, V. I.; Stuchka, V. I., et al. *Soviet Legal Philosophy*. 1951.

Piontkovskii, A. A.; Romashkin, P. S.; and Chikvadze, V. M., eds. *Kurs sovetskogo ugolovnogo pravo*. 6 vols. 1970–1971.

Shveitser, V. L., and Shabakova, V. M., eds. *Bisprizornye v trudovykk kommunakh*. 1926.

K

Kadet. *See* Constitutional Democratic Party—Cadet.

Kaledin, Aleksei Maksimovich (1861–1918). Kaledin was a Cossack* general in the tsarist army and an early leader of the White Movement* in the Civil War in Russia*.

A. M. Kaledin was born into a Cossack gentry family near present-day Volgograd. He pursued a military career graduating from Mikhailovsky Artillery School in 1882 and the General Staff Academy in 1889. Kaledin served as a Commander of the Twelfth Army Corps during the early part of World War I*. He attained the reputation of being one of tsarist Russia's best generals. In May 1916 he was placed in charge of the Eighth Army on the southwestern front.

Following the February Revolution* in 1917, Kaledin's outspoken conservative opposition to democratic reforms in the army led to his dismissal by General A. A. Brusilov*. Returning from the front, Kaledin was elected ataman of the Don Cossacks (*see* Cossacks) in June 1917 in Novocherkassk, which gave him control of the two Cossack divisions in that area. In August Kaledin attended the Moscow State Conference* where he spoke as a representative of all Cossack troops in Russia. His speech was reckoned the most conservative delivered to the conference. He assailed the soldiers' soviets and army commissars and called for their abolition. Although probably privately sympathetic to the Kornilov Revolt*, Kaledin took no active part. When A. F. Kerensky* suspected that Kaledin might have been involved in the Kornilov uprising, he ordered his arrest, but the Cossack Assembly (Krug) refused to obey Kerensky's orders.

Kaledin was a bitter opponent of the October Seizure of Power*. His Cossack district did not recognize the authority of the Soviet regime or any non-Cossack political institutions. In the aftermath of the seizure of power he became active in opposition to the new regime. He was in close contact with other leading conservative military figures and offered use of Cossack lands as a locus for consolidating counterrevolutionary forces, although he found it difficult to rally his own Cossacks to the cause or to come to an agreement with generals like A. G. Kornilov and M. V. Alekseev. Shortly after the Revolution Kaledin ordered the Cossacks to take Voronezh, but they refused to move. On November 7, 1917, Kaledin's Cossack government proclaimed its independence until a legitimate Russian government was formed. That decision prompted the local Bolshevik organization, the Military Revolutionary Committee in Rostov, to move, and on December 9, 1917, it announced that it did not recognize the authority of the Cossack government.

The challenge provided by the Military Revolutionary Committee drew the three most important generals in the White Movement* to unite. Kaledin had already declared martial law on November 26. Now he decided to move on the rebellious Rostov Military Revolutionary Committee, but once again his Cossack troops refused to accept the order. Kaledin had to turn to Alekseev, who provided 500 officers to take the city. This battle on December 9 marks the beginning of the Civil War. Kaledin arrived in the city on December 2 and announced a policy of reconciliation. There would be no retribution against the Bolsheviks. The action not only gave new prestige to the Cossack government but also cemented Kaledin's relationship with Kornilov and Alekseev. At the end of December the three generals, Alekseev, Kaledin, and Kornilov, formed a triumvirate, the leading counterrevolutionary body in south Russia at the time, with Kornilov dealing with military questions; Alekseev with administration, foreign relations, and finance; and Kaledin with Cossack matters.

Kaledin was one of the most enlightened White leaders, despite his conservatism. (see White Movement). He was known for his efficiency as an administrator and for his honesty and integrity. One of his programs involved the sharing of political power in Cossack areas with the numerous non-Cossacks (inogorodnye), although the experiment was ultimately unsuccessful. As the months passed following the October Revolution, problems mounted for the Cossack ataman: he had to deal with the tensions between the Cossacks and inogorodnye, between Cossacks of the younger and older generations, and between Cossacks and the White Volunteer Army. Finally, he had to cope with the disintegration of Cossack unity as the Bolsheviks (see Russian Social Democratic Workers' Party [Bolshevik]) sent in agents from their Cossack Department to seduce the rank and file away from Cossack generals like Kaledin. Even without this agitation, Cossack soldiers returning from the western front saw little reason to fight the Bolsheviks.

In Novocherkassk on January 29, 1918, with the Red Army* on the advance and the White forces preparing to retreat from Don Cossack territory, Kaledin resigned his office of ataman and advised his subordinates to do the same. Two hours later he shot himself through the heart.

Bibliography

Brinkley, George. The Volunteer Army and Allied Intervention in South Russia. 1966.
Kenez, Peter. Civil War in South Russia, 1918–19. 1971.

————. *Civil War in South Russia, 1919–20*. 1977.
Luckett, Richard. *The White Generals*. 1971.
Stewart, George. *The White Armies of Russia*. 1933.

Kalinin, Mikhail Ivanovich (1875–1946). Mikhail Kalinin was a prominent Old Bolshevik leader, who became the President (Chairman) of the All-Russian Central Executive Committee* in 1919 and held that post for twenty-seven years.

Kalinin was born on November 7, 1875, in the village of Verkhniaia Troika in Tver Province into a family of poor peasants. He served as a footman to the aristocratic family of Mordukhai-Boltovskii in St. Petersburg. Kalinin learned to read by attending the *zemstvo* primary school along with the children of the Mordukhai-Boltovskii family. At sixteen his mistress sent him to serve as an apprentice at the Putilov factory where he also attended the factory school in the evening. At the age of eighteen he became a full-time worker at the Putilov factory as a lathe operator.

Kalinin joined the Russian Social Democratic Workers' Party in 1898 and was arrested the following year for membership in the St. Petersburg Union of Struggle for the Emancipation of the Working Class, the organization founded by V. I. Lenin* before he was sent into exile. Kalinin was also sent into exile but escaped to European Russia where he worked in various factories around the country until 1903, when he was arrested again. He spent six months in jail and was then sentenced to exile in Siberia, although he soon escaped and returned to St. Petersburg to take part in the 1905 Revolution (*see* Nineteen-Five Revolution).

In 1906 Kalinin worked for the Bolshevik faction (*see* Russian Social Democratic Workers' Party [Bolshevik]) and on the staff of the Central Union of Metal Workers. Arrested in 1916, he was freed during the February Revolution*. In April 1917 he advocated conditional support for the Provisional Government* along with many other Bolshevik leaders, and he cooperated with the Mensheviks (*see* Russian Social Democratic Workers' Party [Menshevik]), two actions that Lenin would condemn in his famous April Theses*. Despite Lenin's objections, Kalinin continued to call for cooperation with the other radical parties and opposed Lenin's demands for an armed uprising against the Provisional Government. In the fall elections to the Petrograd City Duma he was chosen mayor of the city and proved his mettle in the administration of the city during and after the October Seizure of Power*.

In 1919 Kalinin became a member of the Central Committee of the Russian Communist Party and a candidate member of the Politburo. In 1926 he became a full member of the Politburo. When Ia. M. Sverdlov* died in 1919, Kalinin replaced him as President (Chairman) of the All-Russian Central Executive Committee, a post he would hold for many years. In 1922 the name of the post was changed to Chairman of the Central Executive Committee of the USSR and from January 1938 to March 1946 to Chairman of the Presidium of the Supreme Soviet of the USSR.

Kalinin was among the small group of Old Bolsheviks close to I. V. Stalin*, who survived the Great Purges. Some referred to him as the "Old Fox." But despite his support of Stalin through the struggle for power with L. D. Trotsky*, the Joint Opposition, and the Right Opposition, he was no toady and privately opposed the excesses of collectivization and the Great Purges.

Bibliography

Haupt, Georges, and Marie, Jean Jacques. *Makers of the Russian Revolution*. 1974.

Kamenev, Lev Borisovich (1883–1936; true name, Rozenfel'd). Kamenev was one of the most important Bolshevik (*see* Russian Social Democratic Workers' Party [Bolshevik]) leaders in the October Seizure of Power*.

L. B. Kamenev was born in Moscow on July 18, 1883. His education at gymnasiums in Vilna and Tiflis and then in the Law Faculty of the University of Moscow was cut short in March 1902 because of involvement in radical student activities. For the next six years he worked in the Russian underground as a Social Democratic propagandist in Tiflis, St. Petersburg, and Moscow, with brief interruptions for visits to party congresses abroad and to tsarist prisons at home. In late 1908 he immigrated to Western Europe where, as a member of the Bolshevik "Center" and as one of V. I. Lenin's* closest confidants, he assisted in editing *Proletarian* (*Proletarii*), *Social Democrat* (*Sotsial-demokrat*), and *Workers' News* (*Rabochaia gazeta*). In January 1914 he returned to St. Petersburg as Lenin's personal emissary to oversee the operations of the Bolsheviks' legal daily *Truth* (*Pravda*) and of their six-man Duma faction. On November 4, 1914, while attending a meeting in the village of Ozerki to discuss Lenin's anti-war instructions, Kamenev and the Bolshevik Duma deputies were arrested. Despite his disavowal of the party's defeatist position, Kamenev was exiled to Siberia on February 10, 1915.

On March 12, 1917, he returned to Petrograd in the aftermath of the February Revolution*. By virtue of his previous services to the party and in the absence of Lenin and G. E. Zinoviev*, he and I. V. Stalin* assumed direction of the Bolshevik forces in the Russian capital. Despite the protests of local Bolsheviks who objected to his conduct in 1915 and resented his "strong-arm methods," Kamenev again took over *Pravda* and became the party's chief spokesman within the new Petrograd Soviet*. The policies that he and Stalin pursued were considerably more moderate than those advocated by Lenin in Switzerland or followed initially by the Russian Bureau in Petrograd. They now not only acknowledged the right of the Provisional Government* to rule but also were willing to sanction a defensist war and possible unity with the Mensheviks (*see* Russian Social Democratic Workers' Party [Menshevik]). Despite his unsuccessful opposition to Lenin's April Theses* and particularly to the idea that Russia could proceed directly to its socialist revolution, Kamenev was elected to the nine-man Central Committee of the Russian Social Democratic Workers' Party (Bolshevik) (see Central Committee of the Russian Communist Party [Bolshevik]) at the Seventh (April) Conference in 1917. From then to the end of the revolutionary year, he (with the assistance of Zinoviev) led the right wing of the party in its pursuit of a more conciliatory and cautious policy than that favored by the Leninist majority. Thus it is ironic that he was the only member of the Central Committee to be arrested by the Provisional Government following the suppression of the July Days*.

Kamenev's release a month later coincided with the revival of Bolshevik fortunes. During September and October he again served on the editorial board of the party's newspaper and as its spokesman in the Presidium of the Petrograd Soviet. Inside the Central Committee he opposed Lenin's efforts to boycott the Moscow State Conference* and the Pre-Parliament (see Democratic Conference) as well as Lenin's insistence on the efficacy of armed insurrection. Following the committee's approval in principle of an insurrection on October 10, Kamenev and Zinoviev addressed a private appeal to local party organizations urging restraint. They argued that the party could not count on the support of the Russian peasantry or of the international proletariat and that even the loyalty of the Petrograd garrison was suspect. Given the superior strength of the Provisional Government, it was better, they believed, to wait for the convocation of the Second Congress of Soviets and the Constituent Assembly*. These institutions would not only broaden the party's base of support but would also provide the means for the peaceful transfer of power to a socialist coalition at the head of a "combination-type state." Lenin, who had no interest in sharing power with other parties, responded that the Revolution could not wait. After the Central Committee backed the Bolshevik leader and on October 16 reaffirmed its earlier decision, Kamenev's counterarguments were publicized in Maxim Gorky's newspaper New Life (Novaia Zhizn') as proof of Bolshevik intentions. Lenin was furious at this "strike-breaking." Although his attempt to have Lev Borisovich expelled from the party was ignored, Kamenev's resignation from the Central Committee was accepted on October 20. Four days later, however, as the Provisional Government belatedly started to respond to the Bolshevik "move," Kamenev was back at the Smolnyi Institute helping to direct defensive measures. He was also in the chair when the Second All-Russian Congress of Soviets (see Soviets [Councils] of Workers', Soldiers', and Peasants' Deputies) opened on October 25, and thus it fell to him to announce the capture of the Winter Palace.

Despite his earlier opposition to the October Seizure of Power*, Kamenev was named chairman of the Soviets' Central Executive Committee (see All-Russian Central Executive Committee), or VTsIK, and as such was titular head of the new state. In this position he sought to broaden the political composition of the VTsIK and to admit non-Bolsheviks to the Council of People's Commissars* (Sovnarkom). On November 4, in protest against Lenin's "sabotaging" of the proposed coalition, Kamenev again temporarily resigned from the Central Committee and was replaced by Ia. M. Sverdlov* as chairman of VTsIK. For the next two and a half years Lenin used Kamenev's linguistic skills and quiet demeanor while sparing himself Lev Borisovich's frequent political opposition by naming him his diplomatic troubleshooter abroad.

Kamenev was at the pinnacle of his power from 1920 until mid–1925. In addition to his position as chairman of the Moscow Soviet*, he was elected to the party's five-man ruling Politburo (*see* Central Committee of the Russian Communist Party [Bolshevik]) in March 1919 and frequently chaired that body during Lenin's illness. In recognition of his administrative abilities, he was appointed first deputy chairman of the Sovnarkom and in January 1924 took over as chairman of the Council of Labor and Defense (STO).

Kamenev also made his greatest political mistake during this period. Early in 1922, fearing that L. D. Trotsky* would eventually assume the mantle of Lenin's power, Kamenev and Zinoviev formed a "triumvirate" with Stalin. Kamenev not only proposed this "small-town politician" for the position of Secretary General of the Party, but he was instrumental in suppressing the damning indictment of Stalin found in Lenin's "Testament." Only in 1925 did he and Zinoviev become aware of the immense power now concentrated in the Secretary General's hands and of the doctrinal dangers inherent in Stalin's "socialism in one country." Kamenev's belated opposition to Stalin at the Fourteenth Party Congress cost him his position on Sovnarkom and caused him to be reduced to candidate status within the Politburo. It was only after they were stripped of their real power that Kamenev and Zinoviev finally made common cause with Trotsky and the "United Opposition" in April 1926. This ineffectual alliance, in turn, gave Stalin and his supporters reason to relieve Kamenev of his remaining posts as chairman of the Moscow Soviet and as Commissar of Trade in July as well as of his Politburo membership in October. In 1927, after a year as Soviet Russia's ambassador to Mussolini's Italy, Kamenev was summoned home and was expelled first from the Central Committee and subsequently from the party. Nine years later he appeared in the first of the great "show trials," made a public confession to having been a member of the "Trotskyite–Zinovievite Terrorist Center," and was executed in late August 1936.

Carter Elwood

Bibliography

Carr, E. H. *Socialism in One Country*. Vol. 1. 1958.

Cohen, Stephen F. *Bukharin and the Bolshevik Revolution*. 1973.

Daniels, R. *The Conscience of the Revolution*. 1959.

Deutscher, Isaac. *The Prophet Unarmed: Trotsky, 1921–29*. 1959.

Haupt, Georges, and Marie, Jean Jacques. *Makers of the Russian Revolution*. 1974.

Kamenev, L. B. *Mezhdu dvumia revoliutsiami*. 1923.

———. *Stati i rechi*. 4 vols. 1925–1929.

Medvedev, Roy M. *Let History Judge*. 1973.

Schapiro, L. *The Origin of the Communist Autocracy*. 1965.

Sukhanov, N. N. *The Russian Revolution, 1917*. 2 vols. 1955.

Volin, B. M. *12 biografy*. 1924.

Kautsky, Karl (1854–1938). One of the most famous leaders and theoreticians of the German Social Democratic Party and an outspoken critic of the October Seizure of Power* in Russia.

As one of the principal theoreticians of the German Social Democratic Party, Karl Kautsky had a strong influence on Lenin's thought. Lenin had observed Kautsky in action as early as 1895 when he visited Germany and attended meetings of the German Social Democratic Party. It fell to Kautsky to defend the orthodox Marxist view that a revolution was necessary to achieve a socialist revolution against the contrary arguments of revisionists such as Eduard Bernstein. Bernstein argued on the basis of the political experience of German Social Democracy before World War I* that revolution and proletarian dictatorship were no longer necessary and that the goals of Marxist socialism could be achieved by social reform through the democratic political process. Bernstein argued that Marx's theory of the breakdown of capitalism and the increasing misery of the industrial working class had been proven wrong by the course of European history, and that also made the utopian vision of a future classless and stateless society unlikely. In the end Bernstein abandoned the economic interpretation of history and the Marxist dialectic as well. Kautsky defended the vision of a classless, stateless society as a desirable goal and the dialectic as, in Alfred Meyers' words, a "creative thought process" that enabled one to see the relationship between apparently contradictory phenomena (Meyer 1963, p. 133). In defending orthodoxy, however, Kautsky found it necessary to abandon the whole notion of the inevitability of the proletarian revolution, arguing instead that socialism was desirable and could be achieved by peaceful means. In effect, this meant that both Kautsky and Bernstein believed that socialism would be achieved in Germany by gradual and democratic evolution away from capitalism.

Because the state had developed functions that were crucial to the well being of the industrial working class, Kautsky argued, it was necessary to take over its institutions rather than to destroy them and create an entirely new socialist state. Because the class struggle could take place within a democratic institutional framework, the seizure of power could mean simply winning elections. Having won a respectable place in society, the party of the working class could wage class warfare within the parameters and rules of the democratic state. A radical left wing led by figures such as Rosa Luxemburg* clung to the old revolutionary concepts, but the majority followed either Bernstein or Kautsky.

It is not surprising, given his views, that Kautsky attacked the October Seizure of Power* in Russia. In a sixty-three-page pamphlet published in Vienna in 1918 Kautsky attacked the Bolshevik coup d'état as a new form of Russian absolutism. Lenin replied in an eighty-one-page pamphlet called "The Proletarian Revolution and the Renegade Kautsky," completed on November 9, 1918. This essay opened a debate between the Russian Communist Party and the European socialists that has continued to the present. Lenin contended that his proletarian dictatorship was probably more democratic than any bourgeois state. In an argument laced with sarcasm and name calling, Lenin reaffirmed the old prerevisionist Marxism that called for the exclusive control of the state apparatus by the proletariat (or the party claiming to represent its interests), the destruction of the old political edifice, and its replacement with entirely new institutions. He denied Kautsky's contention that Marx never intended the dictatorship of the proletariat as anything more than a temporary measure. Essentially, Lenin denied the legitimacy of the whole posture of the German Social Democratic Party that socialism could be achieved by democratic means or even that social justice for the industrial working class could be achieved through the institutions of the bourgeois democratic state, arguing instead that the more highly developed the bourgeois democratic state, the closer it would be to civil war. In Russia, he argued, because the old state apparatus and bourgeois political groups had been smashed, there was no danger of compromise with such elements or domination by them.

Lenin's response was surprising in a number of ways, surprising in that the architect of the new Soviet state would take time out of his busy schedule of trying to create a new state in the middle of a civil war (*see* Civil War in Russia) to write a long theoretical pamphlet. It was surprising also in that he heaped praise on dictatorship as a higher form of democracy. But Lenin did not have second sight and could not have forseen the subsequent tyranny of I. V. Stalin* imposed in the name of proletarian democracy. When he wrote his reply in 1919, Lenin almost certainly believed that Germany itself would follow Russia's example, and on the same day that he finished the pamphlet Wilhelm Liebknecht would indeed proclaim a German Soviet republic. But on January 16, 1919, the German army seized Berlin and executed both Liebknecht and Rosa Luxemburg, and on February 9, 1919, a German National Assembly created a democratic government for that country—the well-known Weimar republic—in which Kautsky's German Social Democratic Party would play a leading role. In the end, European socialists would have to choose between the path described by Kautsky and that described by Lenin, and socialism would split its forces between socialist and communist parties (*see* Lenin, Vladimir Il'ich).

Bibliography

Fischer, Louis. *The Life of Lenin*. 1964.
Kautsky, Karl. *Die Diktatur des Proletariats*. 1918.
Lenin, V. I. *The Proletarian Revolution and Kautsky the Renegade*. 1920.
Meyer, Alfred G. *Leninism*. 1957.
———. *Marxism*. 1963.

Kazakhstan, Revolution in. The Kazakhs were a large Moslem Turkic nomadic ethnic group numbering about 3 million people before the Revolutions of 1918 and occupying the prairies of present-day Kazakhstan in Soviet Central Asia.

The territory occupied by the Kazakhs was a million square miles in size and, though mostly steppe lands, graded off into mountains in the North. The Kazakh people achieved some sense of identity in the fifteenth century as a result of the melting together of the Turkic tribes settled in the area since the eighth century and the Mongols from Central Asia who appeared there in the thirteenth century. In the fifteenth century three Kazakh tribes broke away from the Mongol Golden Horde to form their own three hordes (*orda*). By the midnineteenth century most of the Kazakhs were conquered by the Russians, who began to move Slavic settlers into the region.

On the eve of the year 1917 one-third of the population in this area were Russian and Ukrainian peasants, and the rest, the Kirghiz and the Kazakhs, lived a nomadic life outside of the cities. Less than 5 percent of the Kazakhs were literate. Until April 19, 1925, no distinction was drawn between the Kazakhs and the Kirghiz.

In Kazakhstan, as in Kirghiz territory, the land question played an important role because the natives thought they had been victimized during the postemancipation period (after 1861) by the incursion of Russian and Ukrainian peasants. The Russian government denied that the Kazakh nomads had any legitimate territorial claims and distributed more than 11 million acres of Kazakh land to slavic colonists. In many instances this left the Kazakh-Kirghiz tribes without any grazing land for their cattle.

When the Tsarist government began drafting Kazakh–Kirghiz natives for noncombatant duty in 1916, there was a native revolt. The rebellion was put down by force, and 360,000 natives were forced to flee their lands as a result. In March 1917 the Kazakh intelligentsia began to form a political movement. A Duma (*see* Duma and Revolution) deputy, Alikhan Bukeikhanov, although involved in the 1916 rebellion, was appointed a member of the Provisional Government's* Turkestan Committee. A teacher and a writer, A. B. Baitursunov, became editor of a native publication called *Kazakh*. In the spring of 1917 these two men took part in the preparation for the formation of the Alash Orda* Party to represent the interests of the Kazakhs and the Kirghiz. The party was closely allied to the Constitutional Democratic Party and the Bashkir (*see* Bashkiria, Revolution in) nationalists led by A. Z. Validov*.

Clashes between the Russian settlers and the Kazakhs in the autumn of 1917 forced the Provisional Government to impose martial law, but after the fall of the Provisional Government the national parties in Kazakhstan decided that it was time to assert their independence, and on December 5–13, 1917 the Bashkirs and the Kazakh–Kirghiz held national congresses in Orenburg and called for national autonomy. They established close ties with the Orenburg Cossacks* led by General A. I. Dutov*, who promised to support their aspirations with military force. The declarations of the congress were also said to be a way to erect barriers against Soviet or Bolshevik (*see* Russian Social Democratic Workers' Party [Bolshevik]) penetration.

The new Soviet government and the Bolshevik Party did not have much support in this area at first because they aimed their program at those social groups that were primarily Russian in origin, the garrison, and the industrial working class. After the October Seizure of Power*, V. I. Lenin* began to court the nationalist movements in Central Asia (*see* Central Asia, Revolution in). In December 1917 Lenin issued a special appeal to the "Peoples of the East," promising them Bolshevik support for their efforts to establish national self-determination under the protection of the new Soviet Republic. At the same time that they were making an appeal to the nationalists, the Bolsheviks used their strength among the slavic population in the urban centers in Kazakh territory, taking the cities of Orenburg on January 18, 1918, and Semipalatinsk on January 21, but holding those cities against Cossack and Kazakh partisans for only a few weeks. Some Kazakh forces under Amangeldy Imanov and A. N. Dzhangildin allied with the Red Army* against the Cossacks, seeing the latter as representatives of tsarist repression. In the same month I. V. Stalin* attempted to organize a pro-Bolshevik Moslem nucleus under the Commissariat of Nationalities, recruiting a Tatar engineer, M. N. Vakhitov*, to head the so-called Commissariat of Moslem Affairs with Galimjan Ibragimov*, another Tatar, and Sharif Manatov, a Bashkir.

When the Moslems seemed to have succeeded in establishing their own Pan-Islamic movement in December 1917, creating a Moslem constituent assembly established in Kazan (*see* All-Russian Moslem Council) and a Moslem executive council (or shura) in Petrograd, Stalin's organization countered by calling a conference of procommunist Moslem bureaus (*musburos*) in June 1918 to form the Russian Party of Moslem Communists with its own Central Committee.

The threat of a Moslem Communist Party independent of the Russian Communist Party was averted by cooptation. With the coming of the Civil War in Russia*, the Russian Party of Moslem Communists was merged with the Russian Party by the formation in November 1918 of the Central Bureau of Moslem Organizations of the Russian Social Democratic Workers' Party (Bolshevik)* under the Central Committee of the Russian Communist Party, which deprived the Moslems of all genuine autonomy. In any case, during the Civil War it was difficult to see any single force controlling Kazakh lands. Becoming discouraged by the attitude of the White and Cossack leaders, the chiefs of the Alash Orda began to gravitate toward the Bolsheviks by December 1918, and by July 1919 a new Soviet Kazakhstan government, the Kirrevkom, began to take shape. It was called the Kirghiz–Kazakh Revolutionary Committee* (Kirrevkom). Although the Kazakh leaders Dzhangilden and Mineslav were nominally in charge, Stalin's assistant, S. M. Dimanstein, seems to have called the tune. The area they controlled included only a portion of the western half of today's Kazakhstan Soviet Socialist Republic.

When the Civil War began to wane at the end of 1919, it was discovered, not surprisingly, that there was little popular support for the new Soviet regime. Serge Zenkovsky (1960) estimated that no more than 500–700 Kazakhs joined the Kazakh Communist Party formed on January 5, 1920. Early in 1920 this led to one last effort by the native leaders to achieve freedom of action from Moscow and to pursue their own Pan-Turanian goals. In March 1920 Baitursunov and T. I. Sedel'nikov, the Russian who had come to the Bolsheviks from the *Trudoviks* in 1918, wrote a letter to the Central Committee of the Russian Communist

Party (Bolshevik)* asking that the Communist Parties in Kazakhstan, Bashkiria, and Turkestan be given "real guarantees" of national autonomy and that they be allowed to form local economic councils to plan their development. The Soviet government responded to the sentiment expressed in the letter but removed those who expressed it from high office. A Soviet decree of August 25, 1920, recommended Kazakh independence at the same time that Baitursunov and Sedel'nikov were removed from Kirrevkom. Baitursunov was allowed to return later as a contrite token Turk.

Concessions were made to Kazakh national feelings when they did not jeopardize Moscow's political control. Further colonization into Kazakhstan was forbidden, and a decree of February 21, 1921, returned to the Kazakhs land taken from them by the state, the church, and the nobility. Some Cossack land was also returned. In 1921–1922 Kazakh provinces placed under Siberian administration—Semipalitinsk and Akmolinsk—were returned, and in 1924 Kazakh land that had been given to Turkestan was returned to the Kazakhs.

Bibliography

Olcott, M. B. *The Kazakhs.* 1987.
Pipes, Richard. *The Formation of the Soviet Union.* 1954.
Zenkovsky, Serge. *Pan-Turkism and Islam in Russia.* 1960.

Kerensky, Aleksandr Fedorovich (1881–1970). The last Prime Minister of the Provisional Government* in 1917.

Aleksandr Kerensky, the dominant figure in the Russian Provisional Government of 1917, was born in Simbirsk on April 22, 1881. The son of a tsarist official stationed first in Simbirsk and after 1889 in Tashkent, Kerensky acquired the privileged status and developed the political orthodoxy characteristic of the provincial bureaucracy. Upon graduation from the Tashkent gymnasium in 1899, he attended the University of St. Petersburg and in 1904 received a law degree and entered the St. Petersburg Bar Association. By that time Kerensky's parochial traditionalist outlook was so weakened by his student experience that he chose employment in a nongovernmental legal aid organization rather than in the Imperial administration. After witnessing the massacre of Bloody Sunday, he broke with the established regime, participated in revolutionary activities, and was imprisoned.

When Kerensky emerged from prison in 1906, his political attitude had assumed its permanent form. A fervent Populist and nationalist who had shifted allegiance from the autocracy to the people (*narod*), he was convinced that liberation could be achieved only by a concerted national effort. To further that aim, he renounced covert tactics and concentrated upon legal methods of opposition against the government. Using his exceptional oratorical talents, he became a "political lawyer," specializing in cases that would embarrass the regime and call attention to the deficiencies of tsarism. His successes, which reached a high point with a sensational exposé of government callousness in the

Lena Goldfield Massacre of 1912, gained him a nationwide reputation as a crusader against injustice and led to his election in the autumn of 1912 to the Fourth State Duma (*see* Duma and Revolution).

Kerensky's Duma position allowed him to widen the scope of his previous actions, rejecting traditional parliamentary methods, which he thought only strengthened the autocracy. He used his post as a platform from which to criticize the government, conduct inquiries into abuses, and disseminate revolutionary propaganda. As the head of the Labor (Trudovik) Party and the spokesman of the leftist deputies, he tried to radicalize the Duma and prepare it for a revolutionary role; he hoped that when tsarism faltered, the Duma would become the nucleus of a new government. But despite his strenuous efforts, Kerensky failed to move the Duma majority to the Left. Although liberals and moderates respected his eloquence and energy, they preferred orderly political evolution to the uncertainties of violent revolution.

For patriotic reasons Kerensky suspended harassment of the autocracy at the outbreak of World War I*, but he reverted to his previous tactics in 1915, when setbacks in Galicia exposed the government's inability to wage war. Although the Duma majority did reveal a leftward drift after the Galician debacle, Kerensky's influence upon it remained marginal; he stayed outside of the Progressive Bloc*, considering its solutions overly timid, and stood apart from elitist conspiracies against the Crown, for he thought that the age of palace coups had passed. Convinced by late 1916 that revolution was imminent, he intensified his Duma attacks against Nicholas II* and the imperial ministry, exhorted his fellow deputies to lead the struggle against the autocracy, and kept his finger on the popular pulse by expanding his contacts with the Petrograd garrison and various labor organizations.

When the February Revolution* erupted, Kerensky assumed a leading position among his colleagues. On February 27, in an effort to identify the Duma with revolution, he directed insurgent troops to appear before it, ordered the arrest of tsarist ministers in its name, and lodged the newly formed Petrograd soviet* in an adjoining chamber in the Tauride Palace. The pressure of events would probably have forced the State Duma into a revolutionary stance in any case, but the rapidity and ease by which it became the wellspring of a new order were due largely to Kerensky's efforts.

From the first hours of the Revolution, Kerensky's influence extended beyond the confines of the Tauride Palace. Acclaimed as a popular hero by an enthusiastic populace, he was accepted as a leader of the powerful Socialist-Revolutionary Party* and elected to the Presidium of the Petrograd Soviet. Using his formidable power bases, he facilitated the abdication of the Romanovs and participated in the creation on March 2 of the First Provisional Government. When he could not overcome the Soviet Executive Committee ban on participation in the new regime, he personally ignored the ban and entered the government as Minister of Justice, winning approval for his defiant action at a subsequent Soviet plenary session.

Kerensky was satisfied with the terms of the February settlement. The monarchy was disposed of without civil war and the new government, drawn mainly from the Progressive Bloc* of the State Duma, assured the country of experienced patriotic leadership. Admittedly, the socialist rejection of a coalition regime prevented the union of all classes that Kerensky believed necessary to the success of the Revolution. Nonetheless, his presence in the cabinet reinforced the tentative class truce that had been established, provided a channel through which difficulties could be resolved, and established a precedent for the future appearance of other socialist ministers.

As Minister of Justice, Kerensky concentrated upon two major goals: the shielding of former tsarist officials from prosecution in order to convince liberals and conservatives that a reign of terror was not in the offing and the formulation of a model law code that would establish the moral purity of the Revolution. He also took a leading part in the activities of the Ministerial Council, where he usually commanded a cabinet majority on controversial issues. However, Kerensky's intervention in the departmental affairs of his colleagues was less fortunate. By taking public issue with P. N. Miliukov's* traditionalist conduct of foreign policy, he contributed to popular disorders that toppled the cabinet in the April Crisis.

Since the April Crisis demonstrated the weakness of a government lacking adequate socialist representation, Kerensky was able to persuade the Soviet Executive Committee to reverse its stand against coalition. With prominent socialists such as I. G. Tsereteli* and V. M. Chernov* holding cabinet rank, the regime that emerged on May 6 appeared strong enough to pursue a vigorous military policy. As Minister of War in the First Coalition, Kerensky revitalized the revolutionary army and on June 18 launched a series of assaults against the Central Powers. After initial successes, Kerensky's June offensive collapsed. Its failure, which coincided with a cabinet split over Ukrainian separatism (*see* Ukraine, Revolution in) and the eruption of Bolshevik-led riots in the capital, plunged the country into renewed turmoil.

Those somber events provided Kerensky with an opportunity to revive the class truce and place the Provisional Government on a secure foundation. With the entire Left in confusion and the Right angered but leaderless, Kerensky assumed control of the rump cabinet and suppressed the Petrograd disorders. He pressed his advantage on July 22 by forming a second coalition of his own choosing, assuming the title of Minister–President within it and renouncing partisan limitations on his future actions. To all appearances Kerensky was at last able to impose his will upon the course of the Revolution. At the fulcrum of political power, he felt free to pursue the non-partisan policies that could best steer the country through the perils of war and internal dislocation and disorder.

The Minister–President's expectations were not fulfilled. The non-socialist forces had only accepted his leadership under duress, and when he elevated L. G. Kornilov (*see* Kornilov Revolt) to the post of Supreme Commander, they quickly transferred their loyalties to the fiery general. Although Kerensky had striking success in restoring state authority throughout July and August, he experienced a steady erosion of tight support that could not be countered by recourse to the still demoralized Left. The conservative response reached a climax at the Moscow State Conference* of August 12–15 when Kerensky suffered repudiation and the Supreme Commander was given a hero's welcome. A few days after his triumphal reception in Moscow, Kornilov attempted a coup against the government. That ill-considered act shattered the February settlement, discredited moderation, and provoked a radical resurgence of enormous proportions.

Although Kerensky clung to formal power after the failure of the Kornilov Revolt, he was unable to reverse the progressive disintegration of the state. Shunned by both the Left and the Right, he experimented with a Triumvirate, a Democratic Congress, and a third coalition and advanced the date for the convocation of the Constituent Assembly* in vain efforts to restore some political balance to the country. As these expedients failed to arouse significant support, he watched helplessly as the army disintegrated, the countryside was engulfed in anarchy, and the resurrected Bolshevik Party (*see* Russian Social Democratic Workers' Party [Bolshevik]) openly plotted insurrection. On October 23, in a desperate attempt to weaken the Left and rally Right support, he ordered a preemptive attack against the party of V. I. Lenin*. His slender governmental forces were overwhelmed by a Bolshevik counterattack on the night of October 24–25, and he was forced to flee Petrograd. When an attempt to retake the capital with a small mixed force of Cossacks* and artillery failed on October 30, Kerensky went into hiding. In May of 1918 he left Russia aboard a vessel bound for England.

After an unsuccessful effort to influence the course of Allied intervention in the Civil War in Russia*, Kerensky abandoned diplomacy in favor of journalism. As the editor of a succession of Populist journals, the most significant of which was the Berlin-based *Dni* (*Days*), he established a reputation as an acute critic and an informed observer of the Soviet Union. Through articles, memoirs, and associations with universities and emigré organizations, Kerensky defended Russian democratic ideals until his death in 1970.

Michael J. Fontenot

Bibliography

Browder, R., and Kerensky A., eds. *The Russian Provisional Government, 1917*. 3 vols. 1961.
Burdzhalov, E. *Vtoraia Russkaia revoliutsiia*. 2 vols. 1967–1971.
Daniels, R. V. *Red October: the Bolshevik Revolution of 1917*. 1967.
Gosudarstvennaia Duma: stenograficheskii otchet, 1906–17 36 vols. 1907–1917.
Kerensky, A. F. *Iz deleka, sbornik statei (1920–21 g.)*. 1922.
———. *Russia and History's Turning Point*. 1965.
Radkey, O. H. *The Agrarian Foes of Bolshevism*. 1953.
Rosenberg, William G. *Liberals in the Russian Revolution*. 1974.
Stankevich, V. B. *Vospominaniia, 1914–19*. 1920.
Volobuev, P. *Proletariat i burzhuaziia Rossii v 1917 godu*. 1964.

Kirghiz. *See* Kazakhstan, Revolution in.

Kirghiz-Kazakh Revolutionary Committee. A government for Soviet Kazakhstan established in July 1919 with a membership that was drawn primarily from the Kazakh nationalist party, Alash-Orda*. *See* Kazakhstan, Revolution in.

Kirov, Sergei Mironovich (1886–1934; real name, Kostrikov; pseudonyms, Sergei, Serge). Kirov was a prominent Bolshevik (*see* Russian Social Democratic Workers' Party [Bolshevik]) leader.

Kirov was born in a peasant family in Urzhum, a small village near Viatka in the northeastern sector of European Russia. When he was young his mother died, his father abandoned him, and he was reared in an orphanage. After completing elementary school he received a scholarship to attend Kazan. In 1904 he graduated and about that time became a member of the Russian Social Democratic Workers' Party and accepted a job as a draftsman in Tomsk. He was imprisoned in 1905 for revolutionary activities, and in 1909 he moved to Vladikavkaz in the northern Caucasus where he conducted active revolutionary work for another decade while working as a journalist for a Terek liberal newspaper. Kirov was arrested in 1911 and spent several months in jail awaiting trial. He was released after his trial, returned to Vladikavkaz, and married Maria L'vovna Markus, beginning a relationship that lasted the rest of his life. In the same year he adopted the pseudonym Kirov.

In 1916 Kirov was successful in forming a study group in Vladikavkaz. He was an active member of the soviet in Vladikavkaz after the February Revolution* and was in Petrograd during the October Seizure of Power* as a delegate to the Second All-Russian Congress of Soviets. He returned to Vladikavkaz to organize the Soviet seizure of power in the Terek Region, where the Mensheviks (*see* Russian Social Democratic Workers' Party [Menshevik]) were the dominant political group. The chairmanship of the United Regional Committee of the Russian Social Democratic Workers' Party went to a Menshevik, N. A. Skrypnik, but Kirov became the vice-chairman. The support for the Social Democrats came primarily from the city dwellers against the Terek Cossacks and General A. I. Denikin's* White Army. In 1918 and 1919 Kirov served as political commissar to the Eleventh Red Army. During that time he was charged with enriching himself and misappropriating funds by A. G. Shliapnikov, although nothing seems to have come of the charges. In April 1920 Kirov was appointed a member of the Caucasian Bureau* of the Central Committee of the Russian Communist Party (Bolshevik) (*see* Central Committee of the Russian Communist Party [Bolshevik]), and in May he became the Soviet ambassador to Menshevik Georgia, a position he occupied when the Bolsheviks invaded the country in February 1921.

Kirov was not an especially prominent Bolshevik until his collaboration with I. V. Stalin* and G. K. Ordzhonikidzhe in the reconquest of the Caucasus. He attended his first Bolshevik Party Congress in March 1921. By that time he had also achieved a reputation as a tough and relentless leader in crushing the uprising against the Bolsheviks in Astrakhan in March 1919 and in taking Baku in 1920.

From 1921 to 1927 Kirov "ran" Azerbaijan. He became first secretary of the Central Committee of the Azerbaijan Communist Party in July 1921 and about the same time became a candidate member of the Central Committee of the Russian Communist Party and a member of the Presidium of the Central Committee's Caucasian Bureau (*see* Caucasian Bureau). In 1923 he was appointed a full member of the Central Committee, and in 1925 he was placed in charge of the Leningrad Committee of the Party. After two years of struggle he was able to purge the party of oppositionists and was rewarded with an alternate membership in the Politburo. In 1930 he would become a full member of the Politburo and one of Stalin's closest collaborators. In the 1930s he was regarded as Stalin's heir apparent. In 1934 he became a member of the Secretariat of the Russian Communist Party and then was assassinated by Leonid Nikolaev under mysterious circumstances.

Bibliography

Haupt, Georges, and Marie, Jean Jacques. *Makers of the Russian Revolution.* 1974.

Kirrevkom. *See* Kirghiz-Kazakh Revolutionary Committee.

Kokand, the Autonomous Government of. Kokand was one of the two most important cities in the revolutionary movement in Turkestan (*see* Turkestan, Revolution in). Tashkent was the other. Tashkent became the center of Russian communist (*see* Russian Social Democratic Workers' Party [Bolshevik]) strength and Kokand of nationalist Moslem activity. The two leading Moslem groups in Turkestan, the conservative Ulema Jemyeti and the liberal democratic Shuro-i-Islam, mainly Jadids (*see* Jadid Movement), had united and formed Ittifak-ul-Mislimin (Union of Moslems). When the Tashkent soviet called the Third Regional Congress of Soviets and the Third Moslem Central Asian Conference to meet together on November 15, 1917, and proclaimed a Soviet Turkestan and appointed a Turkestan council of people's commissars, the nationalist Moslem groups decided to act.

In November 1917 the Union of Moslems called the Fourth Moslem Central Asian Conference in Kokand. Some representatives of the Russian Right Socialist-Revolutionary Party* groups in Central Asia attended. The largest delegation to the conference—almost three-quarters of the participants—was from Ferghana Province where Kokand was located. On November 27, 1917, the conference announced that Turkestan was "territorially autonomous within the union of the Russian Democratic Republic," adding that the rights of all national groups within Turkestan would be protected. The conference elected a national council to implement this decision. It included thirty-six Moslems and eighteen Russians and an executive committee of twelve, which by 1918 was headed by the Kazakh leader Mustafa Chokaev. The conference called for a people's council to serve as the Provisional Government and for a Turkestan Constituent Assembly for March 20, 1918. This was a direct challenge to the claims of the Tashkent soviet. But the Kokand Autonomous Government represented a small group of Moslem intellectuals and did not have much support from the native Moslem population. Nor was it able to forge alliances with potential friends such as the Alash-Orda*, the Emir of Bukhara, General I. M. Zaitsev, or the chief of the Orenburg Cossacks, General A. I. Dutov*.

On January 29, 1918, the Russian-dominated Kokand soviet, headed by K. A. Babushkin and O. G. Poltoratvskii, that was opposed to the Kokand Autonomous Government, asked for help from the Tashkent soviet. In January 1918 the Tashkent soviet called for the dissolution of the Kokand Autonomous Government, and from February 6 to February 9, 1918, the Kokand Autonomous Government tried to defend itself from the forces supporting the Tashkent soviet and was defeated. The Tashkent soviet sent the Kokand communists armed support in the form of Russian soldiers reinforced with Austrian and German prisoners of war. The communists were victorious, and their commander allowed the soldiers to pillage and destroy the city of Kokand. There were three days of destruction and slaughter of Moslems. At the end of this period one observer described Kokand as "the city of the dead." The fall of Kokand spelled the end of efforts for native rule in Turkestan, but it also marked the beginning of the Basmachi* movement. The leaders of the Kokand Autonomous Government either fled or were arrested.

Bibliography

Pipes, Richard.*The Formation of the Soviet Union*. 1964.
Zenkovsky, Serge. *Pan-Turkism and Islam in Russia*. 1960.

Kolchak, Aleksandr Vasil'evich (1873–1920). Admiral Kolchak became the Supreme Commander of the counterrevolutionary forces during the Civil War in Russia*.

Kolchak was born in St. Petersburg. His father was a naval artillery officer, and Kolchak attended the Naval Academy between 1888 and 1894. At the time of the Russo–Japanese War he commanded the artillery emplacements at Port Arthur. At the beginning of World War I* he led mining operations in the Baltic and Black seas. In July 1916 he was given command of the Black Sea Fleet with the rank of rear admiral. According to one scholar, Richard Luckett (1971), Kolchak represented the best of the Russian Imperial Navy officer corps. Throughout the rest of the navy in 1917, the enlisted men leaned increasingly to the Left, and mutinies were common, partially because of the harsh and authoritarian behavior of their officers. But this did not occur in the Black Sea where Admiral Kolchak was in command. His father had impressed upon him the value of caring for the needs of his men. Kolchak had already achieved a reputation as a scientist, a polar explorer, and an expert on marine mines.

Despite his many accomplishments and a strong sense of duty and integrity, Kolchak was poorly suited to command. According to one of his closest sub-ordinates, Baron A. Budberg, he was prone to fits of temper and easily influenced by those around him. He also proved to make poor decisions in his choice of commanding officers, to have little sense of appropriate strategy in land warfare, and to have little diplomatic skill in dealing with his chief potential allies, the Czechoslovak Legion* and the Western Allied forces.

In June 1917 the mutinies finally came to the Black Sea Fleet when the enlisted men became convinced that the officers were planning a counterrevolution. When they demanded that the officers be disarmed, Kolchak resigned his command and threw his sword into the sea. Prompted by a sense of duty, he offered his services to the British embassy in Tokyo. He attracted the attention of Major General Sir Alfred Knox, the British representative at Allied headquarters in Siberia. Encouraged by Knox, Kolchak came west from Vladivostok to Omsk and was appointed Minister of War in the recently formed All-Russian Directorate (see Directory—Russia) in October 1918.

The fate of the counterrevolution lay in the hands of this weak and disunited Directory, the Western Allies, and the Czechoslovak Legions. With the coming of the armistice in World War I in November 1918, neither the Western Allies nor the Czech Legions were interested in further involvement in the Russian Civil War. A coup d'état occurred on November 17, 1918, and the Directorate was overthrown. Kolchak was asked to assume command of the whole White Movement* with the title Supreme Commander. The new government changed the entire complexion of the counterrevolutionary movement. Between May and October under the Socialist–Revolutionaries (see Socialist-Revolutionary Party) the Directory had been one of the most liberal regimes in Russia, but its members were less interested in the development of a strong and disciplined army than in the development of democratic governments. The new Kolchak government focused attention on military matters and on December 24 achieved a surprising success in the capture of Perm. However, in the absence of strong leadership by Kolchak, the White forces under his command became better known for their brutality and corruption than for their military prowess. His foreign allies were not much help. Although the Western Allies helped to train and supply his troops, they were unwilling to commit any of their own forces to his enterprises, and the Japanese and Ataman G. M. Semenov* tended only to disrupt his rail communications east of Irkutsk. At the same time Kolchak antagonized the representatives in Siberia of those who could have helped him the most, the allied Commander-in-Chief in Siberia, General M. K. Janin, and the Minister of War of the new Czechoslovak government, General M. R. Stefánik.

In the first two months of 1919 both sides tended to wait out the winter snows and take stock. The Soviet Minister of War, L. D. Trotsky*, decided to rebuild the Third Army and to hold back his forces until Kolchak had advanced farther into their midst. By March Kolchak's 120,000 men had advanced and recaptured the city of Ufa, and by April were close to Kazan and Samara. When Kolchak's forces appeared to be overextended, the Red Army* counterattacked on May 14, and by June Kolchak's forces were in full retreat; with them was the Tsar's imperial gold reserve. Desertions began on a large scale. By July the British had become convinced that Kolchak was leading a lost cause and withdrew their support. In November Kolchak lost his capital city, Omsk, and he retreated toward Irkutsk. The Socialist–Revolutionaries and Mensheviks (see Russian Social Democratic Workers' Party [Menshevik]) in Irkutsk seized power on Christmas Eve and created a new government called the Political Center. Kolchak had not yet reached Irkutsk because it had been held up by the Czech Legions who controlled the Trans-Siberian Railroad in that area. By this time he only had the allegiance of General V. O. Kappel's forces, from whom he became separated. On January 15 his Czech guards announced that they could no longer accept responsibility for his safety and turned him over to the Political Center. A unit of Red Guards* escorted the admiral to jail in Irkutsk.

The Political Center interrogated Kolchak, but it was overthrown by the Military Revolutionary Committee of Irkutsk on January 21, which referred Kolchak's fate to the chairman of the Military-Revolutionary Soviet of the Soviet Fifth Army, Ivan N. Smirnov*, who, despite explicit orders to the contrary from V. I. Lenin*, ordered Kolchak's execution. The reason seems to have been fear that Kolchak's survival would strengthen the efforts of his supporters to seize Irkutsk and rescue him. On February 7, 1920, Admiral Kolchak was executed by firing squad.

Bibliography

Bradley, John. *Civil War in Russia, 1917–20*. 1975.
Fleming, Peter. *The Tragedy of Admiral Kolchak*.
Luckett, Richard. *The White Generals*. 1971.
Melgunov, S. P. *Tragediia Admiralay Kolchaka*. 2 vols. 1930–1931.
Stewart, George. *The White Armies of Russia*. 1933.
Varneck, Elena. *The Testimony of Kolchak and Other Siberian Materials*. 1935.

Kollontai, Aleksandra Mikhailovna (1872–1952). Kollontai was a prominent Bolshevik (see Russian Social Democratic Workers' Party [Bolshevik]) feminist who served as commissar of Social Welfare (1917–1918) and as head of the Communist Party's Woman's Department (Zhenotdel) in the first Council of People's Commissars*. She was also a leader of the Workers' Opposition (see Workers in the Revolution, Role of).

Aleksandra Kollontai was born Aleksandra Domontovich on March 19, 1872, in St. Petersburg. Her father, Mikhail Domontovich, was a cavalry officer who later rose to the rank of general. He and Kollontai's mother, Aleksandra Aleksandrovna Masalin, advocated political liberalism. Thus they reared their only child to be critical of Russian autocracy. They educated her at home, employing tutors to keep her away from radical ideas boiling through the student community.

Kollontai grew into a bright young woman with a strong need for independence. Her first act of rebellion was to marry a man of whom her parents disapproved, her cousin Vladimir Mikhailovich Kollontai. Within a year, in 1895, she bore a son, Mikhail. She soon began to chafe at the monotony of domesticity, however, and to escape it she became involved in educational work among the poor. There she had her first contact with the proletariat and with revolutionaries. At the same time, Kollontai was reading Marx, Engels, and Bebel. In 1898 she decided to become a Marxist propagandist; the desire for autonomy that led her from her parents into marriage now impelled her out of marriage and into political activism. She left her husband and son and spent one year in Zurich, studying Marxism. When she returned to Russia in 1899, she joined the Russian Social Democratic Workers' Party.

From 1900 to 1908 Kollontai worked in St. Petersburg as a party organizer and theorist. Her first publications were scholarly studies of the Finnish economy. Later she wrote propaganda pamphlets, and in 1905 she began to concentrate on attracting working-class women to the socialist cause. Kollontai prevailed upon the party leadership to devote more attention to women, and she published articles and a book (*The Social Bases of the Woman Question*) on the issue of female emancipation. Her purpose was twofold: to establish a woman's department within the Russian Social Democratic Workers' Party and to write analyses of the position of women in contemporary society.

In 1908 Kollontai fled Russia to avoid arrest. She remained in Western Europe until 1917, lecturing, writing, and working with German Social Democrats, most notably Clara Zetkin. Her most important publications were three articles on the psychology of women's oppression. Kollontai wrote that in bourgeois society women were trapped by heterosexual love, for men required that their wives subordinate themselves and women accepted that subordination. They, like their men, had internalized society's dictates, so that even the most independent of women possessed "an atavistic tendency to become dependent" (Clements 1979, p. 73). To be free, by which Kollontai meant autonomous, a woman must learn to live alone. Only after the Revolution had destroyed private property that was the basis of male superiority could heterosexual love be based on equality.

In addition to her explorations of female personality, Kollontai wrote a study of maternity insurance in Europe, *Society and Maternity*, published in 1916. She also continued to press the Russian Social Democrats to begin to organize proletarian women. Her crusade was halted, however, by the outbreak of World War I*. That conflict absorbed all of Kollontai's attention and convinced her to leave the Mensheviks (*see* Russian Social Democratic Workers' Party [Menshevik]) and join the Bolshevik faction (*see* Russian Social Democratic Workers' Party [Bolshevik]). She saw V. I. Lenin*, the leader of the Bolsheviks, as more resolutely opposed to the war than were the Menshevik leaders. Kollontai spent the war years in Scandinavia, first Sweden and then Norway, where she served as liason between Left socialists and Lenin, who was living in Switzerland. It was also as advocate of Lenin's antiwar position (*see* World War I) that she made a lecture tour of the United States in 1915. When she returned to Russia in 1917, after the February Revolution* had toppled the Romanov dynasty, she came as an ardent supporter of Lenin's plan to establish a Soviet government. Throughout 1917 Kollontai worked as a Bolshevik agitator, rising to prominence as one of the party's foremost speakers. Accused of being a German spy, she was jailed by Aleksandr Kerensky's* government in the late summer and then released in September. The next month the Bolsheviks seized power in the name of the soviets (*see* Soviets [Councils] of Workers', Soldiers', and Peasants' Deputies), and Kollontai was appointed commissar of social welfare. In that capacity she issued decrees in January 1918 that laid the foundations for public funding of maternity care. Kollontai also acted as advisor on the drafting, by the Commissariat of Labor, of protective labor legislation for women. She took part in the establishment of civil marriage and divorce laws. For her, therefore, the early months of the Revolution were a time of great progress toward the emancipation of women and a time of personal triumph.

The glow dimmed in March 1918 when the Bolsheviks signed the Treaty of Brest-Litovsk* ending the war with Germany at a high price in concessions. Kollontai saw the peace as a betrayal of the international Revolution and a capitulation to the leading capitalist powers of Europe. Furious, she resigned from the Council of Peoples' Commissars.

When Kollontai returned to work in the late summer of 1918, she specialized in organizing proletarian women. She, Inessa Feodorovna Armand*, Konkordiia Nikolaevna Samoilova, and a number of other Bolshevik women managed to convince the male leadership of the party that women could contribute to the war effort if persuaded to do so by people trained for the purpose. Thus Kollontai argued, the party needed a woman's department. Permission to establish this organization, the Zhenotdel, was granted in 1919. In 1920, after the death of Inessa Armand, its first head, Kollontai, was chosen to lead the department. As director of Zhenotdel, she organized meetings, classes, and publications designed to attract working-class women to government projects such as nurseries, maternity hospitals, and public dining rooms. Kollontai also instructed her subordinates to inform women of their rights, to protest against the abuse of women by male workers, and to push for the inclusion of women on decision-making bodies within the party, government, and trade unions.

This advocacy role for the woman's department most communists neither understood nor tolerated. Many would not even accept the existence of an organization for women within the party. Throughout 1921 provincial party leaders, suspicious of the Zhenotdel as feminist and separatist, dissolved local sections without authorization from Moscow. Far from being able to make the bureau into a vital voice for women within the party, Kollontai had to work simply to keep it alive.

Meanwhile Kollontai was also involved in the Workers' Opposition, a group of trade unionists who came together in 1920 to protest against the loss of trade union autonomy and against the bureaucratization of the party. In

1921, in a pamphlet written for the Tenth Party Congress (*The Workers' Opposition*), Kollontai issued an eloquent demand for greater democracy in party and unions. Although the Tenth Congress in March denounced the Workers' Opposition, the leaders of the faction, A. G. Shliapnikov* and S. P. Medvedev, continued throughout 1921 to criticize party policy. Kollontai lent her voice to their efforts at the Third Comintern Congress in the summer of 1921. Fearing arrest in retaliation for the speech, she gave a copy of *The Workers' Opposition* to Bernhard Reichenbach, a German communist, for safekeeping. He sent it to Berlin, and by year's end Kollontai's criticism of her own party was circulating among socialists in Europe and North America. This embarrassing publicity, her continuing contacts with Shliapnikov and Medvedev, and her outspoken demands for reforms for women moved the party leadership to fire Kollontai from the Zhenotdel early in 1922. She made one more impassioned plea for democratization at the Eleventh Party Congress in March, but her life at the center of Soviet politics was over. When she was offered a post in the diplomatic service in the summer of 1922, she took it and fled the ostracism of Moscow.

Kollontai worked as a diplomat until she retired in 1945. She served in Norway from 1922 to 1926, in Mexico in 1926 and 1927, in Norway again from 1927 to 1930, and in Sweden from 1930 until 1945. Initially, she planned to resume writing about female emancipation, and she published a number of articles and short stories in 1922 and 1923. In them Kollontai discussed "The Winged Eros," her concept of love under communism. Based on erotic attraction and shared commitment to the building of a new society, "The Winged Eros" was monogamy purified. It was "free love," not promiscuity but the nineteenth-century vision of heterosexual love "freed" of all material and social considerations. Kollontai prophesied its coming but wrote that it had not yet arrived. In Soviet society women continued to be plagued by the choice between dependent love and autonomous solitude.

Immediately, Kollontai was accused in the party press of being a feminist who concerned herself with trivial personal problems rather than with the great problems of building socialism. In 1926, when she made several speeches on marriage law reform, they, too, were dismissed as feminist, and Kollontai decided to confine herself in the future to writing diplomatic dispatches and memoirs. Although she thought about leaving the party, she could not bring herself to take that final step. Rather, she chose to remain in service at a distance from Moscow. The distance, and her prominence as the only woman ambassador in Europe, probably saved her from arrest in the party purges of 1936–1938, and she went on to play the role of peacemaker in negotiations ending the wars between the Soviet Union and Finland in 1939–1940 and 1941–1944.

In 1945 Kollontai retired. She returned to Moscow, where she lived for seven years as a pensioner. She died of heart failure on March 9, 1952, three weeks short of her eightieth birthday, and is buried in Novodevichii Cemetery, under a white marble statue inscribed "Revolutionary, Tribune, Diplomat."

Barbara Evans Clements

Bibliography

Clements, Barbara. *Bolshevik Feminist: The Life of Aleksandra Kollontai.* 1979.
Holt, Alix, ed. *Selected Writings of Alexandra Kollontai.* 1977.
Itkina, A. M. *Revoliutsioner, tribun, diplomat.* 2d ed. 1970.
Kollontai, A. M. *The Autobiography of a Sexually Emancipated Communist Woman.* 1971.
———. *Den första etappen.* 1945.
———. *The Love of the Worker Bees.* 1977.
———. *Novaia moral' i rabochii klass.* 1918.
———. *The Workers' Opposition in Russia.* 1921.
Palencia, Isabel de. *Alexandra Kollontai: Ambassadress from Russia.* 1947.
Stora-Sandor, Judith, ed. *Marxisme et révolution sexuelle.* 1973.

Komintern. *See* Communist International.

Komsomol. *See* Russian Communist League of Youth.

Komuch. *See* Committee of Members of the Constituent Assembly.

Kornilov Revolt. The Kornilov Revolt was a last-ditch attempt on the part of a member of the General Staff, L. G. Kornilov, to forestall a revolution from the Left by using the army to take over the Provisional Government* in August 1917.

Russia's military woes continued unabated after the failure of the July offensive of 1917 (*see* July Days). A series of mysterious fires in factories engaged in war production, a worsening food situation, and the fall of Riga on August 21 produced near panic conditions. Fearful that the Prime Minister of the Provisional Government, A. F. Kerensky*, was unable to halt the political, economic, and social deterioration because of personal weakness and unwillingness to move against the Left, which they considered the source of the problem, various anti-socialist and liberal groups turned to General L. G. Kornilov as a savior. Included among those who encouraged Kornilov were military organizations such as the League of Georgian Cavaliers and industrial groups, the Society for the Economic Rehabilitation of Russia and the Republican Center. Sympathetic to Kornilov's goals, but not his tactics, were many members of the Constitutional Democratic Party—Cadet*. His allies hoped that Kornilov could restore order at home and discipline at the front; the former goal involved eliminating the influence of radical socialists, especially the Bolsheviks (*see* Russian Social Democratic Workers' Party [Bolshevik]); the latter demanded reimposition of the authority of the officers and the reintroduction of the death penalty for desertion and treason.

General Kornilov enjoyed a reputation as a war hero after his dramatic escape in 1916 from an Austro-Hungarian prison camp. Early in February 1917 he was named commander of the military district of Petrograd, a post that he resigned in April when the soviet countermanded his orders. Subsequently, he was appointed commander of the Eighth Army on the southwestern front where his armies achieved temporary success during the July debacle. His anxieties about the weaknesses of the Petrograd government were encouraged by V. S. Zavoiko, a staff member who wrote Kornilov's speeches and worked to promote Kornilov's popularity as a potential national leader.

Kerensky reluctantly appointed Kornilov Supreme Commander-in-Chief on July 18 because he seemed to have a broader outlook than other available generals who were unacceptable to the Right or unwilling to tolerate the existence of any "democratic elements" in the army, for example, Soldiers' Committees (see Soldiers and Soldiers' Committees) and commissars. That Kornilov was indistinguishable from the so-called hard-liners soon became apparent to Kerensky, when, as a condition for accepting command, Kornilov demanded "responsibility before his own conscience and to the whole people"—a clear challenge to Kerensky's authority (Rabinowitch 1976, p. 103.). This issue and other conflicts about military discipline between the Prime Minister and the general were temporarily bridged through the efforts of M. M. Filonenko, Political Commissar of the Supreme Military Headquarters (Stavka) (see General Staff), and B. V. Savinkov*, shortly to become Deputy Minister of War. They convinced the two leaders that despite differences of opinion, they needed to work together to restore military discipline and the authority of the government.

Subsequent meetings between Kerensky and Kornilov on August 3 and August 10 were strained. Kerensky accused Kornilov of presenting his program for the restoration of military discipline as an ultimatum. Kornilov voiced suspicions that Kerensky was working for his dismissal.

It seems likely that after the failure of the Moscow State Conference* (August 12–15) at which he vainly attempted to find a source of mass support for his government, Kerensky moved toward acceptance of Kornilov's program, which entailed restoration of the death penalty to the rear as well as to the theater of military operations, reduction of the role of democratic organizations, discipline of strikers working in the factories engaged in war production, and strengthening the role of the military command. Kornilov's spokesman, Savinkov, handled the negotiations at a series of meetings on August 23 and 24. Savinkov also asked Kornilov to dispatch the Third Corps to the Petrograd Military District to enforce martial law. Clearly, it was anticipated that implementation of Kornilov's program might provoke demonstrations in the capital; the Third Corps might have to act against the Bolsheviks and other members of the Petrograd Soviet* who joined them.

Unknown to Kerensky, on August 6 Kornilov had unilaterally ordered troops, including the Third Corps, to move within convenient striking distance of Petrograd and Moscow. Kornilov told his chief of staff that it might be necessary to squash an anticipated Bolshevik insurrection scheduled to occur on the six-month anniversary of the February Revolution*. Thus Kornilov was prepared to move against the Left without the government's consent. Following his conversations with Savinkov, however, Kornilov had good reason to think he had secured Kerensky's support, which eliminated the need to act illegally to strengthen the government and suppress radicalism in the capital.

The machinations of a well-meaning, self-appointed middleman, V. N. Lvov, undid the pending cooperative effort of Kerensky and Kornilov against the Left. Lvov's interventions between August 22 and August 25 convinced Kerensky that Kornilov not only planned to purge the Left but also intended to replace Kerensky as head of the government. Jolted by the threat to his own position and panicked by his approval of troop dispositions to Petrograd for his own undoing, Kerensky, near hysteria, dismissed Kornilov from office without consulting the government. That he did not denounce Kornilov as a rebel until later the next day suggests that Kerensky had doubts about the coup theory and may have regretted his precipitous action.

Kornilov was bewildered by Kerensky's telegram of dismissal on August 27, for it flagrantly contradicted Kerensky's recently given assurances that he would support the Kornilov program even if it meant a break with the Left. Moreover, Kornilov's understanding from his conversations with Lvov was that Kerensky was willing to acquiesce to a change of government, a view Kerensky seemed to confirm by agreeing on August 26 to come to General Staff headquarters to discuss details of reorganization. Kornilov refused to capitulate and, through Zavoiko, issued a plea on the 27th to all military commissars to support him so that in victory he could convene a Constituent Assembly* to choose a new form of government for Russia.

By the 28th news of Kornilov's impending attack led all groups to the Left of the Constitutional Democrats (*see* Constitutional Democratic Party—Cadet)—political parties, labor organizations, soldiers' committees—to prepare measures of resistance. The forces of the Left—Socialist–Revolutionaries (*see* Socialist-Revolutionary Party), Mensheviks (*see* Russian Social Democratic Workers' Party [Menshevik]), and especially the Bolsheviks (*see* Russian Social Democratic Workers' Party [Bolshevik])—who were organizing their actions through the Committee for Struggle against the Counter-Revolution were instrumental in the defeat of Kornilov. They armed recruits, constructed defense fortifications, persuaded Kornilov's troops to disobey their officers, wrecked railway lines, and rallied popular support. These actions, and the ineptitude of Kornilov's allies, assured victory without any skirmishes between the opposing sides. Kornilov's forces were cowed into submission when they recognized the overwhelming superiority of the enemy. On September 1 Kornilov acknowledged the hopelessness of his position and surrendered.

The Kornilov affair had important repercussions. It disillusioned the lower classes with the bourgeoisie, who were heavily implicated in the affair. The Bolsheviks could, with evidence, play on the masses' elemental and emotional fear of the counterrevolution and use the theme that the "revolution" was in danger. The unexpected turn of events was an important factor influencing V. I. Lenin* to advance the date for a Bolshevik seizure of power (*see* October Seizure of Power). The new sympathy of the masses for Bolsheviks who had played a leading role in the suppression of the *Kornilovshchina* (Kornilov Revolt) was evident in the majority Lenin's party received in the Petrograd and Moscow Soviets on August 31 and September 6 on resolutions expressing lack of confidence in the Provisional Government. There is also evidence of a generic growth of Bolshevik influence, especially in the larger cities. The Bolsheviks consolidated their control of the military revolutionary committee set up to combat the *Kornilovshchina,* organizations that were subsequently to play a prominent role in directing the October Revolution. It was through these organizations that the Bolsheviks armed the Red Guard* and other militia units that did not disband with the defeat of Kornilov and that later formed most of the troops used in the October Seizure of Power.

Following the *Kornilovshchina,* the Provisional Government was a corpse futilely trying to give the impression of life. When Kerensky attempted to assume control again after the "democratic organs" had smashed Kornilov, it was too late. The "democratic organizations" had proved that they were stronger than the Provisional Government, and the Bolsheviks now dominated them. Also, Kerensky's conduct in the Kornilov Revolt ruled out any support he might have expected from the Right, which now displayed an equal dislike of the Provisional Government and Kerensky. Clearly then, the *Kornilovshchina* accelerated the demise of the Provisional Government by alienating its sources of support while strengthening the hand of its enemies.

Harvey Asher

Bibliography

Chugaev, D. A., ed. *Revoliutsionnoe dvizhenie v Rossii v avguste 1917 g.* 1957.
Katkov, George. *The Kornilov Affair.* 1980.
Kerensky, Alexander. *The Prelude to Bolshevism.* 1919.
Martynov, P. V. *Kornilov.* 1927.
Miliukov, P. V. *Istoriia vtoroi russkoi revoliutsii.* 3 vols. 1921.
Rabinowitch, Alexander. *The Bolsheviks Come to Power.* 1976.
Savinkov, B. V. *K delu Kornilovu.* 1917.
Vladimirov, V. *Kontr-revoliutsiia v 1917 g.* 1924.

Krasin, Leonid Borisovich (1870–1926; pseudonyms, Zimin, Vinter, Iogransev, Nikitich, Nikolaev). Krasin was a former leftist dissident in the Bolshevik Party (*see* Russian Social Democratic Workers' Party [Bolshevik]; Left Communism) who became a prominent figure in the Soviet government with a brilliant performance in the administration of industry and in diplomacy.

Krasin was born in the small town of Kurgan, Tobolsk Province, in western Siberia. Krasin's parents were well educated and familiar with many of the populists exiled to Siberia. Krasin was well educated, attending the Tiumen Technical High School and the St. Petersburg Technological Institute. In the latter institutions he became a Marxist in 1887 and began agitation among the textile workers in the city. The circle that he joined would later become known as the Union for the Emancipation of the Working Class, the organization that V. I. Lenin* joined when he came to St. Petersburg, although Krasin was expelled and jailed before Lenin arrived.

In 1892 Krasin served ten months in Taganka Prison in solitary confinement for his revolutionary activities. He used the time to teach himself German and read in psychology, philosophy, and Russian history. In 1895 he was sentenced to three years in Siberia, where he spent his time in Irkutsk. He returned to Russia and graduated with distinction from the Kharkov Technological Institute, earning a diploma in engineering with distinction. He spent four years working as an engineer in Baku, an experience that would later serve him well as a Soviet economic administrator. Trotsky would later describe Krasin as one of the real founders of the Social Democratic movement in Baku and the Caucasus.

At the historic Second Congress of the Russian Social Democratic Workers' Party in 1903 Krasin supported Lenin and was added to the Bolshevik Central Committee in October of that year. In 1905, at the so-called Third Congress of the Russian Social Democratic Party (actually the first congress of the Bolshevik Party) in London, Krasin was elected to the Central Committee of the Russian Democratic Workers' Party (Bolshevik) (*see* Central Committee of the Russian Communist Party [Bolshevik]). He played an active role in the 1905 Revolution (*see* Nineteen-Five Revolution) in Moscow and St. Petersburg and was elected to the St. Petersburg Soviet. With Maxim Gorky (*see* Peshkov, Maksim Alexeevich) he founded the legal Bolshevik newspaper *Novaia Zhizn'* (*The New Life*) in October 1905. Between 1905 and 1906 Lenin and Krasin disagreed, first, on the question of legal activities and participation in the elections to the Second Duma and, second, on philosophical issues. Krasin became associated with the Vpered Group, which included A. A. Bogdanov (real name, Malinovsky) and A. V. Lunacharskii*, and they became a separate leftist faction in the party. Krasin left revolutionary activity altogether and became general manager of a German electrical equipment firm (Siemans-Schuckert). During World War I* he became managing director of one of the Putilov factories in Moscow and a member of the War Industries Committee*.

Although at first remaining aloof from the October Seizure of Power*, Krasin was persuaded by L. D. Trotsky* to take part in the Brest-Litovsk* negotiations for an end to the war with Germany. Upon return to Russia Krasin accepted appointments as Commissar of Foreign Trade, Commissar for Transport, and member of the Presidium for the Supreme Council of the National Economy* and of the Council of Labor and Defense. In 1920 he negotiated a trade treaty with Estonia and in 1921 a trade treaty with England.

In the inner councils of the party and government Krasin was a sharp and outspoken critic of Soviet economic policy, and he called for massive efforts to bring in foreign capital. Using the debt claims of foreign companies for enterprises confiscated in Russia as an opening wedge, he proposed to give foreign companies long-term leases in return for investment capital. But when he succeeded in reaching such an agreement in the famous Urquhart concessions of 1922, Lenin found the terms exploitative and vetoed the proposal.

In 1924 Krasin served as ambassador to France where he continued his efforts to interest foreign capital to invest in Russian economic development. In 1925–1926 he became Soviet ambassador to England where he continued his efforts to secure foreign capital until his death on November 24, 1926.

Bibliography

Haupt, Georges, and Marie, Jean Jacques. *Makers of the Russian Revolution.* 1974.
Karpova, Rosa. *L. B. Krasin: Soviet Diplomat.* 1962.
Krasin, L. B. *Voprosy vneshnei torgovli.* 1928.
Krasin, Liubov. *Leonid Krasin.* 1929.
Pozner, S. M., ed. *Leonid Borisovich Krasin.* 1928.

Krasnoshchekhov, Aleksandr Mikhailovich (1880–1937; pseudonyms, Stroller, Tobenson, Tobinson, Tobelson, A. S. Tobelson). Krasnoshchekhov was a communist (*see* Russian Social Democratic Workers' Party [Bolshevik]) leader who played a leading role in the Soviet seizure of power in Siberia. (*see* Siberia, Revolution in).

Krasnoshchekhov was born in a Jewish family in Chernobyl in Kiev Province. While preparing to attend the University of Kiev in 1896 he came under the influence of M. S. Uritskii* and joined the "Circle for the Emancipation of the Working Class." In 1898 Krasnoshchekhov was arrested and sentenced to six months in prison. At the end of that term he renewed his revolutionary work in Nikolaev where he may have met L. D. Trotsky*. After doing revolutionary work in several cities and towns in the Ukraine he became a leader of the South Russian Proletarian Association, which Trotsky had founded in 1897. In 1901 he fled Russia to avoid arrest.

Arriving in America in 1901 Krasnoshchekhov remained there until 1917 under the name A. S. Tobelson. He first became a tailor and then a paper hanger. He played an active role in the formation of the International Workers of the World and worked within the American Federation of Labor as a member. In 1912 he received a bachelor's degree at the University of Chicago and then a law degree. He founded and became the head of the Chicago Workers' Institute and served as a lawyer who defended various radical causes.

When Krasnoshchekhov heard of the February Revolution*, he and his wife and two children took a ship from Vancouver to Japan and then to Vladivostok, where he arrived in August 1917 and immediately became a member of the local Bolshevik organization. In the flurry of political activity in Siberia in 1917 a man with Krasnoshchekhov's ability, political experience, and education could rise very quickly, and like the achievements of other Bolsheviks in Siberia, Krasnoshchekhov's success had more to do with personal qualities than fidelity to Lenin's principles and strategies. A separate Bolshevik political party did not really exist in Siberia until October 1917, and it began to appear in central and western Siberia before it was formed in eastern Siberia. Although the First Siberian Congress of Soviets, which met simultaneously with the First All-Siberian Conference of Bolsheviks in October, was intended to give both the Soviets and the Bolsheviks centralized leadership under the new Central Executive Committee of Soviets headed by B. Z. Shumiatskii*, eastern Siberia continued for a time to go its own way. Krasnoshchekhov first became secretary of the local domestic workers' union and was sent by the union to the Vladivostok soviet and elected to the City Council of Trade Unions. Shortly thereafter, he was appointed to the City Council of Nikol'sk-Ussuriiski. Within two weeks he was elected President of the Soviet of Workers', Soldiers', and Peasants' Deputies of Nikol'sk.

But the first phase of the Siberian Revolution in 1917 (*see* Siberia, Revolution in) did not belong to the Bolsheviks. It was led by those non-Bolshevik leaders who sought greater regional autonomy through the new *zemstvo* institutions and committees of public organizations and of public safety. It was they who convened the First Congress of Regionalists (Oblastniki) in the first half of October 1917 in Tomsk and elected the Regional Duma that they maintained would become the supreme political body in an autonomous Siberia. Their response to the October Seizure of Power* was to convoke an extraordinary congress in Tomsk in December and call for the election of a constituent assembly for Siberia in March. But on January 26, 1918, the regionalists were dispersed by the Tomsk Soviet of Workers' and Soldiers' Deputies. The regionalists formed a provisional government of Siberia the following day, and their leaders moved to Harbin until May when they entered Vladivostok with Japanese and American military forces to reaffirm their claim to rule Siberia.

By December 1917 the soviets were beginning to gain ground everywhere in Siberia at the expense of the *zemstvos* and committees of public organizations. When the first convention of workers' organizations in the Far East was called at Vladivostok in October 1917, Krasnoshchekhov was sent by the Nikolsk Soviet and elected as Vice-President of the convention. He was charged with the responsibility of composing the first bylaws of labor unions in the Far East. When the news of the October Seizure of Power in Petrograd reached him, he called a conference of all soviets in the Russian Far East to meet in Khabarovsk on December 11, 1917. A rival conference of Siberian *zemstvos* began meeting in Khabarovsk on December 10. The *zemstvos* called for a continuation of the existing political institutions, and the soviets called for a Soviet government. Krasnoshchekhov attended both conferences and tried to bring about a compromise. When the soviet conference announced the dissolution of the *zemstvo* conference, a Japanese warship arrived in the harbor of Vladivostok.

The push for a Soviet government in Eastern Siberia was at first successful, although the soviets were not at first dominated by Bolsheviks. The Khabarovsk Conference of Soviets organized a coalition government for Siberia, leaving 40 percent of the posts in the cabinet for representatives appointed by the *zemstvos*. The *zemstvos* in the Maratime Province and Blagoveshchensk refused to join in the new government, and the conference dismissed the old *zemstvos* in Blagoveshchensk and ordered a new one elected. The new government created by the Khabarovsk conference was clearly dominated by the soviets, and it was called the Far Eastern Krai (territory) Executive Committee of Soviets. Krasnoshchekhov was elected President. For a few weeks in May Vladivostok became part of the new government after the Vladivostok Soviet overthrew the reigning *zemstvos* and Municipal Council. The Trans-Baikal region also joined the Far Eastern government.

By February 1918 the Bolsheviks had gained control over the soviets in the Siberian Far East. The Far Eastern Krai Executive Committee changed its name to the Far Eastern Council of People's Commissars and claimed that it controlled the Amur and Maratime regions along with Sakhalin and Kamchatka. This placed them in conflict with the Central Executive Committee of the Soviets of Siberia* (Tsentosibir), which had been created in October 1917 in Irkutsk, was lead by B. Z. Shumiatskii, and claimed to control the same area.

The revolt of the Czechoslovak Legion* in May 1918, while in transit from European Russia to Vladivostok on the Trans-Siberian Railway, changed the whole balance of power in Siberia. The Czechs seized control in Vladivostok. Most of the Far East fell under the control of Ataman Grigorii Semenov* with the connivance of the occupying forces that intervened in Vladivostok (*see* Far Eastern Republic; Far Eastern Bureau). All of the gains won by the soviets in Siberia seemed to have been swept away all at once. In December 1918 the Central Committee of the Russian Communist Party (Bolshevik) formed a Siberian Bureau* in the Far East to restore Siberia to Soviet rule. In May 1918 the Far East the Provisional Government of an Autonomous Siberia, which had fled from Tomsk in January 1918, was resurrected in Vladivostok under Japanese and American protection. When Vladivostok passed into the hands of the Czech Legion, the Provisional Government of an Autonomous Siberia claimed control of all of Siberia, but they surrendered those claims to the Directory (*see* Directory—Russia) created in Ufa in September 1918.

Krasnoshchekhov lost all of his power as quickly as he had gained it. At first he withdrew to Blagoveshchensk. He sent his wife and children back to America and then went into hiding in the forests. In May of 1919 he reached Samara where he was arrested as a Bolshevik spy. He soon escaped and made his way to Irkutsk by September, where he was once again arrested. In Irkutsk power had passed into the hands of a coalition of leftist parties called the Political Center, which favored a non-communist state in eastern Siberia. When Kolchak was overthrown on December 28, Krasnoshchekhov was one of the prisoners that was freed, and he began to collaborate with the Political Center. The Political Center was displaced on January 21, 1920, by the Irkutsk Revolutionary Committee. By this time Krasnoshchekhov had accepted the belief of the Political Center that the allies would never accept a Bolshevik government in Siberia and that probably Siberia was too backward for communism. It would have to go through bourgeois democracy and capitalism before it would be ready for that stage. He had, therefore, proposed to the Irkutsk Revolutionary Committee that a mission be sent from Irkutsk to the Military Revolutionary Council of the Soviet Fifth Army at Omsk. He went personally at the request of the Irkutsk Revolutionary Committee before they seized power and argued in favor of an independent democratic republic in Siberia as a buffer state between Soviet Russia and the Japanese. The Soviet chairman of the Military Revolutionary Council, I. N. Smirnov*, received Lenin's approval for the idea on January 21, 1920, and agreed to the notion that the state would include all of the territory between the Oka and the Enesei to the Arctic Ocean.

In effect, Lenin was approving a proposal that was far more modest than the ambitions of most of the Siberian communists because Lenin was convinced that the interventionists would not accept a Siberian Soviet government. Krasnoshchekhov was the beneficiary of Lenin's decisions, but he found that he could not bring his idea back to Irkutsk because the Soviets had already seized power there and immediately proclaimed Soviet power. Therefore, he went to Krasnoiarsk to carry out his plan. He was forced to leave Krasnoiarsk because of the fighting and with six Mensheviks (*see* Russian Social Democratic Workers' Party [Menshevik]) and Socialist–Revolutionaries (*see* Socialist-Revolutionary Party), and he set up his new government in Verkhneudinsk. The new government, which was to be democratic rather than Soviet, adopted the title ''The Temporary Self-Government of Transbaikalia.'' A conference was called at the village of Bicbura for March 28. The conference expanded its membership and moved to Verkhneudinsk where on April 6, 1920, Krasnoshchekhov announced the Declaration of Independence of the Far Eastern Republic*. Krasnoshchekhov had been its creator, and he was elected its first president, a post he kept until July 1921. Although mostly Bolshevik in its composition, the new government maintained an outward posture of independence from the Soviet state to the West. Among Krasnoshchekhov's recruits for the new government was V. S. (''Wild Bill'') Shatov, who had worked with Krasnoshchekhov in the United States. Shatov became Minister of Transportation. The Soviet government recognized the Far Eastern Republic as a separate state on May 14, 1920, and in the same month B. Z. Shumiatskii joined Krasnoshchekhov in the new government as Premier. Shumiatskii negotiated a truce with the Japanese that called for the Japanese to withdraw from the strategically located city of Chita. In August

Shumiatskii returned to Tomsk to become a member of the new Siberian Revolutionary Committee there.

Krasnoshchekhov had been able to achieve power because Lenin had accepted his proposition that the facade of an independent Far Eastern Republic was desirable, and Lenin had, with this thought in mind, put Krasnoshchekhov on the Far Eastern Bureau of the Russian Communist Party created under the Siberian Bureau* of the Communist Party on March 3, 1920, to take charge of efforts to establish communist control over the Russian Far East. But Krasnoshchekhov was a strong and opinionated leader who proved unwilling to accept the views of his fellow commissars in the Far Eastern Bureau. Complaints came from fellow workers that he tended to ride roughshod over opposition and tended to avoid consultation with colleagues. There was also a division in the Far Eastern Bureau that transcended personalities because the committee was evenly divided between the three communists who had established their original base in Verkhneudinsk and those who came from Vladivostok. The three Vladivostok communists, led by P. M. Nikiforov, were more independent of Moscow and favored their city as the capital for any new political entity.

Some Siberian communists, like B. I. Khotimskii and A. A. Shiriamov, had opposed the whole idea of a buffer state from the beginning, whereas others, like Krasnoshchekhov and I. G. Kushnarev, saw the Far Eastern Republic as a genuine transitional state between bourgeois democracy and Soviet government. There were also a number of personal rivalries in the Far Eastern Bureau* that compelled many changes in its membership. In April 1921 the six members of the government of the Far Eastern Republic sent a telegram to Lenin asking that Krasnoshchekhov be removed. As a result Krasnoshchekhov was brought back to Moscow on January 1922 to serve as Deputy to the Commissar of Finance. Even there, all of his new colleagues except G. Ia. Sokolnikov opposed his appointment. Their fears proved justified, and in the spring of 1922 Lenin had to transfer him to the Presidium of the Supreme Council of the National Economy*, and he became head of the National Industrial Bank (Prombank) where he served for two years. In 1924 he was arrested and imprisoned for a few months on charges of irregularities in the performance of his office. He was arrested and imprisoned during the Great Purges and died some time between 1937 and 1939 in prison. He has been posthumously rehabilitated.

Bibliography

Dotsenko, Paul. The Struggle for a Democracy in Siberia, 1917–20. 1983.
Istoriia Sibiri. Vol. 4. 1968.
Norton, Henry. The Far Eastern Republic of Siberia. 1923.
Smith, Canfield. Vladivostok under Red and White Rule. 1975.
Snow, Russel E. The Bolsheviks in Siberia, 1917–18. 1977.

Krestintern. *See* Peasant International.

Kronstadt, 1917–1921. Kronstadt was a naval base located on an island close to Petrograd whose military forces played a decisive role in bringing about the October Seizure of Power* and the New Economic Policy*.

The name "Kronstadt" evokes images of rebel sailors (*see* Sailors in 1917) dying heroically in the snow under the guns of the oppressive, unyielding Soviet power. In more prosaic terms, Kronstadt is the name of a naval base, town, and fortress situated on Kotlin Island, some twenty miles west of Petrograd in the easternmost part of the Gulf of Finland. Kronstadt has figured prominently in Russian naval history since its founding by Peter the Great. It was also the scene of significant revolutionary activity before the events of 1921.

The first manifestations of mass discontent in Kronstadt were naval mutinies during the reigns of Peter I and Catherine II. The first revolutionary conspirators there were naval officers involved in the Decembrist revolt. Half a century later, a bomb made by a Kronstadt naval officer killed Alexander II. Revolutionary involvement among the lower ranks can be traced to the years 1901–1903 with the appearance of small circles devoted to the reading and discussion of forbidden literature. Although the naval authorities and the gendarmes suppressed such activities whenever they were discovered, official prohibitions could not overcome a general dissatisfaction with naval service conditions. When compounded with the tremendous fermentation within Russia in 1905 (*see* Nineteen-Five Revolution), this discontent erupted in a naval mutiny that October. Kronstadt was also one of the focal points of an abortive uprising provoked by the Socialist-Revolutionary Party* and the Bolsheviks (*see* Russian Social Democratic Workers' Party [Bolshevik]) in July 1906. Although the authorities unearthed small networks of revolutionary sympathizers in the Baltic Fleet on several occasions during the next decade, the Kotlin cauldron did not bubble again until 1917.

With the coming of war in 1914, Kronstadt became part of a fortified region established to protect the seaward approaches to Petrograd. Some 8,000 artillerymen manned the Kronstadt fortress and the Kronstadt harbor batteries. Kronstadt Naval Base, which functioned as the Baltic Fleet's training and repair center (and also housed its prisons and penal units), had a complement of roughly 20,000 sailors. Most Kronstadt civilians, who numbered around 20,000, were associated with the shipyard or naval base.

The events of February 1917 in Kronstadt were more violent than in most other parts of the country. The tsarist regime fell with little bloodshed in Petrograd, but the news reaching Kronstadt was intermittent and fragmentary. Perhaps mindful of the punishment reserved for wartime mutineers, the Kronstadters carried their revolt further than necessary to be sure of having gone far enough. The senior naval commanders were killed by a mob on Anchor Square, while other naval officers, senior noncoms, and gendarmes fell victims to the first rush of insurrection or died attempting to combat it. The death toll is estimated at forty for twelve hours of violence.

Having overthrown the old order, the Kronstadters feared punishment for their deeds at the hands of the military high command. Although military officers participated in the first popularly elected institutions to emerge in the aftermath of the February Revolution*, their presence was a reminder that they might execute order to curtail the gains of the Revolution. Within a few weeks, several hundred officers, including Kronstadt's remaining gendarmes and police, had

been arrested on vague charges of cruelty to the lower ranks or counterrevolutionary activity. The Kronstadt Soviet, made up of representatives elected by
the naval and army units and from among the local workers, was functioning
by mid-March. At first a sounding board for complaints, by May it had assumed
control of virtually the entire local administrative apparatus. The Soviet was
continually at odds with the Provisional Government* over questions of discipline
and authority.

The Socialist–Revolutionaries and the Bolsheviks dominated Kronstadt party
politics almost from the beginning. More than half of the sailors were of peasant
origin, and the Kronstadt Socialist-Revolutionary organizations secured a sizable
plurality in the March Soviet elections. The Kronstadt Socialist–Revolutionaries
were drawn to the Left element of their party's leadership. Indeed, the shift
leeward in local sympathies as 1917 progressed gave the Socialist-Revolutionary
Maximalist and Left Socialist-Revolutionary (see Left Socialist-Revolutionary
Party) factions together a majority in the August soviet elections. However, the
Kronstadt Bolsheviks had won a plurality in the May soviet elections and maintained their strength in August. The local Bolshevik organization was extremely
efficient and maintained closer ties with Petrograd than its rivals. Like the local
Socialist–Revolutionaries, the Kronstadt Bolsheviks adhered to a Left position
relative to their party's central leadership, probably because they were closely
associated with the party's Left-leaning Military Organization in the pre-July
period. The Mensheviks (see Russian Social Democratic Workers' Party [Men-
shevik]) and other moderate parties had few followers in Kronstadt after April,
but any radical speaker, particularly an anarchist (see Anarchism), could always
attract a crowd on Anchor Square.

Throughout 1917 Petrograd rightly regarded Kronstadt as a hotbed of radicalism. Kronstadters took part in the April demonstrations that brought socialists
into the Provisional Government. In May the Kronstadt Soviet passed a resolution
recognizing the authority of the Petrograd Soviet* but pointedly ignoring the
Provisional Government. The resulting confrontation, known as the ''Kronstadt
Republic'' incident, ended when the Kronstadters agreed to recognize the authority of the Provisional Government until all power passed to the soviets. Many
thought the time for this had come in early July, and some 5,000 Kronstadters
joined elements of the Petrograd garrison and work force in marching on the
Tauride Palace to demand the transfer of all power to the Soviets. In the aftermath
of the July Days*, the Kronstadt Bolshevik leaders went to jail, and Kronstadt's
imprisoned officers were freed, but leftist sympathies remained high, as indicated
by the aforementioned August elections to the soviet. During the Kornilov
Revolt* Kronstadt sent men to the capital to help defend the Revolution. In
October some 2,500 Kronstadters answered the Military Revolutionary Committee's (see October Seizure of Power) summons to defend the Revolutions
from the Provisional Government, thereby helping the Bolsheviks seize power.

Contingents of Kronstadt sailors helped put down the first opposition to the
Soviet regime and performed many administrative tasks for the new government

during its first months in power. In early 1918, with the evacuation of Reval and Helsingfors, Kronstadt became the principal base of the Baltic Fleet. During the Civil War in Russia* Baltic Fleet sailors formed some of the best units in the Red Army*. Kronstadters fought on every front, often serving as shock troops, invariably displaying complete loyalty to the Soviet regime.

This is not to state that Kronstadters always agreed with the policies of the government and the Russian Communist Party (the name adopted by the Bolsheviks after the Revolution). Some resented the Bolshevik monopoly of power in the first Council of People's Commissars* (Sovnarkom). Many felt betrayed when the Soviet regime replaced the elected Central Committee of the Baltic Fleet* (Tsentrobalt) with an appointed council of commissars. Bolshevik diplomatic maneuvers, together with the attendant loss of territory to the Germans, caused considerable dissatisfaction with the Treaty of Brest-Litovsk* among soldiers and sailors alike.

However, defense of the Revolution remained the first priority. The restoration of hierarchical authority and some measure of discipline was necessary to defeat the White armies (see White Movement). When P. N. Wrangel's* forces evacuated the Crimea in November 1920, seemingly bringing an end to the Civil War, many Kronstadters thought it was time to return to 1917 conditions. But three years of civil war had left Russia prostrate. Peasant revolts flared up all over the country that winter, and factory workers grumbled at scanty rations.

When strikes broke out in Petrograd in late February 1921, the city's party leadership resorted to lockouts and arrests to restore order. Reports reaching Kronstadt were mixed with rumors of troops firing on demonstrators and representatives of the Cheka (see All-Russian Extraordinary Commission for Combatting Counterrevolution and Sabotage) shooting strike leaders. The Kronstadters, who had received bad food, no clothing ration, and little fuel for their barracks that winter, were already disillusioned with the communists. On February 28 a meeting aboard the battleship *Petropavlovsk* passed a resolution that became the political manifesto of the subsequent rebellion.

The *Petropavlovsk* resolution called for new election to the soviets by secret ballot, freedom of speech and press for all Left political organizations, freedom of assembly, release of all socialist political prisoners, abolition of communist political departments and fighting detachments in the armed forces, equal rations for all working people, and full freedom for the peasantry with regard to the land. The economic demands would soon be met or exceeded by the New Economic Policy (NEP), but the political demands were a direct challenge to the party's claim to sole representation of the worker–peasant masses. The Soviet government and the party leadership considered the latter counterrevolutionary.

At a mass meeting on Anchor Square on March 1, some 15,000 Kronstadters endorsed the *Petropavlovsk* resolution by an overwhelming majority, despite warnings and threats from communist leaders. The next day, amid rumors of a revolt in Petrograd and imminent communist reprisals in Kronstadt, a provisional revolutionary committee was formed.

The government made little effort to conciliate the Kronstadters. On March 8, after the last ultimatum demanding Kronstadt's surrender had expired, the Petrograd leadership ordered some 25,000 picked troops to cross the ice and quell the rebellion. Some 12,000 active defenders turned back this force, which suffered heavy losses. Probing operations continued while the government called up loyal units from other parts of the country. L. D. Trotsky* arrived to supervise the pacification operation, and M. N. Tukhachevskii* to direct it. The second major assault, by some 50,000 men, came early on March 17. With their food, fuel, and ammunition almost exhausted, the Kronstadters could not hold out. Their last stronghold fell on March 18. Some 8,000 escaped to Finland; Kronstadt's losses had been about 600 dead and 1,000 wounded, with perhaps 2,500 captured in the final assault. All who survived went to swell the population of Soviet Russia's early prison camps. Government losses were approximately 10,000 dead, wounded, and missing.

Soviet charges that the Kronstadt rebels were the dupes of a White Guard plot, aided and abetted by emigré organizations and encouraged by the Socialist–Revolutionaries and Mensheviks, have no basis in fact. During the insurrection, Kronstadt received no assistance of any kind from outside sources. It is clear that the Kronstadters were governed by roughly the same motives in 1921 as they had been in 1917—a desire for freely elected soviets, made up of representatives from all Left political organizations charged with the functions of local government and safeguarded to a greater or lesser extent from arbitrary demands by higher governmental organs. It was the Communist Party that had changed its perspective toward political power since 1917 and this change that had demanded suppression of the Kronstadt Revolt.

Kronstadt is but the best known of the many contemporary popular rebellions against Soviet rule. In time the NEP would destroy the economic basis for these revolts, and the Cheka and its successors would eliminate the regime's remaining political opponents. The Revolution had in effect devoured its children, leaving the Communist Party free to transform the Soviet state in the manner of its choosing (see also Sailors in 1917; Navy in World War I).

                                                                        J. Dane Hartgrove

Bibliography

Avrich, Paul. Kronstadt, 1921. 1970
Getzler, Israel. Kronstadt, 1917–1921. 1983.
Mawdsley, Evan. The Russian Revolution and the Baltic Fleet. 1978.
Pravda o Kronshtadte. 1921.
Pukhov, A. S. Kronshtadtskii miatezh v 1921 g. 1931.
Saul, Norman E. Sailors in Revolt. 1978.
Semanov, S. N. Likvidatsiia antisovetskogo kronshtadtskogo miatezha 1921 goda. 1973.
Sivkov, P. Z. Kronshtadt, Stranitsy revoliutsionnoi istorii. 1972.

Krupskaia, Nadezhda Konstantinova (1869–1939; pseudonyms, Artamanova, Frei, Gallilei, Katia, Minoga, Onegina, Ryba, Rybkina, Sharko, Sablina). Krupskaia was V. I. Lenin's* wife and also played an important role in her own right in the Soviet government and in Soviet education.

Krupskaia was born in St. Petersburg into a poor gentry family. Her mother was a governess, and her father was a military officer with some radical sentiments. Her father left the military after some legal training for a career in the civil service and became chief of the Grojec district in Warsaw Province in Poland. In 1875 he was tried on vague charges and demoted in grade. Although he won an appeal against that decision in 1880, his success did not restore his now-blunted career. Her mother was a teacher and a writer of children's poetry in Polish. Krupskaia's father died when she was fourteen and the family had difficulty trying to make ends meet. Somehow she managed to finish her education at the prestigious Obolenskii Female Gymnasium from 1881 to 1887 and, after teaching at that school until 1891, went on to teach evening classes to workers at the so-called Evening Sunday School, eventually becoming director of that school's evening programs. She probably became a Marxist in the spring of 1890 when she began to read his books. She joined the Union of Struggle for the Emancipation of the Working Class and in 1894 met Lenin. Both of them were arrested, Lenin in December 1895 and Krupskaia in August 1896. In January 1897 Lenin was sent to Shushenskoe Village in southern Siberia, and Krupskaia learned in November 1896 that she would soon be sentenced to three years in northern Siberia. In January 1897 Lenin asked her to join him, and by March the authorities had agreed to that idea providing they were married as soon as she arrived. In April 1898 Krupskaia and her mother began the long journey from St. Petersburg to Shushenskoe Village.

Although it is clear that the two loved each other, in many ways the marriage followed the conventions at that time of a revolutionary partnership. As Krupskaia herself describes it, "Krupskaia was not only Lenin's wife, but also his collaborator in every circumstance, and especially during her years of exile" (Haupt and Marie 1974, p. 147). In exile she became secretary to the Bolshevik newspaper *Iskra*. In 1905 she became secretary to the party Central Committee (*see* Central Committee of the Russian Communist Party [Bolshevik]). She also wrote a number of articles on the theory of education and a book published in 1915, *Public Education and Democracy*. In 1910 she began to suffer from a thyroid condition that was later complicated by heart trouble.

After the October Seizure of Power* Krupskaia became chairman of the Central Committee for Political Education in 1920 and chairman of the Scientific Methods Section of the State Academic Council of the Commissariat of Enlightenment*, where she played a significant role in the development of education in collaboration with A. V. Lunacharskii*. With Lenin's stroke in May 1922 she had to withdraw temporarily from administrative work to nurse her husband. She attempted to mediate between the ailing Lenin and other Bolshevik (*see* Russian

Social Democratic Workers' Party [Bolshevik]) leaders. One of her confrontations with I. V. Stalin* led to Lenin's harsh criticism of Stalin in his so-called "Last Testament" (*see* Lenin, Vladimir Il'ich) on January 4, 1923. Krupskaia said that she wanted to read that testament at the Thirteenth Party Congress after Lenin's death but that the Central Committee* rejected her proposal by a vote of twenty to ten.

Although she finally spoke out against Stalin at the Fourteenth Party Congress in December 1925, by 1926–1927 they had come to terms, and she joined him in attacking G. I. Zinoviev* and L. B. Kamenev*. There is evidence that Stalin threatened to displace her as Lenin's official widow if she did not give her support to him. She served as Deputy Commissar for Education from 1929 to 1939 and as a member of the Central Committee of the Russian Communist Party from 1927 to 1939.

Bibliography

Haupt, Georges, and Marie, Jean Jacques. *Makers of the Russian Revolution*. 1974.
Krupskaia, Nadezhda. *Reminiscences of Lenin*. 1959.
Levidova, S. M., and Pavlovskaia, A. A. *Nadezhda Konstantinova Krupskaia*. 1962.
McNeal, Robert H. *Bride of the Revolution*. 1972.

Krylenko, Nikolai Vasilevich (1885–1938; pseudonym, Abram). Krylenko was a Left Communist leader of the Bolshevik Party (*see* Russian Social Democratic Workers' Party [Bolshevik]) during the Revolution and became a prominent jurist in the new Soviet state. He was born in the village of Bekhteevka in the Smolensk region where his father, a former official, had been sent into exile for participation in the revolutionary activities of students in St. Petersburg in the 1880s. When he was five years old, his family was allowed to move to Smolensk and then to Lublin. In 1909 Krylenko graduated from the Department of History and Philology at St. Petersburg University and in 1914 from the Department of Law at Kharkhov University. Krylenko became a member of the Russian Social Democratic Workers' Party in 1904 and became well known as a student leader and agitator. In 1905 he was active in the workmen's quarters in the Vyborg District. He met V. I. Lenin* at a meeting of the St. Petersburg Committee of which he was a member. In 1906 he was sent into exile, but he soon returned and became a member of the Military Organization of the St. Petersburg Committee of the Russian Social Democratic Workers' Party (Bolshevik). In the spring of 1909 he was allowed to return to St. Petersburg legally and complete his university examinations where he passed with high honors.

He volunteered to complete his military service in 1912 in the Sixty-Ninth Riazan Infantry Regiment, where he rose to the rank of ensign. He continued to do party work in various cities after discharge from the army. In 1913 and in April 1916 he was again conscripted and was sent to the front where he was elected chairman of a regimental revolutionary committee after the February Revolution* and then of a divisional revolutionary committee; finally, in April

1917 he became chairman of the Revolutionary Committee of the Eleventh Army. In May he became a delegate to the Congress of Front Line Soldiers. In Petrograd (formerly St.Petersburg) he became a member of the first All-Russian Central Executive Committee* of Soviets and in June was elected to the Central Bureau of the All-Russian Military Organization under the Central Committee of the Russian Communist Party (Bolshevik)*. In the same month he was arrested by the Provisional Government* and held until August.

During the October Seizure of Power* Krylenko played an important part as a member of the Petrograd Military Revolutionary Committee. He was elected to sit on the first Council of People's Commissars* as a member of the Committee of Military and Naval Affairs with V. A. Antonov-Ovseenko* and P. E. Dybenko*. On November 9, 1917, Krylenko was named Supreme Commander-in-Chief and People's Commissar on Military Affairs, and V. I. Lenin described him as "one of the keenest Bolsheviks and among those closest to the army" (Levytsky 1974, p. 405). Krylenko had to go personally to army headquarters in Ogilev to relieve General N. N. Dukhonin for refusing to take up peace negotiations with the Germans. Krylenko took charge of the troops while L. D. Trotsky conducted the peace negotiations at Brest-Litovsk*.

After the Brest-Litovsk Treaty Krylenko disagreed with Trotsky's military policies and returned to law. He was state prosecutor in many of the important political trials between 1918 and 1931 and became People's Commissar of Justice in the Russian Soviet Federative Socialist Republic in 1931 and People's Commissar of Justice in the Union of Soviet Federated Socialist Republics in 1934. He was also active in a wide variety of other fields, becoming one of the leading radical theorists in Soviet law and a member of the various commissions that codified Soviet law and composed Soviet constitutions. In 1934 Krylenko received the Doctor of Political and Social Sciences degree. He was the author of a number of books on the theory of law and took part in the preparation of the official *History of the Civil War* and the *Great Soviet Encyclopedia*. He taught at various colleges including the Moscow Institute of Soviet Law and was a member of the Institute of Red Professors. He was arrested during the Great Purges, suffering the fate he had so often imposed on others, and died on July 29, 1938, in prison. He has been rehabilitated posthumously.

Bibliography

Levytsky, Boris. *The Stalinist Terror in the Thirties*. 1974.
Medvedev, Roy. *Let History Judge*. 1972.
Simonian, M. *Zhizn' vo imia revoliutsii*. 1962.
Simonov, E. D. *Chelovek mnogikh vershin*. 1969.

Kun, Bela. A Hungarian Communist (*see* Russian Social Democratic Workers' Party [Bolshevik]) leader who led the first Soviet republic outside of Russia.

Bela Kun was born in a Hungarian peasant family in the village of Lele in

Transylvania, Hungary. He attended a Calvinist school and developed a skill in writing. Kun joined the Hungarian Social Democratic Party in 1902 and wrote for various Hungarian socialist newspapers. In 1913 he began to work for the Workers' Insurance Bureau and married. He was conscripted into the army in World War I* and achieved the reserve rank of lieutenant before he was captured in 1916. He was imprisoned in a camp near Tomsk where he began to learn Russian and lead a Marxist study group of Hungarian prisoners despite severe health problems. After the February Revolution* the Tomsk Soviet allowed him to live outside of the camp where he was interned. He was placed in charge of passes for the other prisoners. He began writing for Russian Marxist journals and in that way attracted the attention of the Bolsheviks (*see* Russian.Social Democratic Workers' Party [Bolshevik]). As a result of his political activities Kun was invited to Petrograd after the October Seizure of Power*. K. B. Radek* appointed him to the International Propaganda Department of the Commissariat of Foreign Affairs. In March 1918 he converted his Hungarian study group into the Hungarian Group of the Russian Communist Party.

On November 17, 1918, Kun returned in disguise to Hungary and founded the Hungarian Communist Party. He called for the immediate overthrow of the reigning Karolyi government. He was arrested on February 20, 1918, along with many members of his party for his role in violent demonstrations on behalf of the unemployed. To some extent his brutal treatment by the Hungarian police made him a martyr at a time when the Karolyi government was already unpopular for its unsuccessful wartime leadership. When Karolyi received an ultimatum that he knew he would have to accept even though it was unacceptable to the Hungarian nationalists, he resigned, and a socialist regime was called to power on the assumption that an alliance with Soviet Russia might stave off capitulation to the Entente. The Hungarian Soviet Republic was announced on March 21, 1919, with Kun as Commissar of War. The creation of the Hungarian Soviet Republic was, however, an act of futile desperation, and on August 1, 1919, Entente troops entered Budapest and brought that republic to an end. But Bela Kun escaped to become a hero in the international communist movement, along with future leaders of Hungarian communism such as Mathias Rakosi and Eugene Varga. As the leader of the first non-Russian Soviet republic, Kun became a prominent figure in the Communist International until 1937 when he was arrested during the Great Purges. He is said to have died in prison in 1939 and has been rehabilitated posthumously.

Bibliography

Borkenau, Franz. *World Communism*. 1962.
Kun, Bela. *Uroki proletarskoi revoliutsii v Vengrii*. 1960.
Levytsky, Borys. *The Stalinist Terror in the Thirties*. 1974.
Pastor, Peter. *Hungary between Wilson and Lenin*. 1976.
Tokes, Rudolf L. *Bela Kun and the Hungarian Soviet Republic*. 1967.

Kuusinen, Otto Vil'gel'movich (1881–1964). Kuusinen was a Finnish communist leader who played an important role in the Finnish Revolution (*see* Finland, Revolution in), in the Communist International*, and in the Russian Communist Party (*see* Russian Social Democratic Workers' Party [Bolshevik]).

Kuusinen was born in the Grand Duchy of Finland in Laukaa where his father was a tailor. He graduated from Helsinki University in 1905 with a degree in history and philology and joined the Finnish Social Democratic Party in 1904. During the 1905 Revolution (*see* Nineteen-Five Revolution) Kussinen led a group of Red Guards* in Helsinki. He became a member of the Executive Committee of the Finnish Social Democratic Party in 1909 and edited party journals from 1906 to 1916. When the Finnish Civil War broke out in January 1918, Kuusinen became People's Commissar of Education. When the Revolution failed, he fled to Moscow and took part in the formation of the Finnish Communist Party there in August 1918 and became a member of its Central Committee. In effect, however, he became a permanent resident of Russia and a citizen of the Soviet Union.

Kuusinen took part in the formation of the Communist International and was elected to the Central Committee of the Comintern in 1921. From 1921 to 1939 he was Secretary of the Executive Committee of the Comintern and took part in the work of its various sections while retaining his post as a member of the Central Committee of the Finnish Communist Party. When the Soviet–Finnish Winter War broke out on December 1, 1939, Kuusinen accepted the post of President of the so-called People's Government of Finland, although that government never came to power.

When the Karelo-Finnish Republic was established on March 31, 1940, Kuusinen became chairman of the Presidium of its Supreme Soviet until 1958. In Russia he served as deputy chairman of the Supreme Soviet of the USSR from 1940 to 1958, deputy to the Supreme Soviet of the Russian Soviet Federative Socialist Republic from 1940 to 1958, member of the Central Committee of the Russian Communist Party (Bolshevik)* from 1941 to 1964, member of the Politburo from 1957 to 1964, and secretary of the Central Committee of the Russian Communist Party from 1957 to 1964.

L

Land Committees. On April 21, 1917, the Provisional Government* formally established the institution that was envisaged as the main instrument of its land policy, the land committees. According to the government's decisions, a chief land committee was to be established in Petrograd, individual committees were to be created at the province (*guberniia*) and county (*uezd*) levels throughout the country, and committees were to be established at the district (*volost'*) level where they were considered necessary. Like the government itself, the committees were to be temporary organizations to carry out the government's land policy only until the Constituent Assembly* was convened and brought about a final resolution of the land question.

The broad tasks of the land committees were twofold. They were to collect information on the state of land relations in the areas for which they were responsible, such information being required to provide the Constituent Assembly with the full data it would need to resolve the land question. The land committees were also to deal with the disputes that developed over land matters, although any settlements that the committees brought about were to be of a provisional nature, pending final resolution of the land question by the Constituent Assembly. The land committees thus did not have the power to bring about land redistribution and thereby satisfy the peasants' demands. They were to conduct a holding operation, implementing the government's policy of retaining the status quo in land relations until the Constituent Assembly could meet to formalize a reordering of property relationships in the countryside.

The Chief Land Committee was responsible for supervising the collection and processing of information necessary for future reform and for devising a general plan of land reform for consideration by the Constituent Assembly. The Committee was also to advise the Minister of Agriculture on legislative aspects of the government's land policy.

Membership in the committee was to consist of the Minister of Agriculture and his assistant ministers, a chairman, a business manager, and twenty-five government appointees (most of whom were members of the Constitutional Democratic Party—Cadet*), one representative from each provincial land committee, six representatives from the All-Russian Peasants' Union, six from the All-Russian Soviet of Peasants' Deputies, three from the Provisional Committee of the State Duma (see Duma and Revolution) and the All-Russian Cooperative Union (see The Cooperative Movement, 1917–1921), one representative from each of the eleven political parties (Socialist-Revolutionary Party*, Popular Socialists, Bolsheviks [see Russian Social Democratic Worker's Party (Bolshevik)], Mensheviks [see Russian Social Democratic Workers' Party (Menshevik)], Trudoviks, Cadets, Octobrists [see Guchkov, Aleksandr Ivanovich], Progressive Party, Center Group, Nationalist Party, and Independent Rightist Party), five representatives from the most important scholarly societies, and experts invited by the chairman with an advisory vote. Representatives of government departments were also able to attend with an advisory vote. In August this membership was supplemented by representatives from the Nobles' and Peasants' Land Banks.

The Committee's membership was too large to work as an effective body; altogether it consisted of 161 members and, with "competent persons," more than 200 attended meetings. As a result, an executive committee was formed, and it was this body that handled most of the committee's business. The Chief Land Committee met in full session on only three occasions. The Executive Committee was largely dominated by Right Socialist–Revolutionaries (S–R's) and Cadet agrarian experts. It was a continuing influence on government land policy, in part providing a conservative bureaucratic counter to the Ministry of Agriculture while it was led by V. M. Chernov*.

The provincial and county committees were meant to be of more practical importance than the Chief Land Committee. They were to be responsible for the collection of the information necessary for the eventual land reform, execution of the decisions taken by the central authorities on land matters, supervision of the operation of state-owned properties, regulation of local land relations within the framework of government policies, settlement of disputes, and prevention of the disruption of agricultural production and the destruction of property. Provincial committees were to consist of four members elected by the provincial zemstvo assembly, one by the municipal Duma of the provincial capital, one representative from each district land committee, representatives from the economic sections of the provincial zemstvo board (to a maximum of three), a justice of the circuit court, a justice of the peace, a representative of the minister of agriculture, and experts invited by the chairman with a consultative vote. Membership of the county land committee was to consist of four members elected by the county zemstvo assembly, one from the municipal Duma of the district capital, one from each district committee, a zemstvo agronomist and statistician, a justice of the peace, and experts invited by the chairman with a consultative vote. In June representatives of the corresponding Soviet of Peasants' Deputies and Soviet of Workers' and Soldiers' Deputies were added to each committee, and in August representatives of the Nobles' and Peasants' Land Bank were added.

Unlike province and county committees, district committees did not have to be established in every district. Where they were established, they were formed on the initiative of the local population or the county committee, and their responsibilities were to be defined by the county committee within the limits applying to province and county committees. Where district committees were established, the April 21 decision specified that they were to consist of five full and three alternate members elected by the district *zemstvo*. In the absence of a district *zemstvo,* which was the situation throughout large areas of Russia for most of the life of the Provisional Government, the procedure for electing members was to be determined by the county committee in accordance with local conditions. It is not clear how many government-sponsored land committees were established. The government allocated sufficient funds for only about 25 percent of all of the districts in Russia.

There were a number of problems with the land-committee structure as established by the decision of April 21. A major weakness was the ambiguous nature of the relationship between committees at different levels. Although each level was nominally subordinate to that above it, little effective guidance was given regarding the limits of each committee's jurisdiction. The powers of the district committee were not even defined. Furthermore, there was no adequate principle of accountability in the structure. When lower-level committees chose to ignore and even directly contradict instructions handed down from above, there was little the higher bodies could do to enforce compliance. This lack of clarity in the formal operating principles of the land-committee structure seriously undermined its capacity to act effectively under the chaotic conditions of 1917. Moreover, this ambiguity within the structure was matched by a similar vagueness in the relationship between the land-committee and food-committee structures. Neither of these types of committees could adequately carry out their functions without intruding into the sphere of responsibility of the other, and yet it was not until July that the government attempted to bring to order the relationship between the two structures by specifying more precise guidelines for their action. Even then, areas of uncertainty remained, impeding the efficient conduct of government policy.

The most serious failing of the land committees was their rejection by the peasantry. The land committees were seen by the peasants as urban bodies, situated in the towns, consisting of urban-based people with few close links with the villages, and unresponsive and insensitive to the needs and desires of the peasants as a whole. This charge was clearly of most relevance in the case of the Chief Land Committee and its Executive Committee. These bodies were isolated in the Petrograd bureaucracy, and their members had little intimate knowledge of or sympathy with the agrarian producers. But this view was also relevant to committees at the lower levels. In both the provincial and district committees, links with the villages were usually weak, particularly among those party activists and intellectuals who tended to dominate the proceedings of these bodies. The effect of this alien urban nature of the committees was reinforced by their inability to meet the peasants' demands. They appeared as bodies designed simply to frustrate the peasants' demands for the land. Consequently, the peasants rejected the authority of the land committees, widely refusing to work with or to obey them and thereby undermining their capacity to carry out the functions they were accorded. Moreover, if the committees could not persuade the peasants to comply, they could not gain such compliance through force. From the outset the committees were powerless. In many areas district committees were taken over by the peasants and transformed from government administrative bodies into revolutionary organizations that the peasants used to destroy the established landholding system. In practical terms, the government land committees were ineffectual in 1917.

In the years following the October Seizure of Power* the land committees established under the aegis of the Provisional Government disappeared from the Russian scene. The Chief Land Committee formally merged with the peasants' section of the Third Congress of the Soviet of Workers', Peasants', and Soldiers' Deputies in January 1918 (*see* Soviets [Councils] of Workers', Soldiers', and Peasants' Deputies). The lower-level land committees ceased to exist as discernible entities as power devolved to popular organs rooted among the peasants themselves (*see* Peasants in the Russian Revolution). It was in these peasant, village-based organs that real power rested in the countryside during the post-October years.

Graeme Gill

Bibliography

Gill, Graeme J. *Peasants and Government in the Russian Revolution.* 1979.
Keep, John L. H. *The Russian Revolution: A Study in Mass Mobilization.* 1976.
Lozinskii, Z. *Ekonomicheskaia politika vremennogo pravitel'stva.* 1976.
Pershin, P. N. *Agrarnaia revoliutsiia v Rossii.* Vol. 1. 1966.

Landlords. The landlords or landed aristocracy of Russia provided the most prestigious group of recruits for the right wing in the unfolding drama of the revolutionary year 1917.

Virtually all large landlords in pre-revolutionary Russia were members of the nobility. Peter the Great, in search of a bureaucracy to run his Western-style army and state, universalized and formalized the service nobility. Ownership of an estate depended on fulfilling one's duty to the autocracy. Thus wealth and status were determined not by ownership of land but by service to the emperor. The aristocracy (*dvorianstvo*) was a traditional order of loyal servitors and not a modern social class, especially not a ruling class. The nobility did not control the state. Rather, this highly privileged, legally defined estate of the realm served the autocracy in the new bureaucracy.

By the end of the nineteenth century, the homogeneity of this estate was disintegrating under the impact of the rapid growth of Russian capitalism. Non-noble elements had come to perform many of the bureaucratic tasks previously carried out only by the nobles. At the same time, many nobles, in the wake of the peasant emancipation of 1861, were leaving the land to seek new careers in the cities. Others simply lived off rents. The decline of noble landowning was precipitous. Between the two universal surveys of 1877 and 1905, the *dvorianstvo* lost more than 30 percent of its lands. Although some estates went to merchants, most acreage was sold to peasants whose acute land hunger was exacerbated by enormous population growth during this period.

If Russian capitalism had led to the disintegration of the traditional nobility and sapped the landlords' economic power, it also created opportunities. As industry and cities grew in the 1880s and 1890s, an internal market finally emerged for an agricultural surplus. Noble landlords who were willing to convert their farms to modern methods could provide this surplus and reap sizeable profits. Late in the century, many nobles left state service to return to their estate and make a go of farming. This trend involved a change in self-image. These activist landlords now defined their special positions not in terms of bureaucratic rank but according to productive role. They were becoming a modern social class of agrarian producers.

This shift did not affect the entire *dvorianstvo*. Modernizing farmers were certainly a minority, and even the most agriculturally advanced landlords never abandoned all of the attitudes of the traditional nobility. Yet this new group of independent gentlemen farmers at last gave Russia a true provincial gentry. However, these men entered the world of modern agriculture just as the state was heavily taxing the agrarian sector to finance industrialization. This approach estranged many landlords from the autocracy. They found a highly imprecise political vehicle for their controlled discontent in the semi-autonomous bodies of local government, the *zemstvos* (*see* All-Russian Union of Towns and All-Russian Union of Zemstvos). Formal political activity, however, was anathema to most nobles. They considered any independent organization to be subversive of the traditional organic unity of tsarist society. Politics and parties were for the members of the opposition. Beyond this, any form of political organization outside state control was simply illegal.

The 1905 Revolution (*see* Nineteen-Five Revolution) changed these attitudes overnight. Massive peasant disturbances galvanized conservative landlords into action. They took over the *zemstvos* and turned them into overtly political institutions. At the same time, the tsar had created a parliament (*see* Duma and Revolution) that required landlords to organize themselves in defense of their interests. The obvious form called forth by the Duma was a modern political party, but landlords faced obstacles in the creation of such a party. First, it took time for old attitudes about organization to disappear. Second, the nearly universal suffrage granted in December 1905 swamped the landlords in a sea of peasant votes. Two radical Dumas were elected under this law before the government, led by the new President of the Council of Ministers, Peter Stolypin, dissolved the Duma in 1907 and decreed a new, more restrictive franchise in the hope of creating a more cooperative legislative branch.

The electoral law of June 3, 1907, made it possible for landlords to elect their own representatives to the Duma. Large landowners were given a majority or near majority of the electors in each provincial assembly that actually chose the deputies. Not only were the landlords able to send many of their own members to the Duma, but they also controlled the selection of those deputies who were supposed to come from other social groups, most notably the peasantry and the clergy.

Duma members made formal choices of party affiliation only after they had arrived in St. Petersburgh for the beginning of the Third Duma in the autumn of 1907. Nearly every Duma faction had some large landowners in its ranks, but three groups were actually dominated by the landed gentry and sought in different ways to speak for it. The Union of October 17 or Octobrists (*see* Guchkov, Aleksandr Ivanovich), the Nationalist Party, and the amorphous Duma group of right-wing deputies articulated a broad variety of landlord viewpoints on political as well as economic issues. No single party emerged as the sole representative of the gentry in the prerevolutionary period. Eventually, the organizational successes of the Octobrists and the Nationalists during the Third Duma gave way to splits and impotence in the Fourth Duma (1912–1917).

The Union of October 17 dominated the early days of the Third Duma. With its 154 members, it was the largest parliamentary faction, and it occupied the Center of the lower house. It was flanked on the Left by the Constitutional Democratic Party—Cadet* and on the Right by the group of Moderate Rights who later became the Nationalists. Despite their early success, the Octobrists were riven with dissension, and party discipline was weak. They hardly ever voted unanimously on any question. Their vaguely constitutionalist program never inspired the loyalty of the entire membership, and their once-flourishing local organization quickly began to disintegrate in the early years of the Third Duma. Led by a combination of landed nobles and wealthy merchants, the Union of October was an attempt to reconcile the interests of all large holders of private property, urban and rural, around a set of conservative constitutionalist principles.

Any such group had to cooperate with the state on a program of limited and prudent reform. In the first session of the Duma the Octobrists worked closely with Stolypin. They supported him during the discussions of his agrarian reform and cooperated on a series of military proposals that would later lead Stolypin into difficulties with Tsar Nicholas II* in the spring of 1909. The crisis engendered by the Naval General Staff Bill led Stolypin to disengage himself from the Octobrists. His tacit partnership with the party's leader, Aleksandr Guchkov, evaporated. At the same time, the Octobrists began to lose important local elections, and their provincial organization all but disappeared. They suffered severe losses in the elections to the Fourth Duma (1912), and in the autumn of 1913 the Octobrists split into a minority Left group headed by S. I. Shidlovskii, the president of the Duma. Guchkov's sympathies were on the Left.

Although bourgeois participation, especially among the leadership, was an important element of Octobrist politics, the party's Duma faction was thoroughly dominated by landowning nobles who had gained their first political experiences in the *zemstvos*. The attempt to find a basis of political cooperation between industrial and agrarian property owners was unsuccessful. Moreover, neither wing of the Octobrists was able to maintain support for the government. On the eve of the war, every element of the party had publicly questioned its loyalty to the state, and by 1917 all Octobrists had moved into the opposition.

At the same time that the Octobrist ascendency in the Duma was slipping, a more conservative party of the landed nobility emerged with the coalescence of the Moderate Right and National Groups in the Duma to form the anti-constitutionalist Nationalist Party in the autumn of 1909. With ninety-five members, it was the second largest Duma faction. It would come closer than any other formation to becoming a true modern political party for the provincial landlords. Stolypin was attracted to the new group, which sought to emphasize its concern for the needs of the landlords in the localities. Beginning with the winter of 1910, the Premier embarked on a program of legislation, called the National Campaign, which was designed to advance the interests of the new party. The central element of this campaign was a proposal to place elective *zemstvos* into six western borderland provinces where they did not then exist (Kiev, Podol'e, Volynia, Minsk, Mogilev, and Vitebsk). It was no coincidence that the Nationalists drew most of their deputies from these provinces, and the peculiarities of this region do much to explain the early success and ultimate failure of the Nationalists' attempt to become a true party of the provincial gentry.

Because of the long-standing dominance of Polish landlords in the region, the aristocracy refused to allow elective *zemstvos* in these provinces. Had the franchise requirements of the 1864 law been followed, local government would have been in the hands of a politically untrustworthy element in a sensitive border area. Stolypin and the Nationalists now wanted *zemstvos* with special national curiae to assure Russian dominance. In addition, these provinces, especially the three southwestern provinces of Kiev, Podol'e and Volynia, were sites of highly successful commercial agriculture. The extensive raising of sugar beets was the particular agrarian distinction of the borderlands. Landlords there, Polish and Russian, had long ago made the transition to modern farming methods. This combination of ethnic, economic, and institutional factors made it possible for the Nationalist Party to evolve in the early years along the lines of a modern political party with local and national organizations capable of representing its constituency. Yet these conditions did not exist outside the West, and in other regions the party was weak. The Nationalists' cooperation with Stolypin to obtain the Western Zemstvo Bill represented a novel form of interest politics in the

Russian political scene. In fact, the newness of this approach distressed many more traditional conservatives who then sought to block the proposal.

Stolypin was forced to precipitate a constitutional crisis in March 1911 to get the Western Zemstvo Bill passed. In the process he lost the confidence of Nicholas II*, who hardly mourned when the Premier was assassinated under mysterious circumstances that autumn. Stolypin's death marked the end of Nationalists' ascendancy. Subsequent presidents of the Council of Ministers were far less friendly to them. Although they enjoyed considerable success in the election to the Fourth Duma, the Nationalists soon began to split over the fundamental constitutional issues they had sought to avoid. They believed in the Duma since its existence had led them to organize and thus gain many demands. At the same time they were loyal to the autocracy, which was the original source of their lands and privileges. This contradiction could be resolved only as long as the state cooperated with society's representatives in the Duma. This was the case under Stolypin, but after his government lost its willingness to take the Duma seriously, Nationalist Party members were forced to choose between their conflicting loyalties. Nearly a third of the party had lost faith in the state and was edging toward the opposition on the eve of the war. The split became formal in 1915 when the so-called "Progressive Nationalists," led by Vasilii Shulgin, joined the quasi-constitutionalist Progressive Bloc* in the Duma along with the Octobrists, Constitutional Democrats, and Progressives. At that point the Nationalist Party ceased to have any independent significance in Russian politics.

The right-wing group in the Duma made no pretense of being a political party. Its fifty members maintained the traditional noble mistrust of parties and instead existed as a loosely disciplined group of arch-reactionaries. They had little influence on the Duma's work. Yet their leaders, V. M. Purishkevich and N. E. Markov, were notorious for bombast and parliamentary scandal. By 1914 even these highly conservative groups had become disillusioned with the government. Although they did not join the opposition, the Right chose not to defend the autocracy that was seeking to ignore or destroy the Duma.

Outside the capital, calm had returned to the land. Peasant disturbances subsided and did not return until the end of Revolution. The Stolypin land reform had little direct impact on landlords, who were not forced to give up their lands. Although the decline of gentry landowning continued, it did so at a much slower rate than before 1905. The more capitalistically inclined landlords used this period to improve their practices and reap greater rewards. This advance did not involve any fundamental concessions to the peasantry whose demands for more land rentals remained unfulfilled. As a result of the failure to meet peasant needs, large landholding came to a sudden and complete end with the October Seizure of Power* in 1917.

Robert Edelman

Bibliography

Anfimov, A. M. *Krupnoe pomeshchich'e khoziaistvo, Evropeiskoi Rossii.* 1968.
Avrekh, A. Ia. *Stolypin i tret'ia duma i sverzhenie tsarizma v Rossii.* 1968.

Chermenskii, E. D. *IVia Gosudarstvennaia duma i sverzhenie tsarizma v Rossii*. 1976.
Diakin, V. S. *Samoderzhavie, burzhuaziia i dvorianstvo v 1907–11 gg*. 1978.
Edelman, Robert. *Gentry Politics on the Eve of the Russian Revolution*. 1980.
Hosking, Geoffrey. *The Russian Constitutional Experiment*. 1973.
Manning, Roberta. *The Russian Gentry and the Crisis of the Old Order*. 1982.
Robinson, Geroid. *Rural Russia under the Old Regime*. 1932.
Pershin, Iu. B. *Agrarnaia revoliutsiia v Rossiia*. 2 vols. 1966.

Latvia and the Russian Revolution. Although representing only a small part of the Russian Empire, Latvia had an important influence on the outcome of the Revolution in Russia and would experience some of the effects of that Revolution as well.

The year 1917 in Latvia was a Bolshevik (*see* Russian Social Democratic Workers' Party [Bolshevik]) year. In the Latvian situation we cannot fully speak of Dual Power*. The Bolsheviks had an edge there from the very beginning, which they enlarged upon as the year progressed. One can say without exaggeration that the Bolsheviks enjoyed a dominating position by June 1917, a position that was confirmed by a series of city, district, and provincial elections during the autumn, when the Bolsheviks won in most cases by majorities over 60 percent. The reasons for the precipitous rise in Bolshevik power were as follows: (1) the control of the Riga Soviet and the Soviet of Landless Peasants in the countryside, which were theirs from the first days of their existence in March 1917; (2) the control of the Latvian Riflemen (*Strelki*) Soviet by May 17; (3) the victory in the elections of the Vidzeme provincial Land Council, which gave them unchallengeable control of that body by October 1917; (4) the establishment of the Iskolat Republic in November 1917, which (except for the Council of People's Commissars* in Petrograd) was the only such territorial Bolshevik government in the former Russian Empire; and (5) the entrance of two Latvian Strelki formations (the Sixth Tukums Regiment and the Special Smolnyi Battalion) into Petrograd in November 1917.

The Riga Soviet was almost completely dominated by Bolsheviks from the beginning of March, and by early summer the Soviet had emerged as the main decision-making organ of the city. The early Bolshevik advantage derived from the fact that by 1917 the Bolsheviks were in control of the Latvian Social Democratic Party and because by 1917 there were no major non-Bolshevik radical parties, such as the Socialist-Revolutionary Party* in Russia, left in Latvia. During the early stages of the Revolution, the main competitor to the Riga Soviet was the Riga Council of Organizations, which in some respects paralleled the Petrograd Soviet*, the main difference being that the liberals were also full participants in the Council. The Council of Organizations was comprised of representatives of all social and political organizations; the Riga Soviet from the beginning consisted only of representatives from workers' organizations. In Riga, as in Latvia at large, the Bolsheviks pursued a two-pronged policy: enlarging the power of the soviets and aiming to obtain legitimacy through elections. Thus the Bolsheviks threw the full force of their influence into resuscitating the Riga Council (dome), the prerevolutionary elected governing body of the city. The elections to the Riga Council took place on August 13. The Latvian Bolsheviks, owing to the numerous non-Latvian minorities in the city, obtained only 40 percent, not a full majority but enough to be in a position to determine the future of the city. The Bolsheviks' success in Riga was spoiled by the German offensive and the fall of Riga on August 20, 1917.

In Vidzeme (Livonia), Bolshevik ascendancy was even more pronounced, although it did take longer. The first to organize in Vidzeme were the non-Bolshevik forces. On March 12, 1917, delegates from all major Vidzeme social and political organizations convened in Valmiera and created the Provisional Vidzeme Land Council, to be legitimized by future elections. Soon thereafter, the Bolsheviks called the Congress of Landless Peasants, which in a stormy three-day session elected the Vidzeme Council of Landless Peasantry. For a number of weeks thereafter, a dispute between the Provisional Vidzeme Land Council and the Council of Landless Peasantry took place. The conflict was resolved by merging the two councils, which in effect gave the Bolsheviks a slight edge. From there on, non-Bolshevik plans and designs in Vidzeme were checkmated. In the election of August 20 that was to choose the permanent Vidzeme Land Council, the Bolsheviks won by a majority of 65 to 70 percent.

From the perspective of the history of Russia and that of the world, a most important development took place in the soviet and the soviets of the Latvian Strelki. The Strelki were Latvian formations (nine regiments with about 35,000 soldiers that came into existence in 1915 after the Germans advanced into Kurland. Contrary to the advice of the Baltic Germans, who, remembering the 1905 Revolution (*see* Nineteen-Five Revolution), feared armed Latvians, the Russian military command permitted the organization of these Latvian units. Until 1917 the Strelki units performed in an exemplary fashion on the Riga front; thereafter their contribution was in the service of the Bolshevik cause, at first in Petrograd in 1917 (*see* October Seizure of Power*) and then on all the Civil War (*see* Civil War in Russia) fronts throughout Russia until the end of the Civil War. Already at the First Congress of the Latvian Strelki Soviet of Deputies, March 26–29, Bolshevik voices were in strong evidence. The Bolsheviks completely dominated the Second Congress of the Latvian Strelki Soviet of Deputies, May 12–17. The Executive Committee (Iskolastrel) that the congress elected consisted only of Bolsheviks, and it passed a resolution that was the most thorough condemnation of the Provisional Government* seen anywhere in the Russian Empire, except for Bolshevik Party resolutions. Thereafter, the Latvian Strelki remained under Bolshevik leadership.

At the same time that the Bolsheviks were pursuing their goals through the electoral process with great success, they were also centralizing and consolidating their power through the soviets. On July 29–30 deputies from all of Latvia's soviets gathered in Riga to elect the Iskolat—the highest organ of Latvia's soviets. After the October Seizure of Power, the Iskolat emerged as the governing body in the unoccupied part of Latvia, nullifying the elected Land Council of Vidzeme. In effect, the Izkolat became the Commissariat of the First Latvian Soviet Republic.

If the Bolsheviks obtained control over Latvia's administrative structure easily, the situation in the Russian Twelfth Army, which was mainly stationed in Latvia, was more complicated. Socialist–Revolutionaries and Mensheviks (*see* Russian Workers' Social Democratic Party [Menshevik]) were in control of the Executive Committee (Iskosol) of the Twelfth Army Soviet of Soldiers' Deputies from the beginning of the Revolution, and they were able to resist calls for reelection until October. It was the task of the Latvian Social Democrats and the Strelki political leadership to spearhead the Bolshevik takeover of the Iskosol. The Latvian Strelki regiments served as the nucleus in organizing the Leftist Bloc of the Twelfth Army, the purpose of which was to unify the Bolsheviks forces in the army. By October the network of the Bloc extended to almost all regiments of the Twelfth Army, and in a stormy session of October 28 the Twelfth Army Soviet of Soldiers' Deputies split, allowing the Leftist Bloc to establish its own Iskosol dominated by Bolsheviks.

During the autumn of 1917 the Latvian Strelki regiments were groomed for service in the Bolshevik insurrection. The regiments were purged of officers hostile to Bolshevism, and strict party and commissar control was established within the regiments. On October 16 on orders from Lenin, V. A. Antonov-Ovseenko* traveled to Valka to meet with the Latvian party and Strelki leadership to coordinate activities in Petrograd with those in the region of the northern front. The Latvian task was to prevent any shipment of troops loyal to A. F. Kerensky* from the northern front to Petrograd and to prepare immediate deployment of two Latvian regiments to Petrograd. The first assignment the regiments carried out with dispatch, but in the fulfillment of the second, delays arose due to the logistics of shipping the Strelki to Petrograd. It was only on November 25 that the Sixth Tukums Latvian Strelki Regiment arrived in Petrograd to perform a variety of guard and military tasks that included the guarding of the Tauride Palace, the meeting place of the Constituent Assembly* to come. On the following day, November 26, a specially selected Strelki formation that came to be known as the Smolnyi Battalion arrived in Petrograd and was quartered on the third floor of the Smolnyi Institute to perform guard duties in Smolnyi as well as in the city. Many of the Strelki serving in the Smolnyi Battalion came to be involved with security work for the new government, frequently performing tasks for the Cheka (*see* All-Russian Extraordinary Commission for Combatting Counterrevolution and Sabotage). These two Latvian Strelki formations were the first to cross the ethnic frontier of Latvia and enter into the struggle for Bolshevism on Russian soil. By March 1918 the rest of the Latvian Strelki regiments were in Russia, fighting Bolshevik battles on a variety of Civil War fronts.

As the Bolsheviks were reaping success in Latvia during 1917, counterforces against Bolshevism were also developing. The non-Bolshevik forces—the liberals and socialists—were to a large degree hampered by their disagreement with the Provisional Government. The main goal of the Latvian Liberals in 1917 was to obtain Latvia's autonomy within the community of autonomous states of federative Russia. Since the Provisional Government was not receptive to an ethnic partitioning of Russia, the attention of Latvian liberals began to shift from Petrograd to Kiev, to the activities of the Ukrainian Rada (*see* Ukraine, Revolution in). From the Latvian viewpoint it is very likely that, had it not been for the October Seizure of Power in Russia, a new federative state with Kiev as its capital would have emerged to replace the Russian Empire.

Although in 1917 it was not anticipated that Latvia should emerge as an independent country after the Revolution, the liberal, political, and ideological activities of 1917—for example, establishing a structure of political parties—helped Latvians to prepare for that alternative. During 1918 Latvia was under German occupation, but then in late 1918 two things happened: on November 18 the Latvian liberals, including the democratically inclined members of the Latvian Social Democratic Party, proclaimed the existence of an independent and democratic Latvia. On December 17, 1918, the Latvian Bolsheviks, under the leadership of P. I. Stuchka*, proclaimed Latvia a Soviet republic. By March 1919 the Bolshevik government was almost in full control of Latvia. The democratic liberal forces, with their backs against the sea, clung to Liepaja (Libau) and a narrow sliver of Kurland along the western littoral. In May 1919 the war effort of the Bolshevik forces collapsed, and the Soviet-backed army threatened the eastern frontier of Latvia. Thereafter, Latvia became an independent democratic republic.

The Bolshevik retreat from Latvia was mandated in part because of a deteriorating military position on all Civil War fronts and in part because by the beginning of 1919 the Latvian liberals and Social Democrats were able to form an anti-Bolshevik coalition, comprising the majority of the population. The cruelty and ineptitude of the Stuchka government that ruled Riga from January to May 1919 also greatly contributed to the Bolshevik collapse. The Latvian Bolsheviks, about 100,000 strong, retreated to Soviet Russia, where they survived as a culturally vigorous community until the Great Purges in 1937.

Andrew Ezergailis

Bibliography

Ezergailis, Andrew. *The 1917 Revolution in Latvia*. 1974.
Ezergailis, Andrew. *The Latvian Impact on the Bolshevik Revolution*. 1983.
Germanis, Uldis. *Oberst Vacietis un die Lettischen Schutzen im Weltkrieg und in der Oktoberrevolution*. 1974.
Kaimin', Ia. *Latyshskie Strelki v borbe za pobedu oktiabr' skoi revoliutsii*. 1961.
Krastin', Ia. *Istoriia Latyshskikh Strelkov*. 1915–1920.
Toman, B.ˆA. *Za svobodniiu Rossiiu, za svobodnuiu Latviia*. 1975.
Vacietis, Jukums. *Latviesu Strelnieku Vesturiska Nozime*. 2 vols. 1922–1924.

Left Communism. The left wing of the Russian Social Democratic Workers' Party (Bolshevik)* that opposed Lenin on several issues during the Revolution and Civil War in Russia*. From the beginning the Bolshevik movement was a union of opposites. As Robert Daniels pointed out in his book *The Conscience of the Revolution*, Left Communism represented one of the two major tendencies within the Bolshevik movement from its inception, and it lasted for the first decade of the history of the Soviet Union.

The Left faction in Bolshevism was drawn to Lenin and his movement because it appeared to be an action-oriented radical movement that would not waver or compromise. The view of politics in the movement was utopian and apocalyptic, with a preference for violence over compromise. Despite signs of intransigence on many issues, there remained a fairly consistent hard core of members who provided the Bolsheviks with much of their zeal and popularity during the first decade of Soviet rule. The right wing consisted of those who followed Lenin because of his strong sense of organization and structure. They saw in Lenin a strong leader who would not yield to the shifting whims of the masses. After the Bolsheviks boycotted the election to the First Duma (*see* Duma and Revolution) they discovered that the boycott was a mistake, but the Bolshevik Left called for a continued boycott of all elections. Lenin sided with the Mensheviks (*see* Russian Social Democratic Workers' Party [Menshevik]) against his own Left faction on the question of participation in the next round of Duma elections. In 1907 the boycott issue was raised again at a conference of the Russian Social Democratic Workers' Party in Finland, and eight out of nine of the Bolsheviks attending voted for boycott. Lenin was the one Bolshevik delegate voting against. Standing with Lenin against the Bolshevik Left were L. B. Kamenev*, G. I. Zinoviev*, and A. I. Rykov*. Among those who voted for the boycott were future Soviet leaders such as A. V. Lunacharskii* and A. S. Bubnov*. In 1909 leftists such as A. A. Bogdanov, Maxim Gorky (*see* Peshkov, A.M.), Lunacharskii, and G. A. Aleksinskii began leaning toward the political theory of Otzovism–Ultimatism and the philosophy of empiriocriticism that Lenin opposed. In debate, some leftists, like Bogdanov and the future Soviet leader L. B. Krasin*, left to form their own faction, which became known as Vperedists after their journal *Vpered* (*Forward*). Although Lenin needed the vision and energy of the Left, he insisted that it overcome its tendency to be too involved in theoretical issues and to be lacking in party discipline and willingness to conduct more mundane tasks associated with political activity. He had the opposite problem on the Right with the so-called conciliationists who wanted to compromise the Bolshevik position in order to return the Mensheviks to the fold and restore the unity of the Russian Marxists. Among the conciliationists were A. I. Rykov*, V. P. Nogin*, and A. L. Lozovskii.

On the eve of World War I* there were two major clusters of Internationalists*, those who gathered around Lenin and those who followed L. D. Trotsky* and his Interdistrict Committee* and their journal *Nashe slovo* (*Our Word*). The latter groups shared Lenin's views on the war but opposed him on organizational matters. They included Trotsky, D. Z. Manuilskii, V. A. Antonov-Ovseenko*, Lunacharskii, M. N. Pokrovskii*, D. B. Riazanov, G. V. Chicherin*, A. M. Kollontai*, M. S. Uritskii*, I. M. Maiskii, A. A. Ioffe, G. Ia. Sokolnikov*, K. Radek*, Lozovskii, and many Menshevik–Internationalists (*see* Russian Social Democratic Workers' Party [Menshevik]). When Lenin espoused the use of national self-determination as a slogan to mobilize those feeling against capitalist government, N. I. Bukharin*, G. L. Piatakov, and F. E. Dzerzhinskii* opposed him, stating that it was contrary to the spirit of revolutionary internationalism.

During 1917 Lenin assumed a leftist revolutionary position, and his opposition came mostly from the Right, first on the issue of setting a date for the October Seizure of Power* (which was opposed by the Right), and second on the issue of admitting other parties to the Council of People's Commissars* (which was favored by the Right). But Lenin's first serious confrontation with his own Left faction came after the Bolshevik Revolution when discussion began in January 1918 on the issue of peace negotiations with Germany at Brest-Litovsk*. Bukharin became the leader of the extreme Left opposing the negotiations and calling for guerilla resistance against the Germans while stirring up the international revolutionary movement. On February 17, 1918 the Germans announced that they were renewing their advance into Russia. The Bolshevik Central Committee (see Central Committee of the Russian Communist Party [Bolshevik])* did not support Bukharin's appeal for revolutionary war but also did not support Lenin's request for peace at any price. Trotsky voted with the extreme Left to allow the Germans to discredit themselves in the eyes of their own workers by renewing their war on the first workers' state in the history of the world. On the next day the seriousness of the German advance came home to the Central Committee, and Trotsky supported Lenin's position on peace at any price. When the German peace terms arrived, Lenin had to threaten to resign in order to persuade the Left to support it.

The second major confrontation between Lenin and the Left faction in his own party came with the onset of the Civil War on the issue of workers' control of industry. Although a decree of November 14, 1917, recognized workers' control over industry, which in most cases was already in existence at that time, Lenin and many Bolsheviks believed that so radical a change in the management of the economy so soon was unthinkable as a practical measure. At first Lenin leaned toward the continued use of bourgeois specialists—in many cases they were the former owners and managers—kept under surveillance by workers' control, in effect a system of state capitalism. The Left Communists wanted to finish the nationalization of industry being carried out by the factory committees and some national body that would represent all of the local organs of workers' control. It was to satisfy this wish that the Supreme Council of the National Economy* was set up in 1917. Although the Left Communists controlled the Supreme Council of the National Economy in the beginning, the Left became increasingly dissatisfied with Lenin's attempt to restore labor discipline and to restore the authority of the bourgeois specialists (*spetsy*).

In March 1918, at the time of the Brest-Litovsk* crisis, the leftist members of the Supreme Council of the National Economy were removed and replaced with three moderates, Rykov, V. P. Miliutin, and Iu. Larin. The result was an immediate call for a stricter worker discipline and an end to workers' control in many areas. The Left faction, the same group that attacked Lenin on the Brest-Litovsk issue, now mobilized against him on workers' control in a Central Committee meeting in April. It even started a new journal, *Kommunist (Communist)*, with Bukharin, Radek, N. Osinskii*, and V. P. Smirnov playing an active role. The ratification of the Brest-Litovsk Treaty by the Fourth Extraordinary Congress of Soviets in March 1918 built momentum behind Lenin for his solution to all other problems. He was loud and vocal in his denunciation of the Left Opposition, and they were made to feel that it was a violation of party spirit that threatened the survival of the party itself. They abstained from voting in the congress and gave up their campaign to change the party's mind on these two issues. They dallied with the Left Socialist–Revolutionaries (*see* Left Socialist-Revolutionary Party), who shared their opposition to the Treaty of Brest-Litovsk, and there is some evidence that this coalition planned to remove Lenin for a few days, place Piatakov at the head of the Council of People's Commissars in which Left Socialist–Revolutionaries and Left Communists would now have a majority, and continue the war with Germany. But the Left Communists abandoned the effort and left the Socialist–Revolutionaries to conduct their own abortive coup d'état in July 1918 (*see* Left Socialist–Revolutionary Party).

The issue of workers' control did not die an easy death, however. It would reappear with Trotsky's efforts to militarize labor in 1920. The Left faction had come along with the centralization of the period of War Communism* and now found itself in support of Lenin's proposals for a continuation of state control over industry, although with more emphasis on persuasion than Trotsky had asked. Bukharin, Radek, Dzerzhinskii, N. N. Krestinsky, and L. P. Serebriakov—all former leftists—thus found themselves supporting Lenin against the Workers' Opposition (*see* Kollontai, Aleksandra Mikhailovna; Shliapnikov, Aleksandr Gavrilovich) and against Trotsky. In the end at the Tenth Party Congress in March 1921, Bukharin and his group joined Trotsky in calling for the governmentalizing of unions, merging the proletarian unions with the proletarian state.

This situation left Lenin with two factions, the ultra-left calling for a decentralized self-government economy, and the moderate Left allied to Trotsky, calling for a continuation of War Communism and centralized economic control, at least until the temporary problems of reconstructing an economy from the ravages of war had been achieved. Once again Lenin, with the help of the Petrograd organization, was able to wage a stubborn struggle against the two Left factions and win by the time of the Tenth Party Congress on March 8, 1921. It was fortunate that the two Left factions were as much at odds with each other as they were with him.

350 LEFT SOCIALIST-REVOLUTIONARY PARTY

The Kronstadt Revolt (*see* Kronstadt, 1917–1921) of March 2, 1921, undoubtedly also helped to discredit the extreme Left within the party and make all too apparent the need for party unity. Unity was the order of the day at the Tenth Congress, and both the Workers' Opposition and the Democratic Centralists* were roundly condemned. This trend also had its effect on the balance of power between the Left and the Right in the party leadership, with the latter gaining over the former. In the end it would be I. V. Stalin* who would most benefit, since the weakening of the Left would make it easier to mobilize the Right against Trotsky's claims to Lenin's mantle after Lenin's death and, finally, to liquidate most Left Communists altogether during the Great Purges of the 1930s. The weakening of the Left would also spell the end of the leftist dream of a self-governing workers' democracy, a dream that had inspired many of the followers of Lenin in October 1917 (*see* Bukharin, Nikolai Ivanovich).

Bibliography

Bagaev, B. F. *Bor'ba s 'levymi kommunistami'' v mestnym partiinykh organizatsiiakh nakanune VII s''ezda partii.* 1961.
Daniels, Robert. *The Conscience of the Revolution.* 1969.
Schapiro, Leonard. *The Origin of the Communist Autocracy.* 1965.

Left Socialist-Revolutionary Party. The Left Socialist-Revolutionary Party was that faction in the Socialist-Revolutionary Party that left to form its own independent movement and joined in the October Seizure of Power* with the Bolsheviks (*see* Russian Social Democratic Workers' Party [Bolshevik]) and became members of the Council of Peoples' Commissars* until the Treaty of Brest-Litovsk* in March 1918. A Left Socialist-Revolutionary faction existed in the party as early as 1904 but did not become a separate party until November 1917. In 1904 the left wing of the Socialist-Revolutionary Party took the form of a group that placed its emphasis on terror as the chief weapon of political struggle with the Tsarist government. In 1906 a similar group separated from the party and formed a Union of Socialist-Revolutionary maximalists. In 1908 another such leftist group separated from the party and published its own journal, *Revoliutsionnaia mysl'* (*Revolutionary Thought*).

The Left Socialist-Revolutionary Party, however, originated under a somewhat different set of circumstances and issues that had more to do with the party's attitude toward World War I* than any other factor. With the coming of World War I the majority of members of the Socialist-Revolutionary Party adopted a "Defensist" (*see* Defensism) position in relation to the war at the Zimmerwald Conference. The minority took an "Internationalist"* position (*see* World War I), calling opposition to the war effort and to support for the army or the government during the war. During the time of the February Revolution* one Socialist–Revolutionary Internationalist, P. A. Aleksandrovich, issued an appeal for soldiers and workers to form a provisional revolutionary government under the Soviets to achieve land and freedom.

The split in the ranks of the Socialist-Revolutionary Party would become more pronounced at the Third Congress of the Socialist-Revolutionary Party in May 1917, and the issue was once again the war. B. D. Kamkov proposed an antiwar resolution, which was not carried, and A. R. Gots* proposed a "Defensist" resolution, which passed. Only one member of the Left faction was elected to the Central Committee.

The events that precipitated the eventual schism in the Socialist-Revolutionary Party were all associated with the war. When the June offensive, 1917 (*see* Army of Imperial Russia in World War I) failed in that effort, the Left faction in the Socialist-Revolutionary Party challenged the Defensist posture of the Central Committee. The Left also opposed the reintroduction of the death penalty for desertion.

From the beginning the left wing opposed the entry of the party into the coalition cabinets of the Provisional Government*. At the Democratic Conference* in September it voted with the Bolsheviks against a continuation of the coalition, and it left the Democratic Council* in protest against the position of its own Central Committee.

When the Military Revolutionary Committee of the Petrograd Soviet* (*see* October Seizure of Power) was formed, many Left Socialist–Revolutionaries joined and took part in the coup d'état. When the Mensheviks (*see* Russian Social Democratic Workers' Party [Menshevik]) and Right Socialist–Revolutionaries left the Second All-Russian Congress of Soviets in protest against the October Seizure of Power, the Left Socialist–Revolutionaries remained behind. They did not, however, seek a coalition with the Bolsheviks but rather sought an all-socialist cabinet that would include all of the non-Bolshevik socialists.

The cause of the final split between the Left Socialist–Revolutionaries and their mother organization was the imprudent decision of the Socialist-Revolutionary Central Committee on October 26, 1917 to expel all of its members who had remained behind at the Second All-Russian Congress of Soviets. The Left Socialist–Revolutionaries countered by holding their own congress from November 19 to 28, 1917, which created a separate party.

When the Constituent Assembly*, the only freely elected representative body in the history of Russia, met for one day in January 1918, its fate was already preordained. Although the Left Socialist-Revolutionaries were not listed as a separate party, they had become one, and there was some validity, therefore, to V. I. Lenin's claim that the weight of public opinion had changed since the original electoral lists were drawn up for the Constituent Assembly. In particular, he argued that Left Socialist-Revolutionary representation (about forty delegates) was far short of its actual popularity, since it had not been able to appear on the ballot as a separate party. The Left Socialist–Revolutionaries joined with the Bolsheviks in the All-Russian Congress of Soviets' Central Executive Committee to approve the dissolution of the Constituent Assembly. One Left Socialist-Revolutionary delegate, A. L. Kolegaev, had been appointed commissar of agriculture on November 17, and on December 9 six others were appointed to the

Council of People's Commissars. There is no doubt that at that time the new Soviet government could give some credibility to its claim that the Soviet government included two political movements that represented the interests of the peasants and the workers.

The basis for the coalition government had been at least, in part, the Bolshevik acceptance of the basic Socialist-Revolutionary position on its Decree on Land (*see* Agrarian Policy 1917–1921). But the Bolsheviks and Left Socialist-Revolutionaries began to move apart in February 1918 on the issue of the Brest-Litovsk Treaty. The Left Socialist-Revolutionary Party was completely opposed to the terms of the treaty and on March 19, 1918, withdrew its representatives from the Council of People's Commissars. Although it left the Council of People's Commissars in March, individual Left Socialist–Revolutionaries remained in important posts in the Soviet government, like the Central Executive Committee. From those positions it continued to criticize the government's policy on agriculture, such as the creation of the Committee of Poor Peasants in June 1918. The Second Congress of the Left Socialist-Revolutionary Party in April 1918 approved the decision to leave the coalition. At the Fifth All-Russian Congress of Soviets on July 4, 1918, 470 Left Socialist–Revolutionaries argued for two hours with 868 Bolsheviks. The next day they walked out of the congress.

It was the so-called July uprising that led to an irreconcilable rift between the Bolsheviks and the Left Socialist–Revolutionaries. On June 24, 1918, the Left Socialist–Revolutionaries had decided to oppose the Brest-Litovsk Treaty by using terror against the German delegation. This strategy was approved by the Third Party Congress meeting in Moscow from June 28 to July 1. A group of Left Socialist leaders headed by Maria Spiridonova decided to assassinate the German ambassador, Count Mirbach, in collaboration with some party members who were in the Cheka (*see* the All-Russian Extraordinary Commission for Combatting Counterrevolution and Sabotage). They hoped the action would cause Germany to resume the war and force the hand of the Soviet government. Count Mirbach was assassinated on July 6, and a group of Left Socialist–Revolutionaries took over Cheka headquarters, arresting the head of the Cheka, F. E. Dzerzhinskii*. The Left Communists had originally expressed interest in the plot, but they had failed to consummate the alliance before the assassination took place.

Lenin put N. I. Podvoiskii* (Commander of the Supreme Military Inspectorate) and I. I. Vatsetis (chief of the Latvian Sharpshooters, or Strelki) in charge of the suppression of the rebellion. According to Podvoiskii's calculations, about 1,800 men took part in the insurrection and had in their possession six to eight artillery pieces and four armored cars. The rebellion was put down in a few hours. Thirteen members of the Cheka were executed, but Spiridonova was only imprisoned and later released. Sympathetic revolutionary actions occurred on the eastern front but were easily put down.

For the Bolsheviks it was a twofold triumph. They had met the first armed challenge to their supremacy in the Soviet government, and they had successfully rid themselves of their only remaining rivals for political power. Most scholars believe that the Left Socialist–Revolutionaries merely wanted to change the policies of the Soviet government, not overthrow it, although there was some talk of arresting Lenin and placing someone else in charge of the government for a few days. For the Left Socialist–Revolutionaries the action marked the end of their participation in government as an independent party. The party was expelled from the Congress of Soviets and its publications banned. Individual members either joined the Bolshevik party or fled abroad. It thus marked the beginning of the Russian Communist Party's monopoly of power in the Soviet government.

Bibliography

Gusev, K. V. *Krakh partii levykh eserov.* 1963.
———. *Partiia eserov ot melkoburzhuaznogo revoliutsionarizma i kontrrevoliutsii.* 1975.
Radkey, Oliver. *The Agrarian Foes of Bolshevism.* 1958.
———. *The Sickle Under the Hammer.* 1963.
Schapiro, L. *The Origins of the Communist Autocracy.* 1955.
Steinberg, I. *Spiridonova.* 1935.

Lenin, Vladimir Il'ich (April 10, 1870–January 21, 1924); true name, Ul'ianov. Lenin was the undisputed leader of the Bolshevik Party (*see* Russian Social Democratic Workers' Party [Bolshevik]) during the October Seizure of Power* and the first head of the Soviet state as Chairman of the Council of Peoples' Commissars* (Sovnarkom), a post that was described in the West as Prime Minister of Russia. Lenin was founder of the Russian Communist Party, which was known as the Russian Social Democratic Workers' Party (Bolshevik) from 1903 to 1918.

Lenin was born in the city of Simbirsk (called Ulianovsk after 1924) in the middle Volga region. His father, Il'ia Nikolaevich Ul'ianov (1831–1886), although of peasant origin, became Director of Public Education in Simbirsk Province (1869–1886) and earned the status of hereditary nobleman through his public service. His mother, Maria Alexandrova Ul'ianova (nee Blank) (1835–1916), was the daughter of a German-born doctor who had also acquired aristocratic status through public service. Lenin had a comfortable childhood and in 1879 entered the Simbirsk gymnasium, where he excelled as a student. In 1887 Lenin's older brother, Alexander, was executed for being part of an unsuccessful Populist (*see* Socialist-Revolutionary Party) plot against Tsar Alexander III. That fall Lenin entered the University of Kazan, but he was expelled at the end of the year for taking part in a student demonstration. While in Kazan Lenin became acquainted with members of both the Populist and Marxist movements. In 1889 the Ul'ianov family moved to Samara Province where they lived until 1893. In 1889 at the age of nineteen Lenin became interested in Marx after reading *Das Kapital* and G. V. Plekhanov's* *Our Differences.* In 1890 Lenin received permission to take law examinations at St. Petersburg University as an external student. He received a Diploma First Class (honors degree) in law in 1891.

Lenin indicated in his own writing that he did not join a Marxist circle until 1893 at the earliest, when he moved to St. Petersburg, ostensibly to practice in the office of a lawyer named M. F. Volkenstein. In 1893 Lenin wrote his first article, "New Economic Development in Peasant Life," a long eulogy of Post-nikov's Populist monograph *The South Russian Peasant Economy*. Lenin found in Postnikov's work convincing proof that capitalism had already penetrated the Russian village and undermined the highly prized village commune. Throughout his career Lenin remained intensely interested in the problem of making a Marxist revolution in a peasant country like Russia, where the industrial working class was small.

From 1893 through 1895 Lenin took part in a Marxist discussion group, where he met Nadezhda Konstantinova Krupskaia* (1869–1939), his future wife. Although only in his mid-twenties, Lenin had already acquired the unique combination of dogmatic orthodox Marxism and tactical flexibility that was to mark his role as a revolutionary leader. He brought to the revolutionary cause the same remarkable tenacity, self-discipline, and drive that had always enabled him to forge ahead of everyone else in his academic accomplishments. Lenin took what he wanted from Marx, placing emphasis, for example, on those passages where Marx intimates that Russia might skip a stage in historical development and, with appropriate revolutionary leadership, pass directly from feudalism to a proletarian dictatorship.

In 1895 Lenin went abroad to meet Russian Social Democratic leaders in emigration and to observe German Social Democratic leaders in Berlin. In Geneva he met G. V. Plekhanov*, the father of Russian Marxism and the leader of the emigré group, Liberation of Labor. When Lenin returned to St. Petersburg, he and the future Menshevik (*see* Russian Social Democratic Workers' Party [Menshevik]) Iu. O. Martov* organized the Union of Struggle for the Liberation of the Working Class. Lenin was soon arrested along with other leaders for agitation among the industrial workers. After more than a year awaiting trial, Lenin was sentenced to three years of Siberian exile in the village of Shushenskoe in Enisseisk Province (1897–1900).

In 1897 he sent for Krupskaia, and they concluded a revolutionary partnership–marriage that would last until his death.

During this interlude in Siberia Lenin wrote some of his most ambitious works, including *The Tasks of Russian Social Democracy* and *The Development of Capitalism in Russia*. The latter is probably Lenin's most comprehensive and scholarly work. Leaning heavily on the work of V. E. Postnikov and the Legal Marxists M. I. Tugan-Baronovski and P. B. Struve, Lenin took up the major issue dividing the Populists and the Marxists, the question of whether Russia was going through the same stages of economic development as Western Europe. Armed with an impressive array of *zemstvo* statistics, Lenin answered with a ringing yes. Russia, he affirmed, was becoming a capitalist country, and thus Russian development conformed to Marx's stages of economic development.

Having completed his term of exile, Lenin left Siberia and Russia itself in 1900. With the older generation of Social Democratic leaders, G. V. Plekhanov P. B. Akselrod*, and V. Zasulich, and members of the younger generation, Iu. O. Martov and A. N. Potresov, Lenin began the newspaper *Iskra* (*The Spark*) abroad to combat Russian revisionism. In 1902 L. D. Trotsky* met Lenin in London and became a major contributor to *Iskra*. As part of the effort to unite the more militant and orthodox Russian Marxists, Lenin published his famous pamphlet *What Is To Be Done?* Most of the important features of "Leninism" appear in this book, and Lenin tried to adapt European Marxism to Russian circumstances. In particular, *What Is to Be Done* is one of the earliest and strongest expressions of Lenin's belief that Russian Social Democrats needed a party that was a tightly organized, highly centralized, conspiratorial elite, a "general staff" Revolution. This has been interpreted as an indication of Lenin's elitist view of Revolution or as a sign that Lenin believed that his tactical formulations were the only ones possible under an oppressive regime such as that existing in tsarist Russia. Certainly, Lenin expressed little faith, in *What Is to Be Done,* in the ability of the Russian worker under ordinary circumstances to develop a revolutionary point of view on his own initiative.

The Editorial Board arranged for a second congress of Russian Social Democrats in 1903. (The first one, in Minsk in March 1898, was very short lived). It was at this meeting, beginning in Brussels and later transferred to London, that Lenin and his faction earned the Bolshevik (majority) label that he and his successors proudly kept until 1939. The historic split between the Bolsheviks led by Lenin and Plekhanov and the Mensheviks (majority), including Martov and Trotsky, was primarily on the issue of party membership. Lenin wanted to require all members to serve the party actively as members of a cadre of professional revolutionaries, whereas Martov wanted a more flexible definition of party membership that would permit contributors and sympathizers to become members. After the congress Plekhanov deserted Lenin and took *Iskra* with him. The Bolsheviks began to publish their own newspaper, *Vpered* (*Forward*), in Geneva.

When the 1905 Revolution (*see* Nineteen-Five Revolution) broke out, Lenin was still living abroad. With the October Manifesto and the amnesty for political prisoners, Lenin returned to Russia for the first time in five years. From November 1905 to August 1906 Lenin was in St. Petersburg. His attitude toward the soviets vacillated—at first he opposed them as organs of revolutionary power, fearing that they would compete with the Social Democratic Party; then he supported them as an instrument through which the party could influence events; and finally, he rejected them. The same ambivalence characterized his attitude toward the Duma (*see* Duma and Revolution) elections—he opposed Social Democratic participation in the elections to the First Duma and supported participation in the Second Duma.

With the decline of revolutionary fervor and the reemergence of tsarist repression, Lenin left for Finland. In January 1912 the final split between the Bolsheviks and the Mensheviks took place when Lenin called his own conference of party members and elected an all-Bolshevik Central Committee. The Bolsheviks began to publish a legal daily newspaper in St. Petersburg called *Pravda* (*Truth*).

Lenin spent World War I* in Switzerland. He joined the minority of European Social Democrats who condemned Social Democratic support for the war and urged industrial workers to turn their weapons against their own rulers and the capitalists. At two conferences of the Social Democratic Left, the first held in Zimmerwald in 1915 and the next in Kienthal in 1916 (*see* World War I), Lenin found himself joining a minority of Left Social Democrats who wished to turn the imperialist war into a class war. Lenin urged his own faction, which called itself the Zimmerwald Left to form a Third International (*see* Communist International) against imperialist war.

In 1916 Lenin wrote *Imperialism the Highest Stage of Capitalism,* borrowing heavily from the British radical John Hobson, to prove that war was the logical outcome of the world competition between capitalist states for colonies. He further argued that for more advanced capitalist states, imperialism brought in profits that could be used in the form of higher wages as a bribe to the working class, postponing the day of proletarian Revolution. But Russia, as a poorer and unsuccessful imperialist country, as the weak link in the chain of imperialistic states, could not use imperialism for these purposes and, therefore, remained vulnerable to revolutionary movements. The less-advanced capitalist countries, therefore, like Russia, might glide through the capitalist stage of development directly to a proletarian Revolution in an ''uninterrupted'' or permanent Revolution.

With the cooperation of the German authorities Lenin was permitted transit by ''sealed'' train through Germany, Sweden, and Finland to Russia. When he arrived in Petrograd on April 3, 1917, he discovered that his Bolshevik comrades in arms had given tacit approval to the Provisional Government* as the necessary bourgeois-democratic stage through which Russia had to pass on the way to proletarian Revolution. They also gave support to the continuation of a defensive war against Germany until Russian soil had been evacuated. Immediately, Lenin rebuked them in his April Theses*, calling for immediate peace, a relentless struggle against the new provisional government, and preparations for a Bolshevik seizure of power through the soviets. Lenin soon seized command of his rapidly growing political party, turned its policies around, and, unlike other socialist leaders, refused to give permission to members of his party to join any coalition governments between February and October. Most Western and Soviet accounts tend to exaggerate the degree to which he was successful in molding his party into a tight-knit conspiratorial elite. Russian geography, an imperfect communications network, and the well-known independent temperament of the Russian intelligentsia probably made that goal impossible to achieve. But Lenin was successful over the long run in imposing a general line, sooner or later, on all branches of the party. The public was somewhat wary of him at first because his open hostility to the war seemed to confirm widespread rumors that he was a spy in the pay of the German government.

Many times throughout 1917, as in the prewar years, Lenin found himself at odds with his own followers, sometimes those on the Right, sometimes those on the Left (see Left Communism), alternately urging a course that seemed too radical or reckless to the Right in the period before the October Seizure of Power (see Zinoviev, Grigorii Evseevich; Kamenev, Lev Borisovich), or one that seemed too conservative during the Civil War in Russia* and the negotiations for the Brest-Litovsk* Treaty. For example, Lenin encountered considerable disagreement in the party from the right wing over the timing of the seizure of power in the name of the Soviet government. The right wing of the party interpreted the extraordinary successes of the Bolsheviks in City Duma elections in Petrograd in August and in Moscow in September as proof that Soviet power could be achieved without an armed uprising. Lenin saw those results as proof that an insurrection should take place as soon as possible. Although forced into temporary exile in Finland after the July Crisis (see July Days), Lenin returned on October 7 and on October 10 persuaded his Central Committee (see Central Committee of the The Russian Communist Party [Bolshevik]) to put the armed uprising on its agenda. One of those who opposed Lenin's timing and wanted to wait to see the mood of the Second All-Russian Congress of Soviets scheduled to meet on October 20, Kamenev published his opposition to the timing of the planned uprising in Gorky's newspaper, Novaia zhizn (New Life) on October 18. Kamenev and Zinoviev wanted to wait for the meeting with Bolsheviks arriving for the Congress of Soviets scheduled for October 20.

The opening of the Second All-Russian Congress of Soviets was postponed until October 25. In the early morning of October 24, the Provisional Government ordered the arrest of the leaders of the Military Revolutionary Committee established by the Petrograd Soviet* and closed Bolshevik newspapers. The October Seizure of Power began as a response to that step. In the evening of the 24th Lenin walked from his place of hiding to the Smolnyi Institute to take personal command of the insurrection, which until then had been organized by Trotsky in the name of the Petrograd Soviet. In the morning of October 25 Lenin announced that the Provisional Government had been overthrown. That night at the first session of the Second All-Russian Congress of Soviets the Bolsheviks proved to have a majority of the votes, and their seizure of power in the name of the Soviets was endorsed, although many delegates walked out in protest. At the same time, the remaining members of the Provisional Government were arrested by Soviet forces in the Winter Palace. The next day the Congress of Soviets approved the new cabinet, or Council of People's Commissars, with Lenin as Chairman, making him Premier of the new Soviet state, a post he held until his death in 1924.

Lenin immediately issued two decrees calling for immediate peace and the nationalization of all land. The latter permitted the peasants to use the land they had already confiscated. There followed a succession of decrees dealing with nearly all aspects of Russian life. From the outset Lenin tried to persuade the Council of People's Commissars to accept peace with the Germans at any price, but he met determined opposition from his own left wing and the Left Socialist–Revolutionaries. It was only after renewed hostilities and a new German advance into Russia that the new Soviet state accepted the terms dictated by the Germans in the Brest-Litovsk Treaty signed on March 3, 1918.

At the end of August 1918 Lenin was shot and critically wounded by Dora Kaplan, a Socialist–Revolutionary, but he soon recovered and returned to work. With Lenin's encouragement a Third or Communist International* was created, and its first congress was held in Moscow on March 2 to March 7, 1919. The destructive period of Civil War and foreign intervention finally came to an end with the Treaty of Riga, signed with Poland on March 18, 1921. After four years of deprivation and suffering the Bolsheviks had lost much of their popular support, as was demonstrated dramatically in the rebellion of the sailors at Kronstadt (see Kronstadt, 1917–1921). Most of the rebellious sailors had fought for Bolshevik victory in 1917. As a result of the desperate situation of the new Soviet state, Lenin decided to compromise with public opinion and to conduct a temporary retreat from his ultimate goals in the form of his New Economic Policy* for Russia.

Lenin suffered his first stroke in May 1922 but was able to resume all of his responsibilities in August of the same year. A second stroke in December 1922 paralyzed his right side. On December 23, 1922, Lenin composed his so-called Last Testament, appraising the ability of his potential successors in the leadership of the Bolshevik Party and the Soviet state. On January 4, 1923, he attached a postscript, asking that I. V. Stalin* be removed from his post as secretary general of the Communist Party. Lenin managed to write or dictate a series of articles criticizing Stalin's conduct as secretary general and commissar and attacking the growing bureaucratization of the state. On March 9, 1923, Lenin suffered a third stroke, which deprived him of the ability to speak. From May 1923 to January 1924 he tried to recuperate at Gorky. On January 21, 1924, he suffered his last and fatal stroke. Lenin's body was embalmed and has been exhibited ever since in the mausoleum built for that purpose in Red Square outside of the Kremlin, where Stalin's body was placed beside him from 1953 to 1956.

Through his strong leadership Lenin made a distinctive and probably decisive contribution to the October Revolution and the character of the Soviet state. The timing and strategy of the Bolsheviks in 1917 was primarily a result of Lenin's actions. He also brought Russia the one-party state and a new and far more oppressive state political police (see All-Russian Extraordinary Commission for Combatting Counterrevolution and Sabotage). Once in power, it was chiefly his decision to prohibit other political parties and even factions within the Bolshevik Party. It was he who encouraged and supported the creation and the strengthening of the state political police. Lenin gave Russia socialism, including free and universal education, national health care, and guaranteed employment, but he also unwittingly laid the foundations for Stalin's tyranny. Lenin's success in conducting a communist Revolution in a peasant country also made the Bolshevik experience seem useful as a model for Revolution in other economically under-developed countries in Asia, Africa, and South America.

Bibliography

Fischer, L. *The Life of Lenin.* 1966.
Krupskaia, N. *Reminiscences of Lenin.* 1966.
Lenin, V. I. *Polnoe sobranie sochinenii.* 5th ed. 55 vols. 1958. (Fourth edition is less complete but is available in English as V. I. Lenin, *Collected Works,* 1960-.)
Lewin, Moshe. *Lenin's Last Struggle.* 1968.
Reddaway, P., ed. *Lenin, the Man, the Theorist.* 1967.
Service, Robert. *Lenin, A Political Life.* 1985.
Shub, David. *Lenin, A Biography.* 1948.
Ulam, Adam. *The Bolsheviks, the Intellectual and Political History of the Triumph of Communism in Russia.* 1966.
Wolfe, Bertram. *Three Who Made Revolution.* 1948.

Literature and the Russian Revolution. In literature, as in Art (*see* Art and the October Revolution) and Architecture (*see* Architecture and the Revolution), the Russian Revolution was bound to have a profound effect, although perhaps only in providing new momentum to trends already under way in Russian culture.

In literature, the years 1917–1921 did not represent a new start but rather a continuation of the Revolution in literature that had begun two decades earlier. The circumstances under which the writers functioned, however, changed radically, for they faced extreme shortages of food and fuel and limited outlets for publication. The state publishing house, *Gosizdat,* had priority in obtaining scarce paper. Private publishing houses closed for lack of supplies. In 1918 and 1919 scarcely any books were published. Some poets managed to "overcome Gutenberg," as they put it, by public declamations at poet's cafes. There were also mass festivals held in the open air or in large auditoriums organized by symbolists, futurists, and Proletcult writers. Modeled on the national festivals of the French Revolution, they were also influenced by Richard Wagner's ideas of democratic theater and of synthesis of the arts. As before the Revolution, afterward realism, symbolism, and futurism remained the dominant literary schools, even though important, realist writers such as L. N. Andreev and I. A. Bunin died or emigrated.

Maxim Gorky, (*see* Peshkov, Maksim Alekseevich), the foremost realist writer, devoted much of his energy to his newspaper *New Life* (*Novaia zhizn'*), founded in April 1917 and closed by the Bolsheviks (*see* Russian Social Democratic Workers' Party [Bolshevik]) in July 1918. He also was involved in practical activities designed to insure the survival of culture. He founded the "House of Art" to provide writers with food and shelter, organized a project for the translation of classics of world literature to provide writers with paid employment, and frequently interceded on behalf of persons in trouble with the

Soviet regime. Important literary works of these years are his memoirs of L. A. Andreev and L. N. Tolstoy.

Many, though not all, symbolist writers accepted the Revolution and found employment in TEO, the theatrical section of the Commissariat of the Enlightenment* (*Narkompros*). Indeed, the most famous poem of the Revolution is Alexander Blok's "The Twelve" (January 1918) about a Red Guard* detachment on patrol in Petrograd. It concludes with Jesus Christ at their head. In his poem "The Scythians" (January 1918), he exalted the triumph of the barbaric East over the decadent West. Opposed to Bolshevik materialism and rationalism, Blok interpreted the Revolution as a spiritual and cultural process that would forge an artistically creative and spiritually elevated new man. In a series of essays, he hailed the collapse of the old order: "Intelligentsia and Revolution" (January 1918), "Art and Revolution" (March 1918), "Cataline" (April-May 1918), and "The Collapse of Humanism" (March-April 1919). Andrei Bely (true name, A. N. Bugaev) expressed his faith in a "revolution of the spirit" in his essay "Revolution and Culture" (Spring 1917), his poem "Christ Is Risen" (April 1918), and the two-volume miscellany *Notes of a Daydreamer* (1919–1922). In 1919 he participated in the founding of *Volfila*, the Free Philosophical Society. Viacheslav Ivanovich Ivanov accepted the Revolution, wrote essays on culture and theater, and wrote *A Correspondence from between Two Corners*, a dialogue with M. O. Gershenzon on Revolution and cultural continuity. But he also contributed to the bitterly anti-Bolshevik symposium *From the Depths* (*Iz glubiny*), 1919. A continuation of *Landmarks* (*Vekhi*) printed in 1909, it included essays by the philosophical idealists and neo-Christians N. A. Berdiaev, S. N. Bulgakov, S. L. Frank, and P. B. Struve. A. M. Remizov's "Lament for the Ruin of the Russian Land" was essentially apolitical, but he considered the Revolution punishment for Russia's sins. D. S. Merezhkovskii and Z. N. Gippius, both adamant opponents of Bolshevism, considered the Bolshevik regime *The Reign of Antichrist* and polemicized against it. They emigrated in December 1919. V. V. Rozanov was horrified by the Revolution, which he described as *The Apocalypse of Our Times*, and blamed Russia's writers, including himself, for it.

Futurists (after the Revolution the term was used loosely to denote all "Left" or avant-garde tendencies in art) saw the Revolution as the future they had been predicting all along and cooperated with the Bolsheviks in building a new society dedicated to the principles of the machine age. Like the symbolists, they were interested in the sound and emotional impact of words rather than their meaning, but they rejected symbolist mystification and considered the writer not a surrogate priest but a worker and an artisan. The art section of Narkompros (IZO) turned out to be their bastion. It published the journals *Art of the Commune (Iskusstvo kommuny)* and *Art (Iskusstvo)*. Futurists' interest in word theory gave them common ground with the Formalists, a group that included V. B. Shklovsky, B. Eikhenbaum, and Roman Jacobson, which stressed techniques and devices in its literary analysis. They published an anthology, *Poetika,* in 1919 and organized the Society for the Study of Language (OPOIAZ) in October 1919.

V. V. Maiakovskii*, playwright, poet, propagandist, was the leading futurist writer. Calling himself "the drummer of the Revolution," he was a master of sound effects, hyperbole, and poetic diction; his theatrical personality was especially suited to public declamation. His important works include the iconoclastic poem "It Is Too Early to Rejoice" (1917), an attack on Pushkin and other classic generals; "Mystery-Bouffe" (1918), a revolutionary mystery play ridiculing Christian concepts of heaven and hell and celebrating workers' determination to build paradise here on earth; and "150,000," a poem about a boxing match between a worker and a bloated Woodrow Wilson, which V. I. Lenin* incidentally, heartily disliked. Another leading futurist, V. V. Khlebnikov, regarded the Revolution as a momentous and inevitable event, interpretating it from the perspective of his theory of history, which was that historical events are governed by natural cyclical laws that can be discovered and used to predict the future. His theory was based on natural science rather than mysticism. Among his important works are "Ladomir" (1920), about a future utopia; "Nocturnal Search" (1920), about an episode in the Civil War (*see* Civil War in Russia); and many other poems depicting the Revolution and contemporary conditions such as starvation.

Other literary groups were related in some way to the major literary schools or political "isms." Proletcult, for example, founded in 1917 by A. A. Bogdanov, was an attempt to develop an authentic workers' culture and to encourage worker literary and artistic creativity in order to liberate the workers psychologically and spiritually from the bourgeois past. In Proletcult schools and studios, workers were taught literary and artistic techniques, often by prominent figures such as V. Ia. Briusov, Bely, and N. S. Gumilev. Their ideal of a new life based on industrialization can be seen in poems such as Kirillov's "The Iron Messiah," Gerasimov's "Song of Iron," and Alexander Gastev's collection *Shock Work Poetry* (1918). Industrial traits such as standardization and synchronization were exalted as the supreme virtues. After Proletcult's activities were curtailed in 1920, splinter groups developed: the Smith (Kuznitsa) group, which wrote poems of iron, and the Cosmos group, which propagated a mystique of science fantasy and pseudo-religion. The unofficial poet laureate in these years was Demian Bednyi (E. A. Prilvorov).

The Scythians were a group of Left Socialist–Revolutionaries (*see* Left Socialist-Revolutionary Party) led by Ivanov-Razumnik (V. I. Razumnik) who went over to the Bolsheviks. Like Bely and Blok, with whom they were associated, the Scythians viewed the Revolution as religious in essence, a purifying fire that would destroy the corrupt old world. Active in Volfila, they also had links to the "peasant poets" S. A. Esenin and N. A. Kliuev, who idealized the traditional village and regarded the Bolshevik Revolution as the triumph of the Russian land over the city. Christian images and themes, especially apocalypticism, permeate their work, as they do the writings of the Scythians Bely, Blok, and

Maiakovskii. Esenin was also associated with the Imaginists, led by Vadim Shershenovich, self-styled successors to futurism.

The acmeists were essentially apolitical. Osip E. Mandelshtam's essays and poems of these years treat mainly a non-political theme, but there are allusions to the Revolution that reflect an attitude of fear more than hope. Boris L. Pasternak's personal lyricism and complex and sophisticated style made him a model for other Russian poets but no spokesman for the new regime. He was forced increasingly to devote himself to translations. Marina I. Tsvetaeva produced major works of poetry, despite great physical suffering: *Mileposts* (1917–1921), *The Camp of the Swans* (1917–1922), and *Craft* (1921–1922). Anna A. Akhmatova wrote poems of love and spiritual themes in *White Flock* (1917–1923), *Plantain* (1921), and *Anno domini* (1921). Nicholas Gumilev was in Paris when the Revolution broke out but returned to Russia out of a sense of adventure, did translations, taught at Proletcult schools, and was executed in 1921 on a charge of counterrevolution. Although he was the only writer actually executed, the literary atmosphere was marred by vitriolic disputes on which literary schools best expressed the spirit of the Revolution or the voice of the proletariat.

The institution during the New Economic Policy* (NEP) of limited capitalism is generally considered the end of the revolutionary period. Private publishing houses reopened, and cultural interaction with the outside world resumed. New faces emerged on the literary scene; among them were the Serapion Brothers, a group of "fellow travelers" who accepted the Revolution but demanded tolerance for a variety of views. Their most famous member was Evgenii I. Zamiatin, author of *We* (1921) and *The Islanders* (1917), a novel critical of bourgeois society in England. Other new writers, including Isaac E. Babel, Boris A. Pilniak, and Fedor V. Gladkov, treated the Civil War as one of their major themes.

Bernice Glatzer Rosenthal

Bibliography

Blok, Aleksandr. *Sobranie Sochinenii v Vos'mi Tomakh*. 6 vols. 1960–1963.
Brown, Edward. *Russian Literature Since the Revolution*. 1982.
Ivanov, Georgii. *Petersburgi zimy*. 1952.
Khodasevich, V. *Literaturnyie stat'i i vospominaniia*. 1939.
Mirsky, D. S. *Contemporary Russian Literature*. 1926.
Nilssen, Nils Ake. *Art, Society, Revolution: Russia 1917–21*. 1979.
Polonskii, V. *Ocherki literaturnogo dvizheniie revoliutsionnyi epokhi*. 1928.
Rosenthal, Bernice Glatzer, ed. *Nietsche in Russia*. 1986.
Struve, Gleb. *Russian Literature under Lenin and Stalin*. 1971.
Trotsky, Leon. *Literature and Revolution*. 1960.

Lithuania and the Russian Revolution. Like all other small nationalities within the Russian Empire, the Lithuanian people took advantage of the revolutionary situation in the rest of the empire to achieve political independence.

At the time of the Revolutions of 1917 in Russia, the fate of Lithuania was shrouded in uncertainty and controversy. As a result of centuries of Polish cultural domination, 120 years of Russian rule, and, more immediately, the past two years of German military occupation, the Lithuanian national movement had no territory or administration to call its own, and it had to struggle even for recognition as a culture.

Until the end of the nineteenth century, the Lithuanian-speaking population, about 2 million people, had been shrinking. Lithuanian had come to be scorned as a language just for peasants. Only in the last generation had the language reversed this trend, but even so the nationality could only watch as many of its young immigrated, especially to the United States. The nationalist Lithuanian intelligentsia spoke of restoring the statehood of the medieval Lithuanian Grand Duchy, but to do so it had to deny centuries of union with Poland, and it also had to find a *modus vivendi* with the other nationalities that lived in the territory the Lithuanians claimed. Even the historic capital of Lithuania, called ''Vilnius'' in Lithuanian and ''Wilno'' in Polish, had a plurality of Jews in its population, whereas the peasants in the surrounding countryside mostly spoke Belorussian.

In 1917 Lithuania, originally just a battlefield on Russia's Northwest frontier with Germany, acquired new political significance, as the Germans, who feared the establishment of a large and strong Polish state, began to encourage the Lithuanians. In September 1917 the German-occupation authorities permitted the Lithuanians to hold an assembly (seimas) in Vilnius, which in turn elected a council (Taryba) that had the charge of leading the Lithuanian people to independence. The Germans, however, had their own designs on Lithuania, and Berlin refused to recognize the Taryba's declaration of independence of December 11, 1917.

In the peace talks between the Bolsheviks (*see* Russian Social Democratic Workers' Party [Bolshevik]) and the Germans at Brest-Litovsk*, Lithuania served as a major bone of contention. The Germans spoke of the Lithuanians' desire to separate from the Russian Empire. The Bolsheviks, who had organized a Lithuanian Commissariat within their Peoples' Commissariat of Nationality Affairs (*see* National Question and the Russian Revolution), contended that the working people of Lithuania wanted to take part in the Russian Revolution. By the terms of the Treaty of Brest-Litovsk signed on March 3, 1918, the Bolshevik Party continued to work among the Lithuanian refugees in Russia.

Upset by the Germans' dilatory tactics, the Taryba had issued another declaration of independence on February 16, 1918. On March 23 Berlin finally recognized the declaration of December 11, which had called for close ties with the Reich. In the summer of 1918 the conservative majority of the Taryba, over the objection of its socialist members, attempted to preempt the designs of the Hohenzollerns by electing Wilhelm of Urach as King Mindaugas II of Lithuania. Wilhelm accepted, but Berlin would not permit him to visit his new realm, and with the collapse of the German army in the autumn of 1918, the Taryba abrogated his election.

Although the Germans surrendered to the Allied powers in November 1918, they were still standing as victors in Eastern Europe; for the Lithuanians this paradox was full of both hope and peril. The German military units, against the wishes and orders of the victorious Western powers, organized themselves into soldiers' councils (*Soldatenräte*) and began to withdraw from their positions in the East. In their wake, following at a distance of some 15 to 20 kilometers, advanced the western Red Army*, bringing Bolshevik rule with it. The Taryba, which still had neither an administration nor an army, claimed to be the legitimate authority in Lithuania, but in the eyes of many it was compromised by its birth under German aegis and by its efforts to find accommodation with Berlin. When the Germans ignored the Lithuanians and turned Vilnius over to the Poles, the leaders of the Taryba yielded their place to a new government headed by Mykolas Sleževičius, a member of the leftist Populist Party, only recently returned to Lithuania from Russia. It was, however, too late to save Vilnius, and the new government had to retreat to Kaunas, 100 kilometers to the West.

The Polish forces were themselves unable to hold Vilnius, and on January 5, 1919, the western Red Army entered the city, installing a Bolshevik government headed by Vincas Mickevičius-Kapsukas. The Lithuanian Soviet Socialist Republic was short lived; the Lithuanian peasantry resented its attempt to keep the large estates intact and its vague national policies. The government, therefore, merged in March with the Belorussian Soviet Socialist Republic (*see* Belorussia, Revolution in), thereby forming the so-called Litbel Republic, but this too, proved to be unstable. With some support from the Germans, the Slezevicius government was able to make a stand with Kaunas, and in April 1919 the Polish army occupied Vilnius, destroying Bolshevik rule in Lithuania at this time.

Under Sleževičius's leadership, the Lithuanian nationalist government was able to consolidate itself, regularizing both army and administration. Three wings of Lithuanian national politics now emerged as parties: the Christian Democratic bloc, led by clerical intellectuals, represented the Catholic traditions of the land; the Populists, claiming to represent the peasantry, took an aggressively anticlerical stance; and the Social Democrats, weakened by the defection of their left wing to the Bolsheviks, claimed to represent the workers. All three favored extensive land reforms, which would be carried out at the cost of a landholding class that was displaying strong sympathies for Poland. Another important party, the Pažanga, or Progress party, was made up of socially conservative nationalists; although its leaders had been prominent in the Taryba, and one of them, Antanas Smetona, had been named President of Lithuania in April 1919, it had but shallow roots as a popular party. When the Lithuanians elected a constituent assembly in April 1920, the Christian Democratic bloc won a majority of the seats; the Pažanga failed to win a single place. The official language of the new government was Lithuanian. The other nationalities living under its authority responded in different ways: the Polish nationalists were hostile; the Jews negotiated an agreement on cultural autonomy; Belorussian nationalists welcomed Lithuanian help in their own campaign against the Poles.

With both the Germans and the Russians neutralized by external circumstances, the Lithuanians viewed the Poles as the major threat to their independence. The

Poles themselves did not speak with just one voice; the "annexationists" favored a large Poland that would probably have to include Lithuania as an autonomous unit so as to keep it from German influence; the "federalists" spoke of organizing a large multinational Lithuania that would enter into some sort of federative relationship with Poland. The Lithuanians distrusted both of these programs, believing that they had to free themselves of any ties with the Poles to establish their own identity and independence. They resented the centuries of Polish cultural hegemony in the land, and they demanded that the Poles recognize Vilnius as the historic capital of an independent Lithuanian state. The Poles, who had their own claims to Vilnius, would not relinquish what they saw as their own historic and national rights, and when a Polish plot to overthrow the Lithuanian government was uncovered in August 1919, there could be no reconciling the two nations.

After the Poles had invaded the Ukraine in April 1920, the Lithuanians calculated that they had more to gain from Moscow than from Warsaw. The Lithuanian government officially adopted a stance of neutrality, but when, on July 12, it concluded a treaty of peace and recognition with the Bolshevik government, it secretly agreed to countenance Soviet use of Lithuanian territory in the Bolsheviks' military campaign against the Poles. Soviet troops took Vilnius from the Poles on July 14, and with them, returned Kapuskas, who was preparing a coup to overthrow the government in Kaunas. The Polish success in holding Warsaw, however, disrupted his plans, and at the end of August the Russian formally turned Vilnius over to the Lithuanians in accordance with the terms of the treaty of July 12.

The Polish government resented the behavior of the Lithuanians, but the Western powers, while understanding little of the conflict, tried to restrain Warsaw. On October 9, 1920, Polish troops claiming to be "revolting" against Warsaw's inaction seized Vilnius, thereby driving the Lithuanian government once again back to Kaunas. The Poles made the city the capital of a state called Central Lithuania, which was incorporated into Poland in 1922. The Polish occupation of Vilnius cut off the Lithuanians from Soviet Russia, and the Lithuanian government thereafter looked to Germany and to Russia for help in opposing Warsaw. When Soviet troops moved into Poland in September 1939, the Soviet Union turned Vilnius over to the Lithuanians, and in June 1940 it forced the Lithuanian government to reorganize. In August 1940 Lithuania was incorporated into the USSR as a constituent republic.

Alfred Erich Senn

Bibliography

Bor'ba za sovetskuiu vlast' v 1918–20gg. 1967.
Lossowski, Piotr. *Stosunki polso-litewskie w latach 1918–20.* 1966.
Navickas, Kostas. *The Struggle of the Lithuanian People for Statehood.* 1971.
Senn, Alfred Erich. *The Great Powers, Lithuania, and the Vilna Question.* 1966.
Vaitkevičius, Bronius. *Socialistine revolucija Lietuvoje 1918–19 metais.* 1967.

Lomov-Oppokov, George Ippolitovich (1888–1938; pseudonyms, Afanasii, Zhorzh, A. Lomov). Lomov was a prominent Left Communist (*see* Left Communist) leader during the October Seizure of Power* in Moscow (*see* Moscow, Revolution in; Moscow Soviet). He joined the Russian Social Democratic Workers' Party in 1903, and at the time of the split between the Bolsheviks (*see* Russian Social Democratic Workers' Party [Bolshevik]) and the Mensheviks (*see* Russian Social Democratic Workers' Party [Menshevik]) he joined the Bolshevik faction. Lomov took part in the 1905 Revolution (*see* Nineteen-Five Revolution) in Saratov. In 1906, while attending the University of St. Petersburg, he began to organize the railroad workers in that city. In 1909 he graduated from the Law Faculty of the University of St. Petersburg and became secretary of the St. Petersburg Committee of the Bolshevik Party.

Between 1910 and 1913 Lomov exiled to Archangelsk for his revolutionary activities where he took part in some Polar expeditions. He returned from exile and then was again sent into exile, first to Saratov in 1913 and then to eastern Siberia in 1916. After the February Revolution* he returned from exile to become a member of the Moscow Oblast' (Regional) Bureau and the Moscow Committee of the Russian Social Democratic Workers' Party (Bolshevik). He also became deputy chairman of the Moscow Soviet and a delegate to the Sixth Congress of the Russian Social Democratic Workers' Party (Bolshevik). He was arrested again in the spring of 1914 and exiled to Saratov. When the October Seizure of Power took place he was one of the members of the Military Revolutionary Committee that seized power in Moscow (*see* Moscow Revolution in).

Lomov was the first People's Commissar of Justice. He then joined the Left Communists in opposing the Brest-Litovsk* Treaty and in opposing the abolition of workers' control. From 1918 to 1921 he was a member of the Presidium and deputy chairman of the Supreme Council of the National Economy*. From 1921 to 1923 he was a member of the Siberian Bureau of the Central Committee of the Russian Communist Party (Bolshevik), a member of the Siberian Revolutionary Committee, chairman of the Siberian Industrial Bureau of the Supreme Council of the National Economy, member of the Ural Bureau of the Central Committee of the Russian Communist Party (Bolshevik), and chairman of the Ural Economic Council. He remained active in economic posts and party posts until his arrest in 1937. He died or was executed in 1938 and has been rehabilitated posthumously.

Bibliography

Levytsky, Borys. *The Stalinist Terror in the Thirties*. 1974.

Lunacharskii, Anatolii Vasilievich (1875–1933). Lunacharskii was a prominent Bolshevik (*see* Russian Social Democratic Workers' Party [Bolshevik]) leader in 1917, although, like L. D. Trotsky*, he entered the party in that year as a member of the Interdistrict Committee*. He played a decisive role in the development of Soviet culture as head of the Commissariat of the Enlightenment* (in actuality the Commissariat of Education; *see* Education) from 1917 to 1929. He was born in a noble family in Poltava. His name is taken from his mother's husband, although his biological father, A. I. Antonov, actually reared him. His mother lived with his biological father, who introduced Lunacharskii to radicalism. Lunacharskii attended the First Kiev Gymnasium where he came into contact with Populism and Marxism, and he was drawn to the philosophy of empiriocriticism as espoused by the German–Swiss professor Richard Avenarius.

Lunacharskii's intellectual outlook was shaped by his wide contacts with European and Russian emigré culture and with the Marxist revolutionary movement at home and abroad. In 1894 at the age of nineteen he went to study with Avenarius in Zurich where he also met the Russian emigré Marxist leaders P. B. Akselrod* and G. V. Plekhanov*. He rapidly became well known as a gifted speaker and intellectual in the emigré community where he associated himself with people of every political persuasion. In 1896 he returned to Russia and became a member of the revolutionary circle of V. I. Lenin's* older sister A. I. Ulianov-Elizarov in Moscow. He was arrested and expelled from Moscow. He returned to Kiev but was soon arrested again in 1899 and was sent into exile in Kaluga and Volgda. In Kaluga he became a close friend of Bogdanov who was a close friend of Lenin's. Bogdanov shared Lunacharskii's enthusiasm for Avenarius. There was also a family connection because Lunacharskii married Bogdanov's sister Anna in 1902. While in exile Lunacharskii wrote one of his most original and important works, *The Experience of Positive Aesthetics*.

After completing his first term of exile, Lunacharskii returned to Kiev in 1902 and became a literary critic. At the historic Second Congress of the Russian Social Democratic Workers' Party in 1903 Lunacharskii immediately joined the Bolshevik faction and edited party newspapers such as *Vpered (Forward), Proletarii (Proletarian),* and *Novaia zhizn' (The New Life)*. Although he became one of the most prominent figures in the Bolshevik movement, Lunacharskii had limited enthusiasm for Lenin. He thought that Lenin was too much involved with the mundane details of party work and regarded himself more as a "poet of revolution." He became one of the leaders of the so-called God-Building faction that regarded Marxism as a new godless religion. Strongly influenced by empiriocriticism, as represented in the work of the German physicist Ernst Mach, and Bogdanov, Lunacharskii tried to reconcile positivism with Marxism. The God-Builders did not believe that there was a God but rather that immortality could be achieved when one's ideas and identity remained in the memory of others where they could live on forever. Marx was not taken to be a repository of absolute truth but rather a hypothesis that worked and was capable of motivating others. It could put an end to the old supernatural faith and replace it with a firm faith in man's ability to employ his own creative powers in a collective environment. Essentially, it was an effort to combine the emotional fervor of religion among the workers with the scientific rationalism of Marxism.

Lenin and Lunacharskii found themselves at opposite poles in 1906 on the question of Bolshevik participation in the Duma (*see* Duma and Revolution). When Lenin decided that Bolsheviks should participate in the elections to the First Duma in April of that year, Lunacharskii joined those opposing that decision. In 1907 he left Russia for Western Europe and remained there until 1917. Those opposing Lenin gathered around the journal *Vpered,* which Lunacharskii edited. There they opposed any kind of legal activity in Russia, preferring instead to focus on illegal agitation and propaganda. Lenin attacked the whole philosophical school on which they built their principles in his book ''Materialism and Empiriocriticism'' published at the end of 1908. Bogdanov was expelled from the party, and empiriocriticism was roundly condemned, but Lunacharskii was not removed and continued to work with both Lenin and the factionalists. Nonetheless in 1909 the *Vpered* Group set up its own party school at Capri to train workers eventually to replace the intellectuals who led the Marxist movement.

With the coming of World War I* Lunacharskii shared Lenin's opposition to participation in the war effort, although he was more inclined to blame the workers themselves, rather than their leaders, for the widespread support they gave to their country's military efforts. On May 22, 1917, Lunacharskii returned to Russia and sought an immediate alliance with Lenin. Together with Gorky, who had been his collaborator in *Vpered* and the Capri School, he joined the editorial staff of the Bolshevik newspaper *Novaia zhizn' (New Life)* and was elected to the Petrograd Duma. In August 1917 at the Sixth Congress of the Russian Social Democratic Workers' Party [Bolshevik], he formally rejoined the Bolshevik Party.

Although Lunacharskii opposed Lenin in his original desire to form a one-party government, Lenin appointed him to head the Commissariat of the Enlightenment* (the first Soviet Ministry of Education [*see* Education]). In some respects Lunacharskii was an unlikely choice. Although he was a distinguished party worker, orator, and writer, Lunacharskii had never revealed any special talents as an administrator. In many ways he seemed the prototype of the old-fashioned cosmopolitan Russian intellectual, more comfortable in the world of lofty ideas than in that of budgets and management. Moreover, Lunacharskii was an eminent figure, and the Commissariat of Enlightenment seemed a minor post. Although he never really succeeded in winning much support for his efforts among other Soviet officials, and his ministry was often inefficient and ineffective, Lunacharskii succeeded at one level that is still widely admired in Russia today. His importance lies less in his efforts in education but rather in his endeavors to use the resources of the state to preserve the creative artistic achievements of the past and to encourage and support the whole range of artistic activity in his own time. His tenure as commissar of the enlightenment is widely regarded by many Soviet citizens today as the ''golden age of Soviet culture.'' He protected artists against the endeavors of his friend Bogdanov's Proletcult to dominate, and he protected Proletcult against the expressed desire of officials like Lenin to destroy it. He encouraged Vladimir Tatlin, the great Soviet architect, in his extreme and radical architectural projects (*see* Architecture and the Revolution) and at the same time appointed Marc Chagall director of the Academy of Arts at Vitebsk. He sponsored S. M. Eisenstein's grandiose and spectacular films (*see* Cinema, 1917–1921) and V. E. Meyerhold's "biomechanical" theater, while also sponsoring the first Hebrew theater in history. An era of tolerance, diversity, and impressive creative energy followed in every area of the arts, which lasted until Stalin imposed cultural controls in the 1930s.

In education Lunacharskii was somewhat less successful. Working closely with Lenin's wife, N. K. Krupskaia*, who knew more than he did about educational theory, he attempted to develop polytechnical education, which would produce the new collective working-class culture he sought to foster. According to Krupskaia and Lunacharskii, this new polytechnic education would provide the people with an understanding of general principles, rather than merely vocational knowledge. They called their model the "united labor school." But the opposition to their plans within the party was formidable. Their opponents argued that there was an immediate need for technical skills, not an understanding of processes, and in 1929 Lunacharskii resigned from the Commissariat. Six of his polytechnical schools were removed from his control and placed under the Supreme Council of the National Economy.

With his departure Lunacharskii's influence and health declined at the same time, and in 1933 he died on his way to his new post as Soviet ambassador to Spain. He left behind a prodigious amount of creative and critical writing and became something of a cultural hero in the post-Stalinist era.

Bibliography

Fitzpatrick, Sheila. *The Commissariat of the Enlightenment.* 1970.
Haupt, Georges, and Marie, Jean Jacques. *Makers of the Russian Revolution.* 1974.
Kairov, I. A. *A. V. Lunacharskii vydaiushchiisia deiatel' sotsialisticheskogo prosveshcheniia.* 1966.
Lunacharskii, A. V. *On Literature and Art.* 1973.
———. *Revolutionary Silouettes.* 1968.
———. *Sobranie sochinenii.* 8 vols. 1963–1967.
O'Connor, T. E. *The Politics of Soviet Culture Anatolii Lunacharskii.* 1980.
Trifonov, N. A. *A. V. Lunacharskii i sovetskaia literatura.* 1974.
Williams, Robert C. *Artists in Revolution.* 1977.
Wolfe, Bertram. *Three Who Made Revolution.* 1964.

Luxemburg, Rosa (1871–1919). Rosa Luxemburg was one of the most prominent leaders of radical Marxism in Western Europe and one of the most influential Marxist critics of I. V. Lenin's* policies after the October Seizure of Power*. She was one of the founders of the Social Democratic Party of Poland and Lithuania (*see* Poland, Revolution in) and of the German Communist Party (the abbreviations in German were KPD as distinguished from those of the German Social Democratic Party, SPD, from which it sprang).

Rosa Luxemburg was born in 1871 in Zamość, Poland, in a middle-class Jewish family. From childhood a hip ailment limited her physical activity and perhaps caused her to channel her energies into intellectual endeavors. She joined a Polish socialist party called Proletariat while she was a young student in the gymnasium. The national Polish Socialist Party (PSP) was founded in 1892 as a result of the consolidation of four revolutionary organizations from Russian Poland. They favored cooperation with Russian socialist movements but refused to be subordinated or absorbed by their Russian counterparts. Russia, they argued, was more backward than Poland and had a destiny different from that of Poland, the former moving toward constitutional monarchy, Poland moving toward a democratic and socialist republic. The new Polish Socialist Party also demanded that it have exclusive rights to conduct all political activity in Poland. In March and July 1893 a group of dissidents led by Rosa Luxemburg and Julian Marchlewski (Karski) seceded from the party and in 1894 founded their own party, the Social Democracy Party of Poland and Lithuania (in Polish, SDKPL).

The debate between the two Polish socialist movements reached its peak at the International Socialist Congress in Zurich in August 1893. The main issue was nationalism. Led by Rosa Luxemburg, the future leaders of the SDKPL opposed the idea of a Polish nation, branding it a bourgeois illusion. They called upon their followers in Russian Poland to work for the incorporation of Russian Poland into the Russian state and collaborated with the Social Democratic movements in the rest of Russia to achieve their goals.

Although she moved to Zurich to study for her doctoral degree in 1893, Luxemburg remained active in Polish politics. At the International Socialist Congress in London in 1896 Luxemburg engaged Josef Pilsudski, the chief representative of the PSP and the future dictator of Poland, in a bitter debate on these issues. One can find some of the reasoning behind Luxemburg's stand against Polish nationalism in her doctoral dissertation completed in 1897 on the industrial development of Poland. There she argued that Poland needed Russian markets and resources and that, therefore, unification with Russia was economically necessary.

Yet in many ways her career was an anomaly. Her unqualified opposition to nationalism was in some ways quixotic. The nationalism among her Polish compatriots was doubly intense because of the cruel subjection and dismemberment of that country in the eighteenth century. It was a political reality that no political movement could ignore if it wished to be successful. But Rosa displayed the same intolerance toward the nationalism of the Jewish Bund*, which claimed the exclusive right to agitate among Yiddish-speaking industrial workers in Russia. No other Central or East European Marxist matched her in unqualified opposition to the spirit of nationalism. She refused to acknowledge any legitimacy to nationalism among self-proclaimed Marxists in Central and Eastern Europe. From her point of view no national self-determination was necessary under a socialist government. In 1898 Rosa moved to Berlin, where she assumed a prominent position in the German Social Democratic Party and adopted the same posture toward German nationalism as she had toward that of the Poles.

Although Rosa Luxemburg opposed Polish nationalism and worked for Polish unification with Russia, she was reluctant to join Lenin's Bolshevik Party (*see* Russian Social Democratic Workers' Party [Bolshevik]) after it was formed at the Second Congress of the Russian Social Democratic Workers' Party in 1903. There was strong support in her own party for unification led by leaders such as Julius Marchlewski and F. E. Dzerzhinskii* (in Polish, Dzierzynski). But Luxemburg was unalterably opposed to Lenin's support for national self-determination in the platform of his party. There were also other differences of opinion. In a pamphlet written shortly after the Second Congress, "The Organizational Question in Russian Social Democracy," Luxemburg joined L. D. Trotsky* in attacking Lenin's notion of a party organized as a tight-knit conspiratorial elite, a general staff of Revolution. She stated that Lenin's attempt to impose socialism on the working class through a band of conspirators was a violation of proletarian democracy and a sign of the backwardness of the Russian Social Democratic movement. Instead, she argued, Lenin should trust the revolutionary instincts of the masses. Although she and Lenin did agree that socialism could not be achieved through the ballot box, they differed on the role of a socialist party in bringing about proletarian Revolution. For Luxemburg a socialist party should be engaged in consciousness raising, preparing the workers to take matters into their own hands. Revolutionary movements, she argued, could only be created by specific historical conditions and spontaneous actions on the part of the working class. They could not be manufactured.

Neither Luxemburg nor the SDKPL played an important part in the 1905 Revolution (*see* Nineteen-Five Revolution) in Poland, although that Revolution tended to support her thesis that the mass or general strike was the most effective weapon in the workers' arsenal. The concessions made by the tsarist government in Poland weakened the efforts of the SDKPL to try to gain support, and it reconsidered the prospect of joining the Bolshevik Party. At the Fifth Congress of the Russian Social Democratic Party in 1907, the SDKPL and many other movements within Russia joined together to form a unified Marxist movement. Luxemburg herself appeared at the Congress, and the ties with the Bolsheviks continued through the October Seizure of Power when SDKPL leaders like Marchlewski, Dzerzhinskii, and Karl Radek* became active leaders in the new Soviet state.

After 1909 Luxemburg devoted most of her energy to the development of the SPD in Germany, where she was imprisoned for most of World War I*. She was an "internationalist," like Lenin, calling upon all socialists actively to oppose their country's war efforts. But when Luxemburg published her views in 1916 in her *Crisis in German Social Democracy*, Lenin mixed his praise for the work with criticism for its hostility to the idea of national self-determination. With the coming of the February Revolution* in Russia, Luxemburg was somewhat pessimistic about its eventual outcome, arguing that only a workers' revolution in Germany would make it possible for her Russian comrades to create a durable proletarian dictatorship. That was a view shared by many Bolsheviks, including Lenin himself. She echoed the same sentiments in a letter to Karl Kautsky's* wife, Louise, when the October Seizure of Power took place.

Although Luxemburg gave approval to the socialist Revolution in Russia, praising Lenin for his courage in leading a socialist Revolution, she expressed grave doubts about its outcome in a public form in an essay published in September 1918. First she questioned the Bolshevik decision to seek peace with Germany at any price, which she described as a "capitulation of the Russian revolutionary proletariat before German imperialism" (quoted in Nettl 1966, II: 696). She argued that Russia's surrender would make the necessary German socialist Revolution impossible. She also indicted the Bolsheviks for weakening their own state by endorsing national self-determination. All of this she said, was a sign of the "moral collapse" of Bolshevism (p. 697). In a pamphlet written in September 1918 but not published until 1922, she criticized the land program of the Bolsheviks as a policy that strengthened the enemies of the Revolution.

Both the land program and the program on the national question made converts to the counterrevolution because they compelled the Soviet government to be ruthless and dictatorial. She opposed Lenin's desire to dissolve the Constituent Assembly* and to limit suffrage. Most of all, she opposed Lenin's dictatorship as an institution that would rob public life of all spontaneity and life and lead to bureaucratization.

Although Lenin had frequently expressed his own belief that the Russian proletarian Revolution would need the support of a German proletarian Revolution to succeed, he found himself and his Revolution under attack from the two German Marxists he admired most, Karl Kautsky on the Right and Rosa Luxemburg on the Left. The attack from the Left was far more serious, because the internationalist left wing of the German party, the Spartacus League, was under the leadership of Rosa Luxemburg, and that was his single most likely prospect for leading a German workers' revolution. Neither Rosa Luxemburg nor her chief of organization, Leo Jogiches, were enthusiastic over the prospect of transforming their organization into a German Communist Party. When the congress for founding such a party took place in December 1918, Luxemburg and Jogiches wanted to call it the Socialist Party. The final vote was four to three with Luxemburg and Jogiches in opposition. She argued that her organization needed to bridge the gap between the radical East European Russian Communist Party and the reformist socialist parties of the West. Adopting the same label as the Russian party would only make that task more difficult. When the new German party had to choose a delegate to attend the founding congress of the Communist International, Luxemburg chose a man who would not cave in to Russian wishes, Hugo Eberlein. She also expressed her desire that he oppose the Russians on forming a new International until all of the countries of Eastern Europe had their own Communist parties. But Rosa Luxemburg was assassinated by soldiers in Berlin when revolutionary outbursts threatened the new German republic. Ironically, it was she who tried to curb the outbreak of revolutionary zeal in Berlin because she thought it was premature. Despite her critical posture toward Lenin and his Revolution, Luxemburg remains one of the revolutionary heroes of German, Polish, and Russian communism today (*see* Poland, Revolution in).

Bibliography

Badia, G. I. *Spartkisme*. 1967.
Dziewanowski, M. *The Communist Party of Poland*. 1976.
Laschite. A., and Radzun, *Rosa Luxemburg*. 1971.
Luxemburg, Rosa. *Gesammelte werke*. 3 vols. 1973–1973.
Nettl, J. P. *Rosa Luxemburg*. 2 vols. 1966.
Wolfe, Bertram. *Three Who Made Revolution*. 1969.

L'vov, Georgii Evgen'evich (1861–1925). L'vov was a Russian prince who became the first Prime Minister of the Provisional Government* on March 2, 1917. He was born in 1861 in Tula Province into one of the oldest noble families of Russia. Although well educated at the law faculty in Moscow University, he spent little time in the city, coming in only to take his examinations. Most of his energy during and after his education was devoted to the management of his estate which he succeeded in making profitable. He became involved in the *zemstvo* movement and was chairman of the Tula Provincial Zemstvo from 1886 to 1893. He did not become partisan and tended to exercise authority in a benign personal way, rather than through the authority of a party or social status.

During the Russo–Japanese War L'vov used his personal influence with the tsar to obtain permission to mobilize the fourteen provincial boards to help the sick and injured in the war zone. In May 1905 he was chosen as a member of the delegation sent to the tsar to request permission to call an All-Russian Zemstvo Congress. He was selected to the First Duma (see Duma and Revolution) as a candidate from the Constitutional Democratic Party—Cadet*. He was elected to the Second and Third Duma and in 1913 was elected mayor of Moscow, although the government nullified the election. From 1914 to 1917 he was head of the All-Russian Union of Zemstvos. During World War I* he again went to the tsar for permission to mobilize the resources of the *zemstvos* to help the sick and the wounded soldiers. A public decree in August 1914 approved the formation of the All-Russian Union of Zemstvos for the Sick and Wounded Soldiers. But the Tsar would not give permission for a scheduled *zemstvo* conference in December.

Because of his vocal criticism of the government's management of the war effort, L'vov came to be seen as a spokesman for the Progressive Bloc* and as the possible head of any government formed by the Progressive Bloc. L'vov himself began to state publicly that the real business of government was being conducted by the Union of Zemstvos (*see* All-Russian Union of Towns and All-Russian Union of Zemstvos). In November 1916 he signed an appeal to M. V.

Rodzianko, the Duma President for a government "capable of uniting the country." P. N. Miliukov* played a leading role in L'vov's appointment as a Prime Minister of the first Provisional Government. L'vov also accepted the post of Minister of the Interior. But he did not prove to be a very decisive or effective leader, failing to make the necessary appointments and failing to recognize the country's desire to end the war. He did, however, succeed in persuading the Petrograd Soviet* to send some of its leaders to participate in a second cabinet, the first coalition government, formed on May 3. When the Cadet Party members resigned from the cabinet in July, L'vov tried to devise a plan for ending the July Days*, but in repudiating the land program of the Socialist-Revolutionary Party* he lost the support of the soviet and with it any possibility of resolving the problem of dual power*. L'vov resigned on July 4, 1917 and Kerensky* became his successor. He was arrested by the Bolsheviks (*see* Russian Social Democratic Workers' Party [Bolshevik]) in 1918, but he escaped and spent his last years in exile in Paris.

Bibliography

Browder, Paul. *The Provisional Government*. 3 vols. 1961.
Miliukov, Paul. *Political Memoirs, 1905–1907*. 1967.
Polner, T. I. *Zhiznennyi put' Kniazia Georgiia Evgen'evicha L'vova*. 1932.
Rosenberg, W. G. *Liberals in the Russian Revolution*. 1974.
Tsereteli, I. G. *Vospominaniia o fevral'skoe revoliutsii*. 2 vols. 1963.

M

Maiakovskii, Vladimir (1893–1930). In the Soviet Union today, Maiakovskii is treated, not only as the poet of the October Revolution, but also as the model for Socialist Realist poetry.

Maiakovskii was born the son of an impoverished Russian nobleman in the village of Bagdadi in Georgia. Throughout his childhood he was impulsive and difficult. Maiakovskii did not complete high school and was expelled from Moscow College of Painting, Sculpture and Architecture in 1912. He was active in the Russian Social Democratic Workers' Party (Bolshevik)* in 1908 and was arrested for his involvement with Bolshevik activities. After 1912 he became one of the founders of the Cubo-Futurist Movement in Russia, having been inspired by the encouragement and ideas of his friend, the Russian futurist painter David Burliuk. This movement, based on the writings of the Italian, Filippo Tommaso Marinetti, attacked all previous literary work and painting as outmoded, and sought a whole new vocabulary for portraying the glories of the new urban industrial society that was emerging. Maiakovskii was opposed to participation in the war, and when drafted into the army actually served as a draftsman in an automobile school in Petrograd.

Maiakovskii idealized the Soviet regime both in art and in poetry. He created a series of posters for the Revolution (*see* Art and the October Revolution) and some of the most famous poems idealizing its goals, which just happened to coincide with the ideals of Futurism, such as "Left March," and "150,000,000." He also created a play, "Mystery-Bouffe," which gives a cosmic perception of the Revolution.

In the mid-thirties he became increasingly disillusioned with the prospects for changing Russian values, and in some poems, like *Agitprop,* he sharply criticized the vulgar propaganda the regime was passing off as art. Although opposed to cultural controls, he joined the Russian Association of Proletarian Writers before he committed suicide in 1930.

Bibliography

Baroolshien, Vaheb D. *Brik and Mayakovsky*. 1978.
Brown, E. J. *Mayakovsky, a Poet in Revolution*. 1975.
Janfeldt, Bengt. *Majakovskij and Futurism 1917–21*. 1976.
Maiakovskii, V. V. *The Bedbug and Selected Poetry*. 1960.
Maiakovskii, V. V. *Sobranie Sochinenii*. 1928.
Staponian, J. R. *Mayakovsky's Cubo-Futurist Vision*. 1986.
Woroszylski, W. *The Life of Mayakovsky*. 1971.

Makhno, Nestor I. (1889–1934). Makhno was an important Ukrainian (*see* Ukraine, Revolution in) anarchist leader who led guerilla forces against both the communists and the Ukrainian nationalist movements in the Ukraine. He was born in a Ukrainian peasant family in the area known as Guliai-Pole in Ekaterinoslav Province. His father died when he was an infant, and Makhno and his three brothers grew up in poverty. At the age of nineteen he was sentenced to be executed by hanging for participating in a robbery (to get political funds) that led to the death of a policeman. The sentence was commuted to life imprisonment, and he spent the next nine years in jail, widening his knowledge of anarchist theory by spending part of that time in a cell with an anarchist named Peter Marin-Arshinov.

After the February Revolution* of 1917 Makhno was released from prison and returned to his native village. He became chairman of the local carpenters' and metal workers' union and head of the local soviet (*see* Soviets [Councils] of Workers', Soldiers', and Peasants' Deputies). In the summer of 1917 he became a popular peasant leader, organizing the poor and landless peasants for armed activities against the local landlords and for the confiscation of their land. With this agenda one would have expected that Makhno would have joined or collaborated with the Ukrainian Socialist-Revolutionary Party. But Makhno was unique in his role as a Ukrainian Populist revolutionary who was neither a nationalist nor a member of any organized political party. In many ways his attitude toward nationalism paralleled that of Rosa Luxemburg*, whom he admired, toward Polish nationalism (*see* Poland, Revolution in). In both cases these two individuals seemed to be riding against the tides of history, emphasizing the primacy of the community of toilers, as opposed to the seductive power of the community of nationality, and seeing the latter as a threat to the former.

When the Soviet government signed the Treaty of Brest-Litovsk* in March 1918, Makhno had to go underground because the Ukraine was occupied by German and Austrian troops. He fled north to Moscow where he met one of his anarchist heroes, Prince Peter A. Kropotkin, and had a personal interview with V. I. Lenin*. According to his memoirs, Makhno chided Lenin for his Great Russian chauvinism in refusing to use the word *Ukraine,* preferring instead to refer to "the South of Russia." Makhno saw in this a nationalism as dangerous and virulent as Ukrainian nationalism. Returning once again to his native village in July 1918, he began to organize guerilla operations against the forces of the

Ukrainian leader General P. P. Skoropadskii and the German and Austrian army of occupation. As his army of peasants grew, Makhno achieved an almost legendary reputation. Peasants began to refer to him as *Bat'ko,* or little father.

When the Germans and Austrians left the Ukraine after the armistice of November 1918, Makhno turned his energies against the new Ukrainian government, the directory (*see* Directory—Ukraine), and its armed forces directed by S. M. Petliura*. In Makhno's native Guliai-Pole region he began to organize an independent anarchist state. After convening a series of regional congresses of soviets of peasants and workers, he created the Regional Military Council (or soviet) of Peasants, Workers, and Insurgents to rule the area. This body was elected by and responsible to regional congresses of soviets from which established political parties were excluded. Despite his anarchist hostility to political institutions, Makhno had created a regional government consisting of his Regional Military Revolutionary Soviet and its hierarchy of soviets. Under its jurisdiction, the Military Revolutionary Council encouraged the formation of local nonparty soviets and peasant anarchist communes, the latter consisting of a few hundred peasants in each unit. Significantly, the first such commune was named after Rosa Luxemburg whose views on nationalism were similar to Makhno's. The communes used confiscated land and tools, sharing in the work and profits, but confining their operations only to those lands they could cultivate with their own labor.

Makhno also began to establish close ties with the anarchist organization the Nabat (Alarm) Confederation, which had spread throughout the Ukraine at the end of 1918. It was founded in Kursk in November 1918 and included the well-known anarchist leader V. M. Voline (Eikhenbaum) and Makhno's old friend Arshinov (see Anarchism). But despite the base that Makhno provided the anarchists, when they moved their headquarters to Guliai-Pole in May 1919, they complained that their ideas made very little headway among the unsophisticated peasant soldiers of Makhno's army. In keeping with his antinationalism, Makhno was also noted for his hostility toward the anti-Semitism* of some of the Ukrainian nationalist movements. Many of the anarchist leaders were Jewish (*see* Jewry, 1905–1921), and they thought that Makhno's military successes and hostility to anti-Semitism promised a secure haven for them and a launching pad for a new anarchist community.

Makhno's army was called the Insurgent Army of the Ukraine and was under the direct control of his Military Revolutionary Council. Despite Makhno's anarchist beliefs, the army was organized with the same hierarchy of authority and discipline as that of any other army fighting during the Civil War in Russia*. The only difference between his army and the others was that his officers were drawn exclusively from the lower classes. During the summer of 1919 Makhno maintained a shaky and uneven alliance with the Red Army* against the counterrevolutionary forces of General A. I. Denikin*. In September Makhno made a significant contribution to the eventual defeat of Denikin by cutting some of his most important supply lines.

Makhno reached the peak of his power and importance as Denikin's campaign began to flag and turned into a full-scale retreat. When he expanded into the cities of Ekaterinoslav and Alexandrovsk in November, he introduced his own anarchist principles into the areas he occupied. He immediately decreed freedom of the press, free speech, and freedom of assembly but forbade organized political parties. He encouraged workers' control of industry but dispersed existing Bolshevik organizations.

By the end of the year Makhno was in open rebellion against the Soviet government, refusing to obey its orders that he move his troops to the Polish front. Although he briefly rejoined the Red Army to defeat Baron P. N. Wrangel* in the Crimea (*see* Crimea, Revolution in) in October 1920, his own forces were defeated by the Red Army in the following months. Makhno escaped to Western Europe where he became a factory worker and died ten years later in Paris.

Bibliography

Footman, David. *Civil War in Russia*. 1961.
Hunczak, T. *The Ukraine, 1917–21*. 1977.
Makhno, Nestor. *Pod udarami kotr-revolitusiia*. 1937.
————. *Russkaia revoliutsiia na Ukraina*. 1929.
————. *Ukrainskaia revoliutsiia*. 1937.
Malet, Michael. *Nestor Makhno in the Russian Civil War*. 1982.
Nomand, Max. *Apostles of Revolution*. 1939.
Palij, Michael. *The Anarchism of Nestor Makhno, 1917–1921*. 1976.
Peters, Victor. *Nestor Makhno: The Life of an Anarchist*. 1970.
Teper, I. *Makhno*. 1924.
Voline, V. M. [Vsevelod Eikhenbaum]. *The Unknown Revolution*. 1955.

Maklakov, Vasilii Alekseevich (1869–1957). Maklakov was the most important leader of the right wing of the Constitutional Democratic Party—Cadet*.

He was raised in a professional family, and his father was a physician. In 1887 he entered the University of Moscow and studied at a time when the ideas and practices of the existing government were coming under critical scrutiny. Although he was not a revolutionary, he acquired a reputation as a radical for his outspoken criticism of the government's policies. In 1889 he was profoundly influenced by the notion of citizenship based on mutual obligation between the individual and the state, which he believed was the secret of the lively involvement of the French people in their politics. He returned to Moscow to become a law student, thinking that it was essential for Russia to build a state where the rule of law prevailed for government officials as well as citizens.

Maklakov began his political life by joining the Beseda (Conversations) group in 1903. The members of this group were drawn primarily from the *zemstvo* movement, in which Maklakov felt at home with their moderate liberalism and emphasis on constitutionalism, and he soon displayed his brilliance as an orator. When the Constitutional Democratic Party was founded in 1905, Maklakov was one of its foremost leaders and was elected to its Central Committee. In many ways he was the leader of the right wing of the party, and P. N. Miliukov* was the leader of the Left.

Maklakov was afraid of Revolution and was more inclined to stress the need for a strong state than was Miliukov. He therefore opposed the party's posture in the First Duma (*see* Duma and Revolution) as well as its policy of seeking alliances with the parties of the Left in 1905–1906. He was more inclined to accept the Fundamental Laws than was Miliukov and his wing of the party.

Maklakov was elected to the Second State Duma in 1907 and the other two Dumas that followed. Until 1907 Maklakov represented a minority wing in the party that sought to persuade the whole party to accept the Fundamental Laws and try to build a new state based upon those laws. When Prime Minister P. A. Stolypin violated that constitution by proroguing the Duma and changing the franchise that was in violation of the Fundamental Laws, Maklakov had to give up his efforts to persuade other Cadets to his point of view. Nonetheless, both as a Duma member and skillful parliamentarian and as a practicing lawyer in many political cases, he continued his campaign to further the role of law in Russia. During the war he was one of the leaders who initiated the creation of the Progressive Bloc* and spoke vigorously against the shortcomings of the tsarist government without, however, advocating its overthrow.

Maklakov did not accept any post in the Provisional Government* immediately after the Revolution. With his own visceral hostility to Revolution and believing that Russia was not yet ready for it, he found it difficult to accept the new government and emerged as a spokesman for those who sought to limit the revolution and create a new and stable government that could impose the rule of law. He spoke with fear of the danger from the "dark masses" and in April 1917 commented that "Russia had received more freedom than she could manage" (Rosenberg 1958, p. 119). He finally agreed to serve as ambassador to France for the Provisional Government and he left for that post just before the October Seizure of Power*. Until 1924 he continued to coordinate the activities of the various embassies of Imperial Russia. In France he organized the Russian Political Conference which tried to influence the development of a broad anti-Bolshevik coalition inside Russia during the Civil War*. In 1924 France recognized Soviet Russia, and Maklakov was forced to confine his activities to Russian emigré life. He remained active in emigré politics and wrote a great deal about his experiences before and after the February Revolution*.

Bibliography

Fisher, George. *Russian Liberalism*. 1958.
Maklakov, V. A. *Vopsmominanie*. 1954.
Rosenberg, W. G. *Liberals in the Russian Revolution*. 1958.

Martov, Iulii (1873–1923); real name, Iulii Osipovich Tsederbaum. Martov, the co-founder of the Marxist "St. Petersburg Union of Struggle for the Emancipation of the Working Class" in 1895 and of the Social Democratic *Iskra* organization in 1900, became a founder and leader of Menshevism (*see* Russian Social Democratic Workers' Party [Menshevik]) at the Second Congress of the Russian Social Democratic Workers' Party in 1903. There he opposed both Lenin's bid for domination of the party and his organizational scheme for a narrow, highly centralized party of professional revolutionaries, advocating instead a broad, inclusive workers' party adapted to Russian conditions.

A champion of the doctrine of bourgeois revolution and of its self-denying ordinance of socialist abstention from power (in debate with V. I. Lenin*, L. D. Trotsky*, and K. Kautsky* in the period from 1905 to 1915) and of socialist internationalism (*see* Internationalists) during the war years, Martov returned to Russia from Swiss exile on May 9, 1917, to head the small group of Menshevik–internationalists who strenuously opposed the coalitionist policies of the Menshevik majority led by Iraklii Georgevich Tsereteli* and its "revolutionary defensism" (see Defensism).

Indeed, Martov's and Menshevism's understanding of Russia's bourgeois Revolution had always envisaged a revolutionary situation and social democratic strategy corresponding to the "Dual Power"* of the February Revolution* during the period of the First Provisional Government* (March 2-May 5, 1917). He expected a liberal bourgeois-democratic government to follow the fall of tsarism, while Social Democrats would entrench themselves as a "militant . . . revolutionary-democratic" opposition in "organs of revolutionary self-government" such as soviets, trade unions, cooperatives, town Dumas (*see* Duma and Revolution), and village councils. From there they would pressure the government to pursue democratic policies and thus realize the minimum program of Russian social democracy, until political liberty and capitalist development together prepared backward Russia for a proletarian revolution and the achievement of the maximum program, socialism.

It was that revolutionary strategy that he urged again at the First Congress of Soviets (*see* Soviets [Councils] of Workers', Soldiers', and Peasants' Deputies) in June 1917, denouncing Tsereteli's coalition of "all the living forces of the country" as a "fundamental mistake" and demanding the recall of the socialist ministers from the coalition government to leave the soviets free to exert the "heaviest pressure" on the bourgeois government and tell it "either forward, or out of the way."

At the same congress, in debate with Lenin and Tsereteli, Martov called for an ultimatum to the Allies: "They must renounce all imperialist war aims and negotiate peace. If not, revolutionary Russia would break with them and wage separate war if the Germans attacked" (Getzler. 1967. p. 152).

It was only on the eve of the "July Days"* during the government crisis caused by the walkout of four Cadet (*see* Constitutional Democratic Party—Cadet) ministers on July 2 that Martov lifted orthodox Menshevism's taboo on power: "Now there can be only one decision," Martov pleaded in the All-Russian Central Executive Committee* of Soviets on July 3 and 4: "history demands that we take power into our hands" (Getzler. 1967. p. 155). But his call for a broadly based "government of the democracy" was drowned out by Bolshevik (*see* Russian Social Democratic Workers' Party [Bolshevik]) shouts of "All Power to the Soviets" of the "July Days" and was skillfully thwarted by Tsereteli.

Martov made another onslaught on Tsereteli's coalitionism at the Democratic Conference* in mid-September 1917 but failed again, although only narrowly, to persuade a majority to vote consistently against coalitionism and for a popular-front government. His defeat underlined his failure during the Russian Revolution of 1917 to free himself in time from Menshevism's doctrine of bourgeois revolution and its inherently oppositionist mentality.

Having failed to provide a viable alternative to the Bolsheviks' "All Power to Soviets," on the morrow of the October Seizure of Power* Martov tried to prevent the Bolsheviks from establishing a minority dictatorship by negotiating the formation of a broad socialist coalition government "from the Popular Socialists to the Bolsheviks" (Getzler. 1967. p. 157).

In the same spirit, and assuming the role of a neutral "third force" during the "democratic" phase of the Civil War in Russia* (until October 1918), Martov and the Mensheviks tried to mediate between the Socialist–Revolutionaries (*see* Socialist-Revolutionary Party) and the Bolsheviks. Neutrality gave way to conditional support during the period 1919–1920, when Martov recognized in the Bolshevik regime the "defender of the revolution" against White (*see* White Movement) counterrevolution and foreign intervention but fearlessly denounced Bolshevik despotism and terrorism.

Martov's and the Mensheviks' attempt to fit themselves into the Bolshevik regime as a semi-loyal, semi-implacable opposition party came to a sad end in 1920–1921 when they were driven into exile or underground. Thereafter, and until his death in 1923, Martov's nightmare was a "Thermidorean, Bonapartist finale of the Red Dictatorship" maturing within the Bolshevik apparatus (Getzler. 1967. p. 217). Mensheviks, he urged, should not only wash their hands of the Bolshevik regime but also should equally shun "Koblenz"—emigré anti-Bolshevik coalitions.

Israel Getzler

Bibliography

Bourguina, A. A. *Russian Social Democracy: The Menshevik Movement*. 1968.
Getzler, Israel. *Martov: Political Biography of a Russian Social Democrat*. 1967.
Haimson, Leopold, ed. *The Mensheviks*. 1974.
Martov i ego blizkie. 1959.

Menshevik. *See* Russian Social Democratic Workers' Party (Menshevik).

Mezhraiontsy. *See* Interdistrict Committee.

Military Opposition. The Military Opposition was the faction in the Russian Communist Party (Bolshevik) (*see* Russian Social Democratic Workers' Party [Bolshevik]) that opposed the reorganization of the Red Army* to make it a more conventional hierachical and disciplined military force. The Military Opposition took shape at the Eighth Congress of the All-Russian Communist Party of the Soviet Union (Bolshevik) from March 18 to March 23, 1919. Part of the problem lay in L. D. Trotsky's* decision to use tsarist officers (military specialists) to train the Red Army that had come into being on January 28, 1918. Some members of the Left Communists (*see* Left Communism) faction wanted to return to the idea of the militia army with the election of officers, the abolition of ranks, an emphasis on partisan warfare, the eradication of military specialists, and the abolition of the death penalty.

At the Eighth Congress the debate was carried on chiefly by one representative from each side. G. I. Sokolnikov* spoke for Trotsky's position, and V. M. Smirnov, with the support of T. V. Sapronov, E. M. Iaroslavskii (*see* Gubel' man, Minei Izrailovich), and K. E. Voroshilov* (all Left Communists), spoke against it. In the debate, resentment against Trotsky's imperious manner was expressed, and there was much difference of opinion about the role of the political commissars. In a separate closed meeting where the debate took place, the Military Opposition won 37 to 20, but in the full meeting of the congress, Trotsky's view prevailed 174 to 95. To placate the strong Military Opposition, however, a committee was formed with I. V. Stalin*, V. M. Pozner, and G. E. Zinoviev* representing the majority view and E. M. Iaroslavskii and G. I. Safarov representing the Military Opposition. The compromise resolution still followed Trotsky's position fairly closely but set up machinery for hastening the training of proletarian officers so that they might take over from the specialists. Despite the size of the vote for the Military Opposition, it was defeated at the Eighth Congress. Its chief significance lay in its cost to Trotsky.

Voroshilov (perhaps at Stalin's instigation) was among those opposing Trotsky's measures, and the debate flared up again briefly at the Ninth Party Congress in 1920 when Trotsky appeared personally to defend his position. At that point the issue was civilian control over the army, in particular of the political commissars in the army. That debate continued at the Tenth Party Congress in 1921, when N. I. Podvoiskii* demanded civilian party control over political work in the army. Although the Military Opposition never won these battles, many army personnel and party figures became involved because they felt strongly about the issues, felt excluded from army careers, or simply disliked Trotsky. He made enemies who would later join in the struggle against him.

Bibliography

Daniels, Robert. *The Conscience of the Revolution.* 1960.
Schapiro, Leonard. *The Origin of the Communist Autocracy.* 1960.

Miliukov, Pavel Nikolaevich (1859–1943). Paul Miliukov was the founder and leader of Russia's major liberal party, the Constitutional Democratic Party— Cadet* (*Kadet*).

Miliukov was considered Russia's most important liberal by his followers and foes alike. A prominent historian and editor of his party's unofficial newspaper, *Rech' (Speech)*, Miliukov led the Cadet delegation in the Third and Fourth Dumas (*see* Duma and Revolution) and also served as chairman of the party's Central Committee. During the 1905 Revolution (*see* Nineteen-Five Revolution), Miliukov sought the destruction of autocracy and the creation of a liberal political system by revolutionary means. Although he viewed the October Manifesto, which produced the Duma, as an insufficient concession by the autocracy, Miliukov never favored the boycotting tactics of some radicals. In the decade preceding 1917, during which he became one of the Duma's leading figures and its foreign policy expert, Miliukov gradually moved to the Right, eschewing revolution as a tactic.

Upon Russia's entry into World War I*, Miliukov abandoned his previous pacificism and emerged as an ardent supporter of the crusade against the Central Powers. The government's unsuccessful prosecution of the war led him to participate in the creation of the Progressive Bloc*, a loose coalition of Cadets and Right-leaning Duma forces. This "loyal opposition" sought the modest goal of a "ministry having public confidence." Miliukov hoped that such responsible opposition would convince Tsar Nicholas II* of the need for concessions and would thus avoid another revolution that the Cadet leader had come to fear. Having failed with the Bloc, and under increasing criticism from left wing Cadets, Miliukov delivered his famous "Treason or Stupidity?" speech to a stormy session of the Duma on November 1, 1916. In the speech he linked the war's misconduct to the treasonous or stupid policies of the Tsar's appointees and Empress Alexandra. This immoderate salvo by a leading moderate became part of the mythology of the Revolution, seen by monarchists as the "storm signal" and by Cadets eager to establish a link with the successful February Revolution* as the "beginning of the Russian Revolution." Indeed, the speech was a symbol of the moderates' total lack of confidence in the government and was symptomatic of the atmosphere in which the monarchy collapsed.

Miliukov played a leading role in the creation of the Provisional Government* and in the formulation of its initial policies. Although viewed as the strongest figure in the first cabinet, he joined reluctantly. He led the Temporary Duma Committee in its negotiations with representatives of the Petrograd Soviet* and even wrote part of the Soviet's declaration supporting the new government. Almost alone amongst the Duma leadership, he sought to preserve the monarchy by convincing Grand Duke Michael to accept the throne. Miliukov argued the necessity of retaining the traditional symbol of state authority as a means of avoiding anarchy and preserving the army's capacity to fight. After five sleepless nights, countless speeches, interminable negotiations, and his failure to persuade Michael, Miliukov declined the position of Minister of Foreign Affairs. He reconsidered only on the urging of a delegation from the Cadet Central Committee.

Miliukov was determined that the Revolution should influence foreign policy as little as possible and made few changes in his ministry's personnel. With the new government in need of Allied recognition and assistance, he quickly assured the Allies of Russia's intention to fulfill all obligations and to fight "shoulder to shoulder" to final victory. Dismissing all revolutionary slogans in foreign policy as German formulations, he was committed to securing Constantinople and the Straits, and his imperialism triggered the Provisional Government's first crisis. Under Soviet pressure for "peace without annexations and indemnities," the government issued to the Russian people on March 27, 1917 the "Declaration of War Aims," which renounced "domination over other nations and seizure of their national possessions." But the declaration also contained the ambiguity of fully honoring all treaties and obligations contracted with the Allies and thus led to pressure for clarification both from Russia's embassies and Soviet leadership. Miliukov, who resented the Declaration's contents and its tacit recognition of Soviet influence, employed a formal note to Russia's allies as a means of "clarifying" the declaration to his liking. Instead of declaring against "annexations and indemnities," Miliukov's note, published in newspaper *Rech'* on April 20, referred to "decisive victory" and "guarantees and sanctions which are required to prevent new bloody encounters in the future." This seeming circumvention of growing public demand for revision of Russia's war aims precipitated street demonstrations on April 20 and 21 against Miliukov and the Provisional Government. Counterdemonstrations led by Cadets revealed the growing potential for social conflict and civil war.

While Soviet and Provisional Government leaders compromised on war aims and began negotiations for a coalition cabinet of nonsocialists and socialists, Miliukov opposed further infringement of state power. He refused the position of Minister of Education and resigned from the government on May 2. He had intended his departure to cause the withdrawal of other Cadet ministers, but the Cadet Central Committee voted eighteen to ten to keep its members in the government. As in March, a Central Committee delegation entreated Miliukov to remain in the government, but this time he remained firm. From its inception, then, Miliukov was against the "rotten compromise" of coalition.

After the April crisis, Miliukov confined his efforts primarily to party work, quickly reasserting his influence at the Cadet's Eighth Congress in early May. In his presentation to the congress Miliukov stood against continuing the Revolution, desiring instead to preserve its gains and Russia's state integrity and to delay further reforms until a constituent assembly could be convened. The combination of Miliukov's opposition to the principle of coalition and his concern for Russia's internal integrity led him once again to initiate withdrawal of Cadet ministers in early July over concessions made by the government to the Ukrainian Rada (*see* Ukraine, Revolution in). Miliukov's strategy of withdrawal was supported by a small majority (sixteen to eleven) of the Central Committee but was heavily criticized by Cadets outside Petrograd.

During the protracted cabinet crisis of July, Miliukov consistently opposed deepening the Revolution, as proposed on July 8 by the socialists remaining in the government. He made rejection of their stance a precondition for further Cadet participation in government. Although a new coalition, including Cadets, was finally created, Miliukov's support was decidedly soft. He began searching for allies to his Right in an attempt to stem the tide of Revolution and to establish a more stable state authority. As conservative forces coalesced around the idea of a military dictatorship under General L. G. Kornilov (*see* Kornilov Revolt), Miliukov and his followers confronted the dilemma of the incompatibility of their desire for firm state authority and their distaste for a conspiratorial coup. As a result, Miliukov's relationship to the Kornilov Revolt was ambiguous. While supporting Kornilov's goals, he was definitely not involved in the conspiracy and tried unsuccessfully to mediate between A. F. Kerensky* and Kornilov. In the aftermath of the abortive rebellion, Miliukov withdrew to the Crimea (*see* Crimea, Revolution in) for a "rest," reinforcing radical suspicions of his complicity.

In the waning days of the Provisional Government, Miliukov continued to oppose cooperation with socialists, even though conciliationists achieved a temporary majority within the Cadet Central Committee. Shortly after the Bolsheviks (*see* Russian Social Democratic Workers' Party [Bolshevik]) took power, they declared the Cadets "enemies of the people" and ordered Miliukov's arrest. One of seventeen Cadets elected to the Constituent Assembly*, Miliukov had gone to N. Rostov to join Generals M. V. Alekseev and Kornilov in their attempt to mount a campaign against the Bolsheviks.

Throughout the maelstrom of the Civil War in Russia*, Miliukov sought a military force capable of countering the Bolsheviks. When Alekseev's Volunteer Army (*see* White Movement) failed, Miliukov astonished his colleagues by attempting to work with German occupation forces in the Ukraine. With the collapse of Miliukov's "German policy" in the summer of 1918, he turned to the Allies, participating in an abortive conference of Russians and Allied diplomats at Jassy, Romania, to discuss the coordination of Allied intervention. Miliukov presented a characteristically archaic proposal, insisting that the Allies back a dictatorship and a regency. With the Civil War lost on the battlefields, and living in exile, Miliukov finally realized the critical error of both the Cadets and the White movement in ignoring popular aspirations. Miliukov proposed a turn to the Left and support for immediate reforms, the tactic of left-wing Cadets in 1917, which he had shunned throughout the Revolution and the Civil War. Miliukov hoped that this "new tactic" would lead to a massive insurrection against the Bolsheviks, but Lenin's own new tactic, the New Economic Policy*, insured that this would not happen. Instead, Miliukov's insistent pursuit of the new tactic permanently split the remnants of his dispersed party. He had gone from being the mediator of differences to being the precipitator of schism; one who had been the consummate politician was now confronted with the political irrelevance of emigration.

In his Parisian exile, Miliukov continued his careers of historian and journalist, remaining a staunch anti-Bolshevik and retaining the hope that his homeland would eventually join the community of Western liberal nations. Although his long political career had been devoted to this goal, in 1917 Miliukov's pursuit of traditional imperialist war aims and his opposition to conciliation with moderate socialists undermined the prospects for a moderate outcome to the Revolution.

Paul E. Burns

Bibliography

Medlin, Virgil D., and Parsons, Steven L., eds. *V. D. Nabokov and the Russian Provisional Government, 1917*. 1976.
Miliukov, Paul. *Political Memoirs, 1905–17*. 1967.
———. *The Russian Revolution*. 3 vols. 1978–1987.
Rosenberg, William G. *Liberals in the Russian Revolution*. 1974.

Molotov, Viacheslav Mihailovich (1890–1986; real name, Skriabin). Molotov was a prominent leader in the Russian Social Democratic Workers' Party (Bolshevik)* who played an important role in the October Seizure of Power* in Petrograd. He survived the political struggles within the party after Lenin's death and became one of the closest colleagues of I. V. Stalin* during his rule of the Soviet Union.

Molotov was born in a middle class family in the village of Kukarki, Nolinsk District, Viatka Province. The family had a high respect for education and Molotov and his brothers were well educated and artistic. Molotov was taught to play the violin and attended one of the so-called "modern" schools in Kazan. The "modern" schools differed from the old fashioned gymnasia in trying to train industrial managers and engineers, rather than the more conventional liberal arts. According to his authorized biography, Molotov became interested in revolutionary ideas in 1905 when he was fifteen years old. He first became involved in student discussion groups. The news of strike activity in St. Petersburg and discussions with a revolutionary named Vasnetsov, who was the brother of a well known artist in exile in Nolinsk, stimulated his interest in revolutionary ideas. But he tended at first to be interested in Marxism, more as a philosophical system than as a program of action. Thus, he did not choose between Bolshevism and Menshevism until 1906, the same year he began collaborating with V. A. Tikhomirnov in propaganda work in the Kazan secondary schools. The two men would remain friends for life.

In 1909 Molotov and Tikhomirov were arrested. In prison Molotov began reading and studying. At the end of that year he was sent to Vologda Province. There he passed his examinations for the seventh form (last year of school) and began to organize among the railwaymen. He finished his term of exile in 1911 and went abroad, where he met V. I. Lenin*. Molotov and Tikhomirov were put to work creating a legal Bolshevik newspaper.

Upon returning to St. Petersburg Molotov completed the preparations for the legal publication of *Zvezda* (the Star) and then of *Pravda** (Truth), becoming editorial secretary of the latter newspaper. At the same time he attended the Economics Department of the Polytechnic Institute. Molotov became secretary of *Pravda* and helped with the work of the Bolshevik Duma* (*see* Duma and Revolution) faction. At some time during 1912 and 1913 he worked with his future patron, I. V. Stalin* on the editorial board of *Pravda*.

In 1913 Molotov was arrested in Moscow and sent into exile in the Siberian village of Manzurka where he met M. I. Latsis. Molotov escaped and made his way back to Petrograd, where, in 1915 he founded a Bolshevik group that included A. Ia. Arosev, G. I. Bokii and Bazhanov. At the end of 1915 Shliap-nikov arrived as a delegate of the party Central Committee (*see* Central Committee of the Russian Communist Party [Bolshevik]). Shliapnikov organized the St. Petersburg Bureau of the Central Committee and made the twenty-five year old Molotov a member. By the end of 1916 Shliapnikov also appointed Molotov a member of the Central Committee's Russian Bureau along with Shliapnikov and P. A. Zalutskii. Molotov's responsibility was publications and after the February Revolution Molotov was put in charge of restoring the party newspaper *Pravda*. It resumed publication in February, 1917 with Molotov as chief editor. He directed the paper to follow a strict Leninist position of opposition to the Provisional Government*. On February 28 Molotov was chosen by the Petrograd Bolsheviks as one of the Bolshevik delegates to sit on the Executive Committee of the All-Russian Central Executive Committee of Soviets. Although Stalin and the other members of the Petrograd Committee tended to be conciliatory toward the other political parties, Molotov consistently opposed any alliance with them. Despite Stalin's deviation from Lenin's directions it was he, and not Molotov, who was appointed to the Bolshevik Central Committee in the April Conference, and it was Stalin that took over the post of chief editor of *Pravda*. Molotov, however, was appointed to the new nine-member Executive Committee of the Bolshevik Petrograd Committee in its meeting of May 10, and remained there throughout the preparations and execution of the October Seizure of Power in Petrograd.

Molotov was destined never to achieve a top level position in the new party or state. He achieved a reputation as a tireless worker, a man with incredible discipline who worked with cool efficiency, but he was not a brilliant speaker, an impressive public personality or a man inclined to be decisive or take his own initiatives. He was widely known by the nickname "stone-ass." As a result, during his lifetime he remained in posts just below the top. In 1918 he was put in charge of the Northern District Economic Council and in 1919 he was sent to the Volga Region to take charge of economic reconstruction and the creation of a Soviet structure of government.

When Ia. M. Sverdlov* died a Secretariat of the Central Committee was created and in 1921 Molotov was placed at the head of it. He was appointed a full member of the Central Committee and a candidate member of the Politburo, though in the following year Stalin would once again take the top position by being appointed General Secretary. Molotov became Stalin's assistant and was appointed a full member of the Politburo in 1925 and head of the Communist International* in 1929 when N. I. Bukharin* was removed from that post. In 1930 he replaced A. I. Rykov* in the Council of People's Commissars where he became Stalin's right hand man, a post he retained until Stalin's death in 1953. During the purges in 1936 he was in charge of the purge of the Ukrainian Communist Party. In May 1939 he was appointed People's Commissar of Foreign Affairs and negotiated the famous Molotov-Von Ribbentrop Non-Agression Treaty with Nazi Germany. Molotov would remain Commissar of Foreign Affairs until 1949. At the end of the 1950s when his wife was sent into exile, it was rumoured that he also would be arrested. Khrushchev would later state that Molotov was saved by Stalin's death, though in 1957 he would be removed from office by Khrushchev as a member of the so-called "Anti-Soviet Group" conspiring against Khrushchev. In 1961 he was expelled from the party with Kaganovich and Malenkov.

Bibliography

Burdzhalov, E. N. *Russia's Second Revolution*. 1987.
Haupt, Georges and Marie, Jean-Jacques. *Makers of the Russian Revolution*. 1974.
Medvedev, Roy. *All Stalin's Men*. 1983.
Slusser, R. M. *Stalin in October*. 1987.

Moscow, Revolution in. As Russia's second city, Moscow played an important role in the outcome of the October Seizure of Power* in the name of the soviets (*see* Soviets [Councils] of Workers', Soldiers', and Peasants' Deputies).

Soviet power in Moscow was not achieved until November 2, 1917, after eight anxious days of street fighting between Red Guards* and supporters of the Old Order. Although the political climate in Moscow had favored Soviet power well before October 25, the seizure of power was delayed because local leaders hesitated to risk bloodshed to attain control. Rather, the moderate Bolshevik (*see* Russian Social Democratic Workers' Party [Bolshevik]) leaders in Moscow hoped to achieve a negotiated transfer of power.

By October 1917 there were several indicators that Moscow had become an important center of opposition to the Provisional Government*. A general strike called to protest the Democratic State Conference* in Moscow had paralyzed the city on August 12. Moscow's workers overwhelmingly condemned the Kornilov mutiny attempt (*see* Kornilov Revolt) in late August, and on September 5 the Bolshevik Party received its first majority in the Moscow Soviet of Workers' Deputies. On September 25, in voting for new district Dumas (local branches of municipal government), the Bolshevik candidates received 51 percent of the citywide vote. In late June the Bolsheviks had received less than 12 percent of the vote in the City Duma elections. The statist Constitutional Democratic Party—Cadet* finished second in the September elections, with 26 percent of the votes, and the moderate Socialist-Revolutionary (S-R) Party* and the Mensheviks (*see* Russian Social Democratic Workers' Party [Menshevik]) received a dismal 14 and 4 percent, respectively. This was a striking reversal of the S-R Party's overwhelming victory in June, when it polled 58 percent of the Moscow vote. The September Duma elections clearly signified the polarization that had taken place between the forces of the Left—the Bolsheviks—and of the Right—the Constitutional Democrats.

In addition, there was increasing sentiment among the Moscow working class for a transfer of power to the soviets as the only way out of a growing economic morass. The soviet vote that gave the Bolsheviks their first majority on September 5 was a call for power to the soviets, and many resolutions recorded for the period September and October echoed this sentiment. Particularly significant was the involvement of hitherto inactive textile workers in the demands for Soviet power. But it is also important to note that these resolutions did not call for a violent seizure of power, and many of them suggested that Soviet power was an interim measure until the Constituent Assembly* could finally be convened.

Given this political background, Moscow Bolshevik leaders were cautious in their response to V. I. Lenin's* call for a seizure of power in early October. Leaders of the local Moscow Committee of the party (including I. A. Piatnitskii*, P. G. Smidovich*, M. F. Vladimirskii*, V. M. Likhachev, V. M. Smirnov, and E. M. Iaroslavskii [*see* Gubel'man, Minei Izrailovich]) worried that they commanded too few arms and too little support from within the local garrison to stage an uprising. They preferred a strategy of soviet power by decree: the Moscow Soviet would issue a series of decrees ending strikes, holding down rents, and then the newly formed Red Guard would arrest those capitalists who violated these decrees. The Moscow committee did endorse V. I. Lenin's famous October 10 resolution on the seizure of power (*see* Lenin, Vladimir Il'ich; October Seizure of Power), but with a significant change: it demanded the "liquidation" of Kerensky's government rather than its "overthrow." But the city committee was continually pressured for more decisive action by the younger and more radical Moscow Oblast' Bureau of the party. This body included V. N. Iakovleva*, N. I. Bukharin*, A. I. Gusev, N. N. Zimin, G. I. Lomov-Oppokov*, and N. Osinskii*, among others. This division within the Moscow party organization contributed to the Bolshevik leaders indecision in response to the Petrograd seizure of power on October 24–25.

The Moscow Soviet received the news from Petrograd that the soviets there had taken power at 11:45 a.m. on October 25. It was time now for Moscow to follow suit, but there had as yet been no concrete preparations. The radical Oblast' Bureau wanted to create a military center consisting only of party members, but the moderate Moscow Committee favored the Military Revolutionary Committee (MRC) sponsored by the Soviet and including representatives from all soviet parties. That evening the Soviet plenum voted on the Bolshevik resolution to create such a committee. The Bolsheviks received 394 votes for their resolution; a counterresolution proposed by the Mensheviks (*see* Russian Social

Democratic Workers' Party [Menshevik]) won only 113 votes. Thereupon the Mensheviks agreed to join the committee, but the Socialist–Revolutionaries refused. The original Moscow MRC, which later grew to twenty-six members, was elected to include seven voting and six non-voting (candidate) members, The seven were the Bolsheviks G. I. Lomov-Oppokov, V. M. Smirnov, G. A. Usievich, and N. I. Muralov'; the Mensheviks M. I. Teitelbaum and M. F. Nikolaev; and the Social Democratic Unityist I. I. Konstantinov. The six candidates were the Bolsheviks A. Ia. Arosev, P. N. Mostovenko, A. I. Rykov*, and S. Ia. Budzinskii and the Unityists L. E. Gal'perin and V. Ia. Iasenev,

On the other side, the S–R-dominated City Duma resolved to oppose the Soviet seizure and appointed its own Committee of Public Safety*. The committee included the Right S–R V. V. Rudnev (City Duma president), K. I. Riabtsev (Moscow military commandant for the Provisional Government*), S. A. Studenetskii, I. N. Kovarskii, I. Sorokin (S–R's and members of the municipal government), Constitutional Democratic Party—Cadet* member P. A. Buryshkin, engineer L. K. Ramzin, Menshevik V. V. Sher (active in military affairs), and Menshevik K. V. Kalmykov and S–R Kamaev from the Soviet of Soldiers' Deputies. Ironically, this committee to defend the Provisional Government refused to admit any representatives from that government to its council.

Neither side commanded significant military forces. The MRC could count on perhaps 6,000 armed Red Guards and the Committee of Public Safety (CPS) an equal number of military cadets (*junkers*). At the outset of hostilities, the MRC halfheartedly seized important communications centers and the Kremlin arsenal but soon lost the latter to troops from CPS. On October 26 V. P. Nogin* returned from Petrograd and attempted to negotiate a settlement with Riabtsev to support Nogin's plea for an all-socialist government. Actual fighting did not begin until late October 26, when a detachment of radical soldiers were fired upon trying to reach Soviet headquarters. From this point the Red Guards were thrown on the defensive. The MRC called for a general strike to begin the next day, but by then most factories were idle anyway, awaiting the outcome of events largely confined to the nonindustrial city center. On October 28 things looked so bleak for the Soviet forces that the MRC prepared to evacuate its headquarters. But the next day there were a series of Red Guard victories; the siege of the Soviet headquarters was lifted, and the Red Guards began to take control of strategic points in the outlying districts of Presnia and Khamovniki. By the end of the day, too, revolutionary soldiers began to arrive from points outside the city to assist the Moscow Red Guards, and armed units of workers were also dispatched by the soviets in the neighboring industrial towns of Serpukhov Podol'sk, Pavlovskii, Posad, Ivanovo, Tula, and Vladimir.

At this point, with the Red forces nearing victory, on October 29 the neutral Moscow bureau of the All-Russian Executive Committee of the Union of Railwaymen* (Vikzhel) appealed for a truce and a negotiated end to the fighting to be followed by the creation of an all-socialist government. Bolshevik radicals were at that time out in the working-class districts, and the moderates remaining in the MRC accepted the twenty-four-hour truce and began negotiations. Although the MRC agreed in principle to a coalition socialist government, final agreement could not be reached. When moderate socialists began to organize a "third element" in support of coalition government, MRC leaders finally abandoned their attempts to resolve matters peacefully. Fighting resumed on October 31, complete with an artillery bombardment of White (*see* White Movement) strongholds. Support from other centers continued to arrive; late on the 31st, 500 armed Kronstadt sailors detrained in Moscow. By late on November 1, the CPS offered to discuss their surrender. While talks proceeded into November 2, the White forces continued to lose ground, and by afternoon, they held only the Kremlin, the Alexandrov military academy, and an outlying officers' training school. At 5 p.m. the CPS chairman signed a mild surrender. The CPS agreed to terminate its existence, and the MRC agreed to end its shelling. The junkers were allowed to keep their arms, and prisoners would be released. Even now, the Moscow tradition of social harmony prevailed.

On November 3 the Moscow MRC and party leaders met to organize Soviet power in Moscow. On November 5 they dissolved the City Duma and the old Soviet of Soldiers' Deputies, both centers of opposition to Soviet power. New elections to the Soldiers' Soviet produced a Bolshevik delegation of 202 out of 296 deputies, and on November 14 the MRC formally handed its mandate over to the first meeting of the now-combined Soviet of Workers' and Soldiers' Deputies.

Diane Koenker

Bibliography

Grunt, A. Ia. *Moskva 1917- i: Revoliutsiia i kontrrevoliutsiia.* 1976.
Koenker, Diane. *Moscow Workers and the 1917 Revolution.* 1981.
Melgunov, S. P. *Kak bol'sheviki zakhvatili vlast: oktiabr'skii perevorot 1917 goda.* 1953.
Moskovskii voenno-revoliutsionnyi komitet. 1968.
Oktiabr'skoe vosstanie v Moskve. 1922.
Podgotovka i pobeda oktiabr'skoi revoliutsii v Moskve. 1957.
Vladimirskii, M. F. *Oktiabr'skie dni v Moskve.* 1927, 1957.

Moscow Soviet. The Moscow Soviet played a decisive role in the October Seizure of Power* in that city and serves as an example of the similarities and differences between the Bolshevik (*see* Russian Social Democratic Workers' Party [Bolshevik]) triumph in Petrograd and in other cities.

The Moscow Soviet of Workers' Deputies originated in the Revolution of 1905 (*see* Nineteen-Five Revolution) as a coalition of committees of five striking trades: printers, furniture makers, metal workers, tobacco workers, and ribbon weavers. The purpose of the Soviet was to coordinate the strike movement begun in Moscow in September 1905. Gradually, the founders sought to include all workers in the city; striking railway workers joined the movement, and the first formal session of the Moscow Soviet of Workers' Deputies met on November

21, 1905. The first chairman was N. I. Chistov, a Menshevik printer. This Soviet was not without rivals for the leadership of the Moscow working class. Many Bolsheviks, for example, perceived the Soviet as a rival institution rather than as one through which the party could work. For a time in early December the Soviet led the armed uprising of Moscow working-class districts, and in the aftermath of the rising's defeat, the Soviet was itself a victim of tsarist repression.

The memory of this first Soviet survived, and when members of political parties and public organizations met in Moscow on February 28, 1917, the resurrection of the Soviet was the first order of business. Twice on March 1, at noon and at 6 p.m., representatives of factories, trade unions, and political parties met to organize the body that would defend the interests of the workers in the Revolution. The first chairman of the Moscow Workers' Soviet was a popular Menshevik (see Russian Social Democratic Workers' Party [Menshevik]) lawyer, A. M. Nikitin. He resigned the next day to take a post in the city government and was replaced by another Menshevik, L. M. Khinchuk, who continued as chairman until September. Within a few weeks, the Soviet regularized procedures: workers sent deputies at the rate of one per 500 workers. Trade unions and political parties were also represented (trade unions according to their size). The plenum of the Soviet, elected as above, in its turn elected an executive committee of seventy-five, which met several times weekly to coordinate soviet affairs and to provide the leadership cadres for the Soviet's many functions. The plenum also elected a seven-person presidium to provide full-time leadership. The first presidium consisted of, in addition to the chairman, A. M. Nikitin and I. I. Egorov, Mensheviks; D. S. Rozenblum', P. G. Smidovich*, and V. P. Nogin*, Bolsheviks.

Initially, political party affiliation was subordinated to soviet activity. Unlike the situation in 1905, in this case the Bolsheviks did not see the soviet as a rival for power. With the fall of the monarchy, the soviet attained instant legitimacy in its own right. Furthermore, the majority of deputies were members of no political party. Only in June, when authorized elections of deputies were finally completed, did the Soviet report on the party composition of its members. The Bolsheviks comprised 29 percent of the deputies, the Mensheviks 29 percent, and the Socialist–Revolutionaries (see Socialist-Revolutionary Party), who coalesced with the Mensheviks, 14 percent. Executive Committee places were allocated so that each of the three parties had twenty representatives. From March until August, the Bolsheviks regularly claimed the allegiance of about one-third of the deputies in partisan voting; on September 5 the Bolsheviks won their first important vote, on the issue of Soviet power. Thereupon, the executive committee and presidium were reelected: V. P. Nogin, a longtime party member and political moderate, was elected chairman. (When Nogin resigned from the party Central Committee (see Central Committee of the Russian Communist Party [Bolshevik] in November 1917, he was replaced as soviet chairman by the historian M. N. Pokrovskii*.) The new September presidium included P. G. Smidovich, A. I. Rykov*, V. A. Avanesov, E. N. Ignatov, Bolsheviks; L. M.

Khinchuk and B. S. Kibrik, Mensheviks; L. E. Gal'perin, Social Democratic Unityist; and V. F. Zitta, Socialist–Revolutionary.

The Soviet of Soldiers' Deputies was organized on the initiative of the Workers' Soviet on March 4, and throughout the year this body tended to follow the lead of the parent Workers' Soviet. Contrary to the pattern in Petrograd, in Moscow the Soviets of Workers' and Soldiers' Deputies maintained their separate identities until after the October Seizure of Power*, although on important issues the two bodies often met in joint plenary sessions. The Soldiers' Soviet officially included about 600 deputies. Of them, 145 had been working peasants before mobilization, 210 were employees, 187 were workers, and 50 had been employed in intellectual professions. The leadership of the Soldiers' Soviet was dominated by Mensheviks. The first chairman was the Menshevik D. M. Krizhevskii. The Bolshevik Party never gained a majority in this soviet, which merged with the Workers' Soviet in November 1917. The Soviet of Soldiers' Deputies published its own daily organ throughout 1917, *Soldat-grazhdanin.* Of the two, the Soviet of Workers' Deputies was by far the most active soviet, both in reflecting political life in Moscow and in mobilizing political activity. Throughout the year, the most important concern of the soviet was the unity of the working class. Its daily organ, *Izvestiia,* which began publication on March 2, was designed to unite the workers of Moscow under the banner of socialism, regardless of party. Unity was important because the Soviet saw itself as representing Moscow's "socialist democracy" before the rest of the Russian public. Therefore, an important function assumed by the soviet throughout 1917 was to act as the spokesman of the working class.

The Moscow Soviet did not play the national role that its Petrograd counterpart did, but it was a major force in local politics and economic life. Almost from its inception, the soviet was called upon to help administer city functions and to provide services for the working class. Chief among these services was the mediation of labor–management disputes, and the soviet eventually created both a conflict commission to arbitrate immediate problems and an economic department to deal more systematically with the problems of wages, prices, and long- and short-term unemployment. Other departments and commissions of the soviet describe its many other activities: agitation-propaganda, local organization, provincial organization, trade union organization, food-supply, labor, military, and artistic enlightenment departments and medical, arbitration, alcoholism, prison, and fund-raising commissions, among others.

The soviet enjoyed wide popularity and respect among Moscow workers, not so much for its political views but as the legitimate representative of working-class interests. This respect waned only once, when the soviet (meeting together with the Soldiers' Soviet) refused to permit a general strike to protest the Moscow State Conference* in August. The strike proceeded anyway, authorized by the local central bureau of trade unions, and the soviet suffered a serious loss of prestige. But it regained its leadership role when all parties united behind the soviet to defend the city against the Kornilov Revolt* at the end of August, and it was sufficiently respected by October for the majority of Moscow's workers to support the transfer of power to the soviets as governing institutions.

Soviet organization in Moscow also existed at the neighborhood level. Again on the initiative of the central Soviet of Workers' Deputies, eleven district soviets were formed to represent the ten major working-class neighborhoods, with the railway workers as an eleventh "district." The ten were Gorodskii, Zamosk-vorech'e, Rogozh-Simonovskii, Blagusha-Lefortovskii, Basmannyi, Sokol'niki, Butyrki, Sushchevsko-Mar'inskii, Presnia, and Khamovniki. These district soviets were far less formally organized; they often consisted of joint meetings of local soviet deputies and delegates from area factory committees, so their mandates were sometimes unclear. They were often used by the Bolshevik Party as a forum for views that were not well received by the more august central soviet. In addition, the district soviets also performed many local administrative functions: conflict resolution, provisioning, and cultural and propaganda work.

After the October Seizure of Power in Moscow, the Moscow Soviet served as the principal organ of municipal government in Moscow. (A council of City Dumas, although possessing an elected Bolshevik majority, lost its administrative power by February 1918.) The separate soldiers' section of the Moscow Soviet was eliminated in March 1918. The first post-October elections to the soviet in April 19, 1918, produced a Bolshevik majority of 491 of 869 deputies (57.0 percent). Another 13.0 percent identified themselves as sympathetic to the Bolshevik Party; 10.0 percent of the deputies were Mensheviks, 4.0 percent Socialist–Revolutionaries; 7.5 percent belonged to other parties and 8.0 percent to no party. The new chairman was P. G. Smidovich*. With the transfer of the central government to Moscow in March 1918 and, more important, with the centralization of power characteristic of the entire country after October, the Moscow Soviet increasingly lost its character as a chamber of discussions and evolved into a purely administrative organ. Following the rise of socialist opposition to the Bolsheviks, on June 28, 1918, the Moscow Soviet voted to exclude the Menshevik and Socialist-Revolutionary factions from participation in the soviet and its executive organ. Only the Socialist-Revoluntionaries were actually expelled and Mensheviks continued to be elected and to participate into the 1920s.

Diane Koenker

Bibliography

Dvinov, B. *Moskovskii sovet rabochikh deputatov, 1917–22*. 1961.
Grunt, A. Ia. *Moskva 1917-i revoliutsiia i kontrrevolutsiia*. 1976.
Ignatov, E. *Moskovskii sovet rabochikh deputatov v 1917 g*. 1925.
Koenker, Diane. *Moscow Workers and the 1917 Revolution*. 1981.
Moskovskii sovet rabochikh, krest'ianskikh i krasnoarmeiskikh deputatov, 1917–27 gg. 1927.

Moscow State Conference. The Moscow State Conference was an assembly called by the prime minister of the Provisional Government*, A. F. Kerensky*, on August 12–14, 1917, to rally support for the Provisional Government*.

About 2,500 people attended the Moscow State Conference. They were drawn from a broad spectrum of Russian political life. Those who were represented were members of the cabinet of the Provisional Government; deputies from all of the Dumas (*see* Duma and Revolution); the top military officers; and representatives of the All-Russian Congress of Workers' and Soldiers' Deputies (*see* Soviets [Councils] of Workers', Soldiers', and Peasants' Deputies), the All-Russian Congress of Peasants' Deputies (*see* Peasants in the Russian Revolution), trade unions, cooperatives, provincial *zemstvos,* municipal councils, institutions of higher learning, and other assorted committees and congresses. The weight of representation, however, seemed to be conservative and moderate, groups that wanted stronger measures to impose order and leadership upon the country. The Bolsheviks (*see* Russian Social Democratic Workers' Party [Bolshevik]) did not attend because they had been threatened with expulsion from the soviets by the All-Russian Central Executive Committee* of the First All-Russian Congress of Soviets if they attended the Moscow State Conference and spoke out without permission.

There was widespread fear in Moscow that a right-wing coup d'état was imminent. In anticipation, the Moscow Soviet* formed a six-man provisional Revolutionary Committee that included two Bolsheviks (V. P. Nogin* and N. I. Muralov), two Mensheviks (*see* Russian Social Democratic Workers' Party [Menshevik], and two Socialist-Revolutionaries (*see* Socialist-Revolutionary Party). The Bolshevik Moscow Regional Bureau organized a protest strike for August 12, the opening day of the conference, despite the opposition of the Moscow Soviet. The strike was an eloquent testimonial to the growth in strength of the Bolsheviks because it was widespread despite the opposition of the leaders of the Moscow soviet.

Meanwhile the Moscow State Conference expressed enormous enthusiasm for the strongest measures recommended by the army Chief of Staff, General L. G. Kornilov (*see* Kornilov Revolt), on August 10 for the restoration of law and order and the repression of the soviets throughout Russia. The Cossack* general A. M. Kaledin* received a loud ovation when he expressed his support for Kornilov's recommendations. V. A. Maklakov*, representing the right wing of the Constitutional Democratic Party—Cadet*, urged those attending to have the courage to take "the daring steps necessary" and spoke with contempt for the "deep, dark masses" (Rosenberg. 1974, p. 216). Even the socialists, like the Menshevik N. S. Chkheidzhe*, seemed to endorse law and order, although they spoke of it being implemented by a government that represented the will of the majority (meaning a non-Bolshevik socialist government). There seemed to be some ambiguity among socialists and nonsocialists about the continuation of support for Prime Minister A. F. Kerensky, but he appeared before the conference anyway, giving a dramatic peroration. The speech was seen by some delegates, like the Constitutional Democratic Party leader P. N. Miliukov*, as an act of desperation rather than of confidence. To climax the turn to the Right, Kornilov himself appeared before the conference on August 13, consummating the new consensus with an elaborate, loud, and enthusiastic reception. He seemed to be sought after by all of the leaders of the Provisional Government, except perhaps Kerensky himself, who only sent his Minister of Transport, P. P. Iurenev, to meet with the general.

The Moscow State Conference gave both Kerensky and Kornilov a false sense of public support for a movement to the Right, although Kerensky seems to have been more aware than Kornilov of the hazards of his own position. The conference closed on August 15, and on August 17 Kerensky asked his assistant Minister of War, B. V. Savinkov*, to draft appropriate measures to restore order in the country. Although decrees similar to many of those proposed by Kornilov were issued and the two men seemed to have worked out a *modus vivendi* that included the declaration of martial law in Petrograd, Kerensky became increasingly wary of the general's actions. There was a growing awareness of Kornilov's plans for a right-wing coup d'état (*see* Kornilov Revolt), and that led to Kerensky's decision on August 27 to fire Kornilov as Chief of Staff, leading to Kornilov's attempt to seize power.

Bibliography

Browder, R. P., and Kerensky, A. F. *The Provisional Government, 1917.* 3 vols. 1961.
Rabinowitch, A. *The Bolsheviks Come to Power.* 1976.
Rosenberg, W. G. *Liberals in the Russian Revolution.* 1974.

Moslem Democratic Party (Musavat). The Moslem Democratic Party was founded in 1912 by a group of Azerbaijani revolutionary intellectuals who had helped form Gummet*, including Karbalai Mikailzade and Abbas Kazimzade. Its members were drawn from the Azerbaijani secularized intelligentsia, and they were wedded to the notion of a Pan-Islamic, Pan-Turkic Azerbaijani state organized along democratic lines and dedicated to modernization. But that program had no central core and was made up of a grab-bag of current popular notions. Apparently, the goal was to win over as much of the Moslem public as possible but especially the new native middle class. In 1913 Musavat acquired a talented leader named Mammad Amin Resulzade.

During the war the party urged its followers to refrain from criticizing the Tsar openly. After the February Revolution* the party allied itself to the Turkic Party of Federalists in late June and adopted the name Turkic Democratic Party of Federalists, Musavat. The new party again strove for broad appeal, calling for democracy and the defense of the economic and class interest of the masses and for federal autonomy for Moslem national groups within the Russian state. At the First Transcaucasian Moslem Congress on April 15–20, 1918, the issue of territorial national autonomy was raised. The All-Russian Moslem Congress (*see* All-Russian Moslem Council) that followed on May 1 called for a federal autonomy and a democratic state and created the All-Russian Moslem Council (Shura). Resulzade moved away from the Pan-Turkic idea to the notion that each Moslem nationality had its own linguistic national identity. In Azerbaijan the

native language was to be taught in the lower schools, and Ottoman Turkish
would be taught in the secondary schools. At the same time Musavat urged
support for the Provisional Government* and the war against Turkey and the
Central Powers. They also called for agrarian reform and protection of labor.
In June 1917 its support for the Provisional Government and for the war began
to wane, as it became clear that the Provisional Government had no sympathy
for the idea of greater autonomy for the national minorities.

When news of the October Seizure of Power* reached Baku, Musavat met
on the next day, October 26, in its first congress and called for territorial autonomy for Azerbaijan. On November 7 the Baku Council of Musavat endorsed
the overthrow of the Provisional Government. But Musavat soon discovered that
the Bolsheviks in the Baku soviet (*see* Transcaucasia, Revolution in; Azerbaijan,
Revolution in) had no intention of granting Azerbaijan federal autonomy. Some
members of Musavat joined the anti-Bolshevik government formed in Tiflis on
November 11, the Transcaucasian Commissariat, or Zakavkom. On November
26 the elections to the Constituent Assembly gave second place in Transcaucasia
to the Musavat with the Mensheviks ranking first. When the Constituent Assembly was dissolved by the Soviet Council of People's Commissars*, the Zakavkom, with the support of Musavat, moved to create its own Transcaucasian
legislature for Transcaucasia, the Seim, on February 10, 1918.

When the Baku soviet took over the city of Baku at the end of March along
with looting and burning of the Moslem quarters of the city, Musavat created
its own government in Tiflis in May 28, 1918, announcing that Azerbaijan was
now a sovereign state. The March Days had convinced most Moslem national
groups that they could not achieve autonomy under the authority of the Baku
soviet. In September 1918 they returned to Azerbaijan, first with the support of
the Turks and then with the support of the English. In alliance with the Dashnaksutiun (*see* Dashnaks) and the Georgian Mensheviks (*see* Russian Social
Democratic Workers' Party [Menshevik]), the Musavat ruled Azerbaijan from
1918 to 1920. When the English withdrew from Azerbaijan in August 1919, the
Musavat were overthrown in April 1920. As the British forces left the Caucausus
the Armenian Communist A. Mikoian went to Baku to resurrect the Azerbaijani
Communist Party. The Caucasian Bureau* had been set up in Moscow under
G. K. Ordzhonikidze* and S. M. Kirov* to strengthen the communist parties
in Georgia, Armenia, and Azerbaijan. On April 8, 1920, the Caucasian Bureau*,
in the name of the Soviet government, the Baku communists, and the Eleventh
Army Unit of the Red Army*, poised on the border of Azerbaijan under the
command of Ordzhonikidze and demanded that Azerbaijan submit to a communist regime. A new Azerbaijani government was set up by the Baku communist
(and former member of Gummet) Nariman Narimanov*. All political parties
other than the Communist Party were banned, and the leaders of Musavat were
coopted, as in the case of Resulzade; were executed; were arrested; or escaped
into exile.

Bibliography

Bennigsen, Alexandre A., and Wimbush, S. Enders. *Muslim National Communism in the Soviet Union.* 1979.
Pipes, Richard. *The Formation of the Soviet Union.* 1968.
Swietochowski, Tadeusz. *Russian Azerbaijan, 1905–20.* 1985.
Zenkovskii, Serge A. *Pan-Turkism and Islam in Russia.* 1960.

Moslem Social Democratic Party. *See* Gummet.

Musavat. *See* Moslem Democratic Party.

N

Narimanov, Nariman Nejefoghi (1870–1925). Narimanov was an Azerbaijan Communist political leader and writer who was born in Tiflis of a merchant family. He graduated from Gori Teachers Seminary and in 1908 from the Medical Faculty of Novorossiisk (Odessa University). He had four careers, as a physician, a teacher, a writer, and a political leader. Before 1905 he was best known in Azerbaijan (*See* Azerbaijan, Revolution in) for his novels in which he called for an end to antiquated customs and religious fanaticism. In 1905 he became a member of Gummet*, and played an active role in the 1905 Revolution (*See* Nineteen-Five Revolution) in Azerbaijan. In 1909 he was arrested and sent into exile for five years. When Gummet was revived in 1917 he became chairman of its Provisional Committee and a member of the Baku Committee of the Russian Social Democratic Workers' Party (Bolshevik)*. Like most of the Baku members of Gummet in 1917 he did not run for elections on a Gummet ticket, and so was not a member of the Baku Soviet. Nonetheless when the Baku Commune was formed in 1918 (*see* Transcaucasia, Revolution in) he was appointed Commissar of the National Economy. When the Baku Commune fell, he escaped to Astrakhan, where he and the remaining members of Gummet reorganized. He deserves some credit for having warned the Baku Bolsheviks against the danger of an "intercommunal" massacre before the March days in 1918.

In June 1919 Narimanov was appointed head of the Near Eastern Division of the Commissariat of Foreign Affairs, and then Deputy Commissar of the Commissariat of National Affairs. In April 1920 he became Chairman of the Azerbaijani Provisional Revolutionary Committee, and in 1921 Chairman of the Council of People's Commissars in Azerbaijan. In December 1922 Narimanov became one of the chairmen of the Central Executive Committee of the USSR. At the Twelfth Congress of the Russian Communist Party (Bolshevik) Narimanov was elected a candidate member of the Central Committee of the Communist Party of the Soviet Union. Though climbing very high in the apparatus of the new Soviet government, Narimanov tried to use his position of power to gain greater federal autonomy for Moslem national minorities within the Soviet state, starting with his native land of Azerbaijan. The decision of the Politburo in July 1919 to recognize Azerbaijan as an Independent Soviet Republic owed much to his influence and that of the other members of Gummet living in Moscow. But the quarrel between the Moscow Gummet and the Baku Bolsheviks ended with a compromise. The Gummet Party would be dissolved along with all other political parties, but there would be an Azerbaijani Communist Party.

Although Narimanov died in bed, he was denounced along with all of the other members of Gummet during the Great Purges of the 1930s. After Stalin's death his name was rehabilitated.

Bibliography

Swietochowski, Tadeusz. *Russian Azerbaijan 1905–1920*. 1985.
Zenkovsky, Serge. *Pan-Turkism and Islam in Russia*. 1960.

National Question and the Russian Revolution. Nationalism was regarded by most Marxists as a transitory bourgeois ideology that would expire as soon as industrial workers and the masses had achieved a "true" consciousness of their position in the world. It also was expected to decline with the spread of a socialist world economy. Despite this persistent belief, nationalism has played an important role in the history of the Union of Soviet Socialist Republics from its inception.

Even before the Revolutions of the twentieth century the Russian state was polyethnic and multiconfessional. The last tsars attempted to attack the non-Orthodox religions and compel institutional and cultural Russification on the one hand and pursue a violently anti-Semitic (*see* Anti-Semitism) policy on the other hand. Coupled with the socioeconomic strains attendant with the development of a modern economy, this situation brought the national question to the fore as a major issue just before and during the Russian Revolutions (*see* Nineteen-Five Revolution; February Revolution; October Seizure of Power). The relationship of the Russian state and the Great Russian peoples to the different nationalities and religions in its midst has at least three dimensions: political, religious, and cultural.

The *political dimension* refers to the questions of the constitutional structure of the Russian state and whether national groups should possess solid legal guarantees of either secession or federal autonomy in order to obtain self-determination. For example, should Poland have legally sanctioned autonomy on either ethnic or purely territorial lines or alternatively enjoy a guaranteed right of participation in a federal union? The *cultural dimension* refers to the right to use the native language in education and state business affecting citizens on an equal basis with Russian control of curricula and removal of discriminatory barriers to minorities. The *religious* dimension, being closely tied to ethnicity among Jews (*see* Jewry, 1905–1921), Moslems, and minority Christians, refers to freedom of worship and observation of rites, for example, religion, education, and marriage (*see* Religion and the Revolution).

During 1917–1921 the main controversies surrounding the national question became political issues because of the chaos and internal strife that offered national minorities the opportunity to give political expression to their desire for greater national self-determination. This was clear immediately after the February Revolution* in the positions taken by both the Provisional Government* and its rival, the Petrograd Soviet*.

The Provisional Government refused to make any decision that might bind the future Constituent Assembly* in deciding the constitutional structure of Russia. This meant that during its entire tenure, despite growing pressure for commitment to autonomy or to guarantees of ethnic participation in future decisions, the government stood firm in support of the imperial status quo and refused to diminish central authority over the ethnic borderlands. In the beginning the Provisional Government issued a declaration of civil rights, guaranteeing full statutory equality and full civil rights to all. It believed that with this declaration it had resolved the national issue and that any future steps toward autonomy or federation not only compromised the Constituent Assembly but threatened the integrity of Russia at a perilous time.

With this in mind the Provisional Government duly rejected Finnish pressure for autonomy, Ukrainian threats of secession if it was not accorded self-government, pressure to recognize a future independent Poland, and the Baltic states' call for self-rule. But by breaking up the old regime's administration, the Provisional Government proved unable to arrest the headlong drift to interethnic violence between Russians and Moslems in Central Asia (*see* Central Asia, Revolution in) or between Armenians and Azeris, (*see* Azerbaijan, Revolution in) in Baku or the ominous signs of range wars between Russia and Moslem peasants along the Volga (*see* Central Provinces), in Central Asia, and in the Caucasus (*see* Transcaucasia, Revolution in). Essentially, the Provisional Government remained bewitched, like the tsars before them, by the belief that it could survive only by ruling over subject peoples.

The Petrograd Soviet's outlook was basically similar. It was characteristically ambivalent about taking power and deciding nationality issues. Neither the Mensheviks (*see* Russian Social Democratic Workers' Party [Menshevik]) nor the Socialist-Revolutionaries (*see* Socialist-Revolutionary Party) ever framed a coherent answer to the political demands of the national question. In the last days before October, V. M. Chernov* and F. I. Dan (*see* Gur'vich, Fedor Il'ich) of these parties announced in the Council of the Republic (*see* Democratic Council) that "the programme of the revolution is to give all the nationalities the right of self-determination. But it does not mean independence. We believe that this right must be used to preserve close links with Russia—having received their right, the nationalities must remain part of a free Russia" (quoted in Ferro, 1976, p. 100).

This essentially was also the Bolsheviks' (*see* Russian Social Democratic Workers' Party [Bolshevik]) policy once they came to power. Whatever their position in theory, in practice the Bolsheviks did not shrink from inventing new political modalities to implement centralization and were much more ruthless in putting them into practice. Their rivals in the soviets (*see* Soviets [Councils] of Workers', Soldiers', and Peasants' Deputies) and the Provisional Government remained impotent and paralyzed by these and other issues, proving themselves helpless to arrest the drift into disintegration occurring in late 1917. This disintegration came about because the breakdown in central authority and its unresponsiveness to local needs forced unwilling radicals among the national minorities—who had no intention of seceding—to take matters into their own hands. The collapse of central authority stimulated groups from Finland and Georgia to prevent anarchy and disintegration by establishing their own self-rule. The memory of Russian misrule and oppression and the obstinacy of the soviets and the Provisional Government intensified their desire to avoid dependency on Russia. What confounded the Bolsheviks was that their victory made no impression on many ethnic groups, many of whom remained hostile to them and did not flock to their banner. But although the Bolsheviks may have been confounded, they were not rendered helpless by this discovery.

As early as 1912 I. V. Stalin* had been commissioned to define the Bolshevik position on the national question. The future Commissar of Nationalities arrived at a formula that would become the cornerstone of Bolshevik policy on the national question, although he always wisely referred to it as an expression of Lenin's thoughts on the subject. Attacking the theoretical writings of the Austrian Marxists, Stalin wrote his famous article ''Marxism and the National Question.'' In it he endorsed the right of national minorities to national self-determination up to and including secession, but it was clear from the outset that national aspirations for political autonomy would be subordinated to the paramount goals of creating a socialist society and state. In its final form after 1925, the official Bolshevik position would be expressed in the formula ''national in form and socialist in content,'' which in effect meant that the Bolsheviks would allow the outward forms of federal autonomy and the expression of national cultural identity without the right of secession from the soviet socialist state. In practice Bolshevik leaders and party members really held a view similar to that of their political rivals, that the national question was a transitory phenomenon of the capitalist epoch and, therefore, subordinate to the question of the socialist revolution. However, the Bolshevik theoretical position gave them a tactical advantage over their political rivals in a period of political upheaval. Bolsheviks could appear to support the demand for national self-determination up to and including secession in multi-ethnic capitalistic–imperialistic states or their colonies and at the same time embrace a revivified vision of the imperial heritage. Thus in 1917 the Bolsheviks could appear to support all national liberation movements while, in the last stage of the struggle, denying that movement the right to secession, a strategy that would permit them paradoxically to use the desire for national self-determination to defeat that goal.

In Finland and the Baltic states the combination of allied military force, Soviet weakness, and lack of support for Moscow-oriented Baltic socialists precluded the reintegration of those areas into Russia. But the Soviet regime made repeated attempts to incite or institute such an outcome during the Civil War in Russia* of 1917–1921. Although ultimately obliged to accept the political independence of Finland, the Baltic, Poland, Bassarabia and Sub-Carpathian Ruthenia, prominent Bolsheviks such as Stalin railed against it and would restore those areas to Russia with the exception of western Poland and Finland during World War II.

Soviet leaders, such as V. I. Lenin*, saw an analogy between the national question and the right of divorce—everyone should have the right but not necessarily be encouraged to use it. In devising policies to hold the embattled empire together, the leadership in Moscow hit on the notion of recruiting native nationalist leaders who would enlist the assistance of Moscow and the Red Army* in support of their cause. In the end the supreme military–political command would come from Moscow. This strategy proved enormously successful in Central Asia, Siberia (see Siberia, Revolution in), Transcaucasia (see Transcaucasia, Revolution in), and the Ukraine (see Ukraine, Revolution in).

The political institutions through which national radicals were led into the Russian Communist Party (Bolshevik) was the Commissariat of Nationalities (Narkomnats). It served as a channel of elite recruitment among minorities' struggle, winning significant beachheads among their elites that would provide the Bolsheviks with access to the masses. In turn, this opened the door to class struggle and revolution within the nationalities. Combined with the use of the Red Army, these tactics proved brilliantly successful, but the cost was the incorporation of all nationality conflicts into central government institutions.

There were essentially two reasons for this. On the one hand, the ethnic radicals placed their highest priority on national self-determination, finding it easy in the beginning to find a response in Lenin's commitment to that cause. On the other hand, once entrapped, the national leaders found that the local Bolsheviks and the central government unanimously opposed genuine political self-determination and set definite limits to cultural self-determination. The struggles over these issues turned every dispute into a major political battle. In 1922–1923 nationality policy in Georgia became tied to the struggle for secession, and nationalists like Mirsaid Sultangaliev* were purged in public party trials. Given these conflicts, it would have been difficult for the regime to prevail had its enemies been more perceptive about the real position of the Bolsheviks.

There were, however, few alternatives. Most of the national minorities were weak militarily and divided among themselves. The Whites (see White Movement) were out-and-out chauvinists who made openly disdainful remarks about the nationalities and imagined the Revolution to be a Jewish–Communist conspiracy. Their commitment to a Russian chauvinist utopia of the past, their virulent anti-Semitism that culminated in terrifying pogroms, their anti-Islamic prejudices all decisively estranged the minorities at a crucial time. Given their numerical weakness, nationalist leaders had no choice but to join the Bolsheviks. This was especially true of the Jews, who had been the most loyal supporters of the Provisional Government because that government had ended discriminatory laws. Lenin at one time remarked that without the Jewish intelligentsia, the regime would have been hard pressed to survive (Dimanshtein 1924). Thus by 1920 the regime had weathered the storm of Civil War and was on the way to achieving reintegration of Russia by exploiting the nationality tactics it had developed to export revolution abroad. During 1920–1921, it sought to do this by wars and invasions in Poland, Transcaucasia, and Iran. Poland and Iran repulsed these attacks, but the empire remained intact.

During 1918 the regime provided a new definition of self-determination, restricting the concept solely to the proletariat and its party and stipulating that the regime would tolerate it only if it was packaged in the soviet form. This definition was announced by Stalin in 1918, and although reiterated candidly by N. I. Bukharin* at the Eighth Party Congress in 1919 for which Lenin rebuked him, it stood as policy. By 1921 the regime, speaking through Stalin, was now ready to redefine the term still further, to prevent self-determination through secession or genuine federal autonomy of Russia's national minorities. Those ethnic minorities that sought to leave the Union of Soviet Socialist Republics found themselves in the eye of the storm. Despite stipulations to the contrary in its successive constitutions, the Soviet Union proceeded to deny genuine national self-determination beyond certain well-defined limits and instead strengthened the centripetal forces of the country through economic and cultural integration. Mass cooptation of obedient national leaders and perfection of the governing apparatus completed the centralization process.

The secession struggles of the 1920s and the long-standing debates over the economic, religious, and cultural issues of that decade are all linked together. This could be seen in the trial of Sultangaliev—Stalin's first show trial—in 1923 in which the regime's top Moslem was purged for nationalism. Perhaps it was destined to be that way, since the Bolsheviks had given highest priority from the beginning to the creation of a socialist state over the goals of the separate nationalities. In staying this course the Bolsheviks demonstrated an aptitude for using the instruments of power to survive whereas their rivals fell before the challenge of nationalism. They were able to use nationalism to defang nationalism, at least temporarily. In the long run, however, they allowed enough expression of cultural nationalism to keep alive the consciousness of national identity. Instead of succumbing to the higher needs of socialism, the nationalism of ethnic minorities has in most cases remained strong to the present, continuing to provide a persistent problem for Soviet leaders.

Stephen Blank

Bibliography

Benningsen, Alexandre, and Lemercier-Quelquesay, Chantal. *Islam in the Soviet Union*. 1968.

Borys, Jurij. *The Sovietization of the Ukraine, 1917–23.* 1960.
Connor, Walker. *The National Question in Marxist-Leninist Theory and Strategy.* 1984.
Dimanshtein, S. M. *Lenin o evreiskom voprose.* 1924.
Ferro, M. *The Bolshevik Revolution.* 1976.
Gitelman, Zvi. *Jewish Nationality and Soviet Politics, 1917–30.* 1973.
Kulichenko, M. I. *Bor'ba Kommunisticheskoi Partii i reshenie national'nogo voprosa v 1918–20.* 1963.
Meyer, Alfred. *Leninism.* 1957.
Park, Alexander. *Bolshevism in Turkestan.* 1957.
Pipes, Richard. *The Formation of the Soviet Union.* 1968.
Safarov, G. I. *Kolonial'naia revoliutsiaa.* 1921.
Tucker, Robert C. *Stalin as Revolutionary, 1879–1929.* 1973.

Navy in World War I. The Russian navy played a crucial role in both the war and the Revolution. In August 1914 the Russian navy was unprepared to fight the scale and type of war that was ahead. In this respect it was in a position similar to that of the Russian army and to most of the armed forces of the other participants. The Russian navy, however, faced more serious and unique problems created by history, geography, and politics. Despite these formidable obstacles, the ships and sailors performed admirably under generally capable officers, compiling an impressive routine combat record. That they could do no more was due to the strategic planning and the domestic conditions within Russia.

The Russo–Japanese War (1904–1905) and the 1905 Revolution (*see* Nineteen-Five Revolution) had already cast deep shadows over the Russian navy. The disaster that befell the Baltic Fleet (Second Pacific Squadron) at Tsushima in May 1905 and the celebrated mutiny on board the battleship (*Poltava*) in the Black Sea the following month had powerful influences on the officers and men and the environment within which they worked. In the interwar period (1905–1914) revitalization was required not only because of the recent heavy losses but also because of the rapid escalation in naval technology that produced a veritable armaments race. But despite the imperative need for construction and the efforts of respected naval strategists such as Nicholas L. Kladko, the government, bothered by a recalcitrant legislative body, the Duma (*see* Duma and Revolution), failed to speed the necessary advances.

The navy in its attempts to rebuild was also hampered by a well-deserved reputation for revolutionary activity. A number of naval ships and bases besides the *Potemkin* experienced major disturbances in the 1905–1906 period, producing in the public mind an image of an untrustworthy force. Duma leaders were thus reluctant to agree on appropriations for new battleships that might be only the vehicles for new "Potemkins." This proved to be a well-founded fear.

Construction, nevertheless, proceeded, at first slowly but then, with the prodding of Naval Minister I. K. Grigorovich after 1911, with greater speed and efficiency. Older pre-dreadnaught battleships (Gangut class) were completed; new battle cruisers, such as the *Riurik,* were purchased abroad; and several new-type dreadnaughts (23,000 tons) were laid down the same time as a prototype of a modern destroyer (*Novik*). Far-sighted innovations in naval aviation, submarines, and mine laying were also extended beyond the experimental stage. By the outbreak of World War I* the Russian navy consisted of 8 battleships (all pre-dreadnaughts), 14 cruisers (of various sizes and ages), around 100 older-type destroyers, and a relatively small number of torpedo boats and submarines. Seven dreadnaughts, 4 battle cruisers, 8 line cruisers, 36 destroyers, and several submarines were under construction. The dreadnaught *Petropavlovsk* and modern destroyer *Novik* entered active duty soon after hostilities commenced.

The Russian navy had followed the patterns of the other great naval powers by concentrating on capital ships to the neglect of submarines and smaller craft. The Russian limitations in these areas were removed in part by wartime construction, by conversion of merchant ships, and by the arrival of a British submarine squadron that successfully ran the gauntlet through the Baltic to the Gulf of Finland in late 1914 and early 1915.

But a major limitation on Russian naval planning was the geographic division of the navy into four separate fleets: Baltic, Black Sea, Pacific, and White Sea, with no way, once the war had begun, to shift units effectively from one area to another. The Baltic Fleet, for example, despite its weaknesses, possessed a decided superiority over the German fleet normally stationed in that sea, but the latter could always be reinforced by the high seas fleet from the North Sea. Even the decided advantage that the Russian fleet had over the Turkish in the Black Sea was drastically altered by the quick dispatch from the Mediterranean of the German battle cruiser *Göben* and light cruiser *Breslau*. Ironically, during the first weeks of the war the Russian navy, which always considered itself superior to that of the Turks, was put on the defensive in the Black Sea by the surprise bombardment of its Black Sea bases and ports by the German ships that possessed superior speed and firepower while in the Baltic a relatively powerful Russian fleet was committed from the beginning to a defensive strategy, subordinated to the Sixth Army of the Russian Northern Front. Under the command of Admiral Nicholas von Essen the ships of the Baltic fleet laid a series of mine fields that would prove formidable defenses for the Gulf of Riga and the Gulf of Finland. Despite its mainly defensive posture, the fleet carried out effective offensive mine laying off the German coast, particularly aimed to interdict traffic into the Bay of Danzig and the shipping routes from Sweden into the winter and early spring of 1914–1915. These daring exploits, coupled with the technical capability of Russian mines, caused the sinking and damaging of a sizable number of German warships and merchant vessels in the early years of the war.

A foolhardy attempt by the German fleet in August 1914 to test the new mine defenses at the entrance to the Gulf of Finland resulted in the grounding and capture of the light cruiser *Magdeburg,* the significance of which was chiefly the discovery of copies of the German naval codebooks on board, a boon to Entente intelligence throughout the war. The Russians also lost a cruiser, the *Pallada,* to a U-boat torpedo in October. These single but striking losses no doubt influenced the cautious strategies employed for the duration of the war in the Baltic. In 1915 and 1916 both sides improved their mine fields and made tentative offensive strikes. The British submarines of the E-class were highly effective in interdicting German-Swedish sea lanes, and in August 1915 a reinforced German squadron attacked the defenses of the Gulf of Riga but was repulsed with losses by a few Russian ships led by the old battleship *Slava* and the mine fields.

The basically defensive strategy and fear of mines and U-boats caused the Russians to keep the new, powerful dreadnaughts, when they were completed and commissioned, out of action and stationed at the main base of Helsingfors (Helsinki) in Finland most of the war. Their crews soon became increasingly untrustworthy and subject to revolutionary and anti-war propaganda, an additional reason to avoid assigning them to combat missions. The effectiveness of the Baltic Fleet was also weakened by command problems. The energetic and experienced Admiral von Essen died suddenly in May 1915 and was replaced as commander-in-chief by the mild-mannered and desultory Admiral V. A. Kanin. His removal in September 1916 raised hopes for a revival of discipline and action under Admiral Adrian I. Nepenin, but the latter was cut down by a revolutionary mob in March 1917.

In the Black Sea, on the other hand, the completion of the first new dreadnaught, the *Imperatritsa Mariia,* in July 1915 changed the balance of naval power decisively in favor of Russia and placed the German–Turkish forces on the defensive. Less use of submarines and mines in this theater made the larger ships more effective, and operational command, under Admirals A. A. Eberhardt and A. V. Kolchak* (from 1916), was more consistent and energetic. The sailors were also more loyal and less contaminated by ideas of dissension and revolution. The Black Sea Fleet, though hurt by an unexplained explosion in October 1916 that sunk the *Imperatritsia Mariia,* effectively prevented the Turkish use of the sea to supply the Caucasian front but still was unable to launch an offensive strike at the straits, which might, in coordination with the Gallipoli campaign, have forced Turkey out of the war and reopened a vital supply line into the South of Russia.

While the Black Sea Fleet gained strength and mastery over limited domain, the Baltic Fleet by 1917 was increasingly contained behind mine fields in the Gulf of Finland, a victim of superior German land forces and increasing domestic difficulties. The officer corps was drastically shaken physically and mentally by the upheavals of the revolutionary year, beginning with the violent uprisings on many ships and in shore units in the February Revolution*. Officers and men still retained the desire to defend the region from German attack, but distrust, disorganization, and the intrusion of domestic affairs made a military posture more and more difficult. Still, in October 1917 a final engagement was fought against a vastly superior German naval force that penetrated the Gulf of Riga and attacked the Russian defenses in Moon Sound and Irbin Strait. The result was the sinking of the battleship *Slava* and a modest victory for the Germans, but they lost even more ships and shifted to a defensive position.

Considering the strategic limitations, the Russian navy had performed credibly at sea, inflicting more losses than were sustained. But the navy also constituted a logistical burden, which the country by 1916 could no longer afford. In the case of the Baltic Fleet, inactivity and proximity to political activism led to the ships and men becoming more of a threat to a Russian government that intended to prosecute the war than to the Germans.

The old Russian Imperial Navy was mostly destroyed by incorporation into the Red Army and by neglect during the Civil War in Russia*, 1918–1920. Many officers joined the White armies and later emigrated, while most sailors became soldiers. The Black Sea Fleet and Pacific squadron fell under White control and were later sold or scuttled. The more revolutionary Baltic Fleet also suffered a disastrous blow as a result of the Kronstadt Revolt (*see* Kronstadt, 1917–1921) of March 1921, and many surviving sailors were killed or jailed. The ships of this fleet were in such poor shape by 1922 that a number were sold to Germany for scrap. A few, such as the cruiser *Aurora,* remained to provide the nucleus of a major rebuilding campaign in the 1930s.

Norman Saul

Bibliography

Graf, H. *The Russian Navy in War and Revolution from 1914 to 1918.* 1923.
Mitchell, Donald W. *A History of Russian and Soviet Sea Power.* 1974.
Pavlovich, N. B., ed. *Flot v pervoi mirovoie voine.* Vol. 1. 1964.
Timirev, S. N. *Vospominaniia morskogo ofitsera.* 1961.
White, Dimitri Fedotoff. *Survival through War and Revolution in Russia.* 1939.

Nevskii, Vladimir Ivanovich (1876–1937; real name, Feodosii Ivanovich Kribokov). Nevskii was a prominent Bolshevik (*see* Russian Social Democratic Workers' Party [Bolshevik]) leader during the October Seizure of Power* in Petrograd, and became an important figure in the new Soviet government, and later an important editor and historian.

Nevskii was born in Rostov on the Don in a rich merchant family. There was some military background in the family as well, since his great-grandfather had been a Zaporpozhian Cossack (*see* Cossacks) and his grandfather a professional soldier in the Russian Imperial Army. In his own autobiography Nevskii expressed some hostility toward his father and his vocation, and contended that it was his mother who gave him some sympathy for the downtrodden and some respect for education. While in the gymnasium in Rostov on the Don in 1894 he organized a study group that read the works of the major nineteenth century Russian revolutionary writers. In 1895 and 1896 he became involved in a Populist group, but after reading the Communist Manifesto in 1897 he turned to Marxism and the Russian Social Democratic movement. By the end of the year he and E. V. Bystritskoi had formed an organization which would come to be known as the Don Committee of the Russian Social Democratic Workers' Party. When he moved to Moscow to attend the university in the fall, he formed a social democratic group that established ties with the Moscow Committee of the Russian Social Democratic Workers' Party. After the Second Congress of the Russian Social Democratic Workers' Party Nevskii sided with the Bolshevik faction, though he did not meet V. I. Lenin* until October 1904. He recalled that Lenin made a stronger impression on him than any other Social Democratic leader that he had met. From 1905 to 1908 he was a prominent member of the St. Petersburg Committee of the Bolshevik Party.

Between 1898 and the October Seizure of Power Nevskii became one of the most active members of the Bolshevik Party working inside Russia, though his career as a revolutionary was frequently interrupted with arrests and exiles. Despite this he managed to finish his degree in natural sciences at Kharkov University in 1911. In addition to his work among soldiers and workers he also served some time as editor of two Bolshevik newspapers, *Zvezda* (the Star) and *Pravda* (Truth). In 1912 he was appointed a member of the Central Committee of the Bolshevik Party (*see* Central Committee of the Russian Communist Party [Bolshevik]) and in 1913 he was appointed a member of the Russian Bureau of the Central Committee. This placed him in the top ranks of the party on the eve of World War I* and the October Seizure of Power.

After the February Revolution* Nevskii returned to Petrograd and with N. I. Podvoiskii* created the Bolshevik Military Organization and edited the party newspaper for soldiers, *Soldatskaia Pravda*. When the preparations for the October Seizure of Power took place he became one of the commissars of the Military Revolutionary Committee of the Petrograd Soviet*. In this position he became closely associated with G. E. Zinoviev and shared Zinoviev's skepticism about the wisdom of a Bolshevik seizure of power, although he was finally persuaded that it was necessary two days before the event occurred. During the Civil War in Russia* Nevskii played an important role in the organization of the new government, first as Commissar of Communications, and then as Deputy Chairman of the All-Russian Central Executive Committee of Soviets*, and a member of the Department for Rural Work. He also was appointed to the Revolutionary-Military Council of the Republic.

After the Civil War Nevskii became more involved with teaching and research in the history of the Russian revolutionary movement. In 1919 he became Rector of Sverdlov Communist University and taught the history of Russian revolutionary movements. He served with A. I. Elizarov and M. S. Ol'minskii as a member of the Commission for the Study of the History of the October Revolution and the Communist Party and became one of the editors of its famous journal, *Proletarskaia revolutsiia* (Proletarian Revolution). In 1921 he moved his activities to Petrograd where he created a branch of the Communist University, and opened a research institute based on the extensive revolutionary archives of the tsarist state security police, the *Okhrana*. In 1922 he published his own archival journal in Petrograd, *Krasnaia letopis* (Red Chronicles). From 1922 to 1924 he represented the Commissariat of Enlightenment* (Education) in Petrograd (Leningrad) and from 1925 to 1935 he directed the Lenin State Library in Moscow.

He taught revolutionary history at a number of educational institutions and in 1924 was named to the governing council of the newly formed Lenin Institute.

Although Nevskii tried to remain above the heated conflicts associated with the struggle for power in the Russian Communist Party in the 1920s, his writings were severely criticized for being out of tune with the latest party "line" in historical interpretation. More seriously, he increasingly came under attack for his staunch defense of scientific objectivity and a balanced approach to the history of Russian revolutionary movements that included the activity of all social groups, including the other political parties. Nevskii's views did not change, but the party line on historical writing did. At the First Congress of Marxist Historians in 1928, Nevskii gave an address on "Party History as a Science," in which he called for party historians to place the history of the Bolshevik movement into the more general framework of revolutionary history. He was roundly attacked by those who argued that party history need not consider the history of either the revolutionary movement in general or even of the history of the working class. It was the latter view which would triumph in the following years, and Nevskii who would be attacked as one of the chief representatives of the opposing view. In 1935 he was arrested, allegedly for refusing to purge the Lenin Library's collection of revolutionary literature of banned books and sources. He died in prison in 1937 and in May 1966 he was officially rehabilitated. (*see* Historiography)

Bibliography

Daniels, R. V. *Red October*. 1967.
Fitzpatrick, S. *The Commissariat of the Enlightenment*. 1970.
Istoriia i istorii. 1965.
Klushin, V. I. *Pervye uchenye-marksisty Petrograda*. 1971.
Medvedev, R. A. *Let History Judge*. 1971.

New Economic Policy. The New Economic Policy (NEP) was a dramatic shift in the general policies of the new Soviet government, which remained in force from 1921 to 1928.

The NEP was formulated when the peasants' unrest (*see* Peasants in the Russian Revolution; Agrarian Policy 1917–1921; War Communism), in response to coercive methods of grain requisitioning under War Communism*, forced the hand of V. I. Lenin's* Soviet government. With the end of the Civil War in Russia*, the peasant no longer feared return of the aristocracy and the reversal of revolutionary gains, especially the restitution of land taken by the peasant from the large estates. Parallel to these rural developments was the revolt of sailors at the base (*see* Kronstadt, 1917–1921) in March 1921. This revolt was considered to be even more threatening to the Bolsheviks (*see* Russian Social Democratic Workers' Party [Bolshevik]) because the sailors had been enthusiastic supporters of the October Seizure of Power*. The sailors sympathized both with urban strikers who wanted bread and with other dissatisfied elements among the working class who demanded the democratization of party organization. At the Tenth Party Congress in March 1921 the Bolsheviks tightened discipline in the party to inhibit challenges to party authority and unity. Toward the peasants, in contrast, the party accelerated reform that would normalize the marketing of grain and increase the availability of industrial products for peasant use. These reforms together constituted the New Economic Policy and, with elaboration and modification, continued through the 1920s.

The NEP was designed to permit the reconstruction of the economy following the years of economic disintegration. In 1921, for example, industry was producing at less than 20 percent of the level of 1914, and urban areas had lost substantial population. Not only had agricultural production dropped, but subsistence farming also had reduced grain availability to the cities. To facilitate rebuilding the economy, the Bolsheviks reinstituted a stable currency, acknowledged the peasants' right to use the land in any form of tenure they chose subject to a tax in kind on their crops, and encouraged the development of privately owned consumer-goods production. A foreign trade monopoly was instituted, however, and the Bolsheviks retained control of the "commanding heights" of heavy industry, banks, and railroads. The economy was mixed, with centralization of control in some sectors and free-market forces allowed to operate in others.

The NEP reforms in the early 1920s were successful in encouraging economic activity, but the political implications confounded many Bolshevik (*see* Russian Social Democratic Workers' Party [Bolshevik]) leaders. Many still looked forward to revolution in the West to save the Bolsheviks from being swamped in the sea of peasants who constituted 80 percent of the population. But the failure of the German communist revolt of October 1923 left serious doubts about any early assistance from friendly socialist governments. Likewise, the mundane character of the NEP did not suit those who remembered the heroic times of War Communism during the Civil War. Lenin's incapacitation and death in the early part of the NEP left many Bolsheviks directionless. Although Lenin had little difficulty persuading the party initially of the correctness of the NEP, there remained difficult questions concerning both the meaning of the Bolshevik Revolution and the character of the NEP.

The Bolsheviks had been convinced both of the rightness of their Russian Revolution and its contagiousness. By 1924–1925 they abandoned in the face of events only the belief in the imminent spread of the Revolution. The rightness of the Revolution remained unchallenged but had to be accommodated with the persistence of the NEP and the belated character of Russian industrialization. At first the NEP was viewed as a strategic retreat on the road to socialism. Indeed, Lenin referred to the NEP as "state capitalism," a stage between bourgeois capitalism and socialism, and he looked forward to eventual electrification of industry and cooperative farming (*see* The Cooperative Movement, 1917–1921) as the prerequisite for socialism. Most of the other Bolsheviks disagreed with Lenin's interpretation of the NEP as state capitalism, and they began to search for other ways to reconcile their belief in socialism with the pragmatic pace of the NEP. Policy dilemmas facilitated that reconciliation. In 1923 a "scissors crisis" unfolded in which the price of industrial goods increased while agricultural products decreased. The peasants resisted selling their grain, and the Communist Party was faced with the prospect of increasing its economic concessions to the peasantry. The party made the concessions but became embroiled in a long polemic about the degree to which the Communist Party would have to make concessions to the peasantry on the path to the development of socialism in Russia.

The economic concessions to the peasantry revealed how difficult it would be to find resources for industrialization. By 1925 industrial production was nearing the prewar levels. To increase industrial capacity required massive new sources of capital in comparison to the requirements of rebuilding older facilities. Identifying the source of savings for expansion prompted what has been called "the great industrialization debate." The leftist Bolshevik economist E. A. Preobrazhenskii launched the debate in 1923 by suggesting that the agricultural sector would be the primary source of capital accumulation. This analysis flew in the face of party concessions to the peasants and to the policy of strengthening the "*smychka*," or link with the peasantry.

Other Bolshevik economists devised an alternative industrialization plan that was more consistent with the NEP. Whereas Preobrazhenskii had placed emphasis on heavy industry and large-scale agriculture, others like N. I. Bukharin* urged stimulation of light and heavy industry through increased peasant demand for industrial goods. Another economist, V. A. Bazarov, tried to combine Bukharin's and E. A. Preobrazhenskii's approaches. Bazarov agreed with the Left Communists' (*see* Left Communism) analysis of the coming difficulties of capital accumulation, and he argued that state planning was essential in stimulating demand for heavy industry. He disagreed with the Left Communists on the need for a fast tempo of industrialization and suggested an alternative that would focus on investments in existing factories and electrification. Bazarov's policy suggestions would avoid the inflationary aspects of Preobrazhenskii's program while seeking a balance between market and planning forces. Although Bazarov's suggestions were never operationalized, his approach and that of others demonstrated a fairly sophisticated attempt to outline a Marxian program for industrialization. Marx had been silent on this issue because of his contention that the bourgeoisie would industrialize societies. The NEP was filled with provocative and necessary discussions on appropriate socialist techniques, patterns, and tempos for not only industrialization but also social organization generally.

Parallel to the industrialization debate was a debate over "socialism in one country." I. V. Stalin* in late 1924 cautiously presented the notion, and Bukharin enthusiastically elaborated on it during 1925 and 1926. In its most elementary meaning, "socialism in one country" referred to the belief that substantial progress toward the construction of a socialist society could be made even in a country that had not experienced full-scale capitalism. The debate over socialism in one country was often confusing. For many Bolsheviks the debate appeared only to quibble over the issue of when the final victory of socialism would occur. For others the debate was about varying assessments for the spread of revolution in the future. The genius of Stalin's introduction of the soon-to-be doctrine was the proclamation of faith in the victory of socialism in Russia together with the implication of the primacy of the Russian experience. The doctrinal debate over socialism in one country, however, confounded the policy debate over whether socialism could be built on NEP conditions.

Three general views dominated Bolshevik thinking about the NEP during the 1920s. The primary interpretation was that of Bukharin who saw the consolidation of the link between proletariat and peasantry as essential to the Bolshevik future. Another perspective, that of L. D. Trotsky* and Preobrazhenskii, saw the growth of planning and state industry as crucial to Bolshevik success along with attentiveness to the world revolutionary situation. These two perspectives were not diametrically opposed because both saw that socialism could be built on the basis of the NEP. The second perspective, like the first, associated the socialist character of the NEP with proletarian control of state industry. There was a difference in emphasis, but each held that socialism could evolve from NEP conditions. Indeed, there was a consistency between the two perspectives that provided a strategy for modernization of Russia under Bolshevik auspices. The first perspective, as articulated by Bukharin, proposed that the link between town and country could be sufficient to prompt the development of state industry and, therefore, insure the slow growth of socialism. The second perspective, as articulated by Trotsky, held that the growth of the planning process would guarantee the predominance of state socialist industry over private capitalism without necessarily disrupting the link between town and country. The two perspectives were complementary with both assuming that the NEP provided an adequate base for the construction of a socialist society.

A third perspective was held by various opposition groups including the Leningraders from 1925 on. Their analysis was that NEP stood for "New Exploitation of the Proletariat" and was, therefore, not socialist, nor could it ever be. The Leningraders in particular saw the NEP as inordinately favoring the peasantry while inequalities were growing between urban workers and managers. A capitalist restoration was feared along with a degeneration of the party apparatus. The goals of a classless, stateless society and international revolution were prominent in this perspective. Although this third perspective never had a party spokesman as talented as Bukharin or Trotsky, its importance can be seen in 1928 as Stalin began to destroy the NEP. In the absence of this third perspective it is difficult to believe that Stalin could have succeeded so quickly in dismantling the NEP.

The urban areas had been very dependent on the lifeline of food from the countryside throughout the 1920s with each winter bringing anxiety about the volume of grain the peasants would be willing to deliver. By the late 1920s the peasants saw their increasing economic power and withheld grain from the market to drive up prices. The political defeat of Trotsky and later the Leningraders had left Bukharin's faction on the Politburo alone in the face of Stalin and his faction. Stalin cleverly used formal party decisions so as to justify both greatly accelerated industrialization and coercive methods of grain collection. By 1929 the Bolsheviks were embarked on the path of ruthless collectivization, and the NEP was dead. Bukharin's policy of accommodation with the peasantry was decisively repudiated. Stalin took leadership of the perspective that the NEP was inconsistent with socialism, but he abandoned the goals of a stateless, classless society in favor of superindustrialization under the auspices of a powerful party–state.

Despite the abrupt end of the NEP it has been remembered fondly by many in the Soviet Union. The civil peace, the social and educational experimentation, and the relative openness of political and public debate during the period impressed a variety of Soviet citizens. There was an air of intellectual excitement as a whole new generation was inculcated in the history of the Revolution and the prospects for a new society. The imposition of Stalin's "revolution from above" in 1928–1929 could not eliminate all memories of the period. For example, as de-Stalinization proceeded in the late 1950s and early 1960s, there were attempts to revive Bukharin's status in party history. He was rehabilitated in 1987. Scholars in the West still speculate on whether the NEP can supply a model of liberalization and reform of contemporary Soviet society.

Patrick F. Drinan

Bibliography

Carr, E. H. *A History of Soviet Russia: Socialism in One Country, 1924–26.* 3 vols. 1958.
Cohen, S. F. *Bukharin and the Bolshevik Revolution.* 1973.
Daniels, R. V. *The Conscience of the Revolution.* 1960.
Deutscher, I. *The Prophet Unarmed: Trotsky, 1921–29.* 1959.
Erlich, A. *The Soviet Industrialization Debate.* 1960.

Nicholas II (1868–1918). The last Russian monarch, Nicholas II, succeeded to the throne after the death of his father, Alexander III, on October 20, 1894.

The preceding twenty-six years of his life included the customary preparation of a *Tsarevich:* closely tutored formal study leading to an education comparable to that provided by a contemporary university and general staff academy, some practical training in military affairs, a very limited introduction to matters of government as a member of the State Council and chairman of the Siberian Committee, and an extended tour to acquire an acquaintance with the Near and Far East.

At the time he assumed power, it was evident that Nicholas II possessed the commendable qualities of intelligence, devotion to Russia, and a sincere sympathy for its people. It was evident also that, like most of his class, he had little conception of the realities of his changing country. Moreover, there was in his makeup a marked reluctance to make firm decisions or to demonstrate the reasoned forcefulness necessary for the head of any state, particularly the absolute monarchy he had inherited.

For a man of that nature to undertake, as Nicholas did, to continue the policies of Alexander III was to face the very problems he was not equipped to handle. Following established policy would require him to resist growing demands for representative government, to support the landed gentry at a time when its privileges were being widely challenged, to force Russification on resistant subjects, to continue discrimination against the Jews, to use police power to crush political dissent, to continue the various phases of economic growth already begun under the direction of Minister of Finance S. Witte. At the same time, foreign policy would be requiring that he maintain Russia's alliance with France and promote imperial interests in the Near and Far East. The complicated realities inherent in the administration of these policies quickly exposed Nicholas's tragic weaknesses as a leader.

By the turn of the century, the growth of dissent among his subjects was becoming an open threat to peace. Nicholas, understanding only that any act of concession to meet popular demand would not accord with his concept of imperial rule, made the worst possible response to it. In 1902 he appointed the harsh, unprincipled Viacheslav K. Plehve as Minister of Interior and confidently left the problem in his hands. The result was that although Plehve's measures subdued some of the dissidents temporarily, the excesses and the cruelty of his tactics actually hardened the opposition's resolve to force change and redress. The emperor remained the focus.

In 1904 Nicholas's misdirection brought criticism still nearer. While promoting Russian interests in Manchuria, he gratuitously provoked Japan into an attack that began the Russo–Japanese War of 1904–1905. The repeated military disasters of that conflict so undermined his deteriorating domestic support that he finally realized the necessity, however painful, to grant concessions of some kind. One of the first came at midyear, after the assassination of Plehve. As a replacement, he chose moderate Prince Peter Sviatopolk-Mirskii, hoping that he could placate the opposition. But the prince failed, and the country moved toward revolution.

Tension was heightened when the Bloody Sunday incident of January 9, 1905 (*see* Nineteen-Five Revolution), which ended in the unwarranted slaughter of innocent petitioners, was attributed to Nicholas, although he was only indirectly responsible for the result. The aftermath of that day put his hope of maintaining the monarchy to painful test.

Seeing the futility of continuing his discredited attempts to continue the war against Japan, he finally accepted the inevitable in that area. He made peace on August 23, 1905, and then turned to face the conflict at home.

In October the unflexed strength of dissenting ranks was demonstrated when a widely supported general strike (*see* Nineteen-Five Revolution) brought the country's essential services to a virtual halt. It was a situation that left Nicholas with no choice but to concede some of his cherished rights. On October 17 he issued a manifesto that in fact, but not in name, converted his realm into a constitutional monarchy.

Between that time and the outbreak of World War I*, Nicholas faced a yet greater challenge: to make a constitutional monarchy work. He responded to it reluctantly and indirectly. He permitted Sergei Witte, his first premier, and Peter Stolypin, his third premier, to initiate some of the needed changes and try to establish a positive policy that would demonstrate good intentions on the part of the government. But in 1911, before Stolypin's efforts could produce any evidence of the anticipated results, he was assassinated, and Nicholas replaced him with a far weaker man, Vladimir N. Kokovtsev.

Again, he had brought upon himself open criticism and even more specific demands for change. In addition, he was now accused of disregarding capable advice and accepting counsel from his wife, Empress Alexandra. The empress was always concerned with any situation involving him, their four daughters, or their hemophiliac son, the Tsarevich Alexis. She often did, in fact, offer opinions on matters of state, an area in which she was even more poorly equipped than Nicholas. Critics, aware of that, were beginning to identify her political judgment with that of the "man of God" Gregory Rasputin*, in whose "special ability" to deal with her son's affliction she had compelling faith and with whom she had frequent consultations. Nicholas did not believe in the man's healing power, nor was he impressed by warning of his putative political influence. But he did see reason to tolerate Rasputin's association with the empress; "better ten Rasputins than one hysterical empress." Actually, Rasputin's presence was a political liability that the emperor could not afford with impunity on the eve of 1914.

Just then, labor was on the march again, revolutionaries were still gaining strength, liberals were beginning to lose hope that the country would ever attain constitutionalism, and conservatives were seriously questioning Nicholas's ability to govern under existing conditions. Crisis was averted only because the outbreak of war and the attendant surge of patriotic fervor supporting emperor and fatherland brought an uncommon sense of unity among the people. The calming sense held until disastrous defeats of Russian forces on the Galician front prompted a public outcry charging dishonesty incompetence, and even treason among the highly placed members of government along with demands for the removal of many ministers and the formation of a cabinet enjoying "public confidence." Nicholas refused to yield on the matter of the cabinet, for to do so would mean renunciation of monarchical power, but he did replace some unpopular ministers and authorize other changes that served to improve public morals for a time and benefit the fighting forces. But then the detracted from those gains when in August 1915, disregarding the urgency of domestic problems and the entreaties of his ministers, he committed the folly of assuming personal command of the armed forces.

If he had responded to the need to form and empower a cabinet under a forceful premier, able to mobilize people and resources behind the fighting man, this act would have been less disastrous. As it was, when he went to army headquarters at Mogilev, he left the premiership in the incapable hands of the superannuated Ivan Goremykin and later chose equally ineffective men to follow him. Soon it was being widely rumored on both the home and the fighting fronts that imperial power was completely in the hands of the empress and Rasputin.

The public's response to this gross exaggeration, widely accepted as certainty, led some of Nicholas's loyal supporters to conclude that his inattention was endangering the country. A few dared to advise him to get rid of Rasputin; others suggested that he send the empress to a convent for the duration of the war. Such suggestions served only to infuriate him, and he responded by becoming more and more isolated, deaf even to the most well-intentioned advice. That attitude, in turn, drove many influential subjects to begin considering various ways, even desperate ones, to save the government. Some tried to organize a coup that would replace the emperor with his brother the Grand Duke Michael as regent, but the effort failed for lack of necessary support. One desperate act was carried out: assassination of the hated Rasputin, in December 1916, but even the removal of that "dangerous influence" did not bring the anticipated results; the government remained unchanged, and that deed only furthered Nicholas's alienation.

He had now become so out of touch with the home front that, after a visit with his family in February 1917, he returned as usual to Mogilev, with no thought of impending disturbance from that source. Even the grim word of mass rioting in Petrograd that reached him the following day did not alert him. He appeared neither to understand its meaning nor to comprehend its threat. His senior generals were equally as unprepared for reasoning about it; when the demand for Nicholas's abdication came from Petrograd on March 1, they advised him that he had no choice if he wished to save the army and the monarchy.

At heart Nicholas believed that there was a choice; but he submitted, abdicating the throne on March 2 in favor of the Grand Duke Michael. On the following day, Michael refused the throne. The role of the Romanov dynasty had come to an end.

Shortly after March 2 Nicholas and his family were promised temporary refuge in England. However, revolutionary workers and soldiers, insisting that the deposed emperor be tried for treason, prevented the departure by arresting him, his wife, and their five children.

The newly organized Provisional Government* allowed them to begin their imprisonment in their residence in Tsarskoe Selo, where imperial amenities were soon effectively displaced by the indignities of their treatment and the prospects of a future as yet unknown. To protect them against threatened mob violence, they were secretly transferred in July to Tobolsk. They remained there while the government was established and began consideration of plans for dealing with them. The procedure finally decided on was to stage a trial of Nicholas for "crimes against the people." To avoid the possibility of his being rescued, he and his family were again transferred—to Ekaterinburg, where security, it was thought, could be more easily maintained.

The outbreak of Civil War in Russian* in the spring of 1918, forced postponement of the trial. When White forces (see White Movement), fighting to overthrow the government, came within striking distance of Ekaterinburg, the local authorities decided, with Lenin's* approval, to have the family executed in order not "to leave the whites a live banner to rally around"* (Trotsky 1963, p. 81). There was no delay. Early on the morning of July 17, 1918, Nicholas, Alexandra, their children, and their personal attendants were summarily killed. Their bodies were hidden, and all evidence of them was destroyed—symbolic evidence of the strength of the monarchical idea.

Sidney Harcave

Bibliography

de Grunwald, Constantine. *Le Tsar Nicholas II*. 1965.
Harcave, Sidney. *The Years of the Golden Cockerel*. 1968.
Kasvinov, Mark. *Dvadtsat tri stupeni vniz*. 1978.
Massie, Robert K. *Nicholas and Alexandra*. 1967.
Nicholas II. *Dnevnik*. 1923.
Oldenburg, Sergei. *The Last Tsar*. 4 vols. 1975–1976.
Pares, Bernard. *The Fall of the Russian Monarchy*. 1939.
Russia, Chrezvychainaia Sledstvennaia Kommissia. *Padenie tsarskogo rezhima*. 7 vols. 1924–26.
Trotsky, Leon. *Trotsky's Diary in Exile, 1935*. 1963.
Witte, Sergei I. *Vospominaniia: Tsarstvovanie Nikolaia II*. 2 vols. 1922.

Nineteen-Five Revolution. The Russian Revolution of 1905 was a political upheaval directed primarily against the absolutist monarchy and aimed at replacing it with an elected constitutional government. Those who take a Marxist view call it the "first bourgeois-democratic revolution" in the history of Russia.

The Revolution grew out of widespread dissatisfaction with the existing order, dissatisfaction derived to a considerable degree from the regime's inability and, in some cases, unwillingness to cope with problems produced by urbanization, industrialization, and Westernization. The opposition was heightened by the adherence of Tsar Nicholas II* to traditionally conservative and reactionary policies while closing the door to peaceful change. Also, the disastrous war with Japan that began early in 1904 undermined the prestige of the government as well as its ability to cope with unrest.

The articulation of dissatisfaction and the leadership for the opposition were provided by the intelligentsia recruited from the gentry and the middle class. On the eve of the Revolution, the organized opposition was divided between liberals and socialists. The former were represented by a loosely knit group of liberals associated with the *zemstvos* (local elective institutions) and by the recently formed Union of Emancipation, which sought to form a common front of all opposition forces. The latter were represented by the Socialist-Revolutionary

Party* and by the Russian Social Democratic Workers' Party (see Russian Social Democratic Workers' Party [Bolshevik]; Russian Social Democratic Workers' Party [Menshevik]).

The preliminary stage of the Revolution began in July 1904 with the assassination of the repressive and much hated Minister of Interior, Viacheslav K. Plehve, while Russia was at war with Japan. Although the Tsar would have preferred replacing Plehve with someone equally repressive, he deferred to those who urged the appointment of a conciliatory minister of interior who would strengthen public support for the government when it was essential. He chose Prince Peter Sviatopolk-Mirskii, who undertook to introduce minor political reform as a means of placating the opposition. Most of the opposition, however, was not placated: it took the appointment as a sign of weakness rather than as a sign of goodwill and simply heightened its efforts to force substantial change. By the end of the year, the opposition was stronger, more vocal, and more defiant than ever before, expressing its desires through illegal meetings and petitions. Sviatopolk-Mirsky had meanwhile lost the confidence of the Tsar. Although many expected and even hoped that the coming year would see even greater political turbulence, no one, not even the most ardent revolutionary, expected a revolution in the near future.

The Revolution came in response to "Bloody Sunday" (January 9, 1905), when troops and police in St. Petersburg fired on unarmed workers and their families, who, led by Father George Gapon, marched toward the Winter Palace to submit a reform petition to the emperor. Bloody Sunday had an electrifying effect: it was perceived by those already hostile to the government, as well as by many hitherto apolitical, as an act of deliberate butchery by Nicholas II designed to teach the folly of opposition, even peaceful opposition.

Virtually overnight the major cities became scenes of turbulence: workers on strike (more on strike in January than in the ten preceding years combined), protest meetings, demonstrations, and schools closed by student protest. In the capital, even so august and unpolitical a body as the Academy of Sciences and ultraconservative newspapers such as Novoe Vremia (Modern Times) called for political reform. In effect, there came into being in those days "a common front" including revolutionary as well as conservative segments of Russian society, united in the belief that to continue as before was impossible but divided with respect to tactics and goals. Zemstvo liberals hoped to achieve their ends through the good graces of the Tsar, whereas the Union of Emancipation sought to overthrow the monarchy by nonviolent, albeit illegal, agitation, and socialists hoped to achieve the same end by political strikes, assassination, and armed uprising.

The response to Bloody Sunday compelled the emperor to make what for him were two major concessions; on February 18 he granted what amounted to the right of petition and promised to establish an elective Duma (see Duma and Revolution), with the right to suggest legislation but not to enact it. Some zemstvo liberals accepted these concessions as adequate, but most of the opposition continued to press for more radical change.

In May a coalition of liberals and socialists formed the Union of Unions, an illegal association of organizations such as the Union of Teachers, the Union of Railroad Employees, and the Union for Equal Rights for Women. Its leader was the fiery liberal P. N. Miliukov*. Its aim was to compel Nicholas II to permit the election of a constituent assembly* that would establish a democratic republic. Insofar as anybody represented the common mood of 1905, it was the Union of Unions.

In the same month the first workers' soviet (*see* Soviets [Councils] of Workers', Soldiers', and Peasants' Deputies) was organized in Ivanovo-Voznesensk; in Lodz there were bloody clashes between strikers and troops. In the following month the mutiny of the cruiser *Potemkin* occurred, the first ominous sign of a revolutionary spirit in the armed forces. By late spring the forces of revolution were obviously growing, but the government, although frightened, was not routed.

By August the government began to feel confident about the future. In that month it made peace with Japan, thus relieving itself of a burden that made the struggle against the forces of revolution difficult. Also in August Nicholas II signed a law establishing the promised Duma in the expectation that the Duma would satisfy the demand for reform on the part of the most reasonable people and in the belief that he had the power to crush whatever opposition might still remain. But he misread the signs, as did others.

The Revolution entered a new phase when, in September, printers in Moscow went on strike; their action prompted other strikes in that city. Then the strike spread from Moscow to the rest of the country with astonishing rapidity, largely through the efforts of the railway workers. By the second week in October the country was immobilized by a general strike that shut down virtually all industry, all communications, and all services.

The emperor would have preferred to end the strike by force, but he was advised that his troops might not obey if used against the strikers and that even if they did, the result would be a prolonged civil war. He was also advised that he could end the strike and restore domestic tranquility by granting civil rights and by granting the Duma the power to enact laws. He made these grants in a manifesto issued on October 17.

The manifesto was greeted joyously, and the general strike came to an end, but the Revolution was by no means over. All socialists and many liberals vowed to fight on until the monarchy was overthrown. Large numbers of workers led by socialists organized soviets, engaged in political strikes, and in some cases used arms against police and troops. Unrest among peasantry and in the armed forces grew rather than diminished after October 17. In some areas peasants burned manor houses and seized grain belonging to landlords. There were mutinies in the armed forces, and in some localities, soldiers' soviets were created. In short, the country seemed in open revolt, but the revolutionaries were inadequately organized to turn revolt into successful revolution, and more important, they lacked a sufficiently broad popular base to enable them to topple the regime. As a result, when the government assumed the offensive in November, arresting the leaders of the St. Petersburg Soviet and dispatching punitive expeditions to curb peasant rioting, the revolutionaries were unable to mount effective resistance. Early in December they tried to rouse the country to armed rebellion, but only in Moscow was the call answered on any substantial scale. The Moscow uprising was spirited, but it failed for lack of support from outside the city and also because the government still had a core of dependable troops. The failure of the Moscow uprising marked the end of revolutionary hopes, even though sporadic disorder was to continue for more than a year.

Although the Revolution failed to overthrow the monarchy, it forced Nicholas II to make concessions that he would have considered unthinkable before 1905. Chief of these concessions was the granting of civil rights and the right of the people to participate in the making of laws. Also, as V. I. Lenin* put it, the Revolution was the dress rehearsal for the October Seizure of Power*.

Sidney Harcave

Bibliography

Akademiia Nauk, Institut Istorii. *Revoliutsiia, 1905–1907 gg. v Rossii: Dokumenty i materialy*. 15 vols. 1955–1963.
Engelstein, Laura. *Moscow, 1905*. 1982.
Harcave, Sidney. *First Blood*. 1964.
Mehlinger, Howard D., and Thompson, John M. *Count Witte and the Tsarist Government in the 1905 Revolution*. 1972.
Pervaia Russkaia Revoliutsiia, 1905–1907 gg.: Problemy i sovremennost. 1976.
Sablinsky, Walter. *The Road to Bloody Sunday*. 1976.
Schwarz, Solomon M. *The Russian Revolution of 1905*. 1967.
Sverchkov, Dmitrii. *Na zare revoliutsii*. 1921.
Trotsky, Leon. *1905*. 1971.

Nogin, Viktor Pavlovich (1878–1924). Nogin was an important right-wing Bolshevik (*see* Russian Social Democratic Workers' Party [Bolshevik]) leader during the October Seizure of Power* in Moscow (*see* Moscow, Revolution in; Moscow Soviet). He was the son of a Moscow sales clerk. Because of the poverty of the family, he had little schooling and began to work in a textile factory in Bogorodsk (now Noginsk) while still a child. He later moved to St. Petersburg where he joined a group called Workers' Banner. In 1900 he was sent into exile for revolutionary activity, but he escaped and fled to London. There he came into contact with V. I. Lenin*.

Nogin served as Lenin's agent to several Russian cities and became a member of the first Bolshevik Central Committee. Although he continued to do the party's work in various cities, in 1905 he settled in Moscow, where he became Chairman of the Moscow Central Bureau of Trade Unions, (*see* Trade Unions), and in 1916 became a member of the Moscow Regional Bureau of the Bolshevik Central

Committee. Throughout his career he was arrested and escaped several times. After the February Revolution* he helped to form the Moscow Soviet and became its first vice-chairman; then on October 2, when the Bolsheviks achieved a majority, he became chairman. He took part in the formation of the Moscow Military Revolutionary Committee, which organized and led the Soviet seizure of power in the city. On April 29 Lenin made Nogin one of the members of the Bolshevik Central Committee (see Central Committee of the Russian Communist Party [Bolshevik]) that would lead the Bolsheviks through the year 1917. Nogin, however, was chosen for this post because he was a member of the Central Executive Committee of Soviets and because he was a representative of the "conciliators," those in the Bolshevik Party who believed that the party should work with the Mensheviks (see Russian Social Democratic Workers' Party [Menshevik]). He often served as liaison to the other political parties. He was in favor of participation in the Pre-Parliament (see Democratic Conference) and was extremely wary about the decision to try to seize power in Moscow and Petrograd. Although he accepted the post of Commissar for Trade and Industry in the new Soviet government, on November 17, 1919, he joined L. B. Kamenev*, N. A. Miliutin, A. I. Rykov*, and G. E. Zinoviev* in resigning from the Council of People's Commissars because no other socialist parties except the Left Socialist-Revolutionary Party* were represented in the government. Nogin also resigned from the Central Committee. He became reconciled with the new government but never recovered his former political position. He held a variety of lesser posts in the government until May 22, 1924, when he died during surgery for stomach ulcers. He is buried in the wall in Red Square.

Bibliography

Arkhangel'skii, V. Nogin. 1964.
Daniels, Robert V. Red October: The Bolshevik Revolution of 1917. 1967.
Deutscher, Isaac. The Prophet Armed, Trotsky, 1879–1921. 1954.

North, Revolution in, 1917–20. The fate of the Soviet seizure of power was determined in part by the outcome of the Revolution and intervention in the northern regions of European Russia. The North was one of the three major entry points for foreign intervention, the other two being the Black Sea region in the South and Vladivostok in far eastern Siberia (see Siberia, Revolution in).

In 1917 the northern region of European Russia encompassed an enormous territory extending southward some 400–600 miles from the Arctic Ocean and eastward from the border of Finland all the way to North Central Siberia. Divided administratively into the Arkhangel'sk, Olonets, and Vologda provinces, the characteristic geographical features of the North were its severe climate and forbidding topography. Although traversed by an extensive network of navigable inland waterways, much of the region was enveloped in an impenetrable forest or trackless tundra that fully justified its general reputation as a place of remote desolation suitable only for the confinement of political exiles.

To a large extent, the economic and social structure of the North in 1917 was determined by its physical geography. Essentially backward, the northern economy was tied closely to the region's natural resources. Most important in this regard was the timber industry and its various subsidiaries, followed at some interval by the commercial hunting and fishing industries. Other sizeable enterprises included flax spinning, some shipbuilding and repair, and an important munitions operation. In addition, beginning in the late nineteenth century, much effort had been expended on the construction in the region of two railroads; the first, completed in 1898, connected Moscow with Arkhangel'sk via Vologda, and the other, built during World War I*, linked Petrograd to the newly constructed, year-round port of Murmansk in the extreme North. Finally, agriculture, though widely practiced, was not nearly so prominent in the North as elsewhere in European Russia. Indeed, in spite of the most intensive cultivation during the brief growing season, agricultural production in the region was insufficient to meet the needs of the local population. This circumstance exerted a powerful influence on the regional history of the Revolution.

The population of the Russian North in 1917 was relatively small (about 2.7 million). Of this total, as elsewhere in Russia at that time, the overwhelming majority (93.5 percent) consisted of peasants. In several respects, however, the peasants of the Russian North differed markedly from their counterparts in central and southern Russia. Primarily descendants of the former state peasantry or of fugitive serfs and schismatic Old Believers, the northern peasantry had long since developed traits of rugged individualism and political indifference generally uncongenial to the revolutionary passions unleashed in Russia by the events of 1917.

By contrast with the peasantry, the urban population of the Russian North in 1917 was numerically tiny and confined largely to the provincial capitals of Arkhangel'sk, Petrozavodsk, and Vologda and a few other centers located along the major lines of communication. At the top of this urban society in the North were the ranking officials of the provincial civil and military bureaucracies and the most eminent local entrepreneurs, many of whom, in fact, were foreigners. For its part, the very small middle class was made up of subordinate officers and civil servants, the lesser bourgeoisie (*meshchanstvo*), and members of the professions (doctors, lawyers, and teachers). In addition, largely due to the region's prominence as a place of exile, there was often among the urban population a small but influential element of the radical intelligentsia. Finally, at the bottom of the urban social pyramid were rank-and-file soldiers and sailors and various representatives of the proletariat, whose ranks were periodically swelled by large numbers of seasonally employed peasants. Of the total northern population about 10.6 percent belonged to minority nationalities including the Komi, Karelians, Nentsy, and Saami. Of them, however, only the Karelians played any significant independent role in the events of the Revolution.

Before 1914 the politics of the Russian North was essentially conservative. This situation, however, was altered by the impact of World War I, which brought to the region a substantial influx of potentially radical newcomers. Chief among these new arrivals were large numbers of soldiers and sailors sent north on military assignment and numerous port and railroad workers attracted to the area by the vastly increased volume of regional trade occasioned by the war. The appearance on the northern scene of these potentially activist outsiders was then compounded by the wholesale conscription of the native population, which had the dual effect of creating resentment among the local peasantry while sharply accentuating the critical problem of food supply in the North.

Notwithstanding the changes wrought by the war, the initial response in the North to the overthrow of the monarchy in February 1917 (*see* Nicholas II; February Revolution) was generally moderate. To be sure, leading tsarist officials—governors and other prominent bureaucrats—were summarily dismissed and replaced by variously titled commissars and provisional committees. Similarly, tsarist police and related coercive institutions were swiftly dismantled. On the other hand, the basic institutions of local self-government—municipal assemblies, town councils, and, where already functioning, *zemstvos* organizations (*see* All-Russia Union of Towns and All-Russian Union of Zemstvos)—were preserved intact. Moreover, with the exception of the Commander-in-Chief himself, the staff of the White Sea Military District remained in place with powers substantially undiminished.

More important than the official changes effected in the postrevolutionary North was the widespread appearance in the region of a whole series of unofficial political organizations. Among them were potentially powerful organs such as the Central Committee of the Fleet of the Arctic Ocean* (Tseledflot) and the Council of Railway Workers (Sovzheldor), the union of railwaymen of the Murman Railroad. Even more significant was the creation in the North of the first Soviets of Workers', Soldiers', and Peasants' Deputies. As initially organized in vital centers such as Arkhangel'sk (March 4), Murmansk (March 8), Vologda (March 9), and Petrozavodsk (March 15), the northern soviets harbored clearly political pretensions and enjoyed widespread popular support. Significantly, however, the soviet movement penetrated only very slowly into the localities of the North.

Despite the participation of some liberals and even a few moderate conservatives, the politics of the North in 1917 was thoroughly dominated by the radical party of the Socialist–Revolutionaries (S–R's) (*see* Socialist-Revolutionary Party). Based first on their appeal to the numerically preponderant peasantry, the primacy of the S–R's in the North rested also on their established leadership of the popular Cooperative movement*. In contrast with the S–R's, no organization of the Marxist Russian Social Democratic Workers' Party (RSDWP) even existed in the North before 1917.

Accordingly, following the Revolution, feverish efforts were made in the chief northern cities to create joint organizations uniting both the Bolshevik (*see* Russian Social Democratic Workers' Party [Bolshevik]) and Menshevik (*see* Russian Social Democratic Workers' Party [Menshevik]) factions of the movement. From the outset, however, these efforts encountered difficulties and began to break down as early as May and June. Thereupon, the Mensheviks joined forces with the S–R's together with whom they soon came to dominate virtually all major leadership positions in the North in both the government and local soviets. In these circumstances, the regional politics of the North during 1917 focused heavily on critical military and economic, especially food-supply, problems.

Not surprisingly, in view of the S–R/Menshevik predominance in the region, the October Seizure of Power* in 1917 was not well received in the North. Indeed, in cities such as Arkhangel'sk, Petrozavodsk, and Vologda, news of the Revolution met with outright refusals on the part of local authorities even to recognize the new Soviet government. In other cases, for example, at Murmansk, the authority of the new regime was outwardly acknowledged but covertly subverted. In no case, at least in any significant instance, did the coming to power of Bolshevism evoke any great enthusiasm or elicit any fundamental changes in personnel or government structure in the North.

In general, the Bolshevization of the North took place only very gradually after November 1917 and was nowhere completed before late 1917 at the earliest. Seen in retrospect, the process was effected first in the cities of the North and culminated, in each case, in the eventual achievement of Bolshevik majorities in the reelection of local soviets. Crucial to this process, which was often accomplished under the guidance of envoys dispatched from the Center, was the preliminary control of influential local organs such as Tseledflot and Sovzheldor. As a result of such efforts, Bolshevik majorities were finally attained in the key soviets in Vologda on December 6, in Petrozavodsk during January 4–5, and in Arkhangel'sk as late as February 17. Bolshevik advance in the localities of the North, where pivotal roles were played by demobilized peasant soldiers, was even slower. In the rural North a strong temporary alliance was formed in November between the Bolsheviks and the dissident Left Socialist-Revolutionary Party, which complicated political developments. Because of this ambiguity, Bolshevik hegemony in the northern countryside was not fully achieved even as late as mid–1918.

No sooner had the Bolsheviks brought the region under their more or less effective control than the North became one of the earliest centers of Allied intervention in Russia (see Foreign Policy, 1914–1921). Ostensibly motivated by the need to protect substantial Allied war stores stockpiled in the North against an alleged Finno–German threat, intervention was initiated by the debarking of a British force at Murmansk in March 1918, followed by a much larger interallied landing at Arkhangel'sk in August. At first welcomed by local authorities concerned about food supply in the region, the northern intervention soon became enmeshed in the trammels of the unfolding Civil War in Russia*.

From the outset, the Civil War in North Russia took on a highly complex character, involving conflicting patterns of Allied motivation, fundamental disunity within the local anti-Bolshevik opposition, and even, on the remote Murman front, the emergence of a Karelian nationalist movement (see Finland, Revolution in). In response, after some initial panic, the Bolsheviks soon reorganized the unoccupied North into a so-called Northern Commmune (April 1918) and took up an essentially defensive position in the region. In the end, although an anti-Bolshevik government was briefly stabilized at Arkhangel'sk, the northern front proved to be little more than an artificial product of Allied intervention. Thus with the final Allied withdrawal from the North in October 1919, the anti-Bolshevik movement found itself utterly unable to elicit any popular support from the independent northern peasantry and soon fell victim to internal disintegration. As a result, a final Red Army* offensive in early 1920 easily recaptured Arkhangel'sk (February) and Murmansk (March) and quickly returned the entire region, with the notable exception of insurgent Karelia, to Soviet rule.

John W. Long

Bibliography

Aksenov, A. N., and Potylitsyn, A. I. *Pobeda Sovetskoi vlasti na Severe.* 1957.

Footman, David. *Civil War in Russia.* 1962.

Halliday, E. M. *The Ignorant Armies.* 1958.

Kennan, George. *The Decision to Intervene. Vol. 2: Soviet-American Relations.* 1958.

Mints, I. *Angliiskaia interventsiia i severnaia kontrrevoliutsiia.* 1931.

Shumilov, M. I. *Oktiabr'skaia revoliutsiia na Severe Rossii.* 1973.

Strakhovsky, Leonid. *Intervention at Archangel.* 1944.

Ullman, Richard H. *Anglo-Soviet Relations, 1917–21.* 2 vols. 1961–1967.

Vetoshkin, M. K. *Revoliutsiia i grazhdanskaia voina na Severe.* 1927.

———. *Stanovlenie vlasti Sovetov na Severe RSFSR.* 1957.

O

Obolenskii, V. V. *See* Osinskii, N.

October Seizure of Power. The Soviet seizure of power in October 1917 represented the second, extremist stage of the Russian Revolution, supplanting the Provisional Government* set up following the fall of Tsar Nicholas II* (*see* February Revolution). Known officially as the "Great October Socialist Revolution," the Soviet takeover was accomplished under the leadership of the Bolshevik Party (*see* Russian Social Democratic Workers' Party [Bolshevik]) on October 24–25, 1917. Its outcome was the establishment of the present Soviet government.

The stage was set for the Soviet seizure of power by a classic process of disintegrating authority and political polarization under the Provisional Government. Despite their setback after the July Days* riots when V. I. Lenin*and other Bolshevik leaders were forced into hiding or arrested, the Bolsheviks won increasing popular support by endorsing the workers' control (*see* Kollontai, Aleksandra Mikhailovna; Workers in The Russian Revolution) movement, peasant land seizures (*see* Land Committees; Agrarian Policy, 1917–1921; Agriculture), and the soldiers' urge for peace (*see* Army of Imperial Russia in World War I; Soldiers and Soldiers' Committees). The abortive right-wing coup led by Chief-of-Staff General L. G. Kornilov (*see* Kornilov Revolt) in August, the *Kornilovshchina*, drove public opinion further to the Left, and the Bolsheviks won control of the key Soviets of Workers' and Soldiers' Deputies, including Petrograd and Moscow (*see* Moscow Soviet; Petrograd Soviet; Soviets [Councils] of Workers', Soldiers', and Peasants' Deputies). This development prompted Lenin to translate his hostility to the "bourgeois" Provisional Government into a direct call to the Bolshevik Central Committee on September 12 to prepare an armed seizure of power in the name of the proletariat and the soviets.

Lenin's demand for an uprising was at first resisted by the Bolshevik leadership, which split between a cautious faction led by L. B. Kamenev*, working for a coalition with the moderate Mensheviks (see Russian Social Democratic Workers' Party [Menshevik]) and Socialist–Revolutionaries (see Socialist-Revolutionary Party), and a more aggressive faction following the newly elected Chairman of the Petrograd Soviet, Leon Trotsky*, who aimed to take power by transforming the soviets they controlled into the actual government. Disregarding party instructions, Lenin returned secretly from Finland to Petrograd on October 7 to insist on the idea of an insurrection before the Second All-Russian Congress of Soviets then scheduled for October 20. On October 10, over the vigorous objections of Kamenev and G. E. Zinoviev*, he secured a vote by the Bolshevik Central Committee to place armed insurrection on the order of the day.

Meanwhile, responding to rumors that the Provisional Government was planning to move to Moscow from Petrograd and possibly abandon the latter to the advancing German army, the Petrograd Soviet under Trotsky's chairmanship had initiated steps to establish its own military headquarters to assume control over the troops in Petrograd in the name of defending the Revolution. This body was officially authorized on October 16 as the "Military Revolutionary Committee of the Petrograd Soviet," nominally chaired by a Left Socialist-Revolutionary (see Left Socialist-Revolutionary Party) soldier, P. E. Lazimir, but dominated by N. I. Podvoiskii and other members of the Military Organization of the Bolshevik Party.

On the same date, amid general rising tension, the Bolshevik Central Committee met again with representatives of the Petrograd Bolsheviks to reaffirm the decision to seize power by force, Zinoviev and Kamenev again dissenting. Still no date was set for the uprising. However, the time for preparing such a seizure before the Second Congress of Soviets was fortuitously extended on October 17 when the Mensheviks and Right Socialist–Revolutionaries controlling the All-Russian Central Executive Committee* of Soviets postponed opening of the Congress until October 25. Nevertheless, apart from activation of the Military Revolutionary Committee on October 20, the dispatch of soviet "commissars" to the various barracks in the capital, and sporadic arming of workers' Red Guards*, the Bolshevik leadership took no overt steps to plan or prepare an insurrection before the Congress. Lenin was preoccupied by polemics against Zinoviev and Kamenev for leaking to the press the fact that the party was considering a coup. At this point, the party was in fact taking the course favored by the Trotsky group, waiting for the expected pro-Bolshevik majority in the Congress of Soviets to endorse the transfer of power from the Provisional Government to the soviets and preparing to beat down any armed effort by the government to avert this fate. Trotsky later contended that this stance, reaffirmed publicly as late as the afternoon of October 24, was a smokescreen to hide preparations for the coup, but available evidence suggests that this argument was an attempt after the fact to make his leadership appear more consistently aggressive.

Events abruptly took a different course in the early morning hours of October 24. Prime Minister A. F. Kerensky*, having secured the Soviet's withdrawal of a claim made on October 22 to review all orders issued to the garrison, nevertheless decided on preemptive action and ordered government forces to close the Bolshevik press. Convinced that this move was the signal for a counterrevolutionary coup on the Kornilov model, the Bolshevik Central Committee meeting in the Smolnyi Institute (headquarters of the Petrograd Soviet) ordered all pro-Bolshevik military units and Red Guards* to assume defensive positions throughout the city. However, so weak were the forces loyal to the government in numbers and morale that almost everywhere they melted away without a shot, leaving most of Petrograd by default in the hands of the Bolsheviks and the Soviet.

Throughout these developments, Lenin, still in hiding on the outskirts of Petrograd, was unaware of any action to implement his wished-for coup. Late in the evening of the 24th—once again ignoring party instructions—he made his way on foot to the Smolnyi Institute, assumed from the furious activity underway there that a deliberate coup was in progress, and took charge of the Revolution. About this time—it is uncertain whether previous to or as a consequence of Lenin's arrival—the troop movements ordered by the Military Revolutionary Committee took on a more deliberate and aggressive character to occupy (again, bloodlessly) key points such as the telephone exchange and the power stations still guarded by government units. Almost everyone, friend and foe alike, thereafter assumed—and Trotsky and the other Bolshevik leaders were content to let the assumption stand—that the Revolution Lenin had called for had in fact been deliberately planned and launched. Absence of any documentation to this effect, however, compels the conclusion that the preemptive coup desired by Lenin to take power independently of the popular groundswell was only the accidental consequence of the government's abortive initiative.

By the morning of October 25 the entire city of Petrograd was under soviet control except for the former Imperial Winter Palace occupied by the cabinet of the Provisional Government. Lenin appeared in public for the first time since July to proclaim the overthrow of the Provisional Government. As the Bolshevik success unfolded, support for Kerensky's government crumbled. He was betrayed on the Right by military leaders and Cossack* units, who hoped the Bolshevik venture would pave the way for a counterrevolution, and was repudiated by the moderate Left, which pushed a motion of nonconfidence through the unofficial parliament, the Council of the Republic (see Democratic Council). Thereupon, Kerensky escaped from Petrograd in an automobile commandeered from the American embassy to try to rally loyal military units at the battle front and lead them back to retake Petrograd.

The remainder of the day on October 25 was consumed by awkward efforts on the part of the Bolsheviks to organize a seizure of the Winter Palace, with the support of the pro-Bolshevik cruiser *Aurora** anchored in the Neva River. Late in the evening, after some desultory shooting and minimal loss of life, the defending units (mostly officer candidates and the "Women's Battalion of Death") surrendered, and the ministers of the Provisional Government were arrested.

Simultaneously with the fall of the Winter Palace, the Second Congress of Soviets was assembling in the Smolnyi Institute. In protest against the violence (corresponding to what they expected of the Bolsheviks) most of the moderate Menshevik and Socialist-Revolutionary delegates walked out, leaving the Bolsheviks and their Left SR allies to vote a series of revolutionary decrees: a decree on the soviets proclaiming them to be centrally and locally the legitimate government of Russia; a decree on peace, calling for an immediate end to the "imperialist" war; and a decree on land, nationalizing the soil and placing it at the disposal of those who tilled it. After two days of meetings, the Congress disbanded, leaving the consolidation of the new regime to the Council of Peoples' Commissars* under the chairmanship of Lenin and the Central Executive Committee, now serving as a quasi-parliament under Bolshevik domination.

Resistance by the partisans of the Provisional Government had not yet been overcome. Kerensky was returning from the front with loyal divisions, and on October 29 the officer candidate schools in Petrograd staged an uprising to coincide with Kerensky's entry. However, Bolshevik forces still commanded by the Military-Revolutionary Committee were able to crush the cadets' uprising before turning to check and disperse Kerensky's troops at the decisive battle of Pulkovo on October 30.

Elsewhere in the country, anti-Bolshevik resistance was considerably more prolonged, but with the capital city and the nominal government in their hands, the Bolsheviks enjoyed a decisive psychological advantage. Bloody fighting erupted in Moscow (*see* Moscow, Revolution in) on October 28, with executions of hostages on both sides; the Bolsheviks finally secured the city on November 2. In most of the industrial and garrison cities throughout Russia, soviet control was asserted swiftly, but in more remote areas the authority of the soviets was not established until the end of the year. In the region of the Don Cossacks, as well as in non-Russian areas such as the Ukraine (*see* Ukraine, Revolution in) and Transcaucasia (*see* Transcaucasia, Revolution in), soviet power was rejected altogether, thereby setting the stage for the Civil War in Russia* that raged for the next three years.

The October Seizure of Power did not immediately establish one-party government by the Bolsheviks. The Left SR's had supported the soviet takeover, and a substantial part of the Bolshevik leadership argued for a coalition government representing all socialist parties. However, the Mensheviks and Right SR's, deeply alienated by the violent overthrow of the Provisional Government, refused to serve in any cabinet headed by Lenin. The outcome, temporarily, was a coalition of the Bolsheviks with the Left SR's as junior partners and, eventually, the suppression of all other parties by a one-party communist dictatorship.

Robert V. Daniels

Bibliography

Daniels, Robert V. *Red October*. 1967.
Elwood, Ralph Carter, ed. *Reconsiderations of the Russian Revolution*. 1976.
Ferro, Marc. *October, 1917*. 1980.
Geyer, Dietrich. *Die russiche Revolution*. 1968.
Melgunov, S. P. *Bolshevik Seizure of Power*. 1972.
Mints, I. I. *Istoriia velikogo oktiabria*. 3 vols. 1967–1972.
Mints, I. I.; ed. *Lenin i oktiabr'skoe vooruzhennoe vosstanie v Petrograde*. 1964.
Rabinowitch, Alexander. *The Bolsheviks Come to Power*. 1976.
Reed, John. *Ten Days That Shook the World*. 1960.
Sobolev, P. N., Gimpel'sov, Ia. O., and Trukov, G. A. *History of the October Revolution*. 1966.

Ol'minskii. *See* Aleksandrov, M. S.

Ordzhonikidze, Grigorii Konstantinovich (1862–1937; pseudonym Sergo). Ordzhonikidze was one of the most prominent leaders of the Bolsheviks (*see* Russian Social Democratic Workers' Party [Bolshevik]) during the October Seizure of Power* in Petrograd. He also played an important role in bringing Soviet governments to power in the Ukraine (*see* Ukraine, Revolution in) and the Caucasus (*see* Transcaucasia, Revolution in).

Ordzhonikidze was born in Western Georgia in the village of Goreshe in Sharapanskii District, Kutaiskii Province. His father was an impoverished nobleman who farmed the land and did some hauling for the local manganese mines. After completing the curriculum at the two year classical gymnasium in 1901, Ordzhonikidze decided to begin the four year program at the *fel'dsher* school provided by the Mikhailov hospital in Tiflis to become a *fel'dsher* or physician's assistant. At the same time he was drawn into revolutionary work with the local railway workers and in 1903 became a member of the Russian Social Democratic Workers' Party (Bolshevik). In 1904 he met and became a close friend of the famous Armenian revolutionary Kamo (S. A. Ter-Petrosian).

When he graduated from the *fel'dsher* school in 1905 he began working in various cities in the Caucasus and continued his revolutionary activities in each one. In June 1906 he met I. V. Stalin*, and a close relationship developed which would be crucial to his future career. In 1907 Ordzhonikidze became head of the Bolsheviks in Balakhova District in Baku. From 1907 to 1909 he was exiled and in jail, but Ordzhonikidze returned to Baku and did revolutionary work in Persia where he acquired some experience in guerilla warfare. During his work in Persia he began to correspond with V. I. Lenin* and in the summer of 1911 he attended the party school Lenin ran in Longjumeau near Paris. In 1912 he participated in the Russian Organizational Commission which made the preparations for the Sixth (Prague) Conference of the Russian Social Democratic Workers' Party (Bolshevik), the meeting which made the split between the Bolsheviks and the Mensheviks (*see* Russian Social Democratic Workers' Party [Menshevik]) permanent. At the Sixth Conference a Russian Bureau was created to coordinate all party work inside Russia that included both Stalin and Ordzhonikidze.

From 1912 to 1915 Ordzhonikidze was in prison and in 1915 he was sent to Siberia where he continued both his work in medicine and his political activities. After the February Revolution* Ordzhonikidze became a member of the Committee of Public Safety in Iakutsk and President of the Iakutsk Soviet. When he arrived in Petrograd at the end of May Ordzhonikidze was immediately appointed a member of the Bolshevik Petrograd Committee and a member of the Executive Committee of the Petrograd Soviet. He tried unsuccessfully to persuade the demonstrators during the July Days* not to conduct an armed demonstration, and he took part in the Sixth Congress of the Bolshevik Party in July. In August he returned to Transcaucasia and did not return to Petrograd until October 24, at the very moment when the October Seizure of Power was beginning. He immediately joined in and persuaded a cyclist battallion to join the Bolsheviks in the fight against the cadet (junker) rebellion in Petrograd on October 29.

In December 1917 Ordzhonikidze was put in charge of the Ukraine as Temporary Extraordinary Commissar of the entire region, but by March most of the Ukraine was occupied by the German army. Ordzhonikidze was given the same title, Temporary Extraordinary Commissar, for the Southern Region, which also included the Caucasus. When A. I. Denikin's Volunteer Army (*see* A. I. Denikin; White Movement) formed, the Bolsheviks were forced to retreat. Ordzhonikidze fled to Astrakhan, where he met S. M. Kirov*, with whom he formed a life long friendship. During the Civil War in Russia* he served as a member of the Military Revolutionary Committee of the Fourteenth Army.

In 1920 Ordzhonikidze returned to the Caucasus where he headed the Bureau for the Restoration of Soviet Power in the Northern Caucasus with Kirov as his deputy. In April, when the Bolsheviks formed the Caucasian Bureau* to direct all party work in that area, Ordzhonikidze became its chief. He proved to be an aggressive leader, pushing the reconquest of Azerbaijan (*see* Azerbaijan, Revolution in), Georgia (*see* Georgia, Revolution in), and Armenia (*see* Armenia, Revolution in). Working closely with Stalin, the Commissar of Nationalities, Ordzhonikidze imposed unification and Russification on the Caucasus. The invasion of Georgia and the forceful imposition of Russian models on Georgia were accomplished against Lenin's stated wishes, and on November 28, 1921 he vetoed the Caucasian Bureau's plans to create a Transcaucasian Federation. Despite that decision, Ordzhonikidze moved on March 12, 1922 to create the Federal Union of Soviet Socialist Republics of Transcaucasia that achieved the same end, and infuriated Georgian political leaders.

While he was directing Transcaucasian affairs Ordzhonikidze's status within the party was rising. He headed the party's Transcaucasian Regional Bureau from 1922 to 1926 and became a member of the party's Central Committee in 1921. In July 1926 he moved into one of the highest positions in the party as a candidate member of the Politburo and head of the Central Control Commission of the Party responsible for weeding out Stalin's opponents. He became a full member in December 1930. He served in some of the top posts in the government, such as Chairman of the Commissariat of Heavy Industry in 1932, Deputy Chairman of the Supreme Council of the National Economy* after 1930, and Deputy Chairman of the Council of People's Commissars.

Throughout the struggle for power in Russia after Lenin's death Ordzhonikidze sided with Stalin, though he expressed some regrets over the expulsion of the right wing in the party. He was an effective and dynamic leader, acquiring a reputation as a political moderate who emphasized the importance of modern technology and skilled managers in the development of the Soviet economy. He lost ground with Stalin when he joined with Kirov and V. V. Kuibyshev to try to moderate Stalin's Great Purges. By 1937 there were signs that he was designated to be purged himself, especially after a long and stormy exchange between him and Stalin in February. On February 18, 1937 he shot himself, though some have charged that he was murdered. He left behind a reputation as one of the most energetic, capable and courageous leaders of the Soviet Union.

Bibliography

Cohen, S. F. *Bukharin and the Bolshevik Revolution*. 1973.
Dubinskii-Mukhadze, I. *Ordzhonikidze*. 1963.
Haupt, Georges and Marie, Jeane-Jacques. *Makers of the Russian Revolution*. 1974.
Kirillov, V. S. *Grigorii Konstantinovich Ordzhonikidze*. 1967.
Lewin, M. *Lenin's Last Struggle*. 1968.
Medvedev, *Let History Judge*. 1973.
Mikoian, A. I. *Dorogoi bor'by*. 1971.
Ordzhonikidze, A. *Put' bol' shevika*. 1967.
Pipes, R. *The Formation of the Soviet Union*. 1968.
Suny, R. G. *Transcaucausia*. 1983.
Tucker, R. *Stalin as Revolutionary 1879–1929*. 1973.

Orthodox Church. *See* Church and the Russian Revolution.

Osinskii, N. (1887–1938; real name, Valerian Valerianovich Obolenskii) Osinskii was a prominent Left Communist (*see* Left Communism; Russian Social Democratic Workers' Party [Bolshevik]) leader during the Soviet seizure of power in Moscow (*see* Moscow, Revolution in) and an economist who held various important posts in the administration of the economy. He was born in the village of Byki in Kursk Province to a family of landowning gentry. He was educated in the gymnasium and in 1905 at Moscow University. He continued his studies in Munich and Berlin.

Osinskii joined the Russian Social Democratic Workers' Party (Bolshevik) in 1907 and worked for the party in Moscow, Tver, and Khar'kov. He became a member of the Moscow Oblast Bureau of the Bolshevik Party and a member of the Editorial Board of the party's newspaper, *Sotsial-demokrat,* after the February Revolution*. After the Soviet seizure of power Osinskii was the first Chairman of the Supreme Council of the National Economy* and director of the State Bank of the Russian Soviet Federative Socialist Republic (RSFSR). But Osinskii was one of the young Moscow Left Communists grouped around N. I. Bukharin*, and during their opposition to the Treaty of Brest-Litovsk* he helped to write their platform of opposition. In 1920 he was appointed chairman of the Executive Committee of Tula Province. In 1920–1921 he was a member of another dissident group, the Democratic Centralists*, and in 1923 he supported L. D. Trotsky*. In 1925 he was a member of the Presidium of Gosplan, and from 1926 to 1928 he was Director of the Central Statistical Administration. Osinskii was arrested during the Purges and died on September 1, 1938. He has been rehabilitated posthumously.

Bibliography

Cohen, Stephen F. *Bukharin and the Bolshevik Revolution.* 1973.
Daniels, Robert V. *The Conscience of the Revolution.* 1969.
Shapiro, Leonard. *The Origin of the Communist Autocracy.* 1955.

P

Peasant International (Krest' ianskii International, or Krestinern). The Peasant International was an international organization created with the assistance and support of the Communist International* to try to attract peasant political movements into a united front with native communist parties.

The inspiration for the creation of the Peasant International was provided by Tomas Dombal (in Polish, Dąbal), a former member of the Polish Peasant Party (Piast) and a former deputy in the Polish Parliament. He proposed the idea in an article in *Pravda** on June 19, 1923, having in mind his own experience in Eastern Europe where the postwar surge in peasant political parties seemed to offer prospects for seduction and infiltration by infant communist parties.

The founding congress of the Peasant International took place on October 10–16, 1923. Forty countries were said to be represented by 158 delegates, although most of the representatives came from Eastern Europe and Asia. They agreed to create an International Peasant Council (mezhdunarodnyi krest'ianskii sovet) and to publish a newsletter, *International Peasant Newsletter* (published in English, French, and German), and a journal, *Peasant International* (*Krest'ianskii Internatsional*). From 1923 to 1928 A. P. Smirnov was first secretary of the Peasant International, although Dombal seems to have been its chief spokesman. From 1928 to its demise in 1939 the Bulgarian communist Vasilii Kolarov was chairman of the Executive Committee of the Krestintern. The Krestintern established a research auxiliary, the International Agrarian Institute (Mezhdunarodnyi Agrarnyi Institut), which continued to publish monographs on the agrarian question until 1942.

In many ways the Peasant International was one of the still-born creations of the Communist International. In most cases it was only able to attract splinter peasant parties that had frequently been created by the native communist party. The only exception was the token adherence in 1924 of the Croatian Peasant

Party under Stepan Radić. Radić impulsively joined the organization on a visit to Moscow but played no visible role after that.

Plenums of the International Peasant Council met in October 1923 and November 1927, and the second Peasant International Conference was held in November 1927, but the organization ceased publishing its journal in 1926 and appears to have died before the Soviet Union and the Comintern abandoned its "united front" tactics in 1928. It seemed about to rise from its ashes with the formation of the European Peasant Committee in Berlin in 1930, but that organization was no more successful than its predecessor. Most of the leaders associated with the Peasant International were executed during the Purges, including A. P. Smirnov and Tomas Dombal.

Bibliography

Goranovich, M. M. *Krakh zelenogo internatsionala, 1921–38.* 1967.
Jackson, George D. *Comintern and Peasant in East Europe, 1919–1930.* 1966.

Peasants in the Russian Revolution. At the time of the fall of the Tsar (*see* February Revolution), Russia was still overwhelmingly a peasant country. Most of its population lived in rural areas, trying to eke out a living from the produce of the plots. However, over the preceding half century the economic basis of peasant agriculture was steadily eroded. A combination of rapid population growth and traditional land-tenure provisions had led to a decline in the size of the peasant plot, while the obligations the peasant had to meet continued to rise. This increasingly difficult economic position fostered among the peasants a belief that their problems would be eliminated if they could gain control of the land currently owned by nonpeasant landowners. After 1905 most peasants also looked to the reabsorption by the communal structure of that land consolidated after 1905 under the so-called Stolypin reforms as a key to the alleviation of their distress (*see* Agrarian Policy, 1917–1921; Agriculture).

Peasant expectations soared with the fall of the Tsar. The peasants hoped that the February Revolution would bring to power a government that was sensitive to their problems and that would act to alleviate their land hunger by passing into their hands the land they desired. But they were disappointed. The Provisional Government* adopted a policy of postponing any major change in the land relations until the whole question could be considered and resolved by the Constituent Assembly* but made little attempt to expedite the convening of that body. In effect, this policy involved a governmental attempt to retain the status quo in land relations. The opposition that such a policy generated among the peasants was reinforced by government action on the questions of local government and food policy (*see* Famine). The local government organs that the Provisional Government sought to create consisted largely of people who had few close links to the villages and little empathy for the peasants and their concerns. Reliance on traditional landowners, former officials, and urban-based intellectuals for the local government organs caused the peasants to view these bodies as out of touch, unsympathetic, and alien to their needs. Finally, the government's food policy not only did not ease the crisis that had developed in the grain market but also exacerbated it. The imposition of a grain monopoly with fixed prices caught producers in a vice. The price of their main commodity was frozen, but the price of most other goods they had to purchase rose alarmingly. As a result, producers widely refused to surrender their grain to the state, thereby creating substantial shortfalls on the domestic market. Even the doubling of the fixed prices on August 27 did not alleviate the situation, with the result that the government's policy frustrated both producers and consumers.

The peasants responded to the government's failure in these areas by unleashing a wave of unrest throughout the countryside. Although the precise dimensions of these disturbances are unclear, what is certain is that they eliminated non-peasant land ownership as a prominent feature of Russian agriculture. In many instances peasants took action to disrupt the working of privately owned estates, particularly early in the year; they seized tools, equipment, and livestock; withdrew their own labor or fixed exorbitant rates for it; and drove off indentured workers and laborers hired from other regions. Land was seized on a wide scale, often initially under cover of offering (but rarely paying) a nominal rental for the land but, increasingly, as the year wore on by direct and open seizure. Crops were seized, and in those areas characterized by woodland, all except local peasants were denied access to the timber. The physical destruction of private property was a frequent occurrence, as was violent personal assault on those who opposed peasant wishes.

The level of rural unrest in European Russia between the two revolutions fluctuated month by month, as the following figures show (in terms of the monthly proportion of all unrest for the period [March-October = 100 percent—each month provides a proportion of that]):

March	1.9%
April	7.1%
May	11.6%
June	16.6%
July	17.1%
August	13.1%
September	16.0%
October	16.6%

Although a number of influences combined to produce this pattern, the chief determinant was the traditional agricultural life-style of the villages. In the early period, the time that the peasants could devote to disruptive activities was restricted by the demands of their rural subsistence. During spring and early summer they had to spend long periods in the fields preparing for and carrying out the spring sowing, tending the winter crops planted the previous year, and gathering fodder. In midsummer the demands of field work declined, thereby creating greater scope for involvement in rural unrest before the busy harvesting and planting period of late July and August. In the late autumn and early winter the demands of field work again subsided. Thus within the context of continuing disillusionment with the government, the contours of rural unrest were determined largely by the traditional demands of agricultural production.

The traditional basis of rural unrest is also clear in the geographical distribution of peasant disturbances. The highest levels of unrest occurred in the provinces of Kazan, Penza, Orel, Riazan, Minsk, Podolsk, Mogilev, Kursk, Tula, Tambov, Samara, and Volynsk, all of which individually experienced more than 3 percent of all unrest in European Russia. The central black-earth area, in which most of these provinces were found, was the bastion of the traditional peasant repartitional commune. The communal structure had more successfully resisted the effects of the Stolypin reforms here than anywhere else in the country with the result that communal sentiment was very strong. Furthermore, these provinces experienced not only high levels of peasant unrest but also severe land hunger. In general, this area was characterized by smaller peasant plots and therefore greater pressure on peasant resources than was the norm for most other parts of Russia. This was reflected in a high level of land rental from private landowners. The effect of this was reinforced in 1917 by crop failures throughout much of this region. As a result, this area experienced not only higher levels of unrest in general but also greater violence and destruction. Wherever the traditional grievance of land hunger was reinforced by crop failure, levels of unrest were high and violence more pronounced.

The traditional nature of peasant unrest was also reflected in the types of organizations that dominated the countryside in 1917. The peasants rejected the authority of urban-based bodies, even those formed ostensibly to represent their interests. It was to the traditional peasant *skhod* (village assembly) and to the commune that the peasant turned to structure their activity. Despite the proliferation of diverse bodies in the countryside in 1917, those that were influential in the villages appear to have been either the traditional organs under a new name or those based entirely on the traditional institutions. The peasant turned away from the towns, rejected their authority, and relied upon traditional village-based institutions, leaders, and mores in this situation of the breakdown of established governmental authority.

Peasant actions constituted a revolution in the countryside. Non-peasant land and land held by those who had separated from the commune under the Stolypin reforms was integrated or reintegrated into the traditional peasant framework. External authority was rejected as the peasants relied on their own institutions for guidance. The domestic grain market collapsed as peasant producers refused to participate in it. But the peasant actions also contributed substantially to the Revolution in the cities. Peasant seizure of timber resources contributed to fuel shortages in Petrograd, thereby stimulating enterprise closures and increasing unemployment. More importantly, the peasant producers' refusal to surrender grain to the state contributed to the serious food shortages being experienced in the capital. This provided a significant stimulus to the move to the Left in the mood of the capital that so aided the Bolsheviks. Furthermore, peasant unrest contributed to the disintegration of the army (*see* Army, Imperial) as troops left their posts to return to the villages to share in the land redistribution. The peasantry was thus a key social force in the events of 1917, which culminated in the October Seizure of Power*.

Upon coming to power the Bolsheviks legally passed the land into the hands of the cultivators, thereby generating a significant level of peasant support for the regime. This support seems to have been maintained during the Civil War in Russia*, at least to the extent that the peasants seem to have favored the Bolsheviks over their White (*see* White Movement) opponents. But this support must be balanced against the growth of resentment and opposition caused by the introduction of War Communism* in mid–1918. This involved, among other things, the replacement of the market by the forced requisition of grain and a centralized rationing system. As in 1917 such an arrangement alienated producers without satisfying consumers. Hunger and famine were widespread, leading to outbreaks of revolt in various parts of the country, the most important of which was Tambov. This sort of response forced the government to reverse its policies through the introduction of the New Economic Policy*.

Graeme J. Gill

Bibliography

Gill, Graeme J. *Peasants and Government in the Russian Revolution*. 1979.
Keep, John L. H. *The Russian Revolution: A Study in Mass Mobilization*. 1976.
Kotel'nikov, K. G., and Meller, V. A. *Krest'ianskoe dvizhenie v 1917 godu*. 1927.
Kravchuk, N. A. *Massovoe krest'ianskoe dvizhenie v Rossii nakanune oktiabria*. 1971.
Owen, L. A. *The Russian Peasant Movement, 1906–1917*. 1963 [1937].
Pershin, P. N. *Agrarnaia revoliutsiia v Rossii*. 1966.

Peshkov, Maksim Alekseevich (1868–1936; Maksim Gorky). Maksim Gorky along with Vladimir Maiakovskii has been hailed by the USSR as the father of the official Stalinist literary style, Socialist Realism. Gorky (whose real name was Peshkov) was already a world reknowned writer before the October Seizure of Power*, and also both a supporter and a critic of V. I. Lenin*. Gorky was one of the major patrons of the Russian Social Democratic Workers' Party (Bolshevik)* and during the first years of the Soviet state he frequently served as the public conscience of the new regime in articles that appeared in his newspaper, *Novaia zhizn'* (New Life).

Gorky was born in a lower middle-class family in Nizhnii-Novgorod (now named Gorky). His maternal grandfather Kashirin, became head of the Dyers' Guild in that town and his paternal grandfather was an officer in the army of Tsar Nicholas I. Gorky's own father died when he was four years old and he had to live with his maternal grandfather who put him out to apprenticeship at an early age. When he turned eleven he ran away from home and became a wanderer, finally settling at the age of fifteen in the city of Kazan where he worked at various manual labor jobs, became a voracious reader, and began hobnobbing with intellectuals and university students. In 1887 he punctured his lung with a bullet in a suicide attempt.

In the 1890s Gorky began to work as a journalist and published his first short story in 1898. In the years before 1917 he became known around the world as a writer, publishing many short stories, plays and novels, most of which dealt with the seamy side of Russian life among the people of the "lower depths" of society's tramps, workers, artisans, and poor. Though he adopted the pen name "Gor'kii," which means bitter in Russian, most of his works are optimistic and hopeful, incorporating a faith that through genuinely good and determined people, and a Russian revolution, the country could be transformed. Among his better known works are the novel *Mother* and the play *The Lower Depths*.

Although Gorky became a member of the Russian Social Democratic Workers' Party before the turn of the century, he did not belong to either of its two major factions, the Bolshevik or the Menshevik (*see* Russian Social Democratic Workers' Party [Menshevik]). There was a close friendship between Gorky and V. I. Lenin*, though there were also long intervals of estrangement. Lenin openly admired Gorky's work, but distrusted his Marxism, especially when Gorky became close to the Marxist faction of "God Builders" (*see* V. I. Lunacharskii). He was especially incensed when Gorky decided to operate his own party training school for revolutionary workers on the island of Capri in 1908. Lenin was intensely and sometimes offensively opposed. Yet Gorky would keep alive his hope in a humane brand of socialism and express it, even as late as 1922.

In 1917 Gorky published his own newspaper in Russia, *Novaia zhizn'* (The New Life). In it he condemned Lenin's efforts to seize power and replace the freedom of political life under the Provisional Government* with a proletarian dictatorship. He warned Lenin that such a coup d'etat would unleash the basest instincts of the mob. After the October Seizure of Power he accused Lenin of a cruel experiment on the Russian people whom, he said, Lenin knew only through books. He was enraged when Lenin dissolved the Constituent Assembly*. On July 16, 1918 Lenin ordered Gorky's newspaper closed.

After the attempted assassination of Lenin in August 1918 the two men signed a truce, but they continued to disagree. Gorky accepted a number of jobs under the new regime to protect art treasures and historical monuments and to provide assistance for indigent writers. His efforts to protect freedom and creative artistic endeavors were only partially successful.

Gorky finally left Russia for medical treatment abroad and did not return until 1929. When Lenin decided to try the leaders of the Socialist-Revolutionary Party* in 1922, Gorky broke off all communication with him. But in 1929 Stalin induced him to return to his homeland where he became President of the Union of Socialist Writers. In his new role he found himself at the head of an organization that was imposing order and conformity on Russian writers, though Gorky had striven all of his life to preserve freedom for artists. He seems to have accepted that role in the hope that he could use the power thus acquired to save writers he

loved and admired from personal extinction. Gorky died in 1936 and there is
some debate about the nature of his death. He continued to be idealized by the
Stalinist regime in Russia, which represented values contrary to those that Gorky
professed during his lifetime.

Bibliography

Gorkogo, A. M. *Letopis' zhizni i tvorchestva*. 4 vols. 1958–60.
Gorky, Maxim (Maksim Gorkii). *Sobranie sochinenii*. 30 vols. 1949–55.
———. *The Autobiography of Maxim Gorky*. 1969.
———. *Days with Lenin*. 1932.
———. *Untimely Thoughts*.
Hare, Richard. *Maxim Gorky*. 1963.
Kaun, A. *Maxim Gorky and His Russia*. 1931.
Levin, Dan. *Stormy Petrel*. 1965.
Weil, Irwin. *Gorky*. 1966.
Wolfe, Bertram. *The Bridge and the Abyss*. 1967.

Petliura, Symon M. (May 10, 1879-May 25, 1926). Petliura was a civic and
political activist, a journalist, an organizer of Ukrainian military units, and the
head of the Directory of the Ukrainian Democratic Republic (*see* Directory—
Ukraine). His parents, being of modest means, sent the young Petliura to the
seminary in Poltava where he joined a secret group of students for which he
was expelled from the seminary in 1901. By that time Petliura was already an
active member of the Revolutionary Ukrainian Party founded in 1900.

After 1900 Petliura spent most of his time editing newspapers and writing
articles for a variety of journals. To be sure, his membership in the Ukrainian
Social Democratic Party was reflected in his writings, which conveyed his profound commitment to social justice as well as the right of the Ukrainian people
to self-determination. As a journalist, Petliura reached his highest point editing
the highly respected journal *Ukrainskaia Zhyzn*, which began to appear in Moscow in 1912. This journal, which published some of the finest articles, was a
Ukrainian voice in pre–World War I* Russia.

The war and the Revolution reoriented Petliura; he became interested in military affairs. As a realist, he realized that during a Revolution the decisive factor
is the army. This realization brought him to the first Ukrainian Military Assembly
(May 18–21, 1917) where he was chosen head of the Ukrainian General Military
Committee. Subsequently, Petliura became Minister (General Secretary) of Military Affairs in the government formed by the Central Rada*.

During the rule of Hetman Pavlo Skoropadskii, Petliura was jailed as politically
dangerous. After his release, however, he joined the national uprising as one of
the members of the Directory-Ukraine. Soon thereafter, he became the head of
the Directory and Commander-in-Chief of the army of the Ukrainian Democratic
Republic (UNR). He remained in that position until the remnants of the Ukrainian
army were interned in Poland in November 1920. The struggle in Ukraine
continued, principally a guerilla war against the Ukrainian Bolsheviks (*see* Rus-

sian Social Democratic Workers' Party [Bolshevik]). Petliura, although in exile, continued to direct the struggle as President of the UNR.

At the request of the Soviet government, the Polish government asked that Petliura leave the country. As a president of an exile government, Petliura had little choice. Toward the end of 1923 he left for Budapest and then went to Vienna and Geneva; finally, in 1924, he settled in Paris where he directed the affairs of the Ukrainian government in exile. In Paris he also renewed his interest in journalism. Besides continuing his writing, Petliura also established a weekly Ukrainian journal, *Tryzub,* which became an important forum for the political ideas of his followers.

On May 25, 1926, Petliura's plans came to an end—he was assassinated by a would-be avenger, Sholom Schwartzbard. Historical scholarship has proven, since the tragedy of 1926, that Petliura was innocent of any wrongdoing against the Jewish people. On the contrary, he always was their friend.

For the Ukrainians, Petliura has become a symbol of a dedicated man who sacrificed his entire life for the cause of national statehood and personal freedom of the Ukrainian people (*see* Ukraine, Revolution in).

Taras Hunczak

Bibliography

Desroches, A. *Le probléme ukrainien et Simon Petliura.* 1962.
Hunczak, Taras. "A Reappraisal of Symon Petliura and Ukrainian-Jewish Relations, 1917–1921," in *Jewish Social Studies,* July 1969.
Ivanys, V. *Symon Petliura: Prezydent Ukrainy.* 1952
Petliura, Symon. *Statti, lysty, dokumenty.* vol. 1, 1956; vol. 2, 1979.
Zhuk, A., ed. *Symon Petliura v molodosti.* 1936

Petrograd Soviet. The Petrograd Soviet was the organization through which the October Seizure of Power* was effected in Petrograd in 1917. Technically, though, the new Soviet government had to be approved by the Second All-Russian Congress of Soviets, in conjunction with the Military Organization of the Bolsheviks (*see* Russian Social Democratic Workers' Party [Bolshevik]) that actually organized the overthrow of the Provisional Government* and the seizure of power in the name of the soviets in October 1917 (*see* Soviets [Councils] of Workers', Soldiers' and Peasants' Deputies).

The Russian word *sovet* means council, and the first workers' councils, or soviets, appeared in the Revolution of 1905 (*see* Nineteen-Five Revolution). Although historians disagree about the location of the first soviet, it was probably either the Petrograd (then called St. Petersburg) Soviet created on October 13, 1905, or the Council (soviet) of representatives elected in Ivanovo-Voznesensk on May 15, 1905. These workers' soviets originated as strike committees when factories decided that they needed to coordinate their activities and provide a united front. In Petrograd the name Soviet of Workers' Deputies was adopted on October 17, 1905. At that time the Petrograd soviet established an executive committee and made plans to publish its own newspaper, *Izvestiia** (*News*).

Once established as a permanent institution representing the working class of the city, the Petrograd Soviet rapidly became a rival government in that city, ordering an end to censorship and negotiating directly with the official government and management. Some members of the Petrograd Soviet even discussed the possibility of seizing power in Petrograd from the Provisional Government. Because it was the soviet of the capital city, it naturally had more influence than any other soviet, although it moved very haltingly to fulfill its role of national leadership among the soviets.

The Petrograd Soviet was crushed by the official government in the city at the end of November and beginning of December 1905. Its first chairman was arrested on November 26, 1905, and his successor, L. D. Trotsky*, along with the rest of the Executive Committee of 200 deputies on December 3, 1905. Although the idea of the soviet as a government in its own right was occasionally discussed in the writings of V. I. Lenin* and L. D. Trotsky, most revolutionary activists thought of it between 1905 and 1907 primarily as an instrument for conducting a revolution. The other possibilities for the institution were not widely discussed during that period.

The success of the February Revolution* in 1917 led to a call for the resurrection of the Petrograd soviet. On February 27, 1917, a group of socialists gathered in the Tauride Palace (the Duma Building) and formed the Provisional Executive Committee of the Petrograd Soviet of Workers' Deputies and issued an appeal to the workers and soldiers of the city to send delegates to the first meeting of the Petrograd Soviet that night. Because of the inclusion of soldiers, the name of the institution was changed on the following day to the Petrograd Soviet of Workers' and Soldiers' Deputies. From the beginning the Soviet once again began to take on some of the characteristics of a government, its Provisional Executive Committee calling for measures to preserve order in the city, to prepare defenses against counterrevolution, and to insure the supply of food to the city. At the first meeting of the Soviet, admittedly loosely thrown together, N. S. Chkheidze*, a Georgian Menshevik (*see* Russian Social Democratic Workers' Party [Menshevik]), was elected chairman with M. I. Skobolev (a Menshevik) and A. F. Kerensky* (a Socialist-Revolutionary [*see* Socialist-Revolutionary Party]) as Vice-Chairman. In the beginning the organization was predominately Menshevik in its membership and primarily consisted of members of the moderate socialist intelligentsia. The Executive Committee elected on February 27 did not include any workers' delegates, although some of working-class origin were brought in on March 1, 1917, when ten soldiers' representatives were added to the Executive Committee.

The Soviet did not have a clear sense of direction or even of identity in the beginning. Despite the famous Army Order Number One issued by the Petrograd soviet on March 1, 1917—an order that seemed to give the Soviet authority over the armed forces superior to that of the Provisional Government and called for the enlisted men to form democratically elected soviets of their own with broad administrative powers—the leaders of the Soviet did not move to act on that assumption and even retracted some of their earlier claims in Army Order Number Two issued on March 3, 1917. In fact, the only revolutionary leader to speak of the soviets as a potential government for Russia, replacing the Provisional Government, was V. I. Lenin, who upon arriving in Russia ordered the Bolsheviks (see Russian Social Democratic Workers' Party [Bolshevik]) in his April theses* to give no support to the Provisional Government and to inform the masses that "the Soviets of Workers' Deputies are the only possible form of revolutionary government" (Lenin. 1967. Vol. I. p. 14).

It was not Lenin, however, but I. G. Tsereteli* who gave the Petrograd soviet its sense of direction after the February Revolution. He and his followers, mostly moderate Mensheviks and Socialist–Revolutionaries, gained control of the Executive Committee at the end of March and held that control until September. This group included Tsereteli, F. I. Dan (see Gur'vich, Fedor Il'ich), V. M. Chernov*, and A. R. Gots*. A large part of their support came from the soldiers garrisoned in Petrograd, who were more moderate in their views than the workers, at least in the first half of 1917. The Petrograd soviet gave its support to the Provisional Government, although at first the members of the Executive Committee refused to join any of that government's cabinets because that would mean that they had been coopted by a bourgeois government. They were also reluctant because they did not wish to join a government that had to commit itself to a continuation of the war. In addition, there was, among many of the leaders, an aversion to the responsibility of governing. They had spent their lives in opposition. It was a more natural posture for them, and, perhaps, they were not even sure they had the ability to govern. They were, in fact, more comfortable in the role of the "loyal opposition" leaving the government to the liberals and the criticism and right to veto to the Soviet.

The leaders of the Soviet were forced to rethink their position after the April crisis led to the resignation of many of the liberals (including G. E. L'vov*). On May 5 the first coalition government was created and a cabinet formed that included ten non-socialists and six socialists. Some historians argue that this decision was a crucial mistake, and the only radical socialist party that refused to participate was the Bolshevik Party. Essentially, it did mean, as the soviet leaders had originally feared, joining a bourgeois government and accepting responsibility for all of its policies, including the continuation of an unsuccessful and unpopular war and the absence of a land reform. It meant also an increasing gap between the leaders of the Petrograd soviet and the rank-and-file workers and soldiers whom they claimed to represent. As the food shortages, the strikes, the failures at the front, and the inflation continued, the patience of the ordinary people in the city wore thin. But now there was only one alternative to the socialist parties in the government: the Bolsheviks led by V. I. Lenin. It was Lenin who was the last remaining leader of a major party calling for Soviet power and a workers' state. The slogan, "All Power to the Soviets" became increasingly popular in midsummer, especially in the July Days*.

One of the questions raised by rank-and-file Bolsheviks when Lenin questioned their conditional support for the Provisional Government and their reluctance to call for its overthrow and replacement by a Soviet government, was their relatively weak position in the soviets.

When the First All-Russian Congress of Soviets was called on the initiative of the Petrograd Soviet in June 1917, representing 305 workers' and soldiers' soviets and 34 army units, the Bolsheviks were able to win only 11 percent of the vote. The All-Russian Central Executive Committee elected by this meeting was controlled by the moderate Mensheviks and Socialist–Revolutionaries. But between July and September all of the pressing issues became more urgent. While the government vacillated, the economy faltered, and the war effort failed, large-scale strikes became more common, peasants seized land, and national minorities began to agitate for separation.

The passage of power into the hands of the Bolsheviks began as early as June when the Bolsheviks gained control of the Workers' Section of the Soviet. But after the July Crisis many Bolsheviks, including Lenin, had to go into exile or jail on charges of treason. The Kornilov Revolt* in August dramatized both the threat of counterrevolution and the incompetence of the Provisional Government in the face of such threats. In the middle of those events on August 31, the workers and soldiers in the Petrograd Soviet voted together in overwhelming support for a Bolshevik resolution that blamed the Provisional Government for the Kornilov Revolt and called for a government of "representatives of the revolutionary proletariat and peasantry." When the Menshevik Socialist-Revolutionary leadership of the Soviet called for a vote of confidence on September 9, it lost 519 to 414 with 67 abstentions. The Presidium of the Executive Committee of the soviet resigned, and a new one chaired by L. D. Trotsky took over.

On October 12 the Bolshevik-dominated Soviet Executive Committee formed the Military Revolutionary Committee (MRC), a committee that included Bolsheviks and Socialist–Revolutionaries and also was chaired by Trotsky. Although nominally formed to protect the capital against the danger of counterrevolution, the Military Revolutionary Committee merged with the Bolshevik Military Organization to become the General Staff of the projected October Seizure of Power. Although, as Robert Daniels (1967) pointed out, the preparations for the seizure of power were woefully inadequate, when provoked by Kerensky's actions, the MRC was successful in taking over the city. The executive organ of the new Soviet government, the Council of People's Commissars, was approved by the Second All-Russian Congress of Soviets that met on October 26. It included about 350 Bolshevik delegates out of 650 and approved the formation of a Soviet government after the Mensheviks and Right Socialist–Revolutionaries had walked out in protest. As the central institutions of the new government took shape, the Petrograd Soviet became less and less important, a mere regional institution, especially after the capital was moved to Moscow on March 12, 1918.

Many historians have posed the question of representation. In the confusion of the period, could any institution effectively represent the interests of the Russian people? Did Lenin pick up power from the streets by a clever manipulation of public opinion, using slogans that appealed to everyone but providing little information about the real program of the Bolsheviks? To some extent that approach ignores the very real failings of the leaders of the Petrograd Soviet both in the Soviet and in the Provisional Government. To deny the legitimacy of Lenin's masterminding seizure of power through the soviets is also to ignore the fact that his party had become the most popular party in that body, partially because Lenin was listening to the demands of his constituencies.

Bibliography

Anweiler, Oscar. *The Soviets*. 1974.
Daniels, Robert V. *Red October*. 1967.
Hasegawa, Tsyuoshi. *The February Revolution*. 1969.
Lenin, V.I. *Selected Works*. 3 vols. 1967.
Potekhin, M. N. *Pervyi Sovet proletarskoi diktatury*. 1966.
Rabinowitch, Alexander. *The Bolsheviks Come to Power*. 1976.
———. *Prelude to Revolution*. 1968.
Tokarev, Iu. S. *Petrogradskii Sovet rabochikh i soldatskikh deputatov v period mirnogo razvitiia revoliuutsii*. 1969.
Zlokazov, G. I. *Petrogradskii Sovet na puti Oktiabriu*. 1966.

Piatnitskii, Iosif Aronovich (1882–1939; true name, Iosif Aronovich Tarshis; also known as Piatnitsa and Freitag). Piatnitskii was a Bolshevik (*see* Russian Social Democratic Workers' Party [Bolshevik]) who took part in the October Seizure of Power* in Moscow and became a prominent leader of the Communist International*.

Piatnitskii was born in the village of Vil'komir in Kovno Province into a working-class family. Piatnitskii joined the Russian Social Democratic Workers' Party in 1898 and became a tailor and worked at that job until 1902 when he became secretary of the Vilnius Union of Tailors. As early as 1901 he had begun to help in the effort to smuggle V. I. Lenin's* newspaper *Iskra* (*The Spark*) into Russia. When arrested for this, Piatnitskii escaped to Germany where he continued in this activity. During the 1905 Revolution (*see* Nineteen-Five Revolution) Piatnitskii returned to Russia and became a member of the Odessa Party Committee. From 1906 to 1908 he remained in Moscow administering the technical affairs of the Moscow Party Committee. In 1912 he helped to prepare the Sixth Conference of the Russian Social Democratic Workers' Party (Bolshevik) in Prague. In 1914 he helped to create the Bolshevik Organization in Samara but was arrested for his party work and sent into exile in Eniseisk Province.

After the February Revolution* the Provisional Government* granted amnesty to political prisoners and Piatnitskii returned to Moscow and became Chairman of the Military Revolutionary Committee of the Railroad District in Moscow. He also became a member of the Party Center, where he took part in the work of the Moscow Military Revolutionary Committee that organized the Soviet seizure of power in that city. In 1918 he became a member of the All-Russian Central Executive Committee* of Soviets and of the Executive Committee of the Moscow Soviet*, and was secretary of the Moscow Party Committee. In 1921 he moved on to the Communist International where he became one of its most important officials. From 1927 to 1934 he was a member of the Central Committee of the Russian Communist Party (Bolshevik)* and from 1935 until his arrest worked in the apparatus of the Central Committee of the Russian Communist Party (Bolshevik). Despite the personal intervention of N. K. Krupskaia*, he was arrested during the Purges, charged with being an agent of the tsarist police, and died in prison on October 30, 1939. He has been posthumously rehabilitated.

Bibliography

Levytsky, Borys. *The Stalinist Terror in the Thirties*. 1974.
Medvedev, Roy A. *Let History Judge*. 1973.
Pitanitskii, I. A. *Zapiski bol'sheviki*. 1925.

Plekhanov, Georgii Valentinovich (1856–1918). The founder of the Russian Marxist movement, Plekhanov is regarded as one of V. I. Lenin's* mentors.

Despite his stature as a revolutionary theoretician and Social Democratic leader, Plekhanov played a relatively minor role in the October Seizure of Power* by the Bolsheviks (*see* Russian Social Democratic Workers' Party [Bolshevik]). When he arrived in Petrograd on March 31, 1917, bringing to a close a thirty-seven-year period of exile, the father of Russian Marxism and lifelong warrior against autocracy was given a tumultuous reception. However, he could not translate gratitude for past contributions and sacrifices into leadership in the unfolding revolution, for his views on the major issues ran counter to the movement of popular sentiment.

At the outbreak of World War I*, believing that German imperialism was at fault, Plekhanov had wholeheartedly embraced the Entente cause. He strove to do everything in his power to prevent German victory, convinced that it would spell disaster for the Russian people and especially the working class. Consequently, he urged the Social Democratic members of the Duma (*see* Duma and Revolution) to vote in favor of war credits, supported worker participation in the War Industries Committees*, and even warned that labor disturbances in the rear of fighting forces would be tantamount to treason. For the sake of winning the war, the old revolutionist advocated a moratorium on political and class struggle. His extreme Defensist (*see* Defensism) position set him apart from the great majority of emigré Social Democrats, and his following in Russia dwindled between 1914 and 1917.

Since it stemmed from antiwar sentiment and worker discontent, the February Revolution* conflicted with Plekhanov's prescriptions and therefore initially upset him. He quickly recovered, however, taking comfort in the thought that what had occurred was the Russian bourgeois Revolution he had long predicted.

His position on other issues remained substantially unchanged. He persuaded himself that the democratization of the political system would facilitate more effective prosecution of the war. His concern to keep a damper on political and social strife that might disrupt the war effort was unshaken. To this concern was soon added a resurgence of the anxiety he had first experienced in 1905–1906 that "utopian" efforts might be made to push the Revolution beyond bourgeois limits.

On the latter score the moderate socialists who dominated the soviets from March to September were at one with him, reflecting the continuing influence of the revolutionary prospectus Plekhanov had worked out in the 1880s. Their conditional support of the "bourgeois" Provisional Government* and their disinclination to put power into the hands of the soviets bespoke an appreciation that the level of Russian economic and social development precluded a rapid movement to socialism. On the war issue, the soviet leaders took a tack different from Plekhanov's. Blaming the conflict on Germany alone, they sought to end by international socialist action what they perceived as an imperialist war (*see* World War I) and meanwhile to support only defensive military measures. Plekhanov inveighed against what in his view was a self-contradictory and self-defeating policy. He attacked the Petrograd Soviet*, especially the promulgation of Order Number One (*see* Soldiers and Soldiers' Committees) for its adverse effects; celebrated the launching of the unpopular and unsuccessful July offensive; and repeatedly called for the restoration of discipline in the armed forces— all in vain. If the somewhat more responsive policies of the moderate socialists proved increasingly unacceptable to soldiers and sailors desperate to end the war, Plekhanov's line was utterly unrealistic.

His ideas on how to deal with other groups that became ever more restive were no more suitable. When peasants clamored for land and workers for better conditions or even control of their factories, he counseled moderation, restraint, and the deferment of solutions. Otherwise, the bourgeois parties would quit the governing coalition, class conflict would be intensified, and the all importance of the "war to a successful conclusion" would be hopelessly jeopardized. On these matters, as on the war question, Plekhanov stood to the right of moderate socialists. In his opinion they were "semi-Leninists" because they yielded to mass pressures, although actually their support was eroded because they were so reticent about fulfilling popular demands. So also were the insurgent masses heedless to Plekhanov's plans for order, class conciliation, and relentless pursuit of the war. Theoretical considerations concerning historically attainable goals made no impression on a populace hungry for peace, land, and bread. By contrast, the Bolsheviks gained popular support by promising everything that the turbulent masses demanded.

By way of the printed and spoken word, Plekhanov waged unremitting war against the Bolsheviks in 1917. He described V. I. Lenin's April theses* as "ravings" and labeled Lenin himself as an "alchemist of revolution" for his seeming disregard of the teachings of Karl Marx and Friedrich Engels. Deeming

Bolshevik promises impossible of fulfillment, he denounced their leader as a "demagogue to the tip of his toenails." After the July Days*, he gave currency to the rumor that Lenin was a German agent, and he later berated the Provisional Government for insufficient determination and vigor in suppressing "anarchy." All his efforts came to naught—he was impotent to stop the Bolshevik march to power.

Despite the great ovation given Plekhanov upon his arrival in Petrograd, he held no important post in the following months. His entry into the Provisional Government as Minister of Labor was canvassed but never consummated. The first cabinet decided against offering him the post, but he was invited to join the coalition government formed in May. He refused to accept without the endorsement of the Soviet Executive Committee (*see* All-Russian Central Executive Committee), but when, as a condition of acceptance, he demanded a seat for the small Edinstvo (Unity) group, an organization of his followers, the committee vetoed his proposal by a narrow margin. He held no post in the soviets throughout 1917 and in the government held only an insignificant position as chairman of a commission to improve the condition of the railroad workers. The stance that alienated him from the Left made him popular with liberal and even rightist circles. General L. G. Kornilov (*see* Kornilov Revolt) expressed interest in having Plekhanov in his cabinet; after the Bolshevik takeover, he was invited to take a ministerial post in a counterrevolutionary coalition. He adamantly refused.

Plekhanov's public activity in 1917 was associated with the Edinstvo group. Shortly after his arrival in Russia he became editor and chief contributor to its newspaper of the same name. Although he wrote a great deal and spoke to public meetings whenever he could, his impact was modest at best. Edinstvo took a strong interest in electoral campaigns, but its candidates in the Moscow municipal elections netted a mere two-tenths of 1 percent of the vote. When in July the Mensheviks (*see* Russian Social Democratic Workers' Party [Menshevik]) sent invitations to all Social Democratic groups to participate in a unification congress, none went to Plekhanov and his group, for they were considered outside the party. The newspaper Edinstvo was suppressed soon after the October Seizure of Power*, and he who had launched the Marxist revolutionary movement in Russia was silenced. In a final indignity, revolutionary soldiers and sailors in search of arms broke into Plekhanov's apartment in Tsarskoe Selo, took him for a member of the hated bourgeoisie, and verbally abused and threatened him. Thereafter the illness that had long afflicted him worsened, and he died in a sanatorium in Finland on May 30, 1918.

Samuel H. Baron

Bibliography

Baron, Samuel H. *Plekhanov*. 1963.
Deutscher, Isaac. *The Prophet Armed*. 1954.
Iovchuk M., and Kurbatova, I. *Plekhanov*. 1977.

Plekhanov, George V. *God na rodine*. 2 vols. 1921.
Service, Robert. *Lenin*. Vol. 1. 1985.
Vaganian, V. *G. V. Plekhanov*. 1924.
Valentinov, N. *The Early Years of Lenin*. 1969.

Podvoiskii, Nikolai Il'ich (1880–1948). Podvoiskii was a prominent Old Bolshevik (*see* Russian Social Democratic Workers' Party [Bolshevik]) who played a very significant role in the October Seizure of Power* and later faded into obscurity.

Podvoiskii was born in the village of Kunochevsk in Chernigov Province. His father had been a teacher, but later decided to become a priest. Podvoiskii seemed to be following his example when he entered the local Nezhin Seminary, and then in the spring of 1904 entered the Chernigov Seminary. However, he was soon expelled for revolutionary activity and entered the Law Faculty of the Demidov Juridical Lyceum in Iaroslav. In that city he became an active member of the Russian Social Democratic Workers' Party (Bolshevik) using the pseudonym "Mironich." In Iaroslav he worked with such well known Bolsheviks as E. M. Iaroslavskii (*see* Gubel'man, M. I.), V. I. Nevskii*, V. R. Menzhinskii and M. S. Kedrov.

He played an active role in the Nineteen-Five Revolution* in organizing the railway workers. He was wounded in a demonstration and went to Germany and Switzerland for treatment. He returned in 1906 and worked in St. Petersburg from 1907 to 1908 in the Zerno Publishing House. In 1908 he was arrested for his revolutionary activities and released in 1910 in order to receive medical treatment. After a short time in the Caucasus (*see* Transcaucasia, Revolution in) he returned to revolutionary work in St. Petersburg where he remained until his arrest shortly before the February Revolution* in 1917. In 1913 he was one of the founders of the Bolshevik (*see* Russian Social Democratic Workers' Party [Bolshevik]) newspaper, *Pravda*.

After the February Revolution Podvoiskii was released and rapidly became one of the most important figures in the Bolshevik movement in Petrograd. From the beginning he was a staunch supporter of the Soviet movement as a deputy in the City Soviet. This made him a representative of the left wing of the party. He opposed the support for the Provisional Government* before V. I. Lenin* returned and called for that stance in his famous April Theses*. The Petrograd Committee of the Bolsheviks appointed him to their Military Commission which was charged with the creation of the Bolshevik Military Organization. At the same time he edited the Bolshevik newspaper for the soldiers, *Soldatskaia Pravda* (Soldier's Truth). Working with Nevskii he was eminently successful in recruiting support for the military organization, and by the end of June he was able to assemble 150 delegates representing sixty military units in the All-Russian Conference of Front and Rear Military Organizations. When the Petrograd Soviet* created its Military Revolutionary Committee (MRC), Podvoiskii was appointed one of its members and helped plan the insurrection as a member of the Military

Revolutionary Committee's governing bureau. According to John Reed in his *Ten Days that Shook the World,* he contended that Podvoiskii "conceived the strategy of insurrection," though that probably overstated his role.

In actuality Podvoiskii seemed to have had more of a talent for insurrection than for more conventional military operations. Though he subsequently received some very high military appointments, he did not distinguish himself in those posts and soon sank into relative obscurity. Lenin described him as a man of "great stature, though an undisciplined energy, gifted with a creative imagination which, it must be said, often meandered into fantasy." (as quoted in Haupt, p. 190).

In early 1918 he commanded the Petrograd Military District, was Chairman of the All-Russian Collegium on the Organization and Formation of the Red Army (*see* Red Army), headed the Commissariat of Military Affairs and had been appointed to the Supreme Military Council. In the autumn he was appointed to the Revolutionary Military Council of the Republic and was Inspector-General of the Armies. When he was appointed as one of the military commissars of the Ukraine (*see* Ukraine, Revolution in) in 1919 his fortunes began to decline, and by the summer he was removed from that post at Lenin's request.

During the next three years he was relegated to posts that focused on military and physical training, and in the late 1920s he began to work with the Marx Engels Lenin Institute where he remained until his retirement in 1935.

Bibliography

Haupt, Georges and Marie, Jean-Jacques. *Makers of the Revolution.* 1974.

Podvoiskii, N. I. *God 1917.* 1958.

———. *Krasnaia gvardiia v okiabr'skie dni.* 1927.

Rabinowitch, Alexander. *The Bolsheviks Come to Power.* 1976.

———. *Prelude to Revolution.* 1968.

Tarason, E. P. *N. I. Podvoiskii.* 1964.

White, D. M. *The Growth of the Red Army.* 1944.

Wollenberg, Erich. *The Red Army.* 1940.

Pokrovskii, Mikhail Nikolaevich (1868–1932). Pokrovskii was the most influential Marxist historian in Russia in the 1920s and 1930s and a prominent Left Bolshevik leader (*see* Russian Social Democratic Workers' Party [Bolshevik]) in the October Seizure of Power* in Moscow (*see* Moscow, Revolution in).

Pokrovskii was born in Moscow. Like V. I. Lenin*, his father had been a state official who had thereby risen into the rank of the heredity nobility. He was trained in a gymnasium and entered the Historical Philological Faculty of Moscow University at the age of nineteen. There he studied with two of the greatest scholars of that era, the Dean of Russian Historians, Vasilii O. Kliuchevskii, and the noted Medievalist, Paul Vinogradov. Although he pursued his master's degree with Kliuchevskii, they had a falling out and Pokrovskii did not continue his studies at the university. He decided, however, to become a professional historian and began to teach in secondary schools and university extension courses. In 1902 he was forbidden by the government to lecture in public because of his revolutionary views.

According to his own recollections he became a Marxist in the 1890s, but according to contemporaries he considered himself a liberal as late as 1905. During the Nineteen-Five Revolution* he did convert to Marxism, and Lenin invited him to participate in the emigré newspaper *Proletarii* (Proletarian). He was made a member of the Moscow Committee of the Russian Social Democratic Workers' Party (Bolshevik) in 1906. In the following year he became a candidate member of the Central Committee of the Party (*see* Central Committee of the Russian Communist Party [Bolshevik]). He also was a member of the editorial boards of the party's major publications.

Pokrovskii was drawn to the left faction in the party headed by A. A. Bogdanov (*see* Lunacharskii, A. V.), and when that faction was excluded from the party, Pokrovskii joined the Factionalists. He took part in the party schools organized by Bogdanov and Maxim Gorky (*see* Peshkov, A. M.), and remained outside Bolshevik affairs until 1917. When he returned to Moscow in 1917, however, he renewed his relationship with the Bolsheviks and became a member of the Moscow Soviet of Workers' and Soldiers' Deputies* which sent him to the Democratic Conference* as a delegate. After the October Seizure of Power he became Chairman of the Moscow Soviet* and a member of the Moscow Military Revolutionary Committee. He edited the *Izvestiia* (News) of the Moscow Soviet and in 1918 was elected Chairman of the Moscow Regional Council of Commissars. He was also appointed to the commission that drafted the First Soviet Constitution (*see* Constitution) for the Russian Socialist Federative Soviet Republic. But in 1919 he would earn the label of schismatic by joining the other Left Communists* in opposition to the Treaty of Brest-Litovsk*.

Pokrovskii's main contribution would not, however, be in politics, but in the development of Soviet historical writing and research. He was convinced that there should be a "proletarian" history of Russia, and he set about writing it and teaching others to follow suit. As Deputy Commissar of the People's Commissariat of the Enlightenment (*see* Commissariat of the Enlightenment), Chairman of the State Academic Council, Chairman of the Presidium of the Communist Academy, Director of the Institute of Red Professors, editor of one of the major journals for the publication of sources, *Krasnyi arkhiv* (Red Archive) and head of the Central Archives Administration, Pokrovskii became literally the tsar of Russian historical writing. Among his many historical writings, he published a large history of Russia, a book called *Outlines of Russian Culture* and a *Brief History of Russia*.

Pokrovskii's theory of history for which he tried to mobilize all of the resources of the Soviet state, was that Russian history should be written from a conventional Marxist point of view, rather from the perspective of Russian nationalism with an emphasis on Russia's unique qualities. He believed that the Russian Empire was an instrument of the Russian bourgeoisie, just like all the other European governments. Unlike his successors, however, he tolerated and encouraged historians who did not share his point of view to teach and publish. With the coming of I. V. Stalin's* cultural revolution in the 1930s Pokrovskii passed into disfavor because of his hostility toward Russian nationalism. He managed to survive by joining in the insistence that all historians write from a Marxist point of view. He died before the Great Purges reached him, with his original approach to historical writing already abandoned. His works were subsequently excoriated and many of those who were close to him were purged. He was rehabilitated after Stalin's death, but his books were not revived as a model for contemporary historical writing in the Soviet Union.

Bibliography

Barber, John F. *Soviet Historians in Crisis*. 1981.
Enteen, G. M. *The Soviet Scholar Bureaucrat*. 1978.
Mazour, Anatole. *Modern Russian Historiography*. 1958.
Pokrovskii. M. N. *History of Russia from Earliest Times to the Rise of Commercial Capitalism*. 5 vols. 1966.
————. *Brief History of Russia*. 2 vols. 1968.
Shteppa, Konstantin. *Russian Historians and the Soviet State*. 1962.

Poland. Because most of Poland was inside the Russian Empire the fate of the Russian and Polish revolutionary movements were closely intertwined with one another.

There was no longer a Polish state in 1917. A large part of what had been Poland lay inside the Russian Empire as a result of the three partitions of Poland in the eighteenth century. That part of Poland absorbed by Russia was called Congress Poland. It contained about nine million Poles out of fifteen million who had lived within the borders of the land that had been the Kingdom of Poland.

Although Poland had a long history of radicalism, very often the idea of national rebellion and liberation of Russian control was more important than social reform. In some respects Poland was more advanced economically than Russia, which made the Polish intelligentsia susceptible to socialism and other political ideologies inclined toward social reform in an urban setting.

In his history of the Communist Party of Poland, Dziewanowski characterized the Democratic Society formed by Polish emigres outside of their homeland in 1832 as socialist in its program. In this case it was influenced by French socialism rather than Marxism. In the 1846 Revolution in Galicia, the followers of the Democratic Society called for an agrarian revolution and thereby gained the endorsement of Marx and Engels. Marx's persistent support for the resurrection of the Polish state made his other ideas more attractive to the Polish intellectuals.

Polish feelings in relation to Russia were often dichotomous—hatred toward Russia for oppression and yet a feeling of kinship for those Russian intellectuals who were also seeking to liberate themselves from tsarist oppression. It was this sense of a common bond that had brought Polish and Russian revolutionaries together as early as the Decembrist Revolt of 1825.

The harsh and repressive measures adopted by the Tsarist government after the Polish insurrection of 1863–1864 stimulated the Polish revolutionary movement to respond to vigorous Russification and the abolition of purely Polish institutions and the punitive measures against many of the Polish gentry. In some ways Poland benefitted from the Russian connection because it began the industrial revolution somewhat before the Russians and could, therefore, take advantage of the vast market in the rest of Russia. By 1890 25 percent of Russia's industrial production came from Poland, although the population of Congress Poland was only 7 percent of the population of Russia.

In 1882 Ludwik Waryński created the first genuine socialist party in Russian Poland, the Proletariat. Dissenters from this group organized a party called the Polish People in Geneva under Bolesław Limanowski. The Proletariat emphasized the need for international social revolution and collaboration with Russian revolutionaries. Limanowski did not reject collaboration with Russian revolutionaries, and even proceeded to establish ties with the Russian People's Will Party, but he placed more emphasis on the need for socialism within a Polish national liberation movement. Like the Russian People's Will Party, the Proletariat began to use terror as a political weapon. In 1885 many of their party members, including Felix Kon, a future leader of the Communist Party of Poland, were arrested as a result of a violent strike. After the Proletariat was crushed, a second Proletariat, generally called the Union of Polish Workers, was formed by three future leaders of the Polish Communist Party: Julian Marchlewski (Jan Karski), Adolf Warszawski (Warski), and Bronislaw Wesołowski (Smulny).

There was an effort to create a unified Polish socialist movement when a Congress of Polish Socialists was called in Paris on November 17, 1892. Their program called for cooperation with their Russian comrades, but insisted that the Russian party remain separate and make no effort to recruit in Poland. They placed equal emphasis on the need for an independent Polish state and the need for social justice and the nationalization of land and industry. The party also accepted the need for terror as a political weapon under certain conditions.

The split that had begun with the internationalist Proletariat Party and the nationalist People's Party continued, however, for those Polish Social Democrats who disagreed with the nationalist Polish Socialist Party. They now formed a party of their own, the Social Democracy of the Kingdom of Poland, a party that branded the Polish Socialist Party as "social patriots." The Social Democracy of the Kingdom of Poland, as its name implied, placed the cause of socialism above the nationalist cause of Poland, and they vowed to confine their political activities to the Congress Kingdom. They called for close cooperation with the Russian revolutionaries and vowed that they would not strive for an independent Polish state. Two of the leaders of the new party were future leaders of the Communist Party of Poland: Julian Marchlewski (Karski) and the famous Rosa Luxemburg*. Under Luxemburg's leadership the Social Democracy specifically rejected the notion of an independent Poland, emphasizing Poland's need for the Russian market. Actually, Luxemburg argued that it would be best for Poland if she were totally incorporated into the Russian state.

In the years between their founding and the February Revolution* it was the Polish Socialist Party that grew, especially because it did not confine its activities to Congress Poland. It was the Polish Socialist Party that dominated the Polish working class movements, but in 1902 a new leader, F. E. Dzierzynski (*See* Dzerzhinskii, F. E.), the future head of the Cheka (*see* All-Russian Extraordinary Commission for Combatting Counterrevolution and Sabotage), took over the party and moved its headquarters to Krakow. Although Luxemburg had originally been in favor of an amalgamation with the Russian Social Democratic Workers' Party, she objected to V. I. Lenin's authoritarian style and his insistence on the principle of national self-determination.

In 1907 the Social Democracy joined the Russian Social Democratic Workers' Party under the assumption that the Bolsheviks (*see* Russian Social Democratic Workers' Party [Bolshevik]) and Mensheviks (*see* Russian Social Democratic Workers' Party [Menshevik]) had rejoined forces. The reunification was never completed and in the next five years the SDKP would sink into a prolonged decline. The Polish Socialist Party did not fare very well either. It split into two factions in 1906—the Polish Socialist Party and the Polish Socialist Party-Left, the latter holding a position close to that of the Polish Social Democracy.

When World War I* broke out the Polish Social Democracy, the Polish Socialist Party-Left and the Jewish Bund (*see* Bund) took a strong stand in opposition to any Polish support for the war, though the two latter parties would withdraw from that position by 1915. The Polish Social Democracy drew closer to Lenin's position on the war at the Zimmerwald and Kienthal Conferences (*see* World War I), though Lenin still found himself under fire from two of the leaders of the Polish Social Democracy, Luxemburg and Karl Radek*, for his endorsement of national self-determination. When the February Revolution came, most Polish socialists hailed it as a major victory for socialism, but neither the Polish Social Democracy nor the Polish Socialist Party-Left were pleased with statements from the Petrograd Soviet* and Lenin in favor of national self-determination.

When the October Seizure of Power* took place in 1917 there were more than two million Poles in Russia as a result of the evacuation of Congress Poland by the retreating Russian army. The new government of Russia, the Council of People's Commissars, created a Department of Polish Affairs and appointed a member of the Polish Social Democracy, Leszynski (Lenski), as its chief. Members of the Polish Social Democracy were appointed to high positions in the new Soviet administrative apparatus, the Red Army* and the new Commissariat of Polish Affairs. The most conspicuous appointment was that of Feliks Dzierżyński, who became head of the All-Russian Extraordinary Commission to Combat Counterrevolution and Sabotage.

At home, however, the Polish Social Democracy was losing ground because of its unpopular stand against national independence for Poland and against land redistribution to the peasants. In effect this meant that the leaders of the Polish Socialist Party-Left and the Polish Social Democracy who became part of the new Soviet administrative apparatus increasingly regarded that position in Russia as permanent. The emergence of an independent Polish state further undermined the position of these two parties on those two questions.

On November 15–16, 1918 the Polish Social Democracy met in Warsaw to prepare ground for a merging of their party with the Polish Socialist Party-Left. A congress of the two parties took place in December and the new party took the name of the Communist Workers' Party of Poland, following basically the policy of the Polish Social Democracy. The new party opposed the formation of an independent Polish state, national self-determination and land redistribution. In all other respects it was close to the Bolshevik position, calling for the creation of Polish workers' councils (soviets), nationalization of land and industry and the dictatorship of the proletariat.

By March 1919 the hopes of the Polish and Russian Communists for a wave of communist revolutions in Europe had been dashed except in Hungary, and that Soviet republic would not last long (see Bela Kun). When war broke out between Poland and Russia in February 1919, the Communist Workers' Party of Poland began to think in terms of a Polish communist revolution with the help of the Red Army. In the industrial areas of Poland the new communist party earned strong support in elections to workers' councils, but the new Polish government wisely liquidated the councils. At the same time the communist party refused to register with the government as required by Polish law for all political parties, and thus the Polish Party became illegal for the next twenty-five years.

Although at first Rosa Luxemburg opposed the entry of the Communist Workers' Party into the Comintern (see Communist International) in 1919, she was involved primarily with the new German Communist Party and the Poles proceeded to become charter members of the Communist International. The last major effort of the Polish Communists to combine the force of the Russian Revolutions with the revolution in Poland took place in 1920 as a result of the Russo-Polish War. When the Red Army successfully counterattacked in that war and recovered territory that had belonged to Belorussia (see Belorussia, Revolution in) before the Treaty of Riga in March 1921, Lenin proclaimed the Polish Soviet Socialist Republic.

On May 5, 1920 Karl Radek issued a proclamation defining Russia's war aims in relation to the Poles. In it he said that Russia would sue for peace with a Polish Soviet government and that it recognized the rights of both the Ukrainians (see Ukraine, Revolution in) and the Belorussians to be free from Russian control and of Poland to be completely independent. The appeal was issued in the name of the All-Russian Central Executive Committee of Soviets*. A Provisional Revolutionary Committee was established on August 2, 1920 in the city of

Bialystok after it had been occupied by the Red Army. Julian Marchlewski was chairman and the members included Feliks Dzierzyński, Feliks Kon, Jozef Unszlicht and Edward Prochik. Although the Communist Workers' Party of Poland had acceded to the twenty-one demands of the Comintern, they continued to oppose land redistribution in the territory won from the Polish state. But their program depended on the success of the Red Army, which again found itself falling back. On March 17, 1921 the Polish parliament approved the constitution of the new Polish Republic and on the following day Poland signed the Treaty of Riga ending its war with Russia and leaving large parts of the western Ukraine and western Belorussia under Polish control. This marked the end of one era and the beginning of another. Although the Polish Communist Workers' Party would finally bend on the national and agrarian questions at its second congress in Moscow in August 1923, it was a decision after the fact. Within a year Marshal Pilsudski would establish a dictatorship in Poland and the Polish Communist Workers' Party would endure a twilight existence as party in exile, interrupted only by the virtual liquidation of the party and most of its members during the Great Purges in Russia in the 1930s.

Bibliography

Dziewanowski, Marion. *The Communist Party of Poland*. 1976.

Pre-Parliament. *See* Democratic Conference.

Press and the Russian Revolution. Although historians are agreed on the importance of the press's role in 1917, surprisingly little has been written on this topic. Before the February Revolution* the press was divided into two distinct categories: the legal and the illegal. Within these categories, further sub-categories or groupings can be distinguished: the "official" or governmental press, the legally functioning press of the various opposition groups and parties, the nonsectarian press, and a clandestine press (published either inside the empire or outside). The official press included organs of the various ministries and governmental agencies but could be understood to include that section of the press that, while ostensibly private, was partially or wholly subsidized by the government. The legal press was shackled by the Press Law of November 24, 1905. This law, together with several supplemental restrictions, provided for the confiscation and suppression of any publication for printing information determined to be in contravention of Russian law, for spreading false reports on governmental agencies and officials, or for promoting discord between groups in Russian society (especially between workers and employers). In addition, publishers, editors, and printers were subject to the imposition of severe fines and imprisonment for any infringement of the law. In a declared "state of emergency," a common phenomenon in the period between 1906 and 1917, officials were given discretionary rights to suspend the publication of any organ. The result was that reports on scandals, corruption, or malfeasance by governmental agencies and officials led to the implementation of these several restrictions.

Within the legal category, rightist and conservative publications such as *Russkoe znamie (Russian Banner)* of the Union of the Russian People or the Petersburg *Vechernee vremia (Evening News)*—which became *Malen'kaia gazeta (Little Gazette)* in 1917 and *Vecher' (Evening)* after November 11—enjoyed a more secure existence because of their support of the autocracy. The major factional newspapers included *Rech' (Speech)*, a Constitutional Democratic Party—Cadet* newspaper published in St. Petersburg/Petrograd; *Pravda (Truth)*, a Russian Social Democratic Workers' Party (Bolshevik)* newspaper; *Den' (Day)*, a right-wing Russian Social Democratic Workers' Party (Menshevik)* newspaper published in Moscow; and *Russkiie vedomosti (Russian Register)*, a liberal newspaper published in Moscow. In addition, there were widely circulated and generally nonfactional publications such as *Petersburgskii listok (St. Petersburg Leaflet)*, changed to *Petrogradskii listok (Petrograd Leaflet)* during World War I* and appearing as *Petrogradskii golos (Petrograd Voice)* in 1917; *Utro Rossii (Russian Morning)*, published in Moscow; and the monthly *Vestnik evropy (Messenger of Europe)*. The legal press also included publications of special-interest groups, such as *Birzhevie vedomosti (Stock Exchange Register)*, published in St. Petersburg, the organ of liberal business groups.

During the war all legal newspapers had to tread a narrow line between the permissible and the impermissible. In addition to the press being restricted as noted above, it was constrained from publishing commentaries or privately obtained information of the actual progress of the war (such as military reversals). Such information was limited to the official communiques issued by the War Ministry. Although the press of the radical opposition—Social Democratic, Socialist–Revolutionary (*see* Socialist-Revolutionary Party), Anarchist (*see* Anarchism)—was able to continue publishing, the longevity of each publication was often dependent upon its position on the war. For example, the Right Menshevik liberal *Den'* published throughout the war as an organ supporting the victory of the Entente, whereas the Bolshevik *Pravda* (and its successor *Trudovaia pravda*) was suppressed in 1914; the editors of *Pravda* were arrested in November. Other socialist publications that tried to compromise on the issue of support for the autocracy were suppressed, for example, *Nasha zaria (Our Dawn)*, which tried to unite Defensists (*see* Defensism) and antiwar Internationalists*, or the Samara-based *Nash golos (Our Voice)*, which called for support of both the War Industries Committees* and the Zimmerwald Conference (*see* World War I). The harassment, exile, or emigration of prominent editors and publishers effected the demise of many other radical publications for the duration of the war.

The illegal press appeared in two distinct guises. The first, published inside the empire by the opposition, while freed from the constraints of censorship was subject to the tender mercies of the Ministry of the Interior, whose agents' success in infiltrating clandestine organizations and groups made the existence of such publications precarious and participation in them dangerous. This part of the illegal press often emerged out of suppressed legal publications but at other times was simply the voice of radical opposition.

The second illegal press, outside the empire, was centered in Switzerland and Paris. During the war these publications were the most outspoken critics of the war and the autocracy to be found in Western Europe. The Paris-based *Nashe slovo* (*Our Word*), a nonfactional daily successively titled *Golos, Nashe slovo, Nachalo,* and *Novaia epokha,* which appeared from September 1914 to April 1917; the Socialist-Revolutionary Party's *Mysl'* (*Thought*), published first in Paris and then in Geneva under the title *Zhizn'* (*Life*); and the periodic publications of the Menshevik and the Bolshevik foreign sections, *Izvestiia* (*News*) and *Sotsial demokrat,* all made their way into Russia by courier where they were passed from group to group in the underground. These publications were not entirely freed from interference and intimidation, however. In Switzerland the initiators of these radical antiwar organs (and especially the publications of the Bolshevik faction) were often subjected to postal surveillance and other forms of official harassment because the neutral Swiss were especially sensitive to the pressures of belligerent powers. In France the Russian-language newspapers were subject to the strictest censorship laws of the French government and to the pressures exerted by the Russian Embassy in Paris on its ally for their suppression (these pressures are credited with having been instrumental in the French censor's decision to suspend *Nashe slovo* and *Nachalo* in 1916 and 1917).

Despite overt and covert activities of the autocracy, the continued military disappointments and reversals, the mounting internal economic chaos, and the shortages of food supplies and war material led to growing criticism of the autocracy's handling of the war in the press. Although the Duma (*see* Duma and Revolution) speeches denouncing the cabinet were forbidden publication in 1916, they were widely circulated in typescript and appeared subsequently in the illegal press.

The February Revolution had an immediate impact on the press. The Provisional Government*, by announcing complete freedom of the press, opened the way for a startling proliferation of newspapers, broadsheets, pamphlets, and journals. These new publications were overwhelmingly political, published by and reflecting the political views of the groups that had initiated them. The only restraints on their appearance were financial and, occasionally, personnel related (as had been true in 1905, the publishers of some conservative publications had difficulty in finding printers and typesetters who would agree to aid in their appearance). Another restraint was the passion of the population more broadly defined. For example, in June 1917 the offices of the conservative *Russkaia volia* (*Russian Will*) were temporarily occupied by anarchist workers who opposed its continued publication. Although the editors of *Russkaia volia* had their offices restored to them (on the order of the Soviet Executive Committee), the Provisional Government was not dedicated to an *absolute* freedom of the press. The presses of the Orthodox Church Synod were "requisitioned" after Synod publications had appeared supporting the return to autocracy and labeling the February Revolution as the work of the anti-Christ. Similarly, the editorial offices of the Bolshevik *Pravda* (which had made its reappearance in March) were raided on July 5, with its latest issue confiscated and its editors jailed for fomenting the July Days* insurrection against the Provisional Government.

The general freedom of the press (a part of what Lenin meant in April 1917 when he described Russia as the freest nation in the world) persisted throughout the turbulent summer months. It ended as the Provisional Government ended— as the new Soviet government assumed power in October. On October 27, 1917, the Council of Peoples' Commissars* authorized the suppression of all newspapers hostile to the new government. This decree was later supplemented by the confiscation of all stocks of paper and private presses. In the months that followed, one after another of non-Bolshevik organs was suppressed or transformed to reflect the government's position. Regarding itself as the voice of the population, the new government justified the suppression of all opposition organs by the simple expedient of charging them with counterrevolutionary agitation. Or as L. D. Trotsky* said in November in answering a critic of the new press law, the Bolsheviks were now in a position to introduce their maximum program, not freedom of the press but truth in publishing.

Michael Shaw

Bibliography

Alfavitnyi sluzhebnyi katalog russkikh dorevoliutsionnykh gazet (1703–1916). 1958.
Baevskii, D. *Istoriia rabochei pechati v Rossii.* 1923.
Beliaeva, L. N., et al. *Bibliografiia periodicheskikh izdanii Rossii, 1901–1916.* 4 vols. 1958–1961.
Beshkina, G., ed. *Legal'naia sotsial-demokraticheskaia literatura v Rossii za 1906–14 gody.* 1924.
Maichel, K. *Soviet and Russian Newspapers at the Hoover Institution: A Catalog.* 1966.
Okorokov, A. Z. *Oktiabr' v krakh russkoi burzhuaznoi pressy.* 1970.
Predvaritel'nyi spisok periodicheskikh izdanii Rossii, 1901–1916 godov. 1949.

Profintern. *See* Red International of Trade Unions.

Progressive Bloc (*progressivnyi blok*). From its beginnings in 1906 and until its demise in 1917, the Russian parliament of State Duma (*see* Duma and Revolution) never enjoyed a significant influence on the government, a government that served at the pleasure of the Tsar (*see* Nicholas II) and felt little responsibility toward the popularly elected representatives. The creation of the Progressive Bloc, a parliamentary coalition of political parties and groups formed out of the moderate wing of the Russian political spectrum, was a serious but largely unsuccessful attempt to strengthen the role of the Duma.

During the years just before the outbreak of the World War I*, leaders of the liberal political groups often discussed the possibility of forming a coalition of the Duma's moderate forces (at that time consisting of the Cadets [see Constitutional Democratic Party—Cadet], Progressists, and Octobrists [see Guchkov, Aleksandr Ivanovich]). The liberal leaders believed that their lack of success in turning political programs into legislation was a direct result of divisions within their camp. Since a bloc of the liberal groups would possess a majority of the votes in the Duma, something that had never before been enjoyed by any Russian political movement, the liberal leaders believed that the unification of the moderate political forces into a parliamentary coalition would place the Duma and, in particular, the moderates themselves in the position of being able to exert a greater influence on the governmental process. However, discussions never led to more than inchoate efforts toward liberal cooperation, since the issues dividing Russia's liberal camp were of greater concern than the necessity of the creation of a parliamentary coalition.

Within a year after the outbreak of the hostilities in 1914, the moderates' attitude toward political cooperation changed markedly as a result of Russia's poor showing in the war and the political environment of 1915. Of particular importance were a series of military defeats in Poland and Galicia, fears of an imminent decrease in the Duma's already limited wartime role, and a broadening of the political opposition to now include elements of the moderate Right. These issues convinced the moderate Duma leaders that the time for effective political cooperation was at hand and that a unified parliamentary front was now an indispensable prerequisite for preserving the young constitutional system and providing Russia with the means to defeat Germany and its allies.

During the first two weeks of August 1915, six Duma factions (the Cadets, Progressists, Left–Octobrists, Zemstvo–Octobrists, Centrists, and Progressive Nationalists), representing a clear majority of the deputies (236 out of 422 members of the Duma), agreed to join forces in what became known as the Progressive Bloc. Believing that the Russian government was not pursuing the war effort competently, the Progressive Bloc declared its intention to prepare a legislative program that would respond adequately to Russia's wartime needs, present the program to the Duma, and gather the votes necessary to guarantee that the program would pass safely through the Duma. Within days of its formation, the Progressive Bloc was joined by three moderate groups from the upper house, the State Council (they were the Center, Academic, and Nonparty groups), which now made the newly formed coalition an alignment of political forces stretching through both of Russia's legislative chambers.

Rumors that Nicholas II would soon prorogue the Duma gave added urgency to the work of the Bloc. The parliamentary coalition, which the press dubbed the Progressive Bloc, quickly prepared a political program and published it on August 26, 1915. The authors of the program believed that only a united country would be able to bring victory to Russia, and national unity was dependent on the elimination of as many of the public's grievances as possible. The program reflected these views. It called for the formation of a new "united government composed of individuals who enjoy the confidence of the country" (Golder. 1964, p. 134). An appeal was made for a "decisive change in the methods of

administration . . . which have been based upon a distrust of public self-help''
(p. 134). Citizens' rights were an important part of the program, particularly in
the areas of labor and religion. Also given a great deal of attention were relations
with the minority peoples of the Russian Empire. Specifically singled out were
the Jews (*see* Jewry, 1905–1921), Ukrainians (*see* Ukraine, Revolution in), Poles
(*see* Poland, Revolution in), and Finns (*see* Finland, Revolution in), all of whom
were to receive significant political and social concessions.

The funding of the coalition and subsequent publication of its program were
the high points in the history of the Progressive Bloc. Within days of these two
events the Bloc received a defeat from which it never fully recovered. On
September 3, 1915, Nicholas II, bowing to the insistance of his aging Prime
Minister I. L. Goremykin, adjourned the Duma without establishing a date for
it to reconvene. The Progressive Bloc was now a parliamentary coalition without
a parliament.

During the period of the Duma's recess, the Blocists held informal meetings,
but without a functioning parliament, there was little hope for them to be effective. As a result, discord became the coalition's most prominent feature. The
political groups making up the Bloc split into Left and Right factions and began
a prolonged argument about whether the coalition should pursue political reform
or only concern itself with military matters. The bickering between the groups
led to erosion within the Bloc. Of particular significance was the withdrawal of
the Progressists, who would not satisfy themselves with anything less than a
strong political program.

When the Duma was finally reconvened in November 1916, the Progressive
Bloc, no longer enjoying a majority of the deputies, had one brief moment of
glory. P. N. Miliukov*, who had always been acknowledged as the leader of
the Bloc, delivered a famous Duma speech in which he criticized the Russian
government by asking whether its actions were ''stupidity or treason.'' As a
result of the response to Miliukov's speech, Russia's new Prime Minister, with
the German name Count B.V. Shtiurmer (Stürmer), was forced to resign. The
Shtiurmer (Stürmer) resignation was one of the Progressive Bloc's few victories.

The February Revolution* of 1917 brought an end to the reign of the Romanov
dynasty, the Duma, and the Progressive Bloc. However, the former leaders of
the Progressive Bloc were instrumental in shaping the form of the revolutionary
or Provisional Government*. Many ministerial portfolios in the new government
were placed in the hands of the former Blocists. Although these men had for
years dreamed of the day they would hold the reins of the Russian government,
they were no more effective as members of the Provisional Government than
they had been as members of the Progressive Bloc.

Lawrence Lerner

Bibliography

Chermenskii, E. D. *IV Gosudarstvennaia duma i sverzhene tsarizma v Rossii.* 1976.
Diakin, V. S. *Ruskaia burzhuaziia i tsarizm v gody pervoi mirovoi voiny.* 1967.

Golder, F. A. ed. *Documents of Russian History, 1914–1917*. 1964.

Gurko, V. I. *Features and Figures of the Past: Government and Opinion in the Reign of Nicholas II*. Translated by Linda Matveev. 1939.

Laverychev, V. Ia. *Po tu storonu barrikad: Iz istorii bor'by moskovskoi burzhuazii s revoliutsiei*. 1967.

Miliukov, P N. *Political Memoirs, 1905–1917*. Edited by Arthur P. Mendel and translated by Carl Goldberg. 1967.

Pearson, R. *A Russian European: Paul Miliukov in Russian Politics*. 1969.

———. *The Russian Moderates and the Crisis of Tsarism, 1914–1917*. 1977.

Propaganda and the Russian Revolution. The Bolsheviks (*see* Russian Social Democratic Workers' Party [Bolshevik]) won their revolution and emerged victoriously from the Civil War in Russia* because they succeeded in imposing order on anarchy and because they won over crucial segments of the population. As V. I. Lenin* well understood, organization and propaganda were not merely connected, they were opposite sides of the same coin: the goal of propaganda was to make possible organization and this organization enabled the Bolsheviks to persuade and to coerce.

Not only historians but also participants in the Civil War conceded Bolshevik superiority in techniques of persuasion. This success can be explained by the fact that the Bolsheviks' past and ideology provided the right combination for the needs of the moment. First Leninism was a theory of organization, and the Bolshevik Party was the embodiment of the central principle of the doctrine. The party was crucial in every aspect of the struggle, but nowhere did it provide a more obvious benefit than in the ability of the Bolsheviks to take their message to every segment of the Russian people. Second, unlike their chief enemies, the Whites (*see* White Movement), the Bolsheviks had an abiding faith in the power of ideas. They learned from Marxism that theory and practice were equally important. But, third, and in this respect they differ from their socialist competitors, the Mensheviks (*see* Russian Social Democratic Workers' Party [Menshevik]), they never believed that the people left to themselves would recognize and remain loyal to the "correct" ideas. The notion that revolutionary consciousness must be brought to the proletariat from the outside is both an essential feature of Bolshevism and a good framework for the organization of successful propaganda.

The communists were inventive in their methods. Some of their ideas were obviously utopian and had few positive results, but others worked well. Most importantly, the leadership had an unflagging interest in this matter.

The party did not neglect the most obvious instrument, the press (*see* Press and the Russian Revolution). In this sphere the Bolsheviks started on a weak foundation. In February 1917 they had not a single paper. During the revolutionary year, apart from reestablishing the main party paper, *Pravda*, the Bolsheviks published separate papers for peasants and soldier audiences. The editors did their work well. They saw to it that authors composed simple articles suitable for mass audiences. Revolutionary soldiers and workers passed these papers from hand to hand, and consequently, the audience was wider than the modest circulation figures would show. However, the enemies of the Bolsheviks were in a much superior situation; their financial strength allowed them to print hundreds of thousands of issues, whereas the communists could never produce more than tens of thousands.

Even before November 1917, Lenin was determined to eliminate the bourgeois papers following the victory of his Revolution. Two days after this victory, the government published a press decree that "temporarily" closed down "hostile" newspapers. The publication of this decree was the first important issue that created discord not only between the Bolsheviks and their coalition partners, the Left Socialist–Revolutionaries (*see* Left Socialist-Revolutionary Party)*, but also within the party itself. Several leaders resigned in protest of an act that seemed to them contrary to what they had been fighting for. (The protestors, however, soon returned to the fold).

Between November 1917 and June 1918 all non-Bolshevik papers operating on Soviet territory were gradually closed down. The victorious revolutionaries had trouble in justifying to themselves the closing down of Menshevik and Socialist-Revolutionary papers. But they reasoned that those who opposed a genuine social revolution were objectively counterrevolutionaries and therefore deserved treatment no different from that of the other enemies. The Bolsheviks confiscated the presses and paper supplies of the defunct newspapers and used them for their own purposes. At a time of great paper shortage, this acquisition was a crucial gain. The key to the success of newspaper agitation was that the revolutionaries, from a very early date, succeeded in establishing a monopoly.

Under the circumstances that prevailed in Russia, oral agitation was more important than the printed word could be. Both sides in the Civil War faced the same problem: how to reach the illiterate peasantry (*see* Peasants in the Russian Revolution). The party network was immensely useful in this respect, but the difficulty was that the party penetrated the countryside very inadequately. The Bolsheviks hit on an ingenious idea: since they lacked the infrastructure and manpower to govern and propagandize in the villages, they decided to send "agitational" trains to different provinces that could do both. The trains included agitators and representatives of Soviet commissariats. When a train stopped at a remote station, the representatives set up shop and established a kind of government in residence. The agitators answered questions from peasants, gave lectures, and printed newspapers and leaflets. They also showed films, which were particularly effective with illiterate audiences. In most instances, this was the first time that the peasants encountered this new wonder of technology. From their bases along the railroad lines, the agitators on small cars and motorcycles travelled into even more remote regions. It is impossible to say how important a contribution these "agit-trains" made to Bolshevik victory. However, it is clear that the followers of Lenin well understood the importance of reaching the people and were inventive in the choice of their methods.

There is another small example that shows Lenin's interest, inventiveness, and thinking in this matter. In November 1917 the demobilized soldiers returned to their villages. The Bolsheviks wanted to use the opportunity to acquaint the peasantry with the recently published Decree on Land (*see* Agrarian Policy, 1917–1921), and they gave every soldier a copy of this document. Lenin feared that at the time of a great paper shortage the soldiers would simply roll cigarettes out of the precious document. Therefore, he personally directed his aides to have old calendars cut up and, together with the land decree, the soldiers should also be given a useless piece of paper. The Decree on Land, among other things, was also an instrument of propaganda.

The authorities examined several ways to reach approximately 60 percent of the Russians who could neither read not write. Lenin clearly saw the political significance of the matter. He believed that the illiterate person stood outside of politics, and, therefore, it was the task of the new regime to draw him in. The simplest method of overcoming the problem was also the most naive. In December 1918 the government published a decree that obliged the literate to read aloud government decrees and other propaganda material to their less fortunate fellows. The task of reading was compulsory and without payment. The local soviets were asked to supervise the work and send monthly reports to the higher authorities. There is no way to establish the success of this undertaking, but there is reason to believe that very little was accomplished. The party lacked the strength in the countryside to enforce this decision.

More ambitiously, immediately after their victory (*see* October Seizure of Power) the Bolsheviks undertook a campaign to eradicate illiteracy. Times were hardly propitious: the country was torn by anarchy, the teachers as a group were hostile, and the regime hardly possessed the vast resources necessary for the undertaking. Indeed, the resolution of this major social problem had to wait for another twenty years. Nevertheless, the remarkable enthusiasm did produce some results. The Red Army* freed its soldiers an hour or two a day for "political education" and literacy work with which it was often combined. The Commissariat of the Enlightenment*, which had a separate department for extramural and political education under N. K. Krupskaia*, commissioned politically satisfactory textbooks suitable for teaching illiterate adults. The literacy work that was accomplished at the time of the Civil War in Russia* served as an instrument of indoctrination and also created a foundation on which the much greater and more successful efforts of the 1920s and 1930s would be based.

In retrospect, it is clear that Bolshevik determination to bring their message to the uncommitted and the ingenuity with which they treated this difficult problem were essential ingredients of victory.

Peter Kenez

Bibliography

Kenez, Peter. *The Birth of the Propaganda State*. 1985.

Provisional Government. The Provisional Government came to power in February 1917 (*see* February Revolution) and was replaced by the Soviet government after the October Seizure of Power*.

It announced its formation and composition on March 3, 1917, following the decisive February days. With assurance of support from the newly organized Petrograd Soviet of Workers' and Soldiers' Deputies (*see* Soviets [Councils] of Workers', Soldiers', and Peasants' Deputies), insofar as it conformed to an agreed-upon set of guiding principles, the government officially assumed the full plenitude of power. Its membership was predominantly from the Constitutional Democratic Party—Cadet, with the notable exception of A. F. Kerensky*, the leader of the Duma (*see* Duma and Revolution) Trudovik faction and a vice-president of the soviet. A nominal Socialist–Revolutionary (*see* Socialist–Revolutionary Party), he had accepted the portfolio of justice despite the decision of the Soviet Executive Committee that its members remain outside the cabinet as "watchdogs" of the Revolution. The Minister–President and Minister of the Interior was the nonparty liberal Prince G. E. L'vov*, chairman of the All-Russian Union of Zemstvos (*see* All-Russian Union of Towns and All-Russian Union of Zemstvos). The Octobrist A. I. Guchkov* became minister of war and navy. In the beginning, the leading figure was Cadet P. N. Miliukov as Foreign Minister, but his expected predominence was soon eroded by the dynamic activity of Kerensky.

The first weeks of the regime were marked by a flood of legislation, in accordance with the "guiding principles," designed to remove the most oppressive and restrictive enactments and practices of the Tsarist government and to introduce a measure of democratization and legal reform. Civil, religious, sex, class, and nationalist distinctions were repealed, the death penalty abolished, and political prisoners released. Local self-government was extended and liberalized. Judicial rights were restored and a special commission appointed to prepare an election law for the Constituent Assembly*. Unfortunately, the implementation of much of this activity was overtaken by political events. German-occupied Poland was promised independence and the ancient rights of Finland restored. Meanwhile, the government had been recognized almost immediately, first by the United States and then by the Allied Powers after receiving assurances of continued vigorous prosecution of the war.

Significantly, the two paramount issues facing the country, the conduct and continuance of the war and the disposition of the land, had not yet been specifically mentioned in the Soviet–Provisional Government understanding, precisely because of the failure to agree on a policy. Implicitly, they were reserved for decision by the forthcoming Constituent Assembly, which was to determine the future form of government and the character of fundamental reforms. Nevertheless the soviet acted quickly, on March 14, to present its views on the war by issuing an appeal "To the Peoples of All the World," calling for a negotiated peace without annexations or indemnities (*see* Foreign Policy, 1914–1921; World War I). On March 27 the government followed suit with the Declaration of War

Aims, drafted reluctantly by the nationalist Miliukov, eschewing "forcible" annexation but vowing continued defense of the fatherland and observance of all obligations to its allies.

Continued evidence of Miliukov's chauvinism disturbed the "democracy," however, and forced the government to dispatch its domestic declaration to the Allies on April 18. But an accompanying explanatory note verified popular suspicions by reaffirming Russia's intention to continue the war to "a decisive victory" with "guarantees and sanctions." Street demonstrations broke out on April 20, which precipitated the first major test of the regime, the April Crisis. Concurrently, Kerensky began agitation for Soviet participation in the government to minimize the conflicts inherent in dual power*. After some vacillation, the Soviet Executive Committee agreed. Guchkov and Miliukov resigned. The First Coalition was formed on May 5, with a new cabinet which for the first time included socialists such as V. M. Chernov*, I. G. Tsereteli*, and Kerensky, who accepted portfolios of war and navy. M. I. Tereshchenko, a Cadet, succeeded Miliukov and remained Foreign Minister until the end of the regime. Promptly, the new government issued a program incorporating the Soviet formula of "no annexations or indemnities" but firmly rejecting a separate peace. The program also called for ending the military stalemate. Accordingly, Kerensky began preparations for an offensive, obtaining, with the exception of the Bolsheviks, remarkable political support for the defense of the revolution against the external threat. He signed the modified Declaration of Soldiers' Rights, formalizing the controversial military democratization and appointing General A. A. Brusilov* to succeed M. V. Alekseev as Supreme Commander, and began touring the front with inspirational speeches. Launched on their southwestern front, the June 18th offensive initially enjoyed considerable success, but victory turned to rout as German reinforcements entered the battle.

Meanwhile in Petrograd the second major crisis of the government began with the resignation of the Cadet members in protest against the agreement negotiated by their socialist colleagues granting a degree of autonomy to the Ukraine (*see* Ukraine, Revolution in). Street demonstrations followed on July 3 (*see* July Days) under the slogan "All Power to the Soviets." Inspired and led by second-echelon Bolsheviks, although viewed with apprehension by V. I. Lenin* as a premature action, the uprising came close to success. But the refusal of the still-moderate soviets to accede to the demand, the unauthorized release by the then Minister of Justice of information suggesting that the Bolsheviks were in German pay, and the news of the German counteroffensive combined to bring some mutinous and neutral troops as well as a substantial number of the rebellious populace over to the government. Bolshevik organizations were raided, L. D. Trotsky* was arrested, and Lenin fled into hiding. Apparently, the threat from the extreme Left was crushed. But the Cadet resignations, followed by that of L'vov on July 7, together with the disruptions of the July Days, required a ministerial organization.

Kerensky assumed the premiership. His attempts at a new coalition failed, however, until in desperation he himself resigned and shocked the contending parties into giving him a free hand to form a cabinet, which was announced on July 23. The Second Coalition was preponderantly moderate socialist. As Minister–President, Kerensky appointed the hero of the brief offensive, General L. G. Kornilov (*see* Kornilov Revolt), Supreme Commander. The death penalty was restored at the front, and Kerensky and Kornilov began increasingly embittered discussions over the latter's insistence upon stronger disciplinary measures in the rear as well as at the front. Kornilov's demands and his colorful personality now became a rallying point for the forces of the Right, which called for firm action to restore order throughout the country and achieve military success. The failure of the government to deal with the pressing land problem (*see* Agrarian Policy, 1917–1921; Agriculture) and the National Question (*see* National Question and the Russian Revolution) before the convocation of the Constituent Assembly, which was repeatedly delayed by a preoccupation with legalism and the recurring political crises and in some quarters by doubts about the advisability of fundamental reforms in the midst of war, had swelled the tide of growing impatience, unrest, and disorder. In hopes of receiving greater support pending the meeting of the assembly, the government convened a congress of public representatives (*see* Moscow State Conference), which met from August 12 to 15. Despite some evidence of conciliation, the principal impression left by the meeting was an upswing in conservative sentiment that looked for leadership to the forceful but politically naive Kornilov, whose impassioned address to the Conference galvanized his adherents, frightened the Left, and led to a further deterioration of his relations with Kerensky.

Whatever the convoluted origins of the abortive Kornilov Revolt, which was launched by the march of troops to Petrograd on August 26 by order of the supreme commander, it clearly hastened the end of the Provisional Government. Although concerted support of Kerensky by the soviets, including the discredited Bolsheviks, subverted the revolt, the government was left in disarray. Opposed by the Right and many liberals who had opted for Kornilov and military dictatorship, and suspected by the Left of weakness at best and complicity at worst, Kerensky stood virtually alone. A wave of anarchy and violence swept over the countryside and through the rest of the forces.

Kerensky placed Kornilov and his lieutenants under arrest, personally assumed the supreme command, declared Russia a republic (in violation of the agreement with the soviet), and established a five-man Directory until the formation of a new cabinet. The socialist Democratic Conference*, convened in Petrograd on September 14, failed after a week of confused debate to frame clear recommendations to the premier on the formation of a government. Further negotiations by Kerensky with the socialists and the Cadets resulted, however, in the announcement on September 25 of a coalition of moderate socialists and Cadets, none of the first rank, and the establishment of a Provisional Council of the Republic (*see* Democratic Council) to serve as a consultative body until the convocation of the Constituent Assembly, for which elections had been scheduled beginning November 12.

The Bolsheviks were the only victors of the Kornilov Revolt and its aftermath. Lenin immediately recognized the opportunity it afforded them, urging preparations for an armed uprising. By mid-September the Bolsheviks had gained de facto control of both the Petrograd and Moscow Soviets (*see* Petrograd Soviet; Moscow Soviet). In the night of October 10, Lenin persuaded the Central Committee of the Russian Social Democratic Workers' Party (Bolshevik) (*see* Central Committee of the Russian Communist Party [Bolshevik]) to approve a seizure of power (*see* October Seizure of Power). Kerensky, aware of Bolshevik activity among the city workers and troops, alternated between hope for a coup that could be definitively crushed and puzzling inaction. On October 24 he demanded of the Council of the Republic a vote of confidence for strong measures but, after prolonged debate, received only recommendations to negotiate for a general peace and to divide the land. That night the Bolsheviks struck. The next morning Kerensky left the city to rally troops at the front. The following day, Red Guards* seized key positions in Petrograd and, in the evening, occupied the Winter Palace, arrested the remaining ministers, and proclaimed an all-Bolshevik Soviet government to the convening Second All-Russian Congress of Soviets. Kerensky, with the few loyal troops he was able to muster, marched towards the capital only to suffer defeat on the outskirts at the hands of a hastily gathered Bolshevik force. Retreating to Gatchina, where his small contingent disintegrated, he fled into hiding and eventually into exile.

The Provisional Government was handicapped from its inception by self-inflicted limited tenure and authority. Idealism, political inexperience, and naiveté prevented its understanding the temper of the masses and taking strong action to meet war weariness and to satisfy the popular demands for far-reaching reforms, especially in land tenure and in the workplace. Excessive legalism and growing factionalism, marked by recurring political crises, delayed the convocation of the Constituent Assembly, which might have addressed these pressing problems in time. The continuance of "Dual Power" even after coalition, the chaos in the administrative machinery, and the staffing of local and central government and the absence of dependable enforcement agencies exacerbated its problems. Allegiance to its Allied obligations exposed it to constant unsympathetic importunities from the West. The lack of continuity in its various compositions and the variety of constituencies clamoring for satisfaction further mitigated against a firm, consistent, and forceful course. Above all, it was unable to surmount the dual demands of war and revolution.

Robert Paul Browder

Bibliography

Abraham, Richard. *Alexander Kerensky*. 1987.

Browder, R. P., and Kerensky, A. F., eds. *The Russian Provisional Government, 1917*. 3 vols. 1961.

Chernov, Victor. *The Great Russian Revolution*. 1936.

Hasegawa, Tsuyoshi. *The February Revolution*. 1981.

Kerensky, A. *The Catastrophe*. 1927.

Lozinskii, Z. *Ekonomicheskaia politika vremennago pravitel'stva*. 1929.

Medlin, V., and Parsons, S. L, eds. *V. D. Nabokov and the Russian Provisional Government, 1917*. 1976.

Miliukov, P. N. *Istoriia vtoroi russkoi revoliutsii*. 3 vols. 1921–1923.

Tsereteli, I. G. *Vospominaniia o fevral'skoi revoliutsii*. 2 vols. 1963.

Vasiukov, V. S. *Vneshnaia politika vremennago pravitel'stva*. 1962.

Volobuev, P. V. *Ekonomicheskaia politika vremennago pravitel'stva*. 1962.

R

Radek, Karl Bernardovich (1885–1939; true name, Sobelson). Radek was a prominent Left Communist* leader who had worked in three European socialist parties before World War I*: the Social Democracy of Poland and Lithuania, the German Social Democratic Party and the Russian Social Democratic Workers' Party (Bolshevik)*.

Radek was a tireless journalist and conspirator who spared none from his wit and venom. Although always at the center of some storm or scandal, he managed to maintain a prominent position in the international socialist movement throughout the entire pre-war period and became an important official in the Soviet government and the Communist International* after the October Seizure of Power*.

Radek's family were Polish Jews. His father died when he was four and his mother was a teacher in Tarnov in western Galicia where Radek went to school. In his autobiography Radek stated that he was more drawn to Polish literature with its Catholicism and nationalism than to the classical German literature that was so popular in his family. The name ''Radek'' was taken from a popular Polish novel. He became involved in Marxism while studying at the gymnasium in Tarnow and continued those activities when he moved on to Krakow in 1902 to study at Jagellonian University. At Krakow he made the acquaintance of F. E. Dzerzhinskii* and Rosa Luxemburg*. In 1903 he moved on to Zurich where he heard G. V. Plekhanov and V. I. Lenin* speak and made the acquaintance of G. E. Zinoviev*. In 1904 he returned to Poland to take part in the 1905 Revolution (*see* Nineteen-Five Revolution).

In 1908 he left Poland for Berlin. He was expelled from the Social Democracy of Poland in 1912 and from the German Social Democratic Workers' Party in 1913. In both cases the cause was primarily his instinct for stirring up trouble and for factionalism. Rosa Luxemburg was a key figure in both expulsions. She was prompted to act against Radek from a personal dislike for him, not for disagreement with his views that were, in most cases, close to her own. She wrote of him in 1912 "Radek belongs in the whore category. Anything can happen with him around, and it is, therefore, much better to keep him at a safe distance" (as quoted in Nettl. II, 471). Lenin, however, sided with Radek against Luxemburg, and offered him work with the Bolshevik newspaper *Sotsial-Demokrat* and some financial support. Since Lenin was at the moment preparing to complete his split with the Mensheviks (*see* Russian Social Democratic Workers' Party [Menshevik]), who were threatening Lenin with charges of scandalous behavior, he may have felt some kinship to Radek.

During the war Radek moved even closer to Lenin by joining him in this "internationalist" position at the Zimmerwald Conference (*see* World War I). Though he did not take part in the October Seizure of Power, he came to Moscow at the end of November and was put in charge of international propaganda in the Commissariat for Foreign Affairs. Although he eventually opposed the peace terms, he took part in the negotiations for the Treaty of Brest-Litovsk* where he frequently served as Lenin's advisor. Radek was involved in the creation of the German Communist Party, and even Rosa Luxemburg felt compelled to deal with him as a representative of the now triumphant Bolshevik Party. After her death he remained in Germany for eleven months serving as an unofficial Bolshevik delegate to the new German government and advisor to the German Communists from a jail cell. While he was in jail the Communist International* elected him to its Executive Committee, and in 1920 to the Presidium of its Executive Committee, a position he held until 1924.

Radek's own position with the Bolsheviks remained on the Left throughout. Before World War I he opposed national self-determination, joined N. I. Bukharin* in attacking the Treaty of Brest-Litovsk, attacked the New Economic Policy* and supported L. D. Trotsky* in the Central Committee of the Russian Communist Party (Bolshevik)* until the Trade Union Controversy (*see* Bukharin). As the struggle for power began in earnest in Moscow, Radek's status began to fall. He became the scapegoat for the Comintern's failures in Germany in 1924, and was removed from the leadership of that organization. In 1925 he was appointed to head Sun-Yat-Sen University in Moscow, a post he held until 1927. In 1927 he was exiled to Tobolsk in Siberia along with other oppositionists including Trotsky. In 1929 he recanted and in 1933 was appointed a member of the editorial board of *Izvestiia*. He gradually became a loyal Stalinist (*see* I. V. Stalin), becoming one of the architects of the 1936 Constitution (*see* Constitution) and a spokesman from "socialist realism" (*see* Literature).

Radek was arrested in September 1936, tried in January 1937 and sent into Siberian exile. The exact circumstances of his death are unknown, though some sources contend that he was murdered by a fellow prisoner in 1939. He was posthumously rehabilitated in June 1988.

Bibliography

Daniels, Robert. *The Conscience of the Revolution.*
Deutscher, Isaac. *The Prophet Armed.* 1954.

Haupt, Georges and Marie, Jean-Jacques. *Makers of the Russian Revolution*. 1974.
Lerner, Warren. *Karl Radek*. 1970.
Nettl, J. P. *Rosa Luxemburg*. 2 vols. 1966.

Rakovskii, Khristian Georgevich (1873–1941). Rakovskii was a Bulgarian communist (*see* Russian Social Democratic Workers' Party [Bolshevik]) who played an important role in the revolutions and the Civil War* in the Ukraine (*see* Ukraine, Revolution in) and became an important Soviet diplomat.

Rakovskii was born into a rich Bulgarian family in Kotel. His father was a member of the Democratic Party in Bulgaria, and his mother was related to a well-kown Bulgarian revolutionary and politician named Savva Rakovskii. Like many Bulgarians he grew up with a strong sympathy for Russia, the country that was regarded by many Bulgarians as their "big Slavic brother" in the struggle against the Turks who then controlled Bulgaria. In his autobiography Rakovskii stated that he became a Marxist in 1888 while attending a gymnasium in Gabrovo. The Bulgarian Marxists always had close ties with Russian Marxists and they tended to influence one another. Rakovskii became involved with the Russian Marxists in 1890 when he went to Geneva to study medicine. During his three years in Geneva he met G. V. Plekhanov*, V. Zasulich and P. B. Akselrod*, and conducted a Marxist study group with the famous Rosa Luxemburg*.

Rakovskii studied medicine in Montpellier, France where he became acquainted with many French socialists. By the time he received his degree in 1896, he was married to E. A. Riabova, a Russian Marxist and friend of Plekhanov and Zasulich. Although he worked primarily for the Bulgarian Socialist Party, he was a citizen of Romania. Until 1900 he served as a doctor in the Romanian army. From 1900 to 1902 he lived in St Petersburg and became very active in the Russian Social Democratic Movement. In 1902 he went to Paris to study law. He returned to Romania in 1903. He was deported from Romania during the 1907 peasant rebellion.

Rakovskii became a foremost revolutionary leader in the Balkans and a leading figure in the Second International. In 1917 he was an important Marxist leader in the revolutionary movements in Romania and the Ukraine and was also appointed a commissar for the Council of People's Commissars of the Russian Soviet Federative Socialist Republic. After various missions for the Soviet government, he was appointed president of the Provisional Revolutionary Government of the Workers and Peasants of the Ukraine. In March 1918 he was elected chairman of the Ukrainian Council of People's Commissars by the Third All-Ukrainian Congress of Soviets, and he became a member of the Central Committee of the Russian Communist Party (Bolshevik)* and for a time of the Orgburo as well. He remained the president of the Soviet Ukraine until 1923. In the inner party struggles in Russia Rakovskii became known as a Left Communist*, criticizing in particular I. V. Stalin's* efforts to centralize and Russify the new Soviet state. In 1927 Rakovskii was expelled from the party as a Trotskyite, and although rehabilitated in 1934, was tried as a member of the right opposition in Moscow in 1938. He died in a concentration camp in 1941 and was rehabilitated posthumously in 1988.

Bibliography

Haupt, Georges and Marie, Jean-Jacques. *Makers of the Russian Revolution.* 1974.

Rasputin, Gregory Efimovich (1872–1916). Rasputin occupies an extraordinary position in the history of the last days of the Russian Empire. Without any distinguished ancestry or important official position, he nevertheless became in some ways the most powerful influence on the royal court during World War I*.

Born in the village of Pokrovskoe in the eastern Siberian province of Tobolsk not far from the Ural Mountains, Rasputin had no surname, as was the case with many peasants. He supposedly acquired the name Rasputin (meaning "the dissolute") because of his licentious sexual conduct as an adolescent. Little is known of his early life, although popular biographers have contrived to fill the void with "events" of dubious authenticity. He apparently acquired no formal education and few social graces, but he was endowed with native intelligence. As a young man he underwent some kind of religious conversion and was later charged with membership in the *khlysty,* an outlawed heretical sect given to sexual orgies. It seems unlikely that he joined the sect in any formal sense, but the peculiar combination of piety and sexual promiscuity that he espoused was akin to *khlysty* practice.

Rasputin married, and he fathered four children, but he was too restless for a conventional life of domesticity. He acquired a local reputation as a *starets,* or holy man, and traveled widely in Russia and abroad while still in his twenties. His religious pilgrimages included a journey to Mt. Athos in Greece and to the holy places in Palestine. He acquired influential patrons such as the Archimandrite Feofan, inspector of the Theological Seminary in St. Petersburg, and Germogen, bishop of Saratov. He also met the Grand Duchess Militsa, a Montenegrin princess married to one of Tsar Nicholas II's* cousins. Together with their sister Anastasia, the Montenegrins had introduced several faith healers and "holy men" to court circles, and it was probably under their auspices that the initial meeting took place between Rasputin and the emperor and empress. Nicholas noted the occasion in his diary on November 14, 1905: "We have come to know a man of God, Gregory, from the province of Tobolsk."

Presumably, Nicholas and his wife, Alexandra, were impressed by Rasputin, but there is no indication that he became an imperial favorite at that time. Nicholas, unlike Alexandra, never became obsessed by Rasputin. Yet as Alexander Mosolov, who headed the court chancellery, so aptly put it, he needed a "typical peasant." Isolated from the masses and with only the most superficial insight into their aspirations, he could, through Rasputin identify himself with them and project his self-image of a kind and benevolent ruler. Unlike his popular image as a sinister and drunken lecher, Rasputin's manner was unpretentious yet impressive, and he had an eloquent tongue and a shrewd if often flawed grasp of human nature. In his relationship with the royal couple he blended familiarity and deference with exquisite precision. He never made demands or presumed too much, but he spoke to them as equals (Nicholas and Alexandra were "Papa" and "Mama") and assumed the role of a wise but humble *starets* with consummate ease. Whether sincere or not, his piety struck an emotional chord, especially with Alexandra, and Nicholas entrusted him with the office of imperial lampkeeper—he was to tend the numerous lamps burning continuously before the palace icons at Tsarskoe Selo. A sinecure, it was, nevertheless, a token of the Tsar's esteem, for he was a connoisseur of these holy images and maintained a rare and priceless collection.

Rasputin's success as a royal favorite would not likely have been sustained, however, without his apparent ability to relieve the suffering of Nicholas's only son Alexis, a hemophiliac. The rare disease, which prevents the normal clotting of the blood, can lead to uncontrolled hemorrhaging and death. On several occasions—the specific dates and circumstances are not well documented—Rasputin seemed to alleviate the pain and to control the bleeding either by hypnosis or by less melodramatic methods of calming the boy. The neurotic Alexandra came to believe that Rasputin was indeed a holy man, an emissary of God, and the overwhelming evidence of his unsavory personal life could not shake her faith in him.

Once he had thoroughly ingratiated himself with the emperor and the empress,Rasputin's conduct away from the court became less circumspect. He often drank heavily—his favorite was Madeira wine—and his sexual prowess was alleged to be such that he became a virtual cult figure to jaded society women in St. Petersburg. By 1910 gossip was widespread about his lascivious habits, and ultimately, the rumor that he and Alexandra were lovers was accepted as fact by a large segment of the population. Although he obviously enjoyed the privileges and notoriety of his position and on occasion went out of his way to express his contempt for the effete aristocrats of the capital by insolence and foul language, he apparently did not seek wealth or political power. But his generosity with money and favors and his proximity to the throne attracted a motley group of "followers" from humble petitioners to opportunists of the most brazen sort. Nor did he refrain from offering counsel to Nicholas and Alexandra on political matters.

Alarmed by the growing scandal, which by 1911 the press began alluding to with increasing boldness, Peter Arkadeevich Stolypin, president of the Council of Ministers, ordered an investigation. His report was damning, but Nicholas declined to take action. "Perhaps all that you tell me is true," he acknowledged. "But I beg you to speak no more to me of Rasputin. There is nothing more I can do about it" (Salisbury 1978, p. 210). Early in 1911 Stolypin saw Rasputin, evidently at Nicholas's request, and demanded that he leave St. Petersburg for his native village. Rasputin did leave, although he probably went on a pilgrimage to Jerusalem rather than to Pokrovskoe. The following September he was reportedly in Kiev at the time of Stolypin's assassination and returned to St. Petersburg in late autumn. By this time several of his patrons in the church had disavowed him, notably Bishop Germogen, but their attempts to ''expose'' him failed, at least in regard to persuading the Tsar. However, Nicholas did receive Mikhail Vladimirovich Rodzianko, the Duma (*see* Duma and Revolution) president, who denounced Rasputin at some length and was ordered to conduct another investigation. A report was sent to Nicholas in March 1912, and unlike the one prepared by Stolypin, this one he read with more than cursory interest. At any rate Rasputin was out of favor for a time and returned to Pokrovskoe. He seems to have regained his ascendancy over Alexandra—and perhaps Nicholas—in October of the same year when Alexis seriously injured himself and Rasputin sent a reassuring telegram that coincided with the boy's recovery.

Rasputin's notoriety, which reached new dimensions in 1912 because of attacks on him in the Duma and by unflattering publicity in the daily press, declined in 1913 because the *starets* spent less time in St. Petersburg. His presence might have proved salutary in the summer of 1914 with the outbreak of war (*see* World War I), for he had warned Nicholas of dire consequences should Russia become involved in an European conflict. But Rasputin was then in a hospital in Tiumen recovering from a serious stab wound inflicted by a mentally unbalanced woman, either a discarded mistress or (according to another version) an assassin hired by one of Rasputin's clerical enemies. He returned to the capital in the autumn. His relations with Nicholas were temporarily strained due to his disapproval of the war; apparently, he saw Alexandra at regular intervals in Tsarskoe Selo. As Russian defeats mounted and the glitter of patriotism grew tarnished, he became an ever more conspicuous scapegoat for the ills that beset the government and the war effort. At first accused only of pro-German tendencies, he (and Alexandra) was elevated to the status of a German spy in the paranoid world of popular rumor. His activities were closely monitored by the secret police, and although they lent no encouragement to charges of treason, his indiscretions, especially semipublic drunkeness, further sharpened his image as a dissolute scoundrel.

The emperor's prolonged absences at army headquarters near the front—he assumed the post of commander-in-chief in the autumn of 1915—allowed Alexandra to play a significant role in governmental affairs. She was widely regarded as a tool of Rasputin, whose taste for political intrigue had become more pronounced during the war. To ultraroyalists it became almost an article of faith that the dynasty would have to be saved in spite of itself. Only the elimination of this ''holy devil,'' a veritable monster of iniquity in the eyes of his enemies, could purify the monarchy and save the country. In December 1916 a group of conspirators headed by Prince Felix Felixovich Iussopov, a nephew of the Tsar by marriage; Vladimir Mitrofanovich Purishkevich, a reactionary member of the Duma; and Grand Duke Dmitrii Pavlovich; said to be Nicholas's favorite cousin, concocted an assassination plot. Rasputin was lured to the Iussopov mansion after midnight on December 17. There he allegedly drank poisoned wine, and when the deadly potion failed to accomplish its purpose he was shot, beaten, and, according to his daughter, emasculated. His comatose body was dropped in a hole in the ice of the Neva River, where he very likely died by drowning, although the absence of an autopsy made the exact cause of death difficult to establish. With the imperial family as the chief mourners, burial services took place at Tsarskoe Selo on December 21. The two most prominent murderers were given only token punishment: Iussopov was exiled to one of his provincial estates and Grand Duke Dmitrii sent to Persia for service with Russian forces there.

The killing of Rasputin was accepted by public opinion with equanimity, even outright approval, but the regeneration of the monarchy that the royalists expected failed to materialize. Nicholas and Alexandra were sunk in apathy, and the emperor spurned numerous appeals for a government enjoying public confidence. As for Rasputin himself, legend, both in his own lifetime and in later decades, overshadowed reality. Sensational biographies strove to satisfy public taste, and even scholars were persuaded that the "mad monk" had been the power behind the throne. Rasputin's political influence was modest indeed compared to his reputation; yet popular perception of his role did much to discredit the monarchy and to bring about its collapse within ten weeks of his death.

Robert D. Warth

Bibliography

Curtiss, John Shelton. *Church and State in Russia*. 1940.
De Jonge, Alex. *The Life and Times of Grigorii Rasputin*. 1982.
Fülöp-Miller, René. *Rasputin: the Holy Devil*. 1928.
Harcave, Sidney. *Years of the Golden Cockerel*. 1963.
Massie, Robert K. *Nicholas and Alexandra*. 1967.
Pares, Bernard. *The Fall of the Russian Monarchy*. 1939.
Salisbury, Harrison E. *Black Night, White Snow*. 1978.
Wilson, Colin. *Rasputin and the Fall of the Romanovs*. 1974.

Red Army. Although the Bolsheviks (*see* Russian Social Democratic Workers' Party [Bolshevik]) came to power in 1917 with a promise of peace, the threat posed by foreign and domestic enemies demanded that the Soviet (*see* Soviets [Councils] of Workers', Soldiers', and Peasants' Deputies) state devote its energies throughout 1918 to creating a Red Army.

On November 8, 1917, the Second Congress of Soviets adopted a decree on peace with all belligerent parties in the imperialist war. Very soon the delegates were bitterly disappointed because the decree neither eliminated the threat of further German advances nor forestalled the emergence of armed resistance to Bolshevik rule across the newly proclaimed Soviet Republic. The leaders—who had hoped to end the war, send the soldiers home, and build socialism—were faced with the task of building a new organization to defend the republic. The Bolshevik–Left Socialist-Revolutionary (*see* Left Socialist-Revolutionary Party) coalition realized the urgent need to organize some form of armed defense, but the first socialist state had no precedents and had to choose among several competing military models in revolutionary practice and in the theoretical writings of Marx, Engels, and Jean Jaures.

The first debates in the Congress of Soviets concerned what to do with the rapidly demobilizing 8 million soldiers of the imperial army (*see* Army of Russia, Imperial) in World War I. The Congress resolved to disband the demoralized tsarist army, but also to retain as many experienced soldiers as possible to fight in a socialist army. Revolutionary soldiers pressed their demands on the new leadership through elected committees. Soldiers' committees, which included Bolsheviks, Mensheviks (*see* Russian Social Democratic Workers' Party [Menshevik]) Socialist–Revolutionaries, and Anarchists (*see* Anarchism), had played a decisive role in the Bolshevik victory, and they voiced strong opinions about what was a just military order. The committees removed unpopular officers, elected new ones, debated issues of army life, and implemented thoroughgoing reforms of the structure of military authority and discipline. There was little talk, however, about abolishing either the standing army or the institution of officers.

The ideological heritage of the Russian revolutionary parties, on the contrary, shared with European Social Democracy its antipathy for standing armies and its preference for a people's militia. The officer caste, barracks insulated from civilian influences, and drill-sergeant discipline carried odious connotations from the era of absolute monarchs and were incompatible with the principles of a democratic socialist republic. Rather, citizen–soldiers would complete minimal universal military training and serve in the people's militia only when national emergencies dictated general mobilization.

Workers and revolutionaries created a version of the militia model in the organizations for armed defense that appeared in 1917 and early 1918. These urban organizations formed under several names: Red Guards*, socialist militias, and people's detachments. The units elected their commanders, stipulated after October 1917 that their members declare loyalty to the socialist Revolution, and strove to adhere to democratic principles of organization. Meanwhile in the countryside, where the Center's authority had virtually collapsed, peasants organized partisan detachments to defend themselves from the depredations of various outsiders who sought to impose a new order on rural society.

Finally, from the first days of the army's existence, a growing number of former tsarist officers and noncommissioned officers joined the Soviet government and proved invaluable for their technical skills, which were in critically short supply among the revolutionaries themselves. The military specialists, as they came to be known, had their own ideas of how to organize an army.

The Civil War in Russia* did not provide a propitious environment in which to resolve most issues of political organization and control. The military organization was no exception to the rule, and the creators of the Workers'–Peasants' Red Army had to improvise in the heat of battle. Thus the army emerged as a compromise among several principles, for each model had powerful advocates among the party leadership and military command. For example, the all-Russian collegium created to organize a socialist army in January 1918 included representatives from important constituences with very different visions—two men from the General Staff of the Red Guards and three from the Bolshevik Party's Military Organization.

From mid-autumn of 1917 to the spring of 1918, the Red Army resembled a socialist militia more closely than it ever would again. Revolutionary soldiers and sailors joined Red Guard detachments to form the first volunteer units in Moscow, Petrograd, Ivanovo-Voznesensk, and the cities in the Urals. The renewed German offensive in February 1918 raised a panic; subsequently, the All-Russian Central Executive Committee* of Soviets decreed universal military training for workers and "peasants who did not exploit labor." The Universal Military Training Administration (Vsevobuch) was established to train all eligible citizens in eight-week courses, with minimal disruption of their workdays. The staff and leadership of Vsevobuch became the most vocal proponents of socialist militia in the debates that divided the leadership until the military reforms of the mid–1920s.

The major opposition to the projects for a militia army came from the military specialists who joined or were conscripted to serve the new regime. On March 19, 1918, after L. D. Trotsky* took command of the army, the Council of People's Commissars* sanctioned the large-scale recruitment of military specialists. By the end of 1918 the Red Army counted 22,000 former generals and officers and 130,00 former non-commissioned officers of the tsarist army. As late as 1921, after sustained efforts to train Red commanders from workers and peasants, 34 percent of the 217,000 command personnel were military specialists. Because these men held critical posts in the military command, the academies, and the supply administration, their views carried great weight. They fought civilians' attempts to interfere in army affairs and sought to reimpose those forms of military organization most familiar to them. In particular, they insisted that the political and military leadership curtail the power of the soldiers' committees (see Soldiers and Soldiers' Committees). Shortly after the decree on the recruitment of military specialists took effect, the Supreme Military Council banned the practice of electing officers.

These measures met with determined resistance from within the revolutionary government. Not only the staff of Vsevobuch but also party workers in and outside the army remained deeply suspicious of the loyalty of the former officers. The Left Communists, (see Left Communism), and later the Military Opposition*, relentlessly attacked Trotsky and the army command for placing increasing authority in the hands of officers who were no longer subject to election in a conscript army. In response to these criticisms, the Bolshevik leadership reformed and expanded the institution of the political commissar, a holdover from the Provisional Government*. Two commissars watched over one military specialist in the three-man revolutionary military councils (revvoensovety) that directed the war effort at all levels of command. According to the principles of dual command, orders were to be obeyed only if they bore the signatures of both officer and commissar. During the Civil War the commissars' responsibilities grew to include supervision of party members, maintenance of troop morale, and organization of political education. The central military and political administration experimented with a range of measures to coordinate the activities of political commissars. The All-Russian Bureau of Military Commissars (Vsebiurvoenkom) was reorganized in April 1919 into the Political Administration of the Revolutionary Military Council of the Republic (PUR).

The Civil War environment demanded, above all, flexibility in response to local developments. A series of military front administrations—the Eastern Front (the Urals and Siberia [see Siberia, Revolution in]), the Southern Front (south Russia and the northern Caucasus [see Transcaucasia, Revolution in]), and the Western Front (the Ukraine, [see Ukraine, Revolution in] and Poland [see Poland, Revolution in])—directed most of the fighting. Despite the center's persistent efforts to assert its own authority in these areas, decentralization was also the rule for most conscription and training. During 1918 urban soviets and rural Committees of the Poor* (Kombedy) recruited soldiers for the Red Army. Although a system of military commissariats was in operation over all Bolshevik-held territory by the end of 1919, the extraordinary commissions for combatting desertion played a leading role in conscription in the countryside throughout 1919 and 1920. According to early Soviet legislation, only workers and peasants who did not exploit each others' labor were eligible to bear arms for the republic. All members of the exploiting classes, including kulaks, faced obligatory labor in the rear services of the army or in the civilian economy. Despite high rates of desertion and failure to appear for induction, Bolshevik conscription registered remarkable successes. At the end of 1919 the Red Army stood at 3 million men. A year later it grew to 5.5 million, of whom 778,000 were actual combatants.

Beginning in the summer of 1918, the Communist Party itself organized mass mobilization of its members to bolster troop morale and fighting ability at the start of every major offensive. During the Civil War, more than 200,000 party members fought in the Red Army. Special assignment detachments (ChONy), comprising only party members and sympathizers, reinforced failing units at critical moments.

To a large extent soldiers' morale depended on the ability of the regime to guarantee its army a constant and adequate supply of food, clothing, medicine, and weapons. Central authorities attempted to coordinate and control local requisition and distribution operations through an elaborate but largely ineffective bureaucracy, the Chusosnabarm. Often regional military councils bypassed the weighty central administration and turned to local handicrafts and rural artels to fill their orders. The breakdown of rail and water transportation served as a boon to small-scale industry; village craftsmen were better able to replace materials in short supply with locally available substitutes than were large-scale enterprises. Regiments also set up military farms (sovkhozy) and cooperatives (see The Cooperative Movement) to provide needed food supplies.

Although the use of propaganda (*see* Propaganda and the Russian Revolution) in armies already had precedents during World War I*, the Red Army embarked on a program of "political enlightenment" to persuade its mostly peasant soldiers that they were fighting a just cause. Alongside teachers and doctors, leading writers and artists brought literacy and culture to the Red Army masses under the joint auspices of the Commissariat of the Enlightenment* and the army's Political Administration. The Commissariat of Social Security also began a program of pensions and welfare for Red Army families. Soldiers and their families were entitled to tax exemptions, special educational benefits, and priority eligibility for other state and Soviet services.

The victory of the Red Army in the Civil War was in part the outcome of a complex and changing mixture of techniques of coercion, moral suasion, and material incentives. Because most Red commanders who served in the first two decades of the army's history began their careers during the Civil War, the legacy of the years 1917–1921 left a long-lasting imprint on the character of the new fighting force. Well into the 1930s the Soviet army remained an institution built on the compromises and improvisations of the immediate postrevolutionary period.

Mark von Hagen

Bibliography

Direktivy komandovaniia frontov Krasnoi armii, 1917–22 gg. 4 vols. 1971–1979.
Erickson, John. *The Soviet High Command.* 1962.
Gorodetskii, E N. *Rozhdenie sovetskogo gosudarstva, 1917–88 gg.* 1965.
Kliatskin S. M. *Na zashchite Oktiabria.* 1965.
Trotsky, Lev. *Kak vooruzhalas' revoliutsiia.* 3 vols. in 5. 1923–1925.
White, Dimitri Fedotoff. *The Growth of the Red Army.* 1944.

Red Guard. The Red Guards were the armed bands organized among the industrial working class in the cities of Russia in 1917 that played an important role in the October Seizure of Power*.

Armed workers' (*see* Workers in the Russian Revolution) bands—soon to become the Red Guard—orginated with the February Revolution*. In Petrograd loosely formed groups of armed workers appeared in the streets as early as February 27, and by the 28th they had become organized armed bands. In the provinces they appeared quickly on receipt of the news of the Revolution and were a part of the transfer of political power in almost every city. Called by various names—workers' militia, factory militia, fighting *druzhina*, workers' guards—they emerged out of the factories and worker districts in one of the clearer examples of spontaneity and worker self-organization. Their leaders were chosen from their own ranks or from local political activists. Their purpose was basically twofold: to maintain public safety and protect the Revolution. This latter function quickly shifted to mean protection of the gains made by the workers in the February Revolution and to further their social, economic, and political objectives. From the beginning, and becoming more emphatic as time progressed, they were a symbol of workers' self-assertion and of the "we–they" mentality that increasingly divided the country. Their importance was not only physical— their fighting capacity was always in doubt—but psychological. To the workers they were extremely important, and various efforts to reduce or disarm them met vigorous resistance. To the propertied classes they symbolized disorder and the danger of anarchistic (*see* Anarchism) violence against person and property. In a situation where the government—national or local—had little ability to use soldiers or police (militia) to enforce its will or laws, they loomed as a major force.

After an initial surge during and just after the February Revolution, their numbers dwindled in late March or April. However, at the same time efforts were begun, usually by local leaders, to organize them into better trained and more cohesive units. At the factory level these efforts had some success; the Red Guard units were intensely local in orientation, based on the factory. In Petrograd and other large cities repeated efforts were made to form larger city wide organizations. These efforts generally failed, in part because of the factory orientation of the groups, in part because of the opposition of the Menshevik (*see* Russian Social Democratic Workers' Party [Menshevik]) and Socialist-Revolutionary (*see* Socialist-Revolutionary Party) leaders of the soviet (*see* Soviets [Councils] of Workers', Soldiers', and Peasants' Deputies) whose attitude toward them was ambivalent. On the one hand, they had a difficult time opposing the idea of armed workers; on the other hand, they were concerned with order and feared that the Red Guard would be used by the Bolsheviks (*see* Russian Social Democratic Workers' Party [Bolshevik]). As a result, it was possible to use the Petrograd Soviet* to assist the organization of the Red Guard only after the Bolsheviks gained control of the Soviet. The same was true of most provincial cities.

The term *Red Guard* was not widely used until April and May. Apparently, the term comes from a "red proletarian guard" formed in Finland in 1905 and first was used in 1917 in an article by V. D. Bonch-Bruevich* in *Pravda,* March 18. As its use developed during the summer it generally implied a more political orientation, a concern with advancing the workers' interests and with furthering the Revolution, and, conversely, a decline of interest in helping maintain public safety and order. In fact, however, the various terms continued to be used, often interchangeably.

As a social and political phenomenon, certain features stand out. The Red Guard appears to have been composed in the main of individuals who were slightly younger than the work-force average, were more likely to be unmarried or without children, but *seem* to have been in the factory a considerable time and to have acquired a sense of working-class identity. In nationality Russians predominated, but the main determining factor was factory composition. In many instances workers of evacuated factories, especially Latvians, played a major role in the local Red Guard. They were mostly working class, although that varied. In Petrograd they were almost entirely composed of workers, but in some areas, such as the Volga towns, they had a large contingent identified as peasant, soldier, "employee," and others, although even these categories may most often have included individuals associated with a factory.

Politically, the Red Guard drew more members from the Bolshevik party than any other but included also Mensheviks, Socialist–Revolutionaries, anarchists, and nationalist groups. Many, often a majority, were nonparty. The Bolsheviks' prominent role reflects, in part, that they were the only major party vigorously supporting the idea of the Red Guard. It also may indicate that the two organizations attracted the same type of people: more radical, more impatient, more willing to resort to organized violence to advance their interests. The Red Guard leadership came from varied backgrounds, but local Bolshevik leaders were especially prominent, and as 1917 wore on, local Bolshevik committees tried increasingly to form or to organize better the Red Guard units. Whatever the background or origins of the Red Guard leaders, they were undoubtedly influenced by the growing prominence and militance of the Bolshevik party. The primary focus of loyalty for the Red Guard, however, was the local soviet, and its political aspirations were best reflected in the slogan "Power to the Soviets," rather than in party programs.

The size of the Red Guard has been much disputed. The estimates for the period just before the October Seizure of Power range from 70,000 to 200,000 for all of Russia. Using the statistics of the soviet scholars V. I. Verkhos (1976) and G. A. Tsypkin and R. G. Tsypkin (1977) and allowing for some adjustments, it appears that there were about 150,000 in organized armed bands, in addition to an incalculable number of small groups and individuals with arms that they were willing to put at the disposal of local soviets or factories in time of crisis. In a sense, however, the exact size is not the most critical issue. Much more important are things such as morale, attitude, and ability to dominate a locality physically or to threaten to do so. They often played a role out of proportion to their size. In Saratov, for example, although much smaller than the local garrison, they provided roughly half of the armed force for the armed showdown leading to the Bolshevik seizure of power and were more determined in forcing the issue than were the soldier participants. Although their fighting ability has been questioned, they represented a potent force in the progressively disintegrating society of late 1917, especially as they were striving vigorously to acquire adequate arms and to gain proficiency in their use.

The formation of Red Guard type units, after a brief falling off in late March and April, proceeded through the summer and fall of 1917. As was the case in so many other parts of Russian life, in the Kornilov Revolt* there was an impetus to their further development. It aroused not only the fear of counterrevolution but, by stimulating the barely hidden—and sometimes open—worker distrust of the soldiers as the guardian of the Revolution, gave an urgency to efforts not only to form but to organize better and arm and train the Red Guard. This impetus, sustained by the alarms in the autumn and by growing strikes and industrial strife, continued on to the October Revolution.

The role of the Red Guard in October compared to that of the soldiers has been disputed. Although lacking the proficiency in arms of even the often ill-trained garrison troops, it generally was more committed and determined. Moreover, there were not any clear-cut garrison versus Red Guard confrontations, and comparative numbers are both unreliable and, to some extent, irrelevant because even when garrisons were large, only a small party usually took place in any conflicts over the Bolshevik seizure of power. Overall, the evidence, and it is imperfect, suggests that the role of the Red Guard, though varying by locality, generally was disproportionate to its numbers (compared to the size of garrisons).

What role the new governors of Russia would assign to the Red Guard and other armed detachments once power was achieved was uncertain. Bolshevik ideology stressed the "arming of all of the people." Concepts of a militia composed of all the people capable of bearing arms, which might replace both the old army and old police, ran through earlier writings. Some Bolsheviks in 1917 saw the Red Guard as an initial stage in that process. These utopian plans quickly were battered by the realities of power and especially by two problems: maintaining public order and the forming of combat units to fight domestic and foreign enemies. The former was easiest. Workers' armed bands tended to take over the tasks of local police immediately after the Bolshevik seizure of power and, in fact, already had done so in some places. Despite some excesses, this system, supplemented by soldiers, worked for the short run.

The use of the Red Guard as a military force was more difficult. In fact, the Bolshevik regime seized upon whatever armed force was at hand: Red Guards, soldiers (see Soldiers and Soldiers' Committees), and sailors (see Sailors in 1917). The last two groups were crucial because of their military experience and numbers, but the Red Guard was considered especially important as a morale factor and as the possible kernel around which a new Red Army* might be built. The central Bolshevik authorities, in fact, tried to draw under their own control the very local-oriented workers' units, with varying success.

The role of Red Guard units in the first months of the Soviet regime, in contrast with that of soldiers and sailors, can be determined only by educated guesses. Much depends on whether one stresses purely military capacity or whether one considers also factors such as determination and enthusiasm. What is clear is that they played a significant role starting with the participation of Petrograd Red Guards in the defense against the Krasnov—Kerensky offensive (see Kerensky, Aleksandr Fedorovich) and continuing through the spread of the Revolution during the winter of 1917–1918, including especially the sending of special Red Guard expeditionary units from Petrograd to South Russia and from other cities to various trouble spots.

As the new Soviet government faced the problems of creating a new army, however, it soon became clear that the type of detachments relied upon in the first weeks of the regime's existence, both Red Guard and military, were not satisfactory. Although the new Red Army created slowly in the late winter and early spring was to rely significantly on working-class recruits, they were to be within a framework much closer to a traditional army than the old Red Guard and workers' militias, with their spontaneity, localism, elected leaders, and strong sense of self-assertiveness. The Red Guard, in turn, lost its importance and then its existence. In some instances Red Guard units were transformed by decree into Red Army units; sometimes a Red Guard group made up a major part of a newly formed army unit; in other cases they retained for a while a separate status as a "reserve" for the Red Army: in yet other instances they became partisan bands.

In all cases the central features of the old Red Guard/workers' militias were abolished or obscured. The essential traits of self-organization and elected leadership ended with the Red Army, and in both the Red Army and the partisan units the tie to local factory and environs that had been so central to their identity was broken. The pressures of Civil War in Russia* led inexorably to their demise, for they were remnants of an earlier stage of the Revolution when the workers organized themselves to defend their interests under a government and social system they distrusted. They were not suited to the new communist order or the demands of civil war.

Rex Wade

Bibliography

Lur'e, M. *Petrogradskaia Krasnaia gvardiia*. 1933.
Pinezhskii, E. *Krasnaia gvardiia*. 1929.
Startsev, V. I. *Ocherki po istoriii Petrogradskoi Krasnoi gvardii i rabochei militsii*. 1965.
Tsypkin, G. A., and Tsypkina, R. G. *Krasnaia gvardiia*. 1977.
Verkhos, V. I. *Krasnaia gvardiia v Oktiabr'skoi revoliutsii*. 1976.
Wade, Rex. *Red Guards and Workers' Militia in the Russian Revolution*. 1984.

Red International of Trade Unions (1921–1937). The Profintern or Red International of Trade Unions was a subsidiary of the Communist or Third International, and was devoted to the recruitment of radical trade unions for the Communist cause around the world.

Like its mother organization, the Red International of Trade Unions was formed in response to efforts in Western Europe to revive the Second or "Socialist" International after 1917. The original Second International could not be revived in its original form because of the deep rifts in the international socialist movement brought about by differences between member parties in World War I*. Though most West European socialist parties tended to support their country's war efforts during World War I, their trade unions moved more to the left and were at best luke warm. Those socialist parties and trade unions that opposed the war gravitated, often reluctantly, toward the Communist International. Most of them objected to V. I. Lenin* and the Russian domination of the Communist

International in general, but felt that if they joined the Communist International in force, they could counterbalance the Russian influence. Lenin met that threat, however, by writing his "Left Wing Communism, an Infantile Disorder" in April 1920 which clearly affirmed his belief that the Russian model of Marxist revolution should prevail for all countries that wished to make a proletarian revolution. He attacked those "Leftists" in the West (as in Germany) who refused to participate in trade unions and parliamentary elections, though he believed Leftists should be seduced back into the fold while maintaining a solid front against those Right Socialists who accepted the bourgeois state and bourgeois trade unions as enduring organizations. Two months later Lenin published an article called "The Tasks of the Third International" that denounced the leaders of Western socialist parties and western trade unions as a "labor aristocracy," lumping all socialist reformers into the same category, that is, as traitors to the working class.

These instructions became the guidelines for the Second Congress of the Communist International, which met in July 1920. To retain membership in the Communist International, member parties had to accept the famous "twenty-one conditions," terms which compelled them to remold themselves after the image of the Russian Bolsheviks (see Russian Social Democratic Workers' Party [Bolshevik]). The result was that member parties were asked to oppose the Right and the Left in European socialist movements, by joining in parliamentary and trade union activity in order to transform them into genuine proletarian organizations. In the case of the trade unions, the Second International had formed an International Federation of Trade Unions before 1914. It seemed to Russian leaders that, if they were creating a Third International to replace the Second, then they should also create their own trade union international to replace the existing International Federation of Trade Unions in Western Europe. The First All-Russian Congress of Trade Unions in January 1918 urged this course of action and called an international trade union conference in Petrograd in February 1918 in order to bring it about. The conference was stillborn. But in July 1919 the International Federation of Trade Unions in the West revived itself and established its headquarters in Amsterdam. G. E. Zinoviev* countered in a speech before the Ninth Party Congress in March 1920, calling for the formation of a Red International of Trade Unions. The following month the International Federation of Trade Unions wedded its activities to the International Labor Office in Geneva, a subsidiary of the League of Nations. Two of the twenty-one conditions of admission to the Comintern presented at its Second Congress in July 1920, the first calling for Communist infiltration of existing trade unions while revealing the traitorous behavior of the leaders of those trade unions and the other calling for struggle against the International Federation of Trade Unions. A few delegations to the congress, including the Russian, Italian, Bulgarian, and some British, joined together to form an International Trade Union Council (*Mezhsovprof*) to organize an international trade union congress. A Russian Left-

Communist (*see* Left Communism) with experience in the French trade union movement, Aleksandr Lozovskii (real name, Solomon Abramovich Dridzo) was selected as head of the new organization.

The strategy seemed contradictory. Western communists were urged to join existing trade unions and transform them, but the idea of a separate Trade Union International seemed to call for the formation of separate trade unions (parallel unionism) loyal to the new Red International of Trade Unions. Despite the contradictions, the Red International of Trade Unions was founded in its first congress in July 1921. It was to be nominally independent of the Communist International, but would accept three members of the Executive Committee of the Communist International as members of its Executive Bureau and, in turn, would send three members of its Executive Bureau to sit in the Executive Committee of the Comintern. The Executive Bureau of the Red International of Trade Unions would have fifteen members and Lozovskii became its chief. Trade unions wishing to join the Red International of Trade Unions could not be affiliated with the rival International Federation of Trade Unions and had to commit themselves to cooperation with their native communist parties. Their major successes apart from the Russian trade unions were the affiliation of the Italian Confederazion General del Lavoro (CGL) and the Spanish Confederation Nacional del Trabajo (CNT).

The Red International of Trade Unions never made much progress in its efforts to win over the trade unions of Western Europe. Its efforts to court the Amsterdam International Federation of Trade Unions were rejected, and it was not successful in courting independent trade unions either. In 1922 it reached the high point in its career by winning over most of the Czech trade unions and the syndicalist Confederation General du Travail Unitaire (CGTU), a group that included the majority of French trade union members. At its Second Congress in November 1922, it marked its first effort to move into Asia, where it would experience greater success in the long run. In 1925 the All-China Trade Union Federation with two million members would join.

Between 1928 and 1930 the Red International of Trade Unions followed I. V. Stalin's* directions that it move to the Left and seek to lead radical trade union members out of established trade union organizations into Red Trade Unions (parallel unionism). The Fifth Congress of the Red International of Trade Unions in August 1930 was its last. The adoption of parallel unionism seemed to have reduced its following to a few radical schismatic groups, and with the adoption of the Popular Front Policy in Moscow in 1935 there was no purpose served by the Red International of Trade Unions. It ceased publication of its journal and had no more congresses or conferences. Its indefatigable leader, Lozovskii, diverted his activities back to the mother organization, the Comintern, where he was a member of the Presidium of its Executive Committee. In 1949 he was arrested, and died in prison as part of Stalin's campaign against Jewish Bolsheviks, in 1952. In 1956 he was rehabilitated posthumously.

Bibliography

Adibekov, G. M. *Krasnyi Internationsl Profsoiuzov.* 1971.
Borkenau, Franz. *World Communism.* 1962.
Carr, E. H. *The Bolshevik Revolution.* III. 1953.
Lorwin, Louis. *Labor and Internationalism.* 1929.
Lozovskii, Alexander (real name Solomon A. Dridzo). *The World's Trade Unions.* 1924.
Olberg, Paul. *Die rote Gewerkschafts-Internationale und die europaischen Gewerk-schafts-Bewegung.* 1930.

Red Peasant International. *See* Peasant International.

Religion and the Revolution. The February Revolution* gave political power to leaders who advocated substantial changes in the legal, civil, and social status of religion in Russia. The October Seizure of Power* was conducted by leaders who were even more convinced that radical changes of religion's status were imperative. The Revolution's impact on religion was destined to be far reaching.

Under the autocracy, there had been clear inequality between the Tsar's subjects who belonged to the Russian Orthodox Church (*see* Church and the Russian Revolution) and those who were non-Orthodox. The former comprised nearly 70 percent of the population and received the favor of the state, which itself professed to be Orthodox. Among the non-Orthodox, about 15 percent of the population adhered to non-Christian religions, 10 percent were Roman Catholic, and 3 percent were Protestant. Recognizing that the religious identity of most of these persons derived from their nationality, the autocracy granted them grudging toleration within their nationality regions, most of which were geographically peripheral to the Russian heartland of the empire. The 5 million Jews (*see* Jewry, 1905–1921) constituted a special case in this category, as the officially encouraged anti-Semitism* left them victims of pogroms and rigid residence restrictions.

Specific disadvantages were suffered by ethnically Russian non-Orthodox religious believers. According to official dogma, the state considered that such persons could be Orthodox Christians only. In this category were more than 5 million Old Believers, Ukrainian Uniate, and a variety of officially designated "sectarians" (Dukhobors, Molokans, Khlysty, Skoptsy, Tolstoyans, Baptists, Evangelicals, Adventists, and so on). Only in 1905 had they won formal legal toleration, under which they still were forbidden to try to convert anyone from Orthodoxy. But the years of reaction before the Revolution effectively abolished what the law allowed. During World War I* Uniate Metropolitan Sheptitsky was imprisoned; more than 1,000 sectarians were under sentence for various offenses associated with their religion, including refusal to bear arms in combat; large groups of sectarians took refuge abroad, including Baptists and Skoptsy in Romania and 10,000 Dukhobors in Canada. Both the autocracy and its opponents suspected that there was potential in revolutionary sentiment among those who had been repressed. In the event, however, most religious dissenters stood aside from the political sphere, supporting the Revolution only passively.

A considerable number of Duma (*see* Duma and Revolution) deputies persistently spoke for a liberal religious policy. In 1916 P. N. Miliukov* led the parties of the Left in repeatedly calling attention to the persecution of sectarians. Even many deputies whose sympathies lay with traditional Orthodoxy found the existing situation undesirable. The Octobrists V. N. L'vov and P. V. Kamenskii, who led the Duma Committee on Religious Affairs, often complained against the enslavement of the Orthodox Church to the bureaucracy. Thus when the revolutionary government created by the Duma to replace the autocracy included Miliukov and L'vov, changes in the religious situation in Russia were to be expected. Specifically, the new rulers intended to organize a nonconfessional state and to implement equality and toleration for all religions. Two days after Nicholas II's* abdication, V. N. L'vov, who became the Provisional Government's* Procurator General of the Holy Synod, announced to the Orthodox bishops that thereafter the Orthodox Church was administratively independent of the state. On March 20 the Provisional Government abolished "all restrictions established by existing legislation on the rights of citizens of Russia by reason of adherence to a particular religious denomination or sect" (Browder and Kerensky 1961, I: p. 211). Already two weeks earlier the government had ordered the release of all persons imprisoned for religious offenses. By special actions the government welcomed the return of Dukhobers from Canada and ordered the release of Metropolitan Sheptitsky.

Despite its professions, however, the Provisional Government moved slowly in changing the pattern of church–state relations it had inherited from tsarism. Appointment of members to the Synod of the Orthodox Church remained the prerogative of the state, which was dramatized on April 14 when the bishops it viewed as uncooperative were replaced. Even after the church met in the Sobor to organize its autonomous administration, the government reserved the right of final approval of decisions reached. In practice, non-Orthodox religions began to exercise more freedom than even the Orthodox had, and consequently, they gave more enthusiastic support to the Revolution than did the church's leaders.

By a decree of June 20, the government removed 37,000 parish schools from the jurisdiction of the church and placed them under the Ministry of Education. The church viewed this secularization of the schools as a hostile act. The government responded that its actions derived from its nonconfessional nature, since the schools received funds from the Treasury. The autocracy, as a confessional state, could reasonably use state money to support parochial schools, but the new government was obliged to administer directly the education it financed.

After Premier Georgii E. L'vov's* resignation, on July 14 the government promulgated a law stipulating freedom of conscience for every citizen that included the right to change religious affiliation or to have no religion. With the formation of A. F. Kerensky's government on July 25, the Constitutional Democrat (*see* Constitutional Democratic Party—Cadet) A. V. Kartashev became

Procurator General; he began immediately to implement the abolition of this office that tied the church to the state. On August 5 Kartashev became the "Minister of Confessions," which extended the purview of the office to the relations of the state with all religions. Among these relations, the government anticipated giving modest subsidies from the state budget to all religious denominations. The Provisional Government, then, brought to Russia legal religious freedom, but this did not mean the introduction of separation of the church and the state.

The earlier near unanimity of support for the Revolution among religious groups disintegrated under A. F. Kerensky. At the beginning of the Kornilov affair in August (*see* Kornilov Revolt), the Orthodox Sobor debated whether to support the general's program, with the majority clearly sympathizing with its counterrevolutionary thrust. Former Procurator General L'vov went to the Winter Palace as Kornilov's representative to negotiate with Kerensky. His arrest spelled the doom of Kornilov's attempt to halt the leftward drift of the Revolution and saved the Sobor from the embarrassment of a futile declaration. The Sobor did, however, appeal to Kerensky to spare Kornilov's life, despite his treachery.

On the other hand, sectarianism aided different political forces. When in a last-minute effort to save his government in October Kerensky ordered the closing of the Bolshevik (*see* Russian Social Democratic Workers' Party [Bolshevik]) newspapers, the Baptist publishing house Slovo istiny printed Bolshevik propaganda. This action did not signify so much sectarian advocacy of Bolshevism as it exhibited radical commitment to freedoms that the Revolution had promised.

After October, the Bolshevik government showed itself much more willing to act decisively in matters affecting religion than had been the Provisional Government. V. I. Lenin* clearly expressed his personal animosity toward religion and was joined in this by many of his associates. Their goal was to eliminate as quickly as circumstances would allow the public influence of religion.

The Bolshevik treatment of religion took shape early in a series of decrees that dealt in whole or in part with church interests. The Decree on Land of October 26 specified "monastery and church lands" among the property transferred to state control. The Orthodox and Catholic churches were hurt by this decree more than the other religions, which had been unable to acquire much property earlier. The "Declaration of the Rights of the Peoples of Russia" on November 2 repeated the Provisional Government's abolition of "any and all national and national-religious privileges and disabilities." (Meisel and Kozera 1953, p. 26). A decree of December 11 nationalized all educational institutions, including theological schools. Marriage was made a purely civil matter by decrees of December 16, removing divorce proceedings from ecclesiastical jurisdictions and, as of December 18, requiring registration of marriages, births, and deaths with government offices. Theretofore, churches had been registering as well as the solemnizing agencies. On January 17, 1918, all teachers of religion were dismissed from public schools, abolishing the Orthodox "law of God" as the obligatory subject of study that it had been.

The Council of People's Commissars* climaxed its legislation affecting religion on January 23 with the decree that has remained to the present as the fundamental law on church–state relations in Soviet Russia. This "Decree on Separation of Church from State and School from Church" abolished all forms of civil cooperation in religion, including financial subsidies and religious rites (e.g., oaths, prayers) in public functions or places. It deprived all religious organizations of the legal rights of contract; consequently, everything the churches owned was declared public property. Items such as buildings, vessels, and icons that religious groups required for "purposes of worship" were to be leased to them, without charge. Although the decree professed to guarantee unlimited freedom of conscience, it actually provided the basis for extensive restrictions on religious practice. The immediate termination of all subsidies threatened to curtail the practical operation of the Orthodox Church inasmuch as it had no readily available alternative sources of financing for its far-reaching activities. The decree prohibited parochial schools. The only organized religious activity that the decree explicitly permitted was "worship." In sum, the decree not only disestablished and disendowed the Orthodox Church, it laid the legal foundations that deprived all religions of participation in the public, social, cultural, and educational life of the country. In the event, some time was to pass before the legal provisions achieved their effect in practice.

The restrictiveness of the decree was not immediately apparent to all. In contrast to the laws of the empire, the decree appeared even more permissive for most non-Orthodox. General approval of Bolshevik actions respecting religion came from all religions except the Orthodox and Catholic churches. After the Bolsheviks prevented the Constituent Assembly from accomplishing any of its purposes, these churches emerged as the chief anti-Bolshevik organizations on Soviet-ruled territory. Orthodox Patriarch Tikhon and Catholic Monsignor Constantin Budkiewicz each ordered their respective faithful to resist state appropriation of church property in accordance with the separation decree. These men were arrested subsequently on charges of counterrevolutionary activity. The last Procurator General, who had been arrested with the other members of Kerensky's government, was elected by the Orthodox Sobor to the church's Supreme Ecclesiastical Council. As another example of the church's opposition to the Revolution, upon his release from prison in 1918 he organized a counterrevolutionary center in Moscow that supported the activity of White General A. I. Denikin*.

Sectarians whose losses under the Bolsheviks' actions were minimal acted differently. Through the mediation of Lenin's personal secretary, V. D. Bonch-Bruevich*, they found the Bolsheviks generally attentive to their wishes. For example, in January 1919 Lenin's government granted pacifist sectarians the right of exemption from combat service in the Red Army*. The regime also encouraged some sectarians' instincts for economic communalism by subsidizing their agricultural and productive cooperatives for several years. A governmental office called the Orgkomsekt was created to supervise this subsidy. Despite the dislocations in Russia in the years of the Revolution and Civil War (*see* Civil

War in Russia), sectarian religious groups generally prospered. As a result, most non-Orthodox religions abstained from anti-Bolshevik activity, thereby, in some measure, contributing to the triumph of the Bolshevik Revolution.

Paul Steeves

Bibliography

Browder, R. P., and Kerensky, A., eds. *The Russian Provisional Government, 1917.* 3 vols. 1960–61.

Gidulianov, P. V., ed. *Otedlenie tserkvi ot godudarstva v S.S.S.R.* 1926.

Klibanov, A. I. *Religioznoe sektanstvo i sovremennost'.* 1969.

Kolarsz, W. *Religion in the Soviet Union.* 1966.

Marshall, R. *Aspects of Religion in the Soviet Union.* 1971.

Meisel, J. H. and Kozera, Edward. *Materials for the Study of the Soviet System.* 1953.

Putintsev, F. M. *Politicheskaia rol' i taktika sekt.* 1935.

Simon, G. *Church, State, and Opposition in the U.S.S.R.* 1974.

Szczesniak, B. *The Russian Revolution and Religion.* 1959.

Russian Communist League of Youth (Kommunisticheskii souiz molodezhi; often known as the Communist League of Youth or by its acronym, Comsomol [Komsomol]). The Comsomol is the youth organization of the Russian Communist Party (*see* Russian Social Democratic Workers' Party [Bolshevik]).

The idea of organizing Russian youth in support of the communist cause goes back to a resolution of the Russian Social Democratic Workers' Party at its Second Congress in 1903, calling upon all such spontaneous youth organizations to seek guidance and supervision from the Mother Party. During the Nineteen-Five Revolution* some spontaneous youth organizations were created, like the Student Organization of the Petersburg Committee of the Russian Social Democratic Workers' Party, which had about 250 members and survived until 1905. A youth organization led by N. I. Bukharin* and G. Ia. Sokol'nikov* called an all-Russian Congress of Social-Democratic Students, but the organization it tried to establish faded away by 1908. More youth organizations sprang up in Russia after 1917, but it was not until the Sixth Congress of the Bolshevik Party in July-August 1917 that a decision was made in a resolution "On Youth Leagues" to urge youth organizations again to seek tutelage from the adult party. The resolution did not call, however, for a single youth organization that would be an auxiliary of the party. The youth organizations themselves took the initiative in Petrograd and Moscow. They formed an organizational bureau that issued an appeal for an All-Russian Congress of Youth, and ultimately the creation of a Red International of Youth.

Such a congress was called in Moscow from October 29 to November 4, 1918. The First Congress of the Communist League of Youth had 194 delegates, and claimed to represent 120 youth groups with 22,100 members. Approximately half of the delegates were Communists, 38 were sympathizers, and 45 were non-party people. The new Central Committee of the organization consisted exclusively of Communists. In its new rules it described itself as self standing and fully independent, but "the League is solidary with the Russian Communist Party (Bolshevik) ("Solidary" meaning completely united. Fisher p. 10). This seemed a somewhat contradictory description of its relationship to the Russian Communist Party. Despite the use of the word "communist" in the name, the speaker at the congress claimed that it would be open to people who were not Communists. The Eighth Congress of the Russian Communist Party gave its approval to the new organizations on March 18–23, 1919, and reiterated the importance of the organization remaining self-standing (in Russian, *samostoia-tel'nyi*) in order to allow the "maximum of spontaneous activity" (Fisher, p. 12). In August a joint resolution of the Central Committee of the Party and the Youth League, however, subordinated the youth organization to the Party, stating in part, "the Central Committee of the Russian Communist League of Youth is directly subordinated to the Central Committee of the Russian Communist Party" and that "the local organizations of the Russian Communist League of Youth work under the control of the local committees of the Russian Communist Party" (Fisher, p. 13). To facilitate this change, all party members under the age of twenty would automatically become members of the Communist League of Youth. Despite these strictures, the resolution still insisted that the League was autonomous (in Russian, *avtonomnyi*). Membership in the organization rose from about 96,000 in October 1918, to about 319,000 in May 1920 and 480,000 in October 1920.

One of the early questions was the intended role of the youth organization. In general terms, its purpose was to train the young for service in the Party and to help the Party to achieve its tasks. The Eighth Party Congress in March 1919 referred to the Communist League of Youth as the "trained reserves" of the Party. But in their early groping for a sense of corporate identity and more narrowly defined goals, a number of ideas emerged. At one point it was suggested that the Comsomol should establish Young Proletarian Homes where all working class youths could spend their spare time and be indoctrinated. That proposal was turned down, but it was followed by the notion of youth sections affiliated with trade unions which was also rejected. On September 15 the Party Central Committee intervened and said the supporters of both factions represented non-communist deviations. The Comsomol would undergo the same kind of purging and discipline as the mother party. Probably the issue was one of control. If the base of membership or activities became too broad it would be difficult to subject the organization to maintain the necessary conformity to party dictates. It was in effect closely patterned on the structural model provided by the party itself, and, whatever the wording, it remained subordinate to the party.

Specific tasks were assigned in practice, and one of them was to encourage military training which meant to volunteer for the armed forces. On May 10, 1919 there was a nation-wide mobilization of Comsomolites to meet the threat from A. V. Kolchak*, providing 75,000 front line troops. Most of the volunteers were not organized into special Comsomol units, but there were a few: a Petrograd unit of bicyclists, a Ural youth detachment and a Ukrainian armed train. At the

Second Congress of the Comsomol on October 5–8, 1919 the threat was A. I. Denikin* and a second All-Russian Mobilization of Comsomols took place. It called up all Comsomols over sixteen years old. By the time of the Third Congress from October 2 to 10, 1920, four more mobilizations had taken place bringing in another 10,000 Comsomolites into the army. By this time the Comsomol had been charged, in keeping with the decisions of the Ninth Congress of the Party in March 1920, to help create a militia army (*see* Red Army) and the Comsomol's job was to provide preliminary physical and ideological training to prepare the young communists for their service in the armed forces. But the party did not move toward the formation of Comsomol cells in the army, because the party was afraid of creating a double apparatus.

Among their other tasks, the Communist League of Youth resolved at its First Congress to create a Youth International, and took a meeting of Russian and Polish young people in 1907 as its antecedent for what it called the First International Congress of Proletarian Youth Organizations. After the First Congress of the Communist International in March 1919, that organization and the Comsomol planned the First Congress of the Communist International of Youth (*see* Communist International of Youth) for November 20–26, 1919.

The values to be held and fostered by members of the Young Communist League were at first stated in a somewhat nebulous fashion, except for those associated with patriotism and production at the workplace. In the factory, Comsomols were expected to make sure the rights of the workers were protected, but also to try to explain to other young workers their role in relation to the new socialist society and state. In the first few years, however, the emphasis shifted away from the protection of young workers to exhortation of young workers to meet production quotas and observe work discipline and socialist competition. When Lenin spoke to the Comsomols in their 1920 Congress, he said that the task of the Comsomol "can be expressed in one word: The task is to learn" (Fisher, p. 69). He went on to point out that this meant learning practical knowledge as well as book learning. He coined the Comsomol slogan "You can be a Communist only when you enrich your memory with the knowledge of all of those riches that mankind has produced" (Fisher, p. 70). A. V. Lunacharskii* added to this definition of education the need for class consciousness and political consciousness. These appeals were translated into a new effort to provide education and indoctrination in the secondary schools which were not being used at night.

By the end of the Civil War in Russia* the Comsomol organization had a membership of about two-thirds that of the party. It had proved its value, both as a reservoir of indoctrinated and disciplined Communists from which the party could draw and as a potentially powerful instrument for the mobilization, not only of youth, but also of the whole society. The New Economic Policy* was a challenge, however, to the new organization. It brought to an end the period of dramatic crusading for the party cause, and ushered in a new period of stark contrasts between the party's stated goals and its present policies, permitting a return to class differentiation, profiteering, and private ownership in some sectors of the economy. In many respects the first phase of the New Economic Policy would test the mettle and the faith of the Communist League of Youth. Although they were informed that this period of strategic retrenchment would pose new challenges for them, such as how to fight bourgeois values, that confrontation did not seem as glorious to them as fighting for Socialism in the battlefield. There was a temporary disillusionment and dropping away of membership. By the Fifth Congress in October 1922, membership had dropped to 250,000. But there would be new challenges for the Comsomol that would cause it to grow and expand its activities when I. V. Stalin* moved Russia into the Second Revolutionary Period, the First Five Year Plan, between 1928 and 1934.

Bibliography

Fisher, Ralph Talcott Jr. *Pattern for Soviet Youth*. 1959.
Kassof, Allen. *The Soviet Youth Program*. 1959.
Mehnert, Klaus. *Die Jugend in Sowjetrussland*. 1932.
Naslednikam revoliutsii. 1969.

Russian Communist Party (Bolshevik). *See* Russian Social Democratic Workers' Party (Bolshevik).

Russian Social Democratic Workers' Party (Bolshevik). The Bolsheviks were the Marxist political party that seized power in Russia in 1917 and created the Soviet state of today. Bolshevism before the February Revolution* had only a few thousand adherents. Its numbers had been depleted by wartime arrests in Petrograd and elsewhere in late 1916. The faction's leaders were in prison, Siberian exile, or emigration. V. I. Lenin* was in Switzerland. A handful of central activists remained in operation in Russia. But contact between Bolsheviks in Russia and those abroad was irregular, and communication in the political "underground" inside the country was almost as difficult. Disagreements about policy were frequent. A faction that gave theoretical favor to discipline and hierarchy was in fact in organizational disarray. Morale was low. Bolsheviks still spoke of the imminence of autocracy's collapse and called on fellow socialists to ensure that the succeeding regime instituted a comprehensively democratic order. But the chance of immediate revolution appeared slim.

The absolute monarchy's (*see* Nicholas II) sudden overthrow in February 1917 (*see* February Revolution) transformed the condition of Bolshevism. Above all, the Bolsheviks at last succeeded in forming a fully independent party. Russian Marxists had fallen into severe internal controversy in 1903. But the two factions, the Bolsheviks and the Mensheviks (*see* Russian Social Democratic Workers' Party [Menshevik]) did not undergo a final practical split (even though separate factional centers had been maintained), and until 1917, the Russian Social Democratic Workers' Party on paper was a single Marxist body. The irreversible division occurred after the February Revolution. Its basis was the difference between the two factions' attitudes to both the Provisional Government* and World War I*. Unlike the Mensheviks, Bolsheviks wanted state power to be transferred quickly to the soviets—and by force. They ridiculed Menshevik hopes of ending the war by getting Europe's socialist parties to put non-violent pressure upon their respective governments. Bolshevik optimism was limitless, and this fact was reflected not only in mood but also in organizational behavior. Initially, some leaders, such as L. B. Kamenev* and I. V. Stalin*, had advocated a relatively cautious policy toward the Provisional Government, but there were others, particularly at the party's lower levels, who intransigently sought the L'vov cabinet's speedy removal. Debate raged. Lenin, returning from emigration in April, backed the radicals. Their campaign triumphed at the Seventh Party Conference in the same month: the will of the party as a whole was duly registered. Throughout 1917, furthermore, the central apparatus had to take account of provincial opinion or else risk its wishes being ignored. Rank-and-file party members in their turn influenced the measures of local committees. Nor was the party introspective. Since three-fifths of the membership were workers, it was not difficult to keep in touch with working-class aspirations, and an effort was made, too, to have as many activists as possible elected into posts in the soviets and other mass organizations. This expenditure of energy was not wasted. The discontent of workers, peasants, and conscripts with the Provisional Government's handling of the war and of economic issues increased. This worked in the party's favor. By August Bolsheviks purportedly numbered around a quarter of a million. Electoral popularity grew. In September urban soviets in Petrograd and elsewhere (*see* Petrograd Soviet; Moscow Soviet) acquired Bolshevik majorities. On October 10, 1917, the Bolshevik Central Committee resolved that power should be seized in the name of the soviets, and fifteen days later this desire was fulfilled.

The new administration's euphoria, however, did not last long. Workers, who supplied the main support for the Bolsheviks, discovered that the country's economic and military dilemmas had no easy solution. In town and village, moreover, opposition mounted to the Bolshevik Party leadership's acts of intolerance and violence. The party's social composition began to change. Reports of factory laborers abandoning local groups and organizations became frequent. In addition, party life was adversely affected by the necessity to transfer ever more Bolshevik activists into jobs in governmental institutions. Above all, political acrimony engulfed the party. The informal freedom of committees in the provinces to set their own policies had given flexibility and dynamism to Bolshevism before the October Seizure of Power* but this situation almost led to a total organizational schism in 1918. The furor over the Brest-Litovsk* Treaty was enormous.

The danger of the party's dissolution was recognized, but little of a drastic nature was attempted until the second half of the year. The incentive for internal party reform became irresistible. The worsening of the food supply problem (*see* Famine) was accompanied by an intensification of the Civil War in Russia* in midsummer. The lines of command in the government structure were chaotic and confused. Party leaders in the Center and in the provinces concluded that a supreme agency of coordination was required and that the party should fulfill such a function. The tug of war in authority between Bolshevik-dominated soviets and the Bolshevik Party was finally settled with a victory for the latter (*see* Soviets [Councils] of Workers', Soldiers', and Peasants' Deputies). Simultaneously, behavior inside the party was altered. There had been moments in the past, such as when the decision to oust the Provisional Government was adopted on October 10, 1917, that witnessed the central party apparatus fixing policy with little consultation with the rest of the party. This exercise of influence now became a permanent prerogative. Local party committees were subjected to real hierarchical control; at the center, inner subcommittees of the Central Committee (the Politburo and the Orgburo [*see* Central Committee of the Russian Communist Party (Bolshevik)] were created in early 1919 to direct the party. At each level of the national structure, power was devolved to fewer and fewer officials. By 1920 a single functionary, with the title of "secretary," held sway in any local committee. Obedience became the key word. The authoritarian trends were strengthened by habits inculcated in the Red Army*. A majority of Bolsheviks served in its forces during the Civil War. The dissenting group known as the Democratic Centralists* called for a return of the internal party freedoms of 1917. Their plea was rejected. Centralism had triumphed, and few local leaders had much sympathy with its critics.

Ideology was a factor in this transformation. Bolshevism before the October Seizure of Power had affirmed the need for a politics of liberation, but there had also been an emphasis upon coercion. The "dictatorship of the proletariat" was eagerly heralded by Lenin and L. D. Trotsky*. After the seizure of power, the inclination in favor of intolerance and violence grew as difficulty after difficulty confronted Sovnarkom (*see* Council of Peoples' Commissars). Workers demonstrating against the Constituent Assembly's* closure were fired upon in January 1918, and by the midsummer of that year, peasants who would not release grain to the authorities had to contend with armed urban detachments. Gradually, the conduct of public affairs became cruder, and this began to affect party life itself. The rigors of Civil War intensified the process.

By 1920 a Red victory over the Whites (*see* White Movement) had become a certainty. The Democratic Centralists repeated their demands, and a new faction, the Workers' Opposition (*see* Kollontai, Shliapnikov, Left Communism), went even further by asserting that workers and peasants should be allowed to control economic decision making in their locality. Such schemes were strenuously resisted by party committees in Moscow and the provinces. The methods of the Civil War were continued. Workers responded by going on strike, and a diminution of the working-class proportion in the party membership was registered. Rural revolts grew in frequency and severity, and a mutiny was brewing in the Kronstadt (*see* Kronstadt, 1917–1921) naval garrison by early 1921. Only under great pressure would the Politburo contemplate altering its practical program. Grain requisitioning was abolished in February 1921. The Tenth Party Congress in March ratified and extended the New Economic Policy.

But there was to be no relaxation of the political regime. Lenin argued that a tighter grip had to be applied even to the party if the concessions in agriculture and industry were not to get out of hand. All of the factions were explicitly banned. The Democratic Centralists and the the Workers' Opposition were instructed to break up their groups or face disciplinary sanctions. The central party apparatus, so far from diminishing its power and ruthlessness after the Civil War, actually became more authoritarian than ever. Circumstances and ideas had combined to yield this result. It surprised most Bolsheviks from the days of 1917 and before. It caused no astonishment to most of their opponents, who had always maintained that the Bolshevik Party had a predisposition toward internal bureaucracy.

The Russian Social Democratic Worker's Party (Bolshevik) changed its name to the Russian Communist Party at the Seventh Party Congress on March 8, 1918. At the Fourteenth Party Congress in December 1928 the name was again changed to All-Union Communist Party (Bolshevik).

Robert Service

Bibliography

Carr, E. H. *The Bolshevik Revolution, 1917–1923*. 3 vols. 1950–53.
Daniels, R.V. *Conscience of the Revolution*. 1961.
Pospelov, P. N., ed. *Istoriia Kommunisticheskoi partii Sovetskogo Soiuza*. 1963.
Schapiro, L. *The Communist Party of the Soviet Union*. 2d rev. ed. 1970.
Schlesinger, R. *History of the Communist Party of the U.S.S.R.* 1977.
Service, Robert. *The Bolshevik Party in Revolution*. 1979.

Russian Social Democratic Workers' Party (Menshevik). The Menshevik Party, like the Bolshevik (*see* Russian Social Democratic Workers' Party [Bolshevik]), grew out of two factions into which the Russian Social Democratic Workers' Party split in 1903 though they did not give up the idea of a reunited party until 1917. The Mensheviks were the major Marxist competitors to the Bolshevik Party in 1917 among the industrial workers in the cities. Although both Menshevik and Bolshevik factions were committed to bringing about a bourgeois democratic revolution in Russia—to be followed by a socialist revolution—they developed different strategies for the completion of this two-stage program.

Menshevik strategy emphasized the need for a prolonged period of cooperation between the parties of the working class and the more progressive representatives of the educated propertied classes of Russia. This strategy also called for—and this was the particular effect of the defeat of the Revolution of 1905 (*see* Nineteen-Five Revolution)—the creation of working-class organizations that would teach the workers the principles of democratic cooperative action, would minimize their sense of isolation, and would prevent the rise of a premature radicalism that would turn against the "democratic" bourgeoisie. In the years that preceded the outbreak of World War I*, the Mensheviks first saw this strategy acquire a widespread popularity among the Russian workers and then lose ground to the more militant, isolationist, Bolshevik strategy during 1913–1914. Similarly, in the months following the February Revolution* the Menshevik Party first rose to the highest level of political influence and then fell to defeat between July and October—a turn of fortunes that closely paralleled the political history of the February Revolution itself.

The events that led to the collapse of the tsarist government found the foremost Menshevik leaders in emigration or exile and the party's central organizations paralyzed by the wartime division between Internationalists* and Defensists (*see* Defensism; Martov, Julii; Tsereteli, Iraklii Georgevich). Nevertheless, by February 27 members of the Menshevik Party and its sympathizers had emerged as the uncontested leaders of the Petrograd Soviet* of Workers' and Soldiers' Deputies. Their rapid ascendance was due to the popular recognition of their Duma (*see* Duma and Revolution) deputies, their close ties with the Labor Group of the War Industries Committee* (whose Secretariat became the administrative apparatus of the soviet), and, most importantly, their readiness to unite around a strategy that suited the political realities of the moment and the mood of the masses. That strategy, known as Dual Power*, envisaged the soviets as separate and autonomous bodies for the organization, political education, and independent activity of the masses and made the soviets' support of the Provisional Government* contingent upon the implementation of specific reforms and policies.

In late March and early April, however, Dual Power came under attack from circles close to the Provisional Government as well as from elements within the soviet, particularly the soldiers and the activists in many of the provincial soviets. This attack coincided with a major realignment that was taking place within the Menshevik Party itself: the majority of the Mensheviks in Petrograd, including many who had supported Dual Power, were rallying around a new "Revolutionary Defensist" faction (*see* Defensism), and together with like-minded Socialist–Revolutionaries (*see* Socialist-Revolutionary Party) they quickly gained a majority in the Petrograd Soviet. Led by I. G. Tsereteli and F. I. Dan (*see* Gur'vich, Fedor Il'ich) the Revolutionary Defensists formulated a novel approach to the most critical question of the time—that of the war. In principle they, like the Internationalists*, denounced the war as "imperialist" and called on all socialist parties of Europe to pressure their governments into concluding an immediate peace without annexation or indemnities. But the Revolutionary Defensists also believed that the Petrograd Soviet had to bear responsibility for the defense of the Revolution until peace could be guaranteed and argued that both the military defense and the goal of democratic peace would be better served by closer cooperation between the Petrograd Soviet and the Provisional Government.

Throughout the month of April the revolutionary Defensists remained opposed to direct participation of the socialists in the Provisional Government on the grounds that during an essentially "bourgeois" revolution no government could satisfy the complete demands of the working class and its party. According to a long-held Menshevik doctrine, the presence of socialists in such a government would give rise to unrealistic expectations among the workers and eventually lead to their disenchantment with the Social Democratic leaders. However, in the wake of the April Crisis the Revolutionary Defensists found themselves compelled to join the Provisional Government, a decision that was motivated both by the need to strengthen the crumbling authority of the government, especially among the soldiers, and by the hope of obtaining greater influence in formulating foreign and economic policies. The establishment of a coalition cabinet was also supported by all Menshevik Defensists as well as by certain Menshevik Internationalists, who believed that a coalition would force the Provisional Government to carry out the Petrograd soviet's program for peace and economic reforms. More importantly, in the provinces, where Mensheviks had been running the local government and the local soviets, the abolition of Dual Power was received with great enthusiasm. At the All-Russian Conference of the Menshevik Party in Petrograd (May 7–13) only the small Internationalist faction, led by Iu. O. Martov*, remained opposed to the participation in the cabinet of Tsereteli and M. I. Skobelev, two of the party's leaders.

The Menshevik Party reached the height of its influence during the two months' existence of the First Coalition. At the First All-Russian Congress of Soviets in Petrograd in early June, the party and its affiliates held more than one-third of the votes and could count on a two-thirds majority for all of its proposals. With the undoubted support of the soldiers and workers of Russia behind them, the socialist ministers felt powerful enough to dictate the government's policies, and in some areas, such as taxation and social security, they were often successful. At the same time, their position of national responsibility in the government added more force to their call for sacrifice and moderation on the part of the workers and soldiers. However, by early July, the failure of the soviet's representatives to achieve a dramatic change in the government's policies of peace and economic reforms had turned the majority of the workers and soldiers of the capital against the policy of coalition. Nevertheless, most Mensheviks continued to support coalition as the only means of preventing the total isolation of the working class, which they believed would result from the establishment of a government based on the soviet alone. Even after the Kornilov Revolt*, when coalition had become all but impossible, the Revolutionary Defensists insisted that the soviet try to secure the consent of all other "democratic organizations— cooperatives (see The Cooperative Movements) and rural and urban self-governments—for the establishment of a "homogenous democratic government." Even the Internationalist minority of the party, which had called in early July for an "all-socialist government" based on the soviets, hesitated to press for it during the last three months of the February Revolution for fear such a government would be dominated by Bolsheviks.

The complete discredit of the Provisional Government and the Menshevik's failure to formulate an alternative to the policy of coalition resulted in a dramatic loss of support for the party. At the Second Congress of Soviets beginning in Petrograd in October 25, Mensheviks of all persuasions accounted for less than one-seventh of the delegates. All of them—Defensists, Revolutionary Defensists, and Internationalists—left the Congress to protest the Bolsheviks' seizing power (that very day) in the name of the soviet. The period of Menshevik leadership of the soviet had come to an end, although the reconstructed party in which the Internationalists held the majority continued its opposition to the Bolsheviks in the soviets.

With the outbreak of the Civil War, the Central Committee, led by Martov and Dan, declared itself against any cooperation with the antisoviet forces. It first advocated neutrality in the struggle between the Bolshevik-led soviets and the Socialist-Revolutionary (*see* Socialist-Revolutionary Party) government of the Volga region and, later, active support of the soviet forces against the White (*see* White Movement) generals and foreign intervention. Right-wing Mensheviks who disobeyed the directions of the Central Committee were expelled from the party. But the Mensheviks were allowed to play the role of an intrasoviet opposition only for a short while. On July 14, 1918, the party representatives were expelled from the soviets, and thereafter Menshevik organizations and newspapers were subjected to increasing repression. By 1922 most Mensheviks had emigrated or left the party, and the remaining loyalists were forced underground and were gradually imprisoned during the 1920s.

Ziva Galili y Garcia

Bibliography

Ascher, Abraham, ed. *The Mensheviks in the Russian Revolution.* 1976.
Bourgina, Anna. *Russian Social Democracy. The Menshevik Movement* (a Bibliography). 1968.
Brovkin, V. N. *The Mensheviks After October: Socialist Opposition and the Rise of the Bolshevik Dictatorship.* 1987.
Galili y Garcia, Z. *The Menshevik Leaders of the Petrograd Soviet: Social Realities and Political Strategies in the Russian Revolution of 1917.* 1989.
Getzler, Israel. *Martov.* 1967.
Haimson, Leopold H. *The Mensheviks.* 1974.
Ruban, N. V. *Oktiabr'skaia revoliutsiia i krakh menshevizma.* 1968.
Wade, Rex A. *The Russian Search for Peace.* 1969.

Rykov, Alekse Ivanovich (1881–1938). Rykov was a prominent Communist leader who took part in the creation of the new Soviet government in its early days and was Prime Minister of Russia from 1924 to 1930.

Rykov was born into a peasant family in Viatsk Province. He graduated from the Saratov Gymnasium and entered the Law Faculty at Kazan University in 1900. He was expelled from school and arrested for his political activities after which he decided to become a full-time revolutionary. In 1902 he became a member of the Saratov Committee of the Russian Social Democratic Workers' Party (see Russian Social Democratic Workers' Party [Bolshevik]) where he supported a Leninist (see I. V. Lenin) position. He was arrested in 1903, and upon release went abroad and met Lenin in Switzerland. He did party work in various Russian cities and in 1905 was a full Bolshevik (see Russian Social Democratic Workers' Party [Bolshevik]) to the Third Congress. Although he disagreed with Lenin on several issues, he became the chief spokesman for those party members who worked inside Russia, as opposed to the emigre leaders, and he was elected to the Central Committee (see Central Committee of the Russian Communist Party [Bolshevik]). During the 1905 Revolution (see Nineteen-Five Revolution) he became the head of the Moscow Committee after the December Uprising.

From 1906 to 1913 he did party work and was arrested and sent into exile several times. He became the spokesman for those who called themselves "conciliators," those who were in favor of reconciliation with the Mensheviks (see Russian Social Democratic Workers' Party [Menshevik]), though otherwise agreeing with Lenin. In 1913 he was sent into exile to Narym Krym where he remained until after the February Revolution*.

When Rykov returned to Moscow in April he was added to the Executive Committee of the Moscow Soviet*, and after the Bolsheviks achieved a majority in that body, he became a member of its nine man Presidium. At the party's Seventh Congress in August, he was elected to the Central Committee of the Bolshevik Party, and along with V. P. Nogin*, A. Lomov-Oppokov*, and N. I. Bukharin*, to direct all party work in the Moscow Oblast. At the Second All-Russian Congress of Soviets, directly after the October Seizure of Power*, Rykov was appointed People's Commissar of Internal Affairs. When he discovered, however, that Lenin had no intentions of inviting the other socialist parties into an all-socialist coalition government, Rykov resigned his ministerial post along with the other members of the Right, like V. P. Nogin, L. B. Kamenev*, and G. E. Zinoviev*.

In April 1918, when Lenin removed the Left Communists* from the Supreme Council of the National Economy*, he appointed Rykov as the head of that organization, a post he kept until the New Economic Policy* was introduced in 1921. From May 21 until Lenin's death, Rykov served as his assistant in the post of Vice Chairman of the Council of Labor and Defense and of the Council of People's Commissars*. He also returned to the Central Committee of the Russian Communist Party (Bolshevik) in 1920 and became a full member of the Politburo in 1922.

From 1924 to 1930 Rykov served as Chairman of the Council of People's Commissars, and with Bukharin, was one of the chief spokesman for the right wing of the party which favored the continuation of the New Economic Policy. When I. V. Stalin* began the First Five Year Plan, most members of the Right were demoted from their party and state posts. Rykov continued at minor posts in both institutions until his arrest on February 27, 1937. He and Bukharin were two of the chief defendents in the 1938 Show Trials. Rykov was executed on March 12, 1938. Like Bukharin, he was not rehabilitated until 1987.

Bibliography

Cohen, Stephan. *Bukharin and the Bolshevik Revolution.* 1973.
Daniels, Robert. *The Conscience of the Revolution.* 1960.
Haupt, Georges and Marie, Jean Jacques. *Makers of the Revolution.* 1974.
Medvedev, Roy A. *Let History Judge.* 1973.
Schapiro, Leonard. *The Origin of the Communist Autocracy.* 1955.

Ryskulov, Turar Ryskulovich (1894–1938). Ryskulov was a prominent Kazakh Jadid leader who was also a teacher and historian. He ultimately became a prominent Communist (*see* Russian Social Democratic Workers' Party [Bolshevik]).

Ryskulov was born into a rich nomadic family in the Semireche Region. His father had been sent to prison by the Tsarist government in the wake of the Kazakh (*see* Kazakhstan, Revolution in) uprising of 1869. Ryskulov himself turned to the struggle for national independence in 1916, and was also arrested for his activities. In 1917 after the February Revolution* he joined the Bolshevik Party (*see* Russian Social Democratic Workers' Party [Bolshevik]). In the spring of 1917, in conjunction with N. Chernishev, a Russian Bolshevik, he helped organize the "Revolutionary Union of Kirghiz Youth" in Merke. He was active in the Tashkent Soviet* and on March 12, 1917 took part in a meeting of those Kazakh leaders who rejected the Provisional Government*. In September 1917 he joined the Bolshevik party and was elected to soviet and party organs. At the end of 1917 he became Chairman of the Executive Committee of the Aulie-Ata District. At the First Congress of Soviets of the Turkestan Republic he was elected a member of the Central Executive Committee and People's Commissar of Health of the Turkestan Autonomous Soviet Socialist Republic. In 1919–1920 he became the Deputy Chairman of the Central Executive Committee and Chairman of the Extraordinary Anti-Famine Commission and the Extraordinary Commission for the Suppression of the Basmachi*.

Early in 1920 he was elected Chairman of the Turkestan Central Executive Committee or President of the Turkestan Republic. He was also a member of the Presidium of the Russian Communist party. Ryskulov was one of the founders of the Moslem Bureau of the Central Committee.

Ryskulov's career was blighted very early, however, because of his strong Pan-Turkic inclinations. Ryskulov ran afoul of the Soviet government and the Russian Communist party at the Fifth Regional Party Congress in early 1920 when he became one of the chief spokesman for changing the name of the Turkestan Communist party to Turkic Communist party, and of Turkestan itself to a Turkic Autonomous Republic (*see* Turkestan, Revolution). In analyzing this meeting Zenkovsky (p. 244) concluded that Ryskulov and the other Jadids* who had taken over the leadership of the Communist movement in Turkestan at the

Third Regional Party Congress in June 1919, had no interest in the class war, but wished to create a giant Central Asian Turkic state with its capital at Tashkent. Apparently the hope was that, not only the Turkic people of Russia, but also those of Afghanistan, China, Persia, and Turkey would be encouraged to join. The Central Committee of the Russian Communist Party (Bolshevik)* itself decided to take action. This was one of the major reasons for the creation of the Turkestan Commission appointed in January 1920, which, after due deliberation and some changes in personnel, met with the Turkestan Central Committee in September 1920 and removed Ryskulov and his sympathizers from the top positions in the government and the party. The Jadid communists were not purged in the 1920's, however, merely reassigned to lesser tasks. This was the first major leadership struggle under Soviet rule in Kazakhstan (*see* Kazakhstan, Revolution in) and Central Asia*, and the primary issue was Russian control over affairs in a national republic, and affirming the primacy of the Communist program over Pan-Turkism and local nationalism.

Ryskulov seemed to have made something of a comeback 1921 to 1924. He was recalled to Moscow in 1921 and became a member of the People's Commissariat of Nationalities, and soon thereafter Second Deputy People's Commissar. He achieved some notoriety at the Eleventh Congress of Turkestan Soviets in 1922 for publicly criticizing the land reforms in Turkestan, which did not follow Soviet laws, allotting the land instead to Central Asian tribes without any effort to consolidate holdings, though he tended to be more positive at the Twelfth Party Congress in 1923 where he argued that the reforms had put an end to national inequality in Turkestan. From 1923 to 1924 he was Chairman of the Council of People's Commissars or Prime Minister of the Turkestan Republic and a member of the Central Asian Bureau of the Russian Communist party and of the Bureau of the Central Committee of the Turkestan Communist party.

But his career slipped after 1926 and he began to devote himself more to scholarly and journalistic pursuits. From 1926 to 1937 he was head of the press department of the Caucasian Regional Commission of the Russian Communist party, chief editor of the Kazakh newspaper, *Enbekshi-Kazak,* lecturer at the Communist University of Eastern Peoples in Moscow, and author of several books on Kazakh political history. During the First Five-Year Plan, which caused severe hardship among the Kazakhs, who were primarily raising livestock, Ryskulov's historical works from the 1920s were roundly condemned for admitting that there had been no popular support for the Bolshevik Revolution among the Kazakh people. His *Kazakstan* would be reissued in 1935 with the newly prescribed thesis that there was overwhelming support for the Bolsheviks among the Kazakhs from 1917 to 1921.

In 1937 Ryskulov was arrested during the Purges and either died in jail or was executed. He was rehabilitated posthumously at the Twentieth Party Congress in 1956.

Bibliography

Bennigsen, Alexandre and Wimbush, S. Enders. *Muslim National Communism in the Soviet Union*. 1979.
Levytsky, Boryus. *The Stalinist Terror in the Thirties*. 1974.
Olcott, Martha Brill. *The Kazakhs*. 1987.
Park, Alexander G. *Bolshevism in Turkestan 1917–27*. 1957.
Zenkovsky, Serge. *Pan-Turkism and Islam*. 1960.

S

Sailors in 1917. One of the most lasting images of the momentous events of 1917 in Russia is that of the Cruiser *Aurora** anchored in the Neva below the Winter Palace, firing a famous signal salvo that ushered in the Great October Socialist Revolution. By most authoritative accounts, including those of V. I. Lenin* and L. D. Trotsky*, the Baltic sailors played a crucial role in the Bolshevik (*see* Russian Social Democratic Workers' Party [Bolshevik]) achievement of power in Petrograd in 1917 (*see* October Seizure of Power). The reasons for this are unique and influenced the whole course of the Russian Revolution.

The explanation for the radicalization of the Baltic sailors is complex but essential to understanding the peculiarities of events. Prewar St. Petersburg was a center of opposition to the authoritarian government, and the nearby training centers and bases of the Baltic Fleet were major targets for propaganda of the revolutionary parties—first, the People's Will; then the Socialist-Revolutionary Party* and the Russian Social Democratic Party. The Kronstadt naval training base (*see* the Kronstadt, 1917–1921), on an island less than twenty miles from the capital, became an especially fruitful environment. Frozen in half of the year, with a high proportion of enlisted men from a working-class background; living under extreme military conditions; and responsive to the conditions of a large lower-class population in the adjacent urban centers, sailors were particularly susceptible to dissident ideas and organization.

The existence of radical, antitsarist agitation in the Russian navy can be found as early as the Decembrist movement in the 1820s, but the real beginning of a concentrated effort to infiltrate a major military force began around 1880. The conservatism and loyalty of the majority of officers and men kept the danger of serious upheaval in hand until the revolutionary outburst of 1905 (*see* Nineteen-Five Revolution). The navy, because of disastrous defeats in the Pacific, suffered a serious decline in morale, which enabled the active revolutionaries to gain footholds on several ships and in shore units. The result was several major mutinies—the battleship *Potemkin* in May 1905 on the Black Sea and the naval bases of Kronstadt, Sveaborg, and Revel in the early spring and summer of 1906. These famous incidents, along with the post–1905 hasty rebuilding of the fleet, provided the fuel for further revolutionary activity.

The proximity of naval bases to industrial and urban areas was only one factor in the development of a revolutionary mood among the sailors. Most of the recruits were specially picked from the enlistment quotas for their literacy and experience in the mechanical skills needed in the modern navy. Moreover, the intensive training in the naval schools produced even more "conscious" workers for the Tsar's navy. On the other hand, the officer corps was divided between the older, traditional, and conservative types and the newer, technical, and liberal officers, a factor that would lead to difficulty in retaining a solid support for the regime in a time of adversity.

The Baltic Fleet during World War I* was particularly susceptible to revolutionary agitation and propaganda. Expanded in number (to almost 100,000), ice bound for several months, and kept mostly inactive behind mine fields, the Baltic sailors at the main bases of Helsingfors (Helsinki), Revel (Tallinn), and Kronstadt grew increasingly disenchanted with the progress of the war. By the autumn of 1916 Kronstadt especially was seething with discontent, and Admiral R. N. Viren, the port commander, considered it a hopeless situation. He felt that one push from Petrograd would turn all of the naval units against him and the government.

As Viren predicted, the demonstrations in Petrograd at the end of February caused explosive developments in the fleet. At Kronstadt, Viren and a number of other ranking officers perished at the hands of mutinous naval units who were inspired by men released from prisons and disciplinary units and by active revolutionaries—Socialist–Revolutionary, Bolshevik, and anarchists (*see* Anarchism). Helsingfors, the base of the larger, capital ships, witnessed even more violence, as Admiral A. I. Nepenin, the fleet commander, and other high officers met their end in the chaos of early March. The regular chain of authority was left shaken and practically destroyed by the upheaval.

The ability of sailor committees to take the initiative in establishing partial control or veto power over the officers was a major factor in the failure of the new Provisional Government* to reestablish decisive control. Under the left-leaning Admiral A. S. Maksimov, "elected" as commander by the sailors, the Baltic Fleet became a fertile ground for revolutionary agitators. Already in March a Bolshevik newspaper, directed especially to the sailors, was being printed in Kronstadt, and the next month an even more important Bolshevik forum, *Volna*, was released in Helsingfors. Under the influence of the unit committees, the local soviet organizations, and the sailors' assemblies, the Baltic Fleet was rapidly politicized in a leftward direction. By the end of April the Central Committee of the Baltic Fleet* (Tsentrobalt) was formed under the leadership of a Bolshevik sailor, Pavel E. Dybenko. All of the adherents to the revolutionary parties in the fleet tended to become more radical than those of the central organization.

Incidents in the fleet further exacerbated relations with government authority. One was the "declaration of independence" by the Kronstadt Soviet in May that created quite a critical stir in the Center and Right press in Petrograd. Although the Soviet eventually backed down, the resulting publicity and the obviously ineffectual "disciplining" of Kronstadt weakened the Provisional Government, at least in the eyes of the sailors of the whole fleet. Every week brought renewed demonstrations against the Provisional Government's policy of continuing the war. By early July these reached serious proportions and culminated in the July Days* crisis in which several thousand Kronstadt sailors and workers (*see* Workers in the Russian Revolution) marched under arms through the streets of Petrograd into several small skirmishes and a final showdown with loyal troops.

Although some units were disarmed and a few leaders arrested during the July demonstration, discipline was never really restored at the naval bases. In fact, an amazing conclusion to the July crisis found the new commander of the fleet, Admiral D. N. Vederevskii, under arrest for consorting with the sailors' committee in protesting a Provisional Government attempt to use naval ships to suppress the armed demonstration in Petrograd. Yet another change in command only weakened the governmental control that still existed.

Disturbances occurred in the fleets during the summer of 1917, spurred especially by agitators from the Baltic Fleet, but they were kept under control. A stronger command structure, a more active combat situation, and less political unrest on shore saved the Black Sea fleet and its main base of Sevastopol from control by the most radical elements.

By August–September the Bolsheviks and their left-wing Socialist-Revolutionary allies were in control of a large number of Baltic crews and shore units. Tsentrobalt was also firmly controlled by the Bolshevik organization. Lenin's awareness of this Bolshevik strength in the strategically important naval centers became a major factor in his insistence on seizing power. The sailors, experienced and well trained, truly devoted to the revolution, could provide the essential firepower and organizational talent for a successful coup d'etat. Much of the planning of the Bolshevik hierarchy and in the Military Revolutionary Committee hinged around making maximum use of the potential in the Baltic Fleet.

Yet that potential was not easy to realize. Many sailors had dispersed to the countryside, while others were deeply involved in local organizations. Logistically, it was not easy to move ships in 1917, given the mine fields, scarcity of fuel, and the condition of ships and units. Even the Cruiser *Aurora,* moored in the repair yards at the mouth of the Neva, had to be towed to its place of destiny by improvised tugboats. Only about 10,000 sailors participated in the October Seizure of Power in Petrograd and the vicinity, but that was a key element, probably of greater importance than the approximately 20,000 soldiers and workers who took part.

The most significant contribution of the sailors came later, however, in the defense of the new Soviet (*see* Soviets [Councils] of Workers', Soldiers', and

Peasant's Deputies) government. Pavel E. Dybenko* from Helsingfors, Fedor F. Raskolnikov from Kronstadt, and a number of other sailor–Bolsheviks and their allies provided crucial leadership and firepower in the initial skirmishes at Pulkovo Heights and Gatchina, in consolidating control of strategic rail lines, and in Moscow and other important centers. The sailors, along with the valuable arms from the warships and the Latvian Rifle Regiment, formed a vital nucleus of the Red Army* in 1918.

Norman Saul

Bibliography

Dybenko, P. E. *Iz nedr tsarskogo flota k velikomu oktiabriu*. 1928, 1958.

Getzler, Israel, *Kronstadt 1917–1921: The Fate of a Soviet Democracy*. 1983.

Izmailov, N. F., and Puskhov, A. S. *Tsentrobalt*. 1971.

Khesin, S. S. *Oktiabr'skaia revoliutsiia i flot*. 1971.

Mawdsley, Evan. *The Baltic Fleet in the Russian Revolution, 1917–21*. 1978.

Mordvinov, R. V. *Baltiiskie moriaki v podgotovke i provedenii velikoi oktiabr'skoi sotsialisticheskoi revoliutsii*. 1967.

Raskolnikov, F. F. *Kronstadt and Petrograd in 1917*. 1982.

Saul, Norman E. *Sailors in Revolt*. 1978.

Savinkov, Boris Viktorovich (1879–1925; pseudonym, V. Ropshin). Savinkov was one of the most prominent members of the Socialist-Revolutionary party* and an active terrorist. During the year 1917 he became acting Minister of War in the Provisional Government* in the cabinet called the Second Coalition under Prime Minister A. F. Kerensky.

Savinkov was born in the Ukraine (*see* Ukraine, Revolution in) in the city of Khar'kov. His father was a civil servant, an assistant prosecutor of the Khar'kov Military District. He was educated in a gymnasium in Warsaw, but was arrested in that city in 1879 for distributing revolutionary literature. In that same year he was expelled from St. Petersburg University for taking part in student demonstrations. At first he became a member of various social democratic organizations and in 1901 he took part in a St. Petersburg group called *Sotsialist* that followed G. V. Plekhanov*. He was exiled to Vologda in 1902 where he met E. K. Breshko-Breshkovskaia* who converted him to populism. He became a prominent member of the terrorist arm of the Socialist-Revolutionary party, the Battle Organization, and participated in the assassination of the Minister of the Interior, V. K. Plehve in 1904 and the Governor General of Moscow, Grand Duke S. Aleksandrovich in 1905. In 1922 he emigrated and began to write, producing two interesting novels based upon his experiences in the revolutionary movement, *The Pale Horse* in 1909 and *What Never Happened* in 1912.

Oliver Radkey described Savinkov's political views as proto-fascist (Radkey, *The Agrarian Foes of Bolshevism,* p. 315), emphasizing Savinkov's identification of himself with the state, his ambivalence toward the masses—contempt for them, while claiming to represent their best interests, and his addiction to violence, rationalized by patriotism and an avowed sympathy for the plight of the downtrodden masses. It is not surprising, therefore, that at the beginning of World War I* he urged an end to all revolutionary activity and enlisted in the French army. He returned to Russia in April 1917 and was appointed by the Provisional Government* to serve as Commissar to the Seventh Army on the Southwestern Front. When the Second Coalition Government was formed after the July Days* A. I. Kerensky appointed Savinkov Assistant Minister of War and, in effect, Acting Minister of War, since Kerensky himself became Prime Minister as well as Minister of War. Savinkov was instrumental in having General Kornilov (see Kornilov Revolt) appointed Commander in Chief, and became one of the chief advocates of a strong government, one that would supposedly be dominated by three men, Kerensky, Kornilov and Savinkov. He was opposed as a ministerial candidate by his own party, the Socialist-Revolutionaries. V. M. Chernov* opposed him because the two men hated each other, but he had also strayed far from the party line long before the Provisional Government came into being. Kerensky probably appointed Savinkov because of his reputation as a man of action, but also because his alienation from his own party made him a man above party considerations. Although in the end Savinkov opposed the Kornilov Revolt*, he was expelled from the Socialist-Revolutionary Party in September for failing to give a full accounting of his own role in the relations between Kornilov and Kerensky.

After the October Seizure of Power* Savinkov joined a succession of counterrevolutionary organizations. His argument in each case was to create a strong anti-Bolshevik front. The tsarist generals needed to strengthen their support among the rank and file by including known socialists in their leadership. At first he placed himself at the disposal of General Krasnov and his Cossacks*. Then he became a member of a group called the Civilian Council that collaborated with General Alekseev; and in March 1918 as a member of that group he helped to establish the Union for Defense of the Motherland and Freedom in Moscow. He took part in the counterrevolution in the Upper Volga Region and in the Ufa State Conference in September 1918, and in January 1919 he would represent Admiral A. V. Kolchak* at the Versailles Peace Conference. In January he moved westward and established contact with Marshal Joseph Pilsudski. He won Pilsudski's support for the creation of a Russian "Third" Army (that is, neither Red nor White) in Poland under a group created by Savinkov called the "Russian Political Committee." In exchange for Pilsudski's support Savinkov accepted Pilsudski's territorial ambitions in the Western Ukraine, and supported the movements for national autonomy in Belorussia (see Belorussia, Revolution in), the Ukraine, the Kuban, and Finland*. With the signing of the Treaty of Riga in March 1921 Savinkov lost Polish protection and by autumn ordered Savinkov to leave.

The end of the Civil War in Russia* and the beginning of the New Economic Policy* did not end Savinkov's intrigues. His Russian Political Committee was renamed the National Union for the Defense of Freedom and the Fatherland and moved its headquarters to Paris. In August 1924 he was arrested trying to enter

Russia illegally. He was tried for conspiracy by the Supreme Court of the USSR and sentenced to death, but the sentence was commuted to ten years in prison. Shortly thereafter he was allowed to publish a recantation explaining why he now recognized the Soviet Union. According to official Soviet reports he committed suicide by jumping from the fifth floor of Liubiank Prison in 1925.

In some respects his career illustrated the ambiguity of revolutionary careers. Savinkov was less a theorist than an artist and activist. His values were in many ways closer to the fascism of Mussolini than the populism of Victor Chernov. This made his shift from revolutionary terrorism to support for a succession of potential military dictators that much easier. In the end he was more successful as a novelist than as a revolutionary conspirator or leader.

Bibliography

Boris Savinkov pered voennoi kollegego vekhovnogo suda USSR. 1924.
Kenez, Peter. *Civil War in South Russia.* 1971.
Radkey, Oliver. *The Agrarian Foes of Bolshevism.* 1958.
Savinkov, Boris. *The Black Horse.* 1924.
———. *Memoirs of a Terrorist.* 1931.
———. *The Pale Horse.* 1917.

Semenov, George Mikhailovich (1890–1946). Semenov was an important Cossack* leader in the Transbaikal Region in Siberia during the Civil War in Russia*.

He was born in the village of Kuranzha near the Mongolian border. His father was a Cossack and his mother a Buriat Mongol. He was chiefly self-educated, though he seems to have had a wide range of interests. He entered the Cossack Military Academy in 1908 and graduated in 1911 as a junior officer. He was assigned to the First Verkhneudinsk Regiment of the Transbaikal Cossack Army. Because of his Mongol background, he was assigned to the Russian consulate at Urga where there was considerable daily contact with members of the Mongol community. In February 1914 he was assigned to the First Nerchinsk Regiment and acquired some experience in guerilla warfare fighting Chinese bandits.

When World War I* began Semenov's unit was sent to the Western Front. There he served under Baron Wrangel* and met Roman von Ungern Sternberg. He was transferred to the Third Verkhneudinsk Regiment where he was serving at the time of the February Revolution* and the overthrow of the Tsarist government. Semenov and Sternberg proposed to the Provisional Government* that they be allowed to go back to Transbaikalia and raise a volunteer Buriat Mongol army. He was appointed Commissar of the Irkutsk and Priamur Military Districts and Commander of the Mongol-Buriat Cavalry Regiment. When he arrived, however, his success in raising a volunteer army was limited. It was a period in which there was a proliferation of political parties and would be governments. Semenov was the only able commander in the Transbaikal Region, but his appeal was confined to the Buriats and Mongols, and some urban middle-class citizens, Britain and France, and Japanese interventionists, all of whom saw in him some hope for curbing the revolutionary unrest. He had little appeal for the mass of workers and peasants and did not seek their support. Semenov began to raise an army which he called the Special Manchurian Detachment and recruited or pressed into service about seven thousand men. Wrangel characterized Semenov as a good soldier, but said he had too much of a fondness for intrigue, and no scruples in the pursuit of his own ends. In many respects he did harm even to his own cause by his violence and ruthlessness.

From February to October 1918 he received support from the British and French and from March 1918 from the Japanese. When Irkutsk fell to the Czechs (*see* Czechoslovak Legion) in the summer, Semenov captured Chita and held it for two years with the help of the Czechs and the Japanese. Chita became the capital of his ''Provisional Government of Transbaikal'' and to all of the other governments in Siberia it became known as the ''Chita Stopper.'' Using Chita as a base of operations, Semenov stopped trains passing through and looted them when he was not raiding villages in the area. He was in control from Khabarovsk to Lake Baikal. Semenov justified all of his attacks by saying that those slaughtered were Bolsheviks, though holding up Czech and White (*see* White Movement) supply trains was a little more difficult to explain. Kolchak would have moved against Semenov except for his Japanese protectors. In the end Semenov did give luke warm support to Kolchak and more or less protected his rear against revolutionary uprisings.

Several months after Kolchak became Supreme Commander Semenov recognized his authority, though he often failed to comply with Kolchak's requests. Semenov changed his official rank in June 1918 from captain to field ataman and remained behind the lines when his troops were sent into battle. When Kolchak found himself in full retreat he transferred his title to Semenov in exchange for passage through Chita into exile for himself and his officers, many of whom became part of the Kappelite movement further east (*see* Siberia, Revolution in; Far Eastern Republic).

When the Japanese began their retreat from Siberia, in 1920, so also did Semenov. He found his way to Port Arthur by September. He briefly appeared in Vladivostok in June 1921 when the Kappelites seized power with Japanese approval. He demanded that they recognize his title as Commander in Chief, but the Vladivostok government asked him to leave. The Cossacks also rejected him and removed his title of field ataman on September 14, 1921. Semenov left Russia for exile.

Semenov found exile difficult, wandering from Korea to Japan, Shanghai, the United States, back to Japan, Peking, and finally Darien. The Japanese did not recruit Semenov when they created the puppet state of Manchuko in Siberia though they asked him to use his influence to encourage the Russian fascist movement in that area. When the Red Army entered Manchuria in August 1945, Semenov was arrested by the Russian State Security Police (NKVD), tried as an ''enemy of the Soviet people,'' and executed on August 30, 1946.

Bibliography

Luckett, Richard. *The White Generals*. 1971.
Morley, James. *The Japanese Thrust Into Siberia*. 1957.
Semenov, G. M. *O sebe*. 1938.
Sherevskii. *Razgrom semenovshchiny (aprel'-noiabr' 1920)*. 1966.
Smith, Canfield. *Vladivostok Under Red and White Rule*. 1975.
Stewart, George. *The White Armies of Russia*. 1933.
Varneck, Elena and Fisher, H. H. *The Testimony of Kolchak and Other Siberian Materials*. 1935.
White, John. *The Siberian Intervention*. 1950.

Shliapnikov, Aleksandr Gavrilovich (1885–1937). Shliapnikov was one of a number of personalities who was lifted from obscurity by the Russian Revolution and who was subsequently destroyed in its aftermath. Born to a lower-middle-class family from Murom in Vladimir Province, his father died when he was two years old, and his mother took in washing to support her four children. He was brought up as an Old Believer in the Pomory sect but was converted to socialism by the turn of the century. He became a lathe operator and worked at the Neva shipyard in St. Petersburg until he was blacklisted. In 1905 he became a Bolshevik (*see* Russian Social Democratic Workers' Party [Bolshevik]) and worked as an underground party worker. He was arrested numerous times and finally left Russia in 1908. In emigration he was deeply impressed by the workers' movement in the West and worked his way from factory to factory in France and Germany.

Shliapnikov returned to Russia in April 1914, and after a brief period of patriotism at the beginning of the World War I*, he became active in clandestine party activity for the St. Petersburg Party Committee. Throughout the war he was one of V. I. Lenin's* principle contacts and informants on the underground party organization in Russia. He traveled several times between Northern Europe and Russia and even made a trip to America where he spoke against the war. The outbreak of the February Revolution* found him in Petrograd. He participated in the forming of the Petrograd Soviet*, and he was elected to its Executive Committee. He was assigned to the task of arming the workers (*see* Workers in the Russian Revolution; Kollontai, A.M.) and participated in forming the Red Guards*. He was reticent about alienating the soldiers from the workers, but was on the left wing of the Bolsheviks. He favored the extension of the imperialistic war into a civil war and was hostile to the Provisional Government*. In mid-March he was ousted from the party committee by the return of I. V. Stalin* and L. B. Kamenev* but was one of the Bolshevik leaders who greeted Lenin on his return at the Finnish border on April 3, 1917. Although Shliapnikov had been a coopted member of the Central Committee (*see* Central Committee of the Russian Communist Party [Bolshevik]) during the war, a car accident prevented him from attending the April Party Conference, and he was not elected to the Central Committee again until the Seventh Congress in March 1918 and then as a candidate member. He subsequently became more active in trade union activities (*see* Trade Unions). He was elected President of the Petrograd Metal Workers' Union in April, and in July became chairman of the provisional committee of the All-Russian Metal Workers' Union. Largely due to his influence, this very important union was won over to Bolshevism and to the principle of industrial unionism. In June he took part in the Third All-Russian Trade Union Conference, and he was delegated as a Bolshevik representative on the All-Russian Central Council of Trade Unions.

During the July Days* his position on the Soviet Executive Committee enabled him to rescue Bolsheviks from arrest and imprisonment. He took part in the Moscow State Conference* and the Petrograd Democratic Conference* and was elected Vice-President of the conference of factory committees of the Petrograd industrial region. Shliapnikov was not enthusiastic about the proposed seizure of power by the Bolsheviks (*see* October Seizure of Power). Nonetheless, during the uprising he enlisted the support of the trade unions and mobilized the Petrograd Red Guard detachments. It was the Petrograd Metal Workers' Union that financed the Military Revolutionary Committee. He attended the Second Russian Congress of Soviets and was elected as a member of the Sovnarkom (*see* Council of Peoples' Commissars, 1917–1922) as People's Commissar of Labor. He was also appointed chairman of the commission supervising the planned evacuation of the capital due to the German threat. In his post as Labor Commissar he directed the struggle against sabotage and strikes by anti-Bolshevik workers and employees (*see* Left Communism; Kollontai, Aleksandra Mikhailovna).

Shliapnikov aligned himself with those Bolsheviks who wanted an all-socialist coalition government, but he remained silent on the Brest-Litovsk* controversy. On November 27 he cosigned with Lenin the statute on Workers' Control, which granted local factory committees complete control over the operation of each enterprise and authorized them to implement the government's economic policy (*see* Kollontai, Aleksandra Mikhailovna; Left Communism; Workers in the Russian Revolution). The factory committees were made the lowest organs of the trade unions and were ultimately brought under their control. But these experiments in workers' self-management were attempted under conditions of almost complete economic collapse. This situation was only intensified with the onset of the Civil War in Russia*. Shliapnikov resigned as Commissar of Labor in October 1918 and became involved with military missions. In early 1919 he became a critic of Lenin's policy of one-man management and on reliance on specialists in industry. He stated that specialists knew how to run industry only on a capitalistic basis and that socialist construction could be successful only if it relied upon the self-reliance (*samodeiatel'nost*) of the working masses. In March 1920 he submitted a set of theses to the Ninth Party Congress: "On the Question of the Inter-relationship of the RCP [Russian Communist Party], the Soviets, and the Industrial Unions" (*see* Russian Social Democratic Workers' Party [Bolshevik]; Soviets [Councils] of Workers', Soldiers', and Peasants' Deputies). This called for a greater degree of equality among the institutions, with each given its own area of responsibility, free from interference by the others.

By the autumn of 1920 the Workers' Opposition constituted itself as a separate faction, being composed of a coalition of unionists, former worker–Bolsheviks, and industrial administrators. The one exception was Aleksandra M. Kollontai, who had been Shliapnikov's lover during the war. Her pamphlet *Robochaia Oppozitsiia* broadened the attack on bureaucracy and authoritarianism in the party. Shliapnikov drafted the Workers' Opposition's contribution to the Trade Union Debate that was published in *Pravda** on January 25, 1921. This called for an All-Russian Congress of Producers that would concentrate the entire economic administration in the hands of the industrial unions. It would develop a single economic plan that would be implemented in each enterprise by elected Workers' Committees, which would involve all workers in the enterprise. The only alternative to the bureaucratic mass created by VSNKh (*see* Supreme Council of the National Economy) was to allow the workers' creative activity to flourish and to remove nonproletarian elements from positions of power. At the Tenth Party Congress in March 1921, in the wake of the Kronstadt Revolt (*see* Kronstadt, 1917–1921) and the general crisis of War Communism*, the party rallied to Lenin and his call to put the lid on opposition. After much lively debate between the main protagonists, the congress passed all of Lenin's resolutions including two direct attacks on Shliapnikov and the opposition. "On Party Unity" and "On Anarcho-Syndicalist Deviation" put constraints on factional activity in the party and damned Shliapnikov's position as a deviation from communism. But an example of Lenin's genius was his support for Shliapnikov's election to the Central Committee, with the provision that he straighten out the deviation in the context of a theoretical discussion.

Following the congress, Shliapnikov continued to criticize party policies as the introduction of the New Economic Policy* (NEP) brought new hardships for the workers. In May 1922, following the rejection of the list of candidates of the Central Committee of the Metal Workers' Union by the party faction, the Central Committee ignored this and appointed its own candidates. Incensed by this assault on his strongest power base, Shliapnikov submitted his resignation to the Central Committee. It was refused, but in July Lenin wanted Shliapnikov out. At a cell meeting in Moscow, Shliapnikov criticized the concessions that VSNKh was making to private capitalists and decried the position of the workers in these enterprises. Lenin convened a joint session of the Central Committee members and candidates with the Control Commission but failed to obtain the necessary two-thirds vote to expel Shliapnikov from the party.

In February 1922 Shliapnikov and Kollontai submitted their "Statement of the Twenty-two" to the Comintern (*see* Communist International), which detailed the harassment of oppositionists by the party. At the Eleventh Party Congress in March, Shliapnikov once again barely escaped expulsion. But at the Fifth Congress of the Metal Workers' Union Shliapnikov and Lenin battled again, culminating in Shliapnikov's expulsion from the presidium of the congress.

Defeated in his party and in his union, Shliapnikov became a bitter man. He disliked all of the contenders in the party struggles of the 1920s but was repeatedly linked to the oppositions and was forced into self-criticisms in 1926 and 1930. He held minor posts with the Metal Import Trust and with the economic organs. But most of his time was spent working on the history of 1917. He wrote numerous articles and the major four-volume study *The Year 1917 (semnadtsatyi god)*. Part narrative and part memoir, *1917* was an honest attempt to chart the events and the actors of the Russian Revolution. In his historical writing he championed the ideals of 1917 and boldly chronicled the diversity of opinions in the parties and social classes. He defied the growing Stalinist dogma of the unity of the party and the working class and revealed the complex contradictions and mistakes that were made.

In 1933 Shliapnikov was expelled from the party as a "degenerate." He was arrested the following year and was "investigated" for three years but was never brought to trial. In 1935 he was reported to be sick and deaf in prison in Verkhne Uralsk. He was implicated in the "Trotskyite-Zinovievite Terrorist Center" (*see* Trotsky, LevDavidovich; Zinoviev, Grigorii Evseevich) during the show trial of August 1936 but was never brought to confess. He was shot in September 1937.

Shliapnikov was never able to make the transition from proletarian revolutionary to party functionary and bureaucrat. He was rehabilitated by the Public Prosecutor's office in 1956 but was denied posthumous reinstatement in the party. His role in the revolution is discussed honestly by Soviet historians, but no honest attempt has yet been made to treat the Workers' Opposition, which is still condemned as a serious deviation. Perhaps the events in Poland foreshadow a new restlessness of the workers in the socialist countries, and Shliapnikov's legacy will be vindicated.

Barry Smirnoff

Bibliography

Bettleheim, Charles. *Les Luttes de Classes en URSS, lere Periode 1917–1923*. 1974.

Bunyan, James. *The Origin of Forced Labor in the Soviet State, 1917–1921: Documents and Materials*. 1967.

Daniels, Robert V. *The Conscience of the Revolution*. 1969.

Haupt, Georges and Marie, Jean-Jacques. *Makers of the Russian Revolution*. 1974.

Kollontai, Aleksandra. *Rabochaia Oppozitsiia*. 1921.

Schapiro, Leonard. *Origins of the Communist Autocracy*. 1956.

Shelavin, K. *Robochaia Oppozitsiia*. 1930.

Shliapnikov, A. G. *Les Syndicate Russes*. 1921.

———. *Platforma Shliapnikova i Medvedeva*. 1927.

———. *Semnadtsatyi god*. 1925.

Sorenson, Jay. *The Life and Death of Soviet Trade Unionism, 1917–1928*. 1969.

Zlobina, V. M. *Bor'ba Partii Bol'shevikov Protiv Melko-burzhuaz nogo Vliyaniya na Rabochii Klass v Pervye Gody Nepa (1921–1925)*. 1975.

Zorky, Mark S. *Rabochaia Oppozitsia, Materiali i Dokumenty, 1920–1926*. 1926.

Shumiatskii, Boris Zakharovich (1886–1943; pseudonym Andrei Chervonnyi). Shumiatskii was one of the most important Bolshevik (*see* Russian Social Democratic Workers' Party [Bolshevik]) leaders in Siberia during the revolution and Civil War in Russia*.

Shumiatskii was born in Verhneudinsk in a large working class family. He spent his early years in a village near Kansk, Enisei Province. In 1897 his family moved to Chita and shortly thereafter Shumiatskii moved to Chita and obtained work there in a railroad workshop. His work for the local branch of the Russian Social Democratic Workers' Party and local strikes led to his dismissal and arrest. After the split in the Russian Social Democratic Workers' Party, Shumiatskii sided with the Bolshevik faction. He moved on to Irkutsk and then Krasnoiarsk continuing his work with the railway workers in both cities. In Krasnoiarsk he met M. S. Uritskii* and began to read Marx, Engels and V. I. Lenin*. During the 1905 Revolution (*see* Nineteen-Five Revolution) a Krasnoiarsk Soviet was created and Shumiatskii was elected to its Executive Committee. When the revolution was crushed in January 1906 Shumiatskii was arrested, but escaped and took up different jobs in a succession of cities in Siberia, including Cheliabinsk, Kurgan, Irkutsk, Sliudanka, and also in Kharbin, Vladivostok and for a time in South America. With the arrival of World War I* Shumiatskii, who was once again in prison in Krasnoiarsk, was compelled to serve along with many other political prisoners in the Fourteenth Siberian Reserve Regiment.

The February Revolution* opened up new opportunities for experienced revolutionary leaders like Shumiatskii. He had taken part in the formation of a Military-Socialist Union in 1916 in Narym which brought together revolutionaries from all political parties into a single organization. After the February Revolution the Military-Socialist Union formed a new Krasnoiarsk Soviet on March 5 and Shumiatskii served on its Executive Committee, on the staff of its newspaper, and in a central Bureau of Trade Unions formed at about the same time to mobilize all of the local trade unions. Shumiatskii belonged to a minority group among the Siberian Bolsheviks who opposed the majority Siberian Zimmerwaldists and followed Lenin's policy of trying to transform the "capitalist war" into a proletarian revolution. Shumiatskii's group formed a Central Siberian Bureau to carry out their goals and by the end of June they had begun to form their own Leninist Bolshevik Party in Tomsk with several other Siberian city organizations following suit before the end of that month. Shumiatskii himself was a delegate to the First All-Russian Congress of Soviets (*see* Soviets) in June 1917 where he was elected to its Central Executive Committee* and he attended the Sixth Congress of the Russian Communist Party in July. He organized the first Bolshevik book publishing house in Krasnoiarsk, *Pristup* (Assault), published a Bolshevik newspaper there, *Siberskaia Pravda* (Siberian Truth), and took part in editing the various incarnations of the Bolshevik newspaper *Pravda** in Petrograd, becoming its chief editor by September.

Lenin sent Shumiatskii back to Siberia in October to help prepare the way for the Soviet seizure of power. The only cities where the Bolsheviks did not control the soviets were Novonikolaevsk and Irkutsk. Shumiatskii took part in the First All-Siberian Congress of Soviets (October 29–November 6) which was called by the Central Siberian Bureau (*Centrosibir*) of the Bolshevik party. The Central Committee of the Bolshevik party had already given Shumiatskii responsibility for Eastern Siberia, and N. N. Iakovlev and V. N. Iakovlev responsibility for Western Siberia. The Central Siberian Bureau was successful in gaining control over most of the Soviets in Siberia by collaborating with other political parties, and the Soviets were able, in most cases, to seize power in the Siberian cities. But Shumiatskii opposed the Treaty of Brest-Litovsk* and, as a result, was removed from the chairmanship of Central Siberian Bureau at the Second All-Siberian Congress of Soviets in February 1918.

In the summer of 1918 the White Movement* began to sweep the Soviets out of power in Siberia and the Bolsheviks had to go underground. Shumiatskii was again in opposition to the Bolshevik leadership on the question of strategy. He urged the Bolsheviks to collaborate with the Mensheviks (*see* Russian Social Democratic Workers' Party [Menshevik]) and the Socialist-Revolutionaries (*see* Socialist-Revolutionary Party) in underground oppositions to the Whites. In the spring of 1919 his point of view was publicly condemned in the pages of *Pravda* and Shumiatskii reluctantly accepted Lenin's dictates.

He continued to be used as a Bolshevik troubleshooter in Siberia, and when the Far Eastern Republic* was created Shumiatskii was sent to Verhneudinsk to become Prime Minister and Foreign Minister of the new entity. In that capacity he was successful in negotiating a truce with the Japanese that spelled out the terms of their withdrawal and their support for Semenov. He also engaged in negotiations with China, laying the foundations for future relations between the Soviet Union and Mongolia. By August 1920 his career was again in an upswing and he was appointed to the Siberian Revolutionary Committee charged with supervising the restoration of soviet power in Siberia. He was a member of the Bolshevik Far Eastern Bureau* under the Central Siberian Bureau and in January 1921 as the Chief Political Officer of the Soviet Fifth Army was charged with the interrogation of Semenov's partner, Baron von Ungern-Sternberg. In the following month he was appointed chief of the Far Eastern Secretariat of the Communist International*, becoming in effect Regional Chief for Comintern affairs in Siberia. In that capacity he organized the Congress of Workers of the Far East in the summer of 1921.

Shumiatskii's background and experience made him one of the Bolshevik's most trusted leaders in Far Eastern affairs. From 1922–1925 Shumiatskii served as Soviet ambassador to Persia. His star continued to rise with the growing strength of I. V. Stalin* and in 1925 he joined V. M. Molotov* in a mission to Leningrad (formerly Petrograd) to root out G. E. Zinoviev's* supporters and put S. M. Kirov* in charge. At the same time he became head of the publishing house, *Priboi* (Surf). In 1926 Shumiatskii was appointed Rector of the Communist University of Toilers of the East, designed to train party workers and Asian Bolshevik activists, and he became chief editor of the major Bolshevik publication for these cadres, *Revolutsionnyi vostok* (Revolutionary East). In 1928 he became a member of the party's Central Asian Bureau, and at the end of the year returned to Moscow to become chief editor of the *Sibir'skaia sovetskaia entsiklopediia* (Soviet Historical Encyclopedia). After 1930 Shumiatskii became chief of the Soviet cinema industry charged with its "Stalinization". In April 1937 he disappeared, and his biographers list him as a victim of "illegal repression." He has been posthumously rehabilitated.

Bibliography

Agalakov, V. T. *Sovety Sibiri 1918–29*. 1924.
Bagaev, Boris. *Boris Shumiatskii*. 1974.
Maksakov, V. and Turuonov. *Khronika grazhdanskoi voiny v Sibiri (1917–18)*. 1926.
Shishkin, V. I. *Revoliutsionnye komitety Sibir v gody grazhdanskoi voiny, avgust 1919-mart 1921 g.*. 1978.
Shumiatskii, B. Z. *The Aims of the Bolsheviks*. 1919.
———. *Bor'ba za russkii Dal'nii Vostok*. 1922.
———. *Sibir' na putiakh k Oktiabriu*. 1927.
Smith, Canfield. *Vladivostok under Red and White Rule*. 1975.
Snow, Rusell. *The Bolsheviks in Siberia*. 1977.

Siberia, Revolution in. Siberia was Russia's frontier society at the time of the October Seizure of Power*. Because of the differences between Siberia and European Russia, the course of the revolution was quite different in the two areas, despite superficial similarities. In many ways events in Siberia had a crucial bearing on the outcome of the revolution in European Russia.

On the eve of revolution and civil war Siberia was a complex society in transition, and the process of change was accelerated by the impact of World War I*. It was an area of boundless untapped natural resources. Although almost twice the size of European Russia, Siberia had six percent of the population of the Russian Empire and was responsible for only 3.5 percent of the industrial production. However, with the opening of the Trans-Siberian Railway at the end of the nineteenth-century millions of Russian and Ukrainian (*see* Ukraine, Revolution in) peasants migrated into this once forbidden region, transforming its western portions into rich, productive farmlands. By 1917 Western Siberia had become the single most important part of the Empire still in Russian hands because it produced seventeen percent of the country's yield of grain for that year. The native population, which was only about twenty-seven percent of the population of Siberia, had been completely overwhelmed by the influx of European Russians. The European Russians had begun their encroachments upon the lands lying closest to the railroad, and the Buriat Mongols situated on both side of Lake Baikal suffered the most, especially during the Revolution and Civil War in Russia. All told, the European population increased in size, not only in the countryside, but also in the large cities, many of which increased their population two, three, and even ten times between 1897 and 1917. These cities, Omsk, Irkutsk, Tomsk, Krasnoiarsk and Vladivostov had populations ranging from 70,000 to 130,000, mostly Russian and not counting the large military garrisons to be found in each.

The social, economic, and national structure of Siberia was, therefore, quite diverse. Despite the impressive growth of some Siberian cities, only about ten percent of the population could be considered city dwellers, and most of the city dwellers were Russian. Even Soviet scholars cannot identify more than 300,000 people who could be considered proletarians, and many of those belonged to different nationalities, some of them, like the Chinese railway workers, neither native nor Russian. There were also by 1917 some 172,000 members of the Siberian Cossack Host (*see* Cossacks), a military force to be reckoned with. Moving from West to North and East the percentage of non-Russians in each area tended to increase. In Zabaikal Province it was 31.8 percent, in Akmolinsk 42.1, in Semipalitinsk eighty percent, in Iakutsk ninety-four percent. Also in some industries the percentage of native population was quite high. In the Lena Goldfields it was fifty percent. The bulk of the population was rural, many nomadic, and only about ten percent of the population could be considered urban by any stretch of the imagination. Essentially Siberia was an agrarian hinterland, supplying, not only grain, but also ninety percent of the meat consumed in European Russia. But the cities were the tail that wagged the dog. The concentration of Slavic population in the cities, because it included a high percentage of political prisoners, war prisoners, and railway workers, tended to make politics in those cities much more radical than in the cities of European Russia.

Despite the significant social and economic differences between Siberia and European Russia, the pattern of revolutionary events in Siberian cities in 1917 was remarkably similar to those in Petrograd and Moscow, perhaps because the Slavs in those cities tended to follow the lead of Moscow and Petrograd. News of the February Revolution* resulted in a remarkably peaceful abdication of authority by Tsarist officials, who, in many cases actually helped Socialist exiles and public figures form various kinds of committees of public safety. Soviets of soldiers', workers' and, in some cases, peasants' deputies were created in all of the major cities, and in the larger villages. By the end of the first week in March a revolutionary order, similar to that in the country at large had been established, with one significant difference. In Siberia all of the Socialist exiles without differentiation by party took part in forming and running the various organs of local provisional government, and all of the politically conscious people looked towards Petrograd and gauged their own activities both by what they perceived to be happening in the capital and their own understanding of Siberian conditions.

From the outset the Provisional Government simply replaced tsarist officials with appointments of its own without radically restructuring the tsarist administrative machinery. Although the Provisional Government had little popular support in Siberia, it did have the power of the purse. The Provisional Government first replaced the provisional governors, announced that existing laws would remain in effect, and then sent several members of the State Duma (*see* Duma and the Revolution) out to survey the situation, such as I. P. Laptev to Omsk, E. L. Zubashev to Tomsk and Krasnoiarsk, P. I. Preobrazhenskii to Irkutsk and N. A. Rusanov to Transbaikalia and the Far East. These emissaries were given the title "Commissars," and they returned to report that there was strong sentiment for regional autonomy in the various new representative bodies springing up all over Siberia. In an attempt to create some sympathetic organs of local self-government the Provisional Government extended the elective bodies known as zemstvos to Siberia by a decree of June 17, 1917. Neither the zemstvos nor the commissars were adequate, however, to the task of controlling or directing political action in Siberia.

There was strong sentiment for a democratic system among the political activists in Siberia, but it was tinged with a desire for Siberian autonomy, and, therefore, tended to deprive itself of the necessary military and financial support it might have received from the Provisional Government. As a result the political organizations created by the non-Bolshevik parties in Siberia tended to drift in a void between the struggling Provisional Government in Petrograd and the emerging menace of the small but militant local Bolshevik movement. The movement of revolution in the larger cities of Siberia tended to follow the pattern of events in European Russia—the April Crisis*, the July Days*, the Kornilov affair*, and the October Seizure of Power* by the Bolsheviks in the name of the Soviets, all had repercussions in Siberia. But, uniquely Siberian conditions and geopolitics were also significant factors in the course of the revolution. In Western Siberia for example there was strong regional hostility to any attempt by the Provisional Government to extend its control over this area, and all the revolutionary leaders had to take this sentiment into account in formulating their programs. In Eastern Siberia there was less sentiment for autonomy, but equally strong hostility toward the Provisional Government. Here the militant antiwar Left Socialists dominated the entire revolutionary infrastructure, and virtually engineered a socialist revolution in the city of Krasnoiarsk during the spring of 1917. Irkutsk, on the other hand, had a fairly sizeable middle-class and became the stronghold of pro-Provisional Government sentiment in Siberia and here the Bolsheviks encountered stiff military resistance during the takeover late in 1917.

Resistance to the increasing strength of the Bolshevik party and the soviets of Siberian cities was organized by the Siberian Regionalists (*Oblastniki*), who created a Siberian Regional (*Oblast*) Bureau in May 1917 to mobilize the anti-Bolshevik forces. An All-Siberian Congress of Siberian Regionalists met on October 8 in Omsk and all the political parties were represented except the two that had taken a stand against regionalism, the Bolsheviks and the Constitutional Democratic Party-Cadets*. The majority, some fifty-two percent, came from the Socialist-Revolutionary Party*. They declared Siberia autonomous and announced that a Siberian Regional Duma* was to be created to become the new government of the Siberian state, and it would call a Siberian Constituent Assembly early in 1918.

The first phase in the struggle for power in Siberia took place between the Siberian Soviets, who stood for the "statist" idea, that is preservation of some form of a centralized Russian state, and the Regionalists, who sought regional autonomy. The Soviets were increasingly dominated by the Bolsheviks and were clearly winning the struggle up to February 1918. The Regionalists were rather weak and disunited and losing ground to the Soviets during the same period.

Soviet sources estimate the Bolsheviks were weak in number at the time of the February Revolution*, only about 24,000 people, but only a small percentage of those were in Siberia, and an even smaller percentage chose to stay in Siberia after the February Revolution. There was some flow back, and Soviet sources estimate that of the total of 200,000 party members claimed by the Bolsheviks in October 1917, only 12,000 were in Siberia. At the beginning of 1917 the Bolsheviks were not very popular or well-known in Siberia except in the cities which served as rail heads. Bolshevik success in winning control of the Siberian Soviets was a result of the efforts of the Siberian Regional Bureau* of the Bolshevik Party created in Krasnoiarsk at the end of March 1917 to orchestrate the efforts of its scattered organizations. Essentially they employed the same strategies that served them so well in European Russia, remaining aloof from the Provisional Government and exploiting its failures and weaknesses and those of the political parties that participated in it, the creation of strong cadres and organizational structures, and greater attention to the demands of local peasant and workers groups in the cities. In Siberia, however, it was also a result of the efforts of such leaders as B. Z. Shumiatskii* to collaborate with Leftists from other political parties in bringing about Soviet power. Throughout the late summer and autumn the Socialist leadership of the local organs of government and the Soviets became increasingly aware of the polarization of European Russia. With the exception of Irkutsk most of the Socialists were anti-war Mensheviks (see Russian Social Democratic Workers' Party [Menshevik]), Bolsheviks (see Russian Social Democratic Workers' Party [Bolshevik]), and Left Socialist-Revolutionaries (see Left Socialist-Revolutionary Party) who supported the idea of a Soviet seizure of power. In most Siberian cities the Soviets would have been able to take formal control almost from the first days of the revolution. When the transfer did take place during the winter of 1917 amidst a great deal of confusion about what was happening in the center, it was almost effortless.

The First All-Siberian Congress of Soviets took place between October 29 and November 6, 1917 in Irkutsk under the supervision of V. I. Lenin's* special emissary, the Siberian B. Z. Shumiatskii*. There were 129 delegates representing all of the Soviets in Siberia. Among the representatives were sixty-four Bolsheviks, thirty-five Left Socialist-Revolutionaries, ten Mensheviks and a handful of Right Socialist-Revolutionaries and Right Mensheviks. A Central Executive Committee for the Soviets of Siberia* (Tsentrosibir') was elected which included three Bolsheviks and two Left Socialist-Revolutionaries. It would last until August 28, 1918.

The Regionalists responded to the October Seizure of Power by calling an emergency meeting in Tomsk, which announced a meeting of the Siberian Regional Duma in January and the election of a Siberian Constituent Assembly in March. When the Tomsk Soviet dissolved its congress on January 26, the Regionalists met secretly and created their own Provisional Government of an Autonomous Siberia, though that body had to move its headquarters almost immediately to Harbin.

In some localities the resistance to Soviet power was strong. In Irkutsk the Menshevik-Right Socialist-Revolutionary coalition refused to recognize the Bolshevik government and the city had to be taken by force in December 1917, using military forces from Tomsk and Krasnoiarsk. The transfer of power to the Soviets, which continued throughout the winter of 1917–18 was greatly facilitated by the return of Siberian troops, most of which were armed, from the various fronts. The Bolshevik government in Petrograd, anxious to establish control over the rich grain stores in Western Siberia, sent into Cheka (*see* All-Russian Extraordinary Commission) units under S. Lazo, who became Commissar of Military Affairs in the new government, to assist local Bolsheviks in ensuring Soviet control over society. By March 1918 the Soviet seizure of power in Siberia was virtually complete in the major cities and larger villages, but already the forces of counterrevolution and foreign intervention were at work, and would soon transform the revolution in Siberia into a terrible and bloody civil war.

The Second All-Siberian Congress of Soviets met from February 16–26, 1918 and announced the creation of a Soviet Government of Siberia. B. Z. Shumiatskii, however, who had led the struggle, would not enjoy the fruit of his labors because he had opposed the Treaty of Brest-Litovsk*. He was recalled and N. N. Iakovlev (often called the Lenin of Siberia), took his place.

The uprising of the Czechoslovak Legion* on the Trans-Siberian Railway in May 1918 opened the second phase in the revolution in Siberia, and the Siberian Soviets would lose power almost as rapidly as they had gained it. The second was marked by the rise and fall of a left-democratic Regionalist movement. In the summer of 1918 political groups opposed to the Soviet seizure of power began to regroup in northern Russia, the Baltic Region, the Ukraine, and Siberia. The Czechoslovak uprising and the intervention by Japan and the United States in Vladivostok provided the opportunity for the counterrevolution to gain some momentum and search for identity because it served the umbilical cord of Siberia—the railroad—and placed military power in the hands of forces that tended to favor anti-Bolshevik political movements.

New anti-Bolshevik governments began to emerge, dominated mostly by Socialist-Revolutionaries. In May the so-called Committee of Members of the Constituent Assembly (*Komuch*) was formed in Samara with Czech help. When the Japanese and American forces intervened in Vladivostok, Derber and members of his Siberian Provisional Government of Autonomous Siberia moved to that city. At the beginning of June 1918 a West Siberian Commissariat of the Provisional Siberian Government was created in Novonikolaevsk. At the end of June five members—they called themselves the Cabinet of Five—of the original Provisional Government of an Autonomous Siberia formed the so-called Provisional Government of Siberia in Omsk and absorbed the West Siberian Commissariat*. On July 4, 1918 it would declare the independence of Siberia.

Yet none of these counterrevolutionary organizations had much staying power. The West Siberian Commissariat retained most of the social reforms enacted by the Soviets, except for the nationalization of businesses and banks. It retained the Soviets, though not as governing bodies, and proclaimed civil liberties, free trade, local self-government and democratic elections.

The third phase in the development of the revolution in Siberia extended from the formation of the Provisional Government of Siberia in Omsk in June to the Creation of Admiral A. V. Kolchak's* post as Supreme Ruler in November. It was still primarily a Regionalist movement, but much more conservative than the preceding regime, and gradually gravitating toward the notion of a strong authoritarian centralized state. The Provisional Government of Siberia in Omsk, for example, was much more conservative than the West Siberian Commissariat and abolished nationalization of land and business, abolished the Soviets and restricted the activities of labor organizations. Though originally derived from Derber's Siberian Provisional Government of Autonomous Siberia, it competed with Derber, who was in power in Vladivostok, in its claims to govern all of Siberia. The regionalist movement was, however, destroyed by the Ufa State Conference in September of 1918 where all of these bodies were compelled to submit to the idea of an All-Russian Provisional Government under the Directory* and in November to Kolchak's dictatorship.

Despite the opportunities provided by the Czechoslovak uprising and Allied intervention the Siberian Regionalists were too divided by internal political differences and the absence of any real control over the instruments of power to create a democratic alternative to Soviet power. Although Siberian cities fell one by one to the Whites (*see* the White Movement) and the victories for Soviet power seemed to have been lost as quickly as they had been won, the Soviet movement simply went underground, deriving its staying power from the existence of a Soviet state in Great Russia. On December 17, 1918 the new Siberian Bureau* of the Russian Communist Party (Bolshevik) was formed to direct underground activity and partisan warfare in the areas seized by the White forces and interventionists. Its efforts were complicated by the decision made by the United States and Japan to intervene by landing in Vladivostok in the spring of 1918, a decision which posed the threat of Japanese expansion into Siberia, increased support for such anti-Bolsheviks as the Cossack leader G. M. Semenov* in Chita and possibly war between the new Soviet state and Japan. In the summer of 1919 the Soviet Fifth Army began its final offensive against Kolchak and the Third Siberian Conference of the Russian Communist Party (Bolshevik) met in Omsk and elected the Siberian Regional Underground Committee of the

Russian Communist party (Bolshevik) to organize new Soviet institutions in areas where the White forces were driven out.

The fourth and final phase in the revolution in Siberia was marked by the gradual advance of the Red Army from the West and the eventual defeat of all Regionalists with the accompanying restoration of Siberia to the Russian state. Along the way, in order to make the restoration of Siberia more palatable to the Japanese interventionists, the Bolsheviks created a semi-autonomous puppet state called the Far Eastern Republic* to be located between the Japanese and Soviet Russia. On March 3, 1920 the Far Eastern Bureau of the Bolshevik Party was created as an institution subordinate to the Siberian Bureau in order to create a Far Eastern Republic as a puppet buffer state to placate the Japanese until they left Siberia. After the Japanese withdrew in the summer of 1922 the Far Eastern Republic was absorbed into the Union of Soviet Socialist Republics.

Russel Snow

Bibliography

Bradley, John. *Civil War in Russia*. 1975.
Dotsenko, Paul. *The Struggle for a Democracy in Siberia 1917–20*. 1983.
Guins, G. S. *Sibir', soiuzniki, i Kolchak*. vols. 1921.
Istoriia Sibir'. 1968.
Safronov, V. *Oktiabr' v Sibiri*. 1962.
Smith, Canfield. *Vladivostok Under Red and White Rule*. 1975.
Snow, Russel. *The Bolsheviks in Siberia*. 1977.
Spirin, L. M. *Klassy i parii v grazhdanskoi voine v Rossii* (1917–1920gg). 1968.
Svetachev, M. I. *Imperialisticheskaia interventsiia v Sibiri i na Dal'nem Vostoke (1918–22)*. 1983.
Zhurov, Iu. V. and Bozehnko. *Souiz rabochego klassa i krest'ianstva Sibiri v period postroenie sotsializma (1917–1937 gg)*. 1978.

Siberian Bureau of the Central Committee of the Russian Communist Party (Sibbiuro). The Siberian Bureau was created on December 17, 1918 to supervise the efforts of the Russian Communist Party (*see* Russian Social Democratic Workers' Party [Bolshevik]) to restore Soviet power in Siberia during the Civil War in Russia*. The members of the Siberian Bureau were appointed by the Central Committee of the Russian Communist Party (Bolshevik)* and included prominent Communist leaders from Siberia who were active with the Soviet Fifth Army of the Eastern Front, with partisan and underground movement in Siberia, and members of the Siberian Revolutionary Military Council. Among its members were V. N. Iakovleva*, B. Z. Shumiatskii* and M. Iaroslavskii (*see* Gubel'man, M. I.) The *Sibbiuro* served as an executive committee for Communist party work in Siberia, establishing ties to local Communist groups, supervising and coordinating their efforts, and providing logistical, financial and propaganda services. In the spring of 1919, during the offensive of the White army (*see* White Movement) under Admiral A. V. Kolchak*, its work was temporarily transferred to the Siberian Regional Underground Committee appointed by the Third Siberian Conference of the Russian Communist Party (Bolshevik) in March 1919 in Omsk. When the Soviet Fifth Army began its offensive in the summer of 1919, the *Sibbiuro* resumed its original role. In March 1920 the Siberian Bureau created a subdivision to coordinate activities in the new and nominally independent Far Eastern Republic. This organization was called The Far Eastern Bureau and it became an independent committee under the Central Committee on August 13, 1920. Until May 1924 the Siberian Bureau functioned as the party's highest executive body in Western Siberia. In May 1924 at the First Siberian Regional Party Conference its functions were transferred to the Regional Committee of the Russian Communist Party of Siberia.

Bibliography

Istoriia Sibiri. IV. 1968.

Siberian Regional Duma (also known by the Russian term for region as The Siberian Oblast' Duma). The umbrella organization for the varied counterrevolutionary regional governments in Siberia (*see* Siberia, Revolution in) during the Civil War in Russia*.

The Siberian Regional Duma was created in the first half of October 1917 as a provisional organization designed to bring together representatives of the Russian Socialist-Revolutionary Party*, the Mensheviks (*see* Russian Social Democratic Workers' Party [Menshevik]) and the Siberian Regionalists* to oppose the Soviet movement in Siberia. The Socialist-Revolutionaries had a bare majority. After the October Seizure of Power* by the Soviets, the Siberian Regionalists called an Extraordinary Congress in Tomsk in December 1917. The congress called for the election of a Siberian Constituent Assembly by March 1918. Although the Tomsk Soviet of Workers' and Soldiers' Deputies forcibly dissolved the Congress of Siberian Regionalists on orders from the Central Executive Committee of the Soviets of Siberia* (*Tsentrosibir*), the leaders of the Siberian Regional Duma movement continued to claim jurisdiction over all of Siberia and the name served as an umbrella for a variety of counterrevolutionary governments spawned by its members until the group was dissolved by the formation of the Directory* in Ufa in September 1918. On January 27, 1918, the day after the Tomsk Soviet dissolved the congress of the Siberian Regionalists, some of those attending the congress formed a group called the Provisional Government of Autonomous Siberia. Some members of this government moved to Harbin and under the leadership of the Right Socialist-Revolutionary, P. A. Derber, called itself the Siberian Provisional Government.

The group calling itself the Siberian Provisional Government of Autonomous Siberia moved back into Russia when American and Japanese interventionists seized Vladivostok in May 1918. They were given protection by the occupation troops, but they were not very successful in winning support from a local population to whom they were literally unknown quantities. On May 8–9 the Committee of Members of the Constituent Assembly* (*Komuch*) was formed in Samara, though it did not claim the Siberian Regional Duma in its ancestry or regional autonomy in its program. The others did. In Novonioklaevsk four Socialist-Revolutionaries formed the West Siberian Commissariat of the Provisional Siberian Government in June and claimed allegiance to the Siberian Regional Duma. Later in June 1918 in Omsk five members of the original ill-fated Provisional Government of Autonomous Siberia who had remained behind formed their own Siberian Provisional Government and absorbed the West Siberian Commissariat. This Siberian Provisional Government abolished the Soviets and denationalized private property. On July 4, 1918 it declared Siberia's independence. It became in actuality a moderate rival to Derber's Provisional Government of Autonomous Siberia, though nominally subordinate to it. Both surrendered to the Directory created in Ufa in September 1918, which in the end succumbed to A. V. Kolchak* in November.

Bibliography

Gudoshnikov, M. A. *Ocherki po istorii grazhdansoi voiny v Sibiri.* 1959.
Turunov, A. N. and Begman, V. D. *Revoliutsii i grazhdanskaia voina v Sibiri.* 1928.

Smidovich, Petr Germanovich (1874–1935; pseudonyms: Matrena, Zybin, Chervinskii, Marselets, and Vasiliu Ivanovich). Smidovich was a prominent Bolshevik (*see* Russian Social Democratic Workers' Party [Bolshevik]) leader who played a leading role in the October Seizure of Power* in Moscow (*see* Moscow in 1917).

Smidovich was born into a noble family in the town of Rogachev. One of his grandfathers was Polish and one of his grandmothers was a Tatar. His second cousin was a well-known writer of that time, V. V. Veresaev-Smidovich. Smidovich graduated from a gymnasium in Tula in 1892 and then went on to study in the physical-mathematics faculty at Moscow University. In 1895 he was arrested and expelled for political activity and sent back to Tula. He obtained a passport and emigrated to Paris where he enrolled in the Higher Electrotechnical School in Paris where he received a diploma in 1897 and participated in student radical groups. He resolved at this point as a matter of principle to become a factory worker so that he could combine his desire to work for socialist revolution with his occupation as an electrician in a Belgian factory, Piper's International, and an electrical company in Liege, and there he participated in the work of the local metal workers' union and became a member of a Belgian Workers' party. He returned to Russia with the passport of a Belgian worker in 1898. After working in various cities and at various jobs he returned to Russia with a Belgian passport in 1898 to work in a Briansk metallurgical factory. Though arrested for revolutionary work and sent into permanent exile he soon returned. He joined the Russian Social Democratic Workers' Party as soon as it was formed and began working for Lenin's newspaper, *Iskra* (the Spark), inside Russia becoming one of its most important agents inside Russia. During the 1905 Revolution (*see* Nineteen-Five Revolution) he took part in the ill-fated December Uprising in that city.

Between 1905 and the February Revolution* in 1917 Smidovich took on a series of jobs throughout Russia while serving as an agent of Iskra and a member of the Moscow District Committee and the Moscow City Committee of the Bolshevik Party. He was arrested and sentenced to two years imprisonment in Vologda in 1908. When he returned he worked in Kaluga and then obtained an engineers job at an electrical station in Moscow. A heart ailment prevented him from continuing to work as a physical laborer.

After the February Revolution Smidovich was elected a member of the Executive Committee of the Moscow Bolsheviks and a member of the Presidium of the Executive Committee of the Moscow Soviet*. He played an important role in the Soviet Seizure of Power in Moscow, although he had opposed the action up to the time that it actually took place. Along with other moderates in the Moscow Committee of the Bolsheviks, like O. I. Piatnitskii* and A. I. Rykov*, he remembered the failures of December 1905. His group argued against the more radical members of the Moscow Regional Committee, like V. N. Iakovleva*, N. I. Bukharin*, G. I. Lomov-Oppokov* and N. Osinskii*, saying that the Moscow workers were unarmed, the soldiers in Moscow were unreliable. When the Bolsheviks began to seize power in Moscow, however, Smidovich became a member of the Military Revolutionary Committee and played an important role in leading the uprising and negotiating the surrender of the opposing forces.

With the victory of the Bolsheviks Smidovich became a member of the Presidium of the All-Russian Central Executive Committee of Soviets*, Chairman of the Moscow Soviet and a member of the Presidium of the Supreme Council of the National Economy*. He also became Chief of Procurement for the Fifth Army and Chairman of the Revolutionary Tribunal for that sector of the front. From 1920 onward he worked as Deputy Chairman of Presidium of the All-Russian Central Executive Committee of Soviets, that is, as Chief Assistant to M. I. Kalinin*, the Chairman, widely regarded as the President of the USSR. Kalinin often praised Smidovich for his intense devotion to the Party and Communism, for his honesty, and for, what he called, his "proletarian humanism" and love for the people. He died in 1935 and was buried in Red Square.

Bibliography

Arenshtein, A. *Rannim moskovski utrom.* 1967.
Geroi oktiabria. 1967.
Grunt, A. Ia. *Moskva 1917-i revoliutsiia i kontrrevoliutsiiia.* 1976.

Smilga, Ivar Tenisovich (1892–1937). Smilga was a prominent ultra-Left Lithuanian Bolshevik (*see* Russian Social Democratic Workers' Party [Bolshevik]) leader who played an important role in the October Seizure of Power* in Petrograd and in the effort to establish Soviet power in Finland (*see* Finland, Revolution in).

Smilga was born in a prosperous family in Livonia. His father was executed for his role in the Nineteen-Five Revolution*. Smilga joined the Social Democratic Party in 1907 and was arrested the same year during a student demonstration in Moscow. In 1911 he was exiled to Vologda Province for three years. When he returned he joined the Petrograd Committee of the Russian Social Democratic Workers' Party (Bolshevik). In May 1915 Smilga was arrested and exiled to Eniseisk for three years. He was in exile during the February Revolution* but returned to Petrograd afterward and attended the Seventh (April) All-Russian Party Conference. At the age of twenty-three he was appointed to the Central Committee (*see* Central Committee of the Russian Communist Party [Bolshevik]). During the October Seizure of Power* he was Chairman of the Regional Executive Committee of Soviets of the Army, Fleet, and Workers in Finland, and, as such, was V. I. Lenin's* chief emissary to the Baltic Fleet (*see* Navy and Sailors) that played an important role in the plan for the Soviet seizure of power in Petrograd and in Finland. During the seizure of power in Petrograd he was one of the few Bolshevik leaders authorized to report directly to Lenin. Smilga also took part in the unsuccessful attempt of the Finnish Soviets to take power between January 28 and May 4, 1918.

He returned to Russia and played an important role as a member of the Military Revolutionary Council commanding troops in Russia and the Ukraine (*see* Ukraine, Revolution in). Throughout 1918 he remained an ultra-militant Leninist leader, critical of L. D. Trotsky* and unswerving in his support of Lenin. In particular, he opposed Trotsky in his efforts to recruit tsarist officers to staff the Red Army* (*see* Military Opposition). At the end of the Polish Campaign of 1920 I. V. Stalin* tried to make Smilga the scapegoat for the failures of that campaign, and Smilga was expelled from the Central Committee despite Trotsky's defense of his actions as political Commissar for M. N. Tukachevskii's* army.

Smilga began an entirely new career in economic planning, rising, once again, to full membership in the Central Committee of the Bolshevik Party (*see* Central Committee of the Russian Communist Party [Bolshevik]) by 1925 and becoming Vice-Chairman of the Supreme Council of the National Economy*. But in 1927 he became part of the United Opposition, a group that included Trotsky, G. E. Zinoviev*, and L. B. Kamenev*. Smilga helped to draw up the economic portions of their program and, as a result, was once again expelled from the Central Committee. He was believed to be the most determined and dangerous opponent of Stalin and N. I. Bukharin* at that time.

In 1927 Stalin sent Smilga into exile in Khabarovsk. His departure from the Iaroslav Station in Moscow became the occasion for one last public demonstration by the opposition. When Stalin changed his economic position Smilga, Karl Radek*, and E. A. Preobrazhenskii applied for rehabilitation and were allowed to return. Smilga was arrested again in 1932 and never seen again.

Bibliography

Haupt, Georges, and Marie, Jean-Jacques. *Makers of the Russian Revolution*. 1974.

Smirnov, Ivan Nikitovich (1881–1936). Smirnov was one of the leading Left Communists* who played a leading role in the October Seizure of Power in Siberia (*see* Siberia, Revolution in) as Political Commissar of the Fifth Army during the Civil War in Russia*.

Smirnov was born in a peasant family in Riazan. His father died when he was an infant and his mother moved to Moscow where she worked as a domestic servant. When he grew older Smirnov began to work in the railroads and factories. He formed a Marxist circle among his fellow workers in 1898 and was first arrested in 1899. After two years in prison he returned and conducted Party work in Tver Province. From 1903–1905 he was again in prison. When he was freed in 1905 he began to work for the Moscow Committee of the Bolshevik party in the Lefortovo District. He took part in the December Uprising in Moscow. In 1909 he was banished from Moscow and began work in St. Petersburg where he worked in the Storona District. From 1910 to 1912 he was imprisoned in Narym in Siberia, and then returned to Khar'kov, arriving back in Moscow at the beginning of World War I*, only to be arrested and sent back to Narym. In 1916 he was conscripted into the army. He and some other exiles began to set up a Bolshevik military organization in Tomsk, and claimed that it reached a membership of 200.

During the February Revolution* Smirnov was elected a member of the Executive Committee of Soldier's Deputies in Tomsk. In August he was ordered by the Party to return to Moscow where he founded the Party journal *Volna*. During the October Seizure of Power in Moscow (*see* Moscow in 1917) Smirnov commanded the Red Guard* on the Kazan Railroad.

At the beginning of the Civil War Smirnov was sent to Kazan to serve as a member of the Military Revolutionary Committee of the Eastern Front, and in December 1919 he became a member of the Bolshevik's Siberian Bureau* and then Political Commissar of the Fifth Army which liberated Siberia. When A. V. Kolchak* was defeated Smirnov became Chairman of the Siberian Revolutionary Committee. From 1921 to 1922 he was in charge of the armaments industry under the Supreme Council of the National Economy*. In 1920 he was elected to full membership in the Central Committee of the Russian Communist party (Bolshevik)*, but after joining L. D. Trotsky on the issue of trade unions (*see* Trotsky and Left Communism) lost his seat in 1922. He became an outspoken oppositionist, and was relegated to Commissar for Posts from 1923 to 1927. As a member of the Joint Opposition he was exiled to Siberia in 1927. In 1929 he recanted and was allowed to return, but in 1932 he contributed an article to the *Bulletin of the Opposition,* and in 1933 was arrested. In 1936 he was put on trial and confessed to participation in the assassination of S. M. Kirov*, though he was in prison at the time it happened. He was executed in 1936.

Bibliography

Daniels, Robert. *The Conscience of the Revolution.*
Haupt, Georges, and Marie, Jean-Jacques. *Makers of the Russian Revolution.* 1974.

Socialist-Revolutionary Party. The Socialist-Revolutionary Party was the party claiming to represent the Russian peasants (*see* Peasants in the Russian Revolution) and, therefore, was probably the most popular party in 1917 and the chief competitor to the Bolsheviks (*see* Russian Social Democratic Workers' Party [Bolshevik]) for political power in 1917.

The Socialist-Revolutionary Party was formed at the end of 1901 as a result of the unification of various groups of neo-Populist tendency that had been formed in the 1890s in Russia and in emigration. The main organ of the party was *Revoliutsionnaia Rossiia* (*Revolutionary Russia*), edited by V. M. Chernov* and M. R. Gots; its theoretical journal was *Vestnik Russkoi Revoliutsii* (*Herald of the Russian Revolution*), edited by N. S. Rusanov (real name, K. Tarasov). Initially, the party was concerned with organizational and propaganda activity among the industrial workers and the intelligentsia. However, with the outbreak of peasant disorders in Poltava and Khar'kov provinces in 1902, the Socialist–Revolutionaries (S–R's) turned their attention also to the peasantry, and the S-R Peasant Union was formed in that year.

From its inception the S-R Party adopted tactics of political terrorism in the tradition of the *Narodnaia Volia* (*People's Will*). The Party's Combat Organization (Boevaia Organizatsiia) was formed in 1901 under the leadership of G. A. Gershuni. The Combat Organization was responsible for several spectacular assassinations: the murder of the Minister of Internal Affairs D. S. Sipiagin by Stephen V. Balmashov in 1902; of the Minister of Internal Affairs V. K. Plehve by Egor S. Sazonov in 1904; and of the grand duke Sergei Aleksandrovich by Ivan P. Kaliaev in February 1905. From 1903 the Combat Organization was headed by E. F. Azef, an *agent provocateur* in the pay of the tsarist security police.

Until the First Congress met at the end of 1905 the S-R Party had no official program or organizational statute. Its ideology, however, was worked out on the pages of *Revoliutsionnaia Rossiia* by V. M. Chernov. S-R theory claimed to be an amalgam of Populism and Marxism. While recognizing the importance of the class struggle in history, the S–R's did not identify the working class exclusively with the industrial proletariat. In S-R theory the exploited classes—the peasantry, the proletariat, and the intelligentsia—formed an alliance against the exploiters, the landowners, the bourgeoisie, and the bureaucracy. The forthcoming revolution in Russia would not be bourgeois-democratic, as in the Social Democrats' view, but anti-capitalist as well as anti-feudal. The S-R's had a maximum and a minimum program: the maximum program was full socialism; the minimum program incorporated the conventional socialist demands for political, social, and economic reform. In the agrarian section, the main demand was for socialization of the land, which was defined as the abolition of private property in land and its egalitarian distribution for those who worked it. The S-R's regarded this as a major step not only against agrarian capitalism but also against Russian capitalism in general.

The S-R Party played a prominent role in the 1905 Revolution (*see* Nineteen-Five Revolution). Although the party aimed for a Constituent Assembly* the leadership welcomed the October Manifesto: terrorism was temporarily suspended, and members of the Central Committee who had been in emigration returned to Russia. The S-R Central Committee opposed the militant tactics of the Social Democrats after October, although some S-R's participated in the Moscow rising of December 1905.

In 1906 the S-R Party suffered two splits: the Popular Socialists (Narodnye Sotsialisty) seceded to the Right, and the Maximalists (Maksimalisty) to the Left. The Popular Socialists wanted to abandon terrorism and illegality to achieve a mass socialist party. The Maximalists favored simultaneous socialization of industry and land to achieve an immediate socialist revolution. They advocated economic as well as political terror and rejected parliamentarianism. Neither Maximalism nor Popular Socialism deprived the S–R's of any significant degree of popular support. As a result of the 1905 Revolution the party expanded rapidly. In 1906 the S–R's claimed a membership of 50,000, with a further 300,000 supporters.

The S–R's boycotted the elections to the First Duma (*see* Duma and Revolution) in 1906, but they contested the elections to the Second Duma in 1907, and thirty-four S–R deputies were elected. The S–R's boycotted the elections to the Third and Fourth Dumas in 1907 and 1912, but some party sympathizers were elected as Laborites (*Trudoviki*).

From 1906 the S-R Party suffered a series of blows to its organization and morale. The Stolypin agrarian reforms, with their attack on the peasant commune (*see* Agriculture), carried a threat to the S-R demand for the socialization of land, and the party responded defensively by placing greater emphasis in its agrarian policy on agricultural cooperatives. At the end of 1908 Azef was exposed as an *agent provocateur*. The resulting crisis in the party led to a reassessment of the value of terrorist activity. The S–R's decided to continue terrorism, but in practice this aspect of party activity ceased to have any major significance after 1908. The last years before the war passed with little achievement for the S–R Party. The organization in Russia was weakened and the emigré leadership was divided into various quarreling factions. On the Left the group based around the journal *Revoliutsionnaia Mysl'* (*Revolutionary Thought*) favored a return to the more exclusive use of terrorism, including regicide, while the Pochin (Initiative) group desired the abolition of terror and the legalization of the party.

In 1914 the leadership of the S-R Party, like that of most other European socialist parties, was divided on its attitude toward the war (*see* World War I). V. M. Chernov opposed the war from an Internationalist* position, but the majority of the Central Committee was Defensist (*see* Defensism.)

After the February Revolution* of 1917 the S–R's played a dominant role in the Petrograd Soviet,* and the S-R Party, together with the Mensheviks (*see* Russian Social Democratic Workers' Party [Menshevik]), adopted a position of qualified support for the first Provisional Government*. After the April Crisis (*see* Provisional Government) the S–R's and Mensheviks joined the Cadets (*see* Constitutional Democratic Party—Cadet) to form the first coalition government. In the first coalition, Chernov became Minister of Agriculture and A. F. Kerensky* was Minister of War. When the second coalition was formed in July 1917, Kerensky became Prime Minister. In 1917 the S-R Party was bitterly divided. From July the major issue was whether the socialist parties should remain in coalition with the liberals or whether they should take power themselves, through the soviets (*see* Soviets [Councils] of Workers', Soldiers', and Peasants' Deputies). In the interests of maintaining national unity in order to continue the war, the S-R ministers accepted responsibility for the policies of the Provisional Government, including the postponement of land reform (*see* Agrarian Policy, 1917–1921; Agriculture) until the convocation of the Constituent Assembly. After the Kornilov Revolt*, with the alleged complicity of the Cadets in counterrevolution, the issue of coalition split the party organizationally. In October 1917 the Left S–R's formed a separate party that called for an end to coalition, an immediate armistice, and land to the peasants. After the October Seizure of Power* the Left S–R's formed a coalition government with the Bolsheviks that lasted from November 1917 to March 1918.

The S-R Party declared its hostility to the October Seizure of Power, and the right wing S-R delegates left the Second All-Russian Congress of Soviets in protest against the Bolshevik seizure of power. Although the party had declined in popularity in the Soviets of Workers' and Soldiers' Deputies since the First Congress of Soviets in June, in which the S–R's were the largest single party, they continued to have the overwhelming support of the peasant majority of the Russian population. In the election to the Constituent Assembly of November 1917—the only free and democratic election in Russian history—the S–R's gained a clear victory. Out of the total of around 700 deputies, about 440 were S–R's (including Left S–R's, 80 Ukrainian S–R's, and 20 S–R's of other national groupings), and the party received more than 50 percent of the popular vote (by contrast the Bolsheviks had 168 deputies and about 25 percent of the vote).

After the dissolution of the Constituent Assembly in January 1918 the S–R's attempted to set up a "Committee of the Constituent Assembly"* (Komuch, or Komitet chlenov uchreditel'nogo sobraniia) on the Volga. During the Civil War in Russia* the party attempted unsuccessfully to create a "third force" between the Reds (*see* Russian Social Democratic Workers' Party [Bolshevik]) and the Whites (*see* White Movement). When by 1919 this policy proved impractical, some S–R's on the Left accepted an accommodation with the Bolsheviks; others on the Right preferred an alliance with the Whites. In 1922 34 S–R leaders were tried in Moscow on charges of terror and counterrevolutionary activity against the Soviet regime. Most were found guilty and sentenced to terms of imprisonment.

Many members of the S-R leadership emigrated after the end of the Civil War. In emigration in the interwar years the party remained divided. In Prague V. M. Chernov edited *Revoliutsionnaia Rossiia,* a party journal of left-wing tendency, while a right-wing group including M. V. Vishniak, I. I. Fondamin-skii, and V. V. Rudnev produced the journal *Sovremennye zapiski (Contemporary Notes)* in Paris. Other S-R groups were based in Revel, Berlin, and Belgrade. The emigré party organizations in Europe did not survive World War I. Some individual S-R leaders, for example Chernov, Kerensky, and Vishniak, spent their last years after the war in the United States. The party archive is now located in the International Institute for Social History in Amsterdam.

Maureen Perrie

Bibliography

Garmiza, V. V. *Krushenie eserovskikh pravitel'stv*. 1970.
Ginev, V. N. *Agrarnyi vopros i melkoburzhuaznye partii v Rossii v 1917 g*. 1977.
Gusev, K. V. *Partiia eserov*. 1975.
Gusev, K. V., and Eritsian, Kh. A. *Ot soglashatel'stva k kontrrevoliutsii*. 1968.
Hildermeier, Manfred. *Die Sozialrevolutionaere Partei Russlands*. 1978.
Perrie, Maureen. *The Agrarian Policy of the Russian Socialist-Revolutionary Party*. 1976.
Radkey, O. H. *The Agrarian Foes of Bolshevism*. 1958.
———. *The Sickle under the Hammer*. 1963.
Spiridovitch, Alexandre. *Histoire du Terrorisme Russe*. 1930.

Sokol'nikov, Grigorii Iakvolevich (1888–1939; pseudonym, Brilliant). Sokol'nikov was a prominent Left Communist leader in Moscow who participated in the October Seizure of Power* in Petrograd.

Sokol'nikov was born in Poltava Province where his father worked as a doctor on the railway. When the family moved to Moscow Sokol'nikov entered a gymnasium and experienced some persecution because his family was Jewish. He joined some Marxist student groups and in 1905 joined the Moscow Bolsheviks (*see* Russian Social Democratic Workers' Party [Bolshevik]). He became director of the Bolshevik youth groups in Moscow and met such Bolshevik leaders as M. N. Pokrovskii*, N. N. Rozhkov, M. S. Mitskevicius-Kapsukas and E. Tseitlin. He also took part in the December Uprising in Moscow during the 1905 Revolution (*See* Nineteen-Five Revolution).

In 1906 Sokol'nikov and N. I. Bukharin called a citywide youth conference, and in 1907 a national youth congress. In the fall of 1907 he was arrested and remained in prison until 1909. He escaped from Siberia after being sent there for a lifetime sentence of exile, and emigrated to the West. There he obtained a law degree and doctorate in economics in Paris, becoming very active in the emigre Marxist movement. Although he was in complete agreement with V. I. Lenin* on the appropriate Marxist response to World War I*, Sokol'nikov was one of the leading members of the editorial staff of L. D. Trotsky's newspaper *Nashe Slovo* (Our Word) and before the war (between 1908–1910) one of the leading advocates of conciliation between the factions in the Russian Social Democratic Workers' Party.

Sokol'nikov was a member of the Bolshevik group that returned to Russia with Lenin after the February Revolution*. He returned to Moscow in April to continue his revolutionary work there, and became a member of both the Moscow Regional Committee and the Moscow Committee of the party. He also became a member of the Executive Committee of the Moscow Soviet*. By September Sokol'nikov was back in Petrograd as a member of the Executive Committee of the Petrograd Soviet*, and after the Second All-Russian Congress of Soviets he would be a member of the All-Russian Central Executive Committee of Soviets*. The party made him a member of its Central Committee and in August he joined I. V. Stalin* and V. P. Miliutin on the editorial board chosen to supervise all Bolshevik newspapers. When the first Political Bureau (Politburo) was formed Sokol'nikov was chosen as a member along with Stalin, Lenin, A. S. Bubnov*, G. E. Zinoviev*, L. B. Kamenev*, and L. D. Trotsky. He and Kamenev were chosen by the party Central Committee to take charge of the important negotiations with the All-Russian Central Executive Committee of Railwaymen* (*Vikzhel*). He was an elected member of the Constituent Assembly* and he and Bukharin were put in charge of the Bolshevik delegation to the Constituent Assembly. In December 1917 he was appointed a member of the Presidium of the Supreme Council of the National Economy*. He was an enthusiastic supporter of Lenin's efforts to bring the war with Germany to an end and in March 1918 he was placed in charge of the delegation to sign the Treaty of Brest-Litovsk*. He occupied important posts on many different fronts during the Civil War*, and in 1920 went to Turkestan (*see* Turkestan, Revolution in) as commander of the Turkestan front and chairman of the Turkestan Commission (*Turkkomissiia*). He played an important role in defeating the Basmachis* and in the Bolshevik conquest of Central Asia (*see* Central Asia). In 1921 he joined with Bukharin in supporting Trotsky's proposals for strict party control over the trade unions (*see* Trade Unions) as part of the struggle against the Workers' Opposition (*see* Kollontai).

   In 1922 Sokol'nikov became Commissar of Finance and assumed responsibility for restoring organization and structure to the financial operations of the Soviet government, one of his major contributions to the new regime. Like Bukharin Sokol'nikov found himself moving from an extreme Left position in the party to the extreme Right, supporting the New Economic Policy* and calling for trade with the non-Communist West and the granting of concessions in Russia to foreign investors. Like Bukharin he also believed that agriculture and industry should receive equal attention in economic development, and that one should not be favored over the other. He also became an advocate of strict accountability for each economic enterprise. They should, he argued, all be run on a strict cost accounting (*khozraschet*) basis, with each industry developing its own self-sufficiency on a profit and loss basis. In 1924 he became a candidate member of the Politburo and a member of the Russian delegation to the Communist International*.

   In 1925, however, Sokol'nikov became a leading member of the Left opposition, joining Zinoviev, Kamenev and N. K. Krupskaia* in the so-called "Platform of the Four," calling for more open discussion of the differences separating the top leaders of the party. The Left opposition was defeated at the Fourteenth Party Congress in December 1925 and Sokol'nikov was dropped from the Politburo. In January he was dismissed from his post as Commissar of Finance, and became a Deputy Chairman of the State Planning Commission. He joined the United Opposition in 1926–27, but was not deprived of his seat on the Central Committee until 1930, though he was reappointed a candidate member in 1934.

From 1929 to 1934 he served as Soviet Ambassador to England. During the Great Purges in 1936 he was tried along with K. Radek*, Iu. Piatikov, and L. B. Serebriakov and sentenced to ten years of prison. He died or was executed in 1939.

Bibliography

Daniels, R. V. *The Conscience of the Revolution*. 1960.
Haupt, Georges, and Marie, Jean-Jacques. *Makers of the Russian Revolution*. 1974.
Sokol'nikov, G. Ia. *Finansovaia politika revoliutsii*. 2 vols. 1926.

Soldiers and Soldiers' Committees. The soldiers of the Russian Imperial Army played a pivotal role in both the February and October Revolutions (*see* February Revolution; October Seizure of Power) and throughout 1917 were an important component in the overall structure of power through their own soviets (*see* Soviets [Councils] of Workers', Soldiers', and Peasants' Deputies) in the urban centers and committees at the front; moreover, with the total collapse in March of normal military discipline, soldiers asserted themselves in countless informal ways— spontaneous arrests of officers, fraternization with the army, desertions, perpetual discussion and flouting of orders—that frustrated the normal exercise of authority not only of the command and the government but also of the Soviet and higher soldiers' committees as well.

The Russian Revolution of 1917 began with the massive mutiny of the Petrograd garrison when the foundering tsarist government called upon it to suppress mounting strikes and street demonstrations. Initially employed only as backup forces for the regular police, on February 26, at the tsar's command, they were ordered to fire on the street crowds. Early on the morning of February 27 the Volynskii Guards Regiment arrested its officers and flooded into the streets, soon to be joined by other regiments of the guards; by the following day virtually the entire garrison of Petrograd and its environs, some 330,000 men, declared themselves on the side of the Revolution. Soldiers took over their barracks from the officers, opened up arms chambers, passed weapons freely among the street crowds, assisted in taking buildings of strategic military importance and arresting policemen, and otherwise lent their support to the establishment of a new revolutionary authority. The soldiers shared with the lower-class population of Petrograd a deep anxiety over the killing inflation, economic disorganization, and protracted war, as well as hostility to the police, ministers, and other representatives of tsarist authority. Political agitation against the "German influence" on the government, the high command, and even the royal couple had reinforced their own desire to finish the pointless war and get back to their families and villages. The "Revolution" and the fall of the dynasty were interpreted as a defeat of all of the forces that had oppressed them in the past—the gentry, the rural police, "*burzhuis*" (bourgeois) officialdom—and the promise of the realization of their centuries-old dream of acquiring land. Thus they would ardently support the new order to the extent that it measured up to these expectations.

The soldiers' power became institutionalized in the Soldiers' Section of the Petrograd Soviet* of Workers' and Soldiers' Deputies. Originally, when a handful of liberated workers and revolutionary intellectuals issued the first call for elected deputies on the afternoon of February 27, they recognized the importance of winning over the soldiers by also calling for one soldier deputy per company; nevertheless, they established a workers' soviet only. On March 1, after the Temporary Committee of the State Duma (*see* Duma and Revolution; Provisional Government) through its "Military Commission" sought to secure the return of the officers to their barracks, a group of angry soldiers from the streets stormed a session of the Workers' Soviet, demanding the formation of a separate "Soldiers' Section" and the proclamation of the famous Army Order Number One* of the Petrograd Soviet. The order provided that in every company or comparable unit there should be formed elected committees to represent soldiers' interests, and in all *political* questions the soldiers should be subject only to the authority of the soviet in which they would be represented through the Solders' Section; orders of officers should be obeyed only "insofar as" they did not conflict with those of the soviet. Control over weapons was to be in the hands of the committees. Finally, the order stipulated new democratic practices between officers and soldiers, such as addressing the soldiers with the formal "you" instead of the demeaning "thou" and officers with "Mr. Lieutenant" instead of "Your Nobility." Although addressed specifically to the Petrograd garrison, the order was immediately printed in thousands of copies and distributed to every part of Russia and the front, where it exercised an incalculable revolutionizing influence. The Soldiers' Section of the Petrograd soviet served as a forum for soldiers' concerns and a locus of political leadership for the entire army. Moreover, the Petrograd Soviet extracted a formal agreement from the Provisional Government not to send soldiers from the revolutionary Petrograd garrison to the front, which had the effect of disrupting the flow of troops from the training camps to the front, and withdrawing the garrison troops from normal military training. The garrison soldiers, therefore, became preoccupied with the political concerns of the capital and viewed themselves as the enforcement arm of the soviet to ensure that the Provisional Government lived up to its obligations.

At the front the soldiers first learned of the full significance of events in the capital on March 4 or 5 with the official announcement of the abdication of Nicholas II* and Grand Duke Michael and the formation of a new Provisional Government. Although nearly all commanders followed instructions precisely, the soldiers were convinced that many of their officers secretly sympathized with the "old regime" and were hiding important pronouncements of the new government, particularly on the burning questions of peace and land. They clamored to send deputations directly to Petrograd or some other urban center. A continuous flow of rumors and vivid accounts by those returning from leave created unceasing agitation and clashes with officers, not infrequently leading to their arrest or forceful removal, even of commanders of regiments or divisions. Most upsetting was the broad circulation of Order Number One by the press, telegraph, radio, and even enemy propaganda. By March 7 or 8 every sector was aware of it, and the command was taking countermeasures. Further misunderstandings occurred over the oath of loyalty to the Provisional Government, Defense Minister A. I. Guchkov's* abolishing of officers' titles and substituting "Mr.," and the saluting and wearing of red ribbons as a sign of loyalty to the new regime.

All of this turmoil led to the rapid, spontaneous formation of soldiers' committees, and in the interest of restoring some semblance of order, the command thought it expedient to authorize and control the committees through official regulations. With the consent of Stavka (General Headquarters in Mogilev), the army commanders on all fronts, by the third week in March in response to official orders, instituted elected committees at every level, also often authorizing deputations to Petrograd and the holding of army and front congresses. Most statutes provided for committees at the company, regimental, divisional, and army levels, usually at the ratio of eight soldiers to one officer at the regimental level and a ratio of four soldiers to one officer at higher levels. Their assigned functions were defined primarily as the supervision of commissary and other routine matters but also often included the mediation of soldier–officer disputes and political self-education in preparation for the forthcoming Constituent Assembly*. The command hoped very much to employ them to restore discipline and continue the war and thus attempted to involve Duma deputies and to forestall participation by the soviet. But as deputations to the capital familiarized themselves with the political situation and the distinctive position of the soviet as an organ of "control" over the "bourgeois" Provisional Government, the front committees lined up behind the soviet. Above all they endorsed the soviet slogan of "No Annexations and Indemnities" rather than the patriotic, middle-class formula of "War to Full Victory." The relationship of the front committees to the soviet was formalized at the First All-Russian Conference of Soviets at the end of March and confirmed by a series of army and front congresses over the next few weeks.

Although elected by soldiers through a series of ascending indirect elections, soldiers' committees at the higher levels necessarily were dominated by educated elements—lower officers, military doctors, clerk and technical personnel of the rear—who tended to be oriented toward one or the other of the revolutionary parties; as such they articulated the political concerns of the latter more accurately than the feelings of the workers and peasants who elected them. Although both elements were intensely loyal to the soviet, the committeemen tended to support the "Defensist" (*see* Defensism) wing of the soviet leadership, whereas the soldiers looked at the soviet for a speedy end to the war and a radical fulfillment of their social aspirations. The committees soon found themselves in the peculiar role of upholding military discipline and obedience to officers, whereas the soldiers expressed their attitudes by engaging in massive fraternization with the enemy and flouting all orders connected with repairing trenchworks and the normal rotation of units on the line. Arrests of both lower and higher officers on various pretexts continued without interruption.

The April Crisis (*see* Miliukov, Pavel Nikolaevich; Provisional Government) and the formation of the coalition on May 5 seriously shook the soldiers' confidence in the revolutionary order, since they had counted on soviet "control" over the Provisional Government to prevent the resumption of major new military operations and to bring about an early negotiated peace. Now with socialists in the government, War Minister A. F. Kerensky* was vigorously promoting a new offensive and the restoration of "old regime" military discipline. Inevitably, a deep split developed between the mass of peasant soldiers and the committeemen and deputies to soldiers' soviets who loyally supported Kerensky and the soviet leadership. In Petrograd the Soldiers' Section, under strong pressure from the soviet Executive Committee (*see* All-Russian Central Executive Committee) consented to the resumption of sending replacements to the front in preparation for the offensive that provoked a response among the garrison troops that was directly connected with the turmoil in the capital leading to the July Days* under the influence of Bolshevik (*see* Russian Social Democratic Workers' Party [Bolshevik])-dominated units like the First Machine Gun Regiment. A similar response was taking place in garrisons throughout the country.

At the front a series of army and front congresses in May, usually attended by Kerensky or authoritative soviet figures, passed resounding resolutions in favor of a new offensive and condemning fraternization and disobedience to military orders. Although soldier committeemen at the front loyally supported the soviet position, they faced considerable disenchantment and hostility in their constituency on the lower levels. In May and June entire regiments and divisions slipped from the control of their regular committees and fell under the influence of "Bolshevik agitators." Only a few of such units, such as the 436th Novoladozhskii regiment, the 169th Division, and the Guards Grenadiers were controlled by identifiable Bolsheviks; most agitators were freshly indoctrinated soldiers of the rear sent up to the front in replacement companies or those who had picked up Bolshevik slogans and arguments from Bolshevik newspapers, which now reached the front in massive quantities. Especially *Soldatskaia Pravda* (*Soldiers' Truth*) and *Okopnaia Pravda* (*Trench Truth*) were written in simple, forceful style for ordinary soldiers, stressing the "imperialist" character of the war, the secret treaties with England and France, and the betrayal of the socialist peace program by the Mensheviks (*see* Russian Social Democratic Workers' Party [Menshevik]) and the Socialist–Revolutionaries (*see* Socialist-Revolutionary Party). They were particularly hostile to officer authority, openly endorsing the election of officers by the soldiers, and promoted fraternization as a bloodless way of terminating the war. The war-weary soldiers, front and rear, disenchanted with their elected leadership, grasped at Bolshevik slogans as a desperate means of sabotaging the offensive. In spite of Kerensky's extensive tours of the front as "persuader-in-chief," from a quarter to a half of the units at the front could not be counted on to carry out military orders connected with the offensive. Under strong persuading by committees, commissars of the Provisional Government (most of them known soviet figures), and various deputations of the rear and with the heaviest artillery support that had yet been employed on the eastern front, the soldiers of the southwestern front reluctantly launched the offensive on June 18, obtaining a limited success in a few sectors; but heavy casualties, renewed antiwar agitation, and the mutiny of a number of Bolshevik-dominated units soon brought the advance to a halt. On July 9 the German army broke through in a counteroffensive at Tarnopol, setting off a panicky retreat a hundred miles or so to the rear. The offensive on the northern and western fronts were canceled because of the heavy inroads of Bolshevik agitation.

In July the soldiers' committees, blaming the Bolsheviks for both the Petrograd uprising and the catastrophe at Tarnopol, cooperated with the government commissars and the command in arresting "Bolshevik agitators" and disbanding Bolshevik regiments. Ordinary soldiers were for the most part sullen and distrustful of their committees and more hostile than ever to their officers. Desertion and plundering by soldiers in the rear now became a mass phenomenon. The appointment of L. G. Kornilov (*see* Kornilov Revolt) as commander-in-chief and the restoration of the death penalty at the front signaled a harsh new regime in the army and the serious intention of the high command to restore officer authority. Commanders now engaged in the systematic harassment of committees, even punishing and disbanding them for real or imagined "illegalities." Alerted to the revival of right-wing political activity at the Moscow State Conference* in August, the soldiers' committees at the front quickly dropped their campaign against the Bolsheviks to wage a defensive struggle to maintain the integrity of the democratic organizations. When they learned of Kornilov's plot to move on Petrograd, the soldiers' committees, now ardently supported by the soldiers, took special measures to take over staff headquarters to monitor staff communications, and to arrest officers, especially higher commanders who were suspected of sympathy with Kornilov. Although the Kornilov uprising temporarily reconciled soldiers with their committee leadership, they immediately became disillusioned again when Kerensky ordered the liquidation of the special controls over military staffs and appointed the known Kornilovite General M. V. Alekseev as his chief of staff (Kerensky himself assuming command of the army).

By this time, totally hostile to the experiment in coalition with "bourgeois" groups, particularly the Constitutional Democrats (*see* Constitutional Democratic Party—Cadet) whom they perceived as pro-Kornilov, the front soldiers eagerly responded to the call for a Second All-Russian Congress of Soviets, which they ardently hoped would assume full power until the convocation of the Constituent

Assembly and immediately resolve the burning issues of land and peace. The Bolsheviks merely articulated ideas that had a strong inherent appeal to the soldier masses. In October the desire for immediate peace before another winter set in overwhelmed all other considerations and gave an irresistable impetus to the surge toward the Bolsheviks and Soviet power on the part of soldiers both front and rear. The higher soldier committees, belatedly yielding to their constituents on an immediate end to the war and a radical solution to the land problem (*see* Agrarian Policy, 1917–1921; Agriculture), nevertheless tended to see the political solution in the immediate formation of an all-socialist coalition government and the prompt convocation of the Constituent Assembly, the elections for which they had carefully prepared and were now under way. They opposed the convocation of the Second All-Russian Congress of Soviets because they feared it would be dominated by Bolsheviks and would represent a serious rival to the Constituent Assembly. Nevertheless, they had to contend with considerable pressure from below to send authorized deputations to the Second Congress, and the Bolsheviks were very active in those same weeks by forcing by-elections to soldiers' committees and calling for new army congresses to renew the leadership of the army committees. The Fifth and Second Armies, as a result of this campaign, held new congresses shortly before the October coup and sent pro-Bolshevik deputations to the Second Congress. In a number of other armies (Tenth, Twelfth) this process was only completed after the coup and in part was a response to the proclamation of Soviet power. By mid-November all armies of the northern and western fronts were under the control of pro-Bolshevik elements, and on other fronts non-Bolshevik elements usually maintained a tenuous control but nevertheless favored recognition of Soviet power and the immediate initiation of peace negotiations. The consequence of this marked shift in control of the soldiers' committees was that Kerensky was unable to find military support at the front to restore the Provisional Government. Thus this ''soldiers' revolution'' was the major reason the Bolsheviks were able to retain power once they had seized it.

Paradoxically, the soldiers did not regard the proclamation of Soviet power as an inherent conflict with the idea of an all-socialist coalition or elections to the Constituent Assembly, and the elections to the latter proceeded smoothly as planned. The northern and western fronts gave the Bolsheviks firm majorities (56 percent and 66 percent, respectively), but on the southwestern, Romanian, and Caucasus fronts, they received more than 30 percent, and the Socialist–Revolutionaries received the largest single vote (approximately 40 percent). On these fronts the Ukrainians were serious competitors, frequently receiving up to 25 percent. The garrisons in October, seriously depleted through desertions and from sending replacements to the front, were more decisively pro-Bolshevik than the front. They very frequently participated in the formation of Military Revolutionary Committees that effected local transfers of power and supplied armed support to the local soviets. But in November and December the soldiers, front and rear, were returning home in massive numbers, so in a military sense they were of little significance to either side in the shaping Civil War in Russia*. Essentially, the soldiers, as Lenin stated, voted with their feet for the Bolshevik program of peace, land, and Soviet power but not necessarily for Bolshevik power.

Allan K. Wildman

Bibliography

Burdzhalov, E. N., *Vtoraia russkaia revoliutsiia. Vosstanie v Petrograde.* 1967.

———. *Vtoraia russkaia revoliutsiia. Moskva, front, periferiia.* 1971.

Frenkin, Mikhail S. *Russkaia armiia i revoliutsiia 1917–1918.* 1978.

Gavrilov, L. M. *Soldatskie komitety v oktiabrskoi revoliutsii (deistvuiushchaia armiia).* 1985.

Miller, V. I. *Soldatskie komitety russkoi armii v 1917 g.* 1974.

Wildman, Allan K. *The End of the Russian Imperial Army. The Old Army and the Soldiers' Revolt (March-April, 1917).* 1980.

———. *The End of the Russian Imperial Army. The Road to Soviet Power and Peace.* 1987.

Soviets (Councils) of Workers', Soldiers', and Peasants' Deputies. The soviets, or councils, were the principal mass organizations set up during the Russian Revolutions of 1917. Such bodies had first appeared in the 1905 Revolution (*see* Nineteen-Five Revolution), notably in St. Petersburg, where for some weeks one representing workers only challenged the authority of the tsarist government. Other soviets appeared in major industrial centers and even in the armed forces. Most acted essentially as committees to coordinate strike action. Delegates were elected directly by workers in the factories and others who saw them as representing their common interests regardless of craft distinctions. They were ad hoc assemblies, and there was no generally agreed-upon procedure for electing delegates or conducting business.

As was the case in 1905, soviets formed spontaneously during the 1917 February Revolution*, especially in and around Petrograd (*see* Petrograd Soviet). They served initially as forums of self-expression for the radicalized elements of the urban population. Soon they proliferated across the country, regularized their procedures, and developed a rudimentary executive apparatus manned by cadres who were often professional revolutionaries of intelligentsia origin rather than ordinary workingmen or soldiers. These leaders strove or felt compelled to expand the soviets' role and to take over state functions that the feeble Provisional Government* was unable or unwilling to fulfill. By the summer of 1917 the soviets had emerged as a major alternative focus of popular loyalties. Delegates to the soviets were chosen directly and informally (by show of hands) in the factories or barracks. Usually, one delegate represented 500 (or in larger enterprises, 1,000) workers and the men in each military unit. Constituency boundaries were poorly defined. Party–political rivalries, at first restrained, soon became important.

Conservatives and liberals (*see* Constitutional Democratic Party—Cadet) deplored the soviets' growing power, whereas socialists generally welcomed it, although with varying degrees of enthusiasm. Most Mensheviks (*see* Russian Social Democratic Workers' Party [Menshevik]) and Socialist–Revolutionaries (*see* Socialist-Revolutionary Party) saw the soviet movement as an adjunct and a counterweight to the existing government, not as a substitute for it. The Bolsheviks and other Maximalists on the extreme Left appreciated that the soviets could prove an invaluable instrument in mobilizing popular support in their campaign to subvert the allegedly bourgeois and imperialistic Provisional Government. In his April Theses* V. I. Lenin* called for a republic of soviets. This slogan appealed to the masses' deep longing for popular self-government but left vague, perhaps for tactical reasons, the actual place that Lenin expected soviets to assume in the forthcoming socialist order. Lenin may not yet have fully clarified his own views, but there was a latent contradiction between his expressed ideas about the democratic, mass character of the future socialist society and the view, which Lenin had propounded since 1902, that the Bolshevik Party (*see* Russian Social Democratic Workers' Party [Bolshevik]) should exercise a vanguard role under a proletarian dictatorship. Would there be a central Soviet government, and if so, how would it impose its will on the local councils?

The Bolshevik Party seemed at first to be in a paradoxical position, demanding political power for institutions in which it was a small minority. Even some other Bolshevik leaders were at first puzzled by Lenin's fundamental opposition to the Provisional Government and his insistence upon Soviet rule. When the moderate socialist-controlled Petrograd Soviet* was formed in March, it consisted of about 1,200 delegates, and by the end of March it had grown to almost 3,000, of whom no more than 40 were clearly identified as Bolsheviks. In mid-April a small soviet was formed in Petrograd out of the larger body to deal with daily business in a more expeditious manner, and an effort was made to tighten control over delegates' credentials, but Bolshevik support rapidly increased. This process was facilitated by the merger of Workers' and Soldiers' Soviets, where the former were more radical, and by the extension of the urban soviets' influence into the countryside, where the peasant soviets lacked such a well-developed institutional structure.

At the First All-Russian Congress of Soviets, which met in Petrograd from June 3 to June 24, there were only 105 Bolsheviks among the 1,090 delegates, and the All-Russian Central Executive Committee* of Soviets, which it formed, included only 35 Bolsheviks out of 250 members. The Mensheviks had 104 members and the Socialist–Revolutionaries 100. The July Days* led to a temporary weakening of the Bolsheviks' position, but they recovered after the abortive Kornilov Revolt* in late August, and their influence began to rise dramatically in most mass organizations. Lenin's party became paramount in the key soviets of Petrograd and Moscow. One popular rallying cry was the demand for convocation of a second All-Russian congress of soviets that would ratify this shift to the Left. The moderate socialist-controlled Central Executive Committee resisted this pressure, but to no effect.

When the congress met in Petrograd on October 25 and 26, the Bolsheviks found themselves with a bare majority, but the moderates walked out and so helped them to present the gathering as an expression of the will of the most revolutionary elements of the population. The delegates endorsed an all-Bolshevik Council of People's Commissars* to replace the Provisional Government, which had been overthrown by a military revolutionary committee (MRC) of the Bolshevik-controlled Petrograd soviet. For six months after the October Revolution the Bolsheviks shared power in the Central Executive Committee of the All-Russian Congress of Soviets with the Left Socialist–Revolutionaries and other Maximalist political groups. More important was the Left Socialist–Revolutionaries' presence on the Council of People's Commissars, which assumed the role of a central executive body and submitted only some of its decrees for endorsement by the supposedly sovereign "workers' parliament," the Central Executive Committee of Soviets, and governed dictatorially. However, the new political system enjoyed an appearance of popular legitimacy, and this proved a valuable asset when Lenin decided to disperse the democratically elected Constituent Assembly* (January 6, 1918) on the grounds that it did not express the will of the most revolutionary elements, which allegedly supported the dictatorship.

Within a few months, however, the soviets' real decision-making powers had been whittled away, and they atrophied into decorative pseudorepresentative organs, cogs in a centralized state bureaucracy. Although delegates continued to be elected, voters had no real choice between alternative candidates, since they were nominated by Bolshevik functionaries and were presented to them for endorsement. Most dissidents were expelled or suppressed by mid-summer 1918. The Central Executive Committee dispatched agents to the provinces who brought the local soviets into line. This centralizing process was facilitated by the formation of intermediate-level (regional and provincial) soviets. However, they were often appointed rather than elective bodies and so lacked authenticity and popular support. Urban, city–ward, and rural district (*uiezd*) soviets mushroomed. In October 1917 there had been some 900–1,000 urban soviets; thereafter, many were just fictions. Elections and plenary meetings of delegates were no longer held, and all that existed was an executive committee acting in the soviet's name. In November 1918 there were 6,550 such committees in the thirty-two provinces then controlled by Moscow. The Civil War emergency accounts in part for this atrophying of the soviets, but there were also ideological reasons. Bolshevik revolutionary theory had always stressed the need for an integral state power combining legislative and executive functions, unrestricted by any formal laws, that could act energetically against internal and external enemies of the proletariat. The first task of the local soviets, the jurist M. A. Reysner (Reussner) argued in 1919, was to strengthen the Soviet state, to which end "it is perfectly natural to resort to extraordinary measures of struggle, and thus partly to terror," aided by the Cheka (*see* All-Russian Extraordinary Commission for Combatting Counterrevolution and Sabotage) and Red Army* detachments. Militant prosecution of the class struggle went hand in hand with efforts to reconstruct the economy on socialist lines.

The formal principles of the Soviet political order were set out in a declaration endorsed by the Third All-Russian Congress of Soviets (January 10–18, 1918), which was later incorporated in the Constitution of the Russian Socialist Federative Soviet Republic* (RSFSR), approved by the Fifth All-Russian Congress of Soviets (July 4–10, 1918). It provided for a pyramid of soviet bodies, the resolutions of the higher being binding on the lower; the most important functions were reserved for the central agencies; the All-Russian Congress of Soviets, the highest deliberative organ, was elected indirectly on an unequal suffrage, a worker's vote counting five times that of a peasant. The congress's role was really symbolic, and it met with declining frequency: four sessions in 1918 (January, March, July, October) and then one each year in December. At the Third Congress, attended by 1866 persons, 1,347 with a full vote, out of 708 deputies polled, 152 were non-Bolshevik socialists and 97 nonparty. Some critics of the regime were allowed to speak, but they were fiercely heckled. At the Fifth Congress the Left Socialist–Revolutionaries, who had split from the Bolsheviks, were expelled. Thereafter the few noncommunist delegates (3 percent at the Seventh Congress) wore a nonparty label. The Central Executive Committee, wholly communist from July 1918 onwards, went over to a sessional system in 1919 that reduced the frequency of election. In local soviets opposition candidates were frequently harassed and sometimes arrested on the eve of the poll. At the end of 1918 communists comprised 93.0 percent of the provincial and 83.5 percent of the district Executive Committee members, but many of them were later purged for moral or political inadequacy. The party sought to exercise its vanguard role by supervising, not supplanting, the work done in soviet agencies and to avoid petty tutelage. But this was difficult when all party members within such bodies had to belong to a faction subject to strict party discipline (Eighth Party Congress resolution of March 22, 1919).

The same principles were applied within the Communist International*, which encouraged revolutionaries abroad to emulate the Russian example of a soviet-based state structure. Such councils did indeed come into being in Germany, Austria, and elsewhere. They were marked by similar conflicts between democratic and authoritarian tendencies and failed to put down lasting roots. Many foreign communists harbored sympathies for those Soviet comrades who objected to increasing bureaucratization of the mass organizations and to the gradual reduction of democratic freedoms even to working men. Such objections stimulated mutinous sailors at Kronstadt in March 1921 to demand "soviets without commissars," that is, a return to the self-government of the early days of the Revolution. The repression and centralization that followed the defeat of the Kronstadt rebels disenchanted many left wingers abroad as well as in Russia and made the Soviet model of political development less attractive internationally.

Whether the soviets could have ever lived up to the responsibility of serving as the vehicle of a new kind of decentralized working-class democracy is a matter of debate among historians.

John Keep

Bibliography

Andreev, A. *The Soviets of Workers' and Soldiers' Deputies on the Eve of the October Revolution.* 1971.

Anweiler, O. *The Soviets: The Russian Workers', Peasants', and Soldiers' Councils, 1905–21.* 1974.

Gimpelson, E. *Sovety v gody inostrannoi interventsii i grazhdanskoi voiny.* 1968.

Gorin, P. O. *Organizatsiia i stroitel stvo Sovetov rabochikh deputatov v 1917 g: sbornik dokumentov.* 1928.

Keep, J. L. H. *The Debate on Soviet Power: Minutes of the All-Russian Central Executive Committee of Soviets . . . October 1917-January 1918.* 1979.

———. *The Russian Revolution: A Study in Mass Mobilization.* 1977.

Moiseeva, S. N. *Sovety krest'ianskikh deputatov v 1917 g.* 1967.

Spiridonova, Mariia Aleksandrovna (1884–1941). Spiridonova was a prominent leader of the Left Socialist-Revolutionary Party* (*see* Socialist-Revolutionary Party).

Spiridonova was born in Tambov into a family of gentry. In 1905 she joined the Socialist-Revolutionary Party and assassinated a prominent provincial official in January 1906. A military court sentenced her to death, but that sentence was later commuted to life imprisonment. Her actions had been taken, by a decision of the Tambov Socialist-Revolutionary party, as retaliation for a punitive expedition by the government against some peasants in the Tambov Region. Spiridonova herself was beaten and abused by the arresting officers and her case received national and international attention. Nonetheless she was sentenced to imprisonment in Eastern Siberia in Nerchinsk, where she remained until the February Revolution* of 1917. She was released by a general amnesty and was elected mayor of Chita where she ordered the destruction of the local prisons.

In May 1917 she participated in the Third Congress of the Socialist-Revolutionary Party in Moscow and became one of the leaders of its Left wing. She moved to Moscow where she became a member of the Petrograd Committee of the Party and edited the left wing journal, *Nash put'* and the daily newspaper of the Petrograd Committee of the Socialist-Revolutionary Party, *Znamia truda* (Banner of Labor). She became a member of the Petrograd Soviet* and of the Central Executive Committee of the All-Russian Soviet of Peasant Deputies. When members of her own party joined a coalition cabinet in the Provisional Government*, and thereby endorsed the continuation of the war with Germany, Spiridonova was one of the Left Socialist-Revolutionaries that rejected their own right wing and moved toward the Bolsheviks who were calling for immediate peace. By October 1917 Spiridonova and most of the other Left Socialist-Revolutionaries supported the Bolsheviks during the October Seizure of Power* and at the Second All-Russian Congress of Soviets that followed. She played a decisive role in the split of the Socialist-Revolutionary Party that occurred at its Fourth Congress on November 26-December 5. In November she was elected Chairman of the Presidium of the Second All-Russian Congress of Peasant Deputies. She took part in the Constituent Assembly as a delegate and in the Third Congress of Soviets in 1918.

At first Spiridonova disagreed with the other members of the Central Committee of the Left Socialist-Revolutionary Party on the question of the Treaty of Brest-Litovsk*. The majority wanted to resign from the Soviet government, but she opposed that step. She gradually changed her mind and in July 1918 during the Fifth Congress of Soviets her party, with her encouragement, assassinated Count Mirbach, the German ambassador to the Soviet Union. As a delegate to the Congress Spiridonova took full responsibility for the action which was designed to nullify the Treaty of Brest-Litovsk and serve as a signal for a Left Socialist-Revolutionary uprising in Moscow. Spiridonova was tried for her role in these events and sentenced to one year in prison. She was arrested several more times between 1919 and 1925, and then sent into exile to Smarkand, Tashkent, and finally in 1930 to Ufa where, according to Soviet sources, she died in 1941.

Bibliography

Radkey, Oliver. *The Agrarian Foes of Bolshevism*. 1958.
———. *The Sickle Under the Hammer*. 1963.
Steinberg, I. *Spiridonova, Revolutionary Terrorist*. 1935.
Spiridonova, M. *Iz vospominanii o Nerchinskoi katorge*. 1926.

Stalin, I. V. (1879–1953; real name, Dzhugashvili, Iosif Vissarionovich). Stalin was born in the Georgian village of Gori. The future dictator of the Soviet state was the son of a shoemaker and the grandson of serfs. He joined the Tiflis branch of the Russian Social Democratic Workers' Party (*see* Russian Social Democratic Workers' Party [Bolshevik]) in 1898 after being expelled from the Tiflis Orthodox Theological Seminary. He was an active underground labor organizer (in Tiflis, Batum, and Baku) who frequently attracted police attention. He was arrested and exiled to Siberia in 1902, 1908, 1910, and 1913; each time he escaped and returned to the revolutionary underground in the Caucasus. Known by his revolutionary pseudonym "Koba," Stalin attracted the attention of V. I. Lenin* as one of the few Caucasian Social Democrats who sided with him in the 1903 party split. The vast majority of revolutionary Marxists in Transcaucasia (*see* Transcaucasia, Revolution in) were Mensheviks (*see* Russian Social Democratic Workers' Party [Menshevik]). At Lenin's prompting, Koba wrote the standard Leninist statement on the nationality question (*see* National Question and the Russian Revolution), *Marxism and the National Question,* in 1912, which established him as the Bolshevik expert on this issue. He was coopted as a member of Lenin's Bolshevik Central Committee the same year (*see* Central Committee of the Russian Communist Party [Bolshevik]).

Stalin's role in the Russian Revolutions of 1917 is extremely controversial. According to latter-day Stalinists' accounts of the October Seizure of Power*, "a party centre, headed by Comrade Stalin . . . had practical direction of the whole uprising" (Istoriia Vsesoiuznaia Kommunistichiskaia partiia [Bol'shevik] 1938, p. 197). Yet N. N. Sukhanov wrote that Stalin "gave me the impression of a gray spot which would sometimes give out a gray and inconsequential light" (Sukhanov 1955, I, p. 230). L. D. Trotsky* concurred with this appraisal, observing that "the greater the sweep of events the less Stalin's place in it." The last half of Trotsky's history, *The Russian Revolution,* mentioned Stalin only in a list of members of the post-October Bolshevik cabinet, and John Reed's eyewitness account, *Ten Days That Shook the World,* did not notice him at all. The contemporary Soviet dissident historian Roy Medvedev wrote that "Stalin's role at that time was relatively insignificant. He occupied a very modest place among the leaders of the party" (1967, p. 10). Isaac Deutscher claimed that "even more than usual he remained in the shadow."

Despite apparent agreement on his unimportance, Stalin was the senior Bolshevik in Petrograd after the fall of the Tsar in the February Revolution*, and in April he received the third highest number of votes in elections for the Central Committee (after Lenin and G. E. Zinoviev*). At the Bolshevik Sixth Party Congress in August 1917 he gave the main political report, received the greatest number of votes for *Pravda's** Editorial Board, and received the fourth highest vote total (after Lenin, Trotsky, and L. B. Kamenev*) for election to the Central Committee. In October he was named to the cabinet of the first Soviet government. Robert Tucker has concluded that although Stalin "did not rise to greatness as a revolutionary leader . . . he gained much influence in party affairs" (Reed 1919, 1967).

In the wake of the political amnesty following the abdication of Nicholas II*, Stalin returned to revolutionary Petrograd from his current place of exile, Turukhansk. In view of this former party service, the Petrograd meeting of the Russian Bureau of the Bolshevik Central Committee decided on March 12 that "it would be advisable to have him as a member of the Bureau of the Central Committee. However, in view of certain personal characteristics, the Bureau decided to give him only a consulting vote" (Tucker. 1972. p. 163). This was a reflection of Stalin's' rudeness to other Bolsheviks during his exile and of the fear of the current Petrograd Bolshevik leaders (A. G. Shliapnikov* and V. M. Molotov*) that Stalin's party seniority would displace them personally. On the following day, however, Stalin apparently asserted his claim over the protest of the members of the Russian Bureau and was made a member of the bureau and one of the editors of *Pravda*.

Before Lenin's arrival on the Russian scene in 1917, Stalin and most of the other Petrograd Bolsheviks favored limited support of the Provisional Government*. Stalin wrote in *Pravda* in March 16, 1917: "Our slogan is pressure upon the Provisional government with the aim of compelling it . . . to open immediate negotiations . . . and until then every man remains at his fighting post (Stalin, *Works*, 3, p. 8). Similarly, Stalin took what Lenin called a conciliationist position on the question of reunion with the Mensheviks: "We must do it . . . We will live down petty disagreements within the party" (Tucker 1972, p. 164). This attitude reflected Stalin's lifelong inclination to take a middle position on most political issues and to attempt compromise wherever possible. It also represented the opinion of most of the "practicals in the party who favored maximum party unity and who could not understand the rather talmudic arguments and theoretical distinctions drawn by Lenin and the intellectuals around him" (Stalin, *Works* I, xiii).

In April Lenin returned to Russia and took a sharply radical stance; he called for overthrowing the Provisional Government, ending the war immediately, and maintaining the break with the Mensheviks. Stalin and Kamenev, as editors of *Pravda*, refused to publish three of the four "Letters from Afar" in which Lenin had set out his positions and published the remaining one in abridged form. Stalin, along with most of the Bolsheviks, was against Lenin's incendiary propositions and published the leader's April Theses* on April 7 only after strong pressure from Lenin. Even then, on April 8 Kamenev (with Stalin's approval) published a harsh criticism of Lenin's ideas.

This disagreement with Lenin was to cause Stalin much embarrassment in later years when Trotsky and others brought it up during the struggle for Lenin's succession. Years later, Stalin would make a rare confession of error on this score:

> It is not surprising that Bolsheviks . . . just able to come together from different ends of Russia in order to work out a new platform, could not immediately understand the new situation . . . . I shared this mistaken position with the majority of the party and renounced it fully in the middle of April, associating myself with the "April Theses" of Lenin. (Medvedev. 1979. p. 8)

After adjusting himself to Lenin's radicalism in April, Stalin did in fact associate himself with most of the leader's positions, at least until October. During the April-October period, Stalin worked behind the scenes in an editorial position, editing and writing for *Pravda* and its successor, *Rabochii put'* (*Worker's Path*). He was not one of the Bolsheviks' fiery tribunes and kept out of the public eye, busying himself with propaganda and organizational tasks. His writings tended to be terse and slogan-like. Deutscher wrote that Stalin's pieces were "the small change of Bolshevik propaganda" (1967, p. 156). As would be the case throughout his life, his work was neither glamorous nor brilliant, but he was adept at the dry and plodding details of office work.

After the abortive uprising of the July Days*, most of the leading Bolsheviks were either under arrest or in hiding from the Provisional Government. Although Stalin was a member of the Central Committee and a leading editor of *Pravda*, the Provisional Government did not include him on the list of Bolshevik outlaws.

He remained at liberty not because he was too unimportant but rather because he was beyond the notice of counterrevolution. Thus he was free to give the main political report to the Sixth Party Congress in August and was the only senior party leader at liberty until September.

A party crisis in October once again demonstrated Stalin's inclination to compromise and his willingness to disagree with Lenin. In mid-October the Bolshevik Central Committee finally decided (at Lenin's insistence) to plan an armed uprising against the Provisional Government and to establish a Soviet government. Much of the Bolshevik Right regarded this as potentially disastrous for the party and the Revolution. Shortly after the meeting, Zinoviev and Kamenev revealed the still-secret insurrection decision by writing a strong criticism of it in the non-Bolshevik party newspaper *Novaia zhizn' (New Life)*. Lenin was furious. He called the two "strikebreakers of the revolution" and demanded their expulsion from the party for breach of discipline. Stalin, separating himself from Lenin's position, published a critique of Lenin by Zinoviev in *Pravda* and, in an attempt to heal the wounds, added a personal comment: "We in our turn express the hope that with Comrade Zinoviev's statement . . . the matter can be considered closed. The harsh tone of Comrade Lenin's article does not alter the fact that essentially we remain of one mind" (*Rabocii put' [Pravda]*, October 20, 1917). Shortly thereafter, at a meeting of the Central Committee, Lenin formally demanded the expulsion of Zinoviev and Kamenev. Stalin opposed Lenin's demand in the Central Committee, apparently more stridently than the others present. He was criticized so sharply that he proffered his resignation from *Pravda*, which, in accordance with party tradition, was declined by the committee. The matter died down, and a reconciliation was achieved, but the incident remains an illustration of Stalin's role and attitudes during 1917.

During the Bolshevik-led insurrection in October Stalin remained behind the scenes, working in the Editorial Offices of *Pravda*. The later claim by his followers that he had "practical direction of the whole uprising" is not true (*Istoriia Vsesoiuznaia Kommunistichiskaia Partiia* [Bolshevik] 1938, p. 197). In fact, in an article after the Revolution Stalin explicitly credited Trotsky with that role, although the piece was subsequently deleted from the later editions of Stalin's writings.

From the proclamation of the first Bolshevik government in October until 1922, Stalin held the position of People's Commissar for Nationalities. During the Civil War in Russia* (1918–1921), however, he was primarily occupied as a political commissar in the Red Army* on the southern fronts. In that capacity, he came into conflict with Trotsky over the question of using former tsarist military officers. Trotsky's view, which was supported by Lenin, was that the Red Army needed the services of those old-regime "military specialists" who were willing to help against the Whites (*see* White Movement). With their assistance, Trotsky built the Red Army into a disciplined fighting force with traditional chains of command and authority. Stalin argued that the tsarist officers were "class alien" and could not be trusted. He favored a popular militia using guerilla tactics and relying solely on the participation and enthusiasm of the proletariat and peasantry. His proposals were, however, overruled by Lenin and the Political Bureau.

In 1922, at Lenin's suggestion, Stalin was named general secretary of the party and assumed responsibility for the party's record keeping, personnel assignments, and communications with regional party committees. Stalin used this office to build up a powerful political machine over which he was boss. This development alarmed Lenin who wrote shortly before his death:

> Stalin has concentrated tremendous power in his hands, and I am not always sure that he is always capable of using this power with due caution. Stalin is too crude, and this defect . . . becomes intolerable in the post of general secretary. I therefore propose, comrades, that we think of a way of removing Stalin from this post and replacing him with someone else. (Medvedev 1972, p. 24–5)

Stalin was not removed from this crucial position because the delegates to the Eighth Party Congress who read the letter decided to ignore Lenin's suggestion. Stalin held the position of general secretary until his death in 1953.

During the 1920s Stalin won political contests against Leon Trotsky (the "Left Opposition") and N. I. Bukharin* (the "Right Opposition"). By the end of 1929 he had no real rivals for party leadership.

In the 1930s Stalin's policies produced the fastest rate of industrial growth in history, but the parallel collectivization of agriculture was poorly handled and led to peasant resistance and a severe famine. His politics dramatically raised the educational and technical levels of a backward society and promoted former workers and peasants into leading positions. However, this period of opportunity and rapid social mobility was also the time of the Great Purges, a confused and violent political warfare in which thousands—mainly from the former elite— were denounced by hysterical militants and arrested, imprisoned, or executed by the secret police. The dramatic economic and social revolution of the 1930s, sometimes called the "Stalin Revolution," traumatized, modernized, and completely transformed Soviet society.

The tumultuous thirties were followed by another shock, World War II. During the war, in which the Soviet Union lost 20 million lives, Stalin functioned as commander-in-chief, supervising military strategy and assuming the title of generalissimo. Under his leadership, the Soviet Union was unprepared for the Nazi surprise attack in 1941 and suffered tremendous reverses and casualties. It was also under his leadership, however, that the USSR defeated Hitler and emerged from World War II as the second strongest power in the world.

Stalin died, probably of a cerebral hemorrhage, on March 5, 1953, and was interred next to Lenin in the latter's mausoleum. Stalin's memory continued to be publicly revered until 1956 when Khrushchev officially condemned the "crimes of the Stalin era" and denounced the dictator's "cult of personality." In 1961 Stalin's body was removed from the Lenin Mausoleum and buried next to the Kremlin wall behind the mausoleum.

Stalin's life was full of contradictions. He was the ruler of the Russian state and an extreme Russian patriot but was not himself Russian. He allowed himself to be publicly adored as a "great and wise teacher," "the greatest human who ever lived," and "father of the peoples" but was shy and uncomfortable in public. He held almost absolute power and sycophants jumped at his every wish, but according to his daughter, he slept on a foldout bed in a bare room and wore the same overcoat for twenty years.

J. Arch Getty

Bibliography

Deutscher, Isaac. *Stalin: A Political Biography.* 1967.
Grey, Ian. *Stalin: Man of History.* 1979.
Medvedev, Roy A. *Let History Judge.* 1972.
———. *Stalin and Stalinism.* 1979.
Reed, John. *Ten Days That Shook the World.* 1919.
Slusser, Robert M. *Stalin in October.* 1987.
Stalin, I. V. *Na putiakh k Oktiabriu.* 1924. (*The October Revolution.* 1978.)
Sukharov, N. N. The Russian Revolution. 2 vols. 1955.
Trotsky, L. D. *Stalin.* 1941.
Tucker, Robert C. *Stalin as Revolutionary.* 1972.

Stuchka, Piotr Ivanovich (1865–1932, pseudonyms: Veteran, "Paragraf"). A prominent Latvian Communist (*see* Latvia, Revolution in) who also played an important role in Russia as one of Lenin's first Commissars of Justice, and a leading figure in the October Seizure of Power*.

Stuchka was born in Lifland and returned to Riga after completing his studies at the Juridical faculty at the University of St. Petersburg. He worked as a barrister in Riga from 1888–1897 while also serving as chief editor of the daily Marxist newspaper *Doenas Lapa.* For his work as editor he was arrested in 1897 and sentenced to five years exile in Viatsk Province. From prison he contributed to the Latvian Marxist journal *Social Democrat* which was published in Bern, Switzerland. After he had served his prison term Stuchka worked in the Vitebsk organization of the Russian Social Democratic Workers' Party. When the split took place in that party he immediately joined the Bolshevik faction (*see* Russian Social Democratic Workers' Party [Bolshevik]). In 1906 he returned to Riga and began work to create a Bolshevized party there, and in that capacity became Chairman of the Central Committee of the Latvian Social Democratic Workers' Party. He was elected to the Second Duma (*see* Duma and Revolution). In 1907 he moved to St. Petersburg where he was associated with a variety of Latvian Social Democratic and Workers' publications, and contributed to the Bolshevik journal *Prosveshchenie* (Enlightenment). After the February Revolution* he became a member of the Bolshevik faction of the Petrograd Soviet* of Workers' Deputies. From 1917 to 1918 he served as one of the Soviet Union's first Commissars of Justice and then moved on to the Commissar of Foreign Affairs from 1918–1919. When the Latvian Bolsheviks declared the creation of a Latvian

Soviet (in Latvian, *Iskolat*) state in the fall of 1918, Stuchka was elected as its first Prime Minister or Chairman of the Council of People's Commissars of Latvia, but that job only lasted until May 1919. He was also a member of the Central Committee of the Russian Communist Party (Bolshevik)*. He was first Commissar of Justice from November 15, 1917 to December 5, 1917 and then from March 18, 1922 to August 22, 1918. In 1923 he became head of the Supreme Court of the USSR and Latvian representative to the Communist International. Stuchka was one of the leading theorists in Soviet law during the early years of the regime. He belonged to the school of Soviet jurists who argued that the creation of a proletarian dictatorship called for the creation of a new kind of working-class law in which the old laws would be overthrown and new concepts applied. Where no revolutionary law had yet been formulated judges were expected to follow revolutionary concepts of justice, especially against the enemies of the revolution. As Stuchka put it in 1927 "Communism means not the victory of socialist law, but the victory of socialism over any law, since with the abolition of classes with their antagonistic interests, law will die out altogether" (Juviler, p. 28). Stuchka died in 1932 and was interred along with the other revered heroes of the October Revolution in the Kremlin Wall. By 1937–1938 however, he would be officially condemned as a "legal nihilist" in the field of jurisprudence.

Bibliography

Juviler, Peter. *Revolutionary Law and Order*. 1976. *Soviet Legal Philosophy*. 1951.
Stuchka, P. I. *Revoliutsionnaia rol' prava i gosudarstva*. 1921.

Sukhanov, Niklai Niklaevich (1882–1940; real name was Gimmer or Himmer). A prominent historian and Menshevik.

Sukhanov was born in Moscow in the family of an official who worked for the railroads. He attended a gymnasium in Moscow while his mother worked in a factory. His mother was arrested when he was fourteen and he began to support himself through tutoring. He joined illegal student discussion groups in the gymnasium and in 1903 went to Moscow University where he became active in student organizations affiliated with the Socialist-Revolutionary (*see* Socialist-Revolutionary Party) movement in Moscow where he was arrested in 1904 for operating an illegal printing shop. He was released in 1905. Sukhanov took part in the 1905 Revolution (*see* Nineteen-Five Revolution) in Moscow as a member of the Socialist-Revolutionary party. From 1906 to 1914 he devoted himself to study and writing while working for the Ministry of Finance. Around 1909 he decided to become a Marxist and member of the Menshevik faction (*see* Russian Social Democratic Workers' Party [Menshevik]). During the war he edited a non-party "internationalist" journal called *Sovremennik* (Contemporary), and with Maxim Gorky (*see* Peshkov, A. M.) helped found the journal *Letopis'* and later the newspaper *Novaia zhizn'* (The New Life). Sukhanov was a member of the Executive Committee of the Petrograd Soviet from the first days of the revolution until June 1918. Sukhanov associated himself with the Menshevik Internationalists (*see* Internationalists) who opposed the leadership of their own party, the Socialist-Revolutionary party, and the Constitutional Democratic party on most issues, but also opposed V. I. Lenin on the need for an insurrection to overthrow the Provisional Government*. Though disapproving of the continuation of World War I* and the entry of Socialists into a cabinet of the Provisional Government*, they were in favor of a Socialist-Liberal coalition of some sort, and continued to oppose the idea of a coup d'etat. They also hoped to revive the Second International (*see* World War I and the Communist International). He was very close to Iulii Martov*.

Sukhanov's wife, Galina Flakserman, was a Bolshevik (*see* Russian Social Democratic Workers' Party [Bolshevik]) which made him privy to many of the most important developments in that party, though on the night of October 10, 1917 when the Bolsheviks met in his apartment to decide upon insurrection, Sukhanov's wife arranged for him to be absent. Because of his unique position, poised between the three major radical political movements in Russia at that time (Bolshevik - Menshevik - Socialist-Revolutionary) and because of his perceptivity, Sukhanov performed a unique role as memoirist of the 1917 Revolutions in his *Zapiski o revoliutsii* (*Notes on the Revolution*), one of the most important personal accounts of the year 1917 in Petrograd. In it one finds vivid and valuable portrayals of events, personalities, and of the city itself during that year. An abridged version appeared in English in 1955 and 1962.

After the October Seizure of Power* Sukhanov resigned from the Menshevik Party in 1919 and became a Soviet official. In 1922 his *Notes on the Revolution* were published in Berlin, probably from a manuscript he smuggled out of Russia during a trip to that city. In 1931 he was arrested and along with other former Mensheviks confessed to participation in an international conspiratorial organization called the Union Bureau of the Central Committee of the Russian Social Democratic Workers' Party (Menshevik) that was supposedly preparing a military intervention in the Soviet Union from the West. Sukhanov received a ten-year prison sentence and apparently died in prison.

Bibliography

Haimson, Leopold, ed. *The Mensheviks*. 1974.
Sukhanov, N. N. *Zapiski o revoliutsii*. 7 vols. 1922.
————. *The Russian Revolution 1917*. 1955.

Sultangaliev, Mir Said (1880–1939). Sultangaliev was the most prominent Volga-Tatar Moslem Jadid* Communist in the early years of the Soviet regime. He was born in the village of Krymyskaly in a family of Volga-Tatar teachers in the Volga Region and studied in the Russian Tatar Teachers' College in Kazan. He began his career as a teacher in a reformed Tatar school in the Crimea, but he contributed to many liberal and radical nationalist journals in Kazan, St. Petersburg, Baku and Orenburg. In the spring of 1917 the Executive Council of the Moscow All-Russian Moslem Congress hired him as a secretary and he became one of the leading members of the Moslem Socialist Committee of Kazan.

After the Bolsheviks came to power in Kazan, Sultangaliev joined the Bolsheviks and became Commissar of Education and Nationalities. In the elections to the Constituent Assembly he ran on the same ticket with M. Vakhitov* and M. A. Tsalikov. In February 1918 he took part in the overthrow of the All-Russian Provisional Moslem National Council (or *Shuro*) in Kazan. (*See* Tatars, Revolution Among the; Turkestan, Revolution in.)

After the death of Vakhitov, I. V. Stalin,* Commissar of Nationalities, made Sultangaliev the most important Moslem in the Soviet state. He became Chairman of the Central Moslem Military College in December, 1918, one of the three members of the Small Collegium of the Commissariat of Nationalities, co-editor of the Commissariat's official publication *Zhizn national' nostei* (The Life of Nationality). For a time Sultangaliev's National Communism was tolerated, and in his own way he provided a foreshadowing of many of the features of National Communism that would follow. Using V. I. Lenin's *"Imperialism: the Highest Stage of Capitalism"* as his springboard, Sultangaliev argued that non-proletarian nations can go directly from precapitalism (or feudalism) to socialism, because the oppressed third world people are in some sense all proletarians. While affirming this notion of a nation of proletarians, Sultangaliev did not argue the brotherhood of all oppressed people, but predicted that national identity would remain. In short, the proletarian revolution in such areas would make the nation stronger, not weaker. But in the absence of an industrial proletariat third world nations could only have Soviet revolutions. They were not yet ready for class war. By mid–1919 Sultangaliev argued that the key to world revolution no longer lay in the advanced West, but rather in the backward East, which he called the "linchpin of the revolutionary process." It would be conducted by an alliance between the Asian peasantry and the revolutionary national bourgeoisie.

In the 1920s he would carry his arguments a step further and argue that the only way to avoid the reappearance of Great Russian imperialism under socialism was to make the oppressed nations the dictators over the Russian people. In some respects this was a response to the New Economic Policy*, which Sultangaliev believed had returned the old ruling classes to power in the East, that is, the Russian merchants and officials and Moslem tradesman and clergy. For Sultangaliev the answer was that Moslem nations should have Moslem leaders, and that Russian Communists should stay in their own territories. He soon began to call for the creation of a Colonial International, a Soviet Turkic Republic, and a revival of the Moslem Communist Party.

When the Communist International conducted the Congress of the Peoples of the East in Baku in 1920, the Russian and Western leaders, like G. E. Zinoviev*, clearly rejected the notion that Asia would call the tune either in its own countries or in the rest of the Soviet Union. In Zinoviev's words "the salvation of the East can come only through the victory of the Western proletariat."

In April 1923 Sultangaliev was arrested and expelled for the first time. He was accused of treason, Moslem nationalism, and collaboration with other Moslem Nationalists at the Fourth Conference of the Central Committee of the Russian Communist Party with the workers of the National Republics and Regions in June 9–12, 1923. In particular he was charged with conspiracy with members of the Basmachis*. He had the honor of being the first prominent party member to be expelled from the Communist Party by I. V. Stalin*, but was released from jail. He was arrested again in 1928 and disappeared into the prison camps. He has never been rehabilitated (see Tatars, Revolution Among the).

Bibliography

Bennigsen, Alexandre A., and Wimbish, S. Enders. *Muslim National Communism in the Soviet Union.* 1979.

Pipes, Richard. *The Formation of the Soviet Union.* 1968.

Supreme Council of the National Economy (1917–1932; Verkhovnyi sovet narodnogo khoziaistva or Vesenkha—VSNKh). The Supreme Council of the National Economy was a department in the Soviet government created for the purpose of organizing the whole economy on a socialist basis.

Three days after the Council of People's Commissars* decreed workers' control (see Left Communism; Shliapnikov, A. G.; Kollontai, A. M.; Workers Role in Revolution) on November 17, 1917, it dissolved existing economic committees and called for the creation of a Supreme Economic Conference. That proposal materialized in the form of the decree of December 5, 1917 creating the Supreme Council of the National Economy. The original decree on workers' control had called for the institution of workers' control within a planned economy—the exact words were "the planned regulation of the national economy." The decree on the Supreme Council of the National Economy said that its function would be "to organize the economic activity of the nation and the financial resources of the government" (Carr, 1952, p. 80).

In the beginning the creation of the Supreme Council of the National Economy appeared to be a concession to the Left Communists* and their version of workers' control, and in the beginning most of the executive staff was drawn from their ranks. N. Osinskii* was the President with the title People's Commissar for the Organization and Regulation of Production. Prominent members of the Left Communists, like N. I. Bukharin*, G. I. Lomov-Oppokov* and V. N. Smirnov were members. But their conception of their role would soon come into conflict with V. I. Lenin's*. The Left simply wanted a central organ to coordinate and implement workers' control and speed up nationalization. Lenin was more concerned with the restoration of labor discipline and the use of bourgeois specialists including former managers. It was not originally intended that the Supreme Council should become the chief planning agency for the Soviet state, despite the wording cited above, since that would be contrary to the intent of the Left Communists staffing it.

During the next three months the pressure of other forces moved the Supreme Council into a different course from that which the Left Communists had intended. It became the general staff of economic planning because of the growing need for a coherent sense of direction in the national economy. The withdrawal of the Left Communists from its executive boards, in protest against the trend toward state control at the top, made the new policy easier to implement through the Supreme Council of the National Economy. At its first meeting on December 14, 1917, the Supreme Council discovered that the Central Executive Committee of the Supreme Soviet* had nationalized the banks and all industrial enterprises. Many of these decrees were more a statement of principal than an actual administrative action. On December 23, 1917 the Supreme Council decided to set up regional agencies (Councils of National Economy, *Sovnarkhozy*) to implement the decisions of the national body. A hierarchy of such bodies parallelling the structure of the Soviets of Workers' and Peasants' Deputies was decreed in May 1918. As E. H. Carr points out, however, the reach of this ministry exceeded its grasp during the chaotic period at the beginning of the Civil War in Russia*, and in the end the Supreme Council would move into the gap created by the demise of, or demonstrated ineffectiveness of, workers' control and the need for some other method for introducing planning, coordination and a sense of direction in the Russian economy during a period of crisis. Thus, its most significant decision was the creation on December 23, 1917 of special commissions for each branch of industry. Essentially, the Supreme Council stepped into a gap created by the intense pressure of the Civil War and the failure of workers' control or any other state agency to organize and direct the chaotic disintegrating economy.

Immediate nationalization of the whole economy was not part of the original Bolshevik (*see* Russian Social Democratic Workers' Party [Bolshevik]) plan. It was to a large extent thrust upon the new government by the failure of workers' control and the pressures of the Civil War. As Carr put it in his *The Bolshevik Revolution*, nationalization proceeded in a haphazard way that was both "punitive" and "spontaneous"; punitive in that it was punishment for the failures and shortcomings of particular plants, and spontaneous in that it was not only decreed by the Supreme Council, but also imposed spontaneously by local organs of political power. In January 1918 the Third All-Russian Congress of Soviets would advance the process by issuing a blanket decree, "The Declaration of Rights of the Toiling and Exploited People," "which proclaimed all factories, mines, and transportation state property" (Carr, III, p. 88). To a large extent this was also an announcement that workers' control had decisively failed to produce the desired results. The process of nationalization began with the sugar industry in May 1918 followed by the oil industry in June.

The Treaty of Brest-Litovsk*, with the hardship caused by its surrender of forty percent of the industry of the Russian Empire, signalled a change of national economic policy. It also marked the departure of the Left Communist majority in the Supreme Council. Bukharin, Lomov-Oppokov, and Osinskii left, and

Larin and Miliutin, both moderates, stepped into their shoes. Larin issued a decree on March 3, 1918 that clearly called for a system of centralized supervision and control throughout the entire economy. At a meeting of the Supreme Council on March 19, 1918 Miliutin called for a complete change in economic policy, and attacked both workers' control and extreme nationalization. In the latter case he argued that any further nationalization should be adequately planned beforehand.

The decisive turning point came with the appointment of a right wing Communist, A. I. Rykov*, as Chairman of the Supreme Council in May and the decrees of June 1918 nationalizing all large scale industry. This marked the end of one phase of economic policy and the beginning of another. A series of articles published by Lenin in April and May identified the next stage in economic policy. Osinskii criticized the new policies, saying that they announced the creation of state capitalism in Russia. Lenin accepted the charge, saying that state capitalism—meaning a concentration of ownership in industry by private capitalists under close state supervision—would be an improvement. In the next stage the emphasis would be on organization. The appeals of the Left Communists for workers' control and decentralization were decisively rejected. The decree of June 28, 1918 on nationalization put the power of administering the nationalized economy into the hands of the Supreme Council.

The nationalization of the Russian economy under the direction of the Supreme Council called for a radical increase in the size of that institution. By November 1920, 37,000 enterprises were under its control, and the administrative apparatus of the Supreme Council expanded from 328 in May 1918 to 21, 261 by April 1921 with local Councils of the People's Economy at every level. But things did not go smoothly. There was considerable opposition to the activities of the Supreme Council from the Left Communists. Moreover, there were frequent disagreements with Lenin over basic policy. There were conflicts between the Supreme Council and the Council of the People's Commissars*, with the latter seeing a narrower role for the Supreme Council—that is, it should confine itself to industry. The Supreme Council did not agree with Lenin on the question of one-man management of industry—they preferred the collegial control—and they were less enthusiastic about planning than Lenin. Finally, the Supreme Council found it difficult to carry out its mission under the adverse conditions created by years of war, revolution and Civil War, conditions which repeatedly forced it to submit to the authority of higher institutions on critical matters because of the urgent need to support the war.

As early as 1919 it found itself increasingly subordinated to other institutions, and losing its function and personnel to other institutions, in particular to the Council of Labor and Defense. With the arrival of the New Economic Plan a host of new institutions began to take over the functions of the Supreme Council, such state agencies as the Central Economic Administration, the Central Administration for State Industry, and finally the State Planning Agency itself, GOSPLAN, which began its work in April 1921. By 1932 the Supreme Council had outlived its original purpose. It was dissolved and its functions were given to three new economic commissariats.

Bibliography

Baykov, A. *The Soviet Economic System*. 1945.
Carr, E. H. *The Bolshevik Revolution*. III. 1952.
Dobb, M. *Soviet Economic Development Since 1917*. 3rd Edition. 1966.
Meyer, Alfred. *Leninism*. 1957.
Nove, Alec. *An Economic History of the USSR*. 1969.
Schwartz, H. *Russia's Soviet Economy*. 1954.

Sverdlov, Iakov Mikhailovich (1885–1919). Sverdlov was a key figure in the organization and preparation of the Bolshevik Party (*see* Russian Social Democratic Workers' Party [Bolshevik]) for the October Seizure of Power*.

Iakov Mikhailovich Sverdlov was born in Nizhnii Novgorod, the third child in a family of seven children. His father owned a small engraving shop in the city and his mother led a domestic life dedicated to rearing the children. Sverdlov's attachment to the revolutionary movement began seriously after only four years of formal education and unsuccessful attempts to secure steady employment. Influenced by his elder brother Zinovii (later Maxim Gorky's adopted godson) and local Social Democrats and Socialist–Revolutionaries (*see* Socialist-Revolutionary Party), Iakov Sverdlov formally became a member of the Russian Social Democratic Workers' Party in Nizhnii Novgorod in 1902.

His exploits at first consisted of mundane tasks: printing and distributing illegal leaflets, speaking to meetings of workers, and organizing underground printing presses. By the end of 1904, however, he had advanced to a position where he directed Bolshevik organizations in the textile town of Kostroma. The tsarist Okhrana (State Security Police), although nicknaming him "the little one" (*malysh*) because of his frail physique, took him seriously as a "professional revolutionary."

The 1905 Revolution (*see* Nineteen-Five Revolution) enabled Sverdlov to make his mark as an effective Bolshevik organizer in the Urals. He and his wife, Klaudia Novogorodtseva, directed the Bolsheviks first in Ekaterinburg and then in Perm. According to both comrades and members of the political opposition, Sverdlov established his reputation as a tireless organizer with a remarkable memory for names and characteristics of those with whom he worked. E. A. Preobrazhenskii, for example, claimed that Sverdlov personally knew most of the Bolshevik Party workers. Sverdlov found that V. I. Lenin* knew him by reputation. Sverdlov, who was known as "comrade Andrei" in party circles, was arrested in June 1906 and imprisoned until 1909. Upon his release Lenin appointed him to rectify the unacceptable operations of the Moscow district *okrug* committee. Arrested again in December 1909, Sverdlov was exiled for three years to the Narym region of Siberia, where he nearly died in the distant hamlet of Maksimkin Iar. Sverdlov first met and then roomed with I. V. Stalin* in Narym in 1912.

Both men escaped in the same year and returned to the capital. Sverdlov found that the Prague Conference of Bolsheviks (January 1912) had coopted him into its Central Committee and its Russian Bureau. In December 1912 Lenin became so displeased with Stalin's de facto editorship of the newspaper *Pravda** (*Truth*) that he removed him and appointed Sverdlov to that position. Sverdlov was somewhat successful in converting *Pravda* into a forum for Lenin's views and in combatting the so-called "liquidators" in the State Duma (*see* Duma and Revolution) before he was betrayed by the police spy Roman Malinovskii in February 1913.

Sverdlov spent the years from 1913 to 1917 in exile in the Turukhansk region of Siberia. He once more was Stalin's roommate, an arrangement that was so unsatisfactory that Sverdlov initiated a transfer to the larger village of Monastyrskoe. There he continued his interest in journalism, becoming a regular contributor to a Tomsk newspaper. He also continued his self-education as a Marxist, took part in local political affairs, and wrote the articles "Studies on the History of the International Workers' Movement" and "The Split in German Social Democracy."

The February Revolution* of 1917 freed Sverdlov, who arrived in Petrograd in late March. Although a Central Committee (*see* Central Committee of the Russian Communist Party [Bolshevik]) member since 1912, he was not widely known within the party, except by reputation as an excellent organizer. He participated as a "personal" delegate to the March conference of party workers and then departed from the capital to the Urals. There he helped organized an all-Ural conference of Bolsheviks, which, however, did not endorse Lenin's "April theses"*. The Ural Conference returned Sverdlov as one of its delegates to the party's April Conference (Seventh All-Russian Conference of the Russian Social Democratic Workers' Party [Bolshevik]).

The April Conference marked the beginning of Sverdlov's rise as a party administrator. Adopting Lenin's political views, Sverdlov helped organize this conference to the advantage of Lenin and was in turn reelected a member of the Bolshevik Central Committee. Following the conference Sverdlov was appointed by Lenin to direct the party's Secretariat in Petrograd. He and his small staff attempted to coordinate information on Bolshevik activities throughout Russia and to increase the Central Committee's authority within local party committee's. Sverdlov also played a key role in negotiating the merger of L. D. Trotsky's* Interdistrict committee* with the Bolsheviks. In addition to performing his secretarial duties, together with Stalin he guided the Bolshevik delegation at the First All-Russian Congress of Soviets in June 1917.

When the disturbances of the July Days* forced Lenin and G. E. Zinoviev* to flee from Finland and landed other prominent leaders such as L. B. Kamenev* in jail, Sverdlov emerged as the interim leader of the Bolsheviks. The Secretariat restored its contacts with provincial organizations, and as a result of Sverdlov's organizational ability, the semi-legal Sixth Party Congress was able to convene in Petrograd in late July. Sverdlov gave the organizational report, which indicated that the Bolsheviks had grown from 78 organizations with 80,000 members in April to 162 organizations with approximately 240,000 members, and he chaired the majority of the sessions. In the debate over the leadership of the Central Committee and *Pravda,* Sverdlov defended both against complaints by provincial delegates and the Petersburg Committee.

After the Sixth Party Congress Sverdlov became a member of the Central Committee's "core staff" and its Organization Bureau (Orgburo), both of which began to function in August 1917. In addition to undertaking these duties Sverdlov also handled a variety of other tasks: mediating between Stalin and the Central Committee's "Military Organization," organizing party work within trade unions, monitoring the party press, chairing sessions of the Central Committee, establishing the basis for party control through the provincial committees, and campaigning for Bolshevik candidates to the Constituent Assembly*. By October 1917 Trotsky considered Sverdlov to be so important that they nick-named him the "general secretary of the October insurrection."

In preparation for that seizure of power (*see* October Seizure of Power), Sverdlov fully supported Lenin and organized the crucial party meetings of October 10 and 16 to the advantage of the Leninists. From behind the scenes he also prepared the important Northern Regional Congress of Soviets (October 11–13), which Lenin had hoped would begin the assault on the Provisional Government*. Sverdlov was the only one of five people on the Central Committee's "military revolutionary center" to work with Trotsky and the Petrograd Soviet's* Military Revolutionary Committee (MRC) before the actual transfer of power on October 25.

Following the October Seizure of Power Sverdlov held positions in both party and soviet organs. On November 8, on Lenin's suggestions, he was elected Chairman of the All-Russian Central Executive Committee* of Soviets (VTsIK), replacing the more moderate Kamenev. As Chairman of this Executive Committee, Sverdlov devoted his main attention to the soviet apparatus until mid–1918. He established himself as a firm chairman overriding the opposition within VTsIK that favored a more broadly based government including all socialist parties. Sverdlov also played a key role in persuading the Left Socialist–Revolutionaries (*see* Left Socialist-Revolutionary Party) to enter the government in November 1917. To circumvent non-Bolshevik opponents in the Executive Committee, Sverdlov began to rely not only on the general meeting of VTsIK but also on its Bolshevik-controlled presidium. By early 1918 the presidium had become the de facto locus of power within VTsIK. The Bolsheviks were thus able to use the authority of VTsIK to justify decisions that had been formulated by their own Central Committee and then implemented by the Council of Peoples' Commissars* (Sovnarkom). The control of the Executive Committee was completed by July 1918, by which time all political parties not agreeing with governmental policy (Mensheviks [*see* Russian Social Democratic Workers' Party

(Menshevik)] and Right, Left, and Center Socialist–Revolutionaries) had been excluded from VTsIK.

The Bolsheviks' victory within the soviets enabled Sverdlov to turn his attention to the party structure. From August 1918 until his death Sverdlov consolidated the organizational structure of the party from top to bottom, based upon party discipline and "democratic centralism." He also began to amass files on party workers and to strengthen the provincial party committee (*gubkom*) system of administering the provinces. When confronted with the problem of bureaucratism, Sverdlov proposed a rotation of workers between higher administrative posts and ordinary rank-and-file jobs. His authority within the party reached such a point that some Bolshevik leaders in the provinces addressed him as "chairman" of the Central Committee.

In the early months of 1919 Sverdlov took on further responsibilities. He served as the government's plenipotentiary to Lithuania and Belorussia, where he participated in the creation of a joint Lithuanian–Belorussian republic and helped select that government's personnel. In March 1919 he traveled to the Ukraine (*see* Ukraine, Revolution in) to mediate the conflict between the "Left" (G. I. Piatakov, A. S. Bubnov*, and others) and "Right" (E. I. Kviring, Ia. A. Epstein, and others) Bolsheviks there. He was partially successful as mediator, but these added responsibilities, lack of rest, and Sverdlov's frantic pace undermined his health. He returned to Moscow with a fever that developed into "Spanish influenza." He died from this disease at the age of thirty-three on March 16, 1919, on the eve of the Eighth Party Congress.

Critics of the Central Committee at the Eighth Party Congress blamed Lenin and Sverdlov for the concentration of power in the hands of the few, for the absence of Central Committee sessions, for incorrect policies, and for bureaucratism. N. Osinskii* even credited the entire organizational work of the party to Sverdlov alone. Lenin and V. A. Avanesov, speaking for the Central Committee, defended the party's organization man and spoke of his extraordinary ability in handling administrative problems.

Sverdlov's chief accomplishments in the Russian Revolution consisted of his adroit leadership of VTsIK, his ability to isolate the opposition both in VTsIK and in the party, and his direction of the Bolshevik Secretariat. Sverdlov as chairman of VTsIK and Lenin as chairman of Sovnarkom constituted the nucleus of the Soviet government during the Civil War in Russia*. By the use of "technical" regulations such as time limits for speakers, the privileged position of the VTsIK presidium, and the chairman's right to recognize speakers, Sverdlov helped insure the dominance of the Sovnarkom (*see* Council of People's Commissars, 1917–1922) over VTsIK and thus helped pave the way for a party state. By July 1918 the Bolsheviks had routed their opponents in VTsIK and were well on their way to dislodging the opposition from provincial soviets.

Sverdlov also used the party's Secretariat to bolster the influence of the Central Committee in local organizations. From April to October 1917 he and his staff compiled information on the political mood in the provinces. During the crucial debate over the October Seizure of Power, Sverdlov used this information to support Lenin's demand that the Bolsheviks take power. After the Bolsheviks wrested control of the soviets from their opponents, Sverdlov returned to the problem of consolidating the party apparatus. From August 1918 until his death in March 1919 Sverdlov and the Secretariat strove to subordinate local party committees to the will of the Central Committee. Sverdlov used Secretariat agents to reorganize recalcitrant party committees, denied funding and literature to uncooperative organizations, and reassigned party members who were hindering the party efforts by personal clashes (the most notable example of which was the so-called "Astrakhan case," in which E. E. Bosh and A. G. Shliapnikov* were transferred to other duties. Sverdlov's death was a great blow to the Central Committee's effort to bolster its influence within provincial committees. It produced a vacuum in the field of party organization that only began to be filled in April 1922 with the appointment of Sverdlov's rival, Stalin, to the post of General Secretary.

Charles Duval

Bibliography

Avdeev, N. et.al., eds. *Revoliutsiia 1917 goda: khronika sobytii*. Vols. 3–6. 1923–1930.
Chamberlin, W. H. *The Russian Revolution, 1917–21*. 2 vols. 1957.
Fedorov, K. G. *VTsIK v pervye gody sovetskoi vlasti, 1917–20 gg*. 1957.
Gorin, P. O., ed. *Orginazatsiia i stroitel'stvo sovetov RD v 1917 gody*. 1928.
Keep, J. L. H. *The Russian Revolution*. 1976.
Kleandrova, V. M. *Organizatsiia i formy deiatel' nosti VTsIK (1917–24 gg.)*. 1968.
Protokolii zasedanii VTsIK sovetov R.S.Kr, I Kaz. deputatov II sozyva. 1918.
Rabinowitch, A. *The Bolsheviks Come to Power*. 1976.
Radkey, O. H. *The Sickle under the Hammer*. 1963.
Razgon, A. I. *VTsIK sovetov v pervye mesiatsy diktatury proletariata*. 1977.

T

Tatars, Revolution Among the. Among the Turkic peoples of Russia, the Tatars played a special role in the Russian Revolution, not because of their numbers, though they counted about three and a half million both before and after the Revolution, but because they were probably the most advanced Turkic group and, therefore, played an important role as teachers and leaders, providing I. V. Stalin* with a cadre of Moslem leaders after the October Seizure of Power*.

Although people of Tatar ancestry are found throughout the Soviet Union, the name "Tatar" is usually applied to two distinct ethnic groups—the Kazan Tatars, who today have an autonomous republic on the Volga and the Kama Rivers, and the Crimean Tatars (*see* Crimea, Revolution in the) who had a home in the Crimea until World War II. About one third of the population of the Bashkir Autonomous Soviet Socialist Republic (ASSR) (*see* Bashkiria, Revolution in) also regard the Tatar language as their native tongue. The Kazan or Volga Tatars are probably descendents of the Volga Bolgars and the Tatars of the Golden Horde who controlled Russia from 1240–1480.

Although the Tatars had originally controlled Russia, they lost ground to their former subjects, the Russians, after Ivan the Terrible took their city of Kazan in 1552. The Russians then began to cultivate the middle Volga plains and today outnumber the Tatars in that area. There were attempts to forcibly convert the Tatars in that area from the Moslem faith until Catherine the Great granted them religious tolerance in 1788. Although the Tatar noble families had long since merged with the Russian aristocracy after Catherine's edict of toleration, the Tatar merchants resisted absorption and began to compete with their Russian counterparts in the economic penetration of Central Asia (*see* Central Asia, Revolution in). The similarities between the Tatars and the native Moslem population of Central Asia in language and religion gave the Tatars an edge over Russian tradesmen.

With the conquest of Turkestan in the 1870s, the situation began to change. Russian merchants then had the backing of the Russian government, and the railroads and cotton growing began to change the whole nature of that economy.

Within this historical context the rise of the Jadid* (or New Method) schools under the inspiration of a Crimean Tatar, Ismail bey Gasprinski (1815–1914), led to the development of a new liberal westernized Pan-Turkic Tatar intelligentsia. Their first significant political actions were the calling of the First All-Russian Moslem Congress in 1905, the Second All-Russian Moslem Congress in 1906 and the formation of the Union of Russian Moslems (Ittifak) which elected delegates to the First Duma (see Duma and Revolution). In the elections to the Second Duma they sent thirty-nine delegates, most of whom voted with the Constitutional Democratic Party-Cadets. As the Jadid movement spread to other Moslem lands, other ethnic groups, like the Kazakhs (see Kazakhstan, Revolution in) and the Uzbeks, began to think in Western political terms.

The Tatars still played an important political role when the First (post-revolutionary) All-Russian Moslem Congress (see All-Russian Moslem Council) took place in Ufa in May 1917 in response to the February Revolution*. The Volga Tatars, disagreeing with the Crimean Tatars, spoke at the Congress in favor of a centralist position, that is, they favored a strong centralized democratic Russian state in which there would be extra-territorial cultural autonomy. The reason for their position was that the Volga Tatars did not have an ethnically homogenous area in which they were the numerical majority, therefore, they wanted a political structure that would accommodate smaller cultural nationalism entities within a larger territorial structure. Surprisingly, this placed them on the side of the Kazan Socialist Committee headed by M. Vakhitov*, which would gain the support of the new Soviet government in the fall, and in opposition to most of the other Moslem national groups. The Volga Tatar delegates lost this round, when the other delegates opted for territorial autonomy with a federal republic. The First Congress created an All-Russian Moslem Council* (or Shuro) to carry out its resolutions. The pan-cultural idea might have succeeded in bringing about greater unity among the Turkic peoples of Russia since they could have borrowed from each other more freely in that kind of setting and perhaps have achieved stronger Pan-Turkic political unity than was possible in separate and competing states.

When the Second (post-revolutionary) All-Russian Moslem Congress met in Kazan in July, the delegates from Azerbaijan, Kazakhstan, the Crimea, and Central Asia did not attend, leaving the field to the Volga Tatars, with whom they disagreed on the question of national autonomy. At the meeting the Bashkirs also broke with the Tatars and left the Congress. Despite the unrepresentative character of the meeting, the Tatars proceeded to declare their program on July 22, 1917, issuing a document calling for extraterritorial cultural autonomy for all of the Moslems of Central Russia and Siberia (see Siberia, Revolution in) as a separate national group. In order to pursue that goal further they called for the convocation of a National Assembly of Moslems in Ufa in the fall of 1917. For the elections to the Constituent Assembly, they adopted the name All-Moslem

Democratic Socialist Bloc for what was essentially only Tatar candidates. A Moslem Military Congress was called at the same time as the Second All-Russian Congress of Moslems and called for the formation of all-Moslem military units. When the Tatar National Parliament (Milli Mejilis) finally met in Ufa in November, there was a new government in Petrograd.

The Volga Tatars had to respond to an entirely new situation when they met in the national Assembly of Moslems of Inner Russia and Siberia in Ufa on November 20th. On November 19, 1917 they abandoned their previous position and declared their support for a large autonomous Idel-Ural Tatar-Bashkir state in which the majority of the population would belong to those two nationalities.

While the Tatars moved slowly toward their goals for a large autonomous Turkic political group, they found themselves outflanked by Stalin's decision on January 17, 1918 to appoint two Tatars, M. Vakhitov, and G. Ibragimov* to head his Committee for Moslem Affairs.

When a Second Moslem Military Congress took place on January 21, 1918, its efforts to create a military force for the projected Idel-Ural state were frustrated by a complete rift with the Tatar socialist faction. The Kazan Soviet used the situation to create a revolutionary High Command which included the Tatar leader M. S. Sultangaliev* as one of its leaders. The new body declared martial law in the city and arrested the leaders of the Congress. Those non-socialist Tatars who escaped arrest fled the city. By the end of the month the city was in the hands of the Soviets and the Red Army*. By the end of March the Soviet Government dissolved all of these political institutions for a large Turkic state which the Tatars had created for themselves.

Efforts by Vakhitov and Sultangaliev to create a large soviet Tatar-Bashkir Republic were also thwarted by the course of events. On February 20, 1918 a communist group in Orenburg proclaimed the formation of the Bashkir ASSR (*see* Bashkiria, Revolution in), the first such national state within Russia to bear that label. They then began to agitate against the idea of a joint state with the Tatars. The Left Communist (*see* Left Communism) also opposed the idea of a large Tatar-Bashkir state. On May 10, 1918 Stalin assembled a large meeting of Moslem Communists and announced his intention to proceed with the formation of a Tatar-Bashkir state. But that statement was made on the eve of the Czech Revolt (*see* Czechoslovak Legions) which would begin the Civil War (*see* Civil War in Russia).

At the same time that Stalin was announcing the prospect of a large Tatar-Bashkir state, other Tatar socialists were meeting in Ufa to lend support to the anti-communist forces that would coalesce around the Committee of Members of the Constituent Assembly*. When this group assembled with other Moslem nationalities in September 1918, they were given support that any new states would be based on national self-determination. Large numbers of Moslems were recruited for Moslem regiments in the Civil War battles in that area, but the question of state structure had to be postponed until the territory was reconquered.

Although the issue of a large Tatar state remained suspended during the period of the Civil War in that area, the creating of the Bashkir Autonomous Soviet Socialist Republic on March 23, 1919 more or less decided the question. Vakhitov was dead and Sultangaliev continued to press for a large Tatar state, but his efforts were doomed to failure. After careful consideration of the dangers posed by a large Tatar-Bashkir state as a potential center of Pan-Islamic activity, the Politburo decided on January 26, 1920 to create a smaller Tatar Autonomous Soviet Socialist Republic that would be about one half the size of the original proposal. In February 1920 a gathering of communists from the Volga-Ural region was assembled in Moscow. Both Lenin and Stalin participated and the decision was made to create an independent Tatar state without Bashkiria. By that time there were nearly 4,000 Tatars in the All-Russian Communist Party (*see* Russian Social Democratic Workers' party [Bolshevik]), though eighty-five percent of them were outside the projected Tatar Republic (many serving in the army). On May 27, 1920 the Central Committee of the Russian Communist Party (Bolshevik)* announced the creation of the Tatar Autonomous Soviet Socialist Republic.

Bibliography

Pipes, R. *The Formation of the Soviet Union.* 1968.
Rorlich, Azade-Ayse. *The Volga Tatars.* 1986.
Zenzinov, S. A. *Pan-Turkism and Islam in Russia.* 1960.

Trade Union International. *See* Red International of Trade Unions.

Trade Unions in the Russian Revolution, 1917–1921. The role of the trade unions in the Russian Revolution must be considered in relationship to other labor and political organizations such as the factory committees, the socialist parties, and the soviets. Also of concern is the relationship of the trade unions to the policy of workers' control in its ideological and practical aspects. They should be considered as political, rather than economic institutions. "Politics," said V. I. Lenin* in speaking of the functions of the trade unions in 1920, "cannot but have precedence over economics."

Under the Provisional Government* the most effective socialist labor organizations seem to have been the factory committees which were attempting to institute workers' control in their own individual enterprises and were opposed to the more moderate trade union organization by crafts. The factory committees, organizations distinct from the trade unions, were legally established in both state-owned and private industry by the Provisional Government acting with the soviets in a decree of April 23, 1917. Unlike the trade unions, the factory committees were organizations of workers in various trades employed at the same factories.

There were obvious concepts of the functions of factory committees. On the part of the Provisional Government in general, it seems that the factory committees were intended to bring about greater communication and cooperation between labor and management and thus maintain or increase labor productivity in post-February (*see* February Revolution) conditions. The committees gave labor greater representation in the life of the factory, as in the determination of wages and hours. The government, however, did not make the committees the sole bargaining agents for labor. The soviets, though heterogeneous in their viewpoints, seem to have intended that the factory committees increase labor's scope in the workplace and under the new bourgeois democratic state, train the workers for future socialism by giving them a degree of control over industry, partially through overseeing management. For the Bolsheviks (*see* Russian Social Democratic Workers' Party [Bolshevik]) the policy of workers' control under the Provisional Government functioned to weaken that government and capitalist industry and to acquire workers' support for the Party. After the October Seizure of Power*, workers' control became an issue among Bolsheviks rebuilding a soviet economy (*see* Kollontai, Aleksandra Mikhailovna; Workers in the Russian Revolution).

Workers' control over industry is of prime importance to an understanding of trade unions in the revolution. Workers' control, already popular among workers, was enunciated as labor policy at the First Conference of Factory Committees of Petrograd, May 30 to June 3, 1917, at which Bolshevik influence was predominant. The Bolsheviks, however, were still not leaders in the soviets or at the Third All-Russian Conference of Trade Unions held from June 21 to June 28, 1917. This Third Conference was the first since the February Revolution*, the Second Conference having taken place in 1906. Many trade unions, like the soviets, emerged in the months after the February Revolution. The workers vigorously took advantage of the freedom to form unions and were encouraged to do so by intellectuals who looked to labor for revolutionary support. Trade union membership rose from three trade unions and 1,500 members before February 1917 to 967 trade unions and five bureaus (coordinating agencies) of trade unions by June. By July, union membership had risen to about two million.

At the Third All-Russian Conference of Trade Unions, the Mensheviks (*see* Russian Social Democratic Workers' Party [Menshevik]), who provided the leadership, constituted 55.5 percent and the Bolsheviks 36.4 percent. If the Bolsheviks could unite the factory committees, as they were doing, they could establish upon industrial lines an organization functioning alongside the trade unions. United factory committees could further influence the soviets and advance socialist goals. One of the most important concerns of the Third Conference was the trade unions' relationship to the factory committees and workers' control. It emphasized the role of the factory committees in enforcing at their factories rights acquired by the trade unions from management. The Trade Union Conference relegated to second place the function of the committees in surveilling management.

According to the Central Council of Factory Committees, close relationships were to be maintained between the Council and the coordinating agency of the trade unions, the Central Bureau of Trade Unions. For example, members of the Central Council of the Factory Committees had to be members of the trade unions in their industry. In contrast to the policy enunciated at the Third Conference of Trade Unions, the Central Council of the Factory Committees asserted that the committees were not merely to enforce the rights of unions, but were to regulate and even take new initiatives in matters of hours, wages, hiring, and firing.

Although not accomplished without opposition in the Party, sometime between the second and fifth day after the October Seizure of Power, a draft Statute on Workers' Control was drawn up by Lenin. In addition, a proposed Law on Workers' Control was submitted to the Commissariat of Labor on November 3 for its consideration. On November 15 the Statute on Workers' Control, signed by Lenin as Chairman of the Council of People's Commissars and by A. G. Shliapnikov* as Commissar of Labor, was passed by the All-Russian Central Executive Committee* of the Soviets. Though there was considerable disagreement among the appropriate policies, the Statutes of November 15 speak of centralizing workers' control in the "interests of a systematic regulation of the national economy."

They tried to balance the factory committees most active in the implementation of workers' control with trade unions. In the All-Russian Council of Workers' Control, each had five out of twenty-six representatives, the others representing other workers' organizations, peasants, technicians, and specialists. Generally, in the constantly changing and uncoordinated conditions of the revolution, it was easier to draw up statutes than to enforce them. Insofar as what the Party declared officially, it appeared that its intention was to deprive workers of control at individual enterprises. Instead, it promised labor a role in the regulation of industry. At the First All-Russian Congress of Trade Unions from January 20–27, 1918, the factory committees were subordinated to the trade unions. It became the task of the trade unions to convince the workers to give up the control of the enterprises they had taken over. Instead, the unions were to guide workers' control organizationally and ideologically for the sake of "universal" rather than parochial class interest. If the trade unions were to take over control functions in a future nationalized industry, it raised the problem of the relationship of the unions to the state and to the Communist Party (*see* Russian Social Democratic Workers' Party [Bolshevik]), for if the October Seizure of Power was to bring about the workers' state, which one of the workers' organizations would have influence in that state?

At the First All-Russian Congress of Trade Unions, there were three principle points of view regarding the question of trade unions as organs of state power, that is, whether they should take over some state functions. A. Lozovskii (Drisdo) proposed the unions remain independent and take over the economic functions of the soviets. The left Socialist Revolutionaries (*see* Left Socialist-Revolutionary Party) proposed the "statification" or "governmentalization" of the trade unions, that is, that the unions become organs of the state subordinated to the soviets. The Menshevik (*see* Russian Social Democratic Workers' Party [Menshevik]) ideological position was based upon their view of the soviet state as a government of workers in a society with a numerically larger peasantry having a bourgeois democratic character. Thus the Mensheviks believed that the unions should remain independent of the state in order to protect and fight for the interests of labor. The Bolsheviks claimed the bourgeoisie was no longer in power and that Russia was "close to the beginning of the socialist revolution."

To bring socialism closer, the task of the trade unions, according to the Bolsheviks, was to support the socialist Soviet power led by the Council of People's Commissars*. Thus the trade unions were made subordinate to the Commissariat of Labor of that Council which, in turn, was managed by the party. The unions could also act as mediators between workers and managers or employing institutions. The right to strike also became an issue closely involved with the relationship between the unions and the state. By February 1918 the Soviet government, as well as the All-Russian Council of Trade Unions had committed itself to a condemnation of the strike. In explaining this condemnation of the First All-Russian Congress of Trade Unions, the Bolshevik Matrozov said: "During the transfer of power into the hands of the workers and soldiers, during the struggle for socialist conditions of life, it is impossible that we [the workers] present demands to ourselves." By 1920 the strike was so far obliterated that the strike funds of the All-Russian Congress of Trade Unions were turned over to the Red International of Trade Unions.*

The question of "statification" or militarization of labor was whether industry and labor were to be directed by state organs or by trade unions separate and distinct from the state. The official definition in 1919 seems to have been that the "statification" of the trade unions presupposed: the existence of the trade unions themselves, the compulsory requirement by the state that all workers serve in some branch of industry, and the regulation by the state of all activity of trade unions. Organizationally, the trade unions and the state were two distinct bodies but the trade unions were, in fact, regulated by the state. The unions were not to be neutral or to oppose the state, but were actively to support the state. They were to implement a program assigned to them by the Commissariat of Labor.

According to statute, the Commissariat could unilaterally determine working conditions and deal with problems formerly settled between unions and employers. Decisions of the All-Russian Central Council of Trade Unions that required enforcement by the state were to be transferred to the Commissariat of Labor to which such power belonged. The local councils of trade unions were transferred intact to the Commissariat.

Attached to the Supreme Council of the National Economy* were *Glavki* (Heads) and *Tsentri* (Centers) formed out of the bureaucratic apparatus of the Tsarist state and the Provisional Government. Each head and center was in charge of a particular industry and allied itself with the union of that industry. This was an attempt to acquire control of the economy from the soviets on the local level, particularly where there was resistance to the party and where the soviets under conditions of the Civil War (*see* Civil War in Russia) had a good deal of independence in 1919. Thus, in 1919 the extension of political control over the outlying soviets may be regarded, itself, as part of the Civil War. The participation of the trade unions in this process of centralizing industry was regarded and represented as providing for proletarian and non-bureaucratic industrial management. The debate on "statification" or "governmentalization" or militarization began at the Third All-Russian Congress of Trade Unions, April 6–13, 1920, and reached its resolution at the Tenth Party Congress in March 1921.

By the end of 1920, when conditions had become more stable and the state more cohesive, steps were taken to undermine the authority of the unions, *Glavki* and *Tsentri,* by increasing the economic jurisdictions of the now reliable local soviets. The trade unions were even accused of capturing *Glavki* and *Tsentri* and advocating or implementing parochial trade union interests in them.

In December 1920 at the Eighth Congress of Soviets, L. D. Trotsky* and his supporters advocated a policy of "statification" that would, in effect, have led to considerable control over the economy by fusing the trade unions with the chief organs of industrial administration. As in all other uses of the concept of "statification" or "fusion," Trotsky too provided for the postponement of the actual goal—complete acquisition of state power by the unions. "It is obviously not a matter of statifying the trade unions in twenty-four hours," said Trotsky. "That is nonsense. It is a matter of actually holding to the course of 'statification'.... " (Kaplan, 1967, p. 284). This promise that some day the trade unions would manage the economic life of the nation was familiar to the unions. It was in accord with the earlier pre-revolutionary promise that the revolution would destroy a political and economic system in which the government and industrial management was in the hands of bodies of officials separate from the "people." It was a promise that had been used before the revolution to manipulate the revolutionary chiliastic mood of labor and which, after October, was viewed as a device to postpone chiliastic goals and project them into the future. The model for Trotsky's fusion of unions with state organs may be found in *Glavpolitput',* the Main Political Section of the People's Commissariat for Rail Transport, and *Tsektran,* the Central Committee of the Union of Workers in Rail and Water Transport, both of which Trotsky administered.

Lenin, backed by G. E. Zinoviev*, opposed Trotsky's proposal saying, "The most correct thing to do about 'fusion' at present would be to keep quiet about it" (Kaplan, 1967, pp. 291–92). He contended that it was the function of unions to draw the millions of non-party workers into unions that should be "schools of communism" (Ibid). "What," asked Zinoviev at the Tenth Congress in 1921, "does 'schools of communism' mean?. ... It means to teach and educate not to command" (Kaplan, 1967, p. 295). The trade unions were to be a link between the party and the masses, but they were not to possess state power. They were to implement policy, not make it. Trotsky countered that unions as "schools of communism" (Daniels, 1966, p. 156) should provide training in the practical work of production by joining with state industrial organs. In the competition for party influence in and through the unions, this controversy continued into 1921 when a new voice was added, that of A. G. Shliapnikov, leader of the Workers' Opposition that proposed industrial control by the factory committees on the lowest level up to the trade unions as managers of centralized industry.

In spite of party conflict over the function of unions, the party retained control of them. Party cells controlled carefully from the center, for example, were established in unions. From the beginning, the function of trade unions in establishing a workers' state was recognized ideologically and organizationally, and struggle for influence in party and state was carried out partially through the trade unions.

Frederick I. Kaplan

Bibliography

Carr, E. H. *The Bolshevik Revolution.* vol. 3. 1952.

Daniels, Robert. *Conscience of the Revolution.* 1966.

Deutscher, Isaac. *Soviet Trade Unions, Their place in Soviet Labor Policy.* 1956.

Garvy, F. A. *Professional'nye Soiuzov v Pervye Gody Revoliutsii* (1917–1924). 1958.

Kaplan, Frederick I. *Bolshevik Ideology and the Ethics of Soviet Labor 1917–1920, The Formative Years.* 1967.

Koenker, Diane. *Moscow Workers and the 1917 Revolution.* 1981.

Lozovsky, A. (Drizdo). *The Trade Unions in Soviet Russia.* 1920.

Smith, S. A. *Red Petrograd, Revolution in the Factories 1917–1918.* 1983.

Sorenson, Jay. *The Life and Death of Soviet Trade Unionism, 1917–1928.* 1969.

Zinoviev, Grigorii. *O Roli Professionalnykh Souizov.* 1921.

Transcaucasia, Revolution in, 1917–1921. The overthrow of the Romanov monarchy in the February Revolution of 1917 occurred just over a century after the Russian state had begun the annexation of Transcaucasia. This region, a multi-ethnic isthmus lying south of the Caucasus Mountains and between the Black Sea and the Caspian Sea, was populated by three major nationalities: the Georgians in the north and west, the Azerbaijanis (usually referred to as "Tatars" before the revolution) in the east, and the Armenians to the south. In the 100 years of tsarist rule, the Russian autocracy had integrated the noble elites of Caucasia into the seigneurial political and economic order of the empire, had developed ties of economic interest with the local industrialists and merchants, but had failed to solve the land hunger of the peasantry or to deal adequately with the material and political demands of the newly-emerging working class in the cities of Baku, Batumi, and Tiflis (Tbilisi).

By the indices of industrialization, urbanization, and literacy, Transcaucasia was a region less developed than Russia proper. Divided from one another by language, culture, and religion, the people of Transcaucasia were also stratified socially and economically. Ethnicity and class reinforced one another, accentuating the differences between the major nationalities. Azerbaijanis, the largest group (1,791,000 or 24 percent of the population), were primarily peasants little influenced by urban culture or secular nationalism (*see* Azerbaijan, Revolution in). The Georgians (1,741,000 or 23 percent) were a people in rapid social transition. Their noble elite had declined as a political and economic force in the second half of the nineteenth century and was displaced as the political guide of the nation by a new generation of Marxist intellectuals (*see* Georgia, Revolution in). The Armenians (1,685,000 or 22 percent) were divided between a majority of poor peasants and a small but powerful middle class. By the early twentieth century the middle class had become the dominant economic force in several cities in Transcaucasia (*see* Armenia, Revolution in). In the ethnic mosaic of Baku and Tiflis, conflicts between social groups often took on ethnic aspects as Georgian or Azerbaijani workers confronted Armenian and Russian employers, or Armenian peasants defied Moslem landlords.

By the second decade of the twentieth century, three major developments were shaping the progress of the revolutionary movement in Transcaucasia: (1) a Marxist-led peasant movement had swept through western Georgia in the first years of the new century, and by 1905 Menshevik (*see* Russian Social Democratic Workers' Party [Menshevik]) intellectuals had become the acknowledged leaders of the majority of the Georgian people; (2) Bolshevik and Socialist-Revolutionary (*see* Socialist-Revolutionary Party) activists were largely isolated in and around the oil-producing center, Baku, where the largest concentration of industrial workers was to be found; in the two years before World War I*, the socialists organized and led two general strikes of oil workers, the impact of which was felt as far away as St. Petersburg; (3) growing as a potent rival to internationalist socialists (*see* Internationalists) were the various ethnic nationalisms of the Armenians, Azeri Turks, and Georgians. Most significantly, the Armenian Revolutionary Federation (or Dashnaktsutiun [*see* Dashnaks]) had effectively monopolized political expression among the oppositional elements in the Armenian communities.

On March 1, 1917, a cryptic message was telegraphed by the Mensheviks in the State Duma (*see* Duma and Revolution) to their comrades in Tiflis: "Mtavrobadze is dead." The Caucasian socialists understood that the government (*mtavroba* in Georgian) had fallen, and within hours the Viceroy of the Caucasus, Grand Duke Nikolai Nikolaevich, called in the Armenian mayor of Tiflis, Aleksandr Khatisov, to inform him of the end of the Romanov regime. Two days later elections to the Soviets of Workers' Deputies were organized by the socialists in Tiflis and Baku (*see* Soviets [Councils] of Workers', Soldiers', and Peasants' Deputies). At the same time, in both Baku and Tiflis, so-called "executive committees" ostensibly representing all classes in the cities were appointed to operate in place of the now-defunct government of tsarist officials. Thus, from the first week of March, in the major cities of Transcaucasia as in Petrograd, two rival organs of power existed—the first, the soviet, the elected voice of the workers; the other, the executive committee, claiming authority from the Provisional Government* and nominally representative of all strata of the towns. But *dvoelastie* (Dual Power*) in Transcaucasia, as in Petrograd, masked only temporarily the fact that real decision-making power was located in the soviets. Only those bodies elected by workers and soldiers had the authority to call people into the streets or to issue effective orders to the garrison. What formal power the executive committees and the Special Transcaucasian Committee (Ozakom) appointed by the Provisional Government enjoyed in the spring of 1917 derived from the sanction received from the soviets controlled by moderate Socialist Revolutionaries (S-R's) and Mensheviks, who wanted to preserve social unity and maintain the war effort. Most Mensheviks conceived of the revolution as "bourgeois-democratic," and this view was accepted by the S-R's. Although suspicious of the Provisional Government, they were willing to support it as legitimate and to restrain workers from seizing power in the name of their soviets.

The one major group opposed, first to "Dual Power" and from May to October to the Coalition Government*, was the Bolshevik wing of Social Democracy. Led by S. G. Shaumian and centered in Baku, the Bolsheviks conceived of the Revolution as developing into a socialist revolution under the impact of events in Europe. They opposed the "defensist" (*see* Defensism) tendencies of the moderate socialists (*see* Russian Social Democratic Workers' Party [Menshevik]; Martov, Iulii), called for a government of the whole "democracy" (the lower classes), and stimulated a formal break with the Mensheviks, which came relatively late in Transcaucasia (June 6 in Tiflis, June 24 in Baku). As a result of the party schism, the Bolsheviks were reduced to an impotent sect in Georgia, where the party organizations and soviets were firmly in the hands of the Mensheviks, led by N. N. Zhordania*.

During the government crisis of April-May, the Mensheviks of Georgia came out against their comrades in Russia on the question of power. Under Menshevik urging the Tiflis workers' soviet voted overwhelmingly on April 29 to keep socialists from entering a coalition government. Zhordania preferred a purely "bourgeois" government but without Cadet (*see* Constitutional Democratic Party-Cadet) leader, P. N. Miliukov* and others who favored annexationist war aims. But the workers' soviet was not supported by the soldiers' soviet, led by the Socialist-Revolutionaries, which on May 16 voted to support the Coalition Government*. The conflict between the workers in Tiflis, largely Georgian and Menshevik, and the soldiers, primarily Russian and favoring the Socialist-Revolutionaries and even Bolshevism, came to a head on June 25 at a demonstration organized by the Bolsheviks. An estimated 10,000 soldiers shouted down Menshevik orators and adopted a Bolshevik resolution condemning the Kerensky military offensive and calling for a government based on the soviets. The Tiflis Mensheviks, sensing a threat from the Left, banned meetings of soldiers in the Alexander Garden, warned the public of the danger of counterrevolution, and made peace with Petrograd by approving the Coalition Government.

In Transcaucasia as in Russia proper, the pace of the Revolution quickened toward the end of the summer as the mood of both workers and soldiers grew ever more hostile toward collaboration with the propertied classes (*tsentsovoe obshchestvo*). On September 2 in Tiflis the Menshevik-led soviet came out against coalition with the bourgeoisie and advocated a "democratic socialist government.'' But it was primarily the Bolsheviks who benefited from the deteriorating economic situation, the inconclusive war, and the increasing suspicion of the upper and middle classes. Industrialists in Baku provoked a general strike of oil workers in September, but in just six days Bolshevik-led strikers forced the industry to capitulate. In the aftermath of Kornilov's (see Kornilov Revolt) abortive attempt to establish a military dictatorship in Petrograd, Bolshevik resolutions found new support in Transcaucasian soviets. As militant opponents of the war, the Leninists gradually garnered support from soldiers, displacing the S-R's in the Baku and Tiflis garrisons and at the Caucasian Front in the autumn of 1917. As the most vocal critics of the feeble Coalition Government and the local executive committees and Dumas, the Bolsheviks gained credence as class antagonisms between the verkhi (top) and nizi (bottom) of society grew sharper. As Shaumian exclaimed in early October: ''Unrest is growing everywhere, and land is being seized, etc.; our task is to stand at the head of the revolution and to take power in our hands'' (Suny 1983, p. 246–47).

The news of the October Revolution reached Tiflis on October 25, and there reports circulated that the Bolsheviks would attempt to seize power in Baku. But in Transcaucasia the Mensheviks proved to be much more decisive than the local Bolsheviks. Whereas Shaumian hesitated to provoke an interethnic blood-letting by instigating Civil War in Baku, Zhordania's forces seized the Tiflis arsenal at the end of November, thus disarming the pro-Bolshevik garrison. With their own Red Guard*, the Mensheviks resisted efforts of the Bolsheviks to propagandize the soldiers. As the Caucasian Front dissolved in December and Russia's soldiers ''voted with their feet'' to end the war and return home, the Bolsheviks lost their most potent supporters in the struggle for power and the key to preservation of the link to post-October Russia. The Armenians in Baku, led by the Dashnaks, voted with the local soviet to remain loyal to Soviet Russia, but the Armenians in Tiflis, also under Dashnak influence, sided with the other local parties and worked within the autonomous and later independent political institutions.

Within the first few months of 1918, Transcaucasia gradually broke its ties to Russia, and on April 22, 1918, an independent ''federative republic'' was declared. Baku remained an outpost of Bolshevik Russia under the Baku Commune until the end of July, threatened by the nationalist Moslems of the Musavat Party (see Moslem Democratic Party) and finally overwhelmed by the Turkish Army (September 14–15, 1918). Shaumian and his closest comrades perished in the deserts of Turkmenia, the fabled ''Twenty-Six Commissars,'' victims of anti-Bolshevik separatists. With the Turks advancing through Transcaucasia, the single republic containing antagonistic Armenians, Azerbaijanis, and Georgians, rapidly disintegrated into three separate independent states (May 26–28, 1918). The intense social and political conflicts of the first revolutionary year had not led to a Transcaucasia united with a democratic Russia but to fragmentation and conflict between socialists and nationalists.

The period of independence for Armenia, Azerbaijan, and Georgia lasted only as long as Civil War and foreign intervention prevented Bolshevik Russia from imposing its authority over Transcaucasia. Georgia, under Menshevik rule for two and a half years, managed to evolve a democratic constitutional political system, though it never achieved full economic stability and physical security. Border disputes with Dashnak-ruled Armenia discredited both republics in Western eyes. Armenia, the least viable of the three states, was inundated by refugees from Turkey, plagued by epidemic diseases and hunger, and threatened by the resurgent Kemalist movement in Anatolia. Azerbaijan gravitated from being a Turkish satellite to being a British ward before falling to the Bolsheviks in April 1920. Its capital, Baku, with its large Armenian and Russian working-class population, never reconciled itself to separation from Russia and dominance by the Azerbaijanis.

Within months of the establishment of Soviet Azerbaijan, the Armenian political leaders agreed to accept Bolshevik suzerainty in order to prevent a Turkish invasion, and on December 2, 1920, a Soviet republic was proclaimed in Erevan. In February 1921 the Red Army* moved into Georgia, ending its brief experiment in independence. The Dashnaks briefly but unsuccessfully revolted against the first Armenian Soviet government, but by April 1921 all of Transcaucasia had come under the rule of local Communists.

Ronald Gregor Suny

Bibliography

Belen'kii, Semen Natanovich and Manvelov, A. *Revoliutsiia 1917 g. v Azerbaidzhane (Khronika sobytii).* 1927.
Hovannisian, Richard G. *Armenia on the Road to Independence, 1918.* 1967.
Kazemzadeh, Firuz. *The Struggle for Transcaucasia (1917–1921).* 1951.
Makharadze, Filip. *Sovety i bor'ba za sovetskuiu vlast' v Gruzii.* 1928.
Mikoian, Anastas. *Dorogoi bor'by.* 1971.
Pipes, Richard. *The Formation of the Soviet Union.* 1957.
Ratgauzer, Ia. A. *Revoliutsiia i grazhdanskaia voina v Baku, I: 1917–1918 gg.* 1927.
Sef, Semen E. *Bor'ba za Oktiabr' v Zakavkaz'i.* 1932.
Suny, Ronald Grigor. *The Baku Commune, 1917–18.* 1972.
———. *The Making of the Georgian Nation.* 1988.
Suny, R. G., ed. *Transcaucasia,* 1983.
Swietochowski, Tadeusz. *Russian Azerbaijan, 1905–1920.* 1985.
Zhordania, N. N. *Maia zhizn'.* 1968.

Trotsky, L. D. (1879–1940; true name, Bronshtein, Lev Davidovich). One of the most important leaders of the Bolsheviks (*see* Russian Social Democratic Workers' Party [Bolshevik]) in the October Seizure of Power*, Trotsky was a Marxist theorist and author.

In 1917 it was common for Russians and foreigners alike to consider both Trotsky and V. I. Lenin* as leaders of the Bolshevik Revolution. As a prolific writer, energetic organizer, and gifted orator, Trotsky made a powerful public impression in 1917, from his arrival in Petrograd early in May to his famous gibe at the Second Congress of Soviets where he consigned Menshevik (*see* Russian Social Democratic Workers' Party [Menshevik]) leaders to the "dustbin of history." Yet the historical record is far from clear as to Trotsky's exact role in shaping the Bolshevik coup of October. The subject is also complicated by the distorted perspectives sponsored by Trotsky's political foes in discussions of the Revolution during the 1920s and after. In defense, Trotsky and his followers responded with sometimes exaggerated claims of their own.

Originally Lenin's protege on the staff of the Bolshevik newspaper *Iskra* (*The Spark*), published abroad, Trotsky became his political opponent after the split at the Second Congress of the Russian Social Democratic Workers' Party in 1903. Until 1917 Trotsky stayed outside of both Bolshevik and Menshevik factions. In 1905 he was elected Chairman of the Petersburg Soviet (*see* Petrograd Soviet). Later, drawing on ideas of the Russian-born German Marxist Parvus (A. L. Gelfand), with whom he had collaborated, Trotsky authored a theory of "permanent revolution" according to which mass rebellion in Russia would inevitably result in state power for the proletariat and in turn generate socialist revolution in Europe. Trotsky's formula seemed to have been an accurate forecast and theoretical guide to action in 1917. But Bolshevik political behavior in that year was more conditioned by temperament and timing than adherence to theory. As Trotsky later wrote: "In the years of reaction [after 1905], one needed theoretical foresight in order to hold fast to the prospect of permanent revolution. Probably nothing more than political sense was needed to advance the slogan of a fight for power in March, 1917."

When tsarism was overthrown, Trotsky was living in the Bronx in New York City, writing, speaking, and editing the newspaper *New World* (*Novyi Mir*) with N. I. Bukharin* and other Bolsheviks. At the outbreak of World War I* Trotsky left Vienna, where he had gone for the twenty-fifth anniversary of the Second International. Trotsky's response to the war was "Internationalist"* (*see* Russian Social Democratic Workers' Party [Menshevik]; World War I), and he campaigned against the conflict in social democratic circles, helping organize the Zimmerwald Conference of September 1915 and drafting its manifesto (*see* World War I). From Vienna Trotsky went to Zurich and then settled in Paris where he was associated with Iu. O. Martov's* newspaper *Golos* (*Voice*), later *Nashe Slovo* (*Our World*), and wrote about the war for *Kievskaia Mysl* (*Kievon Thought*) until he was forced to leave France in October 1916. After a brief stay in Spain, where he was not allowed to reside either, he arrived in New York in January 1917. Characteristically, Trotsky greeted the February Revolution* with the prediction: "an open conflict between the forces of revolution at whose head stands the urban proletariat, and the antirevolutionary liberal bourgeoisie temporarily in power, is absolutely inevitable" (Daniels 1967, p. 28).

From 1914 to the spring of 1917 Trotsky's positions, therefore, were bringing him closer to the Bolshevik Party in general and to Lenin's views in particular. From abroad Trotsky had been associated with the Mezhraionka (*see* Interdistrict

Committee), or Interdistrict Organization of Independent Social Democrats, founded in Petrograd in 1913 and claiming a following of some 4,000 workers by 1917. In the spring and summer of 1917 Trotsky spoke as a Mezhraionets and helped found and contributed to the party's newspaper, *Vpered (Forward)*. Soon after his arrival in Petrograd on May 4, 1917—after detention by British naval authorities in Nova Scotia—Trotsky was collaborating with the Bolsheviks; he was soon to join them, enter their Central Committee (*see* Central Committee of the Russian Communist Party [Bolshevik]), and become their chief spokesman.

With Bolshevik support, and in view of his having chaired the St. Petersburg Soviet in 1905 (*see* Nineteen-Five Revolution), Trotsky was accepted as an associate and nonvoting member of the Petrograd Soviet's* Executive Committee. In his first address to the Soviet, he struck a conciliatory note aimed at unifying the Left but asserted that "our next move will be to transfer the whole power into the hands of the Soviets" (Deutscher 1967, p. 255). In May Trotsky also conferred with Lenin and expressed solidarity with his April Theses*. Over a decade of political combat ended with that meeting; Trotsky was now Lenin's ally and augmented the Bolshevik leader's efforts to put the Revolution—and first of all his party—on the path of Soviet power. Trotsky's most vivid and direct impact on events came from his oratory; he was in constant demand and seemed to be everywhere at all hours—throngs heard him at the Cirque Moderne, at Kronstadt, at Smolnyi. As A. V. Lunacharskii* expressed it, Lenin "directed mainly the work of organization in the Bolshevik camp, while Trotsky thundered at meetings" (Lunacharskii 1967, p. 65).

Speaking at the First All-Russian Congress of Soviets in June, Trotsky argued for an all-socialist Provisional Government*, defended himself and Lenin against charges of being German agents, and held out the prospect of the Russian "citadel of revolution" spreading its influence across the map of Europe. At that Congress the Bolsheviks and Mezhraiontsy opposed efforts to curb armed workers' demonstrations; at Trotsky's insistence the Mezhraiontsy agreed to join a Bolshevik-led demonstration scheduled for June 10, although it was later cancelled. At a June 18 demonstration sponsored by the congress, however, Bolshevik banners and influence were evident. The general Bolshevik position for an all-socialist Provisional Government or even for full transfer of power to the soviets (*see* Soviets [Councils] of Workers', Soldiers', and Peasants' Deputies) was attracting wider circles of the public.

This radical mood swelled early in July when it seemed to many that the Bolsheviks were engineering an assault on the Provisional Government by way of armed street demonstrations. This "July Uprising" (*see* July Days) was probably less an attempted Bolshevik coup than an upsurge of militant feeling on the part of the public, with Trotsky and the Bolshevik Party desperately trying to restrain militant workers and men in uniform after months of agitating among them. Symbolic of the these dynamics was an incident at the Tauride Palace on July 4 when a menacing group of sailors from Kronstadt (*see* Kronstadt, 1917–

1921; Sailors in 1917) very nearly lynched the minister of agriculture, the Socialist–Revolutionary (*see* Socialist-Revolutionary Party) V. M. Chernov*, but for Trotsky's personal intervention. The Provisional Government responded to the July episode with arrest warrants for Bolshevik leaders. Trotsky publicly expressed identity of views with the Bolsheviks and was himself arrested—as a German agent—on July 23. Until September 4 he was confined at Kresty Prison, familiar to him from his incarceration there in 1905, and poured out articles for the Bolshevik Press and Maxim Gorky's *Novaia Zhizn'* (*New Life*).

At the Sixth Congress of the Bolshevik Party opening on July 26, the Mezhraiontsy were formally absorbed by the Bolsheviks; Trotsky was named one of several honorary cochairs, and he was elected to the new Bolshevik Central Committee—he had even been slated to deliver the keynote on the current political situation. In the wake of the Kornilov scare (*see* Kornilov Revolt) Trotsky was released from prison on bail. After the Bolsheviks won a majority in the Petrograd Soviet Trotsky was elected to the Soviet's Presidium and became its president on September 23. Since mid-September Lenin—in hiding—had been calling for armed insurrection, but Bolshevik leaders were divided about what course to take. At a Central Committee meeting on September 15, Lenin's proposal was set aside; some of his articles of this period were even censored by Bolshevik editors. (Trotsky was a member, with I. V. Stalin* and G. Ia. Sokol'nikov*, of the group responsible for editorial supervision of the Bolshevik press.)

Outwardly, Lenin's position won out since his resolution placing the "armed uprising on the order of the day" was passed at a meeting of the Bolshevik Central Committee on October 10. No precise place or timetable was drawn up, however, and despite Lenin's repeated prodding in the weeks following, the Bolshevik Central Committee, Trotsky included, seemed psychologically disposed to wait for something to happen rather than actively prepare for a coup.

Trotsky's public addresses during October definitely called for transferring authority to the soviets, and his militant stances earned Lenin's approval. When Trotsky, unlike many Bolsheviks, came out for boycotting the Council of the Republic, or "Pre-Parliament" (*see* Democratic Conference), Lenin wrote, "Trotsky was for the boycott: bravo, Comrade Trotsky" (Deutscher 1967, p. 294). Yet it does not appear that Trotsky was working toward an armed seizure of power as such; instead, his public statements and organizational work—for example, with the newly created Military Revolutionary Committee of the soviet—seemed defensive, designed to deal with an anticipated counter-revolution launched by the Provisional Government. Leading the walkout of delegates to the Pre-Parliament on October 7, Trotsky declared: "Petrograd is in danger! The Revolution is in danger! The nation is in danger! . . . All power to the Soviets!" (Deutscher p. 297). After the Bolshevik Central Committee Resolution on armed uprising of October 10, confirmed on October 16, Trotsky's public statements had the same tenor. At the Petrograd Soviet on October 18, for instance, he denied that a schedule for armed uprising existed but added, "if in the course of things the Soviet should be compelled to schedule an uprising, the workers and soldiers would go out at its call as one man . . . " (Deutscher p. 302). As late as October 24, before the same body, he made similar remarks.

Trotsky and the other Bolshevik leaders were not sticking to the letter of the Central Committee resolutions calling for armed insurrection. Apparently, they assumed the transition to Soviet power was at hand, peacefully and by simple majority voting at the impending Second All-Russian Congress of Soviets originally scheduled for October 20 and then postponed to October 25. This was precisely what Lenin did not want; he wanted political matters settled by a show of force before the Congress met. But he could do no more than send passionate messages to Bolshevik leaders from his hiding place, urging them to seize power. It was A. F. Kerensky* who came to his assistance.

Early in October the Provisional Government had collided with the Petrograd Soviet over Kerensky's decision to remove most of the garrison from the capital. On the night of October 21–22 Trotsky drafted a statement for the Soviet repudiating the Provisional Government's authority over garrison troops. Such defiant acts, together with rumors about a Bolshevik coup circulating throughout Petrograd, prompted Kerensky to take forcible action. The Provisional Government prepared to arrest Bolshevik leaders, close bridges, and fortify defenses at key centers; on October 25 Bolshevik presses were shut down. Such activity galvanized Trotsky, other Bolshevik leaders, and the Military Revolutionary Committee. From their headquarters in Smolnyi, they swung into action and began to mobilize armed detachments to counter Kerensky's measures. Finally, goaded by Lenin's arrival at Smolnyi around midnight of October 24, they acted to bring strategic points throughout the capital under definitive Soviet authority, leaving the Provisional Government isolated and waiting for their arrest in the Winter Palace. On the afternoon of the 25th at a session of the Petrograd Soviet, meeting jointly with Bolshevik delegates to the congress scheduled to begin that evening, Trotsky made the triumphal announcement: "In the name of the Military Revolutionary Committee I declare that the Provisional Government no longer exists!" (Rabinowitch 1976, p. 278).

Trotsky's enormous and indispensable part in the amazing political denouement may be understood from the testimony of a Menshevik delegate to the congress who heard him announce the death of the Provisional Government: "every word burned the soul, it awakened thought and roused adventure, he spoke of the victory of the proletariat. We listened to him with bated breath and I saw that many people were clenching their fists as they brought themselves to the final decision to follow unwaveringly wherever he might call them."

Clearly, Trotsky was not, as later accusations crudely charged, a crypto follower of L. B. Kamenev* and G. E. Zinoviev*, out to sabotage an armed uprising led by the Bolshevik Party. Nor does it appear, as Trotsky and others countered, that he had a carefully planned strategy for timing the coup to mesh with the congress so as to give it legal cover. Lenin certainly attached no such intent to the Bolshevik Central Committee resolutions on the armed uprising. In all probability, Trotsky shared with other Bolshevik leaders a "passive" understanding of those resolutions, convinced that victory was forthcoming at the congress and that only protective measures were in order before it met. In this light, Trotsky's denials in October that the Bolsheviks intended a coup were probably sincere and not part of some *ruse de guerre*.

When a new Soviet government was formed, named at Trotsky's suggestion the Council of Peoples' Commissars*, Trotsky declined the post of chairman (he deferred to Lenin) and interior head (it would not do, he said, to have a Jew in a position traditionally associated with police functions and repression), but he accepted the portfolio for foreign affairs. He also rejected the idea of a coalition government not dominated by the Bolsheviks. (In a sense, this was the stand that really earned him his Bolshevik spurs at last: it drew from Lenin the compliment, "There has been no better Bolshevik.")

Trotsky introduced a new look into diplomacy. He published the secret treaties between tsarist Russia and the Entente with this announcement: "The elimination of secret diplomacy is the very first condition for an honest, popular, truly democratic foreign policy." At Brest-Litovsk* at the end of December 1917, Trotsky jousted with German and Austrian delegations from the standpoint of revolutionary principles. The outcome of negotiations were, however, determined by the realities of military power; after initial acceptance of Trotsky's temporizing "neither peace nor war" formula, the Soviet government was forced to accede to German terms.

Trotsky resigned from the Foreign Affairs Commissariat in February 1918 and assumed the command posts from which he helped to organize the triumph of Soviet arms in the Civil War in Russia* (Chairman of the Revolutionary Military Council, People's Commissar of Military Affairs, and People's Commissar of Naval Affairs). Stressing discipline and professionalism, Trotsky introduced conscription, integrated former tsarist officers ("military specialists") into the chain of command under the eyes of political commissars, and eliminated partisan units and the Red Guards*. From some 10,000 Red Guards under the Soviet flag in the spring of 1918, Trotsky helped to forge the 5 million-man Red Army of two and one-half years later. He spent a good deal of that time in the famous train traveling from front to front. On several occasions friction developed between Trotsky and I.V. Stalin, a recurring feature of coming political controversies. In March 1919 Trotsky made a brief appearance in uniform at the founding congress of the Communist International*. In the autumn, having just helped stave off N. N. Iudenich's* assault on Petrograd, Trotsky was awarded the Order of the Red Banner. The Revolution was safe; complete victory in the Civil War was in sight; Trotsky was at the summit of his career. The ensuing decade saw Trotsky at the center of every conflict over policy within party and government, and he spoke and wrote widely on politics, international affairs, culture, and the economy.

In his autobiography, written in exile, Trotsky summed up his role in the Revolution as a devoted follower of Lenin: "Lenin was leading [the Party] toward its greatest tasks. I harnessed myself to the work and helped him." As a comment on Trotsky's role in 1917 there is perhaps excessive modesty here, but it suggests a larger truth about Trotsky's general position within Bolshevism: without Lenin he was isolated and incapable of leadership, a victim ultimately to his own incapacities as a politician and to his principled opposition to the relentless pressures of Stalin and Stalinism.

Louis Menashe

Bibliography

Burdzhalov, E. N. *Vtoraia russkaia revoliutsiia: Vosstane v Petrograde.* 1967.
Daniels, R. V. *Red October.* 1967.
Deutscher, I. *The Prophet Armed: Trotsky, 1879–1921.* 1967.
Golikov, G. N. *et al,.* eds. *Oktiabr'skoe vooruzhennoe vosstanie v Petrograde.* 1957.
Medvedev, R. A. *The October Revolution.* 1979.
Melgunov, R. A. *Kak bolsheviki zakhvatili vlast'.* 1953.
Mints, I. I. *Istoriia velikogo oktiabria.* 3 vols. 1967–1972.
Rabinowitch, A. *The Bolsheviks Come to Power.* 1976.
Sukhanov, N. N. *Zapiski o revoliutsii.* 6 vols. 1922–1923.
Trotsky, Leon. *The History of the Russian Revolution.* 3 vols. 1932–1933.
———. *My Life.* 1931.

Tsereteli, Iraklii Georgevich (1881–1959). Tsereteli was the most influential leader of the Petrograd Soviet* from March to October 1917 and the major exponent of revolutionary Defensism*, the political program that dominated the Menshevik Party (*see* Russian Social Democratic Workers' Party [Menshevik]) and the All-Russian Central Executive Committee* of Soviets during that period.

Tsereteli was born in 1881 into a gentry family that figured prominently in the literary and political life of Georgia (*see* Georgia, Revolution in). Like many of the Georgian intelligentsia who were drawn from the impoverished nobility of the countryside, he felt a close affinity with the Georgian peasantry. During his youth in the capital city of Tiflis he also witnessed how the Georgian intelligentsia, which had become overwhelmingly Marxist in the 1890s, joined forces with the Georgian workers against Russian and Armenian industrialists and merchants. Thus Tsereteli grew up firmly convinced that it was the intelligentsia's role to lead the entire nation in the struggle against the oppressive rule of tsarism and in the democratic reconstruction of Russia. This conviction was further strengthened during his student years at the University of Moscow where he participated in the students' campaign for political freedom in 1901–1902.

Tsereteli paid for his activity in the students' movement with exile to Siberia*, where he became a Social Democrat and later a Menshevik. He returned to Georgia in the autumn of 1906 and won a seat in the Second Duma (*see* Duma and Revolution) as the Social Democratic deputy from Kutaisi Province. From February to June 1907 he served as chairman of the Social Democratic Duma faction and was responsible for implementing the Menshevik strategy of cooperation with the moderate opposition parties, including the Cadets (*see* Consti-

584 TSERETELI, IRAKLII GEORGEVICH

tutional Democratic Party—Cadet). This short parliamentary experience established Tsereteli's reputation as a brilliant orator and strengthened his conviction that the "liberal bourgeoisie" had a positive role to play in the Russian Revolution—a conviction that shaped his political course in 1917.

In June 1907 the Duma was dissolved and its Social Democratic faction, including Tsereteli, arrested. He spent six years in solitary confinement, after which he was exiled to Usol'e, a Siberian village near Irkutsk, where he became the center of a group of other Social Democrats. With the outbreak of World War I* this group called itself "Internationalists"*, and its members became known in Russia and abroad as the "Siberian-Zimmerwaldists." They were thought to be unswerving in their loyalty to the principles of Zimmerwald (see World War I) as the emigré Menshevik Internationalists indeed were; that is, they were presumed to oppose any use of military force for national purposes and to insist on the revival of the Socialist International as the only means for bringing the war to a just end. In fact, however, Tsereteli emphasized in all of his articles and conversations during the war the permissibility of national defense in the face of "militarist" aggression such as that being waged by Germany. His objections to the war stemmed largely from his belief that the tsarist government was fighting for territorial acquisitions.

During the first weeks of the February Revolution* Tsereteli and his Social Democratic friends remained in Irkutsk and, together with a group of like-minded Socialist–Revolutionaries (see Socialist-Revolutionary Party), assumed all of the functions of the local and provincial government. This experience in practical administration, coupled with Tsereteli's peculiar "Zimmwaldist" position of legitimizing national defense, laid the basis for the ideas that came to be known as "Revolutionary Defensism": first, that peace could and should be achieved not through separate agreement between Russia and a still-autocratic Germany but through one that would include all of the warring states; second, that while the war continued, Russian socialists should aid the defense of the country and the Revolution; and finally, that the tasks of peace and defense as well as that of transforming Russia into a democracy required the cooperation of the socialist parties and the masses of workers, soldiers, and peasants whom they led, along with the privileged and educated classes of the country.

Upon returning to Petrograd in late March 1917, Tsereteli was able to rally the great majority of the soviet's leadership and constituency around his centrist ideas and became the leader of the "Revolutionary Defensist" bloc of Mensheviks and Socialist–Revolutionaries that held the majority in the Soviet until the autumn of 1917. As the leader of that bloc, Tsereteli exerted a critical influence on the political course pursued by the Soviet and the Menshevik Party, most notably on their decision in early May to join with representatives of the "bourgeoisie" in forming a coalition government. He joined the First Coalition ostensibly as the Minister of Post and Telegraph but in actuality as the leading representative of the Soviet in the Provisional Government* and the chief spokesman of the Revolutionary Defensist strategy for peace. Although he succeeded in gaining the respect and sympathy of the European socialist leaders who visited Russia, the Soviets' call for an international socialist conference to discuss the terms of peace came to nothing. Similarly, he enjoyed the close cooperation of moderate "bourgeois" ministers; yet many of his initiatives were never implemented by the Provisional Government.

Despite these failures and the decline in popular support for the policy of coalition, Tsereteli remained opposed to the idea of government based exclusively on the soviet and sought vainly to promote its cooperation with a succession of nonsocialist parties and organizations: the Cadet Party, the Radical Democratic Party, the Cooperative Movement*, and the national unions of local governments (*see* All-Russian Union of Towns and All-Russian Union of Zemstvos). The strain of his efforts, coupled with repeated frustrations, led to a breakdown of his health, and in early October he left Petrograd for a rest in his native Georgia.

Tsereteli returned to Petrograd only after the October Seizure of Power*. He insisted on the Constituent Assembly's* ultimate responsibility in determining the form of Russia's future government. At the Assembly's opening session on January 5, 1918, he delivered his famous speech attacking the Bolsheviks (*see* Russian Social Democratic Workers' Party [Bolshevik]) for planning to dissolve that body—a plan that he predicted would throw Russia into the arms of counterrevolution—and calling for the preservation of democratic institutions as the only hope for Russia and Revolution. When the Assembly was forcibly dispersed by the Bolsheviks and arrest appeared imminent, Tsereteli escaped to Georgia where an independent republic was declared in the spring of 1918. Although he did not join other Mensheviks in the highest levels of the new government (because he had always opposed Georgian nationalism and saw independence as an undesirable, if necessary, evil), he agreed nonetheless to serve the republic through its diplomatic missions to the Paris Peace Conference and the Second Socialist International. He continued to represent Georgian Social Democracy in the International even after Georgia fell to the Bolsheviks in the spring of 1921.

During the 1920s Tsereteli became increasingly alienated from his Georgian comrades and their anti-Russian nationalism. He was also in disagreement with his former friend F. I. Dan (*see* Gur'vich, Fedor Il'ich), who had become the leader of mainstream Menshevism and who was not prepared to denounce the Bolsheviks as completely as Tsereteli demanded. By 1929 Tsereteli found himself isolated from his former allies and decided to abandon political activity entirely. He lived in Paris until 1948 and thereafter in New York, working on his memoirs until his death in 1959.

Ziva Galili y Garcia

Bibliography

Galili y Garcia, Z. *The Menshevik Leaders of the Petrograd Soviet: Social Realities and Political Strategies in the Russian Revolution of 1917.* 1989.

Roobol, W. H. *Tsereteli - A Democrat in the Russian Revolution. A Political Biography.* 1976.

Tsereteli, I. G. *Rechi (proizvedeny v 1917).* 1917.

Tsereteli, I. G. *Vospominaniia o fevral'skoi revoliutsii.* 2 vols. 1962.

Tukhachevskii, Mikhail Nikolaevich (1893–1937). Tukhachevskii was one of the most prominent military leaders in the Soviet Union. Gaining fame as a commander in several military campaigns during the Civil War in Russia*, he eventually became a Marshal of the Soviet Union in 1935 before his arrest and execution during the purges.

Tukhachevskii was born in a family of impoverished nobility in what is now the village of Slednogo in Smolensk Province. His mother came from the peasantry. He attended a Penza elementary school for the first seven grades and then took an examination that exempted him from the first six years of the Moscow Military School. In 1911 he attended that institution for one year. From 1912 to 1914 he went to the Alexander Military Academy in Moscow. Upon graduation he became a Second Lieutenant in the Semenovskii Guards Regiment and immediately went into battle. He was captured in battle in 1915, escaped and walked back to his regiment in 1917, a distance of nearly one thousand miles. After the October Seizure of Power* he was elected as a company commander, and on April 5, 1918 he joined the Russian Social Democratic Workers' Party (Bolshevik)*.

During the Civil War in Russia Tukhachevskii soon displayed his boldness as a military commander and his remarkable talent for military strategy. As a result he was promoted very rapidly and was one of the top military commanders to rise to the surface during that period, ranking with Iakir, M. V. Frunze*, and Gamarnikov. He became a general staff officer in 1922 at the age of twenty-nine. From 1925 to 1928 he was Chief of Staff of the Red Army*.

He commanded the First Army of the Eastern Front from June 1918 to January 1919, the Eighth Army of the Eastern Front from January to March 1919, and the Fifth Army of the Eastern Front from April to November 1919. During that period he was one of the major military leaders in the successful campaign against A. V. Kolchak*. From February 1920 to August 1921 he commanded the troops of the Western Front in the successful campaign against A. I. Denikin*, and in the war with Poland*. To some extent his stock fell when the war with Poland proved to be a stand-off, but he recovered his prestige when he was given the command of the Seventh Army during its difficult but successful suppression of the Kronstadt Rebellion (*see* Kronstadt, 1917–1921). In April and May of 1921 he was placed in command of the troops that put down the Antonov Revolt. His style of leadership emphasized attack, mobility, and maneuverability. In some respects he seemed an outsider among the new generals of the Red Army* because of his aloof, frequently brusque, or condescending aristocratic manner, and because of his interest in high culture, especially music.

Tukhachevskii's activities were not confined to field duties. In 1918 he played an active role in the development of the new Red Army as a member of the Military Department of the All-Russian Central Executive Committee* of Soviets. In 1921 he became Director of the Military Academy of the Workers' and Peasants' Red Army and commander of the forces in the western military district. From May 1928 to June 1931 he was commander of the Leningrad Military District. In 1931 he became Deputy Chairman of the Revolutionary Military Council of the USSR and Deputy Commissar of Defense, which meant, in effect, acting People's Commissar of Defense. In 1936 he became head of the Directorate for Military Training.

Despite his indisputable talents, Tukhachevskii was frequently at odds with the political leadership in the USSR. During the Military Opposition* debate he joined I. V. Stalin and K. E. Voroshilov* in criticizing L. D. Trotsky* for his reliance on military specialists (from Tsarist officers). Tukhachevskii and Frunze, however, were less romantic than Voroshilov, who still dreamed of an all-partisan army where cavalry charges would solve all problems. The two generals worked out their own "Proletarian Concept of War" which not only called for the development of highly mobile forces able to attack and withdraw rapidly, but also the development of a cadre of international revolutionary communist comanders promoted through the ranks on the basis of ability. They wanted to develop strategy and tactics based on offense, rather than defense. Despite his actions on the side of Voroshilov and Stalin during the attack on Trotsky, Tukhachevskii's relations with them were rather cool because he publicly blamed them for the failure of the Polish campaign in a book published in 1923. More than once he publicly expressed his contempt for Voroshilov's ability and competence as a military leader. That is why after his friend and patron Frunze died in 1925, Tukhachevskii was demoted to command of the Leningrad Military District. But his talent was needed by the new regime and he seems to have bypassed Voroshilov and gone directly to Stalin with his plans for modernizing the Red Army, and in 1931 was restored to a leadership position when he was reaapointed as Voroshilov's assistant in the post of Deputy People's Commissar of Defense. In that post he took many of the steps that made it possible for the Red Army to conduct World War II. He modernized and enlarged the standing army, established many new military academies, wrote extensively on modern military strategy and organization, and sponsored the development of rocketry. On May 11, 1937 he was demoted to the post of Commander of the Volga Military District. That marked the beginning of Stalin's purge of the Red Army General Staff. On June 9 Tukhachevskii, Iakir, and Uborovich were relieved of their commands, and the June 11 *Pravda* (Truth) announced that they were being investigated. On the following day, Voroshilov announced that the accused had confessed to treason and had been executed. Tukhachesvkii was rehabilitated after Stalin's death.

588 TURKESTAN, REVOLUTION IN

Bibliography

Alexandrov, Victor. *The Tukhachevsky Affair*. 1964.
Butson, T. G. *The Tsar's Lieutenant*. 1984.
Garthoff, Raymond. *Soviet Military Policy*. 1966.
Haupt, Georges and Marie, Jean-Jacques. *Makers of the Russian Revolution*. 1974.
Kolkowicz, Roman. *The Soviet Military and the Communist Party*. 1967.
Levytski, B. *The Stalinist Terror in the Thirties*. 1974.
Marshal Tukhachevskii. Vospominaniia druzei soratnikov. 1965.
Popov, A. *Trud, talant, doblest'*. 1972.
Todorovskii, A. I. *Marshal Tukhachevskii*. 1966.
Tukhachevskii, M. N. *Izbrannye Proizvedenniia*. 2 vols. 1964.

Turkestan, Revolution in. The revolution in Turkestan was, in many ways, a prototype for the other economically backward Moslem areas, for it represented the same mixture of tribal, religious, and ethnic conflict that made that part of the world so vulnerable to outside conquest during most of its history. These qualities also made Central Asian people less susceptible to Marxist ideas than the rest of Russia. As Pipes has put it, "Among Moslems in Russia, Marxist influence was very limited, and where it did exist (Vladikavkaz, Baku, Kazan) it was Menshevik in character. In general Moslems had been far more affected by liberal and Socialist Revolutionary thinking than by Marxism . . . ." (Pipes, p. 156).

The name Turkestan was applied by the Russian conquerers of Central Asia (*see* Central Asia, Revolution in) to those lands that were conquered from 1865–1876. Basically Central Asia was placed under the jurisdiction of the Governorship General of Turkestan and included parts of present day Uzbekistan, Turkmenistan, Kazakhstan, Tajikistan, and Kirghizia. The population was diverse, including the four major groups: Turkmen, Kazakhs, Uzbeks, and Kirghiz.

Between the time of its conquest and the February Revolution* Turkestan prospered, especially by comparison to its poorer steppe neighbors. The cultivation of cotton became a large scale business in Turkestan, with the Russian plantation owners reaping most of its profits and the natives doing the work. However, the natives did benefit from the Russian occupation, chiefly in the form of order and security. The new Russian rulers put an end to tribal warfare and some of the benefits of economic development did filter downward. By 1910 there were nearly seven million natives living in the area, and about 400,000 Russians. There were two major cultural groups among the native intelligentsia in Turkestan. The first was the Ulema (*Ulema cemiyeti* [in Russian *Dzhemieti*] or Association of Clergymen) which was a group of conservative scholars who wanted to preserve Moslem courts and religious law (the *shariat*) for the whole Moslem population. The other was the Jadid* movement that wanted to westernize the Moslems and create a lay political and legal system for all led by a Kazakh Jadid named Mustafa Chokaev.

By and large Turkestan remained outside the conflict that swirled around the rest of Russia in 1917. Even where there were some repercussions, as, for example, in Tashkent where a soviet (*see* Tashkent Soviet) was established it was accomplished by Russians, not Turks and Moslems, and by Left Socialist-Revolutionaries (*see* Left Socialist-Revolutionary Party) in collaboration with a small number of Bolsheviks (*see* Russian Social Democratic Workers' Party [Bolshevik]). The Tashkent Revolutionary Committee formed in September consisted of four Russians, four Jews, one German, and one Pole. As Zenkovsky puts it: "This small, but resolute group of socialist adventurers without connections among the natives and unsupported by the larger part of the local Russian population was to rule Central Asia in the name of the Soviet government for the next two years" (Zenkovsky, p. 231). Its sources of support were the railroad workers, some regular troops who became Red Guards*, "internationalist" battalions (*see* Internationalists) recruited from prisoners of war. The Tashkent Soviet was ahead of its time and tried unsuccessfuly to seize power in that city on September 2, electing a new executive committee consisting of eighteen Left Socialist-Revolutionaries, ten left-Mensheviks (*see* Russian Social Democratic Workers' Party [Menshevik]) and seven Bolsheviks. Although that attempt to create a Soviet Turkestan was premature, when they heard the news of the October Seizure of Power*, the members of the Tashkent Soviet began seizing power on October 25 and were in control by November 1. They called the Third Regional Conference of Soviets on November 15, 1917 in Tashkent. But that conference refused to accept any Moslems in their Council of People's Commissars, because, they said, there were no proletarian Moslems. The new Council of People's Commissars for Soviet Turkestan consisted of seven Bolsheviks and eight Socialist-Revolutionaries, all Russian or European, under the chairmanship of a Russian army lieutenant named F. Kolesov. Paradoxically, the members of the Ulema at first decided to meet at the same time as the Third Regional Congress of Soviets in Tashkent in a Third Moselm Central Asian Conference concocted by the Tashkent Soviet. They had intended to support soviet power and participate in the new government, believing the Soviet's promise of regional autonomy for Turkestan. When they were denied a role, they turned to the National Center under Chokaev.

To the native Moslems, intellectuals and commoners alike, this seemed to be only another form of imperialism. In their provincial capital of Tashkent they had only exchanged one group of European masters for another. The leadership of the Moslems in Turkestan had originally been in the hands of the Jadids, the liberals, who had called the First Turkestani-Moslem Conference in April and called for a decentralized federal system in which the Moslems would have a great measure of self-rule and their lands would be returned to them. It created a permanent executive committee, the Turkestan Moslem Central Council (*Shuro-i-Islam*), later called the National Center (*Milli-Merkez*) under the leadership of Mustafo Chokaev, and, although it sent delegates to the All-Russian Moslem Congress in Moscow in May, it remained relatively independent of that body.

At the Second Moslem Central Asian Conference on September 3, 1917, a declaration was approved that called for autonomy for Central Asia in a new democratic federal Russian state.

Rejected by Tashkent, the Moslems of Turkestan decided to create their own form of Dual Power*. They would provide native Moslems with an alternative capital city for Central Asia in Kokand. Under the leadership of Chokaev they gathered in Kokand in the Fourth Moslem Central Asian Conference on November 25 in a city that was the former palace of the Kokand Khans and almost entirely Moslem. The assembly did not break off relations with either Moscow or Tashkent, but on November 27 announced the autonomy of Turkestan within the union of the Russian Democratic Republic. As a rival to Tashkent, which also claimed to rule Turkestan, the Kokand government became known as the Autonomous Government of Kokand. They elected a National Council of thirty-six Moslems and eighteen Russians. The government included Kazakhs (*see* Kazakhstan, Revolution in), Bashkirs (*see* Bashkiria, Revolution in), Uzbeks, and Azerbaijanis (*see* Azerbaijan, Revolution in). Chokaev became its head of state. In December they successfully put down an uprising organized by Russian officers and some conservative Moslems. When the Constituent Assembly* was dispersed, Kokand announced that on January 23 it would convoke a Turkestan Constituent Assembly of its own.

At the end of January the Tashkent Soviet called the Fourth Regional Congress of Soviets and resolved to take immediate action to crush what it called the counterfeit autonomy of the Moslem nationalists. The supply route to Russia was opened up at the end of January, giving Tashkent the opportunity to obtain support from the Red Army*. Tashkent moved to crush the autonomous government of Turkestan and succeeded in doing so by February 19. That day, however, marked the beginning of the anti-Soviet Basmachi* movement, which was fueled by the slaughter of Moslems (14,000 were said to have perished) which followed the soviet seizure of Kokand and the desecration and destruction of its buildings.

Although I. V. Stalin*, as People's Commissar of Nationalities, had already set up a subordinate Commissariat for Moslem Affairs under the Tatar, Mullanur Vakhitov*, that was only the beginning of the Soviet government's efforts to counter the activities of the Tashkent Soviet by courting Russia's Moslem population. Vakhitov set up Moslem Bureaus in many cities in Central Asia in March and April, but not in Turkestan. With the death of Vakhitov in 1918, another Tatar, M. S. Sultangaliev*, took his place and pursued similar policies.

The Tashkent government did not, however, temper its victory with mercy and its unpopularity with the native Moslems began to attract attention even in Moscow. On April 30, 1918 a declaration that had been approved by the Fifth Congress of Central Asian Soviets, V. I. Lenin*, and I. V. Stalin announced the creation of a Turkestan Autonomous Soviet Socialist Republic. Special emissaries came from Moscow to intervene. A new Turkestan Central Executive Committee included ten Moslems (mostly Jadids) out of thirty-six members. On

June 17, 1918 the First Regional Party Congress, under prodding from Moscow, was forced to accept in principle several concrete steps to give more equality and representation to the Moslems, but in practice Tashkent continued to drag its feet. Moscow's efforts to change the leadership in Tashkent was facilitated in January 1919 when the Tashkent Commissar of War attempted a coup d'etat and shot most members of the Tashkent government. Under continued pressure from Moscow, the Second Regional Party Conference in February 1919 counted almost half its members as Moslems, including such prominent former Jadids as T. Hojaev, N. Hojaev and T. Ryskulov*. At the First Conference of Moslem Communists in Central Asia the Moslems voiced their grievances frankly for the first time.

Moscow acquired more influence in Tashkent when Soviet troops captured Orenburg in January 1919, reuniting Turkestan and Russia, and British troops in the Transcaspian were ordered to leave. In anticipation of more direct influence, a Special Commission for Turkestan was appointed which included in its membership Sh. Z. Eliave as Chairman, M. V. Frunze*, V. V. Kuibyshev, F. I. Goloshchokov and Ia. Z. Rudzutak. They arrived in Tashkent in November 1919 and immediately took charge.

Moscow's efforts to bring in Moslem representatives to Turkestan led to a mass influx of Jadids, including T. Ryskulov and N. Hojaev. By January 1920 the Fifth Regional Party Conference elected a Regional Bureau that was primarily Moslem and the former Jadid leader, Tursun Hojaev, became secretary of the Bureau. In effect, the Uzbek Jadids took control and began to make the local communist organization an instrument of Pan-Turkic nationalism, excluding non-Turkic peoples from their organizations. They renamed Turkestan the Turkic Autonomous Republic; they changed the name of their branch of the party from Turkestan organization of the Russian Comunist Party to Turkic Communist Party and they began to talk about the need for a large Central Asian state that embraced all Turkic people. By spring the Turkestan Commission began to understand what it had on its hands, especially Frunze, who was expected to hold power in the area with an army of only 16,000 men. On February 24, 1920 the Turkestan Commissions rejected Ryskulov's changes, and in a resolution "On the Autonomy of Turkestan" on March 8, 1920 the Central Committee of the Russian Communist Party (Bolshevik) endorsed the decision of the Turkestan Commission. In actuality, the pressure was building up from Turkic nationalists in all quarters—the Alash Orda* was fighting for an autonomous Kazakhstan, the Tatar Communists (see Tatars, Revolution among the) had achieved an independent Tatar state, and Ts. Validov was proposing a Kazakh-Bashkir federation. When Ryskulov appealed directly to Lenin against the Turkestan Commission, Lenin upheld the commission and appointed a new Turkestan Commission, not only without any Moslems, but including a Latvian Chekhist, Ia. Peters.

Moscow was encouraged by Frunze's success in overthrowing the Emir of Bukhara in August 1920, scarcely noticing that their allies in Bukhara were also

Uzbek Jadids. But the intemperate speeches of the Jadids that put more emphasis on Turkic nationalism than on class struggle did not escape notice. In September most of the Jadids were removed from positions of power, and the Ninth Regional Congress of Soviets in Turkestan, after meeting in Tashkent, adopted a new constitution accepting the Soviet definition of national autonomy. The new Moslem Bureau consisted chiefly of Uzbeks and Kazakhs who were workingmen, not intellectuals.

On April 11, 1921 the All-Russian Central Executive Committee* of Soviets announced the creation of the Autonomous Soviet Socialist Republic of Turkestan. The new republic did not, however, include Bukhara and Khiva. In 1924, presumably as a further measure to prevent any resurgence of Pan-Turkic sentiment, the Turkestan People's Republic and the Kirghiz People's Republic were broken up into some of its smaller national components. Uzbekistan and Turmenistan became Union Republics. Kazakhstan became an Autonomous Republic along with Tajikistan and Kirghizia.

Bibliography

Bennigsen, Alexandre A. and Wimbush, S. Enders. *Muslim National Communism in the Soviet Union*. 1979.
Park, A. G. *Bolshevism in Turkestan*. 1957.
Pipes, R. *The Formation of the Soviet Union*. 1968.
Zenkovsky, S. *Pan-Turkism and Islam in Russia*. 1960.

U

Ukraine, Revolution in. The Ukrainian component in the Russian Revolution, more properly referred to as the Ukrainian Revolution, came about as a result of the collapse of the central authority and the emergence of the Provisional Government*, which sought to establish a democratic order on the territories of the former tsarist empire. Compared to the other European states, the Ukraine occupied an important place with a territory of 179,614 square miles inhabited by a population of approximately 31 million of whom 80 percent were Ukrainians, 9 percent Russians and 6 percent Jews. The remaining 5 percent was made up of various lesser national groups. In 1916 the Ukraine comprised about one quarter of the Russian Empire.

Taking advantage of the momentary confusion in Petrograd, the Ukrainians hastened to establish a political system of their own. The story of the Ukrainian Revolution from March 1917 tells us of the insurmountable problems facing the Ukrainians who wanted to build a legitimate democratic successor state. Those problems were both foreign and domestic. The greatest obstacle facing the Ukrainian leadership was the reluctance of the Russian Provisional Government to recognize the Ukrainian government as the legitimate representative of the Ukrainian people. Internal problems stemmed from the low level of national consciousness, from lack of administrative and political experience, and from the negative attitude of the national minorities toward Ukrainian political aspirations.

The process of Ukrainian state-building began on March 4, 1917 when the Society of Ukrainian Progressives (in Ukrainian, *Tovarystvo Ukrainskykh Postupovtsiv*), which hitherto functioned as a secret organization decided to form a Ukrainian central body that would represent various Ukrainian organizations. Three days later such a unifying body was created, and it was given the name of Ukrainian Central Rada (*see* Central Rada). This new political body was made up of representatives of the Ukrainian parties, of workers, students, military units, and various civic organizations. To head the Central Rada, the assembly chose Michael Hrushevsky, the most distinquished Ukrainian historian. It was he, together with Volodymyr Vynnychenko, who articulated the Ukrainian social, economic, and political objectives for the rest of 1917.

The Central Rada, which became the focal point of Ukrainian political forces, quickly extended its activities to various centers of the Ukrainian territory. To be able to speak on behalf of the Ukrainian people, the Rada called for an All-Ukrainian National Congress to be held on April 6. The Congress was preceded by a tremendous enthusiasm—it seems that Kiev was treated to an unprecedented national euphoria as successive gatherings, often numbering tens of thousands of people, celebrated the rebirth of a nation that, only a short time before, was declared by tsarist officials to have been non-existent.

The National Congress, which met in Kiev from April 6 to April 8, was attended by some 900 delegates who represented peasant cooperatives, various cultural and profesional organizations, and local self-government bodies known as zemstvos. The Congress over which S. Erast presided dealt with the problem of administrative structure and, more significantly, with the question of Ukraine's political status. After a lengthy discussion the Congress adopted a resolution that, within a federal structure, remanded territorial autonomy as a basis of political order in the Ukraine. Adopting the principle of autonomy within a democratic federal structure was very much in line with the ideologies of the Ukrainian socialist parties, which basically made up the Central Rada. They saw the future of the territory of the former tsarist empire as a voluntary union of free democratic states. Basically, the quest for free development within an autonomous Ukrainian state remained the central point of Ukrainian internal and external policies for the rest of 1917.

Pursuing the concept of autonomy and democracy to its ultimate conclusion, the National Congress expressed itself in favor of granting full guarantees of equal rights to national minorities that inhabited the territories of the Ukraine.

As a last item on its agenda, the Congress conducted an election which provided the Central Rada with the necessary political support to deal with internal and external problems of a newly created state. In a spirit of national solidarity all political parties joined the Central Rada, thus creating a coalition government in which the leading role was played by the Socialist-Revolutionary Party*. The second most influential party was that of the Social Democrats, which was Marxist in orientation and had a higher proportion of intellectuals and professional men than the Socialist-Revolutionaries who were concerned primarily with agrarian questions (see Agrarian Policy, 1917–1921; Agriculture).

After the initial euphoria wore out, the Central Rada discovered that it was difficult to extend and maintain its authority in the provinces. There was simply a shortage of Ukrainian intelligentsia experience in public and political administration. The situation was further complicated by the fact that while the Rada was trying to establish a firm foundation for an autonomous Ukrainian state, the Russian Provisional Government of Petrograd never recognized the Rada as the sole governmental authority of the Ukraine. Despite Ukrainian professions of friendship toward the future federated Russian Republic, the Petrograd government very grudgingly recognized only some territorial administrative authority of the Central Rada.

During the initial period of the Ukrainian Revolution the Ukrainian military played a prominent political and organizational role. Through a process of Ukrainization, entire units of the tsarist army (*see* Army of Imperial Russia in World War I) became Ukrainian. These units organized their own political councils whose representatives held two large congresses (May 5 to May 8 and May 28 to June 2, 1917) during which they expressed an unqualified support for the Central Rada and the political programs it represented.

The political philosophy of the Rada was articulated by the decrees, or Universals, of which there were four. The First Universal was approved by the Central Rada on June 10, 1917. It stated that henceforth the people of the Ukraine shall direct their own lives. "Let the Ukraine be free," the Universal declared solemnly, " . . . let the Ukrainian people have the right to order their own lives in their own land" (Hunczak).

On June 23 the Central Rada (which acted as a parliament) further asserted its authority by creating a governing body that was given the name of General Secretariat. Volodymyr Vynnychenko, a Social Democrat, became the head of the Secretariat as well as General Secretary for Internal Affairs. There were eight other portfolios: General Secretary, Paul Khrystiuk; supply, Mykola Stasiuk; agricultural affairs, Borys Martos; nationalities, Serhii Efremov; military affairs, Simon Petliura*; education, Ivan Steshenko; financial affairs, Christopher Baranovsky; judicial affairs, V. Sadovsky. The Central Rada thus took an important step beyond issuing proclamations. It created a government that would carry out its policies and its laws.

The Russian Provisional Government, faced with a *fait accompli,* decided that it was better to negotiate with the Ukrainians than to fight them. With that purpose in mind, the Petrograd government sent to Kiev A.F. Kerensky* (Minister of War), M. I. Tereshchenko (Minister of Foreign Affairs), and I.G. Tsereteli* (Minister of the Interior). As a result of the discussions between the two parties, the Central Rada on July 3 issued its Second Universal, which declared that the Russian Provisional Government recognized the right of the Ukrainian people to self-determination. Probably the most important point of this entire affair was that the Provisional Government felt compelled to send its representative to negotiate with a de facto Ukrainian government.

The representatives of the Russian Provisional Government also reached an agreement with the Central Rada concerning the participation of the national minorities in the Ukrainian government. In general, this agreement was very much in tune with the previously enunciated position concerning the national minorities by Hrushevsky and by other leading members of the Central Rada. On the basis of the Second Universal, the national minorities were allotted 30 percent representation in the Central Rada, and the Little Rada added eighteen members from the minorities to the forty Ukrainians. Thus the minorities received representation in excess of their actual numbers. The executive branch of the Ukraine's government, that is, the General Secretariat, was increased by two Jews, two Russians, and one Pole.

The agreement with the Provisional Government did not, however, prevent its meddling in Ukrainian affairs, a fact that helps to explain the strained relations between the two countries. The tug of war between the Ukrainian government and the Provisional Government ended when the Bolsheviks (see Russian Social Democratic Workers' Party [Bolshevik]) came to power. From that time on the Ukrainians had an even more formidable opponent to cope with. The soviets (see Soviets [Councils] of Workers', Soldiers', and Peasants' Deputies), while pursuing the same centralist objectives as the Provisional Government, presented them behind a facade of socialist and Internationalist* ideals (see National Question and the Russian Revolution).

Anticipating Bolshevik political claims in the Ukraine, the Central Rada with the support and encouragement of the Third All-Ukrainian Military Congress which met in Kiev (October 20 to 30), decided to assert its prerogatives. It did that by passing the Third Universal on November 7, 1917, which proclaimed the establishment of the Ukrainian Democratic Republic (in Ukrainian, Ukrainska Narodna Respublika). The Universal, which was addressed to the "Ukrainian People and all peoples of the Ukraine," declared the Rada to be the sole repository of authority until the convocation of the Constituent Assembly of the Ukraine which was to take place on January 9, 1918. The document also extended the jurisdiction of the Ukrainian government to territories inhabited predominantly by ethnic Ukrainians. Thus nine provinces (gubernii) made up the territory of the Ukrainian state.

The Third Universal also had several paragraphs that, given the opportunity, would have provided a philosophical basis for the evolution of the Ukrainian state. It proclaimed amnesty for all political prisoners and abolished the death penalty. Furthermore, the document stated that the Ukrainian Republic shall secure its citizens "freedom of speech, press, worship, assembly, association, strikes, inviolability of person and residence, and the right and opportunity to use the native language in dealing with all administrative agencies." In the spirit of toleration, the Universal proclaimed that Russians, Jews, Poles, and other people of the Ukraine were granted national-personal autonomy. By this act the Rada hoped to promote the self-government of the various minorities in the Ukraine. Parenthetically, it might be noted that as a political act the provisions on national minorities of the Third Universal have no equal.

The Universal also touched upon the most controversial economic issue of the time—the land question (see Agrarian Policy, 1917–1921; Agriculture). It proclaimed that henceforth lands of the nobility, the church, the monastaries, and other non-working proprietors were abolished. These lands were to become the property "of the entire working people" without any compensation to the former proprietors. The interests of the factory workers were also taken into consideration—for them an eight-hour day was made mandatory.

Reflecting a popular demand for an end to the war, the Central Rada declared that it would use resolute means and firmly insist "that peace be instituted quickly." This signaled that the Rada was ready to enter peace negotiations with the Central Powers.

While the Central Rada was coping with the Provisional Government and attending to its domestic problems, there began to emerge a new political competitor—the Bolsheviks. Although few—in the summer of 1917 in the Ukraine there were only some 18,000 members—the Bolsheviks were a significant factor in Ukrainian politics because behind them, particularly after October 25, 1917, stood Soviet Russia. However, even though they lived in the Ukraine, the Bolsheviks were members of the Russian Communist Party (*see* Russian Social Democratic Workers' Party [Bolshevik]), and their membership with some exceptions, consisted of Russians, Jews, and Russified Ukrainians.

A lack of native roots of Bolshevism in the Ukraine manifested itself when the All-Ukrainian Congress of Soviets was convoked on December 4, 1917 by the Bolsheviks, and was attended by 2,500 delegates who took a position against the Bolsheviks. Only 80 delegates supported the Bolsheviks. It may have been that the position of the Bolsheviks at the Kiev Congress was weakened by the ultimatum the Russian Soviet government sent the Central Rada accusing it of disorganizing the front by withdrawing Ukrainian troops, disarming Bolshevik forces in the Ukraine, and shielding General Alexei M. Kaledin's* counterrevolutionary uprising in the Don region by preventing the passage of Bolshevik troops. The Ukrainians were given forty-eight hours to cease their practices, or a state of war would follow.

The ultimatum seems to have had the effect of a catalyst in mobilizing the Ukrainians. The Congress, convoked by the Bolsheviks, passed a resolution that condemned the ultimatum as an interference in the internal affairs of Ukraine and a violation of the Ukrainian people to self-determination.

Having experienced this debacle, the defeated Bolsheviks left for Kharkiv where, on December 13, 1917, they formed the People's Secretariat, or the first Soviet government of the Ukraine—a rival of the Central Rada. The new government, headed by the son of a famous Ukrainian novelist, Yurii Kotsiubynsky, was already formed under the protection of and had the support of the Russian troops who violated the border of the sovereign Ukrainian state.

Faced with the reality of a Soviet Russian invasion and an internal rebellion of the Bolsheviks, the Ukrainians abandoned their federalist program and adopted a position of complete independence. This new political stance was articulated by the Fourth Universal on January 9, 1918. It stated: "From this day forth, the Ukrainian Democratic Republic becomes independent, subject to no one, a Free Sovereign State of the Ukrainian People."

Even as the Ukrainians were proclaiming their independence, large portions of the Ukraine were being occupied by rebels and V. I. Lenin's* troops. Devoid of any outside assistance, the Ukrainian government took steps to conclude a treaty with the Central Powers in order to obtain help against Soviet Russia. This was accomplished when the Treaty of Brest-Litovsk* was signed on March 3, 1918. Following the agreement, the joint armies of the Ukraine, Austria, and Germany, expelled the Bolshevik forces from Ukrainian territory and the Central Rada again established its authority over the Ukraine.

The Ukrainian Bolsheviks retreated with the Russian troops into Russia where the first Soviet Ukrainian government was dissolved. To provide an organizational framework for their activities, a framework which would conform to the dictates of the Russian Communist Party, the Ukrainian Bolsheviks held their First Congress in Moscow from July 5 to 12, 1918. The newly established party, which for all practical purposes was a branch of the Russian Communist Party, had a membership of 4,364. At this juncture, more than ever, the Communist Party (Bolshevik) of the Ukraine, CP(B)U, was the least Ukrainian in its membership and political orientation.

The relations between the new allies—Ukrainians on the one side, Austrians and Germans on the other—were not harmonious. The Germans, viewing the Ukrainians as junior partners, began to behave as occupiers violating the sovereignty of the Ukrainian state. When the Rada protested their behavior, the Germans helped General Pavlo P. Skoropadskyi stage a coup d'etat on April 29 as a result of which a new government was established under the leadership of Skoropadskyi, who assumed the historic title of *Hetman*.

Establishing a monarchy after the socialist Central Rada was a radical change. Skoropadskyi's rule from April 29 to December 14, 1918 was a period characterized by a response to the previous Rada policies in social, economic, and political spheres. The Germans, for their part, gained a free hand in the internal affairs of the Ukraine. Knowing that Skoropadskyi lacked a strong basis of support, the Germans almost completely disregarded his government. Indeed, they even issued decrees in different provinces of the country abrogating civil liberties granted by the Central Rada. It would be unfair to suggest that the *Hetman* rule was completely devoid of any positive developments. Probably, its most important accomplishment was the introduction of an era of relative tranquility throughout the land during a most unsettled time.

The opposition of the socialist and nationalist groups to the Skoropadskyi government led to the creation of the Ukrainian National State Union which launched an uprising against *Hetman* Skoropadskyi on November 14, 1918. The uprising led by the Directory (*see* Directory, Ukraine), whose most popular leaders were Volodymyr Vynnychenko and Symon Petliura, gained the support of the Ukrainian masses, and as a result the Skoropadskyi regime was quickly overthrown. This victory of Ukrainian national and socialist forces led to the temporary reestablishment of the Ukrainian Democratic Republic and of the guiding political principles of the Central Rada.

To take advantage of the revolutionary situation in Ukraine, the Bolsheviks secretly established, on November 20, 1918, a provisional Soviet Ukrainian government. It was headed by a Russophile, Georgii L. Piatakov, who, within six weeks, was replaced by an even greater centralist, Khristiian G. Rakovskii*. Thus came into existence the second Soviet Ukrainian Republic in which all important government positions were occupied by non-Ukrainians. But the real source of power was in the hands of Vladimir Antonov-Ovseenko*, the commander of the Russian Red Army* which invaded the Ukraine for the second time, ostensibly to extend fraternal help to the Bolsheviks in Ukraine.

With this uprising against *Hetman* Skoropadskyi in November 1918 the Ukrainian Revolution entered its last and most tumultuous stage. It was characterized by foreign interventions, Bolshevik invasion, internal uprisings, and a cataclysmic agarian social upheaval whose by-product was a state of anarchy that gave birth to a variety of warlords known as *otamans*. Without any assistance from the outside, the Ukrainian state could not withstand these enemies from within and without. Despite the heroic efforts of Simon Petliura, who became a symbol of the Ukrainian national state idea, his enemies, the Bolsheviks, prevailed and after the Treaty of Riga (March 1921), Lenin imposed his rule over the Ukrainian people behind the facade of a Ukrainian Soviet Socialist Republic (*see* Directory—Ukraine).

Taras Hunczak

Bibliography

Adams, Arthur E. *Bolsheviks in the Ukraine*. 1963.
Borys, Jury. *The Sovietization of the Ukaine, 1917–23*. 1980.
Doroshenko, Smytro I. *Istorii Ukrainy*. 1930–1932.
Hunczak, Taras, ed. *The Ukraine, 1917–21*. 1977.
Khrystiuk, Pavlo. *Zamitkyi materialydo istorii Ukrainskoi Revoliutsii*. 4 vols. 1921–1922.
Pidhainy, O. S. *The Ukrainian Republic in the Great East-European Revolution*. 1966–1971.
Reshetar, John S. *The Ukrainian Revolution, 1917–20*. 1952
Sullivant, Robert S. *Soviet Politics and the Ukraine, 1917–1920*. 1962.

Ul'ianov, V. I. *See* Lenin, Vladimir Il'ich.

Uritskii, Mikhail Solomonovich (1873–1918; pseudonum, Dr. Ratner). Uritskii was one of the foremost Left Communists (*see* Left Communism) during the October Seizure of Power* and the Civil War in Russia*. He was born in the town of Cherkassy into the family of a Jewish merchant. He received a strict religious education, but became interested in Russian literature and attended the Belaia Tserkov Gymnasium and then the Law Faculty of Kiev University. He was a member of the Social Democratic movement in Russia as early as 1897 when he was arrested and charged with being a member of the Russian Social Democratic Workers' Party (*see* Russian Social Democratic Workers' Party [Bolshevik]). He was sent into exile a number of times, serving sentences in Iakutsk, Volgda, and Archangel. When the Russian Social Democratic Workers' Party split in 1903, Uritskii sided with the Mensheviks (*see* Russian Social Democratic

Workers' Party [Menshevik]). He was an "Internationalist"* during World War I* and collaborated with L. D. Trotsky* on the journal *Nashe slovo* (Our Word). When he returned to Russia after the February Revolution*, he joined the Interdistrict Committee, and with that group joined the Bolshevik Party (*see* Russian Social Democratic Workers' Party [Bolshevik]) and became a member of its Central Committee (*see* Central Committee of the Russian Communist Party [Bolshevik]). He was appointed as one of the five members of the Military Revolutionary Committee chosen by the Central Committee to become a member of the Military Revolutionary Committee of the Petrograd Soviet* that directed the October Seizure of Power. Some of the documents issued by that agency bear his signature followed by the title President (or Chairman). After the revolution he became a member of the Council of People's Commissars*. But, like many Left Communists, he opposed the Treaty of Brest-Litovsk* and left the government and the Central Committee of the party in order to protest the Treaty of Brest-Litovsk. At the Seventh Congress of the Bolshevik Party in 1918 Uritskii read the declaration of the Left Communists, which included N. I. Bukharin* and G. I. Lomov-Oppokov*, who refused at that time to enter the Central Committee even though elected to it. He finally submitted and was appointed as chief of the Petrograd Cheka (*see* All-Russian Extraordinary Commission for Combatting Counterrevolution and Sabotage). Although opposed personally to the death penalty, he signed execution orders approved by his committee.

On August 30, 1918 he was shot by a student, L. A. Kannegiesser, whose friend had been executed by the Cheka. Because the assassination occurred on the same day as an attempted assassination of Lenin, the two events became the occasion for the retaliatory execution by the Cheka of 500 "counterrevolutionary and White Guards." Uritskii was buried with full honors in the Field of Mars in Petrograd.

Bibliography

Daniels, R. V. *The Conscience of the Revolution.* 1969.
Haupt, Georges, and Marie, Jean-Jacques. *Makers of the Russian Revolution.* 1974.
Leggett, George. *The Cheka.* 1981.
Volkov, P. P. and Gavrilov, L. N. *Pervyi predsedatel' Petrogradskoi Cheka.* 1968.
Lunacharskii, A. V. *Revolutionary Silhouettes.* 1967.

V

Vakhitov, Mulla Nur (1855–1918). Vakhitov was a prominent Tatar revolutionary who as head of the Central Moslem Commissariat, became Stalin's agent for dealing with Russia's moslem population.

Vakhitov was born in the village of Kazaevo in the Kungar District of Perm Province. He attended a Russian gymnasium in Kazan, entered the St. Petersburg Polytechnic Institute in 1910, and the Psycho-Neurological Institute in 1911. He was repeatedly arrested and finally expelled from the institute for his revolutionary activities. In 1910 he accepted a job working as an engineer in the railroad system of Kazan. In March 1917, with M. S. Sultangaliev*, he organized the Moslem Socialist Committee of Kazan. In October 1917 he fought with the Bolsheviks (see Russian Social Democratic Workers' Party [Bolshevik]) and in December joined their party. He also edited a newspaper called Kyzyl bairak. In January 1918 Stalin appointed him to head the Central Moslem Commissariat under the Commissariat of Nationalities and Chairman of the Moslem Military Collegium of the People's Commissariat of War. Vakhitov proceeded to organize Moslem Bureaus in various parts of the provinces of Central Asia and Siberia. He convened a conference of communists in May 1918 that called for the creation of an autonomous Tatar-Bashkir Moslem state. In June 1918 he called a conference of provincial branches of his Moslem Commissariat in order to create a Russian Party of Moslem Communists (Rossiiskaia Partiia Kommunistov [Bolshevik] Musul'man) with its own Central Committee. The new Tatar-Bashkir state would be created by a constituent congress of Tatar-Bashkiria to be called by an eight man commission headed by Vakhitov. These ambitious plans were interrupted by Vakhitov's death before the end of the year. In August 1918 Vakhitov was captured when, in an effort to defend Kazan, he led the Second Tatar-Bashkir Battallion against the Czechs (see Czechoslovak Legion), and after examination by a Moslem tribunal he was executed by the Czechs.

Bibliography

Bennigsen, Alexandre A. and Wimbush, S. Enders. *Muslim National Communism in the Soviet Union.* 1979.
Ishakov, V. M. *Mullanur Vakhitov.* 1958.
Nafigov, R. *Mullanur Vakhitov.* 1960.
Pipes, R. *The Formation of the Soviet Union.* 1964.
Zenkovsky, A. A. *Pan-Turkism and Islam in Russia.* 1960.

Vesenkha. *See* Supreme Council of The National Economy.

Vikzhel. *See* All-Russian Executive Committee of the Union of Railwaymen.

Vladimirskii, Mikhail Fedorovich (1874–1951). Vladimirskii was a prominent Bolshevik leader in Moscow during the October Seizure of Power (*see* Moscow, Revolution in). Later he became an historian of that event and a soviet official. Vladimirskii was born in Arzamas, Nizhnyi-Novgorod Province. He enrolled in the medical faculty in Tomsk in 1894 and then transferred to the medical faculty of Moscow State University, and finally to the University of Berlin in 1903. While studying in Moscow he became involved in a Marxist circle and in the formation of the Moscow Workers' Union in 1896. He completed his medical studies in Berlin from 1900 to 1903 after fleeing arrest in Russia for his revolutionary activities. When the Bolsheviks (*see* Russian Social Democratic Workers' Party [Bolshevik]) split with the Mensheviks (*see* Russian Social Democratic Workers' Party [Menshevik]), Vladimirskii joined the Bolshevik faction and became a member of its Moscow Committee. In the summer of 1914 V. I. Lenin* chose Vladimirskii to serve with Inessa Armand* and I. Popov as the Bolshevik delegation at a conference of Russian Marxists to explore the possibilities of reunification. During World War I*, Vladimirskii worked as a physician in France, and returned to Russia in July 1917. He became a member of the Bolsheviks Party's Military Center and played an active role in the preparations for the Bolshevik Seizure of Power in October (*see* October Seizure of Power). After the Soviet government was established, Vladimirskii became Chairman of the Council of District (*Raion*) Dumas which governed the city. At the Seventh Congress of the Russian Communist Party (Bolshevik), Vladimirskii became a full member of the Central Committee (*see* Central Committee of the Russian Communist Party [Bolshevik]) but was reduced to candidate member in March 1919. From 1918 to 1921 Vladimirskii served as a member of the Presidium of the All-Russian Central Executive Committee* of Soviets and Deputy Commissar of Internal Affairs. From 1922 to 1926 he served in the Ukraine as Secretary of the Central Committee of the Ukrainian Communist Party and Chairman of their Central Control Commission, People's Commissar of Worker-Peasant Inspection and Deputy Chairman of the Ukrainian Council of People's Commissar. He occupied various posts in the central government from 1917 to 1927 and served as Chairman of the Party's Central Auditing

Commission from 1927 until his death in April 1951. When he died his body was placed in the Kremlin Wall.

Bibliography

Haupt, Georges and Marie, Jean-Jacques. *Makers of the Russian Revolution*. 1967.
Slonimskaia, I. A. *M.F. Vladimirskii*. 1967.
Vladimirskii, M. F. *Organizatsiia sovetskoi vlasti na mestakh*. 1921.
Vladimirskii, M. F. *Sovety ispolkomy i s'ezdy sovetov (materialy k izucheniiu stroeniia i deiatel'nosti organov mestnogo upravleniia)*. 1920.

Volodarskii, V. (1891–1918; true name, Mosei Markovich Goldshtein). Volodarskii was a prominent member of the Interdistrict Committee* who became one of the leading figures in the Bolshevik (*see* Russian Social Democratic Workers' Party [Bolshevik]) movement in Petrograd (*see* October Seizure of Power; Petrograd Soviet) in 1917. He was especially known for his oratorical gifts. Volodarskii was born in a poor Jewish family in Ostropol, Volhynia Province. He attended primary school and a local gymnasium and began working in the Jewish Bund (*see* Bund) and then the Ukrainian Social Democratic Party (in Ukrainian, *Spilka*). He was first arrested in 1908 when he was seventeen. After working for a few years underground he was arrested again in 1911 and exiled to Archangel Province. During his exile he completed his requirements for graduation from the gymnasium, and when his term of exile ended he immigrated to the United States. He worked as a cutter in a garment factory in Philadelphia and then in New York, and became an active member of the International Trade Union of Tailors. In New York he worked with N. I. Bukharin* and Chudnovskii on the editorial board of the newspaper *Novyi Mir* (New World). He returned to Russia in May 1917 and in Petrograd became a member of the Interdistrict Committee. Somewhat earlier than the other members of the Interdistrict Committee, Volodarskii joined the Bolsheviks and was appointed a member of their Petrograd Committee. He was put in charge of the Peterhod-Narva District which included the massive Putilov works. He also became a member of the editorial board of the Bolshevik newspaper *Rabochii put'* (*Workers' Way*). When the Bolsheviks obtained a majority in the Petrograd Soviet*, Volodarskii was appointed a member of its Executive Committee. He and L. D. Trotsky* were the most popular orators at the meetings of the Petrograd Soviet. He was a staunch advocate of Soviet power and opposed the party's decision in July to drop the slogan "All Power to the Soviets." However, when the growing strength of the Bolsheviks became apparent, he balked at the idea of insurrection, arguing instead that the Bolsheviks should put the issue to the Second All-Russian Congress of Soviets scheduled to meet at the end of October. When the All-Russian Central Executive Committee* was formed on October 26, Volodarskii was one of its most prominent members and vigorously opposed G. E. Zinoviev*, L. B. Kamenev*, and the idea of a coalition socialist government. After the October Seziure of Power* he became Petrograd's Commissar of Press, Propaganda and

Agitation, and in 1918 editor of the Bolshevik newspaper *Krasnaia gazeta* (*Red Newspaper*). Although he opposed the Treaty of Brest-Litovsk*, he did not join the other Left Communists (*see* Left Communism) in voting against it. On June 20, 1918 he was assassinated by a Left Socialist-Revolutionary (*see* Left Socialist-Revolutionary Party) and his body was buried with honor in the Field of Mars.

Bibliography

Haupt, Georges and Maire, Jean-Jacques. *Makers of the Russian Revolution*. 1974.
Kalashnikov, V. *V. Volodarskii*. 1924.
Kniazev, V. *Volodarskii, V*. 1922.
Lur'e, Ia. *V. Volodarskii*. 1919.
Naumov, I. *Tovarishch Volodarskii*. 1926.

Voroshilov, Kliment Efremovich (pseudonym Volodia; 1881–1969). Voroshilov was a Bolshevik soldier who became a major Party official and in 1935 a Marshal of the Soviet Union.

He was born in a small village in the Ekaterinoslav Province called Verkhenye. His father was a railroad worker and his mother was a charwoman. Voroshilov moved about a great deal during his childhood because of his father's early work as a miner. Growing up in poverty, Voroshilov had little formal education and at eight years old went to work in the mines of Golubov not far from Lugansk where he would conduct much of his early revolutionary work. In 1896 he found a job in Alchevsk as a metal worker. It was here that he became involved with a social democratic circle. He led a strike in 1899 and was consequently arrested.

The strike and arrest in 1899 established a new direction for Voroshilov. In 1903 he got a job in the Hartmann factory in Lugansk and joined the Bolshevik faction of the Russian Social Democratic Workers' Party (see Russian Social Democratic Workers' Party [Bolshevik]) and quickly became an important leader in the local Bolshevik movement. He participated in the strikes during 1905, and in 1906 he became chairman of the Lugansk Soviet and head of the trade union in that factory. Voroshilov attended the Fourth Party Congress in Stockholm in 1906 and the Fifth Party Congress in London in 1907. At the Fourth Party Congress he met I. V. Stalin* and began a long, though uneven friendship with him. At the Fifth Congress he met his future wife, Iakaterina Davidovna Gorbman.

The years after the Nineteen-Five Revolution* were the best and the worst for Voroshilov. Although he was arrested and exiled to Archangelsk, he soon escaped and headed to Baku and the Don Basin in order to engage in revolutionary activity. During World War I*, Voroshilov went to Petrograd where he played a role in the Bolshevik rise to power after the February Revolution*. When the Petrograd Soviet* was created he became a representative of the Izmailovsky Regiment and became more involved in street demonstrations. He was a delegate to the Seventh (April) Conference of the Russian Social Democratic Workers;

Party [Bolshevik])* and the Sixth Congress of the Bolshevik Party in July. In August 1917 he was elected Chairman of the Lugansk Soviet and Chairman of its City Duma. Those two responsibilities kept him so preoccupied that he did not attend the Second All-Russian Congress of Soviets of Workers' and Soldiers' Deputies in Petrograd. Nonetheless he was elected a member of the All-Russian Central Executive Committee in absentia. At the end of the year, he was elected a delegate to the Constituent Assembly*, went back to Petrograd for the Third All-Russian Congress of Soviets in December (where he was elected to its Central Committee) and helped F.E. Dzerzhinskii* organize the Cheka (See All-Russian Extraordinary Commission.)

Voroshilov did not play a decisive role in the Bolshevik rise to power, but he did not try to embellish it later on, as did I.V. Stalin*. In his writings, Voroshilov did not try to imply that his role in the events of 1917 was crucial. Instead, he believed that his greatest contribution to the Party was his military leadership. Today many Soviet and Western military experts would question that judgement as well.

Voroshilov began his rise to power as a military leader after the breakdown of peace talks with the Germans in February 1918 (see Brest-Litovsk). In March 1919 he helped to form military units from Lugansk that participated in the fighting near Khar'kov. In July 1919 Stalin at his own request was placed in charge of the War Council of the Northern Caucasus Military District close by. Voroshilov's 15,000 troops ragged and poorly trained troops moved toward the city of Tsaritsyn to defend it against the German army. His forces were given the name Tenth Army and Voroshilov was appointed their commander. There he proved to be a brave and effective commander. In collaboration with Stalin he managed to save the city, but the casualties suffered by the Red Army* as a whole were estimated at 60,000. The Commissar of War, L. D. Trotsky*, asked for Stalin's recall and wanted to court martial Voroshilov.

Despite the cost of the Tsaritsyn victory, Voroshilov earned his reputation in that campaign. Even Lenin, though praising Voroshilov's bravery, commented that the losses might have been less if the Red Army had more military specialists and well-trained regular troops. Voroshilov thought otherwise, and became one of the chief opponents of Trotsky's effort to create a regular army with the help of Tsarists military officers. Voroshilov's philosophy of constructing an army of partisans or guerillas led to his role in the Military Opposition* at the Eighth Congress of the party in 1919. Voroshilov's insistence that former tsarist officers be refused commissions in the Red Army* brought him into conflict with Trotsky who wanted to create a professional army. Voroshilov once again chose to side with Stalin on this issue. Although Trotsky won the battle, his victory was costly in that it caused Stalin to join forces with Trotsky's other political enemies.

After Tsaritsyn, Voroshilov continued his military career, serving with distinction against A. I. Denikin* and P.N. Wrangel.* In May 1920 Stalin was appointed Political Commissar of the Southwestern Front where the Polish army had advanced into the Ukraine and seized the city of Kiev. When the Polish army was forced to retreat, Trotsky opposed plans to pursue the Poles and to advance on Warsaw. Lenin and Stalin disagreed with Trotsky and approved the pursuit, and by July 1920 M.N. Tukhachevskii* was approaching the capital city of Warsaw. In August the Politburo ordered that troops under the command of Voroshilov (the Fourth and Fourteenth Divisions) and S. M. Budenny* move toward Tukhachevskii to cover his left flank. Stalin refused to accept the order and the Poles moved into Tukhachevskii's exposed left flank. Stalin was recalled on August 17, but the Polish advance had already begun and the campaign was lost. Tukhachevskii never quite forgave Voroshilov and Stalin and in 1923, without using actual names, he would assign blame for the failure in Poland to Stalin, Budenny, and Voroshilov.

As a representative of the First Army to the Tenth Party Congress in 1921, Voroshilov helped to lead troops against the sailors at Kronstadt (*see* Kronstadt Uprising). From 1921 to 1924, he was in charge of the Caucasus Military District—probably another attempt by Stalin to reduce Trotsky's influence in that region. In May 1924 Voroshilov was named Moscow Military District Commander, replacing Trotsky.

With the death of M.V. Frunze* in 1925, Voroshilov replaced him as Commissar for Military and Naval Affairs, a post he kept until 1934. Voroshilov, a man who had no military training and contributed nothing to military science, came into conflict with M.N. Tukhachevskii, possibly the most talented soviet military leader at that time. Tukhachevskii advocated a stronger, modernized Red Army* and often criticized Voroshilov for his casual attitude towards his job. Voroshilov may have refused to help Tukhachevskii when he was accused of treason because he wanted Tukhachevskii out of the way.

Voroshilov is perhaps best known for his intimate friendship with Stalin, which is probably the chief reason for his successful rise through the Soviet system. They were often seen together in public and went on vacation together. He composed fanciful tales of Stalin's role in the military leadership during the Civil War* and also surrounded himself with his own cult of personality, exalting his role as a ''worker-commander.''He was an apparatchiki par excellence who seems to have survived the Stalin era for that reason.

Voroshilov appears to have been well paid for his loyalty to Stalin. In 1926 he was elected to the Politburo and in 1935 named Marshal of the Soviet Union. At the Seventeenth Congress of the Party in 1934, the city of Lugansk was renamed Voroshilovgrad.

There seems to be no direct evidence that he was involved in choosing those to be eliminated during the Great Purges of the 30s. Certainly, he must have sanctioned the purges on the army with no protest. Needless to say, Stalin and Voroshilov paid dearly for the destruction of the office corps in the early years of World War II.

The man who argued for the partisan army in the early years of the Civil War in Russia* did not finish his career in military affairs. Rather, he was involved with the Politburo from 1926 to 1952, where in addition to his political duties as head of state, he was engaged in promoting cultural projects such as films and documentaries. From 1946 to 1953 he was Deputy Chairman of the Council of People's Commissars and from 1953 to 1960 Chairman of the Supreme Soviet, also sitting on the Central Committee of the Supreme Soviet from 1921 to 1961. He was a member of the Politburo from 1926 to 1956.

At one point he fell out of favor with Stalin who mentioned several times that he thought that Boroshilov was a British spy. Somehow he managed to survive Stalin only to be denounced by Krushchev, and in June 1957 he admitted to membership in the Anti-Party Group that attempted to overthrow Khrushchev. His admission saved him from the exile that was imposed on V. M. Molotov and L.M. Kaganovich, but he was already an old man and he faded from the political spotlight. Voroshilovgrad was renamed Lugansk. From 1962 to 1966 he lived in quite retirement, though he was regularly elected to the Supreme Soviet. In 1966 he was once again elected to the Central Committee of the Party and in 1968 his first volume of memoirs was published. Following his death in 1969, Lugansk was once again renamed Voroshilovgrad.

Christopher Mendoza

Bibliography

Butson, Thomas G. *The Tsar's Lieutenant*. 1984.
Daniels, Robert. *The Conscience of the Revolution*. 1969.
Haupt, George and Marie, Jean-Jacques. *Makers of the Russian Revolution*. 1974
Medvedev, Roy. *All of Stalin's Men*. 1984
Tucker, Robert. *Stalin as a Revolutionary*. 1973.
Voroshilov, K. E. *Oborony SSSR*. 1937.
———. *Rasskazy o zhizni*. 1968.

W

War Communism. *War Communism* is a term used to describe the first period of economic policy in the history of the Soviet Union from 1918 to 1921. It was brought to an end in the spring of 1921 with the inauguration of the New Economic Policy*.

The authoritarian and statist economic policy of War Communism was a response to a series of material disasters, each one sufficient to overwhelm and destroy a stable political order, much less a fragile hierarchy of soviets (*see* Soviets [Councils] of Workers', Soldiers', and Peasants' Deputies) controlled at the top by a few hundred inexperienced revolutionaries. Between 1918 and 1921 Soviet Russia was invaded and dismembered by Imperial Germany, torn apart by the Civil War* (*see* Civil War in Russia), weakened by Allied military intervention (*see* Foreign Policy, 1914–1921; Allied Blockade), and deprived of its major grain and fuel-producing territories. The issue of survival became a first priority as citizens of the world's first socialist state died by the millions of starvation, cold, and disease. In this context, the makers of Bolshevik (*see* Russian Social Democratic Workers' Party [Bolshevik]) economic policy came more and more to blur the distinction between their coercive emergency measures and the substance of socialism itself.

Perceiving the food shortage (*see* Agriculture; Agrarian Policy, 1917–1921; Famine) as a distribution rather than a production problem, the Bolsheviks established a Food Commissariat to control the exchange of agricultural and industrial products on a nationwide basis. From the outset, the effort to obtain grain from the peasantry (*see* Peasants in the Russian Revolution) was crippled by an Allied blockade that cut off the supply of imported manufactured goods, as well as the machinery that might have enabled Russia's war-shattered industry to produce them. With nothing to offer the peasantry but promises of a rosy future or payment in an increasingly worthless currency, the new government moved inexorably toward an adversary relationship with the rural populace. In

June 1918 Committees of the Poor* (Kombedy) were formed to forcibly requisition surplus grain from the wealthy peasants who were judged guilty of
creating the food shortage. Although the Bolshevik economist E. P. Preobrazhenskii argued that the Kombedy embodied the highest socialist principle of
taking from each according to his ability and giving to each according to his
need, the more tough-minded V. I. Lenin* admitted that in fact "we really took
from the peasants all their surpluses, and sometimes even what was not surplus,
but part of what was necessary to cover the costs of the army and to maintain
the workers. . . . Otherwise we could not beat the landowners and capitalists."

The peasantry, fresh from the revolutionary struggles of 1917, were unwilling
to submit to authorities who seemed to them as hostile to their immediate interests
as the tax-hungry officials of the tsarist regime. In the summer of 1918 they
took to violent action; between July and September the Commissariat for Internal
Affairs recorded 108 peasant uprisings. The Bolshevik leadership, wracked by
the fear that maintaining the Kombedy would drive the peasantry into the embrace
of the White armies (see White Movement) and that dissolving them would
jeopardize the food supply of the army and the urban proletariat decided to
abolish the Kombedy in November 1918. But in the same month all internal
trade was prohibited, and the Food Commissariat was empowered to confiscate
any stocks of goods still in private hands. Both the principle and the practice of
forced requisition at fixed prices were retained even after the Kombedy were no
more.

In marked contrast to the Bolshevik approach to problems of distribution,
outright coercion was avoided in the sphere of agricultural production. Here
preference was consistently given to large-scale, centralized economic efforts.
State farms were established; some were even "ascribed," that is assigned
directly to a particular urban institution or enterprise for the purpose of supplying
it with foodstuffs or material essential for industrial operations. No aid was
provided the traditional repartitional land commune (the *mir*), which claimed
the loyalties of the majority of the peasantry and provided, however unwillingly,
most of the grain requisitioned by the state. By 1921 the unrelieved failure of
state-sponsored agricultural experiments, the tendency of commune peasants to
curtail production to personal subsistence levels rather than produce for forced
requisition, and the wartime destruction of livestock, machines, and farm buildings reduced the total grain output to 45 percent of its pre–World War I* level.

Productivity in industry declined even more rapidly than in agriculture, with
coal production at 27.0 percent of its prewar level by 1920 and iron ore at an
abysmal 1.7 percent. Under War Communism all large and medium-sized firms
had been nationalized by a Supreme Economic Council (see Supreme Council
of the National Council), which had set up a vertical system of industrial management. "Essential" branches of industry were designated as "trusts," each
one subordinate to a *glavk*, or "center," that might—at least on paper—manage
hundreds and even thousands of factories. In keeping with the tendency of the

Bolshevik leadership to centralize political and economic institutions, a system of one-man management came to prevail in state-owned factories.

In industry as in agriculture, the hopes of proletarians and peasants that their destruction of the old order had put an end to hierarchical and bureaucratic rule counted for little. Instead, new and inexperienced planners attempted to exert unprecedented top-down control over Russia's economic life. In practice, the Supreme Economic Council, despite its stated powers of regulation and supervision, was completely unable to coordinate the efforts of the various *glavki* or to mediate their bitter jurisdictional disputes, and the *glavki* themselves became a byword for bureaucratic incompetence among ordinary citizens.

It may have been that both Bolshevik policy and its failures were unavoidable. In 1918 when one-third of the factories in Petrograd were forced to close for lack of fuel and more people died of cold than of hunger, administrative options were severely limited. It is difficult to imagine how it would have been possible to concentrate scarce resources where they would have done the most good without an extremely centralized planning organization and a more or less bureaucratic chain of command.

Crisis conditions, combined with the belief that a militant socialist state need not fear to use its coercive power to the fullest, came to justify a growing tendency toward direct government supervision of the industrial work force. A central committee on compulsory labor was established under the Cheka's (*see* All-Russian Extraordinary Commission for Combatting Counterrevolution and Sabotage) F. E. Dzerzhinskii* for the purpose of distributing workers to areas of special need. At the same time, the state as chief employer in nationalized industry frequently evaded and undermined the authority of the proletariat's own trade union organizations (*see* Trade Unions). In 1919 compulsory labor was decreed necessary for the supply, loading, or unloading of all sorts of fuel. In 1920 chaos in the system of transport brought a decree mobilizing all railway workers for the labor service on demand. The heroic example of the famous "*subbotniki*," the militant proletarians who had voluntarily undertaken arduous socially necessary tasks in addition to their daily labor, was used to support the imposition of mandatory "voluntary" labor for members of the Communist Party and even for trade unions—a sort of unpaid overtime. By 1921 an absence of more than three days from the job was held to constitute industrial sabotage. As Russia's industrial machine continued to disintegrate, L. D. Trotsky* argued for the militarization of labor as another socialist advance beyond the profit seeking and disorganization of the bourgeois labor market.

Overworked and undernourished, Russian factory workers suffered far more deeply than the peasantry during the period of War Communism. At the same time, they were considered the "Pride of the Revolution" and the state's highest priority consumer (after the needs of the army were met). Favored by the food-rationing system, urban proletarians were frequently granted free

rent, fuel, water, electricity, generous periods of maternity leave, and unprecedented educational and cultural opportunities. In contrast, the more self-sufficient peasant majority was feared as potentially traitorous and used as
a "reservoir" to supply the needs of the social elements judged more strategically and politically significant. In response to such treatment, the peasantry
took the sort of revenge that only majorities are capable of inflicting. With
trade in requisitioned products decreed a state crime, peasant "criminals" began to spring up everywhere. A black market arose side by side with the legal
channels of distribution and eventually eclipsed them in extent and impact. By
the end of 1920 the peasantry had achieved a sort of triumph, as the barter of
all kinds of products for food became so widespread that formal mechanisms
of state control became irrelevant to the process of exchange. In the cities,
where factory managers were in fierce competition for scarce skilled labor,
the practice arose of granting bonuses-in-kind (particularly in food) to make
up for the inadequate and sometimes nonexistent wages promised by the state.
The weakest urban elements—the aged, the sick, and the very young—were
less able to bargain for food. Despite the suffering entailed by the disappear-
ance of any orderly system of distribution, the Bolshevik economist Iu. G.
Larin (M. A. Lure) argued that barter and payments-in-kind marked a still
further socialist advance toward the abolition of a money economy.

Neither Larin's idealization of the deepening economic crisis nor L. D.
Trotsky's arguments for increased coercion of the work force proved politically tenable once the Civil War and foreign intervention were over in 1920.
At that point, the renewal of peasant unrest, the outbreak of industrial strikes,
and the utter failure of the state to check the disastrous fall in argicultural and
industrial production convinced Lenin to call for a strategic retreat in economic policy. In 1921 the Tenth Party Congress and the Council of People's
Commissars*—after (1) crushing the Kronstadt Rebellion (see Kronstadt,
1917–1921) against the Bolshevik monopoly of political power, (2) tightening
the machinery of repression, and (3) reasserting control over the "commanding heights" of industry—resounded with positive concessions. It was decided
that the restoration of a more freely functioning market and the encouragement
of small-scale private enterprise were essential to revive the economy and de-
fuse "petty bourgeois" peasant discontent. Increasing agricultural production
was recognized as a concern more appropriate to the Soviet Union's immediate needs than the thankless task of extracting a nonexistent surplus from a
predominantly subsistence peasantry. Yet it was significant that many of the
most enthusiastic supporters of the New Economic Policy considered it a temporary concession, an unavoidable setback rather than a less coercive approach
to socialism. The belief that in principle efficient and rational management
meant unlimited state power to shape and control the activities of agricultural
and industrial production was not discredited. The war-generated fear that
powerful enemies threatened the world's first socialist state and rendered inevitable the imposition of military-style economic measures did not disappear

after 1921. It was not the New Economic Policy but the heroic and draconian policy of War Communism that would turn out to be the precursor of the Soviet Union's economic future.

Esther Kingston-Mann

Bibliography

Bukharin, N. I., and Preobrazhenskii, E. P. *ABC of Communism.* 1967.

Carr, E. H. *The Bolshevik Revolution, 1917–1923.* Vol. 2. 1966.

Kritsman, L. *Geroicheskii period velikoi russkoi revoliutsii.* 2d ed. 1926.

Kosinskii, V. A. *Osnovnye tendentsii v mobilizatsii zemel'noi sobstvennosti i ikh soti- al'no-ekonomicheskie faktory.* 1925.

War Industries Committees. The War Industries Committees (Voenno-pro- myshlennye komitety) were the last of the major ''public'' organizations to emerge during the war. They were created at the Ninth. Congress of the Association of Industry and Trade in May 1915 to provide voluntary public assistance in the organization of industries for the war effort.

The immediate inspiration for the committees' formation was the shortage of munitions experienced by the Russian army (*see* Army of Imperial Russia in World War I). This shortage, which had existed since the beginning of the war, took on crisis dimensions in the spring and summer of 1915 when the Russian army was forced to retreat from Austrian Galicia and Russian Poland. Raising serious doubts about the tsarist authority's ability to administer the war economy and sustain the war effort, the crisis was at once political and economic, and insofar as it pointed to a need to mobilize the industrial working class for production, it had obvious social implications as well.

Initially, the Central War Industries Committee, located in Petrograd, was controlled by the Association of Industry and Trade, and its relations with the tsarist state reflected the cautious ''businesslike'' approach of the association's leaders. Three delegates from the Central Committee, all long-standing, active members of the association, were coopted by the Special Council for the Supply of Munitions under the war minister, and several million rubles worth of orders were assigned for distribution by the committee to armaments factories. But at the first congress of the new organization in July 1915, its leaders and their policies were rejected by the majority of the 231 delegates representing eighty- five district and local War Industries Committees. In the forefront of this successful challenge to the association's domination were Moscow-based textile manufacturers who had already consolidated their position in the Moscow district committee. Their subsequent leadership of the organization was insured by the election of two prominent Muscovites, A. I. Guchkov* and A. I. Konovalov, as chairman and vice-chairman, respectively, of the Central Committee.

By February 1916 when the committees held their second congress, they numbered 226, divided into 34 district and 192 local committees. With the exception of the Moscow Committee, which could contract directly with the central military departments, orders were obtained by the Central Committee and distributed to district committees and thence to individual private enterprises, those run by the committees themselves, or to their local branches for further distribution. Most of the district and some of the local committees contained sections reflecting the predominant economic activities of the areas in which they operated. Hence, the Ural district committee in Ekaterinburg supported sections devoted to mining, cottage industry, fuel, raw materials and food supply, and the labor question. The Moscow Committee, by contrast, consisted of twenty-one sections, the most active of which were involved with textiles, shell production, and the evacuation and resettlement of factories and equipment located in areas near the front. Presiding over more than 50 local committees throughout the central industrial region* and publishing a monthly journal filled with technical information and reports from all parts of the empire, the Moscow Committee under the textile magnate P. P. Riabushinskii rivaled the Central Committee as the authentic voice of the entire organization.

A survey covering slightly less than half of the committees revealed that 31.4 percent of the members (1,378) were representatives of commercial–industrial organizations, 17.1 percent (751) consisted of *zemstvo* and city officials, and another 16.2 percent (711) represented scientific and technical organizations. The coalescence of these groups around the issue of mobilizing the productive forces of the country for the war effort was significant. Before the war they had been subordinated to, respectively, foreign and state capital, the central state bureaucracy, and foreign technical and managerial personnel. But the war caused a sharp reduction in foreign capital investment in industry while requiring massive industrial redeployment and technological innovation. It also brought on the political crisis of mid–1915 because of the tsarist state's inability to accommodate itself to the new situation.

The emergence of the War Industries Committees, therefore, may be seen as the response of Russia's nascent national bourgeoisie not only to a crisis but to the opportunities that that crisis provided. Provincial producers were attracted to the committees by the possibility of receiving war orders and priority in obtaining raw materials, machinery, and technical assistance necessary for their fulfillment. Scientific, technical, and professional personnel, drawn from the universities and polytechnics, various branches of the Imperial Technical Society, and industry itself, viewed the committees as offering scope for research and development appropriate to war in the industrial age. Indeed, much of the work done during the war in relatively new fields such as pharmaceuticals, telecommunications, and aeronautical instruments was to be the product of this institutional link between science and industry. Finally, the more politically oriented leaders of the organization sought to ally it with other public organizations, the Progressive Bloc* in the Duma* (*see* Duma and Revolution), and representatives of the industrial working class. Their aim was to reconstitute the political structure that they deemed essential for victory in the war, the maintenance of domestic peace, and economic prosperity after the war.

But the forces amassed by the War Industries Committees were insufficient to overcome those arrayed against them. The attempt to assume control of the military procurement system and to determine credit, manpower, raw materials, and fuel requirements accordingly antagonized not only the large Petrograd firms with long established bureaucratic connections but the military departments as well. The campaign for a "government of public confidence," which featured the committees' leaders both as advocates and ministerial candidates, foundered when the Duma was prorogued and the Progressive Bloc split over the issue of whether to engage in extraparliamentary activity. It also ironically contributed to the economic marginalization of the committees, as the government responded by stripping them of many privileges and powers they had initially enjoyed. Hence the various regulatory bureaus and commissions founded by the committees were one by one superseded by state institutions in which the committees' representatives constituted small minorities.

The result was that by February 1917 the Central and Moscow committees had placed orders worth slightly less than 500 million rubles, or only 7 percent of the value of all orders distributed by the military departments. For certain articles capable of being assembled by small and medium-sized enterprises, such as grenades, mortar, and high-explosive shells, the committees' share was considerably higher. But difficulties in supplying skilled workers and the means of production meant that many others were eventually cancelled, went unfulfilled, or were only partially fulfilled.

In many ways the most interesting and revealing failure of the committees was their attempt to exercise hegemony over the working class through their sponsorship of Workers' Groups. Although fifty-eight such groups had been elected by factory workers as of February 1917, relations between them and the committees were, as a rule, stormy. Moreover, the proposals they jointly drafted, such as conciliation boards, factory elders, and the legalization of trade unions, alienated large sections of the business community, exposed the committees and the Menshevik (see Russian Social Democratic Workers' Party [Menshevik])-dominated groups to police harassment and highlighted the Bolsheviks (see Russian Social Democratic Workers' Party [Bolshevik]) as the only party unequivocally opposed to class collaboration and "defensism"*.

Finding itself increasingly isolated from its social base, the central workers' group under K. A. Gvozdev abandoned its opposition to mass action in late 1916 and drew up plans for a march to the Duma to coincide with its reopening. Simultaneously, Guchkov began sounding out various liberal activists and military officers about the possibility of organizing a palace coup. Both these actions were effectively nipped in the bud, the former by the arrest of the Central Workers' Group on January 26–27, 1917, and the latter by the February Revolution*. Yet both the Workers' Groups and the War Industries Committees managed to contribute to the constellation of forces that emerged after the overthrow of the monarchy. The factory cells created by the Central Workers' Group continued to agitate in the factories after the abortive march to the Duma on

February 14 and are generally credited with being among the first to call for the election of soviets* (*see* Soviets [Councils] of Workers', Soldiers', and Peasants' Deputies). Gvozdev and two other members of the Central Workers' Group were released from prison during the February days and subsequently took an active part in the Central Executive Committee of the Petrograd Soviet*. Guchkov, after having obtained the Tsar's signature on the abdication decree, took up his position as War Minister, becoming one of the four members of the War Industries Committees to assume ministerial portfolios in the Provisional Government*.

The committees themselves urged unconditional support of the Provisional Government and its prosecution of the war to a victorious conclusion. They thereby antagonized the Workers' Groups, which, in any case, had been made redundant by the formation of soviets, factory committees (*see* Workers in the Russian Revolution), and trade unions*. As the revolutionary disintegration of industry proceeded in 1917, those industrialists who had earlier placed their hope in the committees turned to the more militant employers' unions to defend their interests. At the same time, there was a shift in the committees' orientation away from mobilizing industry for war production toward questions relating to the demobilization and the postwar economy. By October the dominant force within the organization was the "third element," especially scientific and technical personnel. Having opposed the October Seizure of Power* by the Bolsheviks in Petrograd, the committees were placed under the control of the Supreme Council of the National Economy* in January 1918 and renamed National Industries Committees. In this way, many technical experts made the transition to working as "specialists" in the Soviet state.

Lewis H. Siegelbaum

Bibliography

Haumann, Heiko. *Kapitalismus in Zaristichen Staat, 1906–1917*. 1980.
Katkov, George. *Russia, 1917, The February Revolution*. 1967.
Sidorov, A. L. *Ekonomicheskoe polozhenie Rossiia v gody pervoi mirovoi voiny*. 1973.
Siegelbaum, Lewis H. *The Politics of Industrial Mobilization in Russia, 1914–1917*. 1983.
Trudy vtorogo s''ezda predstavitelei voenno-promyshlennykh komitetov 26–29 fevralia 1916 g. 1916.
Zagorsky, S. *State Control in Russia during the War*. 1928.

White Movement. The White Movement is a label often applied by both communist and Western historians to all anti-Bolshevik political and military movements.

In actuality, the White Movement was born out of the failure of moderate liberals and socialists in 1917 to achieve a workable coalition to defend the democratic Revolution and prevent the polarization that brought the Bolsheviks (*see* Russian Social Democratic Workers' Party [Bolshevik]) to power and provoked a conservative reaction. This fateful division in the ranks of those who stood for democracy and the determination of Russia's future by the freely elected Constituent Assembly* was already apparent in the A. F. Kerensky* and L. G. Kornilov (*see* Kornilov Revolt) clash in August.

When liberals (notably, the Constitutional Democratic Party—Cadet* led by P. N. Miliukov*) supported the demands of the army's commander, General L. G. Kornilov, that Kerensky's predominantly socialist government suppress the soviets and assert stronger leadership to prevent anarchy and defeat, Kerensky suspected a military coup and retaliated by ordering the arrest of virtually the entire High Command. An irreparable split then opened between the two opponents of Bolshevism, with the socialists fearing that the liberals would become pawns of a counterrevolutionary military dictatorship, and liberals convinced that the socialists would simply open the way to a Bolshevik victory and with it a capitulation to the German enemy. Although retired army commander M. V. Alekseev persuaded Kornilov to submit to arrest, and a new coalition was formed, mutual recriminations within the leadership continued, thus facilitating V. I. Lenin's* conquest of power in October (*see* October Seizure of Power).

In the aftermath of the Bolshevik seizure of power in October, and especially after the forcible dismissal of the Constituent Assembly in January 1918 and acceptance of a separate peace with Germany in February (*see* Brest-Litovsk), the country literally disintegrated with numerous national minorities declaring independence from Russia and dozens of local "authorities" springing up across the land. Most importantly for the future of the White movement, the Cadets split into three groups: a Right faction called the "Moscow Center," which now advocated turning to the Germans for aid and openly professed monarchist views; a Left faction, which still believed that the only hope for victory lay in a coalition with the socialists and therefore joined with Right Socialist–Revolutionaries (*see* Socialist-Revolutionary Party) and Mensheviks (*see* Russian Social Democratic Workers' Party [Menshevik]) in April to create the Union for the Regeneration of Russia; and a middle group, the "National Center," which initially rejected both the monarchist and pro-German orientation of the Right and the coalition with the socialists favored by the Left.

The Union for Regeneration, remarkably, succeeded in the spring of 1918 in getting agreement from moderates on both Left and Right, as well as strong encouragement from the Allied embassies, to form a three-man Directory (*see* Directory—Russia)—one liberal, one socialist, and one military commander— to provide all-Russian leadership for the struggle. Key figures in the negotiation of this plan, such as Cadet N. I. Astrov and Right Socialist-Revolutionary (S-R) leader N. D. Avksent'ev*, then set out to win support in the regions of major anti-Bolshevik strength, particularly in the Volga area where the S-R Committee of the Constituent Assembly had been set up in Samara, in Siberia (*see* Siberia, Revolution in) where a regional government in Omsk under the Cadet P. V. Vologodskii was founded by Right S-R's with military support, and in the Cossack* territories in the South where a Volunteer Army was being formed by

Generals Alekseev and Kornilov. When the resulting Ufa State Conference appointed a five-man Directory in September to exercise "supreme authority over all territories of the Russian state," however, its support almost immediately evaporated. Although the Directory included three socialists, Socialist-Revolutionary Party Chairman V. M. Chernov* launched an attack on the collaboration sought by the Union for Regeneration as a betrayal of the Revolution, and liberals, most importantly Astrov who was designated a Cadet member of the Directory, rejected participation after the socialist majority at Ufa committed to reconvening the old Constituent Assembly rather than electing a new one (the Union plan). General Alekseev, originally designated as the military member, declined to serve under any Directory, and General A. I. Denikin*, who had assumed command of the Volunteer Army after Kornilov's death in battle in March, refused to recognize the Directory, and Astrov concurred. Although the Directory was then reorganized (a Left Cadet and liberal, General V. G. Boldyrev, filling the vacancies) and in October, after moving to Omsk, it appointed a Council of Ministers under Vologodskii, its life was short. On November 5 a military coup in Omsk brought the arrest of Avksent'ev and other socialists, after which Vologodskii turned over "supreme governmental authority" to the Minister of War, Admiral A. V. Kolchak*.

The trend to the Right was further revealed when in November 1918 at a conference in Jassy, Romania, intended to unify anti-Bolshevik elements for an appeal to the Allied Powers for recognition and aid, the debate on the issue of national authority saw defeat of both a leftist appeal to retain political leadership in the form of a Directory and a rightist bid to gain recognition of Grand Duke Nikolai Nikolaevich as regent. Rejecting both coalition and monarchist approaches, the White movement now fixed on military dictatorship with advisory political councils (excluding socialists) as the only form of leadership strong enough to conduct a Civil War in Russia* against the Bolsheviks. The "unity" it promoted subsequently was that of unification under Kolchak of the various military commands, principally those under General N. N. Iudenich* in the Northwest, General E. K. Miuller in Arkhangelsk, Denikin in the South, and the armies of Cossack* *Atamans* A. I. Dutov* and G. M. Semenov* in Central Asia (*see* Central Asia, Revolution in) and eastern Siberia*, an effort that succeeded on paper but never in practice. The Allied governments, which had been prepared to recognize the Ufa Directory as the government of Russia, subsequently established close relations with and provided aid to the White armies but declined to extend formal recognition to any government.

After the Jassy conference a delegation was sent to Paris to represent the Whites with the Allied governments, but French opposition to the inclusion of Miliukov (who had briefly advocated seeking German aid in the spring of 1918) and refusal by the Allied Powers now to accept any Russian representation to the Peace Conference frustrated such plans. However, in January 1918 the Russian ambassador to France, a prominent Cadet, V. A. Maklakov*, put together in Paris the Russian Political Council headed by the premier of the first Provisional Government, G. E. L'vov*, and including B. V. Savinkov* (former Minister of War under Kerensky and leader of the abortive Right Socialist-Revolutionary uprising at Iaroslavl in August), N. V. Chaikovskii (a Populist and original member of the Ufa Directory who had briefly headed the government at Arkhangelsk), and S. D. Sazonov (the former tsarist foreign minister who was designated by both Kolchak and Denikin as their personal representatives). Although this body persistently put pressure on the military commanders to take a liberal stand on the issues for the sake of better relations with the Allies, it also operated on the basic proposition that only a strong military authority could win the war and that popular support could best be achieved by commitment to a future constituent assembly rather than premature attempts to impose social and economic reforms in wartime.

By 1919 the White movement had fully emerged as a separate and now more conservative appendage of the military effort chiefly directed by Kolchak and Denikin, whose military-dominated administrations included mainly Right Cadets as political advisors. This development did not mean that Kolchak and Denikin personally stood for reactionary goals or restoration of the old regime. On the contrary, they identified strongly with the February Revolution* and the liberal program of parliamentary democracy and social reform. Although they were firmly set against socialism and any separatism that would divide Russia into its many nationalities (see National Question), their political philosophy (such as it was) included land reforms (see Agrarian Policy; Peasants in the Russian Revolution) and national minority autonomy, as they affirmed in reply to a note in May 1919 from the Allied Supreme Council laying down the conditions for further aid. However, Kolchak and Denikin regarded their commitment to the election of a new Constituent Assembly as overriding all other issues and argued that no "predetermination" should be allowed to prejudice the sovereign power of that body in the future, thus precluding any immediate effort to gain support through such actions as land distribution or declaration of support for a federation.

Given the results of the Constituent Assembly election in 1917, one could argue, as many White supporters did, that a pledge to turn over power to a new assembly elected on the basis of universal suffrage would ensure that Russia would become a democratic federation in the event of a White victory. On the other hand, the White military leadership's refusal to implement reforms and its inability to articulate clearly its intentions, together with clear, if unapproved, violations of its declared goals in practice, led to the belief vociferously expressed by many socialists, and more importantly held by the masses of the people, that the White movement as now constituted would lead to a return of the old regime. Thus although both Kolchak and Denikin consistently resisted demands to raise the banner of monarchism, and in the last months of the struggle Kolchak's Prime Minister, V. N. Pepeliaev, as well as Astrov, acting as Denikin's chief advisor, even brought about a formation of civilian governments that included representatives of the Left, such gestures had a hollow and pathetic quality about them, coming, as they did, only in defeat. The long stand on "non-predetermination" and "One Russia" had created a kind of apolitical stagnation that had not achieved popular support or even respect in Allied circles and could not now be overcome.

Had the White armies won on the battlefield, the White movement might have proved its claims, but the image of restoration that it conveyed only doubled and tripled the enemy to be fought by pitting it against peasants and minorities who otherwise would have had good reason to want the Bolsheviks defeated. Indeed, the White leadership even antagonized its own closest allies, such as the Czechoslovak Legions* in Siberia* and the Cossacks in the South. In the end Kolchak was handed over to the Bolsheviks for execution in January 1920 by the Czechs, and Denikin, to whom he had turned over "supreme power throughout the Russias" just before his demise, was himself forced out in March by General P. N. Wrangel*, an aristocratic rival who called himself regent and used Cossack jealousies against him. As the last of the White generals, Wrangel made more clever use of political slogans and postures, with the skilled advice of conservatives such as A. V. Krivoshein and P. B. Struve, but this epilogue, like that of G. M. Semenov in Siberia counted for little other than the final split between the republican and monarchist elements in the movement. With the mass evacuation of the Crimea (*see* Crimea, Revolution in) in November 1920, following total defeat in Siberia, the White movement came to an end in Russia (although it would survive decades longer among the emigrés). In the final analysis, the militarization of the White movement proved to be a fatal weakness, but, that being the case, its failures can be attributed as much to shortsighted political leaders whose conduct brought it into being as it can to the shortcomings of officers like Kolchak and Denikin who inherited the consequences.

George Brinkley

Bibliography

Bradley, J. F. N. *Civil War in Russia, 1917–29.* 1975.
Brinkley, George. *The Volunteer Army and Allied Intervention in South Russia, 1917–21.* 1966.
Denikin, A. I. *Ocherki Russkoi smuty.* 5 vols. 1921–1926.
Fleming, Peter. *The Fate of Admiral Kolchak.* 1963.
Golovin, N. N. *Rossiiskaia kontr-revoliutsiia v 1917–1918 gg.* 5 vols. 1937.
Kenez, P. *Civil War in South Russia, 1918–20.* 2 vols. 1971, 1977.
Melgunov, S. P. *Tragediia Admirala Kolchakova.* 3 vols. 1930–1931.
Miliukov, P. N. *Russia Today and Tomorrow.* 1922, 1973.
Rosenberg, W. G. *Liberals in the Russian Revolution.* 1974.
von Lampe, A. A., ed. *Beloe delo: letopis beloi borby.* 7 vols. 1926–1933.

Women in the Russian Revolution, Role of. Women participated in the Russian Revolution as members of the mass organizations and mass demonstrations that first toppled the Romanov dynasty (*see* Nicholas II) and then, six months later, brought the Bolsheviks (*see* Russian Social Democratic Workers' Party [Bolshevik]) to power.

Women of different social classes participated in the turmoil of 1917 in different ways. Peasant women remained largely quiet: they, more than city dwellers, considered politics to be a male concern. Sometimes they would go along when their husbands seized land from the local gentry, for they were capable of sporadic outbursts against the authorities, but becoming political activists was too radical a departure from traditional values.

Working-class women in the cities were also more willing to throw rocks at a shop that had just sold out of bread than they were to join a political party. Their avoidance of radicalism was one reason factory owners had been employing them since the 1880s under abysmal conditions and for starvation wages. As was the case throughout Europe and North America, in Russia women were concentrated in the textile, food, and luxury-goods industries, although the exigencies of World War I* also brought them into metallurgy and mining. By 1917 women constituted one-half of the paid labor force; there were 50,000 of them employed in the factories of Petrograd alone. Their growing contribution to the economy was not matched, however, by increased wages, and the tsarist government also suspended for the duration the regulations that protected women from dangerous working conditions. As inflation and shortages grew in 1915 and 1916, there were more and more incidents of angry women lashing out at the government by looting stores or joining strikes. Their anger boiled over again in February 1917, when they learned that Petrograd had only ten days' supply of flour left. Rock throwing gave way to mass violence in which working-class women played a prominent part. On February 23, the day proclaimed International Woman's Day by the Second Socialist International, women marched to demand bread and constitutional reform. On February 24 they were in the streets again, their ranks swelled by male workers and revolutionaries, and the February Revolution* had begun. One week later Nicholas II* abdicated, ending the rule of the tsars.

The participation of women in the demonstrations that brought down the monarchy was typical of their role throughout the revolutionary year. Very few women held leadership positions in the trade unions*, soviets (*see* Soviets [Councils] of Workers', Soldiers', and Peasants' Deputies), political parties, or the Provisional Government*. They, like their peasant sisters, were handicapped by their own reluctance to put themselves forward, and they were also burdened by child care responsibilities and discouraged by male opposition. More women than ever before, however, attended rallies, signed petitions, and voted in municipal elections for the Constituent Assembly*, the legislature called to write a constitution for Russia. At times working class women spoke out for their own rights as well as for general reform. The wives of soldiers fighting at the front held demonstrations in Petrograd in the spring of 1917 to demand an increase in military allotments. Laundresses organized a strike for better wages and working conditions in May and won, after several weeks of bitter confrontation with employers. Factory women drew up their own petitions to the soviets as well as signing those drafted by men, and in their petitions they called for female equality and an end to sexual harassment on the job.

A small number of working-class women, as well as women of the intelligentsia, even joined the radical parties, chiefly the Bolsheviks and Mensheviks (see Russian Social Democratic Workers' Party [Menshevik]). Women comprised about 8 percent of Bolshevik members in 1917. Within the parties they did the same work as men—organization, speaking, writing, and serving as delegates to the soviets, Municipal Dumas (see Duma and Revolution), and trade union committees and congresses. In the middle and lower ranks of the party they led local committees, but they did not achieve national leadership. Only one woman, Mariia Aleksandrovna Spiridonova, played a commanding role in a political party, the left Socialist-Revolutionary Party*. The few other women of national fame—Inessa Fedorovna Armand*, Aleksandra Mikhailovna Kollontai*, and Nadezhda Konstantinovna Krupskaia* among the Bolsheviks, Ekaterina Konstantinovna Breshko-Breshkovskaia* among the Socialist–Revolutionaries, Vera Ivanovna Zasulich and Vera Nikolaevna Figner of the Mensheviks—remained excluded from the centers of power in their movements. Those women who developed the greatest authority, Kollontai and Armand, did so in organizing women workers, an area relegated to women.

Meanwhile non-radical middle-class women were also involved in the Revolution as feminists and supporters of the Provisional Government. The National Council of Women, led by Anna N. Shabanova, and the Republican Union of Democratic Women's Organizations, led by Poliksena Shishkina-Iavein, demanded universal suffrage and obtained it for the Constituent Assembly elections. Their calls for employment opportunities were answered by government decrees that gave women the right to become attorneys, to be admitted to engineering schools, and to be treated equally with men in the civil service. In return for these reforms the feminists rallied around the Provisional Government, joining other middle-class women in organizing charity projects. In Petrograd such women helped soldiers' wives set up cooperative food stores. Others urged the government to increase aid to wounded veterans and worked in settlement houses in the slums. The most famous, and probably least significant, female support for the Provisional Government came from the Women's Battalion of Death, members of which defended the Winter Palace against the assault of pro-Soviet troops during the Bolshevik coup d'état on October 25. Commanded by Mariia Bochkareva, the battalion was a regular military unit that saw service at the front. It was one of a number of efforts in 1917 to enlist women in support of the war, and it, like other feminist and philanthropic groups that worked with the Provisional Government, was swept away in the storm of 1917, which the Bolsheviks rode to power.

The establishment of a Soviet government resulted in more significant changes for Russian women than any other event in 1917, for the Bolsheviks set out immediately to lay the foundations of a socialist society. Included in their program were proposals for full legal and civil equality for women, equal access to schooling and jobs, and social services that would communalize housekeeping and child rearing so as to enable women to take advantage of their new freedoms. To fulfill these promises, the Bolsheviks rewrote the law code, particularly those statutes dealing with marriage and the family, established day-care centers and maternity-leave programs, and decreed nondiscriminatory educational and employment practices. In the 1920s and 1930s quotas were set for the enrollment of women in training programs and directives urged managers to promote women on an equal basis with men. These policies, taken as a whole, comprise the most far-reaching attempt any government had made to that time to draw women into the work force and thereby abolish the traditional division of labor and the female subordination that went with it. The Bolshevik leadership undertook this great experiment because they had adopted the socialist belief that women should stand as men's equals in society and because they had been convinced by Armand, Kollontai and the other leaders of work among women that women could aid the Revolution.

As early as 1905 Social Democrats had discussed the possibility of enlisting women in the revolutionary movement but had dismissed the idea because it took too much effort to reach women. Valuable resources could be more profitably employed organizing male workers. When the Bolsheviks began to govern Russia, their leaders still believed that women were more resistant to their appeals than men, but they also saw that women were an untapped resource in a country short of manpower. All hands were needed to build socialism; yet women's hands were tied by values that commanded them to concentrate on domestic duties. In attacking these values, the Bolsheviks could not only undermine traditions they despised, they could also draw women into the drive to modernization. By 1917 programs promoting female emancipation were seen to have utility as well as virtue.

To what extent were women themselves responsible for bringing the Bolsheviks to power? The evidence is unclear: more women workers in Moscow voted for Mensheviks than Bolsheviks, and generally women do seem to have been more conservative and therefore more anti-Bolshevik than men. But if they did not give overwhelming support to the party, women played a crucial role in persuading the party to act on its pledges of emancipation immediately. The most articulate, determined socialist feminists—Inessa Armand, Aleksandra Kollontai, Konkordiia Nikolaevna Samoilova—were Bolsheviks. They were the architects of the Bolshevik programs for female emancipation and the advocates for women within the party, and it was they who argued so convincingly that women could guarantee the success of the Revolution. Women were working in the factories already, and they were marching in the streets. In the future they could help to build socialism. Thus the participation of women in the events of 1917 demonstrated their readiness for emancipation to the Bolsheviks and played

an important part in setting in motion the program of female emancipation that
would grant Soviet women a substantial measure of political, economic, and
social equality.

Barbara Evans Clements

Bibliography

Clements, Barbara Evans. *Bolshevik Feminist: The Life of Aleksandra Kollontai.* 1979.
Glickman, Rose. *Russian Factory Women.* 1984.
Lapidus, Gail Warshofsky. *Women in Soviet Society.* 1978.
Selivanova, Nina N. *Russia's Women.* 1923.
Stites, Richard. *The Women's Liberation Movement in Russia.* 1978.

Workers in the Russian Revolution. The working class in Russia in January
1917, including all urban and rural nonmanagerial wage earners, is estimated to
have been about 15.0 million (not counting family members) in a total population
of 140 million. But the "proletariat," the conscious and active core of the
working class employed in large-scale industry, amounted to only 3.4 million.
Even if some 830,000 railroad line workers are added, by all contemporary
standards, including the Bolsheviks' (*see* Russian Social Democratic Workers'
Party [Bolshevik]), this seems to be too small a proportion of the population to
have made a social revolution.

It would be wrong, however, to gauge the workers' political importance by
their numbers. Although not as extensive as in the West, Russia's large-scale
industry and railroads constituted a crucial segment of the economy by the turn
of the century, representing the economic heart of the empire, which the workers
were in a position to paralyze. Geographically, too, the workers were strategically
situated to make the most of their limited numbers—Moscow and Petrograd
(with 400,000 industrial workers alone, not including family members, in a
population of 2.4 million) were the nerve centers of Russia.

The development of a militant class consciousness among workers, who,
except for brief periods (1905–1906 and 1912–1914), lacked even elementary
economic and political rights, was facilitated by the highly concentrated character
of Russian industry. A single factory would often employ thousands of workers.
More important was the influence of the Social Democratic movement, which
filled the ideological void left by the weakness of Russian liberalism (which
reflected the social and economic dependency of the bourgeoisie upon the tsarist
state and the monarchy's total loss of credit among the workers after Bloody
Sunday, January 9, 1905 [*see* Nineteen-Five Revolution]). Industrial workers
invariably supported the socialists. The liberals (*see* Constitutional Democratic
Party—Cadet) and parties to the Right were considered *barskie* (upper classes).

The working class first came into its own with the great textile strikes of
1895–1896 in St. Petersburg (renamed Petrograd in 1914). These strikes were
no longer isolated, spontaneous outbursts of rage but part of a conscious, coordinated movement with clearly formulated aims that resulted in legislation

shortening the workday. No other class or group in society had been thus able to force the hand of the autocratic state through direct confrontation.

It was in 1905 that the working class moved to the fore of the all-national movement. A massive strike wave was launched in response to Bloody Sunday. It evoked broad sympathy in the rest of society, even among the hitherto ultraloyal industrialists. The regime was eventually forced to retreat from its autocratic principles and grant society a voice, however limited ultimately, in running the state.

Within this national movement class antagonisms soon began to assert themselves: some wanted to go further along the revolutionary path than others. A major breech occurred in November 1905 when the Petrograd workers launched a campaign for the immediate, universal introduction of the eight-hour working day. Unlike labor's earlier political demands that had been directed against the autocracy, this one was "social" and directed against an industrial bourgeoisie grown weary of strikes and inclined to accept the Tsar's limited concessions. The response was a cooperative effort of private and state managements locking out more than 100,000 workers. Not the only factor in the Revolution's eventual defeat, this marked a definite turning point. Henceforth, labor became progressively isolated as "census society" (the propertied classes), soon followed by the intelligentsia, pulled away from the revolutionary movement. A period of political reaction and economic depression set in, immobilizing the labor movement under their combined weight.

When it reemerged in a sudden explosion of militancy provoked by the massacre of Lena Goldfield workers in April 1912, its fire was directed as much against capital as against the state. The workers' collective economic and political actions became practically inextricable, much to the consternation of the Mensheviks (see Russian Social Democratic Workers' Party [Menshevik]), who advocated a worker–liberal (bourgeois) alliance against the autocracy. On the other side and in parallel fashion, capital and state acted in league in an attempt to suppress all aspects of the labor movement, economic as well as political. Despite renewed growth of oppositional sentiment within census society, in contrast to 1905 there was now no sign of sympathy for labor's struggles. Not surprisingly, the workers turned to the Bolsheviks, whose militancy and irreconcilability toward census society in the struggle to overthrow the autocracy corresponded best to worker perceptions of the situation. The industrial workers' curiae elected only Bolsheviks to the Fourth Duma (see Duma and Revolution), and by the end of 1913 all of the workers' organizations in the capital were Bolshevik led.

The outbreak of World War I* in July 1914, with its accompanying patriotic upsurge, mobilizations, and intensified repression, cut short a movement that to many observers portended a new revolution. But within a year strikes began to occur again, at first mainly economic but becoming more and more political. By the winter of 1916 worker antigovernment sentiment was approaching the explosion point, fired by deteriorating economic conditions due to a war that the great majority now viewed as imperialistic, as well as by the severely repressive politial regime. This culminated in February 1917 in a spontaneous general strike of Petrograd's workers, who managed to win over the garrison and thus bring down the regime. From here the February Revolution* spread rapidly and with little bloodshed to the rest of Russia.

Within census society opposition to the regime, spurred by its inability to pursue the war successfully and hold the restive workers in check, had also been growing. But fear of popular revolution prevented an open rupture. Once, however, the Revolution was victorious and indeed threatened to roll right over them, the census leaders reluctantly rallied to it. This gave the Revolution an all-national character unknown in Russian politics since the 1905 Revolution. The workers, who were not eager to assume the responsibility of running the state, genuinely welcomed this as a guarantee against civil war and of the Revolution's success. But mindful of past experience, they mandated their Soviet of Workers' and Soldiers' Deputies (*see* Soviets [Councils] of Workers', Soldiers', and Peasants' Deputies) to watch over the Provisional Government* representing the propertied classes and (in which there were no socialists in the beginning except A. F. Kerensky*) to insure the implementation of the Revolution's program.

For the workers, this meant a democratic republic, an active policy aimed at a speedy peace without annexations, the transfer of all land to the peasantry (*see* Agrarian Policy, 1917–1921; Agriculture; Peasants in the Russian Revolution), as well as the achievement of certain "social" demands: the eight-hour working day, wages befitting a free citizen, and internal autonomy within the factory. This autonomy, which was designed to correct the worst abuses of the despotic prerevolutionary management, took the form of elected factory committees to represent the workers before management and to oversee hiring and firing, wage classifications, labor discipline, medical care, and so on. None of these measures, including those of a social nature, called capitalism into question. Nor was this the workers' intention.

The radicalization of the working class during the following months found its political expression in the call for Soviet power and for a government without representation of census interests. This demand was based upon the workers' perception of census society's hostility to workers' aims and upon the increasingly counterrevolutionary mood of census society.

It soon became evident to the workers that the government had little intention of abandoning the old regime's annexationist war aims. The famous "Miliukov Note" in April (*see* Foreign Policy, 1914–1921; Provisional Government) affirming this provoked the first anti-government demonstrations, which led to the entrance of the moderate socialists into a coalition government. This, however, changed little. The disastrous June offensive (*see* Army of Imperial Russia in World War I), which broke the de facto cease-fire established by the February Revolution on the eastern front, was perceived by the workers as a betrayal of trust and a blow to the international significance of the Revolution as a model for emulation by people thirsting for a just end to the war. Soon after, the government dropped all pretense of a peace policy. On the third anniversary of the outbreak of war, in a direct affront to the overwhelmingly popular sentiment, Prime Minister Kerensky informed England's King George of Russia's ability and will to continue the war to the end.

At the same time, despite the growing economic dislocation, the government yielded to capital's intense opposition to economic regulation, which had long since been instituted in the other warring states. With the onset of mass dismissals and plant closures, and suspecting sabotage and a "hidden lockout" aimed at defeating the Revolution, the workers moved to establish "control" over management. They were still far from envisioning full takeover and expropriation of the factories, but this movement represented a deepening of the Revolution's social content. (The demand for nationalization came into its own only after the October Seizure of Power* when the economic crisis reached full force.)

Already following the April crisis, census politicians began openly to attack the "pernicious" influence of the soviets on the government. But it was only after the mass demonstration in Petrograd on July 3–4 (*see* July Days) demanding Soviet power that the government dared to use force against the workers and Left socialists. This growing "insolence" of the counterrevolution, as the workers termed it, culminated in General L. G. Kornilov's (*see* Kornilov Revolt) abortive rising in late August aimed at installing a right-wing military dictatorship. Kornilov enjoyed broad sympathy among the propertied classes, and even after his defeat and arrest, P. N. Miliukov*, leader of the Cadets (*see* Constitutional Democratic Party—Cadet), the main party of the propertied classes, insisted that he was a patriot and an honest man.

By late September the Bolsheviks, the only party advocating Soviet power and a decisive break with census society, had won majorities in the soviets of nearly all industrial centers. This was confirmed on October 26, when the Second All-Russian Congress of Soviets endorsed the insurrection in Petrograd (*see* Petrograd Soviet; October Seizure of Power), voting to transfer all power to the soviets. With the disintegrating army thirsting for peace at any price and the countryside in flames, the October Seizure of Power tore Russian society in two, completing a process of polarization whose roots went back long before 1917. The issue of whether 1917 was a workers' revolution is still hotly debated. It was many things—a soldiers' mutiny (*see* Soldiers and Soldiers' Committees), a peasant rebellion (*see* Peasants in the Russian Revolution), and a movement of national minorities (*see* National Question and the Russian Revolution). But although the neutrality, or at best mainly passive support, of these groups was crucial to the success of the October Revolution, it was the working class that gave it direction and provided it with most of its active forces. This was in accord with earlier experience. For only with the appearance of the working class had Russian society been able to assert itself effectively against the state and ultimately, if briefly, gain full control of it.

The tragedy of the Revolution lay in the weakness of the working class, which was virtually consumed, both physically and morally, by the immense task it had undertaken. The hoped-for revolutions in the West failed to materialize, and an economic collapse of unheard of proportions, hunger and disease, the civil war fronts, and, not least, the new state and economic administrations removed much of the former working class from the factories, weakening its coherence and sense of corporate identity, and, therefore, its ability to function as an independent social force. The scene was set for the rise of a new absolute state, albeit one with a different ethos and institutional basis.

David Mandel

Bibliography

Ferro, M. *The Russian Revolution of February 1917*. 1972.
Koenker, Dianne. *Moscow Workers and the 1917 Revolution*. 1981.
Mandel, D. *The Petrograd Workers and the Fall of the Old Regime*. 1982.
————. *The Petrograd Workers and the Soviet Seizure of Power*. 1982.
Oktiabr'skaia revoliutsiia i fabzavkomy. 2 vols. 1927–1928.
Rashin, A. G. *Formirovania rabochego klassa rossii*. 1958.
Smith, A. A. *Red Petrograd, Revolution in the Factories 1917–18*. 1983.
Velikaia Oktiabr'skaia sotsialisticheskaia revoliutsiia. 8 vols. 1968.
Volobuev, P. V. *Proletariat i burzhuaziia v 1917 g.* 1964.
Wildman, A. *The Making of a Worker's Revolution*. 1967.

Workers Opposition. *See* Kollontai and Shliapnikov.

World War I. The outbreak of World War I astonished and dumfounded the socialist and revolutionary movement. In Russia, as elsewhere, the revolutionaries and socialists thought that the war had deprived them of their weapons, their arguments, their legitimacy, and their hopes. The socialist and revolutionary movement refused to use the general strike as the ultimate weapon for persuading countries not to arm because of the illogical fear that in the most advanced countries, where it would have been the most effective, the signs were not favorable for its success. Therefore, the regimes in more authoritarian countries, such as tsarist Russia, and in autocratic backward countries would take advantage of the situation to impose their will, whereas the more advanced countries, those that were the most socialistic, would lose their advantage.

The socialist movement and the Second International (*see* Communist International) had affirmed the power of the economic order to determine everything: they had even assumed, during the Moroccan Crisis of 1911, that the great capitalist powers would recognize their own best interests by saving themselves rather than destroying each other. It was clear that the war was not caused exclusively by imperialistic rivalry.

When it became apparent at the first trumpet call that if socialism, in Benedetto Croce's words, "was an ideal, patriotism was an instinct," all the socialists, citizens or not, despite their former vows, ran out to meet the enemy. The few militant socialists who were the exception ran the risk of being lynched, so powerful was the concept of the "sacred union" within each nation.

The international socialist movement lost all credibility as the war seemed to drag on endlessly, as governments found themselves strengthened by it, and as the military apparatus within each state identified with the response and increasingly gained the upper hand. People going off to war forgot the very idea of revolution; instead, the hope of victory took its place.

In Russia the opposition of a minority to the war and to the "sacred union" was the most extreme in Europe because the militant revolutionaries and the working class were less integrated with society than in the West, and their leaders even less so. Coming mainly from well-to-do families, the revolutionaries could easily lead the revolution from Switzerland, the United States, or Spain.

The obstacles seemed insurmountable. Fifteen million soldiers had responded without fail to the Tsar's mobilization order. Whereas a million deserters had been foreseen, there were fewer than 15,000. Russian public opinion had concluded that the cause was just. The people respected the promise given to their "little Serbian brother." The alliance with the Western democracies led people to hope that after the war Russian institutions would be brought into line with those of the West. Even George V. Plekhanov*, "the father of Russian Social Democracy," believing that the struggle against German imperialism should come before everything else, urged the revolutionaries "to postpone temporarily the struggle against Tsarism" so as not to hinder the war against William II.

However, not all opposition disappeared. From the beginning certain emigrés—V. I. Lenin*, L. D. Trotsky*, Iulii O. Martov*—had stigmatized the war as "imperialistic," calling both camps equally to blame (*see* Internationalists). In an unpublished letter found in the Trotsky Archives at Amsterdam, A. G. Shliapnikov*, a Bolshevik (*see* Russian Social Democratic Workers' Party [Bolshevik]), expressed his surprise: "This betrayal [of the German socialists] untied the hands of the opportunists in all countries. . . . The workers have remained faithful to the principle of 'war against War' but for the moment they are alone. . . . " (Ferro, 1972, p. 331).

Therefore, Lenin's first rallying cry was poorly received. While his comrades were content to call for an immediate peace, Lenin, as early as September 1914, recommended changing the imperialist war into a civil war: for Russia, tsarism was the absolute evil, and the victory of its armies would only strengthen it. Therefore, revolutionaries ought to struggle "for the defeat of their government," a tactic that should be adopted by the revolutionaries of every country. But this "Defeatism"* (*porazhenchestvo*) evoked no response. In Paris, for example, there were some Bolsheviks who responded instead to the call of Plekhanov. They enlisted in the French army, despite the contrary appeals in *Nashe slovo* to which Trotsky contributed. In Russia there was the same patriotic contagion. But the Left socialists (like Liebknecht in Germany) voted against the military budget, and A. F. Kerensky's* Trudoviks even left the Duma (*see* Duma and Revolution), but they still announced that they would contribute to the defense of the country. Only the Bolshevik deputies maintained an absolute opposition to the war. But these eloquent gestures went almost unnoticed. When the government sent them into exile in Siberia, only a few factories went on strike. The war seemed to have tolled the death knell for the revolutionary movement.

In the spring of 1915 a handful of minority party Social Democrats responded to the battle cry of Zaleskii: ''Those elements which united on the basis of the revolutionary action of the proletariat against the War want to reawaken the class consciousness of the workers. Only these elements can oppose the nationalist appeals . . . .'' (Ferro, 1972, p. 332). These Russian emigré revolutionaries ''rejected any attempt to build a bridge between the Internationalists* [who opposed the war] and the social patriots [who supported it]. All Russian revolutionaries of all shades are asked to join the true Internationalists'' (Ibid.). This was Lenin's position, which was opposed to that of the majority of Internationalists, who, following Martov, V. M. Chernov*, M. A. Natanson, and P. B. Akselrod*, wanted first of all to reestablish the International in order to force all of the governments to conclude a peace without annexations.

In September 1915 a conference of those who shared these views was held at Zimmerwald. The call for such a conference was well received, but then a left faction was formed by N.I. Bukharin* and Lenin, who condemned the spirit of conciliation that the signatories showed by collaborating with those condemned as saboteurs of the International and refusing to break with them. Martov and his friends thought that Lenin's position was extreme, since it isolated the leaders from the workers. It was necessary for all groups struggling against tsarism to close up ranks. At the time Lenin's ''sectarianism'' disturbed Trotsky, D. Z. Manuilskii, Bukharin, and I. M. Maiskii, who made up with Martov and his friends.

At the end of 1915, in view of the serious military setbacks suffered by the Russian army (see Army of Imperial Russia in World War I), Lenin believed that the facts were beginning to bear him out. Weariness was overtaking both the front and the rear. He developed the idea that because of the war the Revolution would erupt not in the nation where capitalism was strongest (Germany) but in the one where it was weakest (Russia). Especially in showing the fighting quality of national and patriotic forces, the war led Lenin to believe that the rise of nationalities would help to weaken the great powers. Such a development, he believed, should be encouraged, a point on which he differed from Bukharin and K. B. Radek*, as well as G. L. Piatakov. In Russia itself, the bourgeoisie looked for relief from tsarism. Some of these militant pacifists joined up with them, and there was a regrouping of the internationalists who condemned such collaboration. To their happy surprise, when the elections took place in the factories, to find out if the socialist organizations there accepted this collaboration between the classes to ''save the country,'' the great majority of the workers refused. Despite the war, therefore, hopes for the necessity of a liberating revolution were rekindled.

After the February Revolution* the Provisional Government* and the Petrograd Soviet* were jockeying for power with each other. The former had the power without the substance, the latter the substance without the power (*see* Dual Power). According to the agreement reached on March 1, 1917, the government could act only when its action was endorsed by the soviet (*see* Soviets [Councils] of Workers', Soldiers', and Peasants' Deputies). Thus when the Minister of Foreign Affairs, P. N. Miliukov*, confirmed the adherence of the new Russia to all of the existing diplomatic agreements, he provoked a strong response from the soviet because his actions seemed to confirm Russia's imperialistic ambitions. (He was called "Dardanelski.") There were demonstrations by soldiers and workers. After the April Days (*see* Provisional Government), Miliukov and the Minister of War were forced to resign. It was clear that the policy of the soviet had carried the day, presaging the conclusion of a general peace without annexations or tribute. At that point the leaders of the soviet, notably the Menshevik (*see* Russian Social Democratic Workers' Party [Menshevik]) I. G. Tsereteli*, decided to participate directly in the government. The massive entry of socialists into the government was hailed by democratic public opinion as a second revolution.

Returning from Siberia, Tsereteli was the first of the militants in the soviet to raise the question of the relationship between war and revolution. On the two central issues, those of power and revolution, the Right and the Left gave their answers. The bourgeoisie (Miliukov) said that, "the recognition of his party's supremacy and his party's war slogans was the number one problem of the revolution."

The Left (N. N. Sukhanov* and the Bolsheviks) said the number one problem was the dictatorship of the proletariat and the ending of the war in order to adopt revolutionary measures for the country. The former knew nothing of the problems of the Revolution; the latter knew nothing of its opportunities. Both were heading for Civil War in Russia*. Tsereteli concluded that the Internationalists and the Bolsheviks were more interested in fighting the government than in formulating an alternative policy. It was important that the soviet not appear to trust the defense of the country to the government since the soviet was doing all it could to force the government to make peace. The defense of the revolution had to be linked with the struggle for peace.

Thus the government's declaration of May 3, 1917 marked a decisive change. It was no longer just the Petrograd Soviet but the government as well that adopted the policy of "peace without annexations or tribute." On the other hand, the leaders of the Provisional Government committed themselves to the defense of the country and the restoration of military power: never before had there been such agreement among those in power. In the cabinet the two advocates of the new policy, Tsereteli and M. I. Tereshchenko, were in complete agreement and everyone was confident that Kerensky, the new Minister of War, would reconstruct the army in the spirit of the Revolution.

The workers, the peasants, and the soldiers (*see* Workers in the Russian Revolution; Peasants in the Russian Revolution; Soldiers and Soldiers' Committees) discovered that, whether or not there was a coalition with the socialists, their own situation had hardly changed. Rather than satisfying their demands, which in retrospect seem very modest, the socialist ministers explained that if one imposed measures of reform on management, officers, and landowners by force, they would unleash a civil war. The people needed reassurance. But far from reassuring them, the socialists lost the confidence of the masses. Leninist tradition labeled as "conciliators" those, like Kerensky, who wanted to ease off from military discipline without at the same time displeasing the officers; like Tsereteli, who wanted to prepare for peace while continuing the war; like Chernov, who wanted to satisfy the peasants without breaking any laws; or like M. I. Skobolev, who wanted to get the bosses and the workers to agree on factory working conditions.

These socialists also believed that only a Constituent Assembly* elected by the whole nation could legitimately rule the country. One segment of the citizenry could not vote because they were serving in the armed forces. In March or April this was changed, pleasing a people enamoured with the notion of equity. But the new citizens of the Russian Republic soon discovered that the legalism of the revolutionary ministers had the effect of perpetuating the very order that the popular uprising sought to abolish. Besides, it seemed clear that the leaders who opposed the reforms were the same ones who claimed that peace was impossible and advocated an offensive to end the war. Behind all these conflicts was always the same question: Was the defense of the country's interests a form of deceit? The militant bourgeoisie and the leaders of the advanced proletariat were both opposed to the politics of "conciliation." "While the advanced bourgeoisie," wrote Bukharin in *Spartacus,* "want to prolong the war in order to suppress the revolution, the proletariat wants to end the war in order to prolong the revolution. . . . " Arguing against this position, Tsereteli, chief theoretician of the policy of conciliation, believed that the idea of peace without annexations would win over the whole of Europe. Neither Lenin nor Miliukov shared this illusion, but since in the spring of 1917 their audience was small, people heard only the new leaders, who claimed they were sure to succeed.

The architect of this policy, Tsereteli, believed that the Russian renunciation of Constantinople would serve as an example both to the Allies and to the enemy. At Petrograd the presence of Zimmerwaldians, like Chernov, in the government guaranteed this policy. But one could not be sure of either the Allies or the Central Powers, and Russian democracy had to support the action and the influence of the socialists in the belligerent countries, thus reviving the Second International in which Tsereteli had a "messianic faith." As a preliminary, a conference of all of the socialist parties at Stockholm was to draw a peace proposal that the participants would then try to impose on their own governments. In Russia this had already been done, but success had yet to be achieved elsewhere. The struggle would be conducted at two levels, between governments and between socialist parties, while simultaneously each socialist party would put pressure on its own government.

Neither Kerensky nor Tereshchenko truly believed in the reality of any action by the socialist parties, because they were too divided among themselves. But Prince G. E. L'vov* was confident, and Tsereteli was as much encouraged by Russian public opinion as by the sympathy that the Revolution evoked around the world as shown, for example, by the trip of Marius Moutet and Marcel Cachin, who were sent by A. Ribot to Petrograd in March; by the trip of Daniel Sanders, who was sent by Lloyd George before A. Henderson and Albert Thomas, representing the Allied government, arrived their turn;, then there were the messages from Sun-Yat Sen and from the United States, France, and Germany also in an atmosphere that was still euphoric and full of illusions.

Although skeptical, like Kerensky, and putting more faith in the action of governments, Tereshchenko played the game. He agreed to tie the policy of the government to the decisions of Russian Democracy, even declaring publicly that "the government's policies must come closer to conforming with the hopes of Democracy. To that end, Socialist Conferences will lay down the foundations on which the policy will be based" (Ferro, 1972, p. 236).

In fact, before even being undertaken, this venture was criticized from every quarter, first in Russia itself. Miliukov made fun of the International which, incapable of preventing the war, now claimed it could end it; Plekhanov raged against socialists of the Kaiser rubbing shoulders with true revolutionaries. The Bolsheviks also condemned the proposed conference because they believed a revolution in Germany was imminent and that the success of the Stockholm Conference (if it ever took place) would strengthen the German socialists and capitalists at the very moment when they were about to collapse. Karl Radek showed the dialectical character of the new international relations: "German imperialism wanted peace with Russia," he wrote on May 3, 1917, "in order to consolidate the L'vov/Kerensky regime, but if the Russian Revolution wanted to defend itself against German imperialism, it would have to submit to the bourgeoisie, its internal enemy. But the bourgeoisie must be fought, in order to set the example for the German proletariat to fight its own oppressors . . . Just as we cannot beat our internal foe, Capital, allied to the external foe and the property-owning classes, so we cannot beat the external foe allied to our internal enemy' " (Ferro, 1972, pp. 237–238). Faith in a German revolution and then a European one was shared by all of the Bolsheviks, as demonstrated by a speech of Trotsky's made during the summer: "They say that the hope for a European revolution is utopian, but if it doesn't occur somehow Russian freedom will be killed by the united forces of our allies and our enemies. He who doesn't believe in the possibility of such a revolution must expect the collapse of our freedom" (Ferro, 1972, p. 239). Nevertheless, although hostile to Stockholm, the Bolsheviks decided to go there, despite Lenin. The main thing was to make the decisions of Stockholm binding; afterward, the governments would have to yield.

The first half of the politics of peace—admonitions by the Provisional Government* directed at the Allies—was a total failure. The Russian chancellery did not know the extent of France's and even England's territorial ambitions.

Only Germany's ambitions were greater, and they were likewise unknown to the chancellery.

Therefore, the idea of a peace without annexations or tribute, accepted as "just" in principle, was turned over to the negotiators on the Allied war aims; in short, it was put off indefinitely. The response of Woodrow Wilson, however, threw the Russians into disarray. The American president argued like Lenin, that peace "before victory" would actually strengthen German imperialism, which wanted to conclude a compromise peace treaty. "The ground was cut from under Tereshchenko's feet" observed Miliukov, who, like Lenin, was right in doubting the feasibility of the government's strategy (Ferro, 1972, p. 240). Worse yet and a slap in the face for Petrograd, the Franco-British expedition to Athens showed that the Allies were going to pursue their own interests without consulting the Russians—even in Greece, a zone that was especially sensitive for the realization of the Russian war aims.

Lacking the power to govern, the Soviet placed all of its hopes on the Stockholm Conference. But the majority-party socialists, English and French, refused to sit down with the majority-party Germans. The Belgians followed suit. On the contrary the German and Austrian minority-party representatives—H. Haase, Karl Kautsky*, Victor Adler, and others—agreed to come, as did the Franco-English minorities. On the Russian side, hope was rekindled when the minority party became the majority, and when it seemed likely that the English and Italian majorities would join them. Only the Bolsheviks and the European ultra-left held aloof. The permanent Zimmerwald (or Berne) Committee decided to meet at Stockholm to decide whether or not to participate. The suspense was complete until two events made the Stockholm Conference collapse: first, the communication by the German government of its peace proposals to Grimm of the Berne Committee, thereby lending support to the alleged collusion between Lenin, Robert Grimm and the Germans; second, the response of Robert Lansing, U.S. Secretary of State, who denied visas to the American delegates to the conference. This action encouraged A. Ribot and Lloyd George to do likewise. Despite the meeting of various committees among the Germans, Austrians, and minority-party Russians, this broke the spirit of the conference, which actually never took place.

The Russian public had long since lost interest in the stillborn conference. Pretending to seek peace, the government actually unleashed a new offensive; this was the second half of its policy. This June 16, 1917 offensive failed as did the "Days" that the soldiers of the capital revived in order to stop the process of normalization that the offensive implied.

The state dissolved not just because of the blows inflicted by the society that had produced the new institutional system consisting of the soviets of all kinds (and not just the soviets of deputies) but also by those things that brought an end to the process of normalization. The Bolsheviks made sure that the soldiers understood the role played by the continuation of the war in this context. In fact, only the army could intervene in this sense; the chiefs then tried the putsch of General Kornilov (see Kornilov Revolt). The experience of the Revolution had taught the soldiers to differentiate between the two functions of the military—defense of the country and defense of the social order. When the debate took place on the reform of military discipline and on its necessity, when it was no longer a question of training soldiers for combat, it became apparent that discipline was needed only so that the command could use the army as an instrument of repression. Officers absolutely refused to limit the application of strict discipline to military operations. They also refused to give reasons for their orders. The Kornilov Revolt demonstrated that orders said to be merely operational camouflaged counterrevolutionary orders. Henceforth, the soldiers refused to obey any operational orders whose legitimacy and utility were not demonstrated. If there was no great "desertion" from the Russian army, as the high command liked to imply, there was nevertheless, a large mutiny. It was no longer possible for the government to appeal to the patriotism of the soldiers to cover operations designed to preserve the (old) social order.

The soldiers' "mutiny" made it impossible to continue the war. The failure of the offensive and then the loss of Riga brought the threat close to capital of the Revolution. There was no hope of peace. Kerensky said in 1966 that he counted on the collapse of Austria-Hungary, with which he was engaged in secret negotiations. There are indications that delegates to the soviet who were close to Kerensky had proposed as a basis for a general peace that some way be found to spare Charles I. But there is no proof that the issue was seen in this fashion as a way to strike the "great blow" which would have paralyzed the growing opposition of the Bolsheviks and the soviets and made the October Seizure of Power unnecessary. The paralysis of the state had become total. Failing to make peace or win the war, the February regime lost its legitimacy.

The Great War had given birth to the Revolution, but in its turn, the Revolution, failing to end the hostilities, gave birth to the Civil War in Russia* and foreign intervention. The decree on peace (*see* Foreign Policy) changed nothing. It invited all belligerent nations and their governments to begin negotiations immediately for a just democratic peace. Hence it was to protect the Bolsheviks' ties to its allies that led Lenin and Trotsky to propose peace to *all* the belligerents—the offer was meant to lead inevitably to a rising of the proletariat against any governments that opposed it. "If the unlikely happens" explained Lenin, "that none of the states will accept an armistice, then we shall be able to call the war what will truly be just, defensive. Russia will become the ally of the world's proletariat of all the oppressed of the globe. The Soviet government will be the heart of the world revolution" (Ferro, 1969. p. 208).

The Central Powers answered and began negotiations at Brest-Litovsk*. Nevertheless, in putting an end to the traditional dissociation between foreign policy and domestic policy, the Bolsheviks demonstrated the bond between foreign war and Civil War. After the war had been transformed into the revolution, the latter, in the name of peace, declared war on the governments of the world.

Marc Ferro

Bibliography

Albertini, Luigi. *The Origins of the War of 1914.* 3 vols. 1952–57.
Debo, Richard K. *Revolution and Survival.* 1979.
Fainsod, Merle. *International Socialism and the World War.* 1935.
Ferro, Marc. *The Russian Revolution of February, 1917.* 1972.
Ferro, Marc. *The Great War.* 1969.
Gay, Peter. *The Dilemma of Democratic Socialism.* 1952.
Temkin. *Lenin i menzhdunorodnaia sotsial-democratiia, 1914–1917.* 1968.
Tuchman, Barbara. *The Proud Tower.* 1966.
Wade, R. A. *The Russian Search for Peace.* 1969.

Wrangel, Petr Nikolaevich (1878–1928). Wrangel was a White general (*see* White Movement) during the Civil War in Russia*. He commanded the Volunteer Army in the Crimea after the resignation of A. I. Denikin*.

Wrangel was born in a distinguished noble family of Swedish descent. He received what some would call a liberal education for an aristocrat when, in 1901, he earned a degree in engineering from a technical institute in Petrograd. Wrangel joined the army and served as an officer in the Chevalier Guards where he became a superb horseman. After a few years of service in the army, he worked as a chemical engineer in Siberia. With the outbreak of the Russo-Japanese War in 1904, he rejoined the army serving with distinction in Manchuria. After the war, Wrangel's ability to lead troops in battle enabled him to join the Academy of the General Staff in 1907, after which he was attached to the Horse Guards. In 1916 he commanded a regiment of Nerchinsk Cossacks.

By 1917 Wrangel was a General and in command of the Seventh Cavalry Division, where he saw action against Austria during the summer offensive. He became known as an aristocrat, an upholder of orthodox values, but also one who recognized the need for democratic reforms. Although attempting to appear more responsive to the opinions of his men and the desire of national minorities for more voice in determining their destiny, he was not always comfortable with the results of more democratic methods. This was evident, for example, when, as a brigade commander in Bessarabia, he complained of the rigid system of promotion. When the system was reformed and many junior officers including Wrangel himself were moved up in rank, he complained that the reforms were too sweeping.

After the Kornilov Revolt* in August and the October Seizure of Power*, Wrangel resigned his commission and settled in Yalta where he was called upon to serve in the forming anti-Bolshevik Volunteer Army as a lieutenant-general under Denikin. However, the White forces, while appearing formidable, suffered from rivalry among their leaders. Peter Kenez, in *Civil War in Southern Russia*

1919–1920, argued that perhaps nothing hurt the White Army more than the relationship between Wrangel and Denikin. Although Wrangel was a capable man with a charismatic personality, he was extremely arrogant and ruthless, which is evident by the infamous massacre at Stavropol. In order to recruit new manpower from his three thousand Red Army* prisoners at Stavropol, Wrangel ordered them all out to the parade ground. He then shot all of the officers and non-commissioned officers and informed the rest of the troops that the same fate was in store for those who did not join the Whites. At the same time he criticized Denikin for his "colossal mistakes" and openly regarded him as too weak and too liberal.

Wrangel joined Denikin in 1918 and, once he took command of his division, soon demonstrated his ability to carve a fighting unit out of a ragged group of volunteers. By the beginning of 1919 Denikin put Wrangel in charge of the campaign to clear the northern Caucasus of Red troops, which he succeeded in doing with his usual flair and determination, and he was soon appointed commander of all of the cavalry. In June 1919 he launched an offensive in Tsaritsyn (later called Stalingrad and then Volgograd). Denikin had tried once before to take Tsaritsyn in 1918 and had been turned back by Red forces commanded by S. Budennyi*, K. E. Voroshilov*, and I. V. Stalin*. In the 1919 campaign, reinforcements Wrangel requested from Denikin were late, and, at first, the Whites were turned back by Voroshilov again. The city was crucial to the continuation of the White campaign in South Russia and Wrangel expressed his anger toward Denikin for letting him down. In June 1919 the reinforcements appeared and Wrangel took the city in July. But conflict between Denikin and Wrangel continued and after confrontations early in 1920 finally reached a climax. Wrangel resigned his position in the Volunteer Army in February 1920 and left for Constantinople.

In April 1920 Wrangel was asked to succeed Denikin as head of the White Army in the Crimea (*see* Crimea, Revolution in), the playground of Imperial Russia, in the hope that he could breathe life into a hopeless situation. Faced with the possibility of defeat, Wrangel ignored British demands to cease hostilities, and instead, struggled to build up and train his forces. Although Wrangel did create an effective fighting force of 40,000 men divided into three corps, he was often brutal—sometimes hanging officers in front of troops. At the same time he encouraged the acceptance of deserters from the Red Army, gave attention to the organization of the rear and foreign policy, and courted support from the local population.

He appointed a cabinet of talented men from every political persuasion, including A. V. Krivoshein, formerly P. A. Stolypin's Minister of Agriculture, and P. B. Struve, a Marxist turned liberal. Upon their advice, Wrangel issued orders addressing land reform, administration of the Crimea, public relations in the West, and collection of revenue. He had criticized Denikin for not winning over the West with liberal reforms. He also criticized Denikin for not courting the Cossacks and national minorities with measures that gave them a voice. He suggested that foreign capitalists could be won over by promising them some opportunity to exploit Russia's natural wealth. He was frequently accused of conducting "leftist policies with rightist hands" (Luckett, 1971, p. 360). Wrangel won popularity for his movement in the West by promising that land would be distributed by agrarian assemblies or soviets which would determine who would get the land and the size of the plot alotted. He proposed that the peasants who received the land would have twenty-five years to pay for it through the delivery of a small portion of their yearly harvest. In order to be effective, Wrangel had to make foreign powers aware of the value of his proposed reforms. Wrangel tried to formulate reforms that would undermine the appeal of the major agrarian proposals of the Bolsheviks (see Russian Social Democratic Workers' Party [Bolshevik]). However, Wrangel's reforms failed to attract much support in Russia because they were less revolutionary than outright peasant seizure of land and because he was unable to apply the plan outside the Crimea to areas that faced acute land problems.

In the political arena, Wrangel was aware of the delicate situation in international affairs. He realized that if he succumbed to British pressure it would mean an early armistice. Fortunately, the French government was willing to offer military assistance in the event of an evacuation. At the same time Wrangel's army was given some "breathing space" with the outbreak of the Bolshevik-Polish War. Although there were efforts to coordinate the Polish and White armies, the majority of the Bolshevik forces were pitted against the Poles, which seemed to have enabled Wrangel to win victories against weaker Bolshevik units.

Wrangel decided to attack the Tauride on June 7, 1920 in a campaign that enabled him to break out of the Crimea. The attack was successful and he doubled his territory when he captured Melitopol, capital of the Northern Tauride. Subsequent battles did not prove as successful. His invasion of Kuban in August 1920 was a fiasco. This and the capitulation of Poland ended Wrangel's hope for glory, leaving only an evacuation to save his forces at Sevastopol. Red units (see Red Army) moved into the area by November 7, 1920 and within one week Wrangel fled with 150,000, who found homes throughout Europe and Turkey. Wrangel's military career was over. He worked diligently to help refugees, and later founded the World Organization of Russian War Veterans with the Grand Duke Nicholas. Wrangel wrote his memoirs and worked as an engineer until his death in Brussels in 1928.

Christopher Mendoza

Bibliography

Brinkley, George A. *The Volunteer Army and Allied Intervention in Southern Russia 1917–1921*. 1966.
Chamberlain, William. *The Russian Revolution*. Vol. 2. 1935.
Kenez, Peter. *Civil War in Southern Russia, 1919–1920*. 1977.

Luckett, Richard. *The White Generals*. 1971.

Wrangel, P. N. *Memoirs*. 1930. (A shortened version of his *Zapiski,* which appear in von Lampe A. A. (ed.) *Beloe delo*. Vol. 6. 1926–28.) Issued in America as Wrangel, P. N. *Always with Honor*. 1957.

Y

Yakovleva. *See* Iakovleva, Varvara Niklaevna.

Yaroslavskii. *See* Gubel'man, Minei Izrailovich.

Yudenich. *See* Iudenich, Nikolai Nikolaevich.

Z

Zhordaniia, Noi Nikolaevich (1869–1953; pseudonyms: Kostrov, Dzhordzh). Noi Zhordaniia was the founder of the Georgian Social Democratic movement and a prominent Georgian Menshevik leader. He was born in a noble family and after attending a seminary in Tiflis enrolled in the Warsaw Veterinarian Institute. It was in Warsaw that Zhordaniia first became aware of Marxism. In 1892 Zhordaniia, along with some other Russian-educated Georgian intellectuals, called the first conference of Georgian Marxists in Zestaponi. This first group of Georgian Marxists became known as the *mesame-dasi* (third generation). They developed a program of action designed to overthrow the oppressive tsarist government and permit the development of democracy in Georgia. It would become the most popular political ideology in Georgia. Part of the success of this program was a result of the subordinate position of the Georgians in their own territory in relation to the other two large national groups, the Armenians and the Russians. Because the Georgians, in fact, constituted a proletariat in the Georgian cities, the message of Marxism seemed especially relevant to their plight. In the beginning, the twin goals of the new movement were to eliminate the Armenian middle class and the Russian autocracy. When the split took place between the Bolsheviks (*see* Russian Social Democratic Workers' Party [Bolshevik]) and the Mensheviks (*see* Russian Social Democratic Workers' Party [Menshevik]), Zhordaniia joined the Menshevik faction, and became their leader in the Caucasus. He was one of the chief theoreticians of the Menshevik movement and a critic of V. I. Lenin*. Zhordaniia took an unusual position on the National Question* (*see* National Question and the Russian Revolution). Because he saw nationalism and even the idea of soviet power as potentially divisive in Georgia, he urged the Georgians to place their emphasis elsewhere. Georgia, he argued, should not strive for national self-determination. That, he argued, would automatically flow from the achievement of democratic government in Russia. In 1905 he edited the Menshevik newspaper Social Democracy (*Sotsial*

Demokrat). At the Fourth Congress of the Russian Social Democratic Workers' Party he supported the "municipalization" of land. He was a deputy to the First State Duma from Tiflis and leader of the Social Democratic faction in that body. At the Fifth Congress of the Russian Social Democratic Workers' Party in 1907 he was elected to the Central Committee. In 1912 he edited the Menshevik newspaper *Our Word* in Baku. During World War I* he adopted a defensist (*see* Defensism) position, though after the Kornilov Revolt* he would oppose coalition with the upper middle class Russian parties that shared his defensism. After the February Revolution* he became Chairman of the Tiflis Soviet of Workers Deputies. Throughout 1917 he opposed any coalition at the national level with the "bourgeois" leaders of the Provisional Government*, preferring that the national government remain "bourgeois-democratic." By way of contrast, in Georgia he would argue that the moving forces of the Georgian Revolution would be the proletariat, the army, and the liberal bourgeoisie. To some extent this was a juggling act, since in Georgia the workers were Georgian and Menshevik, the soldiers were Russian peasants with a Socialist-Revolutionary (*see* Socialist-Revolutionary Party) orientation, and the liberal bourgeoisie were Armenian. The coalition failed when the Russian soldiers moved closer to the Provisional Government and Zhordaniia and the Georgians remained intransigent. In September Zhordaniia opposed both Lenin's slogan of "All Power to the Soviets" and coalition with the Consitutional Democratic Party-Cadets* as advocated by I. G. Tsereteli* and Dan (*see* Gurvich, F. I.). Instead, Zhordaniia called for a "democratic socialist government." The Menshevik response to the October Seizure of Power* in Petrograd was to disarm their own Russian soldiers and use the Georgian Red Guard to create a Menshevik city government in Tiflis on November 29, 1917. In April 1918 the Transcaucasian "federative" government was declared. With the formation of the Baku Commune and the invasion of the Caucases by the Turkish army, the federative republic split up into its various national components and from May 1918 to 1921 Zhordaniia was at the head of the Menshevik government of Georgia. He went into exile in 1921, and spent the remainder of his life in Paris (*see* Transcaucasia), Revolution in, 1917–21).

Bibliography

Haimson, L. H. *The Mensheviks.* 1974.
Noi Zhordaniia i tsarskaia okhranka. 1931.
Pipes, R. *The Formation of the Soviet Union.* 1968.
Suny, R. G. *Transcaucasia.* 1983.

Zimmerwald Conference. *See* World War I.

Zinoviev, Grigorii Evseevich (1883–1936; true name, Radomysl'skii). Zinoviev was one of the most prominent Bolshevik (*see* Russian Social Democratic Workers' Party [Bolshevik]) leaders during the October Seizure of Power* in Russia and became an important member of the Politburo, head of the Communist

International*, and one of I. V. Stalin's* chief competitors in the struggle for power for control of the Communist Party in Russia after Lenin's death.

He was born in the town of Elizavetgrad in Kherson Province where his father owned a small dairy farm. Although he never attended school, he acquired enough education at home to acquire a job as a clerk in two business enterprises and by the end of the 1890s became involved in the organization of workers in his home town. In 1901 he fled police persecution and lived abroad until the 1905 Revolution (see Nineteen-Five Revolution). From 1906 to 1908 he helped to organize the metal workers of St. Petersburg. At the Bolshevik Party Congress in London in the spring of 1907 Zinoviev was elected to the Central Committee of the Party (see Central Committee of the Russian Communist Party [Bolshevik]) and remained in that office until his expulsion by Stalin in the 1920s. During World War I* Zinoviev stayed with V. I. Lenin* in exile and returned to Russia with him after the February Revolution*.

For Zinoviev, 1917 was a year of paradox characterized by great achievement of his party and profound personal disappointment, by a position of political leadership in the party and almost total estrangement from it, and by commitment to an international workers' revolution and simultaneous opposition to the October Seizure of Power itself.

The series of paradoxes began with the February Revolution. Zinoviev, second only to Lenin in Bolshevism's "vanguard" in 1917, failed to anticipate or participate in these startling events. From his position as a Swiss exile, he was too poorly informed of Russian developments to foresee the collapse of the tsarist regime. But once the regime fell, there was no doubt about the course the Bolshevik leaders in exile wanted to follow. Their two prime goals were to return to Russia to avail themselves of the new freedoms of their native land and to continue the policy of condemning World War I as an imperialist war that true revolutionaries should transform into a civil war.

Lenin and Zinoviev brought that policy, which was at odds with the one enforced on the party by L. B. Kamenev* and I. V. Stalin, back to Petrograd in early April on the famous "sealed" train. Once back home Zinoviev immediately assumed positions of responsibility in directing the party's course and publications and in doing what he did best—giving provocative speeches and writing inflammatory articles for his party's press.

Although Zinoviev supported a radical revolutionary transformation for both Russia and the world, it quickly became apparent that he was considerably more cautious than Lenin in charting the party's course. Like the rest of the party leadership, Zinoviev was plainly surprised by the vehemence of Lenin's April Theses*, and he hesitated briefly before adopting their message as his own. Moreover, he refused to acquiesce in Lenin's demand that the Bolsheviks withdraw from active participation in the Zimmerwald movement (see World War I), and he was able to carry the party majority with him at the Bolsheviks' Seventh All-Russian Conference in April. Lenin seemed to think that the more narrowly the Bolsheviks circumscribed their program and the more they cut themselves off from allies who did not fully share the Bolshevik position, the greater was the party's revolutionary appeal and strength. Zinoviev, on the other hand, wished to preserve a broader base and some possibility of working with groups that did not have positions identical to the Bolsheviks. He also was convinced that Bolshevik strength could easily be overestimated and that therefore it was possible to expose the party to extreme danger by taking too radical a position and isolating the party from all outside support.

Zinoviev's actions in response to both a pro-Bolshevik demonstration scheduled for June 10 and the July Days* confirmed his cautious stance. Military units sympathetic to the Bolsheviks and anarchists (*see* Anarchism) began to agitate in early June for a demonstration. When the Bolshevik leadership met on June 6 to consider the question of approving and supporting a demonstration, Zinoviev, unlike Lenin and Stalin, spoke against it on the grounds that the Bolsheviks were weak and poorly organized and that the turning point was only beginning. Although he later temporarily yielded to the overwhelming mood in the party favoring the demonstration, at the first opportunity he moved against it, casting a decisive vote against the demonstration.

During the July Days Zinoviev did everything he could to restrain the radicalized Bolshevik sympathizers who now insisted, against the will of the party leadership, on taking to the street. Only when he knew that his and Kamenev's appeal against any demonstration would not be heeded did he switch tactics and seek to restrain rather than prohibit any demonstration. Faced with the certainty that a protest would be held, Zinoviev sought to turn it into a "peaceful and organized armed demonstration"—armed only because it was impossible to disarm it. Zinoviev's main preoccupation was not in inspiring a revolution in July but in rescuing the party from disaster, which he feared would be the consequence of premature, ill-considered action. In pursuing this goal. Zinoviev was, as Trotsky later acknowledged, "extraordinarily active, ingenious, and strong."

Although Zinoviev was forced to join Lenin in hiding outside Petrograd after the July Days as a result of government charges that they were German agents, and although he may have been momentarily disillusioned with the slogan of "All Power to the Soviets," his belief that the Bolsheviks were too weak to seize and hold power by themselves never left him. At summer's end he moved his hideout to Petrograd while Lenin went to Finland. From their respective locations the differences in assessments of Bolshevik strength and appropriate tactics, which had existed between Lenin and Zinoviev since spring, became increasingly pronounced. While Lenin began to press ever more vehemently for more radical action, Zinoviev stressed with corresponding vigor the need for caution and the strength of the counterrevolutionary forces.

After the Kornilov Revolt* at the end of August, Zinoviev compared the situation in Russia to that in France during the period leading up to the Paris Commune in 1871. He predicted that any uprising in Russia might suffer the same defeats as did the Paris Commune. Although there might be debate about what should be done, he said, there could be no question about what should not be done. There should be no attempt at a seizure of power by revolutionary action. What he proposed instead was a defensive "fraternal alliance" of "all revolutionary forces of the country for the creation and solidification of the power of the workers, soldiers, and poor peasants." This was the best hope for defending the revolutionary forces against the attack he saw being prepared by the reactionary forces in the country.

By mid-October these disagreements had reached a crucial stage. Lenin demanded that the party seize power by itself, arguing that recent victories for the Bolsheviks in the Moscow and Petrograd Soviets (*see* Moscow Soviet; Petrograd Soviet) proved that the time was right for initiating an armed revolution. Zinoviev saw these things as only signs of the long-term trends, and he even cautioned against announcing the transfer of power to the soviets (*see* Soviets [Councils] of Workers', Soldiers', and Peasants' Deputies), because that would invite the reactionary forces to respond with bloody repression, which he thought they would be able to do. His program was for the formation of a democratic coalition of the Left, according to which the Bolsheviks would proportionately share the seats of the presidium of the Petrograd Soviet with the Mensheviks (*see* Russian Social Democratic Workers' Party [Menshevik]) and Socialist-Revolutionary Party*. In short, he continued to believe that for revolution to succeed and develop peacefully, the Bolsheviks had to have a broader base for power than Lenin considered necessary or desirable.

This fundamental difference in assessment was the root cause of the violent disagreements that occurred between the time of the Bolshevik Central Committee meeting on October 10 and Zinoviev's letter of November 7, in which he submitted to party discipline. When on October 10 the Central Committee approved Lenin's resolution putting armed uprising on the agenda, Zinoviev and Kamenev responded with an appeal that boldly took issue with the majority by denying that the Bolsheviks had either sufficient support in Russia or from the international proletariat to seize and hold power. Zinoviev held to that position even after the Bolsheviks had seized the reigns of power, and he worked, together with other Bolsheviks, to form a coalition government along the lines he had endorsed in September. Only after numerous strident attacks by Lenin and under threat of expulsion from the party did Zinoviev, declaring that he preferred "to make mistakes with millions of workers and soldiers and to die with them than to stand aside at this historic moment," finally submit to party discipline and resume his positions of leadership in the party (Daniels 1967, p. 213).

Myron W. Hedlin

Bibliography

Daniels, Robert V. *Red October*. 1967.
Protokoly Tsentral'nogo komiteta RSDRP (B), avgust 1917-fevral' 1918. 1958.
Zinoviev, G. E. *Sochineniia*. 16 vols. (incomplete). 1923–1929.

CHRONOLOGY OF THE RUSSIAN REVOLUTIONS

1898

March 1–3   First Congress of Russian Social Democratic Party
                             (RSDWP)—Minsk

1903

July 17–August 10   Second Congress of RSDWP—Brussels and
                             London—split between Bolsheviks and Mensheviks

1904

January   Beginning of Russo-Japanese War
December 19   Surrender of Port Arthur to the Japanese

1905

January 9   Bloody Sunday—Beginning of Revolution of 1905
April 12–27   Third Congress RSDWP—London
August   FIRST ALL-RUSSIAN MOSLEM CONGRESS—
                             Nizhnii Novgorod
August 12   Treaty of Portsmouth Ends Russo-Japanese War
October   FIRST FOUNDING CONGRESS OF THE
                             CONSTITUTIONAL DEMOCRATIC PARTY
                             (CADETS)
October 13   FIRST MEETING OF THE ST. PETERSBURG
                             SOVIET OF WORKERS' DEPUTIES

| October 17 | October Manifesto—Tsar promises constitution and representative assembly (Duma) for Russia |
| Dec 29, 1905—January 4, 1906 | FIRST FOUNDING CONGRESS OF THE SOCIALIST-REVOLUTIONARY PARTY |

1906

January 13–23	SECOND ALL-RUSSIAN MOSLEM CONGRESS—Petersburg
April 10–25	Fourth (Unification) Congress of the RSDWP—Stockholm
August 16	THIRD ALL-RUSSIAN MOSLEM CONGRESS—Nizhnii Novgorod
Nov 3–7	Second Conference RSDWP, or FIRST ALL-RUSSIAN CONFERENCE RSDWP-Tammerfors

1907

April 30–May 19	Fifth (London) Conference—London
July 21–23	Third Conference RSDWP, or SECOND ALL-RUSSIAN CONFERENCE RSDWP—Finland
November 5–12	Fourth Conference RSDWP, or THIRD ALL-RUSSIAN CONFERENCE RSDWP-Helsingfors

1908

| December 21–27 | Fifth Conference RSDWP—Paris |

1912

| January 5–17 | Sixth (Prague) Conference RSDWP—Prague |

1914

| March | Outbreak of World War I |
| December | SPECIAL ALL-RUSSIAN MOSLEM CONGRESS |

1916

| December 17 | Rasputin assassinated |

1917

February 23	International Women's Day—women demonstrate in Petrograd
February 26	Troops fire on demonstrators—garrison mutinies
February 27	Formation of Temporary Committee of the Duma, Petrograd Soviet revived

March 1	Petrograd Soviet issues "Order Number One" to army
March 2	Provisional Government announced; Prince L'vov named Prime Minister
	Nicholas II Abdicates
March 3	Army Order Number Two
March 12	Stalin and Kamenev reach Petrograd
March 18	The term "Red Guard" first used by V.D. Bonch-Bruevich in *Pravda*
March 23	FIRST ALL-RUSSIAN COSSACK CONGRESS—Petrograd
March 25–28	ALL-RUSSIAN CONGRESS of cooperative organizations
March 27	Lenin leaves Switzerland
March 29–April 3	ALL-RUSSIAN CONFERENCE OF SOVIETS OF WORKER' AND SOLDIERS' DEPUTIES—Petrograd
April	First Moslem Central Asian Conference
April 3	Lenin arrives in Petrograd
April 7	Stalin published Lenin's "April Theses" in *Pravda*
April 18	(May 1- new style) May Day: Miliukov's not to Allies
April 20	Miliukov note published
April 20, 21	April Days demonstrations; April Crisis
April 22	Sverdlov's position filled by Stalin as General Secretary
April 24–29	SEVENTH (APRIL) ALL-RUSSIAN CONFERENCE of RSDWP (B)—Petrograd
April 28	First All-Kirghiz (Kazakh) Congress—Orenburg
May 1	FIRST (postrevolutionary) ALL-RUSSIAN MOSLEM CONGRESS-Moscow
	First Congress of the Soviets of the Far East
May 3–28	ALL-RUSSIAN CONGRESS OF PEASANTS' DEPUTIES—Petrograd
May 4	Trotsky arrives in Petrograd
May 5	The Provisional Government reorganized—The First Coalition Government
May 7–12	ALL-RUSSIAN CONFERENCE OF MENSHEVIK AND UNITED ORGANIZATIONS OF RSDWP
May 7	ALL-RUSSIAN OFFICERS' CONGRESS—Petrograd

May 9	EIGHTH CONGRESS OF THE CADET PARTY—Petrograd
May 25–June 4	THIRD ALL-RUSSIAN CONGRESS OF THE SOCIALIST REVOLUTIONARY PARTY (S-Rs)—Moscow
May 28–29	All-Ukrainian Peasant Congress—Kiev
May 30–June 2	First Conference of Factory Committees
June 3–24	FIRST ALL-RUSSIAN CONGRESS OF SOVIETS WORKERS' AND SOLDIERS' DEPUTIES
June 7	ALL-RUSSIAN COSSACK CONGRESS—Petrograd
June 18	Beginning of the June Offensive
June 20	Parish schools removed from the jurisdiction of the church
June 21–28	THIRD ALL-RUSSIAN CONFERENCE OF TRADE UNIONS
July	SECOND ALL-RUSSIAN MOSLEM CONGRESS—Kazan
July 2	Cadet Ministers resign from cabinet
July 3–5	July Days demonstrations
July 7	Kamenev and Trotsky arrested
July 7	Prime Minister L'vov arrested
July 8	Kerensky appointed Prime Minister
July 14	ALL-RUSSIAN CONGRESS OF LANDED PROPRIETORS
July 18	Kerensky appointed Kornilov Commander-in-Chief
July 21–26	Second All-Kirghiz (Kazakh) Congress—Orenburg
July 23	Kerensky forms Second Coalition Cabinet
July 23	NINTH CONGRESS OF THE CADET PARTY
July 26–August 3	SIXTH CONGRESS OF THE RSDWP (B)—Petrograd
July 31–August 6	CONGRESS OF ALL-RUSSIAN PEASANT UNION—Moscow
August 3	SECOND ALL-RUSSIAN COMMERCIAL AND INDUSTRIAL CONGRESS—Moscow
August 3–5	SECOND CONGRESS OF ALL-RUSSIAN UNION OF TRADE AND INDUSTRY
August 7–12	Second Conference of Factory Committees—Petrograd
August 12–15	Moscow State Conference—Moscow
August 25–30	Kornilov Revolt

August 27	Kornilov dismissed by Kerensky
September 1	Kornilov surrenders and is arrested; Kerensky forms the Directory
September 3	Second Moslem Central Asian Conference
	Bolshevik Resolution adopted by Moscow Soviet; Congress of Soviets of Central Siberia—Krasnoiarsk
September 10	Third Conference of Factory Committies—Petrograd
September 14–22	Democratic Conference—Petrograd
September 20	Trotsky said Congress of Soviets must decide transfer of power to Soviets
September 21	Petrograd Soviet resolved against Democratic Conference and in favor of immediate All-Russian Congress of Soviets to settle the question of power
September 23	Trotsky elected President of Petrograd Soviet's Presidium;
	CC selected delegation to Pre-Parliament (headed by Trotsky). Delegation issued call for a revolutionary power.
	CEC convoked Second Congress of Soviets for October 20
September 25	Kerensky formed 3rd Coalition Cabinet
	Petrograd Soviet elected new Exec Comm with Trotsky as chairman; condemns Third Coalition as counterrev
October 7	Pre-Parliament opens. Trotsky reads declaration on bourgeois danger to revolution, and Bolsheviks walk out
October 10	LENIN PERSUADES CENTRAL COMMITTEE OF RSDWP(B) TO PUT THE ARMED UPRISING ON THEIR AGENDA
October 10–11	Fourth Conference of Factory Committees—Petrograd
October 11	Trotsky called for transfer of power to the Soviets in order to save the revolution
October 12	Conservative newspapers report that Bolsheviks plan insurrection for October 20
October 14	Cadet Party Congress
October 15–16	Second All-City Conference of Factory Committees—Moscow

October 16–11	Lenin calls for insurrection
	Party Military Revolutionary Center formed
October 16–23	First Congress of Workers', Soldiers' and Peasants' Deputies of Siberia—Irkutsk
	Meets simultaneously with First All-Siberian Conference of Bolsheviks
October 17	Gorky's newspaper reports on Zinoviev's opposition to the Bolshevik seizure of power
	Central Executive Committee postpones meeting of Second-All Russian Congress of Soviets to October 25, 1917
October 17–22	FIRST ALL-RUSSIAN CONFERENCE OF FACTORY COMMITTEES—Moscow
October 20–23	Conference of Red Guards
October 20	FIRST SESSION OF MILITARY REVOLUTIONARY COMMITTEE (MRC)
October 23	KERENSKY DECIDES TO ARREST MILITARY REVOLUTIONARY COMMITTEE AND CLOSE BOLSHEVIK NEWSPAPERS
11 A.M.	MRC notified all units to be ready for orders. Bolshevik papers resume publication.
12:30 P.M.	Kerensky addresses Pre-Parliament to justify his attic on the Bolsheviks; proclaims state of insurrection and demands extraordinary powers
10:30 P.M.	Lenin leaves for Smolnyi on foot and arrives around midnight
October 24	
11:45 A.M.	Soviets take power
Noon	Democratic Council (Pre-Parliament) convenes for last time; dispersed by Bolshevik forces
2:35 P.M.	Meeting of Petrograd Soviet to endorse uprising; first public appearance of Lenin and Zinoviev since July
9:40–10:00 P.M.	Artillery fire on palace by AURORA (blanks) on Peter-Paul fortress
10:45 P.M.	Second Congress of Soviets opened; Kamenev elected chairman; Martov resolution on all-socialist government passed; anti-Bolsheviks walk out
October 26	Decree on Land
	Decree on Peace
3:00 A.M.	Congress of Soviets resolves to take power recesses at 5:00 A.M.

Noon	Bolshevik CC plans new cabinet; Left S-Rs decline to join it
11:00 P.M.	Congress of Soviets reconvenes, ratifies Lenin's decrees and Council of People's Commissars (Lenin chairman, Trotsky Commissar of Foreign Affairs)
	Vikzhel convenes conference to negotiate a coalition government; Bolshevik CC votes to participate
October 27	Suppression of anti-soviet newspapers
October 29–November 6	First All-Siberian Congress of Soviets meets simultaneously with First All-Siberian Conference of Siberian Bolsheviks in Irkutsk. Forms the Central Executive Committee of Soviets of Siberia known as Centrosibir or Tsentrosibir. It claims to be the true government of Siberia until August 28, 1918
November 2	"Declaration or Rights of Peoples of Russia"
	Moscow Bolsheviks take Kremlin; end of anti-Bolshevik resistance
	CEC votes Bolshevik terms for coalition; Bolshevik CC condemns conciliationists
November 4	Conciliationists resign from Bolshevik CC and Council of People's Commissars
November 9	Krylenko named Supreme Commander-in-Chief and People's Commissar on Military Affairs
November 10	Decree abolishing social classes and ranks
November 12	Election of Constituent Assembly (S-Rs lead, Bolsheviks second)
November 14	Socialist-Revolutionary Party Central Committee expels Left-Socialist Revolutionaries from the party party
November 14	Decree establishing Workers' Control of Industry
November 18–December 12	Negotiations for the entry of Left Socialist-Revolutionaries to enter the Council of People's Commissars and create a coalition government
November 19–28	Left S-Rs hold their own Congress—their first as a separate party
November 26–December 5	Fourth Congress of the Socialist-Revolutionary Party—the first without the Left S-R's
November 30	Extraordinary Congress of the RSDWP (Mensheviks)

December	Bashkirs and the Kazazh-Kirghiz held national congresses and called for national autonomy
	Moslems established a Pan-Islamic movement creating a Moslem constituent assembly
December 1	Decree creating the Supreme Council of the National Economy
December 4	All-Ukrainian Congress of Soviets in Kiev
December 5–31	Third All-Kazakh Congress in Orenburg
December 7	Decree creating the CHEKA
December 11	All educational institutions are nationalized
December 11	Negotiations with the Germans for peace begin at Brest-Litovsk
December 12	First All-Ukrainian Congress of Soviets in Kiev
December 16	Marriage made a civil matter
	Abolition of military ranks and titles
December 20	CONGRESS OF ALL-RUSSIAN UNION OF RAILWAYMEN

1918

January 5	CONSTITUENT ASSEMBLY (the only freely elected representative body in the history of Russia) met for one day
January 7–14	FIRST ALL-RUSSIAN CONGRESS OF TRADE UNIONS
January 10–18	THIRD ALL-RUSSIAN CONGRESS OF SOVIETS OF WORKERS' AND SOLDIERS' DEPUTIES
January 13–18	THIRD ALL-RUSSIAN CONGRESS OF PEASANT'S DEPUTIES
January 15	Decree calling for the creation of the Red Army
January 17	All teachers of religion are dismissed from public schools
January 23	"Decree of Separation of Church from State and School from Church" abolishing all forms of civil cooperation in religion
January 26	Tomsk Soviet dissolves the Siberian Regional Duma but delegates create the Provisional Government of Autonomous Siberia, claiming jurisdiction over all of Siberia
February 8	Red Army seizes Kiev

February 9	The Ukrainian Central Rada signs a separate peace with Germany
February 16–26	The Second All-Siberian Congress of Soviets establishes a Bolshevik government for Siberia
March 2	The German Army takes Kiev
March 3	Treaty of BREST-LITOVSK signed
March 12–16	FOURTH ALL-RUSSIAN TRADE UNION CONFERENCE
March 14–16	FOURTH ALL-RUSSIAN CONGRESS OF SOVIETS
March 19	Left S-Rs (opposed completely to the Treaty of Brest-Litovsk) withdraw its representatives from the Council of People's Commissars
	Trotsky takes command of army
April 5	Allied troops and ships occupy Murmansk
April 13	Trotsky becomes Commissar of War
April 17–25	SECOND CONGRESS OF LEFT SOCIALIST-REVOLUTIONARIES
April 22	Independent "federative republic" declared in Tiflis Georgia
April 22	Decree calling for general conscription
May 14	Shooting incident at Cheliabinsk between soldiers of Czech Legion and Soviet forces
May 25	UPRISING OF THE CZECHOSLOVAK LEGION ON TRANS-SIBERIAN RAILWAY: BEGINNING OF CIVIL WAR
May 26–28	Armenia, Azerbaijan, and Georgia disintegrate into three separate states
June 11	Decree on the Organization and Supply of the Rural Poor—creation of Committees of the Poor (Kombedy)
June 14	Expulsion of most non-Bolshevik socialist parties from the Soviets
June 28	Nationalization of Large-Scale Industry (Beginning of War Communism)
June 28–July 1	THIRD CONGRESS OF THE LEFT SOCIALIST-REVOLUTIONARY PARTY
July	Bolsheviks close Gorky's newspaper, the New Life
July 4	The Provisional Government of Siberia in Omsk declares the independence of Siberia
July 4–10	FIFTH ALL-RUSSIAN CONGRESS OF SOVIETS

July 6	ASSASSINATION OF GERMAN AMBASSADOR, COUNT MIRBACH as part of abortive coup by Left S-Rs
	Left S-R uprising; all non-Bolshevik parties outlawed
	TERROR BEGINS
July 10	Constitution of the R.S.F.S.R. announced (the first Soviet Constitution)
July 16	Execution of Russian imperial family
August 30	Lenin shot by Dora Kaplan
September	Ufa State Conference appointed a five man Directory
October 9	Directory establishes its headquarters in Omsk
October 18	Abolition of Workers' Control in Industry
November	Armistice of WW I
November 5	Military coup in Omsk brought arrest of Avkseent'ev
November 9	French land their troops in Odessa
November 21	Abolition of private trade
December 17	Latvian Bolsheviks, under Stuchka, proclaimed Latvia a Soviet Republic
	The Siberian Bureau of the Russian Communist Party Bolshevik (Sibburo) is formed to direct the recovery of Siberia by the communists
December 18	Kolchak appoints himself Supreme Ruler and dismisses the Directory
December 28	Kolchak overthrown

1919

	Sverdlov died and Kalinin replaced him as President of the All-Russian CEC (post changed to Chairman in 1922)
January 16–25	SECOND ALL-RUSSIAN CONGRESS OF TRADE UNIONS
February 6	Red Army occupies Kiev
March	Lithuanian Soviet Socialist Republic merged with the Belorussian Soviet Socialist Republic to form the so-called Litbel Republic
March 2–7	The first and founding congress of the Communist International

March 6–8	Seventh Congress of the Russian Social-Democratic Workers' Party (Bolshevik)
	Changes its name to RUSSIAN COMMUNIST PARTY (BOLSHEVIK)—March 8
March 18–23	Eighth Congress of the Russian Communist Party (Bolshevik)—adoption of party program
March 21	The Allied forces decide to withdraw all of their military forces from Russia
March 21	The Soviet Republic of Hungary is created
April	Bolshevik rule in Lithuania destroyed by Polish army
April 24	Beginning of Russo-Polish War
May 19	Denikin's spring offensive.
August 31	Denikin takes Kiev
September	Eighth Congress of Central Asian Soviets
September 27	Allied troops evacuate Archangel
October 20	White armies begin massive retreat
November 22	Nationalization of Small-Scale Industrial Enterprises
December 16	Red Army takes Kiev
December 24	S-Rs and Mensheviks in Irkutsk seized power and created new gov't called POLITICAL CENTER

1920

January 4	Kolchak abdicates as Supreme Ruler
January 15	Czech Guards turn Kolchak over to Political Center Gov't
January 18	Bolshevik Military Revolutionary Committee takes Irkutsk and dissolves Political Center
March	Denikin forced out of power by Wrangel
March 3	Far Eastern Bureau of the Russian Communist Party created under the Siberian Bureau of the Russian Communist Party
April	Poles invade the Ukraine
May 6	Polish Army takes Kiev
May 14	Soviet Gov't recognized Far Eastern Republic as separate state
June 6	Wrangel starts his offensive
June 12	Red Army takes Kiev
August 17	Polish counteroffensive

September	Last of Czechoslovak Legion leaves Russia in Vladivostok
September 21	Beginning of Russo-Polish peace negotiations
October 12	Provisional peace treaty between Poland and Russia
November 2	Wrangel begins retreat
November 14	Wrangel forces evacuate Crimea

1921

January 25	Shliapnikov drafted Workers' Opposition contributing to Trade Union debate published in Pravda
February 22	Decree Creating the General State Planning Commission (Gosplan)
March	TREATY OF RIGA ENDS WAR WITH POLAND AND CIVIL WAR
March 2	KRONSTADT REVOLT BEGINS
March 18	Kronstadters' last stronghold fell
March 21	Decree Creating Tax in Kind
	BEGINNING OF THE NEW ECONOMIC POLICY
December 10	Denationalization of Industry

1922

February 6	Creation of the State Political Administration G.P.U. to absorb and replace the Cheka
May 22	The Land Decree of the New Economic Policy
May 22	Decree on the Right to Private Property
May 25	Lenin partially paralyzed by first stroke
December 13	Lenin partially paralyzed by second stroke

1923

March 10	Lenin's third stroke

1924

January 21	Lenin dies from fourth stroke

MAPS

THE BREST-LITOVSK SETTLEMENT

(March 3, 1918)

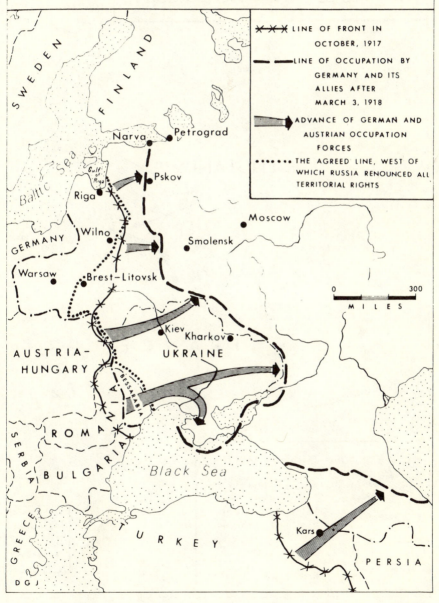

LINE OF FRONT IN OCTOBER, 1917

LINE OF OCCUPATION BY GERMANY AND ITS ALLIES AFTER MARCH 3, 1918

ADVANCE OF GERMAN AND AUSTRIAN OCCUPATION FORCES

THE AGREED LINE, WEST OF WHICH RUSSIA RENOUNCED ALL TERRITORIAL RIGHTS

SWEDEN

FINLAND

Baltic Sea

Gulf of Riga

Narva

Petrograd

Pskov

Riga

GERMANY

Wilno

Warsaw

Brest-Litovsk

Moscow

Smolensk

0   300
MILES

AUSTRIA-HUNGARY

Kiev   Kharkov

UKRAINE

ROMANIA

BESSARABIA

SERBIA

BULGARIA

Black Sea

GREECE

TURKEY

Kars

PERSIA

DGJ

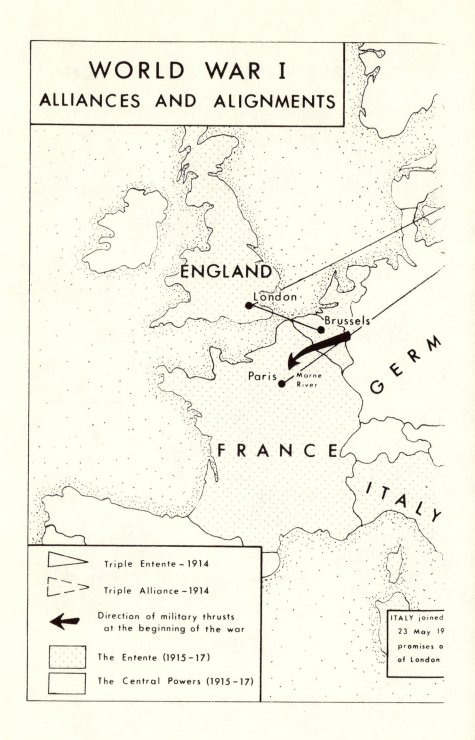

WORLD WAR I
ALLIANCES AND ALIGNMENTS

ENGLAND

London

Brussels

Paris   Marne River

FRANCE

GERM

ITALY

Triple Entente – 1914

Triple Alliance – 1914

Direction of military thrusts
at the beginning of the war

The Entente (1915–17)

The Central Powers (1915–17)

ITALY joined
23 May 19
promises o
of London

664

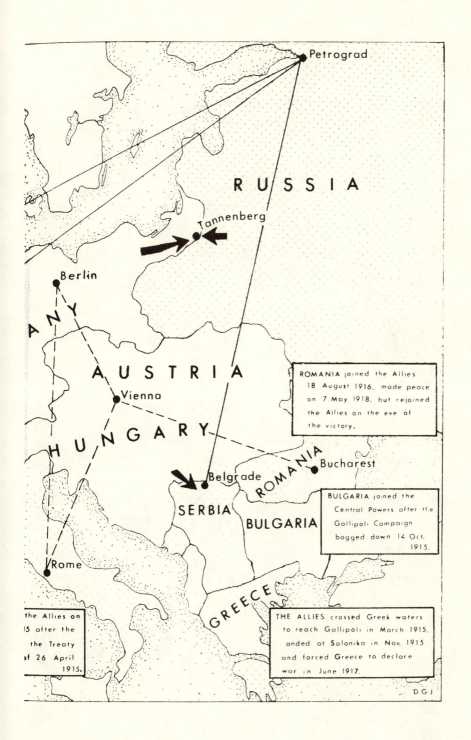

RUSSIA

Petrograd

Tannenberg

Berlin

ANY

AUSTRIA

Vienna

HUNGARY

ROMANIA joined the Allies
18 August 1916, made peace
on 7 May 1918, but rejoined
the Allies on the eve of
the victory.

ROMANIA

Belgrade

Bucharest

SERBIA

BULGARIA

BULGARIA joined the
Central Powers after the
Gallipoli Campaign
bogged down 14 Oct.
1915.

Rome

the Allies on
15 after the
the Treaty
of 26 April
1915.

GREECE

THE ALLIES crossed Greek waters
to reach Gallipoli in March 1915,
anded at Salonika in Nov. 1915
and forced Greece to declare
war in June 1917.

D G J

665

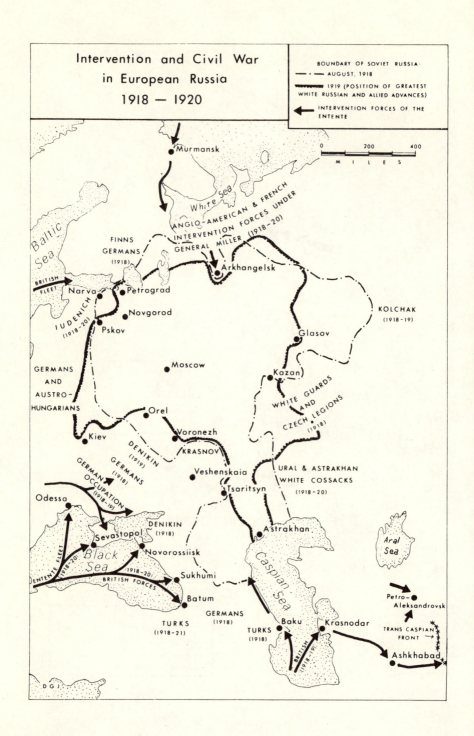

Intervention and Civil War
in European Russia
1918 — 1920

BOUNDARY OF SOVIET RUSSIA:
AUGUST, 1918
1919 (POSITION OF GREATEST
WHITE RUSSIAN AND ALLIED ADVANCES)
INTERVENTION FORCES OF THE
ENTENTE

0   200   400
M I L E S

Murmansk

White Sea

Baltic Sea

ANGLO-AMERICAN & FRENCH
INTERVENTION FORCES UNDER
GENERAL MILLER (1918-20)

FINNS
GERMANS
(1918)

Arkhangelsk

BRITISH FLEET

Narva
Petrograd
Novgorod
Pskov

IUDENICH
(1918-20)

KOLCHAK
(1918-19)

Glasov

Moscow

GERMANS
AND
AUSTRO-HUNGARIANS

Kazan

Orel

WHITE GUARDS
AND
CZECH LEGIONS
(1918)

Kiev

DENIKIN
(1919)

GERMANS
(1918)

Voronezh
KRASNOV

Veshenskaia

URAL & ASTRAKHAN
WHITE COSSACKS
(1918-20)

GERMAN
OCCUPATION
(1918-19)

Tsaritsyn

Odessa

DENIKIN
(1918)

Sevastopol

Black Sea

Novorossiisk

Astrakhan

Aral Sea

Caspian Sea

ENTENTE FLEET
1918-20

BRITISH FORCES
1918-20

Sukhumi

Batum

Petro-
Aleksandrovsk

GERMANS
(1918)

TURKS
(1918-21)

TURKS
(1918)

Baku

Krasnodar

TRANS CASPIAN
FRONT

BRITISH 1918-19

Ashkhabad

D G J

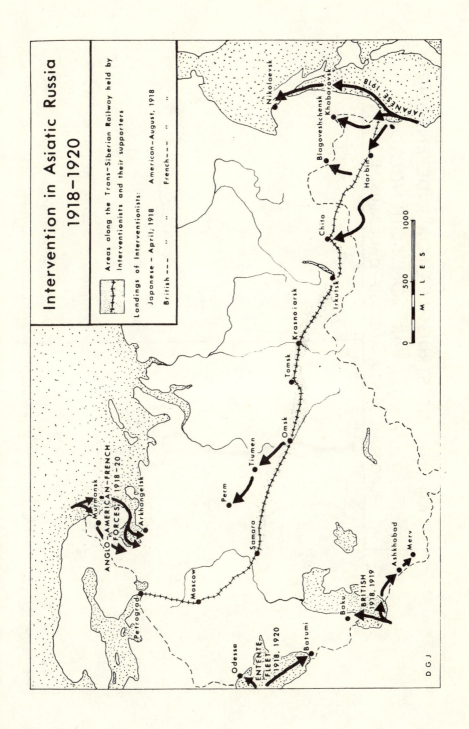

Intervention in Asiatic Russia 1918–1920

Areas along the Trans-Siberian Railway held by
Interventionists and their supporters

Landings of Interventionists:

Japanese — April, 1918   American—August, 1918

British —— " "   French—— " "

Nikolaevsk

Blagoveshchensk

Khabarovsk

JAPANESE 1918

Harbin

Chita

Irkutsk

Krasnoiarsk

Tomsk

Omsk

Tiumen

Perm

Samara

Moscow

Petrograd

MILES

1000

500

0

Murmansk

ANGLO-AMERICAN–FRENCH
FORCES, 1918–20

Arkhangelsk

Odessa

ENTENTE
FLEET,
1918, 1920

Batumi

Baku

BRITISH
1918, 1919

Ashkhabad

Merv

D G J

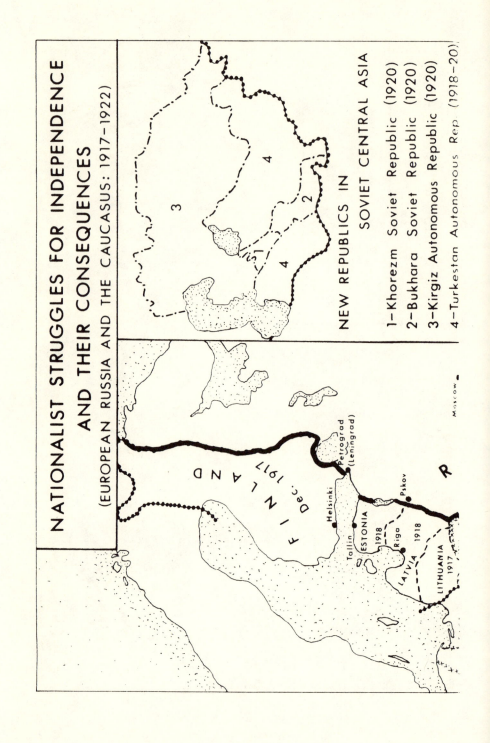

NATIONALIST STRUGGLES FOR INDEPENDENCE
AND THEIR CONSEQUENCES

(EUROPEAN RUSSIA AND THE CAUCASUS: 1917–1922)

NEW REPUBLICS IN
SOVIET CENTRAL ASIA

1–Khorezm Soviet Republic (1920)
2–Bukhara Soviet Republic (1920)
3–Kirgiz Autonomous Republic (1920)
4–Turkestan Autonomous Rep. (1918–20)

FINLAND
Dec. 1917

Helsinki
Tallin
ESTONIA 1918
Riga
LATVIA 1918
LITHUANIA 1917

Petrograd
(Leningrad)

Pskov

Moscow

R

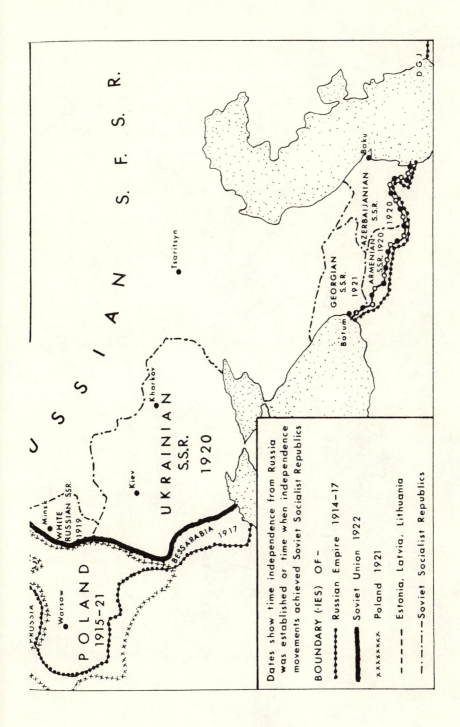

Dates show time independence from Russia
was established or time when independence
movements achieved Soviet Socialist Republics

BOUNDARY (-IES) OF—

●●●● Russian Empire 1914–17

━━━ Soviet Union 1922

×××××× Poland 1921

--- Estonia, Latvia, Lithuania

-·-·- Soviet Socialist Republics

R U S S I A N   S. F. S. S. R.

POLAND 1915–21

Warsaw

PRUSSIA

Minsk
WHITE RUSSIAN SSR. 1919

Kiev

UKRAINIAN S.S.R. 1920

Kharkov

BESSARABIA 1917

Tsaritsyn

GEORGIAN S.S.R. 1921

Batum

ARMENIAN S.S.R. 1920

AZERBAIJANIAN S.S.R. 1920

Baku

D. G. J.

669

SOVIET UNI

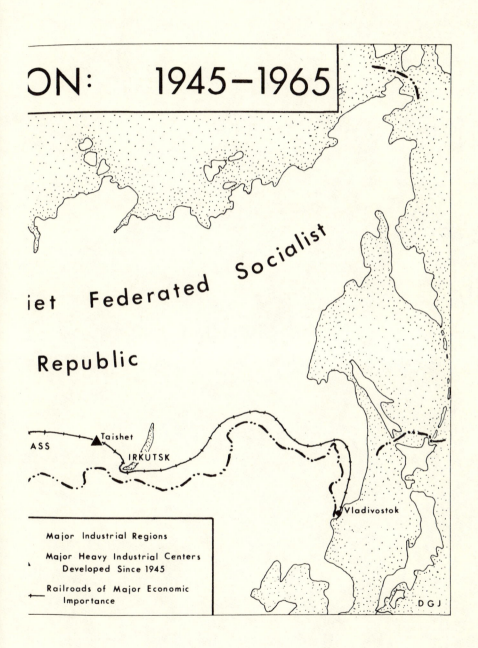

ON: 1945–1965

...iet Federated Socialist

Republic

...ASS

▲ Taishet

IRKUTSK

Vladivostok

Major Industrial Regions

Major Heavy Industrial Centers
Developed Since 1945

Railroads of Major Economic
Importance

DGJ

APPENDIX

SUMMARY OF THE SOVIET (RSFSR) CONSTITUTION OF 1918

I. Declaration of the Rights of the Working and Exploited People (nationalization of land, of natural resources, and of banks, control over the means of production and transport, cancellation foreign debts, establishment of a duty to work, organization of the Soviet Red Army, denial of participation in government to exploiters, the freedom of national soviets to choose to participate in the Russian Federation);

II. General Provisions of the Constitution of the RSFSR (the dictatorship of the proletariat and introducing socialism as fundamental state tasks, a free socialist society where the power belongs to working people united in Soviets, supreme state power in the Congress of Soviets and VTsIK, a bill of rights providing for separation of church and state, freedom of conscience, of expression, of assembly, of organization, and free education—all for the toiling masses, the duty to work and to defend the socialist fatherland, equal rights for all citizens but also the deprivation thereof to all who would use them to the detriment of the socialist revolution);

III. Organization of State Power (All-Russian Congress of Soviets, *VTsIK*, *Sovnarkom*, and federal jurisdiction, local Soviets and their jurisdiction);

IV. The Right to Vote (and to be elected, according to citizens who make their living through labor and to soldiers, as well as to citizens of either of these groups who may have lost the capacity to work, and the specific denial of these rights to seven categories of persons including capitalists, the clergy, and former members of the police and *Okhrana*, the manner for conducting elections and the recalling deputies to Soviets);

V. The Budget;

VI. The State Arms and Flag.

MEMBERS OF THE ALL-RUSSIAN CENTRAL EXECUTIVE COMMITTEE CONSTITUTIONAL COMMISSION (APRIL-JULY, 1918)

Ia.M. Sverdlow,* chairman (Bolshevik); representing faction

M.N. Pokrovskii, deputy chairman (Bolshevik); representing faction

V.A. Avanesov, secretary (Bolshevik)

A.I. Berdnikov, (S-R Maximalist with advisory vote only); representing fraction

D.P. Bogolepov, (Bolshevik); representing Ministry of Finance

N.I. Bukharin,* (Bolshevik); representing Supreme Council of National Econmy

G.S. Gurvich, (Bolshevik as of June 1918); jurist

M.Ia. Latsis,* (Bolshevik); Ministry of Internal Affairs

D.A. Magerovskii, (Left S–R); representing faction

M.A. Reisner (S-R); representing Ministry of Justice

E.M. Sklianskii, (Bolshevik); representing Ministry of War

A.P. Smirnov, (Bolshevik); representing Ministry of Internal Affairs

I.V. Stalin,* (Bolshevik); representing faction

Iu.M. Steklov, (Bolshevik); editor of *Izvestiia*

A.A. Shreider, (Left S-R); representing faction

CENSUS STATISTICS

ETHNIC DISTRIBUTION OF THE POPULATION OF THE RUSSIAN EMPIRE
AND THE SOVIET UNION ACCORDING TO THE CENSUSES OF 1897 AND
1926 (*in round figures*)

Nationality or language group	1897		1926	
	Total within 1897 borders of Russian Empire (by language)	Total within 1926 borders of USSR (by language)	By nationality	By language
Great Russians	55,667,500	54,563,700	77,732,200	84,129,200
Ukrainians	22,380,600	20,232,500	31,189,500	27,569,200
Belorussians	5,885,500	3,570,600	4,738,200	3,466,900
Poles	7,931,300	531,900	781,700	362,400
Czechs, Slovaks	50,400	20,800	27,100	25,100
Serbians, Bulgarians	174,500	70,000	113,800	109,200
Lithuanians, Zmud, Latgals	1,658,500	22,200	51,100	29,800
Latvians	1,435,900	67,900	141,400	115,800
Iranian group	31,700	31,100	51,300	66,600
Tajik group†	350,400	350,400	376,400	390,100
Talyshes	35,300	35,300	77,300	80,600
Tats	95,100	95,000	28,700	87,000
Kurds, Yezidis	99,900	38,400	69,100	34,100
Ossetins	171,700	171,200	272,000	266,800
Moldavians, Rumanians	1,121,700	195,100	283,500	267,600
Germans	1,790,500	1,029,800	1,237,900	1,192,700
Greeks	186,900	151,500	213,700	202,600
Gypsies	44,600	31,500	59,300	40,900
Other Indo-Europeans	44,000	31,800	12,500	11,000
Jews	5,063,200	2,430,400	2,663,400	1,883,000
Arabs, Aisors	7,000	6,500	15,700	16,900

Nationality or language group	1897		1926	
	Total within 1897 borders of Russian Empire (by language)	Total within 1926 borders of USSR (by language)	By nationality	By language
Georgians	1,352,500	1,329,300	1,820,900	1,908,500
Armenians	1,173,100	1,065,300	1,565,800	1,472,900
Kabardians	98,600	98,600	139,900 }	219,300
Cherkesses	46,300	46,200	79,100 }	
Abkhazians	72,100	72,100	57,000	48,100
Chechens	226,500	226,400	318,500 }	396,300
Ingushes	47,800	47,700	74,100 }	
Daghestan Mountain groups	600,500	600,100	574,500	595,400
Finnish group†	143,100	138,700	135,400	153,400
Votiaks	421,000	420,100	514,200	508,700
Karels	208,100	207,700	248,100	239,600
Izhoras	13,800	13,300	16,100	——
Chude (Vepsas)	25,800	25,700	32,800	31,100
Estonians	1,002,700	103,600	154,600	139,500
Komi (Zyrians)	153,600	153,200	226,300	220,400
Permiaks	104,700	104,700	149,400	143,800
Mordvinians	1,023,800	1,020,700	1,339,900	1,266,600
Marii (Cheremis)	375,400	374,700	428,200	425,700
Voguls	7,600	7,600	5,700	5,200
Ostiaks	19,700	19,700	22,200	18,600
Turco-Tatar group*	3,767,500	3,679,000	4,898,800	5,444,300
Bashkirs	1,493,000	1,491,900	983,100	392,800
Karachaevs, Kumyks, Nogais	174,700	174,700	186,000	173,400
Other Turks	440,400	440,400	——	——
Uzbeks, Sarts, Kuramas†	1,702,800	1,702,800	2,440,900	2,497,200
Taranchi, Kashgars, Uighurs	71,400	71,400	108,200	67,500
Kara-Kalpaks	104,300	104,300	126,000	114,900
Kazakhs, Kirghiz	4,285,800	4,285,700	4,578,600	4,673,300
Turkmens (Turkomans)†	281,400	272,800	427,600	426,700
Chuvashes	843,800	840,300	1,117,300	1,104,400
Iakuts, Dolgans	227,400	227,400	214,800	220,400
Kalmyks	190,600	190,500	133,500	131,100
Buriats, Mongols	289,500	289,500	238,100	236,800
Chukchi	11,800	11,800	11,100	11,300
Chinese, Dungans	57,400	57,300	24,800	100,700
Koreans	26,000	25,900	87,000	170,600
Others and unknown	355,800	185,000	326,400	421,700
Foreign citizens	——	——	387,000	——
Total population†	125,666,500	103,803,700	144,327,700	

* Includes Volga Tatars, Azerbaijanis, and Crimean Tatars.
† Exclusive of the principalities of Khiva and Bukhara, and Finland. The total population of the territories of Khiva and Bukhara in 1926 was 2,677,700, among them 1,547,200 Uzbeks, 603,700 Tajiks, and 338,500 Turkmens (by nationality).

NAME INDEX

Page numbers of entries appear in *italic* type.

Buniatzada, D. Kh., 103, 251, 252
Bunin, I. A., 359
Bur'ianov, 207
Burliuk, David, 375
Burtsev, Vladimir L'vovich, *95–96*, 212.
   See also Socialist-Revolutionary Party
Buryshkin, P. A., 390
Bystritskoi, E. V., 408

Cachin, Marcel, 633
Cecek, S. K., 140
Cernich, Bohumir, 174
Chagall, Marc, 59, 369
Chaikovskii, N. V., 163, 619
Chekhonin, S. V., 233
Chelibidzhan (Noman Chelibi Cihan),
   172, 173
Chelnokov, M. V., 33
Cherkezov, V. N., 38
Chernikhov, Ia., 50
Chernishev, N., 503
Chernov, Viktor Mikhailovich, *116–19*;
   agrarian policy of, 118, 336, 534; and
   Comuch, 140; in First Coalition, 305,
   467; as internationalist, 533, 630;
   memoirs of, 256; and nationalism, 401;
   nearly lynched in Kronstadt, 580; op-
   position to Savinkov, 511; and Petro-
   grad Soviet, 444; and Populism, 116–
   17, 532; and Socialist-Revolutionary
   Party, 79, 618. See also Socialist-Rev-
   olutionary Party
Cherviakov, A. V., 70
Chervonnyi, Andrei. See Shumiatskii,
   Boris Zakharovich
Chicherin, Boris Nikolaevich, 119
Chicherin, Georgii Vasil'evich, *119–20*,
   147, 217, 235, 348. See also Foreign
   Policy, 1914–1921
Chistov, N. I., 392
Chkheidze, Nikolai Semenovich, *120–23*;
   as chairman of VTsIK, 22; and Duma,
   198; and Moscow State Conference,
   395; in Petrograd Soviet, 243, 443.
   See also Russian Social Democratic
   Workers' Party (Menshevik)
Chokaev, Mustafa, 309, 588, 589–90
Chubar', Vlas Iakovlevich, *123–24*

Chudnovskii, G. I., 139, 603
Colby, Bainbridge, 19
Copic, C., 271
Czernin, Count Ottokar, 81

Dabal, Tomas. See Dombal, Tomas
Dan. F. I. See Gur'vich, Fedor Il'ich
Degeyter, Pierre, 42
Deich, L. G., 207
Denikin, General Anton Ivanovich, *189–
   90*; in alliance with Red Army, 40; as
   anti-Bolshevik, 159, 193; defeat of,
   86, 135, 137, 236, 377–78, 586; resig-
   nation of, 636; as threat to Second
   Congress of the Comsomol, 494; and
   White Army, 53, 54, 61, 62, 135,
   136–37, 163, 173, 180, 189–90, 201,
   250, 307, 432, 491, 618, 619, 620,
   637. See also Army of Imperial Russia
   in World War I; Civil War in Russia;
   White Movement
Derber, Vladivostok, 524, 525
Diadia, Tom. See Bonch-Bruevich, Vla-
   dimir Dmitrievich
Dimanstein, S. M., 302
Dmitrii Pavlovich, Grand Duke, 476, 477
Dobrogeanu-Gherea, Constantine, 73
Dolgorukov, P. D., 169
Dombal (Dabal), Tomas, 435, 436
Domontovich, Aleksandra. See Kollontai,
   Aleksandra Mikhailovna
Domontovich, Mikhail, 311
Donish, Ahmed Mahdunb, 87
Dosmukhammedov, Kh., 15
Dridzo, Solomon Abramovich. See Lo-
   zovskii, Aleksandr
Dukhonin, General N. N., 241
Dulat-Aliev, M., 103
Dumenko, B. M., 167
Dumsha, Iu., 102
Dunsterville, General L. C., 136
Durnovo, P. N., 39
Dutov, General/Ataman Aleksandr Il'ich,
   200–201; and Kokand, 309; and Octo-
   ber Seizure of Power, 15; and Red
   Guard, 74, 167; and Revolution in
   Central Asia, 100; and Revolution in
   Kazakhistan, 301; and White Move-

Struve, P. B., 354, 360, 620, 637
Stuchka, Piotr Ivanovich, 286, 287, 289, 290, 346, *553–54*
Studenetskii, S. A., 390
Sturmer, B. V., 198, 462
Subkhi, M., 103
Sukhanov, Niklai Niklaevich, *554–55*; eyewitness account of Revolution by, 256; impression of Stalin, 549; and *Izvestiia*, 273; and Left Communism, 631; Lenin's attack on, 258; and Petrograd Soviet, 227. *See also* Russian Social Democratic Workers' Party (Menshevik)
Sukhomlinov, General A. A., 54, 55
Sukhovkin, M. A., 113
Sulkiewicz, Suleiman, 173
Sultangaliev, Mir Said, *555–57*; organization of Moslems under, 102, 103, 272, 567, 568, 590, 605; trial of, 404. *See also* Central Asia, Revolution in; Tatars, Revolution Among the
Sultanov, H. N., 252
Sun Yat-sen, 74, 633
Sverdlov, Iakov Mikhailovich, 24, 106, 154, 295, 297, 387, *560–64*
Sverdlov, Zinovii, 560
Sverianin. *See* Bonch-Bruevich, Vladimir Dmitrievich
Sviatopolk-Mirskii, Prince Peter, 415, 419

Talaat, Pasha, 214
Tarasov, K. *See* Rusanov, N. S.
Tarnovskii, E. M., 286
Tarshis, Iosif Aronovich. *See* Piatnitskii, Iosif Aronovich
Tatlin, Vladimir, 47–48, 59, 369
Teitelbaum, M. I., 390
Teodorovich, I. A., 106
Tereshchenko, M. I.: coup planned by, 248; as Minister of Finance, 268, 269; as Minister of Foreign Affairs, 191, 467, 595; opposed to Defensism, 234; and World War I, 631, 634
Thomas, Albert, 633
Tikhomirnov, V. A., 386

Tobelson, A. S. *See* Krasnoshchekhov, Aleksandr Mikhailovich
Tolstoy, L. N., 360
Tomann, K., 271
Tomsky, M. P., 21
Tönnisson, Jaan, 216
Trepov, A. F., 198
Trotsky, L. D., *577–83*; Antonov-Ovseenko as friend of, 45; and Army, 241, 310, 382, 479, 582, 587; attempt to reconcile the Bashrevkom and the Obkom, 66; and Bolsheviks, 213, 428, 467, 497, 579; Bubnov's opposition to, 86; Bukharin's relations with, 89, 91; and Council of People's Commissars, 168, 170; criticism of, 530; and defeatism, 181; and delegation to Brest-Litovsk, 82–83, 331, 582; and Democratic Council, 185; and diplomacy, 582; financing for, 271; and foreign policy, 235; and free press, 460; Frunze as opponent of, 238; historical writing by, 256; and Interdistrict Committee, 269–70, 578–79; and Internationalists, 347–48; and Krasnoshchekhov, 320; in Kronstadt, 328; and Lenin, 578, 579; as member of suprafactional group for reunification, 212; and militarization of labor, 183; and New Economic Policy, 413; opposition to World War I, 629; organization of Red Army by, 136, 175–76; at party meetings, 28; and Petrograd Soviet, 443, 445; in Politburo, 536; role in release of Chicherin, 119; and Stalin, 549, 551, 552; and trade unions, 536, 572, 611; in United Opposition, 530; in VTsIK, 24; writings by, 507. *See also* Left Communism; October Seizure of Power; Russian Social Democratic Workers' Party (Bolshevik)
Tsalikov, Akhmed, 31, 32
Tsalikov, M. A., 556
Tsederbaum, Iulii Osipovich. *See* Martov, Iulii
Tseitlin, E., 535
Tsereteli, Iraklii Georgevich, *583–85*; ac-

694

Yaroslavskii, E. M. *See* Gubel'man, Mi-
nei Izrailovich
Yudenich, N. N. *See* Iudenich, Nikolai
Nikolaevich

Zade, Asadulla Kafar, 1
Zade, Resul, 62
Zaitsev, General I. M., 309
Zalkind, Ivan, 119
Zalutskii, P. A., 387
Zamiatin, Evgenii I., 362
Zasulich, Vera Ivanovna, 207, 355, 473,
622
Zavoisko, V. S., 166, 316
Zel'geim, V. N., 163
Zenzinov, V. M., 143, 191
Zetkin, Clara, 312
Zhitlovskii, Kh. O., 116
Zhordaniia, Noi Nicholaevich, *643–44*; in
favor of nationalism, 123; and Geor-

gian socialists, 120, 121, 242–43, 244,
575, 576. *See also* Russian Social
Democratic Workers' Party (Menshevik)
Zhukovskii, Vasilii A., 41
Zimin, N. N., 389
Zinoviev, Grigorii Evseevich, *644–47*;
and Borotbists, 78; in Central Committee, 24, 106, 107, 428, 551; in Comintern, 147; in Council of People's
Commissars, 422; and eastern Russia,
556; influence on Frunze, 238; opposition to, 603; opposition to World War
I, 641; in Politburo, 91, 536; and Radek, 471; as right-wing Bolshevik, 85,
296, 297, 298, 330, 347, 357, 382,
409, 502; and trade unions, 21, 486,
572; in United Opposition, 530
Zittd, V. F., 393
Zubashev, E. L., 522

SUBJECT INDEX

Page numbers of entries appear in *italic* type.

Adalet, 2

Agrarian Policy, 1917–1921, *1–5*; collectivization, 2–5%mmunes, 3; cooperative movement, 160–64; crops, 6–13; famine, 219–22; land distribution, 5–12; Land Committees, Lenin, V. I. and, 1–5; livestock, 6, 9, 13; mechanization, 9, 12; output, 8–11; Social-Democratic Workers' Party (Bolshevik) and, 1–5; Socialist-Revolutionary Party, 2. *See also* New Economic Policy; Peasants in the Russian Revolution; War Communism

Agriculture, *5–14*. *See also* Agrarian Policy, 1917–1921

Alash Orda, *15–16*. *See also* Central Asia, Revolution in; Kazakhstan, Revolution in; Moslem Democratic Party (Musavat)

Allied blockade, *7–19*. *See also* Foreign Policy, 1914–1921

All Power to the Soviets, *19–20*. *See also* Propaganda and the Russian Revolution

All-Russian Association of Soviets for Workers' and Soldiers' Deputies. *See* Soviets of Workers', Peasants' and Soldiers' Deputies

All-Russian Central Council of Trade Unions, *20–21*. *See also* Trade unions

All-Russian Central Executive Committee of Soviets, *21–26*. *See also* Soviets of Workers', Peasants', and Soldiers' Deputies

All-Russian Communist Party of the Soviet Union (Bolshevik). *See* Russian Social Democratic Workers' Party (Bolshevik)

All-Russian Congresses. *See names of individual organizations*

All-Russian Constituent Assembly. *See* Constituent Assembly

All-Russian Council of People's Commissars. *See* Council of People's Commissars

All-Russian Democratic Council. *See* Democratic Council

All-Russian Executive Committee of the Union of Railwaymen (Vikzhel), *26–29*

All-Russian Extraordinary Commission for Combatting Counterrevolution and Sabotage, *29–31*. *See also* Dzerzhinskii, F. E.

All-Russian Moslem Central Military Council (Harbi Shuro), *567*. *See also* Moslems

All-Russian Moslem Congresses, *31–32*, *566*. *See also* Moslems

P. B., 14; Chkheidze, N. S., 120–23; Gurvich, F. I., 252–54; Martov, Iu. O., *379–81*; Tsereteli, I. G., 583–86; Zhordaniia, N. N., 643–44

Sailors in 1917, *507–10*; Dybenko, P. E., 201–2

Siberia, Revolution in, *520–26*; Central Executive Committee of Soviets of Siberia (Centrosibir or Tsentrosibir), 107–8; Far Eastern Bureau, 222–23; Kolchak, A. V., 309–11; Krasnoshchekhov, A. M., 320–24; Semenov, G. M., 512–14; Shumiatskii, B. Z., 518–20; Siberian Bureau, 526–27; Siberian Regional Duma, 527–28

Siberian Bureau, *526–27*

Siberian Regional Duma, 527–28

Socialist-Revolutionary Party, *532–35*; Avksentiev, N. D., 60–61; Chernov, V. M., 116–19; Breshko-Breshkovskaia, E. K., 78–80; Gots, A. R., 244–45; Savinkov, B. V., 510–12; Spiridonova, M. A., 547–48

Soldiers and Soldiers' Committees, *537–43*

Soviets of Workers', Soldiers', and Peasants' Deputies, *543–47*

Stavka. *See* General Staff

Strelki (Latvian Sharpshooters), 343–46

Supreme Council of the National Economy, *557–60*

Tatars, Revolution among the, *565–68*; Ibragimov, M. N., 264–65; Vakhitov, 601–2. *See also* Crimea, Revolution in, *for Crimean Tatars*

Tashkent Soviet, 589. *See also* Central Asia, Revolution in

Third International. *See* Communist International

Trade Unions International. *See* Red International of Trade Unions (Profintern)

Trade Unions, *568–73*; All-Russian Central Council of Trade Unions, 20–21; All-Russian Executive Committee of the Union of Railwaymen (Vikzhel), 26–29; factory committees, 568–73;

stratification, 570–73; workers' control, 568–73; workers' opposition, 313–14. *See also* Workers in the Revolution

Transcaucasia, Revolution in, 1917–1921, *573–77*; Armenia, 51–53; Azerbaijan, *61–63*; Caucasian Bureau, 97–98; Georgia, Revolution in, *242–44*

Tsarist Regime: agrarian policy, *1–5*; agriculture, *5–14*; army of Imperial Russia in World War I, *53–57*; Duma and Revolution, *195–200*; February Revolution, *225–29*; industrialists, *265–69*; landlords, *338–43*; Nicholas II, *414–18*; 1905 Revolution, *418–21*; Rasputin, *474–77*; World War I, *624–32*

Tsentrosibir. *See* Siberian Bureau of the Central Committee of the Russian Communist Party (Bolshevik)

Turkestan, Revolution in, *588–92*. *See also* Jadid Movement; Kokand, the Autonomous Government of; Tashkent Soviet

Ukraine, Revolution in, *593–99*; Borotbisty, 77–79; Central Rada, 113; Makhno, N. I., *376–78*; Petliura, Symon, 441–42

Vesenkha. *See* Supreme Council of the National Economy

Vikzhel. *See* All-Russian Executive Committee of the Union of Railwaymen

War Communism, *609–13*. *See also* Economy

War Industries Committees, *613–16*. *See also* Provisional Government

White Movement, *616–20*; Civil War in Russia, 135–38; Denikin, A. I., 189–90; Dutov, A. I., 200–201; Iudenich, N. N., 272–73; Kaledin, A. M., 293–95; Kolchak, A. V., 309–11; Semenov, G. M., 512–14; Siberia, Revolution in, 520–26; Transcaucasia, Revolution in, 573–76; Ukraine, Revolution in, 593–99; Wrangel, P. N., 634–39

Women, Role in Revolution, *620–24*; Ar-